. . . SOME PRAISE IT

"ONE OF THE MOST BRILLIANT STUDIES OF MALE SEXUALITY EVER PRODUCED . . . ABSOLUTELY FIRST-RATE."

> Dr. William Granzig, Executive Director,
> *American Association of Sex Educators,*
> *Counselors, and Therapists*

"WONDERFUL, RIVETING, ARTICULATE, AND INTERESTING . . . PROVOCATIVE AND ILLUMINATING."

> *Cosmopolitan*

"AMBITIOUS . . . A MONUMENTAL WORK."
> *Philadelphia Inquirer*

"THE INSIGHTS ARE . . . PROFOUNDLY IMPORTANT."

> *Newsweek*

"HITE IS AN EXCELLENT SCIENTIST AND SOCIAL HISTORIAN WHO HAS MADE A GREAT CONTRIBUTION TO OUR UNDERSTANDING OF WHO MEN ARE . . . DEMONSTRATES A GREAT HOPEFULNESS ABOUT THE FUTURE."

> Dr. Leah Schaefer, past president
> *Society for the Scientific Study of Sex*

SOME DENOUNCE IT . . .

"ABOUT AS INTELLECTUALLY PROVOCATIVE AS THE PLUMBING IN MY BASEMENT."

The Washington Post

"A SEX BOOK PRETENDING TO BE A SEX STUDY . . . NOT TO BE TAKEN SERIOUSLY."

Prof. Paul Robinson, Dept. of History
Stanford University

"A TRAVESTY OF SEX RESEARCH."

New York Magazine

"HITE HAS TRIED TO MAKE US FEEL GUILTY ABOUT THE WAY WE MAKE LOVE . . . If the clitoris is so important, why don't more women find ways of incorporating it into intercourse?"

Playboy

"ONE OF THE YEAR'S WORST BOOKS."

People Magazine

CONTROVERSY OVER

THE HITE REPORT
ON MALE SEXUALITY

Several years ago, Shere Hite made history with THE HITE REPORT on female sexuality, which revealed for the first time that most women, although they could not orgasm from intercourse, could easily orgasm with more direct clitoral stimulation. The book inspired arguments, discussions, and communication among women who found they shared a great many feelings.

Now Shere Hite has made a study of men. Using the same methods and a detailed questionnaire, she recorded the responses of over 7,000 men from all over the United States, on every question relating to love, sex, relationships, and the nature of masculinity. Hailed as "brilliant" and denounced as "one of the year's worst books," THE HITE REPORT ON MALE SEXUALITY raised new questions for men and women and unleashed a new flood of controversy.

Judge for yourself. And turn the page to see what has been said about

THE HITE REPORT
ON MALE SEXUALITY

THE HITE REPORT ON MALE SEXUALITY

SHERE HITE

BALLANTINE BOOKS • NEW YORK

FOR MY GRANDFATHER,
ALEXANDER J. HURT

CONTENTS

PREFACE

Who are men? Why do they define masculinity—and "male"* sexuality—as they do? It is often assumed that male sexuality, and masculinity, are innate, biological givens. But they have been quite different in other societies and at other times in history. Why do men see them today as they do?

Men in this study generally wanted more sex but were very frustrated with it when they had it—often masturbating alone for a fully satisfying orgasm, even with a regular sex life. Many men spoke of their frustration with the mechanics of the performance they are supposed to give—and yet most did not take steps to change things.

Men's great capacity for sensuality seemed rarely appreciated or allowed to exist—ecstatic experiences were few and far between. The focus on erection and orgasm (with ejaculation†) inhibited many men's ability to continue and go higher. In fact, men's answers implied that "male" sexuality as we know it is only a pale shadow of what it might become: male sexuality is stifled and straight-jacketed by the culture. (See chapter 4.)

Ability of men in this study to truly let go sexually was also held back by lack of information about women's orgasms and by traditional male/female roles. Being told that the man is the "do-er" (he "gives" her an orgasm), while the woman "responds" (she must never show the man how she has an orgasm during masturbation) limited men still more. Men complained over and over that they wanted women to be less passive, to "do more" to them—but at the same time were wary of just this, uncomfortable being in the passive role, being "done to," receiving pleasure, being penetrated themselves. A "real man," after all, is a man of *action*, a "do-er," never one who is merely "done to." In fact, most men had rarely experienced fellatio to orgasm, or anal stimulation by a woman, even though they would like to, in addition to being kissed and

---

* The term "male" as used in this book commonly refers to ideology, not biology.

† Orgasm without ejaculation did not end arousal. See pages 470–472.

caressed more all over. On the other hand, most men still did not understand or take seriously women's needs for clitoral stimulation. Most still believed women should orgasm from simple coitus, and that if they didn't, there was something "wrong" with the woman.*

Many men said that they were deeply frustrated, angry, or disappointed with their emotional relationships with women, at the same time that they treasured these relationships as providing the happiest and most intimate moments of their lives. Many married men were so dissatisfied with their relationships that they resorted to outside sexual encounters to "make the marriage workable."

Most men in this study had not married the women they most passionately loved. Most men did not feel comfortable being deeply in love. Although they sounded very similar to women when they spoke of the first wonderful feelings of falling in love, very soon thereafter many began to feel uncomfortable, anxious, even trapped—and wanted to withdraw. Most men felt very out of control of their emotions when they were in love, not reasonable and "rational," and most men did not like this feeling. As mentioned earlier, men have been taught that the worst thing possible is to be out of control, to be "overly emotional," as this behavior is "womanly" (uncool). Thus, being in love, a man begins to feel out of control, "unmanly," and even worse, he begins to feel that he is controlled by the woman—that is, he would do anything to please her, he is afraid of her displeasure, and so he is "dominated" by her. This is an intolerable situation. Add to this the idea that most men still believe on some level that there are two kinds of women: "good," motherly women, and "bad," sexy women. The man, feeling very attracted when falling in love, is sure that he should not let himself go into his love, trust in it, and count on her. At this point,

---

* In THE HITE REPORT on female sexuality, presenting the statements of over 3,000 women, the majority said that they could easily orgasm during self-stimulation or by clitoral stimulation by a partner's hand or mouth, but very irregularly during coitus. Stereotypes depict women as having a "problem" having orgasm, but this is not true: it is not women who have a problem reaching orgasm, but the society that has had a problem accepting how women do orgasm. The impication of these women's testimonies is that the definition of sex should change so that women's needs for orgasm, usually involving clitoral stimulation separate from intercourse, are accepted as a regular and important part of sex between two people. Further, many women wanted "sex" to be less rigidly defined and not so focused on female *or* male orgasm. See chapter 5 for men's descriptions of clitoral stimulation.

he tends to pull back, to try to provoke a fight or find a problem in the relationship, in order to regain his former stance in life, his "control." He looks for, or believes he should look for, someone more "stable," someone who doesn't put him in a constant position of rethinking his life. Most men described this as a "rational" decision and took pride in having acted wisely, remaining cool and collected, and "using their heads"—even though they missed their lost love.

Most of the men in these marriages were not monogamous. Most marriages based on this "rational" idea tended to develop a pattern (at least in the man*) of extramarital sex unknown to the woman—or, since there was such emotional distance in the marriage anyway, sometimes the wife did know but just did not care, since she herself had little interest in sex with her husband. These ("traditional") marriages, while not close in the romantic sense, could often be long-term: if reasons other than love were the basis of the marriage in the first place, it was not necessary to maintain a high level of communication, intimacy, or understanding to ensure continuation of the marriage. "Newer" marriages in which emotional closeness and equality between the man and woman were goals, tended to be more monogamous and also to have quite different sexual patterns. (See chapters 2 and 5.)

Men in this study also sounded quite irritated with the bounds of how they are supposed to be in society—the role they have to play to be accepted as "real men"; on the other hand, most continued these "standards" because of the prestige and acceptance attached to living within these rules. The principal male value, taught from boyhood on, was that a man should be emotionally reserved, in control at all times—he should not be a "sissy" or in any way "like a woman" (whose domain is feelings). Men should remove themselves from these things, discuss only "important" topics such as business, politics, and sports, and be successful. This tradition continues remarkably strong today: boys now in childhood and their teens are still learning it, under the guise of being "cool."

As one young man expressed his sentiments: "Men are trained at an early age to disregard any and every emotion, and *be strong*. Not only that, they are supposed to be a cross between John Wayne, the Chase Manhattan Bank, and Hugh Hefner. We are only human, for christsake."

* A new questionnaire for women relating to these and other topics can be found on pages 1009–1021.

Men were saddest when talking about their lack of closeness with their fathers. It is impossible not to sympathize with them as they describe their childhoods, filled with the pain of trying to conform to the male role, which demanded complete obedience, strength (or the appearance of it), intense competition, success, and control. This usually was taught by a father who seemed very distant, due to his *own* attempt to comply with the stereotypical male role, which pictures the father as always stable, never showing "weakness" (i.e., feelings), or "burdening" his family with his worries. As one man put it, "My father told me: work hard, never complain, and don't spend all your time with your mother. If I cried, he was humiliated and told me to be a man—or go to my room and stay there until I got control of myself. Other than that, I hardly knew him."

Passion seemed to have been eradicated from many men's lives—except in subterranean form. In addition to "male" upbringing, the twentieth century's increased insistence that a man's nature is to be "rational" (not spiritual or emotional) has turned many men's lives into an emotional desert. There is no longer much trace of the Greek or Renaissance ideal of a balance between reason and the passions*: the success of the Industrial Revolution in the early part of this century created an extreme fixation on "science," which came to mean that men should be as efficient, mentally and physically, as machines.† But this can play havoc with men's emotional relationships‡—and eventually with men's ability to be creative and to have a human perspective on their work.

Are most men changing their view of the world—and who they are in that world—or is it more true to say "the more things change, the more they remain the same"?

---

* Teaching men to obey reason, not feelings, also has roots in Biblical tradition: the ultimate lesson to men to deny their own individual desires and feelings, and to follow laws, rules, and orders unflinchingly, is the story of Abraham on the mountain preparing to kill (sacrifice) his own son, in order to follow the will of God the Father. No more wrenching story of a man learning to kill his own feelings can be found.

† This is reflected even in men's clothing: eighteenth century men's clothing was ornate and flowing, whether the man was rich or poor; twentieth century men's clothing is generally utilitarian and symmetrical, square in shape, resembling somewhat the cutout figures used to represent statistical tables in children's grade-school textbooks.

‡ Not only with women but also with men. Most men did not have a close male friend with whom they could talk intimately. It also inhibited men's relationships with *themselves*—their ability to know themselves.

Is there any difference between how individual men feel about their sexuality and themselves as men—and how the culture says they should feel? It is important to ask what *can* sex and sexual relationships be? What do we want to make them?

"Male" sexuality is central to the definition of masculinity—and masculinity is central to the world-view of the entire culture—in a sense, *is* the culture. Therefore, what we are looking at in this book is far more than male sexuality, it is a way of life, the world itself, a culture in microcosm. To discuss sex is to discuss our most basic views of who we are, what we want life to be, and what kind of a society we believe in.

POPULATION STATISTICS AND METHODOLOGY

Starting in 1974, before publication of *The Hite Report* on female sexuality, questionnaires were distributed to men in various parts of the country. The purpose of this early distribution was to test for errors of fact which might be incorporated into the study of female sexuality, and to see if there was a difference between social stereotypes of "male sexuality" and the way men feel. Quite quickly it was realized that there is much that is not known about men's sexuality, and especially about how men feel about their sexual experiences and personal relationships. Men's replies to this early questionnaire pointed the way to a second version of the questions, which was distributed in 1975. Four complete versions of the questions were undertaken in all, with the final version being the most heavily distributed. (Questionnaire IV appears on page 995.)

Great emphasis was placed on reaching men of all ages, in all areas of the country, in all walks of life, and with all outlooks and points of view. The success of this effort, in most cases, is reflected in the statistics and comparative statistics which are found on the following pages. Basically, the distribution proceeded in three stages. First, the early distribution was done to explore whether men would be willing to participate in such a study and to see which questions had the most relevance for them. Answers to this first questionnaire, and suggestions for further questions, helped make this a questionnaire designed with the help of many, many men. Then massive distribution began in the form of mailing large numbers of questionnaires to groups across the country, including university groups, church groups, and men's discussion groups. The paperback *Sexual Honesty, By Women for Women** also asked male readers to write requesting the questionnaire. Finally, the questionnaire was printed in its entirety in 1975 in *Sexology* magazine with the respondent being requested to return his reply to "Mr. S. D. Hite." The purpose of this was to learn whether any bias was created by replies being addressed to a woman researcher in other samples. In fact, comparison of this sample with others shows that there is very little or no deviation.

After publication of *The Hite Report* on female sexuality in late 1976, distribution intensified. In many interviews given to newspapers, television, radio, and magazines, the address to which men might write was supplied. In addition, a footnote in *The Hite Report* asked men to write for the questions. Many requests for the questionnaires were received from these sources, although not all men who requested them returned the form. Answers from men who had read *The Hite Report* comprise 15 percent of the total sample. In 1977, *Penthouse* magazine and *Houston Breakthrough* (a feminist newspaper) ran the questionnaire in its entirety. The answers from readers of *Penthouse* are included as a part of the 11 percent of replies received from men who learned of the questionnaire through a men's magazine.

Although many answers had been received by 1978, it was felt that certain population groups should be explored more thoroughly. The large numbers of answers received so far had also included significant new areas of interest to question. Accordingly, a new questionnaire was prepared, and distribution carefully planned to emphasize population groups which had not yet been sufficiently examined. These included certain men in certain age, race and ethnic groups, special geographical locations, and educational levels. Once again, distribution through men's clubs, church organizations, professional associations, and sports groups was accomplished by sending bulk mailings of questionnaires for members to individual chapters of these groups across the country, but particularly in the geographical locations which were, at that time, less well represented. This distribution continued intensively for fifteen months, with constant checking of population statistics to

---

* An anthology of forty-five complete replies received from women, published by Warner Paperback Library in 1974.

follow the progress of the samples. Replies were also sought during this period especially from men over sixty-five, black men, and the "disabled" population, whose sexual lives are so rarely acknowledged. Forty-eight percent of the replies received were from this fourth version of the questionnaire; the large majority of those who answered had not read *The Hite Report* on female sexuality.

Each reply which was received was given a number, and then the answer to each question was placed on the appropriate chart, a very difficult and time-consuming process. However, any attempt at condensation or computerization would have defeated the purposes of the study: to find more subtle meanings underneath the easily quantifiable parts of the replies, and to keep intact each individual's voice so that men would retain direct access to communicating their feelings with the reader, thus reinforcing the integrity of the study. After all the replies had been charted, the process of identifying categories was begun, along with the selection of representative quotes. Statistical computation was then possible.

In addition, many of the findings were broken down into several different populations, for purposes of comparison, including the following:

General Sample

    Anonymous   34%
    Non-anonymous   16%

Special Samples

    Forms with return address to a male researcher
    Anonymous   4%
    Non-anonymous   1%
    Men who had read *The Hite Report* on female sexuality
    Anonymous   10%
    Non-anonymous   5%

Men who preferred sex with men	Sex with both men and women
Anonymous 8%	Anonymous 3%
Non-anonymous 1%	

    Military (Answers from men who were in the military service)
    Anonymous   6%
    Non-anonymous   1%
    Answers from men who learned of the questionnaire through a
        men's magazine
    Anonymous   8%
    Non-anonymous   3%

All in all, 119,000 questionnaires were distributed, and 7,239 received in return. The standard rate of return for this type of distribution is estimated at 2.5 to 3 percent. In that this study elicited a return rate of 6 percent,* this was an excellent result, especially since these questionnaires were very long and very personal, requiring an investment of time and thought from the respondent. Even though the forms were demanding, it was felt that this was the ideal type of questionnaire for developing the kind of dialogue which would allow men to speak out and expand on their thoughts in directions which were personal to them—as opposed to being limited by a multiple-choice form, even though that kind of form enormously simplifies the work of the researcher. Although many men did not return the form, this does not mean that the study is "unrepresentative," for two reasons: first, because the majority of the forms were not sent to individual men, but were sent in bulk to groups and organizations, so that many forms may never have reached an individual man and may have been discarded as excess copies by the club or group. Secondly, although some men may have found the questionnaire too personal to answer, or may not have been interested, and therefore not have returned their forms, special care was taken (as just mentioned) to compensate for this by doing especially concentrated distribution in areas where the sample, at the mid-point of the study, seemed lacking—i.e., religious groups, some geographical locations in the south and mid-west, and older age groups, among others. As pointed out earlier, sufficient effort was put into this that the final statistical breakdown of the men who answered *(age, occupation, religion, etc.)* in most cases quite closely mirrors that of the U.S. male population. (See tables beginning on page xxviii.)

A note on "scientific method"

In fact, there seems to be a widespread misunderstanding about the types and validity of methodologies available in the social sciences. Reviews and articles about *The Hite Report* on female sexuality frequently cited the methodology as "unscientific," and yet this is inaccurate, and shows a lack of

* The rate of return is fractionally lower if replies from readers of *Penthouse* magazine are not included, as their distribution was done in a different form.

understanding of the meaning of the term. It is with the hope of clearing up this misunderstanding that excerpts of the following article, which appeared in the *Journal of the American Society of Sex Educators, Counselors and Therapists,* are presented, in addition to some new material.

TOWARD A NEW METHODOLOGY IN THE SOCIAL SCIENCES: IS THE HITE REPORT "SCIENTIFIC"?*

"Scientific" does not mean "representative"

Is *The Hite Report* scientific? This is a question that is often asked. And yet the question itself reflects a misunderstanding of the word "scientific." Having done my master's thesis on the application of scientific method to the social sciences, I am very familiar with the history of scientific method and its various meanings, especially as they have developed over time. Specifically, what this question usually means is, "Does *The Hite Report* contain a statistically representative sample?" To be "scientific" and "representative" is not the same thing.

"Science" is a term which originally came from the Latin root "to know" and means basically systematized knowledge in any field, sometimes as part of a system of general laws. Anything which is investigated carefully and in a scholarly

* Reprinted with permission from the *Journal of the American Society of Sex Educators, Counselors and Therapists,* Vol. 4, No. 2/Winter 1978. This article refers to *The Hite Report* on female sexuality, but is equally relevant to the current study.

manner can be termed "scientific," although the term has many specialized meanings. Scientific method involves the gathering, recording, and analyzing of facts with care and accuracy, the finding of relationships among those facts, and drawing logical conclusions from them. The term "social science" came into common usage in the late nineteenth century when the humanities, overshadowed by the increasing prestige of physics, mathematics, and the advances of the industrial revolution, started to think in terms of applying the same methods to their own work.

Can people be studied "scientifically"?

But is it possible to transfer the methods of the physical sciences to the study of people? To be "scientific" in the study of society has evolved to mean, basically perhaps, to be objective—to see the facts clearly and report them without distortion, with precision. This is important; however, it is a problem in the social sciences, because the researcher is a human being and cannot escape having a point of view, a personal value system. As social scientists from Max Weber to Gunnar Myrdal have pointed out, there is an inevitable relation between the investigator's values and how s/he practices social science. There is no such thing as a value-free scientist, and there is no such thing as a totally "objective" researcher. Those who would imply that they are purely objective are likely to be the least so. It is the responsibility of the social scientist to make her/his point of view ("bias") known from the outset.

In addition to the problem of the subjectivity of the researcher, there is also the difficulty that the "things" being studied, i.e., human beings, are very hard to measure and categorize in the way that classical scientific method did with such success in the physical world. Fortunately or unfortunately, human beings are for the most part more complex than "things," and to try to reduce them to measurable categories is frequently to distort them beyond recognition—and lose sight of the whole person entirely. Even if the measurements are relatively accurate (which is always questionable), there remains the significant question of whether measurement is the best way to understand human nature. Why do we insist on applying scientific method to people in exactly the same way as we have applied it to the physical world? The act of quantifying human behavior into a series of discrete categories reduces a complex whole to a group of oversimplified variables. And, like Humpty Dumpty, can these pieces ever be put back together again?*

Is THE HITE REPORT a statistically representative sample?

There has never been a perfect sample in sex research. In the field of sociology, the two basic methods which have been employed are the taking of surveys, and the building of predictive models, usually based on existing survey material or data banks. Traditionally, the survey—"a sampling, or partial collection of facts, figures or opinions taken and used to approximate the whole"—was the basic method of the sociologists, with a "random sample" being considered the most accurately representative. However, in sex research a perfectly random sample has never been possible on a large scale because most of the people chosen at random would not answer—due to the personal nature of the questions and the lack of anonymity in this sampling procedure.

Was Kinsey representative? . . . What Kinsey did was to question people from as many walks of life, backgrounds, and economic levels, etc., as he could to try to approximate a representative selection. Arguments continued for years as to whether he succeeded, but today his findings are generally accepted as accurate. Of course, Masters and Johnson did not do a survey; they did biological research on the basis of a highly selected population of 694 people. Obviously, a "study" of this kind is just as "scientific" as a survey, as long as it is precise and systematic; not being statistically representative is not the same as being non-scientific.

[*The Hite Report* used the same basic approach as the Kinsey studies, working to include as wide a cross-section of the population as possible, then checking this against the U.S. population statistics, to ensure that the study would be as "scientific" (i.e., representative) as possible. Although there have been assertions made that the women who answered may not have been "typical," in fact, when the statistics are studied, and compared with the U.S. population statistics for women over fourteen, it can be seen that in most cases they are quite similar.

* This is a question that is being asked more and more frequently in the social sciences. See P. Connerton, editor, *Critical Sociology* (Penguin Books, 1976); E. F. Schumacher, *A Guide for the Perplexed* (Harper & Row, 1977); Stephen Toulmin, "From Form to Function: Philosophy and the History of Science in the 1950's and Now," *Daedalus*, Summer 1977.

[*The Hite Report* contained two significant differences in methodology from the Kinsey reports, which were thought to improve the study. First, whereas Kinsey and his (male) associates interviewed women face to face and knew the complete names and addresses of those they interviewed,* *The Hite Report* used an anonymous essay-type questionnaire, believing that women would feel freer to talk about themselves in detail if they were offered the protection of complete privacy and anonymity. In fact, many women who responded said that they had been able to write about things that they would never have been able to tell someone face to face, especially a stranger. The second significant difference is that *The Hite Report* presented not only statistical findings, but also offered many direct quotations from the replies to illustrate the findings—and so gave participants and readers direct access to each other. This was an innovation in social-science methodology. Its purpose was to avoid, insofar as possible, setting up rigid new "norms" which might seem to be telling women what they should feel, and instead, to give women a chance to re-examine and re-evaluate their lives, deciding for themselves how they felt, and what they agreed and disagreed with. In other words, the *Hite Report* methodology was conceived as providing a large forum in which women could speak out freely—giving everyone reading those replies the chance to decide for themselves how they felt about the answers. The methodology was seen as a process, both for the individual woman answering the questionnaire, and for the person reading what the 3,019 women had written —a process of re-thinking, self-discovery, and of getting acquainted with many other women in a way that had never before been possible—an anonymous and powerful communication from the women who answered to all the women of the world.

[As to comments that *The Hite Report* had a political point of view, this is in fact true—as it is true that every research project ever undertaken has a point of view. When this point of view coincides with that which is popularly believed, the point of view often is unnoticed—since it is accepted as "truth." Assumptions made in such studies are often unrecognized, even by the researchers themselves. For example, map makers and explorers in the middle ages assumed that the earth was flat—but no one called this assumption "unscientific." It is only when the point of view is new, or an

* For reasons which were valid at that time.

which had been predominant for so long was the only possible alternative to the standard point of view, that it is considered "biased." In the case of *The Hite Report,* the point of view was woman-oriented, in that it let women define sex as they saw it, rather than assuming that the male definition of sex "correct" definition. For this, the work was described by some as having a "feminist bias." In fact, much of the previous research into female sexuality had been less than "scientific" in that, rather than taking the information that most women could orgasm more easily during masturbation or direct clitoral/vulval stimulation than during coitus, and concluding that therefore this is "normal," instead, previous studies started with the assumption that women "should" orgasm during coitus, and concluded that if they did not, there must be something wrong with them—that they were somehow defective, "dysfunctional," or psychologically or physically abnormal. Research was often geared to finding out what the cause of this "defect" might be. This was a "non-scientific," in that it was not objective, way of looking at female sexuality. No study is free of bias, or a point of view; the important point is to recognize this fact, and to clarify, insofar as possible, just what the point of view is.

[So, finally, is *The Hite Report* representative? I believe that *The Hite Report* represents a broad cross-section of women's points of view, and contains a high degree of representativeness.* Indeed, perhaps since we are trying to avoid setting up new "norms" against which women "should" measure themselves, establishing perfect representativeness may not be the point. However, as mentioned earlier, comparisons of the study population statistics with U.S. population statistics point to a high degree of representativeness. And, on a less formal level, this accuracy is underscored by the fact that, to date, *The Hite Report* has been published in seventeen countries, and in not one country have women disagreed with the basic findings of the book—i.e., that women do not for the most part orgasm via clitoral/vulval stimulation when they choose to; that we must reassess the traditional ideas we have had about female sexuality—and many, many more basic conclusions. In fact, thousands of women everywhere have written publicly and privately that they felt grateful for the book, and relieved to find that they were not "different" from other women, or

* The study of female sexuality now has been replicated in England, Sweden, and Norway; statistics on stimulation necessary for orgasm, and other factors, are extremely similar.

"abnormal." *The Hite Report* quite clearly speaks for many, many women. But most important of all, women of all ages and points of view have found it an invaluable tool in re-examining and exploring not only their sexuality but also their lives as women, and as part of a universe of other women.

POPULATION STATISTICS

Following are statistics presenting such variables about the respondents as geographical location, age, educational background, occupation,* marital status, and other information. Also presented are statistical figures for the general male population of the United States, so that comparison with the population of this study can be made. *It will be seen that in most categories, the breakdown of the male population of the United States and the population of this study correspond quite closely.*

COMPARISON OF STUDY POPULATION WITH U.S. POPULATION BY STATE†

STATE	STUDY POPULATION	U.S. POPULATION	
		1978	1980
Alabama	.9%	1.7%	1.7%
Alaska	.6	.2	.2
Arizona	1.4	1.0	1.2
Arkansas	.8	1.0	1.0
California	12.4	10.3	10.4
Colorado	1.8	1.2	1.3
Connecticut	1.1	1.5	1.4
Delaware	.3	.3	.3

* This chart has been deleted from the present volume, as it was quite extensive. If you would like a copy, please write the author c/o the publisher.

† The city-by-city breakdown of this chart has been deleted from the present volume, for reasons of space. Please write the author c/o the publisher if you wish a copy.

District of Columbia	1.2	.3	.3
Florida	3.8	4.2	4.3
Georgia	2.0	2.3	2.4
Hawaii	.4	.4	.4
Idaho	.2	.4	.4
Illinois	4.7	5.1	5.0
Indiana	2.6	2.4	2.4
Iowa	1.1	1.3	1.3
Kansas	1.0	1.1	1.0
Kentucky	1.0	1.6	1.6
Louisiana	1.3	1.7	1.9
Maine	.3	.5	.5
Maryland	1.9	1.9	1.9
Massachusetts	2.7	2.7	2.5
Michigan	3.9	4.1	4.1
Minnesota	1.7	1.8	1.8
Mississippi	.8	1.0	1.1
Missouri	2.0	2.2	2.2
Montana	.5	.3	.3
Nebraska	.8	.7	.7
Nevada	.7	.3	.4
New Hampshire	.7	.4	.4
New Jersey	3.8	3.4	3.3
New Mexico	1.2	.5	.6
New York	9.0	8.3	7.8
North Carolina	2.0	2.6	2.6
North Dakota	.2	.3	.3
Ohio	4.1	4.9	4.8
Oklahoma	1.0	1.3	1.3
Oregon	1.7	1.1	1.2
Pennsylvania	4.5	5.5	5.2
Rhode Island	.4	.4	.4
South Carolina	.9	1.3	1.4
South Dakota	.5	.3	.3
Tennessee	1.5	2.0	2.0
Texas	5.1	5.8	6.3
Utah	.7	.5	.6
Vermont	.4	.2	.2
Virginia	2.9	2.4	2.4
Washington	2.7	1.7	1.8
West Virginia	.5	.9	.9
Wisconsin	1.6	2.1	2.1
Wyoming	.3	.2	.2

AGE OF RESPONDENTS

AGE	NUMBER OF RESPONDENTS	AGE	NUMBER OF RESPONDENTS
14	2	56	126
15	14	57	82
16	16	58	59
17	35	59	71
18	34	60	99
19	84	61	46
20	143	62	79
21	124	63	47
22	175	64	62
23	197	65	65
24	211	66	36
25	199	67	49
26	288	68	37
27	216	69	40
28	207	70	33
29	203	71	20
30	205	72	28
31	189	73	7
32	162	74	19
33	155	75	18
34	126	76	3
35	192	77	8
36	187	78	8
37	150	79	7
38	158	80	12
39	141	81	5
40	173	82	9
41	102	83	4
42	144	84	3
43	107	85	1
44	151	86	3
45	178	87	2
46	129	88	5
47	135	89	2
48	134	90	2
49	120	91	3
50	161	92	4
51	105	93	2
52	111	94	1
53	127	95	1
54	115	96	1
55	139	97	1

TOTAL: 6,994   *The remaining 245 respondents' ages were not given.*

COMPARISON OF STUDY POPULATION WITH POPULATION OF SEVEN LARGEST CITIES

CITY	STUDY POPULATION	U.S. POPULATION*
New York	3.0%	3.2%
Chicago	1.0	1.3
Los Angeles	1.0	1.3
Philadelphia	1.0	0.7
Houston	0.7	0.7
Detroit	0.7	0.5
Dallas	0.8	0.4

COMPARISON OF STUDY POPULATION WITH AGE GROUPS IN U.S. POPULATION

STUDY POPULATION		U.S. POPULATION† (ages 14 and over)	
Ages	% of Replies	Ages	% of Population
15–21	7‡	15–21	20.7
22–34	35	22–34	27.3
(22–27 17%)			
(28–34 18%)			
35–44	21	35–44	14.3
45–54	19	45–54	14.3
55–64	12	55–64	11.7
65 and over	6	65 and over	11.7
	100%		100.00%

* Based on preliminary 1980 census counts of the population of the thirty largest cities.

† Based on *Statistical Abstract of the United States,* 1978 edition: "The population distribution in the United States of men 14 and over."

‡ This figure is much lower than that of the U.S. population figure because few early teen-age replies were solicited and possibly many young teen-agers were not ready to answer such a questionnaire.

MARITAL STATUS

STUDY POPULATION		U.S. POPULATION*
Single	21%	21.9%
Widowers	2%	2.7%
Living Together	6%	(none given)†
Divorced	9%	4.5%
Married	62%	70.9%

How Long Married	No. of Respondents
1–11 months	114
1 year	116
2–5 years	417
6–10 years	755
11–15 years	598
16–20 years	452
21–25 years	456
26–30 years	468
31–40 years	304
41–50 years	276
over 50 years	51

RELIGION

RELIGION	STUDY POPULATION	U.S. POPULATION‡
Protestant	55%	60%
Catholic	24%	28%
Jewish	6%	2%
Other	4%	4%
No stated preference*	11%	6% (*"no formal religious preference"*)

* Source: U.S. Bureau of the Census, Current Population Reports.

† Current reliable estimates give 3 percent; the *Statistical Abstract of the United States* for August 1978 gives 2.5 percent.

‡ From *Religion in America; Gallup Opinion Index, 1977–78*; published by the American Institute of Public Opinion (Gallup); Survey of Adults (18 years or over) based on their own self-classification, and not on surveys of church membership.

* Religious preference was not asked in every version of the questionnaire; therefore, some men who may have had a preference may not have given it.

RACE OR ETHNICITY (NATURALIZED CITIZENS)

RACIAL BACKGROUND AND/OR ETHNICITY	STUDY POPULATION		POPULATION* U.S.	
White	83.6%		86.61%	
Black	11.9%		11.61%	
Others	4.5%		1.78%	
	includes:		includes:	
	American Indian	0.9%	American Indian	0.4 %
	Hispanic	1.6%	Spanish origin	0.4 %
	Japanese-Chinese-Oriental	1.0%	"Oriental"	0.5 %
	All others	1.0%	All others	0.48%
		4.5%		1.78%
	100.0%		100.00%	

EDUCATION

YEARS OF SCHOOL TYPE OF EDUCATION	STUDY POPULATION	U.S. POPULATION†
8th grade or less	2.0%	*(25 years old*
some high school	6.0%	*and over)*
technical school	14.0%	
currently in high school	1.5%	
	23.5%	32%
high school degree	21.5%	33%
some college	19.0%	
currently in college	4.0%	
	23.0%	15%
college degree	21.5%	11%
graduate work	4.0%	
graduate degree	6.5%	
	10.5%	9%
	100.0%	100%

* Based on U.S. Bureau of the Census, Current Population Reports, series P-20; also see *Statistical Abstract of the United States.*

† Taken from Educational Attainment in the United States, Bureau of the Census, March 1979 Report: P.T. 20, no. 356.

FURTHER STATISTICS AVAILABLE

Note: 103 statistical charts have been deleted from this volume including a listing of occupations of the respondents, the city-by-city geographical distribution of replies, and 20 pages of answers to "Why did you answer this questionnaire?" and "How did you like the questionnaire?" These can be found in the original hardcover edition published by Alfred A. Knopf in 1981, or you can receive a copy of these statistics by writing to the author c/o the publisher.

ACKNOWLEDGMENTS

Many people contributed much of their time, effort, and good will to make this study a reality. Help in tabulating, organizing, or typing the material was provided by Safwan Batayneh, Esther Bonilla, Deborah Farkas, Tam Frankel, Daniel Ginetti, Miriam Hipsch, Frank Martin, Lena Myers, Rosemarie Navarro, Valerie Prescott, Nina Radin, Norma Throop, Sheila Walker, and Betsy West. Other invaluable forms of help, not always directly related to the book itself but without which the book might not have been completed, were graciously given by Dimitri Argyriades, David Bain, John Boys, Andrea Dworkin, Harold Fleischer, Calla Fricke, Joyce Gold, Jay Hughes, Sam Julty, Martha Kaplan, Steve Kaufman, Simi Kelley, Polly Kellog, Richard Kwiecinski, David LaCamera, Ellen McNeilly, Laura Medow, Michael Meller, Martin Oliner, Andrew Peck, Julian Prose, Jean Rosenthal, John-Willy Rudolph, Sheri Safran, Leah Schaefer, Barbara Seaman, Marijan Sinkovic, Charlene Spraetnik, Merlin Stone, Jay Topkis, Michael Wilson, and Shirley and Leon Zussman. I would like to thank Sara Zarem and Martin Sage for their very personal help. Howard Wilson was enormously helpful in ways not directly related to this work, but which, nevertheless, made it possible to continue work. I thank him for his intelligence and his generosity of spirit. Finally, I would most like to thank Edwin Rath for his superb insights and reflections on men and men's view of the world, and for his continuing emotional support throughout all the years of this project.

A most important thanks goes to my editors and publisher, without whom this massive research might never have reached the form of a book. Lesley Krauss and Judy Henry deserve a special credit for their outstanding work in copy editing and design. Regina Ryan performed the formidable task of clarifying, with great intelligence and patience, the early, very rough and oversized manuscript. Robert Gottlieb's intelligence and creative talents were crucial at every stage of the way. Without his intense enthusiasm, insightful criticism, and very hard work, the scope of this work would have been considerably less than it is. Throughout a very long and concentrated period of editing, he remained always wise, challenging, giving, scintillating, and a wonderful pleasure to work with.

Finally, without the 7,239 men who took the time and cared enough to explore their feelings, and had the courage to share them, there could have been no book, and I send my congratulations, personal thanks, and greetings to each and every one.

I would like to add a special note of thanks to all of those who worked so brilliantly to produce the Ballantine edition of this book, especially Marilyn Abraham. I also want to express my deep appreciation to Andrea Mosbacher, Martha Schwartz, Iris Bass, Vicki Spitz, Jo Sgammato, Betsy Elias, Frank Potash, Marion Glick, and Virginia Faber.

1

BEING MALE

"All the time I was growing up, it was funny—I was closer to my mother than my father, she was the one who was more loving—but I knew it was my father's opinion of me that counted, it was his approval that I really wanted. Why? I don't know. But I'm still that way, in a sense: I love my wife, very much, and we are happy together—but to be really happy, I want more than anything to be part of the world of men and to be recognized by other men as a man and successful."

In a very real sense, relationships between men are "what matters" to most men in our culture—even more so than male-female relations. Men look to other men for approval, acceptance, validation, and respect. Men see other men as the arbiters of what is real, the guardians of wisdom, the holders and wielders of power.

But are men able to be close to each other in our society? What do men learn from their fathers about being men, and are they close to their fathers growing up? How do men feel about their friendships with other men?

Paradoxically, even though men regard one another as "who is important," most are afraid to become too close. "Feelings" for other men are supposed to be expressed only casually, and should not go beyond admiration and respect. Thus, men's relationships with one another tend to be based on an acceptance of mutually understood roles and positions, a belonging to the group, rather than on intimate personal discussion of the details of their lives and feelings. As one man put it, "We are comrades more than friends." Our culture simultaneously glorifies and severely limits men's relationships, even relationships between fathers and sons. Still, some men did feel a deep sense of affinity and comradeship with other men.

What are close friendships between men like? How do men like to spend time together? How did men relate as boys—including, for many, physical relationships? Are male friendships important in men's lives?

RELATIONSHIPS BETWEEN BOYS AND THEIR FATHERS

"Are you or were you close to your father? In what way? What is/was he like? What do you think of him? Can you talk to your father?" "What was your relationship to him when you were a child? Were you physically close (affectionate)?"

Almost no men said they are or had been close to their fathers:

"He never shows weakness or strong emotion. I know he loves me but I want a more explicit statement of that. We did not have a physically close relationship. No hugging, kissing, etc."

"He was always busy. He was a quiet man of few words, though extremely witty, and articulate—and very loving and affectionate, which slowly disappeared as I got older to eventually become a formal, stiff, cold relationship."

"I was not close to my father. We never made it."

"Not particularly. We played sports, talked politics. I can talk to him about nonpersonal subjects, but we are not personally close."

"I don't consider that I was close to my father. All that I can remember about my father was that he was always drunk or beating me for something that I didn't do."

"He is quiet and large. I am afraid of him and I don't know what to say."

"I have never been close to my father. He is extremely conservative, status-quo-oriented, successful, and prides himself on not asking for help even if he knows he needs it. Also a big-game hunter."

"I love and respect my father, but am *not* overly close to him. He is reserved, and not demonstrative. He tried to be a good father, and for the most part he was."

"I loved him very much as a boy—now I am ambivalent about him. He is a weak man, dominated by my mother, dependent. I am angry with him because he was not a good model for me—he does not know himself and so taught me to be someone that can't exist—macho."

"I was not real close to my father. He was a hard-working, honest man who liked to drink a little too much on occasion and had a few affairs during his life."

"My father is a dominant, controlling man. He accepts responsibility well, but is inept in interpersonal relationships, except on a very casual basis. I now have a comfortable relationship with him, but very superficial."

"We were never close. He was a weekend alcoholic. When he was drunk Mom would hide upstairs, and he would rant and rave. It was terrifying. The rest of the week he was passive. Did his job, came home, and watched TV."

"We are not close. He is very quiet—distant. I respect his dedication to the family but I never talk to him about important things."

"I don't think of him much. I don't think we were suited to be father and son but I wonder if anyone was."

"My father and I never spent a great deal of time together. He is honest, and loyal, but even now my father and I can go days with saying nothing but good morning or good night to each other."

"I feel cheated because I had absolutely no love from my father for as long as I can remember. He just tried to buy my love with outrageous presents, like a motorcycle when I was twelve and two more before I even had a driver's license. Then a brand-new car, etc. We never talked or did things together."

"Dad was always busy. We saw a lot of him on vacations of a month of camping but little else. He would punish us when he got home from work after talking to Mom."

"My father had a bad temper and did not spare the rod. He was hard to get close to and did not show affection to my brother or me. I liked my dad but doubt that I loved him."

"I don't know a lot about him because he was always traveling, but I feel a lot of warmth towards him and from him. He's dark-haired, doesn't talk much about himself."

"No—but he seemed like a nice man."

"I'm not really close to my father. I respect him more than he knows, and I know that he cares about me. But we did very little together. He is strict, and used to have an explosive temper, which has mellowed considerably in the last few years. He grew up in the depression, and refuses to throw anything away because he 'might need it someday.' I love my father, but I can't talk to him about anything but practical or mechanical matters."

"I was very detached from my father. He was, and is, unable to show any emotion except negative ones, such as anger, cynicism, frustration, etc. He never complimented me or anyone, and never said anything positive to me. I only worked around the house with him as a kind of assistant. He worked a lot on the house, I think as a kind of substitute way of caring for the family and providing for it without ever saying 'I love you' to anyone. I avoided him because he meant more work or criticism. He also worked nights, so I didn't see him as often as others saw their fathers. We were never physically close."

"There were few times of closeness with my father. The occasions of togetherness were generally working experiences, that's where I'd find him. The times of talking in more than just perfunctory ways were rare. I would not say we were especially affectionate. I sensed at times that I was his favorite, but my respect for him bordered on fear. He was a person not easy to know."

Most men are not able to talk to their fathers:

"I am pretty close to my father but more so to my mother. He is a very quiet and simple man, I guess the fact that he is quiet never allowed me to talk to him as much as I would have liked. As a child I think we were pretty close because he did things with me that I enjoyed like baseball, football, etc. We are both very avid sports fans. We would pass time together rather than talk."

"I love both my stepfather and natural father. One is dead but I can communicate with the other—at least as much as is possible with your father."

"I have never been close to my father nor have I ever talked to him really about anything that was bothering me. My father believes in the Catholic commandments, and expects everyone in the family to follow the commandments. If you don't, you pay by having problems. The answer apparently is not to discuss the problems, but to mend your ways and return to the fold. I feel he will treat me like a child for the rest of my life. In spite of all this, I do like my father, as he is very loyal and kind, even if he doesn't talk to me about things that bother me."

"We used to go fishing and crabbing together when I was in my early teens, but we never talked much when we went. Even today I have a hard time talking to him—we're just not on an open, talking basis. My father keeps a lot to himself—he is a loner in his own family, although he seems happy enough."

"I don't remember us having much of a relationship when I was a child. It seemed to me that the only time he would talk to me is when he yelled at me for something."

"I never was close to my father. We just discussed matters of minor importance to us like soccer results or acts of the government. We liked to play chess and sometimes Ping-Pong. I respected him and had fear of his anger."

"I can talk to him but not with him. He is so scientific and cool."

"I respected him. We worked together on the ranch up through my teens. He was considerate of others and squeaky honest. But we could only talk about light matters."

"My father and I rarely spoke about anything. It was basically a yes and no relationship, with 'sir' following each reply."

"We talked a lot about ideas and family history, but we never discussed feelings about anything."

"I've never said anything important to my father."

And even physical relationships with their fathers as very young children seem to have been off limits to many men; when asked whether they had been physically close to their fathers as children, very few could remember being carried or cuddled by their fathers (or sometimes even their mothers)— although they often remembered being spanked or punished:

"I don't remember being cuddled or bathed. Of course, I remember being spanked but my parents only spanked when it was a pure necessity."

"I can't remember being held as a child. About the only thing I remember is once swimming with Dad and, of course, Mom reading a bedtime story to my sister and me. I do remember Mom punishing me for breaking a vase I had been warned about."

"I can remember being punished and corrected with a spanking but I don't recall being held or cuddled. There was always the younger brother or sister, so things were pretty hectic. I do have vague memory of having stories read to me by my mother and sometimes older brothers and sisters."

"No memories in this area, except punishment and spanking, which I dreaded, probably from fear."

"I have no memories of being held by any of my parents. I do remember having my hair washed by my mother, and being spanked with a stick."

"I was always punished."

"No, no conscious memories of closeness. I remember eating soap for cursing, I can still taste it in my mouth."

"I remember being punished and spanked. At least once Daddy tied me to a porch pole when I wouldn't stay in the backyard where he could keep an eye on me. A lot of people think that was terrible but it didn't bother me then and doesn't bother me now. I don't remember being held that much but I'm sure I was never shunned when I really needed to be held."

"Most memories involve punishment by my father. Humiliation was his forte. His classic was when I wet my pants slightly when we were visiting relatives, and he told me to tell everyone present I had wet my pants and to show them the spot of urine near my fly."

"I remember being held very often as a youngster. But as I reached age five or six, it was expected that I played 'boy' games and would not be cuddled nearly as often. I definitely remember being spanked."

"My dad was not physically affectionate, though my mom was. Dad was very severe concerning discipline. The Black Belt loomed in our minds like the Rack in the Inquisition. And he applied psychology that he learned in the military. He would draw back for the first lick, then not deliver. He would repeat that until we were almost relieved to get hit. I don't bear him any ill will over it (I usually had the spankings coming), but I am unable to tell him I love him. I do him favors and give him stuff, but I'll never be able to say the words."

Some men mentioned wanting more affection:

"I think that the reason I value physical affection so much is that during my childhood I didn't have much of it and my relationships with my parents were unpredictable and insecure. I always felt that my father wanted me continually to prove my feelings and loyalty, but I felt that I couldn't rely on my parents to come through for me. I think that I learned early that boys don't show affection and hence stopped being affectionate with my mother also at an early age. Now I see physical affection as a sign of assurance, trust, etc.— the opposite of unreliability. But I feel uncomfortable with it, I'm afraid to reach out and give it—I think it looks inappropriate, too feminine, silly, Maybe this is why I don't connect sex with feelings much—it seems too nerve-wracking and I don't feel comfortable with it."

"In childhood—prepuberty—I always wanted more physical contact than I got: hugging, snuggling, and other kinds of affection. But our family was not very demonstrative, and as I got older, I asked for less."

"I remember my mother always holding my hand or being in her arms. This gave me a strong sense of security. After she died, I tried to be held by my father but a complete sense of apathy was developed by him."

Only a few men mentioned remembering—or assumed that they had had—affectionate physical closeness with their fathers as very young children or babies:

"My father hugged me. My grandfathers hugged me."

"I was cuddled by my father as a baby."

"My father held my hand as a child and did all the things most fathers do for their male offspring."

"I guess my father carried me, and kissed me good night when I was a baby. But I don't remember it."

"I have few memories of physical closeness with my parents, but I remember my mother would bathe me, and my father would, when I was preschool age, teasingly cover my head with his jacket while holding me."

"I remember being tucked in. My daddy did it a lot."

A few mentioned that even though their fathers were not affectionate, their grandfathers had been:

"My grandfather and I used to play silly hand games together and recite funny rhymes. I liked him a lot."

"I remember being cuddled by my grandfather, who had a hard beard that I felt in my face."

Some men developed somewhat closer relationships with their fathers after they grew up:

"I am close to my father now by doing things with him, going to sports activities, doing yard work together, sitting down and talking about problems at school, work, or whatever exists. He is the finest man I have ever known. I don't think I could be as lucky. In my opinion he has never, never done a wrong thing in his life. He doesn't smoke or drink and carries out his Christian life to the fullest and is a great example to others. I used to have problems talking to him because I was scared of him but now I'm more close to him and can tell him just about anything. When I was younger we were not as close as now. He was a strict disciplinarian, since he is a teacher, and I have always tried to stay out of trouble not to disappoint him. We were not that physically close in my younger days, but I was real close in affection to my mother."

"I respect my father greatly, but I would not consider us to be exceptionally close. We have, I think, a mutual admiration for each other, but we don't have very many common interests. I enjoy athletics, and have throughout my youth. My father, on the other hand, does not. While I was growing up, I don't think this lack of common interests bothered me, at least not consciously. As I grow older, I have come to appreciate some of the areas he enjoys more, such as reading, raising plants, and listening to classical music. As to whether I can talk to him, I would have to answer no. He is the product of a large, rural, and impoverished family. He is very conscious of practicality, which prompts him to view many of my activities (going to Florida with a group of friends, taking a date to expensive places, going water skiing or canoeing), if I do them too often, as extravagant and unnecessary. On the other hand, while my father is generally more conservative than I am, I feel this characteristic in him has greatly *helped* me by enabling me to reassess my priorities and often put them into a better perspective. In other words, I don't resent my father's seemingly inhibiting attitude as much as I used to, and I have come to see the benefit such an attitude has afforded me."

"I am now fairly close to my father, but I did not like him growing up. I do not see him often, but we get along superbly and closely when we do have an opportunity to get together. We talk, communicate well. My dad is one of the finest people I have ever met."

"I was close to my father only for a short period when I was about eighteen. Till then his attitude towards me was very autocratic and even tyrannical, I think even distant. I respected him, but mostly I was afraid of him, of his outbursts. Then he approached me and I realized that under the toughness there was a much more gentle and sensitive person; the fear was gone but respect stayed. Later our relationship turned into a more friendly one until the years passed and old age and senility made him more dependent on my presence near him, which in a way turned me off, but, out of respect, I comply."

"My father died last Thanksgiving (1978). I wasn't very close to him until about a month before he died. What happened then was that he and I and his wife of about six months got together and talked at a bar. I had promised myself that I would be completely honest with him the next time we met and that next time happened to be the first time that I met his new wife and the last time that I saw him alive. That night he got kinda loaded on rum and Cokes and laughed a lot but was very nervous inside, he wanted to love me, to reach out, talk to me as a friend, the friends that we never were, but he like me was afraid. I finally broke the first barrier that night and he responded with a note in the mail (*that* he never did before) that said that he had had a good time bouncing ideas back and forth with me and hoped we would do so again. Two weeks later I got a call that my father was in the hospital with pneumonia, and later that night he died. I felt like a huge door had opened in me and a cold wind was blowing through me. I miss my father greatly. I really wanted to get to know him."

A few men said they had always had a close relationship with their fathers:

"I am very close to my father. I still live at home and plan to until I can complete my B.S. degree. We live on a farm, so there is much time spent in working outside and many chances to talk. My father and I have always been very close. When I was younger my father became involved in virtually all of the things I was interested in, Boy Scouting, school, hobbies. My father is very supportive.

"Yes, we were close. He cared for me and took time for me. I respect and admire him. He was much older than most parents."

"My father is dead now. We were very close and I was destroyed when he died of a sudden heart attack. We were both lieutenants in the Army, went to similar colleges, played baseball, and liked the same authors. His only fault was a quick temper. I have tried to take over his role in the family."

"We have many similar interests and mutual love and respect. He is a quiet, hard-working man, who never forced his way of thinking on me. He is a tremendous help to me."

"Although his father was of the school that taught men to hide emotion, my father to his credit always encouraged me to express emotions, and always talked to me and encouraged me to talk to him. We were very close."

"We are physically far apart (two hundred fifty miles), as well as emotionally and intellectually distant. We very rarely do anything together. But we are close. I guess the key to our closeness is, and always has been, our mutual support and honesty. We can talk about anything and there are no judgments, just real concern and support. For example, during Vietnam I was a resister for a time. He disapproved, hated what I was doing, but was there to share my torment—to hold me when I cried, to give me emotional, monetary, and any other support he could. He has also been very helpful in giving me a model of a man who was very masculine (he is a construction worker), but could still be gentle. I recently had a problem with one of my lovers, and while he wouldn't pry, he was willing to talk with me when I was ready, and was very supportive."

But one man probably articulated what many men miss—and long for—when he said:

"I think a relationship between a father and son is one of the most, if not *the* most important in society today. Yet it is probably the most troubled. If only I had a warm, loving, physically affectionate man for a father. A father-son relationship must not be fraught with hatred and a tense tyrant-subject relationship—it cannot work that way; it will ultimately destroy one or the other or both. It must be a wide-open relationship in which a man will give of himself and of all his love so that his son will become the man he wants to become. The father should not be afraid to touch and cuddle his son. His son needs it. Also a father and son should be able to express anger to one another freely as well as love. And either should be able to say anything freely."

And two men voiced the anger many must feel:

"I still have a lot of anger towards my father. He never approved of my career choice or seemed proud of me for what I am. When I got accepted to the most prestigious graduate program in the country he said, seriously, 'You're not going, are you?' I think he always tried to break me down, break my idealism, and get me to accept reality—like money, responsibility, mortgages, and family life. I've had lots of dreams where I scream and yell at my father and tell him I hate him, why did he do this to me. But I feel extremely guilty for harboring this anger towards him, because he was, after all, always supporting the lot of us without complaint—he always did his duty. But he didn't really know who any of us were—myself, my brothers and sisters, or my mother. Weird."

"My father and I still have no relationship, because of all the years I was growing up when I never really had a father—he was always working, even until late at night and on weekends. I almost never saw him. But I sometimes feel guilty for not accepting the psychological realities of why he did what he did, after all, he provided us with all the material benefits we could possibly want. I wonder if I shouldn't feel more for my father than I do—I don't feel much, except anger."

Did most men find the close relationship they had missed with their fathers with a male friend?

FRIENDSHIPS BETWEEN MEN

"Describe your best male friend. What do you like about him?" "Describe the man you are/were closest to in your life. In what ways are/were you close?"

Many men did not currently have a "best friend"; in fact, most men said that if they had had such a friendship, it had been only during school years and that now they and their friend were no longer close:

"I did have a best friend in college. We were very close—worked together on part-time jobs, did our studying together, went out on dates together, and he was best man at my wedding. But due to a difference in geography, our friendship dwindled to nil."

"I was closest to a friend who I grew up with. We've known each other since we were five and roomed together in college. We did all kinds of crazy things together. I liked him very much. We're not as close now because our lives have grown in such different directions."

"My best friend both in and past college was someone I could talk to, sincere, happy, who accepted me without questions and I him. With him I shared my innermost thoughts and dreams (before I met my wife)."

"Best was a friend from junior high school on through college days. I felt we could talk about any topic. I had a similar friend in college. I feel that I could still be comfortable talking with them today although I haven't seen them in ten years."

"My best friend was in college, he was an adventurer, 'let's try anything' type. Fun-loving. We spent much time together. I think he was instrumental in expanding my world. He's dead now."

"The man that has been closest to me in my life was a high school buddy. We did everything together, double-dated, played sports, everything. I could talk to him very easily. We met in junior high school although we didn't start hanging around together until high school. We helped each other through crises, which were mostly girl problems, but there were others too, like family problems and problems in school. We each knew a lot about the other's personal life. I haven't seen him in a long time."

"I had one. I loved him very much."

"My best male friend (and the man I've been closest to) is a college buddy who provided me with an outlet for all my feelings that had been bottled up inside me for my whole life. I talked to him about my fears, phobias, and insecurities. He told me it was O.K. He still remained my friend even though he saw the broken bones of my 'skeleton in the closet.' I loved him for accepting the 'whole me.' I loved him for not shaking his head in pity. I respected him. He helped to show me the way. He set an example for me—something my father was unable or unwilling to do. Now I'm out of school and haven't seen him for years, but I still feel his presence and I hope that one day I can be as good a friend to him as he was to me."

"The closest boy I was with in my life was in grade school. We played together in all kinds of games. We challenged each other. There seemed to be a close tie of love. He was always a little bit more physically adept than I was, but I always came close to matching him. He was athletic but he had a strong overbearing temper. When I got hurt one time he was so mad because someone had thrown a rock at my face, he was crying also. That really meant a lot to me. We spent time practicing pitching and playing baseball, etc. He helped me to enjoy life more by his challenges and playing around. Somehow, over the years we drifted apart, but I always feel close to him in my heart."

Some others mentioned men in their family with whom they were close:

"My three brothers seem to give me a powerful base emotionally."

"The man I am closest to now is my brother although we live far apart. We keep contact by phone or mail and I believe it is a fine relationship because we are completely honest with one another."

"My grandfather. I looked up to him and whatever we did, we did together. He made me feel like I was important."

"That would have to be my brothers. We grew up together. We enjoyed communion and found support in each other. They can't be replaced—we're of the same kind. We won't talk much, we just know how we feel."

But many men did not have, and had never had, a best friend:

"I do not have a best male friend. There is no particular man that I feel close to. I have never talked to any male (other than a brief encounter with a professional counselor) about intimacies of my married life, or otherwise."

Of men who did have a best friend, most described their friend as being very much like them:

"My best male friend is very much like me. Politically active, slow to anger, reflective, very aware of who he is, what he wants to do with himself, not macho, etc. Aside from the fact that we have a similar world view my favorite thing about him is his straightforwardness. We communicate very clearly with each other. No double messages, quick understanding (almost intuitive) of what the other is thinking or trying to say."

"My best friends are fun to be with. We think along the same lines and are compatible. We like doing the same things."

"He is kind of like me. We have common hobby-interests —he is of a similar temperament of calmness and non-excitability as me."

"He genuinely likes me. We've been friends for many years. He's very warm and kind to everybody, including his lovely wife and kids. We have a lot of the same interests, including sports and music. We can talk 'shop' very productively, since he is a banker and I am a financial lawyer."

"He has been a friend for twenty-eight years. He's my age—we like the same things and our families have been close. If I need something he's there."

"My best male friend is a lot like me: quiet, reserved, good sense of humor, a little crazy, conservative, friendly, sensitive, sympathetic. Our reactions and views are quite similar, and we enjoy doing things we both like together, like hunting and fishing."

Many others said their friend had the characteristic of being rather "crazy," wild, or free:*

"I had a friend in school. I liked him, we enjoyed getting drunk together. I thought he was funny, humorous. I liked his brashness and open friendliness."

"He didn't have to go with the crowd. We had our own private craziness."

"He is the true independent. If everyone was as free and creative as him the world would be chaotic. He isn't a macho man and some may even think him unmasculine, but in my opinion he's as much a man as anyone else you could show me."

"Probably one of the few really close friends I have is from high school. He is a very crazy, passionate, self-destruct, anarchist-artist. What I really like about him is his emotions— his tremendous impetus for living dangerously, totally—as honestly as possible."

* Do men's roles in later life become so fixed that this "freedom" or "wildness" is no longer present, and does this inhibit friendships from developing?

"At the present time the man I'm closest to is about seven years my junior. He is very much interested in the same type of church and societal reforms as I am, and we often discuss these issues. We also discuss our children and family, and our responsibility as parents. We enjoy the advice we provide each other, as we benefit from different backgrounds and experiences each of us has had. My friend is somewhat brash and sometimes gets himself into hot water because of it. He has a bit of a know-it-all attitude, but because he has a lot of insight and understanding, people appreciate him. Intimate details about our marriage or personal life we have not really shared except for those that don't pertain to sex. I wonder if this will ever occur."

Some friendships were based on admiration:

"He has 'manly' characteristics that I lack and appreciate in him. We've worked, lived, and dated together for many years. He likes things about me that he lacks. We are complementary."

"He is handsome, athletic, and well-liked. His attribute I like best is difficult for me to define and I've always wondered why. Possibly I like him because I feel if I were a girl, he would be who I'd want. Also, our social interests are very much alike."

"My best male friend is a senior here. I have known him now for over a year. He has style. That is probably the first thing, that he is (or at least seems) tremendously cool, confident, and intelligent. I can do things with him and confide in him. He can keep a secret and he can give me advice. Also he is taller and thinner than I am, and though he is not very good-looking, he has the body I would have liked to have had."

One man described his friendship like this:

"He went through college with me, we met early in high school in a fraternity. We are close in that we confide in each other in matters pertaining to family, social, economic, and sexual matters. We are both very devout heterosexuals but are nonetheless very able to relate to each other's lives. He is presently a law student. I helped him through a difficult period of his life. He could not seem to meet any eligible woman. My girlfriend and I arranged for interesting dates and even put one girl up to letting him seduce her so as to avoid the breakdown he seemed to be headed for. Results were successful and he has regained his 'prowess,' so to speak."

Only a few men mentioned being able to talk intimately with their best friend as one of the important parts of their friendship:

"My best friend is very friendly, talkative, interesting, and actively involved in different things. Something new is always happening with him. Mostly we talk, we can talk to each other. We met in seventh grade. To a limited extent, we help each other through crises by reassuring each other through talking."

"He's twenty-one, white, male, artistic, reasonable, attractive. We share many interests as well as a refined sense of humor, and we go back a ways (six years). We like to get high and listen to or play music together (classical guitar duets). I find that I can talk to him about many things, the exception being the subject of sentiment toward girls. I think he has been victimized by the male 'club' in that he comes across as believing that sex is everything (sometimes). This is unfortunate, for we agree on almost everything else."

"My close male friend is a person who is straight and accepting of me, who will talk with me about anything that is of concern to him and who will listen to me. We share similar interests in terms of music, philosophy, aspirations, friendships, etc. I like him because I sense he likes me."

"He's a good listener, likes to talk about emotions, and tries to understand me and my emotions. He sees my sharing of painful situations as strong, not weak. He's gentle, kind, aware, and has thought about his own actions and motives."

"My best male friend is highly intelligent, a fellow professional with a great sense of humor. We have been good friends for about thirty years but don't see much of each other because he lives in another city. When we get together we talk shop and about everything else. I have helped him a few times through very serious life and marital crises that he had, and he knows intimate details about my marital and personal life.

A few men described very close relationships:

"My best male friend is quite intelligent, has a lot of common sense, and the best part is his honesty and openness. We are able to talk about anything under the sun without embarrassing one another. We have discussed our own masturbatory practices in great length as well as sex with females. He helped me through a divorce which was very hard on me. Another thing I like about him is that he will give me a straight truthful answer even if it means hurting me. He won't snowball the situation. We have hugged each other on numerous occasions and lightly kissed each other on the cheek to express love for one another. We have never had sexual relations with each other and have no particular desire, despite our liberal points of view on homosexuality."

"The man I am closest to is my best friend. He got me through several very serious situations and I helped him in several others. We have a great investment of ourselves in each other. He has been both father and brother to me. I know he loves me deeply. We were college roommates. We don't live near each other and I miss him deeply. When we visit each other or talk on the phone it is as though we have never been apart. I trust him completely with all my feelings. I love him."

Many men said their ability to be close is cut short by fear of "homosexual" feelings:

"In high school and college when our friendships got too close, it was uncomfortable. We did not know how to deal with our feelings, so we let the friendship go. The taboo or fear must still be with me, because from time to time I have been attracted to a good-looking man and the feeling terrifies me. I want to get past that because until I do I may not be able to develop any close male friendships."

"I had two or three close friends in school. I have only maintained a relationship with one. As I think back, we were almost inseparable, but on reflection the closeness became uncomfortable and so we pulled apart. That is sad. There are very few acceptable role models for male friendship in our society. I think we were all afraid of seeming to be gay."

"I wonder if I am in as small a minority as I seem to be in being able to rationally deal with two men having a superb relationship. Men are just so uptight about their bodies and out of touch with their emotions and so incredibly afraid (bring out the cross and silver spike) of homosexuality. I must admit I'm uncomfortable myself about it—strange for someone who thought he was one for a few years—but I am. It's a big stumbling block in male relationships. If we could

open up to ourselves and each other, I think we'd understand
and appreciate women much better."

One very unusual reply was received from a young man currently in college:

"I am twenty, a college junior, from a moderately
wealthy suburban background. Am I in love? Ha—I think so.
Let's just say I have a fascinating and open, affectionate relationship. But nonsexual, we're both men. It feels great—God,
we get along so well and there's no 'feeling bound' and no
sexual side to deal with (except for initially having to talk out
physical rights and limits). The relationship is definitely
heavier on my side, because he's very slow to warm up to people, but it doesn't cause us unsolvable problems. I would like
us to remain in close proximity to each other for years and
years—or until we grow out of it (which could take a lifetime). The best thing about this friendship is that it provides
80 to 90 percent of what I need emotionally, and about half
of what I need physically (touching, hugging—he's still hung
up on kissing, though. Oh well). I 'clicked' loud and clear
the first time I *saw* my best friend."

*But when asked, "Do you value your male friends? Is it important to have male friends or relatives you are close to?
What do you value about their friendship? What do they
mean in your life?" most men answered yes, they do value
their male friends. However, the reasons they gave were
rather brief, emphasizing feelings of solidarity and reliability
based on common interests, companionship, and "being
there"—and often negative feelings toward women—rather
than a desire to explore each other verbally, psychologically,
or emotionally:*

"I like their humanity, and sense of community. They
mean fellowship and communion to me."

"I value men's friendship because they are more even-tempered than women."

"I like their loyalty, and similar interest in sports and
work."

"I learn about myself by having male friends."

"Men can be related to in a way women cannot be."

"Men are strong and self-reliant and they don't have the
petty traits that I often perceive in women."

"I like their sense of humor and comradeship—which I must say seems to be lacking in the great majority of women."

"I like masculine companionship. I like a night out with the boys, getting drunk and talking about sports."

"I like the no-holds-barred competition they provide."

"You can share things with someone who is male like yourself. We get together in a sports club I belong to where we raise money for a sports camp for kids. We drink a little, talk a little about everything."

Similar feelings were expressed in answer to "Do you belong to, or socialize with, a group of men? What do you enjoy/like about it? What do you do? What do you talk about?":

"I socialize in various ways with men. One of them is sports—I enjoy the exercise, dislike the competition. As to poker, which I play, I enjoy the game and the jolly atmosphere, but again dislike the competition. I go to the dinner meetings at the Optimist Club. I enjoy the chitchat, but feel ill at ease at times. Talk in all these settings is about things rather than us as people. Superficial."

"I see fellow craftsmen and fellow businessmen. We talk about sex, among other things. I enjoy their fellowship. The sex-in-common thing is important."

"I socialize with my neighbors (I live in a rural community). I like the shared activities, like hunting, fishing, and getting high. I dislike the superficiality and indirect methods of gaining support and human warmth. We talk about things external of the soul."

"Men I work with. We discuss politics, sports, and theater. Nothing personal."

"Nothing formal. I hang out (drink and chase women) with a few close friends from work, either on lunch hours or after work."

"Well, I socialize with other men—if that's what it's called to sit around and get wrecked all the time."

Other men felt uncomfortable with men in groups because of the kind of male group bonding that often takes place:

"Men together are always trying to be macho and talk about their exploits with women, and how many women they have fucked, and then they expect you to share similar stories with them. Of course, the most self-effacing thing a man can do is to admit ignorance or confusion about sex with women to a group of men. The macho thing to do is to talk about how many women you have picked up and fucked from your local bar, and whether or not she was a great fuck (meaning she did it your way), or whether she was a weirdo in bed (had her own ideas about what pleases *her*)."

Men's friendships were often relatively nonverbal. Although most men enjoyed talking to each other about more general topics, such as business, sports, or politics, they almost never discussed personal problems or feelings:

"My best friend is honest and trustworthy. We talk on many things but he doesn't know the details of my personal life, neither do I his."

"In some ways it's easier to talk to other men because there is no sexual tension, but I really haven't found a man who was good to talk to for me about things that really bother me, because men don't want to appear unmanly to each other by discussing feelings. It's an unspoken code of behavior among men not to show that feelings are bothering you."

"My brother is my best male friend. He is fun to do things with and I love him, but he doesn't know the details of my personal life, and I don't know about his. He has helped me through lots of crises by being a friend, by showing support, by calling me up, visiting me (I live 2,000 miles away), and by cheering me up by making me feel I always have a friend. He never talks to me about my personal problems or helps me solve them, he is just there."

"I have one really good male friend that I've known for ten years. We enjoy doing stuff together, but there are many things it's awkward to talk about with him. There's always a reserve between us."

"Conversations with men usually involve work, politics, economy, or religion—nothing personal."

"We can talk of politics and history, of geography and science, but not of personal relationships."

"I like the chance to talk about things such as hunting, dogs, fishing, sports, work, politics, without some woman complaining about herself or others."

"If I'm building or working on my car, etc., it is very easy to talk to men. But I have generally found it difficult to talk about feelings and problems with other men. I don't know why. Do I see them as somehow 'threatening'? Am I afraid they will belittle me and my 'softness'? I am really curious to see what other men say about this. Do they want to talk, but can't either?"

Especially, men's feelings of closeness and affection for each other were almost never verbalized:

"The closest I have ever felt to another man was at a New Year's Eve party. It was twelve o'clock and I shook the hand of one of my best friends. Then he gave me a big warm hug and I hugged him back. I could feel the brotherly love go between us. I wanted to cry but held it back."

"When my brother came to visit me (we hadn't seen each other for four years, although we were very close when we were growing up), we had a real good time, just like we had never been apart. When it came time to go, I took him to the airport. He never said if he had a good time, and I never said I was sorry to see him go we just said, 'See ya,' and left it at that. It's probably better that way. But I felt really sad to see him go. We never hugged in my family, so we didn't then either. I felt real lonely watching him walk away."

"There's a fellow in my office that I like a lot. I respect his work, and we seem to have a mutual understanding. He has just had a family, like I do (one daughter, one and a half years old), and he comes from a similar background (including the same university). I guess we are friends, although we never go anywhere outside the office together, and of course we have never discussed it. The only conversation we have is about work we are doing together, and a 'how are you today?' kind of thing. But I feel very close to him, and would go quite a bit out of my way to help him, should he ever need it."

But a few men did enjoy talking more deeply with friends:

"I enjoy sharing good news with my friends and they are really supportive when I have 'down' days. I am very open with my friends in telling them how I feel about them, both positive and negative. It's difficult sometimes when I'm angry with a friend to tell them but I feel better about it because I believe that friends can accept your honest feelings without getting too upset."

"One of my most valuable experiences in the past year was a men's group. Several of us who were already friends got together every two or three weeks to talk about common feelings, problems, etc. At first we talked about what prevented warmer relationships among men. Then we moved into our histories and patterns of relationships with women. As the meetings went on, we became aware that there was a dynamic of both warmth and competitiveness operating among us. So we talked out our feelings towards one another and tried to become more conscious of how we relate to men. It was a wonderful experience and opened up new possibilities for all of this is our masculine relationships. We discovered both how difficult and how rewarding it is to be vulnerable with another man."

On the other hand, feelings could be expressed or covered over by rough or combative contact—mock fighting or teasing—so as to avoid any connotation of affection or physical attraction:

"I was in the bar with this guy, and I guess he felt I wasn't part of the group because I wasn't drinking, so he started teasing me and taunting me to get me to do it, and then he said I had to drink with them—why couldn't I just have one drink with everyone—and he got me in a head lock and pushed the glass up to my mouth, and then he pushed my fingers in his drink, and sucked them, and then he said, 'Come on, just lick the inside of my glass, and I'll drink it—spit in my glass—I'll drink it. If you think that's gross you haven't seen anything—I've eaten another guy's puke in the Navy we were so drunk,' I got the sense of it being a big moment of camaraderie, that I would be accepted by him and the group if I would have done it. But I didn't do it, because I thought it was stupid, and I hate being forced to do things. Then everybody started playing pool."

"I may hit another man in the arm, I think that's a sign of affection."

"I have a really good friend I play soccer with every week. Now, I like him, and maybe he's even my 'best friend.' But I sure as hell wouldn't throw my arms around him and kiss him! As long as I pick him up for soccer every week, and try hard to beat his ass, he knows I like him—I don't have to slobber all over him like a girl."

Sometimes communication between men in groups took the form of a physical and/or psychological challenge of an individual by the group, or "teasing":

"A friend of mine in a fraternity told me about the initiation of greasing the fellows in his group. They would wrestle the person down, pull his pants down, and wipe grease up his ass. And they would torture him all the more if he stopped fighting back. The stronger he was, the more respect he got."

"It seems like some men don't understand the fact that I want to be alone a lot of the time, or that I want to be self-sufficient and emotionally free from the group. They seem to have a belief in the male group as a supportive thing to their behavior, and feel more confident as part of the group. They don't want to be different. This is especially true of men who have been in the service, it seems like. Maybe they go through initiations where they learn to accept the idea that the group is more important than they are as individuals. For example, my friend who was a marine told me that you have to conform and obey the rules of being a marine, or else get beat up every day until you understand that you can't rebel against this idea. He said that they beat the shit out of him every day for a while, really violently, so as to make him a tough but loyal marine, afraid to be rebellious against the group. Being a man, they say, is what being a marine is all about—to be macho and unflinching, and able to kill the enemy without feeling anything. He learned how to do it, but he says he always worries if he will be tough enough next time."

Another important nonverbal form of socializing between men is drinking together:

"I had just broken up with my girlfriend. I called up a friend and said, 'Let's go out and get stoned.' We went to a bar and drank until we were falling off our chairs. He never asked me anything, that's why I like to go drinking with him. I felt better."

"To be accepted by certain groups of men (like other salesmen), it seems like you have to get really drunk together to the point of getting sick—like going through similar painful experiences gives you a common bond."

Still, these male friendships—although not verbally or affectionately intimate in the ways relationships with women could sometimes be—were extremely important to most men. Only a few men said they didn't care about having male friends:

"I got left out as a kid. I don't really care about friendships with men."

At the same time, very few men mentioned wanting different or closer relationships with men:

"I have a very large number of male friends, but none that I can really get past discussing sports with. I wish I had a male friend with similar interests I could confide in—one I could be close to and tell how I feel about things, and also my problems with my wife, and hear his frustrations—or at least mine, I don't know if he has any."

"I have never been good at sports and have avoided them. This has tended to isolate me from other men. I socialize with very few men. I wish I knew more men to talk to. As I grow older I am really desiring more male friends but I find it very difficult to talk with men. We are all very guarded. I think we may need male friends to understand ourselves."

And very few men complained about the quality of their male friendships:

"I did have a very close friend—very brother-like feelings. But it was ultimately a superficial relationship."

"Who can say if we are close? He is in pursuit of a female lover and that comes first."

"Knowing other men, it seems to me, is important for self-knowledge, esteem, understanding of similar problems, etc. But I can't find any men here who want to have friendships other than bowling or a beer, or at least I haven't found them yet. I have just been transferred to a new town by my job."

"My best male friend is my age; we've known one another for seven years. Similar background, not so similar interests. He and I have gotten along together due to complementing personalities and sense of humor. But I've always felt a bit removed from him, as if we never truly understood one another. Prototypical drinking buddy, only rarely do we discuss personal matters, but we *do* a lot together. It's not as warm a bond as several of my female friendships. The emotional sides of our personalities are seldom revealed or experienced."

"I have some good male friends, but it's really almost impossible to discuss anything meaningful with them, other than sports or work. If we do talk about anything personal, like sex, it's in a very superficial way. I try to draw out more from them by going into problems my wife and I have had in marriage, or fantasies I have, but they look at me like I was nuts. You *can't* break the ice. I have a friend who's had a vasectomy and I'm very curious about it, but all he'll ever talk about is the clinical operation itself—nothing about the effect it had on his head or his psychological approach to sexual activity. Men never have any intimacy with one another."

"I have no truly close male friendships, and I think the fault is mine. I seem to feel too competitive with men to allow any positive feelings to surface. If they are more attractive than I, physically, then I mentally check out their income or intelligence, or 'station in life,' or the relative attractiveness of the women we are respectively associated with, or our 'power' or influence in the group we are in, or some such B.S. as that—if I 'win' this ridiculous comparison, I feel contempt; if I 'lose,' I hurriedly 'change the subject.' How dumb. I wonder if other people—both men and women—do something like this too."

PHYSICAL AFFECTION BETWEEN MALE FRIENDS

"I do not recall any physical contact with a male in my life other than shaking hands occasionally when meeting someone socially or in business."

Can friends touch? A question which caused a strong reaction was "Do you embrace or kiss men in friendship?" Most men were very wary or afraid of affectionate physical contact with other men—even if it was only friendly contact with a good friend. Expressing affection through physical contact seemed permissible only in the context of "sex" with a woman, and even then some men were uncomfortable with it. Surprisingly, even some men who related sexually to other men also felt uncomfortable with simple affectionate contact with male friends, or even their lovers.

"Do you embrace or kiss men in friendship? Do you enjoy kissing or embracing men?"

MEN WITH HETEROSEXUAL EXPERIENCE

The overwhelming answer to both of these questions was "No!":

"Absolutely not. I never tried it and never want to."

"I can't bear any kind of physical intimacy with a man beyond just shaking hands, and *that* feels clammy enough to me."

"I may be the victim of hang-ups, but I really cannot stand even being *touched* by another male (except for an occasional handshake)."

"I only embrace my father and I don't really like it."

"I prefer not to be touched by another man at all except for handshaking on appropriate occasions. I do not consider this aversion to being touched by men as any sort of latent fear of, or defense against, potential homosexuality on my part. Having lived much of my life in exclusively male company (having been a professional soldier with considerable field and combat experience), I have never felt even the slightest desire to have another man assist me to achieve orgasm in any way—even though we all were undergoing prolonged sexual deprivation. If I simply *had* to get orgasmic gratification, I masturbated. I don't believe I am capable of being physically affectionate with a man."

"I never kiss men. I shake hands. I may grab their shoulders or arms."

"Whatever affection I have towards a man is purely on a mental level."

"I really don't feel comfortable hugging or being hugged by other men. I guess I've been conditioned to feel that way, but there it is."

"Any guy tries to kiss me and I'll bite his tongue off."

Some emphasized that a "real man" wouldn't need affection:

"A real man doesn't need embracing and affection—just sex from *women* (females)."

"I have absolutely no desire to and have never fantasized about kissing another man. It just never turned me on. I used to get into a hugging thing with a close friend but we realized it was a security thing for me, so we quit. I guess part of being a man is being able to be independent, able to stand on my own two feet, the ability to survive. I'm proud that I don't have to be dependent on another person, that I *can* stand on my own two feet."

Several men answered the question by emphasizing that they would kiss only women and girls:

"I only kiss women and little girls. Handshaking is for men. I enjoy men for sports and rapping."

"If I want to caress a man, I could always caress myself. I'm just not intrigued by the male body: women are the great mystery."

"Every touch of grace, beauty, and tenderness in my life has come from women. I've never kissed a man and feel no desire to do so. As a child, being hugged and kissed by male relatives embarrassed me. (Although I remember when I was maybe five or six, I felt protected and comforted when a grandpa I loved hugged me.) I am wary of and uptight about physical affection with men."

"I don't like to get physical with men. I'm very physically affectionate with women only."

On the other hand, given the choice, most men said that embracing is more acceptable than kissing, and a few men did sometimes embrace other men:

"I have certain friends with whom I hug when we meet or on specially moving occasions—maybe after a really nice church service when spirits are high and a feeling of closeness is present. I have never kissed a man except my father when I was a little kid."

"I embrace a man in friendship but usually only if it's a relative and I haven't seen him for a while. It is just unacceptable for two men to kiss and they would only be thought of as queers. But in the Arab world it is quite common and acceptable for men to hug, kiss, embrace, and walk arm and arm with each other. These men are not thought of as queer. So in the States, where everything is so much more civilized, it's taboo. You explain it to me!"

"It's a custom in South America called *un grand abrazo.*"

"I've never kissed a man. Embracing is nice, but embarrassing. I like it but I feel anxious at the same time. I've let a homosexual man move up close to me and touch my arm without running away."

"I enjoy body contact while working, moving furniture,

ladders. I like to feel my strength combined with others' strength—like pushing a car or lifting a long tree trunk with several men. It isn't sexual though, I don't think. I like to hug friends sometimes, or dance with men friends."

"I've never done any serious kissing with a man, but hugging generates warmth or friendship or sympathy and consolations and seems to feel comfortable and kind of rewarding with anyone—man, woman, or child. Even animals get hugs."

Most men were startled, even horrified, by the idea of kissing another man:

"You have to be kidding on this question. To kiss a man on the lips is much too sensual."

"Kissing a man would be like kissing a raw chunk of meat."

"This is America not France."

"I abhor the sight of men kissing or embracing."

"It is not normal to kiss men."

"I couldn't kiss a man because the kiss is a foreplay for me to get ready to fuck."

"I have kissed a man in friendship one time as a joke. It had the desired effect. It mortified him."

But a few were open to the idea (these answers continue to be from men with a heterosexual orientation):

"I have never kissed a man but I wouldn't hesitate to. It's just that it's a taboo in society."

"I could possibly kiss a friend on the lips. It would make me feel very feminine."

"I would find no difficulty in kissing a man if it were not for the massively structured societal disapproval."

"I kissed my father on the lips all his life, and do so now with my thirty-five-year-old son, did same when receiving military decoration from Russian officers in 1945, but in our present society I would expect it to be taken as a homosexual approach, unless done in an encounter group. I do like hugging other men, slapping them on the back, shoulder, or thigh, but I am willing to observe current mores."

"There are certain guys I know whom I *think* I would enjoy kissing."

"I embrace several of my male friends regularly, but only

two have ever felt comfortable about kissing. One felt a little shy about it and it was more like kissing an aunt. The other gave me a good kiss."

"I'm inhibited enough not to want to, but I don't approve of the fact that I genuinely feel that way. I think it's a good idea for men to be tender and loving toward one another."

"I enjoy embracing men. I kiss only my sons, and that is a quick peck, on the mouth. I once did some 'French kissing' with a homosexual friend, both of us having beards, and it seemed very strange, but pleasant."

"I embraced men but never kissed one anywhere. I kiss my son a lot. I would be very uncomfortable kissing a man on the lips but not on the cheeks. I would have to be very close to him and know he could be trusted. I have a male friend I love dearly. I think someday we might kiss."

And a few heterosexually oriented men did enjoy affectionate physical contact with other men:

"I do find men very attractive. It's a sensual attraction to another beautiful, warm human being that I, in my adolescence, mistook for sexual attraction. I did find simple physical contact with the men very enjoyable, simply from the sensual and emotional standpoint. I don't think that I'd ever go to bed with another man, simply because it changes the relationship to an extent that can be hard to deal with, particularly in today's society. I wouldn't think of giving up physical contact with male friends though."

"A man-to-man kiss is exciting. Especially the way men French-kiss. The embrace is strong."

"I like kissing anyone. Men are no exception. I have several men friends whom I kiss on the cheeks. I have kissed a couple of gay male friends on the lips and with the tongue and found it nice, just like with a woman. I love to hug also and do as much as individuals or society will allow me. We too often relate touch with just sex. Body language is eloquent and sometimes we speak our best only by touch. Whether in joy or sadness. So I'm as physically affectionate as my culture will allow me."

"In our church we have a custom that on some occasions we kiss men as part of the kiss of fellowship. It comes out of a European church tradition. It seems to me that it's different when I kiss men because it is more a question of appreciation, while kissing a woman is more mysterious and intense."

"I like to kiss other men although I don't do it if they

seem uptight. If the other man can't even take or give an affectionate hug, then that's usually an indication that they are fearful of sharing themselves in other ways too. My father and I have always hugged and kissed each other as an expression of our love, so it was never wrong for me to do it. Open physical affection is important to me because it's such a clear way of sharing my feelings; this applies to men and women. The important feature here—and in fact, the base line of my sexual responses—is that I'm responding to *people.* The fact that some people live in men's bodies, and some people in women's bodies, isn't of paramount concern. I'm very glad that affection which used to be O.K. with women (if they chose to be affectionate) is now becoming O.K. with men too. It's nice to give a man a hug without both of you going through a crisis of sexual identity right there on the spot—or later on either."

And some men said they would like to become more demonstrative and affectionate:

"I would like to be more affectionate in a friendly, non-sexual way toward my closest male friends. Somehow, a simple handshake, no matter how firm, seems inadequate when greeting *very* close friends, especially if it's been a while since we've seen each other. I feel that this is a real hang-up and would like to get over it. This is obviously simply a result of our upbringing emphasizing that men in our society don't show much emotion or physical affection toward other men. If we do, we feel that we may be ridiculed or ostracized and thus are afraid to do so."

"I get somewhat stiff and awkward if other men come in close physical contact with me, but I am trying my damn best to change in that respect."

MEN WITH HOMOSEXUAL EXPERIENCE

How did "homosexual" (or "bisexual") men feel about embracing or kissing men in friendship? Most gay men enjoyed it:

"I love to kiss and hug in very erotic and intimate ways—even though they are just friends, and we're not going any further."

"I love to kiss and embrace men. Often I feel it's a great release and pleasure for them and I like to help them reach it."

"I enjoy kissing and embracing men a great deal, there is something so manly about it all, it seems so right and so natural. I like to do it forcefully sometimes, and at other times, especially gently. I usually start with a big hug that forms into a full kiss, one hand behind his head and the other on his buttocks—almost a dance position."

"Hugging men, I like the firmness of their muscles that most women don't have, a kind of tightness in the limbs, the back, the chest. Most non-gay men won't let you touch them, though, whether out of fear or just social custom I don't know, but I think it's a shame."

"Embracing men is very natural with me. I embrace men I know well and have strong feelings about. If it's a non-homosexual relationship it's merely an embrace. If it's a love relationship, with sexual feelings, we place our pelvises close together. I kiss three types of men—my father, my son, and the man I love. My father I kiss on the cheek and this is the way I kiss my son. My lover on the lips and we French-kiss. That's an ugly way to describe it. Our tongues dart in and out of each other's mouth. I like to be that close with a man's face. It's an interesting and comforting feeling."

"I embrace men and kiss them in friendship, but let heterosexual men make the first move, since they're such big fools about how much such innocent activities are supposed to affect their 'masculinity.' "

But even some "homosexual" men did not like kissing or even embracing men under any circumstances:

"One of the deepest troubling aspects of my emotional life is my coldness to other men. I would rather suck a friend off than hug and kiss him and even when I want to kiss him or hug him I always freeze no matter how welcome the response. I always feel a deep sadness when I read of cultures where men walk hand in hand or have passionate friendships."

"Although I will suck a man's cock, fuck his ass or in reverse, I detest kissing a man—sexually, that is. I would not think twice about kissing a man, father, brother, etc., on the cheek, but kissing a man sexually seems too faggish. I don't remember hugging either, although a certain amount is involved while fucking another man—that's part of it and it's exciting to feel his body next to mine."

"I would not kiss another man—except on his penis. I do not hug a man during sex with him, nor at any time."

Conclusion

The point of this section has not been to suggest that all men should become more physically affectionate with all other men. It is simply to suggest that the frozen postures which men sometimes adopt in fear of expressing the slightest feeling of physical intimacy are unnecessary and often inhibit the development of closer friendships between men.

It is hoped that the reader will not confuse what has been said here with any intention to push "instant intimacy" on people. The idea current in some quarters that all formal reserve between people is "bad" and all rapid "friendliness" and intimacy is "good" is certainly not the point of view of this book. The tendency to encourage instant intimacy on every occasion, and to consider those who do not wish to behave in this manner "unfriendly," is not a solution for our problems and often only increases alienation. We need to feel more dignity and respect from our society and those around us, not less. And yet we need to be able to touch those we like without fear.

As we have seen, our culture has a very strong taboo against affectionate male physical contact—even in slight, natural, daily ways. We have also seen how many men are afraid to touch and cuddle with their sons after the very early years, or even altogether. Beyond handshaking and some back-slapping, most of society finds male affection, or even friendly patting, shocking. Imagine two male friends walking arm in arm or holding hands. It is simply not done. In fact, men in Japan do not even shake hands on meeting: the handshake originated in the West as a gesture to show that "I bear no concealed weapons."

SEX AND PHYSICAL INTIMACY BETWEEN BOYS

Perhaps surprisingly, given most men's emphasis on maintaining physical distance from other men, many boys—most of them "heterosexual" in later life—had sex with other boys as children or teenagers. 43 percent* of those who answered had had some form of sex with another boy: most of these in mutual masturbation (not touching each other), or masturbation by one partner;† but almost half of these men (20 percent of the entire sample) had masturbated each other; about one-third also did fellatio together; and a few had had anal intercourse, being the active and/or receptive partner. There was no correlation between whether a boy had had sexual experience with other boys and whether he considered himself "homosexual" or "heterosexual" in later life. Many "homosexual" men had never had relations with other boys in youth, and many "heterosexual" men had had such relationships.

Early sexual experiences with other boys, of men who were exclusively heterosexual as adults, were surprisingly common and seem to have been, for most, a lot of fun:

"My best friend and I used to tell each other dirty stories and stimulate each other sexually when we were younger. We started doing so before we knew that society did not approve. When we found out in a fifth-grade sex education class that boys were not supposed to engage in such things, it had little effect on us because we already knew that it did us no harm. We continued these friendly sex acts until we were able to start fulfilling our sex cravings with girls. Our last experience was at

* This compares with A. Kinsey's figure of 48 percent.

† This is in striking contrast to the childhood of girls, who virtually never tell their friends about their masturbation, not to mention doing it together or showing others how they do it.

sixteen. I don't think that either of us had sex with a male again."

"I first experienced intense sensations and my first orgasm at about age thirteen. About this time also several boys and I engaged in mutual masturbation that eventually led to fellatio and anal penetration. As I remember, all I thought about was how good it felt."

"My first experiences were with other boys—we talked about sex a lot, compared organs, masturbated together, and also did have some homosexual sex play—I was jerked off by a male friend when I was thirteen and I jerked him off—we did this occasionally for about one year. At the time I thought it was fun but forbidden fun. The homosexual aspect bothered me but I didn't have the confidence to attempt sex with a girl. The thought during this homosexual play was also heterosexual—the fantasies were always heterosexual. A girl's genitals were a mystery that I very much wanted to solve and a girl's breasts were things I very much wanted to play with."

"In seventh or eighth grade, a bunch of us guys discovered masturbation and then discovered that the others had discovered it, too; we held jerk-off parties, trying to see who could come first and shoot farthest!"

"At summer camp, another boy was proud of 'beating his meat' and one night showed us his 'cream.' I remember touching his cock once, feeling slightly naughty about feeling his cream, and feeling jealous that he had a big cock and could do this trick."

"I remember my older friend's penis was beautifully built, about six and half inches long erect, and would erupt in a white, pearly spray that shot at least twelve inches in the air. It was a beautiful sight, like watching the geyser Old Faithful erupt."

"My oldest brother once had me masturbate him while he was in the tub. He was sixteen. I was eight. I thought his cock was huge and beautiful, and I enjoyed doing it."

"When I was in the sixth grade my best friend and I tried anal intercourse, after a classmate explained how he and his friend practiced for fucking a woman on each other's ass. I don't think we ever got more than the cap engulfed, but I remember it tickling something fierce."

"My first physical experience with a man was with my best friend in high school. We'd go to the state fair together and sleep in the nude. We'd slowly creep ourselves together until our hard-ons touched each other. We'd masturbate each other until orgasm. We'd do this every year, but never thought of having sex with each other at any other time. We just needed the bed environment."

"I used to suck my brother's penis when I was seven or eight. It felt natural and easy at the time."

"When I was age ten, my twenty-year-old cousin and I played around. I liked it and so did he. He called me 'Wanda'!"

"At age thirteen, I had fellatio with an older man. I kept asking myself, 'Am I gay?' I was petrified and didn't tell anyone about it."

"As boys we did masturbation and fellatio with each other. I enjoyed the sexual contact very much—did not include any kissing or embracing."

"There were three boys in my neighborhood (around 1910). We used to play cow. That is, we got on our hands and knees naked and let one milk us and feel our bag of balls just as we saw the man do when he milked the cow. We all had foreskins in those days, so the milker would slide our foreskin up and down sometimes until it got sore. We didn't come off then, we were too young. Another way was for one to lay down on his belly, and one would put his cock in the crack of his ass and rub it back and forth, spitting on it now and then. We never used the anus. We all played with our cocks twenty-four hours a day almost."

"When I was at camp when I was twelve and we were all taking showers, we started masturbating and feeling each other. Then we climbed into the steam room, where we all lay down. I was lying there when my friend jumped on me and started pumping (all the other kids were doing the same), and then I remember very vividly how he went crazy till I think he reached some sort of climax or orgasm. We did that a lot that summer. But in all that time, we never embraced or kissed. We were entirely penis-oriented."

"My first real sexual experiences were mutual masturbation sessions with other boys, individually at first, and then each in turn masturbating the other to orgasm. Going on from that to lying face to face with another boy, with our penises rubbing together to orgasm. Then one boy lying on his stomach with the one on top putting his penis between the cleft of the other's behind until it reached and touched the balls and base of the penis of the other boy, then changing places. There was never actual anal penetration. I don't think we had thought of that or we would have certainly tried. Nor was there any kind of kissing or caressing, we would have thought that most unmanly. Once a boy did take my penis in his mouth, though not to orgasm, but I couldn't bring myself to return it."

"I remember at twelve, with a boy, I sucked him by pure
nstinct. At sixteen, I 'dry-humped' someone else. It was
wicked and wonderful."

And one longer answer:

"At about the age of ten, I made friends with a boy of
ifteen who became quite friendly with me. We spent a lot of
ime together alone, and every opportunity, he exposed himself
when urinating, or just showing me his hard-on. It was twice
as big as mine, and I guess I was a little envious. He talked to
me about sex things, dogs, etc., and if I had seen them, and if
my penis got hard. One day about six months after we started
running around together, we were out at our local park. It was
a fall day, I remember, because I had a long coat on, and a
tam. He had a long coat on also, the style at the time. We were
talking sexy things, and he had his hands in his pockets. He
told me they had holes in them, and to guess what he was
doing. I said something I don't remember, and he stopped,
turned, and opened his coat. He had a royal hard-on sticking
out of his trousers. It was red from him rubbing it, and the
head was wet. I had never had anything come out of mine
yet, so I really did not understand what it was, and he said to
take it out and show it to him. I took it out, and we looked at
each other's penis for a time, as we were all by ourselves.
There were some big green park benches like they used to have
then on the edge of the ball field, and he said to come over
and sit down on them. We went over, and talked about our
penises and sex stuff. He opened his coat wide, exposing his
penis, and started masturbating. He told me to do the same.
This was the first time anything like this had happened
between us. I did like he said, as he said it would feel good.
Well, it sure did. The feeling was just starting for me when he
started coming, and I watched as the sperm shot out onto the
grass, and his hand was flying up and down to make it come
again. The sperm was white and thick over his hand and penis,
as he worked towards another one. Just about the time in my
excitement that I was coming and my little hand was flying up
and down, along came these two old ladies from behind us.
They had seen us, and came over to see what we were doing.
I quickly started to put mine away, but stopped when my
friend kept doing it, and when the old ladies exclaimed, 'My
word!' he said, 'Mind your own business!' and started coming
almost at their feet. I was so excited seeing him shooting, and
I had kept flogging mine, I started to come. It was something

I will never forget, it was great. We finished together as th
old ladies walked away in a huff babbling to each other. W
then very excitedly talked about sexy things. I still had no
ejaculated, but my friend told me I would at eleven or twelve
All we ever did after that was masturbate constantly when
ever we could, and as often as we were able, until sometime
they were sore. We did it on streetcars, doorways, cellars
church, you name it. Sex became the most important thing i
my life, and anyone who wanted to get involved with it, I wa
their boy."

*And one boy of eighteen described the sex he was havin;
with another boy, but said he wanted to have sex with girl
soon:*

"I've only had sex with myself or with my cousin (he'
two years older than me). We are both rather inhibited
neither knows if the other wants sex now, so we usually jus
pull down our pants or something else of this subtle nature t
break the ice. Then we feel each other's body for a while, til
someone gets the nerve to bring mouth and penis together
and then we take turns sucking each other off for about a
hour or two till we've both reached orgasm. We used to experi
ment a lot more a few years ago, that was sometimes rathe
fun. The whole scene is incredibly humorous, the inhibition
and all. I don't really care to change, though I'd mostly lik
to discontinue such things for now. My cousin is definitely ga
and has been trying to find a more permanent partner in hi
own line.

"I like performing fellatio a great deal (even if I don'
do it enough so my mouth gets tired quickly when I do it)
it's one of the few aspects of homosexual sex I like. I like th
sight of a saliva-wet penis, I like the taste once it's in and
like the feel in my mouth. I dislike the hair in the surroundin
area, so I don't feel like roaming away from the penis itself
Someday I'd like to get ahold of a real big cock (partly to se
if I could swallow the whole thing) but I'd much rather tr
cunnilingus even if I'm unfamiliar with it.

"I don't really like kissing a man or hugging them.
definitely prefer a woman (although I've never kissed one)
I like all kinds of kissing including French kissing and ver
gentle tender kissing. As a rule I'm not very affectionate.
would like to show affection to the right people but the righ
times haven't arisen yet. Now things like cuddling are mor
what I want than rocks-off-type sex, partly because of wha

missed when I was younger and also because it's less aggressive.

"I like things up my butt if it's not done too roughly or too often (twice a week at the most?). Fingers are nice and if applied right make me orgasm far sooner. If applied right for a long period of time, when I do cum then it's very violent. A penis is very comfortable. It's quite difficult to describe the sensations.

"In the future I would like extended periods of monogamy I could be mostly isolated with just one woman but have some time of my own, I'm too much into my own things to be totally dedicated to another person. The reason we'd have to be alone is that I'm not monogamous by nature. Casual things are better."

Most gay men's* childhood experiences had not been very different:

"The first time I had sexual physical contact with a man was in fourth or fifth grade, and it was with a kid who explained sex. We went to bed together and later I went to bed with two of his brothers. We used to sleep out in tents in the back yard and switch partners in the course of the night. Some of the kids stayed homosexual and some switched to being strictly heterosexual."

"In grade school—I was picked up by a young dude while waiting for the school bus. He asked a lot of personal questions! He finally put his hand on my leg—when I didn't pull away, he asked me if I would like to go home with him for some 'fun.' I did! We sucked each other off, masturbated—boy did I enjoy this."

"My first experience was with a kid of eighteen. I was fifteen—down by the river we were in the river naked and he was feeling my penis underwater—we climbed out and lay down beside the river. Sucking each other's cock, kissing, then we went off on each other's cock—didn't have intercourse. We didn't know if it was harmful to swallow each other's sperm at that time."

"At age fifteen, another boy said let's go in the bushes and suck cocks and we did, and later fucked. I loved him, and everything we did."

---

* Of those who had had early sexual experiences with another boy; most had not.

*But some boys had refused to have sex with other boys be
cause they didn't want to reveal how much they were a
tracted to other boys and men:*

"I have always felt more attracted to boys than to girl
In high school and junior high school, I knew I was homo
sexual (even before, really) but I was always too shy to d
anything with my friends even when they made the first over
tures. During this time, my sexual activities consisted ex
clusively of masturbation and a once-a-week evening with a
older homosexual man."

"I was not aware of any sexual feelings until sevent
grade. Although I did not discuss it with them, I was intereste
in other boys. I would have liked to have seen their genita
and to have known their sex habits. This continued throug
high school. I was GAY, although I did not then know of suc
words or had only vague conceptions of them. One of th
other students once asked me if I wanted to suck his cock.
really wanted to very much, but I suppressed such feeling
and told him 'no.' "

*And others had never even known of the possibility of a sex
ual relationship with other boys and kept their feelings an
thoughts hidden from everyone around them, feeling ver
isolated and alone:*

"My childhood sexual feelings were not directed toward
other people until I was eleven or twelve. Then I felt a grow
ing attraction to boys my own age or slightly younger—I neve
expressed or mentioned it to anyone; I largely repressed thes
feelings. Finally, midway through high school I talked (ver
generally—not personally) about homosexuality to two friend
in my class (one male, one female) and my father. They didn
say much. I was frightened about the whole subject, and di
not have my first sexual encounter with another person unt
five years after the end of high school. All through junior hig
and high school I was not aware of anyone else who was gay—
I saw my sexual feelings as a barrier between me and ever
one else—and felt completely alone with these feelings. I
my reading I would come across vague (always negative
references to homosexuality, and in my daily life away fro
my family I would hear the ordinary ugly innuendos or jok
that every kid hears. This deepened my isolation; I was ver
frightened of having any of that scorn or hatred directed
me."

"I cried a lot when I was about thirteen or fourteen because I thought I was homosexual. I thought of killing myself rather than admitting to it. I was afraid to tell anyone, and I felt very alone. I didn't know where to find anyone to talk to—this lasted until I was almost nineteen."

"I am fifty years old, 'American-born of Italian descent.' I grew up in an aggressively masculine town—a steel-milling and coal-mining town with very heavy, rigid heterosexual roles. Even at five or six, I knew that men were fascinating to me. Instinctively I knew that if I could survive my growing up I could find a more acceptable world for myself elsewhere. I kept my sexual feelings private. I used many of my school-mates as sexual objects while masturbating, but it was inconceivable that I should actually approach them on any level. When I was twelve the town dirty old man fellated me. I liked it. As far as I knew, we were the only two people in the world who ever did such things."

Some gay boys had been persecuted for their gayness:

"I grew up being called a 'fairy.' I can't remember the first time, there were so many—but I grew 'immune' to it. Until age twenty, I acted very effeminate—and the more people called me a sissy, the more I rebelled and the more outrageous I became. In high school, I had learned I was gay: hated it, flaunted it, defied it—and acted out sexually in angry, frustrating ways. I gave little care or love or gentleness to anyone, including the men I slept with. I also considered myself rather homely and had many hang-ups about my points of unattractiveness. It wasn't until much later that I began to realize how attractive I really was (during therapy), and that many of my 'deficits' were really 'benefits.' "

"In high school being gay was very difficult—as it was the 'worst' thing a man could be—'fags' weren't even men then. I was most definitely closeted in high school. When I was a junior I got very drunk and told a close friend that I had a crush on this fabulous older guy we all knew; from that point on I was not a part of that group of 'friends.' They could not accept me for what I was. Shortly after, I dropped out. This was a shattering experience."

Parents' discussions of sexuality rarely referred to homosexual sex, or if so, only in a negative context:

"My parents told me about the reproductive system and bought a book for me to read. They counseled me always to come to them and not to discuss it with other boys. They warned me about getting someone pregnant (a fear of theirs I didn't understand). But they didn't seem to be talking about what I was experiencing—that is, strong feelings of sexual attraction for other boys. Inheriting their homophobia, I desisted for many years from interpersonal sex altogether. My parents were affectionate towards me and each other, but clearly they were not able to communicate well with a child who was different in a way that they didn't have room enough to allow."

But some boys—both "gay" and "straight"—had had fulfilling and happy relationships with other boys:

"I was happy and content with my male sexual partner in high school, mainly because we entered our affair innocently and remained innocent the entire time. We had no hassles, or guilt, or competition—we didn't know there were supposed to be any."

"The happiest sex relationship I ever had was with a male friend in high school in which we read each other's needs exactly and felt free to express our needs. The sex was erotic, the sleeping together afterwards was peaceful. I felt no guilt and no anxiety and no worry about when we would ever do it again. Our level of verbal communication was very minimal."

And a few boys—both "straight" and "gay" in later life— also fell in love with each other:

"I fell the deepest in love at the age of sixteen. The person I was in love with was another boy, age eighteen. He had no idea that I loved him, just that I liked him a lot. He had become like a brother to me and I guess that's what brought on my love for him. He was the most popular person in my group of friends, the girls wanted dates with him and he was in the position where he just about had his pick of who he wanted to be with, the boys all respected him for his leadership quality and bowed to him as being number one. He stood only five feet ten with long blond hair and dark eyes and he had a smile that wouldn't quit.

"I would hate it when he would tell me about a girl that he was going to have sex with and how he would go about it. I didn't doubt his word, I knew that when he had set his mind on having sex with a certain girl that it would happen, but I hated her whoever she might have been. I remember so many times of wanting to tell him to forget the girl and take me, that I would do anything for him because I loved him and she didn't. I felt fantastic just having him near me and more so when he would shake my hand or pat me on the back for something, just the touch of his hand sent shivering chills of excitement inside my body and many times I had to fight off the urge of an oncoming erection just from his touch.

"I remember one time at an ice rink, all of us had been drinking quite a bit, I was talking to some other people when he called me over to him, then like so many times before he pointed to a car and said that he was going to fuck the girl sitting in the car and he walked over to the car and got in with no trouble as if he didn't think I believed his words. Later that night as I was coming back from my own car he once again called to me, this time I had no idea of what he wanted. We began to walk, making small talk, it was late at night and most of the cars had gone and the rink had closed for the night, we were on the darkest side of the rink talking, still I wondered what he wanted, then without warning he unzipped his pants, pulling out the largest erected penis I'd ever seen and began to urinate. He made no attempt to hide his erection from me, and I couldn't hide the fact that I was staring at it intently. As we walked back and forth a few times I wanted to tell him about how I could physically love him, how I as another boy could take him to heights he'd never know with the girls.

"To this day I still don't know why he asked me to take that walk with him, as he could have urinated at the back of the rink by himself and no one would have ever known. I've thought back about this many times, and I think now that it was his sort of way of letting me know that he knew I loved him, he could tell in my eyes the way I felt about him, but being a very straight boy he couldn't physically acknowledge what he knew, and I didn't want to put him in the spot of defending his sexuality. A year later he went into the Army and I didn't see him again until several years later and by that time he had married and my love for him had cooled off."

"I was most in love with another guy, I *think*. (I say that because I'm not sure if it really *was* love, or temporary infatuation, or something else.) We were roommates at the time, and we just started getting closer and closer, physically and mentally. Finally we ended up in bed together one night. For the next three weeks, we had sex four or five times, I think. I only climaxed twice (he did every time). Then I moved home for the summer, and a few days after I got there I had second thoughts about what I had done. What I really didn't like was the extent to which I had come to depend on him for companionship. It just didn't seem right to be that dependent on *anyone*. Anyway, I broke off anything we had going in a letter I sent him about a week after I got home. He was pretty shook up, I guess. But during the time he and I were really together, I felt like I was on Cloud Nine. The happiest I've ever been in a *short* period of time was with him. But over the long run, I've been happiest, and closest, with the woman I am living with now. Still, there are times when I actually think I'd be much happier spending my life with another *man*. Certain kinds of men really interest me mentally and physically. I guess I'm going to be forced, one way or another, into making a decision sooner or later. Right now I'm still trying to find myself."

WHAT DOES IT MEAN TO BE A MAN?

GROWING UP MALE

What do boys learn from their fathers about how to be a man?

"I used to go hunting with my dad for four or five years, during my boyhood. Unfortunately, I have always been a very poor marksman (my hands shake too much). I gave up hunting after an incident in which my dad and I were duck hunting in a boat with some other men. I had just brought down a duck, and we paddled the boat over to pick it up. As we reached it, I was astonished and delighted to find it still alive and looking well. It seemed so cute and attractive I envisioned taking it home with me, nursing it back to health, and keeping it for a pet. One of the men picked it up and proceeded to beat its brains out over the side of the boat."

"What did your father tell you about 'how to be a man'? Did he tell you not to cry when you got hurt? To be sure to win in a fight? Not to be a crybaby? A sissy? Not to play with girls

or girls' toys? How did you feel? What did he tell you about women?"

Most men had either been told or (more typically) shown by example the traditional male values and behavior patterns, although many men complained that their fathers had not told them enough:

"My father was very concerned that I not grow up to be a sissy. He reacted rather hysterically to signs of weakness (e.g., crying) or femininity (e.g., wiping my ass from the front instead of the rear). His behavior is astonishing to me now, but at the time I felt very deep shame."

"My father said, 'Don't take shit from anybody.' That was about it."

"Dad's idea of a man was someone who hunted, fished, played sports, etc. A man wouldn't be artsy or theatrical (male dancers were fairies). Men speak in deep voices and on and on ad nauseam."

"He told me what was important: $ $ $ $."

"My father taught me the typical macho American male stuff about being a man. Men don't cry. Men don't show emotion. Men provide. Men are the stronger sex. Women are weak physically and emotionally. Honor and duty above all else. Sports, hard work, etc., were masculine. Arts, music, and the fine professions (with the exception of law and medicine) were suspect, if not downright feminine. A woman was to be indulged; was the only 'proper' sex object; was for tending the home and raising the family; worked outside the home if necessary, but never supported a man worth his salt. A real man would rather die than show more emotion to another man than a handshake."

"My father did not tell me how to be a man, I just learned from his actions. He had a pretty much stereotyped masculine/dad image. I didn't buy it all, but I see signs of it in my character: Superior—knows everything—solves all problems—no emotions other than anger. I guess that's Dad's sort of masculine, and to a much lesser degree mine."

"No girls' toys were allowed. I was told not to complain or cry. Be stoic and unemotional."

"Mostly my father told me what *wasn't* a man—and that was just about everything I was . . . in his eyes at least."

"You *show up*. *Be there*—no matter what. Meet your responsibilities."

"My father told me not too much—except the usual

1940's crap: men don't cry and are strong; women are to be taken care of and revered."

"To always provide for your family."

"I was told not to push a baby carriage at about four."

"My father never really told me not to cry—or to cry in my room alone. He told me men had to be strong and make enough money to raise a family. Women had to be good wives and good mothers—if they were 'good women.' The others were all 'trash.'"

"He told me about the necessity of being able to fight for yourself and win. He never said much about women, but it was clear that he considered them inferior mentally."

"He used to tell me to '*act* like a man.' It was because I was enjoying myself, acting silly, and I loved it. When he or my mom wanted me to straighten up, they told me to act like a man. It upset me."

"'Big boys (i.e., men) don't cry.' And by implication: men do the important jobs; women either do trivial things or stay at home where they belong. Work is good; idleness is bad."

"My father always told me to 'be a man'—meaning, don't let the woman run your life or run over you."

"Work hard. Be energetic, don't complain. There was negative pressure about sports—it had no place in our schedule. We were expected to do our part of the work—give a good day's labor for a good day's pay. (I worked for my father in high school.)"

"My father told me to be honest with myself and with others, to be good to others, and that my responsibility in life was in this order—to my family first, to my country next, and to God last. I do not recall much he said about women other than there were good ones and bad ones. He dwelled on staying away from the bad ones."

"Work hard, pay your bills, keep out of debt, owe no man, beat the system, pay cash."

"Be clean, honest, dependable, wise, and hard-working."

"Stand up for yourself—don't be pushed around. Be gentle and kind with women. Protect them."

"Be formidable to one's enemies. Hit back."

"To be a man is to be a success. About women, don't let them get in your way or stop you from being a success, don't let love or a woman dominate your life."

"My father said, 'Don't act like a sissy' whenever I would get on my hands and knees to weed the garden. He told me nothing about women."

"He said nothing on women, except 'dirty' anecdotes, and that he liked legs, tit, and ass. He is very chauvinistic."

"He above all counseled me to be courageous and maintain my personal power."

"My father never told me a damn thing! On the other hand, he sure did expect me to participate in sports as well as get girlfriends."

"Never cry, fight back, be a man!"

"He was always disappointed that I never got into fights. He was probably afraid I was gay (I'm not) because I liked crafts, and weaving, etc."

"He said, 'Quit complaining.' "

"Work hard, never complain, don't spend all your time with your mother."

"If anything, my old man did not prepare me for the 'male' role that I found was expected of me in the Army and in my twenties. He made one attempt, poor man, to play catch with me and it was a dismal failure."

" 'Fight, fuck, make a lot of money.' This was the basic credo. I was humiliated and ridiculed if any 'nonmasculine' behavior was performed—like one time when I was about seven, putting on my mother's makeup with my sister."

Many men emphasized that there had been no father-son talks; that they had learned only from example or from disapproval, condemnation or ridicule when they did something "wrong":

"My father never 'told' me anything. However, the model he presented was one of Prussian arrogance. In his relations with women (mainly my mother), it was clear that they were to be always beneath him."

"Father never said much. But his example was to let women wait on him hand and foot, then belittle them in front of other people."

"My father taught me only by his actions. He tended to just push ahead and not admit mistakes. He implied that most women are basically 'silly.' I do not agree."

"Father didn't really 'tell' me much. In fact he tended to be indifferent to my situation. I think he was bewildered at being a father. He also told me nothing about women, except he gave me the idea that they were just for sex."

"He never taught me anything about 'being a man' directly. What he did teach was by disapproval. Also, he seemed to have the attitude that my mother was helpless and he was supposed to tolerate her. He didn't know how wise she really is."

"He did not stress fighting back but made fun of me when I was beaten up. Lots of disapproval."

"He never talked in general, i.e., a man acts this way or that way. But he tried never to cry and the example was more important than any talk."

"His attitude was essentially disapproving or negligent."

"He never talked much. He just punched me in the face when he needed to straighten me out."

"By example, my father taught me a lot about being a man, although he never talked about it. He was intensely loyal to family, he cared for and protected his children at all costs. He had a bit of macho—had to be dominant or believe he was. He did not hesitate to strike his children or my mother to prove he was boss or to make a point. I believe this turned me away from the macho image. But he was very sensitive and down deep a real 'softie.' "

But a few men reported a different experience:

"He wasn't a man who felt that his son had to be tops, that is, he never pressured me to make something of myself. He encouraged me to *think*."

"By his own interests and actions, my father told me that the artistic side of life is O.K. for men. He was a lover of classical music and enjoyed opera, ballet, and theater. He told me that a more sophisticated manner of life (in contrast to the life of 'peasants') was O.K. All this from a man whose job involved a lot of hard, physical work. This is perhaps an important element in my not associating the artistic with the so-called feminine."

"My father was raised to be and always is the 'Southern gentleman,' both in his life and where women are concerned socially. He spoke to me in actions more than words, in his respect for women. For example, he encouraged Mother to continue going to classes as my brother and I grew up, and backed her 100 percent mentally and emotionally when she started her own business and became active in politics. As to his example of manhood—he was strong, aggressive, a hunter, yet he cuddled me and we still kiss whenever and wherever we meet. I played with dolls almost till high school and Dad accepted it. In fact he used to tell me that he played with dolls as a boy. He is a very heterosexual man, but he accepts and understands my right and need to be a homosexual."

"My father only told me to assume certain responsibilities. On several occasions I've cried in front of my father, but I was never scolded about that expression of my emotions. He also told me never to pick a fight but if I had to fight that I should do my best to protect myself and defend myself. I have played house with my younger brother and sister, and held tea parties with them, with no ill effects. I was usually scolded for misbehaving, but not for expressing my feelings."

A few men said they and their fathers had "done things together," even though they rarely talked:

"My father never really talked to me about being a man, or about women. We did 'father-son' things like go hunting and fishing."

"We went to ball games once in a while, and he asked me to help make repairs about the house. I strived to be like him, to be accepted. But he never *told* me how to act."

"Anytime Dad had a project to do around the house (painting, working on the car, etc.) he'd tell me to help him. I always did when I was there. He was tall, silent, and efficient."

But most boys had not spent a lot of time doing things with their fathers:

"We did not really attend sports events together or play much except to kick a soccer ball around occasionally. Usually I participated in school events on my own, and attended games and sports events by myself."

"We did very little together that I can remember."

"Because of the nature of his business we were not really able to spend much time together except when we were on vacation and the times I accompanied him on a business trip. I don't remember much about those trips."

"We didn't do much together, he said I played baseball like a girl. He liked to go to local baseball games and I hated them."

"I have never been close to my father. He always showed his love by means of materialism versus emotion. My mother died when I was ten years old, so when I was young he spent more time with other women than me. He was a passive individual with me, but acted very masculine among his friends. He got me interested in baseball but just dropped me off at the game and picked me up when it was over. He always seemed to sleep on the couch when a sports program appeared on TV."

One man said what was probably true for many:

"I feel that I really discovered the male role more from watching James Cagney, Humphrey Bogart, Tom Mix, and Hopalong Cassidy than from my father. At least, a male as I would *like* to be."

And another:

"Any male roles I learned were from TV."

Similarly, when asked, "Were you ever called a 'sissy' or a 'mama's boy'? Told to 'Be a man!'? What was the occasion? How did you feel?" most men said they had been taunted and called on to prove their "manliness" in just this way at some point when young:

"I grew up in Detroit where you had your own group or mini gang. I got the brunt of 'sissy.' I was for many years hurt. My father would always call me 'dummy.' I remember that, too well. Him calling me that hurt more than anything. I really thought I was dumb until two years ago."

"As a young boy I was told this by my father when I cried. I remember one time especially when I lost a pet. Now I just don't show my emotions."

"I've been called 'sissy' when I was a kid. I guess it was usually when I wouldn't conform with what the rest of the 'boys' wanted or did. I was told to 'be a man' whenever I cried, for whatever reason. I hated both situations. My older brother would call me a sissy after he would torment me to tears. I felt unaccepted."

"I have never been called a 'sissy,' but I was told to 'be a man' when my mother died. When I saw her in the casket, I started to cry and bawl (almost like a baby). One of my sisters said something like 'Why don't you shut up! You're acting just like a baby.' I felt resentment at not being able to cry for my own mother's death."

"My father told me this stuff during one of my emotional onslaughts when I was a teenager. I kind of agreed at the time. Now I think he should have at least asked me what was wrong. I didn't have anyone I could talk to."

"My father frequently exhorted me to be a man, and

called me a sissy when I had difficulties physically mustering up to his ideal of a man. I felt deeply hurt and bitter and pushed myself even harder to gain the nod of approval. I was doing men's work full measure side by side with them starting at age nine. In the process of this effort I got three permanent physical injuries."

"I have been told this by my father and high school mates very often. I felt hurt and cried, when nobody could see me. Even while I was in the Navy, I was constantly hassled about not smoking, drinking, swearing, or fucking as much as the other guys."

"I am often called a sissy, faggot, etc. I say to myself in a lot of ways I am, but what the hell is wrong with it, and what the hell is their problem in thinking they're any better than I am?"

"While in high school I cried during a very violent quarrel between my father and stepmother. They interpreted my crying to be weakness and told me to stop being a baby, and refused to hear of my frustration and fright at having seen their physical cruelty to each other."

"I remember sissy-baiting. I got it in turn. Then when somebody relatively more of a sissy came along, I gave it to them, you may be sure. One of the boys on our block, a fat one, we often called a sissy. We looked down on him. I once asked him if he took this very badly, and he insisted that he did not. But I think he really did. Now I wish we had left him alone."

"When I was in boarding school riding alone on my horse by the football field—the team was out for practice, and they started calling 'fairy' and 'isn't she sweet' at me. I don't recall being affected by them, as they were not my friends, so I couldn't care less."

"I was called 'mama's boy,' because I did not like to leave the house. I felt odd, and hurt. As a child, being different is a horrible feeling."

"I underwent humiliating ceremonies when drafted in the U.S. Army. Men who are drafted are treated like dirt in the Army by sadistic officers and sergeants. Men are called 'sissies' in training. It was very dehumanizing and degrading in Army basic training and after."

"I was called a 'sissy' by my mother, who wanted me to cut my hair to be like a 'real' man; it made me laugh."

"My peers considered me a sissy in grade school because I played piano. I felt bad but held in my anger."

"In my youth it was very common to call anyone with a

different life style a 'fag.' There were many people who did not accept my life style. Usually a comment like 'Be a man' meant: be like me, value what I value, do what I do, etc. I felt bad about not belonging until I discovered belonging was safe but very limiting."

"Once I ran to my father for having one of the kids pick on me. After the harassment concluded I felt inferior to the rest of my friends for having told him. It made me think that before the incident took place I was one of the gang, but afterwards I was an outsider—maybe a coward too."

"Told to 'be a man'? No. But a 'sissy,' yes, often, by fellow students. The occasion was generally gym class or recess during grade school or, later, in junior high, at the bus stop. On my block, the fellows my age went to parochial school. The public school fellows were a year older, and bigger and cockier. When we all were let off the bus in the afternoon, I was the only one who had to go the same direction as those older kids. Their houses were beyond mine, and they used to taunt me, 'You should be somebody's sister, not brother,' 'You weak coward, you haven't the manhood to stand up to me,' 'Look at him trembling! Ain't it a laugh!' Watta blast. I walked that gauntlet for several years. In the spring of my eighth-grade year I took to walking home from school, a little over a mile, just to avoid it. How did I feel? Are you kidding?"

This was especially true with regard to participation in sports:

"In gym class in junior high (the toiling ground of many) I was called a sissy because I didn't like the organized sports and was not interested one whit in them. . . . When I failed to run a mile the gym teacher called me a sissy and said that there was nothing for me to be proud of. Frankly, I just wasn't interested. But I joined the team."

"I was called a 'sissy' by a P.E. teacher when I didn't want to play football with boys a year or so older and twenty pounds heavier than I. When forced to participate I was kicked in the face and called 'sissy' when I cried! I was humiliated and angry and frustrated in my inability to strike back."

"The only time I can remember having my manliness questioned was in junior high football practice. I tried, but I couldn't see the point in trying to hurt my friends to prove something I already took for granted. I did want to be popular, though, and football seemed to be the way."

"In grade school I was often called a sissy because I didn't like baseball. I felt very hurt, defensive, and confused."

"I was told to be a 'man' not a 'sissy' (=girl) at school during sports, and many times by my father. It hurt because I always wanted to please my dad. My violent dislike of athletics and strong lack of competitive spirit left me open to these charges many times. I felt like a traitor."

"I never liked football, but when I was growing up my brothers used to get me to play to make up a team. I never wanted to but because of being afraid of being a sissy or called a sissy, etc., most of the time I did. I was a cruddy player and usually after every game I would end up fighting with someone. I hated it."

Also, when asked, "Did you go out for sports? If so, did you look down on other boys who didn't? Or if you were not involved in sports, were you made to feel less 'manly'? Were you ever refused admission to a club or a team? How did you feel about it?" most men said there had been great pressure on them to be interested and participate in sports, and compete with other boys in physical strength—and many had resented and resisted this:

"I was never strong in sports. I never liked it very much and I remember at about ten being relegated to an inferior place in our group and looked down on by other boys because of it. I never felt less 'manly' because of that and very soon I found another 'group' I've grown up with, who were not very 'sportive.' "

"I didn't have the internal strength to quit sports teams, even though I grew to dislike them. It wasn't until tenth grade when I was injured in football, and had to sit out most of the season, that I realized that I liked not playing better than playing."

"I did not go out for sports. I didn't feel less manly about not making teams, but I did take a beating emotionally when I would get chosen very close to last when teams were being chosen for pickup street games."

"I was cut from a basketball team once in high school. I kept thinking that I would be missing the crowd applauding as I ran out on the court. My pride was hurt and the thought of being a spectator annoyed me."

"I was an intellectual kid who always had his nose in a book, and as an only child, was driven into a lot of isolation by the demands that I be a jock and good at sports that I couldn't handle at the time. Even now, while I'm able to jog several miles at a stretch, and am in good condition physically, I'm not too big, and get a lot of subliminal flak at the plant where I work because I don't lift things I don't want to lift. A lot of men where I work have developed chronic bad backs because they are always proving how strong they are. What a relief to give this up!"

But some boys reveled in sports:

"I went out for all the sports, playing ball with the other boys on my block, and handball and baseball in school. We boys did somewhat look down on the 'sissies' who didn't play in sports at all or who did very poorly at them."

"I never miss a baseball, football, basketball, or hockey game on television. My whole life is sports, my job deals directly with sports, for relaxation I watch games on TV, and one of my hobbies is collecting sports bubble-gum cards. I identify with them all. Baseball was always my first love. If I'd been given any athletic talent I would have tried to become a major-league player. I have grown to like the other team sports too, like soccer."

"It takes great skill to be a pro athlete; unless you have participated in these forms of sports you have no way to know how it feels. I played college football for four years. To be the fastest or quickest gives self-satisfaction that you have been able to accomplish something successfully. Men who haven't played sports have missed a large part of what it means to be a man."

"When I was in college, one night I had a dream about rugby. It was actually a dream about pirates ravaging coastal towns but later I decided that it was analogous to our rugby team; adorned in black, priding itself as being the roughest in the East. The combination of winning a game of rugby, the sun, grass, sweat, physical contact, and total physical exertion are the best kind of a day one could ask for, also followed by many beers at a nearby pub. The cooperation, spontaneous cooperative effort of any team sport is always satisfying. Extreme mutual admiration always follows a victory. Some people took speed before a game so that their endurance would seem infinite and totally fearless."

There was also pressure to "make it" sexually:*

* See chapter 3.

"At the age of about eleven I remember discussions about girlfriends and about those who were willing to 'make out.' There was pressure to have a girlfriend and it seems to me that we all wanted to at least date a girl who wouldn't mind having her vagina felt or her breasts squeezed. This, however, was not the girlfriend that we wanted to have as a steady. When I was in grade ten, at the age of fourteen, with fellow students who were sixteen or seventeen, I remember notes being passed in class about the availability of certain girls in class. There was pressure on the guys especially to have sexual relations with the girls. Even though I may not have been actively involved in high school, talk like this always turned me on."

"My friends in high school called another guy a sissy when he said he was afraid to ask his girl to go all the way. I hadn't either but I didn't say anything. The idea was that we were all 'men' because we could brazen our way through any girl's defenses—make the tackle and complete the pass, so to speak. What she felt didn't matter (or what *we* felt either, as far as that goes)—so long as we scored. We listened to these stories from each other, secure in our knowledge that we were being men—the others were sissies."

"I guess the pressure to date or 'score' with girls began when I was about twelve or thirteen. It seemed that all the other guys were 'dating' someone at the time; girls were a regular topic of conversation among many of the boys in our grammar school (a Catholic school). How did I feel about it? I enjoyed being with girls, but I did not like being told what I was supposed to 'do' with them. I have always had a strong 'romantic' streak, and idealized notions of 'love' played a very important role in my life. All through high school, whenever I went out with a 'girl' I never felt it necessary to try to act out the fantasies of others (i.e., locker room discussions about women). I just enjoyed being with the individual and doing things together, whether it was going to movies, school dances, or concerts. I never forced myself physically on a 'girl' I might be dating, even for a kiss."

On the other hand, there was pressure not to play with or associate with girls, not to have girls as "friends":

"As a boy, I was always being criticized for playing with girls. I felt that playing with girls was just as much fun as playing with boys, but this attitude always bothered my parents."

"I remember at about eleven my father criticized me for wanting to play with the next-door neighbor girl younger than me, because she was a girl. Another time he blew up at me for spending the afternoon at a girl's house rather than doing something like being out playing football."

Hunting was another testing ground of "masculinity" or toughness:

"I went hunting a few times with other men, with a .22 rifle, when I was eighteen to twenty-two. It was, admittedly, a fun game, feeling the surge of power."

"One time a friend of mine and I trapped a wildcat and beat it to death with clubs. Even now my stomach turns when I think of it. I regretted doing it almost immediately after it happened."

"I grew up hunting and fishing; I dislike fishing but still hunt. I do not like to hunt small game; only antelope on the open range and sheep in the Bighorns really interest me. Most hunters pretend to hunt for something called 'sport.' But I know that what makes hunting of game attractive is the killing of the animal. I *like* to kill things. The very real sense of power over life and death projected through space. A 30.06 or other high-caliber rifle is what makes the sport so popular. Otherwise, why not undertake the hunt with a camera? You have to be even more skillful to get *that* close to the animal you are tracking. Violence is part of the thing. I used to box and shoot pool and all that good ol' stuff, too."

Fraternities and clubs also often involved initiation ceremonies designed to test "manhood"—to see if the applicant could withstand humiliation or "teasing":

"In camp, age twelve to thirteen, our group had a ceremony called a *washbah* in which a group of boys grabbed one of their friends, pulled down his pants, and poured all kinds of shaving cream, aftershave, deodorants, etc., on his genitals. The idea was to make them burn."

"I occasionally enjoyed teasing or trying to humiliate weaker boys—such as one of my classmates in junior high school who was somewhat effeminate. Also later in college in my fraternity we had 'pledge week' during which we were supposed to, and did, humiliate the new guys as much as possible. If they broke down, sometimes we kicked them out. They didn't have what it takes. I remember once when we lowered a German boy out of a second-story window by his heels. He became so frightened that he urinated all over himself."

Some men commented on the effects of equating "masculinity" and toughness:

"Teaching men that masculinity is composed of aggressiveness, destructive competitiveness, and acquisitiveness has led men to value physical aggression and dominance; and has produced the high general level of fear, contempt, arrogance, and paranoia in men, and has contributed mightily to the high general level of interpersonal viciousness in this society. And the role of 'corporate team player' (whose goal must be identification with the company and its goals) has led as many men to self-obliteration and robotization and alienation as the role of 'housewife' (whose goal must be identification with the family and its goals) has led women."

"For me, the most destructive aspect of my 'boyhood' training was competitiveness, which leads to setting impossible goals, which leads to being untrue to yourself—and carries over from sports, where it's most common, into sex, academics, etc."

"In both grade school and high school there was strong pressure to conform, to be like other boys. This pressure came from home and from peer groups, though I never seemed to meet all these demands. I would always find ways around the pressures, or seem to conform when I really wasn't."

Men's training during boyhood to "be a man"—and not be a "sissy"—carries over significantly into later life.

DO MEN BELIEVE IT IS UNMASCULINE TO EXPRESS FEELINGS?

"Men should not hurt, cry, openly display affection, or react to emotion in another. I feel embarrassed when someone shows strong or tender emotions. I feel embarrassed for him."

Boys brought up to be "tough" and not show pain or be emotional often continued to cover over feelings later in life. When asked, "Do you often feel hurt or sad when you don't show it? Do you sometimes force yourself to behave like a robot? Most men said they did try to cover over their feelings, especially of pain or frustration—or even of great happiness or enthusiasm—lest they be teased:

"I was raised to conceal my actual emotions and to display whatever emotion I believed was most appropriate, to maintain or achieve control of a social situation. Since age forty I have been learning to kick the habit."

"Sometimes I don't show my feelings because I say to myself—I can handle this all by myself. I often feel like a robot."

"I sometimes act not hurt or upset when I'm too sensitive. Other times I show it and it bugs me that I do."

"I am forced to wear a mask to protect my professional status. The pressures to keep 'face' are oppressive. I was trained to be this way by the U.S. Army."

"I do mask my feelings and maintain an outward calm."

"Lots of times I feel like a robot or like Mr. Spock from *Star Trek,* not able to show feelings when they seem appropriate. Because of this I find it very difficult to take a lot of situations seriously and I attempt to make light of them or dull their importance. I hardly ever show my true feelings."

"I generally prefer to keep them to myself as much as possible, although I do complain, scream, and even cry when by myself at times."

"I do generally hide my feelings, except with my girlfriend, and even then when I think it would bother her."

"I generally try not to show it when I feel hurt. I can be really mad at something and still turn on charm towards another person."

"Although people tell me I shouldn't hide my feelings, I don't agree. But it does make me feel alienated."

"Social pressure is so enormous sometimes that I do not show emotions and behave like a robot."

"I try not to burden others with my problems or let my feelings show."

"I try to be honest about my feelings. But the greatest difficulty is admitting them to myself—I'm so used to always pretending everything is 'O.K.'—I guess part of the 'Don't cry' and 'Be a man' training."

"I have been raised to not show my feelings. Once when I wasn't getting along with my lover my whole body got sick because I was so miserable. My stomach felt like it got hit by a train. But I didn't tell my friends why I felt so shitty, even though they asked. Sometimes I behave like a robot but I don't feel like one."

"I envy women being able to express their feelings, as this is a very natural (it seems) thing. But myself I *never* express my feelings easily, as I have been raised to control my feelings."

"I do not believe men are cut-and-dried cutouts, but basically we have been taught it is the woman who should have and show her feelings and it is unmanly for us to do the same. This should be changed somehow. I believe men are just as feeling about love, sex, and relationships, but they have become hardened."

"My father taught me to be reserved and not show emotions. Then he committed suicide, which taught me I'd better not be like that."

"I like to control my emotions so that I can make them flow in the direction I want, rather than simply reacting spontaneously. I don't feel like a robot at all. I enjoy my ability to control myself."

A few men did not like the reaction they got when they did show feelings:

"A lot of women pay lip service to the thing going around now that men should be able to cry. But they were brought up with the idea that a man should not cry, and quite frankly, I think women still feel this way. I have seen women encourage their men to cry only to be more attracted to a man that doesn't cry. I have always cried in front of women, but, quite sadly I think, in the last year I have decided not to do this—to do my crying alone. Women should not mistake sensitivity in a man for weakness."

"A lover once complained that I didn't say enough about my feelings, but when I did she was unsympathetic; in fact she usually strongly attacked what I said—'You can become happy if you try. I suspect that you really don't want to be free of your problems.' She may have been correct—it's difficult to know the truth of such matters—but her tone was not the sort which reinforced conversation about what I was feeling. I always came away from these sessions feeling unaccepted (and unacceptable)."

"Sometimes I pretend not to be hurt when I am, but usually I show my feelings. When I don't it is usually because we've been over and over the problem that is hurting me and

I think the best thing is to not make a bigger deal than it is, so I pretend not to be bothered in order to avoid a confrontation."

But not showing feelings is not the same as not feeling them:

"Sometimes I act like a robot when the situation at work has been unhappy, but I can assure you that I never feel that way."

"I've just been fired from the job I had expected to make my career. I'm hurt now, and a little resentful. But expressing such feelings does me no good, and earns me only contempt for whining. (Unspoken maxim: 'Women whine and complain. Men grin and bear it.') I feel like I want to scream, but what's the use of screaming? It would just humiliate me. I may as well get on with the day's business."

And some men did not hold their feelings in, and enjoyed talking and hearing another's feelings:

"I used to hold my feelings in, now I don't. Nothing is worse than to suffer a deep hurt and not be able to express it. It's like bleeding internally."

"I like to talk about feelings and emotions. Society has pushed away the idea that men shouldn't be open. What is wrong with orally expressing an emotion? Many times in the Navy I've seen men portraying their false masculine ways. They won't talk about a problem they are facing at the moment even though it's eating inside of them. I think that if feelings are not brought out between friends or lovers, one often wonders what the other is feeling or thinking. When I speak out, I usually receive a more open rapport with another individual in return."

Similarly, when asked, "Is it easy for you to express yourself, or do you sometimes have trouble talking about emotions or expressing your feelings? Why do you think this is? Does your lover ever complain that you don't talk enough about your feelings?" most men said they often had difficulty:

"I am sometimes not sure what I feel or think, and then it's hard for me to express myself. It usually happens when something is obviously affecting me or her, and I don't mention it. Often I tell myself I should figure this out myself—

'It's my problem.' At that point, I'm often alienated, and there's an element of mistrust."

"I do have trouble talking about my feelings, and my lover complains about it frequently. She feels distanced from me when I don't. It's even harder to talk to other men."

"My wife sometimes feels that I don't communicate often enough about how I really feel. I think this is because I wasn't encouraged to speak openly about my feelings as a child. Feelings were kept to yourself. Revealing them made a person too vulnerable. Sometimes I don't quite know how I feel and at other times I don't quite know how to express the feeling and sometimes I'm ashamed or shy about what I feel."

Others said they had learned to express their feelings only through painstaking effort:

"I talk with my wife very well, although it took me years to develop the capacity (or relearn it?) for doing this. Two years ago, we experienced marriage encounter, which has *everything* to do with communication about feelings. I feel now that we have come a long way since then and that we communicate feelings regularly and effectively. This includes sharing positive and negative feelings about third parties (and our kids), as well as expressing our feelings, positive and negative, about each other."

"I do my best at communication, I must. I feel incomplete if I don't communicate my feelings, but I'm just learning how to do it. It's something few of us men were taught to do, so it's very painful, yet exhilarating to accomplish. I find that I atrophy emotionally if I don't take every scrap of poor or ugly out, and that confusion and tension in the relationship usually are a symptom of not having shared feelings."

One source of this difficulty mentioned by some men is that they feared they did not feel what they "should" feel:

"The clashes between what I'd like to feel and what I do feel have been the basis of my most anguished sexual conflicts. This leads to silence and isolation in me. It has taken much struggle for me to come to terms with my feelings, and learn to have more confidence and practice in expressing and expanding them."

"A woman's questions make me silent. I don't want to answer her because probably what I feel won't be accepted in women's List of Approved Emotions."

But a surprising number of men said they often did not want to share their feelings verbally in any deep way with their lover or wife:

"Generally when I *feel* like expressing myself I find it easy, but I don't believe it is necessary for me to express my feelings as much as some of my lovers would like. I don't *want* to tell them everything."

"Oh boy, do I enjoy talking! But not to my wife. I don't like to express my feelings to her."

"Talking is one of my greatest pleasures. I easily express myself when I choose to do so, and have little trouble talking about my feelings. But my lover complains that I don't talk enough about my feelings—possibly because I don't spend enough time with her, and don't want to talk to her about them."

"My lover does complain, but I generally express everything that I wish to. There are things that I don't want to share for feeling they're unimportant or would cause unhappiness."

"She says I don't talk enough. She is always complaining that she doesn't know how I *feel*—about her, about my day, about everything. Hell! I can't be talking all the time. I work hard, I do my share around the house, what more does she want?"

One man said he did not have many feelings:

"Generally I don't enjoy talking about my emotions. I much prefer current events, work, etc. She often complains that I don't talk about my feelings enough. The problem, I tell her, is that I don't have enough feelings. My emotional response mechanism is turned very low, whether by genetics or environment or both. I'm not a reactive person."

But a minority of men did enjoy talking:

"I am very expressive about these things and usually wind up encouraging my lovers to express themselves more freely."

"I enjoy talking and find it easy to express myself about my feelings about love, dislikes, and personal problems."

"As a psychologist, I've learned to express my feelings. But sometimes I'm very unsure if I'm expressing the feelings I really have, or just being glib. My wife doesn't do so enough to suit me."

"I am quite expressive, especially to close friends and lovers, so communication is *not* a problem for me. The real problem is getting lovers to communicate with *me*. Sometimes I seem to frighten and intimidate some women without meaning to do so."

*Most men said it was more difficult to express feelings to other men than to women:**

"I am a reasonably 'private' person and share little with other people. But my wife would know more of my feelings than my friends. I try not to lose control too often with anyone (especially my family) but have cried with my wife and children."

"There are only a few things I can talk better about with friends than my lover. She and I have explored much uncharted scary ground between us and have a solid bond. I can cry but I still have much trouble showing anger."

"I find it hard to talk to men. It is difficult for a man to establish a trust in another man. But I am not afraid to bare my soul to someone I do trust or know, like my lover."

"It is impossible to talk to other men about feelings and about most problems. It doesn't even occur to me to try. There have only been rare exceptions to this. I find it easier to talk about my feelings with those people who do not seem to have formal or informal authority. I especially enjoy talking about my feelings to many women."

"You can talk to a woman and she will listen to you when a man won't."

*And the great majority of men who answered (who related sexually to women) said they had closer relationships, and were more comfortable being close, to women than to male friends:**

"I believe it is nice to have male friends, and I have several. But I am closer to my wife than ever to anyone else."

"There are many of my friends who like to confide in me and perhaps there are many things that I tell them. However, my closest relationship is with my wife."

"I would like to have a close male friend but find it difficult. I am definitely closer to women."

"I should have male friends because I'm a male. But I am closest to a woman—my wife."

* See also pages 94–96.

"I am not sure whether it is important to have a male friend. I have been closest to my wife, as a friend, of all my friends."

"I very much value male friendships—I have worked hard at them—because they have been harder to come by than female friends. I have been more close to women—I find it real easy to be close to many women."

"My relationships with men have been underscored with an unconscious fear, or at least lack of trust. I find my *close* friends are female. Them I have opened up to. I converse more freely with women and tend to 'shut down' when men are present. I feel like I must be on guard then. The problem with this fear is that there is a backlash. I resent being fearful and therefore don't allow men to touch me, become close, and don't take the initiative myself with someone I know rationally I can trust. I have never felt as close as I would like with men. It is something I would like, but haven't actively pursued it. It seemed like something that should happen naturally. How does one have close men friends? I don't know why this has been so difficult for me. I told myself it's because I don't like sports or cars. But that can't be all there is to it."

HOW DO MEN DEFINE MASCULINITY?

"I've always wanted to be a *man*."

What qualities make a man a man? What qualities do you admire in men?

In fact, most men's early training also taught them that they should be—or appear to be—autonomous, and successfully dominate any given situation without needing help or appearing emotional. They should know the answers to things, and be financially able to provide for a family—unless they choose to be a heroic loner, like Alan Ladd's character in *Shane*, or the mysterious man in the Marlboro ads.

TRADITIONAL DEFINITIONS

Men most often answered that a man should be self-assured, unafraid, in control, and autonomous or self-sufficient, not dependent:

."A man should be self-assured, confident, and in control most of the time."

"Most important are self-assurance and independence."

"Unafraid and self-confident."

"I believe masculinity is defined by presence, confidence, strength, and voice."

"He should have suave control of situations."

"Masculinity is based on a man's ability to control things around him. The ability to move physical objects also."

"A masculine person is a person who is to the greatest extent possible his own person with the fortitude to demand respect, but the sensitivity not to abuse other people in exercising his free will."

"Men are more stable (less overtly emotional) than women in difficult situations, better able to defer their reactions until the trouble is over (or to quell them entirely)."

"A male is a man when he is self-assured, and has strong opinions. He should be willing to be different and stand by his opinions."

"He should be self-sufficient and independent in terms of not having to rely on anyone for survival."

"A masculine person exhibits male traits: aggressiveness, independence, directness, rationality."

The next most frequently mentioned quality was leadership or dominance:

"A man must be decisive, and have qualities of leadership."

"I feel that a man should be strong when he needs to be, yet soft when required. I admire strong leadership in men."

"He must be aggressive and assertive. Protective of women."

"He needs the ability to take charge in a crisis situation."

"A man is a strong, physical, aggressive leader."

"Masculinity to me means being able to be a strong stabilizing force when required, being a good partner to a female, doing most of the heavy chores in a household, and yet being 'soft' and understanding when required."

"Masculine implies strength, not being overly emotional, and decision making."

"Men are usually more aggressive and assertive than women; often view their responsibilities as being broader and more 'important' to the community."

"A man is a strong-willed individual. Very confident in his abilities. A man cannot stand a weak person."

He should also get things done—be "in charge":

"Masculinity means not being pushed around and knowing what he wants and going out to get it."

"Not being wishy-washy."

"A man should be silent and in control."

"A man knows how."

"Emotional strength, honesty, success in all things."

"Things I admire in men are logical analytical ability, grace under pressure, large-scale vision, and persistence."

And be successful, especially financially:

"I admire a man who is best at what he does and doesn't flaunt it."

"Strong, with a successful career."

"Successful in business. Gutsy."

"A man is a guy who makes $100,000 a year, drives an expensive car, and caters to beautiful women."

He should show honesty and integrity:

"My father told me: Mean what you say. Keep your word."

"I admire honesty in men and straightforwardness, integrity, and courtesy."

"The qualities that I admire in a man are strength, assertion, honesty, and integrity."

"Being honest, fair, and considerate."

He should be dependable and responsible and have a sense of duty:

"When a man is willing to accept in full all responsibilities, then he is a real man."

"Steady, reliable, stable, decisive."

"Clean, honest, dependable."

"Good bearing, dependable, forthright, a 'wall' to lean on."

"The ability to carry their share of the load, physical and financial."

"Duty, honor, and courtesy make a man."

"Accept responsibility as it comes to you. Keep your head high and do your best."

And he should work hard:

"I admire men who work hard, either at what they do or at improvement."

"The ability to carry whatever load is placed upon him even if he doesn't enjoy the load."

"He should work. A man can't have much self-worth without it."

"A man is useless if he doesn't work."

"A man without a job is not a man, he is defeated. My conscience would bother me to unbelievable proportions if I didn't have a job."

Some said he should be a good provider and defender of his family, a strong father:

"Strength in time of trouble, the ability to take care of his family, wife, kids, parents, job, country; willingness to serve his country at war or otherwise if called upon. My lowest rating on the scale of a man would be one of the Vietnam draft dodgers."

"Masculine means a defender of home, wife, family, honor, and territory."

"A man should support his wife and family and try to make them happy the best way he knows."

"A man should be the breadwinner and provide emotional stability in the home."

"Support his family and give moral strength to his sons. Be protective of women. I see the role of the father as an authority, a kind of discipline, not of the autocratic disciplinarian variety, but a contrast to the maternal love provided by the mother. As such it gives a balance to the child, which when lacking due to death or divorce, creates conditions of instability in the child."

"A man should have a family and be its rightful head. When my wife told me that we were going to have a baby, it gave me a feeling of satisfaction as somehow it made me feel justified. Now I could take my rightful place in society."

He should participate in men's activities and be accepted by other men as "one of them":

"Masculinity is acceptance by male peers. I am well accepted."

"Masculinity is a way of relating to men which bypasses women entirely. It is the measure of respect you have for other men—identifying and comparing on an ego level. Strong.

"A man is one who enjoys male company as friends."

"Enjoys masculine activities—not a slob."

"Interest in male activities such as hunting, camping, fishing, and exploring."

Or simply look physically like a man:

"Muscles where it counts—between the legs, buttocks, chest, legs, arms, hands, neck, head."

"The quality I think that makes a man are: a manly voice and mannerisms, walk, etc., and one that carries a nice bulge in front of his blue jeans."

"A masculine man is one with a good build, not fat, good muscle structure, and well kept."

"Hairiness. No thinning scalp."

Others said he should know how to handle a relationship with a woman:

"Knowing what you want in relation to women . . . when to be strong and when to be gentle. To be someone who women and children and pets like and respect."

"A man is a person that shows he can keep a woman good and build himself up."

"Knowing how to handle a woman, and keep her happy."

Or be dominant in the relationship:

"A man should dominate the relationship, especially in marriage. Guess who I think should wear the pants? This should make the woman the happiest, proudest woman ever. This is being a man."

*Some men put it in sexual terms:**

"I define it in terms of female orgasms. Not in Don Juanist pussy-counts, please understand, but with respect to

---

* "Sex drive" was an essential component of masculinity for many men; see chapter 3.

satisfaction of a partner. After all, fucking is the whole point of maleness and femaleness, isn't it?"

"My sexuality is masculine. I am attracted to women."

"My definition: (a) Fifteen-year-old girls *always* look the best. (b) All men want to subjugate a woman to their will. (c) Men will never understand women; women will never understand men."

"A masculine man has a drive for sex, and will work at having sex with women."

"I guess a penis counts."

"Masculinity to me means someone who is not 'gay' or 'queer,' and who appreciates women as objects to love and adore."

"It is my opinion that a man cannot be a complete man, feel his strength as a man, unless he has a woman or two that he is pleasing to the maximum, fucking into a coma, every time she gets horny. Success as a man with his woman provides a platform from where he can be successful in other facets of life."

WHAT IS MACHO?

A macho man, on the other hand, was defined as having the following qualities:

"Doesn't giggle, gets respect, and controls his woman."

"Toughness, accepts responsibility, and willing to go to war."

"Macho to me is super-masculine, strong, silent, and having much assuredness in oneself. Macho seems the highest degree of masculinity. I don't consider myself macho per se, although I like the 'look,' and often dress in boots, plaids, leather, etc."

"Macho is brutal, forceful masculinity. Some Latins consider it a form of honor, I guess."

"I think macho is now interpreted to mean 'hairy chest,' daring, brave, strong, and 'hero.' I rate myself middle of the road or moderate."

"Masculinity is having a penis. Macho is trotting around like a rooster advertising it."

"Macho means originally 'death before dishonor,' macho is an exaggerated role type in which certain characteristics are emphasized such as competitiveness, physical courage, and virility."

"Macho refers to men in blue jeans, black leather jackets, peaked caps, black boots, chains, etc. This ties in with sado-masochism."

"Very hairy, with beard, mustache, and long hair."

"Macho is a swinger. Aggressive at women."

"Macho—The 'looking good,' 'feeling good,' well-mannered, clean-cut male, with a high ego."

"A daredevil, chip on the shoulder."

"Macho loves himself more than others."

"Masculine means being a man. Macho means *appearing* virile and sexy to others."

"Macho to me means someone who uses women, but to whom women are somehow attracted. Like the moth attracted to the flame."

"Macho is a ludicrously exaggerated form of masculinity which emphasizes all of its worst aspects and makes life a living hell for all those who have to suffer its effects."

"I was on a construction job with my friend. I said, 'Isn't it great we have such a macho job?' He said, 'You call this macho? Macho means *steel*-workers!'"

But perhaps surprisingly, most men stated that being "macho" represented affected, artificial, and insecure behavior:

"Macho is phony, masculinity is real."

"'Macho' is a state of mind, consisting of insensitivity, competitiveness, conceit, and self-worship, whereas masculinity is more subtle, secure, and understated. I admire guts and determination when it is required to accomplish a particular end, but you don't have to be macho to do that."

"The men who do their best to look macho, sound macho, and act macho are the ones who are the most paranoid about coming across as a sissy. I laugh at these 'macho men.' I don't need bulging muscles and fishnet shirts, my personality speaks for itself."

"Being masculine is part of being a man; being 'macho' is being an ass—it degrades oneself and every female on the earth."

"A macho man is callous, and manipulative. I don't enjoy exploiting, conquering, using, or ridiculing other people."

"I think of 'macho' as being the stereotype form of 'masculine' as opposed to being oneself."

There were many anti-macho statements:

"I think the 'macho' image is really dead. (The guy who makes love to a girl once and then forgets about her.) I like to be tender with the people I make love to . . . I am under the impression that the more kind you are when you love someone, the more they will come back to you and return the sincerity. I have a kid brother who is sixteen and he always calls me about his problems with girls and the like . . . he is really fascinated by my attitudes about loving and I think he is now in the process of experiencing his first love. Whenever he is having problems, I just tell him to be himself, don't try to make showy displays to impress people, etc. The other day he called and told me about his first sexual intercourse. He said he had taken my advice and was very tender about everything and that I had given him the best advice anyone had ever given him. That really made me feel good inside."

"I believe, based on my own experience and in talking with other men, that most of us would rather be with one woman we care about than a dozen we don't. I don't know of a man who really wants to be a satyr, we just want to be comfortable. The macho stud image hasn't done us a bit of good. We either have to fight that image internally or fall short of that ridiculous performance standard. This is our parallel to the objection the women have about being obligated and pressured to have sex."

"Using bravado and humor to get a job done effectively is masculinity. Using the same bravado to oppress or run roughshod over someone is 'macho.' 'Macho' is not considering another's opinion, not being gentle."

"What is a man? I used to identify with the image of the artist as a weird, nonconformist individual who didn't fit into society. I didn't feel like competing in sports, academics, business, driving cars, competing for women, being a hero, or being aggressive. I hated the system and was afraid of it and wanted to be left alone. But this image is still a very masculine, even macho, one—the idea of the 'anti-hero' like *Midnight Cowboy*. In fact, it is macho to think of yourself as negative and hardened, a loser. It means, 'you're so tough, you can take it.' Now that I feel more accepted, I try to avoid these stereotypes."

IS MASCULINITY THE OPPOSITE OF FEMININITY?

Most men said, in addition to the characteristics already listed, that "masculinity" was the opposite of "femininity." The real way to be a man was not to act like a woman:

"It's the opposite from femininity."

"Knowing that you are not a female and should not act like one."

As one man put it:

"I still can't help but think masculine means unemotional —not unfeeling or unreceptive, but visibly unemotional. Like Gary Cooper."

Feminine traits were considered to be loving, caring, and being supportive (see pages 111–113), whereas male qualities as we have seen, were active, independent, doing, creating, and being in charge, dominant.

Most men, when asked, "How would you feel if something about you were described as feminine or womanly?" said they would be angry:

"Enraged. Insulted. Never mind what women are really like—I know what he's saying: he's saying he thinks I should be submissive to him."

"Outrageous demand. I may not seek to dominate, but I shall never submit when I'm not shown wrong."

"To be called 'like a woman' by another man is to be humiliated by him, because most men consider women to be weak, and a man doesn't want to be considered weak."

"No matter *what* it was or *who* was making the comment, I'd be hurt, angry, and insulted."

"Chagrined. I may appear soft, but I carry a big stick, so watch out."

"When a man compares another man's behavior to a woman's, he's looking for a fight."

"Very nervous, tense, threatened—as if I were going to be singled out and ostracized for it."

"If I was described as having something 'like a woman's,' I would be outraged. I would defend my masculinity almost automatically. I wouldn't like being compared to a woman's *anything*."

But some men pointed out the stereotyping contained in these remarks, or said they wouldn't mind:

"I'm sure some of my behavior is thought of as 'like a woman's' and I feel fine about it. I think it's unfortunate that men have been conditioned to think that they cannot have any feminine qualities or they are thought of as being sissies. Men have feminine qualities and women have masculine qualities. It's as simple as that. Denial and repression of these only leads to tension and I think it's too bad that men are so instilled with the idea that they have to be '*men*' all the time."

"I feel that women's characteristics are usually soft, caring, gentle, etc., and I hope people will find them in men."

"Since women are stereotyped as showing their emotions very readily, if someone said I was like that, I would be proud to have overcome my macho training."

"To be honest—I would not feel bad. If men had more characteristics of women, the world would be a better place to live. Men hate to admit to this."

"Proud. I've always admired women for their freedom to be emotional. There's absolutely nothing wrong with showing our feelings. If males tried to deal with their emotions instead of suppressing them, we'd all be better off."

And some men, in answer to "What qualities make a man a man?," said masculinity is a physical/biological characteristic only, and has no definition other than physical attributes; so-called "masculine" behavior is learned:

"A man is a biological male. I cannot think of any quality which is unique to either sex except the capacity to have children."

"From the purely physical standpoint, men seem to have more muscular strength than women. I tend to think that all other distinctions between men and women (women are more emotional, etc.) are more cultural and social orientations than real characteristics."

"To me, masculinity is a question of a 'Y' chromosome. Whatever men do is by definition 'masculine.' I cannot ever remember worrying about my masculinity, and so I have trouble relating to others' fears about theirs."

"I have no idea what 'masculinity' is aside from mere gender."

"Masculinity is a physical definition, not psychological."

"My masculinity is a biological accident, nothing to my credit."

A few said the qualities they admired were the same in women as in men:

"I admire the same qualities in men that I do in women rationality, independence, integrity, honesty, justice, produc tiveness, and pride."

"I look for the same qualities in men and women—honesty, reliability, independence, etc."

"I admire personal qualities which apply equally to mer *or* women, like the twelve points of the Boy Scout oath (trust worthy, loyal, etc.)."

"I admire the same qualities in men and women—honesty, loyalty, intelligence, kindness, friendliness, creativity helpfulness, knowledge of self-worth, insight, flexibility humor, and broad-mindedness."

"Same as in women—courage, love, perseverance."

"Same qualities as in women, no kidding. Doing good caring."

"I'm not convinced that there are characteristics that are particularly 'masculine' . . . other than those we teach as such I believe that masculine characteristics are potentials in al people . . . not just men . . . and the same for feminin characteristics. I admire strength, character, integrity, a self assurance, confidence, sensitivity, softness, tolerance, assertive ness, flexibility, perceptiveness, objectivity, subjectivity emotionality."

REBELLION AGAINST "MASCULINITY"

"Men are trained at an early age to disregard any and every emotion, and *be strong*. You take someone like that and then wonder why they don't and sometimes can't expres feelings. Not only that, they are supposed to be a cros between John Wayne, the Chase Manhattan Bank, and Hugh Hefner. We are only human for christsake."

Many men said they did not feel comfortable with the male code:

"I've never considered myself a typical male. I don' identify at all with all the traditional stereotypes of men. personally have problems relating to many men. It will be very interesting for me to read what other men have to say and to see if the male stereotype is at all accurate, and whether I am as abnormal as I would guess."

"I am not a 'man' as society says I should be: I don' like to fight or play sports, and I have *feelings*."

"I prefer activities that are avoided by the general public; that's why I want to know how 'average' men really feel about things. I suspect that my feelings are unusual."

"Whenever someone would tell me to 'be a man' I would wonder if that is what being a man is; if that is part of being a man or becoming one, and what the hell is being a man anyway."

In fact, it might be said that most men did not feel that they were "typical" or "average"—not the stereotyped image of what a man should be. Perhaps this is not surprising, since the male role involves so much suppression of feeling and so much conformity; it is no wonder that underneath the outward conformity necessary for personal survival (in most cases), there lurks a man who feels he is not really quite "what a man should be."

And many men, when asked how they would define masculinity, said they knew how it had traditionally been defined, but weren't sure how they themselves wanted to define it; some were engaged in rethinking what it means to be a man:

"They say masculinity is someone who thinks he is superior to the opposite sex. That masculinity is easily defined by muscle, or masculinity is someone who never cries, is always tough. Let's face it, I'm so full of this 'masculinity' crap, it is sickening. I consider myself ¼ masculine, ¼ feminine (oh, if those jocks could hear me now), and ½ fighting for something in between. I cry when I feel like it, yet there is pressure to *not* cry ('Young man, men don't cry'), but then I tell myself, the hell with everyone else, I feel sad and crying is the only way. The other part of me says, 'Boy, you are a real sissy crying, you are showing a weak character.' The other part (feminine) says, 'Who ever claimed that if a man cries, he is weak? It takes a stronger person (man) to cry, you know.' That kind of thing I'm fighting, not daily, yet the questions are always there. The answers, I am trying to find them."

"I guess deep inside, on one level, I believe that a man is big and tough, has power, is insensitive to pain, not afraid, and solves problems by being aggressive, etc., etc. Yet I know better than that—how could anybody think about things for five minutes without seeing through it? That's not masculinity, that's a masculinity problem! So I do what I suppose most

men do: take a little pride in 'masculinity' where I can manag
it, and scorn the idea where it's out of my reach. But what a
hell of a way for us to live. Our sexual definitions and ideal
are a mess, and they bring pain and sorrow to us all."

"I don't know. I know what I am told makes a man, bu
I am not sure at all that those are real. In men, I admir
openness, sensitivity, strength of character, kindness, all o
them the same things that I admire in anyone, male or female
I am proud of my effort to redefine for myself what mascu
linity, or perhaps better what humanity is, without listenin
to and buying all the stuff I have been told by society ove
the years."

"I can't say. On the one hand, I would say forcefulness
and on the other, tenderness and affection and openness. I'n
confused about my masculinity."

"Masculine is a term for arbitrarily determined socia
behavior. The definition is now in flux, so I have no firm guide
line as to whether I'm masculine or not."

"Masculinity is a term I have trouble responding to
objectively. I know what it is in my head—but in my guts i
stirs up a lot of connotations like 'be tough,' 'be aggressive,
'be self-reliant,' 'a cocksman,' 'be John Wayne,' 'be a jock,
'be a rescuer of damsels-in-distress,' etc. I struggle not to le
that ingrained feeling control me, because to the extent i
does, I'll always feel I am 'not man enough.' "

"I'm not sure what 'masculinity' is. I believe I'm mascu
line in that I recognize in myself the intellectualized, non
emotional, self-depriving, rigid behavioral characteristic
currently used by some to define 'masculinity.' I am in the
midst of reassessing myself and I am not sure what a 'man' is
I am sensitive to those characteristics in men which demon
strate a mentor quality and generosity. I believe that I am
compassionate and am proud of being this way and also bein
male. I equate 'macho' with behavior toward women which
places them in a servile position."

"When I think of men I admire and what it is abou
them I admire, I find that it has very little to do with th
traditional conception of manliness. It would include: sensi
tivity and gentleness, humility (real humility is openness and
acceptance of others, even though different, the ability to se
oneself and one's ideas and opinions as limited, as non
absolute, as penultimate), artistic ability, humor, especially
dry humor, intelligence and knowledge, being open with
others, i.e., allowing oneself to be vulnerable, strength to
carry on despite disappointment, etc., genuine concern fo

other people, appreciation of beauty, the ability to express affection verbally and physically (this is something I rarely see). I like those qualities in men which awaken a certain vision within me. They are not, however, things I would envy a person for, as I might envy a stereotypical masculine quality (a larger, more muscular build, for example)."

And a few mentioned traditionally "feminine" qualities in their definition of masculinity:

"Masculinity is the ability to feel good, bad, sad, angry, anxious, and then to acknowledge those feelings to yourself and then to show them to others, without 'masking' or 'filtering' them for content."

"The qualities I admire in a man are: gentleness, strength in personality, good sense of humor, caring, loving nature, and easygoing and obliging."

"Doing for others with grace and dignity."

"Having the strength to be gentle and loving."

"I'm masculine. Very. Love to cook, can cry, feel deeply, care a lot."

"Compassion for others—gentility, poise, savoir faire, self-respect, and creativity."

"Just maturity, and caring."

"A person who has become 'free to be.' A humanistic person, open, giving."

"Understanding others and how they are feeling—making people feel warm and wanted and accepted."

"I admire gentleness, understanding, rational strong will, alertness, sensitivity, honesty of expression, the ability to initiate wise changes."

"Masculinity is first being a person. My definition is loving, caring, sensuous, strong."

"Warm, kind and tender, sensitive."

"Warm, tender, responsible."

Some said, with a sense of regret, that there is no longer a place for the traditional male qualities in the modern world:

"Masculinity is the male role as it has always been defined. But society doesn't value these qualities so much anymore. We are not needed."

"Machismo doesn't have much of a place in the modern world for most of us. Even the few people I know who really need a somewhat macho attitude—principally policemen—

today are supposed to also be capable of soft and poignant feelings."

"I like Westerns and war movies because I admire the independence and freedom and the courage to fight injustice that men had in those movies. Seems like these attitudes don't fit in so much anymore. If you fight for what you believe in, you get called a redneck and laughed at."

In fact, many men today feel that they are under attack and unappreciated, even humiliated, as will be discussed in chapters 2 and 5.

Two other men gave longer replies about growing up male, and being a man:*

"I was very close to my father. When I was little I used to help him work on his car (hand him tools, etc.) and we would play ball, listen to the radio, play cards, and build things together, etc. When I got older he always made my friends feel welcome at our house. He could discuss many things with them such as baseball, football, and cars. My father was a man among men. He was loved by all who knew him and he didn't ever run around on my mother. He was ruggedly good-looking with a barrel chest (from wrestling) and huge blacksmith arms. My goal in life is to be as good and honest a man as he was. I guess I was closer to my father than I will ever be to any other man in my life. We did so many things together. We spent much time together fishing, going to car shows, stock car races, and other things. He was very valuable to me because he, more than anyone else, taught me the values I believe in.

"My best male friend now is fourteen years younger than me, has coal-black hair, and is a singer in a band. He talked me through the low time in my life, right after my breakup with my first wife. I like spending time with him because I can be myself and him and I act crazy together. We act like a team of comedians on the radio and joke around a lot. On the

---

* Other questions answered here include, "How can a man distinguish himself today?" and "What is heroic in our time?"; also "Do you have any strong resentments against women?" and "What do you think of the women's liberation movement?" (see chapter 2).

more serious side, we try to give each other good advice (when asked), and are always there when one of us needs the other. Being close to a friend is like having a brother, which I never had. We talk about music, cars, women, troubles in government and the world, and many, many other things.

"Masculinity is a very hard term to define. I would think it would be always being in command of yourself, dressing neatly (not sissy-looking), and treating ladies like ladies. I consider myself very masculine. To me 'macho' means a man that is a show-off. I can't stand what is known as a 'macho man.' I don't consider myself a macho man at all. A man is someone who doesn't brag a lot, is quiet, never starts trouble but is there when needed. I don't think hairy chests and big muscles make a man. I admire men who stand behind their convictions and who are thoughtful to others.

"My father told me never back down from a fight. (Which I have never done.) If there are more of them than you, pick up whatever you can get your hands on and even the odds as soon as you can. I was called a sissy once when I let a bigger boy push me around and I cried. I was told to be a man and not let that happen. I grabbed a broomstick and cracked him on the head several times. He never pushed me around again and as a matter of fact we became very good friends. I didn't like being called a 'sissy.'

"Also once I got into a fight with two guys who tried to rob me and I put one in the hospital (hit him in the side of the head with my fist) and was working on the second one when the police came and pulled me off. It was exciting to beat off these creeps.

"A man can distinguish himself in 1979 by being good at whatever he is doing. Be honest and be himself. To me heroic is having a bad disease such as cancer and not being a baby about it. John Wayne is the best example of heroic I can think of.

"My biggest worry in my life is having the company I work for close down and having no job. I guess problems are something everyone has but my biggest one seems to be not being able to acquire enough money to be able to go into business for myself. My job is just that, a job. It is not satisfying because I have to work for someone else instead of myself. If I could finish my college and get my degree in psychology I would like to become a marriage counselor. Now that would be (I think) very satisfying and rewarding work. On the job I have now I have the recognition of being a very good driver (over 1,000,000 miles accident-free) but that isn't really very much recognition.

"I would say my duties as a man are to work and support myself and my wife. Take care of her, protect her, comfort her, and make her feel loved. Also my duties as a man should include treating everyone with respect and staying within the law. It is very important for a man to work. He has to take care of his obligations by his own toil" (age 27).

"I have not achieved what I personally want; nor am I making the kind of money I want to make. I've won awards, and I consider myself somewhat successful, but my work is not what I visualized and my family hasn't done the things I wanted. My house is modest, whereas I really wanted an elegant town house. Yet I have a meaningful job, and my children are A students—dope is not a problem and they seem to want to be home. Yet, my bankbook barely balances, my wardrode is shabby, and I cannot pursue my hobbies for lack of money. Since I must moonlight in summer and on the winter holidays, I always feel slightly tired. My wife often tells me, 'Money may not be as important to you as you think it is.' It's important, all right, but only for spending. Once I played tennis with a female student, and she said I wasn't aggressive enough. I think that sums up how I am. I wish I were ruthless—aggressive—then, perhaps my life, including my sex life, would be more varied and I wouldn't live in such a fantasy.

"My dad was sure I was a 'sissy' because I couldn't pass the football he bought me in 1941. He didn't bother to show me how, nor did he realize that a full-sized football in a seven-year-old's hand is not a skilled craftsman's tool. I felt so frustrated then that I never learned to pass the blamed thing—and now I don't care. I think I was hurt most when my father's co-workers would make smug comments, such as 'What's it like having a *son* like that?' I knew what 'like that' meant. I felt my father's embarrassment. I didn't know what I did that was so awful. My older sister and her husband gave my brother and me gifts on Christmas that told the tale. He was given a Scout knife and I was given a box of handkerchiefs. Because of my interest in theater, fashion, art, and music I was 'sissy.' Interestingly enough, it may be overcompensation, but now I lift weights with regularity, jog, play tennis well, and have a very active sports life and keep trimmer than my outdoor brother.

"My father never spoke to me in positive ways. He belittled much of my youthful efforts at manhood. He never discussed my body changes when I was an adolescent; he never talked about manly values. When I joined the Navy, he wanted to talk about sex and to warn me about 'the meat eating,' or homosexuals. What I could not reveal then—or now even— was that at college, I had already 'eaten meat,' and I had had my meat eaten. At the time I did not consider myself homosexual, and I still do not feel that I'm driven that way. In any case, my father's sexual information was embarrassing, late, and inadequate. I learned little about women from him and that may be the reason I have troubles in my marriage—I don't view them as impossible problems, but I think if he had been the family manager and had not abdicated all responsibility to my mother, I would have had a better adult model from which to grow.

"A man distinguishes himself today by surviving the death of the family. Perhaps the heroic act of today will be his tenacious belief that the family must survive. A heroic man is the man who holds onto his children after his wife abandons the home to 'find herself.' A heroic man is the man who survives the selfishness of the women's movement and still believes in the equality of women, the truth of the family, and is willing to fall in love again. He's the *real* hero!

"Men as a group can be proud of the fact that they have survived feminism. I find the modern women boorish, rude, and anti-civilized. I deplore their outfront language. I cheered when Bella Abzug was sacked. I don't like the idea that women can say, 'We need a man the same as a fish needs a bicycle.' Perhaps I've been insensitive to women's needs, but I've *never* treated a female with rude and garish disdain. I dislike macho men. To me 'macho' is a guy who throws his prick around like a bull in heat and is insensitive to the needs of others. He uses women and men for his own needs, as he does the world's natural resources, with no regard for pollution, etc.

"As a man, I like softness and romance, where the female plays the part of being vulnerable, and I must defend and protect her. I like looking after the welfare of women and that's what annoys me most about modern life. I like the feeling of being the protector of home and hearth. I wish my wife didn't work. I wish women needed those things that make us men . . . not just our cocks to make babies.

"I like being a father, but sometimes the stress is more than I think I can handle. I went to the Red Cross baby class, the Navy expectant-parent school, etc. I want to be a loving authoritarian. I'm not very good at that, but I do have a sense of devotion to them and try not to be abusive, although I find I take out my frustrations on them and then regret it. They tell me I frighten them when I'm angry. Our relationships, nevertheless, are solid.

"I don't feel guilty about the way I've treated women—now. The women in my life have been professional and important in my growth as a man. I've had a genuine respect for the humanity of all people—I would never view a woman as inferior.

"I'm glad I'm a man; I'm happy that the breadwinning role falls to me. I wouldn't want it the other way around, I don't mind the pressures my wife and children put upon me. We are a two-income family, which creates more pressures, e.g., the absence of mother during working hours and since I work closer to home I often go to school and pick up ill children, etc.

"A man should be strong, both physically and emotionally. He acts in mature ways and is gentle. A man does not hurt people, but helps. He is strong and can be self-sufficient. He understands music, poetry, literature, theater, dance, and politics. He can be graceful in sports and can work in nature with ease. He is a protector of those who are vulnerable. I need to work very hard at being strong—I don't always feel mature. I try not to hurt people but I do. I'm not as self-sufficient as I want to be. Yet, I feel masculine."

CONCLUSION: WHAT IS IT LIKE TO BE A MAN TODAY?

Many men today—men of every age, not just younger men—are privately anguished over how to define their own masculinity, what it means to be a man. The majority feel an enormous amount of pressure, anger, and frustration in their lives, but usually focus on women as the cause of it, rather than the values of the society we live in. Most men, also, feel that they cannot talk to other men about their frustrations with "masculinity"—because to do so might make them look less "masculine" to other men, as if they couldn't "make it" as a man.

While masculinity as currently defined has good points, such as its grooming of men to face life with fortitude, knowledge, and skill, it also unfortunately teaches men to repress and deny their emotional sides to such a degree that they often wind up feeling isolated and upset about their personal relationships—or cynical about them, saying that emotional relationships are a woman's domain, something they would rather not give too important a place in their lives (see chapter 2).

A boy's relationship with his father—how the father presents himself to the son, what role he takes in the family—is crucial to the concept a boy learns of masculinity. Most men as boys had a very distant relationship with their fathers, and therefore got a very hazy and unrealistic picture of what it is really like to be a male human being, member of a family. Most fathers feel that their role is to appear to be a rock of strength, capable of handling anything, never shaken by fear or emotion, never uncertain or in doubt, always able to provide for the family. Most fathers did not talk intimately with their sons. Boys, knowing their fathers from such a distance, seeing them so reserved and unemotional, rarely passionate or "overly" affectionate, frequently grew up believing that it is not "masculine" to communicate openly or spontaneously about feelings. We have seen, and will see, that this affects men's relationships with other men and with women very profoundly.

Although it is often said that "younger men" today are different, that they do not follow the old stereotyped masculinity, this is not the case, according to this study. Younger men, as well as older men, are just as likely to be caught up in the traditional pressures on men not to be a "sissy" or "uncool"—to stay "in control." (However, younger men often *believe* that they have transcended the old stereotypes.) It is, in fact, unique, individual men of every age who have thought more deeply about who they are, begun to change, and communicate more completely.

If men are questioning their lives privately, why aren't they changing more quickly? First, many men are held back by the idea that changing, allowing feelings to have a more important part in their lives, will mean seeming "feminine," always having to be "gentle." Men fear that they will have to repudiate all the old ideas of strength, having power, being in control, getting things done, and so forth. The fact is, this is not true—men do not have to be one-sided. The idea is that both men and women can be strong and powerful, and at the same time have the capacity to feel vulnerable and in need of comfort and help. Secondly, many men are held back from changing their lives because they fear that other men—perhaps their employers—who have not changed, will no longer respect and associate with them if they do not stick to the old masculine stereotypes.

The men in this study who most accepted traditional stereotypes of masculinity were those who were most unhappy with their lives. There has been a built-in contradiction between the so-called male lifestyle and human closeness. The lack of emotionality and closeness makes men feel isolated, angry, and cynical. Men today are faced with the rather formidable choice of either continuing to live their lives as in the past, saying personal life isn't important, feeling torn apart by constantly having to suppress and deny their own needs (and suffering with their early death rate and illnesses)—and creating something new.

2
RELATIONSHIPS WITH WOMEN*

* Women reading this book may want to answer the questions about relationships with men (see pages 1009–1021), or they may write directly to S. Hite, P.O. Box 5282, F.D.R. Station, New York, N.Y. 10022.

HOW IMPORTANT ARE RELATIONSHIPS WITH WOMEN TO MEN?

How do men see women? How are men's relationships with women different from their relationships with other men? Where does a man's relationship with a woman fit into his overall life? What is it men want from a relationship with a woman?*

WHICH DO MEN VALUE MOST—THEIR FRIENDSHIPS WITH MEN, OR THEIR LOVE RELATIONSHIPS WITH WOMEN?

"How do your friendships compare with your love relationships?"

Most men said that friendships with men were nowhere near as fulfilling as a sexual relationship with a woman they loved:

"My relationship with my wife, whatever its flaws, is central and bears no comparison to my friendships. All my friendships, however pleasant and fruitful—and they are—are very subsidiary. While I enjoy them, they're not in the same ball park as my relationship with my wife."

"Friendships to me are nowhere as close and intimate as

* Answers in this section are only from men with a heterosexual orientation.

love relationships. Friends are easy to talk to, you confide in them, once in a while tell them some of your fears and fantasies, but they still do not compare to the intimacy that a love relationship has."

"There are five people who truly matter to me: we've been close most of our adult lives, and I'd have difficulty thinking of life without them. Yet were a choice forced upon me, I would give them all up to keep my lover. Sex is probably the difference. Through sexual love, we've grown intimate on so many levels that the rapport we have is richer, more palpable than any friendship."

"My wife is also my best friend; I know of no one with whom I would rather go on a trip or attend a movie than my wife. So we manage to have a physical relationship, an intellectual relationship, a social relationship—in short a partnership. I can talk shop with her and do. I am also fortunate in that I have a best male friend, whom I have known and loved for nineteen years. Our relationship is the second most important relationship in this world to me."

"The most satisfying part of my life, although it isn't what I envision as ideal, is the special relationship that I have with my wife, and our sharing in caring for our two-year-old child."

"Friendships don't seem to mean a hell of a lot to me when my love life is fucked up. With certain select friends, I can rap it out, but mostly when I'm down, the way that only love can get me down, I see most of my 'friends' as meaningless casual acquaintances. I reflect on all the times that they seemed to prevent us from becoming true friends, all the times that they have 'shut me out,' and I resent the fact that they will probably never call on me in need, and I resolve to never call on them."

"My wife has been a better and more loyal friend than any other person I've ever met. Friendships with men are not as deep or intense."

"Most of my friendships are very satisfying, but on a different plane. When I have a physical relationship with someone, I have a tendency to allow all my true feelings to emerge. If you can take your clothes off in front of someone, you can allow yourself the liberty of being totally candid, undefensive, and yourself. With my lover, I have to be honest. With friends, even the best, I always have an 'out' and can play the role, a bit. With my lover, I've got to be myself, or it doesn't work. She knows it and I know it."

"Friendships are made for convenience, and fill certain social needs. My lover fills a deeper part of me, a part I didn't know was there and I don't ever want to lose. Such a close relationship makes me feel that life is more precious and worthwhile to live."

Similarly, when asked, "What was the happiest you ever were with someone? The closest?" most men mentioned their intimate lives with women:

"The happiest and closest moments I have ever experienced have virtually all been with my wife—our courtship, our traveling, our building a house together, our having a child."

"On our honeymoon."

"With my wife after an affair was ended."

"I have been happiest with my wife. Many times stand out in my mind—our early courtship, the first time we had 'sex,' our engagement, when she was pregnant, the wedding, various outings, the birth of our children—and so many things."

"My happiest moments are with my wife after a mutually satisfying sexual experience, this is also my closest moment."

"The person I feel closest to and most comfortable with is my mate. Our love relationship, time, and our togetherness has transcended a lot of limitations."

"The happiest I have even been and am is with the woman I love."

"I felt the closest I have ever been to anyone recently, when I was in bed with the woman I love, just talking, and she opened up about her needs, our relationship, and her love for me. At the time she was having a lot of problems and needed someone to be near and concerned."

Only a few (8 percent) mentioned time spent with other men:

"I have not been in love with anyone for a year or two now. Right now the closest times I have are with my friends in our CR group, with whom I share a great deal of time and feelings, also one man whom I have great love for, and with whom I have shared, and been shared with, a great deal."

A few mentioned that both friendships and love relationships are important and satisfying, but in different ways:

"Friendships are not more satisfying, or more exciting, or more loving, not even more long-term, and yet they are important. I have one male friend that I can communicate with on an intimate level like I can with my wife. In some areas, sex for example, I can be more honest with him than I have been able to be with my wife. On the other hand, I can confess weakness more readily to my wife."

"My friendships and my love relationships are both quite satisfying. I have good friends and a good lover. Both may be quite long-term, but so far, I've had my friends longer than my lover. My lover is more loving than my friends, but my friends are generally more exciting, because we do a lot of crazy things together."

"Male friendships are close, but different. They are earthy, warm, fun—especially poker, trout fishing, backpacking, etc. My love relationship with my wife has replaced to some degree previous male friendships. I spend less time with them now."

A few men (especially younger men) said their friendships (usually with other men) were more satisfying, especially over a long period of time:

"I find friendships very important because I can relate to my friends without all the complications of living with them. I love my wife more than my friends, but running a household and a family often seems like a hassle."

"My friendships are much longer, mellower, and steadier than the love/sex relationships. While they may be less exciting, they are more satisfactory and rewarding. I think there is far more mutual respect in my friendships than there is in my love affairs. There is also more space and freedom in friendship than in love as far as restrictions are concerned."

"I have had better luck with all kinds of friendships than with close love relationships. The love affairs are more exciting, but they trigger my feelings of inadequacy. The friendships are probably more loving in the best sense of that word as well as more long-term."

"The friendships have definitely been better than the love relationships because there is no bullshit 'heaviness' involved, no romantic games, which is what love relationships often turn into. Friendships can last a lifetime more often than romantic relationships. However, I think the most satisfying relationship, overall, or ideally, would be a romantic one, it's more physical and intimate. It's just too damn hard for me to combine physical love and friendship, I wish it wasn't so difficult."

"I love my friends in the sense of Christian doctrine: I feel responsibility for their well-being and happiness. These can be long-term (forty-six years in two cases). Love relationships are more volatile, short-term (but exciting) than friendship."

"Friendships can be just as fulfilling if I feel I've really related to the person or communicated with them. Like the time I told one of my best male friends that I was going for counseling and found out that he was also. It was so relieving and brought us close together."

"I don't have too many friends, but they've treated me better than the women I've loved."

"Friendships (no sex) are much longer-lasting in my experience and much less devastating than love relationships."

—Or that they could be more honest in a friendship:

"My friendships are more honest."

"Both friendships and love relationships are satisfying, but I am generally more honest and open about my feelings and opinions towards close friends than in a love relationship, probably because I'm still touchy about laying my soul open to another person, after once having my soul and psyche trampled by an unfeeling woman. So far, my friendships have been more long-lasting."

—Or that they were more comfortable around other men than around women, or a woman:

"With men, it's easier to make rude jokes without worrying about being offended. In mixed company, you have to pretend that genitals don't exist, and you're always thinking: 'If I mention sex the women will think I'm crude and I won't get a lay.' When a man *does* mention sexual feelings in front of women, within the space of a few minutes one of the women often goes out of her way to put him down. Many men may not consciously realize what's happening, but once you look out for it it's obvious. As a consequence, men very sensibly decide not to pay too much attention to women's opinions."

"I went through a period where I felt more comfortable

with men. Getting to know men was less threatening than women. Dating always seemed such a pressured situation. I guess it took me longer to discover that you could get to know a woman as a human being, as a friend. I always had assumed there would be 'expectations' of dating with a woman. With men I could just get together and have a good time."

"Doing things with men gets in your blood, especially outdoors, like hunting, fishing, camping, cutting down trees. So every fall when the leaves hit the ground you feel like hiking and hunting in the woods. Walking through the brush and feeling the cold fall air is exhilarating. It's an escape from all the emotional tension that you get wrapped up in in your regular routine. Doing things outdoors with men is fun because it's friendly—competitive. If it is physically hard, you share the struggle, which feels good. It's sometimes fun to do things with the group especially if you're depressed or lonely, because it takes your mind off it. Doing things with other men is fun because I feel confident I can succeed or at least get respect for trying to succeed in whatever the activity is.

"Spending time with a woman is different. Being alone with a woman makes me nervous, because I'm never sure of what's going on. I'm very often unsure how to behave, or I miss signals, cues, misunderstand or don't feel the way she feels, or don't express my feelings to her. Sometimes it can be very relaxed and close, but the next minute I alienate her or hurt her without knowing why. This is very frustrating because I like it when it goes smooth, but inevitably I do something insensitive.

"I sometimes feel guilty when I want to do things with my male friends, and not invite my lover to join us. So I usually don't tell her when I do these things, and I very often don't do them at all. I pretend like it doesn't bother me, but it really does. So I get depressed about it, and then resentful of her, even though I'm the one who created the situation. I try to do things that I think she wants me to do. Of course, this creates confusion and mixed feelings. I don't think she wants me to do things I want to do, like watch sports on TV, go fishing, things I do with other men or alone. This may be the cause of a lot of fights we have."

But, once again, the great majority of men who answered (who related sexually to women) said they are closer, and more comfortable being close, to women (especially women to whom they are relating sexually) than to other men:

"It is nice to have male friends, and I have several. But I am closer to my wife than ever to anyone else."

"I think it is very important to develop male friendships. I find it very difficult, however, to be as intimate with a man as with a woman."

"There are many of my friends who like to confide in me and perhaps there are many things that I tell them. However, my closest relationship is with my wife."

"I would like to have a close male friend but find it difficult. I am definitely closer to women."

"I should have male friends because I'm a male. But I am closest to a woman—my wife."

"I am not sure whether it is important to have a male friend. I have been closest to my wife, as a friend, of all my friends."

"I very much value male friendships—I have worked hard at them—because they have been harder to come by than female friends. But I have been more close to women— I find it real easy to be close to many women."

"My relationships with men have been underscored with an unconscious fear, or at least lack of trust. I find my *close* friends are female. Them I have opened up to. I converse more freely with women, and tend to 'shut down' when men are present. I feel like I must be on guard then. The problem with this fear is that there is a backlash. I resent being fearful and therefore don't allow men to become close, and don't take the initiative myself, even with someone I know rationally I can trust. I have never felt as close as I would like with men, but it doesn't seem to happen naturally. How does one have close men friends?"

Men want to be close to women to express their emotional lives. This is especially true since, as we saw in chapter 1, men learned from their fathers that closeness, personal talks, and affection were not an appropriate part of a relationship with another man; men feel they can only express this part of themselves with a woman—and even then, all too many men have mixed feelings, believing that these feelings, these needs, represent weakness, needs they should not have.

IS TALKING INTIMATELY AND EXPRESSING FEELINGS AN IMPORTANT PART OF THESE RELATIONSHIPS?

Most men said that it was easier to talk to women (especially a lover) about personal topics than to men:

"I am a reasonably 'private' person and share little with other people. But my wife would know more of my feelings than my friends. I try not to lose control too often with anyone (especially my family), but have cried with my wife and children."

"There are only a few things I can talk better about with friends than my lover. She and I have explored much uncharted scary ground between us and have a solid bond. I can cry but I still have much trouble showing anger."

"I find it hard to talk to men. It is difficult for a man to establish a trust in another man. But I am not afraid to bare my soul to my lover."

"I find it easier to talk about my feelings with those people who do not seem to have formal or informal authority. I especially enjoy talking about my feelings to many women."

"You can talk to a woman and she will listen to you when a man won't."

But most men also said that, even with women friends or their wives and lovers, they feel some difficulty in talking deeply about their personal feelings*—once again reflecting their early "male" training not to be "too emotional":

"We have been married eight years. The biggest problem in our relationship is communication. We communicate well on levels of our relationship other than the 'intimate sharing' aspect. We seem to be unable to keep the feelings flowing back and forth in that area. Honestly, I feel very uncomfortable with those subjects."

"I am twenty-one years old, and a junior in college. I have trouble communicating my feelings. I wish I was better.

* Some of the following replies also answer the question, "Is it easy for you to express yourself, or do you sometimes have trouble talking about emotions or expressing your feelings? Does your lover ever complain that you don't talk enough about your feelings? If so, when does this happen? Why do you think it is?"

Many people have complained, including my girlfriend. I guess this is so because I come from a family where there is not much touching or talking."

"The biggest problem in our relationship is my hesitancy in saying what is on my mind."

"She complains about my not talking enough about my feelings when there is a problem between us. But this is improving."

"I am articulate, that is one of my greatest assets. But I confide my personal feelings less and less, as I find my life easier and easier to handle by myself. In fact, I've always kept my emotions to myself, and been raised to believe that feelings are to be mastered and controlled, and I can do it. That is the area where I have contempt for people who can't do as I do."

"There are times when I enjoy talking, but it is often difficult to express myself openly with people who are new to me. It took me a long time to learn that it's O.K. to express feelings. It has not been easy to get in touch with my deep feelings and longings, let alone express them. I was very shy as a youngster. My wife has often wished for more expression on my part . . . but to express is to be put down, in my experience."

"Sometimes I have trouble realizing what I am feeling. My lover complains that I don't talk enough—but she has helped me—by questioning and insisting. I must be afraid that I'll be overcome by or lose control of my feelings."

"I do enjoy talking but it is not easy to express my feelings. I believe I got this from my father because he hardly ever expressed his feelings only what was right or wrong. My wife does complain that sometimes I do not talk enough about my feelings, my mother complains about the same thing to my father."

"I communicate fairly well but I do reserve a large part of myself for myself. I dream that one day I will meet the person who will make me want to give more, although I feel I always will have a great deal I will withhold."

"No I don't like to talk very much. I have extreme problems trying to talk about my feelings. I don't have much feeling about a lot of things. My ex-good friend asked me lots of times about my feelings, especially towards her. I didn't elaborate very much or very easily. She wanted to know what my feelings toward her were. Often after we were resting after making out she'd ask me. Sometimes she asked me to say good things about her. This was usually when she was down in the dumps. She'd call me sometimes when she was depressed or anxiety ridden and ask me to come pick her up and bring her back to my apartment. What I liked most was just to lay there and hold and hug her. I didn't like to say anything."

"Sometimes my girlfriend gets upset with me because I don't talk to her or don't express myself. Sometimes I am quiet and don't feel like talking—usually I feel alienated or mad at her for something at these times, but I hate to admit that. Especially to her. I feel a loss of self-respect when I get emotional, especially if I get mad. I don't like to admit that she can make me mad. It's like she has power over me because she makes me feel excited, aroused, nervous, insecure, wonderful, and confused, all at the same time. It seems humiliating."

Many men thought of having sex as a substitute for talking, as will be seen in chapter 3:

"I just don't get into much talking, especially while making love. We talk some between kisses sometimes, but I feel our heads should be so close that talking is superfluous."

Two men commented on their discomfort revealing their feelings in answering the questionnaire itself:

"I just reread all my answers, and it seems I found it easier to answer the physical questions as opposed to the emotional ones."

"I just reread parts of *The Hite Report* for the first time and it seems that many of the women's descriptions of feelings of orgasm are so much more explicit—have been verbalized better than I have verbalized my feelings of orgasm here. Maybe I have not been able to let myself go—explore my own feelings. I do believe that it is men who need to be awakened, much more so than women."

A few men had the reverse problem—in which the woman would not communicate freely or openly with them:

"I am very happy with the undemanding love, the caring and companionship my wife gives me. But we have a problem communicating: she is often unwilling to really consider what my feelings are, and after considering it, tell me honestly and openly how she feels about it, not agree if she is internally rejecting it. And the reverse of this, her apparent unwilling-ness to explain voluntarily, without pressure from me, things that are important to her, her wants and needs, her side of a situation, how she feels about it, so that I can consider and put myself in her place, meet her if I can, and if not tell her my feelings, let her make a choice that meets her priorities.

"And as a necessity for all of the above, to deliberately find the time to be able to do this, to portion her energies, so that there is time for her to think and consider, time and energy to spend on our *relationship*, not just the day-to-day part of living together, so that I wouldn't feel her time and energy can always be found for other people, her projects, hobbies, or career, but not for time between us."

A very few men placed a high value on talking:

"I feel that problems should be discussed and not swept under the rug—if something bothers my girlfriend, I'm in-exorable until I find out what's wrong and set it straight as soon as possible."

"I believe in showing anger but I rarely do. I usually will go for a walk and scream at the top of my lungs at the air and the parks, and say everything that I wanted to say to that person's face, then I will go back and explain my feelings and how and why they hurt me."

Not only was talking or expressing feelings a problem (and usually the corollary, making a comfortable space for the other person to express her feelings)—but also controlling feelings was such a habit with many men (see chapter 1) that they often felt uncomfortable with physical expressions of affection:

"I force myself to reveal my emotions at times, but usually don't. There's usually a good reason (at least it seems like there is) for not being vulnerable and revealing my feel-ings. (I do equate revealing feelings with vulnerability.)"

"My wife is very affectionate towards me—I've certainly never felt neglected or unloved. As far as how I am towards her, I'm getting better. I used to be a typical male, fairly unemotional and unexpressive. I felt a prisoner of that role, but rather than break out of it, I more or less succumbed. Lately, though, I'm beginning to realize that there's nothing wrong with kissing her for no reason, or saying 'I'm happy with you,' or other mushy stuff. I like to do things for her that make her happy. It's a good feeling. The times that I'm cold towards her are if I'm tired, in an owly mood, or just want to be left alone. It passes."

"My experience shows me that I am quite inhibited about expressing affection. My only lover gave me more than I could handle and asked for more than I could give, which left me feeling extremely tense, somewhat trapped and even schizoid. I am trying to deal with this now."

"My lady shocked me recently by saying I give too much intimate love and not enough social love. For me, showing love or acting out in public is sycophantic. This is becoming a real problem for us."

"I think it's pretty sickening to see a couple fawning and falling all over each other just because they're in love. Love is pretty sickening sometimes."

Anger was often expressed by a lack of communication:

"In my first marriage, I sublimated my anger into working hard. In my second marriage, I sublimated it into physical illness. Now when I am hurt, I just say to the person that I am feeling hurt and want to explore what the hurting is about."

"In my case, when I am mad, even very mad, it tends to be internalized and becomes an unwillingness to communicate. Maybe I get maddest at insensitivity because I feel I am guilty of it so often. Maybe my anger is a form of atonement. I really don't know."

Some men did not like expressing much love and affection:

"I get all of the love and affection I can stand. I don't want much of this. I probably don't give as much as the women would like but they demand too much."

But another man said:

"I'm just now realizing how much real affection I've withheld from other people because I thought it wouldn't be manly. It was real easy to be critical, to be brusque, but not to be affectionate, generous, and kind."

One man pointed out that "showing feelings" is not an automatic equalizer of men and women:

"There is this new perversion going on—what somebody called the 'New Machismo'—that is, being 'man enough' to talk about your feelings, or strong enough to be gentle, or all this kind of thing—it's no real change, it's only an adaptation of the old come-on for a good fuck, with some new, sexually semi-sophisticated jargon thrown in about liberation and sexual politics."

Another added:

"I hate the current trend toward 'discussing your personal *feelings*' endlessly. In northern California, where I live, I consider that the disease of Marin County is the me-decade. It's infuriating."

Sometimes men feel pressure to "show feelings" when they in fact do not have many feelings for the particular woman, or might even dislike her:

"I feel guilty about my treatment of my girlfriend, who seems to feel more for me than I feel for her. I don't want to tell her that I can't devote my life to one person."

"Sometimes I feel that if I'm sleeping with A., I should care more about her than I do. Sometimes I feel love for her, mostly I don't. I'm trying to be free of guilt trips, but it's hard."

"We aren't living together. We see each other every two weeks or so and everything is peaches and cream then. We don't have time to get into hassles. When she leaves me, we both go our own ways. The worst thing is that she gets too serious. I mean, she wants to marry and doesn't realize I have doubts. Even after I tell her, she seems to ignore it."

"My partner is a good friend. We've known each other a long time and understand each other, probably better than anybody else we know. But we live together, and I don't think I love her enough for that. I am trying to figure out how to move out."

"It's important to like the woman but I don't see why you have to love her. It's horrible when women try to pin things down. They say: either you have a deep committed loving relationship, or else you're a brute who's just trying to use a woman as a sex object. What's wrong with that—as long as she can treat you like a sex object too? This doctrine that you're not allowed to 'treat a woman like a sex object' is very similar to the old idea that you've got to 'respect' a woman. I don't think that men should try to make themselves think like women on this issue, though perhaps they should enter into loving relationships more often. I hope that women will be able to move towards men's viewpoint. They should at least accept ours as valid."

"My friend complains sometimes that I do not give enough—that I am unsteady in my affections for her, which is true. Sometimes I find her just too much for me—she is vivacious and energetic, whereas I am low-key and inclined to be retiring. Sometimes I feel like I am drowning in the almost incessant flow of words and ideas that come from her, and I freeze up. At such times I am inclined to be suspicious and irritable, and volatile. I find her fullness of herself very obnoxious and I feel correspondingly worthless. At such times I feel that too much love and affection is being demanded."

Others said they don't want to show their feelings for fear the woman may hurt them:

"The trouble with letting a woman know you are too much in love with her is that she takes advantage of it."

"I feared the fact that I loved this woman so much that she could (and she did) injure me. I'm not sure if she did it on purpose."

Most men, when hurt, said they did not cry, they drank:

"I never cried myself to sleep or contemplated suicide because of a love relationship. I drank a lot."

"My whole world revolved around this girl and she left me. I got drunk and got in a fight and was arrested."

Or suffered silently:

"I should be so lucky as to be able to cry. Lucky to sleep too. It would be more likely for me to spend the night without sleeping and drag my way through the next day until sheer fatigue causes me to physically collapse."

Conclusion

Men *need* women, especially since they cannot usually talk to other men—but many men resent that need, believing that to need affection and to like talking about feelings is a sign of weakness. Sometimes a man, once having opened up to a

woman, will later become angry with her for the very closeness that they had shared. He may feel uncomfortable, that
he has somehow been humiliated, or that now she will not
respect him, or might even "use it against him." This frequently closes a man off from building an ongoing, workable,
enjoyable emotional relationship with a woman—and also
makes it difficult for a man to feel comfortable when a woman
opens up and discusses her own feelings. Of course, these
"feelings" need not be only about each other, but can include
all parts of a person's life, not only positive feelings, but also
ambivalent or mixed feelings, complex feelings—all the perceptions of life, the small anecdotes one can share with another person.

HOW DO MEN SEE WOMEN?

CAN MEN AND WOMEN BE FRIENDS?

"I couldn't see having a relationship with a woman if sex
wasn't involved."

*Even though most men said they were closer to a woman
than to anyone else, men often saw women only in a very
limited way. When asked, "Do you have close women
friends? Do you have more male or female friends?," most
men said they did not have close women friends with whom
they did not have sex, and that a friendship with a woman
would (more or less) inevitably lead to sex:*

"My main problem is that if I am attracted to a woman
by her competence or for some other facet of her being, then
I will also be attracted sexually, since the two are very closely
related in my mind. It causes problems sometimes. I am
presently working on this with some success in a couple of
cases, but it is very hard."

"A man who tells a woman that he wants to be 'her friend' is just looking for someone to jerk off into. This sort of lie is told all the time. And women believe it. The Raggedy Ann and Raggedy Andy act can only be practiced by a man and a woman who are too shallow to be able to feel anything else. I can't do this, and wouldn't want to if I could. I'm an old-fashioned romantic."

"*Lots* of people these days want to avoid feeling. I don't. I let it happen."

"My friendships with men have nothing to do with love. My friendships with women other than my wife lead eventually to bed. If she had a satisfying relationship, she would not have needed my friendship, and if I had a satisfying life with my wife, I would never have looked forward to friendship with another woman."

Or thoughts of sex:

"I might pretend to ignore a woman's sexuality but I cannot do so. I may never make a pass at her in any way, but that doesn't prevent me from fantasizing and mentally seducing her in every manner possible."

"I *feel,* in friendship, like doing acts associated with love. *But I don't do them.* There are restraints which are not necessarily unpleasant. If I like a woman a little bit, the circumstance might happen that we could 'go all the way.' It probably won't happen. But if I really like a woman, I can imagine that I would like to have sex with her. Sometimes I may touch her, on the shoulder, on the arm, on some other always acceptable place. That's friendship, isn't it? And on arriving at or leaving the home, there may be a kiss, usually not on the lips. If the kiss were occasionally passionate, I suppose that wouldn't be friendship. But if the kiss happened because both people really liked each other, rather than happening because the kiss is socially required, that's still friendship, isn't it? In any community, there's a definite, clear line between what is acceptable and what is 'going too far.' As for loving men, well, yes, I sure feel a strong affection for some. If they were in women's bodies, I would like them as I like women, but in a man's body, I love them, but I sure don't want to go feeling around their bodies."

"Most of my very close friends are male. I find it difficult to win the trust of women enough to be close friends. I find that I eventually get turned on, even if I didn't particularly want to."

"I've met some really special women that I could honestly talk to, and I really enjoyed it. They didn't make any pretense. I might have even got laid if the circumstances were right."

"I don't know what to do with my attraction to other women. I like women. There's something I feel when I relate to an appealing women that I just don't ever feel toward a man. But I don't want to fuck a whole mess of women, or have them fall in love with me to bolster my ego. I just like women. Should I hate them or ignore them? Is that the alternative when you've got a mate? I hope not. I can't figure out what to do with this attraction when you are already in a relationship. Do you relate to women only in dreams or as illusions? Do you subvert this attraction? Is it a good idea over time? Am I immature for wondering?"

And one man said:

"All girls are to be fucked. They are made to be fucked."

Another stated that women will always be "sex objects":

"In recent years the women's movement has been attacking the idea that women might be thought of as 'sex objects.' Well dammit, when I am horny, and when I need sex, a woman is a sex object and any man or woman for that matter who denies this is fooling themselves. The story of Jekyll and Hyde is not fiction. There are times when a man gets so horny he would fuck the nearest knothole. He will say and do things to achieve his objective which he believes he means sincerely. He may have regrets later, but at the time anything is acceptable in order to achieve the end. A woman can be very desirable to me before sex and repulsive to me immediately after. By immediately I mean a minute after I get my rocks off. This is not a premeditated charge or a calculated strategy. It is simply a biological fact: it is sad but true—when sexual desire is present, reason temporarily recedes. Women should not blame men for something over which they can exercise no control. To a horny man, a woman can be the same as food is to a hungry person. Yes, an object. For a woman to deny her status as a sex object is for her to deny her femininity, her womanhood. A woman who is not a sex object is a freak."

But some men enjoyed friendships with women, and found it easier to talk (as seen earlier) or relate to women than to men:

"I find it easier to talk with women. With men, you are always tripping up their egos. I don't enjoy competition, and in relationships with men, no matter how subtle, there always seems to be competition involved. I find it much easier to talk about emotional things with women. Men clam up. Women just seem to complement my personality better than any man I have ever encountered."

"In my late twenties I started having continuing friendships with women. I discovered that I often felt more comfortable with women than men. It's easier to find sensitivity and gentleness in a woman, and most women appreciate these qualities in a man."

"My closest companions seem to be women. I've pondered the reasons why this is the case. Apparently, I'm more comfortable with women than I am with men. Why??? Generally, it's more difficult to talk to men about my feelings and problems."

"I have more female friends because I frequently learn more from them, communicate better with them, find them warmer, and more understanding. It's hard to talk to other men because we (men in general) don't like to admit to others that we are having a problem, whether it be sexual, physical, or whatever."

"It is my impression that women are less reserved than us men, more demonstrative and freer to express, show their real feelings. Therefore, they are easier to get to know. The men I feel closest to reflect some traditionally feminine traits —gentleness, consideration, etc. But, Jesus, they are reserved. I suspect I am too."

WHAT THINGS ABOUT WOMEN DO MEN ADMIRE?

Further reinforcing the idea that most men see women basically in terms of their potential as sexual partners are men's answers to, "What things about women in general do you admire?"

Most men answered in terms of women's physical characteristics, or parts of the body they liked:

"I enjoy very much looking at attractive women. I especially enjoy it if they are bra-less. I believe the most beautiful object in the world is a beautiful woman and the ugliest is an ugly one."

"I'm turned off by bad smells, loose folds of fat, ugly blemishes, warts, and disfigurations. Perhaps I could get over looking at a girl with a breast removed. Dressed nicely O.K., uncovered it would as of now turn me off. I like girls or women to be healthy, not really thin but nicely fleshed, not fat."

"I like their cunts and breasts. I like the back of the necks, armpits (especially unshaved), back of the knees, buttocks, and I really like bellies. Taste and smell are some of the most important parts of sex. I like body odor rather than artificial smells. If I suddenly discover an enormous wart or scar on her body—I cry off."

"Some years ago an article in *Esquire* magazine was titled 'American Men Don't Like Women.' The author observed that men's activities are mostly with men, and to them women are wives, housekeepers, mothers, and mistresses. *But not people or friends.* I DO like women as people and friends, but I am unable to look at a woman without looking at her *all over.* Was it Kate Millett who was complaining about men liking tits and asses? Well, whatever was responsible for perpetuation of the species homo sapiens knew what to design when he made men aware of tits, asses, clitorises, vaginas! I love the human female!"

"If I could make my ideal lover, she would be a free swinging woman of intelligence and good health, especially of moderate weight—I don't go for too much fat, which my partner now has. She should not have to spend much time on makeup or dress, or getting ready for going out or sex; should be quick to smile and enjoy life . . . I know several model-like-looking women who have rather dead pans and little expression, which turns me off. She should have the physical flexibility to be good in any position in bed within reason—mine can't. And ability to change to any kind of clothes or style without a hassle. The same hairdo, dress style, etc., gets boring."

"I like women who are just plain soft and cuddly. I love breasts of course but I'm even more turned on by nipples. They're like little penises."

"I like very feminine women, graceful, thin, lithe, etc. (I dropped one lover I once had mainly due to the fact that I didn't like her perfume.)"

"I like a woman's ass and tits."

"I like perfume, but it has to be subtle. I don't like rigid hair or hair spray. I like soft hair. Continental women achieve a disheveled look that I like."

"Starting with externals: Boots. There is something very sexy about girls in boots, even with long skirts. The best effect is with bare knees in a few inches of thigh and calf. Long hair is much sexier than short, hanging free, some of it over her shoulders in front. The shape of a woman's legs touches a man in a way that no man can explain, or woman understand. When they're right, there is no anatomical feature more beautiful. Nice legs are much more attractive to me than breasts. More girls have good legs than good breasts; and good is not the equivalent to huge. Big tits are as unaesthetic as thick thighs; small-breasted girls are not losers, either. But breasts that are of size and shape proportionate to the girl's general physique are relatively rare; they do draw the eye, and invite the hand. The right-sized breast is one that fits a man's hand. A well-turned ass gets to my penis quickest of all. She doesn't even have to walk to give me an erection. If women want to dress to attract men's erotic interest, make it snug across the loins and don't worry about stuffing the bra. And ignore the commercials about panty lines under your clothes. I, for one, look for them; they stimulate the imagination. To give a particular man the green light, give him a view up your skirt; there are many ways you can arrange it."

"I love a well-developed body. I do not smoke, so my sensory perceptions are more vivid and pleasurable. I have only had one turn-off: my partner had long pendulous nipples that were three-quarters of an inch long. They did not seem sensitive or arousing to her and certainly weren't to me. But we made beautiful, beautiful, alive experiences together and still do whenever we get together. She is planning on beginning her family soon, so I am looking forward to see if this changes her nipples and their sensitivity."

Men often sounded as if they owned women's bodies, discussing their merits and demerits* as they might an automobile's or stereo's—presenting a kind of shopping list for the ultimate consumer:

---

* As one woman remarked, "Men think they have a right to pick and choose, like at a beauty contest—or a slave market." John Stuart Mill has written in great detail about women's status as property in the nineteenth century, showing how early laws pertaining to slavery were fashioned from existing laws regarding husbands' rights over wives.

"Here are a few things about women that turn me on: Weight average or a little above. Lips medium-sized or larger, both oral or genital. Generous behind. Breasts not too small or too large with pronounced areolas. Lots of good bushy pubic hair. Armpits shaved or unshaved, but not in between —not bristly. Good complexion. Clean washed head hair and genitals—all over while she's at it. Intelligent, independent, assertive, and initiative, and with a sense of humor. Nails not bitten. Not a high or whiny voice. Hair undyed unless it's a skillful job, otherwise let it go as it will."

"A woman not more than five feet five approaching the 36-24-36 numbers or exceeding them (breasts only, as long as they don't hang). Ass should be firm and round, I dislike flat asses. I don't like white skin, and I like big nipples."

"I like women's breasts, but I prefer that they not be too large. When they hang down into her armpits when she's supine is too large."

"I don't like droopy breasts. You can be top-heavy and sag and look attractive. But saggy breasts are unappealing sexually."

"I like moderate-sized boobs on ladies. I don't like the model flat-chested look, but I don't like cow udders either."

Many of these men justified this attitude in terms of being a "mechanism" or an "instinct"—certainly not an attitude for which they are responsible—as seen in the following two men's replies:

"Someplace deeply within my mind-brain is the ability to find the female form attractive. I find I both recognize and like even the subtlest cues of shape or form that are characteristically feminine. These are visual cues I'm talking about, mostly outlines.

"I am often fascinated with how small a cue is effective. Passing by the entrance of a garage, I catch for half a second a glimpse of a figure in the shady interior, clothed in overalls, bending to adjust a carburetor, and in that instant am aware of that slight but distinctively female line of the silhouette. Or, going jogging in the hills, I catch a glimpse in the distance of another runner away between the trees, and in a quarter of a second have absorbed and noted with pleasure just the hinted contour of a breast within the sweatshirt that she wears.

"Let me illustrate that last point. I remember having gone to give a lecture in a distant city, and being taken afterwards to the airport by a man who was on the local arrangements committee. He didn't know me, I didn't know him. We chatted casually in the car. At a street corner, we stopped at a stop sign and a woman crossed the street in front of us. In an instant I was aware that her form was beautiful, and that my companion glanced at me without saying anything, but simply to share that appreciation. This is the sort of thing that, I believe, often angers feminists, who resent being 'regarded as meat.' I understand (I think) the anger. I regret the crudeness with which it is sometimes by some men expressed. But I do very strongly feel the presence of that underlying mechanism in myself. I keep wanting to explain that this isn't necessarily sexy or exploitative; I repeatedly note the same response (for example) to co-workers with whom I've collaborated for years without the least sexual involvement."

"I was conditioned very early in life to sexy clothes—tight skirts, tight sweaters, girdles, garter belts, stockings, high-heel shoes, dresses, petticoats, etc.—and that conditioning has never changed and can't be changed. Women in sexy, feminine clothes excite me—women who wear pants or slacks or pant-suits or flat shoes disgust me and make me impotent in my relationship with them.

"I consider the recent period since the beginning of the women's liberation movement to be the period when the American woman has been uglier and more unattractive than at any other time in our nation's history. Future historians could honestly call it the era of the Ugly American Woman.

"All my life I have had a basic instinct towards women which I don't have towards men. Clothes and certain physical characteristics such as long hair and breasts trigger the feeling —a feeling of deference and respect and a desire to protect and elevate all women. It is not an animal-like sexual response but a very deep respect and feeling that women are different, they are to be treasured and protected and treated fundamentally different than men. I am combative and aggressive towards other men but not towards women. This instinctive feeling toward women occurs instantly whenever I see a woman or girl. It is completely automatic. I have no control over it."

Age was mentioned quite frequently, with most men saying, predictably, that they did not like older women, but preferred younger women:

"They're really nice and fuckable all the time, but when they grow old, they are not worth looking at. Only between the ages of sixteen and twenty-five. Beyond that she is finished." (Age forty-nine.)

"I am definitely attracted to younger women and repelled by older ones. Why? The young ones have fresh, beautifully formed bodies with firm flesh and skin, and the older ones are not nearly so attractive. Wrinkles and sagging breasts repel me, as do overweight bodies. This is strictly a matter of sexual attraction; I certainly admire and respect many women who are older than myself. In fact I have found that 'mature' (over forty) women make better social companions than the empty-headed teenager with her glorious flush of youth. But the young ones arouse my sexual desires—not the older ones." (Age fifty-three.)

"I only like young women, if possible untouched virgins with young pretty innocent looks." (Age fifty-one.)

When personality or character traits were mentioned, they most commonly involved women being helpful, loving, docile (sweet), or nurturing (a good mother); leadership or autonomous qualities were almost never mentioned—such as being heroic, loyal, brave, intelligent, or strong:

"Warmth, kindness, gentleness."

"Their femininity and loving attitude."

"Intelligence, stamina."

"Gentleness, sensitivity, emotional aspects, insight."

"Tenderness, adaptability, they seem quicker in comprehending reality."

"Sensitivity to others, and to nurture others."

"I like the way women instill love into their families; and I like what they've done as far as breaking into new fields. I think it's healthy for society."

"Their warmth and the sacrifices they are capable of making."

"I think women are (usually) more giving than men. They don't seem to suffer as much from cheap ego-tripping, and can take small defeats and frustrations better. Either they are slightly less prone to power-tripping or they do it in less obvious ways."

"Women are more likely to be simply interested in things (and me), less likely to be using me for something else."

"Gentle non-pushiness, minds, talents."

"First off, women are much more sensitive by and large. I think they are not as headstrong and are willing to compromise more than men."

"Their ability to smile and go along with it."

"Their patience, love, caring, etc., and all the little things."

"Ability to make a man feel good and wanted. To help and take an interest in my work."

"Sensitivity, people-orientation, practicality."

"Women are raised to be caring, open, and emotionally stable. I admire these qualities along with their unselfish ability to put others first and their sense of harmony with their surroundings."

"Women are more sympathetic and understanding than most men."

"They are generally more sensitive. But they are often too emotional and unpredictable."

"I admire women who are feminine, not loud and flashy, and who are ladies. At least until you and her are in bed having sex. Then I like a woman who is uninhibited and likes sex as much as I do. I dislike phony women. The kind who pretend to be something they're not—like the typical 'disco queen' type of cheap-looking, foul-talking, painted-up phony that seems to be prevalent now."

Similarly, answers to "What do women contribute to society?" emphasized helping, supportive qualities, especially connected to the home:

"Motherhood, softness, caring."

"Women contribute tender loving care and sex, to me. To society they contribute children. Without them we'd have no ancestors. (Joke.)"

"They hold society together."

"Humanity. I think they will be better politicians."

"The only thing that women *as a group* can contribute that men cannot is babies."

"Much motherly love."

"Humanizing element."

"Children."

"They contribute companionship."

"Social and home stability; a softness of attitude in the business world."

"*Children* and home and the *better* things in life."

"Compassion, but I really think they're individuals, as men are, and contribute accordingly."

"A hell of a lot of love and supportive energy."

"They contribute much as far as all areas go, but more so in areas of human worth and human development."

"At this moment it is women who contribute most of the compassion to society."

"Women in our society contribute a majority of the kind of strength that holds families together. They are and always have been spiritual leaders, teachers, supporters, and appreciators. They have provided energy and influence that has led away from war and destruction and toward values and nurturance, sustenance, and confirmation."

Some men said women didn't contribute anything, or almost nothing:

"If they make any contribution to society, it is minuscule."

"As for woman's accomplishments in general, except for babies they're fairly unimportant over long-term history in general, but women have scarcely had the opportunities to do much. In the future I think women will play a much greater role in our destinies (for better or worse). Over day-to-day living many women are inspirational and a stabilizing influence to men."

And one man added:

"I wouldn't be a woman for all the tea in China. Anthropologically, they just don't have the drive to do what men do. I have done all the things I've done *because* I am a man."

Women were disliked when they did not fit these "supportive" (or self-effacing) stereotypes, as seen in answers to "What things about women in general do you dislike?":

"Cattiness."

"Fat, dumb, and frigid."

"I dislike it when women play their traditional role of passive, dumb, and sexless."

"Their big *mouths*."

"Stuck-up women."

"Bossiness."

"I dislike dominating masculine-type women, I dislike hysterical women."

"Hardhearted, masculine girls."

"Being cynical and bossy."

"Hate coldness."

"I dislike vulgar talk and not being clean."

"Conceit."

"I dislike the tremendous fluctuation of body temperature. It's either too hot or too cold in any room. They're always changing the temperature setting on the thermostat. It can drive you crazy. Women are slightly more emotional than men, they jump to conclusions too quickly."

"Bad humor."

"Their dependence."

"Showing their emotions, and touching a lot."

"Using men, slovenliness."

"The things I dislike about women are—they like to think they are superior to men. They are always on the defensive— ready to mow a man down in front of his friends."

"Coquettishness."

"Deception and bad breath."

"Materialistic women."

"I despise women when they use their magic to destructive ends."

"Loud women."

"Stupidness, slovenliness, cattiness, coyness."

"Women especially who think their looks should avail them the benefits of life, without further contribution on their parts."

"Almost all women are illogical in normal decisions in life."

"Fat, cheapness, insecurity, dependency."

"Their general propensity to think they are the chosen creatures."

"Princess qualities."

"Weakness."

"I don't like their confusion."

"Nagging."

"Trying to be like men."

"Their attitudes about men and money."

"I dislike their pettiness, vengeance, cattiness, ruthlessness, and masculinity."

"Pettiness, concern over trivialities."

"I resent very much the way women are always trying to boss men, make them feel small, and the way they think they're so superior."

"I dislike the fact that women usually approach almost everything from an emotional point of view, which makes communication between us difficult, as I approach most things from a much less emotional point of view."

"The unreasonableness that verges on abject madness that can ascend upon them at any given moment—usually just before each menstrual period lasting several days."

"The lack of curiosity and general lack of belief in their own abilities are two of the most disturbing qualities of women in general. Beyond that they find telling lies too easy and convenient and they are always looking for options, i.e., better relationships as far as the material stipends of a relationship are concerned."

"What I dislike is their tendency not to think for themselves, but to follow the judgments of others, let others decide their own value—more pathetically, the people who sell them stuff on the TV. But I dislike that about men, too."

"Irrationality, lack of faith in their own intelligence ('I couldn't possibly understand . . .')."

"Men haven't been happy with the world since they stopped wearing swords, and women won't be happy until the world is covered with indoor-outdoor carpeting. Men want things to be functional and exciting, women want things to be safe and predictable. It's the 'high heels and long fingernails' syndrome that does the social and psychological harm to women. The next fashion will probably be to wear a blindfold and earplugs; then women will have effectively cut themselves off from physical activity and a healthy attitude toward their own bodies and capabilities."

"Men are great. You can trust them. They don't judge you the way women do."

"I have the very deep feeling that men are more loyal to friends than women are."

"I admire women's loyalty, their gentleness, affectionately outgoing manner. Women are, however, more likely to lie and falsify their feelings: they usually feel no guilt in prevaricating, providing they do it for someone they like or in a cause they favor. They are more timid and do not feel bravery is called for; they are emotional and prone to exaggeration or dramatization, hence less reliable as to matters of fact. It is hard to say whether these female qualities are innate or are developed through upbringing—I suspect both factors play a part."

"I believe a man would have to look far and wide to find one who will really stick by you. They all are slightly dishonest."

Similar answers were given to "Do you have any strong resentments against women, or against ways any women have hurt you?":

"Women have suckered me into being interested in them, and then dropped me flat to move on to another victim. Women have acted snobbishly and coldly to me when I didn't think I deserved that treatment."

"As a child I used to resent girls' snobbishness and 'don't touch' attitude."

"I don't like their game of playing 'weak' and 'helpless.' "

"My only strong resentments are against 'pushy' women. Men can be 'pushy' but I probably define it differently."

"I think that womanhood is up on a pedestal too much. Everywhere a man has to be aware and warned not to be impolite around ladies—hardly any mention ever that women should be ladies around gentlemen."

"My resentments against women have been with the ones I have loved. Probably the fact that they have chosen to reject my love and that I haven't been able to keep them happy and satisfied. Along with women's lib, today's woman seems to be somewhat of a snob. Maybe they are afraid of the same things I am, of being hurt or taken advantage of and then left cold, so they put up a stiff front and no one is willing to get close and make a move."

"Many feminists, especially radical and militant ones, make me nervous and uncomfortable (even though I consider myself to be a feminist), because I feel that they dislike me or see me as a man, and not a unique human being. (I hate being stereotyped by anyone.)"

"To really understand male sexuality, women must be constantly aware of the *very destructive* effects of personality defects of the woman upon his desire, his enthusiasm, his sensitivity to arousal, his erectile ability, his sexual capacity, and his sexual satisfaction. *Some* of the most damaging personality defects of a woman are among the following: irresponsibility, nagging, quarreling, domineering, criticism, emotional instability, compulsive overspending, letting her beauty and figure proportions deteriorate, laziness, etc. Criticism about anything (non-sexual), nagging kills all my sexual desire for a woman. The atmosphere must be congenial and compatible at all times. Harmony must prevail. No woman should expect a man to function sexually when she is guilty of any of these."

"If a woman is bitchy, I don't even *want* to get aroused with her. If she's understanding, then I'm more aroused, satisfied, and feeling beautiful. Her psyche may even be—hell, *is*—more important than her body."

Some men did give a different kind of answer with regard to what they admire in women:

"I admire women who aren't afraid to assert themselves."

"Their ability to cope better than most men."

"I admire the idealism women manifest."

"Poise, sophistication, warmth."

"In a woman I admire honesty, sincerity, and being oneself, with no put-on."

"I admire their ability to function with the problems, both psychological and sociological, which they face in our society."

"I like women who don't take any shit."

"I admire women who are exciting, intelligent, and bound for glory."

"I admire the fact that, in general, women are more receptive to new ideas, new ways of doing things. Perhaps because they are a 'minority' fighting for recognition, they have to be and *are* by nature more receptive toward a lot of things."

"I admire women's ability to open up quickly and easily, and the objectivity they seem able to attain easily."

"I have always felt that, physically, women are stronger than men. Not from a muscular power standpoint but from an ability to withstand adversity, to maintain persistent effort, to work with dogged determination. They seem to be able to face up to situations and overcome difficulties. Maybe it's their maternal instincts that give them the incentive to succeed. The weepy meek types seem to be very much in the minority."

"It would seem to me that there are a greater proportion of intelligent women than men. Many fields that women are now entering are reaching unexpected heights. They seem to put more effort, initiative, and aggressiveness into their work and are determined to succeed."

"When my women friends have taken to writing me sexy notes and love letters, I have to say that I've always been totally astounded by the level of wit, humor, and sensuality that they can express so easily . . . they take it for granted and don't develop it, or follow it up professionally, they don't take themselves seriously. But many of them are superbly talented."

"Women seem to think more positively than men, and are more gentle. I admire women for being able to know how others are feeling, and for knowing how to make others feel better. This is something I am trying to learn. I also admire women professionals—artists, writers, politicians—many of whom have been underrated very unfairly. I admire the courage that women show in facing the male-dominated world. Women are making very important contributions in this society, which needs a lot of change. Women are strong. If I were a woman I'd be a feminist, because it means to not accept being a second-class citizen."

"Men have taken thought and developed the Mack truck, the atom bomb, the wing-tip shoe, the freeway, and now he's stuck in it. Spiritually I think women have (many of them) a lot to offer the world. It seems to me that the demand on men to produce material results has resulted in a concentration on the materialities and a total unawareness of the spiritualities of the world. I hope that as women break away from the restrictions that have been placed on them, they will retain and develop their spiritual values."

BOYS' RELATIONSHIPS WITH THEIR MOTHERS

Most men did not admire their mothers; in fact, when asked, "Are you or were you close to your mother? How?" men often responded with the same stereotypes as just seen, frequently picturing the mother as "weak" or negative, or looking down on her for accepting a subordinate status:

"No. She is too weak, and refuses to assert herself. She lets my father treat her like dirt."

"I have an oppressive Jewish mother. I love her, but think she wasted her life and is a vegetable."

"I was close to my mother until I realized she is Mrs. Mean/Guilt."

"In a conventional sense, very close, but not in an emotional sense. My mom is about perfect except for three things. She is kind, devoted, practical with time and money, unselfish, an excellent driver, kind of interesting, just the right intelligence for a woman, cooks enough, and puts work in its proper place (well, almost). She's even a bit handy without acting like a man, but she has three faults. She complains too much; that's not important, but what is important is that she's not emotional enough ('warm enough') and she is too domineering toward Dad. I love both my parents very much but I respect Mom much more, she earns it."

"No, my opinion of her is a little higher now, but she's too loud and nagging."

"Never! She was a dried-up old witch who gave me laxatives because *she* was full of shit!"

"I guess I don't think much of my mother. She is a very narrow person who has made most of her life's decisions, and all the important ones, out of fear. I know she loves me, and gave up a lot for me, but I would rather have had her be her own person."

"No. I always wanted to leave her, she was so dominating."

"I am not close to my mother. I am distant in all ways: physically, emotionally, intellectually. She is an honest, kind person who works hard. I consider it strange that whenever I think of her, I don't think of warmth or closeness or the popular notions of what a 'mother' should be."

"I'm not now or was I ever close to my mother. She is a typical mother, a martyr. I don't see her too often, but I speak to her regularly over the phone. She's a product of her times and upbringing, selfish and very unhappy."

"My mother was cold and domineering. She punished me when I was in high school for having dates with my girl."

"I don't get too close to Mother—she's the 'clinging' type. She is like all women—can be nurturing if kept in her place."

"I saw my mother as weak when growing up, crippled by her over-emotionality. My mother would cry on any occasion, good or bad."

"We were never close. Mother was a leftover from the Victorian period—an uneducated know-it-all who didn't know much of anything except mopping, cleaning and scrubbing. But I was with her more than my father. The only time I remember seeing him was at the dinner table."

"My mother is a very kind and gentle person who at the time believed religion was her security. She was afraid of my father and seldom was able to stand up for us. My father never used physical force on her but was very domineering."

"Love and affection came from Mother only, but she could not be counted on for anything else. If Dad was angry at us for something, she would never intercede or express an opinion. She was only good for crying too."

And a few longer answers of this type:

"I'm still in high school so I still live at home (with my mother only). I like to define a strong sense of personal masculinity for myself, and this has led to a very distancing effect from my mother. We're sort of close and sort of distant. My mother is very cold to me, at least that's the way I feel. She's never been neglectful, just not affectionate. I'm always trying to stimulate a communication between us, and sometimes if I press her she will talk a little bit about herself—but only if I press her, otherwise I wouldn't know anything, it would be like two strangers living in the same house. Her favorite things are coffee and talking on the telephone to her friends. We live in two worlds. I tried to make her realize this, but she just thinks because I'm younger, I don't understand anything. Like she always says, 'When you get older, you'll learn.'

"It seems like whatever I do, she finds something wrong with it so that it serves as an escape valve for her own frustrations. I think she is mad because she was never able to carry herself as far as she sees other people carrying themselves in the world. She had kids when she was young (me and my sisters), so she had to stay home and take care of the family, then especially after she got divorced, and especially after my father died, she always had to work, she always had to take care of the family and provide, etc., so she was never able to expand her horizons or go to school or establish a career. I can see that that's a logical frustration, so I really don't blame her—I can see how she could develop the reasons in her own mind for being angry and frustrated. Sometimes that makes me feel guilty for being a burden to her, but I don't let it get me down. Anyway, I think if you have some sort of goal, you should be able to achieve it and not let obstacles stand in your way.

"Sometimes she really takes her frustrations out on me, though. Like once, she asked me to bring her a glass of juice. I try to be nice, so as not to stimulate her hostility. That's how you should treat your mother anyway—you know, you get things for them. So I got if for her, but meanwhile there were some remarks passed, and I made a joke. The joke obviously aroused something within her to such an extent that she threw the orange juice into my face. Was I mad. I was steaming. She makes a lot of cutting remarks that I just let pass. I say to myself, I'll let myself recuperate from that one, but it seems like whatever I do, she still finds something wrong with it."

"My mother was always nice, and always listened to my problems when I was very young, in grade school. I didn't see my dad too much, because he was always working, but my mother was always home. I thought my parents were the greatest and had a great marriage. As I grew older, I realized I didn't know my father very well, and later, I realized I didn't really know my mother either. I thought I knew her, but it was more like she knew *me,* or at least I used to talk to her a lot.

"But at one point, I began to feel angry at my mother because I began to realize that in our long conversations I would be the only one talking. She would listen, and act interested, but I began to feel strange talking to someone who didn't really talk back to me about what I was talking about. So I stopped talking to her pretty much. She never offered any information about how she felt about anything or gave any opinion of anything I might say. So I withdrew and became very reserved and unemotional. I tried to sympathize with my parents—they were really struggling with a large family, money troubles, and life's hardships—but I felt like baggage to them. The only things that made me feel good were rock and roll, pinball, fishing, candy and building things with my tool set. I hated school, life and the future.

"When I went away to school, I didn't really miss them, because I didn't really know them. I thought my father was an idiot, and my mother even more of one for not asking more out of life. All she ever did was passively listen to the rest of the family and my father's complaints, and act like a maid around the house for us. I think she originally wanted to be a lawyer, and she was always reading books about law, etc., but she never did anything about it. After awhile, I couldn't sympathize or identify with her anymore. About this time in my life I realized that my problems were my own. I had decided on a profession, but my parents weren't interested in it—I was someone else to them—perhaps an extension of themselves—and if that's what they wanted to believe in, they could. I decided just to sneak out and become myself while they went on believing in their own fantasies of who I am."

"I don't know how to answer whether we were close. I couldn't talk to her about things on my mind, nor to my father.

She was concerned and caring, we just didn't talk about things. But I was closer to her than to my father—I had no meaningful relationship with him at all. He worked from 11 a.m. to 11 p.m., his obsession in life being not to undergo another Depression, etc. My mother accepted this as the way he was, and felt it was not her place to try and change him. She said he was a product of his times and his environment and he couldn't help it and after all he was providing material comforts for me, so we all had to bear with him.

"I thought my mother was weak to let my father get away with this nonsense. She was weak to put up with it. Maybe they fought about it in private, or talked, but if they did I never heard it, and if they did, she lost. It's still the same even today, although they are in their seventies and he is retired. He still does only what *he* wants, and she lets him get away with it. She won't do things or say things which might provoke him, get him angry, or create problems. Once I said to her, 'Why don't you stand up to him?' She said, 'You can't change an old horse.'

"Although my mother was always loving, concerned and considerate, and worried about us, she was also overbearing— 'you gotta eat,' 'what are you wearing, it's cold outside.' But she's still a weak person. She's weak in the larger context, and overbearing (at times) in small stuff. She never stands up to people and things that are stronger than she is, but she's overbearing when it comes to people who are weaker than she is. I wish this weren't true, but it is."

"I was closer to my mother than my father. My mother took me a lot of places while my father was working before I started school, then, as I got older, my mother was easier to talk to than my father—she is just more verbal than he is, more eager to converse. I remember when my father would come home from work, he would say hello, then go out to the garage where he had a shop, his world, and he would spend his time out there until dinner was ready, then come in.

"My mother never complained, she wanted to please him. She could be very aggressive and ambitious where her children were concerned, but she was not outspoken when it came to him. During high school, she helped research and write papers for me and my brothers, it was her way of being connected to the larger world, growing, I think. Looking back now, I wish that she had had more outlets for her intellectual ambitions. I feel she's in a relationship where she is not with a peer. She is an avid reader, but her education was cut off too early in a really awful way. She also has an outlet through the church where she uses some of her intellectual abilities, but I wonder if it's enough. I think her frustration is not very conscious to her, but it affected her life in lots of ways. I think there's a kind of unhappiness that she masks by going through all the motions of being a good wife and so forth. She's hungry for meaningful talk, and she doesn't get that kind of companionship from the man she lives with—this is not his nature, and it very much is her nature. If I could have changed her, I would have made her more able to reach out and get what she needed, more active somehow for herself—not just in the traditional areas women are allowed to be active in, i.e., their children's lives and church work.

"Many times when I was growing up I looked down on her for this. At times I felt a deep aversion, even a physical aversion: I was afraid I could become passive and false like her, and I didn't want to."

"I was close to my mother until she died when I was eleven (sixty years ago). She was a schoolteacher. She had to walk to the school where she taught. One winter when she was thirty-two she developed pleurisy and died. My father was a disciplining school principal who only valued rules and duties, not understanding. At the dinner table, my father would tell the children what to eat—'take this, don't take that.' When we would ask for more of something, he would usually say 'no more.'

"My mother was composed, quiet, never loud, and always showed affection to her children. But she was too submissive, she never complained. If she had complained, she might have lived for many more years. She should have been more aggressive. She should have had transportation to that far-away school in the winter. She thought she should be a good wife, a good wife never complained. Her worst quality was that she did not stand up for herself, and she did not demand much of life."

Interestingly, many of these answers contained a great deal of anger, anger not seen in men's descriptions of their fathers, even though they had generally stated that they had not felt very much love from them. (See chapter 1.)

But others had had a different relationship:

"Mother confided in me, believed in me, supported me, loved me, respected me."

"We were emotionally close. She was loving, strict. Instilled hard work. Taught me to be self-sufficient. I love her very much."

"When my mother was having hassles with her boyfriend, she would just hold me and cry and cry. She was always open and honest. I give her credit for making me what I am today."

"Yes, I loved her deeply. She was an understanding confidante and adviser, and she provided the impetus and direction that put me on the road to a good life."

"We're quite close—we talk and see each other pretty regularly. I like and admire her a lot. She's generous with her affection, honest about her feelings, willing to stand up for herself, and has a good sense of humor. We share a similar passion for music, metaphysical ideas. Lately we have a nice type of sharing where we help each other, see the humor of our various struggles and reverses. Like me, she has trouble releasing angry feelings."

"My parents almost always got along very well. They worked together, though I never saw or imagined any great passion. I was always closer to my mother and respected her much more than my father. I think she is tremendously strong and intelligent. I envy her moral and social judgment and her impressive collection of friends. I also think she has much more passion and drama than my father, and she and I have always had an understanding beyond words. I really know her as a person, her romanticisms and frustrations."

"She's intelligent and independent and I admire her."

"My father died in the war when I was four. My mother and I were very close. She told me her troubles and I told her mine. She worked as a stenographer. She had an enormous enjoyment of life, an ability to be truly joyful, and a great sense of caring for people. I wasn't jealous of the other boys who had fathers, I felt lucky not to have one, because I had no one to tell me off! I couldn't figure out why the other boys stood for their fathers telling them off. I always asked them why they put up with it. When I lived with my mother, she didn't go out nights too much, but now she goes out almost every night—she has lots of friends and has a lot of fun. All in all, she's one of my favorite people."

And some men had developed better relationships with their mothers after they had grown up; usually they said their mother had changed:

"I am closer to my mother now than ever, emotionally and intellectually. It is easier to be friends with her now that she feels no responsibility for me. I love and admire my mother and enjoy her company. She was pretty uptight when I was growing up, but has changed with the times and accepts me now for what I am. And she is stimulating company."

"I was close to my mother only in the traditional sense. She cared for me, listened to my problems, and was a good mother. But I could never talk to her about my relationships or questions of sex. I respect her more now because she has broken away from my father's overshadowing personality and become an independent but caring person in her own right."

When asked, "What did you learn from your father was the proper attitude toward your mother? Respect? Looking down on her? Pity? Love? Disdain? Hostility? To help her? Other?" most men answered that there had been a double message: on the one hand, they were told to respect her, but on the other, their father had looked down on their mother or dominated her:

"There was a dual attitude. He always taught me to love, respect, obey, and protect my mother. However, my father is intelligent although uneducated. My mother is more simple and parochial. My father often acts in a pitying and superior way toward her. He is fairly careful about this but it has increased over time. He does feel superior to her and does feel pity toward her. We have spoken of this and he realizes that it is his fault as well as hers."

"A mixture of love (because it's the Catholic duty), pity, look down (because my mother is *not* an intellectual and has no personality), help (kitchen and so on), but also expect many sacrifices and support from her. My father told me once never to marry a woman like my mother—this instance I will never forget."

"I learned from my father to live in a state of confusion. He constantly professed his love for my mother, but was not averse to beating the hell out of her."

"I guess he looked down on her, but was not hostile."

"He seemed to have the attitude that my mother was helpless and he was supposed to tolerate her. He didn't know how wise she really is."

"My father punished me if I did not listen to her or if I talked back to her, but he himself treated her in a very verbally abusive way. I never believed that that was the proper way to treat her or any other human being."

" 'Don't talk back to your mother!' 'Do as your mother tells you.' 'Go help your mother out!' On the other hand, her job was to take care of him, his needs and wishes. Everything revolved around him."

"Occasionally I was encouraged to help her out or obey her when I was a child. Today, my father sometimes ridicules her for nagging, mismanagement, and general foolishness."

"Respect was the key word. If he ridiculed or talked down to her, it was not to be a model for how I was to behave to her."

"My father's attitude toward my mother was that he had a wife and she was there to help him, but I should always respect her."

"For relaxation, Dad went hunting with his friends; Mom stayed home and cooked, cleaned house, and took care of the children. She did not have similar time for outings with her friends, but no one thought this was anything unusual."

"He does look down on her somewhat (when she does really dumb things) but then so do I at times. But I always feel guilty when I talk bad to her or mistreat her or don't thank her for things she does for me."

"My father treated my mother like a saint—a saint he took for granted. Sometimes she would act moody and annoyed, but he would just sort of keep on going to work every day, and wait for the problem to go away. His attitude was that she was being silly and over-emotional, childish, and that he would wait until she came to her senses, and that he as a man was above these kinds of things. But I was always supposed to obey her."

"The strongest impression I got of my father's attitude toward my mother was that he looked down on her, that the major decisions were all his, he ran things and she was supposed to accept this and help him in what he wanted to do. This was apparent in large and small ways. For example, if we were going out to dinner, and I put up a fuss about dressing up and my mother insisted, my father would go change into his old denim jacket and come back, as if to say, more or less, 'you can't tell us what to do.' "

"My mother ran the household budget out of a fixed amount he gave her every week, she didn't work. (She was sixteen when she married him.) She had to buy her clothes and everything out of that. It was very important to my father that she look well. If she wasn't absolutely perfect, there would be an argument. He used to criticize her clothes all the time: her dress was always too flamboyant or something. He didn't want other men to look at her, but he wanted her to look perfect, so of course they looked, so she couldn't win either way. Usually my mother tried to please him, and just did what he said, but I remember once she rebelled—she put on a big Hedy Lamar hat to wear to a wedding, and when my father said he didn't like it, she said like it or not be damned! That was great, but usually she was just docile. Another example is, she almost never drank, but if she did, she didn't like rye, she liked Scotch. But according to my father, Scotch was too expensive, he didn't want to spend that kind of money. If she would order a Scotch, he would look at her and say accusingly, 'You want nothing but the best.' Almost every night at dinner, he would find something wrong with the meal —it was either too hot or too cold. His attitude was that she was a dependent or something he owned that could be ordered around at will, and something he could take all his frustrations out on. The worst thing was that she accepted it for so many years, until she finally got a divorce. It gave me a terrible impression of how a man should treat a woman in marriage."

Others mentioned being taught respect:

"I learned to respect, love, and help her."

"If anything, love and respect."

"My parents have one of the best long-term relationships I've seen—my father loves my mother very deeply. I was taught to respect and obey my mother, with no variance allowed."

"I saw love and respect through thick and thin. He never said anything bad or distasteful in front of anyone about my mother."

"Respect. To help her."

"Much respect."

"My father taught me not only to love but to respect my mother. When I was young I was always to help my mother when she asked for it no matter what."

To what extent do these attitudes, learned as a child from observing the position of the mother in relation to the father (usually subordinate), carry over into men's later attitudes and expectations of women and marriage in their own lives? We will see many parallels in men's attitudes in the sections on marriage and monogamy, later in this chapter.

LOVE

Since so many men have the feelings we have just seen about women, and fear being "unmanly" if they are "too emotional," do they fall in love? Yes and no.

"Dad's idea of a man was someone who hunted, fished, played sports, etc. Love was not to be taken seriously or given free rein in your life."

FALLING IN LOVE

"Describe the time you fell the most deeply in love. How did it feel? What happened?"

"When I met my wife, it felt wonderful. I was never tired nor angry, I brushed her hair, kissed and sucked her whole body, gave her baths, we took showers together, as much as I gave she gave back."

"I was most deeply in love when I was around twenty-three. It was an incredible experience, and I would have done anything for her. I couldn't sleep, I couldn't study. I was as aware of my existence as much as I've ever been since. This was even far before any sexual activity became apparent, and when we finally consented to have sex, it was the damnedest thing we ever shared. We lived together for about a year and a half, and we had our friends, and our work. The apartment was a cross between our own peculiar tastes, and it was lovely. I did the sound, she did the light, and we loved it there. Later, when I was commuting in the service, when I came home on weekends I really appreciated our home. Then I was transferred and I lost her. I cried myself to sleep more often than not."

"I fell most deeply in love with my wife when we were in our late twenties, after we were already married. It had little to do with sex. It was the first trimester after we knew that she was pregnant. There was nothing I wouldn't do for her. Suddenly she was a new person. I remember a special day in particular when we went to a motel and had a nice dinner, then went swimming, and had an evening of dancing and fun. Then we went to bed and to sleep just holding each other. The sex wasn't important anymore."

"I fell in love with my wife when I was seventeen. It was exciting. It made life beautiful. It made me feel like Superman. Later, it made me feel awful when I thought the love might be withdrawn."

"During my recent affair I fell deeply, madly in love. I found it difficult to think of anything except my lover. I was continually keyed up, 'buzzing,' on cloud nine. Always planning and looking forward to our next meeting, etc. When we broke up, I went into the depths of depression. I began getting traffic tickets, had an auto accident, experienced all kinds of anxiety attacks, sometimes worried about having heart attacks, went temporarily blind in one eye, fell into a concrete drain and seriously injured myself, etc."

"I had known this girl for some time and developed a fondness for her which turned into a very deep love for her. I wanted to marry her and had it bad. There was such a terrible yearning, a sort of heart sickness. I dreamed of her, had wet dreams, masturbated with her in mind, had a hard time falling asleep at night, was just plain miserable and sick. Wanted to be with her or near her and took every opportunity to be around her. My appetite dropped off and I lost weight and was on the verge of a nervous breakdown. Seeing that the situation was hopeless, I moved away and became interested (in fact drove myself) in other things and went all out to date many girls. But in the back of my mind, she was always there. Even after I got married I thought of her and had fantasies about her, especially at times when my wife and I had sex and intercourse. This lasted for many years, but finally, during my second marriage, wore off."

"The air did breathe her scent and her touch was tattooed on my flesh and her warmth was near. The roses did give off more scents and the magic innocence of youth was everywhere and the world was at peace."

"It was the most draining and growing experience I've ever been in. We went through all my sexism and all her dependencies—I think I almost drove her insane at times—but we're still friends. Our sexual life was profoundly satisfying for both of us—even when we were raging at each other."

"The time I fell most deeply in love occurred via cross-country telephone calls and many letters from a woman with whom I had spent two nights on a business trip to the West Coast. It was a very traumatic experience that left me almost unable to speak and virtually overcome with emotion. It came about because the woman recognized qualities in me that I had almost lost touch with, of creativeness, affection, and a desire to reach out to others. She was offering me love in return and encouraged me to communicate my feelings to her. I made subsequent trips to California to be with her, broke out of a marriage that I felt was causing me to stifle the feelings that I wanted to bring out. We continue to be very special friends to each other, love each other and spend as much time together as we can. Our lives keep us on separate coasts, and we have moved from a feeling of romantic love to being loving friends. She was the catalyst in a period of tremendous change in my life and will always hold a special place in my life. Loving her has brought me to a position where I can love myself as I have never before been able to do."

"It was a reprieve from death and slow descent into a loveless aging. It was fully living again. I knew it could be a disaster in the end, but I thought, what the hell, everything ends badly, if you wait long enough. Falling in love you notice the sky, how beautiful it is, the clouds. All your senses seem superartistically alert. Food tastes good and the small details of life which you never notice when not high on love, seem poignantly significant. Being in love is operating at 100 percent capacity on all cylinders. It cannot last, of course. You subside into a more normal glow . . . or you plunge into the depths of feelings, the pits. Having been that high, you have farther to fall. I know the feeling, the long free fall, no parachute, waiting to hit bottom. You survive, but sometimes you are broken inside and never quite the same."

"The time I fell most deeply in love was the last time, with the woman I now live with, and am married to. This is tricky too, because I've only learned to associate the word 'love' with other things than infatuation recently. About the infatuation, though . . . It felt wonderful. There are no words for it. I went around for weeks and months seeing the world as a place of beauty and hope, rather than ugliness and despair. I spent hours being enchanted by the presence of the woman. Every little nook and cranny of my head was comprehended fully and cherished for the first time in my life.

Now there were two of me. It was as if the One decided to give itself a rare treat, by splitting into two, then seeing how tenuous it could make the split. What happened? I would like to know myself what happened. What always happens. I suppose the nature of infatuation is transitory. Anyway, we went through a lot of bad times, and came out the other side intact. I'm still learning to call what we have now 'love.' "

Others described the pain of breaking up:

"A couple of years ago, when an affair came to an end, I retreated into a shell for a long time. Thankfully, I was doing then the kind of work which is best done alone; I found myself avoiding others and working through breaks and lunch . . . this was something to 'hold on to' while I picked up the pieces of my life. I felt very empty during that period."

"I did cry (in private) when I realized that our relationship was dead. Contemplate suicide? No. If I was going to kill someone, I would have killed her. As it was, I punished her mercilessly with apathy. Ignoring her also makes things considerably easier in life."

"My freshman year in college my girlfriend broke up with me. It destroyed me. I thought she was the one I was going to marry. I have never loved anyone as much as her, and this includes to this day. It took about six months to get over it but still today I think about it and it bothers me some. I was bitter to her for two years and I went through a period where I even went so far as to hate her for what she had done."

"I was most in love with the gal I married, who bore my two children. It was great for thirteen years and then it was gone. Night after night, day after day I used to cry, and try to figure it out. I didn't want to live with the loss of her love plus the loss of my children. I felt shame and disgust even with my own body since it had been rejected. Now I still feel a loss but have put it in the past. I know I'm capable of deep love again, maybe different. But the first time is always special, I guess. I understand better now that relationships require lots of active work. I think now I try harder to keep my end of the relationship alive. But you can't do the other person's work for them, so if they let their part die you can't resurrect it for them or you. You have to accept the facts of life. Now I rely heavily on my friendships. I have fewer friendships but they are deeper and more meaningful. They involve people of all ages and both sexes. I need both the primary relationship like my marriage, and friendship, but since I have only one I draw heavily upon it. My friends understand it, and they listen and feel with me."

"During it all I cried myself awake and shaking through crawling, dark hours. Yes, and walked miles and miles, and actually drank myself into stupors. And pictured myself dead and her remorse-drowned. Why? What else can you do when it's here in you and not there in the other? I guess I've cried for release from the pain, for attention and sympathy if not love, and because I knew I had to change again to stay with someone. Probably the most hurt has come from the set of unrealistic expectations I have about love and marriage. I wish I'd been told the truth, or if there is no timeless truth, at least the tools to find my own truths."

DO MEN LIKE BEING IN LOVE?

But many men, when they fell deeply in love, felt it was not good, that it was something to control or flee from:

"One fellow recently told me he was glad he wasn't in love because it takes up too much energy, and that one is 'blinded' (can't be objective) about one's lover. It leaves you too out of control of your life. I agree."

"I've fallen in love four times. It is exactly the feeling of fear—the pang in the solar plexus. And the other symptoms are the same—the giddy disorientation, the shaky hands, the wild surmises. I've talked to several people about this in deep, careful conversations, and have come to believe that for lots of people this is the feeling of 'falling in love'—we just have a different, positive category for it than 'fear.' I'm describing something, not trying to make a point, let alone 'prove' anything. But what does it mean if, basically, one's *body* responds to dread and to 'falling in love' the same way? And why do we prettify this?"

"I've fallen in love many times. I don't know which time I fell the most deeply, but recently I've decided not to fall in love again. It's a foolishness because I always dream too much, and it's too difficult to find the right person. It's impossible. Thus, today I have a girlfriend whom I like very much but really I keep her only in order not to feel alone. I don't need anybody to live, but I want someone because I believe love is the way to go, although I haven't found it yet."

"I'm not really clear in my own mind about what love is. When I feel a really strong feeling for somebody at the beginning of a relationship I tend to write it off as my laying on this person all the expectations and illusions I have about love; my looking to them to be the whole answer to my loneliness and insecurities and so on. And to a certain extent that's true. But maybe that's part of love? I'm too rational(izing) a person to let myself flow with the feeling—it scares me."

"I try to avoid it like the plague. I don't need jealousy, anger, bitterness and deceit in my life."

Or held themselves back from falling in love:

"I do not fall in love very easily. I am very defensive about my freedom and really fight my feelings when I feel like I may be falling in love. This is something I would sort of like to change. I want to be able to open myself up more. If I am truly in love, I want to express it more than I can now. I have nothing against being in love, I am just not looking for a long-term commitment. I guess this is why my mind will not let me be in love as much as I sometimes want to be."

Many mentioned that they did not like feeling out of control:

"I don't trust falling in love. I used to say that it's nice to be in love, but it's not something I would care to act on! However, now after twelve years of marriage, I'm not sure that I mean that anymore. I think I used to be afraid of being out of control—of being in her control. But now I think I would be able to let myself follow the feeling—that is, now I could handle it rationally, I think. Now I could fall in love because I don't have the same need for security I once did. To be really in love, the problem is, what if she leaves you? You're afraid of being hurt."

"To be in love is to be uncomfortable because you are out of control, you do things you wouldn't normally do. Women are more willing to be dependent, or part of another person, than a man—who wants to keep a separation, keep himself for himself, who fears losing his independence. Women are better at love anyway, because they are more trained to adapt, to negotiate, to be patient. Of course, one does sometimes start to fall in love, but you can always stop it before it's too late. It will be nice in the future if they invent a pill to neutralize you if you fall in love—to alleviate your dis-ease!"

"Before I fell in love, I felt invulnerable—or at least, my success or failure in life was defined by the work I did and the effort I put into it. Now, I feel that I can be rejected and hurt by her. I hate feeling so vulnerable and uncertain about where I stand. I have tried to break up for this reason several times, but we always got back together. Not being able to solve this problem has made me feel very inadequate and uncomfortable, because I still cannot feel free of emotions for my lover. But at the same time, I guess the good things that can come from being in love outweigh the difficulties and pain that can happen. You just have to work hard at getting to know the other person."

In fact, most men said they preferred a more daily, loving relationship to being "in love," or a more volatile, even if exciting, relationship:

"I did not marry my greatest love. My relationship with my wife does not reach the heights of ecstasy that my first love did. But remember, where there are heights, there are depths. I've known my wife since she was twelve. How's that last sentence for a wise old man saying?"

"I had just broken up with a girl I had loved deeply, about two months before I met the woman I lived with. I was new to Berkeley, a little lonely; she felt used by people, no one was kind to her, she said. I said I'd care for her, without making any commitments to love her, and without asking anything in return. I needed someone to love, I guess, and she needed someone to love her, someone she could trust. I just surrendered to the feeling, and it worked out fine for about two years."

"I want the security that she loves me more than I love her. I want the control in the relationship. I've been in the kind of relationship where I loved *her* more and I was in her control. It was awful. I never want to be part of such a thing again. I don't mean I don't feel love and affection for the woman I am living with now, I do. In fact, maybe I love her better than I loved the other woman, maybe it's more enjoyable for her."

But relationships of this type usually also eventually contained secret extramarital sex—that is, men who defined love as less passionate, less "out of control" were also most prone to having sex outside of marriage unknown to their wives (or *outside of a relationship)—as seen in the following man's reply:**

"Love is such a cruel and irrational emotion that I really do not trust it. I have deliberately turned away from women who showed symptoms of love toward me, and have not looked for 'loving' relationships in later years. Too much trouble is involved—gifts to buy, compliments to endlessly provide, dates to remember, calls to make, careful attention to clothing, priorities to rearrange all over the place—too demanding.

"I am fifty-five years old, semi-retired on a police pension. I am married and have been since 1948. I like the convenience of being married, i.e., the homecooked meals and tidy house, but my wife and I are not very compatible.

"I think I have my most contented sexual relationship going right now with a woman I have known for eighteen years. She is one of three I associate with but is certainly No. 1, and I would abandon the rest to keep her. Yet I do not feel that crazy emotion called 'love' in regards to her. I respect her greatly and would do anything reasonably possible to assist her. We have much in common and similar objectives in life—i.e., get through it as easily as possible, grab the pleasure you can, and do not be too critical of the other guy. We both know what most pleases the other sexually and unstintingly strive to satisfy each other. There is never any unreasonable demands one upon the other, and actually I only go to bed with her about once per week in winter—much more in summer, when we can manage weekends away together. I would miss her very much."

HOW DO MEN DEFINE LOVE?

"Is love the thing you work at in a relationship over a long period of time, or is it the strong feeling you feel for someone right from the beginning, for no known reason?"

Similar replies were received when men were asked their definition of love: most did not accept a feeling of overwhelming passion or even transcendent emotion as "love," if

---

* See also pages 150–243.

it came suddenly. Most preferred to define love as a long-term
stable relationship, which did not threaten their definition of
masculinity, or their need to be "in control."

*Most men said that love was only real, or best, when it was
developed over time as a part of a steady, reliable relationship:*

"Am I in love? This depends upon the definition. Using
my own definition, I have a relationship where I love my
partner and she loves me, I am therefore 'in' love. I am not
however, in an ecstatic, romantic, infatuated, pedestal-placing
euphoric, and slightly unrealistic state which in my teens I
called love and to which many people still refer when they
use the term. My term 'love' means friendship, caring, acceptance, a great depth of intimacy (communication), and a
certain degree of commitment (the commitment being the expression of the other terms in action)."

"Love takes a rather long time. Otherwise, it's mostly
imaginary: you *think* the other person has these wonderful
qualities, but maybe they don't have."

"I have not fallen deeply in love for a long time except
with my children. My recollections are of first loves being
intense and preoccupying. I had no idea what was happening
to me and saw this as a loss of control, which was unacceptable
to me. I could not decide whether I was overcome by sexual
lust or by pride in experiencing something that went with
'growing up.' The first loves were sexually enticing but frustrating and disappointing because I wanted to engage in all
the sexual activities I could think of and invent those I did
not know about. The girls were scared of pregnancy and
God knows what else—the issues were not discussed, which
led to further frustration and alienation. Then I fell most
deeply in love with my wife years ago, and through a year
of engagement and courtship with much petting, could hardly
wait to be married for full intercourse. We enjoyed each
other then, and we still do."

"When I was younger, I would have defined love as the
initial strong reaction I felt for someone, but I now think
of it as something that has to be worked at to achieve understanding. Love and friendship go together. I do not feel
sexually attracted or involved with most of my friends or
those I love. Eroticism and sexual activity are exciting, necessary interludes of play, sharing, unique intimacy reserved for

only a few of the people I love. I am most loving with my wife and children but my wife is only incidentally a sexual partner."

Only a few said real love was the unexplainable strong feeling felt for another person almost immediately:

"I've known both kinds of love. I work at the one in my marriage, but once experienced the immediate flame over which I had no control. I suspect the former is more loving (maybe healthier), but the flame is really love."

"It is the strong feeling you feel for someone right at the beginning, reasons unknown. I have observed couples that worked at their relationship, some successfully and others not. I am glad I don't feel a need to work at my marriage. It just happens along. Basically I think we just happen to like each other, and find only a few things that need much altering."

"If I do not feel love for a person right from the beginning, I will never feel it. You can work at being loving *to* someone, but not just plain loving someone."

"About love—sexual attraction can be felt for many, many women—but every once in a while there is that strange, almost overpowering feeling that makes you want to be with a person all the time—through good and bad—just because it is inside you. I don't think you work at attaining this—it's just there. I'm not saying that two people don't have to work at staying in love—quite the contrary—but you do it because of that feeling you have for each other."

"There are two kinds of love, crazy love when you are just zapped when you first meet someone and then the deep love that may develop after you get to know the person. They are not the same. The first kind sends you into the clouds, you feel as if you are walking on air. Even negative experiences don't bother you. At times when you would normally lose your temper, you just smile and forget it. It is as if you are in a dream. This slowly develops into the second kind, or evaporates with a poof because it was unreciprocated. The second kind comes of knowing someone very closely, of becoming superfamiliar with her, of trusting her implicitly and always feeling at ease with her. It is a relaxed and comfortable feeling, not as exciting and heady as the first kind but far more rewarding and secure. I suppose I've fallen the most deeply in love in the first kind. I was crazy about her, she was the ultimate, the person I had always been looking for, my dream woman. Unfortunately she didn't feel the same way. She sure was a dream woman! Poof and she was gone.

"In fact, it seems every time I meet someone I feel that crazy about, she doesn't feel the same way. So I make do; I settle down to a relationship where I feel she isn't really the person I want, but what I want I can't have. After a while I finally acknowledge what I really knew right from the start, and we break up. Ugh!! I went through a cynical stage of trying to dismiss 'love,' but right now I accept that it exists even though it doesn't seem to favor me, in this respect."

Some said that both feelings were important—the initial intensity had to be there, but this feeling had to be nurtured and allowed to mature over a period of time to be considered "real love":

"Love starts from some inexplicable attraction which allows for more intimate understanding and caring. The initial infatuation isn't really love, but without it, I don't think love can really develop and mature."

"I think love arrives for no particular reason. That is, there are a lot of reasons, but they also apply to a lot of people, until this not known reason sets up the feeling. However, that feeling, and the relationship that gets established on account of it, will not endure forever all by itself. I think a lot of attention has to be given over the years to keep the love going, and to keep all the little relationships within the marriage in the right order. I am sure the only way I could have maintained the very fine sexual relation I have with my wife is that this mutual regard we have for each other, which we call love, has stayed strong, has matured with our age, and has kept us wanting more and more of sex as the years have rolled by."

" 'Love at first sight' is when you 'see' the beloved as a lover for the first time. There is also a kind of brief but intense intimacy that happens which I cannot describe as *anything but* love and trust. The long-term sort of love comes with a genuine understanding of the other on all levels of personality. It is definitely work. In a loving relationship, sex has an element of possessiveness about it which is unavoidable. It's *human.* A time comes when casual and shallow sexual affairs are no longer desired. This is the time when one is ready for real intimacy, and has the need for it. But this need can be greater than the other person is willing to give. It's just difficult and that's why it drives people crazy. Me, anyway."

There was a tendency to denigrate and discount passionate or romantic attractions as unreal or undesirable:

"I have loved many people; I have been 'in love' with only a couple of people. The people I loved, I still love, feel very close to, and will always love and care for; I would do almost anything I could for them. The people I have been *in* love with I don't feel that close to, though I still carry that feeling for them somewhere deep inside me. That state is one that seems to me a very selfish one, that is, I was in love with my image of who and what they really were, and naturally found out later how destructive that image was for them and for myself. Being in love, I think, is to be self-centered and selfish with another person's being, you leave them no time to be themselves, you have no room for their needs, but only care about your image of that person."

Some men had very deep questions about what love is:

"Is love this—or is it that? I just don't know. Devotion and commitment? Passionate infatuation? I know them both. I also know that a mixture of resentment and dependency is often confused with and mistaken for love. Perhaps especially in long relationships and marriage."

"I am forty-two, married for sixteen years and the father of four. You ask me if I am in love. I can honestly say that I don't know. I don't know if I have ever been in love. It is easy to love someone who always responds in a loving and caring way. But it takes a lot of effort and hard work to love deeply and to get someone to respond to your caring who has a low self-esteem. I don't think you can love at all unless you can love yourself first. I don't think I'm in love, just used to living with my wife."

"Being *in* love is the strong feeling you have from the beginning, and love itself may come later with work. I don't know much about love. Being in love hasn't done much for me; at one time I thought that being in love was the only thing that gave meaning to living, and everything else was merely a means to that end. This has never produced very satisfactory results in my life."

Others had very cynical feelings:

"Love is a storybook fairy-tale word. 'Falling in love' to me is getting a hard-on and wanting to fuck somebody. Crying over a relationship is childish nonsense for emotional women."

"Love is a very misused word. The best relationships are the ones that result in a good piece of ass."

Or said love wasn't important:

"I once contemplated suicide because I was not a monetary success. I doubt I could ever get that involved over another person."

"I don't think that being in love is necessarily the most important thing in the world. I do believe that the concept of love is an important one, but I think that people should work to develop a more general love for themselves as they relate to everything else in the universe instead of getting totally hung up in personal relationships to the point where it becomes more of a problem than anything else. However, I am in love and have been for several years."

"Love is very unimportant to me. I don't need it. Right now the thing I most want to strive for is a good job. Tennis is the most important and satisfying part of my life."

Some men mourned the loss of romantic love in their marriages:

"We lived together a year before we were married, and had nothing else to do but make each other happy. Then after marriage and the kids came there were just too many other responsibilities to fulfill each other like we used to. This all doesn't happen overnight. It's like one day you remember how it used to be—leisurely fucking, taking baths together, fucking in the living room, etc. Now sex is late at night when we're too tired to really communicate. You get baby-sitters so you can go to the show, but *I'd* really like to get away, just the two of us, or fuck in the car like teenagers. We really love each other even though most of our sexual activities are pretty predictable. We really care and respect each other. The worst aspect of our relationship is the routine we've gotten ourselves into. Much spontaneity disappears with the arrival of security. But love is very important to me. Love changes a lot. It's easiest at first. Then as the relationship grows in a lot of different directions and you're really testing the durability of your love, that's when it's most meaningful—it has *quality*. It's a strong tie that hopefully continually re-defines itself."

Some men believed in loving more than one woman at a time, and defined that love as follows:

"I've always said that the hardest thing a guy ever does is staying married. And this still is true. I don't love my wife any less because I love two other women also. Hell, I love half the world, and it does not decrease my love for any one person. Love grows, goes through stages, and develops just like the people who love.

"With my deepest love, we knew everything about each other from the moment we met. We fell instantly in love, even though each of us was married, and so-called happily at that. And we both respect society so much that divorce is out of the question for either of us. But we have all kinds of mental telepathy and other means of communications.

"Our first sex was such an emotional binge we were both drained. We had engaged in oral, vaginal, and anal intercourse and she had achieved orgasms during all three, and felt such a drain that she was too shaken to walk. I told her that finally I had fucked her cheese-kneed. We went to the basin and she washed me off and I had to urinate and she held it and rubbed my penis as the urine washed over her hand and she just melted into a pulp in my arms. I had to help her back to the bed to rest. Fabulous. Not just the orgasmic sex, but the totality of the commitment and the unity of feeling. Great.

"The best thing about my situation is that sex and love are available from a variety of partners. The worst is the charade of monogamy which all three of us play. But another nice thing is that all three of my sex partners are also my best friends. How about that for luck. All exciting in different ways, all satisfying, all loving, all long-term."

"I am just learning what 'love' is. I would say my mate loves me more than I love her, as I am her only lover, whereas I love many other people in my way. I love her very much, though, especially for allowing me to be who I am as freely as she does. Number one is we have companionship. We live together twenty-four hours a day in a remote one-room (24' × 24') cabin in northern California. Five years! We have a good sex life and regular orgasms.

"My sexuality is the biggest problem in my relationship.

I have always (all five years) insisted on my sexual freedom, and that has caused some rough moments. I enjoy the non-sexual companionship of women—more so than men. But friendships with women often lead to sex. I enjoy talking to women. It is not always easy to express feelings but I am learning. I believe it has a lot to do with trust. When I say I love you, I don't mean forever, I mean now. Also when I get angry I have a loud voice which scares women. And my emotional vocabulary is very poor, which doesn't help. Saying 'I love you' gets repetitious, a good back rub says a lot more."

"At present I love several women. Love for me is an emotion that has to be cultivated, like any good growing thing. It does take a great deal of time (two and a half years for two of them) but if it works out, the wait is well worth it. I think the strong feeling some feel for others at the beginning is just a good dose of lust.

"My relationships now include:

"*Olivia:* She is bright, effervescent, cheerful, hesitant to get involved, a great kisser but very independent, and delightfully outspoken. I enjoy her company, she makes me laugh, the worst thing about it is that she will not see me enough and is extremely reluctant to get involved.

"*JoAnn:* Good in bed from the neck down, a lousy kisser, bright, witty (on occasion), but very involved in what she can get from men. See her infrequently.

"*Brenda:* This little thing is the prettiest girl I think I have ever met. So far we have only necked, but I am hoping to go a lot further in the near future. She makes me feel the most masculine any woman has ever done.

"*Mary:* She is my wife, and I love her. We have a real good home life, and she does everything she can to take care of me and our kids. She never complains and is a good sport, always there to comfort them or help me when I need it."

LOVE STORIES*

The following replies represent a minority of men. Is this because only a minority truly had serious love stories to

* These answers also include some answers to "Have you ever cried yourself to sleep over problems with someone you loved? Contemplated suicide?"

relate—or because the majority felt uncomfortable relating them, even in writing, anonymously? Did the majority of men believe that these were inappropriate things for a man to say? Or had they closed themselves off from ever feeling them?

"I've been infatuated, turned on, or swept away on various occasions, but I think that I have only been deeply in love once—with my wife. It started off with attraction but has developed into admiration, respect, caring, hurt, laughter, crying—the gamut of all emotions. I have flown to the heights of exhilaration with her—both in her own personal triumphs as well as in her positive feelings toward me. And I have plummeted to the depths of depression with her—both in her failings as well as in her negative feelings toward me. I have ached to reach out and help and I have ached to be reached out to. The times we have touched each other's lives have had enormous impact. When things are good, my world is happy. When we are not communicating our love (and that's not just through sex, by any means) I have been immobilized—unable to function professionally or socially.

"If I haven't actually 'cried myself to sleep,' many's the time I have fallen asleep depressed as hell by something which has occurred between us, and awakened with the same depression and have carried it with me through the day—lasting for days. Though I've never seriously considered personal suicide, I considered killing the relationship time and again. I can't help but wonder if it's worth all the pain or wouldn't it be better to be over and done with it—let both of us go—out of this cage which surrounds us.

"Yet I've had greater contentment with her than in any other relationship. Outside sexual affairs have been more intense and even more pleasurable sexually, but at the basis of them all has been a basic discontent with my marriage—and my marriage is such an important part of my life that problems with it have an overriding effect canceling out the positives of the extramarital affair. I suppose it all boils down to the feeling of commitment we have toward each other, and the reassurance that this commitment gives us.

"And in these very strengths lie the roots of unhappiness. All my vulnerabilities lie open to this woman I love—she knows my weaknesses and insecurities—and I hers. And we both can be cruel in exploiting the other. If only we could learn to reinforce ourselves not at the expense of the other but through our own and the other's strengths and positive qualities, our lives would be near bliss (I guess). As I reread this I sound like a naive blithering romantic, but within reason I think it is possible."

"I could not get the girl out of my mind. Every moment was taken up with thoughts of her and fantasies of her. I wanted to be with her, in close physical contact, every minute. It was different than other relationships I had had—they had been challenges to 'make out'—but when I met the girl I married, it was different. There was a compulsion and a freedom involved, not being possessed but at the same time belonging. A good feeling.

"After twenty-six years we are beginning to know one another. Being able to read one another's signs but not having to use signs. No demands are made and we can approach one another on an equal basis. I think love must grow in strength. People change, I am not totally the same as I was twenty-six years ago. Many of my values have changed and certainly my goals. There are times when a constant love relationship can reach a low point, it comes under a strain, children, job, changes to the body, health, etc., and even boredom with one another. It can reach one level and never go beyond it. At one point I had some deeply emotional feelings of wanting to be close to someone else but at the same time guilt because I was committed to my wife. I was depressed enough to contemplate suicide, but I knew enough to get some help. I thought I had made a mess out of my life and that if the one I loved most, my wife, found out, it would hurt her. The greater hurt would have been the suicide. There is no living mess that can't be overcome. So I believe love needs work and constant reevaluation, to see one another in a new light, and to challenge one another to grow."

"We had become lovers with the understanding that there would be no emotional involvement. We played it light-heartedly, much laughter, real affection, fantastic sex. I fell in love long before I admitted it to myself or her. I had been one of the walking wounded for so long, and had felt so little for women and so superficially, that spontaneous *joy* came as a rejuvenation; I felt as if I'd burst out of a cocoon, open to life, joy, grief, beauty, etc., as never before. And she became the center of my feelings. At the same time we were learning how easy we were with each other, that we needed no defenses or masks and that whatever we were doing, we were happy just being together. So into a supposedly cool relationship crept an insidious tenderness and awareness of each other. At first, when we finally dared use the word (it seemed like a breach of contract) we called it our 'now' love, a subterfuge that didn't last very long. We are now in our fifth year. I don't know how to tell you what it felt like except to say that to find the existence of another person who was dear to me reawoke a long-buried joy for life and the desire to give myself to whatever life, through her, had to offer."

"The time I fell most deeply in love two extremes happened to me; on one hand I couldn't sit still, I jumped up and down and danced, I felt like running places instead of walking, I looked in the mirror and laughed with glee, tears of joy would come to my eyes, my heart pounded and I couldn't breathe, I wanted to let everyone know. I wanted to give. I wanted to share. I wanted to tell all lonely people to hang in there it would be along. Then sometimes I could just sit for hours and thank god for putting this person in my life. I always had the feeling that something in the universe had clicked when I had met this person—that for some beautiful mutual reason we were together. It's an honor and a privilege to be in love. It demands my honesty and courage. Above all it's a time of soul searching, a type of respect and I have to stand face to face with my own selfishness, anger, false pride and just make sure I don't fuck any one over, I don't hurt me or her.

"I cried when she was out making love to other men. I would wait and wait for her to come home, but she didn't, not til the morning. She did this a lot and I was hurt, scared, crushed, threatened. If this happened I'd still get hurt. But I understand her a little better today (in retrospect). Very simply she was an oppressed woman, a low opinion of herself was forced onto her, she was taught to be destructive. She always hated what she had done. Sorry that she had hurt me. She would become so guilty that all she could do was lay in bed in a sense of depression. I cleaned, cooked, took care of the kids, then she'd go out and do the same thing. Again I'd cry myself to sleep. Neither she nor I understood what was happening, how to stop it. It was sad. For a whole year I put up with it, thinking that I'd be called a male chauvinist pig or a sexist if I objected. It was a year of pain and frustration.

"But there were wonderful times too. For example, the best time was a Sunday morning, beautiful morning, coffee perking in the kitchen that I, not she, was making. We were in bed and her kids jumped in bed with us. There was lots of laughter, talk, playing, closeness, love. We were in such a position where my penis was gently rubbing against her vagina under the covers. It was secret and sensuous. I felt so loved, with her and the kids. I felt like a husband, like a father, showing love and being loved by my family. It is that sense of belonging, of closeness and comfort, of security that gives me the greatest happiness, being able to love my woman, being able to surround her as a person and as a mother with my life."

"I fell most deeply in love with the woman that eventually became my first wife, and the mother of my three daughters. I met her during the war, and almost from 'first sight' we were inseparable. Our likes and dislikes were similar, our goals exactly alike. While we were married and together, I felt fulfilled and complete. I loved her very much in every way. We became a team both at home and in business, and were very successful. I was *almost* completely satisfied.

"The one fly in the ointment was her possessiveness and jealousy. Strangely enough, this was not directed towards other women, since during the years of my marriage, there were no 'extramarital' affairs . . . but the jealousy was directed at my activities, my dogs, my love of reading, my friends, or whatever seemed to take me away from her side for even comparatively short times. I lost my freedom to be *me,* and after eight and a half years, we were divorced. Now, twenty-five years later, and after dozens of other women with whom I have had relationships of one manner or another, no one has ever been able to replace her."

"I'm in love now, have been for over a year. The woman has rejected me and nothing takes away the feeling of isolation and loneliness. I wish that it would be over with so that I could feel good about myself. 'Love' is not sex. Sex may be involved or not. Love necessitates sex, but sex doesn't always or may never make love a possibility. For me, love is in the head. It needs the physical resolution of sex with the other, and if this is not possible, all one can do is stew in his own juice and hope it goes away.

"There is the good kind of love, but then there is the *other* kind, the kind that can't or won't work for whatever reasons. The reasons don't make sense. *Nothing* makes sense. It's not like a form of mental illness, it *is* a mental illness— something completely unexpected, even unwanted. Who in hell would *want* to feel sick or crazy? Or jealous? Or possessive?

Or greedy to usurp another's time? But that's all part of it. The dark emotions *do* exist, and all the peace, sex, dope shit will never change that . . . *never*. Whole men will always be able to feel these things. A half-man can't. The dark emotions have a *right* to exist *because they are there*. I can't be a good little counterculture freak and sit around drooling in my shoe, and on the nod. I want this person so much it makes me feel guilty for wanting too much—guilty and *bad*. But this is what keeps me going, oddly enough. It's what I live for and think about every day. I think maybe today will work, even though I know that that is foolishness. And *that* makes me feel *bad* too. Makes me feel wrong, like I'm feeling something I'm not supposed to because it isn't shared, but I feel it anyway, in *spite* of what I am *supposed* to be allowed to feel.

"Well, this is Confession City, so I'll tell you that occasionally I still cry myself to sleep over it, or in the middle of the day I think about her with other men, laughing at my needs. Once in a while I have to hold down a crying jag because I'm at work, but it happens then too. But normally, I don't try to hold the crying jags back. Holding a crying jag back is worse than letting it happen and getting it over with. I know it won't last forever (the present crying jag, that is). I get the crying jags when I cannot be consoled, everything is hopeless. Asking the big question in life, the Big Why, asking 'what if . . . ?' is always worrying about death. 'Never' is thinking about death, too, and I know all of this isn't supposed to be involved in a loving situation, but it is. That 'never' *is a very long time* and the thought of it hurts like hell, there are no easy answers: I can't be consoled, nothing does any good, I feel worthless—like shit, and all these things make me mad, mad that someone has this power over me against my better judgment. Against My Will. Mind rape, the kind that women do.

"I have had thoughts of suicide, of my two arms opening up like vaginas with the blood flowing out and, with it, my life and the pain. But I have never picked up the knife. There is always one little bit of brain left during these bouts with the Black Thoughts that says, 'No.' That little bit of brain paralyzes my ability to move toward the cutlery. It has saved my life more than once. I'm a survivor. The Black Thoughts can come around during a crying jag, or in just silently thinking about 'it' and what just exactly 'it' is and what 'it' is doing *to me*. I tell these things here because it is necessary for men to know that it happens, that a man *can* be *that* weak and *that* vulnerable and know *that* capacity for hurting. *And that crazy,* because that's just exactly what it is: crazy. But knowing that won't make it go away either. This kind of craziness isn't in the textbooks. But it is as real as a rock or a tree. It exists. It's *there,* and nothing can be done about it, not really.

"This is written for those who are not expecting the *other* sort of love and what it can do.

"Anyway, I *am* engaged in a relationship now, and the best thing about it is that my woman friend understands my need to talk about my problems (all of them). I also feel that I can understand her life situation. I am learning about 'women's things' from her—stuff I never knew before. The worst part is the fact that I can't return her love, a love which happens to be the good sort."

And some men described love they had felt as a teenager or when very young, often with a great feeling of poignancy or irreparable loss:

"As a freshman in college I met a girl who was and still is my ideal. The entire world revolved about her and I was crushed when we broke up after six months. The breakup destroyed my ability to have a warm relationship with a girl for about two years, and has made it difficult to really give or receive the same love again. The closest I have approched it is with my children."

"I was really in love with a girl in grade 13—tall, with freckles, nothing that anyone would consider outstanding, but I loved her voice and hair, smile, nose, eyes, everything about her. I never told her, even though I sat beside her for a year and a half. Anyway my heart beat fast, I wasn't hungry, didn't eat for days, sleep was restless, and when I ate it was with no appreciation, I just knew I needed energy. So one night after work I wrote a letter to her—twelve or thirteen pages long, about three in the morning. I knew where she lived roughly but didn't know her address, so I tore it up. This feeling lasted for a few months (two or three), finally it died away. I still love her, though, and I doubt if she ever knew or ever will know how I felt. Sad!"

"When I was seventeen and still a virgin, I was more in love than I have ever been, before or since. The girl was also a virgin. We went on a picnic in the mountains and were together alone all day. Though we didn't have intercourse or even heavy petting, we were both highly satisfied emotionally. Each of us felt as though we had made love on the mountain —although our intimacies extended only so far as my resting my head on her lap (which stimulated me) and a single tongue kiss (which stimulated her). I think that that first experience in love has colored all my relationships with women I have known since then and has made me more interested in long foreplay, tenderness, and seeking the ultimate pleasure of my sex partner."

"The time I fell most deeply in love, the only time I have been in love, I was eighteen and she was sixteen. I had not had sexual intercourse with anyone yet, and during our relationship of six weeks, I did no more than kiss her and hold her near to my body. She gradually became cool toward me and I at the same time was falling helplessly in love with her. When she finally broke it off it was as if I had died. It was the only time in my life that I ever cried myself to sleep at night and this I did frequently. I did not actually consciously think about suicide but I considered myself already dead. A greater emptiness and sense of loss I have not known. Since that time I have not been able to love a woman with such utter abandonment of my feelings; I just haven't been able to do it. This happened twelve years ago and I can still feel the pain. If I were to see her right now I know my heart would jump into my throat."

Conclusion

Most men were cautious about falling in love. Men's first feelings on falling in love were as joyous and ecstatic as women's—in fact, this is one of the only parts of this book which could have been written by women—but after their initial feelings of happiness (and erotic attraction), most men ironically backed off or distrusted their feelings, the very feelings that had given them such pleasure. In fact, most men distrusted these feelings so much that the majority of marriages were not based on this kind of emotional intensity—at least as men in this study described their feelings about their marriages and their wives. Most men did not marry the women they had been most "in love" with, although they emphasize that they love their wives and do not want to leave them, even when they are having regular sex with someone they care about outside the marriage—as we shall see in the next section.

ARE MEN MONOGAMOUS IN MARRIAGE?*

The majority of marriages were not based on the kind of emotional intensity, the feeling of being "in love," seen in many of the answers in the preceding section—at least as men described their feelings about their marriages and their wives. But most men said they definitely loved their wives and had no intention of leaving them, even though most also had sex outside of their marriages, unknown to their wives.

MOST MEN HAD SEX OUTSIDE THEIR MARRIAGES

"Do you like extended periods of monogamy? Why or why not? Have you had 'extramarital' sexual experiences? If so, how many and how long? Did/does your partner know about them? What was/is the effect on you as an individual and on your marriage?"

The great majority of married men were not monogamous. Seventy-two percent of men married two years or more had had sex outside of marriage: the overwhelming majority did not tell their wives, at least at the time. By far, the most typical answers to this question were like the following:

"I have been married eighteen years. I like it, very much. We have a very good sexual relationship—I could not ask for a better sex life. I believe in monogamy. It is the moral and the religious thing to do. My outside sex has been unknown

* See pages 267 and 276 for men in relationships, and p. 267 for single men's expectations regarding monogamy.

to my wife. It had no effect on my marriage. The only problem is it costs too much money to support a family and a girlfriend."

"Married to the same woman thirty-nine years. Never more affection and pleasure than this morning. As far as extramarital, yes. Unknown to my wife. It has broadened my understanding of life."

"Married seven years. I greatly enjoy being married. Marriage has given me a regular sex partner and opened more doors for us sexually. I love my wife very much. My love has gone from one of selfish, possessive love to a feeling of need, sharing, communication, protectiveness, and mutual enjoyment of our child and life. I do not believe in total monogamy. I feel that there are times in every person's life when they need outside input, even to the extent of intercourse, to renew their sexual feelings and stimulate their fantasies. I feel that it can improve the marriage relationship under the proper circumstances. I have had ten 'extramarital' experiences and they were of the one-time type. I do not now have one planned. I feel that these exprinces greatly increased my sexual feelings for a while and added to my passion with my wife."

"Married thirty-six years. I like being married. Good sex in marriage can't be beat. It is the most peaceful and natural kind. Yes, I have had extramarital experiences. They were mostly unknown to my wife. They made my marriage more workable."

"Eight years. I don't like being married. I'm still married because of our kid. I've had affairs and they were very satisfying to me. They were unknown to my wife. At first I was bitter, to be out in the street doing something which I'd thought I would be doing home with my wife. But I've resigned myself to her being as she is, and I try not to make comparisons between the women in my affairs and my wife. I just enjoy them. Even prostitutes."

"Married fifteen years. I like being married. I'm just as sexually attracted to my wife, or more so, as ever. But monogamy doesn't agree with me. I think perhaps if I had a different wife or a different relationship with the wife I have, monogamy might be more acceptable. I love my wife tremendously. After fifteen years of marriage, going through a lot together, losing a child, and having a third to replace the second, things got a little shaky this year. I hope they're settling down again. We just are not balanced in sexual desires or needs. My extramarital sexual experiences were unknown to my wife. I think they were a necessary experience for learning and growth to me, and I think it helped rather than hurt my marriage. I had no less feelings for my wife after having affairs. I've been having affairs all through my marriage, and I love my wife more than ever. Casual sex relationships are O.K. once in a while, but I prefer more meaningful or permanent relationships. In a way, all of my relationships had a meaning. I have some beautiful memories of being close to someone for just a time or two. I still remember and respect in a special way almost every woman I've made it with. Why does sex have to be treated so much different with rules and regulations than anything else?"

"Married twenty-five years. I like being married. We do not both get into the mood for sex at the same time as often as I would like, but when we do, it is great. There have been very few times that I have not been potent with my wife. She is a fantastic lover. When we married I had the optimistic expectation that I would (1) never be lonely again, (2) never hurt for want of sex. In the first case this has been at least 95 percent true. In the second case, maybe 70 percent. On the other hand, I have had several sexual encounters with other women. Most of these have been casual, one-night stands, in which both of us realized that there would be no lasting emotional involvement. They were precious and I hope to have others. I once had an extramarital relationship, unknown to my wife, that lasted two years. I was very fond of the woman and enjoyed sex with her very much. I had a great deal of trouble with my guilt feelings. I ended the affair partly because I grew tired of it, partly because I decided it was destructive to my relationship with my wife."

"Married six years. It's super—my wife and I talk a lot about our feelings. However, I wouldn't tell my wife I was having sex (not love) with another woman. It bothers me, but the woman I am seeing is separated and horny and she has some techniques my wife does not."

"I have been married twenty-nine years and I love it; I only wish I could have another wife or two. It is the best way to have a sexual relationship. I always have one or two lovers because my wife doesn't totally satisfy me. I don't like casual sexual relationships—I like to know the woman and feel warmth for her."

"Married over three decades to the same spouse, whom I love deeply, but with whom the sexual relationship seems much less than it should be. We are both gravely inhibited about talking the problems out, and so an unsatisfactory sex life is tolerated as a side issue of what in all other respects is a great and permanent love affair. All of my extramarital experiences have been without my wife's knowledge, with the exception of one concerning which she had her accurate suspicions. I regret the need for secrecy, but the need for the sex is great, and I accept and can handle the problem of the concealment and caution that must go into the preservation of such affairs. My partners all understand and assist in this, some of them being in the same situation vis-à-vis a less than satisfactory home sex life."

"I was married two and a half years to my first wife with no children, and thirteen years to my second wife with three children. I love being married: my woman is always there and I can usually interest her in sex every third or fourth night, while I can still take care of other women and it does not affect my sex life at home. I love my wife and am actually monogamous for long periods, but if the opportunity for sex with a woman I like comes along, I will take it. I will even pursue it because I like sex for fun, it puts spice into my life. But I would *never* get so involved with another woman as to leave my wife."

"I have been married five years. I married at thirty-one. I have ambivalent feelings about it. I am married because I favor the family unit as the proper environment for my sons. I love my wife. Ideally, monogamy is best, but I have had extramarital experiences. I do not know why I have had them. My wife is devoted and a good lover, and faithful as far as I know. But I enjoy developing more than one relationship. My affairs were more than just casual. They were slow in building up and I became deeply involved. My wife became aware of them by discovery. She was deeply hurt. She favors monogamy and does not understand the reason for the affairs. Monogamy has the advantage of allowing the partners to be completely honest with each other. This is very important. But because I feel that monogamy is best and that honesty is extremely important, and because I may have an affair in the future, this conflict can only be resolved by divorce. I have considered divorce for this reason."

"Married thirty-two years. It has been a good and rewarding marriage. My wife is a fine person. We were married very young and probably for all the wrong reasons, but I like being married and I probably will always be married. Sex with my wife was never great and it's been deteriorating. I would prefer monogamy but right now I'm deeply involved in an extramarital affair that my wife is unaware of (I hope). This may destroy my marriage, which makes me sad because I really care for my wife. The affair does make me feel great, however, and I don't want to give it up. I love the new woman very deeply and with all my heart."

"I've been married to my wife for twenty-six years and it's been good. Wouldn't want it any other way, nor do I desire any other woman as a wife. But I would like an occasional affair. Just for a change. To break the monotony. Living together, day in and day out, can't possibly be a constant high. Sexually, I enjoy my wife as much now as I ever have, though I'm not sure she enjoys it as much as she used to. At twenty-four she was pretty and slender. Now her figure has matured and her face has character. Yes, I've had extramarital affairs. They were not of the open marriage type, though I have given her the same opportunities and would give her the same considerations. I've told her about them. Not at the time, but later. She was terribly hurt and I felt awful after each time. She doesn't believe in having affairs and believes in one man at a time. I can't seem to convince her that the affairs have no effect upon our marriage. We're still in love and our marriage, though shaky after each affair, has lasted."

"I have been married for twelve years and we have gone through the entire gamut of experiences from really being in love to near-divorce, to growing to maturity with each other's help. We have had a near-perfect sex relationship up to five years ago when my wife seemed to lose the intense, unconditional feeling she had for me. I try to accept it but fluctuate from tolerance to despair, anger, and back to an understanding that perhaps she may have just entered a new phase. Suddenly she is the Divine Harlot and then for a month it's as if my desire annoys her. I have had many 'extramarital experiences,' mostly favorable and without my wife's knowledge. They were very good for me because I never get involved with immature or bitchy women and therefore avoid personal tribulations or possible damage to my wife. I only like affectionate women with no hang-ups, who would never think of hurting me, themselves, or my wife."

"I have been married almost twenty-four years. I like it . . . the sense of family community is one of the cornerstones of my life, and I love my wife very much. But we were separated for about seven months recently. We married originally because of the desire to have children while we were young. Married sex was not good for a long time, and then we started working on it, got some counseling, and it got good. My wife still turns me on more than any other woman, and when we discovered marijuana in our mid-thirties we became a sensational sex team. But my wife has given up the weed (a few bad trips, a frequent hangover), and she has lost a lot of her sex drive because of her unhappiness about my other women. I find monogamy barely tolerable but I'm trying it again now for the fourth or fifth time, because I'd rather save my marriage than insist on having other women."

"My sex life with my wife is excellent. It was not always so. In fact, during the years when my wife was subject to pregnancy, sex was a chore for her. The fear of pregnancy was always with her and this had a disturbing effect. I began to stray with other women, finding the guilt feelings less powerful than the pleasures found. Through these alliances, I learned more about sex and began to do things away from home that I had not done at home. Much later, I was able to introduce some sexual dramatics into my home life and it was then that sex became great at home. I still engage, but infrequently, in sexual encounters, but they do not interfere with my love and caring for my wife and home. My wife is subliminally aware that I need extra excitements and she is not pleased by it. Not at all. But, being bright and logical, she realizes that my attitudes toward out-of-the-home sex are, after all, pleasure-seeking ventures, and do not pose a threat to her security. I suppose, in fact, that I am at odds with the folkways and mores thrust upon me by a hypocritical society which tells me to abstain from earthly pleasures while it is fucking its collective head off."

"Married nineteen years. I like married life. I'm still married because it's an insured, convenient, and stable life. Originally I married for romantic love. But after eleven years of marriage I started, unbeknownst to my wife, and have continued ever since. I'm most involved with a gal I have loved completely and intimately for the last two years. She has created a contrast in my mind compared to my wife. My lover and I have much more spiritually in common; she is not any more of a 'lover in bed' than my wife is. Still, if she were not also married, I would leave my wife for her."

"Married thirty-five years. I like being married but find it a bit too restrictive at times. I married because I love my wife and feel a strong need for closeness, partnership, love, affection, and sharing. Being married restricts my desired sexual activity. Monogamy is good because of the security it affords, but I have had extramarital sexual experiences including intercourse with at least five other women, one of whom was a young client who became too amorous. All these experiences were unknown to my wife, although she knew there was a social relationship with the other women. I know the church does not approve, but I don't really care, although there is still some residual guilt. I have never had a really casual sexual relationship except one. I prefer a closer, longer-term, more intimate relationship, but these are harder to break when the time comes to do so."

Some answers seemed very self-contradictory:

"I like monogamy. If I were real rich I would have a harem."

"Married twenty years. I like it. Marriage fulfills my needs more than any alternate life style I can think of. I like monogamy. The one-to-one relationship for me is the only way to share fully without constant manipulation. I have had extramarital relationships. They have increased my self-awareness and confidence. My marriage has improved. It would not exist otherwise."

"I prefer one very deep and meaningful primary relationship with as many others as time/circumstances permit. The secondary relationships may or may not involve sexual encounters."

"I like sex three times a week at least. But as I write this it has been a dry spell for us, sexually, as my wife has been away on a long trip; my lover on a film in New York. And me—I'm faithful to both. So it's been two months. But today I made contact with both of them, so I think we will be in the groove for a while."

"Married five years. I think being married is more interesting than being single, plus, since I move often, it is nice to have a constant in my life. My wife is also my best friend. Monogamy is O.K. simply because I don't think I could love more than one woman equally and that would cause jealousy which would cause more problems than it is worth. I have had three extramarital sexual relationships. A casual sexual relationship is great as long as you do not get emotionally involved if you are married."

"I believe monogamy should be, however both of the partners should be free to live their own lives and have a sexual experience with whoever they want as long as it does not interfere with the relationship with the marriage partner. What is good for the goose is good for the gander."

Although most men had sex outside of marriage only after several years of marriage, this was not always the case: 16 percent of married men had outside sex within the first year of marriage and 23 percent within the first two years:

"My second marriage now is nine months. (I was married the first time fourteen years.) I like being married. The excitement of sex decreases but it is good, stable, warm, etc. As far as being monogamous, though, I'm not really—I get bored! I enjoy the excitement of the chase, and new personalities—interesting new areas of interest. These are definitely unknown to my wife! I have guilt at times, and I have to do lots of covering up. But I am happier in our relationship this way because I don't feel 'trapped' or 'tied' on one lady. I feel relatively free."

"Married one and a half years. Like it very much. She is the greatest in every way. Sex with her is good. I have had sex with other women. She doesn't know about it. It really didn't affect me that much because I just want physical satisfaction and nothing else. It has not affected the marriage one bit. I have a very strong mind and I wouldn't have done it if I knew I couldn't handle it. But sometimes I wonder if I should have had more women to satisfy my ego before I got married. It will not affect the marriage, though, I strongly feel we can and will live a lifetime together."

"Married not quite one year yet. We married because we love and need each other. Because I wanted a wife and a home and someone to take care of and raise a family and watch them grow up. It's just great. As to monogamy, I'd like to be married to five different women at the same time, and legally. My sex outside is unknown. It was and is very helpful to me as an individual, and it's helping me to understand married life more freely."

"I have been married for two years. I got married because I wanted to live with the girl I loved, but did not want to hurt either set of parents. Also the marriage ceremony provided us with many gifts, essential items as well as luxuries we would not have been able to afford. Sexual techniques have improved with practice and regular use, but some of the excitement has gone. I find myself fantasizing more during sex. I fell in love with a woman I met less than a year after I was married. We were both happy with our respective marriages and in love with our spouses as well as with each other. A sexual relationship followed quite naturally from that love.

We both chose not to tell our spouses. I knew it would only hurt my wife, she wouldn't be able to see that I did not love her less . . . just as I would be blind if the roles were reversed."

However, a few men who were not monogamous had had outside activities only once or twice during very long marriages (1 percent):

"I was married for twenty-eight years. Sex was disastrous but I had only one evening of extramarital sex. I was foolish enough to confess it to my wife—which was partly due to guilt from my religious upbringing—and partly a little punitive on my part. That one night with my former lover, even though the sex wasn't great, rejuvenated me, and sex with my wife became possible again—whereas it had been falling apart—and it got very much better."

"Married seventeen and a half years and I like it. Marriage gives a couple the opportunity to build a good sexual relationship together if they work at it. I had one extramarital affair but it was disappointing. Due to the guilt feelings I had after doing it, I admitted it, in writing to my wife. Its effect on our marriage was that it almost ended in separation and possible divorce. My wife and I had temporarily lost our ability to communicate with one another."

"I have lived in an extended period of monogamy for over twenty-five years. I had two brief encounters in a time when I was just not thinking well, my head was not on right. At the same time these encounters were significant and in their context very meaningful, they were not casual."

"Married twenty-three years. My one infidelity was a ten-minute period with the wife of a friend of ours—ten minutes of heaven on the floor of our living room, about six or seven years ago."

"I was married thirty-three years. The first thirty years before my wife became ill I liked very much indeed. The effect on sex was an understanding and appreciation of each other, and happy sex. I had no 'extramarital' sexual experiences for thirty years. Then when my wife developed serious physical problems I had a relationship with one other woman. I was most careful. My wife never knew and I discontinued it and lived constantly with my wife through the last six months of terminal cancer. I had very little sex and used a lot of barbiturates and my first tranquilizers."

HOW DID MEN FEEL ABOUT HAVING SECRET SEX OUTSIDE OF MARRIAGE?

Most men, as we have seen, expressed few feelings of guilt or regret, nor did they connect outside sex with problems in their relationships with their wives:

"I have been married thirty-five years to the same woman. I would have it no other way—although there is room for improvement in our sex life (and I am working on it). We are doing quite well by modern standards. I have had several extramarital sexual experiences unknown to my wife. I realize no bad effect and realize some good effect—as each experience taught me something 'extra' that I could use to advantage at home."

"I married for love, for secure sex and for companionship. Sex with my wife is good but I like variety. I do not like monogamy. It is too confining and too one-sided, in favor of the wife. In my extramarital experiences, the only effect on me was sorrow at parting. It never had any effect on marriage as I never was stupid enough to tell my wife."

"I have sex with other women unknown to my wife (I think). It really hasn't affected my marriage. I've never felt guilty about it in any way. I'm a hopeless romantic. I don't think I've ever been in love, and I want to find out what it's like."

"I've been married almost twenty years. Sex gets better as time passes. I have had extramarital affairs, unknown to my wife. I fell head over heels, sophomorically, daisies in my hair, birds in the trees, mindlessly in love with the first girl. This experience made me understand, for the first time, what it's like not to mind-control the emotions. I finally really felt what poets had been writing about. I've not been the same since. I don't know what effect the affair had on my marriage, I never thought of my relations with my wife and the girl as having anything to do with one another."

Most said that the effect on them of secret extramarital affairs had been good:

"In my first marriage I did have sex outside. My wife did not know. The effect on me was great and it had no effect on the marriage."

"I have had extramarital involvements for twenty years. Many occasional and long-term, up to three to four years. She is unaware, and I'm having two now. It's been good for me!"

Some said it was good because it was an ego boost:

"It can be a wonderful experience, a boost to one's ego."

"I have had extramarital experiences unknown to my wife. They pulled me out of a mental slump that seemed to be destroying me. They didn't affect my marriage in any way."

"My affairs, unknown to my wife, had a good effect on me—a nice change, and increased my self-esteem in that other women found me attractive. As much as I enjoyed going out, I enjoyed coming home that much more."

"For two years I lived away from my wife and had an extramarital relationship, which I enjoyed; it made me feel better about myself as a sexual man; it was an ego booster. Years later when I told my wife about it, she considered my telling her as a hostile act on my part, and said I shouldn't have told her. But I really don't think it significantly affected our relationship or marriage."

"All of my experiences have been unknown to my wife. (If she had these experiences I would immediately divorce her.) These experiences were great for my ego, three of the women were the aggressors."

"About four years ago I found myself less than satisfied with our sexual life, when the opportunity for an extramarital sexual experience presented itself. The affair lasted for two or three months at the rate of a couple of times per week. My wife was never aware of it. From a psychological standpoint it gave me a tremendous lift and consequently improved my mental outlook. I am more sexually satisfied now, but still feel an occasional affair, as long as no one is hurt, can be extremely satisfying."

"When I was married I had some extramarital experiences. They were unknown to my wife. I don't believe they affected my marriage, because she was convinced 'I screw everything that walks.' For myself it was very satisfying because it proved to me that most of my wife's criticisms of me were wrong."

As one man put it:

"The effect on me is one of a macho-type thing. That is, to prove my masculinity, probably to myself."

And others said it had helped them preserve or develop a more independent identity:

"Monogamy is a riddle. Now I've come to believe that, for me anyway, there had to be some openness as far as extramarital sex. Extramarital contacts have helped me to know myself deeper, to prove to myself what I really am as a person, to understand new dimensions in myself."

"This present experience is very good for me—has shown me who I am sexually and emotionally, in ways never experienced in my marriage."

"The effect on me as an individual has been delightful. I found out that I had forgotten what love and intimacy and caring is all about, and how to give it and receive it."

"I have had extramarital sexual experiences. They were a part of me trying to find myself, where I wanted to go as a person, etc."

"I have been married for the last six years. I have intact almost all the notions of trust and commitment that I was raised with, but if you really want to know, I prefer extended periods of bigamy. I have had three extramarital relationships in the last three years. These relationships have happened not quite openly and not quite in secret, but with some things ignored, and many things unsaid. They have not improved my marriage, because they are not part of it. But they have improved *me* by nurturing my independence and self-respect. Although I loved this 'mate' of mine, and still do, our sex life has been pretty bruising and has often spilled over into other areas. I do not know whether the tendency of these other relationships to become more open means that my marriage is becoming more open or that it is dying."

"It was too hard to choose which kind of a life to live —conservative, part of the establishment, or 'free,' not caring what people think of me. In the end, I have a staid, respectable life with my wife, the life my business associates see— but having a long-term affair outside my marriage has enabled me to have another complete life (the 'real' me?). I know it's cheating, but I don't know how to be true to myself any other way."

Others gained sexual experience:

"When I was younger I would neck and pet heavy a lot, but I had a moral line against intercourse for unmarrieds. After over twenty years of marital fidelity, I had my first affair, and for the first time (excluding my marriage) did not discontinue lovemaking after the woman was aroused, but went ahead—for her and for me—it felt great! I felt better about myself as a man and a lover. I had very little guilt vis-à-vis my wife and marriage (she didn't really want me anyway). And it's like my sexuality began to develop again from a level it had been arrested at since my teens."

Or simply enjoyed it:

"Married four and a half years. Marriage causes sex to be very restricted. I've had two extramarital experiences which my wife does not know about. It was satisfying, exciting, and emotionally fulfilling for me."

"I was happy to get what I wanted away from home, and enjoyed the excitement and adventure."

"The effect of my extramarital affairs upon me was reassuring, rejuvenating, and exciting."

But outside sex was not always a positive experience:

"Although some affairs were more definite ego builders, others were damaging to my ego."

"I have had affairs that were unknown to my wife. These affairs taught me that my marriage isn't good but it's better than being lost and lonely."

"I have been married for five years and enjoy the relationship. My wife and I have each had an affair during the low point of our marriage when we were working opposite shifts and never saw each other. One thing I found odd was the fact that the other woman that I was in love with during my affair, and I only went to bed with once, but being so used to my wife, I found it hard to be free and open sexually with this woman, and ended up not even being able to have an orgasm all night. I don't know if it was guilt, or just the physical differences in this woman, but I sure felt odd."

A minority of men expressed feelings of guilt:

"Ten years. I like it very much. I have sex outside of marriage very infrequently. Outside sex is followed by considerable guilt. It doesn't do much to strengthen a marriage."

"The effect of my current affair on me is a guilty feeling. That is why we are going to have to talk."

"I cheated on my wife some, unknown to her, most of them anyway. I felt guilty—cheap and sneaky."

"I think outside sex might have been suspected, but not confirmed. I felt guilty, and it was largely because I wanted to be honest with myself that the marriage ended. In any case, the marriage had faltered before the extramarital sex began."

"Married for five years. I like it. Extramarital sex activities, yes, but kept from my marriage. I felt guilty but felt I needed the change."

"Married to my second wife three years now. I love being married. The way my wife and I screw, there just isn't anything better anywhere else. But, on the road, and unknown to my wife, I did have sex with another woman. I felt crummy and it nearly broke up our marriage because she sensed it."

"I had extramarital sex in my first marriage (unknown?) to my wife. It didn't hurt my marriage but it didn't do me any good psychologically—my conscience beat me every time. In my current marriage I have never had an extramarital affair—not once. Now as I look back the most I ever got out of an outside affair is an orgasm."

"I am not proud to say I have had extramarital sexual experiences, and, even sorrier to say, unknown to my wife. I have suffered strong pangs of remorse, and have been plagued with guilt, but go right on, anyway . . . always afraid of being caught, and losing everything (which I would deserve). Except for near-brushes with disaster, I have managed to keep them entirely out of my marriage, and I must acknowledge that sometimes, after a troublesome period of some length, with an intervening affair with the other woman, I have renewed the bonds of my marriage—undoubtedly from guilt, but renewed them, nonetheless, and in doing so, have felt in some small way that I have paid a little of my debt. I have always treated her with compassion, and have tried to care for her sincerely. All these guilt complex reactions by which I can justify my wandering!"

"I've been married for twenty-years. I like being married, but regret the loss of freedom. I really do believe in monogamy, but my natural instinct is definitely not monogamous. I had some extramarital experiences. Although they were unknown to my wife, she still felt some things were happening. It had a bad effect on me, as I do not like to be unfaithful. I was not happy, but I felt I had to have more sex, as I needed it, and I don't want to be frustrated. I have a terrible ability to be seduced by a woman. It seems I could fall in love with all the interesting ones I meet. But then soon

I do not care for them as much. My wife is the only one whom I feel deeply attached to, because of her talents and personality, and in spite of our different characters."

But for some the feeling of guilt was temporary:

"At first, I hated myself, then I got used to it and liked it."

"Sixteen years. I have had a very casual, uninvolved, extramarital sexual encounter, not known to my wife. I felt really bad about it for a few days after ('how could I,' 'what if she'd get pregnant,' 'what if I'm infected,' etc. etc.). I have stopped feeling bad about it, however."

A few men had tried extramarital sex, but didn't like it:

"I prefer monogamy purely because the head hassles and guilt trips I put myself through when I'm having sex with more than one woman are too much to take."

"I don't care for a lot of relationships at the same time. I've found it's too much for me to handle."

"I cried myself to sleep while I was in another woman's bed, when it finally hit me how I had hurt my wife. Then I went home where I belonged."

"I have been married twenty-nine years. I like married life very much. I am married because my wife and I both love each other and when we got married, we made a vow, *no divorce.* We got married because we wanted to be together and also raise a family. Marital sex is harmonious—no fear of V.D., no fear of intrusion, so our sex is great. With monogamy, you have only one person to love, satisfy, and cherish—physically, psychologically, and sexually. I was unfaithful only a couple of times early in my marriage; they were just plain sexual bouts. They were not known to my wife at the time, but I confessed to her later. To me as an individual, I felt empty and lonely, and it almost was disastrous to my marriage."

"In the last analysis, I have decided, outside sex is boring and not fair to either wife or casual partner."

"Married over thirty years. As to extramarital experiences, I've had two—one during my first marriage, and one in my second. Sexually, both affairs were brief—a matter of perhaps three to six encounters. The effect was bad on me. There was much guilt and a feeling that I had been a damned fool. I still think I was. The extramarital affair is not for me."

"Only one extramarital or adultery type of sexual experience. With a friend's wife. It was very morally degrading to me."

"I much prefer a high-quality meaningful monogamous relationship. I have had extramarital sexual experiences but they were always tainted due to being outside my marriage and they were an emotional and physical drain."

"Ten years. I had one extramarital sexual experience. I felt guilty because I should have sex only with the woman I'm married to. Never did it again."

"Right now I'm wrestling with the question if I can truly enjoy the trials and assets of monogamy. Frankly, I think that I'll probably opt for that rather than a continued life of casual sexual relationships. The latter tend to be shallow and unsustaining. While monogamous relationships, if built on mutual growth, sharing, and sustaining, really add more depth and substance to one's life. At least this is what I am beginning to experience in my own life."

WHAT WAS THE EFFECT OF OUTSIDE SEX ON THE MARRIAGE?

The most frequent answer to "What was the effect of extramarital sex on your marriage?" from men who had not told their wives, was "no effect":

"I have had sex outside of marriage, which satisfied my curiosity and desire for variety as an individual. There was no effect on me or my marriage, except possibly some improvement in my sexual technique."

"I have been married for seven years. I don't like monogamy. It can become a sort of imprisonment too easily. I have had sex outside. They have remained totally unknown to my wife. It hasn't made any difference in the marital scene."

"I have been married five years. I had one extramarital homosexual experience. It was unknown to my wife. It had no effect on me or my marriage."

"I have had sex unknown to my wife. It made me feel O.K., and didn't have no effect on my marriage as I love my wife, I happen to be too much in the bedroom anyway."

"Twenty-nine and a half years. I have had extramarital sexual experiences, and my wife does not know about them. They had no effect on me nor on our marriage. As long as I don't feel guilty and need to confess and ask forgiveness from my wife, it does not hurt me or her, provided I am just as tender and loving to her in a deep and sincere emotional way as always. The extramarital affair is like stealing a few moments out of one's life and spending them with someone else one is attracted to for that moment."

"It has neither helped nor hurt the marriage, which was dead years ago, except that knowing I'm not shut off from human relations has made me less bitter with my wife—in fact, I'm not bitter now at all."

"I have not experienced extended periods of monogamy even though I have been married for twenty-five years, nor do I think I would. It would have no meaning for me as an intelligent being. I like casual sexual encounters, they are stimulating, rewarding, and adventuresome. My 'extramarital' sexual experiences are unknown to my wife and it has not affected my married life one bit."

"Married life has been a great joy for all the twenty-six years, the frustrations were far outweighed by the joys of companionship and compassion, early married life was a joy, with excitement that was unbelievable. My partner was (is) sweet, understanding, and for years was more active sexually than I had expected any woman on earth would ever be. Casual sex relationships turn me off as a whole, but I had some delightful experiences when traveling alone and lonesome (and luckily could often recontact these partners on later travels) but by and large found sex away from home from my wife to be a sort of relief, not much better than masturbation at best, and a great disappointment and waste of time and money at worst. I far prefer my wife assuming she is available. The other sex had no lasting effect on myself or my marriage."

"Twenty-one years. Marriage grows old and sours after a number of years—especially when the wife's childbearing years are over. And one person gets boring after a while. I like casual sex relationships to add the 'Spice of Life.' These are always unknown to my wife. No effect on me or my marriage."

"Twenty-seven and a half years. Marriage and sex is more beautiful each year. I did have sex outside, unknown to my wife. It gave me a guilty feeling—but other than that, it had no effect."

"I have had many affairs—not known to my wife, as many are her close friends and associates. They have not had any effect on my marriage or on me. We still have sex an average of five to six times a week."

Almost as many said that sex (unknown to the wife) outside of the marriage had helped the marriage, or made the marriage "workable," since it enabled them to continue in the marriage:

"Married twenty-one years. I can take marriage or leave it. I think of myself as monogamous, but I have one lover, unknown to my wife. It changed my life. Kept me going. Kept me responsible to my family. The best thing that ever happened to me. My lover also has a family. She loves her husband, too, and her children. We have an honest, open relationship."

"Married twenty-six years. Sex is probably the most important part of my life, but there is too little of it with my wife. Therefore, I have sex outside, unknown to her. It keeps me functioning as a member and head of my family—and gives me the ego satisfaction that I need."

"I've had extramarital experiences unknown to my wife. It has made life better for me and easier to stay married. It made me more relaxed as a person, especially in the area of being a father to my children."

"At first I felt somewhat guilty about extramarital sex, but justified it to myself as being good for me and harmless to my marraige. I think it has been good for my marriage because it allowed me to stop being irritated at my wife for not having as high a sex drive as me. It acted as a tension release."

"I have had several extramarital relationships. As far as I know, my wife has never known of them—in any event, she has never actually caught me. The effect of my extramarital relationships has been to keep my marriage together. I don't believe that I could have stood twenty-seven years of an unsatisfactory sex life. If anything, extramarital relationships have improved my marriage, and I have good reason to believe that some of the married women with whom I have had extramarital relationships have also improved their marriages."

"I have had 'extramarital' experiences unknown to my wife. I'm afraid it helped me as a person in my ego problems and helped me weather the bad times in my marriage. I believe it preserved my marriage, as without these interests and pleasures my marriage would have been over. Instead, it continued and survived and improved. I don't need these affairs anymore, but I am glad I had them. They were casual, safe, and always with married women who were horny and who were friends, and some still are."

"My wife and I had a poor period for many years and we were heading for splitsville when I met a woman who thought I was terrific, a great lover and a super human being, besides loving to fuck. I became sexually satisfied and it wasn't necessary to force my wife to screw. This helped our relationship."

"For at least twenty-five of my thirty-five years of married life I have not liked being married. In fact, I have never liked the sexual part of my marriage, which has rarely been fulfilling. To the best of my knowledge all my extramarital relationships were so fulfilling that I was a much happier person and could play my other marital roles much better. On occasion I think my wife suspected something or may even have been jealous, but since our relationship was under strain most of the time anyway, it didn't matter much. I was faithful for the first twenty-five years, and miserable long before starting to 'step out.' As far as I was concerned, the unhappiness could not get worse, nor the deprivation."

"I have had sex with women other than my wife for many years. My wife knows vaguely about it—she doesn't like it, but as long as I keep it out of our home and don't talk about it (pretend it doesn't exist?), she goes along with it. I think also that she realizes that sex means more to me than to her. The effect on me is to keep me 'young,' physically as well as mentally, make me more attractive, and more alert. It's nice to be desired and appreciated. The effect on my marriage has been excellent because without the extramarital sex, I couldn't have stayed with my wife."

"The first seven years (classic!) of my marriage were monogamous. Then for several years I led a fairly active extramarital life; I think I learned a good deal about women in their many varieties; I got a good deal of ego support for myself at a time when I needed it; I recognized that there is more to marriage than sex; and it took some of the pressure away from my wife. On the whole, the effect on the marriage has been salutary."

"Twenty-two years. About monogamy, to be succinct—yes and no. Yes, because from time to time monogamous relationships do it all and handle it all and that special closeness is all I need or want. And no, for the opposite reason in that a monogamous relationship doesn't do it all. It's a relief, after a hassle with the wife and/or kids, to go to a different relationship that is quiet, hassle-free, and non-expectant. My outside relationships have been both open and unknown. As an individual I felt much better and usually performed as a husband and a father at a more civilized level after sex with someone else. I've never had guilt feelings because it's never taken precedence over my home life. If anything, the effect on my marriage has been positive."

Others said secret outside affairs made them more attentive to their wives:

"I like being married. But once in a while a little change helps. I have had some extramarital experiences one or two times. Once it lasted for eighteen months. It started when my wife told me we were all through with sex (argument). This woman was twenty-one years younger and it was quite an affair. My wife did not know, and it turned out that it helped our sex life because I tried harder with my wife, either because of guilt or to cover up, I don't know which—maybe both."

"Married eleven years in October. Sometimes I like it, sometimes I don't, it just depends—but I would rather be married than divorced. My affairs are unknown to my wife. During the sex act I enjoy it, but later I feel guilty, as I know my wife is straight as an arrow. I must say, though, that outside sex has made me appreciate and love my wife better. Why? I am not sure."

"It made me appreciate my wife more. That's something a woman just can't understand."

"If she makes me really feel good then I am nice to my wife."

"I have been married for twenty-five years and like being married. My extramarital sex activity heightens my relationship with my wife and keeps me in full vigor, we are content and happy in our sexual union. If my wife has had extramarital sex, that is her private affair. We still enjoy each other and that is all that matters."

"It created a more respectful admiration toward my wife. I would see how I was acting with the 'other women' and realize how I had been treating my wife. Needless to say, I would change my attitude at home. But this way she guessed I was having an affair."

"These experiences greatly increased my sexual feelings for a while and added to my passion with my wife."

Others implied that their affairs, when they became known (or the threat of future affairs), kept their wives sexually active with them—a sort of sexual blackmail:

"My outside sex had been unknown for the most part. Later on I found that telling her about them after a span of some years made her very sexy for long periods of time, so I even made some up just to turn her on just to satisfy my physical hunger instead of resorting to prostitutes or one-night stands. We went through some marriage counseling and she shaped up for a few years sexually, but then went into a decline with 'I don't have to do this or that anymore.' "

"I had one extramarital experience, unknown to my wife. I later admitted my indiscretion as I felt guilty, but the effect it had on my marriage was dramatic. My wife turned into a sexual tiger for a while, and our relationship improved."

Almost no men mentioned that the secrecy involved, or the dishonesty, had hurt them, or had hurt their relationship with their wives:

"I am a monogamous person in that carrying on a relationship with more than one woman is confusing to me and unsettling. I'd rather direct my energies toward one person. I had two extramarital sexual experiences. They were unknown to my wife. It had a confusing and unsettling effect on me and made parts of our marriage strange."

And only a few said it had damaged the marriage because it had subtly alienated them from their partner:

"The effect of my extramarital sex has been to restrict rather markedly my communication with my wife, probably because of the underlying guilt feelings I have, and to put us further apart."

On the other hand, some men said that outside sex had damaged the marriage when it became known, although the effect on them personally had been good:

"I have been married ten years. I enjoy marriage, we have a content marriage. I have had several extramarital affairs. The effect on my marriage was an adverse one, when I was found out. My wife felt threatened, and talked about leaving me."

"My extramarital relationships have been very good for me; I have learned and grown through every one. And as long as my wife didn't know about them, they were good for her, too, because I became more loving, more giving, and more humane. But when she knew, it was disastrous. Alas, I had never made her secure enough in my love to enable her to tolerate knowledge of the others."

Others said it had improved the marriage after talking about it when the situation became known:

"Married twenty-three years, I love being married. I got married because I met a terrific girl who is still terrific today and I loved her so much that I didn't want to lose her. Sex is great with her. I love and respect my wife very much in every way.

"I have had extramarital relationships, many times. A few, two, lasted a little longer than they should have. (I'm not going to give any details. My wife is liable to find and read this, and I don't want to hurt her.) I'm not having any now and I'm not likely to ever have one again. My wife watches me like a hawk and doesn't trust me for a minute. I'm trying to regain her trust.

"When my wife found out about one, this was the beginning of our working things out, repairing our marriage and building on it. Presently I'm the happiest man alive. Our sex life is improving greatly, because we are both working at making the other person happy. My wife is less inhibited now but I don't believe she can totally let herself go or completely understand my sexual desires even yet. Still, she is a marvelous person, she puts up with me, she loves me, she keeps me stable. She is everything a man wants in a wife and wants to spend the rest of his life with. But I believe every married man should have at least one good love affair at some time in the middle of his married life."

"Because of my wife's 'hanging in there' and trying to understand, our relationship was strengthened, and it brought us closer together. But during the process it tore me up as an individual and wreaked havoc on my job and ability to function normally."

Only a few said that their wives, on finding out, had nearly divorced or did divorce them:

"I had hundreds of affairs unknown to my wife. They led to slight guilt on my part—and divorce on my wife's part."

"The only thing I have done outside my marriage was touching other girls' breasts, kissing, hugging, and rubbing girls' buttocks and backs. My wife didn't know about it until recently. When she found out it had been going on for two years, it almost ruined our marriage."

"I have had numerous 'extramarital sexual experiences' during all four marriages. Each wife found out, eventually. Each wife reacted similarly and divorced or threatened to divorce me. In discussion with them any explanation attempted as to the cause of the experience resulted in their refusing to consider why the affair took place."

"I have been married twice—the first time for twenty-four years, the second for one year. I had extramarital sexual experiences in my first marriage. They were unknown to my wife. The effect on everyone was bad and ended my first marriage."

"I told my wife about it over the phone. She was very upset, and told me later she went into analysis because of it. It led to the divorce, although it was not the grounds."

In fact, other men said that extramarital sex had been a very valuable experience, in that it had helped them change and get out of an unsatisfying marriage:

"I had extramarital sexual experiences when I was married. At first they were unknown to my then wife but ultimately she found out. These 'experiences' helped me to find myself as an individual based solely on me, for me, and not tied to an unrealistic relationship (my marriage) which by then was no longer based on individuality but rather on a contract."

"I got married again at twenty-eight. We are currently breaking up. The effect of my affairs was to remind me how hypocritical my present situation is."

"I was married for eight years. I liked being married but I hated being nagged. Had two affairs. The first almost sank my marriage but it kept popping back up like a bar of Ivory in the bathtub. The second affair did the trick, and now I'm among the happily divorced. I am still involved with the lady who helped me shed my wife. She shed her husband at the same time. She's the best friend I have. I'll probably get married again; if I don't like it I'll get divorced again, now that I've found out how easy it is."

"I have been married to my wife three years, and I really like being married to her. We are married because we love each other. Being married has made our sex life very good and enjoyable. I prefer monogamy. It seems to be the right way of life, provided the right mate has been found. I had extramarital sexual experiences in my previous marriage. They were unknown to the wife I had at the time. The effect on me was a great awakening, and it led to the ending of a tedious, uninteresting, and frustrating marriage."

"In my first marriage, I had sexual relationships unknown to my wife. I wasn't getting any enjoyment at home so I went elsewhere. It didn't affect me as a person, I felt I just needed to love someone. Guess it helped bring about the end of a poor marriage. Seems like it was good all the way around."

"I've been married three years. I love marriage. I plan to do it again after this one fizzles. I found that my sex life regressed after marriage because she chose to stay still while I had hoped for experimentation. Now I've found someone that speaks my language. I am in the midst of an affair with her. My wife does not know about it. It's killing my marriage because I'm a one-woman man. I give all my love to my lover. I haven't had sex with my wife in three months. My marriage is over. Whether or not my lover and I get together after I leave my wife remains to be seen, but she has made me realize just what my relationship with my wife is lacking."

"I was married for about eighteen years. I did like marriage—until the end. In my next marriage I hope sex will not be diminished or deemphasized, or I will have erred in remarrying. My extramarital sex was instrumental in the demise of my (first) marriage. It was not known to my wife. I found this sex outstanding by comparison. With my need and ability in good sex to open up and express feelings, I could never accept the emptiness of my marital relationship again. I had changed, facilitated by the extramarital sex, but my wife had not."

"Married for twenty-six years. I like being married, although my wife and I recently agreed to separate. Our divorce, however, is not the result of an unhappy sex life; in fact, the good quality of our sex life maintained our married relationship far beyond the point at which other factors would have sustained it alone. I had two 'extramarital' sexual experiences. At the time of each, approximately ten years apart and both at critical points in my life, I was overwhelmed with a sense of guilt, and so I told her. In both outside relationships, there was considerable self-discovery and growth for me, which made me realize there was a deficiency in my primary relationship. Both relationships involved shared activities and interests which were important to me but of little interest to my wife. Attempts to involve her produced conflict, and eventually a power struggle over the time and energy I devoted to these interests. This clarified for both my wife and myself the major unresolved emotional and intellectual issues in our relationship and produced a mature agreement, with resignation, to terminate our marriage."

But others said that affairs had only encouraged them to continue longer in a relationship than they later wished they had:

"Outside sex kept me alive and content enough to stay in the marriage (my wife's 'goal at any cost') until I felt too tired to keep myself fragmented in that way, and felt I was not being fair to anyone, including myself, and left."

"I had very few extramarital experiences, all unknown to my ex-wife. I didn't really enjoy them, there was rather a sort of desperate excitement about them. I felt kind of hollow and cheap afterwards. They may have kept my marriage together longer than it should have been because they were a release from tension. At last, stopping the outside games and facing my life ended in divorce."

HOW DID MEN FEEL ABOUT THEIR LOVERS?

Most men felt an outside sexual relationship was more acceptable if love was not involved—that is, love which would compete with their love for their wives:

"I do not consider monogamy to be as important as emotional fidelity. Outside sex is O.K. as long as it is not serious."

"Twenty-nine years. My affairs are only physical and the women are told that at the beginning, and that either of us can call it quits with no questions or strings. That way there is no involvement of a serious nature."

"Married sixteen years. The happiest moments of my day are with my wife and kids. My relationship for many years was purely monogamous but now I don't want it that way. The last year or two it's been a casual thing, if I hit it off with someone, sex just makes it better. I don't want any serious affairs other than my marriage. My wife doesn't know about my casual sex. It bothered me some with a case of guilts but never too seriously. Somehow it seemed to strengthen the marriage on my side."

Most men did not describe their affairs as times of falling deeply in love; most felt that "love" for an extra partner should be subordinated to love for one's wife. One man's description of his relationship with a lover is worth quoting at length to show a typical level of involvement, and overall tone:

"Married fourteen years. It's had its ups and downs but as we mature it seems mostly up. One of the real strengths of my marriage is sex. Sex is mutually important to us and we often try new ideas, read articles or books on sex, and generally try to improve the state of the art.

"Eight months ago my marriage was pretty stale—in-law problems, wife's weight problem (I am slim and loathe obesity), arguments about bringing up our child, etc. I was not *actively* seeking an outside relationship, but one presented itself. The administrator of our club fell ill and we had to replace him. M. seemed to be the only candidate for the job. She was twenty-seven, divorced, and had one child, who is now with her ex-husband. She is pretty, slim, sophisticated, and urbane. I interviewed her and she seemed to have the requisite qualifications. She was hired.

"A week or so later, I intimated to her that my marriage was 'stale.' She expressed interest. Because of my business travel schedule, I was able to spend a lot of time with her by 'extending' my trips by a night, either at the beginning or end of the trip. She had no money and no car, and loved to drive my expensive imported car. It wasn't long before we found ourselves in bed. Meantime, I loaned her the car while I was out of town. All this was unknown to my wife.

"M. was a contrast to my wife. She had had a liberal sexual initiation at sixteen, started living with her now ex-husband at seventeen, got pregnant at nineteen, married in the eighth month, and divorced at twenty-five. She told me she's been to bed with fifty or sixty men. My first sexual experience with her was at her apartment one evening when I was 'at a meeting.' We had a drink or two. I started to hold her hand, and told her (quite honestly) that I really enjoyed her company. This led to a lot of kissing, caressing, and attention by me to her breasts. She had her period, however, which (she said) precluded intercourse. It didn't occur to me to ask her to suck my cock. The novelty of the whole thing overwhelmed me.

"The following week I loaned her the expensive car again and went on a two-day trip. She picked me up at the airport and we went to her apartment. It seemed like sex was foremost in the minds of both of us; I took a shower and found her in bed, nude. We had terrific intercourse. This was repeated the following morning. At the time, I felt she had had orgasms both times; later she told me it was 'only a climax.' A week later we repeated this scene after another business trip, and the next week we went to a club convention in a distant city. It was really fun to share the driving with M., an excellent and aggressive driver, who coaxed every ounce of performance out of my car.

"After the convention, our sex life deteriorated; one evening I tried to hold her hand and she seemed turned off to me physically, for some reason I didn't understand. But we continued seeing a lot of each other because her job required daily contact, and I still loaned her the car. At the beginning or end of my trips I would stay overnight at her place, hoping our relationship would improve. We shared her small bed, but never went any further than some modest kisses.

"Finally, an ex-boyfriend saw her in the car and blew the whistle on our relationship by calling my wife. My wife was just leaving on a three-week trip out of the country; she called me at 4 a.m. and confronted me; I admitted loaning the car but nothing else. I really needed M.'s moral support but it wasn't forthcoming. This was a tremendous disappointment to me, but she just didn't want to get involved. We grew further apart. At Christmas I gave her a small gift which she really liked . . . 'You didn't need to get me a Christmas present.' She had two new boyfriends—one twenty-two ('but he's very mature') and a college student about nineteen.

"Early in the new year M.'s performance in the job was such that I *had* to make a change. It was a very unpleasant scene. She thought this might be revenge for her inattention to me. I did not talk to M. for about a month, then I *had* to call her to settle up how much we owed her. I was pleasantly surprised that she was civil, even pleasant on the phone. We quickly settled the financial part of our conversation and then turned to our emotional feelings. We agreed that it would have been much better if we hadn't tried to combine a business and a personal relationship. She reminded me that she hadn't 'blown the whistle' on me by publicizing my gifts to her, sex with her, etc. I said I had expected that she would react with such discretion.

"I didn't speak to her for another month or so, then one morning I came into the office and was surprised when my secretary told me she had phoned. I called her back. She said she was about to have major abdominal surgery, was still unemployed, and would I do her tax return? I agreed. When I stopped by her apartment for the tax information, we kissed lightly and she seemed to have forgotten the bad scene when I had fired her. The following Monday we had lunch in the country—she drove my car on a brilliant spring day. We discussed sex but didn't have any.

"Three days later we had another nice lunch. She then had to visit her surgeon about the impending operation. I suggested 'sex in the afternoon,' but she showed little interest although we still had a good time (it was my birthday). She wished me a very happy birthday over the lunch table with a kiss, and we had a feeling of real euphoria. Then we began to discuss sex very carefully—her relations with P. and with G. and with me. I rated somewhere in the middle when it came to communication during sex; P., her ex-husband, was very communicative, while G. said almost nothing while he was fucking. She seems to take pleasure in showing she has relationships with other men. One night when I was at her apartment she left from 1 to 4 a.m. to 'visit a friend.' On another occasion she picked me up at the airport (late) with her nineteen-year-old boyfriend in tow. Most recently, we were at her place and she phoned her current friend—and let him know she'd be over as soon as I left.

"Yet the effect of all this on me as an individual has been very positive. M. has added a completely new dimension to my life. My relationship with her has caused me to have a new, more positive outlook toward women. She also gave me the first new and significant sex relationship I've had in years. Yet we realize that we don't love each other and that a long-term relationship isn't in the cards for us. We continue seeing each other; I hope we have more sex because for one thing I owe her a couple of good orgasms and know I can bring her to them.

"As for the future, since M. is far from forming any permanent relationship, needs money, and can use my moral support, I will probably continue my relationship with her. Right now I am trying to help her make some money from her considerable talent. She needs a plan for merchandising her talent more than she needs money. This all gives me a tremendously satisfying feeling. I really want to help her. She is a person who has been treated roughly by life. Even though I have a satisfactory marriage, I think I can help her and derive pleasure from doing so.

"The effects on my marriage? My wife does not believe for a minute that I didn't go to bed with M., despite my denials. However, she is beginning to forget about it and concentrate on me instead. The whole sequence of events has had a very positive effect on our relationship—emotionally and sexually.

"Postscript: Today M. picked me up at the airport. She had had an awful day—must vacate her apartment, her electricity is being turned off, and she got a parking ticket. Then she phoned her ex-husband about seeing her seven-year-old son, and he refused. She and I had a drink, then went to her place. I told her to have a good cry, and she did. I felt very badly for her but did feel I finally broke through her shell and was able to give her some real emotional support. It was a good feeling just to help someone who had given me a lot of help and who is a good friend. There was nothing sexual to all of this although I did hold her and caress her. I'm sure we could have had sex if I'd insisted but it didn't seem like the right time or place to be aggressive about it."

In fact, the preceding reply was not the only one received in which there seemed to be some pressure on a female employee to have a sexual relationship with her married employer, as the following reply demonstrates:

"Francine used to work for me before she moved. I trained her and we always had a good working relationship. She is now in another town working for a man that she cannot tolerate, although she originally moved away to follow her boyfriend of the time. She is very enterprising and now wants to move back here. (This is the main office.) There may be an opening, my supervisor is quitting and I am the most likely to take his place of everyone else in the state.

* See also chapter 6.

She qualifies for my job and it would not only be a promotion for her but the big move here to boot. My administrator trusts my decision and I could be very influential in getting her the position offered. By way of background, we have had a totally platonic relationship until just recently when we took a trip to San Francisco for four days. It took two nights for me to get into her trousers and the last night I was there, she stayed the night with me. We however did not have intercourse, or anything else past petting. How do I feel about it? I resent it.

"There is another girl in our company I've become interested in more recently. She is the most adorable thing I've ever seen. One day I had to visit our branch offices in a nearby town, and I found her working there. During the course of the day, she mentioned that it was her birthday. Since it is my custom to take my people out when I go to their area on business, I made the arrangements for a nice Italian dinner, birthday card, birthday cake, wine, lots of compliments, the whole shooting match. What it got me was a thirty-minute kissing bout (precipitated by a back rub of course) and a case of the 'blue balls.' I'm a sucker for a line, intentional or not, and she makes me feel warm, masculine, and needed. What I don't like about the relationship is that we are very different people, she is shy, doesn't smoke pot, dates state troopers, and doesn't talk.

"My relationship with my wife is good except she isn't as sexually expressive or innovative as I would like. But she is my wife, and she makes many concessions to me—let's me watch what I want to on TV, talks to me, shares my problems, loves me and tells me so often, is there when I need her, and offers me good advice. And thousands of other good things. The worst thing is I currently feel like a juggler with three balls—one slip could cause me a great deal of trouble and hurt my wife very much, which is something I do not want to do."

But a small minority of men felt having sex outside of marriage was more acceptable or justifiable if love was involved:

"I feel sex outside of marriage is O.K. when my feelings of affection for a woman become so strong that to deny them would be more dishonest than to follow them. I have been married sixteen years, and this past year I fell in love with another woman. We had sex. It seemed so 'right' to be with her, so emotionally transcendent, that it did not seem to have anything to do with my marriage. I love my wife too, but that is a different love. My new love didn't change that."

A few of these unusual replies described deeply emotional feelings for the lovers:

"My greatest one and only love affair was a couple of years ago. It reminded me of when my wife and I first started going together, but on a more mature, open, and fulfilling level. We had known each other and worked together for several years—enjoyed one another's company both at work and socially. We were both fond of our spouses, but would share our minor annoyances with each other. Both have similar-aged kids, of which we're equally proud. Her husband was forced to move to another part of the country for his job; she stayed behind to finish the school year and sell the house. One day while talking about the future and how we would miss one another, we found ourselves holding hands. After that, our relationship became more intimate. I was very depressed when the affair broke up. There still is the hope that someday, somehow, it will all work out."

"Married eighteen years. One extramarital experience was shattering. I loved her (I think I still do) far more deeply than any other experience I have ever had. Naturally, it almost destroyed my marriage. But my wife never knew why—she just thought I was naturally turning into a complete shit. I don't know what would have happened if I had not been separated from this woman by a job transfer. Now I have made the decision to love my wife and 'do right' by her, so the marriage is once again strong. Other extramarital experiences had no particular effect—they were just fun."

"I've only had one affair—now. The effect on me is to terrifically enrich my life—it's wonderful. I love the woman more than I ever have anyone. She is exciting and interesting, both pyssically and intellectually. She is beautiful and an incredible lover. Since I try to be a mature individual, I must accept the fact that there seems to be no way I can be married to her. So I am grateful for any time I can spend with her, under any conditions. This relationship has increased my happiness and pleasure. I love life better—therefore it even makes my marriage better."

"The most deeply I felt in love was with my lover of four years. I was strongly attracted to her physically for a long time before I actually met her. She did more for me than any one person has a right to expect of another. She was at once a lover, friend, sister, mother, confidante, and adviser. For the first time in my life I felt important and capable. I don't mean in the macho sense. It was a feeling that we belonged together and that I was *the* person who could please her. I enjoyed most, and still do, doing things that would make her happy. When I first knew I was in love, I felt very excited, a little scared, and very, very happy. The problem is that I am still married and have young children—with all the difficulty and anxiety for both of us that this situation creates."

"I am currently involved in two relationships, one with my wife and the other with a woman lawyer who is a member of the same firm I am and with whom I have been having the most (by several orders of magnitude) serious affair I have had in twelve years of marriage. The situation is incredibly emotionally confusing to me. My wife and I have been having 'trouble' for two or three years and I am not sure our marriage is salvageable. At the same time, I am not ready to abandon it. Also at the same time, there is no doubt in my mind I am more in love with the woman in my office than with my wife right now. I have discussed this frankly with the woman in my office, who is in much the same position with her husband, but have said nothing to my wife. If my wife suspects I am seeing anyone else, she has not let on.

"The best thing about my relationship with the woman in my office is the crazy, teenage-intense infatuation I feel for her; being with her is a constant emotional high. She is the most sensual woman and has the greatest sexual appetite of any woman I have ever had any extended relationship with, and sex with her is the best I've ever had. She has a delightfully quick mind, and a sense of humor that perfectly matches my own.

"While feeling all those things (and much more) about her, I am conscious, realistically, that someday our infatuation must cool to some reasonably sustainable level (we have been seeing each other for four months). I can't figure out how I should be handling it all. I can't see any resolution that is totally satisfactory. I feel great affection, concern, and regard for my wife, and the thought of abandoning our relationship is very painful to me. But I love the woman in my office intensely, and can't think of going on forever sneaking around, not being able to share each other's company openly."

But only a few of the men who were so in love were contemplating leaving their wives for their new relationship:

"I've been married twenty years, and generally like it, despite my current marital problems. I've had one recent affair of five months' duration. It was an extremely emotional experience. I had forgotten how powerful intense love is. It was a real mind-blower. I wound up discussing divorce with my wife, although I didn't let her know about my lover. We're discussing divorce still."

The great majority, even when in love, did not consider leaving their wives for the new lover:

"I have been deeply in love with my lover for seven years. I have grown as a person. I am much happier for having known this person. I feel that I have a right to enjoy my life and if I can't find happiness inside my marriage I will find it outside of marriage."

"I am fifty-eight, white, brought up in a fairly strict puritan family, church and church-related activities very important. About a year after our marriage (thirty-three years ago), I found myself seeking pictures of naked women, to fantasize to along with masturbation. Around the sixth or seventh year, I began to fantasize about another woman, my wife's close friend. About the tenth year, another close friend took a shower with me, and this led to occasional petting, mutual masturbation, but no insertions. During the eighteenth year I set about to seduce a twenty-seven-year-old single woman, secretly. It took almost a year before she was ready for a complete surrender. Our encounters were always clandestine, fraught with the danger of discovery, but the rewards were worth far more than the costs. It was an idyll that must rank with the highest in the annals of love. As far as we know, no one else ever knew about our relationship. After sixteen years and three children, she has decided to marry another man, partly for the children's sake, so that they will have a father, and partly for her own sake, as our secret meetings have had to become less and less frequent, and more dangerous, and her sexual appetite knows no bounds. During this entire affair, my relationship with my wife continued evenly. She probably appreciated the fact that I made fewer demands on her, sexually. The affair with the other woman probably saved me from going crazy."

"When I married my wife, I was not in love as I had been with other women in my early life. We were neither of us emotionally in love, but we were 'comfortable' with each other, had balanced personalities, temperaments, and characters. We fell more emotionally in love with each other after we were married, our love grew stronger for ten or fifteen years. When our four children became teenagers, we seemed to crest in the growth of our love. Now, we are professional, old married hands who have learned to love and live with each other over a long life. We rarely fight but sometimes argue. We love to be in each other's company and our friends, our children, and our children's friends all seem to enjoy being with us for celebrations and family occasions.

"I have had several extramarital sexual experiences which I took great pains to keep from my wife. Fourteen years ago I had an affair with a single woman that lasted six weeks. She is the only woman I have ever loved as much as my wife. We seemed to be much more evenly matched in our sexual appetites than my wife and I are. I also loved her character and intelligence. It was one of the most tremendous episodes in my life, but it had no effect on my love for my wife. And it had no effect on me in terms of guilt, deceit, etc. In fact, for years I tried to find another woman like her to have a similar affair.

"During the time we were having our affair, I should add that, although I was having sexual relations with the other woman that were as frequent as three or four times a week, sometimes lasting for hours and with as many as three or four orgasms by me, I was also having regular intercourse with my wife and felt no change on my part in our relationship. As far as I know, my wife never suspected I was having an affair. I was in love with both my wife and the other woman."

A few men had outside affairs with men only; most felt that this was less of an "unfaithful" act than sex with a woman would be:

"We have been married ten years. I definitely like being married. I like extended periods of monogamy. My wife and I have a 'good' sex life, and I have had only a few 'extra-marital' sexual experiences. They were very casual episodes with male friends. None was an 'affair' in the sense of turning away from my wife and finding 'love' elsewhere. My wife did not know about them. As an individual, I was surprised that the episodes could happen, and I felt 'guilty' about being 'unfaithful' to my wife. At the same time I felt pleased to learn that I am in charge of my sex life and that a sexual foray does not destroy my psyche or my marriage. Our marriage is held together by love, not sex."

"The only 'casual' sex relationships I tolerate are with male strangers for the express purpose of physical sex release —otherwise it's a very straight married sex life for me heterosexually—I know it seems stupid, but so is much of life."

WHAT REASONS DID MOST MEN GIVE FOR HAVING OUTSIDE SEX?

The most frequent reason men gave for having affairs was because their sex life at home was unsatisfactory, usually because sex was too infrequent; however, these answers may be superficial because they do not address the reasons for this lack of sex:*

"I am married, five years. I like being married, but my wife does not like too much sex—once or twice a month will satisfy her—unfortunately it won't satisfy me. I do not like extended periods of monogamy because monogamy is too constricting especially if my partner is not too sexually inclined."

"Married thirty-two years. Before marriage, sex was free, good, and we all enjoyed it. Since marriage it seems to cost. Cost more and I get less sex. Marriage is unfair to a man to have to pay all the bills and work, and still have to do his own sex by masturbation or sex outside the home— the sneaky kind. But if I need sex, I feel no guilt. My wife has her physical self and I have my needs."

"Married forty years. Like it. But sex depends on her health. Old wives get tired, worn out. I had extramarital sex unknown to my wife. The effect on me was I was healthier, less angry."

"Thirty-three years. I like being married. I have a passable marriage, but my real sexual satisfaction has always come away from home. Since my wife originally believed in sex only for children, outside of about once a week throughout my married life, I have always found fulfillment outside my marriage. In the last four or five years, my wife has become more aroused, but though I am more active at home now, my main activity is still away from home."

* See chapter 5 for a discussion of these issues.

While most men complained of not enough sex being available in marriage, many others complained that sex in marriage was too available and thus became boring—leading to a desire for outside sex:

"I am married and have been for three years. I like some parts of being married, but the effect on sex is frightening. I mean, I can go for months without being sexually attracted to my wife. We make love, but it isn't with the same spontaneity as it is with other girls. I have more fun when I have a variety of partners. I find that when I am monogamous, I get easily distracted from sexual encounters, but when dealing with several different people during the course of a month, I can better enjoy each one of them. I thrive on casual relationships. Surely she knows I am seeing other women but she doesn't know who. The effect on me is that it allows me a freedom of expression I don't feel at home. Being a sexually oriented person, if I didn't have the opportunity to screw other women, my sex life would be a disaster and I would probably leave my wife."

"Sixteen years. I don't know how to ward off the ever-lurking feeling of staleness and habit from our marriage. I imagine a new sexual relationship would electrify me out of the habit. But I don't feel this is available to me without great cost in my relationship to my wife. I do now realize how difficult it is to keep a relationship exciting. I have had other sex but I would not tell my wife. There is a certain injury to the ego and the psyche if one is made to feel, directly or indirectly, that he or she is inadequate. On me as an individual the effect was unpleasant, as I do not like deviousness and I would rather raunch it up in my own home, but I believe it saved, if that is a correct word, the marriage. I have tasted variety and I like it."

"Twenty-four years. I like it but it has its bad side—it's like being in jail. After three months there is a need which grows for an occasional strange piece of ass. I don't know why, it just happens."

"It gets pretty dull, doing it with the same one all the time (thirty-nine years). I have intercourse with my wife about three times in two weeks. I have been having an affair with another woman for the last nine years and, when I could be with her, intercourse took place at least twice a day."

*However, as we have seen, most men were not considering ending their marriages, despite infrequent or "boring" sex, which they felt they could supplement outside the relationship; most said they stayed married to retain the benefits of a domestic/family arrangement:**

"Married twenty-three years. We got married because it seemed like the thing to do, plus the benefits of regular sex and a stable home life. But I am not faithful—not at all. Why? I asked her several years ago for sex twice in the same month, and she said, 'Go find somebody who likes that stuff,' and I did. She's still a good cook, housewife, and mother— but I need more. I've discovered what I was missing, but I don't want to jeopardize my home life."

"I am married five years. I got married because I thought it was the right thing to do at the time (I was twenty-five). As far as the effect on sex, I got to know myself sexually very well after I was married, and my sexual self is basically incompatible with her sexual self. Different needs entirely. So I am pursuing my sex life elsewhere, while still relating to my wife on other levels. We enjoy doing things around the house together, having friends over, etc."

"Monogamy? I have had several extramarital experiences, unknown to my wife. I have a much greater drive than my wife, thus this did away with the problem of not enough screwing, etc. However, there was one time when I seriously thought about leaving my wife for one of my lovers. Basically, I am too comfortable with her to leave her."

"I've been married thirteen years. Do I like it? The answer weighs hundreds of pounds. I have stayed married because, for better or worse, etc., the relationship is far richer than any other I have had or am likely to know. I got married originally to join the great stream of life. As a further joining of the great stream of life, we had a child, and the system has been kicking shit out of us ever since —though most people would say I have a good job, good house, good car, and no cause to complain. And it's true. I eat good too. But the whole thing seems pretty hard on sex because pleasure is replaced by duty and plenty of it. But I will stay married."

"I have been married thirty-two years, a marriage I have stuck with because of a deep admiration and affection

* See pages 216–225 for reasons men gave for liking marriage.

for the woman I married. She is charming, personable, warm, and affectionate. On top of all this, it may sound like a contradiction to say I am bitterly disappointed in this marriage, but the marriage has been devoid of sexual understanding and communication. For thirty years, I have tried, in a kind and gentle way, to bridge the gap, but our sex life will always be a disaster area. I have offered medical brochures on sex, but she always knew more than the doctors, so they were never read. I am a monogamist at heart, and I like being married, but in another life, I would never repeat this one. It is a sure road to a shattered sexual ego. My extramarital experience has been heavy petting, masturbation (with a couple of women), and one homosexual experience. At least they kept me from going off the deep end completely, because they let me know that I am no sexual freak and that I am sexually attractive to others, even though my wife has found it something of an ordeal to touch and look at my penis."

Another frequently given reason for having sex outside of marriage was no reason: many men did not believe that monogamy was "natural," and therefore felt that they needed no "reason" for having extramarital sex, although they still preferred to be married (rather than "free") and did not tell their wives about their outside sex:

"I have evolved to the position where I believe monogamy is an unnatural existence for anyone, especially by legal coercion. Other women excite me and I enjoy sex with them. It has nothing to do with my marriage."

"The institution of marriage needs radical restructuring. Monogamy is stultifying and unnatural. There are relationships other than the primary which require nurturing and development, and sexual relations are part of this."

"I don't believe in monogamy. I believe man is biologically suited to desire and fuck many different women in his lifetime. I also like one-nighters. I had many that my wife did not know about."

"I don't believe in monogamy for me, because I like to screw other women. I love to make love to and taste other female bodies. I've had many extramarital experiences."

"I have been married for eleven years. Marriage provides stability in my life and helps prevent loneliness, but I do not believe in monogamy. There is a lack of excitement and adventure with it. The lure of the new and unknown is very strong and appealing, and I can't resist it when the occasion arises. I love my wife but another woman is great too."

"I like having several sexual relationships going at once, and generally bring them to an end after several months. This is because the more people I get close to, the larger, grander, fuller I become. More fulfilled. I get to be me in more different ways. I like to keep them short, because the magic is strongest in the beginning. But I like my home for its calm and constancy."

And one man said:

"I know my sentimental nature well enough to realize that if I were not married I would probably marry the first available woman who came along. Undoubtedly I have used my marriage, without even thinking about it, as a safe refuge from which to make occasional sexual forays on the female population. It's a comfortable arrangement."

Many men separated sex and love, or saw no contradiction in loving more than one partner at a time:

"She doesn't believe in having affairs and believes in one man at a time. I can't seem to convince her that the affairs have no affect upon my love for her or our marriage."

"I have told her for many years that just because you're fucking another woman for the pure pleasure of the act itself, it doesn't mean that you're in love with that woman, but she can't see where there is any separation between sex and love. I told her to look at the thousands upon thousands of guys who go out with call girls and visit whorehouses. They aren't in love with them at all, it's just the pleasure and enjoyment of the sex act. This never made any sense to her and still doesn't till this day."

*Many men "explained" their extramarital activity in terms of the male "sex drive":**

"I believe there is a bit of 'tomcat' in me because I like an occasional affair. I still believe in the family unit that our society calls for, but I do like a casual sexual relationship. A woman can never completely domesticate a man."

* See also page 351.

"Monogamy is a difficult thing for me to live by. When I was married I went five years without another woman and it almost drove me crazy. Even with a good sex life at home I desire other women. Maybe it's fuel for the ego. The relationship I'm in now is being jeopardized by the same problem. And it is a problem. Much like an alcoholic."

"Married twenty-five years. I had extramarital experiences—like all men do. Of my male friends, I only know of two that have been faithful to their wives and one of them is now in the process of getting a divorce because his wife proved unfaithful."

A few men mentioned social pressure on them to have affairs —pressure to be "lusty," to prove masculinity by showing a strong "sex drive"—especially since "all men do it":

"I have been married for almost seven years. I have never strayed. Sometimes I think I'm the only man in the world faithful to my wife."

"I sometimes think I'm not with it if I stay monogamous. If I had a stronger lust for women I'm sure I would be less faithful to my girl."

Very few men connected their affairs during marriage with increased alienation from their wives—the affairs, they most often implied, were a result of lack of sex or boredom with sex at home; there was little discussion of possible underlying stresses in the relationship which could have led to feelings of boredom or disinterest in sex. On the surface, at least, many men seemed to accept women's lesser interest in sex, and their own desire for outside sex, as "just the way things are," due to men and women's supposed different "sex drives."

A handful of men, represented by the following man, made the connection between subtle changes in the relationship with their wives (or their feelings toward their wives, or their feelings about marriage) and their own extramarital sex:

"I guess I had built up feelings of resentment and anger at her, all along. There were things she did that made me mad, that I never told her about, etc. But even more, I think I resented her for the feeling I had of being 'tied down'— even though I had wanted to get married very much. It seemed like all my angers and all my frustrations could be blamed on her rather than asking myself why I didn't feel free. All the negative parts of my life could be blamed on the 'marriage.' But at the same time, while I felt 'unfree,' I was afraid to leave the security of marriage and get divorced. This depedency made me even angrier, as I didn't like the cowardly picture it presented.

"One 'solution' to all this was to have affairs—escaping, but not escaping. To have a fantasy life of being a different person—a 'freer,' more 'independent' person, one who was liked and admired by another woman.

"Finally, of course, all this blew up in my face. As my wife felt that I wasn't all 'there' with her, she became more and more distant, she wanted sex less often (in some ways I was relieved), and our resentment and hostility against each other solidified, until it became a wall between us. My increasing anger and frustration, even desperation (I was feeling so ego-less, so bad about myself), led me to the point where I became less and less careful about hiding my affairs, and my wife confronted me with it. We separated. That was eight years ago.

"Two years ago, after a lot of thinking and talking with each other, we are back together, this time much happier. This time I *appreciate* and enjoy being married. I see it as a chance for growth together with another person, a free (even though monogamous, this time) situation which gives me a broader context for my life. I am more honest. When I am angry (or I notice she is), we talk about it. We have a good thing going. I notice, too, that our really good sex seems to follow times of talking, or sharing time together, especially when we divulge our secrets and dreams to one another. I am just getting to know my wife—I never did before—and she is great!"

"A few years ago, I was having affairs on my wife right and left. I felt guilty, and didn't know why I was doing it— I just thought I was 'male' and that's how we men are. Thought I needed variety. Now, after counseling, I realize our marriage was not good before I was unfaithful, I just did not realize it. I did not connect the stresses and strains in our relationship—how we both felt tied down, especially by the kids, and blamed each other for it!—with my 'desire' for other women. I did not see it as a form of hostility to my wife—I thought it was just my 'sex drive.' I see things different now, we have changed our marriage a lot for the better and are much happier."

Many of the men throughout this section have sounded very angry with their wives. Was this anger only because of the denial of sex? Or were there other basic conflicts in the marriage, of which the lack of sex—or even the "boringness" of sex—was only a symptom?

Only a few men directly mentioned a connection between being unhappy in marriage—other than sexually—and having affairs:

"Sometimes I had had extramarital sexual experiences when I felt unhappy in marriage. They were not of the 'open marriage' type. The effect was rather negative, but it was mostly the beginning of seeing if I wanted to change the partner."

Or thought of it as a way of expressing hostility or anger:

"I have had several extramarital affairs, not of the open marriage type. My wife suspects that I have strayed. However, I have never even hinted at my infidelities and have been as discreet as possible. My outside affairs have left me without the vigor or interest in her, and now as I think about it, I was probably punishing her with rejection for the ways she was a threat to me. What a waste."

Similarly, only a few men made the connection between less sex and tensions in the relationship:

"When we're not feeling close she doesn't feel sexy and like doing anything. I usually don't either."

"If there is the slightest weakness or insecurity within a marriage, extramarital affairs can cause disaster, sometimes irremediable disaster. The possible breakup (as in our case) might not be caused by the affair in question, but by far more subtle psychological and emotional factors which have been simmering for a long time."

"Relationships are invaluable for working through hostility, hatred, fear, along with those joys that we all know and love. My point is that regular sex with another person, with yourself, or no sex at all isn't good or bad as far as I'm concerned. What really matters is how you react to what's happening, and *why* it's happening."

Conclusion

The most frequent reason men gave for having sex outside their marriages was sexual rejection by their wives,* or
the boring nature of repeated sex with the same person in
marriage. But since these two statements practically cancel
each other out, are there other reasons? Why do men need
to bolster their marriages on a continuing basis like this? It
would seem that there may be hidden tensions or anger between men and women in long relationships which are focused on sex. We will continue to look for possible causes of
this in later sections of this chapter, and of this book.

**"How does marriage affect sex? Does sex in marriage become
boring eventually?"**

Most men said yes, it did become less exciting:

"The effect of marriage on sex? It goes stale!"

"I have been married thirty years. I like it, but time tends
to degrade sexual relations because of the million and one
things that occur in your lives."

"Married three years and sex seems to go downhill."

"I was married twenty-three years (six kids). It's tough
on good sex. Lots of boredom."

"Married eight years and I love it, but sex is not so exciting as before we were married. Then we weren't together
all the time and whenever we were, the atmosphere was
charged sexually. Very titillating. Now that we sleep together
every night, we aren't so turned on. But I like it."

"I think marriage interferes with the enjoyment of sex.
'Life is too daily.' All the household chores get in the way
and confuse the sexual relationship."

"Eight years. Security replaces excitement."

"Before we married, I think sex was more fun. There was
so much more anticipation that was never fully satisfied.
Every touch, every kiss, every message had much greater
effect than it does now."

"Married forty-one years. I sometimes believe that marriage means taking a long-term lease on a vagina. In time
sex becomes a humdrum exercise of getting it in and pulling
it out to achieve relief from mental and physical tensions."

* This topic is addressed in chapter 5.

"Sex in a relationship always becomes stale—the crush can't last forever. There must be some meaningful way for a man and woman to relate sexually over a period of time, but neither my lovers nor I know what it is."

But is boredom the inevitable result of knowing another person—or can this imply stagnation or problems in the relationship? And, did the traditional marriage contain such great inequality that this alienation, these stresses, were built in?

For some, marriage had had both good and bad effects on sex; it was, as one man put it, a "double-edged sword":

"I guess, overall, marriage removes a degree of mystery and courtship which is both bad and good—anxiety goes away, but to some degree probably also passion . . . you know there's a pretty good chance you'll get laid tonight . . . but you also know pretty much what's gonna happen and how it'll feel . . . a double-edged sword."

"The good effect on sex in any extended relationship is that we gradually become aware of each other's needs and we feel safer in communicating our needs. But damn! It shouldn't take twenty-one years to reach that point. It should be natural to start with. The bad effect is we often bore each other and also we know there are areas of need where the other will never be able to respond and that need will never be satisfied in the relationship. That is very frustrating knowledge."

One man said the problem was lack of time:

"*The main problem today is that there is not enough time for a couple who has children to have free time alone together.* By the time a man is home from work, the dinner and cleaning up completed, and the children finally 'scraped off of the front' of the TV and put to bed, the couple is too tired for much more than basic intercourse, then off to sleep themselves. There is so very little time in the morning or during the day when a couple can be alone. Children are the greatest blessing a couple can have, but there must be some way a couple can have some time alone."

Many men said an "effect" of marriage was, as men discuss in chapter 5, the simple lack of sex:

"I have been married to my second wife for thirteen years. I have had less sex in marriage than I ever had when single."

"Before marriage, she was horny almost all of the time. I'd take her home, be kissing her good night, and we'd get so horny we'd just have to go out and fuck someplace. After marriage, she was only interested when Jupiter was aligned with Mars and there was a total eclipse of the sun. I always like the Woody Allen joke from *Sleeper*—where he was asleep for a hundred years, and he said he hadn't had sex for one hundred years, one hundred and twelve if you counted his marriage. It's true once you're hooked, they aren't interested. And then you are supposed to be 'faithful.' They got to be kidding."

Others pointed out that marriage per se had no effect on sex —or rather, it is only the state of the relationship (whether bad or good) which affects sex:

"Married five years. It's up and down. The effect on sex is good and bad depending on where we are in our relationship. If my wife and I are tight, it's really neat."

"The effect of marriage on sex depends on what's happening in the marriage—it can make it either great or terrible."

"You can't generalize about the effect of marriage on sex—it depends on the characteristics of the marriage. I think anyone will be sexually inhibited in a situation which is inequitable and where they feel insecure or worried about performance. Marriage has put many women in that position; my wife was in that position for many years and it affected our sex life. I am sure this effect is not inherent in all marriages. Also I suppose that sex becomes dull and unattractive in a marriage where there is no development (if there is such a thing). I believe a good marriage has a fine effect on sex."

And a minority of men said that sex in marriage had always been very exciting, or had gotten more exciting over time, as both people gained confidence with each other and felt freer, and as the relationship gained more layers of meaning:

"I have been married for thirty years to my wife. My marriage has been the most successful thing in my life. I doubt that there is more than one marriage in a thousand that has been as happy and fulfilling as mine has. We are having more sexual encounters now than at any other time in our marriage. This has been going on for four or five years."

"I am not currently married but I loved it while I was. I got married because I was totally in love. Sex was fantastic right up until the time of our divorce and was not changed in any way from what it had been prior to getting married."

"I was married twenty-four years, enjoyed almost all of it; sex was better the last year than the first, though it was pretty damned good from the beginning."

"Married eighteen years. I like it. The effect on sex is terrific. I don't need to prove anything, so I can relax and enjoy it. I'm a lot better at it now than before I was married. My wife takes all the credit for that and she's probably right. She showed me a few things that nobody ever bothered to before."

"Three years. We know what turns each other on, what feels good, and we use that as a base to explore and expand. We have tried acting out her fantasies and mine, and done things that I would never dare to do with someone I didn't know quite well—you have to work up to non-standard things, feel the other person out. And when we do them, they are more enjoyable because they are laden with a symbolic meaning, we feel, at least I feel, that doing these 'forbidden' things together makes us closer, symbolizes that we are willing to go to the further reaches with each other, how deeply we trust each other—and how close we want to be. There are a million fantasies that I still haven't told her about. This is the wildest sex I have ever had."

"I like marriage. In it, each sexual experience builds, so that the next is even better. The most beautiful sexual experiences I ever had were in marriage."

"Being married definitely has had a good effect on sex for me. Barriers drop away and we are a lot freer emotionally to explore each other's sensuality in a leisurely way. Sexual communication is terrific and caring. It's hard not to feel hesitant, rushed, and embarrassed with someone you don't know so well."

"I got married because we were in love. I wanted to marry my wife and have a family. Sex with the same partner is beautiful. We each know what the other likes. Communication during sex is usually only a touch of the hand. It's great."

"Married thirty years. Wonderful so far!"

Conclusion

Does sex automatically become boring in marriage, or in a long relationship? Is the constant repetition of certain activities with one person inevitably less interesting as time passes?* One way to answer this is to ask, is it less interesting to have dinner and a conversation with a friend you have known for twenty years, than with a friend you have known for one? Obviously, it depends on the friend, and on the status of your relationship at that particular time. But usually one can talk more deeply to an old and good friend than to a new one—although there is fun and excitement in discovering a new person.

Part of the reason for the "inevitable boringness" of sex in many of the marriages of men in this book is the fact that they have frequently shied away from marrying the women with whom they were most in love, the women who most excited them, to whom they felt the most open and emotionally vulnerable (as seen earlier in this chapter). Men have tended to base their marriages on practicalities, more on a "rational" feeling of being "in control" over their lives, being able to foresee a stable and predictable future—than on a feeling of being overwhelmed by the sudden beauty (in manner and thought, in a total sense, not just physically) of another. But to be so totally in control is boring, eventually.

Another reason repeated sex with the same person may become "boring" has to do with the repetitive nature of the way we define sex"—i.e., as "foreplay," followed by "vaginal penetration," and ending with intercourse and male orgasm in the vagina. This was discussed in *The Hite Report* on women's sexuality, and will be discussed in following chapters. If the definition of sex is constantly static and filled with performance pressures, perhaps the only way to find variety is to change partners.

In some ways, also, the alienation that has been built into marriages, due to the inequality between men and women legislated by our society, can also lead to a feeling of "boredom"—as boredom often represents built-up and unexpressed anger, rage, or hopelessness. Men often feel this rage against their wives, and marriages often contain decade-long cold wars. Most men's reaction to this situation is to search secretly for an interim relationship outside of the marriage. But men

* See also page 461.

seeking emotional intimacy and fulfillment through sex—first with one partner, then another, as a pattern throughout a marriage—were not, in this study, very happy in the end because of it. Much more rewarding was, as some men did, to seek out the causes of the "boredom" or lack of closeness, whether they were bottled up anger or something else. To deny that there are problems, to describe "male sexuality" as if it were a mechanical "drive," with a built-in need for "variety," as if men were inevitably "biologically programmed" to go from "blossom to blossom" spreading their "pollen," is only a way to increasing loneliness and isolation.

HOW DID MEN FEEL ABOUT THEIR WIVES HAVING EXTRAMARITAL AFFAIRS?*

Most men did not believe their wives had extramarital sex; however, of those who had considered the idea, or whose wives had had extramarital sex of which they were aware, most were negative:

"If I had a wife who had sex outside of marriage, I am sure I would be terribly depressed and outraged. This is the worst thing that can happen to the male ego. (I am not unaware that the female has an ego also and that learning about an extramarital affair would be a sorrowful event.) In my experience with 83 women with whom I have had sex outside of marriage, I had several experiences when jealousy nearly killed me. These were occasions when I learned that lovers had had sex with other men when they were ostensibly my women. Each time it was an almost unbearable affront to my belief that I am the greatest thing that ever happened in bed. One I 'forgave' and took back (we had then been lovers for five years) and we remained very close until her death a dozen years later, but I never forgot. There was still a poignant hurt."

"The one extramarital experience I found had the most profound effect on me was *hers.* I just wish I could be as secure about myself as she is herself. I was hurt, to say the least. I've gotten over it, with only some hurt feelings remaining, in fact I'm now glad she did it. I don't want to know if she is still seeing the same person or any other persons,

* See also pages 199–209.

though. We had a shaky summer that year, I think we are both happy it's over now and we came through it."

"I'd be jealous as hell if she was sleeping with someone else. Angry, too. She'd be out in the cold. I wouldn't want any details. I'd cut her off cold turkey, with no regrets except anger at myself for being taken in by such a castrating bitch. By the same token, any woman who tries to make a man jealous is a sadistic little bastard. She can take a walk."

"My wife had several extramarital experiences; I had none. She told me about them individually after the fact and I was really shaken—more because of our dismal sex life and the feelings of inadequacy which were multiplied 100 times. But her affairs had no great long-term effect on the marriage—we separated for other reasons."

"My first wife had one serious extramarital affair about a year and a half after we were married, and that was one of several major reasons for our divorce. I didn't want to be jealous, but I was anyway. I felt rejected even though, until other troubles developed, she continued to sleep with me as well as him. I told her I suspected, but actually I was already pretty well convinced; and finally she admitted it."

Some men were beyond caring, as they were already very angry with their wives:

"My sex life, the one I feel is really me, has been extramarital. My wife knows and she has a very low sex drive if any at all—she has her own lover. I don't care if she does. I really don't care at all that much about her. Confusion is the effect on me, torn between so much—I'm really trapped by it all. Eventually I plan to be out of all this shit, but for now the kids know about us (both partners). They don't always approve but they know why I have a lover. I've been honest with them. It isn't easy sometimes but I do it and it seems to be O.K. for now. I'd love to be single."

"I was married for sixteen years and found it stifling to life in general, including sex. My wife had a brief affair with a young man she worked with. She didn't know I knew about it and flew into a rage when she found out I did. I didn't let it bother me. I really was glad someone was giving her some love because I sure wasn't."

But a few men accepted it:

"Been married seven years. I really do like being married. Marriage is the framework of my life. Without my wife

I wouldn't have gotten very far in life—either emotionally or intellectually. I've had one 'extramarital' experience. I told my wife, and it gave her a bit of a shock, I think. But she took it in stride. Now my wife has had a sexual relationship with a friend of ours for the last two years. My wife became more and more attracted to him, and I encouraged her to become involved with him. Believe it or not, she seduced him. He would never have made the first move. So for the last two years, two nights a week when I do volunteer work in the community, she has been spending the night at his house. It doesn't bother me in the least. In fact I find it sexually exciting to know she is sleeping with another man: it has enhanced my sexual appreciation of her. All throughout this relationship there was never any question of my wife leaving me. She loves this man but in a different way than me. She can live with me but wouldn't be able to with him. I was never worried about it overshadowing our relationship. My wife and I know one another very well. I've never taken advantage of this openness in our marriage to pursue an extramarital affair. I've just never met the right person. If it happens, it will happen. I'm content."

"OPEN MARRIAGE"

As we have seen, the overwhelming majority of men's extramarital sex was unknown to their wives, or at least the men did not tell their wives. However, a few men (3 percent) had "open marriages"—that is, marriages in which both partners agreed in advance that each could have outside sexual relationships.

Many of these men were still trying to decide how they felt about it, as one man's reply shows:

"Married for eight years, I like being married. It has been a bond—no matter how artificial it might seem—which has kept us working at our relationship and maintained our commitment to each other. I'm not sure we would have lasted if it were not for the 'legal technicalities.' I'm not even sure it will last even with them.

"Now, with problems surfacing, sex has become stale—more, I think, because of a stalemate we've reached (temporary?) in the growth of our relationship than because of disinterest. If the relationship holds together, the sex will (I sincerely hope) improve with the growth and improvement of other aspects.

"Both my wife and I have had extramarital sexual experiences (six to ten apiece). We both know of all the other's experiences. The effects have been variable. My wife was a virgin when we first slept together, and had had sex with no other men before our marriage. It was absolutely necessary for her to experience sex with other people—we both knew and accepted that. In addition, she needed to determine the course of her own economic life—therefore we have spent a great deal of time separated while she has pursued her career. During these times, obviously, new friendships would develop and sexual urges would build. We both recognized the inevitability of 'extramarital' sex and accepted it as a part of the life style we agreed on.

"On two occasions, such affairs have had deeper effects. Twice my wife has become involved quite deeply with other men and 'fallen in love' with them. On both occasions, the sex she enjoyed with them was far better than the sex we have shared. On both occasions I was deeply hurt—not because sex was better with the other men (sex is usually better for me with other women) but rather that she could feel things for the other men that she could not feel for me.

"Such experiences have been very difficult, and forced us to analyze more carefully our relationship. This has led to benefits as well as problems. Sometimes I wish that this added complexity had never been introduced . . . but it's too late now."

Three men explained in detail the conflicting emotions that arose in them when their wives became emotionally attached to another person during an open marriage:

"My wife and I have both had lovers, never unknown to the other; the effect on our marriage has been very positive, and likewise on us individually. I'm not sure what 'open marriage' means but I am probably against it, certainly if it means chasing after 'experiences.' And in the conditions that prevail in many people's lives, and sometimes in my own, I think monogamy is the best one can do.

"The time I fell most deeply in love was with my wife, after we had been married for ages, during her one serious love affair with someone else, around and after its beginning.

Just at that time she was changing rapidly, in fact reaping the benefits of years of struggle. The changes in the relationship between us were so big that a whole new fit was involved.

"For most of my life jealousy has been so remote that I had no comprehension of it. However, after the happy start of my wife's one relatively long affair, the later turns taught me a few things—or at least made me aware of a few things. For several months she had two lovers (I was one) and all was blissful. Then her affair went awry somehow, and she became so preoccupied with it that she rejected me as a lover. (Not as a person, and not even as the most important person in her life, but as a lover. Not just physically—she accepted me physically—but as a lover psychologically.) I think I understand now what happened. Through almost all the years of our marriage I had been the stronger person; almost every clash would work out with me in the right and her in the wrong. Among other effects, this inhibited her sexually with me. Far from completely; she was not inert, and was sometimes quite active. As she gained more independence and more individual success in her life, our sex life continued to get better, but the pattern established over the many years still set a certain barrier. She warmed to her lover and was active toward him in a way that was impossible with me, and I believe that when problems arose, in her effort to maintain her splendid experience with him, she had to be unencumbered of the persistence of the old pattern with me. Her rejection of me as a lover made me profoundly miserable, and gave me some glimmering of what jealousy is all about. A long time later, I still respond with a feeling of some alarm at any hint of a repetition. I still don't understand the whole jealousy syndrome. I've spent hours now trying to put together a coherent answer to this question, and I am giving up.

"Except, I think I should complete the story. Ironically, what went wrong with my wife's affair was that her poor guy couldn't take a warm, active, uninhibited woman. She couldn't be that way with me though that was just what I craved, while he somehow felt dominated by it."

"I really think it would be a dull and undersexed, unimaginative person who would not think that a change would be pleasant after having sex with the same person for twenty or thirty years—however handsome, beautiful, inventive, imaginative, and sexy that partner might be. But when the thing actually happens, all sorts of emotions come into play which I think are underestimated.

"In my own case I was entirely faithful to my wife for fifteen years, never having sex with anyone else at any time. Then, one day my wife in casual conversation with a friend and his wife agreed that they could see no reason why a partner shouldn't have sex occasionally with someone outside marriage. A little later, she told me that the woman who had been present at the conversation strongly fancied me. Shortly afterwards, I approached her, she reacted, and we began a sexually highly charged affair. After six months or so my wife asked me whether I had slept with the other woman and I admitted it. She seemed to be pleased rather than anything else. However, she insisted on being told the details, and when it became clear that I had been making love to the other woman regularly over a period of months— her attitude changed; and changed again when she came to believe that the other woman was *emotionally* committed to me, and had told me she loved me.

"I think it was perhaps my own dismay at my wife thinking that she was in any way endangered, *as* my wife, which prompted me to behave brashly, blaming the whole affair on her (while I would never have started it without the circumstances set out above, I *did*, however, begin it, and am wholly responsible for it). I was aghast that she should be so upset by what I saw as an extremely pleasant sexual affair (our own sex life had improved more or less as a direct result of the affair).

"However, my perplexity has lessened within the past year, because my wife has become emotionally very attached to another man, with whom she has not had a sexual relationship, but whose character and personality fascinate her. She at one point became very concerned about him and the way his life seemed to be going, and I felt at that time as though her love had been withdrawn from me and was directed at him. (I guess that while one has given up the idea that any woman need or should be exclusively one's property sexually, there is still a feeling that emotionally she should be fully committed to one; just a silly belief, but difficult to give up, perhaps.)

"I wonder whether the *emotional* side of promiscuity may not be far more difficult for people to cope with than the simple physical infidelity. I can absolutely honestly say that I wouldn't object to my wife sleeping with anyone, perhaps even however often; though I suppose one might begin to feel jealous if the incidence was too frequent, and I don't think one can lay down a rule—once a month's O.K., once a week's too much. But I can see that I would be concerned if I thought the *emotional* relationship was getting too great.

"Perhaps, then, monogamy *is* still the answer, though I think it's a pity; in our marriage, the fact that after twenty years the sex is better than it ever was is a splendid thing. But in a marriage in which custom, or lack of experiment, or whatever, has meant a thoroughly stale life, how (assuming that release of sexual tension is important, as I believe it is) is either the husband or the wife to survive without extramarital sex, except by a total dulling of the senses and a state of utter boredom? Is there an ideal situation which is reachable?

"I hope I'm not sounding too anguished; I'm *not* anguished. I have—we have, I think—one of the happiest marriages I know of, and an enviably satisfactory sex life, I think. The most strongly I would put it is that now and again I feel I would like a change of sexual experience which can't be satisfied by pornography or masturbation or whatever. It's a very strongly felt need, because I seem to be strongly sexed, so it's stronger for instance than the need to buy new clothes or eat at a new restaurant or whatever. It is, however, controllable; I suppose I only feel that it's an appetite I would be happy to satisfy if that could be done without hurting anyone. But that's an important facet of the situation, and in the final analysis I happen to believe that it's the *most* important."

"Married fifteen years. In the first ten years, I had extramarital sex unknown to my wife. Then in the last five years we have been trying open marriage. I think the effect on both of us of our *own* affairs has been very positive. But the effect on me as an individual of my *wife's* involvement with another man was very harmful and negative. Despite reading very widely, and hours, days, months of very intense talking with each other before we decided to change to an open marriage, my wife and I had very different, opposing, internal to ourselves, conceptions, views, pictures of, and goals.

"My aim in open marriage through all our previous-to-adopting-it talking, was to develop a more intense sexual relationship between my wife and me, while still acknowledging that both of us could be attracted to, and enjoy sex with, other partners. So entering into an open marriage was an impossible dream come true; now I could express my sexual feelings with other women without sneaking behind my wife's back, and I was more than happy that now she had developed to the point where she could admit to herself *her* sexual feelings for, and need for experience with, other men. I was eager for her to have that variety of sexual experience; it didn't seem fair that I had had premarital experiences, plus extramarital, while she had only made love with one man, me, in her whole life.

"My wife's view of open marriage did not stress or even include the enhancement of our own sexual relationship. She *did* want sexual experiences with other men, partly to find out if what we had together was 'what sex was all about,' partly to 'grab at life before it was too late,' and to have a variety of sexual experiences. But her priorities were all for her own, individual, personal growth.

"The type of sexual relationship I had for so long desired between my wife and myself developed between her and another man; with *him* she wanted, and did, everything I had always hoped for in *our* sexual relationship. Perhaps my ego could have withstood that, if she had been willing to accede to my entreaties, even begging, and invest as much time and energy into our *own* sexual relationship.

"Even more importantly, I think I could have accepted it if she had shared her outside activities with me. But she was most unwilling, let alone eager, to do either. And of course, the more I pressed, the less she wanted to. The full sharing, the sense of 'coupleness' was perhaps more important than the actual activity, or at least *as* important, to me, but to her was just the opposite, to her anything outside our marriage was for her alone, private, something to 'hug to herself.'

"The result of my crashing dreams was actual physical illness, massive depression with all the usual physical and mental symptoms accompanying it, much anger at her for 'doing such a thing' to me, often repressed or directed elsewhere such as at myself or at our kids, loss of nearly all my joie de vivre, and enevitably, sexual impotence in varying degrees.

"Despite all this, I still worked very hard to make her 'see,' to cooperate with me to get us 'together,' not just living in the same house. I must stress that her love and affection and what she put into our nonsexual relationship remained relatively unchanged throughout.

"For years, in fact until the last few months, I thought the sexual legacy this left would always be with me, I would never recover my normal self. But most of the nonsexual trauma I got over in two years, and now after another two years I'm much more hopeful."

Some felt "open marriage" had put too much of a strain on the relationship, or presaged the end of the relationship, reflecting deeper problems that had already existed:

"I had a few extramarital 'one-night stands' and so did my wife. They came at a time when our marriage was breaking up; it was a way of attacking each other, especially on her part (i.e., she selected one of my close friends and fucked him in the living room while I was sleeping nearby, etc.). The effect of all these extramarital activities upon me was a terrible one, mostly because of the malicious intent behind them."

"I was essentially entirely monogamous for eight years, while being involved with a woman who didn't believe in it and constantly sought other lovers. I think I was monogamous in order to hold on to her and in order to be able to say, 'You have no right to do that because I'm not doing it.' Then for two years I tried to do it her way, meeting a lot of people and having a lot of experiences I would not have had otherwise, sexual as well as nonsexual. The 'extramarital' sexual activity on both sides hurt us both a lot, and eventually created an atmosphere of hurt so deep-seated that the relationship was impossible, in spite of the love which persisted. It was always complicated and very painful. The people we slept with never had the benefit of really being involved with either of us because sleeping with them was always part of our relationship to each other, not to them. I'm not sure that being monogamous is the right way to deal with possessiveness and jealousy, but the strain that having other lovers puts on a relationship is not worth the benefit of sexual and emotional closeness with other people."

But a few said that "open marriage" had benefited their marriage relationships:

"I've been married thirteen years. I enjoy my marriage very much. I don't like monogamy. I think it oppresses people—makes possessions of them. One's self-identity, creativity, independence, and opportunity to know and love others are squelched. My extramarital experiences are known to my mate. My mate was the first to have an extramarital experience. I was depressed for days. I was quiet. I think I was threatened by it. She really went ape over the guy. I felt she told me too much about the relationship. I was jealous. We had many discussions and gradually I worked out my feelings. I still have twinges of jealousy about other men in her life. She has the same feelings about the other women in my life. She was jealous during my first. It was a real barnbuster. I think I was really in love for about three months. It was an exhilarating experience to be so intensely excited about another person. I leveled off, however, and I became even more intense about my mate. (I'm still very close friends with the first woman I had a loving extramarital experience with.) We both handle the sexual openness in our marriage extremely well now. I look back on it all sometimes and wonder, why all the ruckus?"

"My wife and I have been married for thirty-three— count 'em, thirty-three—years, and I can't imagine (or bear to think of) not being married to her. Our sex life has been good or better than good, in the various moods of different life stages. For long stretches, I didn't feel like looking at anyone but my wife, because she and I love each other a lot and usually have a great deal to communicate. But then again, I (or she) may temporarily go ape over some other person, or have a quickie or more prolonged affair with someone just for fun. Until a few years ago, I had had only one or two brief extramarital adventures, on the sly, and I hated the lying and secrecy I then thought necessary. Since we went into open marriage, each of us has had quite a few outside experiences. It's been liberating for each of us, and contrary to conventional notions, has made the marriage even warmer and stronger."

In some cases, "open marriage" meant both partners participated in outside sex, but in many others, it was really only the husband who practiced it:

"Twenty-three years. My wife is very fat and has turned me off to sex with her. The old story. She knows I have other relationships—she likes being married—and that it cannot be everything—get the most out of it and seek what it lacks elsewhere."

"Eight years. I've had several extramarital experiences. At first they were unknown to my wife, but now she knows that I'm going out with other women and that I'd like her to do the same. But she won't—she's not interested in men— or women—or dogs—or . . ."

"I'm a happily married man, married to a wonderful girl that would never think of making love to another man. However, I will make love to anybody that turns me on, and my wife knows all about it, and cheers me on. Honesty has been the foundation of our marriage."

In a very few cases, represented by the following man, only the wife actually practiced "open marriage":

"I am thirty. I have been monogamous for ten years now, I have never had extramarital sex. My wife is at present having an affair with a young (nineteen) fellow who works for me. She tells me we have been so emotionally dependent on each other that it has stifled us. She has broken from this mold and says I should feel free to also. I am trying to adjust to this idea.

"The advent of my wife's lover caused me some sleepless, teary nights. I felt that her relationship with him was a negation of me. She told me this was not the case and she loves me, but at the moment he gives her something that I can't. At first this seemed totally contradictory to me. If you love me I must be able to fill all your needs. But now I am more optimistic about our future together outside this classic 'be all, do all' concept of marriage.

"I like being married. But the effect of marriage on sex in our case was disastrous! The relaxed spontaneous atmosphere faded in a clutter of role-playing obligations, and responsibility. All too often, sex consisted of a feel or two—penetration, my orgasm, and that's it. Right now my wife is living in the basement of our house, I live upstairs with our child.

"Monogamy makes me feel safe and loved. But I think my wife is right that this situation creates an emotional dependence, which is unhealthy. I would like to be able to have and feel comfortable with a casual relationship. Maybe someday I will. Right now I am trying to fight my way out of this emotional dependency but I still find that the person who interests me the most sexually is my wife."

A handful of men had marriages which included "swinging," or group sex:

"Ten years this time, fifteen the first time. I like to share my life with a woman. We have our up and down periods. In sex you get stale and the newness and excitement wears off.

I have done away with jealousy. I enjoy sex with my girlfriend and my wife both just as much. I have watched my wife perform fellatio and sex with another man and it was a giant 'turn-on.' My wife knows about my current girlfriend (who is married), and does not object. I have the problem at the moment of loving two women at the same time, and would like to have them both under the same roof as wives. I am working slowly toward this goal."

"I've been married for twenty-seven years. I like being married and I wouldn't have missed that part of life for the world. I had a lot of extramarital affairs, which until 1970 were pretty much unknown to my wife. In 1970 we got into swinging and I believe it has actually saved our marriage. I was seriously contemplating either separation or divorce because my life had become rather dull and stale. It changed my outlook and I have a much deeper appreciation of my wife now and a much stronger love. Early extramarital affairs put a very bad strain on our marriage, as the secrecy was difficult to live with."

"Our open marriage experience consisted of two partner swaps. I was happy with them but my wife felt I didn't respect her when I offered her to other men, even though these men were very good friends of hers and mine. She said I just wanted to swap so I could get the women. I didn't need to swap to do that but I thought I might uninhibit my wife, but it didn't work."

Some men, after trying "open marriage," decided against it:

"I have been married three times. During the first marriage, I had an affair which was unknown to my wife. The second marriage was an open marriage, and the third marriage was a 'swinging marriage.' I did not enjoy the aftermath of the affair during the first marriage, as I felt guilt about it. During the second marriage, the open marriage relationship removed the guilt feeling, and both my then wife and I enjoyed doing our thing, but we were not close. The 'swinging marriage' was by far the worst, and we both felt that there was no marriage at all. 'Extramarital' relationships may not do a good marriage any harm, in fact the openness and freedom can be beneficial. But as I found in the third marriage, when two people who are married can fuck anyone they want whenever they want and as often as they want, there is really no foundation for a marriage."

"I was married twenty-five years the first time, and sixteen the second. In the midst of my life, I had four years of polygamy. As an individual I felt like a Ping-Pong ball. Strained relations. The world, at least the one around me, isn't ready for this type of relationship yet. I am through!!!"

"I was married for a period of five years. It was a disaster and at the end we tried an open marriage. The fact is that it's really hard to relate to a spouse totally while going about and affairing everything in sight. Emotionally it just doesn't work in the long run. Down deep I think all of us really wish we could find one person to relate to."

"I have been married three years. We did have brief relationships with other people but it seemed to take place in an atmosphere of distrust and defensiveness. It made me feel threatened and defensive. I feel more comfortable and secure in a monogamous relationship."

"Married eight years. It's wonderful having a strong mutual love, trust, respect, shared experience, companionship, and concern. In the past, I had sex with several others. My wife knew about them entirely. She had sex with others too. We probably learned a little bit about ourselves, each other, and a lot more about other people, but it didn't really change things in any way. Although there is a certain excitement getting involved with someone new, it's not worth all the hassles, and a similar feeling can be experienced just by getting to be close, sympathetic friends. No one has ever aroused me or pleased me as well sexually or as much as my wife, and sex has a lot more meaning with her as well, as it is connected with very deep love."

And a few men spoke out against the "open marriage" concept:

"Open marriage is a crock of shit. I know a lot of people who claim to be open to other experiences, but who haven't done it yet. I don't believe a truly deep relationship is possible with several people simultaneously. Someone doesn't get all of you."

"I'm living with a woman now and I wouldn't think of betraying her. Apparently she feels the same. We know a couple who have an open marriage. We call them predators during our bedtime small-talk sessions. It's so hard to feel comfortable in their presence. They seem to be on the lookout for 'fresh meat' wherever they go. Sex is great but we both feel there's more to life."

MEN WHO ARE MONOGAMOUS

Some men were monogamous; 28 percent of the men who had been married two years or more had never had sex outside of marriage (33 percent of all married men).

Some of these men who were monogamous did not like it:

"Married thirty-six and a half years. Love the home life, service, companionship, but think I'd like to be free to court (chase) the single women and shack up with variety. Sex at home seems uninteresting."

"I've been married to the same woman since December 1939. We have never stepped out on each other, but I am beginning to believe we have been wrong. Being married is right, but sex is fun and pleasurable, why should you save it just for one another? I don't think one should sneak out on a marriage partner, but have a mutual understanding to do so."

"This is a tough one, because I'm sure my wife will read this, but to be truthful monogamy is not my favorite role in sex. I have had no extramarital sex and won't, but I really don't equate sex with fidelity in love. Just as change is exciting in other things, change of sexual partners before marriage made things more exciting. Monogamy takes out the suspense."

"I've been married nine years. As long as I've been married, things are discussed and rediscussed that only bring heartache, I would like someone new so my memories would go away. Sex does get boring with the same person but no deficiency shows up if your imagination is strong. I wish she would go have sex with other men so she'd enjoy sex more than she does. I think she really doesn't like sex. I would like to have sex with other women because I would get a thrill out of making them cum and not having to hear about bills, housework, or bad memories."

"I have no desire for sexual relationships without an emotional or personal involvement. However, I have thought about the idea of enjoying a sexual relationship, other than the monogamous one I'm in, with a few other women in my life. I am married fourteen years. I like being married, and our sex life has improved and matured. But I feel that there should be nothing wrong with a casual sexual relationship with a woman who is a good and meaningful friend."

"I have been married for twenty years. I got married originally and I am married now because marriage is the conventional form of corporate life of two persons. I have no extramarital sexual experiences and I don't want to have, but I don't like monogamy. It is the only way not to be in trouble with my neighbors, however, and besides, I have two healthy hands."

"Married sixteen years. It's O.K.; if my wife and I were sexually compatible it would be great. I have never been unfaithful in body but may not be able to say that tomorrow. In the marriage vows I didn't say 'if she satisfied me.' I also didn't realize how badly we could be sexually mismatched."

"I have been married for five years and love being married. I wouldn't want to become involved with anyone else like I am involved with my wife. However, I have my doubts about monogamy. I deeply love my wife but I miss the extreme excitement my wife and I had during our dating period. Sometimes I would like to make love to another woman on a 'one-night stand' basis to re-experience the excitement."

"I crave to be loved just for the real me. Not as a pretend person. I have a lot of love to give, but nobody seems to want it. I guess women stay away from me because I am the 'good family man.' I do not want to hurt my family by causing a problem, but my thinking has been changing recently in that given the chance for real love I would take it. I think I have sort of went through the 'change of life,' realizing I'm not going any place fast. It amazes me that persons like me with this great longing never get together, as I imagine there are quite many of them."

"I have been monogamous for the last twenty-six years. My father had a relationship outside of the family and I saw what it did to my mother, therefore have decided to keep a happy family by not engaging in any relationship outside of the family."

"I love my wife—she's not well-read, which I don't like, but she is an intelligent college grad. I feel she is not as compassionate or charitable as I am and I don't like it. We have been married two years. The effect on sex is bad. She doesn't orgasm with me, but I bring her to orgasm by cunnilingus. She knows and detests that I masturbate. But I am a traditionalist, and believe in monogamy. I'd never have an extramarital affair."

But some men (20 percent) had always *liked and practiced* *monogamy:*

"I have been married for thirty-six years. I wouldn't live any other way. Once we became educated sexually it has been superlative!"

"I have been married five years. I like and enjoy being married. The total effect it has on my sexual life is that it went from masturbation between marriages to the most fulfilling sexual relationship that I've ever known and God forbid I can even handle! It's fantastic. I obviously enjoy monogamy after five years. It is really wonderful to come home to a wife and family who not only recognize me but take care of my every need. Some people have told me that monogamy is boring. However, they just have not lived with *my* wife."

"Married four years. I prefer monogamy over everything else, and for extended periods of time, because I am very intense and loyal in my relationships, and when I get into one, I very rarely get bored with them. On the contrary, I get more deeply involved as time goes by."

"Married almost thirty-two years. I married for companionship, love, sex, and mutual interest. Our sex has always been great. I prefer monogamy because I am fortunate to have an almost perfect mate and we complement each other. I have had no extramarital sexual experiences."

"I have been married eight years and I like it very much. I wanted to live with my partner, but society dictated that we get married. It has worked out very well. I like monogamy and I've never had extramarital sex, though I don't condemn it, I just haven't needed any."

"Been married fifty-nine years. It is fine. I like it. We were married because we have liked each other's company since we were eight years old. Married sex is best. Also, monogamy is the best plan, in my opinion. I have no extramarital experience. I could not enjoy anyone else half as much as my wife."

"I like monogamy because I feel it's required for depth in myself and my closest friend, my wife."

"My marriage has been a beautiful era to me and my wife. We have always been true to each other. So many of my friends have had extra sex on the sly—but when you come right down to the fact, the grass is just as green on your own side of the fence. I still believe in marriage—can't see these people living together today without it. I was brought up in a Christian home and was taught that there is a right and a wrong."

"Married twelve years. It provides a more natural sex life and better social life as well. I have never had extramarital sexual experiences, do not believe in it. I believe in being true to another human being."

"I like monogamy, one woman at a time is enough to cope with."

"I believe that monogamy is and was the best for us. I don't believe that in any other situation there could have been the wholehearted and enduring love we have known."

"Married four years. I love it, and I like monogamy. It takes real commitment, real balls to love one person and fight to make the relationship work. I like the challenge and the rewards."

"Four years. I love being married! It makes sex very intimate and beautiful. I would not like casual affairs . . . it just would not be the same as when love is present."

"Married forty-one years to the same woman. I like being married. She's a good housekeeper but not exciting in bed. She was taught by her mother to 'be available, and put up with sex.' She's a better mother than a mistress. She's not affectionate. But I like monogamy, it gives me a feeling of security. No extramarital sex. Almost, once, but I told my wife everything. After that my wife was more affectionate for a while. But it is fun flirting with other women."

"Married twenty-five years. I love being married. I was single until I was forty-five, and though I had many lovely affairs with women, it is nothing compared to married life. I married because I fell in love the most deeply in my life, and because we both wanted a family life and children. The effect on sex is to make it most beautiful of all. Although I have been tempted, I have remained faithful to my vows and have had no affairs outside of our marriage. I tried it all before marriage; now I want to give everything to my mate and our marriage."

"I have been married twenty-five years. I like being married. I am married because I like my wife and family and find satisfaction sexually and emotionally and economically and psychologically and socially—why should I not want to be married, with all our good times together and the support we gain from each other? The effect on sex—it has improved it! I like monogamy—I think I would be terribly guilty and dysfunctional as a person were I otherwise—

simply too taken up with guilt, with self-justification, etc. etc., to make extramarital sex very much fun. I have had no such experiences."

"Married over forty years, no extramarital experiences. I have been attracted to a large number of women at different times, but over the years, my wife has been the most interesting woman I have known, we have had a good marriage, she has always been a cooperative and enthusiastic sex partner, interested in my pleasures as well as her own, so that I have never had any justification for seeking other women. Further, we have marriage vows, and I respect her and our children, as they have respected me, and I have always believed a tranquil and stable home and family life are of basic importance. As I cannot easily engage in lies or deceit, I have not been willing to pay that price for short-term excitement and stimulation. Finally, all the women who have attracted me are either unmarried or married! Affairs with the unmarried would seem exploitive and selfish on my part; with the married, disruptive of households, unfair to innocent children and husbands. Perhaps this is a rationalization; theoretically, I regret the lack of experience with a wide array of sexual partners, but practically I doubt that I have missed much beyond some occasional excitement; I am sure I have missed a lot of complications in my life."

"I am forty-two, a high school teacher with a master's degree. I have been married over twenty years to my wife. I enjoy my marriage very much. It is the most important thing in my life. Marriage has affected our sex life by making it progressively better the longer we have been married. I think sex is more physically and psychologically fulfilling within marriage. I am quite satisfied with the monogamous arrangement shared by my wife and me. There is stability within a marriage for raising children, for loving each other, and living together. I would care little for casual sexual relationships outside of marriage. If I had a lousy marriage, I might think differently, but we are very happy together."

"In both of my previous marriages (thirteen years and six years) I have had affairs. The effect on me was of guilt, feeling sorry for myself—wondering what it was that those 'happily married men out there' had that I didn't have. It hurt my marriages in that one just *has* to act differently if he (or she) is having an affair. I'm sure there were many times I did not get angry when I should have, but I didn't because . . . 'Who am I to get mad when I'm doing what I am doing (having an affair)?' That certainly isn't going to lead to a very healthy give-and-take marriage situation. So, for me, affairs were very bad on my marriage. I should have either tried harder to straighten things out or gotten a divorce *much earlier*.

"Now I have been married again for two years. I like being married. Sex is much better since it's based on love, trust, and being exclusive. The affairs before were never very much fun, not really satisfying, left me feeling guilty, and never fulfilling. I'm enjoying the peace of mind of not wanting to fool around for the first time in my life.

"For the first time I see that once you've found someone you love—are happy with in and out of bed—then having any kind of extramarital relationship puts a permanent chip in your relationship that can never be replaced. It's like we both know if we keep together sexually—exclusively—then we are special to each other—but if we (either one of us) did *anything* of a sexual or intimate nature with another person, then our special relationship would end. I wouldn't do it. A truly nice relationship is rare indeed—and once you've found it, you should hold on to it."

"I am thirty-two years old, a management official in an engineering firm. I am fairly young for such a position, but I busted my ass to get here. I graduated from engineering school by going in the evenings, but now I am very satisfied with my life and all my hard work is beginning to pay off.

"I have been married for nine years. I enjoy being married. Having people around you that love you is a very secure feeling. I love my wife and children and they love me. My life is devoted to making their lives full of love, happiness, and satisfaction. The closeness of the family is most important.

"Sex with the same partner is beautiful. We each know what the other likes. Communication during sex is usually only a touch of the hand. It's great. In today's world, monogamy is the only way. Can you support two or three families? Can you love several people enough to live with them all at the same time? Can you or would you share one of your mates? I am a jealous person. I would be hurt if my partner had sex with another person. To say I would be angry is an understatement. However, I trust my partner and don't believe it would happen. If a man or a woman is happy with their mate or the person they are living with I don't see any reason for finding someone else.

"When I met my wife, it was great. I knew her for a few years until finally one day I took her out to a formal party and as we got home I kissed her. She was the only woman I was afraid to kiss. After that kiss I was finished. To this day her kisses always thrill me. She loves me and what can be better than that?"

Of younger marriages that tended to be monogamous, most had a much stronger feeling of equality than in the traditional marriage; perhaps this is a trend for the future (see also pages 970–979).

One man's reply illustrates this feeling:

"Married nine years and I like married life. I love my wife as a person. She is very intelligent, warm, and we usually communicate very well. Monogamy is necessary only because it is a commitment to one person and demonstrates her worth to you—which is necessary to create a life together that has more than enough difficulties without creating a triangle or worse. I have never had extramarital sex during my marriage, but had lots of sex with lots of women when I was not married. Love is mostly a situation where I have a strong desire to make someone happy because my happiness is dependent on making them happy—strange but true."

WHY DO MEN GET MARRIED, AND WHY DO THEY LIKE BEING MARRIED?

We have seen in many of the preceding answers in this chapter that, even though men have many complaints about marriage and frequently have additional sexual relationships outside of marriage, they also frequently say they like marriage and, whether they like it or not, almost always intend to stay married.

Why do men prefer to stay married when they have so many complaints about it? When they find it so unsatisfactory that they have to seek a large part of their fulfillment elsewhere? And when they so often complain of an intense feeling of lack of freedom?

MOST MEN SAY THEY LIKE MARRIAGE

"If you are married, how many years have you been married? Do you like being married? (Why did you get married originally? Do you love your wife? In what sense?)"

Most men—even though they had many complaints about marriage and frequently had sex outside of marriage—basically liked marriage and wanted to stay married:

"Married twenty-seven years. Even though we have a lot of problems, marriage is satisfactory at worst and better than satisfactory most of the time; I strongly suspect I'd be very lonely if I became single now, and more so the older I became; I suspect overall my sex life would be less satisfactory if I became single now; separating now would probably raise hell with me emotionally and also my wife, and even though perhaps less, with my children. For all these reasons, I stay married."

"I have been married eleven years. All things considered, I apparently prefer being married to not being married, for it would appear that, despite occasional feelings that I cannot, within marriage, be the person that I imagine I could have become if I were left to myself, my marriage will continue for quite some time to come. We have weathered some difficult times in our relationship and seem only to draw closer and become more emotionally dependent upon each other."

"I have been married to the same woman for thirty-two years. Do I like it? Yes and no. Yes, because of the being part of a family, the social acceptance, and convenience. No, because I do not get enough sex from my wife, she refuses to communicate about it, and I am not at times able to meet her expectations in other areas, like my auto driving the way she wants it done. But I have no desire to get divorced."

"I have been married twenty-three years and I like being married on balance. There are many things I dislike about it, but more that I like, like the sharing of common interests, the pleasure of children first, and now grandchildren, and the enjoyment of sex on a regular basis. On the other hand, there are limitations on freedom to go where one wants, when one wants, and to do what one wants, for whom he wants to. But I am happy with my life pretty much as it is."

"I have been married for ten years, and like it. I have some mixed feelings. The overall effect on sex has been good —we are having more fun now that we are done having children. The one thing I hate about marriage is its restriction on freedom and mobility. Decisions involve two or more persons, and this often causes problems. But I'd rather be married than not."

"Seventeen years. Why did I get married? I don't know, to avoid loneliness, perhaps. There are moments of great love and beauty interspersed with hate in marriage. But the solution to the stresses and strains is not to get divorced—you have to take the good with the bad. When sex gets too infrequent, there is always sex outside."

What are the basic reasons men give for wanting to stay married or for liking marriage?

Most men liked marriage for the domestic warmth and security, and the stability and regularity of home life,* having someone there to help and care for them; sex was mentioned only infrequently, and then as a minor reason:

"I'm married because that is probably the best thing for me—especially the stability of the relationship."

"I want and need the warmth and comfort of relationships—a home around me. The give-and-take, communicating, growing together, working on problems, enjoying things, nurturing—and receiving. I have only lived alone during my separation and one or two other short periods in my life. It's not for me!"

"I have been married twenty-eight years and I like it. I like the familiarity, the friendship, having someone special to love. It's fun, healthful, and keeps things in perspective. It softens difficult times. It is nice to be wanted and needed."

"Yes, I like marriage. I need and depend upon a wife, good or bad."

"Yes, I need another person to bounce my deeper feelings off of."

* Is there necessarily a conflict between this and a desire to feel "free"?

"I love being married. Having a life partner is exciting, fulfilling, and comforting."

"I like being married. My wife is my backbone in my business. She takes care of everyday problems that I do not want to handle. She is a very good mother to my children, even though she does not turn me on sexually anymore."

"Having people around you that love you is a very secure feeling. I love my wife and children and they love me."

"Home serves as a 'secure' base of operation, a place where I can be me, a place I can always come back to, and a place where I can share my successes and failures. Of course it's a give-and-take process, and much of the importance is my part in listening to my wife."

"It's the best arrangement for maintaining security, sanity, child raising, and economic well-being."

"Most times I like being married. (Married thirteen years.) Why? Because it is physically and psychologically stabilizing."

"I like marriage because there's a sense of family and permanence most of the time."

"I am married because I like the companionship it provides, I usually enjoy being around and talking with my wife, it seems to be a sound financial arrangement, and it is usually a convenient sexual arrangement."

"The most important thing about our relationship is the stability that we have because of our affiliation. Being married is good for both of us."

"Marriage gives me a deep feeling of being needed, of comfortableness with each other, and a feeling of commitment and trust."

Many men stressed the aspect of security:

"Sixteen years. I am happily married and think it is the greatest. I have one partner ready to do anything for me, whom I so deeply love. I know she will be there so long as we both live. It gives me a great feeling of personal security."

"Twenty years. I am married for the security it gives, the pleasure, and the convenience. A framework to live my life in."

"Twenty-nine and a half years. Marriage is restrictive in one sense, but gives a secure feeling in another."

"I've been married thirteen years. I like being committed to one person. It gives me a good feeling and I feel secure about at least one part of my life."

"I have been married almost twenty-four years. I like it. The sense of family community is one of the cornerstones of my life."

"I've been married six months. I like being married. I like to share my days with someone and to share her days with her. I like to have someone to make long plans with and to look forward with someone to fulfilling those plans. I suppose that the feelings of security, the feeling that I am not alone in facing the risks and dangers and problems of the world is the best thing about having a long-term relationship."

"The most important thing I get out of the relationship is structure and continuity. I have a fear of the unknown after a divorce."

"The best thing about marriage is the security and the worst is the security also."

Or having a companion, someone to be there:

"I have liked it, and needed, being married. I guess I need someone to be there when I come home, to be a good companion with me, to share lots of life's experiences with, to confide in and be with me taking care of our children."

"I like knowing I'm not alone, that we are a unit. She depends on me, and I know I can always count on her to be there, whether it's as my companion at a social or business affair, or to comfort me when I'm feeling low."

"I've been married for nineteen years and love it. In times of strain it has been the plaster cast which has kept things in place so that any strains or breaks could heal properly."

"I like extended periods of monogamy, but the advantages thereof have nothing to do with sex. It has to do with building an intimate relationship in which someone really knows you, and having strong psychic communication, and having someone to talk to, not being lonely, caring and being cared for, knowing that there's someone there if you need someone, sharing experiences, and always having someone else to bounce things off of."

"After twenty years, I think the best thing is that, although I have put her through many bad times, she has always remained loyal to me. She wants to be married to me and to me only, and she is willing to do anything to keep the marriage going."

"I like the fact that I get a stable, ongoing relationship where I really can trust and rely on my partner."

"I like the constant, loving companionship. She is devoted to me. I also have a reluctance to terminate the marriage because so many divorcees are unhappy, insecure, and lonely."

Or the sharing:

"I would not want to be single. I am married because my wife and I are good friends and I like sharing my life with someone who I know cares about me and likes me as a person. I would much rather spend my time with a person who I can talk to and who I am not afraid to tell my most personal secrets to. I enjoy the closeness both physically and psychologically. I would not want to be married to anyone else. There are other women who I find more sexually attractive than my wife but no one I respect more. My wife cares about me and we share everything with each other—all our secrets, desires, and feelings. That is more important than sexual attractiveness any day. Don't get me wrong, however. I find my wife to be attractive also and enjoy having sex with her."

Including children:

"Marriage has had its good points. We have a child that we're both devoted to and we've loved sharing her growth. The experience of establishing a single household and building it up has also given us a sense of family and of love almost like brother and sister. Still, I miss the frequent sex and romance."

"I am married because we share a common ideal of raising a family in our tradition."

"Twenty-one years. The best part of marriage is our children. We have three. I wanted them, as I enjoy the idea of procreation. I was proud when my wife was pregnant. But I love my wife more as a helpmate than passionately."

"Family is the most important reason for being married to me. I like helping and caring for others, because it makes me feel needed, loved, and important to them. This includes my children, their spouses, my in-laws, and my wife."

Some said that having a family, or being head of a family, had social and career benefits:

"I had to sacrifice some things to be married but it's worth it. I believe that had I not married I would constantly be on the prowl, and I could not have devoted the time to business that I have in the last twenty-three years."

"Eleven years. Having a family has helped me in my work, as it has caused me to take my job responsibility in a more serious light. I think my acceptance of responsibility would have been less without marriage."

"I gave up a free-wheeling, self-centered life to get married, and I sincerely believe my marriage added a stability and a sense of purpose and direction to my life that played a major role in my maturation and my career in business. We have been married forty-one years."

"Social pressures from her family and mine kept us together originally, but now I see that this was a good thing. We have learned to accept each other for the children and those things we like in each other. You are more accepted in the community when you are married."

Some cited the practical, traditional domestic conveniences of marriage for men—having services done for them, such as laundry, cleaning, and cooking:

"I've been married fourteen years. I like all the advantages of having a woman cooking for me, cleaning my house, washing my clothes, caring for my offspring, and doing the bookkeeping."

"Married eight years. I enjoy all the 'benefits' of marriage, i.e., good food, clean house, clothes, etc., as well as having a child around. Sex too is better, more satisfying, with someone I really love. Marriage simplifies living by having most of one's needs met in one single institution."

"I have been married forty-one years. I love being married although recently my wife indicated she would prefer to live alone. If she persists in her no-sex attitude, which she has maintained for four years now, I think I might agree to a divorce. But there are so many advantages to living together, even without sex—regular meals, laundry, companionship, plus my handiwork around the house and car. It makes my life more regular."

"I have been married thirty-one years as of now. I very much like the healthiness and convenience: as my wife has never worked out of the home, she does all the homework, shopping, cleaning, cooking, washing, etc."

"Sometimes I have my doubts about marriage, but I guess I am lucky to have a beautiful wife, willing to please, with cooking ability and patience and understanding."

A minority of men mentioned finding marriage a convenient sexual arrangement:

"I have been married for almost five years. I like it because it is not as much of a hassle as dating."

"Married eleven years. I greatly enjoy being married. Marriage has given me a regular partner and opened more doors for us sexually."

A few mentioned a feeling of duty or social pressure:

"I stay married because I am a responsible person, and take my responsibilities seriously. I have people depending on me."

"I have been married seven years. I don't like it as much as I first did, but I firmly believe that you should stick it out for as long as possible until it has become obvious that there is nothing left to stay married for."

"I have been married only once and that was twenty-one years ago. It may not always be the greatest, but I accept my fate in stride."

"Reasons for staying married: strict upbringing, taboos, feeling of accountability to God and to my wife and children. Also, a desire to be an example."

Or financial reasons:

"I fear the drop in material wealth that would result from a divorce."

Only a few men mentioned liking being married because of their interest in, and love/liking for, their specific marriage partner as an individual:

"I am married six years. I enjoy being married. I am married to my wife because I love her. She has many outstanding qualities, and I admire her, both in her work and how she thinks about things. She is a very interesting person to be around."

"I've been married for fourteen years, and it is the most important thing in my life—my wife, our life together—my wife is pretty much the center of my life, or the basis for my happiness. We enjoy doing many of the same things, including traveling, and we often just sit and talk to each other. She is very exciting and interesting, always has something new to say."

A new conception of marriage was emerging in a few men who said they enjoyed and valued marriage because of the possibility of growth through such a deep relationship:

"Our relationship provides a place for both of us to be secure and to grow. And to be in love."

"Married for ten years. Marriage has been my best life experience, especially with my one and only partner—I love it. I feel that I have been molded into something more than I really am by family life—grown as a person."

"Married over thirty years. I wanted a 'total' life partner for sex and everything else. That's why I got married originally, why I remarried after my first wife's death, and why I'm married now. Marriage combines stability with (if you make the effort) the sauce of enough change to add spice to your life. People change and even grow in marriage. It's a process, a journey together, and you never quite know what's around the corner. Even conflicts can be enriching. And if you have children you learn—you learn! The hard way, to be sure. But you learn what society means—a society —for you helped to create and sustain one (the family). And you see, you experience at first hand all that's right and wrong with it, its problems, contradictions, and dilemmas."

"Eleven years. Being married has enabled me to get fantastically close to another person, and to learn about parts of myself in ways I never would have done otherwise."

"I have been married two years and yes I like it. It has forced me to deal with other people on other than superficial levels. It has made me come to grips not only with my feelings for my wife, but has taught me to develop deeper and more meaningful relationships with other members of my family, as well as friends and acquaintances. Sex in marriage is another thing that I have been forced to deal with. It has been painful at times but the end results, those already achieved and those that will be, have been well worth it."

Or, finally, because they loved their wife:

"We have been married for ten years. Why am I married? My life seems incomplete outside of marriage. I must interject that marriage is a deeply felt personal commitment to the well-being of my spouse. It is not a matter of sexual convenience, nor meal convenience, nor housekeeper convenience, but is to me the following: 'You are the part of me for which I have been searching for eternity. My heart is no less important to me than are you and though we are separate physically I wish for us to become one in mind, spirit, and goal in life. I seek this form from you and am willing that perfection is neither yours nor mine. I will at all times care for you as I care for my own being in all ways. Should you not be able to respond in like manner I will look for someone else. Should you accept what I have to offer and then find you have erred, I will gracefully release the commitments of the past, trying with all that is in me to allow the parting transition to be as pleasant as the coming-together transition was.' "

Some men did not like their marriages in any way, but remained married anyway:

"I have been married eighteen years. I don't like being married—or rather, I have grown not to care for this particular relationship (the feeling is reciprocated by my wife, though we like each other as individuals). We have stayed married over the past few years so that my daughter could finish her high school education and go away to college, and so that my wife could at the same time finish her advanced degree."

"Twenty-five years. I'm not crazy about our marriage, but she depends on me."

"I have been married unhappily for fifteen years to a cold-natured bitch. If I go, the courts will screw me so bad that it's not worth it. We married because of a mistaken pregnancy. Sex with her is when I am so fucking horny I'd fuck a telephone pole."

"It's not the greatest marriage, but she lives up to my minimum expectations and I am used to her."

"Married nineteen years. I don't like it, but I have stayed married because of the children. I came from a broken home and I don't want my children to go through the same thing. I want to be with them even though at times our home life is a little rocky."

"I have been married twenty years. I don't like it, but could with the right person. I only stay married because of the last child and I don't love anyone else I would rather be with. Also I am very much afraid of loneliness. I got married because she was pregnant."

"I have been married seventeen long, aggravating, boring, depressing years. I don't like being married. Its effect on my sex desire for my wife is deadening. I have had about a dozen extramarital sexual experiences. They were unknown to my wife (I think), but she suspects, and its effect on our marriage is yet another irritant: she considers *my* penis *her* property! Outrageous!"

"It's a demoralizer."

"I have been married twenty-one years! I hate being married. It has a dulling effect and it leaves one hopeless. One should not marry for *sex,* that's one thing for sure."

"I've been hooked (seven) long *miserable* years, and the way I look at life, I wish I had the power to turn back time."

"Ten years. It has become worse because of my dissatisfaction. The feeling burns out trying to get her to change. My wife seems content with our sex life."

"I have been married for seventeen years because being married is the acceptable standard in American society. My wife and I have no sexual contact now. I have casual affairs, unknown to the wife. Our household is more competitive than affectionate. Here is a list of what I would like to tell my wife or any woman about how to treat a man:

"1. If you think it—don't say it.

"2. Stop complaining about frivolous, insignificant things.

"3. Trust him: he is an individual—different than you.

"4. Let him have friends—accept them even if they drink and you do not.

"5. Refrain from making nasty statements and remarks, about your husband, especially in front of the child/children.

"6. Be kind towards each other.

"7. Respect each other's principles.

"8. Why be sick all the time?

"9. Is tranquilizers necessary and other barbiturates?

"10. Why arise at the time the daughter arises in the morning—to then say you're arising to avoid conflicts?!

"I feel that if I were treated with greater respect at home, I would be an entirely new different individual. The saying that women rock the folds of civilization is true. A good woman can either make or break a man."

"WHY DID YOU GET MARRIED ORIGINALLY?"

Reasons most frequently given included because it was "the thing to do," to get a regular sex partner, having a feeling of love, and (less frequently) for companionship or to avoid loneliness:

"I originally got married because it seemed like the right thing to do and the right time to do it. The woman was there, we were in love, and so we did it. Without either of us thinking about it very much, I think."

"Married sixteen years. I got married to avoid loneliness with someone I liked, and to fulfill my sexual desires. I was lucky and fairly satisfied with the first one of these two."

"I can't say why I got married: it was the 'thing to do,' it was time to settle down and raise a family, she was available and cute and thought I'd make a good father."

"Forty-one years. I got married for the most part because I was in love, partly because I wanted companionship, partly because most of my friends and acquaintances were married and it seemed the 'normal' thing to do in those days (the thirties) if one could afford it, and partly, I suppose, because I needed a regular sexual outlet."

"Thirty years. I got married because I did really fall in love with my wife the moment I saw her. She blew my mind. After all the traumas of our lives, it worked. We have a fantastic relationship, caring and sensitive to each other's needs. But I am sure that I married not only because I loved her, but also because it was expected of me that I would marry, and any suggestion that I wouldn't was frowned on, and suspicious."

"Married nine years. I got married cuz it was a good idea at the time. As for its effect, I have a steady piece."

"I married because I liked being loved by the one I love. We got married to be with each other."

"Truthfully? I got tired of shooting in my shorts and having to go home."

"I have been married forty-two years to the same lady. Marriage is a perfect life with the right partner. We married because my wife wanted to. She really loved me and I was fond of her."

"I married because I wanted to have a happy family, a woman (sex partner), and last, because I have been afraid of being alone."

"I got married originally to relieve loneliness."

"I am married so that my lover can inherit and be my wife legally—it avoids hassle from society. We got married after living together for nine months for the above reasons and to please both sets of parents, who were not aware of our arrangement."

"In my first marriage—she showed a strong interest in me, and I in her, and the relationship grew. Second marriage —a compelling attraction that had me moving against obstacles that my brain was telling me to respect. A compelling push from loneliness that had built for close to ten years."

"Why did I get married originally? Romantic love, sexual attraction, I wasn't 'getting any younger,' social and parental pressure, vague visions of loneliness in the future if I didn't. I found somebody I figured my parents would approve of."

"Married twenty-six years. I was ready to settle down."

"Twenty-one years. Marriage was then my goal, and when I met a woman I could be pleased with, we got married. I was in love, at least I think so, but not passionately."

"I married in order to have an attractive, permanent sex partner, emotional security, and a family."

"I have been married twenty-two years. Had the society been more open to sex than it is now I possibly would not have married at all and stayed single."

"I got married because I was thirty-two and felt like settling down. I guess it was sort of preordained that you meet a woman, raise a family. I was lonesome, and wanted the warmth that I was told a marriage would bring. I also wanted a more frequent sex life."

"Married forty-two years to the same woman. Perhaps I married to get away from my dominating mother, and I was in love."

"I got married for a steady lay. I was in love, but that doesn't have anything to do with getting married."

"Married eight years. I got married for regular sex and because I wanted someone to take care of me."

"I got married when I was twenty, and she was twenty-one, and as I now realize, because she was an innocent virgin that I taught to masturbate and fellatio me when we were dating. She was a very happy, serious girl, who fell deeply in love with me. I guess at the time, I loved her in my way, and when it got serious, I felt that it would mess her head up traumatically, after all we had done, if I broke it off. I believed she could not have handled it. I still think I did the right thing, and the first ten years were good."

"We have been married thirty-two years. It's not paradise, but I still prefer being married. The reasons I married in the first place were, in order of priority, desire for a sexual partner, curiosity about women, attraction toward my wife-to-be, creative, experimental urge, curiosity about fatherhood, loneliness, and a feeling that marriage is the only way to fulfill all of a person's aspirations."

"I was married for four years. We got married because we were good friends and she was pregnant. I didn't like it, because she didn't excite me. As a result, I wasn't interested in learning anything about her or solving any of our problems."

"She was certainly not the best fuck I've ever had, but she was a good cook and would be true blue to me."

"I married because there was no alternative; I was in love and wanted to live with a woman, and my life style wouldn't permit any deviation from the norm, which is, I suppose, a way of saying 'peer pressure,' which, under the circumstances, is ridiculous."

"A variety of reasons: (a) it was normal, (b) I was tired of broken relationships, (c) I was very fond of my wife."

"I'm not sure why I originally got married. I remember my wife (then girlfriend) pressuring me for a ring, so I guess one thing led to another."

"I married because I fell in love and stayed in love."

"Marriage seemed like just a formal social step when we already felt emotionally committed to each other for life."

"We were originally married because she was pregnant, she asked me what I wanted to do, I asked her what she wanted to do, and we did what we wanted to do."

"This person was exceptional in my life and I wanted to exalt the situation and celebrate it. It was symbolical rather than practical, comfortable, necessary, or religious."

REASONS MEN DON'T LIKE MARRIAGE: MEN'S ANGER AT WOMEN

Although most men said they liked marriage, or at least wanted to stay married (and, as we shall see, divorced men said they wanted to remarry), still there were deep undercurrents of anger toward their wives—and the institution of marriage, as well as men's own traditional role in it—in many men's answers. In a way, some men's extramarital affairs, kept secret from their wives, can be seen as a form of (perhaps unconsciously) expressing that anger at their wives, "getting even," "showing her"—a private kind of revenge, removing oneself from the relationship and "rising above" it.

But what, underneath it all, are men angry about? Is this anger basically only about sex or lack of sex—or even lack of "sexual freedom"? Or lack of the affection and love that goes with sex? Or are these feelings, valid as they may be, also reflections of other problems in the relationship? And perhaps also, in a larger sense, of cultural problems in the relationship between men and women in our society? It would seem that "sex" easily becomes the focus for repressed or unexpressed tensions in a relationship—whether it is the woman not being interested in sex, or the man finding sex with his wife "boring." To see sex as separate from the larger framework, or to expect sexual relations not to be affected by all the other aspects of a relationship—although men have often been taught that their sex drive is merely a simple biological phenomenon—is unrealistic.* Sex and sexual feelings are affected by the entire spectrum of a relationship, and that relationship is created not only by the two individuals involved, but also by the society and the roles it has tried to assign to both people.

Feelings of anger at women surface again and again in men's replies—in the portraits of marriages, in divorced and separated men's replies (later in this section), in men's attitudes toward women (pages 278–303) and in their opinions of the

---

* Perhaps when some men say they find sex in marriage "boring," they really mean that they do not get an erection. If so, perhaps this is due to the fact that they are responding to a lack of closeness *in the relationship*: male "sex drive" is emotional and not mechanical, after all.

women's movement (pages 303–333).* It seems clear that most men frequently feel ambivalent and sometimes hostile toward women, or perhaps, more correctly, toward their own role as it has come to be defined vis-à-vis women, whether in traditional marriage or not. The basic feeling that comes through is that men feel they are not getting enough love, affection, or appreciation.

But there are other possible explanations as to why men so frequently seek affairs outside of marriage. The reason in many cases may not so much be anger or alienation from the marriage as the fact that after marriage men often begin to see their wives more as mothers, "good women," than "sex objects," who were traditionally "bad women." A woman in a traditional marriage assumes the role that the man's mother once had—that is, caring for his physical needs, taking care of the house, cooking for him, taking care of children. She becomes a "mother." Remembering his childhood, he feels that it is taboo to have sexual feelings for a/his mother, and our culture further reinforces the idea that "good women" (mothers) are not sexual. Sex in marriage may become a duty, or something that is permissible only in the most traditional way, for example, only as standard intercourse. In addition, since as a child he probably was not informed that sex was something that his father and mother enjoyed together, he may have never been able to accept and integrate this fact into his view of the world; many boys and even men find it hard to believe to this day that their mothers ever had sex, or enjoyed it, or that this could be a natural part of the life of a "good woman." "Mothers," for many men, simply are not sexual. In this pattern, the man hides his "escapades" from his wife in much the same way that he did from his disapproving mother—although he feels his true loyalty will always remain first and foremost to her.

But hidden anger, or anger that cannot be expressed, is a cause of many men's secret outside affairs; and there is no question that men do have many angry feelings toward women. After looking at how divorced, separated, and single men feel about marriage and their relationships with women, we will again return to the question of men's anger toward women. (See page 278.)

* See also the opening sections of chapter 5, and many other sections throughout this work. Chapter 5 also shows how men's lack of information about women's orgasms, and our society's definition of sex which did not take into account women's needs, contributed to many women's lack of interest in "sex."

PORTRAITS OF MARRIAGES

How do these contradictions and paradoxes in men's feelings about women and their wives work out in an individual situation—how did men present their feelings about their marriages, overall?

"I am now thirty-seven years old. An area of current turmoil for me is that I am presently involved in two relationships, one with my wife of sixteen years and one with my woman friend of just over three years. There are a whole host of problems connected with this situation. First of all, in the past year and a half I have gradually come to terms with the reality of mutable relationships, marriages included. I used to think that all marriages were 'made in Heaven' (residual Catholicism) and that separation or divorce was a sign of personal failure, and probably a 'sin.' I know that if our current marriage breaks up, many of our relatives on both sides will see it that way.

"Since my entry into graduate school, the pressure on our marriage has grown considerably. It is the old story of a husband who obtains more formal education than his wife, thus producing a situation in which they grow away from each other rather than closer together. Not surprisingly, my wife became aware of this much earlier than I. I guess I was just too wrapped up in what I was doing to sit down and look at the situation. When she would press me to quit my studies and just get a 'normal' job, I would react in a hurt manner, pleading with her to 'understand' that what I was doing was 'for the good of the whole family.' This went on and on, until finally my wife decided she wanted a divorce. She had everyone in agreement with her, both my parents, my sister, a close aunt, etc. I fought it, not with logic but with pleading—'How could she have so little faith in our future?' We left it unresolved and I returned to the university to find a room for myself, since we had decided I would live down there alone over the spring and summer in order to get a good start on my dissertation. This was in January, and I would travel back home on some weekends to spend time with the family.

"In early March, during one of these visits, we had a very heated argument about whether or not to continue the marriage, and in frustration at her lack of 'understanding' I slammed my right fist full-force into a chest of drawers, breaking the hand in three places. This intelligent act resulted in my having to wear a hand-to-elbow cast on my arm for almost two months, thus putting a terrible crimp in my ability to write anything on the dissertation—a sort of poetic justice, one might say. I returned to the university, cast and all, determined that this was not going to stop me, and I managed to make some small progress. The act of breaking my hand served to put discussion of divorce on a back burner, since my wife took that act to mean that I really wanted to remain in the marriage. Is that what it meant? At the time, I thought it was true, but now I think it meant something else, though I'm not sure what. I think it might have been (continues to be?) a distorted sense of male pride that would not (will not?) allow me to admit 'failure' or 'defeat.'

"Soon after this episode and after the cast had been removed I met this very special woman friend, who happened to be a doctoral student in a discipline different from mine. We seemed able to converse on a level that I had never before experienced with anyone, man or woman. Less than one week after we met I found that I opened myself to her completely, holding nothing at all back. We were not physically involved until much later; she also had another relationship, ongoing, with a man who was away from the university. During that summer she went to his home in another state to visit him and his parents a few times. He and I were acquainted, and she told him of our friendship. On a verbal level, at least, he accepted our friendship.

"There was no way I could tell my wife of this new friend, however, since it was clear early on in our marriage (even before) that I was not to have friends who were women. This was one of the inequalities in our marriage, since I never denied her the right to have male friends. Thus, if I felt the marriage to be salvageable, I had two choices. Either give up this new friend, who quickly became very important to me (now, it seems, even more important than the marriage), or keep up with the friendship, though 'underground,' and hope that my new friend would agree. Well, for the past three years we have held on to this relationship, which had become emotional and physical over time. Even though we are now separated by a great geographical distance, I still feel closer to her than to anyone. We continue to write each other a few times a week, at least, and are now planning to be together at a professional conference next year.

"It is very likely that my present marriage will not last another couple of years, and the biggest problem I must deal with is the ultimate reason for its breakup. Basically, I have come to feel that the marriage was a mistake, a feeling my wife had very early (but does not express now). Further, I need to know that the marriage is breaking up because of its own internal dynamic, that it is not because of an outside relationship I might have. In fact, I have made it quite clear to my special friend that she would not be the reason for the breakup, and that I would not expect to jump into another marriage. I have told her that, because I love her so very much, I would hope that we could remain close, but I was not interested in tying her down to any single relationship. In effect, she will be the one to define the parameters of our future relationship. I merely want to be close, within her reach if she should need a very special friend. I know that I need her friendship, but I refuse to attempt to control anyone anymore.

"Though my wife and I continue to tell each other that we do share love, I am just not sure if either of us really means it. I think we care for each other at a fundamental level; we care what happens to each other and to the children. I just think there has been too much pain and bitterness over the years for much in the way of 'love' to remain. This may well be simplistic rationalization, I don't know, but I have no reticence about saying that I *do* love this special friend of mine. Sometimes my ego gets in the way and I wonder if she loves me as much as I love her, or I wonder if she loves me more than she loves the men in her other relationships. I quickly get beyond this, however, and I feel confident that we do actually love each other and that no measurement is necessary in that knowledge. What do we get out of the relationship? We get each other and a greater sense of just who we are, greater self-knowledge through clear awareness of the other. We do not 'play games' with each other; we are always open and even vulnerable. These are things I have never before experienced in any relationship. I refuse to be put into a position of possibly ending what we have found through each other.

"It would be very easy for me to say that I feel (and have long felt) dominated by my wife. Truthfully, I don't feel that to be the case. That would merely be an excuse for not taking responsibility for my own life decisions. I was not forced into marriage, I was not forced to have a family, I was not forced to seek out new relationships, and I am not being forced to maintain any situation I might presently be in. It is possible that both my wife and I feel dominated and that we might blame it on each other, but the decisions we made early on were in many ways expected of us. I think we have grown out of those decisions but don't really know what to do about it at the moment, especially when it concerns two other individuals we brought into the world and to whom we have a deep responsibility."

"When I hit college at eighteen (nine years ago), I believed women were my servants and protectors. Therefore, a high priority for me was to find a woman to take care of me. I was too far from home to send back my laundry, and didn't know how to do it anyway. In keeping with my traditional good luck, I found such a woman the first day.

"My future wife had all the credentials: good breeding, good looks, intelligent, good cook, etc. She was also a virgin, and spunky enough to *not* be looking for a man to tend. Therefore, it was not until six months later, after she was deflowered by some Michigan mystery man, and had heard news of her parents' impending divorce, that I wore her down to marriage. During this period our sex was generally good. It was what I call 'clinging puppy' sex: we were both lost and alone, disillusioned with our parents. The act had an intensity altogether unattainable now in our blasé thirties. She would get soupy looking at me, and vow eternal fealty. For my part, I had the staying power and undirected energy to (almost) fill her needy-ness.

"I achieved some classic low points, too. High on the power of my ability to penetrate (I'd been with only two or three girls before) and ejaculate, once when her period arrived, I announced my sexual appetites were so enormous that I must look elsewhere for a week, or not see her, or both. I am humiliated to think of it and apologize to her, and all women, for such brutal lack of sensitivity. Another low point was the time she got stoned with the girls. I needed to talk to her about something, and looked all over campus. Rapidly, I devised some acute paranoia; so that when I found her (too loaded to care about my trivial problem, and most likely wanting a night out with her friends) I freaked, crying hysterically most of the night, until I achieved the security of being inside her body. Only then did my manipulative despair lift. My fear was that, not being able to communicate with her (i.e., talk), I would lose my power (control) over her and therefore lose her love. This is very important: the reason to control is to make *her* love *me*, not because my love for her depended on it. The natural me couldn't be good enough to make her come back again and again; I had to manipulate, control, delude, in order to be loved. This feeling still lingers a dozen years later, much modified by an increased ability to trust, and seriously increased self-confidence. When it rises in me, I try to understand it and direct it, but usually wind up fighting it and losing.

"I loved being married. We were and are an excellent match. For me it was validation of the security I craved, and a certainty of having a woman to take care of me so I could get on with being a success. I prided myself on having a more enlightened relationship than many of our married friends: doing more around the house, not making unreasonable demands, etc. Bullshit!!! I no more knew how to make a marriage work than she knew how to tell me what was really on her mind. It's a tribute to our persistence and love that we muddled along for several years, when we ended that phase of our relationship. (As an aside here, I just called her after writing the above and told her again how much I appreciate her and enjoyed being married to her. Five years after our divorce we are beginning to reestablish closeness and trust—it feels great to have such an important friend.)

"Our sex during marriage was good, for the most part. Being young and living in a not very adventurous part of the country, we confined ourselves pretty much to missionary sex. I enjoy cunnilingus, so there was that, but she was not into fellatio (at least not with me), so we skipped it. As might be expected, the quality of our sex was a pretty good barometer of our relationship. My sexuality is quite sensitive to stress, and during stressful times our sex was nil. Again, I was pretty self-centered about this, much to the long-term detriment of our 'thing.' I always get sexually supercharged when business is good or I score some kind of coup. And my sexiness fades with my lessened self-image. In my next serious relationship, I want to work on this, since it seems to me a couple could be a sanctuary from daily life, not necessarily victimized by it.

"When things were good (60 percent of the seven years) we'd have sex three to five times per week. When things were great, we'd fuck, screw, and make love ten or more times.

When things got bad in the last year, we copulated thirteen times in twelve months. (This according to her calendar, which I'll believe, since she was curious about who might be the father of the child she was craving. It seems like too many episodes to me, as I was pretty upset and found her repugnant.) I never masturbated in front of or with her, nor she in front of me. Our perpetually infantile midwestern mores and my unwillingness to talk about sex didn't leave much space for things like that. However, I believe she rarely or never faked an orgasm for my benefit and I appreciate that.

"Children may be at the root of my marriage's breakup. I'm afraid of them. I really don't want the responsibility either, at least not until I have so much money I don't have to be a proper father. (I suspect that attitude will change, though, as I become more secure.) I don't like the mess, trouble, inconvenience, and I don't like not being the baby myself. Unlike many men I know, I have no urge to foist a tiny replica of myself on the world. My immortality hangs in the wind, not on the head of an unsuspecting infant.

"Anyhow, she was approaching a late-twenties crisis about it's getting too late to procreate. One day she said she wanted a baby because there was nothing else in the world she was fit to do. My (unproductive) reply was 'What a rotten burden to put on an infant. If you feel that way about yourself, then you're not fit to be a mother either.' What a prick!!! Of course I didn't believe she really felt that way, since I knew how smart and competent she was (is). But one more nail in the connubial coffin.

"I believe monogamy is the preferable circumstance for a marriage, mainly because it's complicated enough to handle things as it is. When I was married, I had no affairs until the last year, when it got apparent that she had been unfaithful for some time. Even then I felt terrible about them, real guilty, y'know? My style was to put my wife on such a pedestal that for most of our years together I felt guilty about looking at another woman. When I started having a couple of affairs, I didn't talk to her about them, presumably because I didn't want her to tell me about hers. But when I fell in love with a devoted twenty-year-old, it scared shit out of me and I told her. One of the saddest times in my life was the moment I did that and she replied, 'How nice for you; do whatever you want, I don't care.' It still hurts to think about it. When we did marriage counseling (at her insistence) she wouldn't speak of her affairs, so I didn't speak much of mine, so it didn't work.

"I didn't lose anything by being married, only gained. My bachelorhood has been made much more enjoyable by starting it at twenty-seven. I don't say 'If I knew then what I know now . . .' because then is now and I know it. I also have a very high understanding of the potential of relationships, so I don't mess with casual sex or women who are not 'uncommon.' I can't and don't imagine my life any other way than it is . . . it's been agonizingly perfect!"

"I am thirty-six. I am an evangelical minister who is conservative in the basic beliefs about Jesus Christ, but liberal in other areas. While my wife and I were engaged, we both attended a fundamentalist Bible school (Pennsylvania Dutch). Even though we were engaged to be married, we were not allowed to hold hands.

"We have been married for sixteen years. We have five children. Generally, I enjoy being married. There are certain minor aggravations in any relationship, but I have come to accept these. I wish there was more love and affection that flowed between my wife and me. I often fantasize about being married to a particular woman friend of mine with whom I have a close relationship (but nonsexual). I haven't the faintest idea why I got married in the first place. Then, I would have said love, but I am just learning what real love is.

"When I first got married, I was the king of the castle. My wife was the slave. My fundamentalist upbringing made me the head of the home. This created an affection division between my wife and me that has not been totally resolved to this day. I cannot say that this is totally my fault. My wife felt the same way when we were first married. I treated her well, but as a lesser person. We have tried to get this straightened out, and have made quite a bit of progress.

"Although there is one person in my life that I love more than my wife, I could never leave my wife for her, since I love my wife too much to hurt her. I think the basic difference between my love for this other woman and my wife is that I have a much deeper romantic and emotional love for the 'other woman.' I am very deeply in love. But we have both consciously chosen to not express our love to each other in a romantic or a sexual way because of the harm it might do to our families. We are at the status of 'best friends' and I don't know where all this will end up—it may pass, and it may develop into something more serious.

"I believe that God designed monogamy as the best way for man to achieve the highest happiness. If things go wrong with your partner, work them out rather than run off to have a surface experience with someone else. You never can get deep enough if you don't stay in some place long enough.

"I have never had an 'extramarital' experience (but I am not totally averse to such an experience). Sometimes I feel I want to make love to my closest woman friend. It's not that I want to get it off with her (masturbate inside her vagina), but I want to be as close to her as I possibly can and express love and tenderness to its fullest extent. Right now, I wouldn't even care if I ejaculated or not—just as long as I could show love to her in the most intimate ways possible.

" 'What are the reasons why many women traditionally have not wanted sex as much as men. What kind of sex do women want most?' is one of the most severe problems I encounter in counseling (I am a minister/counselor). For example, right now I am counseling a couple (members of the church and my closest friends) who are probably going to split up because she feels 'screwed.' She feels that sex to him is just a means of getting it off for himself. The only important thing to him seems to be for him to be able to ejaculate through intercourse with her. She feels used. On more than one occasion, she told him to go over to the door and use the keyhole.

"I don't think that men necessarily want sex more than women. It's just that women don't want the same kind of sex that men do. Too many men just want to ejaculate inside a vagina (or, more realistically, masturbate inside a vagina). I fully believe that this problem is psychological, because I have been able to easily adjust my mentality to enjoy sex the same way my wife likes it.

"With most women, sex is a much deeper experience. It's not so much climax-oriented, but intimate-sharing-oriented. I believe that women are right. Part of being a real Christian is expressing love to others—getting all I can get for myself is contrary to true Christianity.

"To summarize, I am basically happy with my life as it is. The only thing I wish for is to be married to someone with whom I can have a much deeper love relationship than I am having now."

"I will be married twenty-four years next month. Overall I like it. I still love my wife in many ways. She does not like sex—she probably never really did—We still sleep together in a double bed. In all these years I don't think she ever has asked for sex, in any form, and invariably has seemed relieved when I didn't want to. There is still a feeling of warmth and partnership, and we love our kids, but the spark, the magic, has long departed. She has her hobbies, I mine, and we don't communicate much except about routine matters. Yet I do not ever intend to leave her. I have many failings but I am loyal.

"I was happily monogamous for the first sixteen years of marriage. Then I fell in love and have experienced the heights, and the dregs, through two long extramarital affairs. (Is this very typescript proof that I am, in cold fact, *disloyal* for putting all this into words?)

"My affairs are unknown (insofar as I know) to my wife. The effect on me has been internally shattering; psychologically it has changed me in many ways, both for the better and worse. Perhaps it has saved the marriage. What happened was that it was a reprieve from death and slow descent into a loveless aging. It was fully living again. I knew it could be a disaster in the end, but I thought, what the hell, everything ends badly, if you wait long enough. Falling in love you notice the sky, how beautiful it is, the clouds. All your senses seem superartistically alert. Food tastes good and the small details of life which you never notice when not high on love, seem poignantly significant. Being in love is operating at 100 percent capacity on all cylinders. It cannot last, of course. You subside into a more normal glow . . . or you plunge into the depths of feelings, the pits. Having been that high, you have farther to fall. I know the feeling, the long free fall, no parachute, waiting to hit bottom. You survive, but sometimes you are broken inside and never quite the same.

"I fell in love twice with the woman I have loved the most. The second time was twenty years later and we were both married. The first time I loved her, but being young, I didn't realize how much I would miss her in particular. I thought somebody else would come along shortly and it would be the same. It wasn't. Breaking up was the feeling of utter loss, irreplaceability, and the damn memories.

"The best thing with my wife now is that we are comfortable as old shoes together, and we have learned to survive economically. But we no longer generate any passion for life together. But I feel fit to survive with what I've got, whatever that is."

"I am thirty-three years old, white, college graduate, the product of sixteen years of Catholic education, from a blue-collar family. My biggest problem is having two relationships in my life—one based on habit and children, the other founded on enjoying each other, emotionally and physically—having two relationships and not being sure I can handle even one. What I'm afraid of is this: have I confused loving my lover with loving the independence and freedom she represents? I don't know.

"I'm a mess—not sure that I can or want to be an integral part of anyone's life. Sounds trite and 'mid-life' as hell but I need a rest, half time, whatever.

"My wife dominated me for years, used sex in the process of domination. I don't think she did it on purpose, but she realized it worked. Love and dependence are easily confused by me. I *needed* her—whatever that means—and she knew it. Her affection toward me (both sexual and nonsexual) was a function of keeping me in line. We never fought. We simply decided what *we* wanted by doing what *she* wanted.

"Now I think *the most important thing in my life is the minutes that are mine—the ones I do not have to account for*. People around me think I'm a work freak. If you get to know me you realize that working is for ego and diversion. But the *most* important thing is time—not having to be somewhere soon. *Then* I can think about sharing the time or devoting the time to work or play . . . but I've got to have the time first. What I'm going through now—which can affect a dozen other lives—is a tug-of-war that I don't know if I can handle."

"I'm thirty-nine, Jewish, middle-class. I went to a fine college, have a Ph.D. in English, and I am a full professor at a small college. Although only nominally Jewish when I was growing up, lately I have become more interested in my Jewishness. I have learned Hebrew, and become a regular participant in services at a Conservative congregation. My wife, less observant, respects my religious feelings, though we don't obey kosher laws, nor do we observe any purification (menstrual) customs. Our daughters do attend Hebrew school in addition to their secular school.

"We've been married for fifteen years. My wife is the best friend I have ever had and the best lover. We have two beautiful girls, nine and twelve, and, all in all, a damn good marriage. We both have professional lives. My wife also happens to be the best sexual partner I've ever had. I think we've improved in our sexual life in the last three or four years—as we've gotten older and have fewer hang-ups about things. We've talked more.

"We married when my wife was twenty-one, I twenty

four. Although we were very turned on, I had impotency problems. She was extremely patient, and though I knew she was worried, wasn't overworried. At the end of a year of marriage, habit, if nothing else, began to harden my cock for us. My guilt decreased. Oral sex became more of a joy in itself and less of a curtain raiser for the main, and rather short, act. And, if with some setbacks, things have improved, I've gotten older, I've had a few rather casual affairs. These have given me perspective on my chief sexual delight—my wife and me. I've stopped feeling guilty about masturbating, and the pleasures of mutual masturbation have opened up for us new possibilities.

"All in all, everything is good. There are little frustrations. I wish sometimes I had a more "open" marriage—about the masturbation and the affairs. But other times—currently—I think it's best that we do *not* know certain things that might hurt. My wife has become fairly feminist in recent years—though not militant and she hasn't joined any organizations. And this attitude reflected itself for a while in her growing consciousness of her body and her ambitions in her professional life. All for the good and almost no conflict. I say almost. We've had theoretical discussions of the direction of the women's movement—some of them heated. I am against some aspects of militancy, for instance. She's theoretically for them even if not involved directly in them. But the sex life is good.

"I try not to withhold the idea of sexuality from my daughters. When we are nude in the house, we make no attempt to disguise it. (In fact, we all go nude bathing every summer on a public nude beach.) My children are, as far as I can tell, both uninhibited about their sexual feelings, however incipiently developed. I would never have thought of discussing anything with my father after several rejections of the subject. My parents had never heard of sex, no doubt I was conceived by the rays of the sun. When I asked my father about sex once, he turned bright red, looked angry, and said we'd discuss it someday. We never did. Poor man. My mother was a little more adventurous; she smiled and said my sister would discuss things with me. Most of the information, though, came from my earliest friend, and mutual masturbator—some of it accurate, some of it monstrously mythical. ('Like—did you know that on the wedding night the rabbi had to watch your parents fuck?)

"I haven't had an extramarital affair for two years. It

happened by buildup at a few parties with one woman, who was about ten years older. She made the advances. We met for lunch to discuss an academic matter, then at her place, then sex. But adultery is very scary to me. It is a sin; there is a commandment against it in Judaism. And for reasons that aren't to be dismissed by any sexual revolution. Disturbing family peace can be disastrous. I love my wife very much and don't want her hurt. So nothing has happened since. But I enjoy being attractive and attracting. I do enjoy being made love to—in the old sense—being made a pass at.

"Although I've had those few affairs, they haven't been threatening—emotionally—to our relationship. Frankly, one reason that I'm fearful of any more liaisons is that if I should fall in love that would wreak havoc on my wife's life and mine. I and she don't need that. If she should fall in love and leave me, I think I would be devastated. I don't want to think about the effect on our children, especially since we're so close to them. I don't think separation is likely. I think if I discovered she had a lover—or she discovered I had a lover—that was casual and "purely sexual"—then I could recover and so could she, though we might feel hurt. But no affair is very satisfying to me over a long run—all my encounters have been very short-run, for thrills. And really unsatisfying emotionally. Impotency problems emerge. I also feel as if I'm doing something secretive, forbidden, and I admit that this is probably one of the chief thrills. The sex part of the affairs is indeed exciting. There is nothing quite like seeing a woman go naked for the first time. But I am not a man who relishes diving into a motel room with a rigid cock and sticking it in somebody.

"I can honestly say that my wife and I are deeply, have been deeply, and I pray will continue to be deeply in love. It grows, it recedes, it has pettinesses, but it seems to be not only flourishing but making us better. I've been on a high with my wife for two years. I'm married because it's—for me and I think for my wife—the best way to ensure security, long-lasting friendship, raising of children, good developing sexuality, security in old age, comforting of each other during crisis and sickness."

SEPARATED AND DIVORCED MEN

Men's reasons for getting divorced

Men who were now divorced (or separated) gave the following reasons, when asked, "If you are divorced, what are your reasons? How do you feel about it? How did you like being married?":

"My wife was a vegetable. It was a disaster."

"Incompatibility. I accept it."

"The problem was our mothers. The only way to a successful marriage: be an orphan and marry one. I used to say, 'I'm married, she's not.' Now I no longer care."

"I felt like my wife was another one of the kids."

"Infidelity. I felt rotten. I did not feel wanted or needed by her."

"Personality differences. I feel fine now."

"My wife's infidelity. I fell out of love."

"I see no reason to give some female a free ride through life in exchange for sex and maid service, both of which are available on a pro rata basis. I spent two years being used and don't intend to do so again."

"I've been separated two and a half years and married for ten years before that. It's real good to be out of that relationship. We got married to her self-concept, i.e. *wife*."

"Married thirty-five years, recently separated. It became a tremendous and continuous responsibility to others rather than happiness for myself."

"I am divorced because she walked out. I would not marry again; three tries is enough. Now a woman cooks for me five days a week, and I take her to dinner the other two days. This has been for nearly six years. She is a widow—loving, friendly, a great companion, loves theater and dancing, and we get along well. She is rather close-mouthed while I tell all I know and then some. This is the closest I have been with a woman, although I was happiest with my first wife before I married her. All in all, what I have now is the best."

"I was married for ten years. I loved being married. I married because I loved the woman. She married for security. Even though we were good in bed, she'd stymie sex about 90 percent of the time because, as she said, I was a pervert, wanting to perform cunnilingus on her. I've gone through the majority of a divorce now. When married I didn't stray, even when she ceased being a sex partner. Towards the end I strayed, but by then I'd been celibate for two years. The sex was a physical need. She never knew."

"I was married for five years. Sex with my wife was fantastic for the first two years, but after we had our daughter I guess my wife decided that now that she had the child she wanted I was no longer important enough for her to worry about pleasing me. From then on it went downhill till she finally just went."

"At age eighteen, I married my high school girlfriend, who was four months pregnant. I thought I was doing the right thing, but the financial struggle, the children's diapers, and the realization that I had to accept being tied to her for the rest of my life were all too much. I began looking for some new and exciting fun, and I found it. The result, when she found out, was not a solution, but the beginning of some hard learning experiences. After four years together, I have become totally separated from my wife and children."

"I just ended a twenty-year marriage. I loved her for nineteen years but didn't feel she cared that much about me. I did not feel wanted or needed by her. I was never unfaithful. When we had kids, I just took it as a responsibility and did my best to make them good citizens. As my kids got to be sixteen or seventeen, I wondered whether it was worth it since they did not show any affection or love for me."

"I got divorced because of sexual incompatibility. I know I should be talking about compatibility, both intellectually and personality-wise. But I cannot be happy and content without a, to me, satisfactory sex relationship, and I don't want to go outside the marriage to get it. I am ashamed to say that I put sexual compatibility first, before other things, but this is how I feel. After marriages to two bright girls, intellectual compatibility alone is just not enough. In the long haul, I'm a goddamn caveman."

"Married ten years. Sexual involvement outside of marriage virtually blew our marriage apart. I have always loved her and always will, and if she will take me back, my pants will only come off at her bed. Meanwhile, there are many personal things I am catching up on while I am alone—like a summer of sunshine and good times. Because my children are financially secure I do not have that area to contend with. I would remarry the same woman *only*. She has my money, my children, my dreams—I could not invent another life style—my children are mine alone, I don't want to start another family. If we do not get together, I am quite content to remain alone and a father (not necessarily without sex) until such time as my children are able to make their own decision, and I will continue my relationship as a family then."

"One of my most deeply held hostilities towards my ex-wife (married six years) is rooted in the awareness that she mostly had sex with me because it was the 'expected' thing for a beautiful, successful functional lady to do. I took a few years to get smart, but a sexually functional woman does not regularly need to use Vaseline in order to avoid pain in sex. Nor is she so structured that it is difficult or impossible for her to bear the full weight of a man between her legs. I suspect she married me because I looked like a 'likely prospect'; a young man on the way up, who would one day 'amount to something.' But when I chose a full-time Air Force career, and then chose to extend that career in order to extend my schooling, she was bitterly disappointed. I did not live up to her idea of what I was supposed to amount to."

"I was married seven and a half years and absolutely loved it, but my wife thought someone else less stable, terribly romantic, and erratic was more fun, so she left with him. I got married in the first place because of family pressures from both sides. About sex, we had a whole lot of it, and it was great for me (same for her, so she said many times). I prefer monogamy. I just haven't found anyone who wanted to keep it up that way."

How do men who had been married like being single again?

Most men liked it only as a temporary condition; when asked, "Do you plan to marry again?" most said they wanted to remarry, or live with a woman, in the future:

"It's about six weeks since my divorce. I was married twenty-one years. Now I am getting an opportunity to find myself as an individual for the first time in my life. But eventually I'll remarry, I think."

"So far I like being on my own—and the independence. But deep down I feel that one plus one equals more than two. A bond of commitment really gives one more freedom because it opens more possibilities for self-knowledge than when you are not attached. So, most likely, I'll remarry."

"I have been divorced for six months. I miss my son a lot but to be away from all the hassle my wife gave me is sure worth it. I will remarry eventually."

"I have been single for nearly six years. I like it and at other times I don't. I oscillate between wanting to be married and staying single. I feel a pressure from somewhere to get married. All men do it, so I should, etc., etc. But I find it fun to live alone, although I have a girlfriend most times, even living with me sometimes. Perhaps I should face the fact that maybe I won't marry again. But so what, as long as I am happy? I suppose I am still hoping that the perfect woman will come along, but I seem to pick the wrong ones."

"I have been single for eight years. Yes, I like it, because right now, at least, I can handle loneliness better than the kind of sexual deprivation I felt during my marriage. My priorities may change in the next few years. I will probably either marry or live with someone—in, say, five years or less. I already feel the stirrings of desire for the kind of intimacy that living with somebody brings."

"I have been 'single' for the past two years. I've really enjoyed this time, they've been my very best years. I filed for and obtained an uncontested divorce and also received custody of my three children. So my 'single' state is somewhat unique: single parent (and male!) with three kids, ages twelve, eight, and seven. I have really liked this time because I'm out of a ruinous and oppressive marriage relationship and I'm free to be my own person. I've experienced and learned a lot. I would rather now be married, but only to someone I really loved and liked, my current partner. I hope we can be married within a year or so."

"There is a great, warm feeling in marriage in knowing there is someone who cares about you and who accepts your caring in a loving manner. I'm single now and content, but I won't be truly happy until I'm either married again or at least in a very strong, long-term relationship with a woman."

"I am forty-seven—divorced twice; I don't want it to happen again. My personal goal is to be self-sufficient . . . to be able to have a happy life with friends and doing a decent job in my career, and as lovers come into that life, to make room for them. Maybe when I am sure I am self-sufficient, a self-sufficient woman will come into my life and I into hers, and we will decide that it is to our mutual benefit to live together and be sexually exclusive. That's what I would like to have happen. But I am prepared to be satisfied with life even if it doesn't."

"I've been single for almost eight years. I like the independence it offers me but hate the loneliness and boredom. I would like to get married again if the right lady crossed my path and it all clicked together. I'm certainly not actively looking for her, because I really don't know what to look for. I know there must be a lot of beautifully compatible ladies out there somewhere, but it beats hell out of me how to find one."

"Divorced eight years. I like it most when I get to screw around a little, but I'd like to get married if I could find a woman who dug me. But I think I'll die alone."

"I have been single since the break up of my marriage in 1975. I like being single in some ways—I have freedom to be as cultured/barbaric, lazy/hard-working, rich/poor, as I choose to be. But I want to be married again, to my regular partner now, who is very special. I want to help her raise her two kids. We can both have one weekend a month of total freedom."

"I've been divorced for four years. Marriage was that time of life when we fucked less and argued more. But I liked being married. I don't like being single about 60 percent of the time, because of the loneliness. I'd like to get married, but with someone with whom I could have a spiritual relationship."

"Divorced two and a half years ago. It's O.K., and I'm learning a lot about taking care of myself without depending on a woman for household cleaning, cooking, marketing, etc. I like feeling more capable of taking care of myself. Maybe I'd remarry or live with a woman in the future. I don't know."

"Been single for almost three years. Love it. The independence is great. I have a feeling of individuality I never had while married. I like the lack of responsibility for anyone's ass but my own. None of the games that got so heavy in my marriage. Space! Eventually I probably will remarry."

"I've been single for fifteen years. At first I hated it. No one to talk to, meals by myself, the wee-hours-of-the-morning blues and no one to turn to (sob). But I was also very young. Now I like the freedom, the tranquillity, the ability to pursue my own interests without conflicting with the needs of another person. As I write this, I've almost finished a fascinating book, so tonight I'll probably stay up late reading . . . etc. etc. *However*. Last year, through a combination of circumstances too involved to go into here, my lover was able to move in and stay, with interruptions, for several months. I looked forward to her arrival with some trepidation. It turned out to be the best time of my life. We got along beautifully and I rediscovered all I had lost despite my *freedom*. I felt infinitely freer than when I was alone. We didn't have to function as a couple. Yet I found her presence put more excitement and fun in my life, and she began to share some of my love for music and poetry. Now I think I would like to be married to *her*. I could not have said that sincerely before we had the experience of living together."

A few said they would not remarry:

"I've been single for one week. I don't like it. It's too lonely. But I'll probably remain single. I couldn't go through the pain of another marriage."

"I have been 'single' for four years. At this moment I should rather be single. Maybe it is because I am incapable of fully loving again. Maybe it is because I cannot bring myself to commit fully to another woman after the trying, horrible, destructive experience I went through with my wife."

"Married at age twenty-two, divorced at twenty-five, single for five years. I enjoy the independence, living for myself, being responsible only to and for myself. And frankly, I do not know anyone who could stand living with me."

"I intend to stay single for a while for a chance to breathe. If marriage is in store again for me it's going to take a special person."

"I've been married twice, eighteen years and four years. I'm now divorced. It's better than being married. Single and married people move in entirely separate social circles. One has to give up most of one's friends and social life to make the change. I have a strong need for privacy—I want to lead my life without having to coordinate with anyone. I want to mess up my life my own way."

"Two years. I would never marry again, I am a fast-moving loner, business and sex do not mix. I often don't have time to explain every item."

Longer replies from divorced or separated men

"I am thirty-nine, quite in love (perhaps for the first time), and have very recently separated from my wife and child. The reasons for having left the family are manifold and of long standing; my feelings for the other woman are very new and very strong (five weeks). I've learned much from her and my feelings for her, much that was never experienced in thirteen years of marriage.

"The last three years of my marriage were difficult and unhappy. We married because we had known each other for two years and because of a pregnancy and miscarriage—it seemed the thing to do. Marriage soured me on sex. It became terribly repetitious, uninspiring and uninspired. It was a task that I increasingly wanted to avoid, while my wife's appetite continued undiminished. I had had sex experiences outside the marriage all along, but they were, for the most part, unknown to my wife. I was exhilarated by one more lengthy liaison; the 'quickies' left little or no impression. The marriage was questioned during the one longer affair.

"I left my wife for reasons other than the new woman— she was a wonderful coincidence. I had known and respected her as a fellow worker. I wanted her and found my feelings were responded to positively. My feelings are still too much in a state of development to describe them accurately. I do feel extremely liberated of many restrictive attitudes with her. I enjoy talking, holding hands, kissing—showing affection in ways that were impossible for me in marriage. I also find myself able to tell her—and mean it for the first time—that I am in love. She has given meaning to that word. Being with her has such a liberating effect on me and an educational aspect—what she is teaching me about myself and my feelings. I'm sorry that it had to coincide with the end of my marriage. There is no direct relationship but my wife thinks there is, and perhaps my lover does as well. We should have met under less trying circumstances."

"I am married but have been separated from my wife for the last year. I was married twenty-two years. I liked being married (even though I think we maybe embarked on it too soon). I like the sense of commitment and continuity, the feelings of a lifetime laid out, stretching from dimly remembered early adventures on into a still remote future and old age.

"I fell much in love with two other women, but I've often found this difficult, since I've been married for a long time to a woman who feels deeply (in some internal, unarguable way) that for me to love more than one person (that is, anyone but her) demeans and hurts her. But over the last few years I have seen more and more people 'come out' and try to deal openly with their sexuality in one way or another, and so, at least partly, I too have come out and recognized my own clear ability to be deeply involved in concurrent, non-competing love relationships.

"So the consequence of 'coming out' is that my wife has asked me to leave; she finds my divided affection too humiliating, too much of a strain to bear. Now I live alone, seeing one or another of these people singly, fleetingly. It is not what I would wish; I think people need stability, permanence, commitment.

"At first I found living alone hard to get used to. Then I began to enjoy the autonomy. I get up when I like, sleep when I like, eat what and when I like, etc. (I also work alone, largely at home, and can keep my own hours.) Gradually, I've found myself taking more pride and interest in keeping the place nice, and especially in cooking. But I don't really like it. I have the constant feeling of wanting to share my thoughts and feelings. In the long run, I'll probably live with someone on a long-run basis, and quite possibly marry again."

"I am divorced. I married the 'Miss One and Only.' We dated for six years, then she said either I marry her or she would find someone else. Next she got pregnant and I decided to do right by her. The society's demands on the male (two kids, the right church, home in the country, good job, build a name in the community) made it difficult to slow down and deal with a relationship. I succeeded in all but the relationship. Then comes the mistress and the 'My wife doesn't understand me.' Looking back, it all seems like a soap opera.

"I now have joined the men that want to get back to feelings. I am dating now and putting myself together one day at a time. Besides my job, currently I am rebuilding a house and enjoying the accomplishments with that. I am good-looking, in good physical condition. I enjoy being single except when it is lonely. It is exciting to be alone and read, bake, or whatever, but to be lonely is shattering. Generally when it happens I start with depression and go downhill from there. But I like the freedom to do exactly as I want to.

"I do plan to marry again. However, there will have to be a very solid relationship and I would like a woman that is independent, caring, loving, and free. I was hurt so bad by rejection that I cried for long periods of time. Lately I have found people I can talk to that will help relieve the pressure from these situations and provide an atmosphere that allows me to put myself together again."

"I have been married twice, the first time for nearly twenty years. I seem to have personality traits that do not wear well in a marital situation. At some point or other the women always say: 'You don't really *need* me.' That's true, except that I like them and need (even now) their affection. Curiously, they say things—ultimately—like 'I'm nothing but a maid and occasional bed partner for you.'

"I think about my marriages, that I surely could have done better in some way. And, yet, I cannot divine precisely *how*. For instance, I have done housework and laundry (all of the cleaning) through graduate school and two marriages. I fed the babies at night. Both wives started out enthralled by this behavior. But by the end of the marriage each was behaving as if the sharing of labor was really some sort of a 'cop-out.' I am too self-sufficient (they'd probably say too complacent) perhaps. And my tendency to control the appearance of the environment I live in is probably overwhelmingly inconsiderate. I might have done better by the ex in terms of letting her have more of the house than a study and bedroom. But she hated the modern design and perhaps that wouldn't have worked out, either. (Actually, I am always feeling responsible for others' sorrows; both wives thought that was another evidence of my desire to dominate and control them by means that appeared non-directive and open.)

"I dearly wish that my ex-wives still were as fond of me as I am of them. I want very much to be a helpful friend to my last wife now, but she seems curiously suspicious of my solitude and forced cheerfulness.

"I am single now, but my lover spends at least a couple of nights a week over here at my house. (I prefer my relationships to occur here because I like my house. I designed it and it is truly 'mine.' Drives wives up the wall after their initial fascination with a male who understands form and color.) I really am a 'loner.' But I don't appear to be that way to other people."

"My age is forty-eight. I am a blue-collar worker from a family of six children. I was adopted, child of an unwed girl in the Kansas state orphanage. I dropped out of school at ninth grade, went in the military at sixteen, then working—

janitor, police officer, carpenter, plumber, electrician, truck driver, butcher, aircraft assembler, factory worker, lumberjack, etc., etc. Methodist.

"My marriage was a constant battlefield—you pinch me, I get even, I pinch you. We couldn't get along or agree about nothing. One would take a stand, the other wouldn't budge an inch. I was bad as her. We was married fourteen years. I did love. I did have outside sex—only during the first two years while separated so as not to violate the contractual law of marriage. My desire to have children, to have my own children to love, was big. She didn't want any or so she told me. When she said she was pregnant I was overjoyed that from the love a life was created that was part of us. My career in the military was foreshortened for the sake of being home so the child would know its father. After the one she refused to have any more, I broached the subject of adopting one, she said no way. All with other problems too, we got divorced 1968. I have two grandchildren.

"I have a greater understanding of nature, my pets and music and religion since I've lived alone for ten years. But with the right gal I'd chuck it in a moment's notice. I have ten dogs, one cat, one rat, twelve goldfish, one hamster, one gerbil. I have never been lonely, for I have always got God and Jesus. I had no one after the divorce, I turned to God and Jesus Christ and have never felt lonely, only the loneliness of others.

"I paid my child support and debts from the divorce by working sixteen hours a day seven days a week for nine years, and now I'm working twelve hours a day seven days a week to pay my bills which will be paid in December 1981, then I'll get me a whole lot of loving from a young thing (looks like I'll have to settle for over thirty-five though)."

"I cried often when I went through my affair and divorce. The conflict was overwhelming . . . married to one woman, loving my four children deeply, and being so much in love with another woman. It was a gut-wrenching experience. I cried a lot. The thought of leaving my children left me sick and empty inside, but the thought of losing my lady was unbearable and brought me to tears. The day that I left my first wife and told my children I was leaving was the worst day of my life. This was also the time I was closest, actually I am closer now but it is a closeness that comes with the growth of a relationship. For pure concentrated closeness and happiness my trip to New England with my lover (now my second wife) was without parallel. We spent one week in October when the leaves were in full color, we were together day and night and could go out in public without fear of discovery as we were 1,500 miles from home. We made love, discovered the joy of sleeping together all night, and all in an extremely beautiful almost fantasy-like surrounding. It was just the ultimate.

"When I was very involved in my affair and very much in love, I was often impotent with my wife and could not become erect . . . and sometimes even when I became erect and had an orgasm it was almost unpleasant, somewhat painful. These episodes embarrassed me because it was so patently obvious that I did not love her, did not want to be with her and did not want to have sex with her yet I was not honest or straight enough to tell her. It was a *very* difficult time with all the social and religious pressures and the sick feelings the thought of separation from my children gave me, contrasted to the feelings in my body which told me the marriage relationship was dead.

"I miss my children. Divorce is hard on everyone, and they are still working through their anger. I miss seeing them daily, watching them grow, sharing their joys and problems, touching them. I enjoyed rocking and feeding them as infants and now I enjoy hugging and kissing them even though they are teenagers. I am more vocal toward them, and let them know how I love and miss them. My time with them now is usually more meaningful.

"One thing I learned from the whole experience: it is important not to bury my feelings. I did in my first marriage and I felt smothered, stagnant, and 'like a robot.' I conformed to a certain mode of behavior and life style because it was expected of me. Now when I am hurt, angry, or sad I express it one way or another. My partner is very aware of my feelings and intuitively able to bring them out. That helps."

"A virgin at twenty-one, I was married to someone whose upbringing had been even more repressed than mine. I, her folks, and friends *talked her* into marrying me—rather than someone of her choice who turned her on more. We were married for twenty-five years and did a good job of raising a family. We worked at it but never achieved a full-blown, adequately satisfying sex life together. It was almost satisfactory, but never great or even good. I longed for it, wearied of frustration, torment, temptation. Finally had my first affair at forty-two, and it was great. Another and another. Great. No guilt! Then a divorce (her choice). Born in Arkansas, of the fundamentalist religion, I'm still religious (spiritual) but don't have any truck with pews, pulpits, or church houses.

"The reason why I got married: I didn't want to be alone, or a little person like many bachelors, historically. I wanted the warmth of wife, children, and home around me.

"I'm giving some quotations from letters my wife wrote a month before she filed, and because of which I agreed to respond cooperatively. I think they are a beautiful, succinct, honest core statement of the real reasons for the divorce:

" 'I cannot love you and want you the way a wife should love a husband and I feel very strongly that I never can and I don't want to live the rest of my life that way and I'm sure you don't either. It isn't something someone has done or caused nor is it something that can be fixed up or redone. It was just a mistake that was made many years ago and I want to correct it in my life and try to make my remaining years as happy as possible. I finally want to think only of myself and find out what makes me happy and go for it. I just can't do that with you. I feel that I would go to great lengths to keep from hurting you. I can only do that up to a certain point and that is the point that I would hurt myself. I have thought and thought and thought about all this but always come back to the same answer, that we would not be happy together. At times this makes me unbearably sad but I must be honest with you and myself. You see, I remember very well how miserable and unhappy you were for many years, and how in our talks you would beg me for the love and affection you were entitled to. I would give anything if those true feelings could have been there—I tried with all my being to make them be there but I could not create them—if I could I would gladly do so now. Thus, I lived for years feeling incomplete myself and guilty for not letting you be complete either.

" 'I want you to know that I do love you and care very much for your happiness. What we have missing in our relationship is just too important for either of us to go on without. I remember how I never wanted to do things that you enjoyed and you went on alone. That's not right—you need and deserve someone to be a willing companion who enjoys you and things you love. I cannot be that person and I'm sure we would just be unhappy trying any longer. Believe me, and I say this with all my heart, I don't think there is a relationship on this earth that I wouldn't give up for you if I could have the feelings I need to go on with you. There's just a cold spot where there should be physical desire and oh, how sorry I am.'

"How do I feel about the divorce? A lot of pain, grief, working-through for two years. But now I feel good about it. We're both good people, did a good job raising a family. But it shows a lot of masochism in each of us that we stayed in that relationship for twenty-five years!

"I am living with someone else for three and a half months now. I didn't realize it till I just thought about it, but I would rather be married. We both feel it's not the time for either of us to do that right now. Yet we each have made a strong commitment and feel we want to have a long-term monogamous relationship."

How do widowed men feel about being "single"?*

"We were married forty-three years. We liked it. Monogamy was the best for us. I don't believe that in any other situation there could have been the wholehearted and enduring love we have known. It has been about three years since my wife left this life. I still love her. I don't like being alone now. I am living alone and do not find it generally pleasant, but the matter of remarriage would depend on finding a compatible and acceptable mate."

"I was married twenty-one years. My wife died in 1970. I did not like it. I do not miss 'Where were you?' or 'What took you so long?' I don't miss being married. I do miss the cooking. Now I have more freedom of partners for sex and socializing. I also like the quiet. I like to be free—if I come home late my dog does not say, 'Where have you been?' "

"Married forty-seven years. The good years made up for the bad. I was deeply in love with my wife. She told our daughter that our sex life together was perfect. I am single (widowed) six years now. Don't like it. I would prefer to marry but I am too old, seventy-eight, and certainly a candidate for death or a disabling illness. I wouldn't want to inflict any of these on a woman I'd want to marry."

"I am a widower, thirty-five years. I liked being married, and had a rather open relationship with my wife, which was unusual at the time. I do not think that monogamy is necessarily the answer to the problem of relationships. It is better to have open relationships with or without marriage. Too many

* See also chapter 8.

people claim to be monogamous and then cheat behind each other's back. It is preferable to be honest about it and face up to the facts of life. I have had extra relationships, but never without my partner's knowledge. I have lived with women on two occasions for five-year periods while my wife was institutionalized for severe physical illness, and after she died. It worked out well, but I did not desire to get married. Still am very good friends with the person I last lived with. I rather enjoy living alone now."

"I was married for twenty years until my wife died. She was a very pleasant but not very sex-oriented woman, and sex with her was run-of-the-mill. I married her because she was charming, well balanced, and nice to live with. I have had extra affairs, especially after her long illness began. She didn't know or at least never complained, as I was discreet. They were great for my sexual life. I've been on my own for nearly twenty years. I never plan to remarry. I like being single, as I have more freedom."

"I was married for sixty-five years, until she died last month. I liked being married, I was in love with her when we married. Marriage transforms sex into a joyful part of God's plan for Creation. Marriage isn't an easy life. You have to work hard at it, and subordinate your ego. I was not monogamous, but each of my 'affairs' has been convertible into a triumphant spiritual growth because I *willed* it so. Now, since my wife died, I don't like my loneliness. I do miss the love she gave. Why? God made human beings that way. He said, 'It is not good for man to live alone.' "

"I am a widower. I was married three years and before that to another wife, thirty-one years. I liked being married. I miss my wife greatly. Why? Because we had a good marriage, a rarely beautiful one, especially toward the end of her life. I'm not sure whether I'll marry again; it's too soon to think clearly about it."

"As a widower I suppose I'm single. I like the freedom in my daily routine—no regular mealtime or household-chores schedule; I can be a slob about the house, as in 'The Odd Couple.' I hate the loneliness (I don't often play poker), and would rather live with someone, preferably someone I love. Yes, I'd rather be married and I plan to be. I think it makes the woman feel more wanted and secure. It also simplifies settlement of my estate. I think, though I'm not sure, that marriage makes *me* feel more secure too. It's a nice compliment, and a major gesture of affection, at the very least, and I appreciate these."

SINGLE MEN (NEVER-MARRIED)

"If you are single, how long have you been single? Do you like it? Why? What are the advantages and disadvantages? Do you plan to get married eventually, or will you remain single?"

Most never-married (single) men were in their teens and twenties; most liked being single, but—perhaps surprisingly, given the cultural mores of the last twenty years—almost all considered it temporary and eventually planned to marry:

"I've always been proud of the fact that I have friends who I feel very open and close to. But even though I have excellent relationships with my friends and I can talk openly with them about almost anything, I still have this gap in me that needs to be filled. Actually, I want to fall in love, get married, adopt children, and be able to put food on the table, a roof over our heads, and live peacefully ever after. Sounds corny maybe but I do."

"Single is where it's at—at least that's what they say—but I'd like to marry someday."

"I've been single for twenty-two years. I like it for the freedom to come and go. But I intend to get married as soon as I'm discharged from the service."

"I have been single all of my life and like it, but I think I would like the security of marriage."

"If the chance comes and I can economically afford it I will marry."

"There are times when I'm bored and lonely, but generally I'm very happy with my life. I enjoy the variety that the single life allows, and I find that the freedom and independence that comes with it are still important to me. But I hope to someday get married and have children."

Many younger men (including those who enjoyed being single), contrary to popular stereotype, expressed frustration with being "free," saying it was not as much "fun" as it was *supposed to be—perhaps a romantic reaction to the "free love," "Playboy philosophy" of the last two decades:**

"I'm nineteen . . . single too long. I don't like it. I need to show my affections to make people happy. I'm tired of living a life by myself. I want a wife and a family. I love kids, they are so innocent and free. I'll get married, and it will be marriage for *love,* not sex, not convenience, or because we *have* to, but *love.*"

"I've been single for twenty-nine years. I'm ready for marriage. I did my thing. I like long periods of monogamy. I like involvement. I want to know her, not just 'fuck her' and then forget her. I don't care for casual relationships."

"I've been single all twenty-one years of my life. I don't really like it. I want a female companion that I can cherish to myself and be able to make her happy in all ways. I also like the thought of being tied down, the fun in being free anymore has died with me. If I ever find a girl that loves me the way I love her, yes I'll get married."

"The older I get, the more I can see marrying. I settle and get conservative in my old age (twenty-five), wanting security and peace. But a paper won't do it, you know."

"I think that being single is not all that it is made out to be. I'd prefer to be married—but thus far, I have not been dramatically successful at developing the type of relationships which I feel should move naturally to marriage. I chronically feel lonely and as if something is missing from my life. But I do not want to marry out of desperation."

"I'm not crazy about being single, and I'm not an advocate of the swinging bachelor life. I definitely dig my freedom and privacy, but like living with someone I love, who is not an intrusion on my life but an extension of it. I'd love to be in a relationship of commitment again; right now I'm working hard, going to school, and changing—learning more about how I relate myself to people—I'm not sure I want a heavy relationship at these moments, but I definitely do in the future."

Single men were often lonely:†

---

* As one man noted, "When I am talking to married men, and they discover I am single, they seem sort of jealous. I really get the feeling most married couples are unhappy nowadays. They tell me I should cherish my freedom to do what I want to do."

† Divorced, now single, men were also often lonely, as seen in the preceding section.

"I have been single all my twenty-one years. It's O.K., but it's awfully damn lonely at times. I'm not living with someone, but I sure wish I was."

"I am twenty-three and unmarried. I would rather be married since I am lonely; also I would like to stabilize my sex life."

"I've been out of a relationship for about two months. Generally, I don't like it very much, although there are times when I enjoy my privacy and freedom. I don't like the social games involved in being single and on the 'market.' My major problem is learning to be alone, but not lonely."

"I have been single ever since I can remember. The only flaw to being single is that you constantly are feeling alone. You walk those lonely boardwalks in the evenings contemplating on Rod McKuen poems that tell of walking the lonely beach in search of last night's love. You learn the lonely stanzas of the songs on the radio and watch so much TV on Saturdays it seems you were born with a TV next to you. Backpacking becomes your only escape—for there in the mountains with my banjo I'm content. Before I crawl into my sleeping roll and I'm watching the fire, I think maybe next week after work I'll run into someone. Or I say, next month I'll go to more parties—or maybe even hold one myself! And I'll find a lover, one that'll last. I always hope."

"I have cried over my general inability to meet women —once even in my car in the parking lot of a disco in L.A. after having an extremely difficult time conversing with a number of girls who I was really attracted to (which is rare). I have been intrigued with the subject of suicide and realize that it is the most effective way to cure one's depression. I'm also saddened, though, to think that it is the *only* way to cure one's depression. Sometimes my depressions are just so bad that I'm ready to do anything to cease it. When I'm in that mood, I don't want to 'wait it out.' I can't bear to endure it for that period of time—but I always somehow manage to. My depressions always center around my inability to meet women. Period. I really envy guys who have the 'gift of gab' and who can just walk up to strange women and start a conversation. If I had that ability, it would solve all my problems, I'm convinced of it."

"I've been single all my life thus far. I enjoy the non-guilty feeling of going out on someone. I'm free to do as I wish. But I'd rather be married so I won't have to be lonely. At times I wished I had someone. Plus I love children and would like to go home to someone every night. Being single is O.K., but you never know when you'll have someone to be with."

But a few said that being single was also a good time for growing, having energy and attention for oneself:

"I enjoy being single. The advantages are primarily in the freedom it affords you. The disadvantages are there is not anyone around all of the time to support you when you need it, you must go and find that person, also there are some neat sharing things that people who are committed to each other have. I may eventually marry, I don't know yet, but I would probably live with them for a couple of years first. My sex life at the moment consists of masturbation. I have been doing a lot of growing in the last year, and having a lover would distract me, and camouflage what I need to finish, as well as tap some energy from where I need it, that being myself. At this moment I am living with my parents, but I had three and a half years on my own, and I may come and go as I please, but no sex at home. I can live with the rules, as I know they are temporary. They don't talk about my sex life, it isn't 'nice,' and I respect their feelings."

"Someday I will get married but there are some things I want to do while I'm still single. I want to meet other women, I want to travel, get my master's degree, and live by myself for a while before I settle down and raise a family."

"Right now I'm not encouraging relationships. One reason is that it's nigh unto impossible to have a satisfying, non-oppressive relationship. Also, being preoccupied and self-absorbed with a very demanding career has a lot to do with it. I have little energy to look for the signposts, for devotions towards a relationship. I'm *re-creating* myself."

Or for exploring many friendships:

"I've been single all my life. I like it. I made the mistake of latching on to one person five years ago and not developing other relationships. Since breaking up two years ago, I've been developing friendships with a number of people, some just platonic, some becoming sexual. I'm not ready to 'latch on' to just one person again. There's too many different people, and I'm having fun just dating around. Even when I become infatuated with one person, I still want to continue to see other women—I don't want to be 'exclusive.' I suppose I'll get married eventually, or at least settle down with one person for an extended length of time, but I'll know better than to cut myself off from having women friends."

*Quite a few men who were single were also celibate, or had frequent periods during which they had no sex with another person:**

"I am currently uninterested in sex and have been of that state of mind for seven months. I have been celibate since breaking off my previous relationship. I did so to allow myself the time to figure out again who I am, what I can give, and what I need from life. I was living with a woman for six years that I loved very much. She wanted me to be her provider, and keeper, mother and father, but she also wanted no responsibilities toward the relationship. She is a charmer, sweet-talker, liar, deceiver, and very lazy person. Yet I hope that she will become a person in her own right even though no matter how she matures or changes I could never go back with her. I am more aware of everything around me now —plants, animals, sunsets, blue skies, stars, and mountains, I feel closer to all of these things."

"My sex life alternates between activity and celibacy. A period of celibacy follows the end of a relationship. Celibacy is O.K., in spite of the popular image that a 'swinging bachelor' should be 'getting some' every night. In fact, sex can be a hassle at times, and celibacy can be a welcome relief. During the past year, I have been celibate longer than I have been active and I've enjoyed it. While celibate, I can have periods of 'horniness' (solved by masturbation) alternating with periods of little sexual desire."

"I don't have a sex life. I feel that premarital sex is wrong. It is just to show off, or to help someone brag about how 'cute' they think they are."

"I was raised Catholic. According to our belief, men and women are supposed to be celibate until after marriage. It appears other religions neglect this part."

* Of course, some married men, as seen on pages 184–187, were also celibate; see also chapter 5. Some replies in this section also include answers to the question, "If you are currently uninterested in sex (except perhaps for masturbation), how do you like this way of life? How long do you plan to remain 'celibate'? How long have you felt this way? Do you think this could be beneficial to other men?"

"Sometimes I've found that periods of celibacy are necessary to clear up my expectations regarding sexual relationships. It also frees up a lot of otherwise unfocused, confused energy. I write poetry, commune with nature, go fishing, travel, read. I do things I couldn't do with someone else because they may want that attention."

"My sex life at the moment consists of masturbation. I have been doing a lot of growing in the last year, and having a lover would distract me, and camouflage what I need to finish, as well as tap some energy from where I need it, that is, becoming myself."

But a minority of men who planned to marry eventually implied that it was more a question of duty or necessity than a pleasure or a benefit—in fact, it could be something they dreaded or felt would mean the end of their freedom to explore life or develop themselves:

"I have been single for twenty-seven years. I love being single and there is no life like it. I am certain in my mind I will not marry in my remaining twenties. When I am in the mid-thirties I may consider. I will certainly have to be a lot lonelier than I am now. Unless my attitudes change drastically in the future, I will be free for a long time."

"I am not married and rather enjoy single life. I don't want any commitments or major responsibilities to or for anyone but myself. When my father died his roles were put to me. I'd like to make up for the lost time for a while. I do plan to get married but there's plenty of time yet."

Or saw marriage principally as a necessary career and life decision:

"I have always been single, but will get married within five years for its benefits—kids, home, a partner, etc.—and because it will be expected for me if I want to fit in in business, etc."

As two men pointed out, being single could be a drawback socially or lessen one's social status:

"Being single works out fine for me, although sometimes I feel I have an inadequate social standing due to my single status. I feel like, to be considered a really serious and substantial member of the community, I should be married and have children. I would like to be married someday but sound reasons for marriage appear limited."

"I have always thought that being single would be much better if society were more willing to accept it as a valid alternative to marriage and/or family. The last few years have seen the marriage age pushed back a few years, but it is still the ultimate fate for most of us. I myself expect to get married around the age of thirty."

Some worried about the amount of responsibility marriage would entail for them:

"Single all my life. I like it. There are no ties. I don't think I'm ready at this point to be responsible for another person. But someday I really want to get married and have five children. I'm just not ready yet. I need to be alone sometimes and go inside myself—you can't do that with someone living with you."

"I have been single all my life and I like it a lot. I love the freedom in a way, but really I am far too fucked up to even consider marriage. I would like to spend several years with a woman and raise a family, etc., but not until I feel I am settled and mature enough. I can barely be responsible for myself, never mind someone else."

"I have always been single, and have no marital intentions. I don't see myself as mature enough to assume such broad contractual obligations. Neither do I feel mature enough for the responsibility of raising children in this society."

Many had mixed feelings about marriage—once again, centering on the seeming conflict between freedom and the need for security, and human affection:

"I am thirty years old, single, never been married. Occasionally a fantasy of some imagined marriage moves through my mind; sometimes it's a pleasant fantasy of conjugal bliss, sometimes an unpleasant fantasy. The point is: I'm not putting any energy into looking for or making a marriage. I respect this in myself. I am concentrated on other relationships: close friends, my writing, my lover, my work. In a very real way I feel totally married to my personal growth. Marriage to another person could augment my growth but I don't view it as essential to my growth."

"I was 'unalterably' opposed to marriage for many years but I am reexamining my attitude now. Somehow it represents taking one's place on the great assembly line of conformist adult society, something which I never want to do, but since I can't (and don't want to) father children, there is the paradoxical possibility for me that marriage wouldn't be such a prefabricated horror. 'Marriage is a great institution, but would you like to spend the rest of your life in an institution?' I may continue to prefer to abstain from it, even though the illusions of stability and security are very attractive."

"I am an only child, so being alone is both natural and very important to me. I crave my freedom and independence and oftentimes wonder if I can give it up. I cannot imagine being married, although I love the companionship of women. My problem is, career-minded, successful women (what I like) don't like to be tied down with one man either. It's a corner I backed myself into, but I don't like casual relationships, so I'm stuck."

"I would like to get married, but my basic distrust of women makes me afraid of marriage. I realize this distrust is not quite rational, but it does have some basis in that I believe society encourages women to wear masks and cover faults in order to trap a man into marriage. For some women that may be the only way to survive, but the possibility makes me wary nonetheless. But it could be great if it were really a partnership."

A few mentioned looking for, or having, a different kind of marriage:

"I don't know what I want. Marriage has always seemed to be a corral for two people to go stir crazy in, to my mind. I certainly don't envision a traditional marriage in the nucleic mode—but would like to try to create something unique that wouldn't fall into the pattern readily. Knowing my lover has completely turned me around in many ways on this subject, in that I have a desire to stay with her exclusively for the rest of my life. We talked about marriage early on, and have at times said that we'd do it immediately if the repressive and anti-woman marriage laws weren't on the books. But the problem is extremely complicated, because there are many other impulses, needs, and necessities involved. Enough to make my head swim when I try to think about it."

Finally, a few single men said they liked being single and would never get married:

"Single forever!"

"Been single twenty-three years. I like being single—no responsibilities, hang-ups, or fights (or kids). I like meeting new chicks. I probably won't get married. I lived with one chick for six months. It was all right but you can't bring somebody else home. I don't like being committed."

"I'm nineteen. I like being single. I have no personal ties, I can come and go as I please, no bitching. I'll stay single for a few more years, like a hundred."

Most men who were "single" were in their teens and twenties; however, some men of all ages had always been single:

"I have been single all my life (seventy-one years). Presently I do love being single, no responsibility and no one to nag me or pester me for any reason. When I was younger I was looking forward one day to get married and raise a family. Presently I rather be single, I have no intention of getting married, I will remain single. I am living alone now and have a beautiful well-furnished two-and-a-half-room apartment. I work at home and keep the apartment clean. I don't think I would like to live together presently. I rather not being married, even though I have plenty of opportunities."

"I have been single all my life. I don't like it. I would like to be married but I have no plans at this time. At fifty-two it is not so easy to find a woman that is not all tied up with her past family."

"I've been living alone sixty years. I'm single and will probably remain so. Single life has its advantages. It's hard to find a woman to tolerate me."

"I've been single thirty years. It is nice being independent and struggling for oneself but I think I would like to try sharing a lifetime with someone. But if not, I think I shall survive quite nicely."

"I have been single all my sixty-three years. I like being single because I have more independence. I would like to get married if I meet a woman that I feel is right for me and if we love each other. Although I am not married, I favor monogamy. I prefer a sexual relationship with a steady partner but a casual relationship is better than none. Two times I came close; both wonderful girls. If it's any problem at all that I could isolate, it's fear of intimacy (and of failure in an intimate relationship) that has prevented me from continuing the kind of intimacy a relationship needs to lead to marriage. Anyway, knowing your faults is half the battle."

"Why am I single? I get asked that all the time. I'm thirty-two, good job, obviously available. I could give you the usual load of statistics, philosophy, politics, etc., but they are just rationalizations. In women of my generation there was (is?) a widespread fear of independence, leading to flight from freedom, often to marriage, while in men of my generation there is a fear of commitment. Where does this fear of commitment come from? From an essential emotional cowardice? A weak ego? On the other hand, maybe I'm doing a stronger, more just thing than most men. When I see the number of men of my acquaintance who have been divorced, and twice divorced, and the consequences to these men, and the women, and worst of all to the children, I am appalled.

"But there are other reasons why I am not married or living with someone. Sometimes, one time in particular, I felt like I wanted to be in love with a woman. But the fear (I guess it must be fear) gets in the way, and strangles the feeling in its crib. It's an automatic reaction. I am not open enough, I don't give enough. I want to give, I want to, but I fail. I fail to feel enough, to express enough of what I feel. I'm not open. Beyond a point, I clench. Does it include fear that openness may mean rejection, hurt? Or that openness may reveal my innermost self as only a howling void, nothing, a hollow man, a non-person? I think so. 'The lack of love in my life is not so much rejection from others as it is my own fear of giving myself fully to anyone.' I forget who said that, but it seems appropriate."

How do single men feel about monogamy?

Many more single (never-married) men were in favor of monogamy than married men; in fact, the majority of single men planned to be monogamous in their marriages, or were currently monogamous in their (non-living-together) relationships. Is this a reaction to the "sexual revolution," and the lives of their parents, or are younger men more idealistic—or both? Or had married men also intended to be monogamous before they were married?

"Ultimately a monogamous relationship would be the most fulfilling to me. I think everyone should play the field for a while, if for no other reason than to find out that fucking around becomes self-defeating and finally a humiliation to oneself; who wants to admit to having dozens or even hundreds of lovers, and not being able to make one lasting relationship based on something other than physical attraction (a very temporary thing anyway)?"

"I think monogamy is the *only* way to be married. I think this 'open marriage' business is nonsense. I would like to be married, but as yet I've never been really confident as a *date,* let alone as a husband. I tried to envision what it must be like, but it doesn't ease my fears about whether or not I'd be good. I'm not living with anyone yet."

"Yes to monogamy. It must be the romanticist in me, or my upbringing, but when I marry it will be to one woman and I shall be faithful."

"I've been single eighteen years. To be close to someone, to build their trust, you have to make them feel more wanted, needed, and loved than anything, and really mean it. If you mean it you wouldn't want two women."

"I do not believe in divorce or extramarital affairs. My word is as good as gold and whomever I marry is stuck with me and only me 'till death do us part' and vice versa."

"I've been single all my life. I plan to get married, but enjoy my freedom first. I would prefer monogamy because I am by nature jealous and insecure, unable to handle the worry of other relationships."

"Even though I'm not married I support monogamy. I don't feel you could establish a great relationship with many partners. One at a time is hard enough to keep up for me, never mind many more. I think history has proven that one man—one woman has worked out better than several relationships at once."

"I have always been single, I don't like it, but probably would not like being married. I tend to think of marriage as an insufferable submission to highly controvertible authority of the state. But I believe in monogamy between two people. It seems to me I could not endure anything but monogamy. I like the idea of one true lasting marriage."

"For me, monogamy is the only way to go. That's me and the relationship I have with my lover. This is very important to me. I may look at a woman and feel aroused, but really I hope never to have sex with anyone but my present partner."

"I like monogamy because it allows energy to go to other things in life. It is stable in many ways, intensifies living and sharing and working, makes a family structure possible, feedback about myself is stronger, and having a child is more feasible. It adds a very lovely element to life."

"Monogamy generates high emotions. I like it. You get more tuned to that woman's habits, character flaws, strong points, traits, etc. I have no use for casual sexual relationships."

"I prefer monogamy—anything else just screws up too many people."

"My religious background and training and my present beliefs prevent me from being immoral."

"Although it is said that: 'Monogamy is a capitalist invention,' I think it is the only form of relationship that really works."

"I like extended periods of monogamy because that gives me the time to get closer to somebody, to know her better. It is more comfortable. Being with someone a lot makes you sort of a part of them and they of you. I get more security out of a steady monogamous relationship. I feel more steady, and people say I am easier to get along with, in better spirits, and more responsible. I mostly want to stay home and drink beer and watch television and be with the woman I like."

"I prefer monogamy over everything else, and for extended periods of time. I do not enjoy casual sexual relationships. I am very intense and loyal in my relationships, and when I get into one, I very rarely get bored with them; on the contrary, I get more deeply involved as time goes on."

"I like monogamy. You need a lot of time to build a good relationship. The building is important to me. I feel that I want and need to give my all to one person. I have to be attentive to her needs and feelings as well as my own. In my opinion, great things come out of monogamy, something like a birth. I can love other women, but I have to have just one lover. That's good for me. I can only hope it's good for her. I like the feeling of commitment. It makes me feel secure, loved, healthy, strong, and kind of sexy too. Because I know that I have a partner. I can give 100 percent to that person and she can give 100 percent to me. Maybe I'm old-fashioned, but I never could get into casual relationships and I don't think I ever will. I don't want to be a part-time thing. I don't want a woman that's a part-time thing. A lot of my inner stirrings don't get expressed in casual relationships. In short, casual relationships for me, suck! However, if everything is aboveboard and honest and both people agree that they will see other people, well that's okay. I could handle that, but my ideal is a non-oppressive, honest, monogamous relationship."

Are younger men more interested in monogamy and idealistic about it as a result of—or a reaction to—the "freer" sexual mores of the last twenty years, or of their parents? Or does being married or living with another person bring about a change in feeling?

A minority of single men did not believe in or practice monogamy in a relationship:

"I'm deeply committed to my girlfriend, but I also like casual sex; I care for my casual mates as much as (or slightly more than) I care for my tennis partners, my other big sport. Others can be monogamous if they want but I don't understand it as anything but an expression of insecurity and possession."

"I think ideally I would like a relationship with one person, but that both of us would have other friendships and that they could include sex. I realize how difficult this is emotionally, though, on both people. I have had one relationship where my lover lived with another person. (The three of us were aware of the situation.) I often felt frustrated in the relationship, but I always felt good during the time spent with my lover. I think it helped me get over the idea of a lover as personal property, and that is a very positive step. I'm not sure how I would react to a monogamous relationship now, or what I would do if I wanted to have a serious relationship with a woman who insisted on monogamy."

LIVING TOGETHER

A few single (never-married) men—surprisingly few (only one-fifth of never-married men) considering the amount of public discussion the concept has had in recent years—said they would like to live together with a woman, but not marry:

"I've been single since I've been born: 20 years, 5 months, and 27 days. I enjoy it. I'm not ready for marriage, but I'm trying to get my girl to move in with me and we can try to make it. If things don't work out, then I'm going to have to find another girl that's willing to be my roommate as well as my bed partner and lover. But no marriage. Out of the question."

"I would rather live together with someone than be married, because marriage is a kind of legal imposition upon my life and an intrusion of society into my private existence. Marriage becomes *plausible* only when you are going to start having children, for obvious reasons. Apart from this, it has always seemed to me a kind of socially accepted and encouraged sex market. There are so many *wives* who are really prostitutes to their husbands. They marry for protection and money. The other prostitutes are cheaper and sometimes more attractive."

"I'm single, and I plan to stay single. I don't want to be married, because I think the family is an economic unit used to oppress people. In the typical family, the man works hard, and he gets paid less than what he's worth. But he has to work to survive, to make enough to feed his family, clothe them, pay his rent, enough to heat the house. He's got to get that money, if he's married, bring it home, let his family survive on it. That means in most cases the man has to work all the time, and gets nothing but the right to survive. It's equally hard for the wife, because she stays at home, and she has to live off the meager income of her husband, has to do all this work and not get paid for it; she has to produce the family, raise them, and in the end, all this does is repeat itself: the family dies and the children are alive and go to work, they replace their parents, and they work—and it just keeps going like that. The only way it's going to change is with the class-conscious movement—a revolution to change capitalism into socialism. That's why I wouldn't want to get married, because it's just a certificate which says you have the right to be with this person, you *have* to do it, it's a bond, you've got obligations, and she's got obligations. I want to love someone, I want to live with someone; but I only want to live with someone because they *want* to love me; I don't want a deal for life. If it only takes a week, and the other person gets sick of me or I get sick of them, bingo, end it, that's it—I'll be content with that. I don't want a lifelong commitment. You don't need a license to say you love someone."

Six percent of the men who answered, including single (never-married), divorced, separated and widowed men, were currently living with a woman. But most saw living together as a step toward marriage:

"I have been living with my girlfriend for about four months. I like living with her very much and we are going to be married in six months. Living with her has been really good because we have been much closer since she has lived with me. Also I think we have learned a lot more about each other than we could have if we hadn't lived together. The reason we are getting married is because it makes our relationship seem more like a permanent thing. I think that being married will be a commitment to each other to always love each other, and to making our relationship continue to grow and work, in spite of possible problems that could come up."

"Though there are no bands on our fingers, we consider ourselves married. Getting married, to the extent that we have done so, has developed gradually over four years. In the next few months, we hope to make it official. One reason is so we can live together without parents and other relatives getting upset. She has said that marriage per se should make little if any difference, but I do like the idea of partaking in a legal, if not religious, institution. Also, I wonder what actual marriage may hold for us of which we are now unaware. Let's find out! For me, monogamy is the only way to go."

"I like living together but I'd rather be married. I want more depth. More commitment. More security."

"I've been living with her for about two years but want to get married soon. I don't want to live alone, there's too many things I need and want that I get from interacting with another person. I get warm inside, and a little sexually aroused, when I think of getting married to her. It has something to do with a feeling of security that I want."

However, one man objected to the idea of living together before marriage:

"I'm old-fashioned and want marriage first. I won't have to 'try it out,' because when I get married I'll be sure of myself."

The concept of living together as a permanent arrangement (not leading to marriage) was more popular with divorced men, some of whom found living together an improvement over marriage, or who thought they would prefer living together:

"I am divorced. Finally my second lover after the divorce moved in and took over. Living together without being married, I feel more unrestricted. My substance is safer. The threat of a future possibility of being left bereft by an angry wife plus attorneys, plus judges, plus customs and traditions that favor women, heavily, under divorce conditions—all that not hanging over my head is a big help."

"I was previously married for almost ten years. My present 'marriage' is by mutual consent without the legal or clerical blessings, and I prefer it. Marriage is simply a relationship, more intense and extensive than most, and therefore more satisfying and more disappointing. But a man must relate more to one person than another; sheer demands of time and energy force this. Being married is simply being alive and forming relationships; one eventually emerges more important. Unfortunately 'being married' to most of us means being married to somebody besides your partner, a clergy or J.P., etc. Also, unfortunately, if you don't have a marriage contract, the law makes one for you anyway—'common law' laws, etc."

"I was married thirty-two years, divorced eleven. Overseas in WWII was the only time I was unfaithful. Being single now I do what I want to when I want to, but I often feel lonely. No partner to sleep with or to hold or to hold me. No support (as in reinforcement) when I need it. No one *cares* about me. But I'd prefer to live with a woman without marriage. If we had a good thing going we'd each be more aware of and more considerate of the other's feelings and needs, and knowing that one could walk out the door at any time, we'd *work* to keep it good."

"I would not rather be married again. Marriage is a confining, strangling, often ridiculous state of affairs. People should live together and remain together because they want to, and if they don't want to they should be able to split without the legal hassles that are so expensive, unfair, and very often harmful to the parties concerned."

Many widowers also found living together to be more convenient than getting married again, and a happy and satisfying arrangement:

"I am now living with a seventy-two-year-old woman. We enjoy each other in many ways. Especially in bed. She likes fucking fully as well as I do or ever did. I wish I could do it as often as she would like. We don't plan to marry, but it is not dissimilar to when I was married."

Some men described their living-together relationships with great pleasure:

"I've been with my partner in different circumstances for a year, traveling and camping by highways, and living in houses in various conditions of disrepair. I have been supporting her for the past six months. Before that, we traveled on her savings, and lived on her wages as a grill cook in a hotel. This is the best relationship I ever had and I think it will last, mainly because we communicate so well."

"For five months, I have been living with a woman whom I have been dating for three years. We get along much better in the same house together than I had originally estimated. I enjoy living together with her—I especially enjoy sleeping with her every night (not necessarily for sex's sake) and I enjoy having someone to talk to all the time. I love her, I think, mainly because I know *her* so well and she knows *me* so well. It's a special oneness that I've never experienced with another person to date."

"I have now been living with my girlfriend for nearly seven months, and we are both very happy. I like having her know that if she should become bored or restless, she need simply move out. We stay together because we want to, not because we have to, and it's beautiful. We try really hard for each other. At this point in my life, I'll have a monogamous relationship, for as long as it contains more joy than sorrow, or no relationship at all."

"I'm thirty-three years old, and have no plans to get married in the near or distant future. Marriage seems to change people's relationships. I have been living with someone for over a year. I like it very much. Although both my lover and I have complete freedom to pursue other relationships, we are at present basically monogamous. My present relationship started out as being the most casual relationship I had ever had. It has grown to be the most intense loving situation of my life."

Others were not enjoying the experience so much:

"I did live with a woman for a period of time. It had its points but got to be like being married with all the possessiveness and jealousy. It might be a little better than being married but not much."

"Nine months now. I feel like I'm already married, as I've lost a lot of my freedom."

"About six months ago I was living with a woman who I lived with for one year. Living with her had moments of joy, but many times she put me through hell with her bitching. I am very glad we are no longer living together. I think I would not mind living with a woman who I could get along with better."

"I'm not living with someone right now. We did for a while, and it was O.K. except that it can become a drag having to think about someone else every time you want to eat or make an orange juice or whatever."

"I lived with a woman for nine months last year. It had its likes and dislikes. It was advantageous for companionship, someone to talk to, and sexual availability. She was only going to 'live together' for a year before leaving and going on to further her education. I thought it would be fun. My mistake —she got serious and wanted to get married. I did not want to get married to her. I was not in love with her. She was a nice lady, I just didn't love her. After a while I didn't think we were all that compatible, either. The last few months of living together were very uneasy as she 'tried to help me overcome my fear of marriage and recover from divorce.' I tried to be 'diplomatic.' Finally, I just asked her to move out. Never again."

"I lived with my girlfriend until recently and enjoyed it, but we are both people who enjoy our privacy sometimes and enjoy being alone, and for this reason I have moved out. I feel that this has helped our relationship."

One man explained some of the difficulties he encountered in trying to work out a way of living happily together, eliminating the traditional stereotyped male and female roles:

"I've had six relationships where we have lived together. These were for periods of from two months up to three years. I think the hardest thing about living together for me is finding a little time to be by myself at home. Since I work nights, the woman I live with is usually asleep when I get home, so I end up staying up for an extra hour to be by myself, even though I don't like to stay up late. When I am with someone I am living with in our waking hours, that person seems to automatically enter my consciousness at all times. Also, when women were living with me at 'my' place—a house that was under my name or where I was paying the rent—they would invariably feel that things were not 'equal.' This means that they felt the rent, responsibilities, and control of the living place should be shared 50–50. A couple of women moved out because they felt they were ending up following my life style too much and didn't really want to do this. But I like living with a woman that I care a lot for."

Are men in living-together relationships monogamous?

Most were not, or were not planning to be:

"We've been together for five and a half years now. Being married is not important or necessary, although both families would prefer it. I like having one very strong relationship, but with an openness to having other close friendships or 'extra-living-together' experiences. Since being with my partner, we've each had these, always known to the other although after the fact (she told me after). For me, the woman I had the sexual experience with was a very close friend of my partner's who asked her (before approaching me) if it was all right! It was during a short restricted time period and was very exciting to me. It had a positive bringing-together effect on my partner and me. However, when my partner told me about some experiences after they'd happened (which she had before my experience) I was pretty upset for a while. To me, unfaithful was having a secret life, not simply having sex with another person. Going to the outer limits of open marriage nevertheless contributed to our feeling somewhat estranged and unfriendly. In a new relationship, I would not expect either of us to go forever without sex with someone else, but I wouldn't want either of us to have frequent affairs. As a fling now and then, I doubt there would be an adverse effect; as a common situation, love would suffer."

"Living together for more than two years. I like it, but sex tends to become too 'known,' too predictable, and it takes a lotta energy to change that. I do believe in monogamy, even though I tend to look for some novelty outside after a while. Despite all the new tendencies I think there's something very primal about it. But we've been talking about 'open marriage,' mainly because of my urge. I don't want it to happen secretly."

"We've been living together for about two and a half years, and it is generally very satisfying. We have a commitment for the two of us to be together for a long time. I'm trying to develop a reasonable alternative to marriage. I prefer monogamy, because relationships grow from the accumulation of experiences over time. The investment of that time and energy makes understanding, trust, and sharing really possible. On the other hand, casual sexual relationships are acceptable now and then, as long as we both are well aware of the extent of each other's commitment or lack of commitment."

"I am twenty-four. I didn't feel guilty about sex until I started relating to my present girlfriend on a permanent long-term basis. I don't feel ready to make a commitment to her. Right now I have been feeling the need to live by myself. I get uncomfortable living with my girlfriend. I like to be alone a lot. This is so despite the fact that I care for her more than anyone in the world. Basically, I enjoy my relationship with her and feel it is worthwhile despite the difficulties we encounter. We both feel that the rapport and understanding that has developed over the years are incomparable to even the most fantastic initial love experiences. However, because we are growth-oriented, we enjoy exposure to people of different characters in order to increase our own understanding of human nature and enrich our personal repertoire. So we have started seeing other people. However, what appeared fine on the drawing board ended in violent argument and feelings of betrayal and jealousy. I feel caught right now."

One man had very mixed feelings:

"I've been living in a monogamous relationship with a woman for two and a half years. Sometimes I wish for some affairs as an escape, an escape from what, I don't know. Were I inhabiting Paradise I'd still think of going to 'California' sometime soon (and probably wouldn't go), but when I was having a lot of one-night stands and such I wasn't happy or satisfied with my life."

But a few men were monogamous and liked it:

"At this time I like monogamy. I have been living with a woman for two years. I feel satisfied. I am constantly meeting attractive women and I enjoy it, but I have no desire for it to go any further. In a way, when this happens, I appreciate my partner even more, sort of glowing in my satisfaction."

"I like monogamy—I don't even have enough time now for my lady, or myself, or my work. I really couldn't work in another person. But I was desperate for 'extra' experiences in my current relationship during the first couple of years, and I acted that out. I ended up moving out from my lover for three or four months. I have given up a lot of that desperation, recognized it, and don't sense myself really ever doing that again. I believe the energy put into casual sex would be better used for looking at the desperation in a person that I believe is the cause of casual sex."

MEN'S ANGER AT WOMEN

Having looked at men's feelings about marriage—married, divorced, and single men—we can now return* to our question about why men so frequently seek sexual relationships outside of marriage, unknown to their wives. In one sense, it can be said that perhaps many men see it as their "right"—something they are privileged to do when they feel like it; in fact, some men may even feel pressured to have extramarital sex by a culture that implies that all "real men" do it. Other reasons men gave earlier in the chapter included maintaining a separate identity or individuality, getting affection or an ego boost when they needed it, or getting out of a marriage they wanted to end. But the main reason for most extramarital sex, the reason most men gave, was that it "made the marriage workable"—that without these affairs, they would not be able to continue in the marriage. And, in fact, some of the longest marriages did seem to have survived in just this way.

But why *were* these marriages "unworkable"? Is lack of sex, or "boring" sex the reason,† or is the trouble men so often describe as sexual merely a reflection of larger unresolved issues in the relationship? Are these unresolved or unacknowledged issues unique to every relationship, or are there also larger culturally created problems between men and women? Of course, there are always individual conflicts or problems unique to any two people that can lead to fighting or alienated

* See pages 230–231.

† See chapter 3 for a discussion of what sex means to men, what they need from it, and what they get out of it.

feelings; but there are also problems common to many couples, problems which therefore take on a larger meaning.

On one level, as mentioned earlier, many men find that they cannot reconcile in their own minds the idea of loving their wives as the mothers of their children (and the woman who has, in a sense, the role of "mothering"—taking care of, feeding—them), and seeing her as a sexual being. Many men, raised to think of the mother as asexual or sexually taboo, find that they begin to have similar feelings about their wives, soon after marriage or after children arrive. This may be especially true of men who complain that sex with their wives has become "boring."

But another, perhaps more hidden or underlying reason, is unexpressed or unrecognized anger. In fact, many men's extramarital affairs, kept secret from their wives, can be seen as an escape valve—a way of secretly or unconsciously expressing anger at their wives, "getting even," "showing her"— a kind of private revenge that does not on the surface disturb the relationship, but gives a feeling of relief, allowing one to return refreshed, feeling more loving than ever, now that the anger has been expressed.

What, underneath it all, are men angry about? Were there any underlying themes in the complaints men presented—any complaints which reemerged again and again, which could be, on a larger scale, an underlying cause of much of the anger? Or was most of this anger hidden, even unrecognized? In fact, in many, many replies, hidden anger, guilt and ambivalence that men seemed to feel about women was blocking relationships, especially long-term relationships, allowing resentments to grow and solidify. However, some men were aware of these feelings, as seen in the following pages.

There are probably many reasons for men's anger, but two are very basic, and built directly into the culture. The first involves the way men are brought up to see women, and the distance this creates. (The second reason will be addressed on page 284.) Earlier we heard men talk about their need for women, describing women as their only real source of warmth, intimacy, and affection; but then many men went on to say that they saw women in a very limited way, that is, either as potential sexual partners, or as (ideally) nurturing, approving, and encouraging, motherlike figures. They did not picture women as brave, courageous, independent, or intellectually stimulating. In fact they learned from their fathers' attitudes toward their mothers to see women, all too often, as weak and overly emotional, dependent, able to gain "power" only by relying on psychological domination and manipulation to get what they wanted, using men for their own economic advantage. As one man put it, "My father taught me (by implication) that women are traps and burdens, but the best that's available for overcoming loneliness." It is remarkable, given these views—and sadly, the fact that, due to cultural and economic pressures on women, these stereotypes have, at times, been true—that any relationships between men and women have ever managed to succeed.

MEN'S PERCEPTION OF WOMEN AS WEAK

But why does men seeing women basically as "sex partners" or mothers, and looking down on them as generally weak and inferior, make men angry with women? In fact, we saw just this combination of feelings when men described their feelings for their mothers.* The first reason is that this makes men feel guilty and conflicted in their loyalties, and angry with women for making them feel guilty:

"Sometimes I feel 'guilty' when I catch myself thinking that I am more intelligent or can do things better than my girlfriend. There are areas where I have had more experience than her, but there are equally as many things that she excels over me in. But still, I catch myself making this assumption all the time."

"Since she loves me so much, I feel guilty that maybe I don't love her as much. She really looks up to me. Sometimes I feel like she worships me. This makes me feel funny. I know that as a man it is my duty to help her, but sometimes I feel funny. And then I feel annoyed with her. Why can't she stand on her own two feet?"

"I feel guilty when I treat women as women rather than people. It is so much easier with many of them, though."

"I feel most guilty of my behavior towards my sisters and mother as we have all grown. I keep holding back and am unwilling to share myself closely with them, especially my two youngest sisters. I want to get close but don't know how without losing most of my privacy."

* See pages 118–128.

"I can't help looking down on women. You can get anything you want from them by telling them they are 'special.' They love to be told they are 'special.' "

"I guess what makes me maddest about women is when they lack pride, underestimate themselves, and are over-careful. When I see a woman with intelligence and abilities take a passive role in life because she lacks self-confidence, it upsets me and I tend to become critical and to provoke her. Some women do *act,* but in a subservient manner—because they want to 'win' and please a man (to gain security?). In sex this is especially frustrating, even if it is easy to see why they act that way."

"Women often treat me like a *brain* object. I get the feeling that they feel more admirable if they go out with me than with another woman, or alone. If a man admires them, they are worth more. This happens all the time, it seems inevitable almost. But it makes me feel distant from the woman, I don't feel like talking to her."

"I prefer to call women's liberation 'women's empowerment,' which is more accurate. I am 100 percent for it and actively campaign for it. When women are empowered, they won't have to relate to men through manipulation, and the world will be a happier, more honest place. I insist on treating women as equals and being treated by them as equals, and if they don't like it, I pretty much dismiss the relationship as one not holding much promise for me. I am not rescuing any more maidens from railroad tracks; they can gnaw through their own bonds."

A great deal of the alienation between men and women is caused by men's knowledge, on some level, of their superior, privileged class status over women—or at least the difference in status. This is an unspoken issue, too emotionally charged to discuss in most cases, whose existence is taken for granted between most men and women, but which has a diffused effect over the entire relationship. Although men felt somewhat free to voice these feelings about their mothers, and to recognize their mothers' subordinate position vis-à-vis their fathers—often calling them "weak" as seen earlier in the chapter—many men did not feel free to express, or perhaps even recognize, some of these same feelings about their own wives and lovers.

Closely connected to the view of women as "weak" is men's anger at women whom they see as "overly emotional" and *emotionally dependent. Men often perceive women's love for them as an almost parasite-like emotional dependence,* leaving them feeling almost engulfed by what men see as the woman's desire to merge, to gain absolute approval and acceptance, or to live through the man, become his appendage, even own his very identity in a sense—i.e., be Mr. and Mrs. John Smith; this was traditionally described by the derogative phrase "clinging vine":*

"My relationship with my wife is the worst drag in my life after sixteen years of marriage and two kids. But a divorce will certainly destroy her socially and personally, as she depends on me totally. She has been enjoying my loyal love and support for a long time, it gave her her ego, her happiness, her social life, her economic security. She took so much out of me that she has simply enslaved me. Now I have to save what is left of me. The hell with love."

"When I was involved in my last relationship I felt like I was being suffocated because I was supplying security to the woman that she had not developed within herself. I often wanted more time for myself. Now I am alone and happier. I will be very careful about who I get involved with in the future."

But this also, in equal proportion, represents men's own intense fear of becoming emotional themselves—"like a woman" —losing themselves in their emotions.

One man described his ambivalent feelings in detail in a longer reply:

"I was most deeply in love when I was eighteen, more than forty years ago, with an English girl with a very proper, well-bred upbringing. She was a virgin. When we were apart she wrote me nearly every day, great long letters proclaiming her love. We were powerfully attracted to each other physically. I think I was the happiest in my life in those years with her, I was delirious and enthralled by her love for me. It was

---

* Whether or not this perception is correct often involves, once again, men's definition of their own masculinity as separate or different from so-called "girlish" or "feminine" behavior; in fact, many men feel uncomfortable when too closely associated with a woman, or "identified with" a woman, as seen in men's replies related to fear of being in love. (See pages 132–142.)

unequivocal, accepting, warm, and passionate—very passionate—all of which I reciprocated.

"But as time passed, her devotion to me evolved into an emotional dependency which scared me. I began to feel I had too much responsibility as the sole source of her well-being. It was her first affair and I think her background suggested to her it would be permanent. She assumed it was forever. There was a question in my mind about her being too feminine and perhaps believing the male role entailed his responsibility as her sole emotional caretaker, her sole emotional support. I was unable to accept it. I grieved inwardly at this turn of events.

"In the end—and this has always struck me as strange, it bugs me even today—I met and married a girl who was no-where near as beautiful or feminine, or as warm and loving, but far more self-reliant, emotionally independent, the capable sort, stronger, intelligent. Maybe this, without my knowing it at the time, is what attracted me. I probably sensed that this woman, incidentally not unlike my mother, was far less likely to become emotionally dependent on me and thereby relieve me of a responsibility I didn't feel up to. Why else—and this is what bugs me—would I retreat from so enchanting and blissful of a relationship with such a beautiful and lovely woman, to court another who was no match for her as a woman or lover? Why? Simply to avoid responsibility and maybe hoping for some emotional support for myself from a stronger woman? In all these years, I still feel a twinge of regret, and wonder what the outcome might have been had I stayed with her. It took me a whole afternoon to burn her letters, a painful private ritual."

MEN'S ANGER ABOUT WOMEN AND MONEY

Closely related to men's ambivalent feelings about women's subordinate status, letting themselves go to their own emotions, and their fear of women's "emotional dependence" were men's feelings about most women's economic dependence. More men voiced these feelings than feelings about women's supposed emotional dependency, perhaps because economic problems were easier to acknowledge.

Married men, single men, divorced men, and men of all ages spoke out against women's economic dependence,* or, as many men put it, the way women use men, for economic security or gain—leading many to conclude, angrily, "you can't trust a woman":

"I think girls use guys. They have sex to get pregnant and then married."

"I really hope we'll reach a point in time when women will come to be more independent and autonomous. The old idea of marriage solving all of their emotional and financial problems throughout life needs revision. Maybe throw out that proverbial 'happy ever after' Cinderella jive."

"I dislike the acceptance of an inferior role that many women have been taught. I would like to see more women assert their intelligence, dignity, and independence."

"I am not interested in the 'standard' woman who, in effect, uses her pussy to capitivate a meal ticket."

"I find non-liberated women boring generally, as I couldn't stand to be 'responsible' for a woman's life. I get sick when I run into the delicate, eye-batting little girl from the farm. They're playing me for a sucker."

"Women don't seem to look at men as people, women look at men more as robots, or as 'success objects,' and virtually even possessions of theirs for their own economic benefit."

"I'm afraid women are still rather foolish. They don't look at men as if they were people like everybody. They're easily impressed by clothes, cars, and money."

"I think all women are whores, which is not a knock, but they realize that they have something a man wants, and they have things they want and trading pussy is as good and easy a way as any. It doesn't hurt, you can't use it up, and in some cases it actually gets better with use. So if it can buy a piece of good hash, or a three-bedroom house in the country, or a sexy male, or a ticket to a Stevie Wonder concert, why not? (Men are no better. They promise women things or relationships in exchange for sex, then don't hold up their end. Both sides are always working a hustle. That's why I got married—to slow the game down.)"

---

* And yet most men were not wholeheartedly in favor of the women's movement, which could make a change in this dependence possible; women's dependence is linked to very real economic and social discrimination which still persists. (See pages 316–17.)

"Most women search for security and compromise themselves this way. Usually after the failure of an early 'great love story,' they lose confidence in love and try to find a good man who can provide them with material security. Most of them spend many years of life after that without sensing they have lost one of the most valuable things of life, real love. Men are just as bad—after their 'great love' fails, they try to find a good mother, a good housekeeper, and a woman who can understand the problems they had in the office. Real, complete excitement is something they will try to fulfill somehow, 'somewhere' (outside). But after years of such compromise, if they are sensitive enough, they will both face the problem of life's 'black hole,' or meaninglessness. Maybe they will get used to it, maybe they'll get a divorce."

"For several reasons (some personal, some due to society's attitudes) I often distrust women. Maybe they just want me to support them, etc. I think it is extremely important that a woman have her own means of support so that she and her partner know that she is economically independent. I have discussed it with my younger sister because I feel she ought to keep that as a consideration in her own life. Also, I have decided that I should encourage my partner (whoever she may be) to build and maintain her own career. If she did, I think there would be very little chance that she would have sex with me for any reason other than love, or that I would feel beholden to her if I didn't love her."

"Women's economic position in society makes her dependent in the relationship and therefore the weaker part in the relationship. This is very banal, but a fact nevertheless. It makes them afraid of telling: who they are, what they want, what they don't want. Afraid to show what they think or feel. Too conventional. Don't say when they're angry or dissatisfied. I hate playing games, having to guess, not knowing."

"In my marriage, sometimes I feel I have been a means of providing a house, a baby, clothes, expensive car, and escort service to certain social occasions—all of which she seems on occasion to value a good deal more highly than me as a person. Possibly she could just go out and buy these things on her own, but somehow it wouldn't be legitimate to her without a husband there to provide it. She also relies on me for a great deal of the housework, child care, all of the gardening, a lot of cooking, etc. That is, I am a general convenience to her and a sort of slave. In return she gives as little sex as possible. This is in addition to working; she works, too, or I wouldn't be willing to take on so much drudgery. I am generally a good-natured and cooperative person, but she tries to take too much advantage of it."

"You've got to wine and dine them; show them you've got money and status, a new car, and a great future with a fine house (neat)! Then, they open up that little crack between their legs which all of us men came from and which we all try like hell to get back into (God I love it). Hey—hey—"

"It makes me mad when women go out with men that they don't like, and he pays for the whole date. My sister did that a few times, and it really seemed mean to me—sort of dishonest and manipulative. I guess women must feel that they must have to pay for the 'date' with sex. It's really a lousy system."

"I have been married two times. The first time from ages twenty to twenty-nine, the second from thirty-one to now. I like the marriage idea, but I have never been successful with it. My first wife fell in love with somebody else, and the second is miserably frustrated sexually, but needs the financial security this thing provides. I have lost the illusion that I could find a happy marriage. I feel inadequate and project this onto my partner, then destroy it and her. And her feelings about financial dependency don't help either. I think she resents me for it, even though I bend over backwards not to hold it over her. When one partner is dependent on the other, it is not good for a relationship."

"I think it's high time that women are speaking out against the injustices perpetrated on them by the system. But I see women who say they want more sensitivity, etc., turn around to screw some macho superstud or other—a guy who is taller, stronger, earning more, having greater accomplishments in whatever field, or more power (e.g., Wayne Hays) than the women do. I feel that if I (a communications student) and an M.B.A. were both interested in the same girl, I know who'd get left. Women are still being swept off their feet by assertive men and are even eager to have sex with men who are insensitive, self-centered, and brutal, just so long as they project a feeling of strength."

And one cynical and sad young man described his anger about relationships:

"I am twenty-four years old, typical lower-middle-class, a postal worker (for lack of anything better to do; besides, the money is good), high school grad, college dropout, brought up well by my parents but I've managed to change all that, living alone, being totally free and unrestricted to do anything I please in the confines of my house, and outside too the majority of the time (until the useless authority comes down on me). And an unmistakable honky. White as snow. Unable to tan without peeling, unfortunately. Since day one of my life, until I'm dropped in my grave, I will be single. I love it. No restrictions, no responsibilities, no one bitching at every little thing I do, and best of all, no fucking children.

"I lived with a lady for one year and it was nice, but too confining, too many demands, and there was the constant question of marriage, an extremely obscene word. I don't like the idea of answering to anyone, as I had enough of that living at home, at school, and at work. The last cunt that lived with me lasted only a couple of months before the big take-over started, and she thought it was her house, her car, her phone, her bed, her stereo, her guitars, etc. She found her ass out the door.

"I sometimes go quite a while without sexual contact with women, even over four months. Masturbation is a relief, when I feel the need for companionship. Marijuana is a nice replacement, as is a guitar, a nice trip up the coast, or even reading, or anything to occupy my mind. There is so much in the world to experience, I see no point in wasting my time thinking with my pecker. Also, I try to make sex unimportant, because I've been burned too many times. I'm extremely protective with my emotions.

"Initially, women seem to be quite affectionate, concerned, loving, and entirely capable of taking all that I'm willing to give. But once the taking starts, it never ends. And then comes the taking without reciprocation. Nothing for everything is an unfair trade, and too demanding for my fragile mended heart.

"Economic advantages are probably all I get laid for. I've never felt that a cunt has wanted just me, because eventually, they've all gotten too demanding. The status is having an old man, a car, a house, nice furnishings; but this is one old man that can't be manipulated into the rut that has destroyed so many.

"I hope the sexual revolution leads to complete role reversal. I would like the women to be the aggressors, spend the money, and be rejected.

"When I was eighteen my first love was sweet. I think I actually felt love, but it is something that has yet to repeat itself. I lived with *and* for this lady for a year, only to be turned away for newer blood. This was the happiest time I had ever known. If I never know love or sex again, this one time was worth a lifetime of celibacy. I cried many times after that breakup. Suicide I have contemplated into futility. Life is never so bad that I want to die. I'm not afraid of death, but I love life; my only love, now, outside of a six-string guitar.

"Monogamy is the only way I am able to comprehend a relationship. Anything more would damage me more than has been done in the past. One at a time, or no time at all. I've seen too many of my buddies lose sweet ladies because of their lack of control of emotions, and inability to be satisfied. I'm easy to please. One lady is enough, sometimes too much. I detest casual relationships, unless it deals with prostitution. An hour with a pro would be as casual as I'd want to get. (If I had the bucks to spend, I would love to be done by a pro. I find that I pay for sex in one way or another anyway, prostitute or not.)

"Occasionally, I fantasize being able to fall in love. I feel alienated by my inability to feel love and emotional involvement. But somehow this alienation gives me a sense of well-being, self-sufficiency and power. I feel strong because I can't be tied down or controlled. Sometimes, I dream (daydream?) of being with foxy ladies I can't have; my filmdom idols—Karen Black, Lola Falana, Jean Harlow, Mae West, Tina Turner. Forbidden fruit seems sweeter.

"Friendship is all right, but I am a loner. Friends, to me, feel more for me than I do for them. I can take them or leave them. Often they just get in the way of my solitude. I would prefer friendship to love relationships because of the lack of emotional responsibilities; however, neither excite me that much, or prove to be long-term. I am a very cold person."

Some older men pointed with anger to the traditional exchange of sex and domestic upkeep for marriage and economic support, feeling they were shortchanged:

"Women's lib is off the beam. Women have been as liberated as they wanted. They have held men in slavery to their vaginas for a long time. Women seem able to live without sex better than men, and that gives a woman a lot of power. They live longer too, which seems to indicate that men run into the ground while women thrive on the situation. Where else can a person lie around the house and be supported to the style she'd like to become accustomed?"

"I don't mind if my wife works. I encouraged her to get her present job. In fact, she doesn't know it, but I put in the word that got her the job, not because it was going to make my life any better, but because I thought it'd make hers happier. She keeps all her money, except for taxes, and occasionally gives me a present. Pays none of the grimy upkeep expenses I work to cover. If she wants to be liberated, she's free to leave. I think men are fools not to encourage ERA. If liberation means a man can get sex without marriage, it looks like a fool's paradise for me."

"For a couple of months toward the end of the relationship I grew suspicious and resentful of women. Not only was my former partner callous and deceitful, but other women that I talked to would at the time boast of how they had hurt the man they were involved with. Then I realized that these women had several things in common: a desire for marriage to gain property, money, social standing, and power, a lack of education, a lack of desire for knowledge, and a generally selfish and callous attitude. They wanted men for what they could get from them."

"I got married when I was thirty-seven, married twenty years. I like being married, but would like to be married to a more loving and affectionate woman that felt like I was good enough for her and wasn't always complaining because I don't have a million dollars for her to spend. I am married now because of obligation to my children. Once you're married and have children, they have you her slave forever."

"I feel that it has been necessary to compromise my values to insure financial support for my family. The biggest thing I had to give up was freedom in the type of work I wanted to do. But I love my children very, very much."

"I feel I gave up the best of my career to be a parent/husband. I didn't feel this until I got past my fortieth year. It was in that year that I felt angry and jealous."

"It's sort of a truism that when people don't see any hope of change, they adapt to their situation, but when they begin to see hope of change they get unhappy. That's about where I see women's lib now. Most of them are unattractive women, many are probably lesbians. (But I personally know a woman's libber who's married and attractive, who gets her women's lib point in as often as possible, but doesn't seem hostile.) I tokenly say my wife is for women's lib; she wants her freedom to do what she wants, which is definitely *not* work. She fulfills herself by some self-chosen enjoyable activitites. I think it's very important for a happy marriage for a woman to be fulfilled, however that's achieved, as long as she has time for love, and is interested in the husband's self-fulfillment. It's been observed lately that as women become freed of many home responsibilities (children grown), men still feel trapped in jobs that are no longer challenging. How about men's lib?"

"She gets pleasure out of spending money, discarding everything that is slightly used, keeping an ultra-tidy house, dressing fashionably. She is apathetic about sex, can't stand radio music, abhors nudity. These traits are all opposite to mine, so we try to concentrate on a few things on which we agree, and hang on to our marriage for God, country, and children."

In fact, many men felt that if their duty to the marriage was financial support, the woman's duty was to provide sex whenever requested, no matter what the state of the relationship; many men, as seen earlier, were very angry when this expectation was not met and therefore felt fully justified in having sex outside the marriage; they did not see this as a warning sign that they should work on the relationship. They were especially angry when women used sex to get "favors," etc., even if they themselves saw sex in economic terms, feeling they "deserved" sex if they paid the bills:

"I've been married since I was twenty (fourteen years). I like being married in a lot of ways. I enjoy the children, and love my wife when we get along. I enjoy doing things as a family. But the effect on sex isn't good. It seems like after you are married a while, the woman tends to use it as a lever. If you're a good boy you can have some tonight. If you're a bad boy—jack off for a week. Anyway, that's the way it's been with us. I know my wife really likes sex . . . but she doesn't show it or want me to get the idea that she needs it. Living together without the bond of marriage is most likely the best way to go. Then people (man or woman) wouldn't take each other for granted and know they have each other by the ass if one wants to leave. Especially if the man wants out. It is unfair. The woman has the upper hand in just about everything. It's no wonder men take off and never pay support. The woman on the other hand decides to go . . . What happens? She has an attorney kick your ass out of the house and the court awards her a grand a month on top of it."

"I have *never* met a woman who loved sex, simply and straightforwardly. Instead, sex seems to me to be, for most women, a way of manipulating men, getting them to do what they want, etc. This destroys the joy and goodness of sex, and makes it into something sad. I guess this was why I never felt bad going out on my wife. If I supported her and the kids, and then she wasn't even affectionate enough to want to have sex with me (at least more often than once every two weeks or so), then I had no obligation to her at all. I guess I felt totally justified in going out and having sex whenever I wanted to. I fulfilled my part of the marriage agreement, but she didn't fulfill hers."

And yet, if women do sometimes seek economic security in marriage, or use sex to gain "favors," how can they do otherwise, in a society in which they have been more or less forced to see marriage as their only means of financial security? How can they be blamed, since the society has forced them into this position by not giving them equal access to education or employment, and in fact, not paying them equally even for work equivalent to men's?*

One man explained these dynamics in his marriage:

"I am forty-one, recently separated from my wife. We have three children who share time between us. During my marriage, I clearly dominated my wife, even if I didn't want to. She was introverted and passive in many ways, although definitely not submissive. In fact, she was an extremely strong-minded and stubborn person, but in a passive way. It was difficult to find out *what* she wanted in different situations. I would take an initiative, and little by little she would clarify her position in a reaction to mine. Often her reaction would be negative—when it at long last came—and she gave me the feeling that I was consciously trying to dominate her. Of course, by being the one who most often *took* initiatives, that in itself—taking her passive attitude into consideration—became an act of domination.

"We often had conflicts about groceries. At certain times in our marriage, I was extremely busy, and shopping became her task. She would complain about pain in her arms from carrying groceries home. I asked her to give me a list of what was needed, and promised to do all the shopping on my way home from work. She could, however, never get around to writing such a list. Later she found out that the pain in her arms came from playing the piano.

* U.S. Census Bureau statistics for 1980 show that for every $1.00 a man makes, a woman makes $0.59 for the same work.

"During my marriage, I was the sole breadwinner most of the time, while my wife studied for her Ph.D. Since she worked at home a lot, responsibility for our children and our home fell more heavily on her than on me, even if I always have done a lot of housework, and have spent much time with the children. Somehow we never managed to cooperate on economic matters. Money was not talked about much, it was a far too conflict-laden topic. Consequently we never managed to save any money.

"I attempted many times to get my wife to share responsibility for our overall economy, but she refused to do that. Probably she felt it was too complicated. If I tried to regulate our spending, she would accuse me of dominating her.

"She also often said she felt it humiliating to have to use the money I earned on herself. In that relationship a lot of things could have been better if we both were earning money and were economically independent. When we decided to separate, I think money was her greatest worry.

"But generally I do not think economic imbalances per se *have* to affect relationships negatively—if the person earning the most does not use that position to force on the other person decisions and situations. Men seem, however, to have a strong tendency to do exactly that, as part of the traditional male role. Therefore financial independence on the part of women seems crucial if relationships are to function today."

Younger single men often made this same equation, expecting to provide an exchange of "dating" courtesies and payment of expenses for the woman's sexual favors or attention; they often felt that they were being shortchanged:

"I sometimes find myself becoming very bitter towards women. It seems like the more I give and the nicer and more considerate I try to be, the worse I get treated. I've spent a lot of time and money on some of them and received very little in return—and I don't just mean sex. Most women seem to think what they have is so valued that men only want that one thing. Women are brought up to believe that if they were to lay on the sidewalk and hike up their skirt, and spread their knees, men would line up to screw them. A lot of men aren't out just to 'get laid.' Incidentally, I've been picked up by women who just wanted sex, and afterwards just rolled over and went to sleep—I don't like it any more than a woman does. I don't like being just a cock—like women don't want to be just a cunt. But I won't stop trying to get along with women."

"Here is an example of the kind of resentment I have. I am in Austin. It is a strange city to me. The convention is about over. I have met an interesting woman. She lives here. We will have dinner. At dinner I suggest that we go drinking and dancing at a tavern she has mentioned several times that week. More for conversation than anything else I ask her how much drinks are there. She answers naively, 'I don't know.' She had never paid for even one drink! Needless to say, I paid for dinner."

"I sometimes joke to my close friends that all they have to do on dates is ride in the car, respond to conversation, enjoy the meal and show, and later, perhaps, just lay there and enjoy. Women are greatly pampered by the male populace in general."

In fact, when asked, "Have you ever had sex with a prostitute? How did you feel about paying for sex?" many men, shockingly, said, "You always pay anyway":

"I feel you pay for sex every time one way or another."

"I don't like to pay for sex, but sometimes it is cheaper than wining and dining a female with the anticipation. So you spend twenty or thirty dollars and then have sex, so what is the difference?"

"Women talk glibly about love, as if it were only within the woman's province. Hokum. I've reached the conclusion after all these years, men marry for love. Women marry for convenience—for a meal ticket. Starry-eyed females are a tremendous act, a rip-off. Women are devious and conniving. Men are pricks, but at least they are honest."

"I have had sex with a prostitute. I have no feeling about paying for sex. After all, marriage is a paying for sex by contract."

"A prostitute is a hell of a lot more honest than the domestic prostitutes that go under the label as wives, at least you get what you pay for."

"I feel a man is *always* paying for it one way or another."

"I have had sex with a number of prostitutes over the years. I have felt many times that there is little difference in paying a lady fifty dollars for sexual entertainment and spending fifty dollars on meals, etc., and then receiving sexual entertainment. One does it for a living and one for fun."

"I am a firm believer that all women, once they pass eighteen (some even before), are prostitutes at one time or another. All wives are prostitutes, that's for sure. Just let them want something that a man doesn't provide and see how soon the sex is cut off until they get their way."

"You pay for it one way or another—actually it's cheaper with a whore! Also she is a pro, doesn't play coy games, and no pretenses."

"I don't like paying for sex, but really what's the difference if a guy pays twenty-five or thirty dollars on a date, then 'maybe' has intercourse, or just picks up a prostitute off the street and pays her the same? Actually a person is money ahead with a whore."

"Paying for sex never made any difference to me. You pay for *all* of it."

Many men gave similar answers to the question "Did you ever feel a woman was having sex with you because of something you could give her—your prestige, position, or economic advantages?":

"I sure do, in fact in just about every relationship I try to fathom what the woman thinks I am going to do for her. At this point in my life I am well used to being used."

"After about two years of marriage, I came to realize that my wife had used sex for a home and security. We separated and I made up my mind it would never happen again."

"In my opinion a wife makes a so-called professional prostitute look like an amateur!"

"My first wife would say, 'If you do this or that (housework, or take her somewhere), I'll let you love me.' If I didn't, I just got horny. She used sex to get what she wanted. If we argued I was cut off for a week or so. She is no longer my wife."

"With my wife, I felt she only did it as payment for the security I supplied. It took a lot away from our relationship."

"Economic advantages are probably all I get laid for. I've never felt that a cunt has wanted just me, because eventually, they've all gotten too demanding. The status is having an old man, a car, a house, nice furnishings; but this is one old man that can't be manipulated into the rut that has destroyed so many."

"I have felt a woman has had sex with me because of what she thought I could give her—and I resented being like a piece of meat or a land deal, so many dollars per square foot, and bought and sold—also it cheapened the woman."

"Sometimes I have felt this way, and wondered if it was true or just my imagination. It does piss me off that women bitch about being used, but at the same time acknowledge that their man is also their meal ticket."

"My wife. All I meant to her was security and an anchor to hold on to. It has to be the biggest turn-off. I want her to want me for myself."

"During the whole dating game, with a lot of heavy petting stopping just short of sex, I was very, very sensitive to cock-teasing women, who were playing everything but the last giving of sex, because of prestige, position, economics, marriage, or something like that. That's been a heavy, sometimes very bitter feeling. Women in my experience, as I was growing up, submitted to sex because that was the way that you got what you needed—money, prestige, whatever else— and this I found very demeaning *to men*—quite aside from the women's side of it. (There's no question as to the oppression of women in that regard at the hands of men.)"

"A man is kidding himself in his relationships if he thinks he is getting something for nothing—in the end the man *is* paying for something: namely, her sweet ass—because of other financial particulars spent during the course of the relationship! Any man who thinks otherwise is a complete unadulterated fool!"

"Don't we pay for our sex in varying ways almost all of the time? Where a man is 'animally' attracted to a 'pussy,' the woman looks for more than just the act, she looks for image building (vanity), home and security, an ego trip (making him jump through a hoop), political, economic, or social advantages, or revenge on another woman or man/husband. Many of the women I have really talked to can't have sex just because they like to be fucked by some good-looking stud, they *must* have another reason (rationalization): 'I *love* him,' 'He's rich,' 'He's famous,' 'He's a good catch.' How wonderful it will be when women's lib is here and society will allow all women (not just the thinking-liberated few) to pursue sex for what it should be in most cases . . . fun!* Good 'clean,' non-game-playing, non-manipulative, open, spontaneous, and free sex."

* This is a confusion of the "sexual revolution" with the women's movement.

"I am a twenty-nine-year-old, single, black male. The product of professional parents, I was educated in public schools until college. I pursued and completed both my B.A. and M.D. degrees—an Ivy League nigger. I am currently involved in the practice of gynecology and family medicine. No doubt, an eligible black physician would be quite a catch, but I can honestly say (naïveté aside) that I have never gone to bed with someone who had dollar signs in her eyes, that I was aware of. Though I regard myself somewhat as a commodity, when it gets down to the crux of things, I do not like appraisal."

"I have had sex with people where we 'wanted' something from each other besides sex—affection, intellectual stimulation, insights into feelings, admiration, attention. I think there's a prostitution going on in these cases where you attempt to possess a person by trading a commodity (money, dinner, social favors) or accepting one. It's the old slave trade, and the recurrent lesson is: it doesn't work. You can't possess or be possessed. Sex gets political when it is used as a bargaining tool, is not an expression of spiritual caring freely given and shared."

*But one man thought it was his own fear of being "used,"
rather than a real situation he had encountered with a
woman, that caused these feelings:*

"I have felt many times that a particular woman had some sort of ulterior motives; something that she wanted to get that I could give. When I've investigated these feelings, they have usually proceeded much more from my private paranoia than from the woman herself. I've discovered that I have some profound fears of being taken advantage of by a woman, or by a man. These fears are expressive of my distrust in loving others. I also resent the constricting role of supporting a woman at least as much as many women resent being dependent on a man for income. It's often a bummer both ways. No woman or man, however, has ever demanded or even suggested seriously that I support them. I feel like I'm working with largely unconscious fears which need to be revealed—reality has helped me a lot. I am exploring these fears as destructive forces in myself so as to acknowledge them and transform them into a more loving energy, rather than fear my feelings and overreact with self-anger, projected anger, disappointment, and self-righteousness."

Many of these men said that they now insisted on sharing the expenses:

"The women's movement has affected my relationships by making me feel that a woman should share some of the expenses, the responsibility, and the initiative. Most of them depart quickly when these expectations become known."

"I think I am probably a combination of liberated man and MCP. One of the things I like about my current relationship is that she knows she is equal to me emotionally, intellectually, etc., and I know it. But we also insist that we go dutch. (I believe a woman should want to go out with me, not because she's getting a free meal, or a movie, etc.) But occasionally I take her to dinner, bring her flowers, and things like that. I am not intimidated by the fact that she has been to bed with a lot of men or that she has a master's degree in psychology. I like someone I can teach and learn from, and joke around with."

However, to achieve perfect equity, perhaps these expenses should be shared in proportion to the income each receives, since most women still make much less than men.

And one man said:

"I often distrust women. I think maybe they just want me to support them, etc. I think it is extremely important that a woman have her own means of support so that she and her partner know that she is economically independent. I have discussed this with my younger sister because I feel she ought to keep that as a consideration in her own life. Also, I have decided that I should encourage my own partner (whoever she may be) to build and maintain her own career. If she did, I think there would be very little chance that she would have sex with me for any reason other than love, or that I would feel beholden to her if I didn't love her."

On the other hand, a minority of men said they felt just the opposite, and disliked women who were not dependent:

"My personal preference concerning women that I would like to make a permanent bond with runs toward what I call femininity, even though when I was called upon to describe my definition of femininity, I failed. Yet I still think of a woman in my arms that is dependent on me for numerous things that have been traditionally expected of the male partner. However, I will never again say to a girl that she should stay home, even if youngsters are involved. I don't believe in mothers leaving the raising of their kids to others, but my own marriage was to a girl that was far more comfortable out in society than she was when confined to home. Unfortunately it was only after she passed away that I realized that I was a stifling influence in her life. Her talents were immense but not fully developed, partly because I showed a preference for her to be at home. I have had the opposite experience wherein the girl wanted no other influences in her life besides my own, and that situation, while it lasted, was far preferable to me. That is what I would prefer again, if I ever again find myself acceptable to that kind of woman."

"I think the woman should be paid the same as any man, she should have the same rights he does, but the woman should always try to be feminine—even though she can do the job or fix a lot of things. She should always call in the man to do the job for her so he won't feel the woman is superior to him. This is the trouble with a lot of marriages, maybe he's got a job that's making less money and she's making more than he is. That gives him a bad feeling, that she's superior over him, so then when there's anything to be fixed around the house, she goes ahead and fixes it, instead of calling on him to do it, then she's superior over him there in the home too, and he gets the feeling that what the heck, this woman don't need me, what the heck am I married to her for. I'll go divorce her and go marry someone that I can wait on—I want a woman that's—a woman. The man gets to feeling after a while that a woman's superior over him, that they're equal, and a man don't like this."

A surprising number of men prophesied that women would not have the courage to stand on their own when times got rough (perhaps hoping that this would be so):

"I think that many of the women in the movement are there with the good intentions of standing up and holding their own in our male-oriented society, but they are failing. They are trying to play the game from both sides. When things are going good for them, they are good little libbers doing everything for the movement, practicing all the principles and really making a good show of it. But when times start to get tough, women's liberation will be the first thing that gets forgotten about. In rough times, many women will forget about standing up on their own and taking the lumps that are coming, and fall two steps behind their man, who will take care of everything for them—they fall back into the woman's role and coast along. Most women don't have the guts to really stand on their own, through thick and thin. The women who do stand up deserve all the respect and equality they are asking for."

"My wife is a 'liberated' woman and believes very much in the cause of women's liberation. But in my opinion, there's one area women are making a very serious mistake—and that is—they want their cake and eat it, too. They want the 'freedom' to pursue whatever career they want—whatever activity they find intellectually or spiritually challenging—the freedom to work in a job up to their potential. I agree that they should have all of those things. *But—men do not have them and never will. Men have to work whether they want to or not. They cannot learn a skill or profession and then when they get tired of it, just quit—they have to continue for all their lives.*

"But women want it both ways—when they find out that the real world of work is actually a bore after a while, they want to quit, return to the home—learn something else —do something else. *But men cannot do that.* And men are going to resent it more and more. And men *do* control most of the jobs, etc., in our world and *they are not stupid.* When they see the trend going too far they will, in my opinion, *overreact*—and women are not going to like what happens. In other words, the women's movement must be *very* careful not to overstate their case—some way or another they *must* face up to the fact that they *cannot have their cake and eat it, too.* Men can't, and they won't let women do it either.

"*True* education of women would involve letting them know just how difficult it is out there earning a living every year, and if they want those jobs, *then they should be willing to make a lifetime commitment* to them, just as men have always had to do. Anything short of that is pure fraud—and men will react, or more seriously, 'overreact,' and that'll be the end of a lot for both sexes. We love women, and want women to love us, too—but it doesn't work to have *either* sex feeling like they got shortchanged."

And there was some all-encompassing anger. Many men seemed to feel that they would get shortchanged with women no matter whether women were more independent or less independent: they would never be loving enough to men, who need them so desperately:

"What I cannot stand are the mugwumps who like talking about their liberated life styles but fall back on their sugar daddies for little goodies, fall back on sex manipulation to accomplish their ends, and most of all, who decide the best way to deal with roles is to shut men out of their personal lives for good."

But since the society has kept women economically, socially, and even emotionally dependent on men, is it any wonder that men feel "trapped" in marriage, unfree? And yet, most men did not explicitly connect problems with the social and legal role assigned women (or their own role as "caretaker") and their own feeling of lack of satisfaction in marriage, or suffocation. Most seemed to feel that their own wife as an individual was being unreasonable and making too many demands—and that she was not responding with a sufficient amount of affection (gratitude?) by participating in more frequent or "freer" sex. She was not being "giving" enough. Thus, men felt perfectly justified in going outside the marriage for sex and pleasure, since they felt they were being cheated inside the marriage.

However—even though most men did not connect society's assigning women a second-class or dependent role with their own feelings of dissatisfaction, accompanied by their endless search for a gratifying "sexual" relationship with a woman— a majority did recognize the bad effect that being supported or dependent could have on one's spirit.* When asked, "Do you envy women the choice of having someone support them, or the seeming lack of pressure on them to make money?" almost no men said they envied women, and most stated strongly that they would not like to be supported by someone else:

"I don't envy women's option to have someone support them. It is not a very nice option to become economically

* This is not to say that some men or women would not enjoy working in the home while their spouse "supported" them; rather that when this position is not taken by choice, or agreed to by choice, on the part of either the one supported or the one doing the supporting, it can be negative.

dependent on someone else. Also working is probably more fun than staying home, and taking care of a home is certainly work."

"Financial support doesn't interest me, because I value my independence too highly. These choices and lack of pressure only exist through marriage—or, less respectably, 'mistress-hood'?—what a rotten reason to assume the pressures of marriage!"

"No. I couldn't stand to have someone support *me*."

"If a man could take the letdown in his pride, he probably could find a few women to support him, but I know I would not like such a life. Neither would my girlfriend, which is one of the things I like about her."

"Rather than envy a woman's choice to have someone support them, I pity and sometimes get angry with their lack of independence."

"I enjoy supporting my family and I am proud of being able to make enough money to do so. I don't want to be supported."

"I do not envy women. Women work for their husbands, they just don't get paid."

"I don't envy their being supported, as they work hard as housewives or in the job market anyway."

"No. I am my own person and don't think I could ever put up with having to 'answer' to someone who was supporting me."

"I don't envy women or men who have no pressure to make money, because I think that is the worst kind of boredom there is, and to fight and conquer this is an admirable thing."

"No. Most women work very hard for the support they get—work I wouldn't like to do (housework, child-rearing responsibility, and having to accept the hegemony of the man in the house)."

Only a few men envied women for being supported—usually presenting unrealistic stereotypes of the nature of home-making, etc.:

"Sometimes I imagine what it would be like to be in the role of homemaker and have a woman support me. I could whisk through the housework in a couple of hours after I saw my wife off to work, and then have the rest of the day for myself. I could run and lift weights again, and get into really great shape. I could go to school for a couple of hours every day. It would be great! But the way things are nowadays I think there is pressure on everyone to make as much money as he or she can. I know when I get married, my wife will have to share the monetary burden, and I will have to be willing to do my share of the household upkeep."

"I feel if I had been a woman I would be happier because I could be lazy and satisfied and dominated and pampered too."

"It must be nice to be *kept.*"

"Yes, I envy the role of dependence that women have. I wonder what I might feel by being dependent and not having to be judged by how much money I earned."

"I envy their lack of pressure to make money. I would love to have someone support me for a while."

Some had begun to realize the difficulties of a financially dependent role:

"I used to envy women the advantages of their 'role' until I learned the price they paid for these seeming advantages. I still envy anyone the ability to cry, something I unlearned in my early teens."

"I used to envy their ability to choose to be supported, but now I recognize the trap of not being financially independent."

"I used to, but today most of my women friends have the same financial pressure on them as men."

"I used to envy women for 'not having to work,' but am aware they increasingly are forced financially to do some work away from the home, and that housework itself is pretty grueling. I suspect some unconscious resentment toward women exists."

Conclusion

The inequalities between men and women's traditional roles have placed a tremendous burden on relationships between men and women, often creating an adversary, distrusting situation. If individuals were free to choose their role in a relationship, to create new types of relationships with each other, and especially more equal relationships, there would be less need for distrust and more mutual respect and communication possible.

Unfortunately, our society has kept women in a second-class position, economically and socially, and so most women remain dependent on men.* Traditionally, a woman with children had to depend on the good will of her husband for her and her children's support. This may have created a subtle pressure on her to fear her husband, and to cater to his wishes, no matter what her own feelings—thus inhibiting a free and spontaneous relationship between equals. This pressure has also in many cases kept women from telling men about their need for clitoral stimulation, or their type of masturbation to orgasm, as discussed in the chapter "Sexual Slavery" in *The Hite Report* on women.

Clearly, men have cause to be insecure about women's motives in loving them in a society in which women are dependent on men's good will and financial support for survival. Thus, keeping women economically dependent places men in a position in which they may sometimes wonder if they are loved for themselves or because they are, as one man put it, "a meal ticket." This is a tragic consequence of the system as we have known it—both women and men have had, in many ways, to distrust each other, and this distrust can permeate even deep and committed relationships.

ARE THINGS CHANGING? DO MEN WANT TO REDEFINE THEIR RELATIONSHIPS WITH WOMEN?

Many men did not see the relevance to them of the women's movement; they did not see the connection between their own feelings of being trapped and alienated—in their

* According to U.S. Bureau of Labor statistics, women in 1980 still earned only 59 percent of what men earn for the same work.

role in marriage, in their jobs, in their lifestyle, their lack of closeness—and the critique of society and relationships which the women's movement poses, the suggestions the women's movement has made for improving things. Many men tended to see the women's movement more as "women complaining, raising a ruckus" than understanding how both men and women, working to change and restructure their relationships (and the family) could make increased happiness for both. In fact, many men were angry that now women might be "getting ahead," because their own lives had often left them feeling unappreciated, unsatisfied, angry, and stifled.

WHAT DO MEN THINK OF WOMEN'S LIBERATION?

"I think women's liberation is great. It has not affected any of my relationships."

"A man and woman can't live and love each other as husband and wife unless the man is the head of the house and the wife considers her husband as the master over her in everything."

"I can't respect women, because why did they *let* themselves be subjugated, owned, and ruled?"

"I think it's important to mention the guilt I sometimes feel very acutely when I realize the privileges I enjoy as opposed to what the majority of women enjoy. I think of all the hidden ways that this privilege is handed to me by the culture in which I live, and the ways women are shortchanged of those same privileges. It makes me uncomfortable to be given extra points for being a white, middle-class male with an education, but the ingredient that provides the most credence in this society is gender."

Many of the answers to the question, "What do you think about women's liberation?" brought out a huge amount of anger at women, or anger with men's own situation, their own role in society and tremendous lack of fulfillment. Many men felt that now, with the women's movement and the emphasis on women achieving more independence and equality, they were being falsely maligned and misunderstood:

"All I ever hear about these days is how brutal men are, how women are always getting fucked over by men, and how the sisterhood is gonna go it alone. Well, men get the same kind of shit, and I do not like being put in a category. I'm no better or no worse than anyone else, regardless of gender. Just like a woman, I want to be loved and give love in return."

"There seems to be a growing stereotype of what bastards men are. Although I suppose some do live up to this stereotype, I know many men who don't (including, I believe, myself). I don't like this trend and find it similar to the black backlash against all whites once they achieved greater control over their lives . . . alienating even those whites who had fought alongside them for equal opportunities, etc. Some men are stronger feminists than many women. Why condemn all of us? Society has dictated not only to women the roles they should play but also to men. Men have been stereotyped and enslaved into following traditional approaches to life just as much as women, and the more moderate feminists are willing to accept this and seem to be turning towards a cooperation with men in changing society."

"*All* males do not oppress *all* females. I feel that females are probably as often responsible for bad relationships as are males. I may not have the natural talent or the physical endowment to make me a great lover, but I will try with all my effort to sexually please any female I go to bed with, and keep trying, as long as she gives me the opportunity, to please her. It seems to me, however, that most women would rather go with the good-looking, rich, super-stud types who drive Porsches or Corvettes. I guess it is assumed that anyone like that can get a woman off with a wave of his giant prick or a touch of his talented finger."

"I think that men are being overlooked these days. The women's movement may be very necessary, and liberating to men as much as to women, but the focus today is very much on women. Men are being 'blamed' for a lot of the trouble women have had sexually. But I don't think that we are directly at fault for this; the stereotypes and role models we were conditioned to follow from birth are more at fault. It's going to be hard for men to overcome their machoism, because we are conditioned to be tough, unfeeling . . . big boys don't cry . . . if you cry, you're a sissy . . . men don't touch each other. In order for any 'minority' to overcome its oppression, it has got to find a common cause, a common 'enemy,' something that it can identify with. For women, we men have become the scapegoat. It's true that many of the things that have kept women down are the attitudes of men. In jobs and sex, everything women do is supposed to be less than what men do. Women have been considered inferior, so it's no wonder that they are bitter towards men. I would be too. But what we must realize is that we all have been put through the same bullshit, and that men have got a lot of 'unconditioning,' unlearning to do. It's easier for a woman to get fed up and let her emotions fly because she's always had permission to be angry, to get upset, to cry. Men are conditioned to hold things back, to be cool, not to get upset, to be logical. Have you ever tried being logical about an emotional trauma? It's ridiculous."

"What American men need in the way of liberation is not from the macho syndrome, but from the stereotype of the sweet bungler, saved by or bossed about by a clever woman—like Dagwood, Jiggs, or the silly Darrin in 'Bewitched.' "

"I'd like to say that men have recently been put down. The media, the porno rags, TV, and everything have served to give men the image of being inhuman, self-serving, self-indulgent slobs who don't have any decent bones in their bodies. I can't believe this is true. Men are as stereotyped as women, if not more so. Everybody's brainwashed. I think the answer to this is obvious. Why not follow your heart? I really don't think we're monsters, and I don't like being thought of as a monster."

Many men were very confused about the meaning of the women's movement and gave contradictory answers:

"I hate militant women. I hate women who do not recognize the differences between men and women. I hate women who maintain there is no need of the male sex. I hate women who in the name of former repression are exclusionary and even more repressive than any man I know ever was. I find affirmative action non-affirmative. I don't like the things that women's lib has brought into our lives, that is no different than the mind benders of oppressive, dictatorial societies. I believe women's lib is capable of being the new tyranny. But I like strong women. I like tall women. I like women who are fashionable. I like most women. I like women who can do things with their hands. I like women with stamina. I dislike women who play on the weak side of their femininity. I dislike 'dumb blondes.' I dislike women who swear worse than sailors. I dislike women who want to be men and always dress as men. Women contribute motherhood, vast intelligence, the softening of civilization. And, when women don't put the check on the grossness of living, the civilization will crumble. For example, I do believe men should drop their barroom language around women. I believe men *should* open doors. Men *should* protect women, not for their egos, but to soften the brute in them so we are not on the level of the beasts. Yet, I don't see women as chattel or less and inferior. I see them as superior and important. I do believe we must protect motherhood. I believe in the family and the gentle/strong role mothers play in bringing up children. But this does not preclude or excuse the father from participating in the family. I believe women belong in the business world because of the changes in our society, and the business world is better for it."

"My age is forty-one, master welder, white, my background is that I have always worked hard to help this country and was damn proud of it. I think every woman has every right as men do. I say let all women have their freedom. I grew up and was always taught that all women were good to have sex, cook, clean up, and raise children. And women have every right to be gentle or emotional. The reason I say this is that you have to treat women with respect and kindness and love and if you don't, you don't get anything from them. I think that a man that has done a woman wrong, he should have to support them. I support anything a woman does in trying to support herself. I think a woman has just as much knowledge as any man and can work just as hard. I have felt guilty for a lot of ways that I have behaved. Like getting drunk or embarrassing them. I admire women in every way that you can think of, I don't think I dislike women. Women do contribute more to society than men do. My wife can be a lot of fun if only she would not sleep all the time. She can be sweet when she wants to and that is very often."

A large number of those who answered confused the women's movement and "sexual freedom," or the sexual revolution:

"I like the part of women's lib that says *yes* to sex more frequently."

"Women's liberation is a personal preference for each woman. If being liberated is what she wants, it's her option to have as many or as few lovers as she wants."

"It's good. Women should be entitled to sex as freely as men."

"I have yet to meet and be involved with my concept of the truly liberated woman, who could just as soon pick me up and take me home as I could her, who would be just as active, inventive, and energetic in bed as I am, who has overcome her penis envy (no pun intended). Rhetoric in a studio and marching in demonstrations is a good start, but when I find a woman who has forsaken chivalrous chauvinism and is just a purely human lover, I will be happy with the liberated status of women."

"I'm for liberation, after all we are all humans even if of a different sex. I think it could make for a better sex life for all if a girl felt she was free to make a pass and not feel someone would think she was fast as well as being better in other ways as well."

"I wonder if there really is such a thing as women's liberation or does a few think there is. If sex with every Tom, Dick, or Harry is women's revolution, they have missed the boat. It appears that men gained more sexwise than women."

"I'm for women's liberation. However, practically, I still have a hard time convincing some women that it's O.K. to call me, to ask me for a date, or to offer to pay (or go 'dutch')."

"Everyone's talking about women's liberation, but it seems men have never been liberated from the sexual deprivation, the role playing, lying, and cheating necessary to obtain the most minimal satisfaction. I think much of this comes from a lack of understanding on the part of women. If I could address the women of the world, I'd say this: 'We don't want to hold you down, rip you off, or make your lives miserable. We want to enjoy you, make you happy, and be made happy by you. You complain that we are dishonest and profess love when sex is what we're after. Give us a choice. Accept us and yourselves for the sexual beings we all are. And enjoy sex for the wonderful experience it is.' "

"Unfortunately, even *with* women's lib, I've usually had to initiate all sexual response. *Even with the girl* I'm having a relationship now with, even though she is a sex 'freak,' I've still got to initiate response! It's amazing, and it's depressing. How do I feel about it? I hate it, but as much as I rail against it, nothing ever changes. If I desire a sexual contact, I'd damn well best initiate it, or we'll both wind up with cobwebs in our crotches. It is an axiom that no woman will initiate sexual contact, for fear of being cast as low, wicked, bad, harlotous, etc., etc. If sexual response has begun, and I'm turned down, then my response is hurt; massive hurt, leading to intense nervous anger."

"Women are too liberated. I want romance back, and more love."

Several pointed out that they thought women would always remain "sex objects" anyway:

"Women's lib can't make a woman less soft, curvaceous, and desirous to the male. So why try? Any more than a man can prevent a beard growing on his face and chest and having coarser features and bony muscular frames!"

"I think women's lib is great in a lot of ways—especially in cases of inequity regarding jobs, credit, and housing, I'm all for it. But I don't think they will ever get away from men naturally being the 'hunter' and women the 'hunted.' "

A few men insisted that there is no oppression of women in society; individual women themselves are to blame:

"Women have had their rights for a long time, but failed to exert these rights. What they do with them is up to them."

"Liberation from what? I never knew they were enslaved."

"Women's liberation is an individual accomplishment. Legislation can assist but it can never attain it."

"Freedom depends on the extent to which an individual person chooses to exercise it. Liberation movements are a bunch of shit. To immerse oneself in a movement is to sacrifice one's liberty."

"Women control 53 percent of the vote and almost every major corporation in the U.S., they can make things change if they want to. But, apparently, the majority of women don't feel like it because they sure aren't organizing, or doing anything noticeably at all."

And a handful of men said they were not interested in the issue:

"I don't think about it. It is a problem women must resolve. It has no effect on me."

Very few men seemed to have done any reading or real studying of what the women's movement was saying; this was one of the few answers of its kind:

"I have different feelings about it at different times. I used to spend every Sunday night listening to the radical left of women's rights on the radio. It was very interesting and at times very informative."

Many answers seemed to imply that the women's movement is merely something having to do with women's "self-esteem," rather than being a fundamental critique of the society and both men's and women's roles in it, suggesting and looking for new ways to live—and therefore something to which men must address themselves directly, as it involves a basic readjustment in "their" world:

"The 'movement' has not affected my relationships because the women I like do things as individuals, not as part of movements. However, if some subtle change in the general atmosphere has helped them to reach a more open state, that's good. Most, though, still want the man to take the initiative in the early stages of dating and sex. So it has not changed my relationships."

"I feel that it has helped my wife."

"Women's liberation provides a medium of support for women who can't otherwise feel good about their womanhood. As such it has its benefits to our society."

A minority of men, still misunderstanding it, said they were totally against women's liberation:

"It stinks. Women should be feminine, but with equal rights. American women should make men feel like men, not competitors."

"I believe men and women are not equal. They each have their own jobs in life. Let me explain. First of all, a woman can have a child, a man cannot. He doesn't even have to be there for conception. A sperm bank can do that. A woman's skeleton matures faster than a man's. Women have faster reaction times in general. The list is endless in comparing men and women. They were each put on this earth with all their differences. However, if men and women stopped competing with each other it would be a better world."

"It made women feel like they can do it all, as if they don't need men to keep up a house. I think being pregnant should be the woman's natural desire."

"I think it's the worst thing that ever happened to women and their relationships with men."

"Ridiculous."

"I don't like it. The vital role women play as mothers who mold the future generation has been deemphasized. We are on a self-destruction course. If you think we have a lot of crazies now—you ain't seen nothing. Day care centers are sadly run by people who raise children as a business. The children are second-class children, they are entitled to more. Up with Mother Power. It's all marketing and media hype. If some women want to work in this cold, often boring life outside the home, fine. But never degrade the role of the mother. Also, some women are getting socially aggressive. I'm flattered and respond—but if they didn't make advances to me I probably wouldn't go after them, therefore after the initial thrill is over I dump them, and I got a depressed liberated broad to deal with."

"Women just need to sound off. The greatest people alive have been men, including Jesus Christ Himself. *No woman has yet lived* and been great enough to be the Daughter of God! Print it."

"A farcical gyration of dykes. It has afforded me many laughs."

"I think women's lib is bull crap. My wife and daughters are caught up in it. They want the best of both world's. It's causing tension between my wife and myself. She announced that she is resigning the job of housewife. I told her that she can't resign until she finds me a proper replacement."

"I detest the philosophy that men and women are equal. Women have something which is extremely desirable to men, which they can and do use to get what they want and/or need. If the female so desires, she can offer and give something which the male is not capable of. Even without the sex, women are prettier and nicer to have around them than men."

"Women's liberation is exploited by the Communists to undermine our country and its basic values. Although I believe women should be afforded the same opportunities as men and treated in a sense like men, but also in certain cases treated like ladies, I also believe a woman should continue her obligations as a woman—to rear children and to do the things expected of a woman around the house."

But the largest number of men said they were "in favor of women's liberation, BUT"; these answers also continued to misunderstand the ideas of the women's movement in the most fundamental ways, or frequently to give a very shallow interpretation to the women's movement:

"Women need equal rights but not as a man."

"It's O.K. but I wouldn't want a woman for a boss."

"It is righting some wrongs, but also causing disruptions in established patterns which have been beneficial to society."

"Women's liberation is a just cause when it pursues equality of opportunity in life, and the desire to be judged as a person first, not on a prejudicial basis. But the women's movement is unjust when it chooses anti-male attitudes instead of the pursuit of justice. Anti-male is no better than anti-female."

"I'm in favor of it when it comes to getting rid of discrimination, but it's overblown. Women have always been able to get what they want."

"I think that women's liberation is good and healthy, but there has been some backlash and reversal of roles, so that women, in action if not vocally, say, 'O.K., I'm wearing the pants now; you grovel.' Any slaves are bound to take some revenge when they have overcome the odds; it's human nature, but it's not pleasant for me as a man."

"I am all for women being equal, but nothing they or I can do will change biological differences. It is wrong when women 'want to be men,' and I feel sorry for those who do. The world would be a miserable place if most men and women were not happy to be what they are. But basically I am open-minded and want to be fair, so I can't say I'm against women's liberation, but women's liberation turns me off when it becomes hatred of things masculine."

"I am grateful for their telling me how I've unthinkingly been insensitive to women's needs. They've made me aware of my own inflated male ego, which has caused me to make an ass of myself more than once. But I happen to be fairly handsome and have been used as a sex object on a number of occasions, so I get sick of hearing that 'women are treated as sex objects.' That whole game is a *two-way* street. I'm also turned off by all the unthinking propaganda. I also don't like it when women close their own eyes to their own nagging, bitchiness, hypocrisy, cheating, castration complexes, superficiality, etc."

"I welcome it except as it is manifested by the lunatic fringe of women who are using the movement as a vehicle for venting all the ire and frustrations of their lives, and using me as their whipping boy."

"Any kind of liberation is good; however, large segments of the women's movement have nothing to do with liberation but are concerned with juggling statuses within a system which will not permit an overall net gain in freedom."

"Now you are going to see just how much of a chauvinist I really am. I think the women's liberation movement has many good and worthwhile points like equal pay for equal work and abortion on demand (in moderation, not as a form of birth control). But there are some points brought up by the movement that I think are pretty stupid, like the exploitation of the female body *(Playboy)*. Exploitation to me means taking something and giving nothing. Those women are paid pretty well for disrobing, and nobody is forcing them to do it, it is her choice. All in all the principles of the movement are good, women standing on their own two feet and being given credit for it. The principles are good but I don't think women are up to it yet."

"I am 100 percent in accord that women should be paid the same wages for same performance, but I also believe that there are many things men can do better than women, and women in other countries love to have their men do them. Women say that they are liberated here! That's a joke! They are completely unfeminine, competing with their men to down them whenever possible, and then they complain that American men prefer to marry women from Latin America, the Orient, etc., because they are more loving and caring. I love to make a woman feel like a woman, and I want her to make me feel like a man, regardless of whether this is a one-night stand or a lasting affair or marriage. I envy the Islamic people and the Mormons who were able to have several wives."

"I like it, but let's face it, we are not equal. I'm not saying men are superior, it's just that we are all superior in different ways, and to try to make us equal is a farce. I like for women to get equal pay for equal work, and for them to be able to do any kind of work they want to, but I'd hate to see them in combat, or doing extremely dangerous stuff like that. We need our women, they help carry the species. One man can supply millions of sperms, but a woman has only thirty years or so of childbearing potential. So women are important and should be taken care of for that reason. Right on to the feminists—but don't try to castrate me (my hormones make me act this way, you know)."

"Part of it's all right, but it's being overdone and there's too much lesbianism and pathological man-hate connected with it. It is also leading to too much anti-maternalism. And it is castrating too many men."

"I'm all for ERA, for complete equality of opportunity for women, and I deplore the discrimination to which women have been subjected in our society. But at the same time I don't like to see women 'liberated' to become the slaves of the illusions, social pressures, role playing, and game playing that corrupt me."

"I have supported women's liberation all the way as a voter, as a teacher, and in my own home. I strongly believe in equal career opportunity, equal pay, equal political power, and equal participation in all aspects of society. But I part company with the women's movement over its tendency to want men and women to be *alike*. Equal, yes—alike, no. Perhaps the main reason I like sex with women is that they are not men—they are different. They are not inferior, only different. If men and women became alike, if Yin and Yang were homogenized into a gray featureless paste, much of life's meaning would be lost for me. I would hate a society where women tried to be tough and ruthless, and relied entirely on electric vibrators and lesbian relationships to satisfy their genitally dominated sex needs, and where men adopted a non-orgasmic pseudo-feminine role in their relations with women. When men lose their assertiveness and will to dominance, they seem to lose whatever it was that made them attractive to women. I think this kind of thing has already gone too far. Let's get back to basics, like economic and political equality, better jobs, day care centers, and better medical treatment. There I can support the movement all the way."

"I approve of the concept of women's liberation. I truly believe a lot of women have been literally cheated out of a full life due to traditional, backward views of what a 'woman's role' is in life. There is one thing, however, that I notice. A lot of women seem to be going at women's liberation with a belligerent attitude. Women I have known well enough to call 'my lovers' have told me such things as 'I don't want to be liberated. I like being a woman. I like for you to hold the car door for me. I like for a man to pick up the check. I'm getting as much as the guy sitting next to me at the office.' My women have always been very feminine, loving, caring people, and that is why I have loved them. But if women want to be liberated, I'm all for it; they have that right."

"I was brought up in the traditional 'woman's place is in the home—wife and mother' atmosphere. While I don't think this is necessary anymore, I tend in that direction. I have nothing against women working, my bosses for the past few years have been women, but I like women to be women. Still dress like them and be feminine. I enjoy being a gentleman—holding doors, helping with coats, etc. It's the way I was brought up. I may be gay but I'm still male and I still expect men to be gentlemen and women to be ladies."

"I feel a woman has a right to hold down any kind of job she wants, but always be the feminine woman and let the man feel that he's superior to her—even though she may know how to do the job as well as he does. Women's lib has put a bad label on sex life and on men's lives too. A woman asks too many questions, she wants to know why, she asks a thousand questions. If you used to call her darling or honey, she'll ask you why you callin' her honey and go into every little thing that you say and break it into a million pieces. A man don't like this. A man wants to feel superior and masculine around a woman. But in a women's lib, they give a man the feeling that they're superior to the man—the woman becomes masculine and a lot of men don't go for it—the—don't like the women's lib. They don't like the women that belong to the women's lib."

Two radically oriented men also had a "but":

"As a social force it has great potential for fundamental change. But, while widespread consciousness raising has gone on, most of the benefits have accrued to middle- and upper-class white women (i.e., the bourgeoisie) to the exclusion of working-class white women and racial minorities. I support lesbians and women-controlled (corollary of worker-controlled) work spaces, and while I see separatism as physically and psychically often necessary, in the long run it is self-defeating and alienating to other people. At the end of the road (wherever that is), I'd like to see a humanistic, integrated (non-alienated), socialistic, possibly matriarchal society, and think that women's liberation can possibly show the way."

"Of course I am for the women's movement. However,

I think many employers discriminate against women not because they want to keep women down, but simply because they don't want to give expensive training to staff who will leave. So it's up to women to show that they are responsible employees. I don't think women should expect all the maternity grants and maternity leave immediately on joining a firm. This follows my general view that women should not just drop babies whenever and wherever they like, but have some regard for the rest of society. Including the male part of society. It's easy to cloud the issue by talking of women being forced to 'mold their lives to the needs of Big Business.' However, I would think that a workers' cooperative would also want its workers to be reliable in this way."

Some men said women's lib was acceptable if women did not become superior or get privileged treatment; many felt angrily that women were getting ahead of them or that women were getting more than they were (especially economically) since the women's movement began:

"I think this women's lib thing is good. But it is going too fast for most men to adjust to. It becomes very confusing at times because it is so hard to understand a woman's way of thinking. They want to be free and liberated, but they also want to be protected and taken care of. I see so many of my friends' marriages going down the drain because of the jobs their wives have. Some women can't cope with this newfound freedom with high-paying jobs. This is why I am against ERA. Basically I think it's a good thing, but today it's too much too fast. Also, women's lib is really threatening to a man. It presents a real threat to jobs for men who want to support their wives and children. I know it sounds corny but we really think this way."

"Women's liberation is O.K. with me, as long as that's *really* what it is! My general attitude towards women in business and/or pleasure is: *Equal pay and privileges for equal work and responsibilities!!* Anybody who shares this with me gets my vote, but—by God—it had better be *real!* When the ceiling is coming down and doom approaches, if *I* have to stay in it, *then so do all the equal-pay broads!* I don't want to have to listen to a lot of excuses like: 'My period is giving me cramps' (she seemed fine up to now), 'I have to pick up my kids' (even though her kids don't even want to leave what they're doing *anyway*), *or the best of them all:* 'It's not a woman's job; it's a *man's* job.' (Who-ee! What a rip-off.) I can sum this up crudely: 'Shit or get off the goddamned pot!' If *any* female, young or old, gets paid like me to do the job like me, and she *does it*, then *by damn* she can stay! One more item: I have heard so much *crap* coming out of the liberationists' mouth about the 'degradation' of women by *men* that I am sick of it! I agree with it, but *why* does any human being degrade another? It's just plain old *fear* stemming from massive inferiority complex on the parts of males. Personally, I feel like a drone bee in a giant beehive."

"I am against all the publicity and the way the pendulum has swung to favor them in an effort to show no prejudice."

"I believe in equal rights for women, but something has happened to the women. Unfortunately, they tend to use women's lib for their own purposes instead of working with it for the good of all. (Despite ideas to the contrary, it's very hard for a young, single man with no connections and little money to make it by himself in this world.)"

"I like equal rights for women but I don't like *more* than equal rights."

Other men were angry that now women would seem to be getting the "best of both worlds":

"I'm all for *real* equality, but I think women want to eliminate their disadvantages and keep their special privileges and morally superior attitude."

"The 'liberated woman' has become just another role for women to hide behind. Liberation has become another means for women to get what they want. Now, if her family or her man don't treat her right, if accepting her fate or buttering them up doesn't work, she can put on a smart-ass expression and demand her equal rights. Like passive compliance and desireless seduction, 'liberation' now means that the average woman believes it is her *right* to change things to whatever she believes to be to her benefit."

"It seems women *use* 'women's lib' to take unfair advantage. I light a woman's cigarette. She condescendingly calls me a MCP, but she takes the light I've offered. She smirks at me and leaves. This woman uses women's lib to boost her ego, give her a disproportionate sense of pride (for what she really has accomplished), and cover up the passive nature that she once thought of as her own but now shuns. When real trouble comes, she will collapse because she has nothing solid to hold her up. Why does she pick on me? I cannot and will not bear the responsibility for the past enslavement of women by men."

"Women use today's questions on women's lib to fit any situation they want. A lot of women take advantage of men opening doors, carrying things, paying for almost everything . . . then turn around and use that as an example of how they are treated as sex objects. They walk around bra-less, or in see-through tops, or in skimpy bathing suits—then complain that they are considered sex objects."

Many men who said they were basically in favor of women's liberation also said they were angry at "loud" or "militant" women, who were the opposite of "supportive" and "loving" women (see pages 111–113).

"I have mixed feelings about women's lib. On the one hand it seems to be a collection of unhappy, hostile females—unkempt, dressed in dirty old jeans and U.S. Army battle fatigues. Some are interested in power politics, but most are interested in angry confrontations with males. They make me angry. They are my adversaries; they must be stopped from destroying too much with their crass self-interest."

"Liberation is too strong a word. I think that women today are saying that they should be considered as human beings, with the same desires and capabilities that men have. I agree. I am glad that such things have been pointed out to me. From time to time, I regress and appreciate gentle reminders. But militant women merely antagonize me. I think these women are bitchy to begin with. If they would not be bitchy about women's lib, they would be bitchy about something else."

One man was struggling with this issue:

"I appreciate it when women who are not satisfied with their lot still have the love and patience to communicate with me. They may get furious at what I do, but they nonetheless respect me as a fellow human being. Angry women's libbers make me lose my own temper. I am contrary enough that angry arguments tend to freeze me into taking positions I'd rather not take. Away from the heat of argument I ask myself if my opponent had anything useful to say to me. I try to respect them and see their anger as a sign that something is terribly wrong, but not to take it too personally. I change my habits and my life style when I'm convinced the world would be a better place for it. In fact, I admit that, often, anger and unpleasantness are necessary to make it plain enough for me to see that a major change is worth the effort."

But one man thought women should be more aggressive:

"Women's lib in the media has an aggressive, pushy image that is salutary, but I haven't felt this attitude among women acquaintances or in my personal relationships, unfortunately."

Some men felt the point of the women's movement should be for women to "reeducate" men regarding their attitudes toward women:

"I am forty-nine, a physician, white. I believe in a fifty-fifty relationship of sharing with my partner. I feel with a working woman—one of my friends is a physician—we just share everything. She likes to cook, so I do the dishes. She doesn't like to clean house, so I help with housecleaning. I don't like to do the laundry, she does that. And we just feel that we're both putting time in—I don't mind it a bit. I feel that it's an important part of the attraction we have for each other. But I think the battle of the sexes is a very poor expression as far as I'm concerned. I feel no battle, no threat, I enjoy women. I like being with women and I feel I get along with them and try to understand them as much as I can. I agree many men need reeducation, but I think it's not because men are bad or unwilling or mean or just bastards; I think it's because men have not been educated. The persons to educate them are the women. Women should educate men. This is where the revolution comes in more than anywhere else."

But another man pointed out:

"I used to complain that women ought to share their feminism with men and teach us what they wanted. I now feel that men must seek their own liberation from sexism, and that we must do it among ourselves. Feminism has both personally and socially set the ball rolling, and we must take it from there, and forge new identities for ourselves."

Some men seemed to feel that since their own personal behavior or point of view had changed somewhat, equal rights had arrived:

"I think the main reason why women felt the way they do is because of the way men treated women years ago. All men wanted to do was to screw them and not respect them as a woman instead of a quick piece of ass and that was all. But I don't treat women that way."

A few men thought the fight for women's rights was hopeless:

"I think the gap between men and women's rights is closing, but I don't think it will ever totally close . . . men will always have a few more privileges and economic advantages than women."

Or at least going very slowly:

"This here women's lib is long overdue, if it is indeed happening at all. I guess women are getting a better shake, but, until they have exactly the same opportunities, respect, and considerations that men have, the old Revolution has absolutely no meaning. Talk about exploitation! The media is the strongest force in America, and it's also the most detrimental force against the women's movement. Advertisements continue to define women as the basic homemaker and detergent specialists. This business of 'You've come a long way, baby' is the worst crap I've ever heard of. What kind of society can this kind of shit produce?"

Some men prided themselves on "giving" women their liberation, not realizing that they are falsely taking credit for women's own achievements:

"I am white and a Ph.D. When married, I had a B.A. and was working on my M.A. My wife helped me with that and then insisted I get the doctorate: my daughter was my reward. My wife had only a high school education: since I earned my Ph.D. she has earned her B.A., her M.A., and has over thirty hours beyond the M.A. She is an elementary-school teacher. Originally wholly dependent on me and anxious to please me in everything, she is now an independent woman. I made her this—and am satisfied, though at times I find it a bit 'rough.' "

Many men mentioned that they disliked the equalization process as applied to the language:

"I think women's liberation is a big joke. In their so-called rights they are trying to change things that should have remained. For instance calling a chairman a chairman and not a chairperson. The use of Ms. instead of Miss. What the hell is the big deal about these things are I'll never understand. I can see equal pay for equal work, but changing words to something that sounds stupid is very unnecessary. Most of the women appear to me to be failures as women and now want to be failures as men."

"I object strongly to the current lobbying to change titles and pronouns to do away with sex references. It isn't sexist, it's convention to use the male pronoun in speaking or writing."

"The worst thing that bugs me is that business of changing *male words* in songs, the Bible, and any area of conversation you want to have. This bums me up. I'm not against women's lib—as far as equal rights equal pay goes, etc., etc. —but this is ridiculous."

"The women's movement caused me to watch my terminology around women—I don't say 'chick' around them anymore. But I use these terms around other men, and I have also used the terms girl, broad, piece of ass, etc., in my answers here. They are universally understood, and until we invent a new vocabulary, I'll be forced to use them. Besides, I don't know what's so wrong with them."

*Some men were in favor of the "equal but different" formula:**

"Men and women are different and always will be because of their innately different natures. This, to me, also means that neither is superior to the other. It's regrettable that such differences have been interpreted into a 'more and less' way, rather than recognizing that differences are enriching. I don't believe a woman should be denied the opportunity to express her uniqueness, nor should a man."

But finally some men were one hundred percent in favor of the women's movement—for women's and their own sakes:

* The equivalent of this point of view in the movement against black civil rights was the argument in favor of "separate but equal" facilities.

"I'm black. Ask me what I think of black awareness and consciousness. I think of women's liberation (awareness) as the same. As long as its purpose is good for humankind, I think it's good for me too."

"There's no doubt about the fact that Western culture does not and has not treated women at all fairly. I've supported women's liberation since the late sixties. It started in 1967 with equal pay for equal jobs when I saw how my wife, an intelligent and well-educated woman, was exploited when she went to look for work. I don't feel there should be antagonism between the sexes, though there are times when I do get those kinds of feelings. Kind of a damn shame it's had to come to women's liberation for women to get equal rights and some form of positive self-image. In some respects, this is a reaction to the over-domestication of women beginning in the postwar period. I've spoken with many older women who feel they were more free than their daughters."

"It's a good thing. Women's liberation is really human liberation, because the male roles have been confining for men as well. I don't mean to say that men have been as oppressed as women have; far from it. I do feel, however, that the removal of artificial barriers to employment, housing, everything, will result in a healthier society for everyone. Women will gain the largest benefit, but men will benefit too."

"Long, long overdue. I think of all the minds and lives wasted with that tired line of shit bringing up baby, etc."

"I cannot be free if those around me aren't also."

"Women's lib is great. A man has enough of a burden. With the technical advancement of mankind, society gets more intricate and people grow more alone. It is nice that women want to share the burden too. I hope the ERA goes through. Women have been repressed too long, and it is nice to see them assert themselves. We need to help one another, no one should be repressed. I hope to God my great-grandchildren can grow up loving one another, and not mistreating members of the opposite sex or referring to them as 'bitches,' 'cunts,' or 'bastards.' I hope they would treat others as they themselves would want to be treated, regardless of their sex."

"Women's liberation is the best thing that has happened to the human race. I do not feel that my rights as a male are threatened by it."

"It's about 5,000 years late, but better late than never."

"It's long overdue. Think of all the valuable contributions that have been lost because of the suppression of females."

"I think women's lib is long overdue. I support them totally, and as for the effect of their liberation on me, only positive."

"I think it's great. I'd rather work with women anyway. I think women should keep on challenging the male's 'superiority' myth."

"It is in the vanguard of finding out what life really means, and choosing the life you really want, without listening to a lot of shoulds and oughts."

"I think it's wonderful and I'm all for it. I encourage my two daughters to achieve as much as they are capable of."

Many of these men pointed out that the women's movement had many benefits for men, too:

"I'm for women's liberation. The issues raised by women's lib have caused me to reevaluate many of my opinions and values. This reevaluation has been for the good. I understand myself better."

"It's good. I think people should act as equals. I would be glad to have the pressure off my shoulders."

"I am glad, and indebted to the movement. If there had not been one, I probably would have still been buying all that garbage that society gives us about what we should be. Now I am more interested in finding someone who will share and grow with me, and with whom I can share and grow."

"I owe much to the women's movement for helping me sort out my head about my own sexuality. The conventional/macho/sexist approach is bankrupt. It has never done anything for me and I will not do anything for it. I have used the feminist movement as a touchstone for judging other things."

"I like it. It's been good for women, good for the world, and has been good for me. It had the effect of moving many people's lives off dead center, forcing them to take an active part in living again."

"I feel the women's movement is the most important fundamental movement since recorded history. Maybe it should be 'people liberation,' but most of the work comes from women, so women's liberation is probably a good term. Whatever its name, I think it's a process which will revolutionize our existing social structure."

"It's great. I wish men had the same thing going for them, too. It's about time men started looking at how binding and restrictive our lives have been and are being controlled."

"The feminist movement has transformed my consciousness about relationships with both men and women, family expectations and sex roles. It has made me take on the goal of equal relationships with women and men, and made me more aware of how culture has influenced my personal development. It has made me more aware of power struggles within relationships and how to deal with them. Through my association with feminists, I have also become aware of limitations about closeness, tenderness, and congeniality in male groups, and the importance of severing the link between reproduction and female value, allowing women to seek non-reproductive fulfillment with integrity."

"I think women's liberation is human liberation! It means men can re-examine their roles, question their own stereotypes imposed on them (example: men don't cry . . . they just have heart attacks), a greater stimulation of ideas and feelings between men and women, so that I can be friends with a woman not my wife, and my wife can too, so that what one female friend once told me can be more generally accepted, 'I like to talk to other people's husbands.' It is unfortunate that voices of fear and doubt are arising to cloud the issue of ERA with witches' tales of common toilets, women in the front lines, housewives being forced to take jobs outside the home, etc., etc. As a Christian person, I am appalled at the 'fundamentalist' branch of the Church opposing this humane and timely advance."

Most men, however, could not see how the women's movement could affect their lives and their relationships for the better; when asked, "What do you think about women's liberation? How has it affected your relationships?" most men said not at all:

"Women's lib is fine and it has not bothered me in my relationships one bit."

"I am in favor of it. It hasn't affected any relationships."

"It hurts women. It has not affected my relationships."

"Women's lib has had no effect on my relationships. Sometimes it's amusing, but mainly comical, particularly the strident behavior of the lesbians in the vanguard."

"No effect. I avoid 'pushy' women."

"It has not affected my relationships with any of my women friends because we don't let it get in our way."

Other men said that the women's movement and the critique of society which it poses had improved their relationships:

"Women's liberation is a good thing. It has opened women's and men's eyes to the fact that basic rights and needs apply to all people, and that self-sufficiency and self-love must exist before people can hope to find security and completeness in a relationship. I think that humanity and relationships will benefit from the women's liberation movement—mine certainly have. I think my wife and I have gained a new respect for each other. This was a direct result of my understanding how my expecting her to still be responsible for all the household upkeep, entertaining, etc., in addition to a full-time job, was unfair. Since I have begun taking as much responsibility for it myself—and it's hard, I have never done it in my life before—she seems to have opened up to me more, to *like* me more, and we have more *fun* together! We're more of a team now than we were."

"I like feminist women. Feminism is non-sexism—to me, it frees me from being forced into the role of rough and tough, provider, insensitive male. I went with a feminist for a while, and we worked through (translation: *fought* through) a lot of this. I have noticed that my relationships with the women I have dated since then have been more relaxed, I don't assume what they want, I ask, and they in turn respond by a greater degree of openness and spontaneity than I used to notice. It's a question of seeing women as equal human beings, not as inferior, or out to get me."

"Women's lib—great. My wife is more independent and more aggressive—more fun to be with."

"It has given me more opportunities to relate positively in a nonsexual way to women."

"My relationship with my wife and family has definitely improved. Basically I was trained to 'take care of' a family, to be head of a family, and to provide for my wife and children's physical needs. Now I am working at learning how to *care for* others, to show my caring in small ways, to listen to them and share myself with them. I still think it's important for me to support them, but I certainly would listen if my wife decided she wanted to talk about working too, or how she felt about my earning all the money. Funny, but before the last few years, we had never discussed it. I think we will probably discuss it some more, though—maybe we haven't talked about it enough. I have found it hard to believe that small things I do could matter as much to my wife as my supporting her and our home. It makes me feel more human. More loved."

"Since I first became aware of women's liberation, a few years ago, I have been consciously, forcefully, amending the way I think and feel, trying to unlearn the subtle and not so subtle sexism of my childhood (and adulthood!), and trying to treat women as people. It all started one day in my office. I am the supervisor of the duplicating machine floor of a large corporation. Most of the people who come to use the machines are women—secretaries, etc. I always thought of them as the 'enemy' somehow, the ones who broke the machines, ran them wrong, and made me seem inadequate in maintaining the equipment (since they were always breaking it). Of course, those machines just break anyway, but I was ready to blame it on them. One day, I was bawling a woman out and she started calling me a sexist pig as loud as she could. I noticed some of the other women were glaring at me in agreement, and some seemed gleeful that she had said it. I was mad as hell but it really made me think. A little later than that, the corporation had a one-day seminar on office skills, like getting cooperation from others, etc. The woman in charge of the day included as part of the course a role-reversal exercise, during which I had to be a woman asking a man's cooperation at work. Then I read a couple of books my sister gave me. All in all, I learned a lot. I see those women a lot different now. In fact, I married one of them. I'm not perfect (and neither is she), but we have a lot of close times working it all out."

A few men were finding it more difficult:

"Women's liberation has fucked up a number of relationships with women for me. I am generally in sympathy with the women's movement, but relationships are difficult to begin or maintain when the parties to them are at different points on the continuum of liberatedness. What women's liberation has done is change the possible range of expectations on the part of *both* men and women, so now, rather than reacting to safe stereotypes of what both men and women 'really are,' we have to discover what's expected of us as individuals. We have to communicate a hell of a lot more than we did before—not just sexually ('a little more to the left'), but every time we interact as individuals ('Do you want me to come around and open the car door for you?'). The result is that it's gotten a lot easier to offend people."

"In any situation where economic and social power differences are present, sex is political—inevitably so, which pretty much affects all male/female relations since I see almost all women as disenfranchised. Redefining the sexual relationship with my wife is difficult and painful but I am determined to stick with it. I don't foresee any quick solutions."

"I have felt affected by women's liberation through my choice of words in speech and not being so lonely (in a general sense of people seeing each other clearer now), and in support for my own movement toward liberation. I also feel scared, feeling separation, fearing being left out, worrying I'll do some 'dumb' thing that isn't liberated enough and a woman (women?) will go away. The most genuine fear comes when I come in contact with a woman or group I perceive as separatist, and hostile towards me or men. I feel personally affected. My stereotypes come immediately into play, I make judgments about the 'way they look and act' and my reaction is to withdraw and get away. Which can be O.K., and that's just the way it is sometimes. I guess I want to point out the fear I feel (of being physically hurt? or being left out, rejected?) and my sense that somehow what I perceive as happening, this separation, isn't right and isn't the thing to do in the long run. I could let in more, I suppose, that sometimes I need space, that I get hostile to anyone trying to enter or invade my space, and that maybe this is what is going on in another form. I also think it's good to let in, though, that I figuratively spend a lot of time in closets with the door closed, but that when somebody finally does knock, and I let myself open the door and find out who's out there, I tend to wind up having a pretty good and personally expanding time."

"I am in favor of it. I consider myself a feminist, although I don't dare tell anyone for fear of ridicule. I am in a relationship with a woman who is a radical feminist. She is physically attractive to me, extraordinarily independent, and hypersensitive to real or imagined put-downs. It remains to be seen how many microseconds this relationship will last. But she is only the second woman I have met in my life who I would seriously consider as a marriage prospect. She is intellectually active, has a sense of humor, a social conscience, a pleasant personality, physical attractiveness, and a tolerance for other people."

Finally, one man made the important point that equality in a relationship between a man and woman did not mean that the man had to be less strong, or "weak":

"Since feminists are interested in the idea of women being assertive, I'll add something about that. I *used* to be rather frightened about it but have lost this fear and indeed rather like it. The fear in my case (and I suspect for many other men as well) arose because I saw the issue in terms of domination. *Either* I dominate her *or* she dominates and I have to feel submissive and worm-like. For me, this idea stemmed from childhood—if Mother is assertive, then the young boy really *does* have to submit. Quite often parents actually try to prevent the boy (or girl, for that matter) from being assertive in replying to them: 'Don't answer back,' 'How could you say that sort of thing?' etc.

"But *not dominating a woman does not mean being weak and spineless*—nor does it mean always being 'gentle.' It just means respecting her, and giving her an equal right to be assertive, maybe taking turns being 'dominant.' I don't think women want a man to be 'weak' so they can be 'strong'—I think they just don't want to be oppressed. I've seen some men on television talking about how 'liberated' and 'feminist' they were, and I got the impression that they thought it meant wearing beards and speaking softly, looking 'gentle.' But I've found in my own life that my woman gets impatient with me when I'm not assertive (and also when I don't take her opinion into consideration, when I'm 'macho'). We've worked it out now so that the important thing is we both say what is on our minds, and both give each other the right to do what we think best. I don't try to control her anymore, and I'm just as strong and forceful (more) as I ever was."

CONCLUSION: TOWARD A NEW UNDERSTANDING OF MALE/FEMALE RELATIONSHIPS

If there was great confusion over the definition of masculinity (chapter 1), there was also great confusion over relationships with women. Traditionally, men have been taught not to take love that seriously—not to "let a woman run your life," or "don't let love have free reign in your life." But most men did fall in love, and experience all the feelings of ecstasy and abandon, all the happiness that goes with it—for at least two weeks. At this point, many men unfortunately became very confused and apprehensive. Being brought up not to let themselves be "out of control," or "overly-emotional," most men mistrusted the excitement, the feelings, the rush, thinking that feeling that much could not be good, could not be relied on, was not "rational"—and therefore not "masculine" and "strong."

Men's comments about these feelings were quite illuminating. "To be in love," as one man in his early 20's wrote, "is to be uncomfortable because you are out of control, you do things you wouldn't normally do. Women are more willing to be dependent, or part of another person, than a man who wants to keep a separation, keep himself for himself, who fears losing his independence. Of course, one does sometimes start to fall in love, but you can always stop it before it's too late. It will be nice in the future if they invent a pill to neutralize you if you fall in love—to alleviate your dis-ease!"

The fact that most men do not marry the women they are most "in love" with, tending to distrust the feelings and run from their own emotional openness and vulnerability—added to the fact that most men are brought up not to respect women, other than as mothers or mothering-type helping figures—puts most marriages in a very vulnerable, problematic position. An additional problem is most men's training, as seen in chapter 1, not to talk about feelings or to solve emotional problems by discussing them, talking them out: most men's reaction to a dispute would be, to retain "manly" objectivity by going for a walk, etc., expecting the air to have cleared on their return, and to feel proud of this solution, since they had not "lost control."

Most men said they had great, or good, marriages *outside of sex:* "Outside of sex we get along great. We cooperate and are compatible. My wife is a good friend of mine and is easy to talk to about everything except sex. I think outside of sex we have a fantastic marriage." How you interpret this statement depends on what your concept of marriage is. This was a perfectly acceptable statement for a traditional marriage, which was not based as much on a deep emotional and sexual intimacy, but more on children, homemaking, and family life. Newer marriages tend to include the desire for greater emotional intimacy, which brings with it needs for more equality in the relationship to make that emotional closeness possible.

The traditional marriage, in which the man controlled the money, while the woman's domain was the house, was the type of marriage most likely to include a pattern of extramarital sex for the man.* Newer marriages, struggling to create more equal relationships, were more likely to be monogamous—with the partners also being more likely to end the marriage if the closeness dissolved, rather than patching it up with outside sex. But "newer" marriages were not necessarily between younger men and women, by any means; a more equal marriage could be something a couple of any age might strive for.

The happiest men in this study were those with the closest, most functioning relationships with women—that is, a minority of (in most cases, married) men. Trying to live by the male code, being totally self-sufficient, emotionally and economically, always *providing* shelter and food (or sex and orgasms), never receiving or needing anything, never needing a woman's love more than she needs the man's—all this hurts and stunts men.

Some men were beginning to see how their own welfare is tied up with women's fight to restructure their lives and relationships for the better—to redefine themselves above and beyond the traditional confines of "femininity." "Masculinity" can be just as much of a pressure on men as an enforced "femininity" can be on women.

But one of the deepest problems still prevalent in many men's minds is the connection they made between money and sex with women. Most men believed that women were somehow for sale. When asked, "How do you feel about paying a woman for sex?" meaning in prostitution, many answered, "You always pay anyway"—explaining that whether it is in marriage, where the man provides support in return for (what he considers should be) domestic and sexual services, childrearing—or on a date, in which the man pays for dinner, expecting sex in return, he is always paying. Many said that it was more honest, and more of a bargain, to actually pay a woman outright. In fact, the number one reason given by most men for being angry with women was financial support, mentioning frequently that you can't trust women, that women often "use" men to get financial support. Many men feel they can never be sure that a woman

---

* Studies have implied that women's extramarital sex is somewhat less; many men have outside sex with unmarried women. Actually, women's traditional patterns of extramarital sex are largely unknown.

loves them just for themselves—as many men said, "Maybe she is just staying with me as a meal ticket."

The most unfortunate part of all this is that most men did not accept the women's movement, which could change things. If women had equal rights with men, equal access to jobs and education, and equal pay (in the U.S., women make only 59% of what men make for the same work), then men would not have to fear that women loved them only for their money or for financial support. Most men gave lip service to women's rights, saying that women should be "equal," but disapproved of most of the ways that this could be brought about. Most were afraid that women's liberation would mean less love: if women got equal rights, and especially if they were financially independent, they would not love men any more. Most men did not seem to feel secure that they were worthy of love on a deeper level. And most men did not want to give up their so-called masculine privileges, even though these "privileges"—as we saw in chapter 1—had not made them particularly happy. Perhaps the less happy some men are, the more they cling, paradoxically, to the very ideas and beliefs that have left them so unfulfilled.

3

INTERCOURSE AND THE DEFINITION OF MALE SEXUALITY

How important is sex to men? We have seen, and will see again, that it is very important. Why is it so important? What does it mean to men? What do men mean when they say they want and need sex?

To answer these questions, we must look at what intercourse (coitus) means to men, since this is one of—if not *the*—basic ingredient of sex for most men: in fact, the overwhelming majority of men did not want to have sex that did not culminate in intercourse and male orgasm (although there was very little experimentation with other means of having orgasms with women).

But what is the point of studying intercourse and how men feel about it? Hasn't everything been said about it that could possibly be said? Or is that the point, that intercourse is such a dominant symbol of our society that its actual identity has not been studied, and the right questions not asked?

Why is male sexuality defined as so intercourse-oriented? Why is what we know as "male sexuality" so identified with intercourse? Is it for reasons of physical pleasure, or are other, more symbolic, cultural forces also at work?

The standard interpretation of male sexuality says that intercourse is the greatest pleasure that a man can have. Is this true? How do men feel about intercourse? What do they want from it? Do they always find it satisfying? And do pressures on men during intercourse, and to have intercourse, in fact inhibit men's sensuality?

Just as most men both loved and wanted women, yet often hated this need in themselves, just so most men both wanted more intercourse but also felt relieved when it was over—and said that they could have stronger orgasms *physically* through masturbation.

The old mechanistic definition of male sexuality as basically a question of getting an erection, penetrating the woman, and reaching orgasm is in large part a pattern created and perpetuated by our culture—not an inevitable reaction to the "male sex drive." Men are more complicated than that, and male sexuality is just as much tied to emotions as is female sexuality. Is it possible that men are missing out on a large part of their sexuality/sensuality, and their enjoyment, by focusing so totally on intercourse? How *do* men feel about intercourse?

WHY DO MEN LIKE AND WANT INTERCOURSE?

Almost all of the men who answered who enjoyed sex with women said they liked intercourse. However, what are the reasons? It is almost universally assumed that what men like/want from intercourse is their orgasm. And yet, as men have pointed out over and over, they can easily have an orgasm from their own stimulation. In fact, most men say that they achieve a physically stronger orgasm during masturbation. Why then, do men like intercourse?

I: PHYSICAL PLEASURE

Orgasm

Only 3 percent of the answers to "Why do you like intercourse?" mentioned orgasm at all; the following are quite atypical answers:*

"Stated in simplest terms, the greatest pleasure is shoving a good hard penis into a lovely tight vagina and experiencing the consequent orgasm."

"Intercourse is the ultimate sensual pleasure for me . . . . that is, the *orgasm* during intercourse. No other sensual pleasure is as good."

* Although most men may not have given orgasm as a main reason for liking intercourse, many men did like intercourse because it was the "right" (that is, culturally approved) time to orgasm. See page 352.

336

"I enjoy intercourse mostly on a physical level. I fuck for release. The good feeling is the stimulation of my penis. Close physical contact is only necessary during foreplay to get both parties ready for intercourse."

"I have avoided emotional contacts with women and use intercourse to gain the physical contact with them I need for my orgasm."

While it is possible that men did not give orgasm as their reason for liking intercourse simply because they were aware a woman was asking the question and they wanted to appear more considerate, even in the replies received from men who believed that they were writing to another man,* the same low percentage appeared.

The pleasure of the vagina on the penis

One might assume that even if it were not orgasm itself that made men like intercourse, it might be the good physical sensations of the vagina stimulating the penis. But although men did like the feeling of the vagina very much, this was almost never given as the reason for liking intercourse. Nevertheless, it is interesting to note some of these answers to the question "How does the vagina feel to your penis?" as a way of understanding how intercourse and the vagina feel to men.†

Most men enjoyed the feeling very much, describing it very emotionally:

"A beautiful embracing organ."
"Welcoming."
"Comforting."
"Loving, warm, and secure."
"Just right, pressing gently all around."
"Wet, soft, resilient, alive."
"Home."
"A feeling of being held closely and warmly."
"Warm, close, sensual, beautiful, light, sunny—an incredible, wonderful feeling, when things are right."
"Like a velvet glove, a loving hand—a security blanket."

* See page 1009.
† See also pp. 451–56.

"Delicious."

"Warm, moist, and a place of great security."

"Tight, warm cream."

"Like a collar or ring."

"Like an absolute friend. Physically and psychologically gorgeous."

"A cocoon of utter warmth, well-being, and love."

"Hot, moist—strong."

"Fantastically soft and fleshy, almost baroque, a lush overabundance of sensuality, a primeval quivering wet mass."

"Like hot velvet; it's addicting—I surrender to it, I'm powerless to resist."

Closeness and full-length embracing*

Most of the men who answered gave physical closeness and overall body contact—full-length embracing—as the most important physical element of their liking for intercourse:

"Even more important than the orgasm is being able to wrap your arms and legs and whatever else around another human being. It makes you feel less alone, more alive. There's just nothing like it."

"It's beautiful. Two people together, naked, touching, feeling, kissing, sucking, licking, teasing, caressing—aw, come on—why shouldn't I love intercourse?"

"When I am inside her, simple things like her arms wrapped tightly around me, or her hand stroking my hair, or my back, are what really get me off."

"I love the closeness that intercourse brings. It feels good whether you are emotionally involved or not. It feels good to be close to a bare body locked tight together like that."

"To lie upon her and feel her body against mine with the warmth of her and the feeling of her soft belly against mine. Wow! It's hard to explain! I feel an ache for her just thinking about it."

"I like the feeling of the upper half of our bodies pressing together, of my chest and nipples pushing into hers."

"The warmth, the sight, smell, sound, feel, and taste of her body is exquisite. I'm sure I sound like a broken record to her, but every one of my senses all over transmits wonder-

---

* Full-length embracing is an important activity which our language, however, oriented as it is around reproductive activities, fails to recognize with a word.

ful feelings to me when I'm inside her. Many times I lie still inside her so that my movements will not disturb my ability to fully savor the feelings my senses are sending me."

"The being close to another is more important than orgasm. Orgasm can be had through masturbation if that were all one wanted. The close physical contact one has during intercourse is similar to the closeness of holding each other or talking intimately. I have known men who could only be close during intercourse and I feel they were closing themselves off."

"I like intercourse for all of its human contact—touching, looking at, holding, stroking, texture, response."

II: EMOTIONAL AND PSYCHOLOGICAL REASONS

The most important real pleasures men said they get from intercourse—aside from body closeness and feeling validated as "men"—are psychological and emotional. These involve both a giving and a getting of acceptance and warmth, validation—and in addition, many men said that only during "sex" are they allowed to be totally out of control, to release the pent up emotions they are taught they "should" repress at all other times. (See chapter 1.)

Feeling loved and accepted

The psychological/emotional reason most men gave for liking and wanting intercourse was the feeling of being loved and accepted that intercourse gave them:

"Intercourse with my lover gives me a warm and wanted feeling. It makes me feel valuable to someone."

"Having sex and intercourse with a woman revitalizes me. It gets me back in touch with myself and the pleasures of the world around me. It makes me feel clean and whole—a part of life, not just a wanderer."

"I like intercourse for a hundred reasons. Most important, it's the end of loneliness. It's an ego boost—knowing you are loved, knowing you can love."

"Intercourse is the point at which I feel she totally loves me."

"It is the closest you can be to a person, and for a moment or an hour it overcomes the loneliness and separation of life."

"When I really want to be close, when I am feeling alone, alienated, I want intercourse."

"More than a physical trip, lovemaking leading to orgasm, to me, is a mind healer. It erases all the tension and conflict built up between you and your partner during the normal course of living. It also strengthens your image of yourself, as an acceptable, lovable person, so that you can go back out and keep up your identity in an alien world."

"Intercourse is the ultimate acceptance. It's as if she is saying 'I accept you totally and unconditionally.' Even if she is not a long-term lover or even very fond of me, during intercourse she is giving me complete approval. I think it's a very psychologically significant act for me, and probably for most men, because of this sense of ultimate security and total acceptance. And then these feelings are amplified if she is already very close to me."

"I like the feeling of the sexual contact but also the feeling of someone liking you enough to give their body to you. I appreciate the confirmation I receive. It is a wonderful feeling."

"Giving me her vagina represents my partner's desire to satisfy and love me, to become part of me, to be dominated by or dominate me."

"My lover's vagina feels warm and smooth. With my cock deep inside her, I feel totally secure and loved."

"Like fitting two pieces of a puzzle snugly together, intercourse feels psychologically like acceptance of me."

"Intercourse continually reaffirms my close attachment with my mate. It tells me she loves me. It gives me confidence, despite the fact my performance ability is waning. It makes me feel wanted."

"Intercourse is the exact opposite of war, famine, disease, and death. When men are most afraid and fearful of death (such as in *The Naked and the Dead*, by Mailer), they either dream of "Mommy" or of sexual intercourse, which, I think, are the two times that males feel safest and most secure. It is possible that, in some way, these ideas are one of the deep psychological bases for satisfaction in intercourse."

"I don't know how better to explain it, but intercourse is the ultimate experience. It doesn't feel that good to me for orgasm—masturbation is better. But I love the closeness to a woman, it is fulfillment. It is the ultimate *acceptance* that's important to me."

"In analyzing my own sexuality, I started to see that sex took on a symbolic value which was in some sense far more important to me than the sexual act itself, or anything which went on before or after it. A woman's willingness to have intercourse with me was a symbolic expression of her *acceptance* of me, and conversely her unwillingness to have intercourse with me symbolized *rejection* of me by her. Within this context of sexuality (and I have every reason to believe that it is common among males) climax during intercourse becomes extremely important, indeed everything. It is the 'score' by which we measure ourselves as being *acceptable* to others (women in my own case). *Intercourse, in my own case, is important in direct proportion to my inability to perceive a woman's acceptance of me in other ways.*"

In fact, in many of the replies, there is less a feeling that men enjoy intercourse than that they *need* it, sometimes almost desperately. Sometimes there is a feeling that the implications of the act, combined with the affection, the laying on of hands, add up to a kind of acceptance, affirmation, and even benediction which almost transcends words.

Further, a large part of the feeling of loving acceptance many men experience after intercourse/orgasm comes not only from the individual woman, or from the good physical or emotional feelings, but also from the deeply engraved cultural meanings of the act. Through intercourse, a man participates in cultural symbolism and gains a sense of belonging to the society, with the status/identity of "male." (See page 346.)

Expressing feelings, being out of control

Some men also mentioned that they felt intercourse allowed them to be spontaneous and emotionally expressive as at no other time:

"Intercourse is such a real experience, such a change from life's everyday bullshit. I seem so much more myself then. I feel uninhibited, talkative."

"Intercourse proves I'm alive, relaxes me utterly, and lets me act natural. Other times I feel just like a robot."

"Its purpose in my life is to make me feel more. It is a

tool for interpersonal communication, at which I am not very good on any but a superficial (e.g., job) level. It lets me express feelings of affection, warmth, tenderness, and appreciation of a woman that is meaningful, and may even make her feel more. When not perverted by hostility, it's a nice warm refuge in a cold, cold world."

"When we are naked, conversation very rarely centers on the weather or trivialities. Emotions are bared and truths are revealed."

"I think I use it primarily to establish a relationship—it makes it possible for me to be free and open, to a degree that I can't attain otherwise. It's fun, too. I notice that while sex* doesn't solve any of life's other problems, it often acts to take the edge off them—sort of a tranquilizer."

"I like intercourse especially for its opportunity to communicate to another human being the deep messages that surface from within me."

Giving love

For some men this expression of feelings was verbal, while other men felt that the act of intercourse and then their orgasm itself served as a kind of statement, communication, or "emotional expression"—a substitute for verbal communication.†

Some men seemed to feel that the very act of orgasming into the vagina was a way of stating love or caring, usually better than verbal statements:

"An orgasm is a physical and emotional crescendo—a release of withheld expression, things I cannot tell her any other way. During lovemaking I exercise extreme control so that when the right moment for ejaculation comes, I can experience it as fully uninhibited giving and taking."

"During sex, I can express the feelings I have for another person that I can't express verbally. To me sex is important. I don't communicate good verbally, so sex is one of the ways in which I can tell and show another person that I care about them."

---

* Men often used the words "sex" and "intercourse" interchangeably in their answers; however, all answers in this section were given in response to the question "Do you like intercourse?"
† See pages 62–66.

"Sex is really a neat way to express my strong feelings for another person. I guess it's about the only way I feel comfortable doing it."

"Men have this sexual drive, as having sex (intercourse) is their only way of releasing their emotions. Society has put men in such a hole, that's why men are dying young while women are living longer. Intercourse is the closest one has to express how one feels—the ultimate expression of love."

"I have the feeling that intense physical contact, which most of the time leads to intercourse, is the only method of communication that goes to the basics. With men I can only communicate on a business level (science, social problems, etc.) but not about deep feelings. Intercourse says, 'I love you'—unless it is performed as a part of a marriage contract and love has gone out of the marriage."

"I generally feel a tremendous joy, triumph, and desire to, or feeling as if I were expressing myself to my partner when I come in her."

"Humans are islands. The problem is communication. Intercourse is natural communication without words. I just don't get much into talking."

"How else can you show someone you really love them?"

What exactly do men mean when they say that they express their love through intercourse? For some men, this may mean nothing more than their good feelings when they ejaculate, the temporary wave of emotional intensity or euphoria created by arousal and orgasm, followed by a feeling of warmth toward the person who shared/created it:

"Naturally intercourse is most appealing on a physical basis. It's a relief of the pent-up sexual drive. One is relieved of the 'load' of sperm and semen. Without the emotional level, however, it would be less satisfying. Love is the emotion, and it is an act of love. It may be love just during the act, however. But it is still love of one's partner, even though it may be fleeting. If it isn't good (a good fuck), the person may never, intentionally, be contacted again, in a sexual way."

Or it can have a symbolic meaning:

"Intercourse to orgasm is the ultimate expression of how much I love my wife at that moment. I want to be deep inside her and put my body and sperm in her."

But many men mean that they feel they are providing her with the type of stimulation she needs, and thus "giving her love":

"Intercourse is the most satisfying sex act for me both physically and emotionally. The emotional level is so satisfying to me because of the equality of the act. Both of us getting pleasure and stimulation simultaneously without any connotation of one person 'doing something' to someone else. That equality is very freeing for me."

"I get the most indescribable joy squirting a dozen jets of cum into the woman I'm with and feeling immense relief and satisfaction, especially when I know that I've pleased her as much as I've pleased me. I am what you might call an equal opportunity lover."

There is a great deal of confusion here on the part of many men who feel that having intercourse to orgasm with a woman is also giving her an orgasm, or the chance to have an orgasm—and thus giving her love. Of course, our culture had told men that this is, or should be, so; however, most women in fact need more specific clitoral stimulation to orgasm.* On the other hand, many women generally enjoy intercourse very much, whether or not they reach orgasm during it, especially when they have strong feelings for their partner. Thus, men may be right, in one sense, in believing that they are giving women "love" during intercourse. On the other hand, many women, left without orgasm and feeling that they have no way of asserting their own needs, are left not with a feeling of love but of being used.†

In conclusion, it seems that sex and intercourse are almost the only times when many men feel free, or that they have the right, to be emotional and expressive. Similarly, many men feel that the only appropriate way for a man to ask for love and affection is by initiating sex and intercourse. Traditionally, our culture has taught that women can and should be emotional, and have a right to need and ask for affection, while men should be objective, rational, self-sufficient and not emotional—in fact, for a man to be overly emotional or expressive or to need love is to be a "sissy," "girlish," "weak,"

---

* See *The Hite Report* on female sexuality, chapter 3.
† See *The Hite Report* on female sexuality, chapters 3 and 6.

or unmanly. For all these reasons, men look forward to sex and intercourse as providing an appropriate time and place to be emotional. The fact that this is almost men's only time to be emotional and "let their hair down" may account in some measure for men's feeling that they rarely get enough sex and intercourse.

The culturally created dichotomy between many men's emotionality and expressiveness during intercourse and their relatively non-emotional stance in daily life—often going so far as to make jokes about emotional feeling or to ridicule others' expression of it—has confused and disoriented many women, who are left to wonder: Which are the real feelings? The feelings during sex, or those expressed (or not expressed) on a daily basis? This has often led to a tremendous amount of frustration on the part of women, while the men involved cannot understand why the women are frustrated, and become angry, thus leading to a cycle of alienation and problems in their relationships. This is only one example of how the culture, by its frequent insistence on teaching diametrically opposed values and psychological needs to men and women as children, can often lead to a lack of understanding later on.

Celebrating emotional closeness

Some men said intercourse was important as a way of maintaining emotional closeness in a relationship, in addition to talking:

"Not for the orgasm, because I am quite confident I can do that myself, but for the incredibly close feeling possible between two people making love and after making love. Those feelings continue through times of not making love and help to keep a relationship whole and healthy. It's not just for an hour or so of pleasure that I make love. It's for a total feeling of love, friendship, respect, interest, and caring which makes a relationship with another person worth it all."

"I like intercourse more psychologically than physically. If the physical sensation was all I wanted, masturbation would be enough. There is a joining of spirits and souls when intercourse is good that is hard to describe, but is marvelous. Good intercourse usually means things are going well in the relationship, we are happy with each other. When intercourse is not good, it means we are not close in other ways for some reason, and it is very depressing."

"Intercourse makes me feel human. It brings a closeness with my wife which is very consoling—a confidential feeling. You know how frustrating it can be to be unable to find someone to talk about things with—well, intercourse is the very antithesis of that—you're with the person to whom you can say, and from whom you can hear, the things that other people are no use for."

"How I feel about intercourse is, I love her so much I want to get all the way inside her. And intercourse to me is being inside her. I know I am in her vagina but I don't mean that, what I mean is we are one, really one. When I hear her heart beat and her breathing, I don't hear mine, so it's my heart and my breathing. My penis is attached to me, but when we're together it's part of her too. That's why when I come I don't like to take it out. I like to stay one as long as I can."

"Do I like intercourse? And how! But it has changed for me. It used to be sex for the sake of sex—I wanted to get my rocks off. Kissing, petting, intercourse were frantic quests. But now it has become a blend of the physical and the emotional. With marriage one quickly learns to put your wife on a par with, if not ahead of, oneself. Sex now is a mutual affair, give and take, sharing, belonging. The thrill is still in the penis, but the satisfaction comes from loving and being loved."

III: IDEOLOGICAL AND CULTURAL REASONS

Validation of masculinity

Perhaps the most important reason why men continue to define sex as always including intercourse is the pressure of tradition—and the traditional symbolism of intercourse. The culture has taught men and women that intercourse symbolizes masculinity and male identity; the historical reason for this (as discussed in the conclusion to this chapter), which was to create a social system that would maximize reproduction, has long been forgotten, but the symbol continues to be glorified. That is, in a patriarchal society, intercourse (or the erect penis, ready for intercourse) *symbolizes* masculinity. More specifically, just as the erect penis symbolizes masculinity, intercourse symbolizes the *acceptance* of the erect penis—i.e., the validation of masculinity by both the individual woman and the entire culture. How much of men's desire for, and identification with, intercourse is due to a culture which tells men that this is what they *should* want?

Many men mentioned this connection in one way or another. Some men did not answer whether they liked intercourse, or why, but simply stated that intercourse is what men do—the natural and inevitable expression of an "instinctive" male "sex drive"; for these men, intercourse is a way of verifying their male identity:

"Sex* identifies me to myself as a man; sex admits me to full citizenship in my species and my world. Without sex I would regard myself as somewhat less than a man and somewhat less than a person."

"Masturbation is more satisfying but intercourse makes you 'one of the boys.' I love it."

"I consider myself very broad-minded and liberated in *most* ways concerning sex, but I feel that our Creator made men with a penis and women with a vagina for a reason, and that's for intercourse."

"Intercourse is a natural instinct and it proves your manhood."

"Penis-vagina intercourse is the only real sex act. The other acts may be fun, but they are not sex."

"Intercourse fulfills my ego and the fantasies I have picked up from my macho culture and men's magazines."

"Basically, I enjoy coitus for the 'selfish' reason of getting rather than giving pleasure. That's the fundamental characteristic of the primal sex drive as built into males by nature."

"I feel great, I feel powerful, I feel manly . . . excitable, uncontrollable. . . . I have a sense of success, manly fulfillment, extending joy to my partner, acceptance by my partner, something has been exchanged (enjoyed and shared) by both myself and partner."

"Sex is important to men because it releases the pressures of male desire. Many criminals and misfits are the result of no outlet for these desires. Sex is a normal body need."

* Once again, although this answer uses the term "sex" instead of "intercourse," this was given as the reply to "Why do you like intercourse?" Many men used these terms interchangeably.

"Intercourse is the most important thing (physically) in life. Keeps a man young. God gives men the drive which knows no bounds other than the penetration of vaginas. One cannot get enough of it."

"It is a very important expression of masculinity for me —emptying myself into a woman is what it's all about."

"Sex for me is unfortunately inexorably bound up with my view of myself as a man ('a man has sex, period')."

"She is *mine*. I have a right to orgasm through intercourse, God gave me this right when he made women for men."

"Being a healthy male, sex is very important to me. The purpose of sex is a normal function of the human mind and body."

"The purpose of sex is procreation. It is a biological function which our bodies are programmed to need. I have sex because my body craves sex, not because I am in love or because I want to be close to someone or because I wish to dominate or humiliate or be dominated or humiliated. We are all animals first of all and we are bound and ruled by animal needs."

"Big Point: Some/most women do not realize that men get aroused over little things *very* easily. And this arousal is, in a sense, not controllable. *It controls us.* That's why men are like they are, and we really can't help it. It's not an excuse, it's a reason. It's built in physically. By the way, guys get this way in cars driving fast, and other macho ways. I get a semi-erection if I peel out in my car. Seriously, don't let them fluff you, we're all like that. Sexual rushes are everyday to us."

"Men are simple. Men want pussy. Women have it. Women are devious. Thus the accommodations and the costs and the trade-offs."

"My appetite for sex and food are similar: the more you gorge yourself, the more often you must have it! My attitude is healthy, a healthy male."

"I feel a woman wants satisfaction and a lot of loving 'cause she gets more out of a lot of foreplay and loving than the actual climax. A man is like a male animal and has no real desire for all this loving 'cause he is hard and wants to get his rocks off and get it over with. Then for her to get away from him and leave him alone."

"Most men are grown-up boys and love to be held, cuddled, stroked, and told they are grand. Sex is the ultimate in an ego trip, when told of one's strength and masculinity. Intercourse is the way to prove one's maleness. It makes me feel very high to see her smile when I have my penis inside of her—it verifies my male qualities in a very heady way."

"I like intercourse, it makes me feel manly. I believe I feel a deep calling from my wellspring to pursue my sexual life. It pleases me to be a man, and to do these things men do. I like my erect penis. I think it looks good. I know it feels good. I know my partners like it, and it gives me pleasure when I know I have pleased them. It helps me sleep when I've had trying and difficult times; it's like frosting on a cake when there are good times; it validates me and affirms us."

"To penetrate a vagina is the male's reason of existence. It's a strong, driving force that cannot be lessened except by the act of copulation itself. I think it's the greatest thing on earth, a God-given wonder. Physically, it's driving continually. A male is *always* looking and wanting."

Some men used the concept of male "sex drive" to differentiate themselves from women, and define themselves as active and aggressive, stronger, etc; as opposed to passive ("female"):

"We (and here I mean all of us, both sexes) must come to terms with this underlying buzz of sexual awareness. I simply accept that it is there and live with it creatively. It is so deep-seated that there is no prospect of extinguishing it or driving it away—even if we wanted to! I feel the need to explain this because my sense is that women may not share this response, may not understand it in me, and may very well resent my feeling it."

A few men answered this question by saying that intercourse is "automatic" behavior for men, caused by the biological "drive" for reproduction, part of natural or divine law designed to ensure reproduction of the species:

"Sex just 'is.' We 'are,' sex 'is.' It's a drive. Native and all that. The desire to copulate is the ultimate drive among all living things, not only humans."

"It's in my genes, remember? I was born with a desire to reproduce my own genes. It comes naturally and is *not* a learned desire, like beer."

"I like intercourse because it is part of God's plan to procreate children and (it used to be) a sharing of love and sex between two people. Of course it feels good too and it is nice to 'screw' a naked woman."

Intercourse and male dominance: intercourse as a symbol of male power

For some men, part of this validation of themselves as men involves not only "performing" intercourse but more importantly "having" or "conquering" the woman, feeling dominant, superior:

"I like intercourse because of the good feeling I get from it. I feel more of a man than at other times. A woman's body is always a challenge; you never know how it will respond, nor to what nor when. It's like a good game of tennis; you hit a hell of a good shot, and whammo, it comes back twice as hard. A woman's body is a mountain to be scaled, a house to be inhabited."

"It makes me feel good to know that a woman thinks of me in this way. It's like saying 'I think enough of you to allow myself to be put in a vulnerable position.' An ego trip."

"Intercourse gives me physical pleasure, release from sexual tensions, and perhaps a degree of possession (which I'm reluctant to admit). It's a sense of superiority."

"I like intercourse for the possibility of impregnation. (Chauvinistic, isn't it?) I guess it's 'macho,' but it gives success as a man if he is not successful in other things."

"I must admit that intercourse, to me, is tied in with a subsidiary feeling of power over the woman, like that of a master and slave; it means to me that I have conquered all of her resistance."

"The penis has classically been viewed as a weapon and I must admit that I at times feel that I am wielding an instrument of destruction. Little squeals of pain on those days I am feeling hostile and aggressive. Power for power's sake but also a way of reasserting oneself to compete within and face the world."

"Intercourse means I've gotten the woman. I enjoy a woman's subservience."

"If I am going to have sex with a woman, I prefer to have her hunching under me, legs apart, vagina full of my penis, thank you. Also, I confess to deriving a certain amount of pleasure from the fact of inseminating my partner, or leaving her carrying a cache of my semen between her legs wherever she goes and whatever she does for the next day or so. Kind of a caveman sentiment, I grant you."

"Intercourse has a relation to planting something strong

in a woman even though I am not violent with women. Like wounding her with a weapon—very deep within her, reaching the deepest part of her and giving her my very 'macho' power."

"I used to feel super-powerful if I were fucking a woman while she was in a helpless position, i.e., her legs on my shoulders, bent over while I fucked from the rear, etc. It was exciting in a sadistic kind of way. A violence/lust/rape kind of feeling—utter subjection. Power during sexual activity stopped being a thrill when I realized how weird I felt afterwards. It's a strong conditioning for males that they must 'triumph' when fucking. It's like making hate rather than love."

"When I have intercourse with a woman for the first time, it is a feeling of having wetted her with my sperm, or conquered her, and becoming sure that for later meetings she is now my girl. After a while, intercourse with the same girl gets boring."

"I feel stronger than I am during sex. Like I'm some macho, virile man. Like a Greek warrior. Like an Indian warrior. I feel I can do anything and everything I want to her."

"I like everything about sexual intercourse but do not feel it is an act of love. In fact I guess I would be inclined to feel it more an act of domination of the female partner. There is very little tenderness mixed into my emotions concerning intercourse."

"Usually when inserting my penis into a vagina, there is a rush of powerful, God-like feeling. I exalt in my maleness. This, and the thrusts that follow, make me feel fully alive. Much of the male sexual drive seems to me to be to master the female physically: hence rape. I do not want to hurt or be hurt, and so have not messed around with that, but the idea is, I must admit, sometimes exciting."

MALE "SEX DRIVE" AS AN IDEOLOGICAL CONSTRUCT

In fact, the term "male sex drive" is part of the larger ideology of our society; there is no biological or physical proof of a male "sex drive" for *intercourse*. Although both males and females do have a need (or "drive") for orgasm from time to time, there is no evidence that men biologically "need" vaginas in which to orgasm, or that there is anything hormonal or "instinctual" which drives men toward women or vaginas.

Many kinds of physical contact are enjoyed by the other mammals just as frequently as, or more frequently than coitus, which is practiced only when females are in estrus. Most mammals spend more time on grooming and petting each other than they do on specifically sexual (genital) contact, as many primate researchers have described. Mammals and other animals also masturbate and quite commonly have homosexual relations. Among the animals for whom these activities have been recorded are the rat, chinchilla, rabbit, porcupine, squirrel, ferret, horse, cow, elephant, dog, baboon, monkey, chimpanzee, and many others.

Our culture seems to assume that since (theoretically) sexual feelings are provided by nature to ensure reproduction, therefore intercourse is (or should be) "instinctive" behavior. Yet when one looks at other animals it is obvious that other forms of touching and genital sexuality are just as "instinctive." Masturbation may even be a more natural behavior than intercourse, since chimpanzees brought up in isolation have no idea how to have intercourse, but do masturbate almost from birth.

And finally, if (as is so frequently asserted) intercourse really is "instinctive" and all else "unnatural," why do we need laws and social institutions that both glorify and require intercourse (especially in marriage), while setting up grave penalties and taboos against other forms of sexuality?

Social conditioning

A few men pointed out that desire for intercourse could be influenced by cultural training:

"It seems to feel good physically, but I think in actuality it is all in my head, and results from what everybody says I should feel. Before ever having intercourse, I believed that orgasm inside a woman's vagina was supposed to be the best feeling in the world. It was so built up that I was disappointed when I finally did experience it."

"Psychologically I enjoy it because of the tightness and closeness of the interlocked bodies. But I realize how conditioned I am to respond to the intercourse position because of cultural influence, not pure pleasure."

"It is all right and can be satisfying if done with meaning —but after thirty-five years of experience, I feel it is much 'overrated' by our culture. It does not always lead to orgasm —yet our culture impresses upon us that it 'should.' Whether one likes it depends upon many things—the persons involved, their physical and mental makeup and attitudes, the meaning and purpose, and whether one is tired, depressed, or feeling good. A couple can have other means of complete satisfaction without intercourse."

"Two reasons—it gives me physical pleasure and it makes me feel like I'm getting as much sex as everyone else. The latter reason is purely generated by societal (especially peer group) pressures. It is a bad reason to have intercourse and it's caused me lots of pain and anguish afterwards. I'm trying to ignore these pressures but it's hard."

"I like intercourse sometimes, but I really can't respond in a knee-jerk way. Sometimes I think the definition of the All-American Boy is someone who likes baseball, chocolate ice cream, fucking, and cheap gasoline prices. I guess I'm just not normal—thank heavens."

"The vagina is the most stimulatingly desirable place in this world for me to put my penis. It is also the most 'socially acceptable.' "

"Intercourse by insertion has something to do with role playing learned as teenagers. Both males and females play their roles for many years, accepting the lies they tell one another in a sort of passion of ego, males strutting for other males and females increasingly confused, wondering what the hell sex is all about. I went through this stupidity for many years, trying to believe (and succeeding) that it was great to ejaculate as often inside as many women as possible."

Boys are brought up to equate intercourse with manhood:

"I felt (and still do, to a lesser extent) incredible pressure on me to prove my manhood by screwing women. This pressure made it harder on me to meet women and have sexual relations with them. I had to do it; if I didn't there was something wrong with me. Also, it was supposedly so great, look what I was missing. This pressure bred its own miserable rationales, e.g., 'women always want it, even when they say "no." ' Thus, I had *no* excuses. If I couldn't find a woman to fuck, it was my fault I was a failure. I feel this pressure helped retard my sexual growth and experience and placed undue importance on fucking; even all those fuckless nights in college when I and my partner would fondle each other to heaven were not enough for me; they gave others the right impression (I'm 'sleeping' with someone) but covered up the sad truth of my virginity."

"I feel there were many other men (a minority, to be sure) who were unable to compete for fucks, and to make men of ourselves in the sexual Olympics, who found it hard to not be part of this insane scheme and yet have an enjoyable sexual experience with a woman. I think this ties in well with the feminist theme of 'machoism has hurt us'; if my feelings are fairly widely shared by men, it can only serve to show that the male-dominated sex scene also hurt a lot of men who couldn't play the game."

"In high school, there were certain girls who were known to 'put out.' If you couldn't get your date to 'go all the way,' you were supposed to go to them. They would 'lay anybody,' and existed in the scheme of things because boys *had* to 'get laid.' I was turned off by all this, but the pressure was enormous. The lying was insane. The essential hostility and competitiveness of it all depressed me even then. But you couldn't stay accepted in your clique (and I was the third-smallest boy in a gym class of 150 and did much of what I did with boys to compensate) without participating in this disgusting charade. If you didn't do it, you had to pretend, and lie. I guess it was about 90 percent lies. But I wasn't so sure of that then. I felt driven to 'do it.' We all did."

PRESSURE ON MEN TO HAVE FREQUENT INTERCOURSE AND PROVE THEIR SEXUALITY

HOW OFTEN DO MEN HAVE INTERCOURSE? HOW OFTEN "SHOULD" A MAN HAVE INTERCOURSE?

"One thing I don't like is the 'stereotypes' about men sexually, especially the stereotype that a man is always ready for sex. It's like I must be ready to 'get it on' with anyone at any time."

There was a great deal of anxiety on the part of most men about how often they had intercourse, and, in fact, most men felt that they were not having it often enough. For some, this reflected their feeling that a "real man" should have intercourse very frequently; as one man put it, "I have to take to bed the most women I can, as often as I can, the more often the better, to be a real man. I think most men act like this." For others, it reflected a need for more affection and closeness; as seen earlier, most men did not need or want intercourse basically for orgasm, which they could have by themselves, but rather for physical or emotional closeness (or to gain a feeling of masculinity). Perhaps it could be said that, if most men are brought up to channel their needs for closeness and affection mainly through "sex" as seen earlier, then the less closeness and affection currently present in a relationship overall, the more a man may be likely to complain of lack of sufficient sex.

"How often do you have intercourse?"

Most men felt—regardless of their actual frequency—they did not have intercourse often enough:*

"I am ashamed to tell you how often I have intercourse, it is so infrequent. The only time we have frequent and satisfactory intercourse is when we are away together on vacation, or when we are free from family stresses."

"I don't have intercourse enough even though I have a steady girlfriend. I would guess we have it about four to eight times per week."

"I rarely have intercourse lately (about once every two to three months) since I am having marital difficulties. When my marriage was good, we had intercourse about once or twice a week. I would want sex four or five times a week, but we never could agree on this."

"The frequency of late is rare, as my wife does not have the drive I have. In my thirties, there were periods when frequency was two to four times a day, and periods of going without for months. If I get it once a month now, it is often. It is frustrating to say the least."

---

* See also chapter 5.

"Before I joined the army, I had sex about three to four nights a week. Since then not nearly enough, on account of where I'm stationed, about once a month."

"Once a week if I'm lucky."

"I have intercourse two to seven times a week. Generally, I would prefer to have it more often, but sometimes other things seem to interfere."

"I have intercourse whenever a partner is available. With H. it was at least three times a week during weekdays. Weekends were many, many times. On the weekends we were alone we spent much of the time sexually. Since her death, I have been forced to have sex much less than I'd like."

"I have intercourse as often as I can find a partner other than my wife (which isn't often enough)."

"I would have intercourse at least every day or more if I were living with or close to my lover and if she were to lose her inhibitions or fear of commitment. The frequency is generally and mostly her interest or availability of twice a week. If I had no financial or other worries, I would be capable of and desirous of at least four orgasms a week with her."

"The damnedest part of our marriage is that intercourse is seldom more than once a week, except for our honeymoon or now on vacations."

"I have it as often as I can conveniently get it. My wife doesn't like it more often than every third or fourth day. When I approach her the day after, she gets upset, so I wait, or masturbate."

"I generally want intercourse at least once a day, but due to living conditions (college dorm) it is reduced to three or four times a week."

"I would like to have intercourse at least once a day. However, it averages out once or twice a month due to my work hours and that of my wife."

Only a few men did not say they wanted it more frequently, and seemed satisfied:

"We have intercourse once or twice a week. There's part of me that judges me, saying I should fuck more. But one thing I'm aware of is that even if the quantity is less than part of me wants (whether I have the energy or not to do more is another question), the quality is better, I believe, than it was, say, ten years ago. Or even less—three or four years ago."

"How often do I have intercourse? Well, my girl gets here after work on Friday; we have dinner and go to bed and usually make love; if there's nothing pressing on Saturday morning, we may well do it again; if not, it usually happens Saturday night, and almost always happens Sunday morning (I'm rested and lecherous!). And sometimes Sunday night, if she feels like it. Call it three times a week."

"My wife and I have sex about once to three times a week on average, and I doubt that we have intercourse 25 percent of the time if that often. She is more often up for it than I am."

"We usually have intercourse once a week—Saturday a.m. when we have a little extra time and no other demands."

"With my present partner I have intercourse about two or three times a week, but some other kind of sex (cunnilingus, fellatio) almost every day."

"I have intercourse about once every three days with my girlfriend, but when we see each other we do it as much as possible. Once, thirteen times in one night. I am twenty-eight. She is twenty-one."

"I have intercourse whenever I wish to, which is not really too often, about two or three times a month."

"Frequency—well, right now, with my lady, it's usually every other day. And we don't take time out for her period, menstrual fucking doesn't turn either of us off. In the past it's been daily, with one partner; once a week or less with others. The frequency is sort of a natural thing, sometimes you just don't feel like it, other times you can't get enough. Our every other day right now seems fine."

Many men mentioned that their frequency varied greatly depending on circumstances:

"It's hard to say how often I have intercourse. It can vary from none for long periods when I have no partner, to four times a week in a steady relationship, to fifteen times in the space of five days with a lover."

"Sometimes daily over a period of weeks. Sometimes a few times a month. Once I chose to be celibate for several months."

"I have gone as long as four months without intercourse because I haven't felt that way towards any woman I've met. But I have gone two weeks straight of lovemaking each night with someone I had a heavy relationship with."

"When I'm enjoying a stable relationship, the frequency of intercourse depends on both parties—three to five times a week has been my experience. Between stable relationships I'll go three to nine months without intercourse."

"Usually my wife and I have intercourse once or twice a week. Sometimes it stretches out; other times we'll fuck at lunchtime, at night, and upon waking. It depends on the mood or pressures of work, etc."

A few men described periods of no sex with another person —celibacy—and how they felt about it:

"Sometimes I go for weeks without sex and I like that sometimes. I can't explain why because I don't know."

"Celibacy was often more the rule than the exception during thirteen years of marriage. I found it more emotionally than physically frustrating."

"I haven't had sex in four months, because my wife isn't that attractive to me, and I work nights. I masturbate at least three times a week."

"Right now I haven't had sex in a few weeks, but I'd rather masturbate than become involved in what I know will be a short-term sexual relationship just to satisfy my needs. This makes me lonely more than horny."

"I was celibate for two and one-half years following my divorce. Just didn't feel like sex."

"My junior year in college I was having trouble dealing with my sexuality, especially feeling uncomfortable about uncontrolled sexual thoughts arising in my mind and hassles about trying to get a sex life, and I just 'turned off' my sexuality and even masturbation for about a year. (This was not without effort—but it was a rather sudden change.) I liked it then—it simplified my life—but I don't think I would like it just now. Maybe sometime again in the future, though."

"I'm going through a period of celibacy right now, and I rather enjoy it. I've gone two years without sex, but I masturbate at least once a day. I'm a twenty-seven-year-old Vietnam veteran, now a construction worker, and this period of time (I lived with a woman when I got back from the service) gives me a chance to think about who I am and what I want to do with my life. To spend all my energy on me, explore me. But sometimes I feel, or society makes you feel, that if you don't have a woman by your side, if you're not getting laid, then you're unhappy, you're not making it as a man. I love sex, I adore sex, but I can function rather well, be happy and fulfilled (right now) without it. I don't need a woman and sex to give me a sense of worth, of manhood. My celibacy is in no way a dissatisfaction or disappointment with women. Also, a single man or woman, if loneliness is not too oppressive, can make rather big contributions to, say, the community. A single person has time to do things a married person can't."

One man who had always been celibate described his life:

"I am a member of a Roman Catholic religious Order. I have enjoyed living in small groups of religious men all my life. I am fifty-two, middle-class, M.A., stern upbringing, now a high school principal. I feel I'm very successful in my many relationships with people, which have made my good academic background and my administrative skills meaningful to thousands of people.

"Having never had intercourse, I have had masturbation only as my sex life. I had strong desires for intercourse but refrained through fear and guilt feelings. I masturbated irregularly with guilt feelings until age fifty, when I stopped feeling guilty.

"I have 'fallen in love' with both of my parents, each and every one of my brothers and sisters (I have ten), and dozens of men and women. I feel a sexual attraction to some of my female friends and visualize some of them as sexual partners but have found minimum physical intimacy and deep emotional intimacy with several of them so satisfying that I don't feel sexual intercourse would add anything to our relationship. While the enjoyment of sexual intercourse is a worthy activity in itself, I feel it falls far short of the enjoyment I find in my intimate sharing with some of my friends—male and female. Sex is important but overrated and is unnecessary to real happiness. I share more intimately with some of my female friends than most married couples I know.

"The women's movement made me more aware of the equality of my women friends, more respectful of them, and improved my relationships. Until about age forty-five I had more male friends—none really very close—because I was afraid of close relationships with women. Since then I've rid myself of my fears, and have deliberately and persistently developed dozens of close friendships with women, and I enjoy them immensely."

Other men replied with boastful stories of how many women they had "had":

"I've fucked about 3,000 to 4,000 times with twenty-five to thirty-five different women and limit myself to four to six partners in a year while retaining one to two from the previous year. In a year's time now I have eight to ten different partners that have been acquired over a period of years. I turn down 40 percent of the offers I get and avoid or delay 20 percent of the rest. I have been told too many times that I had the 'finest dick in the whole world' or that 'I could make a pork chop come' to ever feel inadequate or badly about myself."

"When I was twenty-four (sixty-five years ago), I played football. Just a hard fucker I was. I had girls all kinds. Streetwalkers, whores, call girls. We used to go into a hotel, get a room for two dollars, tell the elevator boy to send up a girl, and give him a buck. We had more fucking than we could handle. And some nice girls too, not whores. I had one corker from the same school I was going to. And was I in heat. We had it every time I came in the house—on the table, in the chair, on the floor, in the backyard in daylight or at night, we just stayed horny."

Or how early they had started sexual relations:

"My first sexual 'mistress' was my age at five. At nine, I obtained a second 'mistress' my own age and the three of us always had sex together. I've been fucking like that all my life—never could get enough."

"Well, there was Judy down the street in Chicago, we were both about five (not much success but a lot of hell got caught), then there was Connie in Kansas City, I was in third grade, she in fourth (I always liked older women). We had a whole lot of action, we even had penetration. But my first real honest to goodness (oh so good) sexual experience was when I was a freshman in high school in Davenport, Iowa. I had a six-month-long 'affair' with a widow on my paper route, she was an 'older' woman of thirty-five and I was a youth of thirteen or fourteen. Well, I've gone on like that all my life, I could tell you enough to write a book."

Or how much women enjoyed sex with them:

"I'm highly sexual and easily turned on. I'm twenty-three and have no problems whatsover sexually. I always achieve an erection when I want one—and often when I don't! The women I have known have been pleased with my sexual expertise too, one woman calling my penis a 'penile institution' and took a picture of it which she carries with her. Another girl wrote my mother to congratulate her for having a son with 'the nicest penis she had ever been fucked with.' I've never had any complaints with women, or trouble getting them to have sex. One girl recently took me to her bedroom, took off my clothes, and began fellating me. I had a fantastic erection and she sucked my cock with such energy I told her I was about to come. This made her even more enthusiastic and she closed her mouth over the whole length of my cock jerking me off with her hand. It seemed like I came for an hour, and we were writhing all over her bed but as I moved her mouth never left my cock. I was so excited we even fell over the side of the bed together but she never stopped sucking until I calmed down a few minutes later. Then we relaxed awhile, but I still wanted to fuck her so we got back into bed and I did for her what she had done for me for about thirty minutes, giving her the best fuck of her life, as she told me later. I have had many women recommend me to their friends. I have more offers than I have time for."

"Women have always been attracted to me. When I kiss a *woman* even her pussy knows it. When I kiss a *girl* her *mother* makes apple dumplings and invites me to dinner. To me love-making is a duet—my tenor melting into her alto, though soprano can be mighty sweet, too. I have a hunch I could teach a city girl how to enjoy herself like a country girl. Judging from some of the reactions I've had, I believe if Marilyn Monroe had known me, she never would have committed suicide. I know what to do to make a woman happy."

Conclusion

No one can say how often a man "should" have intercourse. It seems logical that a man would want to have intercourse when he was feeling close to a woman, or especially attracted —not as often as some inner hormonal blip made him feel he would enjoy an orgasm. How often a man has or wants to have an orgasm is a separate matter from how often he has or wants to have intercourse.

In fact, the cultural pressure on men to have frequent intercourse seems to be based on a purely mechanical defini-tion of masculinity, in which the desire/"need" for intercourse is related solely to a man's supposed inner hormonal cycles, or some other mysterious "innate" sexual urges. (See page 351.)

Since whether or not a man is having "enough" intercourse has very little to do with whether or not he is having orgasm enough, each man will be able to determine for himself if he is having intercourse frequently enough, based on what it is he needs and gets from intercourse. Certainly it is possible to have sex without having intercourse. And certainly, men have the right to go without sex entirely or not have sex with a partner (celibacy), if they want, as almost all men in fact do for certain periods of their lives. Men should not be made to feel that they "have to" have sex/intercourse to prove they are men or for any other reason.

PRESSURE ON BOYS TO HAVE FIRST INTERCOURSE

Not only do men feel pressured to have frequent intercourse, but also boys, to prove they have become "men," feel pressured to begin intercourse as early as possible. This theme was often repeated in men's descriptions of their first intercourse.

Many men's first experiences with intercourse left them feeling glad they had done "it," but also feeling unskilled and unknowledgeable:

"I was twenty-one years old, if you mean with a woman. It was a failure, I didn't know much and I was selfish but not knowingly. She never gave me a chance. I guess she expected me to know all about sex because I'm a man, but I was not any different than any woman virgin at that time. I felt bad that she did not enjoy it very much. After that I met the woman of my life, my present lover (there were about six or seven other women), and she made me a man, so to speak. She took the time to teach me—I didn't know a damned thing about how to please a woman until she taught me."

"My first intercourse was with a woman four years older than myself (I was sixteen, she was twenty), who had some sexual experience. It took place in the room she was staying in at a hotel where I was working. I enjoyed it, but felt very tiny compared to the big world of sex and women that had been opened up to me. I was bewildered. That is the first time I was aware of a woman as being 'mysterious' and 'different.' Up until then I thought a woman was the same as me, just a different sex. She initiated all the activity. I was greatly excited because I was thinking that now I was finally doing *it!* I remember that I started thrusting very fast, because I thought that was what I was supposed to do, and she slowed me down with her hands. I was used to masturbating, and suddenly being inside her everything felt so soft, it took me a while to reach orgasm. I don't know if she had an orgasm or not, but she made many sounds of pleasure (maybe she felt that was what she was supposed to do, even after having had some experience!)."

"My first sexual act with anyone occurred when I was twenty-four. I held myself up with straight extended arms because I was afraid that my slender body would crush the girl. This happened after I had quite a few drinks. It took me a long time to climax. I was relieved when the ordeal had ended."

A few had felt only relief and pride to finally "be a man":

"Age eighteen. I remember thinking to myself, 'Wow, this is unbelievable, what is happening to me!' It was the most intense feeling I ever had, and it made me really proud of myself. I even took the filled rubber over to my friend's house to show him that I had actually screwed a girl."

Some were surprised that the experience had not been greater than it was:

"The first time I made love with a woman was when I was twenty-two. I had carried this fear of making love (would I perform well, would she purposely try to get pregnant and hope to marry me, an aspiring medical student?) and so there had been lots of petting and orgasms with maybe ten girls/women, but no intercourse. When she indicated that she wanted to make love, and led me to the bedroom, I was scared. When I entered her, I remember thinking, 'Is that all there is?' It didn't feel much different than masturbating. I came in a minute or two and was rather disconcerted that this wasn't the terrific, star-filled experience I thought it was to be (from information from my male friends). What was missing was love and caring."

"After my first ejaculation during intercourse at age nineteen, I thought, 'Is this all there is? It's just a sexy way to masturbate and make babies.' "

"My first intercourse at fourteen left me very confused because I wasn't sure if I enjoyed it so much after hearing so much about it. I was wondering if it was overrated."

Many men had had their first intercourse with a prostitute:

"My first experience with a woman was a prostitute in a border town in Mexico. I was in the service and took a lot of ribbing because I was a 'virgin.' I went along with a group, determined to shut them up by 'getting laid.' What they didn't know was that I was unable to orgasm with her. I worked and worked to no avail. Finally she said 'too much fucky, no come,' and I gave up. At least she only charged me half price, and it shut the guys up. I was nineteen, but I proved (to them at least) that I was now a man. As for what I thought of it, I detested every minute of it and, for that reason, I suppose, I have never gone to a prostitute again."

Or with someone they did not particularly care about:

"On vacation from college—I can't remember but probably sophomore year—I was determined to find out for myself what was so wonderful about every man's Topic A. I'd heard the reputation of a hometown girl I normally wouldn't even say hello to. When opportunity gave me the chance to drive her home from town, we made a date for that night. I decided on Redemption Rock, an old Indian meeting place. When we got there, I found a romantic pine grove, spread my Indian blanket, and without delay began rolling on the ground. Our passion was soon disturbed by swarming mosquitoes, so we retreated to the back seat of my car. Fumbling for a rubber and trembling with anticipation, I twisted and turned with determination until we were in a comfortable position. The event didn't last long, but I realized I had found a new world of pleasure."

Some boys did it in groups:

"By the time I was seventeen, I was under a lot of peer pressure to 'do it' and get it over with. Three of us (it took three of us to muster enough courage) took out one of those girls known to be willing even with the likes of us. We drove out and parked. We drank (very manly to drink). We all knew what we were there for. We broke out the rubbers (that was very manly, to carry rubbers), and one of us went in the back seat with the girl. The other two stayed in front and pretended nonchalant sophistication. I went last. I would certainly have chickened out if the others hadn't been there. (We reinforced one another; together we made one huge male chauvinist pig.) Amazingly, my penis was stiff as a rod. The seventeen-year-old male mind may be a stinking swamp, but the seventeen-year-old male body is a marvel. The girl was stretched out on her back with her skirt up around her hips. She had continued drinking (wisely) and was completely indifferent. None of it, the depressing sordidness, the total lack of caring in all of us, her indifference, my quaking, the palpable hostility under it all, none of it turned me off. And my penis was ready. God, it was awful, all of it. I climbed between her legs, pushed them up and out, and penetrated. She had to help. I then engaged in a parody of violent masculine battering thrusting, at which I lasted maybe ninety seconds, then came. She pushed me off. I was briefly out of it. She lit a cigarette. I threw out the rubber. The boys passed the bottle. I vomited out the window. We drove back. And that was my first 'real' sexual experience with another person."

And for only a few had it been a loving and mutual experience:

"My first intercourse occurred almost exactly when I was nineteen. The girl with whom I was with, luckily, decided to spend the night in my bed with me. It was absolute ecstasy sleeping the whole night naked and warm together."

"I had my first intercourse with my girlfriend in college. We were in love. We were in bed and had been caressing each other for over an hour when we both decided to make love by having intercourse. We proceeded, and upon feeling my penis enter her vagina, I hallucinated vividly. It was like a flashback of being born: an intense surrounding sensation of soft, pink vaginal walls without the contractions or pain which are also a part of birth. My admiration for women's bodies—the rightness of their construction—and men's bodies too, overwhelmed me. It was very significant to have shared this with her; I'm sure that our love helped us to relax and be conscious of the new steps we were taking."

MEN'S FEELINGS ABOUT PENIS SIZE

"Do you think your genitals are beautiful? Do you think your penis is a good size?"

Closely related to the pressure on men to be sexually active on a frequent basis, to "do it" as often as possible (and on boys to begin "doing it" as early as possible), is the emphasis on penis size—that is, not only must a man have a large appetite for sex, but he also must have a large penis—the idea being that the larger penis a man has, the more of a "man" he is, and conversely, the smaller penis a man has, the less of a "man" he is.*

Most men, in answering this question, wished over and over again that their penis could be just a little larger:

"Beautiful? Well, I'm not used to giving many psychological strokes to myself, but I do think it's good-looking. It would be truly beautiful, perhaps, if it were larger. That is something I've fought back and forth in my mind trying to get my inner self to accept that fact that my penis only rises to the national average—if various studies on the subject are to be believed. An extra inch would be appreciated, but I'm maturing to the point that what I've got is quite adequate for the task."

"I wouldn't call my penis beautiful, but I enjoy looking at it. It's big enough, but I'd like it to be even bigger, so that a woman would gasp when she saw it."

"My cock is too small to suit me when it's soft."

"I do not think my penis is beautiful. It sure can shrink to a very short stub. Extended, I believe my penis is medium length but quite thin. Maybe it is long, but it is not what I call powerful. I've seen some powerful penises."

"I think it is a good size when by myself, but in the presence of other men I feel self-conscious as if they all have huge cocks. It is as if I am underdeveloped. Intellectually, I know I am good-looking and have average secondary sex characteristics. Emotionally, I feel I am a boy in a world of men."

"I'm O.K., my balls are not as big as I wish they were."

"Well, I suppose everyone wants to be tremendous, so I guess a little larger wouldn't hurt."

---

* Also, some men believe that a larger penis will make a woman orgasm during intercourse, as opposed to a smaller one.

Many other men were extremely proud of their penises, frequently because of their size, sometimes giving their measurements:

"I think my penis is very well proportioned and a beauty to look at when compared to others. It has been circumcised, is smooth and flawless, and it has a large head which is well appreciated in sexual intercourse (contrary to the adage that size does not matter), or fellatio for that matter, which can be grasped nicely by the mouth, hence I believe its fascination to others. It stretches to 7¼ inches when normally erect and slightly more on full arousal. It has a circumference of 6¼ inches at the base and 5¾ inches around the corona of the head."

"Yes, I think my penis is beautiful. I take good care of it. It is bathed every day, kept nice and clean, lotion used on it to keep its skin smooth, and powder to keep it dry. My penis has given me very much joy and pleasure, and has given the same to many girls and women. It has seldom failed me, so I'm proud of it. I think it is a nice size, there are larger and there are smaller ones, but it made me happy and seemed to satisfy the women. Only a few times some of my lady friends seemed to think they couldn't take it. One of them measured my penis just before ejaculation; it was about 14 cm in circumference at its widest part and a little over 17½ cm, not quite 18 cm long. Marked it down in my diary."

A few men said they liked their penis because it was aesthetically beautiful, or otherwise pleasing to them:

"I think my genitals are exceptionally handsome, especially in comparison with any that I have ever seen. I have what I consider the most beautifully shaped head, whether soft or hard, that anyone could have. Even the meatus is more than a mere slit since the head curves gracefully inwards to it on either side"

"I think a penis is beautiful, including mine. I am still amazed at how it changes in size and texture. When my penis is very hard I think it is very powerful and sexual-looking. I sometimes glance down and look at it."

"I think my penis is beautiful and I'm proud of it. I think when I die I'm going to have it bronzed."

"I take great pleasure in my genitals, especially when erect. I like to walk or run or jump especially in front of a mirror and watch my penis swing and bounce in front of me.

I also take great pleasure in feeling my testicles, hefting them, and being continually amazed at how heavy they feel and thinking about how such a small part of a man's total body could hold the future of mankind within it."

A few men pointed out that they thought male genitals looked good only when aroused and erect (and probably many of the replies to this question refer to the penis when erect):

"Sometimes they look funny and ugly. Let's face it, those wrinkled-up sacs and sausage are silly."

"I think 'male genitals' look their best when erect—otherwise they are a rather sorry sight dangling around there."

But one man saw it the other way:

"My penis flaccid looks attractive. Erect and bulging with arteries it is somewhat less. I don't find it ugly, but still far from beautiful. The scrotum, as it varies with the changes of temperature and mood, also varies in attractiveness. I am embarrassed by it when it dangles and is baggy. But when it is contracted and pressing the testicles against the body, all appearances are much better."

A few men compared their feelings about their genitals with their feelings about women's genitals:

"Like most men I guess I've been conditioned since birth to regard the erect penis as a strong, aesthetically pleasing symbol, an expression of pride, manhood, and all that crap. Conversely, I regard the female genitalia as a far more mysterious and intriguing set of plumbing—if somewhat less impressive externally."

Only a few men were not concerned with size, or felt they were just right:

"I think my penis is beautiful and the right size for me. I've never understood why men have a hang-up about how big —how small. Who cares? It's not going to alter the size anyway."

"I think my penis is beautiful, and not too big, nor too small. Just right and I am happy with it."

"I haven't ever measured myself since I was a kid, but I think my penis is of good enough size—who cares what size it is anyway?"

"Yes, I like my penis, which is a good thing since it's attached to me. I would not say it was beautiful, nor particularly big. As for being big enough I'm not sure what you mean. It is plenty big for me, and as for somebody else—well, I don't know nor do I care."

And a few men, very atypically, did not like the look of male genitals or their genitals in particular, or had mixed feelings about them:

"I think my genitals look fine, although as a whole I think the male body would look better without the penis dangling around down there."

"When stiff, my cock has a slight bend to it which I probably should take in to a body shop to have hammered out."

"One ball is too big."

"I don't think male genitals are particularly pleasing to look at. The penis itself isn't too bad, but the testicles flopping around the way they do aren't the most gorgeous sight in God's creation."

"Male genitals are kind of dumb-looking. Very exposed and vulnerable."

"The male genitals look absurd. They are. God could have found a better way."

Most men in the United States* are circumcised, and appear to give it little thought—other than finding a circumcised penis more acceptable and being generally glad that they are circumcised:

"I am circumcised, and have no ideas about it—it has never occurred to me to like it or dislike it."

"I am circumcised and I like it. I think uncircumcised penises are ugly."

"I am circumcised, and am glad I am. I think my cock looks prettier that way."

* European, African, Chinese, and South American men are frequently or almost always uncircumcised, while men in the United States are almost always circumcised. There is an organization of men in the United States trying to stop the practice of circumcision on the grounds that it is unnecessary and dulls sensation.

"I was rather surprised and disbelieving when I first found out about circumcision, as I thought I had been born the way I was. I still did not want to be uncircumcised, it seemed natural."

"I like the look of a circumcised penis, the uncircumcised ones look like a piece of meat."

But uncircumcised men generally preferred being uncircumcised:

"I feel well off and more fortunate than many men I've met who have small sex organs and who have been circumcised (I have not, I am happy to report)."

"I'm not circumcised. I like it and may be able to achieve more stimulation because of my foreskin. My son is circumcised. I thought it to be more 'healthy,' more 'hygienic,' according to what I had read. Now, I am not so sure there is any data which proves this, and would not have any of my sons circumcised. I think it's fun to have a foreskin."

"I am not circumcised and consider myself very lucky not to be. I got a terrific amount of flak in the hospital when I refused to have my son circumcised . . . you'd have thought I was a pervert. Finally the pediatrician, very annoyed, told me it would have to be done because it wouldn't retract. I consented, but I now think he was full of shit. My youngest son was routinely circumcised without anyone asking permission. I was really outraged. But I don't suppose it matters. I wonder at the arrogance of the damn doctors, though!"

Uncircumcised men usually said they had more sensitivity:

"My glans is more sensitive this way, but I can't hold off very long."

"I'm glad I'm not because I believe I have a more sensitive penis. I'm glad I talked them out of circumcising my son (with their fabulous cancer statistics)."

But some circumcised men also believed they had more sensitivity:

"I heard that being circumcised made the penis more sensitive and enhanced sex, and that this was one of the reasons for doing it. Is that true?"

Many stressed that they strongly preferred to have sex in an emotional context:

"I have sex with this woman because I love her. I don't think I could screw any woman with any amount of success or satisfaction unless the act was the culmination of a very happy personal relationship. I don't say I necessarily would have to be completely in love, to the exclusion of all other women, but I would have to feel that this was a very close friendship which was becoming even closer by this sexual act."

"I have had relations with women where I was being used just as a 'phallus symbol.' I enjoy sex more thoroughly and it is more stimulating where there exists a feeling for each other. At times, I resent the idea of being used as a 'quickie,' just because a woman needs (mostly single women) to relieve her frustrations or sexual fantasies."

Some remarked on the despiritualizing of sex in current society:

"A lot about the present state of sex and sexuality bothers and disappoints me. Sex has been materialized; it has become a commodity. Millions of dollars are made and spent annually on sexual advertising. It's a 'come-on' and a prick (pussy) tease. Sex has descended from being a natural expression to being a competitive and materialistic ('How many chicks have you scored with?') commodity or endeavor."

"I wish there were more spirituality not only in sex but in ongoing relationships. We are all luminous beings, but it is damn hard to remember that."

Others said the sexual revolution had been dehumanizing in its separation of sex and feeling:

"There may be a lot more information, but I think most young people are still getting introduced to sexuality on a sink-or-swim basis. We need to be more supportive of each other. Put a human face on sexuality rather than making it a competitive, high-pressure commodity. Sex is not a primary, sole and single goal of life . . . but it should not be neglected thereby. We need a greater acceptance of diversity—less sexual fads and fashions."

"I think there's too much emphasis on sex, and not enough on love."

"I don't think a greater sexual freedom will make a better society for us. The people who can handle sexual relationships in a mature manner, and who are considerate of the people with whom they deal, are just as few and far between as they ever were. If the new attitude toward sex doesn't end up bringing about better family life, then it is no gain over the incompetent way I was educated sexually."

"My impression of the people I know is that they do it more, hear about it more, see it more, talk about it more, but find it emptier and more meaningless. Am I cynical? Maybe, but I also see more potential for change now, if we learn to love."

"I have teenage daughters, and the sexual revolution is disquieting. I think it may have been somewhat overblown by the media. A good many kids remain virgins for some time, even today. Sex has powerful implications, and really should be engaged in only by relatively mature persons who have some idea what they're about. Introduction to sex should be fairly gradual, while one is growing up, and pressures to go all the way (while inevitable) are to be deplored. The 'revolution' clearly implies such pressures, and true freedom of choice is lessened. Puritanism was defeated long ago, and the emphasis now should be on responsibility rather than self-centeredness."

"I have noticed something change, over the years, that is not exclusive to homosexuality. When I was out and around in my twenties, there was a great deal of romantic feeling among singles. (Call it old-fashioned flirting?) Now, things are reduced to 'My place or yours?' A feeling of real happiness seems to be gone out of it all. Perhaps this is why I avoid tangling with young things. What happened to 'little gifts'????? I seem to be one of the very few who still give them on no-occasion occasions. Love and romance and sharing and release and reward and communication are things that must be tenderly (and sometimes invisibly) worked at, *steadily*. I find this quality in short supply. It's more like a scorched earth policy that burned out the loving heart."

"I'm twenty-three, white, a college-educated musician, 'on the road' right now. I come from a very tight emotional family. My parents are religious and so am I to a point. God exists to me. Sex is an extension of emotion through physical action. It is very important to me. I think the sexual revolution has created more hassle for people than pleasure. Getting laid nowadays is like playing chess or something. Move the right way and you score. A lot of people have had their emotions get crusty because of prior hurts, etc. It's hard to be *real* to people. More and more people are becoming less and less emotional. It hurts me to see it happening. As I travel all over the U.S. with my band, I see it in different degrees in various parts of the country. Sometimes if you even speak to a stranger, it's like you say 'hello' and they feel like 'Well, what do you want, buddy?' Trust is fading fast, and you can't be a true human without being able to be honest and trust, not only others but yourself as well."

However, some men who were critical of the "sexual revolution," as we have seen, sounded more like they were angry at their idea of women's new "freedom" than at the pressure on men to be "sexual," or "sexual freedom" for men, as seen in the following man's reply:

"Back in the fifties when I was a teenager, L-O-V-E and devotion, devotion to one another when you had a love affair, made love with someone, it meant something, it wasn't like relieving yourself like it is today. Going from one bed to another just relieving yourself. Our country was built on God and trust and believing in truth, and that's why we rose up above all these other countries, our technology is unequaled because we believed in God and stuck to the truth and hung together and fought for what is right. God, family life, and freedom were the first things in life.

"But as time went on we got away from that and we turned women into sexomaniacs. That's what's the matter with today. You got a lot of broads running around with no bras on, with no panties on, they're saying, 'Hey, I'm ready. Any number, any time. No matter who you are or what you are.' Today, now, it's harder to find those good relationships—because you're only next . . . *next*, mind you, not first, not last, *next*. There was someone ahead of you and there's going to be someone after you. That's the way it is, but I don't like it, because now you've got nothing. Absolutely nothing.

"See, our women we used to fight for, keep them pure, keep them honest, the kids the same way. Now we've put out all these books—smut books, and all these gadgets to be sold in public, and we've allowed them to print all these magazines —hey, we didn't need that when I was a kid, we didn't read none of that, my parents didn't read none of that. They had four kids and they stayed married the whole time when mother was alive. Like my mother said, never once did it enter her mind to be unfaithful. And you talk about reaching climaxes, and all these women have to masturbate. Today they're corrupted because we've allowed all this smut and crap we put in the streets. Our country never used to allow that. We were brought up on a religious basis, a God-fearing country.

"I'm old-fashioned. I gotta have a relationship. I gotta be able to know she gives a damn a little bit about me. I've never needed no book before and I don't think anybody else does. It's all bull crap."

Others said that there had been no real "revolution":*

"The sexual revolution is mostly on paper. Everybody seems to be talking and writing openly about sex these days. One is assailed by sex on all sides of all media, the whole culture is saturated beyond the point of absurdity. And yet I can't see that basic sexual attitudes and behavior have changed. Sex roles are defined in the same way they were in my youth: boys are encouraged to 'score' and girls are encouraged to trade their 'favors' for the best possible advantage. Men's magazines are still selling the idea that the ideal woman is a playmate—i.e., not a serious human being—and she is portrayed, as always, as a nymphomaniac with big tits. The women's magazines are still retailing the same old bilge about how to please your husband and how to be a sensuous woman—the whole fulfillment through submission fairy tale. The only thing new is that there is evidence that people are engaging in sex at an earlier age (increased pregnancy and VD among younger adolescents)."

Some men said the "sexual revolution" had been created by men to further exploit women:†

"Lust is legitimate, natural, and inoffensive. It's a good idea for men and women to believe that. The trouble with

---

* These answers also confuse, to some extent, the sexual revolution and the women's movement.

† In fact, most women in *The Hite Report* on female sexuality said they did feel pressured and exploited by the so-called sexual revolution; as one woman put it, "If the Sexual Revolution implies the attitude that now women are 'free' too, and they can fuck strangers and fuck over the opposite sex, just the way men can, I think it's revolting. Women don't want to be 'free' to adopt the male model of sexuality; they want to be free to find their own" (p. 303).

this idea 'whose time has come' was that all the desperate guys saw it as a new strategy for the macho males to use. They tried to shame women into sex by claiming resistance to be symptomatic of being 'hung up' about sex. They professed abolishment of the double standard until satisfied, then reinstated it, much to the pain of the women victimized."

"If the *Playboy* 'seduce all women' philosophy is what is referred to, that was no revolution. It means women were expected to have sex more with men, on men's terms. There was no revolt or change in that. Men have always been using all sorts of devices and force to fuck women."

"It's great for the men but how about the women? They're supposed to put out at the snap of a finger or they're not with it. How many single girls tell me their problems every day where I work. I'm glad I was born when I was. At least we had some respect for women. Today the guys think the girls are to be used and abused."

Some men said it put pressure on men:

"One odd aspect of the whole thing is that now I feel like I'm *expected* to make sexual advances toward any woman I take out. Whereas I'm just not comfortable doing that until I know her well. This has led to some very uncomfortable situations. A friend told me once that 'nothing pisses off a girl as much as not being taken up on it when she wants to get laid.' I don't believe that on a *rational* level, but it adds to the discomfort and embarrassment at times. I feel like she'll think I'm not much of a man."

"The sexual revolution put more pressure on me to fuck women, if the sexual revolution means 'dudes balling chicks.' It's intimidating to me. I think it's important for people to feel free to express themselves sexually, not be pushed."

A few said they liked the openness, but didn't like non-monogamy:

"I like the openness. But I'm a 'one-woman man' and I expect the same in return, so the new freedom is threatening. I'm possessive about my own happiness. Who isn't?"

"I'm in favor of sexual enlightenment. I'm not in favor of sexual promiscuity. To me, I find after a tough, full, and perhaps to you, a long life, that selfishly running around for new thrills, new pussies, outside diddlings (as opposed to cultivating that which you have) only establishes the fact that one has really failed at the challenge of making life on a one-to-one basis, which, when done properly, gives you all in return that you can either absorb or handle and with the greatest satisfaction to enjoy while waiting to see what comes next. Those who have not reached this point of agreement, to my mind then, have yet to grow into maturity. Good luck! I think a lot of nonsense is talked and written about the new sexual morality and 'open' relationships and the like, which totally ignores some very deep-seated human needs for security, stability, and long-term emotional satisfaction. I can sound rather old-fashioned if I don't express myself carefully."

But some men said they were totally in favor of the sexual revolution:

"I think the sexual revolution is the greatest thing that could have ever happened to this era. From a sexual viewpoint, it has begun to release women from their 'closet' and enables them to be more free in their lives. It enables women to 'go after' the female/male they choose, without fear of reprisal or shame."

"I think if handled properly by the individual it gives them much more sexual freedom. They are free to indulge in the pleasures of sexual relationships no matter what the involvement; i.e., a purely physical need. Some women say that the sexual revolution has made it next to impossible for them to say no. In my mind these women really have nothing to bitch about, they are making the revolution a problem. It is obvious to me that these women do not have confidence in themselves, they have no self-esteem. What is so hard about saying, 'No, sorry, but you just don't do it to me and there is nothing you can say to change my mind'? It is not really that hard, believe me. Nobody can say honestly that the *sexual revolution is open season on women*. This only happens to the women who haven't got the guts or the wisdom to know what they want and say no to the rest."

Many of those in favor of the "sexual revolution" said they felt left out:

"The sexual revolution is maddening because there is still no more sex for me—but the media says everyone else is having it."

"I find the sexual revolution fascinating. I listen, for example, to the popular songs of today giving open sexual permission which was taboo twenty years ago. In some ways, I feel I missed out by being born too soon."

"I suppose I'm envious. When my eighteen-year-old grandson can have a mistress, I'd like to be eighteen again."

DO MEN LIKE CASUAL SEX?

Similar answers were received when men were asked whether they liked casual sex.

Most men made a great distinction between "casual sex" (one-night stands, or sex purely "for sex's sake") and relationships which, though brief or transitory, still contained friendship or emotional feelings:

"I no longer like casual relationships. I had enough of them when I was younger and I felt that I had to prove myself. I no longer feel that I have to keep any type of score. But I don't like periods of monogamy, either, though I've certainly had such periods. I like caring about someone and I hope that there is someone who feels that way about me. It doesn't matter if you only see her once, as long as there is a warm feeling between you."

"I like having a relationship with one girl for extended periods because you can really get to know another person intimately, share and care with her, and that feels good. But I like casual flings too—they have their advantages. If she's worth going to see again, she has some personality, some value as a person, that takes her out of the casual category—for best results, you should ball only with good friends."

"When I have sex with someone it is because I care for that person as an individual. Even if I have a casual and infrequent affair with someone, I still care about them and their overall welfare. I'm sure this sounds old-fashioned, but it is true."

Surprisingly, most men, whether single, married, divorced, monogamous or not, and of all age groups, were basically against "casual sex"—as opposed to the stereotype which says that men should always be ready for sex in any form:

MARRIED MEN:

"I am very uncomfortable with casual sexual relationships, for the expectations of the two people (as to the casualness) invariably differ and leave one person feeling guilty, used, or some such."

"I have had a very few casual sexual relationships and have found none of them satisfying either to myself or to my partner. I advocate strong emotional and what I consider active relationships."

"I do not like casual sexual encounters as they do not build to an emotional or spiritual plateau. I have been married for thirty-four years and prefer it."

"I have to get to know someone. I've never picked up a gal, took her home and balled her, although I did once or twice do it on the first date. But we were friends before that."

"I think the only thing I'm 'casual' about is my dress (bib overalls). I don't like casual relationships. I need to know the person."

"I like casual relationships more than I used to, but I always get frustrated and desire something deeper after a short while. I just need real affection and caring, and that rarely comes from a casual sexual relationship."

"The emotional content is more valuable than the physical release of orgasm. Since I can masturbate to orgasm, why bother with casual sex?"

DIVORCED AND SEPARATED MEN:

"I guess I think that love and sex are too powerful, too intense, too special to be dispensed casually."

"I'm not really a philanderer but it seems one is almost expected to be if they are divorced. I try to disappoint that expectation as much as possible! Casual relationships get boring and dangerous. I don't like the picture I get of myself or others so involved."

"No, because casual sex degrades people into using someone else's body for selfish reasons. To me, it is only an indulgent form of masturbation. The woman's vagina is only a surrogate 'palm.' Casual sex seems machine-like to me. Perhaps I'm rationalizing, but love and sex do seem to go together."

"I would like to enjoy casual sexual relationships but I simply find I am the kind of person who requires a long-term involvement or a close intimate type of relationship to really get it on with a woman."

"Besides the clap, one-night stands are the way to depression."

SINGLE MEN:

"I do not get off on casual sexual relationships although the idea has attracted me at times. In order to feel comfortable making a sexual advance to a woman, I need to know her as a friend and know she likes me. I guess that's unusual and a little weird, but I've given up trying to do things any other way."

"I don't care much for hit-and-run occurrences."

"I don't like casual sex. I have to feel a special closeness to the person I am having sex with, get to know them first. If a woman (stranger) promiscuously approaches me I turn away. When it comes to sex I'm not an animal, I'm a human being. I don't fuck, I make love."

"I've had one casual sexual relationship, if you want to call it that. I did it out of curiosity to see what it's like. I found out that it was unsatisfactory psychologically. It just didn't ring a bell in my head. I realized that I enjoyed sex with my girlfriend not just because it felt good, but because I love her. I had my orgasm but it was simply physical. There was nothing deep about it. It really wasn't fun. Sex with someone you love is tops, simply unbeatable."

Quite a few men said that the problem was that "casual sex" didn't stay casual:

"I find it difficult to achieve a casual sexual relationship. In the past I've had a few and they've been all right, but I most often find that I get too involved with the person to remain casual. Sex has that kind of effect on me."

"Casual relationships intrigue me very much, but I tend to get too involved, at least in my head. A fatal flaw."

"It's O.K., as long as it stops after the first night. But I've found that, as they progress, one of us gets more sucked into the relationship than he or she had planned, and so one of the two winds up getting hurt."

"I would love to like casual sexual relationships. But I tend to become very heavy with a woman who goes to bed with me."

"The emotional involvement deepens, even though you think it won't. I think that if I could screw around among my

friends on a casual basis, I would like it. But I don't like
rootless people; and people with roots—that is, homes,
husbands, children, and who stay in the same place for at
least five or ten years—they have roots, and they aren't about
to risk a casual sexual relationship which might be discovered
or frowned on."

And many had not had any "casual sexual relations":

"I have not really had any. My insecurity tends to make
me shy away from casual sexual relations."

"I've never had a casual sexual relationship and I think
it would be difficult for me to deal with one in a sane mind."

"For me—an emphatic no. Morality aside, it seems that
the one-night stands going on around me simply don't work."

*But some single men did have good things to say about
casual sex:*

"I like monogamy if I am in love with my lover, not
because I am a one-at-a-time person. Casual sex can be fun
too, but it's hard to find women who feel the same. They
seem to feel that what they have cannot be used for casual
purposes."

"Casual ones do have an intriguing element of mystery
and abruptness that says you don't have to see each other—
mutual masturbation."

"Although I prefer serious ones, there is a certain nice
feeling from having made love once or twice with someone
who is a friend or acquaintance, but not a serious or regular
lover. The feeling of a brief shared intimacy is a very warm
one, I find!"

"Casual sexual relationships are very novel and exciting,
but I get much less out of them. My more satisfactory casual
relationships are usually with friends—women who I have
known for a while and enjoy being with, but have never been
'involved' with. Once we discover that we can enjoy sex with
each other without becoming deeply attached, but still caring
for each other, it adds a nice extra dimension to a friendship.
We can call on each other sexually a couple of times a year
for a change from our ongoing relationships or if we are
feeling lonely. Again, with someone I know it is more comfortable—I can relax and *enjoy* more easily."

As did some married and divorced men:

"There's nothing intrinsically wrong with casual relationships, as long as neither party is operating under any illusions as to the nature of the thing nor is anyone being put upon by it. Some casual relations are merely a relief (or not) from boredom. Some are brief and shining spots of harmony."

"I enjoy occasional casual sex but only if it is mutually understood to be casual. It is always of the 'fuck' variety and for the fun of the moment. Basically, however, I am a one-woman man."

"Casual relationships have an awful lot to offer a person. You can have a lot of fun and get to know a person pretty well without getting all tangled up in their problems. Non-casual relationships are better overall, but they require much more time, trouble, and analysis in the selection of a partner. But I wouldn't go to bed with a woman I didn't at least like."

"I have not experienced extended periods of monogamy, nor do I think I would, it would have no meaning for me as an intelligent being. I do like casual sexual encounters, they are stimulating, rewarding, and adventuresome (unknown to my wife)."

MEN'S FEELINGS ABOUT BIRTH CONTROL AND ABORTION

Do men feel responsible for birth control?

"Do you feel responsible for discussing birth control before intercourse? If you are having a sexual relationship with a woman, do you protect her from becoming pregnant? Do you ask a woman if she has taken measures to prevent conception before intercourse? Who is responsible if she does become pregnant?"

Most men, especially younger single men, said that birth control was the woman's responsibility:

"Nope. If she doesn't know about something that is so important, then that's her problem. It seems a lot don't want to know, or even care about it."

"I know she does or I don't go out with her."

"I don't sleep with unprepared women."

"I assume the female will say something if she feels I need to know, since about all I can do is use a prophylactic or withdrawal. I more or less assume it is the woman's task to avoid pregnancy."

"No. It would be her child. She should take care of it."

"If a girl is over eighteen, she should protect herself from getting pregnant. If she wants to get fucked, she should know the consequences. If she is dumb enough to get pregnant, it is not the fault of the man. She is responsible if she gets pregnant. If the man *loves* the girl, he may either marry her or pay for her to have an abortion."

"It is usually the woman's job to worry about contraception. I am always ashamed to bring it up, because it's not official that we're going to fuck until I plunge my cock in. If I ask her if she takes the pill or something, I am always afraid she will say something to the effect of 'Why do you want to know? I'm not going to bed with you.' "

"I usually don't ask about birth control before intercourse. In a sexual relationship I would bring up the subject and see if we can find a mutual understanding. Otherwise I assume she knows the risks too and she knows if she has a chance of becoming pregnant or not. I am not afraid of getting someone pregnant as long as I love her and I can see we have a chance of staying together for a long time, possibly marriage."

"I used to but I found most women don't want the man to ask or worry about it. I wanted to be a gentleman but by their apparent choice I leave it up to them."

"I'll admit that several times I have just begun intercourse without inquiring about birth control (at least one of the times the woman wasn't using any). I didn't ask in these cases because I was afraid that I'd be turned down. Once I get into a relationship with a woman, I am always careful to protect her from getting pregnant."

Most married men, too, although they were more concerned about the type of birth control used, still considered it basically something the woman should take care of:

"When we were first married, she wasn't at all organized about birth control. I made her go to the doctor and get fixed up. If she loves me, she should think of these things and not stop me in the middle of fucking with 'But I could get pregnant.' "

"After we had been married a few years, I began to worry about the possible side effects of the birth control pills on her, so I suggested she switch to the diaphragm or IUD."

"My wife used to use the diaphragm, now she uses the IUD. I like it better because it doesn't interrupt lovemaking—it's just there, all the time, making sex more available."

"I don't have to ask her, because we are married and I know she will take care of it. (We have three kids, and I know she doesn't want any more now, because she is working full time.) Over the years, she has used several kinds. I don't bother her about it—it's her business, not mine."

But others, especially married men or men in long-term relationships, felt that the responsibility is mutual, at least insofar as discussing it—although the actual method of birth control still most often involves the woman's body:

"I always felt responsible for birth control. I don't know why, but it's related to helping with the housework. In this way, I wasn't merely a taker, but a real participant in the responsibilities we had."

"I think before you have intercourse for the first time with a woman it should be discussed. Decisions should be made about it before tumbling into bed. I have always protected the woman. If she does not use a pill or some other device, I see to it that I use a condom. I think both parties are jointly responsible."

"With a new partner I always discuss birth control. I never have sex with a person not using birth control—it's irresponsible. If she was to become pregnant obviously we both did it."

"Sometimes it admittedly interrupts the mood to talk about birth control, but it's important. I think psychologically most women are reassured about men if the men care enough to talk about preventative measures beforehand. Wouldn't anyone want to hang around a responsible person?"

"I feel responsible for making *sure* we're taking preventive measures. I've had partners who'd always forget if I didn't stop the proceedings just before entering her, and remind her or put a condom on."

"I wouldn't leave it entirely up to the woman—that is exceedingly stupid."

"Most men assume birth control must be the responsibility of the woman, and I used to feel this way too. Now I feel responsible, and I ask my lover about her cycle. If she becomes pregnant it is the responsibility of both people for not preventing it or discussing it. It is fun sometimes when I know her period is coming, and she has forgotten."

"What contraceptive methods (birth control) do you use? Who decides what contraceptive will be used? Which kind do you prefer?"

Most men preferred the birth control pill:

"I prefer the woman to use the pill as it is the best for me. The physical dangers are something an individual must figure out for themselves."

"I like the pill, for my convenience, if she doesn't mind, but I would never tell a woman to take it."

"We use various ones now she's off the pill. I miss that freedom."

"I have been with girls on the pill but I've also had to use condoms. The girl usually decides on what type, but if she decides none, I decide condom. I prefer the type which is always ready—especially the pill, or secondly, IUD."

"I prefer the pill, but I will use a condom (natural skin). Foam is O.K., but it sometimes provides too much lubrication and I loose a good contact with the walls of a vagina. Also foam tastes terrible! I have had no experience with IUD's or diaphragms. I let the woman decide which kind of contraception to use."

"We started using a rhythm method, then used condoms, and now she takes the mini-pill. I prefer the pill methods over all others we have used. I think for a young woman the benefits outweigh the risks."

"I prefer the convenience of the pill. Rubbers are a pain in the ass."

"My wife takes the pill. Until they come up with a better method, we will stay with that. I am aware of the side effects of the pill but, it is the only game in town. The pluses far outweigh the bad points. I wish to God they would invent a pill for men. I would take it and then maybe we would stop hearing this shit about how bad it is for women. No one forces them to take it, they do so by choice. If you follow everything that is said to cause cancer, you might as well not eat or drink anything. It is bullshit."

"I hate condoms. They make intercourse useless. I offer as much advice as I can, but in the end it is the woman's decision. I prefer the pill. I ask, and if she says she is not protected, I don't have intercourse. Two people are responsible."

*Many had heard of the possible side effects of the pill:**

"My wife did take some pills at first and it caused pain, dizziness, etc. I'm glad she's not taking them and I'd rather take a rubber or pill myself before she was to use the pill again."

"I don't believe in women taking pills. I know several friends who suffered from a variety of side-effects. These included nausea, loss of visual acuity, feelings of lethargy, arthritic attacks and increased susceptibility to infections."

"Mostly women I know have used the diaphragm, which is okay by me. I've been aware of the dangers of the pill for quite some time; apparently so have most of the women around me, for I don't know *anyone* who's still on the pill, whereas in college everyone was on it."

"My mother had a pulmonary embolism as a result, we believe, of taking estrogen. Therefore I don't want my wife taking the pill."

Other forms of birth control men mentioned women using, and their feelings about them, included:

"I was allergic to one of the foams. That stuff would take the skin from a stone. Wow! Now she uses a diaphragm most of the time (unless she's having her period, so she can't get pregnant)."

"Of all she has used, I prefer the diaphragm. I have been poked in the penis by the wire of her IUD, and have had burning sensations from foam suppositories. That stuff gets very hot—besides, all chemical contraceptives taste bad."

"I don't like it when a woman has to get up and go into the bathroom to get her diaphragm and then put it in. It breaks the mood for me, and sometimes she seems too businesslike too by the time she comes back. The IUD at least only has to be inserted once or twice a year—although I hear it can have some side effects."

"We went to the doctor together and discussed different forms of birth control she could use besides the pill. It seemed like overall the best was the diaphragm, and he

* These are discussed in detail in the book, *Women and the Crisis in Sex Hormones,* by Barbara and Gideon Seaman, 1977.

explained that it did not have to be unsexual if I helped her put it in. This is what we use now, although I wish we didn't have to use anything."

"Foam causes the vagina to be too slick, and it seems to burn me if I go bare skin, which is one of the reasons we don't use it more often, plus our son is a 'foam' baby. She uses the IUD, even though she doesn't really like it."

A few used the rhythm method:

"I am in college. I have intercourse as often as possible, which is usually about every other day during the 'safe' days. She does not want to use the Pill, because she's afraid we'd do it so often it wouldn't mean as much, and I don't feel as much with a rubber, so we try not to do it when she might get pregnant. Sometimes we can't keep from doing it, and we usually sweat out whether or not she's going to have her period. So far she always has. If we do it during a time when she might get pregnant, I try to pull my penis out just before ejaculation. (That doesn't always work, either.)"

Or the newer forms of the rhythm method:

"We use natural family planning—temperature, mucous, charts, etc. We also occasionally use condoms. Other partners in the past have used the pill."

"Currently basal temperature method (condoms in unsafe periods). It was mutually decided. I preferred this method as there were no associated health risks and it meant I was involved in it too. I had to be aware of my wife's cycle."

Most men disliked condoms:

"I don't like condoms. Any birth control device which does not interfere is O.K."

"I hate condoms and they cause me some pain for they are made for the average penis. What about us men who happen to have big ones? They are just too small for me. The feeling is bad too."

"I dislike rubbers—only used one in my life and the damn thing remained inside and I had to draw it out. The whole experience was unedifying indeed."

"Condoms are too tight at the base and they do desensitize your feelings."

"Condoms deflate my erection, and quickly."

"I used a condom before marriage. I found it very unsatisfactory, it was like the male role, responsible for everything—*all* the initiatives belonged to the man. I can understand that a cooperative woman can make a condom and its application a very sexy and delightful part of the whole thing, but that did not exist for me way back then!"

Some men used them, but without enthusiasm or with active dislike:

"We use rubbers mostly and I hate them—you know the old sensitivity argument about how it feels like taking a shower in a raincoat—but I feel I should do my share. It's easier for me to slip one on my cock than for my wife to get the diaphragm in and all the psychological hassle that involves. It does definitely cut down on my feelings, but it's better than going without sex at all—or putting my partner through extra pressure."

Others had mixed feelings:

"We use condoms, withdrawal, rhythm method. The pill is very harmful and upsetting to a woman's system. I like condoms because they are safe and have no side effects. They don't hurt me or her. Condoms are *not* uncomfortable —they just dull the feeling a bit, and are a hassle to put on when I want to get inside her fast. But I don't want to get my lover pregnant—it annoys me to have to put the condom on at the sensitive moment—I never want to stop and do it nor does she, but I worry if I don't, because she can get pregnant even if I don't ejaculate inside her. I don't feel as excited when I worry about this."

"Back in the days we used condoms, it became part of the lovemaking. The condom only was a discomfort if it came from a machine in a gas station. They're too brittle. The 4X or skins of any kind were so natural I often had to withdraw to check to see if it was still there. The rubber can be burdensome, but it beats pregnancy and the pill."

"We use rubbers about 95 percent of the time. The other 5 percent we use nothing, but this is only during her safe time. Also very occasionally we will use a spermicide foam only as a change of pace. I prefer nothing, but rubbers are better than other kinds of birth control. About fourteen years ago my wife took the 'pill' for a period of time, but both she and I feel it had a negative effect on her."

But some men liked them:

"I like condoms because they delay orgasm for me usually."

"To someone who grew up in the fifties, condoms have an association with sex. I still like the thought of a woman putting a condom on my penis, and using it, even though the pleasure is lessened, because of that very real association with the sex act. However, I also love the thought of depositing my semen in my wife's vagina."

"I like condoms. Condoms are very, very safe. I am a careful character. Besides, the expensive kind made of real skin you can hardly feel at all. It's fun to see the semen caught in the bottom when you take it off."

Finally, some men weren't really satisfied with any of the forms currently available:

"Most often women I have slept with were either on the pill, or had a diaphragm. I haven't used a rubber in so long I can't remember what it's like, although I often have one or two with me. Both partners should decide what contraceptive should be used. The pill is, of course, the best for smooth uninterrupted sex, but I'm not crazy about what it does, or might be doing, to a woman's body. Foam I don't trust. IUD's I don't trust, for what I think it might be doing to a woman's insides. I guess I trust rubbers and diaphragms most for effectiveness and safety, but I'm not really crazy about any of them."

"I've used all kinds. There doesn't seem to be much of a decision point at which the methods are selected. Usually the intimacy is just swept to the point where it becomes necessary to consider birth control. If one or the other has the means at hand, those means are usually adopted. I have been only marginally involved in acquiring birth control materials. I've discussed methods with my partners, and bought condoms when they were decided on. I've helped people with their prescriptions for the pill. I still don't feel terribly involved in the process. I suppose I prefer the rhythm-based methods. I've never used them, but it seems like the absence of hardware and chemicals and operations is the nicest one."

"I pass on a 'modest proposal' made in a letter to the *Times* (by a woman): 'Why not have every man bank some of his sperm and then have a vasectomy? Then he could have convenient sex for the rest of his life and if he wanted to impregnate someone, he would only have to make a trip to the bank.' "

"I'd like to see a concentrated effort on developing a male contraceptive pill: it seems it should be a lot easier to alter male chemistry without side effects than that of women . . . also, it should be a mutual responsibility and not only the woman's burden—I've seen too many people screwed up for life by pills or IUD's or abortions not to be concerned . . . vasectomy should be an answer, but as I understand it now it's only about 50 percent reversible . . . at this point in my life it's not very likely I'll ever have kids, but I don't want to gamble on that option . . . there's always an off chance my dream-lover really exists, right??? In the meantime, a male pill seems a lot more viable—and fair—"

A few men had had vasectomies.* Several of them are quoted here,† as this information is so new. In fact, surprisingly, all men who had had them said they were very happy with them:

". . . I would not have wanted to miss having children—I love my kids and the many good times we've had and will always remember even the bad times—that we successfully pulled through—but, there comes a time that we no longer wish to raise a baby—and perhaps don't feel we ever will again—and I for one, felt the time had come for me to become sterile. It's a big decision for a guy (at least it should be) and, while I wouldn't tell anyone to do it, I would like to convey to anyone that has hesitated because of a fear of pain, or a diminishing 'sex' drive, to stop worrying. It has done only one thing to me, physically—and that is to stop the sperm from reaching the semen—other than that, I had no pain— and my sex life has been revolutionized. It was very quick, relatively inexpensive and my peace of mind is priceless—a very important thing to a guy who loves sex and wants no more children, for the couple's sake and for the sake of future children."

* There have been approximately one-half million vasectomies per year performed in the United States for the last five years, according to the Association for Voluntary Sterilization.

† These replies answer the question, "Do you have a vasectomy? How has it affected your sexual activities? What do your partners think about it? Have you ever wished to have it reversed? Would you recommend it to other men?"

"Yes, I have had a vasectomy. This was after we had had four children. Since I had it, our sexual activities have been more relaxed, more fun and therefore more frequent. My partner loves it (the vasectomy). She thinks it is definitely the smartest thing I have ever done. Wanted it reversed? Hell, *no*. I would certainly recommend it to other men, although a lot seem to be afraid of the idea."

"I have had a vasectomy. I have two children that were adopted during my third marriage. It has not affected my activities in any way. My partner is happy that I have done it. I have no wish for a reversal. I would recommend it to anyone."

"Our current method of birth control is vasectomy. Early in our marriage as a result of religious pressure, we relied on the rhythm method. It not only didn't work, but it led to a lot of frustration (very bad for my wife, who could never have sex at all when it was the time of month when she most felt like it), and kept us apart when we needed each other and imposed a lot of unnecessary physical and emotional stresses. It is a sick way of doing things anyway. Then the pill arrived on the scene, and it was marvelous in many ways. It gave tremendous peace of mind, and my wife began to enjoy sex quite a lot. Fear of pregnancy had almost completely spoiled it for her (we had four kids in as many years as it was). After we had used the pill for several years, there began to be a lot of news about possible side effects of the pill, so we decided that the real answer to the problem was sterilization, and I had a vasectomy. It was a bloody marvelous idea!"

"I have a vasectomy. I decided on this after a discussion with my wife eight years ago. We used rubbers for a long time, but they worried me because I didn't want to be a father again, after both my daughter and son were born. The pill was always a concern. I am very happy with my vasectomy. I have two children. It has only enhanced my sexuality and my wife feels happy that it has liberated her. The operation was *fun!* I thoroughly enjoyed myself and I never felt so whole, as I made the decision without coercion and it provided a happy future at least as far as my sex life was concerned. I would never want it reversed and without equivocation I recommend it as the best possible means of birth control. I do recommend it to other men; those who reject it, reject it from fear. They think it changes the male anatomy. Nonsense. My biologist told me that the only significant change would be that I'd disclose 25 percent less semen. Since I don't know what 25 percent looks like it ultimately did not matter."

"Two children. Vasectomy takes the worry out of being close. I no longer even think about impregnating women; the decision of the sex merely depends on if we want to or not. It's beautiful. Partners love it. Once or twice I thought of reversal but now I've decided *no*. I recommend it highly."

But most men, when asked, "Would you be willing to get a vasectomy?," were horrified by the idea:

"No one is going to cut my cock off. Over my dead body."

"Tubes cut & tied, *never*!!!"

"No. I'm still together."

"Got as far as the doctor's office for the 'interview' and he noticed that my 'view' (expression) was one of mild horror. My revulsion also had to do with my egotistical and philosophical perspective of the importance of knowing one's own generative powers are intact. There is an extreme power, in the sense of carrying the seeds of life within one's self that may have to do with respect of life itself. Handling it is a judicious matter."

"Are you in favor of abortion? Have you ever impregnated a woman who subsequently had an abortion?"*

Most of those who answered had mixed feelings about abortion:

"I am not in favor of widespread abortion but I do believe it should be used when absolutely necessary. I do not believe the law has a place in abortion. It is something to be worked out between the woman, her doctor, and her minister. Back in my early days I was ready to help a young friend who was in trouble but not by me. However it was not necessary as nature took care of the problem in her second month. Another young friend got pregnant by a bum who deserted her without marrying her. She committed suicide. This left a sadness with me for fifty years because I did not know that anything was wrong until it was all over. She should have been able to get help."

* This topic, although important, can only be discussed briefly here for reasons of space.

"I don't think abortion should be outlawed, but I'm not sure how much in favor of it I am. Particularly with the number of contraceptive devices at the disposal of both parties to the act."

"Twice I have been through abortions with partners in the past decade. In both cases, the abortion was the best thing to do and was the result of carefully thought out mutual decisions. I am a strong advocate/supporter of abortion/ reproductive rights and have marched in protests, etc. Still, I wish the abortions could have been avoided."

"I have helped a girl get an abortion and another girl had an abortion when pregnant from me. I am more in favor of abortion than against it, and feel that ending a pregnancy is much better than having an unwanted baby. I also think the logic of the anti-abortion group is incontrovertible: killing a fetus is killing a human. Two incompatible ideas, I guess, but nonetheless true for being incompatible."

"I *personally* am not in favor of abortion. In a pregnancy that I helped create, I'd try to persuade my partner to try some other avenue. However, I recognize that this is an issue where you simply cannot legislate morality. So I am in favor of freedom of choice. I am opposed to abortion being used as a method of birth control. I consider it an extremely drastic step that ought to be used as a last resort. People should be taught to use birth control material correctly, and they ought to be available *everywhere* to *anyone* who wants this."

A few were totally in favor of women's right to abortion:

"I am in favor of abortion. Everyone makes mistakes. We shouldn't compound the problem."

"Yes I am in favor of abortion. A woman should have control over her own body. However in a marriage I think the husband should have a right to voice his opinion."

"I am absolutely in favor of abortion. In the practice of law in past years I often gave women the identity of persons doing abortion clandestinely."

"It's an individual decision. It shouldn't be outlawed at any rate."

"I think abortion should be legal, safe, and clean. The decision to have an abortion is hers. However, I would want to have some part in the decision-making process. I would be angry if I were ignored and left out."

". . . I approve of abortions when the woman wants one. I helped a girl I was living with get an abortion seventeen years ago when they were back-door operations. She was pregnant from another man and told me this two weeks after we started our relationship. I borrowed the money, found a competent doctor, and took her to the doctor and stayed with her afterwards. She was naturally desperately afraid of internal infection even though the doctor had given her a penicillin prescription. I worked extra that summer to pay a friend back the 300 dollars (which was a great deal of money then). Abortions should be a medically safe operation available to any woman."

And some men were totally against abortion:

"I sort of compare abortions to being rich. I can see the practical advantages of them however aesthetically and morally the idea to me of either is deplorable. To me abortions and rich men step on others to get where they are. But welfare taxes are high, environments are needed to raise a child properly etc. To me a more logical but I think illegal solution is to set up with a comfortable-to-rich couple with a good family environment to adopt the baby unless the impregnated woman wanted it. In exchange they pay the bills plus something for her for her suffering. They can afford it. It would get us off the hook. Protect the fetus's rights and make deserving people happy."

"When I was sixteen I got my girlfriend pregnant. I took her to the doctor when he confirmed it. Then we told her parents and her father arranged for an abortion. I offered to pay for the abortion and to tell my parents but he said no. I really didn't want her to get an abortion but at the time I was powerless. I was young and stupid and I'll never let it happen again. I am only in favor of abortion in cases where the mother's life is seriously jeopardized and then only after all other courses of medical treatment have been tried."

WHAT DON'T MEN LIKE ABOUT INTERCOURSE? PRESSURES ON MEN DURING INTERCOURSE

How do men feel during intercourse? Are they enjoying it as much as the popular culture says they should? What are their main concerns? Do men consider themselves "responsible" for women's pleasure during intercourse? Does society's pressure on men to express themselves basically through intercourse limit their own sensuality and excitement?

Although men had many reasons for wanting/liking intercourse, at the same time they also found many things about intercourse not pleasurable. In fact, there are many pressures on men during intercourse:

"Although I like intercourse, psychologically, intercourse for me is work; it's not a pleasure. It's pleasant work, of course, but it is still work. The orgasm I get is always the same and is over very soon, so it's not really an overwhelming sensation to look forward to. And the immense pressure to (1) get an erection, (2) keep the erection, (3) thrust *exactly* the way my partner likes it (with no help from her telling me how she likes it), (4) last longer than ten to fifteen minutes without prematurely ejaculating, and (5) thrust without hurting my partner when I do ejaculate—is just too, too much to do right each and every time out. Women don't realize that men do *all* the work, are expected to know how to do everything well, and are expected to read their partner's minds all the time. Well, it's just grossly unfair if you ask me. Too many women just lay there and silently look up at you as if to say, 'Okay, make it happen.' "

"Now, although men are initially pleased at the opportunity and the challenge, it can get pretty tiresome afterwards when they're chastised for blowing it again. Intercourse is a two-way street. If women would tell men how they want it, when they want it, and open up the communication 199 percent more than they do now, the act of physical love would be something men would not fear as much as they do now. Men would go into the bedroom knowing that if they do something wrong, the girl will help them through it. But that's not the way it is now. I fear the act of sex so much that sometimes I physically shake all over. It's all up to me, and I know it (and she knows it). Men are lousy lovers, are unbelievably inept at it, and I've heard this from countless women before I ever read *The Hite Report*—which confirmed it. But for chrissakes, nothing will ever change unless women take up their share of the responsibility. Sex above all needs to be more of a relaxed act, but I have never met a girl who was able to make me relax yet. Never. When I do, I'll probably marry her. And if you knew my views toward women, you'd know how much of a rarity that would make her."

"You know how I feel? Sometimes I feel like intercourse and sometimes I don't. I feel like, what does she want? If I'm not sure I can get it up right then, I sometimes think it might be nice to lay around together, but usually decide I'd better act cold and say no because I don't know what she wants. I don't like feeling called upon to respond as a male— this has happened a few times—I don't want to feel called upon to do whatever a man 'should' do—you know (grunt, grunt) me man, you woman, I fuck you—etc."

"More than anything else, I associate sex with anxiety, fear of failure, of coming too soon, of being impotent, of being laughed at, compared, abandoned."

"During the buildup stage, it can be like a rocket waiting to go off. Very suspenseful. Will the rocket go off? Will it go straight? Questions like this are what I think about."

"During the buildup I feel frightened that I will not be able to deliver to the woman what I implicitly offered, i.e., an exciting, satisfying sexual experience. This results, I am sure, from my own feelings of insecurity. I am primarily conscious of what I think would be pleasurable to my partner. I am seeking some gesture or signal from her that I am doing the 'right things.' My intellectual preoccupation undoubtedly distracts and detracts from my own enjoyment, however, my dignity may be at stake with this woman, or with women. But during the climax I forget to worry, as I feel the ultimate surge of physical pleasure which is all-consuming, a total body experience which carries me far away. But after—I tend to mentally criticize my own performance and seek some form of acceptance from her. I frequently feel guilt and shame, yet somehow also as though I were physically fulfilled."

Many men had these worries especially after their orgasm:

"Post-coital thoughts: (1) Did she come and if not should I feel responsible? (2) Fears of obligation ('Now that we've had sex this is more serious'). (3) Disappointment when a sexual exchange still leaves me and my partner far from true intimacy."

"Sometimes I get depressed, and have feelings of failure and self-hatred. It could have been longer, bigger, better, etc."

"I get paranoid. Did I please her? Was I good enough? This makes me mad. Why is it that the burden of pleasure is always on the man?"

"Somehow I feel almost guilty that I'm satisfied afterward. There seems to be a stigma now for men to be super cocks—continue, continue, *do* for the woman. I love giving —yet I must do for me. I know I'm being defensive, probably against an unseen enemy, yet the pressure *is* there. Sex is also for *my* enjoyment. I must 'perform' for myself, too."

One reason for men's mixed feelings about intercourse is the enormous amount of pressure on men during intercourse to "perform" correctly: "Will I do it right?" Specifically, the patriarchal model of sexuality puts four pressures on men: to become erect ("get it up"), stay erect ("keep it up"), make the woman orgasm, and do all of this as frequently as possible.

I: PRESSURE TO HAVE AN ERECTION ("IMPOTENCE")

"Have you ever had difficulty having an erection at a time you desired one? When does this happen, and why? How do you feel?"

Indeed most men had experienced difficulty having an erection at *some* time (39 percent infrequently; 17 percent sometimes; 13 percent frequently, regularly, or always).*

* It is noteworthy, however, that very few of the men who had difficulty with erection with their partners had these problems by themselves during masturbation.

But worse than the actual loss/lack of erection, perhaps, is the *fear* of lack of erection (and the outdated disgrace which this implies) which most men carry with them throughout their lives. Almost all men expressed this (unnecessary) fear in one way or another.

Most men had it happen only infrequently or irregularly, although the fear of it happening was always there:

"I have a periodic inability to 'get it up.' Those times sex has still been fun (usually oral sex), and if the favor were returned, then the feeling was good. But there has always been a certain uneasiness on my part, since I felt the whole thing was essentially a failure. Sex happens when the man gets it up. Without that, the whole thing is more or less an undress rehearsal, if you will."

"The only time I am anxious that I am not '*man* enough' (hate that juvenile, macho expression!) is when I have inexplicably lost my hard-on and cannot continue. What the hell happened? I ask myself. How come? How delicately am I balanced, anyway? It is frustrating and embarrassing. It makes me feel like I am a little helpless boy, guilty usually. I feel ashamed."

"A few weeks ago, three or four times the erection just wouldn't come. It happened when we were angry at each other and I was tired of being married to her. I was willing, but my penis was just tired of living a lie. We were as close to divorce as we have ever been. I was being rejected night after night, and when we did do it, it wasn't satisfactory because she was giving no response. It was the classic masturbation in the vagina—and would have been a lot more satisfactory if I had done it in the bathroom, by myself."

"I have sometimes had difficulty achieving and/or keeping an erection when I wanted it. It happens most often during intercourse, but it has happened during masturbation too. It happens more often lately than it used to, and I think that tension, fatigue, and a lack of desire for sex play a large part in causing it. It makes me feel the same way that I feel when I lose in some kind of competition, but it is worse because it disappoints and frustrates my wife too. I usually just give up trying and hope it will not happen next time."

"I have what is called secondary impotence. Sometimes I can, sometimes not. To deal with this, I need a woman who cares, but I would feel I am imposing on her. I'd like to be able to deal with my impotence with the help of someone I was attracted to but could let go of if she wanted out. Most of my recent (last five years) intercourse has been oral."

"I get frustrated and mad at myself when I can't get an erection. I feel that I should have erections whenever I 'command' them. And I worry that the woman takes it as a sign of her lack of desirability. My former wife cried and made me feel terrible."

"Failure to get a full erection (and thus be able to satisfy a woman) is what males generally fear. In fact, the pressure that women feel to fake orgasms is probably their response to the male fear. This includes me, because since I'm big and strong, I'm expected to be the Super Sex Stud of the world. If I'm not ready, the demands come fast and furious. I don't fear this so much as I used to, but it makes me mad that men have to worry about such things."

"Yes, who hasn't? Why? A million reasons. Fatigue, concern over other things. Often overstimulation sexually before fucking—foreplay went on too long and too hot (but sometimes I fuck better when that happens). Often there is a subtle but clear antagonism over something with my wife— we've had an argument or are bothered by something. And sometimes it just seems unexplained. It used to happen every time—when I had my first few experiences, for the first year of marriage on and off, every time I have sex with another woman during the first time or two at least. The few homosexual experiences I've had I've also had erection problems, though it's been less crucial there since I don't have homosexual intercourse. What do I do? Worry as little as possible. Usually I just chalk it up to fatigue or irritability or too much sex on the head."

"It is very embarrassing when it happens. I was relieved to discover from a good woman friend that it is not a problem unique to me. But the pressure is still on the man to perform. Men are horny, lustful beasts, why aren't you tearing at me with a giant erection? It's a myth, but still one that haunts us from over our shoulders."

Some men had it happen more regularly, so that it was an ongoing worry in their lives:

"I've always had difficulty having an erection, even at age twenty-four when I had my first coitus (I'm sixty-nine now). Perhaps it was because I was taught if it's fun it's bad, and that sex is *sin*. Maybe it's a feeling of guilt. I'm trying to rid myself of this feeling."

"When I was a teenager, I used to have to go through mental gymnastics (like thinking of my mother) to keep from having a hard-on in church or at the beach, etc. Now the activity is minimal. Partly, I'm not excited genitally by my wife. I don't know how it would be with other people. As it began to happen more and more, I felt almost suicidal. It's self-defeating—caused by fear of impotence. I feel depressed and resigned about it. Also, sometimes I get angry at my wife, as though I'm her captive, and an impotent one to boot. I don't talk to other males about this (or sex at all). It's very threatening. Also I feel that many women are secretly scornful of impotent men, even though they act understanding."

One man said he had overcome his feeling of shame and embarrassment:

"I've been impotent or partially so for most of my life. That's because I drank too much, also because I was afraid. Once I was having intercourse with a woman I loved and respected. She was about to orgasm. I was just thrusting because I felt I had to. I really didn't want to. It does nothing or very little for me sometimes. I could feel my erection going soft. I got scared. I fell out of her vagina. She, who was about to come, roared up, called me a fucking bastard, and punched me a few times in the chest and stomach. I was so scared and angry at myself—I felt subhuman, a total, miserable failure, the worst lover and person on earth. I went into a catatonic state, I was numb with fear and pain for hours. And why? It really wasn't that serious, it was a bummer, but she got over it in a matter of minutes. The reason why I felt this way was because I wasn't measuring up to the image of what a real man lover was supposed to be. I was taught that women are supposed to cry and scream and have five or six orgasms, scratch my back, and then pass out from ecstacy. And if this didn't happen it was the man's fault. It was my fault. And I couldn't even keep it up long enough to give her one orgasm. I was dirt. I deserved to die. I really felt suicidal. I was conditioned to put a woman's pleasure before mine. My 'job' was to get her to come. After she had her orgasm then it would be okay for me to have mine. I remember that if she didn't come then the man failed and he would lose her to another man who was better, who would make her come. Very competitive. Very sick.

"Now I've learned that I've got a right to be me. I haven't lost the ability to make love at all. I just like to go to bed with my woman friend, just me and her leaving the rest of America out on the street, *Playboy*, Madison Avenue, the shrinks, the Generals, the teachers, Hollywood, the Priests, the rich-powerful men and all the rest of the myth makers. Get out of my bed, get out of my head and let me be the lover I'm supposed to be, let us make love the way we need to make love. The best sex for me is not entirely orgasm or intercourse, but those long hours of closeness, kissing, holding, working back and forth that produce arousal. Long periods of arousal are better than anything for me. There is such a grand feeling of closeness, comfort, and sharing. I guess what I'm saying is that most of the time I get a greater thrill out of foreplay than intercourse. This is true and everything is fine for as long as performance anxiety over intercourse doesn't raise its head. One thing about impotence, it certainly is interesting. Every sexual feeling can be a mystery for us. Every single moment in the arms of a lover, an adventure. If I, the so-called impotent man, can learn to forgive myself, I will never be sexually bored, we can invent a whole new sexuality."

What are some of the reasons men gave as causing lack or loss of erection?*

Perhaps the most commonly cited causes of lack of erection were alcohol, drugs, and/or fatigue:

"When I drink a lot of booze, I have a very hard time. I try not to let it happen because it's a drag. I feel very embarrassed."

"It happens when I'm drinking—but when drinking, I could care less!"

"It's occurred when I've had a few drinks or smoked too much dope. It messes me up. So when I desire sex I lay off booze and weed."

"This just happened to me a week ago. I couldn't get an erection because I hadn't slept in twenty-four hours. I apologized and told her I needed some sleep before I could get an erection."

---

* Persistent erection problems may be an early sign of blood sugar problems, which might not be discovered in a routine sugar test, but would require a five-hour sugar curve test. Also, some medications for high-blood pressure decrease erective ability.

The second most frequently cited reason was emotional upset or anxiety:

"I had a very depressing period when I had some severe marital problems (infidelity on my wife's part). The shock of her withdrawal of any lovemaking from that time to now caused me to seek intercourse elsewhere. I experienced impotence for about a year and periodically for the next couple of years thereafter. I have worked through the impotence problem and now I satisfy the partner orally or digitally."

"If I don't trust my partner or am afraid of getting too emotionally involved, I can be impotent."

"When I am insecure with a partner: I'm not sure she's anxious to be with me. It happens often when the relationship is ending, when mutual interest is waning, etc."

"When I'm angry or mad at my partner, I can't get it up. I have to wait until it passes."

"Fear, anger, humiliation, all cause me to lose my erection—or never get it."

"Most important is a lingering resentment against my partner for some prior event. It may be nothing to do with sex, or maybe I think she is too passive. 'Hell, why doesn't she show more enthusiasm?' But then, what am I doing to fail to enthuse her?"

"I couldn't get it up while trying to have an affair, because I felt guilty."

"I have to feel loved and to feel love for her, which I don't after an argument."

"It only happens when I feel unwanted."

"Mood has an effect. Maybe I need to be just held and caressed."

"I have had difficulty getting an erection when there was extreme frustration in my outside life, especially when I felt deeply that I was defeated badly in one or another way in life. My explanation is that my male behavior in sex is associated with feeling strong beside my tender woman. And when I am badly defeated subconsciously, my sexual strength is turned off."

Many men mentioned that it often happened with a new partner:

"That one nervous bout of impotence caused by over-anticipation and anxiety in connection with a girl I had lusted after for many months and finally got into bed. On this occasion I also drank too much. It was tragic—the harder I tried, the softer it became. I knew what was causing my impotence (overexcitement) but could do absolutely nothing to cure it. I was finally all right in the morning after fitful rest, but it took several meetings before all problems were cleared away between us."

"It happens when I'm having sex with a woman for the first time, usually because I'm nervous and I want very much to please her. I make love to her anyway and hope I can bring her to orgasm in ways other than fucking."

Other men said it happened when they didn't really want to have sex:

"There are times when just a touch or even the thought of sex will bring an erection. There are other times when all the kissing and hugging in the world still have me limp, and it takes direct stimulation of the penis to get it up. I probably don't get erected cuz I'm not interested in sex at the time, or at least not in the orgasmic aspects."

"If I am ever bored during intercourse my penis is the first to know; the erection cannot be maintained."

"Last summer it was so hot that I wasn't in the mood for anything. My wife tried quite hard several times to make me get an erection but nothing happened. Finally I stopped faking it and told her I just was so hot I wasn't interested. She thought it was the funniest thing she ever heard!"

"Sometimes I have had difficulty having an erection. It is not so much that I desired one and couldn't get it but that what I desired was not sex at all. Such situations create great inner turmoil. The cultural bias tells me that 'men' *always* can get a hard-on near an available and eager woman, and that the power of the 'sex drive' is greater than any inhibiting factors. Meanwhile, I know from experience that *I* cannot perform sexually so long as a strong 'negative' feeling is directed toward my partner. What I need to do is to deal openly with the 'negative' feelings and *then* to proceed to sex, if it is appropriate. What I generally *do*, however, is to either shut down to the point of appearing exhausted or muster enough fantasy material to overcome the real feelings and do some perfunctory sex. Such episodes do not happen very often, and when they do I have learned to accept it. My identity and self-worth does not need to depend on the hardness of my penis."

Or if they had no real feelings for the woman they were with:

"For the past nine years an erection has become very unpredictable. The emotional factors are the most critical; i.e., strong desire for the individual female . . . and either the possibility or the reality of emotional involvement, too. Sex for the sake of sex only is no longer possible, apparently."

"After some good therapy, I decided, 'If I don't get hard then I really don't dig this girl.' "

"If I'm not emotionally involved with my partner, it's much harder for me to get an erection."

"My sexual machine works only if there is the proper feeling for the partner."

Or if the woman acted bored or uninterested:

"Difficulty with erection: Ahh yess. It can happen any-time. It will always happen when I feel the woman loses interest or does not wish to proceed. It started when my wife (ex-wife) seemed to be 'putting up with her husband's overtures.' "

Sometimes simple worry over "performance" could create the problem:

"Sometimes if I am too involved with her demands, I lose my erection. I back away emotionally a bit so I can be more concerned with myself—it works."

"Sometimes it happens when I'm worried that I might not last long enough for my wife."

"Something that tends to inhibit an erection is a feeling of uncertainty as to how I am seen, or what is expected of me; or most of all, worrying about whether I am going to have an erection."

Some men connected lack of erection with age:

"When I become anxious about losing my potency with age, my partner reassures me and it goes away if she's understanding—most women are. In a way, these sessions are the best because it takes a while to get it up. Also women seem to enjoy rubbing their clitoris with a soft penis."

"I'm sixty years old. Sometimes I achieve erection but can't *keep* it long enough for either my partner or me to have orgasm. This is more frequent than failure to achieve erection. Re erection: It happens irregularly but on the average half the time I want to have intercourse. Why? Partly because (I'm told; I'm not sure it's true) the aging process includes loss of erection capability. Partly it's because usually I'm easily distracted from the 'core' business at hand—by conversation, music, unidentifiable noises in the house or outdoors, television, etc. Partly because I smoke. Partly because I drink (I don't mean I'm drunk when I'm impotent). How do I feel? Terrible. Ashamed. Old. What do I do about it? Leave my partner (if she's had her orgasm; otherwise, bring her to orgasm with fingers, tongue, or my hand-operated cock); have a cigarette, take sleeping pills, read. But: we don't always try to have intercourse when we have sex; often it's not intended to be anything more than play, from the beginning. In such circumstances, there's no disappointment—just fun."

"For most of my life, I have not had difficulty achieving erections, quite the other way around. But for the past half dozen years (I am now in my sixties), erections are occasionally more difficult to achieve or come more slowly, and are never as hard and full as in my younger years. Age is the obvious reason, though medication (I am obliged to take it to maintain normal blood pressure) can also have this effect. I now simply must have much more stimulus to erection, both physical and psychological. I am no longer automatically aroused by the sight of a nude woman or a bit of pornography. I almost never have morning erections, as I did most of my life, or nocturnal emissions."

This important topic will be discussed more fully in the chapter related specifically to age; but in fact, not all older men had difficulty having erections; physical erection ability may be as much related to general state of health than to chronological age.

But 31 percent of the men who answered said they had never had a problem having an erection:

"My friends tell me that they've had trouble when drinking heavily or doing drugs (other than pot), but I've never had such problems, and I don't really know why."

"What do you do at such times?"

Some men practiced oral sex or some form of sex other than intercourse on their partner to orgasm:

"When it happens, I know in advance it's going to happen and avoid raising any expectations. I've had delightful sex without an erection—cunnilingus, etc."

"I almost always need help from her (which is always forthcoming) to get and maintain an erection. Usually I keep trying and if nothing happens, I try to make her come and then cuddle for a while."

"I lick them to several climaxes until the situation is broken and it'll usually come around—it's embarrassing but all the women concerned were most understanding—all gave me great head to start things off."

Some continued foreplay until erection occurred:

"I just try to keep my partner interested with extended foreplay and usually the problem solves itself eventually."

Many men stimulated themselves, either physically or mentally:

"I get frustrated when I can't bring it up when I really want to. I make an extreme muscular effort, fantasize widely, try to remember which of my wildest fantasies will work, posture my body in stretched-out erotic ways, make love in a variety of ways with increasing rapidity to my partner. It is a mental effort that I put a lot of energy into—success about 90 percent of the time."

"I occasionally masturbate to arouse myself prior to sex when I feel unaroused but want to make myself available for my wife. I also psych myself up for the occasion."

"At the times when I have trouble getting it up I'll masturbate—discreetly so that my partner is not particularly aware of what I'm doing."

Or the woman stimulated them:

"My love is a genius at correcting this situation."

"Manual stimulation helps. Otherwise, lying close helps. In difficult cases I try to shove it in anyway. My wife learned how to hold it so it can usually be pushed in even soft."

Some stopped to talk about their feelings, or whatever might be bothering them:

"Sometimes I'm mad or bothered by something, and getting out what's on my mind usually works wonders on stiffening my dick. If I'm angry and say so, it may seem like a contradiction, but right after that, I can feel really loving (now that I've said it) and be dying to screw."

"I used to feel like my penis was a different part of me— a sort of mechanical thing, not part of *me*. Now that I have done a lot of thinking and working on myself (maybe not necessary if it weren't for this crazy culture we live in), it feels very much a part of me. And I no longer have problems getting an erection. If I don't get one, I know that it's just not what I want at that time, and I look deeper into my feelings at the moment."

A few men were not greatly bothered by it:

"I never gave it too much serious thought. If I'm tired or something is on my mind, anything really, our bodies reflect how we feel emotionally, so I can't expect to have my body perform all the time. It's just accepted. At least by me!"

"Erections are desirable but not required. With this attitude they're allowed to come and go."

"It used to bother me not to have an erection and at first my partner blamed herself. However, we can talk to each other and now it does not bother either of us."

"Men, I think, tend to worry too much about impotence —which, I'm convinced, is temporary if nature is permitted to take its course. An example is a trip that I made to Ireland with my wife. For a while our sex had not been good. We were installed in a luxurious hotel overlooking the lower lakes of Killarney. The view was spectacular. The amenities were superb. The bathroom was huge and sybaritic. It had a fine bidet. My potency returned in a rush. I couldn't even wait to take my clothes off. I took them off later that afternoon, and the next few days were devoted almost entirely to lovemaking. I was a man again—though no longer young."

And one man questioned whether lack of erection was a problem at all:

"In order to avoid this problem, it is essential to eschew an attitude of 'I must perform,' which leads to anxiety, which leads to off-turning. That's why I had the problem more often as a teenager. When I learned to stop thinking in terms of pursuit and performance, to start feeling sex as a process, this problem largely solved itself. Anyway, it is a 'problem' only if we so define it. If (as is true) I don't need erection for arousal and orgasm; and if (as is true) the woman doesn't need my erection for her arousal and orgasm; then why is it a problem? A rigidly erect penis has no other use but penetration and thrusting. It is only a problem if we are blindly insistent on penis-vagina intercourse as essential."

A few men said that they enjoyed sex without an erection:

"Hugging, kissing, and feeling up of each other is great. If the penis does not get hard, don't worry about it. Sex is great any way, without actually having intercourse."

"Sex without an erection feels good in a more concentrated way—and usually doesn't last long for that reason. I'm not in the least embarrassed. We can't all be men of steel."

"It is O.K. to have sex without an erection. Some women don't want to have a big hard penis stuck in them all the time."

"Both my wife and I can have an orgasm if I'm not erect; if I become soft after intromission I can continue with intercourse—if before, my penis can rub against her clitoris from the outside."

"It is difficult to have vaginal intromission without an erection, but I still enjoy doing the kissing, licking, and sucking as much, and I can still get pleasure if she does the same to me."

"I'm not embarrassed by losing my erection, as it happens all the time and adds to the variety, because intercourse with a non- or semi-erect penis feels good in a different way. The sensations are concentrated differently and the stimulation usually brings back a full erection."

And a few pointed out that an erection usually comes and goes during sex:

"It is a natural thing for an erection to change in size during sex."

"My erections wax and wane throughout the session. It isn't disturbing."

"I hate to lose my erection; it's much sexier when it's hard than when it's soft. Come to think of it, though, it's a lot more fun to go up and down a few times rather than going up just once and staying rigid."

Men with homosexual sex lives were much more likely to feel comfortable with the changes in state of erection during sex—although of course they valued and enjoyed erections as much as other men:

"If a partner is a compassionate and smart partner, he could care less whether you might be occasionally impotent. That is the time for tactile sensation, cuddling and fondling. I am not embarrassed to have sex without an erection. Sometimes I can feel very aroused with an erection, lose the erection, but still be in a highly aroused state."

"There have been times when I have immensely enjoyed sex and remained unerect—there is still a sensitive feeling in the penis and an emotional feeling within the mind."

"Having my penis played with is fun, erect or not—and it is fun to play with someone else's."

"I often feel sexual without an erection. I can see an extremely sexy man and feel inside and not get an erection. It does not bother me, but it bothers my lover sometimes. I have to reassure him that it's all right."

"Sometimes if I want to be submissive in anal sex, I don't need an erection. It doesn't bother me if I don't have an erection. It only bothers my partner if he's new."

"I've felt sexual without an erection. In that case I use another part of my body, my tongue, or my fingers, or my foot, as a substitute for an erection. So far everybody's reaction to a pooped-out penis has been O.K. and surprise and enjoyment when I have found and used a substitute."

Conclusion

The demeaning term "impotent" has usually been applied to lack of erection, and means, of course, "lack of power"— i.e., lack of ability to impregnate a woman, the basic "power" of patriarchy. Many beautiful types of closeness have been given second-class status by a social structure which once wanted and needed to increase reproduction. Even though the idea is now so antiquated that birth control is practiced almost universally, we still insist on describing a man without an erection as "impotent," a "failure"—rather than seeing the appropriateness of many degrees of physical arousal. After all, a penis is related to a whole human being and his feelings; it is not a mechanical device, separate from a man's whole body and person.

Of course, erection and intercourse are pleasurable to both men and women; however, it is one thing if a man cannot get an erection when he desires one, and another when he feels he *must* produce one. In fact, a man need not have an erection to give a woman an orgasm, since orgasm in women is usually created by manual or oral stimulation of the clitoral and vulval areas.* The need for erection to "satisfy a woman" has been greatly overemphasized. And most men fear "impotence" more because they think they will appear unmanly, or a failure, than because of any fear of loss of pleasure or because they cannot (or it is more difficult to) orgasm this way.

The cultural emphasis on erection, which leads to an ever-present fear of lack of erection, forces most men to become focused on getting and maintaining an erection during sex. This in turn forces the activities to revolve around the erection, influencing the timing and sequence of events. Physical relations could develop a more spontaneous feeling if the importance of erection were greatly deemphasized. Older men, who *may* have trouble achieving or maintaining an erection (but not always), have been ridiculed and made to feel "less than men" by the society; in fact, often their diversification and rethinking of sexual pleasure has made them "better" lovers than younger men. (See chapter 8.)

II: PRESSURE NOT TO ORGASM "TOO SOON" ("PREMATURE EJACULATION")

"Do you ever orgasm 'too soon' after penetration—that is, find you are not able to continue intercourse as long as you would like? When does this happen? Why? Does it bother you?"

"Years ago I used to think that 'premature ejaculation' referred to spontaneous, unstimulated male orgasm before or just at intromission. Then I began to realize that some writers were using the term 'premature ejaculation' to denote male

---

* Although a minority of women do orgasm during intercourse itself, as they explain in *The Hite Report* on female sexuality, this is most often due to friction between the two pubic areas or other such exterior contact, which can accompany penetration.

orgasm taking place during coitus but prior to the woman experiencing orgasm. No time data were (or are) ever included in these references. It seemed (seems) that some fault lay with the male if he were unable to time (i.e., delay) his orgasm and/or 'manage' his coital movements until her orgasm (uncertain) had occurred. But all this assumed that otherwise unassisted female orgasm during coitus was 'standard' and probable under all normal circumstances if only the oafish male could 'hang in there' long enough. I am now fully persuaded (both from latter-day literature and my own observations) that female 'vaginal' orgasm is the exception rather than the rule—regardless of how long and how cleverly coitus continues—except in those cases where the prior arousal of the woman (both psychological and physiological) has attained an unusually extraordinarily high level and the 'excitement' combined with the most minor motions are sufficient to trigger orgasm upon the onset of 'triumphant' intercourse. I now tend to the belief that the most ordinary, the most routine, and the most reliable way for a woman to achieve orgasm during coitus is either for her or her partner to finger the clitoral area. On the other hand, perhaps I am only rationalizing away my own failure to induce female orgasm with regularity during coitus."

A constant source of anxiety among men is whether they continue intercourse long enough, remaining erect, or whether they reach orgasm "too soon." (Most men, although they sometimes used the term "premature ejaculation," did not in fact refer to its standard clinical meaning—i.e., orgasm before or just at the moment of penetration—but rather referred to very varied amounts of time of intercourse. In fact, most men who expressed this concern felt that this was probably the reason why a woman might not reach orgasm during intercourse with them; this thinking is inaccurate, however, as discussed in *The Hite Report* on female sexuality.

Seventy-four percent of the men who answered expressed concern over whether they continued intercourse long enough:

"Sadly, so far, I have been climaxing too soon to suit me. I can't control it. And I feel as though I haven't really done much for my partner even though I do try to continue stimulation somehow. I consider it a failed test of virility."
"I have to use extreme control to keep from coming too

soon, and this often makes me lose my hard-on. It sure does disturb me, because I know that then I'm not going to come and I'm going to be frustrated."

"I sometimes orgasm too soon after penetration. Anytime before my partner has at least one is too soon. But it can vary from two to five minutes. It usually happens when I have allowed myself to become too aroused or it's been a long time since I've had an orgasm. Of course it's a bother when it happens. It makes me feel I've lost control, and worse, that I'm something of a *weakling*."

"I feel like I'm cheating her."

"I feel guilt, anxiety."

"To come or not to come, that is the question. Whether 'tis nobler of the man to suffer the slings and arrows of prolonging the act to see if your partner is going to orgasm, or ejaculate into a sea of troubles and by orgasming, end them. I try to prolong the act, that is to say, refrain from coming too soon (i.e., before my partner), but sometimes this seems like a waste of time. Most women seem to think that a 'real good lover' would be able to 'make them come.' In my opinion, no one can 'make' a woman come. She has to be able to tell you what she wants before you can give it to her. And so many of them are either unable or unwilling to do this. If they would tell me how, I would do my damnedest to make sure that they reach orgasm. I usually try to think about something else to hold off from coming too soon, but this is by no means easy. And it kind of spoils it for me. I try to please my partner either orally or manually before I enter her. That way at least she has something."

"Oh Lord, is this a problem. I just happen to be one of those people who need very little stimulation to have an orgasm. Like maybe after a minute at most, I come. This is extremely bothersome to me because I can never really give my girlfriend an orgasm since I come so soon. I guess I usually leave her hanging, which really bothers me, not to mention her. Though she rarely talks about it, my coming prematurely is the biggest problem in our sex life and possibly our relationship, since I'm sure she's never satisfied (which means that I'm never really satisfied)."

"It has happened all too many times in my life, especially when my wife and I have gone for a long period without intercourse or a happy relationship. I blame it on my built-up-tight emotions and lack of love and acceptance, then there is sex immediately in front of you and I get uncontrollably excited and go off. Does it bother me? Yes, it makes me hate myself and my wife just that much more. It makes me feel very inadequate, unmanly, makes me feel like a wasted sexual experience, not satisfying to myself or my wife. I went to the physician twice about this problem and both doctors said and laughed, yes, you have a problem, but so do many other men. Nothing can be done about it. Ha, ha."

"One of my most common problems is premature ejaculation. It's just so hard for me to control. I haven't had that much experience or that many partners to try the technique of stopping my thrusts just before ejaculating, but I intend to in the future. I think it's the only way. It's very hard for me to continue for more than fifteen minutes, I would like to continue indefinitely (as any man would), but the stimulation is so great that you just can't imagine it. It bothers me greatly because it hinders me from helping my partner reach her orgasm, which is my main concern during intercourse."

"I have never (last twenty years) made my partner climax. Many times it is my fault, coming within fifty to seventy-five strokes. Other times I can go for many hundred strokes and still she won't even be approaching her orgasm. It is probably simply a matter of will power. But if I had a dollar for every time I have counted numbers or gone over plans in my head, anything to avoid thinking about what I was doing so as to squeeze out ten to twenty more strokes, I would be wealthy. It is interesting to me that many times I don't feel at all like orgasm as we screw, then she makes some physical or vocal actions and this causes me to come very quickly. It is a drag."

"Damn it all: Often! I think a butchered circumcision may have been at fault in part. But still, often I can hold off too. Or *did*. By the way, females must bear some of the responsibility. Those who excite quickly and start saying 'Come in me, please; come in me quickly' are asking for early or premature ejaculation. (So are those who ask for hard rutting.) But let me take the blame; yes, I often let go before I want to."

"It happens every time—probably because of a physical defect. I am always anxious about it happening, concerned about my partner's reaction, embarrassed, depressed after it because I know the women are far from being satisfied."

"Anticipation feels so good, but I feel really bad about coming too quickly and usually try to fake orgasm some time (up to five minutes) after I've actually had an orgasm. Then I feel like an s.o.b."

"Out of the thousands of times I have screwed, I have

made my partners climax only *two* or three times. I climax too soon. Usually the accentuated breathing, or some other action related to increased feeling on the part of my partner, makes me climax too soon."

"My climax comes rapidly if I perceive the lady really at a height. If she is out of control, really feeling 'good,' I lose my head and go. I've had to learn that what I thought was ecstatic for a gal really was nothing at all and she had a lot longer yet to go. My being fast bothers me like hell!"

"At times I have had premature ejaculation. It always happens at the beginning of a sexual relationship, I think because my anxiety level is so high. And the anxiety itself comes about because I have begun the sexual aspects of the relationship before I feel emotionally safe and secure. Again, I think that a cultural bias pushes me toward the sexual activity before the relationship itself is stable, under the pretext that sex *is* intimacy and that being a 'man' *means* being hungry for and competent at sex."

"Recently (the first time in my life, believe it or not) I walked into a porno movie. Besides being shocked at the real thing in living color with close-up camera lenses, I could not believe the *staying power* of the men. They were hard as a rock and lasted two or three women in regular and high-speed-fast anal sex and vaginal sex. If this is *normal* my wife is right. I am in trouble."

"Unfortunately, the more she excites me and the more I want her, the more liable I am to come too soon. I've naturally thought a lot about this and it seems to be almost a case of not believing she's going to stay with me or let me complete the act, like I feel she's going to pull away from me, so I come right away so she can't leave me before I'm finished. I have never had it happen when we spend time fondling each other before intercourse—that is, if she sucks and kisses and plays with me long enough, I seem to get over the anxiety."

"I often orgasm too soon after penetration—within two to four minutes, I expect. It bothers me when this happens . . . not because I see my penis as an engine to bring her somehow to orgasm . . . not because my manhood would be enhanced if I demonstrated staying power . . . but because I love her and love her body and enjoy being inside her. I'd like it to last longer. I don't know why it happens that soon each time (not *every* time, but frequently), but don't toss and turn on a shrink's couch wondering why. I *do* see the lack of control as my dysfunction no matter what books say about normal duration—at least for me it's a dysfunction, because it is counter to what I would like to have happen, and depends too much on my confidence, mood, and what's been happening between D. and myself over the last few hours or even days."

How soon is "too soon"? Answers varied from one minute to a half hour:

"A very bad 'too soon' would be before she is satisfied and I am mentally so, the shortest possible time for this being ten minutes, but usually around half an hour. I'm physically satisfied, but not mentally. This usually happens when I'm particularly horny. It's a case of matter over mind. It bothers me, but certainly doesn't shatter me."

"Regardless of the time (one minute to fifteen minutes) if it is not when I want it, most of the normal bodily sensations are lost."

"I have had an orgasm too soon during intercourse. By time, I mean a minute or two. The feeling during orgasm is the same as if intercourse had gone on for some time, but it is not satisfying to me."

A few men resisted feeling inadequate:

"For a while in the 'good old days' when I fantasized myself a stud and read all the sex manuals, coming too soon was like flunking an exam. I really worked to keep from ejaculating until after the woman, or at the same time, but that really took concentration. This kind of mechanistic concentration and concern with technique I think is a bummer and makes for very unloving sex. But then the women shouldn't be left without resolution. Somewhere there is a compatible middle, and finding it is the quest of good sex. After I cum and if the woman hasn't yet, I still like to keep up the lovemaking. This is not strictly as a matter of good conscience. I like to prolong it as much as possible and do feel warm and loving after orgasm."

Men could also experience this when having sex with another man:

"When orgasm is achieved simultaneously, it is a very intense bond. An auxiliary reason for wanting to come within a close time period of my partner is that after I have come

I go, for a short period—five to ten minutes—into a very uninterested phase. Out of courtesy to my partner, I continue to manipulate him toward orgasm but it is without the same degree of enthusiasm. Intercourse (anal) should last however long the two people desire it to. In instances of extreme excitement, it can have a duration of five minutes or less. It is more meaningful to me if it lasts longer. Already excited, 'horny' or near my threshold, I have experienced coming too soon. It bothers me if I am very much out of 'synch' with my partner; it is somewhat disappointing if the intensity of the orgasm is under par due to lack of control."

How men control ejaculation

Even though it should not be considered "mandatory" for a man to have a long erection/intercourse, here are the means some men used to control ejaculation.

Some men learned through masturbation:

"If anything, I control my orgasm too well sometimes. I think masturbating has given me a good sense of my body and how to control the pleasure, so that if I feel myself coming too close to an unwanted orgasm, I know how to relax and let the tension go down. To extend the time before I have an orgasm, I don't use any artificial method, just relaxing, stopping heavy thrusting, and enjoying quiet times just hugging or kissing or going down on my woman."

"I think I trained myself during years of adolescent masturbation. My purpose was never to just come and be done with it, but to prolong arousal and enjoy the feeling of a hard-on and my entire hungry body. I know and feel when I am about to orgasm, and I back off. I have control over myself. In fact, I often have to exert some effort to orgasm and ejaculate in intercourse. There is as much pleasure in resisting orgasm as there is in orgasming."

Some said masturbating to orgasm before intercourse was the answer:

"If I masturbate three or four hours prior to intercourse, I can continue for a longer period of intercourse."

"If I masturbate before a date, it makes sex last longer, takes the urgency off."

Or having a second intercourse or orgasm:

"I had a continuing problem of sustaining an erection during intercourse when married. Premature ejaculation would give her the chance to say her duty was done. That would end the sexual encounter. I was pleasantly surprised to find that when my current sexual partner asked for and waited for a second penetration, I was able to sustain an erection for fifteen to thirty minutes. Our normal solution now is, if I have not had an orgasm in the prior twenty-four hours, to be brought orally to orgasm. We then continue after about ten minutes with more stimulation, followed by penetration and usually a very mutually satisfying time."

Some men used ointment—not always with positive results:

"I used to have premature ejaculation fairly often. I found it embarrassing as hell and did not really know what caused it—it's equivalent to rejection of your partner. I used to control it successfully with Nupercainal. (Available at any drugstore without prescription—allegedly a hemorrhoid treatment.) A very small piece of that salve rubbed around the head of the penis an hour or so before intercourse will make the head insensitive and prolong an erection—if the general emotional atmosphere is reasonably O.K.—for a very long time. Wash off *with soap* and *warm water* before intercourse, so nothing gets on her! Works, but when things are really right I do not need it."

"I used Delay, a pink ointment you can get in service station rest rooms for a quarter. After using it, it numbed my penis, I couldn't feel a thing, so I didn't use that or anything else anymore. I believe in natural sex."

A common method is to stop moving:

"I slow my movements, and breathe more naturally."

"An experienced man can fuck for hours without coming. When you are ready to come, you move differently to put less pressure on the head of the cock and other 'trigger' areas."

Or to find a less stimulating position:

"The method I use to delay orgasm is to move 'up' on the woman a little and slow down and move less. Moving up tends to provide her with better stimulation of the clitoris (and she doesn't lose her high) while it allows me to move in a manner that is less stimulating for me. That and the slower movement tends to bring her to orgasm 'quicker' and me 'slower.' "

"I try to avoid stimulating the glans. Prolonged deep thrusting increases sensitivity and increases the likelihood of orgasm whereas short thrusts decrease sensitivity. When the woman is on top I can last the longest because she makes more of a rubbing motion to bring herself pleasure compared to the thrusting I make. Her movement extends the time of my pleasure."

"If I rub the shaft of my cock against her and avoid causing any friction to the head, I can keep this up indefinitely. This is more easily accomplished if the woman is on top. It does dull the sensitivity, and I won't lose the erection but I'll find it difficult to come."

Or withdraw completely:

"The only thing that works if we want to continue intercourse for more than five minutes is withdrawal, and concentration on her body while avoiding stimulation of my penis. This often allows me to back off from orgasm while remaining aroused, and then we can resume intercourse."

"Mental control":

"The feeling is so mind-blowing that it is hard not to climax. What helps? Well, thinking about how nonsexual it would be to be cleaning out a cesspool with a shovel."

But as one man said:

"I try to dampen my excitement mentally by thinking unexciting thoughts, but it bothers me that this seems like a betrayal of the occasion and my partner (even if in a good cause), and besides it doesn't work very well, because the sheer physical presence of a woman makes it difficult not to be absorbed."

Some men said they could continue longer when they cared more about the woman:

"It seems to be correlated to my feelings for the particular lover. That is, when the payoffs for holding out a long time are greatest, it's not difficult at all. But when I am some-what indifferent, I suppose my subconscious doesn't allow me to try very hard, even if I tell myself I 'should.' "

"A few years ago I had a lot of trouble with premature ejaculation. I read some sexual shop manuals that didn't help a bit. Then I fell in love, and it went away just that fast. Sometimes it's back when the relationship isn't good. Are other people like that? Nobody talks about it."

"I come too fast when not interested in loving the woman."

"Usually I come too soon when I don't find the woman very attractive and I'm afraid that if I don't come now I'll lose interest."

But other men felt the opposite:

"I can hold off indefinitely if I'm not very excited."

A few men liked the "squeeze technique":

"I slow down the pace of the strokes to a very slow move-ment, think of something else other than fucking, and will sometimes withdraw it for a second, pinch the head hard and shove it right back in, this will usually delay the orgasm for a few more minutes."

"If a guy does have trouble ejaculating too soon, there are a couple of techniques that can be used to cure this. One is the squeeze technique. The girl can help the male with this. She places her hand around the tip of his penis using her first two fingers and thumb. She will place her thumb on the back side of his penis, and when he feels he is going to orgasm, she can apply the squeeze. This will stop him from ejaculating too soon. He might also lose his erection. She can help him get that back."

But most didn't like it:

"If I'm having intercourse and don't want to come, but feel myself starting, I either slow down my tempo or with-draw completely and wait for a few moments (twenty seconds or so) until the feeling has subsided and then start thrusting again. I'm familiar with the 'squeeze technique' but I really don't like the idea. It's too technical for me and makes sex too mechanical."

"That method in whichever of the sex manuals of

squeezing the penis is a total washout for me. Usually the best way for me to cope with it is just stopping for a while."

"I've, or we've, tried the so-called squeeze technique, but it's too much of an interruption, too cumbersome, and doesn't have any more delaying effect than just stopping the movement. Maybe we aren't doing it right."

Some men contracted (squeezed) their muscles voluntarily:

"I contract my muscles, allowing me to ejaculate at a later time."

"Holding back with all my might as if I'm holding urinating helps."

"I tighten my penis muscles."

Drugs and alcohol were sometimes mentioned:

"The best way for me to 'delay' orgasm is with about three ounces of whiskey just before penetration. I can do a certain amount of 'holding back' with my mind also—but need some chemical help."

"I use drugs and alcohol to keep from coming too soon. Also if I keep my legs pulled close together so that the muscles around my anus are not taut, I last longer."

"Take morphine."

One man explained how diet can make a difference:

"The thing that ended my 'premature' orgasms came quite by accident. I changed my diet for health reasons, and began eating *no* sugar. This was six years ago. After about six months I found that in intercourse I could concentrate on a woman's feelings and my own feelings without coming to orgasm too quickly or losing my erection. Since then I have been able to continue intercourse for as long as I want with no great effort. It could be something else but I attribute this to my diet."

Many found that condoms had the effect of delaying their orgasms:

"Condoms are safe and have the effect of helping me to control my orgasms; they reduce the oversensitivity of the cock's head. My wife likes the neatness of using the condom by catching the come and allowing a convenient method of disposing of it and not having to clean up afterwards."

Some men said getting older helped:

"The older I grew, the longer I could hold an erection before ejaculation. And I believe the more skillful I became in giving her enjoyment. In fact, as I get older, what used to be 'holding off' has evolved into 'catching up.' "

"This was a big question once. It tormented the hell out of me. My premature ejaculation, or my worrying that I didn't hold out for a half hour at a time, or whatever, used to worry me, but not my wife or any other woman I was ever with. I used to think I was perverted, basically homosexual, or of weak character. It has decreased in importance and, ironically, I now perform—what a word—longer."

Other men spoke of achieving a new attitude toward inter-course and sex in general:

"I have orgasmed before I wanted to on many occasions, and I think it was most closely linked with the idea I had that sex was a *process* toward orgasm and not something which was valuable in and of itself. As I've learned more that *sex is petting,* and that orgasms are only equal and different manifestations of sexual communication, a more satisfying balance seems to have evolved."

Lest one think that men only wish to hold back their orgasm for the benefit of the woman, it is interesting to note that men often hold off their orgasm during masturbation to pro-long the pleasure and for a stronger orgasm:*

"When masturbating for pleasure I delay orgasm as long as possible so as to enjoy the feelings of arousal. I build up to 'almost,' then stop or change the action until I'm no longer 'almost,' then build up some more. This makes things much more exciting, I get a good inner feeling without being through, and the eventual orgasm itself is much more intense than if I'd come right away. Moral: the more effort you put into something, the more reward you get back."

"To delay orgasm during masturbation makes it more exciting. I delay orgasm by changing rhythm or type of motion (squeezing, rubbing, jerking, tickling); or by stopping

---

* Some men could also avoid ejaculating but still reached a peak which they felt was an orgasm—thus enabling them to have more than one orgasm. See pages 607–609.

action altogether if I have found myself getting too carried away too fast—changing rhythm and/or motion is always much more satisfying."

"I can delay a very long time, I'm in control. I usually just stop the stroking, and just rub my fingers around my penis, or wiggle it between them. That way I build to a more intense peak."

"Delay makes it much more intense. I do it by stopping for short periods and delaying the inevitable. A real quicky orgasm is almost not worth having."

Still, worrying about prolonging intercourse for the woman's supposed orgasm can interfere greatly with the man's pleasure during intercourse:

"After we're both undressed, usually I fondle and caress her all over with a lot of kissing. I like to concentrate on her neck, breasts, waist, and thighs (leaving the genitals until the end), working up her body intermittently to resume kissing every so often. It's at this point that I would like to have more nerve to suggest new and erotic things I've always fantasized about doing—like giving her a baby oil rubdown and admiring her body just for voyeurism's sake or bathing her or just playing with her (wrestling). By this point I'm pretty tense and nervous. I feel like an athlete just before game time wondering 'How good will I be tonight?' The moment is approaching. She's getting very hot and so am I. Just before I think she's ready, I usually will go down on her and remain there until I think she's *really* ready (again, neither time am I positive that she's ready, but by her actions there seems to be no denying that she is). It is then when I penetrate her and have intercourse. Afterwards, I remain in her and thrust until my penis is so limp that it just shrivels out of her vagina itself. I have never pulled out the moment after I've ejaculated. I can't conceive of anyone doing that. When I thrust during intercourse, I try and do it gently and very slowly, trying to go as deep as I can and also as far out as I can without actually going out (once I came all the way out and immediately lost my erection and then had to wait quite a while before I was able to get hard enough to penetrate again. Remember, girls, this ain't easy!). Oftentimes during this period, the girl will shiver or suddenly start to 'feel' something and wriggle all over as if what I'm doing is just right. So I'll try like hell to not change one thing and keep going just like I'm going. And then she'll just freeze or seem to lose all interest all of a sudden as if I threw her off or somehow blew it. At that point I'll usually try something else or change my softer thrusts to stronger ones or speed up or slow down or move around in a circle or do something to 'bring her back.' Well, after reading *The Hite Report*, now I know I *really* blew it. Men think that a girl moans and groans during orgasm, but *The Hite Report* said women usually froze during it. So, being ignorant, I thought her 'freeze' was disinterest and *changed* my technique when in actuality she was probably just about to orgasm and so my change of movement probably *ruined* her orgasm. I think a lot of men mess up out of sheer ignorance—so let them know! Enlighten them."

"I want to definitely continue intercourse longer than I am able to. I would like to penetrate and thrust for five to ten minutes if I can. But I seldom am able to thrust beyond two to four minutes. I don't like making love fast and when my loved one has orgasmed through cunnilingus she asks me to enter her as soon as possible. I want to please her, so I become erect and enter and thrust to climax. Bother me? Yes, it sure as *shit* does! I rarely feel really satisfied after orgasm through intercourse—there's still more water waiting to be wrung from the sponge. I would really like to be able to hold off longer while inside her; also, I am concerned with her satisfaction and end up getting myself partially excited while stimulating her, but not enough to have another orgasm, so that residue is left unsatisfied. During manual stimulation to orgasm, on the other hand, I often do feel satisfied."

Some men realized, quite correctly, that it is not necessary to hold back—at least not for the traditional reasons:

"Premature ejaculation is not one of my concerns and it hasn't been a problem for many, many years. We both know that my orgasm—ejaculation—is my responsibility and she is ready and eager for me to come whenever and however the two of us together let it come. She always knows that she can have at least two or three *more* orgasms if she wants more, because of my ability to 'buckle' my penis to give her more clitoral stimulation. I also do not use any method of holding back my orgasm or delay it in any way, because there is no need to—and it is too good an experience to suppress in any way."

"I usually cannot control when I come to a climax. I'd better satisfy her first with my tongue. How long I can hold off without losing my erection is always different. Since she has had a climax from cunnilingus, I usually just have slow, steady thrusts during intercourse until I climax."

"I used to think I came too quickly (within one to two minutes) but that is only attached to intercourse. Since there are such a wide variety of ways of relating sexually, I no longer attach any value to this. That is not how she obtains orgasm anyway."

"Since there are a variety of ways to bring a woman to orgasm besides intercourse, coming 'too soon' doesn't seem important to me. Why not cunnilingus her to orgasm and then have intercourse? Or, if you come too soon, cunnilingus her afterward (who cares about the taste of semen, presuming you don't use a rubber?). Personally, I just don't find this important."

"The old myth was that you were supposed to stay erect until your partner succeeded in having a vaginal orgasm by clubbing her clitoris to death on your mons. Hard task for a person who can come by masturbating in a minute or so. Variously I tried thought diversion, positioning so as to keep the end of my penis from so much stimulation. (A double lotus with the woman facing my lap was good for this.) Also tried Arabian Nights Hand Cream, etc. That puts the nerves to sleep, sort of like going to the dentist. But if she started to thrust and pant like she was coming, the excitement always caused me to come in spite of myself. Now I see it was all counterproductive. I would more or less insist on the superiority of my tongue or fingers if I had my life to live over."

And a few men could control not having orgasm too soon, but then could not let go after waiting so long:

"I frequently hold off until I'm too pooped to pop. That's O.K."

"I can hold off climax as long as I want to. When I am ready, however, I have to wait for it to occur. I have held my erection for more than one and a half hours."

And one man said:

"How long is a long fuck—ten minutes maybe? I've fucked longer and it was great. But it can be just a bore and an endurance contest. I'm not interested in 'proving' myself. The athletic analogy is important to a lot of men; how far they can run, how much weight they can lift, how long they can fuck. It's just part of the whole machismo tradition."

Conclusion

The popular media are constantly warning men against "coming too soon," insisting that this is the cause of most women not having orgasm from intercourse (coitus). Thus most men feel it is their duty to the woman to have intercourse for as long as possible, so that the woman can have a chance to orgasm too. However, the results of *The Hite Report* suggest that this is a fallacy, since whether a woman has an orgasm is usually not related to length of intercourse. In fact, most women do not orgasm simply as a result of intercourse;* and the minority of women who do, do so not so much from long thrusting as from individually created ways of getting specific clitoral stimulation during intercourse.

But the amount of pressure on men has been enormous. Even the term "premature ejaculation" is negative, giving a man the implicit message that no matter when he orgasms, it may be too soon, "premature," unwanted, or out of place. Men have been getting a double message: on the one hand, they are told that it is very "virile" to become erect and excited and thrust home to orgasm; on the other hand, they are told not to orgasm "too soon." Since most men get rather good stimulation during thrusting, this provides a contradiction —leaving most men feeling slightly uneasy, guilty, and inadequate.

Although extending intercourse can be a pleasure in itself for both men and women, this guilt is unnecessary—as long as women's needs are acknowledged in a realistic manner at some time during sex, or any special needs of women desiring to orgasm during intercourse are fulfilled in a mutually agreeable fashion.

III: PRESSURE TO "MAKE HER COME"

Closely linked with the traditional pressure on men to maintain long erection and thrusting during intercourse is the idea that it is a man's role to "give" the woman an orgasm during intercourse. Just as the man has traditionally been considered the "provider" economically—the man should "bring home the bacon" or buy the house—he has also been

* See chapter 5.

given the role of "providing" the woman with sexual satisfaction. A "real man" should "make her come."

In addition to the pressure created by this role, this idea also often puts the man in a no-win situation since the information he has been given—that thrusting during intercourse should bring a woman to orgasm—is faulty.* This places him in a vulnerable position, leaving him to doubt his masculinity whenever female orgasm does not occur, and also possibly pressuring the woman to fake orgasms. Thus this needless pressure alienates men and women, as each blames the other when expectations are not met.

"Do you feel there is something wrong with your 'performance,' technique, or sensitivity if the woman does not orgasm from intercourse itself? That you're 'not man enough'?"

A few men insisted women never fail to orgasm with them:

"Are you kidding? I never had a complaint."
"I never have failed a woman yet to achieve orgasm."
"Never had the problem."
"Experience has shown that if a woman can't orgasm with me, she can't with anybody. I have brought out the first orgasm in several."

But the overwhelming majority of men realized that women often did not orgasm during intercourse, and found this a source of pressure. Many felt it was their fault:

"If anything goes wrong, I'm blamed for it. Girls always seem to just lay there and say, 'O.K., make it happen.' I feel an immense pressure to perform and feel that it's all up to me."

"The main demands made of me during sex are to hold off ejaculation and to stimulate the right 'spots' on my partner without much trying on her part. I feel a woman has to concentrate on stimulation and learn to receive it as well as the man performing it. If a woman doesn't try, then she blames the man for failure, he is going to have a guilt feeling and then shy away from sex because he thinks he will fail next time."

"Her not having orgasm during intercourse bothers me in a deep-seated way, but I don't dwell on it. I used to feel

---

* See chapter 5 for a discussion of ways men had of stimulating a woman to orgasm.

'not man enough,' but we got over that childishness long ago. There's no doing right or wrong, it has to do with conditions, environment, emotion, and physical strength. We can't win every skirmish, but if we're winning the war in our win/win conflict, that's all that counts."

"I do feel inadequate because she doesn't cum through intercourse. That's when I long for a bigger penis; it seems like the obvious answer, though she tells me it is not. I try to convince myself of it, but it always returns."

"I have to fight this feeling (something wrong with me if she fails). I know rationally that there have to be more reasons than my performance if a woman who wants to make it doesn't. Ignorance and failure in this area plagued the first twenty years of my marriage and left my wife and me both with permanent scars in the inadequacy category. We both know better now, rationally, but there are enormous sore spots in our psyches which may never go away."

"When I come too fast before she can build to a climax, I feel apologetic. I do wonder if some other guys couldn't help her make it every time."

"I feel threatened if I can't please my love ever or give her a climax—the impotence with my wife is a good example. I'm not neurotic about my manhood, though at this time—I have learned and am continuing to learn that I am a worthwhile person in my own right and no longer have to prove myself by conquest—I prefer to share in bed, *not perform*."

"The woman not orgasming? No longer bothers me at all when I realize she either doesn't want to while we're fucking or can't because I have come too fast. If this should persist—over a series of lovemakings—then I worry. Something is bothering me, I'm too wrapped up in myself, too masturbatory while lovemaking, whatever. But I now know from years of experience with my wife, with a few other women, and from, frankly, *The Hite Report*, that women don't have to come like crazy during intercourse in order to have pleasure. Neither do I. Men can have a great time with lovemaking without having to shoot their wad every ten minutes, or have a mammoth hard-on for their precious big cocks. Manliness does have other meanings, after all. Like being tender, good, courteous, etc. And orgasm isn't everything, for a man or a woman. It's great. But so is filet mignon, and I don't eat that every week."

"I feel selfish. I have not come up with the answer or solution yet. Maybe I should prolong the fucking for a longer time."

"I feel a little incapable not being able to make her orgasm during intercourse. I don't see how any male can go on long enough to do this."

"I have always thought that if a woman didn't orgasm, it was the man's fault. That doesn't mean he wasn't 'man enough'; in fact, it means he was too much man. I think it's easier for a woman if a man really cares about her and she trusts him."

"I'm afraid I'm not sensitive enough. I am usually in too much of a selfish rush to get my own rocks off."

"Since I'm currently having problems sustaining erection, I am quite aware of 'performance' pressures. I lay the blame for the woman's lack of orgasm with me. But I've tried everything, what else can I do?"

"Not that I'm not man enough, but that I did not do it right. I'd feel that I should have done something more, such as a longer foreplay. But my greatest displeasure in sex is the feeling that I must *perform* (a concept with no place in sex— leave it to the National Football League), that aggressive thrusting in penis-vagina intercourse produces skyrockets for all, and that my manhood will be judged on that basis: 'If he doesn't get it up, stick it in, orgasm, and make her orgasm, well, shit, he's not a *man*. Not in his eyes, not in hers.' "

But quite a few men reacted strongly against the use of the phrase "man enough" in the question itself:

" 'Man enough' is macho bullshit."

"This question is loaded."

"Insulting question."

"Sometimes I feel I'm not giving her what she needs, or she's not into it. But *No* to 'man enough!' If she likes, I'll go down on her until she orgasms and can't take it anymore."

"Man enough? Fiddlesticks."

"I don't identify my manhood with any ability to 'make' women come!"

Some men felt that women do not orgasm during intercourse with them because their penis is too small:

"I *used* to worry about my ability to make her come, due to the small size of my penis. I thought if it was larger, she would come more often. Now I know it doesn't have anything to do with my penis."

"I feel very much inadequate if a woman doesn't orgasm

from intercourse itself. I have a smaller than I'd like penis. This makes me feel that I'm not man enough."

"If a woman believes that she didn't orgasm because my penis was too small or I'm not hairy enough, then that's too bad, because that's the way I'm built and I can't do much about it. She might as well look elsewhere for what she wants."

Happily, penis size has nothing to do with whether or not women orgasm during intercourse (see chapter 5). It is unfortunate, however, that many men still continue to hold this misconception. Some men also mentioned that they wished their penis could be larger for the same reason, in answer to "Do you think your genitals are beautiful? Do you think your penis is a good size?":

"Sometimes when I'm really horny I wish that the erect penis was larger. Longer and thicker. I measure 6½ inches long and 2¾ around—not too long or too short, just right. But sometimes I wish it would be larger to give the lady a bigger 'O'—a more enjoyable experience."

"My penis seems small in comparison to others in the shower without an erection, but it seems to be about standard size when it is erected according to what I have read in medical books. I don't worry about its size, but if I knew it would satisfy a woman more when bigger, I would certainly like to be bigger to please her more."

Often men felt it could be their fault if the woman did not orgasm from intercourse, simply because they were not "sensitive" enough:

"I'm enlightened enough to realize that maybe I did something wrong. Maybe I wasn't considerate enough that day. Maybe there are certain things she likes that I didn't do. Or things she doesn't like that I did do."

"My performance is O.K. if I stay sensitive and don't get too rough or crude."

On the other hand, some men did not blame themselves. Although still believing that a "normal" woman should orgasm from intercourse, they felt defensively that if she didn't, it was her own "fault," and not theirs:

"It's her fault. I am man enough."
"The woman's mind is at fault."

"She ain't woman enough."

"Your orgasm is your own responsibility. I never claimed to be perfect when I hired on."

"There is no blame—maybe she is just too tired or worried about something."

"Sometimes your medicine works and sometimes it doesn't."

"It's impossible to make a woman orgasm if she does not intend to."

"*She's* not woman enough generally."

"I don't feel something is wrong with me if I think she hasn't orgasmed. My first thought is that she is or has become frigid."

"It's her responsibility."

"If I make an obvious mistake, yes, I feel responsible. But if she isn't up to achieving orgasm, all the loving in the world isn't going to make any difference."

"There is nothing wrong with me at all. It's *her* responsibility."

"I believe that if some women can do it, then potentially all can. We are *both* responsible if she cannot orgasm from intercourse."

"I would think it's her fault. Her anatomy prevents her from adequate clitoral stimulation. Or it might be psychological with her. It can also be lack of communication between both of us as to how she could arrive at orgasm through coitus. But if nothing works it's her fault."

"Maybe she wanted sex, but had something on her mind. Maybe she can't get it on with men who wear wire-rim glasses. If that's the case, then it's her problem. I may be able to help her solve the problem, but it's basically *her* problem."

"That's the way I come. She should do likewise."

"She and she only can psych herself to these heights."

"I believe we are all responsible for our own orgasm. If we need help we should ask."*

"I would question my performance if my partner doesn't orgasm from it. But I would also question her state of mind. I wouldn't question my masculinity."

---

* Of course, the social definition of sex as basically intercourse puts women into the position of having to "ask for help" all too often, since clitoral stimulation to orgasm is not usually included; men are not put into this position—as both women and men assume that intercourse is part of sex and that women do not have the right to withdraw during intercourse until the man has had an orgasm. On the other hand, men feel free to discontinue clitoral stimulation.

"Usually I think it's her problem, but I do realize that I'm a pre-ejaculator and must be careful."

"She may not be conditioned to respond to intercourse orgasmically."

This pressure to orgasm from intercourse has been very oppressive to women, and has often led to faking orgasms. And, in fact, although men here say that they do not feel guilty, there is a tone of defensiveness. The unrealistic goal of women reaching orgasm simply from the rubbing of the penis in the vagina has placed undue pressure on both men and women, and left both vulnerable and defensive before each other—creating, all too often, an adversary situation.

A few men focused clearly on their feelings of discomfort if they usually had orgasm and the woman did not:

"I'm usually a little disappointed if she doesn't orgasm. I know goal-oriented sex is tough on both parties—but it is difficult to detrain/unlearn, especially if you know your partner wants relief and between the two of you, you can't. I frequently get a 'You go ahead, dear, I'm too tired or I can't,' etc. This usually leaves me feeling out on a limb—as if I'm using her. I frequently will say, 'That's O.K., I'll wait too,' and stop—it depends on how much pressure I feel. If she were really excited at times like that we might make more of a joint 'no goal' play session out of it. But usually when she says something like that it means 'I'm not very excited and I'm not going to be—do your thing alone and get it over with.'"

"Unless I feel capable of imparting some satisfaction to my partner, I'd rather abstain."

"I'd lose interest in her as a sex partner if it is permanent. If she enjoys the act without orgasm, I'm happy for her. But it is uncomfortable to think that you can't do anything that will please her. Let's face it. It's a handicap."

"I have trouble with this one . . . if she is merely accommodating me and doesn't want sex, I'd rather masturbate . . . if she *wants* to give herself to me because she cares about me, then I can appreciate the fact (intellectually at least) that this can also meet needs she has . . . 'a gift of love' . . . and enjoy the experience as much for the fact that she cares that much for me as anything else."

"I used to worry that my lack of experience would minimize her possible pleasure, but after finding out how dismally the typical male performed, began smugly to polish my technique, which I thought excellent, if only by comparison. And then I grew up some, and found that a simpler repertoire with my huge soul behind it was good enough, that the critical factors in my partner's orgasms or lack of orgasm were beyond my control. I'm man enough, but all too often, the human being in bed with me is too crippled to play 'man and woman' with me. So we play 'old soldiers,' and bind each other's wounds."

"I'm sorry for her, especially if she has come to believe that she's not whole for the lack of ability. I also wonder whether I should be sticking myself in her, or not. Should I accept graciously what is offered, or insist on some sort of quid pro quo of pleasure? And how do I know she's not taking pleasure on some ethereal inner plane, as she claims? And why *is* she spreading for me? What's in it for her? Is this some sort of martyr shtick? And what does that make me?"

Others said it was nobody's fault if it didn't happen "this time":

"I'm not the best, but I'm not the worst either. Next time it'll be better is my attitude, and also hers."

"If my partner does not have an orgasm, it does not make me feel that it is my fault in any way—only that on that occasion she was not up to it for some reason."

"I used to worry about it more; now I realize we all have our 'off' days."

"At one time I did feel it was my fault, but with conversations with my partner and knowing that I have done all the things I could to bring about orgasm, if she doesn't, now I don't worry about it."

Although certain of these answers suggest that from time to time one partner or the other may not want orgasm, many of these appear to be cover-ups of the real situation, in which the women were almost *never* having orgasms. Surely, it is better to face the issues directly, to be angry even, so that a real understanding of the situation can develop. In fact, the most suggestive reaction to this question was that many men ignored it or answered in such vague terms as to make their answers ambiguous and meaningless—another indication of the tremendous pressure our society has placed on men to "make women orgasm" from intercourse with the penis.

For example, what does the following mean?:

"I used to not much understand what a woman got out of sex, I knew it wasn't the same ka-bam that I felt when I orgasmed. As time went by I got some smarter and realized that at least half the problem was mine 'cause I was a dope. Then things got a lot better."

Why did things get better?

Or the following:

"Different strokes for different folks. Everyone's different. I just have to learn the key that unlocks the woman's passion. It takes time to learn to properly fuck a woman."

"When I started out on my sex education adventure with females I felt disappointed and puzzled if my partner did not orgasm. Now it doesn't puzzle or disappoint me, as the feeling of closeness achieved is more important."

But does *he* always expect to orgasm? If there is a discrepancy, does he mind?

Or finally:

"It depends on the situation. I always try to improve my techniques, but I don't always feel there's something wrong because I suppose certain women can't orgasm from intercourse itself. They need previous stimulation."

And quite a few men, disturbingly, had heard the information that most women do not orgasm as a result of intercourse, but had misunderstood this to mean that, since it was "impossible" for women to orgasm anyway, they need concern themselves no further with it!*—making no attempt to learn how women do orgasm or to see that the difference in men's and women's needs implies a redefinition of sexual relations:

---

* Not a few men said that they had been relieved to "learn" this from *The Hite Report* on female sexuality—a particularly frustrating comment to hear, as one of that work's main points was that it is wonderfully easy for most women to orgasm during adequate stimulation, usually clitoral stimulation, and that sex now should be redefined (or undefined) away from such a strong focus on intercourse and to include more of the stimulation women need.

"I do not feel something is wrong with me if I don't bring a woman to orgasm. Men's release is a lot easier to come by than a woman's and I know that every time a man has intercourse that the woman does not always come. I prefer to bring her to it though, and that is my desire, although I am not always successful."

"I felt in my marriage that there was something wrong with my performance since she didn't orgasm, and suffered greatly. It deprived me of much enjoyment and made me guilty and uncomfortable. But now I know a woman's orgasm depends largely on herself, her own response, body, mind, interpersonal relationships."

Finally, some men had come to terms with the fact that many women didn't orgasm simply as a result of thrusting, but did orgasm easily in other ways—and were beginning to see the benefits to them of this information, trying to integrate it into their lovemaking:

"Since reading *The Hite Report*, I have changed my thinking about women and penetration very much. It proved that my wife was *much more normal* than she thought, in needing clitoral stimulation. I found it hard to believe. We had a long talk and she convinced me that most women were sensitive this way. Stimulation through the clitoris is the way we have had to go most of our marriage anyway. I have always enjoyed this foreplay very much anyway. So this won't change a thing. I was very surprised to find out that so many women felt this way about penetration and clitoral stimulation. So if a woman didn't climax from penetration only, I would really understand. I wouldn't be stimulating her the way she needed to get going."

"I might have felt bad at one time, because I think the sex manuals of my youth (1940–1955) may have tended to place too much burden on the man's technique, but I just enjoy seeing a woman get hot and come. Regardless of how it is achieved (usually clitorally), it will be fun, and so if there is that attitude, there will be more times together of relaxed and happy feelings, so everybody wins."

"My wife rarely has orgasms from penile stimulation. I used to feel badly about this but now take pride in the other nice ways of bringing her off. I love oral sex and also enjoy and take pride in my finger work."

"I don't think there is something wrong if a woman does

not have orgasm from intercourse. I ask her if there's anything I can do to please her, if I took enough time, if she wants to be touched in a certain place, if I was going too fast. I'm the first one to admit that if I attempt to figure out what feels good for her I'll fail, so I tell her to tell me right out, what feels good. It works that way."

" 'From intercourse itself'—no! I adjust to her apparatus, that's all. I'll always find a sweet way to 'get her off.' If I like her for what I see in her, then I want the intimacy of our bodies to be shared, since we've shared inner minds. I never ask myself if 'she is *woman* enough.' Enough for what? Certainly she's not abnormal, apparatus-wise. Only if I'm not person enough for *her* will she not be woman enough for me."

"Manually stimulating the clitoris during intercourse used to strike me as unnatural, but now I recognize the need and even enjoy it. I'm concerned that she orgasm, and giving her pleasure fulfills a great desire of mine. Usually she reaches orgasm in this way; occasionally she has orgasmed without any such manual stimulation, and that was good, too."

"Lately I've come to feel that since there is a cooperative venture taking place, both people must work together. Who's to say intercourse is the only (or best) way to stimulate a woman? My current lover uses a vibrator and can only orgasm with it. We've tried to make it an integral part of our lovemaking."

"My delicate male ego is not affected on this point! I stimulate them to orgasm *before* intercourse."

"For years I thought it was my fault if a partner did not come during intercourse, and I am sure that was true in some cases, since I was more ignorant than I am now. Also I felt that my penis was not long enough or thick enough. But after reading some books and articles and talking to women on the subject, I no longer feel that is true. Now my wife seems to accept the fact she does not orgasm through intercourse."

"It doesn't bother me if a woman doesn't have an orgasm during intercourse, because with most positions your penis can't contact the clitoris and bring about orgasm. It's O.K., especially if she has a climax some other way and is not disappointed. There is something lacking between us if a woman never has an orgasm, and that will bother me."

"I was pretty much a rabbit until all the recent information on sex. Fortunately, even before that we had discovered the clitoris and used it for her relief at times. But for years

I didn't understand that she didn't enjoy intercourse as much as I did. Since then I have made it a project to learn and become proficient in whatever is published. In my case, it is a case of 'there is no one so eager to please as a reformed *lousy lover!*' Believe me, the rewards are supremely rewarding for both of us."

"I think that many demands are made on men. Our penises do not seem to be the right tool for producing feminine orgasms, our capacity for orgasming in a short time is a hassle, our interest in penetration is not really shared by most women . . . still, if one talks about it, and is willing to feel free and friendly, there are no problems: I have nothing against using my mouth, fingers, or a vibrator to make my partner have an orgasm. It's also fun to take turns being 'selfish' once in a while, i.e., making love in a masculine way and, later on, on another day, in a feminine way."

This pressure on men is both unfortunate and unnecessary, as hopefully more and more men will realize. How men feel about clitoral stimulation, as separate from intercourse (penis in the vagina), will be discussed in more detail in chapter 5.

MEN'S ORGASMS DURING INTERCOURSE

Let's look at some of the stereotypes we have about men's orgasms during intercourse to see whether these are based on fact.

Do men have their best orgasms during intercourse?

"Do you have your best orgasms during fellatio, masturbation, intercourse or some other activity? Which activity do you find overall the most enjoyable?"

Although stereotyped thinking would lead us to believe that men have their strongest orgasms during intercourse, this is not true for many men. Although most men enjoy their orgasms during intercourse the most overall, most men usually have their strongest orgasms during masturbation because they can give themselves exactly the stimulation they need:

"Fellatio is fun, intercourse is rewarding in many ways; however, the strongest orgasm still comes with masturbation, as you control it entirely and are best able to fantasize during this time."

"My best orgasms have been from masturbation with intercourse a close second. This is due to the refined techniques I need for which most women do not have the patience, skill, or interest."

"In masturbation the pleasure is more intense, as I am concentrating a good deal more on my own pleasure, that little ol' button-pusher, me. My best orgasms have always been privately conceived."

"The joys of masturbating a cock allow you many alternatives, you can develop a technique that allows you to give yourself all sorts of good feelings. In fucking you ejaculate because the head of the cock is stimulated by moving back and forth in a vagina. There is no change in pressure, no bending, and movement is slower than the hand or head —you don't have the variety. But when you masturbate you can grab the cock in many different ways, with different pressures, you can slide your hand over the head for one sensation, or you can use the skin that forms a movable sheath over the head for another. It gives me the opportunity to enjoy many sensations missed in fucking. Masturbating gives me my greatest orgasms."

"My best orgasms are masturbation with simultaneous rectal stimulation by penis or dildo."

"The stimulation during masturbation is more concise; also I can fantasize during masturbation. The vagina actually is not much stimulation for me. Then too I don't have to worry about satisfying her. I can be selfish. If I try to cross over to the masturbation habits in lovemaking, I'm going to be a bad lovemaker because I'll just be trying to get my rocks off. I love the initial penetration into the vagina, but it's just not enough friction. Probably because I'm so used to masturbating."*

"I have two distinctly different types of orgasm. One is produced by penis-vagina intercourse, the other by masturbation. My first and favorite type of orgasm is produced by masturbating with anal penetration which results in a very different buildup and climax. The entire process is less frenzied, less penis-centered. The sensations are less localized, more diffuse. I feel sensations in my nipples, my inner thighs, the soles of my feet more intensely, and throughout the buildup, rather than only transiently as in the 'usual' thrusting orgasm buildup, where they are quickly overwhelmed by penis sensation. The climax too feels more global, less acute, and its sensation is one of sweet, wonderful *melting*, suffusing out from the genitals."

"I would like to differentiate between the kind of orgasm I feel when I'm masturbating versus the kind of orgasm I have when I'm having vaginal intercourse. When I'm masturbating I usually have a very strong orgasm. Also, I can have several mini-orgasms (orgasms with contractions but without ejaculation) before I finally want to have the ejaculatory orgasm. I've rarely had those kinds of mini-orgasms in vaginal intercourse. I can't control it that closely. Also, if I'm masturbating I can feel all the accessory organs—the prostate, the urethra bulb, all those contracting. In the penis itself I can feel the muscles contracting. When I have the orgasm, it's much more something flowing from inside my body out that feels very nice. There were times when I had a really, really strong orgasm during masturbation that I felt like a velvet rope was being pulled through my body and through my penis."

But the same men who said that orgasms from masturbation were the most physically intense also frequently pointed out that they received more pleasure from intercourse:

"My most intense orgasms have been from masturbation because I can effect stimulation with greater pressure on a

* This statement somewhat parallels women's past fears that possibly they couldn't orgasm during intercourse because they had masturbated too much or too well. See chapter 3 of *The Hite Report* on female sexuality to see why just the opposite is true.

specific area (the one that responds the best on that occasion). However, the most satisfying orgasms are those shared with my lover after I have brought her to satiation."

"Masturbation is exciting and pleasurable and it has the advantage that I can regulate the experience to suit myself, but it can't compare to coitus in warmth and total satisfaction."

A minority said they had their strongest orgasms during intercourse:

"I have my best orgasms by intercourse with a woman, of course. The activity I find most enjoyable is my female mate and I in a dark room, with a soft bed, exploring each other's bodies, doing everything from oral sex to finger sex, and ending up in intercourse either dog fashion or me on top of her."

"I probably have the best cums from being sucked off if the woman is also enjoying it. The next-best is a good fuck and I guess overall I find this best, especially if the woman is desirable."

Many men, while they enjoyed intercourse greatly, were pre-occupied with trying to give the woman pleasure during intercourse, and therefore found that their own orgasms were affected, often adversely:

"I prefer fellatio orgasms, because during intercourse I am preoccupied with her having an orgasm and rarely orgasm myself. During fellatio, I am not concerned for the moment about her orgasm, and if she is at ease about fellatio, I can have a good orgasm."

"I have outstanding orgasms during fellatio *and* intercourse, but in different degrees of concentration and awareness. During fellatio attention is centered totally on my pleasure (the reverse of cunnilingus) and I have more awareness of my own ecstasy. During intercourse I am conscious of my wife's ardor and growing passion and want to effect, insofar as I am able, a consummation that is pleasurable and satisfying for both of us."

Finally, a few men said that when they remained passive and concentrated on themselves during intercourse, they could often have orgasms as strong as those during masturbation:

"When I concentrate on my orgasm, it is almost always great. When I am on the bottom during intercourse and can concentrate on myself (she does the moving), my orgasms are physically as intense as during masturbation but are even better because of the emotions being expressed and experienced."

"The most fantastic orgasms of all, which combine the psychological excitement and overall release of intercourse with the genital awareness of masturbation, are when I remain motionless and my wife sort of massages my penis with contractions of her muscles in the vaginal area."

"How do you orgasm during intercourse?"

We think it is "automatic" for men to orgasm during intercourse. But looking more closely, *why* do men orgasm during intercourse? Is it from the general "in-and-out thrusting" movement, as intercourse is traditionally defined? Or from rubbing the tip of the penis against an interior surface of the vagina? Or stimulating the tip or base by pulling it in and out of the *opening* of the vagina? Or by fantasizing?

Of course, it is different things for different men:

"I guess because I am used to reasonable pressure on my penis from masturbating so much, if the woman has little vaginal control, or is as we say 'loose,' climax can be difficult. I use erotica of the mind to combine with the sensations to achieve orgasm. I do not have to ever use this with my mistress, only with my wife. I usually think of some bottom I would love to explore at work, or being fellatioed by two women at once, etc."

"The best stimulation for me is the slapping of my scrotum and testicles on the woman's groin. That is the part that is most stimulating. It's easier when I'm on top, because of the force of gravity on the scrotum and testicles."

"I need concentration on the underside of the glans. I usually move around until I find the right feeling."

"Usually I've got to move all the way out, so I can feel the mouth of the vagina on my foreskin. It helps to tighten my leg muscles."

Most men said that, although the vagina in general did not automatically provide optimum stimulation, the opening of the vagina, combined with in and out motions, did provide good stimulation for orgasm:

"The most distinctive feeling I can describe is during the later stages, when the deeper part of the vagina has billowed out longer. Then the part close to the entrance feels like a tight ring clasping my penis. This invites a very long stroke, to feel the tightness squeezing me along the entire length. I'll withdraw almost to the point of losing contact, because it feels so good to slide the sensitive part of my penis (around and below the rim) back and forth through that tight ring."

"A woman's vagina feels warm and smooth and sometimes very snug, but except for the opening, doesn't always create much sensation for my penis. If I move in and out very rapidly, I can feel the walls of the canal pulling at the skin of my penis, but to get a lot of feeling at the tip, I have to pull nearly all the way out each time."

"In the aroused level, when the innermost part balloons, I feel a void around my penis with full penetration. The answer I have found is not to push for full penetration, but rather to keep the penis in the first half, where it feels hugged. This, alas, is the opposite of what a man feels like doing instinctively."

"Most vaginas are such that the only sensation is around the lips, with some sensation on the sides if I 'point' that way during fucking. The others, I can feel some of the wall as I thrust, or feel the top against the top of my prick. The softness of the vagina and the caressing of my prick in that softness is particularly pleasureful."

"The movements that bring my lover to orgasm, while they excite me, are not the same movements that bring me to orgasm. My lover likes me to be deep inside her so that she can rub her clitoris against my pubic bone and stomach. I find this movement very pleasant in a 'blissed out' way. I also find that I can maintain an erection this way for long periods of time while my lover gets maximum stimulation. But when I want to come, I have to thrust in and out."

"The entrance to the vagina is a constriction, a jacket that holds me in. The act of rubbing against that constriction is often what brings me to orgasm, backing the glans up against it. It's usually the time spent near the entrance that is the most insistently exciting. The deep penetration is more quiet and comforting, more tender. Deeper, more resting strokes can act to calm me down and keep me from orgasm for a little while."

Many men described the generalized sensation of being inside a vagina, saying that they could not feel the vagina that clearly with their penises:

"The vagina feels very liquid and present on all sides of my penis, and yet I really feel no distinct pressure along the length. It is like being in very deep water and feeling that undiversified pressure of the water from all sides. There is no focal point of pressure. However, I do feel the opening of the vagina slip up and down my penis as I move in and out. That does have a distinct, tight pressure, like a band, or ring."

"I only really feel the entrance and the cervical area with intensity. I know objectively that the walls are there, but the feeling of the entrance sphincter on any part of my cock is more intense than anything that happens with the interior walls."

"The penis is relatively insensitive to feelings. The pressure of introduction is clear, and the warmth, as the first penetration occurs, is wonderful as it encloses more and more of the shaft. But after temperature equilibrium has been reached, there is just a sliding sensation if lubrication is adequate, and irritation if it is not. . . . Sometimes her vagina expands so large as to effectively disappear and I am forced to alter the angle of thrusting to reestablish any stimulation."

Most men described the feeling of the vagina in very emotional terms, as seen earlier in the chapter, not mentioning the physical sensations in great detail:

"It is a warm, lubricated pressure which gives a feeling of security and increases my own blood circulation to my penis. The lips of the vagina feel soft and fleshy against the base of my penis and pubis, and the skin of the vagina is creamy, warm, and accepting. It feels *deep*. Vaginal warmth and holding is most important."

"Vaginas are always, to me, deep, wonderful, warm, moist, magical, intimate."

A few men, however, said the physical sensations of the vagina were very good stimulation for the penis:

"There is no greater feeling in the world than my penis inside a tight vagina. It's absolutely indescribable. It's the lubrication that does it. It's like every square inch of my penis is given the most minute attention by a most understanding pleasure instrument. It's like a monstrous tongue wrapping itself around my penis and squeezing and sucking it as I move around it."

"There's no feeling in the world like a woman's vagina on my penis. It's so voluptuous. It feels like thousands of tiny moist, warm folds and rivulets forming an infinitely variable tunnel to apply just the right caress to every single surface of my penis. When I move, the surface of the vagina seems to move ever so slightly with my penis; and then as excitement proceeds, the upper part of the vagina expands as the lower part becomes somewhat more slippery and firm so that I feel as if I'm thrusting through a wonderful velvet clasp and into infinite space."

A few men had no good feelings:

"A vagina as far as I'm concerned feels no better than putting your cock in between two wet towels."

And one man reacted against the question itself:

"It isn't a vagina that I'm feeling. I'm feeling inside another person."

Is thrusting important for male orgasm?

Intercourse as traditionally defined meant the man on top, thrusting into the vagina until his orgasm. But intercourse need not involve thrusting as its main activity, although thrusting can be part of what is enjoyed. In fact, thrusting may not be so much "instinctive," as has often been asserted, as physically useful for many men so that men can get the rhythmic stimulation which the up-and-down motion of the hand provides during masturbation;* in other words, since there is little or no thrusting involved in masturbation for most men, it is invalid to say that the male "sex drive" or "male" hormones *make men* "mount and thrust." In fact, of the minority of women who did orgasm from intercourse, most of them preferred no in-and-out movement while they were trying to orgasm, but more a kind of pressing together (with the penis inside) so the clitoris could get the kind of continuous stimulation necessary.

Of those who mentioned orgasm, most men said that thrusting is necessary for male orgasm:

"As regards making thrusting movements into the vagina, it's the only way! Unless the woman is on top and you are lying completely passive, that is. But there *has* to be movement of the penis inside the vagina, or I should say in relation to the vagina. Otherwise, it's not intercourse!"

But a few said that thrusting is not *necessary:*

"I was always under the impression that in order to be any good for the woman I'd have to thrust like a madman for half an hour. If I could do it for two hours without stopping that's better. So this was my goal, to be the nonstop stud. There have been times when I was thrusting away and felt I could go on all night. But I didn't like it. I felt *alone*, I just didn't like doing it. One of the greatest orgasms I ever had only entailed about nine seconds of thrusting. At that it wasn't thrusting, it was more like pressing inside her vagina. It came after a long period of holding and kissing. It just seemed so correct, so natural that at a certain point my penis should be inside her. The important thing was just to be inside her. I guess thrusting happens when you don't know what else to do, when that communication, that special intense moment is past or lost."

A few men held the misconception that thrusting was the best, most efficient way for a woman to orgasm:

"I feel like I'm stimulating her clitoris."
"It's the best way for most women to have an orgasm."

* See chapter 4.

Others described it as a "very manly" activity:

"It feels great. I'm the boss on this job."

A few men stated they preferred gentleness or slow rotation to thrusting:

"I think it's specifically penetration and thrusting that give penis-vagina intercourse its aura of conquest and abuse, and that express the male cliché of domination and possession. I think both men and women are turned on by precisely that aura and that cliché. I have the feeling we can't afford to be."

"Sometimes the sense of dominance with heavy thrusting, and even violence ('Take that!'), is overwhelming. More frequently, I prefer deep tenderness and gentle motions."

"I never liked the thrusting part. I got a much better feeling just letting it soak until the urge or thrusts came involuntarily. When I could just plug in and soak while my emotions built up, I felt better about intercourse than when I had to get in quick and go to work; then I didn't get anything at all out of the experience."

"I don't like to be a jackhammer and thrust in that manner; I prefer slow, dreamlike movements."

But one man concluded:

"I used to be careful and hesitant because I thought it must hurt. Then I learned that a lot of women seemed to like to be 'fucked.' Liked to have me take charge and 'take' them. So now at some point in most of my lovemaking I'll adopt that posture and let myself feel dominant and put power (not force) into 'thrusting' and really get into it. It seems to work within the context of generally compassionate and loving lovemaking. The whole idea goes contrary to my ideas about sex-role liberation, but I don't think all this is only me exercising my fantasies. As a matter of fact, the more egalitarian and sharing the lovemaking, verbally as well as in fact, the easier it is to fall into that kind of dominant posture. I think it may be because those roles are culturally deeply inside of us, and the more trusting the relationship, the easier it is to try them out and enjoy them without losing trust and without getting locked into it."

Basically, it is not thrusting itself that has been sexist in the past, but some men's use of thrusting in a sexist way—

that is, in a context of proving masculinity and expecting the woman automatically and in all cases to orgasm from this. If thrusting is a mutually enjoyed *part* of intercourse, and if there is real freedom for the woman to control the course of intercourse for a time, and to have the kind of movement, etc., she wants, thrusting is of course not sexist. Thrusting per se is intrinsically neither "good" nor "bad"; however, like intercourse itself, thrusting belongs to the stereotype of sex that has been glorified.

What positions and movements do men prefer?

Slightly more than half of the men who answered preferred the traditional position of the man on top:

"Not too long ago I was likely to feel more passive and I preferred to have the woman on top of me. I believed I could control erection longer on the bottom. I still enjoy this position, but I believe now I enjoy being on top more. Why? A combination of things. If the woman is really into it, there is great pleasure in seeing her being pleased, in experiencing the power of taking, in seeing her enjoy being taken. Despite the feelings this word 'taking' connotes, I find both of us are equally active."

"I like to be in a position where I can thrust my penis the way it feels best—on top."

"Top, because I have more control and because I can be more aggressive."

"During orgasm I prefer to be top. This position allows me the greatest control of my penis and its activities and sensations."

"On top—I don't feel like it's natural any other way."

"I've always been on top; I did the moving mostly. It's kind of embarrassing."

But a surprising 35 percent of men preferred to be on the bottom:

"She sitting on top—I like to watch her masturbating herself while she is sitting on top of my cock. Besides, the one on the bottom (me) is usually the *receiver*—a very pleasurable place to be."

"I like the bottom. That lifts from me the distinct responsibility to achieve something for her. She is then more involved and can respond to her own physical feelings better.

If I'm on top, I'm constantly wondering if I'm doing what she wants, and worrying about it. When I'm below, she does virtually all the moving; I'm almost afraid to intrude on what she has going. I love it."

"I prefer to be on the bottom, for several reasons. For one thing, I come much faster when on top. There's some difference in the way things rub together. Also, when on top I feel like I'm crushing my partner (I'm a fairly large person, 6'2" and 175 lbs.). I feel like I have to support part of my weight on my arms, which makes it harder to relax and enjoy things."

"If I am on the bottom, she does most of the moving, and gets very involved and excited; I think it is best for both of us."

"I do not like to be on top for several reasons. First, I have to thrust. I find thrusting very distracting, difficult and tiring in this position, and rarely get to orgasm. Second, I'm sure my lover did not really enjoy this position but only did it because she thought that was how I enjoyed it most. Being on top is thus the least desirable for me. For a long time I thought I was abnormal because society expects men to be on top, yet I don't like it."

"I prefer the bottom because I have better orgasms on the bottom."

"On the bottom is less intense and builds more slowly, which leads to much more satisfying orgasms."

Of course, most men liked all the positions:

"We love to use as many positions as suit our fancy. In bed, before sleep comes, we like to lie facing in the same direction with the penis entering from behind. But when a long period of fancy love-play occurs, we like sitting in a chair and she astride, either facing me or facing away. Me lying on my back and she riding me like a horse with many motions, around and around and back and forth, using most of the effort, which conserves my strength, but I still need to take nitroglycerin tablets to ease the heart pain. Sometimes she stands, leaning on a chair, while I enter from the rear, and squeeze her breasts as I plunge into her. A most passionate conquering position is for her to be on all fours and I enter from the rear—then during the climax she extends her arms behind her back, I grip her wrists and drive into her as though I were raping her and she was helpless. This is very exciting to both of us. Or she lies on her back with her hips elevated by two pillows, I enter her and she clasps my neck with her feet and loves me with her feet while I kiss her heels and toes while enjoying the throbbing motion. We kiss each other in any place handy, and enjoy that double sensation of loving. I try to draw out the time of being in the vagina before ejaculating as long as possible."

One man mentioned leg position:

"I was intrigued in reading in *The Hite Report* that so many women can only orgasm with their legs pressed tightly together. I myself can only orgasm with my legs spread far apart. If this situation is common for other men and women, then the traditional coital position with the woman's legs spread apart, and the man's legs pressed together, would be the exact opposite of the optimal sexually gratifying leg positions."

"Do you ever have trouble having an orgasm?"

Men rarely mentioned having trouble during masturbation,* however, they might during sex with a partner. The basic cause suggested was lack of emotional involvement,† either by the woman or the man himself:

"Sometimes when my heart wasn't in it, I couldn't come. When no emotional transaction was taking place, when no mental excitement was present. When I really didn't want to be there. Erection is not necessarily arousal. Arousal is in the mind and without it, erection is unlikely to be maintained and even if it is, orgasm is not apt to be forthcoming. When I have tried to meet felt expectations for performance without being really involved, I have had trouble."

"There are times when I have trouble having an orgasm. Mostly if my mind wanders or my partner just lies there without any emotions. On these occasions the penis will start going flaccid and the excitement is lost."

"At these times I don't feel wanted by my wife. I feel that she is just 'putting in time.' "

---

* Similarly, very few women had trouble having orgasm during masturbation; the problems usually occurred during sex with a partner.

† However, there are organic causes which affect a small minority of men and which should receive medical attention.

Some men had felt so pressured to orgasm during intercourse that they had resorted to faking orgasms at one time or another:

"I have faked orgasms several times—primarily because the partner was a very enjoyable person, a lovable and excellent personality that I truly liked. She had reached her own orgasm two or three times and I felt she would be disappointed if she knew I had not, so I faked it. I keep her confidence up by thrusting deep into her faster and faster until she thinks I have ejaculated, then I hold her in that position with my penis still deep in her until it grows limp."

"I fake orgasms when I have 'prematurely ejaculated,' have continued to thrust in a semi-hard state, and am losing my erection entirely. I continue after the orgasm to prove myself, but when it becomes obvious that I'll soon be totally limp, I'll fake an orgasm. That way it looks like I've lasted longer than I actually have."

"Sometimes during intercourse, if I have ejaculated shortly after entering, I try not to react to this but continue the motions for a while, then act like I'm climaxing."

*Sometimes men did it, they said, to excite their partners, or "make them orgasm":**

"I have faked orgasm to assist my partner to climax."

"Some women only have an orgasm when I have one. To make them come more often, I sometimes fake an orgasm."

"I have faked orgasm when I was having sex, and had already come, but my partner hadn't come yet. As she's coming I'll fake one in order to enhance her orgasm. I'm not sure that this really does enhance hers, but when I'm coming, if my partner is apparently as excited as I am it makes for better sex than if one of us is just laying there waiting for the other to get done."

Some men said they did it when they were bored and couldn't orgasm:

"I fake orgasms on occasion when I'm bored with what is happening and want to make a stop to get it over with."

"When I'm not interested in my partner, I do it the same way a woman does it, dramatically and with feeling."

* It seems doubtful that this would be the stimulation a woman would need to reach orgasm; in fact, many women have faked their own orgasm when the man had his—so as to "make the man feel better."

"I've done it when I found myself with a woman I didn't want to be with after all. Such women never know very much about it anyway, so it takes no particular technique to fake an orgasm. I'd never do it or have to do it with a woman I have a real relationship with. It's a great way of terminating a bad scene quickly."

And finally:

"I can think of three reasons: (a) to convince a non-acceptable partner that she is more than she really is, and (b) to enhance a situation which is not so great because of my momentary lack of arousal, and (c) after some introspection would you believe the infamous male ego response which is—*I'm good in bed and no cold broad is going to convince me otherwise. She's going to get the best piece of ass in pants she ever had.* As for *me* that's probably the real truth but I'm not going to admit that to you."

DOES DEFINING SEX AS INTERCOURSE TO ORGASM INHIBIT MEN'S SENSUALITY?

MOST MEN STILL DEFINE SEX AS INTERCOURSE (AND THINK OF INTERCOURSE AS THE HIGHEST EXPRESSION OF "MALE SEXUALITY")

Lest there be any doubt that the traditional pattern of sex is far and away the most usual type of sex—that is, "foreplay," followed by intercourse, ending with male orgasm in the vagina—following are some highly typical descriptions men gave of their sexual relations; no matter how different some of the replies may sound, they all contain the basic sequence of events:

"My wife doesn't like the way I like to make love. I will tell you how I like to make love to a woman. First I like to take a good shower and brush my teeth and put on my after-shave and cologne and then get in the bed and kiss and play with every part of her body, kissing and licking her all over, and then start eating her love box until she gets good and hot and then start having intercourse. This is my way of making love. My wife doesn't like my way of making love. I think a man should want to make love the way I do to the person he loves."

"I like considerable foreplay. I like a romantic setting—candles, music, wine. Most importantly I just never push or rush. If someone doesn't want to have sex, she doesn't want to have sex and no amount of pushing or urging is going to change her mind and it would just be a foolish thing to do. Then we just undress, go to bed, and play for quite a long time. Then I mount and we have intercourse. Mounting—usually with myself on top, pillow under the woman's head, and then we have intercourse and that's it."

"The pattern of my lovemaking is the following: When I meet a girl that is willing to go to bed with me I take her to my studio or any other place, then I invite her for a drink(s) (not alcoholic). Right there I turn on the soft Latin music which I call the tropical fire, we dance real tight, she moving her hips, undulating her body, kissing her mouth and especially her nipples, breasts, her belly, caressing her thighs, when I get there she starts undressing piece by piece, and after we are all naked, I kiss her vagina, suck it, introduce my tongue and slowly tease her clitoris and right there she starts moaning and asking me to penetrate my penis into her beautiful vagina—*chochita* (Spanish name for vagina)—and after a few minutes we have that beautiful orgasm and ejaculation. So then we take a little rest in order to be ready for the next one."

"Most of the time it starts off with heavy kisses, then I feel her breasts and thighs down while I'm kissing her face, eyes, lips, neck, ears, sometimes nibbling her neck with small love bites. I'm still rubbing her all over (when the girls let me I sometimes get too rough, I guess, 'cause not all of them let me finger them). She is kissing me back, blowing in my ear and making me hot as hell, usually rubbing my dick, then we start to position to screw with me on top. I try not to put all my weight on her (although sometimes my arms get tired). I sometimes kiss her face all the way to her pussy (I only ate a girl once) then come back and suck her breasts. Sometimes she sticks it in, sometimes I do. If she is tight, I start off slow (most of the time) all the way in, as action picks up I start moving in different directions up, down, left, right. Sometimes she raises up to meet me then I come after. It gets feeling nice and I'm almost ready to come. I kiss her face all over, then I usually come."

"After getting into bed usually nude, I generally reach over and draw her to me, pressing her body (genitals to genitals) close to mine while passionately attempting to devour her tongue. I may remain in this position or roll over on my back with her lying on top. After sufficient stimulation and lust, I usually indicate that I would like to be fellated—if she has not already initiated such a move. I could allow the enjoyable sensation of being fellated to go on interminably but it usually ends after a near orgasm, after which I turn my active attentions to the source of my pleasure. I love simultaneously sucking breasts while fingering a clitoris/vagina. Both my partner and I derive a lot of pleasure from this. With one thing leading to another, I soon find my face buried in her 'cunt' (that is, if I desire oral sex at the time). If I can bring the woman to orgasm in this manner, I do, and as many times as I can, resist the temptation of having one with her. When my own passions are uncontrollable, I mount her. I either continue to orgasm in this fashion or change positions. Generally though, I do not allow our genitals to be unconnected for too long a time before I (hopefully we) explode in orgasm. Whew!!! What a good feeling, you know what I mean?"

"After extensive kissing I usually always undress her or we both undress ourselves (I've never been undressed by a woman). I have never petted a girl prior to undressing (before we come to the conclusion that we're about to have intercourse). Also, I don't like petting because the girl might not want to go on to intercourse after it's started, and that just doesn't make too much sense to me. If we're going to make love, we'll make love. If not, why get worked up over nothing and waste our time with the preliminaries? We'll end up both frustrated. I'd rather not get either of us turned on extensively—only to have it cut off at the last minute if she suddenly decides she doesn't want to have sex. I can tell as we kiss whether we're going to have sex or not. That's all I need to know."

"The woman is the pipe organ and the man is the organist. If he plays on his instrument with no skill, he gets very little music in return. If he plays the organ with skill and training, he can bring forth beautiful music from his instrument which in turn delights him. So must the man be the one to lead in the art of love, though the woman responds to his wooing techniques in the many ways of a woman's lore. In answer to the question which way I prefer? It all depends on the mood of the moment. All positions are enjoyed and we try everything we hear about in sex manuals, culminating in intercourse."

A somewhat new pattern seems to be emerging in some cases, in which the man stimulates the woman to orgasm "first," then enters and has his orgasm during intercourse:

"The girl I am with always orgasms first, as I usually have cunnilingus with her until she has a climax, or a series of climaxes. I then have a climax during intercourse that follows. Some of my partners then have another climax."

"She usually orgasms first, during cunnilingus. I usually come when all that there is to be done is done."

"I let my wife orgasm first by way of finger, oral, or vibrator and then me."

"Normally I bring her to orgasm first because after orgasm I'm not in the mood for a while."

"I try to bring her to orgasm by clitoral stimulation before having intercourse and usually succeed. I then feel more relaxed and do not have the need to perform and bring her to orgasm with my penis—and feel bad if I can't keep my erection long enough for her to orgasm."

Another pattern some other men reported was that they stimulate the woman to orgasm manually or orally before intercourse, and then she has another orgasm during intercourse:

"I like to stimulate my partners to orgasm before I penetrate and then bring them to orgasm again when I penetrate. I had to learn this routine because for a long time I was unable to control my orgasm and would lose control too soon."

"Sex usually takes place in bed (but not always), more often it's at night shortly after we've gone to bed. Without any special planning, kissing, hugging, or talk may somehow lead to arousal—more readily in my case than in my wife's—and we'll begin hugging and kissing harder or generally caressing our bodies—with me usually caressing hers a good deal more than she mine. Then, usually, I'll begin caressing her genital area generally and then concentrating on her clitoris until she has an orgasm and then immediately insert my penis and we'll have intercourse till I have an orgasm. Occasionally during intercourse she'll have a second orgasm. This usually occurs when she's especially emotionally 'high.' From her outward reaction, I'd think that her orgasms from intercourse are more profound, but she says they're less intense and more diffused over her body, with sometimes a very light-headed feeling. In any event, it's disappointing they (orgasms during intercourse) don't happen more often (only about one time in ten, I'd guess)."

Another pattern is "foreplay" followed by intercourse but with the addition of manual clitoral stimulation during intercourse, and orgasm for both people.

Other men said that they would always offer manual or oral clitoral stimulation after their orgasm/intercourse if the woman had not had an orgasm during intercourse. But as some men pointed out, this plan could be less workable if the man was fatigued or happily lethargic after his own orgasm, and no longer felt inclined to stimulate the woman:

"I finish intercourse and then (since she might not have come) I continue with my finger around the clitoris (or what I *think* is the clitoris) without a word until she says, 'I'm cold' or 'Well, I've got a nine o'clock lecture tomorrow morning.' There's got to be a better way."

"During intercourse, all my attention is centered on release and getting the right kind of stimulation to get a climax. I usually inquire if the woman wants clitoral stimulation—but if I don't inquire, it's because I can forget about it, after getting release—I don't think too straight sometimes after a climax. I get absentminded, not inconsiderate, and these things should be talked about and recognized for what they are. After climax, 'feeling close' is the main feeling. This 'afterglow' feeling is somewhat self-centered. Well, actually, *quite a bit* self-centered."

"Usually she has the orgasm after I do. This means manual stimulation and is not wholly satisfactory for me. It's too messy and I feel tired."

Conclusion

However, the point here is that—no matter what (slight) changes in the pattern are taking place, and beneficial as they may be for women's orgasms—basically sex is still defined as intercourse, and still, in almost every case, centered on intercourse.

This is not strange, given the many pressures to think of intercourse as *the* sex act. However, it would be understandable if men were to become somewhat less interested in intercourse, since they feel so pressured to have it and so pushed to "perform" it "successfully"—and since they are very attracted to other activities, as we shall see in chapter 4. In other words, if men feel pressured by intercourse—pressured to perform, pressured to "make the woman come," to make the "act" a successful event, etc.—and if they enjoy other activities as much or more, do they always *want* to express themselves basically through intercourse?

In fact, do men feel pressured during sex to have intercourse? Do they sometimes initiate it because it is expected?

DO MEN FEEL FREE DURING SEX *NOT* TO HAVE INTERCOURSE?

"After sex has begun, do you feel pressured to initiate intercourse? Do you always want intercourse, or do you sometimes initiate intercourse because it is expected?"

The standard answer to this question wondered about the meaning of the question: how could one not want intercourse during sex, since sex and intercourse are one and the same? That is, most men said, to want sex is, by definition, to want intercourse:

"Sex *is* intercourse, and I always want it."

"I think that question is turned around. If sex is begun, one is already moving toward intercourse."

"Well, for women this may be true, but I consider that sex is intercourse. So, if this question means 'after sexual *activity* is begun . . .' I can say that I have never felt any pressure to do something I didn't want to do. The women that I have had sex with were supportive of my needs and wants."

"When I'm with a woman, I want to end up covering her,

because that is the cream on the cake, the highlight of the evening."

"It seems to begin because we are both ready. The act of penile penetration is expected of me and by me."

"Once I begin sex I go right for intercourse. I play for real."

"I assume intercourse is the final step in sex and that it is the thing to be built up to."

"After sex is begun, there must be some mutual understanding of what will result, and if I have an erection I am in arousal and therefore I expect full intercourse to its conclusion. There is no turning back at this stage and I therefore do not feel pressured into intercourse—*I want it.*"

"Intercourse is part of sex. To me it's not separated. It feels so-o good to be joined to her and to feel her body from mouth to tit to cunt to toe. I like it. I think she likes it. It's just part of the natural flow of sex done according to passion—although I guess conditioned somewhat by habit."

But some men said they did sometimes feel pressured:

"After sex has begun, I feel compelled to have intercourse. In most cases, I also want it, but at times I feel as though I have to perform because the woman has been aroused."

"Pressure to initiate intercourse? I've never found a woman who didn't want sex ultimately to culminate in intercourse; some sooner than others; some later than others; once I've started sex, she is waiting for this."

"Yes, once sex is begun I feel I must 'put it in' and come."

"After sex starts I have found myself initiating intercourse seemingly because I want to. I do, in fact, enjoy having orgasm in a woman's vagina. However, there have been times that I think I have gotten into intercourse because it is 'the way' to have sex. I *try* to look at sex as a broader range of activities including masturbation, oral and manual stimulation."

"The only pressure for intercourse during sexual activity comes from my conscience, because I feel it is sinful to ejaculate anywhere but in my wife's vagina."

"Society has long taught males (and females) that intercourse is the be-all and end-all of sex. I do feel pressured to go to intercourse quickly. This attitude has engendered considerable anxiety in me because it is extremely restrictive if taken at face value. I put pressure on myself to have intercourse which often makes the woman I am with uptight if that isn't what she wants."

"Something's wrong if I don't have intercourse, I think. A lot of it is psychological pressure to have the orgasm, to get it 'out.' But much of the improvement in my sex life in recent years has been the freedom—relative—from the pressure to always have intercourse every time we make love. Or even have orgasm."

"I like 'foreplay' (I'm not too fond of the word). I know where it leads and I hope there will be more afterwards and more after that. I enjoy touching, kissing, and teasing as much as the orgasm. Some women are attuned to this. But many, more than half, think I am weird because I don't press to get on with coitus. I arrive for dinner and they want to know if I want to fuck first. What's the hurry? This is how I feel pressured."

"I believe my wife assumes that after I have made overtures, that intercourse will always follow. I would like to feel that it doesn't have to unless it comes naturally. However, men are expected to be ready for it."

"Except with my present partner, and even some with her, I do feel pressure on me to initiate intercourse. Sometimes I just don't feel like having intercourse itself even though I do want, as my partner puts it, to 'play around,' or engage in other activities. Usually, though, I feel as though the woman will think we haven't really 'made love,' haven't really done the genuine article, unless intercourse is involved."

"I myself would prefer to feel aroused indefinitely and to extend foreplay for as long as possible, but I am not that experienced and often feel my partner is ready when perhaps she's not. I'm continually worried that the girl will wonder 'When is he going to get on with it?' or 'What is he waiting for?' so perhaps I don't extend foreplay as long as I want to. Most men (me included), I think, feel that after a fair amount of foreplay (fifteen to thirty minutes), the girl will be 'ready' and we should get on with it."

Sometimes another kind of pressure men felt was pressure from the woman to "get it over with":

"After it has begun, I do feel pressure to initiate intercourse. She always says, 'All right, hurry and get it over with.' I get on top—in and out—a wham-bam job and it's over. I often wonder about me as a man. What have I done to make this person react to me this way? Would she react to any man this way? Am I the cause of the situation? Are the parents? What is wrong with this situation when she sleeps in the house and doesn't do anything but wash, iron, cook a meal, and that's about it. What can be done? I wonder. Divorce seems not to be the answer. Group therapy? A job? She refuses to work, says she does not want to do anything to help me out. I don't really want sex, it just becomes available for me, and since I have not had a close, intimate relationship, then I take advantage, or should I say my anxiety takes over for the two minutes. 'Thank you, ma'am.' Sometimes I feel like a vampire. By this time I would like to really be in love again."

"After sex is begun I never feel pressure to initiate intercourse, except when my partner just wants to get it over with (this is often). The pressure I feel is to prolong foreplay long enough so my partner can get orgasm along with myself. Most of the time this is in vain because my partner isn't trying to have orgasms anyway, she just wants me to get finished. This isn't very satisfying when we only have sex once every two weeks."

"At some point I begin to feel with my present wife that she's getting bored, so hell, let's go on and do it."

"I like sex even without intercourse, but my wife prefers to go ahead and get it over with so she can rest for a while without my bothering her."

And finally, a few men said they sometimes had sex without intercourse:

"I used to feel intercourse was expected, but anymore I don't. Until about two years ago, I assumed that women were enjoying intercourse as much as I was. Not until studies started being published (or until I started reading them and talking with women more openly about sex) did I realize that most women don't receive as much stimulation as they need for orgasm through intercourse. So, I no longer feel that intercourse is expected. I don't always want intercourse. Often I do, probably as often as not. I enjoy intercourse very much, but am happy to perform other variations such as oral and manual sex."

"There's never any pressure to initiate intercourse. In fact, I've enjoyed making my lover come orally without ever having entered her."

"It depends on the woman. Some women like to have something in their vagina very quickly; some like to be worked up slowly; some like prolonged clitoral stimulation by a finger; some like cunnilingus, etc. Since attending my daughter's birth (Lamaze) and after my wife miscarried several times and elected an abortion once, I have grown to have very strong feelings about pregnancy; especially that it should not result casually or accidentally. My feelings about this are such that even were I with a new partner that was very attractive to me, I think I would avoid intercourse if she and I had no protection against pregnancy. There are many other ways to have pleasure, after all."

"In bed I fondle my wife a lot without actually having intercourse. I also fondle myself whenever and wherever I desire. I've never felt pressured."

"Sex shouldn't be a set pattern. The element of surprise, the unexpected, should always be there. I used to think sex meant intercourse. Now I just enjoy all facets and love it."

"It always feels good to have intercourse, but sometimes I feel I would be satisfied just kissing and showing affection."

"I don't always want to fuck, sometimes I just want to be loved."

Conclusion

Why should men feel that if they don't want intercourse, they are not "real men"? That only by having intercourse will they have "true sex"? Most men have felt resentment at the many pressures on them to perform, but have rarely revolted against the pressure on them to have intercourse itself—a pressure which makes having intercourse during sex more an inevitability than a choice.

This is not to suggest that intercourse is not often a great, powerful experience. But as one man said, "Unless the woman and I are both really desiring intercourse in particular with each other, then the lovemaking act tends to become a dull ritual. Sometimes I think it should be saved for special times."

Without the cultural insistence that intercourse *is* sex, and that it is the most desirable activity in the world and especially that a *man* should always want intercourse, how important would intercourse be to sex? Would it remain the dominant activity of sex, or would it become simply one of many possible ways of relating, something done sometimes and not other times?

WOULD MEN LIKE TO DIVERSIFY THEIR SEXUALITY BEYOND INTERCOURSE?

"What is the place of intercourse in sex? Would you like to change the definition of sex so that it was not so rigidly focused on erection and intercourse? Would you like to replace intercourse with other activities at times? Or do you prefer always to define sex as intercourse?"

The largest percentage of men did not seem to understand this question.* However, of those who did, most reacted against the (new) idea of making intercourse a choice during sexual relations:

"I'm all in favor of making sex more varied and interesting. *However,* I do think that any attempt to *replace* intercourse with some of these other activities would meet with extremely strong resistance on the part of men. For me, sex *is* intercourse (with ejaculation); you can add more to it, but you can't take away this essential part. And I rather suspect that most men will agree with me!"

"It is a disaster to suggest a 'change' in the concept of intercourse. Intercourse is an act of nature, you cannot change it by scientific theory. Science may only try to understand and interpret nature, and it could change nature in limited cases for the benefits of humans, but it should do that very cautiously in order not to generate wild side effects of interference with the delicate complicated structure of nature."

"I'd be willing—but my track record in reaching orgasm in other ways is poor when I have tried."

"Not really. Sex is intercourse. I always want it to culminate in intercourse."

"After twenty years, we seem pretty set in our ways; in some ways it's nice not to have to worry about what to do next!"

* However, if men find intercourse so unendingly appealing, why do they complain in chapter 2 that intercourse with the same person becomes boring? Perhaps it is not "sex" with the same person that becomes boring, but the constant forced repetition of a pattern that causes lack of interest. If "sex" could be un-defined to become an individual vocabulary of many ways to relate physically—including activities which express anger, tenderness, passion, and love, depending on the current feelings of the two people—perhaps its "boringness" would disappear.

"During sexual encounters I enjoy adding other activities such as kissing the girl's breasts, petting and kissing her body, but I want the intercourse too. It's the central part of 'making sex.' "

"If I'm into balling, I enjoy intercourse. If I'm not, it's probably the easiest way to end it—by coming in her. So either way, if I'm sexually involved, I want to fuck and come."

"I don't know—the current definition seems good for a few more laffs."

"I want intercourse when my penis is erect and begging to enter the sacred sheath of love. I don't want to be told no."

"No—because, although it's often perfunctory, there are those occasional times of pure ecstasy—the ultimate sharing of one's self. Those times make up for all the rest."

"No—intercourse is the highest form of sex—complete physical union."

But some men said that they would be interested in making, or were in the process of making changes:

"I've found that sex is much better for both of us if we don't always have intercourse in our minds as the final act. Most of my partners have appreciated this state of mind, once they got used to the novelty of, they said, 'a guy who doesn't include fucking as a non-negotiable.' By not having intercourse as a preconceived ground rule, sex is so much more natural-feeling, variations seem to stand out, and each thing we do has the same weight and importance. Perhaps four times out of ten there is no actual genital-to-genital sex."

"I don't often have sex without intercourse, but am learning that it can be very nice. It's hard to unlearn the pressure. I am trying to just go with the flow when a sexual event is shaping up. I enjoy it much more when I do that."

"Intercourse by insertion has something to do with role playing learned as teenagers. Both males and females play their roles for many years, accepting the lies they tell one another in a sort of passion of ego, males strutting for other males and the females increasingly confused, wondering what the hell sex is all about. I went through this stupidity for many years, also trying to believe, and succeeding, that it was great to ejaculate as often inside as many women as possible. I don't think I gave too much consideration to the thought that it was anything having to do with close personal relationships."

"I want to let the world know that vaginal penetration is not the full answer. To both male and female only the orgasm is what really counts. Vaginal penetration permits closeness and affection and love and whispers, but so do the alternatives, when the people lay in each other's arms. I feel strongly that masturbating with my partner is important—the best way to teach and learn how to properly and fully stimulate the other!"

"I like intercourse because of the ecstasy involved in all stages of it, yet I place coitus well down the line in preference. My order of preference is: cunnilingus-analingus, then masturbation (solitary or mutual with a woman), then fellatio, then anal intercourse, then fucking."

"Sometimes I'd rather not even have intercourse but would just like to lie close side by side and give each other warm soft kisses all over. It's *good* to know now that women don't get all that excited about intercourse. It takes a lot of pressure off. I feel more flexible. But there's always the haunting thought that she may think I'm not masculine enough to 'do it.' That's a sad state of affairs."

"The simplest gesture at the right time can give me as big a psychological thrill as I've ever had from intercourse. It's true that intercourse is when I usually have my orgasms, but I object to holding up intercourse as some sort of supreme act of love—*love*, yet!—when what it usually turns out to be is two highly specialized organs performing a natural function. There are still people who believe that lie they tried to feed us way back in junior high about intercourse being some kind of ultimate 'test' or 'proof' of love. This is not to deny that intercourse *can* be a very intense and pleasurable form of love, depending on who's doing it and how and sometimes why, but the act itself is no guarantee of pleasure, psychological or physical, since the depression of fucking somebody you don't really like very much can outweigh the pleasure of having an orgasm. So to hell with the glorification of intercourse. Maybe I'm beginning to feel more this way right now because living with my partner has sort of freed us from the *obligation* to have intercourse every time we have sex; we are free to enjoy other activities and not have intercourse at all if we don't feel like it. Intercourse is just one of any number of delightful sexual activities that humans can engage in. Although in any given sexual encounter you may eventually get to doing it, and it is a unique activity, it's just part of a larger range of activities, a larger whole."

"Intercourse is too high in importance in a lot of people's minds. Sex should be defined with a more all-encompassing meaning. Sex is *anything* that one or more people do to become sexually aroused, to orgasm if necessary. I have made changes intellectually, but gut-level reservations may be a part of my anxiety. I *think* that I would like more oral sex to orgasm for both of us, leaving out intercourse."

"Sex without penis-vagina intercourse is strongly appealing. I often want intercourse as *part* of sex but not always —although I do always want (need, for my satisfaction, too) for her to have several orgasms—and am willing and eager to learn what produces them and to take whatever time is necessary to give *(share?)* them. Too bad so many women still are reluctant to show or tell what it does for them."

"I am not very much interested in intercourse (particularly to ejaculation) anymore, and I don't think I ever put it down as a 'must' to experience my orgasm by 'coming' into the female vagina. Hell, there are a lot more interesting things to do than that. In fact, it has been a long time since I have completed an act of sexual intercourse with my wife (and with one other woman thirty-three years ago). In my early married years (we are married forty-one years), I always orgasmed in intercourse with my wife being satisfied by my masturbating her. This developed into mutual masturbation, with sometimes closeness, as putting the penis in the vagina without intention of intercourse but only to 'feel good' and sometimes (in younger years) sleep that way. Only recently has my wife consented to fellatio, which I love. As I suppose, in the most ideal marriages, we seem to continue to learn. From the wedding night, when my wife masturbated me to orgasm just to see how things worked; through our trial of all the positions of intercourse except the more acrobatic—sitting with her on my lap, standing, with her on top, with me on top, with one of us on our left side and the other on our right side—to our latest experience with fellatio (I started cunnilingus with her many years ago and she loved it then and still does—I've now added analingus to the repertoire), we continue to grow sexually."

"I am intensely ambivalent about penis-vagina intercourse. My feelings about it have been undergoing change. I once thought (and having grown up in this culture, it's no wonder) that I needed it, and accepted that, and pursued it. And with that as a basis for relating, the hostility all around was appalling. A combination of personal experience and exposure to the women's movement led some years ago to a 'raised consciousness' that led to some altered perceptions and new perspectives.

"It bothered me to perceive that I had believed I authentically felt things (like the desirability of penis-vagina intercourse) (like the desirability of women??) which upon examination I discovered I only believed I ought to feel in order to fit cultural norms. I began to suspect that the great unspoken truth of our time is that men don't need women—and sure as hell women don't need us. Sexually (physically), there's nothing you can do for me I can't do better for myself —and any woman can make the same statement. Surely the penis is a clumsy tool (how much better fingers, lips, tongue) for anything but baby making. I suspect that penis-vagina intercourse is first-rate procreation, second-rate sex for men, sixth-rate sex for women. I suspect we can both do better, for each other, or for ourselves.

"When I pursued it I thought I liked it, but now I think that was mostly because I was supposed to like it. Physically, it was seldom better than masturbation, often enough not as good. That's for me. What right do I have to believe it was any better for the woman? Psychologically, I am appalled at what it meant to the woman. How can you feel good about what has become the central metaphor of what's sick in our society, the 'making it' metaphor, conquest, domination, and competitive performance crushing all possibility of cooperative mutual enjoyment. There it is summed up in that image —rigid penis, thrusting in vagina. More: penis-vagina intercourse is psychologically repellent because men and women (have been conditionel to) measure a man's masculinity in terms of that act. If he doesn't get it up, stick it in, orgasm, and make her orgasm, well, shit, he's not a *man*. Not in his eyes, not in hers.

"Psychologically, the only saving grace of penis-vagina intercourse is the sense of closeness and union it can produce, but frankly, I wonder if that's enough. 'Does it lead to orgasm . . . ?' Whose orgasm? It usually led to mine, except when I really was unable to get my heart into it, in which case I had no reason to expect one, and what was I doing there then, anyway? When the woman had orgasms, which was not often enough, I doubted then, and doubt now, that it was the penis-vagina intercourse that led to them.

"In the last year, I have become reluctant to initiate it.

If women want it, let them pursue it for a while. If they don't and I don't, then who the hell does, and how did it become the ne plus ultra of sex?

"To the extent that it still appeals to me, it's definitely on an emotional level (physically other things feel good too), but even there, as a means of achieving closeness, people are so dissociated from their genitals that it doesn't work as well as nongenital physical affection. Aside from anything else, it's been devalued as much as the lira, and certainly I helped to do it. It just doesn't mean what it's supposed to, what we hope it will. Although its potential is to effect a unity of two individuals, in a very real sense it distances the participants even as they conjoin. Still, there's the sense I mentioned, of feeling strange, yet natural, like coming home again after a long absence. I think that's unique to penis-vagina intercourse, and you'd have to call it emotional more than physical. But it's mutual affection that joins persons closely with one another, not intercourse."

"I am a nice-looking man, I am two hundred pounds, brown hair, gray eyes. All the women I've ever had sex with enjoyed making sex with me—I am very sensitive in those places.

"You ask me about marital problems. Well, the most problems that women have is having an orgasm. I'd like to comment on this a little, how women have been taught not to masturbate themselves or do anything that's not nice. Women have been told all their lives not to play with or touch their vagina. But I think when women or men get up in the morning they should touch their bodies wherever they want and they should love it. They should find out where all the beautiful spots are on their body and everything, love their body and touch their body and make them feel good in every way and this will cause them not to be so bashful. A woman that masturbates when she is a little girl till she becomes grown and all—and even on the day she gets married and even *if* she gets married, a woman that masturbates herself makes a good marriage partner, in bed, having sex. Women and men should always talk over their sex problems, and tell each other where they like to be touched. Then they will have a good marriage life, by being honest with each other.

"Another point is, make sure both parties are free with each other in lovemaking, and having sex. Let the woman have her fun, let the woman do whatever she wants to do, to the man, and this is also for the man. Let him do whatever he wants to do to her, but both agree on what they want to do to each other. Both parties should always tell each other how they like to have their sex. If one of the partners does not like the things that one partner's doing to the other, they should stop and talk it over and one should compromise— they should always compromise with each other. Now when it comes to lovemaking, a man should always—always—let his partner—his woman—get into the act and do her thing when making sex—let the woman have freedom too. Let her be dominant over the male because sometimes when you have sex she doesn't really get satisfied and the man leaves her high and dry. He gets up there for a couple of minutes and he has his orgasm and the woman doesn't have an orgasm. He just gets his load off and leaves her high and dry.

"To have a good marriage and make a good sex life is to do the right thing by touching each other's parts in the right place. They both can—both partners can get very hot and have a wonderful beautiful sex relationship. Another thing is very helpful. Going—taking a vacation from children, if you have children, and if you don't have children go out alone together and talk about things, walk along the beach, and in the woods and parks, go on vacations together—because this gives a woman and man a chance to talk about small things that bother the woman, also bother the man, to make their marriage—to make a good marriage life by talking together and taking vacations together. Going out alone every chance they get. This makes a beautiful marriage life. I feel another thing women and men should do when they're married, even young boys and girls, should find out about their body and themselves in every way by touching their bodies themselves, all over their body, and should love their body— they should never be made fun of, small children shouldn't be made fun of if they touch their body, and the parents shouldn't have any bad feelings toward their children when they do catch their children touching themselves. And I feel if a man and a woman do this too—touching themselves by themselves, not having a partner doing it, but touching themselves—sit in front of a mirror or something, touch themselves and see and like their body, love their body, praise their body, finding all the nice places on their body, this will help them to have a good marriage."

DO MEN ALWAYS WANT ORGASM DURING INTERCOURSE OR DO THEY SOMETIMES JUST WANT THE PLEASURE OF INTERCOURSE?

Is male orgasm an essential part of intercourse?* Do men always want to orgasm during intercourse? Intercourse can be considered in two ways—as a kind of "foreplay" not leading to orgasm, or in the traditional way, as the culmination of sex.

Can men receive more pleasure from having orgasm during intercourse, or from using intercourse as a means to heighten their own arousal and excitement? Have most men tried approaching sex as a quest for arousal and excitement, instead of looking for orgasm?

Most men who responded felt that male orgasm is the point of sex and intercourse:†

"Got to have an orgasm. No point in starting anything without the expectation of the complete thing. I will avoid intercourse rather than risk an incomplete climax. Isn't sex orgasms? I never heard of any other kind."

"I've never had sex‡ without orgasm. If I were to stop having orgasms, then I would probably stop having sex."

"Being a man, ejaculation is the ultimate of intercourse. I have had times when I did not have orgasm. It just leaves me uptight and dejected. I would say, definitely, that 'good sex' does by all means end in a great orgasm."

"Having orgasms is the most pleasant physical experience in my life, bar none, and as far as enjoying sex without them, how can there be sex without orgasms? An orgasm is the logical culmination of sex, and the two, orgasm and sex, cannot be differentiated."

"Is there any other way to finish up but to orgasm?"

---

* Some men, by avoiding ejaculating, could have multiple orgasms during intercourse.

† However, this contradicts the answers most men gave when asked their basic reason for liking and wanting intercourse (see pages 336–354), and also many of their answers in chapter 4.

‡ Here again, the terms "sex" and "intercourse" are frequently used interchangeably.

Sometimes men felt pressured to orgasm by their partners:*

"I do feel pressure to have an orgasm whenever I have intercourse because it is expected. It just seems like that's the way it's supposed to go (I know that sounds dumb). Also in my experience, women seem to really get off on having a guy blow his rocks inside them, and while doing so, just letting go, indicating by sounds, movements, etc., how good it feels."

"Sore point!! *Why* does everyone feel if you don't have an orgasm, you haven't enjoyed yourself, and they have 'failed' by not bringing you to orgasm? When going with a new lover, I try to work around to the subject prior to getting into the heavy stuff—'Let's just lie here awhile . . . this is nice . . . who cares if we come? I'm a hard come, so don't worry whether I do or not, because I still really enjoy it . . . so you just enjoy'—to try and set the other person at ease and erase any guilt feelings they might otherwise have later because they didn't have me shooting to the ceiling."

"I definitely feel a pressure to have an orgasm. At times when I haven't had orgasm, I've felt that the woman misconstrued this to mean that she wasn't attractive to me or that she had 'failed' to please me. It's hard to explain to a woman that I've enjoyed sex even if I haven't had an orgasm. I usually do have one with sex, but there are times when my orgasm isn't ultimately important to me and I don't think I should have to prove myself by having one any more than a woman should have to prove herself by bringing me to orgasm."

"I have, infrequently, felt pressured to have an orgasm by a woman, many times a second or third one. They (the women) are blown away if I don't—internalizing it as a performance failure on their part. At that point I attempt to reassure them that 'Hey, it's O.K.! I can enjoy stimulation and stimulating without orgasm.' But women have a difficult time accepting this, and I have, *rarely* but I have, faked one to ease their assumed burden, and they appear noticeably relieved."

"I almost always orgasm during intercourse—if I do not, she may feel that she's not exciting enough to me. (This *sounds* ridiculous, but it's the way I feel.)"

---

* These replies answer the question, "Do you ever feel pressure to orgasm—otherwise you have failed?"

"The girlfriend I have now wants me to have 'a vortex of purple ecstasy' every time. I sometimes have to reassure her that I had a great time and feel good anyway."

A few men mentioned social pressure:

"I do go after orgasm most of the time—but I wouldn't doubt that there is some unconscious social garbage operating that orients me toward orgasms or goal-oriented sex. I am intrigued with tantra and have gotten into it some—having intercourse without orgasm on purpose—to get into the feelings of intercourse themselves—rather than just hurrying through them on the way to an orgasm."

"If I don't have one, I feel something's wrong. 'Men always come' (if I didn't come, I wasn't a man)."

But one man observed that men as well as women could enjoy sex without orgasm:

"I used to feel pressured to have an orgasm and always did. But sometimes when I am tired or when I have recently made love, I am quite content to end when she is ready to end. It is not a threat anymore, because I am secure in my ability to be a good lover. However, I have noticed one very strange phenomenon. It appears that women have been indoctrinated somewhere in their youth to believe that unless the man climaxed he would be in bad shape. So I have often discovered that the woman gets into some heavy trip about making sure the man is O.K. I personally think that is bullshit. That must surely be a male chauvinist trip laid on them through the mores of society, maybe in high school. After all, what is so different about a woman being left high and dry. Men can take it too, and it is sort of fun too. Then you will be ready again after a while and in future she won't feel so much 'duty.' "

DRY ORGASMS WHICH DO NOT END INTERCOURSE OR SEXUAL AROUSAL

Are ejaculation and orgasm the same thing? Although our culture has generally equated ejaculation with orgasm, some men made a distinction. Many of the men in this study reported at times having ejaculation without orgasm; another small percent reported having orgasm without ejaculation from time to time; and an additional handful said that they could have several of what one called "dry orgasms," or "mini-orgasms," in a row.

When asked, "Can you orgasm without ejaculating? If so, can you have multiple orgasms?" one man responded, rather typically:

"I was rather surprised to see this question. Orgasm in males *means* ejaculation unless they are very young (prepuberty). If you know of a way we can orgasm without ejaculation, every male on this planet wants to hear it."

A small minority of men mentioned being able to orgasm without ejaculation.*

"I'm not at all certain of this, but I have, while masturbating slowly and deliberately, stopped stimulation just before the onset of ejaculation, in order to delay it, and experienced a series of small contractions. These contractions are not as strong as the contractions of ejaculation, and nothing comes out, or at most a very small drop of semen will appear. After such an aborted ejaculation, I seem to enter onto a new plateau of arousal, in which the inevitability of ejaculation recedes, at the same time that my penis seems guaranteed to remain fully erect for as long as I might want to play, or almost. I have no idea if these are orgasms in their own right, or arrested ones that were incomplete without ejaculation. I would like to think that they were orgasms in their own right, and ejaculation a function of the most intense orgasms, even though I have always been told that ejaculation and orgasm are synonymous in the male. P.S. Since writing this, I

---

* This is, of course, not the same as the phenomenon mentioned by many men of, after having several orgasms in an evening or a day, no longer ejaculating semen: "If I have ejaculated within a few hours there is little or no semen available—this does not preclude or reduce the intensity of the orgasm."

"I very seldom have an orgasm without ejaculation except after the fourth or more time in one evening. The sensation of ejaculation appears to continue during successive orgasms even when the ejaculate has been used up. And the quality of the orgasm is independent of the amount of seminal fluid ejaculated. If it is the latest of a series of ejaculations, there may be very little fluid actually released, and yet the orgasm may be very, very good."

There are also medical reasons for not ejaculating, which include prostate surgery, which can result in retrograde ejaculation (ejaculation directly into the bladder, so that it can be seen in the next urine, either as a cohesive denser liquid or causing the urination to appear foamy). Other causes of retrograde ejaculation include the nerve damage and muscle deterioration characteristic of some forms of diabetes and low blood sugar.

have experimented in masturbation with these non-ejaculatory orgasms and found myself capable of several of them a few minutes apart, connected by a plateau of extremely high arousal. I am now firmly convinced that 'the poor male, he has only one orgasm' shtick *is a myth*."

"I used to think orgasm was ejaculation. Recently, though, my wife and I reached a state where I exhibited all the most intense signs of orgasm—except ejaculation, which seemed to take an eternity to begin. It was most incredible and felt like falling straight over from standing and stopping instantaneously an inch before impacting the floor prone. It's only happened three times, but I think it might be possible to reach this state and not ejaculate if I could figure what gets me there."

"At one period I developed a technique to combat premature ejaculation—I was able to have a 'semi-orgasm'—I don't know if I really ejaculated or not, but it would take the top off the tension without losing an erection and I could then go ahead and have prolonged intercourse leading to subsequent full orgasm."

"I have two types of orgasm. The first type is what I call a 'dry orgasm,' which is a pleasant series of muscle spasms or contractions in the pelvic area, primarily in the crotch and penis, but without ejaculation. The second type is what I call a 'wet orgasm' or orgasm with ejaculation. After a wet orgasm, arousal usually goes down to zero. Sometimes I can become horny again after fifteen to thirty minutes but I am not nearly as inclined to have prolonged arousal on a second time around as with dry orgasms."

"I almost always ejaculate when I orgasm. But sometimes with my lover I can come very, very close to an orgasm by concentrating on having one while we are fucking, without ejaculation. The buildup is the same as for an ejaculation, but I just try not to ejaculate. It doesn't always work, and it gets me so excited that I can only do it once. The next orgasm will invariably be accompanied by ejaculation."

Many men mentioned the opposite phenomenon: they ejaculated but did not experience full or complete orgasm—they did not really enjoy it:

"Anybody can ejaculate. You just do the physical thing and you ejaculate. But to orgasm, you must follow an emotional scenario. Orgasm is satisfying; ejaculation is not. In orgasm, there is a gap, a moment where you lose consciousness, a break."

"When she wants to fuck and I'm just too high, or too uninterested to respond, I ejaculate but I don't come."

"Orgasm and ejaculation are not the same thing. I can and sometimes do ejaculate without having any orgasm or even the normal pleasure of the buildup if my partner, after having been satisfied, is eager for me to be finished. Orgasm is mostly a mental state with the body usually following along. You may not appreciate a sunset unless your mind is into it."

"An ejaculation without orgasm is a nothing—no feeling of any sort except the wetness and the muscle contractions. It usually occurs after I have foreplay sessions in which I do not pay enough attention to my own body needs."

But several of the men who did report non-ejaculatory, dry orgasms said that they could be multiple or sequential:*

"I have had a different kind of orgasm, which is sort of a prolonged series of very small orgasms, without ejaculation, which may go on over a period of one to fifteen minutes and ends when I decide to finish it and go for the final orgasm, and ejaculation. This is achieved only by masturbation, as it requires very delicate control."

"I can have an orgasm without ejaculation, if I'm careful. It requires stopping just before orgasm—the contractions will come, but weaker, and no ejaculation. I can have more than one, sometimes within a minute or two, sometimes only after a resting period. I sometimes feel even more aroused after orgasm, particularly if I haven't ejaculated."

"I feel that I could have multiple orgasms during sex with a partner because I have done this during masturbation on many occasions. One way I do it is to withhold stimulation a split second before orgasm. When this works well the ejaculation is only a few drops accompanied by several 'dry' contractions. It is then no problem to have another orgasm within moments."

"I have experienced this only a few times and it's really a fantastic feeling. It's not that I stop ejaculating and then start

---

* Boys who masturbate to orgasm before being physiologically able to ejaculate quite often continue after their first orgasm to restimulate themselves several times to repeated orgasms, as of course women do also. (See page 607.)

again, but it's like the buildup stage occurring all over again. When I first experienced it I couldn't believe it was happening. I told my partner, 'I am coming again.' It was extraordinary."

Still, most of these men said that the best orgasms were those with ejaculation:

"I do not ejaculate each time. Successive orgasms vary in intensity. Sometimes they are stronger, at other times weaker. Always the best orgasm is the one with the ejaculation."

But one man disagreed:

"A dry orgasm lacks the gratification of feeling the semen squirting through (this is a soothing sensation), but can be just as intense—or even more intense. In fact, it can be achingly, agonizingly intense. Possibly it is the very lack of the soothing feeling of the semen which gives it the potential to feel more intense."

This technique was also discussed in ancient Sanskrit and Hindu literature, which said that men could achieve the greatest pleasure by the continual maintenance of a high level of arousal, by refraining from orgasm during some periods of sexual arousal.

A few men described the increased intensity they felt, sometimes avoiding orgasm altogether to increase their own pleasure:

"I love to luxuriate in all the feelings of intercourse—all the little nuances, different feelings in just slight changes in angle, seeing how deep I can get in, feeling driven to craziness by the sexiness of it, teased to the brink of orgasm over and over—wow! Who cares about orgasm? It's better if I never come!!!"

"I enjoy being inside her *so much* for its own sake that I have changed my conception of intercourse to something that doesn't necessarily lead to my orgasm."

"I feel wonderful during the buildup to orgasm. The height of ecstasy is before the orgasm, which is an explosion that puts an end to the feeling of ecstasy and spoils all the fun. After is a letdown; the fun is all over until you can get another buildup. Unless I want to impregnate a woman, I do not try to have an orgasm; it is far more fun and lasts a lot, lot longer without one. I use mind control over my body to just stay at the brink of orgasm for a long, long time, increasing the pleasure indescribably and leaving one on top of the world!"

"I think my enjoyment of intercourse has changed over the years as I have changed in personality and emotional maturity. In the earlier years, my primary purpose was to produce pleasure for my partner and me as soon as possible, assuming that maximum pleasure was associated with genital orgasm for both of us. In later years, we found through experimentation and exploration that a whole sensual range of pleasures were possible beside orgasm. Today, the physical intimacy and expression of love, mutually shared, is easily as important to me as the momentary physical peak of genital orgasm. In fact, sometimes I don't even bother with orgasm."

One man described discovering entirely new facets of his own sexuality:

"Three months ago my nine-year marriage ended. I never could let loose and really enjoy sex with my wife. I was *performing* sexually as I thought I should, all right, but basically it was a very one-two-three routine. She did orgasm occasionally during sex, but to be honest, sex with me was no joyride, and as it grew more and more infrequent (to practically nil) she learned to suppress her desires as a defense.

"The first time I got horny with my girlfriend (the second woman I've had sex with) I thought I was being very 'manly' because I was being forceful about the kiss/feel/fuck routine. A very understanding woman and a great friend, she did not at that time correct me or try to slow me up. But after a couple of her orgasms, I thought: 'This has been long enough. I guess now it's my turn.' It so happens that I orgasm by penetration very deeply (approximately eight inches) and slowly, rhythmically rocking or grinding. It also happens that this particular action drove her wild with delight and she'd squeal and squirm all over uncontrollably instead of lying there like I thought she 'should,' and I'd lose the right position and pressure necessary to come. I was really getting mad when suddenly she took over, sat atop me, and did excruciatingly delightful things that gave me sensations I've never had before. Do men need orgasm to enjoy sex? Hell no, not every time! We continued to fuck/play/laugh/scream/groan/flail/gasp for three more hours. She lost count of her orgasms after ten.

I had none. Exhaustion stopped us. She felt bad that I hadn't come. I said, 'Listen, I can come by myself in fifteen seconds any day of the week. What I just experienced with you I could never do to myself. It was the thrill of my lifetime.' Two nights later we kissed/stroked/licked/danced/fucked/played/laughed/screamed/groaned/flailed/gasped for four more hours, and I still didn't come and *didn't care!*

"So you see why I want to yell out to all men, 'Come on, you assholes, get with it! There is so much more than fuck 'n' come for both you and your woman.' I don't believe that I am God's gift to womankind. This is not just an ego trip (though it *is* terrific for my once-shot ego!). To me it's a mission to inform men so that they in turn really please their women and enjoy their manhood in the fullest sense. After all, one of those guys may someday become my ex-wife's lover, and I owe it to her for the nine years of her life, womanhood, and sexuality that I robbed and wasted. I want to help prevent another occurrence of so cruel a crime."

For other men's descriptions, see pages 508–515.

CONCLUSION

WHAT IS "MALE SEXUALITY"?

Once again, we must ask, what *is* "male sexuality?" Is it intercourse? Why is it so closely identified with intercourse? Have men missed the boat because of the total focus our society teaches them to have on intercourse, on an always aggressive, dominating, goal-oriented definition of their sexuality?

To always assume that "sex" equals "foreplay," followed by "vaginal penetration" (why not call it "penile enfolding"?), and ending with male orgasm in the vagina—even if now clitoral stimulation to orgasm is included before intercourse

—means that sex will still be focused on intercourse and retain its overly structured definition.

Defining sex as basically intercourse holds men back from getting to know and appreciate their own sensuality, forcing them into an unnecessary, anxious preoccupation with erection: focusing on (what he believes to be) his responsibility to achieve erection and perform coitus, "to perform his duties as a man," tends to cut off many men's erotic responses before they even get started. For example, many men cut short "foreplay" and physical affection because they are afraid they may lose their erection—which they have been taught is necessary to enjoy sex (and which it would be "shameful" to lose). But men could reach much higher peaks of feeling and arousal if they did not feel anxious about how they "should" behave sexually, and if they did not focus so much on reaching orgasm.

Men's denial of their great sensuality is significant because it is part of the overall denial by men of their feelings and emotions: a "real man," it is said, should learn to always be "in control" of his emotions, as we saw in chapter 1. Thus the traditional definition of masculinity tries to close men off from their full capacity to feel joy, sadness, love, the world, life.

Men have everything to gain from leaving behind the old mechanical definition of "male sexuality" and at the same time developing a greater appreciation of their great sensuality, their own capacity for enjoyment and expression. Men's experience of their own bodies has been cut off and limited, falsified, by the culture's insistence that "male sexuality" is a simple mechanistic drive for intercourse.

"Sex" could be un-defined to become something with infinite variety, not always including intercourse or even orgasm (for either person). It can become part of an individual vocabulary of many ways to relate physically—including activities which express anger, tenderness, passion, and/or love, depending on the current feelings of the two people—a way of expressing a thousand different feelings, saying a thousand different things.

Can men imagine a new conception of male sexuality and sensuality not necessarily focused on intercourse or orgasm? Would men like to diversify and expand, eroticize their sexuality—become less constantly active and doing, and sometimes be more passive, more receptive to feelings and attention? Have most men ever experienced sex as less orgasm and more passion? These subjects will be discussed in chapter 4.

ORIGINS OF THE DEFINITION OF SEX AS INTERCOURSE (AND THE IDENTIFICATION OF "MALE SEXUALITY" WITH INTERCOURSE)

Historically, sex has not always been defined as we define it. In fact, the current definition of "sex"—basically, "foreplay" followed by intercourse and ending with male orgasm in the vagina as the "right" way to have sex—has not always been the definition of sex. Everything we see in this book, and what we think of as "male sexuality" is in very large part a reflection of the values and needs of the society we live in, and the culture we have inherited. The definition of sex as we know it was begun approximately twenty-five hundred years ago for the purpose of increasing reproduction. It was at this time that the Hebrew tribes returned from the Babylonian exile, a small, struggling group. These tribes passed a law, the first such law we know of, saying that henceforth, all sexual activities other than heterosexual intercourse would be illegal. The Old Testament constantly warned against other forms of sexuality, including "spilling one's seed" (masturbation), oral sex, and the sexual practices of the "heathens" (surrounding tribes), especially the Babylonians. This officially promoted focus on reproductive activities (and glorification of intercourse) was important for the small tribes, since only through increasing their population could they become more powerful, consolidating their hold on their territory, cultivating and harvesting more crops, and maintaining a larger army to defend themselves.

This definition of sex also reflected a new male ascendancy in society, in that henceforth, the children were to belong (along with the wives) to the fathers (or husbands), which had not previously been the case. The Hebrew tribes (possibly influenced by traditions of invading Indo-Europeans or Aryan tribes) were organized with a patriarchal social structure—that is, ruled by men: women and children were owned (legally) by an individual man (husband or father), who in turn owed his allegiance (legally) to a male king, who in turn owed his allegiance to a male priesthood and a male god. But the Babylonians, like many other societies of the time, for example the Canaanites, did not worship one male god, or even one god; furthermore, many of the gods they did worship were female, and indeed it was women who were the priests. Queens in these societies were frequently more powerful or as powerful as kings—going back to an earlier nonpatriarchal tradition, which was probably very widespread throughout the entire Middle East at that time, and even more widespread during an earlier period.

The exact nature of this tradition is still a matter of debate,* but many scholars now agree that, based on archaeological and written evidence, very early periods of history—often called "prehistory"—had quite a different form of social organization from our own. Some scholars refer to these early societies as "matriarchies," although very little is known in the popular culture about them; other feminist scholars have objected to the term "matriarchy," since it implies that these societies were the simple reverse of "patriarchy," that is, that women owned the children and ruled men, rather than having a more complex tradition of their own, possibly more egalitarian. However, although there was a great variety of social organizations among these groups, it does seem clear that women were held in higher esteem than men, and that women were usually in charge in general of the temples and distribution of food and goods. Whether women also were warriors is not known—although many goddesses were addressed as warrior-goddesses. But these societies were certainly not male dominated. And the "sex" (i.e., physical relations between individuals) and family structure were in all probability quite different in these early forms of social organizations than in the later patriarchal structure.

Following is a simplified version of some hypotheses of the changes which seemed to have taken place over a period of a thousand or more years, perhaps sometime around 8,000 to 5,000 B.C.†

---

* Books related to this subject include *Egypt and Chaldea*, by W. Boscawen (London: Harper, 1894); *Ancient Israel*, by Roland DeVaux (London: Darton, Longman & Todd, 1965); *The Lost World of Elam*, by Walther Hinz (New York: New York University Press, 1973); *The Splendor that Was Egypt*, by Margaret Murray (London: Sidgwick & Jackson, 1949); *When God Was a Woman*, by Merlin Stone (New York: Dial Press, 1976); and *Prehistory and the Beginning of Civilization*, by Jacquetta Hawkes and Sir Leonard Woolley. Also helpful is the extensive bibliography contained in *When God Was a Woman*.

† At present, we do not know the exact dates of the changeover from pre-patriarchy, or "matriarchy," but we do know that the struggles went on for many years, even centuries, and in many separate locations.

The very earliest societies may have worshiped/venerated women because it was thought that only women could bring forth new life. In very early societies, much earlier than the Babylonians or the Egyptians, some scholars believe that the relationship between intercourse and pregnancy was not known, and so the male role in reproduction was unknown. Additionally, the earliest families we know of did not consist of the mother, father, and child as we know them today, but rather a group that included the mother, sisters, brothers, aunts, uncles, and children; children could be brought up by various members of the group—the biological mother having had the choice of whether to "stay at home" with the child or not. In other words, there has not always been the close tie between the biological mother and child (nor the father and child) we consider "natural" today; children of many mothers mixed together and were brought up by many members of the group. In fact, the concept of private property may not yet have existed, or may have been very weak or unimportant to the society; certainly children were not "owned."

It has been theorized that when the male contribution to childbearing became known, possibly around 10,000 or more years ago (this knowledge coming at different times to different societies), there began a gradual shift to more male involvement in religious functions, and gradually to the system of patriarchal social order in which men now are almost entirely dominant. Scholars are only slowly piecing together fragments of records to understand what happened in these early times; much remains to be understood. However, some scholars see the Old Testament as, among other things, representing the story of the early patriarchal struggle against goddess worship and female-oriented societies, and the transition to a male-dominated, "one-god" society. The history of Greece, also, and the chronological changes in Greek mythology, have been seen as representing a changeover in thinking from goddess worship to God ascendancy.* A similar change from the ascendancy of queens to the ascendancy of kings can be seen in several centuries of early Egyptian history. The transition from Cretan culture to later Mycenaean/mainland Greek culture

---

* See Jane Harrison, *Prologomena to the Study of Greek Religion,* Cambridge, 1903, and E. A. Butterworth, *Some Traces of the Pre-Olympian World,* Berlin and New York, De Gruyter, 1966.

is another example. However, these interpretations, while steadily gaining adherents, are far from orthodox. On the other hand, scholars generally agree on a recent revision of the extent of our fully human ("civilized") history: according to latest estimate, complex human societies existed as far back as 40,000 years—quite an increase over what had previously been thought.

What was the role of intercourse in pre-patriarchal or "matriarchal" societies? Even in early patriarchal or transitional times, intercourse was not thought of romantically, or in terms of being the greatest physical pleasure there is, more pleasurable than other forms of intimacy and sexuality, but basically was practiced for reproduction; this was true, for example, in most periods of Greek and Roman history. What must sex and physical relations have been like even earlier, then, 20,000 or 40,000 years ago, when it may have been believed (at least for some time) that women became pregnant simply by lying in the moonlight? When intercourse was not an especially noted symbol in the society? Were sexual feelings tied to religious ("fertility") group activities, rather than "romantic" personal activities? Or were sexual feelings and orgasm linked to "romantic" personal feelings, while fertility activities (whatever they may have been) linked to group or religious activities? There is some evidence that the latter may have been the case, but we honestly do not know what people did.*

But to return to the present, it must now be clear how completely sex as we know it is tied to our own history and social organization. This definition has come down to us from the early Judeo-Christian laws,† which became, in fact,

---

* However, women then, as today, must have known about the importance of the clitoris, since, as discussed in *The Hite Report* on female sexuality, women in the twentieth century, without being given any information whatsoever on how, begin to masturbate quite early in their lives; for the great majority of women this has meant manual clitoral stimulation. Therefore it is logical to assume that if women do this "instinctively" today, women must also have done this then, and known that this was a pleasurable area to have stimulated. Was this stimulation part of sexual institutions or customs at that time? Was masturbation considered private? What other activities were considered important?

† These laws may have stemmed from certain Indo-European or Aryan ideologies—the same ideologies which influenced early religion in Iran, Turkey, and India.

the civil code of the entire West, and whose laws are still basically those of our present civil code; in addition, old church laws are still enforced by many churches today. For example, the Catholic Church says that women should not use birth control, since the purpose of sex is reproduction, and since women should make their bodies available to their husbands for this purpose at all times; and further, that the fathers will own the children. It is also important to note that other societies, like those of Japan, China, India, and the Arab world, once they became patriarchal, also defined sex in much the same way—that is, regulated physical relations so that maximum reproduction, with the children being owned by the father, is the rule;* in other words, the reproductive definition of sexuality is an inherent part of a patriarchal society—i.e., in order for men to control a society, it has been essential for men to control reproduction and to own the children.

But sexuality today is changing—probably largely due to the fundamental changes brought about by the industrial revolution. Increasing population is not as necessary to the power of a society as it once was, since we now have very large populations and even more importantly, machines (and computers) can now do much of the work large populations once performed, from farming to defending a country. Therefore, as society feels it no longer needs to encourage reproduction to the extent that it once did, birth control is becoming more and more acceptable (legal), and male ownership of children (and marriage) less crucial, with "living together" arrangements more accepted.

However, this change has not yet deeply affected our idea of what "sex" is or could be. Even though we frequently use birth control, we still generally follow the traditional reproductive definition of physical relations, centered on intercourse. But, as seen in this book, some men are beginning to question the assumptions of our culture about "male sexuality" and our definition of sex: even though the issues are just beginning to surface, there is a gut feeling on the part of most men that something is wrong—that although there are beautiful elements to sex as we know it, somehow there are unnecessary problems, too.

---

* Most of these societies also had early non-patriarchal traditions, traditions which are just beginning to be studied and understood.

THE TRADITIONAL MEANING OF INTERCOURSE: THE POLITICS OF INTERCOURSE

How much of men's desire for intercourse is due to our culture's insistence that all men "should" seek and want intercourse, that it is "natural" for men; and how much is due to an individual man's desire to have intercourse with a particular woman, for his own personal reasons? We can never know exactly. But it does seem clear that, without the accompanying cultural symbolism and pressures, intercourse would become a matter of choice during sexual activities, not the sine qua non, or denouement toward which all sexual activities move, which it now is. This is not to say, of course, that men and women will not continue to enjoy intercourse with each other when they want, but simply that sex could be more enjoyable for both people if intercourse were not a "requirement"—if intercourse were a choice and not a given. Sex does not always have to include intercourse, and sex would become much freer if intercourse were not always its focus.

Intercourse is at once one of the most beautiful and at the same time most oppressive and exploitative acts of our society. It has been symbolic of men's ownership of women, as just described, for approximately the last three thousand years. It is the central symbol of patriarchal society; without it, there could be no patriarchy. Intercourse culminating in male orgasm in the vagina is the sublime moment during which the male contribution to reproduction takes place. This is the reason for its glorification. And as such, men *must* love it: intercourse is a celebration of "male" patriarchal culture.

Surely the definition of sex as we know it (that is, intercourse) is guaranteed to make a man feel that his needs are serious, worthwhile, and important—at least his need for orgasm and his need for stimulation of the penis to reach that orgasm. This fact is so obvious that it is usually overlooked, or taken as a "given," a simple "biological" imperative. However, our definition of sex is, to a large extent, culturally, and not biologically, created. Women's need for orgasm and for specific clitoral stimulation to reach that orgasm is not honored or respected in the traditional definition of sex. Certainly it is not enshrined within an institution, as is male orgasm. Although perhaps the institution we know as "sex" was created to lead to male orgasm in the vagina not because of male dominance but only because of the society's desire to increase reproduction, nevertheless, the man himself, as eventual owner of the child (should pregnancy occur) and of the woman, must surely feel secure in the knowledge that this ritual honors him and enshrines and venerates his orgasm. Thus men feel that their orgasm during intercourse is *good*. However, men usually do not attribute creation of the institution to man-made society; they look, rather, to biological or religious sources—i.e., "It's just the way things are," or, as one man said, "Intercourse is a heavenly blessing which God created for man."

In addition, this cultural institution, this symbolic rite, is aided and attended to by another person, a woman. If male orgasm is the sacrament here, the woman functions as the priest. This woman not only gives the man a sense of being accepted and desirable on an individual personal level, but also gives him a further sense of acceptance by joining in and catering to the sequence of events which culminates in his orgasm. This woman, with perhaps varying degrees of enthusiasm, but almost never with withdrawal once "sex" (the ritual sequence of events), and especially intercourse, has begun, helps him along towards his orgasm and a sense of pleasure.

Both men and women feel that this is a woman's role. And yet most women still do not feel that they have a similar automatic right to clitoral stimulation to orgasm—and even less do they feel they have the right to touch or stimulate themselves to orgasm—and still less do they feel they have the right to insist that men cater to their needs (especially if the woman is not also catering to the man's needs). Why does our society consider it perfectly acceptable to assume that "sex" can be defined as intercourse to male orgasm "every time," with clitoral stimulation to female orgasm included only "sometimes" or not at all—while considering it outrageous to define "sex" as clitoral stimulation to female orgasm "every time" if it almost never or only rarely included also penis stimulation/intercourse to male orgasm?

In addition, in traditional intercourse, the man was on top of the woman, adding to the symbolic impact of his culturally decreed superiority. Also, the fact that he almost always had an orgasm and she did not further encouraged him to think of himself as superior, more successful, healthier, and more sexual (more fully evolved, as some contemporary psychiatrists have recently asserted)—as opposed to the "weaker" woman, who was not able to have a similar climax (despite the fact that she almost certainly was not getting the right stimulation).

In other words, during traditional intercourse, the ancient patriarchal symbolism of the man on top comes to the fore: the man on top, "taking" his pleasure, the whole force of the social structure behind him, telling him that what he is doing is Good, Right, and that he is a Strong Male—with the woman looking up into his eyes, not resisting and hopefully celebrating these feelings with him, saying yes, you are great.

And there is yet another point: the symbolic acceptance of the sperm by the woman. As the woman accepts the semen, she accepts an intimate part of the man and, at least symbolically, she accepts the idea of carrying the child for him. Intercourse in patriarchy, as we remember, means power because a man can say, "I own this woman. I can make her pregnant." This was equated with power in early patriarchy, because earlier societies had not known the connection between intercourse (sperm) and pregnancy; they thought women reproduced by themselves. After this connection was discovered, the erect penis gradually became the dominant symbol in society that it remains today. Before this, the female body, and especially the vulva and breasts (as seen in the thousands of "fertility goddess statues" that have been unearthed), was the primary symbol.

This is not to say, of course, that intercourse does not feel good to both women and men in its own right. However, superimposed on these basic feelings is an enormous cultural symbolism which has become so ingrained in all our minds, both male and female, that it is hard for us to be sure just why we do like intercourse.

Another implication of patriarchal ideology is that intercourse makes a male a man before other men; intercourse is a form of male bonding. Boys are told that they cannot have intercourse; only men can. Thus intercourse becomes a test of status and dominance through which males prove their membership in the male group—not only the first time, but over and over. One basic definition of a man is "one who has intercourse with women." Why is this? Would this be a test of "masculinity" (whatever that may be) in a society which did not hold reproduction as a primary value? Historically speaking, men's identification with intercourse (and the emphasis on "performance") grew out of a social system which wanted more soldiers and farmers. In fact, for quite a long time, intercourse was not connected with love or romantic love, nor was it even considered necessarily the main thing a "man" would want to do: Greek men, for example, often seemed quite happy having sex among themselves—considering intercourse with their wives a duty necessary basically only for procreation. No doubt this was the way the wife viewed it as well, since her orgasm was not a consideration. (Was she having orgasms through masturbation? Or with her women acquaintances with whom she spent the day? No one knows.) And even earlier, Hebrew men had to be admonished in the Old Testament not to "spill their seed" —i.e., masturbate—or practice sodomy, but instead to have *vaginal intercourse*. This implies that they may have found it more pleasurable or convenient to masturbate or to have other sex for orgasm, and that in fact this may have been their custom.

In patriarchal society, then, intercourse for a man has the whole force of a society's approval behind it: he is doing what the entire society says he should be praised for doing, and the woman's acceptance of him functions as a symbol of the acceptance of him by the entire social order—and especially by other men. However, intercourse does not bestow the same feeling of social acceptance upon women; the meaning of sex/intercourse for women is quite different. Although the woman, as agent for the society (fulfilling her socially dictated role as nurturer, helper), is bestowing acceptance and approval (and the stimulation for male orgasm) on the man, she is frequently not getting any of these in return. In addition, society does not praise *her* for having intercourse. Her orgasm is not enshrined, and she may be looked down on by the man for having "given herself." This is another issue, one which was covered in *The Hite Report* on female sexuality—but it is well to keep in mind how differently our culture has chosen to reward the two sexes for the same activity.

Still, women do enjoy intercourse, and women and men do often transcend these cultural meanings in their personal lives. Although intercourse has been a symbol of masculinity and male power, it need not continue to be. As women gain equality—economic, social, and legal—intercourse can lose these exploitative connotations to become once more a simple thing of beauty and freedom—and above all, a choice.

Finally, the point here is not that men are wrong for liking and wanting intercourse, but that they should be freed from feeling they must have intercourse to have true sex—and to be "real" men. It would be senseless to "blame" anyone, either men or women, for traditional and stereotyped attitudes and behaviors which we all learn every day and endlessly hear repeated around us. The point now is to re-examine the part intercourse plays in our lives, to reassess our personal definitions of sex, and try to create more individual, and more equal, forms of physical relations.

In fact, it may be, on some level, just this cultural catering to men during intercourse which also makes men feel uncomfortable, uneasy, and ambivalent about it. Do they want to feel the object of so much unequal attention? Do men want to feel that the success or failure of the whole ritual rests on their performance? The ideal of masculinity glorifies men at the same time that it would dehumanize them. We will see in the next chapter the sense of release and spontaneity which pervades men's answers to questions about activities other than intercourse, suggesting that men do feel the weight of these symbolic pressures very deeply.

4

MALE SEXUALITY AND SENSUALITY— BEYOND INTERCOURSE

"I never really understood how a woman could let a man enter her until I was entered myself. I enjoyed the feeling. It's an experience or a feeling, a state that most men never have. To be penetrated is very different from penetrating. I realize now that this applies equally well to nonsexual things. To let someone into your life, into your heart, into your fears and desires is a quality that is much more highly developed in women. Perhaps this difference in men is what makes it difficult for men to love. I know my fear of love is like a fear of letting in."

There was a strong feeling expressed by many men in this study that they would like to diversify and expand, eroticize their sexual activities. When discussing activities other than intercourse, many replies sounded much freer and more spontaneous. It was almost as if a burden had been lifted, a tension released—a new expansiveness and enthusiasm filled the air. Men loved, without exception, every one of the activities they spoke about in this chapter.

"FOREPLAY,"*
TOUCHING, AND
AFFECTION

Stereotypes of male sexuality say that what men want from sex is their orgasm, especially through intercourse—and that they find "foreplay" something more necessary for the woman (to "get the woman ready") than something they want for themselves. Is this true? Further, did they like "foreplay" that was "done to" them? Or did they prefer "foreplay" that they "did to" the woman? What kind of "foreplay" did they like for themselves?"

WHAT KINDS OF "FOREPLAY" DO MEN ENJOY RECEIVING?

"What kind of 'foreplay' is important to you for yourself? Do you like to be embraced? Kissed? Petted? Are your breasts sensitive? Your buttocks? Your testicles? Your mouth? Your ears?"

* As one man said, and as was emphasized repeatedly in *The Hite Report* on female sexuality, " 'Foreplay' is a word I don't like. It brings to mind the sex-manual blueprint for sex and its artificial game plans—as if making love were a game in which the major objective is to move on to 'the main event,' intercourse and penetration." And another: "I don't believe in the concept of 'fore' play. It's *all* play, and it's all delightful, and it might go on to intercourse and it might not." However, our language, oriented as it is around intercourse, has, for the moment, an amazingly undiversified vocabulary to describe physical intimacy.

Men's answers to this question were very varied, but almost always enthusiastic:

"I'd really love it if some woman would run her hands all over my body and blow in my ear and run her fingers through my hair and kiss my neck and tickle me with her fingertips and scratch my back and lay on my back, with me on my stomach, and whisper sweet nothings in my ear and finally, penetrate me with her finger. Most women however cannot relax enough to be able to do that, nor has it ever crossed their minds."

"Those special little spots are from the bottom of my ear down my neck, eye contact, my breast, my stomach, around the genital area, the small of my back, the back of my knees, down the inside of my thighs, and my toes. My testicles are very sensitive. My mouth is perhaps the greatest turn-on in foreplay as I am very aroused by touching lips together or French kissing, etc. But I hate someone to put their tongue in my ear or kiss it, etc."

"I like to be kissed on the mouth. I like to be licked in the ears. My nipples are sensitive. My ass is sensitive. My hips and thighs are sensitive."

"I would like to have my whole chest kissed and rubbed—then touched and massaged all over, and especially to have my penis played with. Playing with the balls is great too if the woman knows how to do it. It requires instruction and practice. Those things are so sensitive."

"I must admit I'm a sucker for good nails with a gentle touch scratching my back."

"I love to be kissed, touched, petted, slobbered on, nipped, fucked, and any other thing that feels good."

"Kissing, mutual tickling, mock wrestling, little slaps, hugs, stroking our entire bodies—plus, I enjoy having her stroke my nipples with her fingernails, or have her on top letting her breasts dangle so that her nipples brush against mine. What I would like most, that I don't get, would be walking around both nude, playing or working around the house, taking time out for sex play at intervals, frequent erections, and giving her orgasms in this context."

"In addition to genital fondling, I like to be kissed vigorously with her tongue inside my mouth. I like my nipples sucked to erection. I like my testicles nibbled at. I like my buttocks gently stroked. I like to hear and use tender words like I love you, you're beautiful/soft/gentle."

"Hugging makes a warm full feeling in my chest that almost nothing can match."

"I love my ass to be touched."

"I like mental stimulation (sexy conversation), being touched all around my groin area, my rectum, my balls, my dick, my lower stomach, and my upper thighs. I like the same areas kissed and licked."

"A very erotic place is between my testes and backside, between my legs. I also enjoy being kissed on my neck, ears, breasts, stomach, penis, testes, and thighs, massaging, cuddling, petting. Manual stimulation of my penis and anus, as well as fellatio, could go on forever."

"What is important is for the foreplay to be centered around my big, beautiful dick. Talk to it."

"Hugging is the most important. Soft mellow hugs alternated with some tight meaningful squeezes are fantastic. I'd even rather do that with a woman I love than have intercourse, contrary to the male sexuality myth."

"Kissing, touching all over, rubbing up against the other person and licking. I prefer gentle, feathery touching on my breasts and abdomen, and the inside of my thighs. I have found that my entire body is sensitive when I know I am sharing that space with someone whom I care about a lot. When I have had sex on an anonymous basis I have become very cold and blunt."

"When I'm hot and horny, my entire body is supersensitive, especially my back and feet. I love to massage and be massaged during this period, before heavier things."

"I don't like it. I love it. Touch me everywhere."

"The whole realm of 'touching' is most important. I like to be worked over by the woman. One wishes that the beloved would ravish him."

"I love to be kissed, petted, touched—you name it. Why are women so hesitant?? The best thing is to be kissed on the back of the neck—that absolutely destroys me!"

"Just slow dancing or necking."

"I like to shower with a woman. Washing, scrubbing each other, toweling each other off. It is more of a sharing, caring experience than sexual. I enjoy being undressed."

"Full naked body to full naked body in a deep embrace. With my back being lightly touched, deep French kisses."

"Long stroking and massaging is the foreplay I like. I particularly like to be stroked lightly from stomach down to knees, on the sides next to my ribs, and on the neck. Most women fondle my prick too damn hard, although this hasn't been a problem with the last three to four women. I like women to moan in pleasure during foreplay and during sex."

"I love to be kissed and petted. I especially love rimming, perhaps because I considered it taboo for so long. I like massage with oil or cocoa butter. I enjoy light caressing of my penis, balls, perineum, and anus, caressing of my entire body, sucking of my toes and fingers. And I get great pleasure out of doing all of the above to my partner."

"Full body embracing in the nude."

"I like to feel my lover's entire body over me."

"I like to have my back massaged, sometimes it feels like it is one big penis. I can feel every stroke on my back as though it were directly on my penis."

"Gentle caresses, softly spoken thoughts of the moment, mutual smiles and eye contact (I don't always enjoy it serious and deadpan), grunts and moans. Exploring hands, not leaving a cuticle of body hair and flesh untouched or unkissed. Nudging, pushing and pulling, tickling. Wet, sloppy kisses. Gently kneading muscles of my arms, buttocks, chest, and abdomen. Gentleness about my face and hands."

"I love to be touched and often go for a straight massage in order to be touched. I love to have my hair touched and have the hair on my chest pulled gently."

"Even more important than the orgasm is being able to wrap your arms and legs and whatever else around another human being. Makes you feel less alone, more alive and I mean that in a positive sense."

"I *love* hugging and snuggling. Slow soft quiet kisses are romantic as hell. I can *never get enough*. Would like more of everything. The breasts are super-sensitive. But like with the penis, women think they are hunks of wood. (I'm beginning to think *men* are *more* sensitive than women.) I like them softly kissed and caressed with the tongue."

"The touch of a woman's hand on mine, the slightest touch can give me pleasure. Let a woman touch me anywhere, eyelids, forehead, chest, breast, leg, foot, toe—anywhere. Kiss me, stroke me, slap me on the butt, tweak my nose, put a finger to my lips, blow in my ear, touch the back of my scalp, cut my hair, pick a hair or a piece of fluff off of my clothes, take my pulse, temperature, blood pressure. Dress me. Help me on or off with my shirt, coat, jacket, tie, or pants. Wipe my face with a hanky or damp cloth. Tickle me with a feather. Hug me. Kiss me. Suck me. Do something, anything."

"Homosexual" answers were little different:*

"I like him playing with my ass, sucking my cock, licking my ears, and lots of kissing. I like it to go on forever. It is very exciting and satisfying."

"If I'm with a very exciting and energetic man I like foreplay, especially kisses and nuzzling on my scrotum, penis, buttocks, armpits, and ears. I never liked kissing on the mouth."

"Everything. I need strokes. If somebody dives straight for my prick I feel deprived."

"I like him to hold me tight around the chest, squeezing me to him."

DO MEN FEEL THEY GET ENOUGH "FOREPLAY" "DONE TO" THEM?

"Do you get enough 'foreplay' from your partner? Does your partner touch and fondle you enough?"

One of the biggest complaints of men with heterosexual experience was that women didn't touch them enough, or if they did, they didn't do it "right"—either they didn't seem interested or they lacked the know-how:

"Women seem to want to take more than they give in the way of making love. I love anything a woman does that takes her off her back."

"To me it seems that foreplay is mostly for women. I would like it much better if the woman paid more attention to caressing and teasing me."

"I get almost none. What I do get is lousy as she doesn't make the effort often enough to learn how. A very few times I've started to enjoy sensuously what she was doing just in time for her to quit. She did once generate feeling in my breasts that somehow reached into my genitals but quit just about then. I would like to experiment with it a little more, but it takes two."

"Most women seem to expect foreplay done to them; it is very rare when I have had a woman give *me* foreplay. I

* See also chapter 7.

would like my partner to excite me, but it would be a rare woman."

"I get virtually no foreplay from my partner, even when I ask for it. She however demands lots of foreplay for herself. All women I have been involved with have been the same way."

"Too many women seem to think they're doing me a favor by just letting me touch their sacred bods. What a turn-off!"

"Foreplay for myself that I don't always get are tonguing and kissing of my ear and earlobes, eyes, nose, and the neck and the nape of the neck, the breasts, the navel, the anus, the buttocks, behind my knees, toes and entire feet. Most of these I never get from my lovers, but I enjoy them as much as I do sex itself."

"I like a woman to feel free with my body and caress it as she would like her own caressed. The more I give, the more I get. Some women however appear very inhibited."

"Of course I like to be kissed, hugged, petted, and generally touched. Women seem to be so frustrated when I want more 'foreplay.' They want more, but I don't rate somehow!"

"I like to be kissed and have my body stroked, although not many women know that. They are so used to being the center of attention."

"Why don't the women do some of what I do to them? The answer is they don't know how and couldn't put any feeling into it if they did."

"Most of the girls seem to think 'Oh, typical guy. I'll stick my tongue in his mouth and jerk him off and he'll be all set.' I just want to be held and touched and loved."

"The woman should treat the man as she would want herself treated."

"Prior to my present lover, I never felt that I received enough petting, caressing, and body contact via tender touching and the like. I always felt that I was giving a great deal more than I ever received and was hurt by it."

"I like a lot of kissing, touching, and exploring. I love the feel of soft female skin, and I'll get to know every square inch of her, by sight and touch, every mole, bump, scratch, hangnail, and scar. I have always wanted a woman to take the interest in me that I take in *her*. No woman has *ever* asked me about the scars on my shins, or asked why my circumcision scar is different from others she's seen, or noticed that my front teeth are off-center. A bunch of things. Women just don't seem to notice, and it's important."

Several men stressed that receiving foreplay was emotionally satisfying, and led to a great feeling of acceptance and being desired or wanted:

"Foreplay means physical expressions of caring and an assurance that my partner wants me."

"Foreplay involving the whole of my person is important in making me feel liked for me and not just being a piece of meat."

"Physical affection, touching and kissing take the nobody-loves-me feeling away. It's easy to find people who hate you in this world, just as easy as it is to find trouble, these things are as close as the air you breathe, but love, caring, sympathy are like looking for a needle in a haystack."

One man gave an explanation:

"My partners assume that because I'm a man, I'm ready to have intercourse before they are and they initiate intercourse because they feel pressure to please me. I've found this attitude often in women. They have been conditioned to believe that they should 'please' a man, which they think means intercourse, and that if they don't they have failed in some way. This attitude is changing along with so many others, but it is still there in a lot of people."

Another said women didn't touch and stimulate men more because they were afraid of causing men to orgasm too quickly:

"Never get enough. I would like her to play with my genitals more and with my rectum, but she won't—because she's afraid of making me come. She wants me to come *in* her always. I'd like to be embraced, petted, and kissed more. More tender kisses, back rubs, fingers on my chest, a hand in my hand."

This fear seemed to be quite realistic in some cases:

"Arousal for me can be nonsexual, meaning I feel pleasurable sensations and I enjoy them for an extended period of time. However if I receive direct stimulation of my mouth, penis, ear, nipples, or balls by my partner's mouth, I quickly feel intense arousal and the desire for an orgasm. Arousal of this second kind is purely animal. I close my eyes and only experience sensations of an urging, nonrational nature, and go on to orgasm."

But quite a few men also had mixed feelings about being passive or "done to," especially nongenitally, and questioned their own role in not getting enough "foreplay" and petting from the woman:

"In fantasy I enjoy foreplay tremendously. In practice it's not so good. I worry about whether she's going to let me get there (and perhaps also have guilt feelings for letting her do it) and whether I will lose my erection. After a bit, I get bored and dissatisfied and want to get on with it. Perhaps I'm too goal-oriented!"

"I am still opening up to being touched, and experience myself as somewhat fearful in this area. I have always (to date) been called on to exercise the most active role in foreplay; in recent years, I have found myself wanting more touching and kissing, but am not quite sure how to 'get' that in a spontaneous way. I would like to find a woman who has a natural skill for deep massage; and who is solid enough as a person to ask for whatever she feels she likes in mutual sex, therefore solid enough not to be panicked by my wanting to experiment. This is a combination I haven't come across yet. Probably because I have not yet developed enough myself."

"If I had the nerve to sometimes, I'd ask my partner to do something I'd like done to me, but I'm always afraid that she might think badly of me. The trouble with me is that I've never had a relationship last long enough for me to get to know whether the girl would accept that or not. Someday . . . someday . . ."

"Do you do most of the 'work' in lovemaking? If so, do you dislike this, or do you prefer to take the lead? Are too many demands made on you in sex?"

There was an overwhelmingly positive response to this question. Almost every man who answered said that he had to do all the work in sex, and that he resented this:

"You have hit a nerve. This is my biggest gripe when it comes to sex. I feel I do most of the 'work' in lovemaking. I'm 'supposed to.' I'm the man; or so most women think. I dislike having to do most of the tactile and kissing portions of lovemaking. The woman is usually content to just lie back and let the man work on her. Whenever he's getting tired, this is usually when intercourse begins. Well, I am ready for a woman to just lay me on my back and do some 'work' on me. I happen to like my nipples kissed and nipped at, foreplay is not just tugging at my penis, I want the woman to 'feel' my penis and balls and tickle me. I want the woman to just explore this man's erotic zones and find out what drives me crazy besides kissing my ears. Here is the crux: I have had maybe three women out of maybe twenty-five ask me what do I like, what turns me on, etc. Well, I certainly have asked them what they like, but this is one place where women are not known for reciprocating. So, as far as demands go, I feel that the man definitely comes out short-changed."

"It is too bad that so many women just 'lay there' and expect the man to do everything. I remember one who acted that way—*undressing alone,* lying on the bed in the *dark,* no effort or communication on her part. I suggested she get dressed and go home."

"I do seem to do most of the work in our lovemaking. Once I determined that I would not initiate sex with my lover for two solid weeks, to see what she would do. We didn't talk about it, but she would press herself against me violently every night and seem very disappointed in my lack of response. She can so arouse me simply by lying quietly that I couldn't hold out, and I begin to offer sex to her again. I do enjoy leading the act, but sometimes I would like for a chance to follow her lead and let her take more of the responsibility for the act."

"Yes, I do most of the 'work.' It bugs me. It makes me goddamned angry. There seems to be the assumption that men don't need to be stimulated actively—they just need an occasional stroke on the cock. And rarely does a woman caress the rest of my body, though I'm not fat, bad-looking, or deformed. Men are supposed to be built 'ready.' If only I could explain that 'my cock is standing up, but I'm *not* ready!' Women have often *faked* taking the lead with me—that is, they've let me know they want to, then have sat back expectantly. That is not liberated—that is like paying for half the dinner bill only when we've gone to McDonald's . . . I wanna be *taken* to the party too. In summary, yes, there are too many demands made on me in sex."

"Many women seem to think they only have to lie there and the magic will happen. Perhaps they're afraid to act too sexy, to carry on, but what ends up happening is that the man doesn't like to think he's just there manipulating this lifeless body, just to get himself off. I don't like doing everything. I like the woman to initiate things periodically. And responsiveness is more than an occasional 'That feels good.'"

"I almost always feel that I'm being saddled with all the work of having sex. I would like my partners to sometimes take the lead. I like to feel that I'm being made love to as much as I'm making love to my partner. I have more respect for women who are a little aggressive. It's the silent demands that bother me the most. The woman who wants to orgasm but is either afraid to tell you how to go about it, or thinks that you should just know."

"After 'sex' is begun—say, cuddling or caressing or dry-humping—sometimes I'll just wait, to see how long it takes before the lady will actually touch my genitals, and more, I'll judge her touch by whether it's a flutter, to direct my attention to it, or if she means it, if she likes cock. Well, some women think that intercourse is initiated by passive supinity. I don't always want intercourse, but sometimes I'll screw because that's easier than explaining. My heart won't be in it, but that doesn't seem to matter."

"I have never had sex with a girl who moved a great deal. Why is that? They always expect me to do it all. I was once asked by a girl, 'What makes a girl a good lover?' I honestly had no answer. I never met one, was all I said. Girls never do anything, I said. *We* do it all. She was shocked that I had such a low opinion of women as lovers. But it's true. Girls never move, take the initiative, or become aggressive in bed. I'm sure some do, but I've never met one. I think I understand why they do that, though. They're so often unorgasmic (and know that men are orgasmic) that they feel they don't *have* to do anything to help the man reach his. And that's probably true. They don't have to do anything and we will still get ours."

But a few men expressed more mixed feelings about whether they minded the work—and whether they wanted to be more active or passive:

"I've always done most of the 'work,' but I enjoy it. Part of the reason is I automatically start doing it, which hardly gives the woman an opening to do more of it. To some extent, I have difficulty accepting physical affection and touching that I enjoy bestowing on a woman. So obviously it's my doing. Still, I sometimes feel it would be nice to let someone else be in control (Where are you, strong woman?), create the feelings, and set the mood and direction, while I passively accept them."

"Usually I do most of the 'work,' but if my partner is active, I relax and enjoy it, although this makes me passive—which feels strange, and sometimes uncomfortable."

In fact, at the same time that most men resented having the responsibility for doing all the work, many of them also felt uncomfortable or embarrassed by the idea of being petted or aroused, since usually in our society this is something done by a man to a woman. Some men felt it wasn't "manly" to be petted:

"To tell the truth, I would like stimulation of my dick. Tender kissing and stimulation of my ass, stomach, and thighs. But I don't believe that I would enjoy those things from a girl because she might consider me to be less than masculine."

"I just need my wife to be turned on. If she does *anything* to me, I feel like I must need it, and then I get worried."

"All of my partners have been passive, so I don't know what I like. But really, I think I would feel guilty just accepting stimulation and affection."

A few men did not want the woman to be active at all:

"Being in charge builds the ego up . . . I have asked a girl to keep still."

"As a man, I feel it is, so to speak, my duty."

"In general, I prefer to take the lead. A woman is more 'receptive' than a man and whatever he does she can accommodate herself to it."

The concern about the possible lack of "manliness" in being petted was especially noticeable in the answers to the question "Are your breasts sensitive?" Many men felt uncomfortable or resented being asked about their breasts:

"My breasts—you mean rudimentary male nipples?"

"A man doesn't have breasts. I thought this form was for males."

"There is nothing erogenous about my chest."

"I've had two women try to 'activate' sexual feelings in my nipples. Frankly, it's never really worked. Too much is concentrated in my penis. She can touch my erect penis and forget the rest."

Finally, some men were so used to thinking of "foreplay," as something for the woman that even when asked what they wanted done to them, they told that what they did for her:

" 'Fore-play' is mainly to get the girl hot. I like kissing all parts of her body."

"I have always found women like to be sucked off and/

and I become sort of a 'sex slave' for her pleasure—that's fun!"

"I enjoy both being aggressive and doing the work and I also enjoy laying back and letting my partner do most of the moving. Sometimes I'm expected to be more aggressive than I care to be. We have too often defined aggressiveness as masculine and passiveness as feminine. I don't go along with this and am very happy that these stereotypes are changing. I find that many women today are becoming more aggressive and letting me know what they want and getting it."

And, of course, roles could be traded back and forth:

"I give women the space to do as much of the 'work' as they want. Many times women who are used to just lying back are unsure at that point. Other times I feel really aggressive and prefer her to let me do it."

"I prefer to share sexual activity with an 'equal'; obviously my partner may be more or less experienced/skilled than I in technique, but in terms of attitudes I want no absolute roles based on leader/follower, active/passive, etc. The roles taken at any time vary according to what we feel like and may reverse several times during sex. Sometimes I feel like just lying there and not doing anything at all while she stimulates me, or the opposite, or anywhere in between."

or fucked after ... ...is most important to me is the stimu-
"...foreni kissing a girl's body, the parts I relish—
get the throat and shoulders, legs, feet, and thighs.
...to rub my penis against parts of her body in a posses-
way. Somehow it proves that she belongs to me."

Similarly, some men said that the "foreplay" they liked best for themselves was to stimulate their partner:

"I think the kind of foreplay I like for myself the most is watching the woman get off on the foreplay."

"The only kind of foreplay important to me is to have a willing partner that wishes to be fondled and caressed. My pleasure is giving her pleasure."

"Men get aroused by what they do to women, not vice versa. Just from the sight and feel of my wife's naked body and the touch of her breasts I can get a powerful erection. I really need no further stimulation."

"Foreplay is a pleasure for me, and exciting, as something I do to or for my partner: I find pleasure and excitement in stimulating her, rather than having her do things on me."

DO MEN ENJOY GIVING "FOREPLAY" TO ANOTHER PERSON?

Despite the fact that men complained about having to do most of the work in lovemaking, when asked if they liked giving foreplay to women, most answered very enthusiastically:

"I think that foreplay is the most joyous and intimate part of the whole sex act. During this time, I concentrate totally on my partner's satisfaction. I don't feel 'obligated' to perform extended foreplay, but rather strive for fulfillingness and comfortability, no matter how long it takes."

" 'Foreplay'—a very sweet occupation—means to me: getting close to her; getting her aroused, by any and every means, feeling her responding to me. It can take ten minutes or it can take an hour; I don't care. When it takes ten minutes, I know that she has been thinking of me, loving me, getting ready for me. When it takes an hour, I just enjoy worshipping her body, caressing her, teasing her a bit (she likes that), being close, stroking her all over, until she catches up with me and off we go together."

"Although foreplay is not necessary to me in order to achieve orgasm, it is extremely important to me in psychological and emotional ways. Orgasm is apt to be very self-oriented because it requires and encourages intense concentration on one's own genitals. Foreplay of any type (touching, kissing, caressing, holding—anything) provides an entirely different dimension to making love because it is very much other-directed. When I caress my lover, I get quite a bit of emotional pleasure if I see that my caress gave her pleasure. I am beginning to realize that the activities generally considered foreplay are really what lovemaking is all about. This other-directed dimension can only be obtained with time, practice, real emotional commitment, and the fullest possible communication between two people. When viewed this way, genital sex becomes icing on the cake."

Many men pointed out that they enjoyed foreplay not only because of the pleasure they gave the woman but also because of the close affectionate body contact they received:

"I think it's hard, *very* hard ever to get enough warm bodily contact, caressing and hugging. I would like to make love, complete with enough time, every other day on a regular basis. There is not enough time in twenty-four hours to get and give enough. I need more closeness and the wonderful body warmth I feel during foreplay more frequently, more readily, so for that and many other reasons we are going to be married."

"Touching and hugging are important for me. . . . different ways of saying 'I love you,' or 'I want you,' or 'I think you are beautiful,' or 'You excite me.' . . . to give and receive. And to share it regularly during sex is an important part of our communication, since I am not a very verbal person."

A few men said the woman did not seem to want their "foreplay":

"Sometimes my wife wants me to get on with it, but I'm not ready."

"In prior relationships, the tendency of the woman wanting to get a little warmed up and then jump on it was very depressing."

"She is always a bit in a hurry."

Men often mentioned that they would like more feedback during foreplay:

"Foreplay is a nuisance if my efforts on my partner are not producing the desired responses. It can happen if a woman is not communicative either by telling me what she wants me to do or not to do. One example is the wanting of varying degrees of pressure on the body, on the clitoris, with fingers or tongue. If what I am doing is not producing results, I often ask why not and the best partners will explain why not. If they cannot or do not help me in this manner then foreplay is a nuisance."

"I would like more openness from women. Women seem to enjoy overdoing the 'misunderstood female' role. I hate their secretiveness."

"Foreplay and postplay is usually the largest problem I have. I have no idea when the woman is ready or when it is all right to disentangle. I seldom know whether I continue foreplay longer than necessary, or dismount before it is good for her. I feel obligated to perform longer foreplay than I like, but this may be because of age-old strictures on getting a woman ready and on women needing more time than men. The problem is that I don't get messages in this area."

Of course, men who had sex with other men enjoyed giving them "foreplay" too:

"I luxuriate in long slow periods of arousal for my sake and in order to please my partner as much as possible. I must admit that I get a great kick out of watching my partners as they experience the feelings going through their body. Of all the parts of having sex, my favorite is watching, savoring, and sharing the pleasure of my partner. The visual and auditory stimulation is for me the most exciting and arousing thing. In a way I guess I am very voyeuristic."

But in homosexual relations some of the same complaints could be heard:

"I greatly enjoy 'foreplay,' but there seems too often to be a compelling urgency in homosexuality that wants to skip the preliminaries and get down to business. I'd like more kissing, more affection before jumping into bed."

(The subject of sex between men is discussed more fully in chapter 7.)

A small minority of men didn't like giving foreplay, and in fact said they resented it because they felt they didn't need it but just had to go through with it for the woman's sake:

"I feel like the stereotype male when it comes to foreplay—'a little dab will do ya.' I know that I don't use enough foreplay with my partner, and then I hate the idea I'm supposed to do more of it when I am inside of her during intercourse."

"My greatest shortcoming is my preference for rather abbreviated foreplay. Several partners have expressed a desire for more extended foreplay. I have difficulty ascertaining exactly what they want sometimes. I try to prolong it."

"I understand that women need more than me, but it's hard to keep from forging ahead."

"I like it for two microseconds (ha ha ha)—no, I don't really mean that. About five to ten minutes."

"I get fed up with masturbating my partner to orgasm. The ideal would be to have her masturbate (in front of me) until she's ready."

"I think most men don't need as much foreplay as women. I can get in a 'fuckable' frame of mind in seconds, practically, whereas it takes my wife a lot longer to get into it. I think it's part of male conditioning to be always ready."

"Foreplay for me is a tedious nuisance that she apparently needs before she is ready for me to get in so I can prove myself a man by fucking her and ejaculating. (I deliberately put that in the bluntest, most honest terms I can, to reflect my attitude as of the present.)"

"I'm sorry to say foreplay isn't very important to me. I usually have an erection before I get my clothes off so I don't need much playing around. This is not to say I don't like hugging and kissing. I do. But damn it when I have a hard-on I want it stimulated not tickling my ears."

And a few seemed to be angry with the woman for not being "ready" faster and making the man do the "work" of foreplay:

"I hate being expected to arouse a woman. If a woman isn't wet in her cunt within sixty seconds of my stroking, I get angry and would just as soon stop—but this hasn't happened within the last two years more than once or twice—although it used to happen a lot."

"I guess I'm selfish and don't like to play nurse or mother to some girl. Sometimes I feel obligated because some girls seem to need it to make them hot enough to come, without it they don't climax. I think girls should be 'ready' sooner. Five minutes of foreplay is long enough for any man to have to wait."

"I don't like and never did like long-drawn-out foreplay. Most women used to expect it because they were reading those crazy old sex books which said that the man had to spend so much time on this erogenous zone and so much time on that one to get the woman properly prepared. It wore me out. When the woman is doing the foreplay bit I can take it longer."

"I reject the concept of 'foreplay' on the firmly held opinion that a woman who really digs me will be ready for me quickly, sometimes even before I touch her."

DO MEN LIKE LONG "FOREPLAY"? PHYSICAL AFFECTION WITHOUT ORGASM?

"Do you like feeling aroused for a long period of time, or do you prefer to go to orgasm relatively quickly?"

The majority of men said that they greatly enjoyed feeling aroused for a (reasonably) long period of time, before going on to orgasm:

"If I want to get it over with quick, I'll masturbate. When I'm making love with my wife, I like for it to go on for a while. There's an awful lot of pleasure in the arousal period, so why get it over with? Touching, caressing, caring, being close are all pleasurable experiences—if only most men would take the time to enjoy them. What's the big hurry about ejaculating anyhow? It will eventually come, and in the meantime you can have a lot of fun, and get a lot of pleasure out of expressing love to the other person. Besides, when I have taken much more time, the ejaculation which I eventually got was much more pleasurable and lasted about twice as long."

"I like to have it established that we are going to spend a long time having sex, get undressed, play for a long time, have sex, have a great deal of afterplay, nap, wake up, play, maybe have sex, wake up in the morning, have sex (again) after much foreplay, stay in bed, and *then* and only then feel I have to do something else."

A minority of men did not like long periods of arousal at all and wanted to orgasm quickly:

"I get animalistic when I'm aroused, and I don't like it too long. I get frustrated easily and can't seem to keep my cool. I think of what would feel good at the moment and the urge to demand it comes close to the surface then. I get anxious to reach orgasm quickly. I think of nothing else until I am satisfied one way or another."

"I do not like feeling aroused for long periods of time without relief. Once there was a school of thought which believed that the longer you delayed intercourse, the better. The pleasure of *anticipation* was thus prolonged. For me, that would be sheer misery."

"When I was a teenager, I liked the pleasures of arousal very much and, when nearing an orgasm, would stop masturbating for a few minutes so that I could continue the pre-ejaculation pleasures of stroking my erect penis. I now enjoy the ejaculation the most and like to come to it as quickly as possible."

Some men thought the question implied they would be "teased" by the woman, which they did not like:

"I can wait if I'm sure she wants to, but not be teased."

"I don't like to be prick-teased, but I can wait. When she's ready I'm ready."

"I hate being 'teased,' I want to get the sex act over with once I'm hot and ready. Teasing is aggravating. Arousal (a minimal amount) feels good and warms you up until you're hot—then it should cease and the act should take place."

A few men said they felt uncomfortable after long arousal with no orgasm:

"Mild arousal is euphoric—but intense arousal causes much pressure which after a while causes aching in the testes and orgasm is the quickest way to relieve the pressure."

"I do not like to be highly aroused for long periods of time—an hour of foreplay is fine. After too long, my balls begin to ache."

And some men were afraid of losing their erection during long arousal:

"I prefer to go on to orgasm relatively quickly because I am afraid to lose my erection."

"Women must realize that men have external sex organs which can be stimulated very easily, as they are so much more prominent than women's sex organs. When a man has an erection during the sexual play it is more or less a physical impossibility to maintain the erection beyond a certain point. All men have a different time length, depending upon his muscle strength in the penis. That is why men cannot play for too long a period of time. When a man is at the peak of his passion in foreplay, the woman should take his penis in her hand and guide it into her vagina to its fullest depth for complete pleasure. Otherwise he may lose his erection."

But most men said longer arousal usually made for a better orgasm:

"I find that the longer the period of arousal, the more intense and satisfying my orgasm."

"Orgasm restraint/control is more pleasure-producing than not. The holding back makes the ejaculation more intense when it comes, although after an unusually long time (I can't say how long) it may decrease the pleasure."

"The longer, the better. Arousal is best when slow and easy—up and down—over a long period of time to build to a great climax."

"The longer the arousal, the better the excitement has a chance to grow to its full intensity. After a long arousal I find my orgasms *much* stronger. Arousal feels like my body is *ultra*-sensitive."

"I really like feeling aroused for extended periods of time. Sometimes my lover will tease me with her hands and her mouth for long, ecstatic periods of time. If anything. I would rather abstain from sex than have quick orgasms."

And some men liked extended arousal very much:

"I like long periods of foreplay. When would you end Paradise?"

"I would like to feel aroused for *days!!!* I think one of the nicest parts of being in my forties is that I can be aroused and make another person happy for a long long time and not have it end abruptly with an orgasm, conk out and call it a night."

"With one woman I managed to refrain from being physically stimulated (I wouldn't let her touch me) for several days while I masturbated and sucked her to orgasm at every opportunity. Finally, while playing with her, I had the most explosive orgasm I had experienced in quite some time. I could tell it was going to be a good one because my skin was bumpy and alive, and my balls had been aching. My cock had been at full erection off and on and finally the lights started going up and down, etc., and my partner said she had never seen me ejaculate so violently. Arousal feels like you are super-charged and have seven-league boots on that could enable you to do anything."

"I like being aroused for a *l-o-n-g* time. Like for one or two hours, kissing, stroking, body contact, feeling great, and really getting excited about getting closer."

"What does it feel like? Exciting, romantic, full of anticipation of things to come, nirvana. This is what living is for. There's nothing in the world that feels this good, or commands as much attention or concentration. At a time like this, there is absolutely *nothing* else worth doing instead. It is the ultimate living experience."

"In periods of infatuation I have refrained from actual penetration for eighteen hours or so. To me it is almost orgasmic. During this state I can have multiple mini-orgasms. It is sweet torture."

A few men said that they had such strong feelings of excitement when aroused, and enjoyed so many sensations—which orgasm ended, at least for a while—that sometimes they chose not to orgasm at all:

"I love feeling aroused. I could go on forever as long as the pleasure is trickling into my brain. Arousal feels like a dreamy pleasant high. I can think of nothing more pleasant except orgasm—but orgasm is so short that I prefer to have it only after a long buildup, or maybe only every other time we have sex. That way, during the day I still feel high from the sex we had—more alive, more happy, everything interests me more, I am more stimulated!"

"Orgasm terminates the arousal, at least in its intense (great) state. The picture I have is of Icarus falling out of the sky; personally, I'd prefer to sail around up there, fly on the warm updrafts, and come in for a leisurely landing. Orgasm would be an abrupt landing—too abrupt, most of the time."

Some men, after long or intense arousal, could have non-ejaculatory orgasms, which did not diminish their excitement (see pages 470–475 and 607–609).

When asked, "Are physical affection and touching important for their own sakes, not leading to orgasm or even necessarily to sex? How important is hugging? Talking? Kissing?" a few men answered unequivocally yes, that affection and touching are very important and enjoyable even without leading to sex; many of these answers are given here because of their rarity:

"Physical affection and touching are incredibly important to me. Hugging and back rubs and kissing and snuggling together and stroking and just touching are important and pleasurable in themselves and need not lead to intercourse. This is something that has to be talked about and understood between me and the lady I'm with, though. In some contexts with a woman I didn't know very well I might assume that her wanting a lot of physical contact indicated an interest in having intercourse."

"Physical affection, for me, *is* the sexual relationship. Touching and kissing and eye contact are overwhelmingly important. Sometimes this leads to sexual relations, more usually not. I can't imagine wanting sex every time I kiss the person I love. Kissing is valuable in and of itself. So is touching. To want all affection to conclude with orgasm or sex is obsessive, impossible, and sad."

"Physical affection, touching, and the various ways of being intimate are what making love is all about. To me the most important part of sex and love is intimate contact with another individual in as many ways and as deeply as possible."

"Kissing and petting can be an end in themselves. I have had one- to three-hour sessions of kissing and petting that left me as content and as tired and drained as if I had had intercourse to orgasm."

"I'd rather have closeness than sex if I had to choose."

"Yes! We are often affectionate, even in the presence of our children. Moreover, since we sleep together nude, we cuddle at night when we go to bed and in the morning when we wake up. This is our 'way of life'—in a sense; it sort of sets the stage so that when either of us feels the need, urge, or desire for more intimacy (sexual intercourse and orgasm) we read each other's body signals and just 'drift into' (spontaneously) more pleasure tension—right on through to orgasm. For the majority of times, physical affection and touching are sufficient."

"Physical affection and touching are *essential* in really good sex, but even more important in daily life. They convey much more than words can, and are very important in a really satisfying relationship."

"Physical affection shouldn't always lead to sex; after all, it's just an expression, not a command or invitation. Hugging and kissing are really neat and I enjoy them."

"Hugging! The most important common physical exchange in my life. Whether it be with men, women, my daughter, the hug tells it all. I never could ask a woman to go to bed with me—I just 'listen' to her body when I hug her, and I know. Kissing too, on its own, is great, if it's with someone I really enjoy kissing, not just anyone, not most people. Hugging, talking, kissing, making love. Anyone of these is as highly satisfying and exciting as the next—as long as it is a true exchange of pure love between two people. Love meaning giving up yourself to another, giving your best to that person."

"With a woman I love, I want a lot of affection apart from lovemaking. Maybe for days at a time, depending on our moods. Sometimes it's just nice to neck for a long time like old-fashioned teenagers."

"Physical affection and touching are really important to me for their own sakes, especially from other men, and not necessarily leading to sex or orgasm. I would like more with both men and women, especially with the understanding that touching and sensuality are not necessarily preliminary to genital sex."

"I think the drive to touch is much stronger than the drive to have orgasm, for me."

"There is one thing which has always been significant and deeply pleasing to me, which does not seem to be generally celebrated for itself—sleeping with a woman. I do not mean fucking but simply going to bed together, spending the night together asleep, usually in close and relaxed contact, and waking together. In terms of trust, acceptance, and mutual experience it is really quite special. It is pernicious that 'sleeping together' is understood as a euphemism or particular way of saying that two people fuck together."

"What does arousal feel like?"

"Arousal is a quickening of the heart, the exhilaration somewhat like that feeling in the pit of the stomach as you go down the incline of a roller coaster. It courses through your body from your lips and tongue, down through the gut to the testicles, penis, and prostate."

"It's extremely enjoyable. I have gone for hours just making out, caressing, fellating, licking each other. It's a complete abandonment to physical stimulation and when I get aroused like this, nothing else matters. It's like a mutual adoration of each other's bodies to which we do what we want to. Like having someone's power at my disposal which I can guide along lines to give me maximum pleasure and of course in cases like this it's mutual. I love it."

"Being aroused is an incredible high. The body tingles. There is a feeling of 'aliveness' and vitality. A feeling of fullness. I feel sexy and attractive. There is a sense of maleness, a feeling of pride."

"Arousal feels like security with yourself and the person you're with. It is the feeling of communicating with your body and emotions that which words fail to express, it is feeling loved and loving in return."

"Arousal feels hot and tight. That's the best way I can describe it—a feeling of heat coursing through my body and a feeling of contraction like a spring being tightened."

"Arousal is better than anything, it's a keen interest, a gaining of momentum, a prolonged level of extreme pleasure before the final plunge into the other world—one foot in and one foot out of that world."

"Feeling aroused is a delightfully exquisite torture, a hot, disconnected feeling where my thinking muddies up and I become almost painfully aware of my entire body."

"Arousal is an 'emotional lust' for the woman, her mind, her body, her closeness, to get into her totally."

"All my senses elevate. My thighs become sensation-hungry."

"An electric feeling of rapture."

"I feel *strong*."

"Arousal is all the savage desire turned on, breaking of moral restraint, exquisite anguish."

"Sexual arousal is a whole new state of consciousness—my partner is magically transformed into something so deliciously desirable that for the moment all other reality is secondary and the whole meaning of existence is eroticized."

"Volcano-like. Pistons churning faster."

"As if my whole self could perform fantastic feats, climb Mount Everest, cure the cold, and overrun Moscow single-handed."

ANAL STIMULATION AND PENETRATION OF MEN

THE IMPORTANCE OF ANAL PENETRATION TO MEN

As one man commented earlier in a magnificent statement which has both a larger, symbolic meaning, and also a very specific sense, "I never really understood how a woman could let a man enter her until I was entered myself. I enjoyed the feeling. It's an experience or a feeling, a state that most men never have. To be penetrated is very different from penetrating. I realize now that this applies equally well to nonsexual things. To let someone into your life, into your heart, into your fears and desires is a quality that is much more highly developed in women. Perhaps this difference in men is what makes it difficult for men to love. I know my fear of love is like a fear of letting in."

Anal penetration and stimulation is an important subject which has received almost no attention in the literature of sex research. And yet, it is a real chance for men to have another, completely different type of experience in sex.

Although anal penetration is usually thought of as a homosexual activity, with the anus being used only as a substitute for the vagina, in fact receiving anal stimulation or penetration by a finger is an important activity for many men. Most men, of either heterosexual or homosexual experience, who have tried being penetrated (either by a finger or a penis) said they enjoyed it: it brought feelings of deep pleasure and fulfillment. The main characteristic of being penetrated described by men was an extreme feeling of emotional passion —followed by a feeling of peace and satisfaction. Many men said that orgasm, when accompanied by anal stimulation, could be physically exquisite.

Why, physiologically speaking, does being penetrated and stimulated anally feel good to men? There are two possible reasons. First, the feeling of being penetrated itself is rewarding. In fact, many men described the pleasurable feeling of being penetrated (whether by a finger or a penis) in words similar to those used by women to describe the pleasure of vaginal penetration—feeling "full," "complete," and emotion-

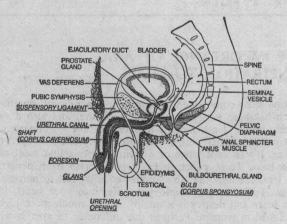

Parts of the penis system are underscored.

ally satisfied. Penetrating and being penetrated can be important emotional statements from one person to another.

A second reason is that men's prostate gland is located just inside (approximately two inches) the anal opening. Stimulation of this gland can cause a man to orgasm, if done properly. However, most anal penetration does not stimulate the prostate directly, since it is necessary, once inside the anal canal, to press against the anterior wall of the anus and down slightly to locate it (it may feel about one inch in diameter), and then continue concentrating the stimulation there to bring on orgasm. Most anal penetration, whether by a finger or a penis, passes over this gland and only stimulates it slightly and indirectly. This explains, perhaps, why so many men say that the feeling of being penetrated anally is one of being almost, almost, almost ready to orgasm. This is also interesting in light of a similar phenomenon with regard to vaginal penetration: that is, that during intercourse for most women, the clitoris is almost, but not quite, stimulated sufficiently for orgasm, giving women a feeling that they could almost orgasm—almost. But the feelings in both cases are often beautiful beyond description, and quite inimitable.

Thirty-one percent of the men in this study with a heterosexual orientation had tried being anally penetrated by a finger (either during masturbation or by a partner), and another 12 percent had tried being penetrated by a penis or penis-sized object (often as a teenager). Eighty-six percent of the men who considered themselves homosexual had tried being anally penetrated, either by a finger or a penis. Most of the men (both heterosexual and homosexual) who had been penetrated by a finger, whether by themselves or by another person, liked it. Many of those who had been penetrated by a penis or penis-sized object had also liked it, although penis penetration was not a daily activity for most men who liked it, including gay men. On the other hand, finger penetration—whether heterosexual, homosexual, or during masturbation—could be practiced daily. Not all men who considered themselves homosexual engaged in anal penetration, and some had tried it but did not like it. Of all the men who answered who had not tried it, 10 percent said they would be interested in trying it, in some form.

DO MEN LIKE BEING PENETRATED ANALLY?

"Do you like, or would you like, to be rectally penetrated? By a finger? By a penis? How does it feel? Do you orgasm this way?"

Finger penetration by a woman*

Many men, as seen in the section on masturbation and elsewhere,† enjoyed having their anus penetrated with a finger or other small object, and described great feelings of pleasure; here are their feelings about having a woman do it:

"When my girl goes down on me or when she is on top during intercourse, she reaches over or under and puts her finger about one or two inches up my rectum and makes low round movements. It drives me crazy. I never thought I would tell anyone this but I'm trying to be as honest as possible."

"I enjoy rectal penetration by a finger . . . the most intense orgasms I recall were by either oral or genital contact coupled with finger penetration . . . it feels like a delicious pain, an openness, a vulnerability, a focusing of all my energy and desire."

"I had a partner for a while who sometimes inserted a finger in my anus during intercourse. At first I was very skeptical, but she seemed to be able to put pressure on my prostate gland and it was actually quite exciting. I am ashamed to admit that I have been too shy to ask other partners to try this."

"I enjoy very much being anally penetrated and I also like doing it to her. We usually do it with her finger, although a few times we have used a vibrator, a douche nozzle, etc. It feels very, very erotic when she does it—she takes her time and always moves her hand in the most provocatively, fantastically sensual ways. Once she undressed me (I wasn't

---

* Penetration by a finger was more typically done by a woman, or by a man to himself, than by a man to another man, except as preparation for penis penetration. See chapter 7.

† Quotes concerning anal penetration during masturbation will not generally be included here, as they appear in the section on masturbation.

allowed to do anything but feel) and made love to me with her finger for what seemed like hours; she gradually found my prostate and massaged it until I had an orgasm—which had never happened to me in this way before! I felt like a fresh virgin all over again—it's something that I'll never forget. It was very different than a penis-oriented orgasm— came from a deeper, different place. Strange and beautiful."

"Often I have used a candle or similar object to penetrate my rectum, and also a vibrator can produce exquisite sensations. Occasionally I have used my own finger, but find this too awkward and not satisfying. One of my lovers does this for me, including massaging my prostate, sometimes when she masturbates me, and on occasion while I masturbate myself."

"Anal penetration is a strange mixture between pain and a very fulfilling joy. Fellatio with a well-oiled finger in my anus just drives me wild. The sphincter muscle is so tight that it takes time to relax, but when it does it feels as if I'm being invaded by an entirely new set of sensations and I can then overcome the slight pain with pleasure."

"Yes, by my woman. It's beautiful. She is taking me, having me, possessing me. I love to give myself to her in this way. There is no orgasm, but it is very exciting. New to me, us."

"I like it, but I am always fearful and sometimes feel guilty. But the more she does it, the more I want it."

"My lady has penetrated me rectally with her fingers and the pleasure was exquisite. The feeling was like being constipated at first, but I enjoyed the feeling of being loved by her and became enchanted. Orgasm—not yet but I hope it will come."

"Once a friend and I sat in the bathtub and put each other's fingers up each other's assholes. I loved it. It didn't feel anything like I thought it would. It felt clean and pink and soft and beautiful—healthy. I had thought it would feel dirty."

"It feels absolutely great to have a finger run up my ass and be sucked off. Or a finger and be fucking away. I come like crazy. Total orgasm. It feels great—I get more feeling in my genitals and I come more totally satisfied—in other words, I achieve total orgasm."

"I like a finger. It feels like internal pleasure, exploring a secret or unfamiliar hidden place."

A few men liked it only if they did it to themselves:

"I don't enjoy the feeling of being anally penetrated by anyone, other than myself using my finger. My ass is very sensitive to pain and the few times that my wife has tried to put her finger in it hurt."

Many more wanted to try it, but worried about what their partner might think of them if they requested it:

"I have never been anally penetrated. I would like to explore the sensation of light pressure or touching during intercourse but have so far not encountered a lover with whom I felt sufficiently trusting or at ease to request this kind of thing. Nor has any volunteered."

"I would love to rid my love of some of her ideas about what men like! I wish I could risk revealing my need for anal penetration (which I do during masturbation), but it's a danger I can't face. The last time I tried I never saw or heard from her again (not the same person obviously). Scientifically the asshole is 'cleaner' than the mouth; who ever objects to kissing?"

Others worried that it would make them "homosexual":

"I guess that if I accept a woman to penerate my anus it's probably part of a homosexual tendency. I don't want to get started down that road."

"It's basically a homosexual act and I would feel queer."

A few who had tried it had more mixed reactions to finger penetration:

"I had a finger—during intercourse. At first it bothered me that she would want to penetrate me, but I did enjoy myself, feeling some suggestion of what she experienced (penetration). I felt a lot of energy in me, pulling in from behind and pushing out up front. But I wouldn't care to have this done too often."

"It's O.K. when in the proper mood. A finger feels like taking a shit and is uncomfortable unless I take my mind off it. Once I mentally convince myself I'm not defecating and stop worrying about it, the movement of the finger creates a tightness and pressure which feels terrific. At the same time, it almost feels like the root of my penis is being pushed, and my erection gets *very* hard."

"I have sometimes, while bathing, placed a finger up my rectum. The sensation was not a turn-on, but it was also not unpleasurable. This does not mean that I'm one step away from boycotting Florida orange juice."

"One time while my partner was sucking on my cock, she put her finger up my ass just before I came in her mouth. She asked me if I liked it and I told her yes—but I didn't tell her that I was concerned that her finger might smell bad!"

"A finger, yes, but I have hemorrhoids."

"How many years of toilet training and sexual channeling come in to play. My lover would try finger penetration and I would resist. I'd like the experience but the muscular reactions seem almost involuntary."

"I vary a lot in this. Sometimes it drives me crazy to have a woman penetrate my anus with a finger (finger only, please) and it brings me to orgasm quickly with other stimulation. Other times it is more of an annoyance. It distracts my focus and I can't decide what to concentrate on. When I do like it, the psychological effect is Being Fucked. It's nice to play it both ways. When I'm in a passive mood, it's nice to lie back and be stimulated. The time I'm not inclined to enjoy it is during fellatio."

"Once, when I was masturbating in the shower, I stuck a finger up my ass to see what it was like. It brought me to orgasm real quickly, but I felt kind of funny about the whole thing. I'm not ready for rectal penetration, I guess."

"The idea used to be repellent. I was shocked on one occasion when fucking to suddenly feel my partner's little finger there, penetrating as deeply as she was able, but I bore it without comment, carrying on with the main event. But I did not enjoy it. Lately, with two of my partners I find they allow their fingers to caress the area and I am growing to tolerate it, though it is still more of a turn-off than a turn-on."

And some men only liked external stimulation of the anal region, without penetration.

A few had tried it and found they did not like it:

"When my girlfriend penetrated my rectum, I thought I had to do number two."

"I do not like to be rectally penetrated, even by a finger. The idea is very sexy. The reality is not. It is painful."

Penis penetration or penetration with a penis-sized object*

Many men who had tried it had had very positive experiences with penetration by a penis or a penis-sized vibrator:

"Stimulation of my prostate is a newly discovered thrill, accounting for much of my enjoyment of anal penetration. Also having anal intercourse with my lover is an extremely emotional experience. To feel someone you love inside you is incredible. (Perhaps like intercourse feels to a woman.) I often feel satisfied when my lover has orgasm in me, without having achieved ejaculation myself."

"I love being rectally penetrated, especially by a cock. I love having them plunge it in deeply. I have orgasmed in this way, but usually not. Often it gets me horny and I end up fucking my partner after he has fucked me. It's very stimulating, you feel great pleasure from having someone in your ass, it's a very passionate experience. I enjoy having a man reach orgasm within me, it also releases tension within my own body."

"I enjoy it if a penis is introduced slowly, giving my anus a chance to relax and to accept it. I find the subsequent feeling extremely pleasurable and stimulating. The pressure of the penis inside me helps increase the warmth and tightness I normally feel in my crotch during arousal, and the push on my prostate from inside usually causes me to orgasm very quickly when my penis is stimulated and makes the orgasm very intense. It seems to fulfill my fantasy of being taken by someone."

"Having it done is different from a finger because there's a man behind that penis who is intent on literally fucking me until he comes. Even though there's some pain involved, I really get turned on because I know I'm pleasing him the way a woman pleases me. His breathing, his touch, his penis plunging in until I think it'll come out of my mouth, and then pulling out slowly and finally his surge when he comes, all of it gives me pleasure physically, emotionally, and mentally. Psychologically I inevitably have guilt feelings—not from the pleasure, but because of the man, but the price is worth it."

* Not all of the answers in this section were from men with a homosexual orientation; some answers refer to penetration by a woman using a penis-sized object.

"Anal penetration is a great sensation. It arouses me. I've often masturbated while I had something stuck in my rear. It adds to the sensation of orgasm."

"I love getting fucked in the ass. To be fucked thus feels solid. It gives a strong feeling of brotherhood with another man."

"I prefer cocks, which feel downright marvelous once I've accommodated them. Oftentimes it hurts at first, but usually it stops hurting and then it's like . . . it's indescribable."

"I have an almost uncontrollable desire to be ravished anally. Sometimes my wife straps the dildo to her pelvis or holds it in her hand. I want to be fucked hard. I want it to plunge in and out until my anus is hot, wide open, and not resisting at all. When the rectum has been completely ravished and can't take any more, then is the best time to have an orgasm. Being fucked in the rectum can be built up into a profound sexual experience engulfing the mind and body and completely blotting out everything else to the point where the sexual feeling is no longer localized, but the whole body feels it—and nothing else. What I am trying to achieve is the same total involvement of mind and body at the same level as the orgasm, but for a much longer period of time. If the events I have described are paced properly, sexual feeling can build up until it becomes so strong that it is like a continuous orgasm."

"Anal intercourse is a feeling of fullness, warmth, being possessed, cuddled, explored, manipulated, loved, used, needed, and surrounding another man with your own warmth, love, usefulness and needs, etc. . . . I feel when I do the fucking I am giving myself to another man. It is a two-way avenue where we meet each other."

"Of all other sex life—putting my penis in the anus of another person, having sex with my wife or prostitutes or oral sex by a prostitute or masturbating by hand or putting something like a penis in my anus for masturbating—I enjoy being fucked by a strong male man the most."

"My wife and I tried a dildo and I did orgasm. It sent chills all over my body. She used a strap-on dildo and we 'traded sex-places.' It was an emotionally delightful experience."

"Whatever she does to intensify the pleasure is acceptable. A vibrator makes me harder, and if she stabs it in my rectum, I'm destroyed—but it's a great destruction."

"I like it with the right fellow after plenty of lovemaking.

When I have a cock in my ass I feel curiously complete. Anal sex is the big number—a man's cock belongs in a man's ass— the way God meant it."

"Oh yes, I love it. Makes me go nuts. But unless I've smoked some dope/drank some liquor or been prepared before entry, a penis makes me tense, tightens me up—but I orgasm great, much better than standard. How does it feel? A stiff rod inside me is heaven."

"I just recently learned how to enjoy it. After ten years of being the active partner, I can now be passive. Anal intercourse feels like you are being filled up by your partner."

"The first time I was with a man I was scared—I never knew an erect prick looked that big, I dug the fear a lady could have. But I stuck it out (or his in) and it was great."

"Every once in a while I take time out and stimulate myself rectally with a dildo. The sensation is something like the sensations of an orgasm except not as intense. It's as though the dildo were massaging the organs which produce the feelings of orgasm. Sometimes I develop a craving for my wife to fuck me in the ass. For this, I like to lie on a low ottoman so that my body is in the form of an upside-down V, my behind raised up high with my anus in the most vulnerable and available position possible. I spread my legs so my anus is exposed. There is a wonderful feeling of anticipation which is focused entirely on the anus and also a feeling of complete submission to one's sex partner. I like her to keep plunging the dildo in and out until I feel I have really been fucked good."

Other men were less enthusiastic about their experiences with anal penetration by a penis, or had more mixed feelings:

"Do I like being fucked? Yes and no. In sex with other men, this is usually the lowest on my list of preferred activities. It is rarely physically pleasurable and often mildly uncomfortable and sometimes quite uncomfortable or painful. Penetration by a finger is less uncomfortable physically but lacks almost the entire quotient of psychological pleasure, which is the main reason to allow myself to be fucked. What does it feel like? Usually, after an initial spasm of discomfort, it doesn't feel like much of anything. I have never felt the pleasures said to come from the prostate gland while being fucked. Most of the physical sensations arise from the immediate area of the opening, the anus. So why do it at all? The answer is entirely for the psychological pleasure. As with doing fellatio, there is substantial vicarious pleasure to be derived from a man enjoying intercourse and experiencing orgasm. There is additional pleasure in the contemplation of the idea that you yourself or at least your body is so enjoyable and pleasure-giving as to induce these sensations in your partner."

"Anal intercourse itself is not a thrill for me; I do it only to indulge a male lover who wants to and only then with someone I like and trust."

"I have never had an orgasm from anal penetration alone, and don't know anybody who has; the stimulation for it just isn't there because the sensations go from mildly pleasing or very mildly painful to nothing at all, numbness (after a minute or two)."

"I like it if the penis is not too large. It feels moderately painful and gives a sort of stretching full feeling while entry is being made. Once penetration is made and stroking action starts, the sensation is pleasurable, and if my genitals are handled at the time of my partner's ejaculation, I reach a strong orgasm."

"Sometimes I orgasm this way—with masturbation, but I have ambivalent feelings about being fucked. I enjoy it and am also ashamed of it. I worry that the man who's fucking me will use the occasion to feel superior to me, dominant."

"Frankly, to be penetrated by another man feels good, but I couldn't come that way. The big thing is, that I'm accommodating my friend and doing what he wants. Of course, the idea is exciting, too, to feel him rising to a crescendo—feel him big and hard in my rear and to feel him finally come in me. The desire to please (most men couldn't care less), the desire to be desired, the desire to have my back to him while he goes in me (trust?) and after he pulls out of me, the feeling that it was good for him and that now I have his semen inside my body."

"I have been penetrated by a penis; again, the pain outweighed the pleasure, but like fellatio the experience gave me a new perspective on how it feels for another person to relate to my body."

"I have been anally penetrated and it hurt. I have given it up. I have even come with a stud working me over and I didn't even have an erection but it felt great. But my butt isn't big enough and my intensity won't allow me to relax, as I have been told is the method. Still, the several times a stud fucked me were the highest moods of sexual excitement I have ever experienced."

"I only like it with a very special partner. It is always painful at first for me—full enjoyment is a gradual process—ideally there is slow penetration, accompanied by circular motions to limber up the rectum. The feeling of anal intercourse is a very 'hot' feeling, and after the penis slips out there is a very warm peaceful sensation. The only trouble is maybe half an hour afterward I feel some pressure and gas rectally. It is like a mini-enema, because when defecating, the semen is expelled too, like a short episode of the runs. Psychologically the union is superb. I feel incredibly high and tender from the whole experience."

Some men were plagued by feelings of guilt, shame, or fear after they did it:

"I can't take the guilt and self-hate the few times I have done such things. It's rather nice to be filled up that way though."

"I can only enjoy being penetrated if I'm very loaded and/or drunk and/or on a Quaalude. I think this is because when I was a child my mom told me about child molesters and homosexuals (notice she categorized them together) that 'they put sticks up your tushie (ass) and hurt little boys.' "

Some who had tried it found that they did not like it at all:

"It can hurt, sometimes very much so. I do not have the ability to relax as the entry is made, sometimes not at all during the whole act. I have found very few male partners that really can relax me and turn me fully on, without pain, in anal intercourse."

"I enjoy the active role. I would enjoy the passive role, but the pain experience upon penetration is not compensated for by the pleasure afterward."

"I would like it psychologically but have found it too uncomfortable physically (by a penis). It feels like you need to take a shit. I had orgasm (once) while being fucked."

"It's painful. I hate it."

"I don't like it. I feel violated and very vulnerable."

"It hurts. Being speared."

"I've tried with my best friend once, but it didn't agree with me psychologically. The penetration hurts like hell but after the muscles relax, it's a lot of fun. I didn't orgasm in my anus but it did feel good and stimulating. I did orgasm in his anus, but it was the thought of having sex with a guy that bothered me. So it didn't go any farther. Men do not turn me on, women do, by sight, touch, and smell."

One man had just recently learned to enjoy it:

"My greatest sexual fears, until recently, involved anal penetration. These fears were matched by a conscious fantasy life that this should happen. I had to work through all sorts of negative feelings about shit, sodomy, and pain (I knew that being hurt had no sexual payoffs for me). I had never rectally penetrated anyone myself, although I was clear that I would be gentle while doing so. Also, I had a fistula for some months in the rectal area which made me feel guilty that there should be an infection there. With such an attitude, something had to happen. It did. First, the fistula was surgically cleared out and afterward—you've got to take this on faith—I had some dynamite talks with my asshole. Turns out that a lot of my sexual uptightness was lodged there. My rectum, naturally, resented this so it was no accident that it felt unwanted and got sick. My desires/counter-desires were really destructive to my person and that's when I decided that rectal sex was going to either be O.K. for me or I should just forget it (which seemed impossible except through increased repression). In the last year, I've started having anal sex with male partners—rimming, penetration by finger or penis. Also I've gotten into doing it to my lovers. The secret is—relax. Sexual caring, as always, makes all the difference. Orgasms are easy since the prostate gland is directly stimulated. Some of my most intense, heightened awareness of what sex can be occurred during anal penetration. I'm sure this is because it unites two fundamental desires—to learn from and love my male body. Being rectally penetrated has helped to put me in touch with the male/female spirit living in my male body."

A few men with heterosexual experience, who had never tried penis penetration, expressed an open attitude toward penis or dildo penetration:

"I would try a penis for the experience. It's all the other freight that would necessarily accompany it that turns me off."

"The only desire that I have in the way of homosexuality

is to feel a penis in my anus. For a long time I've wondered how it would feel and maybe one day I'll get the chance to find out."

"At this point in my life I've only been penetrated by a finger. I'm a little afraid of being penetrated by a penis only because of pain, but if I was with the right partner who really knew how to do it right, I would like to try it."

"I probably would enjoy being penetrated by my wife if she wore a dildo. I realize that if I admit that much, I should like anal intercourse with another man, but my cultural conditioning shows up there and I feel quite blocked regarding that idea. Men are just not it."

"I have never been rectally penetrated by another person, only by me with my fingers. Part of me is afraid of somehow ruining my insides. But I would like to be penetrated by a penis. I have been penetrated by my lady's fingers and by a man lover's fingers. I want more."

"Any homosexual activity by me could cost me my job since the Army frowns upon it; however, I would like to try a well-lubricated penis slipping in and out of my ass and driving hard into me when he ejaculates."

"I fantasize a lot about being taken in this way by another man. Given the proper man and occasion, I would try it."

"I would do it with a man that I felt safe and equal with."

"From a physical point of view I don't think anal intercourse would give that much pleasure, but psychologically it could be thrilling to feel a man come inside you."

"The sensation would probably be nice, as I like digital anal stimulation, but I can't get over the 'dirty' phobia associated with even an immaculately scrubbed and polished anus."

"I have often wondered about it, but I don't think I could ever bring myself to submit to it (finger or penis). Some of my fantasies concern other men penetrating me, but I really couldn't let it happen."

But most men who had not tried either finger or penis penetration stated, in no uncertain terms, their antagonism to the idea of being penetrated by anything:

"I would rather die. I think being fucked in the ass is the most disgusting and humiliating thing a human being can be exposed to."

"Positively not. Because I am 100 percent of a man."

"Hell *no!*"

"Nuts to this question. I do not."

"My only sexual areas are my back and genitals. My breasts and asshole could disintegrate for all I care."

"I am not a homosexual!"

"My anus is paranoid."

"I hate bisexuality. Penal penetration would be rape. I'd have to kill over that."

"Disgusting."

"Revolting."

"No, it hasn't been done. One guy who tried lost an ear, another spent time in the hospital. It must feel lousy—judging by the screams of guys having it done to them."

"This question gives me the creeps. I've never been able to comprehend why any man, woman, boy, or girl would desire or even tolerate sex in the rectum. Revolting."

"Ye Gods no!"

"Ugh!"

"My king-sized homosexual hang-up is accompanied by a king-sized anal hang-up—any anal approach, heterosexual or homosexual, turns me off completely."

"I never experienced it except in a medical situation. Even then I felt outraged and had to suppress feelings of violence toward the doctor."

"No, no, no. It is bad for your health. Ask the homosexuals who have rectal problems about the hazards of butt fucking. Ask the prison medical personnel."

"No. This is humiliation, this is filth."

"Try to stick a dick up my ass and I cut it off."

PHYSICAL AND EMOTIONAL FEELINGS DURING ANAL PENETRATION

Physical feelings

"An aura of sensuality seems to spread around my anus, a pleasant tension. The sensual experience which is usually concentrated in my penis seems to spread out to my anus and the periphery area of the butt aches sweetly."

"Having something in my behind is great fun, partly because it is such a fulfilled feeling, partly because it is so deliciously wicked. Best is a finger or a small vibrator, well oiled. I don't really come from it, but it excites me so much that only a small touch to my penis is needed to blow every nerve in my body. It's the most intense feeling I know, much more exciting than pleasant."

"The anus is a very sexual part of the male body. Deep contact feels wonderful there, particularly with movement. Direct stimulation of the prostate (through my anus) sometimes triggers me to an ecstatic feeling level that makes me feel maybe I am going further than my body should be expected to endure. It's like I want to orgasm, but I can't. It's a little scary."

"The sensation is not in my rectum but in some internal area between there and the root of my penis."

"Penetration feels like a continuous urge to come."

"The only time I ever was penetrated was by a Japanese masseuse who inserted a finger into my ass while she was manually masturbating me. It was one of the greatest experiences I ever had. It felt like the base of my penis was suddenly extended all the way down to my anus. Instead of all my sensations being centered only on the top of my penis, it was now simultaneously centered in both. I would feel a spasmodic twinge of pleasure as her finger penetrated and my anal muscles closed in and grabbed it, and then the feeling would sort of pop and shoot all the way up my penis as it was being stroked. Incredible sensation."

"The area around and just inside one's anus is one of the most neglected and maligned erogenous zones both for me and for my female friends. It's a vital part of the body."

"The feeling on my prostate makes me feel like I am about to come for the longest period of time—after a while it is too intense and I can't stand it any longer."

"A very excited and full feeling—the sensations in my penis take a back seat to those in my prostate and tubes."

"A finger up your ass feels like your penis has support."

"The feeling of a finger during intercourse is one of being full, similar to descriptions I often hear women relate about their vaginas during intercourse."

"I do like getting fucked. I understand better now how my wife could like it. A gentle and careful lover can give you a deep and sustained feeling of being near orgasm that is unique. This afterglow of a good ass fuck can last for days."

"My anus is *very* sensitive to touch, and is a class-A erogenous zone for me. It forms a second and nearly equal locus of sexual pleasure, the other being, of course, my penis.

When my desire is inflamed, I sense a dumbbell-shaped long-ing running all the way between my legs from the tip of my penis to my anus, and from which my balls dangle like a glorious afterthought. One of the principal elements of my confusion around the age of twenty, when I was actively bisexual for a while, was that although I enjoyed females, I saw no way of ever deriving *real* sexual gratification from them—meaning, of course, uninhibited sex play involving a lot of anal teasing and penetration. The pleasure of penetra-tion is largely psychological, I suppose, because the intromis-sion of a penis into my rectum usually hurts, at least at first. Most men are too large. Once I sufficiently relax, however, I succumb to an exquisite pleasure. To think that this other fine man's (they are always fine men) penis is actually inside me . . . ! When he moves, the massaging action sends a radiant pulsating warmth throughout my body, which I find very exciting. It is a delicate question of rhythm at this point, whether things go well or not. If the man is sensitive, relaxed, and can move with an easy, confident swaying motion that does not vary too much, I will soon be in a transport of pleasure. Each man has his own personal rhythm which is a revelation of his own intimate spirit. I adore that gift of himself that a man makes when he fucks me, and I am very proud to be able to enjoy men in this way."

Emotional feelings

"It feels like the other person is 'with in' me. I only let people I love fuck me. It is like someone physically putting their love in me."

"It makes me feel joined and part of the man I am with, having him inside me. This is an act with my body which I give the right to very few—it is my way of showing total trust and unity with the lover and a time when I can enjoy the feeling of total passivity and what society terms femininity. It is that feeling of masculinity and femininity combined which makes me feel complete inside my body and mind."

"I feel like I'm wanting a person in me. I mean deep like in soul or something."

"It's a feeling of surrender, but I know I won't be hurt by my lover. It's a feeling of fullness and power in my lover."

"All of my defenses are gone and I have to trust in my lover completely."

"Emotionally it is the ultimate in intimacy I can offer. It

can be spiritually close or degrading on my person, depending upon with whom or where it is done."

"Penetration is yielding up to an emotionally important person."

"It's a tangible way of expressing an inner feeling."

"I only like to be penetrated if I really feel care and emotionally involved. Otherwise I feel it's for a woman to be penetrated."

"Very satisfying—it makes me feel warm and possessed."

"It's indescribable. A feeling of being filled, not just by a cock, but by warmth and pleasure and something awfully close to enlightenment, a better high than drugs have ever given me."

"It feels like two people become one being sometimes."

"I don't know how to describe that feeling. Emotionally, I know my partner is getting off, and I'm getting off knowing that."

"It's a feeling of fullness and loss of control. It's a very trusting time for me."

"Is anal intercourse more satisfying physically or emotionally? Probably emotionally, although I feel somewhat strange admitting that. Because after the act is complete what I remember most vividly and savor long afterward was the union, the tenderness, and the language that was established between my partner and myself. The good physical feeling derives more from the close physical contact with my partner."

"Anal penetration can be absolute *ecstasy*. I really enjoy it, if it's done gently and with someone I love. In fact I don't feel fulfilled unless I've had that too during sex. I never had an orgasm as a result of that but it gives a feeling of such closeness and intimacy, it's more than completeness."

"Emotionally, it makes me feel dependent and I like being dependent instead of offering the stimulation to her or him all the time. It means I'm getting something instead of giving."

TECHNIQUES FOR BEING PENETRATED ANALLY

Some men gave information about how best to receive anal penetration, especially by a penis, and body positions they liked to use:

"I have been penetrated rectally a few times. If done while I am lying flat on my stomach, it can be pleasant, if done very slowly and carefully with proper lubrication. Psychologically I can get a very 'full' satisfied feeling. I do not tend to be aroused, penis-wise, by this. If penetration is done while my legs are over the guy's shoulder, I find it tends to be very painful."

"In anal intercourse, there's three basic positions I use. One is belly down, which gives the receptor more control of how deep the penetration is and, if you're me, lets you masturbate on the bed while being fucked. The second is face-to-face with the receptor's legs thrown up over the other guy's shoulders. This is good for super-deep penetration and if I can take my partner's deepest thrusts, this is paradise. If I'm having trouble getting started as receptor, I use a third position: I have my partner lie down on his back and I straddle him, kneeling with one leg on either side of him. Then I can lower myself onto his cock. This gives me the most control and makes for the most comfortable entry if there are entry problems."

"Sometimes my wife does this to me when she masturbates me. It can be anywhere from mildly pleasant to really fantastic. She uses a finger in me slowly at first until my anal muscles accommodate to penetration. Next she will sometimes use her (our) vibrator to penetrate deeply into me. Or she will use one or two fingers inserted all the way and bent up to push against my prostate gland. That feels really intense and is great to have done just before coming to give me a big extra push."

"I am laying on my back and he can put all his penis in me as I am kissing him."

"My girlfriend has fallen into the habit if inserting her forefinger (wrapped in a condom) up my anus. One more equalizing factor. In her nakedness, she walks to the bureau from the bed (across the room, literally) and picks out a rubber from the top drawer. She can see me watching her bounce back and forth on this errand (the rubber is to prevail against all scratches—true, it can prevent any dirt but that isn't essential). The mirror over the bureau shows both of us ('The Rover Boys in School and Out') in detail. She works that finger, covered by rubber, in and out of the rectum approximately ten times until she quits. With her other hand she reaches underneath (I'm always on hands and knees for this act) and jerks me off a bit (ten strokes usually), because my penis is always dripping (if I let go, I'd shoot the semen into the bed instead of herself)."

"Fingers tend to be less comfortable than cocks because of the nails, calluses, hangnails, although sufficient lubricant (K-Y's the best) usually solves the problem with all but finger-picking guitarists' hands."

"I prefer to be lying on my back with the other person up over me so I can watch them as they screw me. I find the sight of a male screwing me very stimulating. It seems to fulfill my fantasy of being taken by someone."

"Sometimes I'll be penetrated by a penis by straddling the man and lowering my ass onto his erection. It always needs lubrication. Part of it could be, too, that this act is frowned upon and so is thereby enjoyable. The thrusting in and out (not completely out) of the penis into my rear is very exciting and has never been painful, particularly when you control whether it's going in you, and how. It's one of those times that I lose my erection while I'm being screwed, becaues my mind is on my partner and what he is feeling. My anus is quite sexually stimulating to me, and during the thrusting in and out, it is, of course, stimulated, as is the surrounding area, my buttocks (which are slammed against by the thrusts) and the whole general genital area. It's great."

Men who did the penetrating also had information to share:

"Into an asshole I tend not to *thrust,* but more enjoy stimulating the head of the penis just inside the opening."

"I like being on top, since there is maximum body touch in that position. Most movement is from me—just enough from my partner so that I know that he is responding."

"During anal intercourse I prefer to be on top with my partner face down—deeper penetration is possible this way. This is more physically satisfying. With my partner facing me with his legs on my shoulders—the effect is more psychologically fulfilling. I prefer to make the movements. I prefer to start anal intercourse making small thrusting movements deep inside and then gradually start pulling out further and going deeper and faster closer to climax. I achieve a more satisfying climax than with oral sex. On an emotional level— I feel my partner is really giving something to me."

"I get on top of the guy so he is on his stomach, his legs are spread wide with my legs between his. I prefer this position but I also enjoy having him sit on it upright while I'm on my back. I can look at his body, and facial expression while I fuck him. Also I enjoy it when he leans back a bit, putting more weight on my pelvis with his buttocks. It's a rush. I don't get as much control this way, but it's a great sensation, feeling the guy slam down on my cock. With my partner prone I like both of us to move together in rhythm, but with me doing most of the moving."

"I enjoy variety to achieve orgasm. I use all kinds of positions. Dog fashion—hands and knees—standing up; lying down flat, reversed in various ways; legs up or down; sideways too—both my partner and myself moving—or one still and one moving. There is so much we can do to make our sexual love stimulating and I do my best to keep the anticipation of what will take place a mystery—small though it is, yet a gentle, familiar joy. *No matter what the variables the sexual gymnastics take on, it must remain a loving, warm, emotional encounter.*"

Orgasm from anal penetration

Some men could, at times, orgasm from anal penetration— although in many ways orgasm during anal penetration is besides the point:

"Once, I orgasmed solely by means of rectal stimulation. My partner's penis was fairly small, so that he could move very freely without causing me any discomfort. He moved nicely, sometimes meditatively, sometimes with a rapid ecstasy, and although he was a casual encounter, I had a very good feeling about him, and he was having the time of his life fucking me. As he continued I became more and more absorbed in the rhythmic pulsations I was experiencing in my rectum, and as I lay there on my stomach feeling his hot breath in my ear, I felt to my astonishment the slowly gathering sensation that precedes the onset of orgasm. Perhaps my own penis was rubbing somewhat on the bedclothes, and perhaps this contributed, but the effect was minimal in any case. I was psychologically excited to the greatest possible extent. Orgasming as he continued to thrust was incredible. Because my anus contracts with every pulsation of orgasm (I can feel this with my finger anytime I want to), my rectum spasmodically gripped his penis which resulted in a sensation of utter bodily abandon. I felt that I was coming, shitting, pissing, crying—every single sensation of release and letting go that I have ever felt, all at the same time. Unfortunately, I was blessed with this experience only once, although I have come close to it at other times. I confess that although I love to make love with my woman, the desire for a man comes up very strong in me at times."

"Once she put me across her lap, put her finger up my ass, and felt around until she found my prostate. She said she could feel it—it was flat and round like a quarter—she asked me if that was it, or if I felt anything when she pressed there. I sure did—I felt like I was going to come any minute. She started kneading it with her finger—it was a sensation I wasn't used to—very compelling but it wasn't in my penis. It took a while, and finally I came. I never really got an erection, and there wasn't much fluid either. But it was great."

But most men needed manual stimulation of the penis as well in order to orgasm:*

"I like to be penetrated rectally by the woman's finger or a vibrator, while being fellated or while being masturbated. I like the feeling, but being penetrated alone would not bring me to orgasm."

"The greatest stimulation is the penis or dildo moving in and out (not all the way out, just partially out) rapidly while I move my other hand up and down on my penis."

"I orgasm this way, but only if I am also being masturbated at the same time."

"I like a woman to put a lubricated finger up my ass and gently and rhythmically press down on my prostate area. It feels very satisfying, and causes my penis to throb, sometimes with a burning sensation. Although I have orgasmed with a finger penetrating my rectum, I have never been brought to orgasm solely by it. I believe I could be, though."

How does orgasm feel while being penetrated anally?

"Orgasm this way is a totally different kind of orgasm— orgasm of the entire body. It centers mainly in the testicle area and is intense."

"Only three times have I orgasmed during rectal penetration without the help of masturbation. They were among the most memorable climaxes I've ever had. Feelings vary from a desire to defecate to a feeling of swimming in the rhythm of masculine power."

---

* There are some similarities here to the fact that, while some women can orgasm from intercourse, most women need additional manual clitoral stimulation to orgasm.

"Prostate orgasms are more internal and all around the whole pelvic region. They may or may not result in ejaculation from the penis. I like them, but still I'm not completely satisfied by them if they don't go along with a penile orgasm. It seems like, after eighteen years of masturbation, I'm just very used to orgasms via the penis and anything else seems 'less' somehow."

"My wife sometimes inserts her finger into my anus and massages my prostate gland during intercourse with her sitting astride. When I orgasm this way, the feeling is fantastically ecstatic, usually intensifying the orgasm, and sometimes causing my orgasmic contractions to continue longer than usual."

Whether a man enjoys being penetrated or not seems to depend in large measure on its being done carefully and correctly, with sufficient lubrication. With regard to creating orgasm during anal penetration, it is important to note that prostate massage during anal penetration is by no means automatic. If the aim of anal penetration is to massage the prostate and not simply to stimulate and give pleasure to the other person, one must feel specifically for the prostate and ask one's partner for guidance—watching for signs or reactions. Otherwise, the chances of orgasm are quite slim. Men also said that an orgasm from prostate massage is quite different in feeling from an orgasm caused by stimulation of the penis; prostate orgasms are described as being "deeper" and "more generalized." On the other hand, as with vaginal intercourse, perhaps in many cases the feeling of penetration itself is so beautiful and so intense that orgasm is simply not the point. In fact, most men actually preferred complete penetration without orgasm (by a penis or finger) to a direct prostate massage (usually by one or more fingers) for the purpose of orgasm.

FELLATIO

"My first encounter with this came in my mid-twenties when a good friend surprised me by licking my erect penis. It was dark in the room. I didn't know what she was doing or would do next. It was extremely exciting and I promptly had an orgasm. I was embarrassed at the situation and pulled her head away so as to conceal my vigorous reaction. I was at a point in life when I still felt an orgasm ought to occur in the vagina or if out of it, at least without it being right there for her to see in every detail of semen spurting forth and the penis caught up in its uncontrollable convulsing. Later, soon, I found this kind of 'ultimate disclosure' a sort of final intimacy and revealing everything about myself, even this *most* private and supposedly 'shameful' reflex—very very exciting—especially with the woman's head on my chest, hearing my racing heart at orgasm's approach and arrival. I think it is as close as a man can come to being 'raped' by a woman in that nothing is held back from her hand and eyes and ears. He is totally hers, totally passive and surrenders to her completely."

"I enjoy performing fellatio on other men. The physical sensation, particularly when the phallus is thrust entirely down the throat, is unexplainably exciting. Psychologically it can be anything from an expression of love, to the humiliation of submission, to the worshipping of virility."

MEN'S FEELINGS ABOUT FELLATIO WITH WOMEN

"Do you like oral stimulation of your penis (fellatio)? To orgasm?"

Almost all men said that they enjoyed, or would enjoy, fellatio tremendously:

"My favorite thing? Blow jobs!"
"Fellatio is the high point in *every* man's sexual experience, surpassed only by fellatio to *orgasm!*"

"I believe every man's dream is to have a woman who would, if you'll forgive the vulgarism, suck him off. If I could find the woman who would suck me off in the morning to wake me up, I would lay my life in the mud at her feet, for she would be one woman in a million."

"Are you serious? To come in a woman's mouth is the most intense, pleasurable sexual experience to me because I can surrender totally and focus on the sensation. The sperm seems to come from my 'source,' it intensely drains me of everything. And I like to see myself making love to her, watch the joy in her face."

"This is by far my favorite sexual activity. I always orgasm and it is more intense for me than an intercourse orgasm."

"Oral stimulation of my penis!!! Ah-h-h, one dreams about it!!!!! By this, you may get the impression that I *l-o-v-e* it, and rightly so!"

"I enjoy doing it and having it done *very* much in all ways. I like feeling my cock go inside someone's mouth and that beautiful sucking."

"Fellatio is great. A loving and ardent mouth is more stimulating and exciting than a vagina any day."

"I like the *idea* of it—I feel she is bestowing honor upon my manhood."

"Between cunnilingus and fellatio, you could dispense with contraceptives and copulation entirely, in my opinion."

"Fellatio is the best. Besides the physical sensations, I feel that the woman really loves and appreciates my body—the real me. Also I don't have to perform—I don't even have to have an erection."

"Fellatio! Oh yea!! I have never had a time when I couldn't orgasm this way—even when maybe I wasn't sure whether I should or not."

But most men did not have regular or frequent experience with it, especially not to orgasm, and most complained that women didn't do it very often or very well:

"I enjoy very much to have fellatio performed on me. However, I have yet to find a woman who can do it properly. I have orgasmed like this only once, and one other time with the help of masturbation. Many times I feel I could orgasm this way, but something in the way she does it turns me off, either it's getting too repetitive, I hear a sigh, she bites, or I can tell her heart's not in it."

"My impression is that either the woman I have slept with were afraid because they didn't know exactly what to do when they got down there, or they thought it was dirty and would only go down there as a matter of requirement but that's all."

"Fellatio is most often foreplay to intercourse. Fellatio to orgasm could be more often but my wife doesn't attend the corona of the glans for very long at a time which is my most sensitive spot. Although she fellates me without my asking the last few years, she is really not into it and may never be. Her interest, curiosity, creativity, and technique could be better. She could use lessons in technique but one does not look a gift horse in the mouth."

"My greatest displeasure? A female who must analyze in Freudian terms just exactly why it is that I want her to suck me off, calling it 'infantile' or some other bullshit."

"Most women ain't good at it."

Further, most men said that they felt they should not allow themselves to orgasm during fellatio because of fears of the woman's reaction: women didn't seem to like to perform fellatio to orgasm, and didn't like to swallow the semen, although men wished that this were not so:

"Sometimes I can orgasm this way but most women do not enjoy fellatio to orgasm (at least that's been my experience) and I really don't know how to bring it up. ('Excuse me, dear, may I come in your mouth?') I would like a woman to do this to me."

"I enjoy fellatio very much and can have very strong orgasms. My wife has fellated me to orgasm only twice—I would like it much more often. This is an area where anxiety builds up between us."

"I love it but at the same time I'm not really at ease with it. I usually pull her away although deep down I really don't want to. I've got a hang-up about coming in her mouth. Also, no woman has ever pressed the point, and I've always had the feeling they aren't really into it. I'd like to be wrong."

"I enjoy fellatio but women are usually so afraid of it or don't want to do it or they are afraid you'll come in their mouth or something."

"I have grown up believing that women do not like having men come into their mouths, which is true of many women. But some do like it and that does make it easier to really relax and enjoy."

"What is really unsatisfactory is when a girl removes her lips at the moment of ejaculation, leaving my penis out in the cold air."

"It's terrific. I can always get highly excited this way, but rarely climax as a direct result due to an unfortunate experience inside a girlfriend as a teenager. I was appalled almost as much as she was when I did it in her mouth. So now I prefer it as a preliminary only. Need I add that my wife abhors it and hasn't tried it since the honeymoon, when one taste induced tears?"

"I am inhibited because I don't want to have an orgasm this way, due to the negative feelings I gather most women have about semen in the mouth and throat. I think it certainly can't be fun for the woman—rather a chore actually."

"My wife performs fellatio on me but refuses to bring me to orgasm this way. I don't believe she has ever tasted my come, and thinks it would be too strong and would make her sick."

"I fear coming in her mouth . . . or that she isn't really enjoying it . . . just doing it for my pleasure . . . and I am self-conscious if my cock is pleasing or not."

"I like it, but I am reluctant to ask my lady—she may think me 'dirty' or perverted."

"I like having my parts nuzzled, yes. But I've never come that way. There is this thing about swallowing or rejecting the ejaculate: it hangs me up to see apprehension in my partner, so I usually call a halt to cocksucking well before I reach a pre-orgasm stage."

"My fear is that I will orgasm in my partner's mouth and choke her, so I retreat from the situation."

How do men feel about swallowing the ejaculate? See page 588 and pages 548–51. Also, see pages 587–90 for men's feelings about their own ejaculation and wetness during masturbation.

Some men resented the woman not liking it, especially if the woman liked cunnilingus:

"There is one thing that has amazed me. A lot of women will beg you to go down on them but they make you feel you are unfair to want them to go down on you. It has got to the point that I don't even bother asking, if she does go down on me then she is really thinking about me and wants to please me. This type of woman I get off on."

"Some women don't like men to come in their mouth but they want you to suck on their wet cunts. Be fair, ladies."

"I like a blow job but only if it's *her* idea. I feel disappointed though, if she won't swallow the semen. After all, I've swallowed a lot of *her* juice."

"She does not like me to come in her mouth. But once again women like me to slurp up all of their juices."

But others disagreed:

"Let me say if I have just completed cunnilingus for the one I'm crazy about, that does not necessarily imply that now she has to perform fellatio for me. It is strictly a voluntary act which I do because I enjoy it and because I love making her feel that great pleasure of orgasm. If she also voluntarily eats me, it is an inexpressible thrill, especially if I know that she loves doing it, loves to have my penis and my ejaculation in her mouth, and is not just doing it to please me. But I am doubtful whether most women really *love* fellatio, as men do *love* cunnilingus, with the same urgency and appetite."

"I like fellatio sometimes. A blow job every now and then is very stimulating but I do not like it on a real steady basis. I can orgasm this way, but my wife does not like the semen to end up in her mouth. I can't blame her, I think it would be about like eating snot. I know some women supposedly like to swallow semen, which I think is okay, but if my wife doesn't like it I say 'great'!"

Many men said that a woman's not liking fellatio or their ejaculate made them feel as if their genitals—and therefore perhaps they themselves or their sexuality—were not acceptable or were even disgusting to the woman:

"It gives me a feeling of complete acceptance when she likes to take me into her mouth and have me come. It is very disturbing to upset the emotional moment by running to the bathroom to spit it out, or into a handkerchief, even when done adeptly. It always makes me feel distant. Maybe there is a little hang-up because of the penis being used for urination."

"My wife thinks my semen is nasty. Sometimes I think that about my whole sex drive too—and that I am nasty for wanting to do the things I do."

"There are sometimes negative psychological aspects as when I doubt that the woman really wants to do it, especially if I ejaculate. If I'm afraid of ejaculation there, then there's an unpleasant tension—I feel she doesn't accept me and I resent her."

Or remarked that a woman doing fellatio, especially to orgasm, made them feel greatly accepted:

"If she lets me come in her mouth, that means that she is not afraid of me and that she really accepts me. Wow."

Some men mentioned that they liked fellatio but felt uncomfortable being passive and doing nothing but receiving stimulation:

"I enjoy fellatio but feel mentally uncomfortable about being on the receiving end of any stimulation. I have the feeling that I ought to be doing something instead of just lying there. I rarely orgasm this way although it feels very good. I just hold back and then switch to intercourse when I can't hold back any longer."

"I often have trouble climaxing due to a number of factors—my partner's inexperience, the difficulty of fantasizing, and perhaps most importantly, the knowledge that the woman is not being sexually satisfied by the act; I feel somehow I should be stimulating her too—otherwise, how can she enjoy it?"

"It seems too passive. I want to keep my erection for other things."

"I like fellatio and cunnilingus together because I like to feel that I am doing something for her, too."

Some men said they felt it was a degrading act, especially for the woman:

"I do like it, but I do not like my woman doing it, because in the back of my mind I think she is degrading herself for my pleasure, which hurts me. She has explained to me that she really enjoys it, so we do it once in a while but I never ask for it. I never go all the way with it, I pull away before I come, and I would not like to come in her mouth under any conditions. Somehow it hurts me to think I could even think about it."

"I've had it done to me but it never 'felt right.' A woman shouldn't feel obligated to perform this. It is totally unnecessary for a man's orgasm. I've never met a woman who truly liked doing this. Although I've met several who were willing to. I just feel that this is degrading to both parties."

"I do not enjoy fellatio at all psychologically; I do not enjoy seeing a woman trying to denigrate herself in front of me, which is what fellatio seems to suggest."

"My lover did try fellatio several times but I didn't get off on it. I felt somewhat put off because it seemed that she was 'going down on' me. I am very much in favor of the liberation movement, and her attempts somehow conflicted with my thoughts."

"Only prostitutes and whores go down on guys—my wife would never do it."

But others said it was not degrading, it was a form of love:

"Coming in a woman's mouth and having her swallow it is something special. I don't associate fellatio with the 'degrading of woman' aspects that I have heard about it. A man in love loves his woman's cunt and a woman in loves loves her man's cock and the oral caresses are just a magnificent way of expressing it."

One man said he only liked fellatio with a woman as "foreplay," since he wanted to kiss and hold and be held by his partner during orgasm:

"Usually I'll stop her short and try for intercourse since there isn't a feeling of oneness with oral sex. I want to hold on to someone when I'm close to coming. I recall (fight the embarrassment now) once in a massage parlor nearing orgasm from oral sex, sitting up, reaching out, trying to hold her. She didn't understand what the hell was happening. I also recall (keep going now) conveying this need in a massage parlor and the understanding girl abandoned the oral sex, held me, French-kissed me, and simply masturbated me to orgasm. It was the only memorable experience I've ever had with a prostitute."

A minority of men had an overall dislike for fellatio:

"I don't really enjoy fellatio. I've never had an orgasm by this method. I guess I'm too uptight about those big sharp teeth moving back and forth across my 'manhood.' And I've always had this suspicion in the back of my mind that the guy who gets off on fellatio is secretly a classic male chauvinistic pig who likes to see the submissive female down on her knees. But then again, I may be wrong."

"I do not like people sucking on my penis. Too many other sexy places."

"If a woman knows how to do it well, it's O.K., but it is very easy to lose an erection as an incisor tooth runs along the penile shaft. I prefer it with a sympathetic hand."

"Except for the novelty it is overrated."

"I prefer intercourse. Fellatio is one of those monstrously oversold sex acts peddled by male chauvinists who just don't know better and extol it to heaven. *Deep Throat*'s idiocy notwithstanding, any woman's vagina must be a better place."

And some men had never tried it:

"I have never had fellatio. I have no desire to have it done, it is repulsive to me."

"I think I would like it but I haven't had any experience with it. Probably because I think she would expect me to reciprocate, which I find distasteful."

"I don't know if I like it. She has never even kissed it."

"I dream about it, but can't convince my partner."

"Never experienced it—but I'm waiting anxiously."

Finally, one man expressed his mixed feelings at length:

"Fellatio always scared the hell out of me. If a woman had her mouth on my penis, I thought that I had better have a hard-on and I had better come in her mouth. This is supposed to happen. It never did. Not only did I never come but rarely held the erection. Holy fuck, did I ever feel fucking torment over that. I like to be touched by a woman's hand or mouth. I don't get a hard-on but the feeling relaxes me, I feel literally hypnotized. On the other hand I would like to come in a woman's mouth. I think it would be the height of liberation for me. It would indicate that I had the ability to let go, to surrender, to be swallowed up by another human. It could mean that another person has loved me enough to accept me completely. I could only have an orgasm by fellatio if I knew the woman wanted to do it, wanted to do it because she loved me and willingly wanted to share this form of pleasure. A few women have felt that they were doing such a marvelous and important thing by blowing me, "You'll love this." They think that my penis or a penis has a life of its own, do certain things to it and certain things will happen. The only life *my* penis has is my life and that comes from *my* brain and *my* heart. Sucking on a piece of skin that is only a small fraction of myself won't work. That penis is only a small part of a much, much larger human being. Some women I've been with ignore that.

"This woman and I were talking about *The Hite Report* and the part about fellatio. She likes it, but most of the women in the book said they hated it. 'Like having my face raped.' 'Like hot snot being shot in my mouth.' I feel strange about this. I say that those women who said their face was being raped, they were sucking hot snots, well I have to respect their feelings. But my feelings are that these women miss the point as far as I'm concerned *about me*. For my sake and their sake I would not go to bed with a woman who felt that way. I would not let her come near my penis with a ten-foot pole. For me fellatio, like cunnilingus, is an act of love. The day I can love enough and be loved enough to come in a woman's mouth (I'm not talking about *any* woman, but the person I'm sharing a relationship with) will be the day I cry tears of happiness.

"It's also very hard to tell a woman who thinks she's doing you such a great service, making such a sacrifice, that she is doing it wrong. They talk about the fragile male ego. From what I've experienced you *never, never* tell a woman who is blowing you that she is not doing it well. The female ego would likely get very pissed off. But the fact is that in my experience most women don't know how to give fellatio. Because we've been conditioned to concentrate on the prick and we ignore the rest. And how the hell can a man (myself) deal with a situation where the woman says 'Okay, I'll make the supreme sacrifice and blow you but you better not come.' What it all boils down to for me is that you just don't go to bed with anybody who doesn't love you. If you do then you'll have to be happy with settling for less, and maybe you will feel like your face is being raped, and maybe you'll feel that the best thing that can happen, the only thing that can happen, is that you just fuck and hope you both fall asleep at the same time. As Steve Martin says, if my semen feels like hot snot well then '*excuse me!*' Women are coming to a liberated notion about their vaginas, how they look, how they smell, etc. And I'm coming to a liberated notion of my semen. It's good. It's the most potent, most precious, most life-affirming substance in the Universe. All of humanity depends on it, generation after generation. I will not apologize for it. I will not hide it inside my body. If women would take the time to notice that a head and a heart and a sensitive, feeling human being is attached to that semen and penis things will be better. The pressure and stigma will be removed."

FELLATIO BETWEEN MEN

Fellatio is the most popular form of sexual activity between men. Although a majority of gay men also enjoy anal sex, and some gay men only wanted mutual masturbation and embracing, oral sex is still the daily staple which most gay men enjoy most frequently. This subject will be treated in more detail in chapter 7.

Men were much more likely to receive fellatio to orgasm from another man than from a woman, although many men together used it only as "foreplay":

"Of course I love it!! I can and do orgasm this way about 65 percent of the time I have sex. (The other 35 percent of the time is in anal intercourse.) I like it to be done soft and smooth, no teeth please. There are few things so good as a warm, wet mouth ready and willing."

"I like being passive in fellatio. I usually like it as a foreplay to anal sex but I do like to orgasm this way. I orgasm about once a week or less this way. Many guys do this because it's fast."

"The greatest pleasure from sex that I get is from someone who takes the whole length of my cock in his mouth where I can feel the whole thing enveloped by a warm moistness and where I can feel his throat with my cockhead."

Although men had far fewer complaints about another man's performance of fellatio, there were some worries similar to those expressed about heterosexual fellatio:

"If someone sucks my cock, I keep worrying whether he is doing it only to be nice."

"I have to be relaxed and feel trustfully supported by my partner in order to come this way. I cannot feel that I must perform, then I can't. If he is impatient with me or is easily bored, then I don't want to be sucked off. I enjoy it greatly when someone knows what they are doing and are in no hurry to have me shoot cannons and raise flags. They have to do it with some finesse. If they've got a good technique, right on, suck away. But I prefer not coming that way. It's a very smooth feeling, but I prefer to have access to my partner's lips and face during the last stage before orgasm—it makes the contact with him more personal and more fulfilling to me."

"I love oral stimulation of my cock—but I find it hard to go off in someone's mouth, because most guys I've met don't want to take your juice. It's disappointing to come to a climax and have someone pull away—I would much rather butt-fuck."

"I like fellatio very much. It's my favorite warm-up to fucking a man. I sometimes orgasm this way, but usually it takes a lot of time and I do have some problems reaching orgasm. However, I have been getting better at it lately. Maybe once a week I orgasm by fellatio. But I prefer 69, because I love losing myself in another person's body. I love the taste of cock. Mutual sucking is really something special. It can prolong orgasm indefinitely. I could suck for hours (69)."

DO MEN LIKE PERFORMING FELLATIO TO ORGASM?

"Do you enjoy, or would you like to try, performing fellatio on another man? What do you, or would you, like or dislike about it?"

Answers in this section are not only from men who consider themselves "homosexual"; other men also answered, offering opinions regarding experiences they had had, or their thoughts about how they would feel about such an experience with another man. Nineteen percent of "non-gay" men had had fellatio with another man, either as a boy with another boy, or at some time in their lives.

Most men who had tried performing fellatio were extremely enthusiastic about it, although not all mentioned whether they liked to do it to orgasm:

"I like giving head. It makes me feel as if I'm part of him. I like the smell of him, and my face in his pubic hair is comforting. I don't hesitate to swallow the semen, since it has a taste of the sea."

"I enjoy and will continue to enjoy both sides of fellatio with another man. Physically it feels great to have a hard throbbing cock in my mouth with my chin and lips pressed against his pubic hair and my hands pressing his body right up against my face. Someone's sexual essence in my mouth is like having the person's entire beauty in my mouth—very intimate—unexplainably beautiful."

"I enjoy it very much. I like it because I love cock, especially that of the person I love. I love the feel of it—the look of it, the smell of it. I love it because it is part of the person I love and it is so easy to make him happy that way."

"I enjoy it and I have engaged in it many times—especially with those I really care about and love. It is the ultimate in mental and spiritual communication of one's feelings and caring. I can never understand why any man thinks it is fine for a woman to engage in such an activity, but not for him to do it with a man or to have a man do it with him. Being against fellatio with a man is not loving one's own body nor the body which God created as good."

"In a way, I feel like I *need* to get fucked in the mouth or ass. It's receiving—which I need just as much as ejaculating."

"I like the feeling of his dick sliding down my throat, and the jerking movement a man's dick makes when he comes in my throat."

"I enjoy fellating other men purely on a physical level. I like the feeling of the penis in my mouth, the idea that it is taboo, and the control I have over him (in the sense that I am giving him pleasure and that his pleasure depends upon my actions on his penis—which is the symbol of his manhood, identity as a person). The jerking, throbbing of the penis in my mouth during ejaculation, the warmth of the fluid in a copious discharge (I don't like the bitter taste of some semen), and the knowledge that I have brought about the orgasm are extremely satisfying."

"That's my favorite activity—I even prefer it over being sucked off. I enjoy the taste. I would consider non-consumption of his cum as a lack of acceptance of his whole being. It's simply part of the act—the natural result."

Some said it would depend on the partner:

"I certainly enjoy taking the active role in fellatio but only with a fellow that I am attracted to. I would not do it to just anybody and I'd hate to be forced to do it. While doing it, my penis gets so hard that it hurts. At times I masturbate while doing it, and when I have my orgasm, I feel that I want to swallow his penis whole. I guess this can be described as feeling 'I'm gonna blow my mind.' "

"I like it if it is with an emotional partner rather than a physical partner. Caressing and fondling are important contributions during oral stimulation (by both parties)."

"I like the sight, feel, and taste of him and his sperm. It's beautiful, its size is hard and great. But it's him, not his penis I love."

"I enjoy it when I get exceptionally turned on or if I am emotionally involved. I don't like it when I'm only moderately turned on and when I have no emotional involvement."

"If the person is someone I particularly like, a cock down one's throat is one of the most comforting things I have ever experienced. As I fear claustrophobia, or being deprived of freedom, this is a paradox I can't explain."

Some men who had performed fellatio expressed mixed or negative feelings about swallowing the ejaculate:

"I enjoy giving fellatio. I swallow the seminal fluid. In most cases I like it. I did once get and swallow a mouthful that was more bitter than any other I had had but I swallowed it anyway. I think it's an act of courtesy to swallow it after giving fellatio."

"Sometimes I enjoy giving a man fellatio. I don't usually swallow the semen, sometimes it is quite bitter."

"I love sucking men. I think it's not satisfying to the man if you don't take the cum. It's a form of rejection not to take the cock when it is at its peak, so I always try to keep it in my mouth. It doesn't always taste the greatest, it depends on the man and whether he has good hygiene. But some cum tastes great. I highly recommend it."

"I enjoy giving fellatio and I swallow the fluid. As to liking it, yes and no. It depends on the person's bodily chemistry. There is a chemical in the fluid that makes it peppery-tasting and sometimes it can be quite strong and sort of burn in your throat. Other people have rather sweet-tasting fluid. It varies."

"I like giving head and I like swallowing the seminal fluid. Anyway, I think it's squirrely to spit it out. It's part of life (and has few calories)."

"Only if I really love the partner do I swallow the fluid."
"Fellatio is O.K. only if he wears a rubber!"

A few men who had not tried giving fellatio said they would like to:

"I would like to try fellatio on my own terms, mainly to know what the feelings are to fellate a beautiful hard penis. I would prefer to fellate my own penis but since this has been found to be impossible it would have to be a guy with a cock essentially like mine. I think my cock is beautiful and extremely enticing and I have seen none in my long years that can match its beauty, even though I have seen bigger, fatter, smaller, etc. It would be strictly a sexual act of myself and a cock and the cock alone. The person would not come into the act."

"I could do it if it was with someone I really cared about, and I have two people in mind when I say that, but I would have to be sure that they would enjoy it. I don't think I would find it really sexually exciting to do but it would definitely be an intimate way to show someone your feelings. I would be comfortable doing it if I knew that the other person was comfortable having me do it. Some men have very strong feelings about homosexuality. But if you love someone and want to express it, what does sex have to do with it? What I'm talking about is the physical expression of an emotion."

"I know what I would like—and therefore think I could really please another man with a great blow job. I'd like to try."

A few men who had tried it only once or twice expressed mixed feelings:

"I have done fellatio on another man. The pleasure seemed far more psychological than physical. It seemed *interesting* to have a penis in my mouth but not strongly pleasurable—it made my jaw hurt. The psychological pleasure came from participating in male sexuality in a way different from what I myself can experience; same sex, different body, new perspective."

"I have performed fellatio on a man. I like the male body but I am a well-trained male of my society. I feel guilty admiring men's nude bodies, even aesthetically. After I performed fellatio and had it done to me by a man, I felt sheepish and immature like an adolescent. Although I feel sexual affection between men can be a healthy part of one's total sexual experience, for me I just found it depressing. I am suppressing my interest in men until I can deal with it without the subsequent loss of self-esteem."

"I have tried it once. I barely put his penis in my mouth and it wasn't what I thought it would be like. It was saltier than I thought it would be, and I wasn't relaxed enough to truly try it. I have received blow jobs from other men on two widely separated occasions. Both times were essentially experiments. I have less desire to try fellatio now than before I tried, however feeble the attempt was."

Others said they had such mixed feelings that they would not try it even though it sounded interesting:

"I would like to fellate a man and have a man do fellatio to me. But I will never do it, because although this would be a wonderful physical experience (probably *the* best, if he loved·me), I know it is not for me. I know that I would become emotionally involved with a man who would give me such intense physical pleasure and I do not *choose* to feel this way for a man. I wish I could separate sex from my feelings, because then I could enjoy superb sex, wallow in the pleasure of some man really *loving* me, which would be extremely satisfying. No woman could give me the equivalent pleasure because I would have to train, train, train her!"

"Given the fact that I enjoy fellatio with a woman, if I were not uptight about it, I'd probably like fellatio with a man just as much. I'd like to try it on him, too. But it would mean starting a whole new life style and I don't have the time."

But most non-gay men gave a violent No!!!! to the whole idea:

"I would not and could not perform fellatio with another man. That is *queer* and *sinful*. God didn't put people on His earth to do that. It's nasty."

"I regard any type of sexual activity with another man as repulsive, totally *abnormal* and *unnatural*—in the extreme —*depraved*. Only the mentally retarded or borderline mental cases must be so inclined."

"No! Would you like to suck on the penis of a bull, a

pig, a dog, or an elephant? Why not? I wouldn't want to suck a man's penis any more than a dog's ear, or a horse's tail! What the hell for?"

"I don't enjoy even thinking about fellatio with another man. No way. It's about as interesting to think of as taking a swim in a septic tank. I can't explain what I dislike about it—it's just the social conditioning I've experienced, no doubt. Sex between two women is beautiful to think about, but between two men it's revolting and disgusting especially if I'm involved in the image. I hold no ill feeling about anyone who likes it—if it feels good do it if they're consenting adults (or juniors for that matter)."

"Gross me out. I am a complete heterosexual."

"It's against God's laws—immoral and disgusting. 'Women were created for men.'"

"Physically it wouldn't bother me but I could never consider a man as a loving partner. Men just don't give a shit about each other."

WHAT KINDS OF FELLATIO DO MEN LIKE?

The ways men liked to be stimulated during fellatio varied greatly—which may not be surprising if we recall the variety of types of stimulation men described in the section on masturbation:

"The way that turns me on most is to have it done so I can watch. However, I don't remain passive very long, and usually end up wrapping my legs around her and and caressing her hair and shoulders while thrusting myself into her mouth."

"Fellatio is superb when the tongue tip touches the frenulum. It makes me crazy."

"I am usually on my back, legs spread, and she is crouched between my legs. My knees are bent or pulled up. Sometimes she not only tongues me but also works my shaft up and down—especially if she's tired and wants to bring me off sooner—which is super-O.K. with me! She keeps busy, moving the shaft, sucking, and with her other fingers she caresses, pokes, and strokes my anal area. My anus is extremely sensitive and she will dart her tongue over it too which sends me into orbit."

"How? As lasciviously as possible."

"I like her to start slowly, licking my balls and licking, kissing, and sucking my penis all over. During the course of fellatio I like her to rub my penis all over her face. I like to feel my penis growing harder in her mouth while she just holds it. I like to be sucked more firmly on the up stroke than the down. When I am coming I like to simply have my penis in her mouth firmly but most women think it feels better if they suck harder. Maybe it does, but it also drives me crazy and makes me somewhat uncomfortable."

"I like it when she holds my mushroom in her mouth, her hand up against me holding and squeezing my balls. Just the right amount of pressure needs to be exerted on the area just below the mushroom, and this is not usually possible with the mouth—thus the need to put her hand there too. It's also important to know that she really enjoys it (she says she loves my dick). To know that she is doing it because *she* wants to—that really turns me on."

"I like it done with a lot of sucktion. *Artistically.* Also, no blow job is at its best without a lot of attention to the balls."

"I am difficult to bring off by mouth because of my need for pressure along the full shaft. With my partner's hand moving over the base of the shaft and his mouth over the head, orgasm is more easily achieved."

"I like her to caress my nipples or hold my buttocks while she does it. Put her mouth on it and suck and lick the underside. Then when I orgasm and come I want her to swallow that and keep sucking and licking it clean. That's love!"

"I like her to remain passive, lying under me with me 'fucking her in the mouth' and pushing my member in as deeply as possible."

"I like to have my penis very wet and a firm but gentle mouthing of the entire length at first . . . As orgasm approaches, my partner should concentrate on the head alone with firmer sucking and tonguing motions. It also adds to the pleasure if he uses one hand at the base of my penis and masturbates me. As I begin to ejaculate, I enjoy a well-lubricated index finger penetrating my rectum."

"Many partners have seemed unsure about how to give good head. It is a stereotyped idea that they have to suck the whole penis and stick it down their throat. The most important thing about good head is that they enjoy doing it, and be loving, curious, and playful, regardless of what it is they do."

MANUAL STIMULATION OF THE PENIS BY A PARTNER

MEN'S FEELINGS ABOUT BEING STIMULATED BY HAND

"Do you like manual stimulation of your penis by a partner? Do you often orgasm this way?"

Many men said they loved to be caressed and fondled on their genitals—penis and testicles, and also thighs and buttock area—as part of foreplay or caressing:

"It feels nice when my partner strokes my penis. I like it a lot. It gives me a cozy feeling, a feeling of total acceptance and comfortability. I'm ready to give myself more to her then."

"I love light, caressing stimulation, especially with her hand extending to my testicles, every now and then. Once I get started, all of the area around my genitals becomes sensitive."

"I enjoy just having my penis held by my partner's hand, or having her touch my penis as we happen to pass each other around the house."

"I like her to hold and massage my testicles. This gives me a very firm erection for intercourse."

"Once, years ago, I had a gorgeous girlfriend who used to just run her hands and fingers all over my penis and balls, and my thighs, sometimes pressing, sometimes teasing—while we were just lounging around, talking, etc. I felt she really loved me. She made me feel really good."

But most men felt women were uninterested in touching their genitals and/or unskilled at stimulating them with their hand:

"I like it but I almost always have to ask her to do it, she rarely comes up with the idea."

"I like to be touched on the penis, but it seems few women know how to or even want to."

"Sure, I like it, but sometimes a woman has a tendency to do it too fast or she holds it too hard and causes pain."

"I feel awkward about her manually stimulating my penis. I feel like she doesn't like or want it."

"I like her to touch my penis but she rarely will. After sex therapy last year she would touch it and fondle it gently after touching me all over. But now we quit that and she hasn't touched it for over a year."

"Most of my partners grudgingly rub me a minute or two, as if they feel they 'should'—rarely does their hand stray below the top or middle of my penis. Heaven forbid that they reach on down and grab my sweaty, hairy balls! (That would be too good to be true.) Another thing, they don't caress me *hard* enough—as if they don't want to get too involved."

However, as seen earlier, recognition and affection shown to a man's genitals in this way had an important psychological significance for many men—that is, it brought about a feeling of acceptance:

"I love when she touches me deliberately for her own pleasure. When she touches my penis, I feel she accepts my body and understands our physical differences. I also feel she loves me."

"It's very nice to feel a different touch than my own and it makes me feel wanted."

"I love it when she holds and fondles me. It's not the kind of thing that we could do if we're not feeling really loving towards each other, like when we're not getting along. I couldn't imagine somebody masturbating me that I didn't like, or that I felt really alienated from. When she does it I know she's feeling very loving and loves all of me."

Or lack of it brought a feeling of rejection or alienation:

"It's not too important, except that my wife never touches me. I guess she doesn't want to. I would prefer a partner who liked to touch and feel it in a nice sexy way. After all, it's part of me too."

"I like my sweetheart to stimulate me in every way she will, but she doesn't explore my genital area. It's quite a complex mechanism and the root of the shaft gets unbelievably engorged even inside my body . . . Why doesn't she like it?"

Still, some men felt a woman fondling their genitals was being too "forward" and usurping the male prerogative of being the "aggressor":

"What am I supposed to do while she's doing that? Lie back and look sweet? I think it's silly, all this talk about how the woman's gonna be the aggressive one, she's gonna make love to *me*—I never knew a woman who could do it as good as I can, for starters, and anyway, I don't want to have some female pushing me down on the bed while she does her thing with my body."

"I don't mind if she has her hand down there, just touching me, but I don't want to be worked over, with her trying to make me come just by her efforts alone. I *like* feeling I'm the one handling things, that I'm going to show her just how much pleasure she can have."

One man described a fear of having another person in control of his body:

"It seems to me that one of the reasons certain men don't get as much pleasure from a woman fondling their genitals as they get from masturbating themselves is a deep (and hidden) fear—the same kind of fear that expresses itself in disgust of the vagina or other kinds of castration anxiety. To have the penis in the control of another person may be appealing and pleasurable in many ways, but it also can be inhibiting—particularly to the kind of man with a profound distrust of his own potential passivity."

Very few men said women knew how to stimulate them to orgasm. In fact, most heterosexual men had very little experience with being manually stimulated to orgasm by a partner:

"I like manual stimulation of my penis by my wife and she does this sometimes if I ask, by way of foreplay. I remember only twice when I orgasmed this way."

"The few times she's stimulated me by hand it's been in the shower and I got sore before I orgasmed."

"I have been manually stimulated to orgasm only twice. Once, quite by accident, when I was in the hospital and my girlfriend was stroking my penis through the covers. Rather unexpectedly I ejaculated. The other time was when a girlfriend and I were in the shower. She soaped me up and continued washing my penis to ejaculation."

"I've never been stimulated to orgasm by my female partner."

"I never orgasmed this way. I never really enlightened them on it. I was a little embarrassed to get analytical about it, because it was like masturbating. I didn't think they could possibly know how to do it well, even if I did try to explain."

"Women usually don't know how to provide stimulation manually, just as men usually don't know the best way to manipulate a woman's clitoris."

"I orgasm this way occasionally but it lacks real excitement because most persons are not familiar with how to do it. I like it with soft squeezes. *No rough* stroking. Some women think it is a piece of wood for carving or something. They don't realize how sensitive my best buddy is."

"I do not care much for manual stimulation of my penis by someone else, they just do not do it right. It is either too roughly done or not held properly for the skin to come up over the head to spread the lubrication. Most men I know feel the same way."

"It is hard to show her how to do it right. But it's fun trying. The girl who can even approach my own expertise in giving me a hand job does not exist."

"Most of my partners do not know how and are not anxious to learn. Most partners think that their hand wrapped around the shaft is good enough and are hesitant to put their hand close to the end or head of the penis."

"My experience has been that women think lightning-quick jerking is what's called for, and stop because they get tired."

"My wife refuses to do this because she thinks it will excite me to the point where she will be 'cheated' out of an orgasm when we get around to intercourse."

"Girls usually don't move their hands fast enough when they whack off a guy. Maybe they think they will hurt it or are embarrassed. Actually the cock can take a good beating—excuse the pun. Girls should be firmer with a cock."

"Most girls treat it like a rope in a gym and damn near either pull it off or rub it away, so I usually don't like it."

"I guess I would enjoy having a woman stimulate me up to a point. But actually, I don't need her to mess around with me—I'm hard anyway. Maybe she would pull it the wrong way and hurt me—or cause me to lose my erection by tickling me. I'd rather play with her—she's the one who needs the work, anyway. Then I finish inside her."

In fact, these answers sound very similar to what women in
The Hite Report *said about men giving manual clitoral stimu-*
lation. As one man said:

"It seems women have as much trouble with stimulating
penises as men have with stimulating clitorises."

But a few men had found women to be good at manual
stimulation to orgasm:

"My partner is the first woman I've met who could masturbate me. She's beautiful. Don't ask me why, but her touch
is right, her stroke is right, her timing's right, and I'll come
every time."

"My wife does this better than any woman I ever knew.
She has a delicate touch I've never experienced before."

"I love manual stimulation and my wife is a master at
it. She can stroke a penis in more ways (as well as scrotum
and surrounding area) than I thought possible."

"She lies down, her full body cuddled next to mine, her
lips on my neck or my ear, and I am kissing her, and then
she rubs my balls very lightly until I am aching with desire
and then slowly, very slowly, she starts to touch my hole, the
top of my penis, where a drop of fluid is coming out—and
then she starts to stimulate my cock, up and down, up and
down, gripping more and more firmly, kissing me harder,
saying 'Ed, Ed I love you . . . I love you . . .'—and I come.
We have developed this as I am a disabled vet and can have
my best orgasms this way."

"When my wife first masturbated me it was just a wild
experience that added a new dimension and enhanced my love
for masturbation. I wish my wife would masturbate me more
than she does. Also, my looking at her masturbating is a
tremendous turn-on for me and this is a basis for my fantasies when I masturbate alone. There is just something
fascinating about it all."

Men knew how to stimulate another man more easily;* as
one man said, "I like manual stimulation, but only a man
seems to know how to bring off another man." But even men
giving manual stimulation to another man often could not
duplicate the perfect stimulation a man could give himself:

* See also chapter 7.

"Some men I have no trouble coming with, but lots of times I have to reach down and help jerk myself off at some point during sex because they're just not doing it right."

"I have been told that I am good when I masturbate others, at least they have liked it. It may be said that I give good hand! I find when others have tried to masturbate me, their grip is too loose, their strokes are too indifferent, and the rhythm is not steady."

"Nothing illustrates the point more clearly that only you know what's best for you. I can stimulate myself to orgasm three times faster and more pleasurably than he can."

Still, as one man said:

"My partner often beats me off and I love it. Even though he does not do it exactly as right as I do it when I masturbate, my orgasms when he does it are twice as good."

HOW DO MEN LIKE THEIR GENITALS TO BE TOUCHED?

In men's descriptions of how they would like a partner to stimulate them manually, there was no set formula; the needs of different men are quite individual and vary considerably:

"What I like best is a light touching of my inner thighs, a light touching of the hairs on my balls, a light touching (almost teasing) of my penis, and a hand around my hard-on moving the skin gently up and down the shaft so the skin of my uncircumcised penis covers and uncovers the head of my penis at a moderate speed. I also like manual stimulation mixed with fellatio."

"I like it done slowly and gently—primarily at the top of the penis and around the rim."

"I like manual stimulation, especially if he holds the skin tightly enough that the skin slips over the internal structure. Otherwise, the touch must be fairly light, with an open hand, usually on the bottom of the penis."

"I like to be touched with a medium to light pressure, stroking with her fingertips buried softly in the skin below the rim, letting the surface of her fingers rub a little on my penis at the same time."

"I like her to touch, push, squeeze, and run her fingers up and down my penis as they are wrapped around it. I do not like too much stimulation directly on the glans penis as I orgasm too quickly and only locally at that spot, not reaching a full arousal."

"It feels best if it's prolonged, with very light, teasing touches along the underside of the penis."

"I need definite rhythm with a strong grip, slowly."

"It feels best if the skin of the penis is rubbed over its head very gently but firmly and regularly until to the point of ejaculation. And with open-mouth kissing at the same time, that feels best."

"It feels best if lots of lubricant is used and if most attention is paid to the glans region, gripping the penis like one would grip a baseball bat."

"It's better when I'm on my side, and he leans over me from behind. This way he can begin stroking along my thighs and move over my testicles, right up my prick. It's exciting anticipating when his hand will arrive at the right spot."

"A very soft, gentle playing up and down my penis with the tips of the fingers at first, then slower, more deliberate and firmer touching with the whole hand. The absolute best is when his fingertips are firmly pressing on one particular spot near the middle of the underneath side of my penis, just at the moment that I come."

In general, it would seem that men like gentle touching for arousal, but need a stronger or more steady and often precise stimulation to reach actual orgasm.

Many men also stressed the importance of having their testicles caressed and touched:

"What I especially like is soft stroking of my balls, sort of tickling the hairs."

"I like her to touch my entire genitals for pleasure, especially the scrotum."

"Talk about going through the ceiling, that will drive you crazy: her tickling your testicles either with her hand or something else while you jerk off."

"I like her to suck my testicles at the same time because it's so warm."

"I do enjoy having her play around with her finger in the area between my anus and scrotum—that's a hot spot!"

"I like my wife holding my bag while I hold both her 38's."

"If a girl wants to make a guy orgasm quick she should play with his balls. He won't be able to control himself."

"I enjoy having it done slowly and gently while my testicles are being played with and there is a great deal of suggestive sexual talk."

"I like a lot of attention to my balls. Most women seem so involved with the penis that they forget, if they understand at all, that the balls are the essential male organ for both sperm and hormones. Orgasm depends on the balls, not the cock. Balls are important to all sexuality, are highly erogenous, and of much ego concern to males."

MASTURBATING WITH A PARTNER

"Do you enjoy masturbating with another person present?"

Since it is so difficult for another person to know just how to stimulate a man manually to orgasm, men might enjoy stimulating themselves at times when with another person. However, most men (especially heterosexual men) said they had rarely or never done this:

"I have not masturbated with anyone present."

"We have never masturbated in each other's presence. I don't think I could enjoy it."

"It feels best if I do it, but I never do in front of a girl."

"I may have done it a few times with the other boys when I was younger, but I would never do it now."

However, some did enjoy it, and were very enthusiastic about it:

"I enjoy having my partner watch as I play with myself, and it is absolutely fantastic if she will play with me at the same time. Doing this, I feel very close to her and satisfied."

"Sometimes I orgasm when I masturbate while receiving anal penetration. It used to embarrass me to do this until I did some very deliberate work on my own sexual attitudes.

I even photographed myself masturbating, and through looking at the pictures desensitized myself to embarrassment about
it so that now I can share it with her."

*And one man found masturbation with his wife had greatly
improved their marriage:*

"As I am on the road a lot away from home for weeks
at a time, my wife accused me of going out with other women.
But I honestly can say I never did, because I masturbated
instead. One time I got mad at her for accusing me and told
her to sit at the foot of the bed and stay there silently watching me. I proceeded to masturbate myself like I usually do
while this time she was watching me and did not realize that
I did it every day even when we did have intercourse to satisfaction. She sat there watching with a fascinated look on her
face, never seen a man masturbate himself or my having
anyone watch me, turned us both on very strongly. Later, she
told me that she masturbated men before but never saw what
actually was happening to a man's body during the process
because she was either kissing him or looking into his eyes.
This time she was just observing and seeing how a man can
enjoy himself without having intercourse. How he gets excited,
how his testicles shrink and harden and move up toward his
body at the excitement stage and finally the ejaculation where
she made a remark how high I shot up into the air. To me
this was also very exciting and one of my most intense ejaculations I had ever experienced in my life, that I was even surprised. From this moment on, she knew I have not cheated
on her. Our sex life improved all the time. When she was
not in the mood she wanted me to masturbate in front of her
whenever I had the desire and always was as fascinated as the
first time and I at the same time was just as excited in being
able to share with her."

Pressure to follow the pattern of "sex" is so strong, and the
status accorded to intercourse so great, that self-stimulation
with a partner is considered rather unacceptable. And yet
men (and women) are able to have such strong orgasms from
stimulating themselves, and sharing this activity with another
person is so deeply intimate, that it would seem to be a good
way of relating to each other from time to time. Sharing
masturbation with a partner could bring about one of the
deepest forms of change in our definition of sexual relations.

MASTURBATION

"I have more or less two sex lives, one with my wife and one with myself. I have masturbated for many years, but I now enjoy masturbation very much with no guilt (that I can consciously identify). I hope to discuss this with my wife someday, but free as I think I am with her, I can't bring myself to that point yet. I get pleasures that are deeply solitary, 'forbidden' so to say, from masturbating, that are different from person-to-person lovemaking. I make love to myself. Most men won't admit that. But it's been a gradual lessening of guilt. I still have, in fact they're stronger, definite religious feelings. But I have now accommodated my religious feelings with my sexuality, and no area is more important here than masturbation. I find masturbation very healthy to my sexuality. I'm more in tune with my body and a better lover as a result of feeling freer, less guilty."

DO MOST MEN MASTURBATE?

When asked, "How often do you masturbate?" almost all men, whether married or single, with or without an otherwise active sex life, said they made masturbation a regular part of their lives:

"I have masturbated since I can remember—began probably around eight or ten. Now at thirty-five I masturbate on the average of four times a week. It almost always leads to orgasm because I stick to it until it does."

"I don't masturbate any set number of times, just when something stirs my imagination or I just get an itchy sensation. About two times every ten days to two weeks."

"When alone, I usually masturbate about every day, or ten to eleven times a week."

"I enjoy masturbation, especially physically. Sometimes I feel a tinge of guilt about it when I haven't had sex with my wife for a few days, but nothing serious. I masturbate about five times a week."

"I probably masturbate one a week. Some weeks I don't at all and another week I may do it two or three times depending on how horny I am or how horny she isn't. In the back of my mind I'm probably thinking it's more fun because of the danger of getting caught."

"If I'm not seeing a woman I masturbate one to two times per day. Weekends can be as much as six."

"Once or twice a week. I enjoy those intimate moments alone with my body and dreams. I am pleased and satisfied."

"I was taught that masturbation was bad, and that there were only a thousand orgasms doled out to each person and not to waste them. I have found both to be untrue. On the average I masturbate two or three times a week, and have even all during my married life for twenty years."

"I masturbate once a day, even with regular sex. I consider it sexual exercise."

"I don't really enjoy masturbation. I much prefer actual intercourse, but sometimes out of loneliness, frustration, or sleeplessness I feel it is necessary to maintain my sanity. It's a rush, but psychologically I feel disgusted for not having more self-control. I didn't consciously masturbate until I was nineteen. The first time was during a three-month hospital ordeal after a surfing accident. I was guilty and scared. I didn't know how to do it properly without hurting myself. I know now how foolish I was (I'm twenty-five). Now I masturbate maybe a dozen times in the course of the month, especially in the summer."

"I enjoy masturbation immensely, but in moderation— about once every ten or twelve days. It helps me come to terms with my own sexual makeup and what turns me on, and I always have a hearty orgasm."

"I masturbate from four to ten times per week. I enjoy it more than I used to. I used to be ashamed of it but I am beginning to get in touch with the idea that my body is just fine and it's fine to feel sexual and sensuous about me. Soon I hope to be able to masturbate and enjoy it with my wife watching."

Only 1 percent of the men who answered did not masturbate:

"The premise of this question is unacceptable. I know what the books say, but I have never masturbated, that is, never brought myself to orgasm. I have sometimes played with my penis, stroked it, manipulated it, but without much pleasure. And I have never felt the need to complete such an act just to prove to myself that I can do it. Perhaps I may someday. I have no scruples about it. It simply doesn't interest me."

"I don't masturbate and never have. Other than exploratory touching when I was a child and some recent stroking to discover what I like or what excites me—because I never knew before—and it didn't lead to orgasm. I've read a number of statistical studies on it and noted the degree of masturbation in men and women but I never have. Perhaps I'm just that different. There does exist a moral inhibition based on religion or religious education that may be pretty strong within me. I've never felt the urge."

And two men said they could not masturbate to orgasm:

"Sigh. Masturbation is a hang-up with me. Intellectually I see nothing wrong with it, but unconsciously I must feel otherwise. I *cannot* masturbate to orgasm. It just doesn't work. For this reason I don't try very often. It still feels good, but it's frustrating. I guess I try once every two or three months when I haven't been having sex and am very horny."

"In all my twenty-nine years, I can't remember a time where I've orgasmed from masturbating. I'd sure like to. Maybe I don't do it right. Maybe I'm not patient enough. Since I've had a steady partner for the last nine years and a good sexual relationship I guess I really haven't had to."

HOW DO MEN MASTURBATE? WHERE DO MEN STIMULATE THEMSELVES BESIDES THE PENIS?

There is a wealth of detailed material offered in these answers. In fact, the question "How do you masturbate?" brought out some of the longest and most specific answers of any of the questions. This is important material because there is very little general understanding of some of the things men enjoy, particularly the importance of anal and scrotal stimulation. Many men uninhibitedly touch themselves in many ways during masturbation that they do not feel free to do or ask for during sex with a partner. In addition, many men's answers contain a great sense of freedom, fun, and pleasure.

Where do men stimulate themselves besides the penis?

One of the most important facts to emerge from the responses to this question is the importance to many men of stimulating areas other than or in addition to the penis. Most men at times accompanied their masturbation with stimulation of their testicles, anus, or other generalized body stimulation.

A significant and often overlooked fact is the importance to men of massaging the testicles and entire genital area, in addition to the penis; 37 percent of the men who answered mentioned including this in their masturbation:

"With both hands, lying down or standing, I touch my balls, rub or squeeze them, or push them back up in me. Both the head of the penis and balls and my feet, butt, hole, stomach—all are stimulating."

"The base of the penis is especially sensitive on the lower side, where the sac (I don't like that grating word 'scrotum') joins it. This is the area which feels so good when you thrust your penis as far into a woman as is possible for you. The sac itself and the cords of the balls are responsive to this pressure. I often place my free hand beside the base of my penis and along the left side of the sac, and just touching the sensitive area where the anus is located through which the cords (or tubes) from the balls go in to join the prostate and internal tubes."

"It is almost impossible for me to masturbate satisfactorily if I am not simultaneously holding my testicles in my left hand. I use my right hand, moving up and down, on my penis."

"I like to keep something (wadded T-shirt) between my legs. This stimulates my scrotum and inner thighs."

"I usually masturbate in bed lying on my left side. I like to roll up my pajamas and hold them between my legs to increase the pressure against my testicles."

"Sometimes rather than placing my hand on my scrotum, I will take my two middle fingers and rub them up and down over the skin between the two testicles, separating the two testicles with this motion and just rubbing up and down between them."

"As I arrive at ejaculation, I place my left palm on my scrotum, and jiggle it up and down at the same rate my right hand is going up and down on my penis."

"When I near climax I scrunch up the sheet and blankets between my legs under the scrotum and give a good squeeze with my legs so that pressure comes to bear."

"I press a pillow between my legs on my balls."

"I like my testicles pulled between my legs."

"I like one of my balls to receive a little sensation or slight pressure by being between my thighs while jacking off."

Some men mentioned that the area between the scrotum and the anus is also quite sensitive:

"I touch myself in the crease where my balls meet my legs. Touching is very important in that crease."

"I need pressure on the skin between the scrotum and the anus."

"Sometimes I press on the tube behind my balls while I'm ejaculating—that has a nice feeling."

"I place my left hand with the thumb at the base of the penis to be able to stroke the skin between the scrotum and the asshole."

An equally important finding is how pleasurable anal penetration is to many men; 24 percent of the men who answered sometimes included anal penetration in their masturbation; another 23 percent also often used exterior anal stimulation (see also pages 515–38):

"I use the middle finger of my left hand to massage my prostate gland in the anus while masturbating my penis with my right hand."

"Sometimes while in the shower I slip one or two (or more) fingers of my left hand up my rectum and move them, usually in a wiggling motion, while I stroke my penis with the right hand. I move my fingers towards the front of my body while they are inside of me, because it feels best there (maybe that's where the prostate is). The orgasm, a crashing, intense one, is centered in my body where the fingers were moving. (There is very little sensation in my penis.) When I come, I can feel something swelling against my fingers. It's kind of exciting. I've tried using anal stimulation alone, but it seems that I can't orgasm without stroking my penis too."*

* This sounds very similar to descriptions women gave of feeling extreme pleasure from vaginal stimulation, feeling almost, almost, almost as if they would reach orgasm, but not being quite able to get there without clitoral stimulation.

"I like to stimulate myself all up and down my penis and scrotum and between the scrotum and rectum. Sometimes I stick my finger in my rectum, and that gives a harder quality to my orgasm . . . shakes me up more."

"My wife has a vibrator which I use. I insert the vibrator in my anal canal, then put plenty of saliva on the head of my penis and take the head in one hand while moving the vibrator in a forward/backward motion. I always climax immediately."

"I've found that rubbing and stroking my anus gives me a faster and harder erection, and many times a powerful ejaculation and orgasm. When I do this I usually lubricate my finger with Vaseline or cream so that my finger can slide in and out of my anus."

"The head of the penis seems to be the center of the stimulation, but I get very aroused if I insert my finger in my anus and massage my prostate—which causes a deeper, fuller orgasm, and is wonderful."

"Lightly touching only the hairs around my anus and scrotum is one of the best things."

"If I'm stuck, frustrated, or feeling particularly crazy, I put Vaseline on my cock, pull with my left hand, and put a lubricated finger of my right hand into my ass. I've tried using surrogate cocks and fucking myself as I masturbated, and these orgasms have been the most powerful I've ever had. The climax is strong and long."

"I spread my legs wide, bend the knees and draw my thighs up to my chest and play with my asshole while masturbating. I get tremendously excited fingering my ass. Sometimes I dildo myself with whatever's available. I masturbate my ass until I can't stand it any longer then grip my penis and jack to orgasm."

"I often place my finger down at the opening of my rectum with Vaseline on it, and massage the opening, inserting one or two fingers as deep inside as I can reach. This is highly stimulating, and accelerates the climax. As the contractions of the orgasm start, my fingers are forced outwards from the rectum to near the opening. I finish a very powerful orgasm by rubbing the rectum and spreading the sperm over the penis until all the contractions are over."

"The most enjoyable way I masturbate is by placing a pillow and blanket on my cellar floor if I am in my basement, with a rubber dildo shaped exactly like a penis. I am fully dressed in case someone in the house would come down. I usually stand up away from the steps, and read some porno.

I open my fly and reach in and place the head of the dildo at my rectal opening, and lean back on my workbench, which is just the right height. This maintains the position and attitude as I slowly start a rotating motion with my buttocks to force it in. The feeling is out of this world and is tremendously exciting. I then lay down on the floor on my right side, holding the dildo as deep as possible, and slowly fuck my hand. The combined sensation is mind-blowing. I gently rotate the dildo, increasing the tempo as the orgasm approaches. I am at a fever pitch and I don't feel like I am on this planet. At the climax, the dildo is drawn deep into my rectum, and stays there throughout the climax, until I start pulling it out. This type of orgasm leaves me completely satiated and weak. I rest much longer, and feel very exhilarated when I get up. The next day after the rectal orgasm, I feel very horny, and sometimes masturbate again at work."

And one other similar answer:

"My very first feelings of erotic pleasure when I was about five years old were when I would receive enemas when I was constipated. I would get strong erections and pleasurable sensual feelings in my throat and a rush of blood to my head. Then around the age of twelve I was introduced to masturbation by a school chum. I would then masturbate to orgasm regularly, almost every day, although I did not yet ejaculate. After that I would combine self-administered enemas with masturbation, which to this day have been the most sensual, explosive, and exciting orgasms I have had. I say this even though I have a relatively regular sex life with my wife— we are married sixteen years, and I am the father of four. About two times a month I lie on my back on the bed or a soft bathroom rug and give myself a full warm enema. Other times I will pull a lubricated condom over the rectal syringe tip and insert the full length of the tip into my anus. As the condom slowly fills with water it presses against my prostate gland and also feels like a full enema. My penis, which is fully erect by now and fully engorged, is almost ready to explode with an orgasm. I then lubricate my hand with K-Y jelly. I put my hand on my penis and gently rub up and down, usually around the glans area. My heart begins to pound harder, my throat seems to constrict, I almost stop breathing and my mouth opens wide. At the same time there is a rush of blood to my head and my balls pull in tightly against my lower penis. Then my penis begins to orgasm and ejaculate in powerful streams of come. The sensations emanating from my pelvic area sweep over my entire body in waves of pleasure. I gasp for breath to refill my lungs. A warm glow covers me and I just lie there—my heart slowing down—my breathing quieting—in relaxation. After a few minutes more I remove the syringe tip and condom and expel the water."

Although many men touched their testicles or anus, surprisingly, most men felt great shyness about caressing their own bodies in general, other than their genitals:

"I almost always do it lying on my back, holding the penis in my hand, and rubbing my hand up and down. Sometimes I may run my other hand over my stomach or thigh, as it is very sensual, but the narcissism of that frightens me."

"I never thought of touching myself anyplace other than my penis. I guess I always thought the point of masturbation was to 'get on with it,' or 'get the job done.' To stop and 'play with yourself' would be strange, especially if anybody knew you did it. Do other guys do it?"

But some men did give themselves more "foreplay":

"I love to fool around for hours. I am not a rabbit. I love being naked, and I massage the head of my prick with all kinds of creams, my nipples too. That's what arousal means to an old man who has time on his side with no regular partner. It's a sure thing when you're alone, no one to say *no*. I like to walk around naked with a good rod on. Where I live I can go outdoors anytime that way. I like to wave it in the air and feel the wind on it. If I get hot enough I can just caress the head gently and off it goes right there in the grass —just wonderful."

"When I am by myself and have time, I enjoy a slow, erotic type of masturbation. I lay back on my bed with a towel next to me, just gently caressing myself from my breasts to my thighs in long, soft strokes while I close my eyes and dream one of my fantasies, sometimes switching between several. I always like the lights off because then I don't get distracted or feel I am being watched. After I've become aroused, I start lightly stroking my balls and manipulating my penis in slow, long strokes. Moving slowly along my penis seems to deepen the clarity of sensations and vividness of images."

"It wasn't until about a year ago that I began touching myself in places other than my genitals. Since that time I've found spots on my body that are very sensitive that I didn't know were there, such as my breasts. Sometimes I kiss my shoulders, I stimulate my mouth and lips with my fingers, or hold a pillow in my arms to feel the fullness. I do to myself what I want women to do to me, and what I do to them."

"I completely disrobe and lie in bed on my back with half-closed eyes. I think of a situation with girls, then lightly rub one hand over the breasts, down over the belly, over the abdomen, rub around the hair, etc., to the base of the penis, down the inside of the thighs and back up to the crotch, then with feather-like touches with fingertips, gently caress the testicles. Then I rub the tip of my penis with my finger until there is some juice, then rub this down on my penis with my hand in long slow strokes until ejaculation on my belly."

Although popular stereotypes hold that men need and prefer to reach orgasm as quickly as possible (and that it is women who "make them wait"),* many men frequently enjoyed holding off orgasms during masturbation, increasing the pleasure by stopping and starting stimulation, prolonging the feelings:

"I love to masturbate slowly and deliberately and stop short of ejaculation several times. To me it's a very pleasant sensation. I bring myself as close as possible, then stop. When the peak subsides I slowly manipulate the top of the penis to regain and maintain the peak just under the ejaculatory state. Sometimes I stop there—after an hour or so—or else go on to a great orgasm."

"Sometimes I stop when I'm near coming, and start the whole process of getting excited again. I feel my balls and just behind them, my asshole, stomach, nipples, and press my groin, going gradually faster."

"When I masturbate I hold my penis at the base with one hand and stroke around the head with the other. I do this a while, then let my penis go to a semi-soft state, then start to rub it again. I like to do this for a long period of time before I come."

---

* Possibly the reason is that in this process of slow arousal men feel comfortable with the erection coming and going, but during sex with a partner, men feel they are under performance pressure to keep the erection up.

"I like sometimes to bring myself right to the edge and slow down. My penis throbs in expectation when I do that, and successive peaks seem higher and higher until orgasm."

"Sometimes it's fun to build it up and hold it, then let it go down, just to tantalize yourself and make you hungry like an animal."

And some men did not always masturbate for orgasm; sometimes it was simply for pleasure:

"Sometimes I beat my dick just 'cause it's hard."

"Sometimes I just want to play when I'm reading a book, or watching TV. It's less fattening than popcorn, and twice as handy."

"I masturbate differently all the time. Sometimes I 'come,' sometimes I don't; I love going to the woods and touching myself. I make love to the woods, the plants, the animals, the sky, the earth. I love to feel my genitals dangle freely! I hate underwear especially but all clothes are a hindrance except maybe very loose and baggy pants or something. I like to feel the wind, water, sun on me."

Some men enjoyed looking at themselves in the mirror:

"My favorite masturbation is kneeling on the bed, in front of a mirror. I love my body and like to watch it move as it does when I masturbate. I like to watch myself in the mirror. I like to see my erection and my whole genitalia bobble as I masturbate. I hold my penis with my right hand, erect shaft in closed hand, and pump up and down."

"Usually, I go into the bathroom and watch myself masturbating. When I come, I watch the ejaculate and how the rest of my body reacts. I find watching myself really interesting—greatly exciting. I used to feel guilty a long time ago but now I enjoy it. Still prefer making love with my wife. It's the real thing."

"Sometimes I stand in front of a mirror and slowly fondle my body with both hands. I wear stretch-type swimming trunks which exactly fit over my underpants. My swimming trunks are multicolored and glow under black light. I use a 15-watt black light and a 25-watt shaded bulb at a greater distance from the black light. This makes excellent lighting."

Types of masturbation

By far and away the most frequent form of masturbation for men is direct stimulation of the penis by hand. Most men accompanied this with some variations or additional actions, such as stimulating the testicles, penetrating the anus, or other generalized body stimulation. One point which is quite striking in this type of masturbation is that it almost never involves thrusting, as does intercourse, despite the fact that thrusting is often said to be a "biological" male "instinct." In masturbation, however, it is the hand that moves and rarely the body. It would therefore seem likely that thrusting during intercourse is due to the desire to cause an up-and-down motion on the penis—and not to any biological need to "mount and thrust" into a woman.

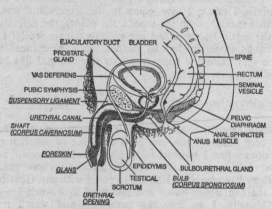

Parts of the penis system are underscored.

Here are men's descriptions of this type of masturbation:

"I masturbate in a number of ways. The usual way is the hand job, which I began masturbating by when I was eleven or twelve. I usually grip down at the base, gently, and stretch my cock very hard. I enjoy seeing it at full length very much and I enjoy the reddening of the glans. I am circumcised. Sometimes I just pull the skin tight down at the base and the tenseness and hardness makes me come, with only the subtlest motion of the hand. I usually watch myself in a mirror. When I release my hand, the cock 'springs' and the come shoots fairly vigorously. I enjoy doing it standing in front of a bathroom mirror by the sink, letting the come spill into the sink. I must emphasize, though, that it's the *base* of the cock I enjoy holding the most. I enjoy the smoothness and the texture and color. I fantasize a lot while doing all this and talk dirty to myself."

"I feel a strange delight in becoming hard and swollen and really wanting to cum. I cross my ankles and my body becomes rigid. The head of my cock is much harder than the shaft and I love it when it is fully swollen. I usually spurt out in streams. I use hand movements until I feel the cum in the shaft and I can no longer hold it, then I do not move my hand, I just squeeze the hardness and watch the cum spurt out."

"I masturbate with my right hand, with my thumb on top and fingertips on the bottom—pumping up and down, taking care not to touch the glans with my thumb until ready to trigger ejaculation. Occasionally I masturbate with a condom on because of the sexy, slinky feeling of the rubber on my flesh. This gives me the most exquisite orgasm."

"After forty years, my favorite is lying nude on my bed with the middle of my top sheet and blanket under my ass and the two corners pulled up and around my legs. I grip my penis with my right hand and grip the corners of the sheet and blanket with my left hand and pull towards my head to increase the pleasurable pressure on my crotch and anal region. Since my enjoyment of masturbation is greater if I shoot over myself, I wear an undershirt which I ejaculate on and wipe myself on when I've done. Sometimes my ejaculate travels farther and hits my neck or the headboard of the bed. I masturbate frequently to pornography but also from mental images of girls I know or have seen during the day either in person or in a movie, TV, etc."

"I usually start masturbating in a standing position because it is harder and the pleasure greater when I cum. I use soap to lubricate my penis then start to read a sexy story or make up a story in my mind. I stroke my penis very lightly with short strokes so the feelings build up slowly in a teasing manner. Sometimes I play with my balls or asshole as I masturbate. As I approach orgasm, my knees feel weak. When I finally ejaculate, I sink down to a sitting position totally drained but left with a relaxing glow."

"Generally my masturbation routine when I'm doing it purely for fun is as follows: I get into bed naked, take a couple of hits and wait a while for the grass to take effect. I have a small towel that I drape across my abdomen and upper thighs to catch the ejaculation. I then either read a bit from some porn or look at photos, trying in one case to visualize the scene described so that it flows like a movie, and in the other to fantasize the still photos into some kind of continuity so that the girl in the photo reaches orgasm when I do. By this time I am hard, so I begin stroking my penis with my hand. There is more sensation at the tip than at the base and for some reason more on the underside just behind the head than anywhere else."

"I have two methods. One is with manual labor of the hand and two is by rubbing Jesus against something, such as fucking the bed. Usually I employ oil in my skilled palm, take a firm grip of Jesus and stroke him lightly and gentle, regulating the speed according to my desire. Sometimes I am deeply turned on and reach a satisfactory orgasm and ejaculation from long deep strokes to the very base of the penis shaft; other times short quick strokes around the glans bring forth a sudden onrush of hot sticky sperm."

"I masturbate with pleasure, softly, sometimes quickly, other times slowly, lovingly, and always with gentleness, with oil, soapsuds, with my right hand or left hand or both hands, or a whirlpool bath, in the dark or the sunlight. I enjoy touching myself all over and sometimes enjoy massaging myself with the wetness of my ejaculation. I feel that there are many unexplored areas of making love with myself."

"When I first began to masturbate, I held my penis in the thumb and first two fingers (same way most people hold a pencil when they write) and moved my hand up and down at the center of the penis. Later, after I heard some of the boys at the school locker room joking about some guy's girlfriend being 'Mary Fist,' I started enclosing my penis in my full fist and pumping up and down, and have done it that way ever since. This use of the fist gives stimulation at both the top and the bottom of the penis. Every stroke moves the foreskin (circumcised) up and down on the head to give stimulation at the top."

"I usually lick my finger and run it along the underside of my penis especially just below the head. Then I rub my hand over the length of it with moderate firmness. My thumb and index finger wrap around the top, sliding over and beneath the corona, while my last finger and palm slide to the base of my penis pushing down on my pubic area. Once in a while I flick my finger over the tip of my cock and the part just below the tip on the underside. When I approach orgasm I alternate between rubbing the entire length of my cock and concentrating on the head in short intervals. When I come I usually stop all movement. I like coming all over my chest and stomach and seeing myself shoot cum out of my cock. Once in a while I eat my cum. I usually masturbate on my back with my head propped up so I can see. The visual stimulation of my engorged cock is very important. Once in a while I masturbate on my hands and knees. I use one hand and I feel like a dog or some other four-legged creature."

And one longer, enthusiastic reply:

"I like lying on my back in bed wearing my white boxer shorts and T-shirt. I like the feel of a good semi better than a hard-on so I try to keep it that way as long as possible. I feel my big smooth nuts through my shorts and that gets me sort of turned on. Sometimes I'll get my pecker and nuts out of my shorts, and other times I'll get both hands down in my shorts. If I've still got a semi on, I'll hold the outer part of my pecker with one hand and with the other grab the upper part and move the semi hard inside in and out. If I'm really horny, I get turned on by the clear lube stuff that comes out of the tip of my pecker. I often stop for a while and let it go soft and that seems to generate a lot more of the lube.

"If I'm wearing tight shorts like jockey shorts, I'll pull them down so the band is behind my nuts putting pressure on and pushing them up. When I finally decide to blow my load, I get one fist around my meat and start beating off while the other hand feels my nuts and the part of my hard-on directly behind them. I generally use long strokes covering the whole length of my wang, but I can get off by just playing with my nuts or just rubbing the tip.

"I usually blow my load right in my shorts, but if I'm running low on clean shorts, I'll use a safe. I don't mind the wet load at all. Sometimes I even rub my wet shorts all over my head. Requires a good shampoo after though.

"Also I like whacking off in the shower. Start with my pecker soft and stand with my legs apart facing the shower, but far away. I swing my pecker and nuts up and down so they flop against my ass and then my stomach. On the up-swing the shower hits my balls and the front of my wang. I'll put a loop in the cord of the soap-on-a-rope and slip it over my wang and balls and let it hang there while I'm shaving. It keeps me turned on. Sometimes use the massage position of the shower—turned on high—and just let it blast over the underside of my pecker and nuts until I blow my load."

Uncircumcised men frequently had a slightly different technique:

"Good God this is getting complicated. Generally, manipulation of the foreskin back and forth over the glans, with full fist and hard and fast if I want to do it quickly, with fingers for greater refinements. Most of the stimulation seems associated with the glans. Since my penis comes in the original factory-prepared wrapping, the glans is sensitive to the touch of anything but mucous membrane tissue. Thus I never directly rub the glans during masturbation. As I approach orgasm, I generally grab my testicles. Usually I squeeze them during orgasm. I am turned on by the sight of my ejaculation; it makes me feel very much alive."

"I am uncircumcised (perhaps a fashion to which we should return) and have an effective stimulator in the form of a foreskin. I usually recline on my back holding my erect penis with my right hand while at the same time cradling my testicles with my left hand. I begin slowly sliding the foreskin back and forth over the head of my penis, certainly the most sensitive part. For my technique, the foreskin is of obvious value to achieve the necessary stimulation."

"Masturbating is easy for me. I am not circumcised and have a full foreskin that easily goes over the whole of the head of my penis even when erect. My hand does not have to move against the skin then, but rather I move the whole skin back and forth."

"I grasp my penis midway down to secure as much loose sliding skin as possible and execute forward and backward movements up over the glans and back down to the base of my penis in a slow rhythm, always making certain that the *sliding skin always remains between the hand and the penis.* The hand never moves across the corona of my glans without the sliding skin beneath it. Full-length strokes are best."

Many men added lubrication to their manual stimulation:

"The only way I can masturbate is to hold my prepuce with thumb, forefinger, and second finger of my hand and work the skin back and forth over the head of my penis. Lubrication is necessary so as not to irriate my tender penis head. I am uncircumcised."

"The most typical method for me is simply with my right hand, moving it against my penis. I usually use hand cream as a lubricant. I cannot 'dry' masturbate because I get sore and swollen."

"I use coconut oil on my hand and move it over my penis."

"Many times I anoint my cock with a slippery lubricant, keeping the friction down. This way I get a softer sensation and can last longer."

And a few men used a vibrator in addition to manual stimulation:

"If time is not available I like to use a vibrator. I place the vibrator pad about midway between the head and my belly with the skin pulled back tight. I use the vibrator to try to pull it back even tighter. Within a minute I have climaxed. I also use a hand-held water spray to bring a climax by holding the skin tight and spraying the underside of the head with warm water. I find the use of a vibrator or water spray helpful in reaching a climax in later years. I never used anything until after I was forty."

"In my teens I discovered the joys of my father's massager. It was the type of massager that fits over the back of the hand. Two springs go across the massager and one's hand can slip into it leaving the hand and fingers free. Turning it on produced a very strong vibration of the hand and then I was free to masturbate by gripping the penis and rubbing up and down until ejaculation. It is more intense because of the vibration and is very pleasurable."

"I can masturbate by just putting the vibrator in my genital area. At climax it feels like the tingling comes from all over my body. It's as good or better than penetration especially since I have a spinal-cord injury which makes orgasm by other stimulation difficult."

"I have a vibrator. The most powerful orgasms I have had have been obtained with this device. I press the vibrator against the top side of the shaft and pull in the direction of the base without actually letting the vibrator slip in that direction. This stretches the skin on the upper section of the shaft taut and magnifies the vibrations."

For other men (15 percent), masturbation meant lying on the stomach and rubbing or thrusting against the bed (many more men had masturbated this way when younger):

"I like pumping away against the bed same as if I was screwing. I have my pecker lying flat against my belly. Meanwhile I like getting the band of my shorts down behind my nuts so I can feel the pressure on them too."

"I lie on the bed nude and feel my full hard-on against my body. I simulate missionary-position intercourse and come against the bed by pumping and moving around."

"I discover that wedging my pillow under my belly and on top of my penis provides the greatest possible envelopment. Lying under the covers, my motion provides friction on the top of my buttocks, which is nice. I don't really thrust under the pillow. I sort of push, varying the pressure with a slow rhythm. There's too much irritating friction if I slide in and out. I find just the right squeeze to send me, then squirm on it till I climax. Then I collapse, rest my head, and feel my feet and legs glowing for a while."

"When in the service, the close quarters made it difficult to masturbate in the bunk, as they were suspended three vertically, and too much penis movement by hand was too obvious. Many of us lay on our stomachs, with the penis over in the hollow of our legs, with the organ outside of our shorts. By controlling the pressure of the penis against the sheet, a great sensation could be obtained by slowly fucking the cloth. When the climax approached, it was very easy to pretend restlessness and turning, as we really got into it. After the climax it was very pleasant to drift off to sleep gently working the penis through the sperm flood."

"I caress my tits with my fingertips while simultaneously rubbing my penis along the bed or floor. I've never been able to figure out how somebody can masturbate while holding his penis."

"How do I masturbate? My principal technique—originating in childhood—is to lie face down in bed (I never wear pajamas), with my penis between the sheet and my lower abdomen, and then rock from side to side."

"The best way to jack off is to lay an old T-shirt on the bed, lay flat on your stomach and hug your pillow and start moving your body back and forth on the bed while looking at pictures of guys' big cocks or pictures of gays fucking each other."

"My main method is humping the bedclothes. The first time I ever had an orgasm (I think I was about eleven) I had arranged the bedclothes into the approximate form of a female body and humped it (practicing!); that has remained my favorite device. Rubbing the balls also makes me come very fast and very excitingly."

"Sometimes I fill a condom with lotion and lying on the bed face down make as though I was in a vagina. It's more work, but a better orgasm."

"It starts by fondling my penis and squeezing it until I am fully erect. Then I put on a lubricated prophylactic and begin rubbing against an object such as a pillow or the mattress. My penis being contained between my stomach and the pillow receives sensations and warmth very similar to vaginal intercourse and very stimulating. It often takes as long as forty-five minutes."

Sometimes some manual stimulation was included:

"I rely on the floor for stimulation rather than my hand for the simple reason that it seems less 'sinful' than an out-and-out direct 'touching myself.' I don't feel as 'guilty.' I don't know where along the line I got this guilt complex (I am now twenty years old). I lie on my stomach, the underside of my penis stroking gently against the carpet, propped up on my elbows, or sometimes with the shaft of the penis pointed toward my feet, I lie on my stomach and grind my pubic area on the floor. Meanwhile, leaning on my left elbow, I reach behind me with my right hand and stroke the underside of my penis lengthwise, stopping every once in a while so that the stimulation doesn't get monotonous."

"I lie on my stomach, embracing a pillow under me. This is my lover. One hand goes under my penis. The base of the penis rests on the heel of the hand. The shaft lies upwards between my stomach and the towel or T-shirt I am using; it also rubs against my wrist and arm. For this to be comfortable and give the right stimulation, a partial erection is best. I hug the pillow and move up and down on it, deep in fantasy, with her head near my shoulder and my face in her hair."

A few men masturbated by pushing their penis down, holding it between their legs and grinding or rotating their hips:

"I lie in bed with my head on a pillow. I pull up my knees and reach under my thigh and grasp my penis from below my legs. Then with my penis pulled down and backward, I put my legs back down and close them on it. By squeezing and flexing my leg and especially my thigh muscles,

I get the feeling someone else is stimulating my cock. Another reason I think masturbation with the penis pushed down between the legs is good is that it holds the balls away from the 'high' position and so keeps me from ejaculation so soon. But of course eventually I do orgasm and it's great."

"Sometimes I sit or half recline with my legs crossed with my penis sticking down below them. Meanwhile I use both my hands to gently push my nipples or caress the rest of my body while I stimulate my penis only by squeezing my legs and sort of writhing around while in that position. It takes a long time to come this way, but it is quite pleasurable. Also the orgasm by this method is more diffuse, seeming to spread over my entire body. If while climaxing I squeeze very tight, I ejaculate a minimal amount of sperm, and my whole body seems to tingle. It is actually almost painfully pleasurable for me to touch myself anywhere for a short time thereafter."

A few masturbated by water massage:

"I can have orgasms in a Jacuzzi whirlpool bath by holding my penis next to the jet with the underside facing the stream of pressurized bubbling hot water. This is the quickest orgasm I've ever had. The total elapsed time from initial erection to ejaculation is no more than fifteen to twenty seconds (versus about five minutes otherwise). It feels so strange because everything is so speeded up. There is an accelerated tightening up of my thigh and pelvic muscles and the orgasm feels like it's being pulled out of me whether I will it or not. I don't do this very often, because it's *too* compressed, but it's definitely an interesting variation."

"A good way to masturbate is to sit close to the tunnel of the Jacuzzi whirlpool bath. It gives a great feeling with the jet stream of warm water pounding against your balls and cock and thighs."

"I masturbate under the shower by running a fine spray of tepid water on my penis. I guide my penis by letting the water hit the bottom, middle, and head. This is usually preceded by soaping up the penis with a good lather of soap. I am not circumcised and keep the foreskin separated from the head. After five, ten, or fifteen minutes of continuous water spraying on my dick, the nerves in my body are begging for release. There is a further stiffening of my penis and finally a pleasant release of sperm."

And a very few men could masturbate by self-fellatio:

"When in my twenties and thirties I could sometimes reach my mouth. My lips and tongue could stimulate the glans while my hands stroked the base. I bent over or lay on my upper back and shoulders with my legs back over my head. This was sometimes hard on my back but it felt good. I've never heard of anyone doing this self oral stimulation of the penis. Mine is only eight inches when fully erect and I am not a contortionist. It was more of a backward somersault and I ended up on my neck and shoulders. There were times when I could just bend over standing and orally stimulate the glans; but now in later age, I am afraid I'll slip a disk or something."

"Did you know a guy can give himself a head job (fellatio)! I've done it to myself twice. One time I was real drunk and wondered what it would be like. It was great. But it's a lot of work. Kind of awkward. I would lay on my back in bed and flip my legs over my head. You have to be very loose. I was really surprised that I could bend my body enough to reach my penis."

"What happens is that my fascination with my own penis grows until eventually I find myself trying to put my face down where my cock is. At this point I lie down on my back, and then throw my knees up around my ears, propping my feet against the wall or any other conveniently immobile vertical surface. In this position my genitals are hanging but a few inches above my face, and with a little effort, by putting my hands on my ass and pushing down, in the direction of my face, I can take some of my erect penis with my mouth at least. This is a truly incredible sensation. On the one hand, I love to suck cock. On the other hand, I love to be sucked. When I suck myself I can give myself the best of both worlds."

Which part of the penis is most sensitive to stimulation?

Most men felt that the top of the penis and/or the glans are the most important to stimulate for orgasm:

"The last two inches of my penis are the most sensitive erogenous zone on my body. The glans penis and the final inch of the shaft must have direct stimulation in order for me to orgasm. The corona of the glans seems to be the most acutely and strangely sensitive area of all, while the area just beneath the glans, on the front side of the shaft, is the most acutely sensitive to conventional touch sensation. The lower part of my penis, closer to my body, is no more sensitive than is the skin of my scrotum—very sensitive to conventional touch sensation, but lacking that final quality which leads to orgasm."

Many of these men mentioned that the most sensitive spot is the frenulum/meatus, that is, the point at the lower base of the head, away from the body. Some men found this spot too sensitive to stimulate, others found it exquisite to stimulate, and others would stimulate it or not, depending on the type of sensation they were trying to achieve:

"There is a point at the lower base of the head of my penis that is the most sensitive. I imagine the local feeling is rather like a woman's clitoris and wonder if there is a name for this spot. Direct stimulation at this point can cause irritation so it is best to move the hood of my penis (I am not circumcised) back and forth over this sensitive place."

"Stimulation is important all along the shaft but specifically the head of the penis. But to achieve orgasm I must be sure to rub the portion of the penis just at the base of the head."

"The most sensitive place is under the cock near the head."

"The most sensitive part of my penis is the little area just below the hole in the head where the skin grows to the head. Stimulation here causes me to come. And no matter how hard I try, if this spot does not get action I will not come even though it may feel really good. I imagine it is like clitoral stimulation to most women."

"The area of most important contact is the head, especially the knobs on the underside (I am circumcised)."

"You can get an extremely sharp, poignant orgasm that's almost painful if you stimulate only the glans. In fact it's hard to stay still for it, but if you can last, there's a special brand of orgasm waiting at the end. It's not as smooth as the *big bang*, so I guess it would be better to describe it as a supernova (explosion of a massive star)."

But a minority said the base of the penis could be better for stimulation—especially to prolong the buildup of sensation before orgasm:

"I firmly grip the base of the penis in one hand and usually stimulate the testicles with the other. By stimulating the base of the penis, this avoids the sensitivity of the head, allowing longer stimulation. Then as orgasm comes closer, I increase speed and grip to the point of orgasm, then grip the head of the penis which is so sensitive at this point it triggers orgasm and ejaculation."

"The most sensitive part of my penis is the front (lower) side of the shaft. I am circumcised, and I've often wondered if the doctor didn't nick a nerve or something, as I have heard that the head is more sensitive for most people. The head of mine is fairly insensitive until it's been rubbed a lot."

"The bottom of my penis near the middle of its length is the most pleasurable spot and this is where my two fingers are. The tip is super-sensitive but it is almost unpleasant to stimulate it too much. If I want to prolong the erection and increase my arousal, I may move my hand down to the base of my penis or rub my balls or my anus or put a finger in my anus."

Some of these men said that although stimulation of the base of the penis could take longer, it could lead to a deeper, stronger orgasm:

"Usually I stimulate the upper portion of my penis, the tip, which is most sensitive. But for variation sometimes I rub just the lower portion with one or two fingers after a hard erection, just at the base. This takes longer to orgasm but climax is much stronger."

"If I'm in no hurry and just getting into it, I stimulate the lower shaft most. It takes longer but the orgasm is closer to being the real orgasm. If I'm in a hurry and just want to come, I stimulate the glans most, and come fast."

It should be noted that a large number of men, although they required stimulation at the top of the penis to cause orgasm, actually felt the orgasm and contractions not only somewhat in the tip of the penis but also deep in the base of the penis, and in the area from the testicles to just inside the body:* (The relevance of this point to women's needs for stimulation is explained on page 684)

"The feeling seems to start in the head of my penis and goes to the prostate and then throughout the entire body."

* Answers here refer to the question, "Exactly where do you feel the sensation of orgasm? Is it in your penis, or inside your body, or exactly where?"

"It starts with a good feeling in the glans, progresses until it overwhelms the penis, then focuses somewhere beneath the balls."

"The major orgasms emanate from my post-scrotum region (the root of the penis between the scrotum and the anus) and proceed at high speed through my penis and throughout my body to my heart, my head, and all limbs to the very tips of my toes."

"Although I feel strong sensations throughout the genital area, the feeling of orgasm is quite centered in the base of the penis, from the testicles to just inside the body."

"The initial sensation begins right at the tip inside the hole. As the orgasm progresses, the feeling extends down the swollen organ on the underside of the penis (I sure don't know my anatomy). There seem to be feelings that come in blasts like waves of the ocean. The intensity is greatest in the tip but travels down the underside to the base of the penis and is transmitted to the rest of the genital area and the inner thighs more as a tingly sensation or ache rather than the orgasmic feeling."

"Down the back of my legs to the knees, up around my anus into my deep insides. The penis is only the focus for all this, the trigger."

"I feel like my cock has roots that extend down the backs of my legs, and coming draws juice from clear down there."

"As the orgasm builds, a pressure starts above the mons and between my legs, and I start to stiffen my legs, and close them. I need a reasonable pressure around my penis, whether masturbating or during coitus. The pressure continues in a most pleasurable way, and I feel everything focusing in my groin, as my heart rate and breathing ascend quickly, muscles are tense before the orgasm. Then at the climax my head feels light, all the pressures are rushing from between my legs, like my insides want to come out of my penis, but so pleasurably. There is a slight hesitation just before the contractions start, then that feeling that almost defies words like Wow, Fantastic, Rockets. The strength and duration of the climax depends on the length of time given to the foreplay. You never want it to stop when it is going on, but when it is over, strangely, it is O.K. Coming down after is very pleasant with the diminished contractions continuing less quickly, but strongly, and very deep from the root of the penis. The head is reasonably sensitive, depending, again, on the length of foreplay. A feeling of peace, serenity, tiredness pervades and, depending on frequency, satisfaction. The best moment is before the hesitation and when the contractions start. The sensation of orgasm is felt from my rectum to just above my testicles."

While body position is not as crucial to male orgasm as to female orgasm (due to the exterior vs. interior nature of the genital structures*), some men did find body position could make some difference:

"The pleasure seems to be connected in some ways with the base of the spine when I am upright. I also like to press the legs together."

"I have jerked off in a sitting position or on my back, even driving my car, but kneeling is the most intense."

"I like laying on my back and at the moment of climax I bend my legs at the knees and spread the legs. I've already noticed a much more complete and satisfying climax in this position."

"After reading how important leg position was to women, I tried lifting my feet off the bed and extending my legs. This is very tiring so I only do it when already quite excited. There is no question but this position leads to the best orgasm because it causes the muscles at the base of my penis to remain completely relaxed until orgasm, while all the other muscles in my legs, hips, and abdomen become quite tense."

How do men feel about the wetness of ejaculation?

Many men were very enthusiastic:

"I love the feel of my cream splashing all over my body, or shooting on the floor, wall, blankets, etc."

"I love the wetness. Even before I come, my cock head starts to get creamy. I use my finger to wipe the head of my dick then suck my finger."

"Wetness is fun to play with and slide around my penis, or just feel warm against my groin. Sometimes I try to aim for my mouth but I have never scored a bull's-eye."

"I like to touch it and put my finger in my mouth to taste it. It's me and I feel it's all right. Part of the acceptance of myself."

---

* Women often need their legs to be in a specific position to reach orgasm, either apart or together. See *The Hite Report,* on female sexuality, pages 52–54.

"Perhaps I am abnormal but I like to see my semen spurt out, see and feel it flow down over my fingers as I hold it straight up. There is an atmosphere of daring in this, somehow, and I have never told anyone that I do that."

"Sometimes when I come back from jogging and my body is all sweaty I like to masturbate and smear the semen all over my body."

"I love come; I think it's beautiful. I like to rub it into my skin, or leave little gobs of it in strange places. I don't often swallow it, however, because I find the taste a little unnerving, but I am getting over that."

Some men ate it:

"Occasionally I eat it because it is so sweet and creamy, coming from one's own body."

"I prefer to lie on my back with my legs raised up over my head, so I catch the semen on my face, and can swallow it. This really turns me on."

"I like to feel the ejaculate and sort of smear it around my cock and balls, and put some of it in my mouth and smear it around my face and nose."

However, a few men mentioned they had tried this and didn't like the taste:

"If I throw my legs over my head, I can get the tip of my cock to within a half inch of my mouth. I've ejaculated about eight times in this position because I was curious as to the taste of semen. I can't stand the taste: I've never been able to swallow it."

"When I was younger, lithe, and into yoga, I once managed to come into my mouth. I did it because I wanted to experience what my lover experienced when she sucked on me. I didn't like the taste of my own come. I told her what I had done and that I didn't expect her to swallow my come, but she insisted that she likes the way I taste. At first I couldn't believe that, but then she can't believe that I like the way she tastes!"

Some men had reservations about the wetness:

"The wetness of ejaculation is a minor nuisance, perhaps the stickiness more than the wetness. As a boy I always expected my mother to embarrass me about seminal stains on my sheets (which she never did). I was also concerned about sheet stains in the military and would ejaculate into a sock, hoping that the dried semen would not attract anyone's notice."

"Do I mind the wetness of the semen? Not at all, though sometimes it can be revealing to my wife if I stain the sheets, so I put tissues underneath me when I come by the bed method. Once late at night, I ejaculated off the balcony of the apartment where I lived and watched till it disappeared."

"I usually avoid the wetness. It lingers around and reminds me of my loneliness after orgasm. But sometimes I squirt all over myself—sometimes I just need to bathe in it. (Not very often.)"

"I keep sperm trapped in my penis as I come by gently pinching the top of my penis together. Then I head for the bathroom and spurt it into the toilet."

Some men thought of the ejaculate not as "wet" but as proof of manhood:

"I view my come as a great physical feat and exciting."

"The record, and every man maintains a memory record book, is thirteen shots. I have been known to spurt far enough to hit my sex partner in the eye at a distance of five to six feet. Other times, rather than distance, I'll get off one blast and then the secondary shots are not as forceful or intense. It may ooze up and over my hand and into my pubic hair. I do not mind the wetness, after all it is a sign of my manhood and my body went to some trouble to make it."

"The truth is, when I ejaculate now, I can't jerk it halfway across the room like I used to (I exaggerate of course), but to me, a sign of masculinity is how far I can send the sperm when I ejaculate."

"The wetness of ejaculation is visible proof of virility."

And some men found it quite unappealing:

"I never cared for ejaculation, it just seems smelly and sticky, and requires care not to mess something up (floor, clothes, books, pictures, etc.)."

"I don't care for the wetness of ejaculation, I wish it was in powdered form."

"The wetness seems dirty, disgusting, and I hate it. Messy too."

"It's like some damn glue. It takes concentration to remove it and get free of the stuff."

"Masturbation ejaculation calls for a towel if you have any respect for yourself."

"I find my own semen to be foul-smelling, paltry, unpleasant."

"I always ejaculate into the toilet or on the ground out in the bushes. I don't get it on my body."

"Kind of a blobby mess, like an egg white . . . as when you poach the egg for breakfast. Icky."

"It gets cold and sticky and smells like Ajax. Hate it."

Thoughts during masturbation

Fantasy, as mentioned earlier, is also very important to many men during masturbation:

"Usually it's very difficult for me to get excited if I'm not thinking erotic thoughts regarding a woman. If I'm just aware of my hand on my penis moving up and down, it doesn't excite me and I begin to lose the hard-on. If I think of past experiences of fucking or being masturbated by a woman, then I become harder and acquire the tension in my penis that's necessary for the ejaculation."

"The use of fantasies is essential to masturbation for me. I don't get aroused unless I think about sex while masturbating. I think how a women looks, her hips, breasts, legs, pubic hair, labia, vaginal opening. One of my favorite fantasies is sliding my hand in her panties and stroking her mons until she gets wet."

"I usually make up semi-elaborate scenes in my head to stimulate me during masturbation. They are always everyday happenings. Sometimes they are recreations of times I've been with my wife. Other times I think of her wearing an article of clothing and standing a certain way and that is enough to bring me to orgasm. Before I met her I used to dream up little scenarios involving me and perhaps a woman I had seen on a bus and with whom I flirted; other times about women I worked with or knew in or around the neighborhood. These little scenes were dependent, oddly enough, on continuity— and if my mind suddenly thought of something incongruous such as a work problem, I would blow the whole thing and have to start all over at the beginning."

"Pictures get boring after a while—so I usually just close my eyes, and use my imagination on some guy I've just seen on the street or something or some past fucks I've had."

"Sometimes someone at work hands me a sex magazine, and I take it to the men's room along with the hand lotion in my desk. As I get about halfway through the pictures I take my penis (the head) in my hand, sliding my hand in downward strokes only. This feels wonderful. As climax approaches, I sit back on the toilet and hold the penis downward, thinking about the pictures, my middle finger at the opening, and then jerk it quickly as the climax occurs. Then I work the sperm over the whole organ, and rest briefly before returning to my area."

"I prepare my mood by the use of pornographic pictures. I may have two or even three pictures arranged so I can view them closely. Sometimes the entire masturbation process is preceded by erotic or obscene literature. I have employed 'stag' films of the 8-mm. variety, but soon tire of a particular film and seldom go to the trouble of viewing them just for a single masturbation session. I will employ the same still pictures fairly often—maybe for two or three months or until I happen across a more stimulating series."

Pornography and male fantasies will be discussed in more depth in chapter 6.

HOW DO MEN FEEL ABOUT MASTURBATION?

Most men felt guilty and inadequate about masturbating, at the same time that they enjoyed it tremendously (many had their strongest orgasms, physically, during masturbation), and seemed to have a great sense of freedom and fun while doing it. Most men seemed to feel freer to stimulate themselves in ways they liked, and to experiment, than at other times—to simply play around and be affectionate with their bodies. Almost no men told anyone else that they did this.

Most men, even though they continued to masturbate regularly throughout their lives, including many times during which they had an otherwise active sex life, felt that they should not masturbate, and that masturbation was basically acceptable for a man only as a substitute for sex with another person—many adding that they felt defensive, lonely, or guilty about doing it:

"If I don't get what I want from my wife, I masturbate. It leaves me depressed and lonely."

"The last ten years I hate myself and my wife whenever I found it necessary to masturbate. I feel cheated psychologically. It makes one feel alienated."

"I'm still hung up on the idea that though there is nothing *wrong* with masturbation, a sexually successful person shouldn't need it."

"I do not enjoy masturbation. It's kid stuff. It means you just struck out."

"I mean, if you're out camping and know you won't see a woman for weeks or months then it's psychologically matter-of-fact. But in civilization it's a small admission of defeat—of inability to share what was meant to be shared."

"If I could have sex with a partner as often as I wanted, I would not masturbate."

"I'm an 'honest masturbator'—I masturbate *only* when the *real* thing is not available (which is lately unfortunately most of the time). When I do, I come and I enjoy it. The *sensation* of 'coming' is very often *more* intense than during normal intercourse—as no other person can *know* what and how you enjoy better than *you* do—but there is *more* to 'making love' than just to come. I'd *much* rather have *one* good fuck than ten 'good jerking-offs.' "

"I masturbate when my schedule is unusually busy, and I can't find time for more relaxed sex with another person."

"I prefer sex with a partner, but if that isn't possible for one reason or another, then 'jacking off' fills the bill. It also feels great. The orgasm is usually more intense."

"If my wife and I were alone more often or didn't have children, we'd probably fuck more like when we were first married. We screwed so much and often for the first year or so we got sore. But I guess even then I masturbated."

"I use it to enjoy an orgasm when it's not likely I'll have sex in the next twelve to twenty-four hours."

"Masturbation, regretfully, still plays a part in my sex life. Though I believe that even if I found no need for it, I would find a need for it. The act brings pleasure and I'm sure if I had a regular sexual relationship with one person I would still find time for my hand to meet my cock. After all, they have been the best of friends for a long time."

"It's good to get unemployment when you can't find work, right?"

"Masturbation feels good and I am in complete control of

the sensations, but I feel that I am somehow cheating on my mate by doing it. If she ever caught me at it I would be terribly embarrassed and she would be thoroughly pissed."

"I feel guilty for not being with someone."

"Masturbation is important for me because it keeps me from adultery. My wife would be happy with sex about once a week. There's no way I could survive that without masturbation."

"I need it if I don't have a woman within three days. Also if I'm out with a girl and I get aroused but no sex."

"Since I am involved in a beautiful affair I may masturbate monthly. I feel good about it, but I regard it as a piss poor substitute for the real thing. But there have been times when I masturbated in the bathroom minutes after orgasm in a vagina. I have never told anyone this."

Similarly, many men said that they enjoyed masturbating physically, but that emotionally it was depressing:

"It is physically enjoyable, but it can leave one emotionally empty or lonely for the real thing. You can do it when you feel like it, come when you want, bring up your own images, but there is no warmth or closeness, no one to share pleasure with, no companionship, and it leaves crusty little stains."

"Masturbation has probably kept me alive, and certainly has played a large part in maintaining my sanity. But its soiltude often depresses me because I want to be with someone."

"I enjoy masturbation physically, but it's a lonely business if you don't ever get anything else. I think, 'Hey ho, another orgasm and no partner.' "

"It is to sex as fast food is to a real dinner—fast, unemotional, and only briefly satisfying. It's bad because you know it's not in the best interests of your psyche."

One man had a different way of thinking about it:

"Masturbation is my staple diet. I probably average it once a day. Genital sex functions like dessert—a luxury once a week or less which I enjoy, but don't put aside the time and energy for. But if I didn't know that I could have 'genital sex' at least that often if I wanted it, I probably would want it more. Knowing it's available makes a difference."

Some men, feeling defensive or guilty about masturbating, justified it in terms of male physiology or the male "sex drive":*

"I masturbated in my former marriage when my wife would not engage in sex and my testicles would hurt so bad—they needed to be emptied and into my wife was the proper place, that is what God intended them for."

"If you neck and pet with a woman without release, you may become so loaded with semen that the pressure actually is painful. This is known as 'stone-ache,' as it is felt most painfully in the balls. In such a case you just about have to masturbate as soon as you have the opportunity, unless you can get home quickly to your wife and if she isn't sympathetic then dash to a 'respectable' whorehouse (few of those are available anymore) or else the bathroom."†

"Maybe this is good for me physiologically because it generates male hormones, testosterone, that get into my system."

On the other hand, other men worried that masturbation, or too much masturbation, might adversely affect their health:

"I like masturbation, but I fear if I do it too much I'll jerk myself out of whack."

"Can someone masturbate too much? I could enjoy it two or three times a day, every day! but I try to restrain myself. Maybe it's not good for me, or maybe I'll damage myself."

There is no basis in fact for these fears. A man can safely enjoy all the orgasms he likes. There does not seem to be a similar fear of having too much intercourse to orgasm; on the contrary, most men felt that the more, the better. Physically speaking, there is no difference to the body between an orgasm produced by masturbation and an orgasm from intercourse or any other means; therefore, there is no need to worry that orgasms produced by masturbation could damage the body.

* See chapter 3, page 351–52.

† There is no term for "blue balls" in the medical vocabulary; women too have pelvic congestion if they are frequently aroused without orgasm, but men have more commonly talked about the feelings connected with an unfulfilled desire for orgasm; however, most men in this study did not mention any physical ache or pain connected with not having orgasm when aroused.

Some men said that they had only masturbated when young:

"Masturbation is a holdover from when I was young. Now I am satisfied with a woman."

"I used to when I was young to relieve the agony of cramped nuts."

"Masturbation used to be extremely important to me because I had very little genital sex. I also learned a lot about the rhythms and sensations of my body and what turned me on by masturbation. Now I have grown out of that, and I prefer genital sex to masturbating. I masturbated once while I was with my partner to show her how I did it."

But another man commented on his doubts about this:

"We know it's 'wrong,' still taboo—nobody admits they do it. Men admit they 'used to' when a boy but 'not now.' Ha."

Another man's statement corroborated this, at least for him:

"I am not bothered psychologically but I am self-conscious about how others feel about it. I have had only two girlfriends who I ever let know that I did it, and I have never told a male friend—other than talking about how we did it as *kids*. That was O.K. because 'all little boys do it.' But there seems to be a big taboo about doing it as an adult, so I don't tell anyone."

A few men said unequivocally that masturbation is bad and disgusting:

"It is a bad habit—a crutch."

"I feel that it's sinful. There's got to be something wrong with it. I pray to be able to stop."

"Now you are really hitting, ma'am. No, it is not good for me. I first did it when I was eleven. I thought myself lost. I thought about it too much, with too much guilt and foreboding. I have complete control now but I haven't stopped entirely and I don't know if I am in reality failing. I must have done it about two thousand times I am estimating. I didn't want to admit and relate this, but it is the truth, although I am willing to call it sin when insisted upon. But I hope I will go to any afterlife as worthy as the next. Christ have mercy, if it is really necessary."

Many men said they had grown to accept it more with time:

"As a high school boy I felt guilt in doing it and wished I had a partner. I wondered if it interfered with partner sex. Now, however, I feel it is O.K."

"I seem to feel more liberated psychologically about masturbation than I used to. When I found out my wife masturbated, I began to feel freer about masturbation."

"I'm beginning to realize that masturbation is necessary for everyone's own sexual independence and that I shouldn't always have to rely on my mate to satisfy or arouse me. I used to never masturbate (stimulate myself) because she always did such a good job on me. Also I guess all the things drilled in your head before you can think made me think that it was degrading, selfish, a waste of time, and why do it yourself when a woman is much better. Lately I've been doing it more, mainly for arousal purposes. It feels so-o-o good."

"Masturbation has been a major part of my sexuality since early teens. I was always curious about what books said about masturbation—years ago it was *at best* seen as a childish activity to be properly outgrown when one became an adult; lately it is seen as ranging from quite O.K. if no sexual partner is around to a fully legitimate part of one's sex life. The changed attitude toward masturbation has made me feel much more comfortable about this part of my sexuality. I am rather proud of myself for not having been intimidated into abandoning the practice—though I used to try to give it up, the way people try to stop smoking. Now I suspect it is healthful (perhaps reducing the likelihood of prostate problems) and clearly a means of my wife and I dealing with our substantial difference in interest in sexual activity."

"I masturbate essentially openly now. Meaning I do not attempt to hide it. My previous wife felt if I masturbated I'd waste a good potential fuck, so I had to slink around and hide to masturbate. Now I feel that masturbation has a real part to play in people's sex life, not necessarily a replacement for partner sex or a substitute, but a part of your life."

"I used to feel guilt because I should be out hustling girls and getting laid instead of jerking off. However, I reason now that it can't do me any harm, I might as well enjoy it."

"When I became a teenager I began to have bouts of guilt about this which I had been doing ever since I can remember doing anything—but I went on anyway through my teen years in spite of attempts to feel I should stop or limit it or feel badly about it. Now as a middle-aged person I enjoy it psychologically as well, having gotten over the guilty feelings. My masturbation has always been accompanied by rich mental imagery and has improved my lovemaking with my wife for the simple reason that fantasies in masturbation then get tried out with her and it's fun."

*But regardless of their frequency of masturbation or their attitude toward it, the overwhelming majority of men were secretive about the fact that they did it:**

"Masturbation is not as satisfactory as intercourse. I guess I am ashamed since I hide to do it."

"I have masturbated on the average of almost twice a day since age fifteen. I am quite secretive about it and haven't talked about it to anyone, not even my closest male friends. I think the main reason for this is my frequency, which I believe is much higher than average."

"I am probably a little secretive about it, but who isn't? I masturbate on the average of about two times a week and sometimes if I am aroused by some woman that I have met during the day, say, I might masturbate twice a night. I feel quite happy about it, if it is a particularly satisfying one. Occasionally I am ashamed about it."

"I'm not secretive but I don't think my wife has ever seen me even though she knows I do. If she ever wanted to watch me she'd only need to say so.

"Whether I talk depends on to whom."

"I am secretive about it. My wife could not emotionally handle this."

"I do it by myself, so I guess you could say I am secretive about it."

"I am usually in bed with my partner when I am masturbating, but I hide it slightly. I hide it mostly so as not to wake up my lover. Maybe they think it's perverted, so I'd just as soon they not know what is going on, but if they do discover it, I'm not going to quit."

"I masturbate every other day. I'm satisfied but a little ashamed. Very secretive to my family. My dad always accused me of being a homosexual because he thought I masturbated."

"I like everything about masturbation except the fact that you have to hide."

* This section includes answers to the question, "How do you feel about masturbation? Are you secretive or open about it?"

Only a few men were not secretive:

"Sometimes I carry on masturbation 'shows' with my lover."*

"I masturbate at least several times a week—generally each night when I don't have sex with my wife. She knows this, and we've often discussed the matter and she came to understand and approves of it. It has had a very beneficial effect on my marriage because I desire and need sex much more often than my wife, so my being able to masturbate with her approval and understanding, it eventually eliminates the pressure that I would otherwise exert on her to satisfy me. It means that I don't have to be nearly as disappointed if we don't have sex together on a particular night, and my wife doesn't have to feel that she has to have sex with me or I'll be 'frustrated.' I love my wife so much, in part, because she understands this and understands me and my needs and desires. She's a great wife!"

Many men said that orgasms during masturbation were physically the strongest orgasms they ever had, since there were no performance pressures, and they felt free to give themselves exactly the right stimulation:

"Masturbation is the most intense method of sex. I have been disappointed in a partner because it was not as intense in physical feeling. In masturbation, pressure and rhythm are ideal, in intercourse, less so."

"I can give myself better orgasms by far than I can have with another person, since I know exactly what I want and when. I like to prolong the time just before orgasm by 'teasing' my body with very light pressure and slight movement. This produces a tremendous buildup of nervous energy and results in an almost shattering orgasm, but the process is so finely tuned that it is almost impossible to get it from another person. Therefore I can be physically most satisfied by far by masturbation, although sometimes oral sex approaches the feeling. But neither of these ways is my favorite by which to come, because they seem so solitary."

"I am quite conscious of a different quality in my experience of masturbation than in my experience of coital sex. I permit myself greater 'selfishness,' speed, and explosive power in masturbation than in most coital sex. I also can

* See also pages 562–63.

seem to have more different types of orgasms during masturbation. On the other hand, I have many times during sex experienced a quality of contact which goes far beyond 'getting off' and seems to involve my whole psyche, my whole soul."

"Physically it's tremendous and there is no question in my mind that the best orgasms, at least in terms of pure intensity, result from masturbation. But psychologically a masturbation-induced orgasm can't hold a candle to orgasm resulting from intercourse with a woman I respect as a person, feel attracted to, and have at least some degree of emotional involvement with."

A few men even masturbated to a second orgasm when alone, something they never did with a partner:

"I only have one orgasm during sex, but several (three) when I masturbate within an hour's duration. With a live woman, once is all I can muster up."

Many men mentioned that they felt freer—less inhibited or less pressured—when alone:

"I prefer having sex with myself in one way—when I masturbate, I feel as though I am under little or no pressure, and I do not have to be afraid of being criticized."

"Masturbation's greatest advantage is that one has only one's own pleasure to think of (except during mutual masturbation). I can do it almost any time for any period of time (usually ten to twenty minutes) and afterwards I can go right to sleep or go right on and do something else and not worry about my partner's needs or desires."

Many men said that it is a good time to fantasize:

"As far as thoughts and fantasies, I have more than *Yellow Submarine* and *Star Wars* put together. This is what masturbation is all about."

"I enjoy masturbation especially when I use it as a love session with my memories or my fantasies, a time now and again to be completely narcissistic. What's satisfying is conjuring up good fantasies, which are fun in and of themselves, and could maybe become reality; and maybe finding a buried treasure from the past."

"I like to fantasize during masturbation—don't during intercourse. Masturbation allows for fantasy without concern for your partner."*

Other men liked the independence of masturbation:

"Emotionally and physically I like masturbation. I like not being dependent on others for my orgasms, so I don't have to be demanding about sex. I have told some women not to feel they are obligated to provide me with sex just as an accommodation, because I have a good right hand; sex should be something we both want together. I miss not having another person to share with when I masturbate sometimes, but I like myself too and being alone is also good."

"Masturbation is very important because it allows me to satisfy my sexual needs without imposing my needs on a non-receptive partner. It also allows me to enjoy myself without going through all the steps necessary to try to interest my wife —and with an approximately 60 percent rejection rate sometimes it just isn't worth the frustration."

Some men were simply extremely enthusiastic about masturbation, and thought it was a lot of fun:

"Do I enjoy masturbation! *Yes.* I would die if I couldn't whack off."

"Masturbation is a great joy to me. I have told my boys to enjoy it and revel in it."

"Masturbation is an emotional outlet, a spirituality of the senses. I practice masturbation at least once every day. It gets me going, gets me motivated, it rejuvenates my system."

"I adore it. I was told that if you have sex you won't masturbate—not true. I think it is a good sexual outlet for men."

"I enjoy jacking off. Fucking is fine but I do enjoy beating my meat. It's been part of my life since age thirteen."

"Damned right masturbation is important. It's the only way of my true total sexual relief—during sex I'm too busy worrying about her to really get my rocks off right."

"Better than Bayer. Also, due to my need for strong stimulation, it often provides the grand finish to a sex session for me."

"I think every guy's first love is his own cock! You start

* See also chapter 6.

playing with it as a little boy and you learn to hold it and squeeze it and grip it in the most pleasurable of ways. No other person in your life will ever be more in tune with your sexual responses than you yourself. I love sexual activity with women, but masturbation with fantasy is just about unlimited in its creative potential. You can really enjoy it at your own pace and never be embarrassed. You can stand on the sink and jack off in front of the mirror if you like, or anything as outrageous as you can think of! And you don't need to wait to pace yourself for your partner. I masturbate every couple of days, usually in the bathroom while I get ready for work. It doesn't matter if we've had sex the night before or not. It's a pleasant way of waking up. Sometimes I do it in the shower— just put some soap or shampoo in my right hand and then imagine I'm showering and some fantastic woman slips into the shower with me and demands I fuck her. I bet more married men jack off than twenty-two-year-old bachelors. Maybe we need the fantasy of it more. Marital sex can get pretty routine. I masturbate more if my wife is sick or if she's having a heavy period. I bet you'd be surprised how many married men you'd find every morning lying on their bathroom floors with a *Playboy* foldout in one hand and their prick in the other."

"Masturbation was always one of life's little free pleasures, like sunsets and butterflies. All boys love to jack off. I've been doing it since about seven or eight years old, without ejaculation of course, and since thirteen with ejaculation. I don't see how you can stop after doing it daily until about twenty-one or so. The only reason you stop or become secretive is the society pressure. As you get older, you are not supposed to masturbate. However, I do, I like it and I think I would go blind (contrary to past rumors) if I stopped (ha ha). I wish the amount of guilt associated with masturbation was ended. Also, it is used as a real derogatory reference, i.e., 'he's a real jerk-off,' etc. I object to this."

A few described it as a form of self-love:

"I do it when I just feel like touching myself and making myself feel good."

"I enjoy it physically and emotionally because I'm giving pleasure to someone I like and care about."

"I masturbate even though my sex life has been happier each passing day. I enjoy and always will, I hope, self-love. You have to have love for yourself before you can have a good sex life with someone else. Until you have love for yourself, you will never have good love to give."

"Masturbation is a form of meditation, profoundly honest. I masturbate almost every night before I go to sleep. During this time I resolve a lot of things. I'm in that state between the conscious and unconscious where major insights occur. It's a special time of day for me."

BOYS' FEELINGS ON FIRST MASTURBATION AND ORGASM

"How old were you when you first masturbated to orgasm? How did you feel about it, and what did you think about it?"

Most boys had had their first masturbation and orgasm alone:

"I had my first orgasm before I was aware of sex in any form (I led a very sheltered life), at about age twelve as I was climbing a tree. For almost two years I 'made love to trees' in that I would climb trees just to get that good feeling. I was about thirteen before any juice would come out. To keep from staining my pants, I would go into the woods where no one was around and take off my clothes and climb around trees until the juice came. I didn't know what the juice was, but I knew that I wasn't just leaking pee. In the wintertime, I would go into the bathroom, take off my clothes, and pretend that I was climbing a tree by hanging on the closet door and pressing my penis against the edge. I would juice within several minutes of this activity and would experience a delightful sensation all over my body."

"My first experience with masturbation was by accident. At age twelve I pressed my penis flat against the mattress, then began pressing a bit more and came. I didn't realize what happened. It just felt really nice. For some time I masturbated by rubbing my penis against the mattress. Then I tried to stop it when I found out what it was. I'd do it in my sleep. After hearing about it from others, I masturbated by holding it in my hand and sliding the skin up and down."

"When I first began masturbating at age eleven or twelve, I had no idea of its connection with 'sex,' and simply thought I was a unique human who had been given this special ability to have pleasure which seemed mystically connected with ladies and flying."

"I was in seventh grade when I first masturbated (eleven or twelve years old). It was to orgasm. I learned by myself. I had an erection and it felt good to touch and rub it, so I went into the bathroom (which was the only place where I could have the needed degree of privacy), sat on the toilet, and rubbed my erect penis because it felt good. I didn't know that it would lead to an orgasm (ejaculation), but it did and that felt great, too. After that, I went to the bathroom nearly every day after I got home from school and sat on the toilet and masturbated."

"When I first ejaculated a few squirts of sperm, I was surprised—I expected it to stream out like urine if anything came out at all. That was a great feeling that I was able to bring to myself although it did hurt a little the first time."

"I was thirteen and had been having wet dreams for about four months before learning how to masturbate. I was daydreaming one afternoon, absentmindedly massaging an erection, when I had an orgasm. It completely blew my mind. I felt expanded, wonderful, and very secretive. It was the first time I felt *adult*, as if I'd been invested with responsibility. Briefly, I thought about babies. I kept all these feelings to myself because I was certain, at that time, that I shouldn't speak to anyone about this."

"At one point normal washing of my genitals (which I had been doing for a long time) caused a 'good' feeling in my penis which then proceeded to erect itself with repeated washing strokes. So I continued and after a short while the 'unbearable' and ever mounting pressure resolved itself into bursts of ejaculating semen. I thought the sensation was incredibly pleasurable. After that, I'd rush home from school at least three days a week, dash to the bathroom, turn the water on in the sink, drop my trousers, grab the soap, and jerk off wildly."

"I first masturbated about the age of twelve. Like most boys, I discovered it was pleasurable to rub my penis—one day I kept on doing it while looking out the window at a well-built young construction worker across the street at a building site. The next thing I knew I started to experience waves of pleasure—then I came. At first I thought I was sick. But after asking a few other guys I discovered they did it too. From that time on I jerked off every night, sometimes three or four times a day. I guess I have not missed too many days right down to the present. Of course, being Catholic I soon was told it was a 'mortal' sin. So I tried with little success to refrain. It never worked."

"I had my first orgasm when I was nine years old. I can remember exactly what happened. I was sitting in class in school, and I felt as though I had to go to the rest room to urinate; but my teacher would not let me go. I put my hand in my pocket, and, through my clothes, I held on to the head and upper part of the shaft of my penis. When I moved my fingertips, it made my penis feel good, so I kept moving them. Finally, my penis got hard, felt real good, and started throbbing. Something wet squirted out of it, and, at first, I thought that I had urinated in my pants. I soon realized, though, that the liquid was sticky and different from urine. For a long time after that I did not understand what was happening, but I started doing it more and more often, except I did it in private from then on."

"The first ejaculation, masturbating in bed at night, was a wonderful feeling and I wanted to tell my friends all about it the next day."

"I remember my first orgasm (age twelve) with ejaculation very well. I had been reading one of my brother's 'dirty books' and had had an erection for twenty minutes before I began to masturbate. When I orgasmed I felt for the first time as if I had committed a grievous sin, and went into the bathroom and laid down on the floor, lightly banging my head on the floor in time with the words 'I won't ever do this again.' The promise to myself lasted about two days. No one ever gave me the information that what was happening was normal, beautiful, and delightful. I couldn't share this experience with anyone at the time. I finally talked about this experience with one or two people when I was in my late twenties."

"I had my first orgasm at age twelve, masturbating, and I was racked with guilt. That 'guilt' has always intrigued me. Nobody ever told me there was anything wrong with masturbating, *ever*. In fact, my father had told me that it was perfectly normal and not to worry about it if I should do it. Still, when it happened, when, without meaning to, I did this *thing* to myself (which, I suppose, *might* barely be masturbation), I was sure that I had somehow ruined my sex life, perhaps damaged myself irreparably, certainly done something disgusting. Never again! Until the next day. And so forth. Where did this feeling come from? The Freudian idea that violent fantasies, especially patricidal ones, cause masturbatory guilt just doesn't ring true—I was thinking about girls. I suspect that the intensity of the experience was frightening, and the fear, combined with the sense that it wasn't proper to be in the bathroom rubbing your 'private parts,' produced a sense of having really done something wrong."

Many boys who had their first orgasm alone were alarmed and terrified by their first orgasm or ejaculation, as no one had prepared them for such an occurrence:*

"At ten I was masturbating and I came. I thought it was blood. Punishment from God for doing this filthy and unnatural thing. When I turned on the light, I saw this funny creamy white stuff."

"I began masturbating at sixteen. I thought I was bleeding."

"Age fourteen. I thought something had broken inside but it felt wonderful."

"Age twelve. I was riding my bike and I came. I thought I had damaged myself. I went to a doctor who diagnosed me as 'getting old.' "

"At thirteen I had a wet dream. I was frightened, I thought my insides were coming out or I was dying. No one had told me what to expect, even though Father was an M.D.!"

"I had heard about 'jacking off' but I didn't know quite what to expect. I was horrified when this thick fluid came out of my penis in spurts. I thought I had harmed myself and was very distraught. I felt very evil and promised God I'd never do it again, a promise frequently remade and broken."

"As a boy I came only in wet dreams, and didn't know *what* was going on. Nobody explained. I thought I was wetting my bed!"

"I thought I had broken something and was squirting blood or urine. My parents were close-mouthed and didn't talk about those things. I didn't even look at my parents for a month afterwards."

"My first ejaculation came a few months after I started masturbating and I was afraid I had made myself sick by doing it too much. I wondered if I should tell my mother."

"When I first masturbated, I thought I had killed myself."

"I remember fondling, rubbing, stroking my penis under the covers for quite a while, until one day I orgasmed. I was incredibly ignorant and fearful. Even though it was weird, I

---

* The confusion and fear caused by this lack of information is similar to girls' first feelings on beginning menstruation when they have not been told that this will happen.

was all right afterwards. It felt like something breaking, but nothing was broken. I hadn't ejaculated yet. And then one night when everything was going as usual, I orgasmed, and this sticky gooey whitish stuff spurted all over me and the bed-clothes. I thought that whatever had felt like it was breaking, had broken. I'd ruined it forever. I was scared and felt guilty and sinful. Plus I had to clean it up or my mother would find out. I swore to all the powers that be, if only it would be all right, and no one would find out, I'd never do it again."

Others were more surprised than frightened:

"I was a little afraid when I saw the few drops coming out of the end of my penis. I got down real close and examined it. It amazed me."

"I thought it was wonderful. I remember I was quite shaken the very first time. I thought I had unloosed something which was hitherto unknown to mankind. I thought I was losing my mind, and so reported the sensation to a friend, who thought I was a riot."

"I can still remember the first time I masturbated to ejaculation. I was thirteen and was overwhelmed by the sensation. I just couldn't believe it was there for the pumping."

Some boys, who had been prepared (usually by other boys) for ejaculation, felt they had achieved a new status as a man:

"I felt that I had arrived and now I was one of the 'big guys' too."

"When I finally ejaculated at thirteen, I felt great! 'Hooray, I'm a man!' The world was complete."

"At eleven after masturbating I came. I felt now I was a 'man' and could do anything."

"With my first ejaculation at fifteen, I thought of it as a big thing, quite macho. Something to brag about to the guys."

"The first few orgasms were dry, so I had to wait even longer to ejaculate semen (I was sixteen). Having an orgasm improved my self-esteem; I had a late puberty and it annoyed me not to have pubic hair like my peers in the gym shower."

"At first I was surprised at something coming out, then happy to be 'a man.' "

"After I came while masturbating, I thought I was a great guy who was gonna lay every chick in sight."

"One day I was masturbating and noticed hair around my cock. Instead of just climaxing, I shot a wad—a totally new experience for a fourteen-year-old, I tell you. I felt like a man, heh-heh."

Many boys had first masturbated to orgasm before they were physically able to ejaculate (usually for approximately six months to a year, but sometimes longer):*

"If 'first orgasm' means when I first ejaculated, then I first ejaculated when I was eleven. But I had been masturbating to orgasm since I can remember—I guess five."

"Orgasm and ejaculation are synonymous for me now. But before puberty I regularly had orgasms without ejaculating. It was a slightly different sensation but quite remarkable. When I talked with my friends about this when we were kids, we referred to it as that 'funny feeling' . . . and we all used to try to get that 'funny feeling.' "

"I used to play with myself all evening long and would beat off in the shower with the stream of water. For a while, I would come without ejaculating and it was incredible—like nothing I'd ever felt before. Then when I started ejaculating I was really amazed. It was really neat."

And one boy said:

"At twelve I was masturbating and ejaculated. Being able to come was great until I found that repeated climaxes were more difficult to obtain after ejaculation."

But perhaps a surprising number of boys had had their first masturbation with other boys or learned to masturbate by watching other boys:†

"This classmate, thirteen years old, showed me how to jack off by sitting on a toilet at school. He sat there beating his meat, which was a lot bigger than mine, until he was ready to come and told me to watch while he shot. That evening at home, in the bathroom, I did the same. I didn't orgasm by masturbating until two months later. I loved the idea of being grown-up enough to come."

"I was twelve years of age when I began to masturbate.

* With no ejaculation there is no refractory period; thus several orgasms in a row are possible. (See also pages 607–609.)

† See also chapter 1.

Guys from school, groups of six to twelve, used to go to one guy's house, after school, whose parents worked and didn't get home until about 6 p.m. We had jack-off contests like: who could squirt the farthest, who could last the longest, the tempo of the stroke being set by following the beat of a song on a record. Who could come with the most-quantity into a Mason jar; who could come the most-number of repeat climaxes in measured time. There was mild homosexual contact: touching another guy, never actually stroking another guy to climax; checking out each other's equipment. Group nudity and checking out asses."

"My first orgasm was with another boy, between fifth and sixth grade. We were masturbating in a tree behind his farmhouse. Really was something. I couldn't wait to show my other friends. We had jacking-off sessions all the time after that. I used to double-date with several friends, we would take the girls home, then jack off together afterward, eventually working up to blowing each other."

"When I was about ten or eleven, an older boy (about fourteen) showed me how to masturbate. I recall being amazed by the amount of hair he had and by the size of his penis, and also amazed by his ejaculation. He didn't describe his orgasm, however, or indicate that it felt any different from pissing. At that moment all I did was watch, but later the same day at home I locked myself in the bathroom and looked at my penis—I was disappointed to find no hair—then I tried masturbating in the way I'd seen. It felt good so I kept on; when the orgasm hit, I was shocked, alarmed, and extremely gratified all at once. There was no semen at that age. From then on I masturbated several times a week."

"I was around thirteen, at Boy Scout camp. After the taps the guys used to talk about fucking, blowing your guts, etc. I didn't know what they were talking about. Then one afternoon when we were supposed to be writing letters home or resting, and the counselors were off swimming, two of the guys had a contest to see who could 'come' the fastest. They took their pants off and started working their limp pricks up to a boner. (That's what they called it—beats me!) Well, that was the first time I'd ever seen a boner or anyone 'come.' It was amazing. I started playing with myself and have masturbated ever since."

"A boy two years older showed me how to masturbate by having me stroke his penis until he ejaculated. I was horrified. A short time later I tried it out on myself with some timidity and a lot of curiosity. It was a revelation."

"I shared a bed with my older brother, who was twelve years old, when I was six. We used to manually stimulate each other. I reached what I remember as a terribly hot pulsating feeling."

"I heard a song about masturbating at summer camp, to the tune of 'Finiculi, Finicula.' I only remember a fragment, but here it is:

'You should see me on the short strokes,
*   I use my hand, it feels so grand!*
You should see me on the long strokes,
*   I use my feet, it feels so neat!*
Bash it, smash it, beat it on the floor,
——— it, ——— it, ———! (forgotten)
Some people say this intercourse is GRAND,
But for all around enjoyment I prefer it in the hand!'

CONCLUSION: TOWARD A NEW MALE SEXUALITY

Men loved almost all of the activities in this chapter, and felt that they did not get enough of them—including fellatio, being stimulated and caressed on their penis, testicles, and anus, perhaps masturbating with a partner, and general "foreplay" and touching. Why are these activities so unexplored? Perhaps many men would like to end the focus on intercourse as being "*the* sex act," but cultural pressures (both internal and external) are such that they feel that they have no right to do so, as "men."

In our definition of sex, men have always been the "doers," and women the "done-to." Although men like this in some ways, in other ways they often resent it. As one man put it, "Doing all the work makes me feel precisely that I am less desirable to her than she is to me." One of the most important themes of men's replies is their desire to sometimes be the receiver during sex, to feel *wanted*, acted on, given to—as if the other person really wants to make love to them. At the same time, many men jealously guard their prerogative of being "in charge" and dominant in the male-female relationship, and resent any attempts by women to become more assertive or active sexually.

Many men seemed to feel on a gut level that somehow they were missing out—and yet our culture's prescriptions about sexuality (and "masculinity") have been so strong, that only a few have been able to go past them and follow their own feelings, create their own personal sexuality.

Most men in this study did not want to be penetrated, either physically or emotionally—and yet *did* want it. Just as in love and marriage men believe they will be happy dominating the relationship, controlling it, rather than risking their guts to a more equal, give-and-take relationship (see chapter 2)—just so in traditional sex men say they want to penetrate the other, thrust, be in charge, in control, and define the end of sex, the goal, as their orgasm, and yet they long for the opposite, to be out of control, also dominated by the other. To control something, whether it be sex or a relationship, is boring in the long run. And yet most men *do* want to be in deeper contact—to feel more—to not only take, but also be penetrated and taken.

What would this kind of sex be like? "Sexuality" as we know it has usually had orgasm as its object; but sensuality, being without an object, would allow you to go beyond the bounds of everyday existence to experience an end to rational awareness, a losing of the "self"—to feel, to be, in a pure state, to renew yourself, to reach a stage of intensity, letting layers of feeling penetrate deeper and deeper, until you feel yourself transformed. As Isolde sings to Tristan, as they are making love, she wishes "to live and die in eternal night— in the heaving swell, in the resounding echoes, in the universal stream of the world breath, to drown, to founder, unconscious, in utmost rapture."

Passion is one of the most beautiful parts of all sensuality— the desire to possess, to take, to ravish and be ravished, penetrate and be penetrated.* But is physical love real love? While love is caring, love is also passion and desire, the desire to belong to, mingle with, be inside of another. Part of love is a sheer physical feeling—a desire not only to have orgasm or "sex," but to lie close while sleeping together, to inhale the breath of the other, to press chests (and souls) together as tightly, as closely, as possible; to lie feeling the other breathe as they sleep, their breath grazing your cheek and mingling with your own breath; to smell their body, caress their mouth with your tongue as if it were your own mouth, know the smell and taste of their genitals—to feel with your finger

---

* See also some of men's answers on pages 794–804.

inside them, to caress the opening of their buttocks. What is love? Love is talking and understanding and counting on and being counted on, but love is also the deepest intermingling of bodies. In a way, body memory of a loved one is stronger and lasts longer than all the other memories.

5

MEN'S FEELINGS ABOUT WOMEN'S ORGASMS

Me: 'Would you like to make love tonight?' Her: 'No, not really—do you mind?' Me: 'Oh no, that's all right, just a thought.' "

"I'm twenty-five. Was a guitar player and still am I guess, but now I'm married and have a daughter and a foxy wife I love. Our sex life, it's great when we have it. It's just my wife's sex urge just isn't as big as mine. I guess I'm a pig, I think!"

"I could never understand how someone I loved as much, my wife, could go to sleep or ignore me as much as she has done. It hurt me for fifteen years until I just sort of gave up. I begged, pleaded, cajoled for her to show her feelings more for me but nothing worked. It could have been due to her home life as it seems that we are repeating it. But not to the degree her parents did because I am different than her father. He gave up a lot sooner with her mother and probably quit going to bed or caring after the first ten years, although they lived under the same roof for forty years in different bedrooms. My wife (forty-five years old) still reverts back to a teenager in the presence of her mother who hates me for marrying her. Thankfully she lives 250 miles away. I do not cry anymore because I don't care anymore."

"I think I possibly have a sex problem—that is, being oversexed, because of my constant fantasizing about sex. My wife just doesn't want to like I do—too tired, headache, ceiling needs painting, wrong time, kid crying, don't mess my hair, go ahead if you want to."

"As one writer (male) very correctly said, a man is always *depending* on the 'good will' of a woman. There is not a man in the world who can get out of bed in the morning and say for *sure: today I'm gonna get laid*, while *any* woman who is not actually a 'monster' *can* do this *any day*. If I could be born again I'd like to be a *gorgeous redhead*. I could fuck all I want—when I want—without having to get up on my two hind feet like a little poodle for a piece of sugar: 'Can I have a piece of ass *pleeease?*' "

"I would like to have a wife that was *interested* in sex, more often, more variety, more time. I tell my wife this constantly. It took threatening to leave her to get minimal satisfaction. In fact, as long as I treated her politely, she treated me, sexually, like dirt. After I started to demand things, and treat her like a chattel, I got a lot more action (not enough) out of her. Fear of being abandoned does a lot of good, I find."

618 THE HITE REPORT ON MALE SEXUALITY

"It is a fact that many women look upon sex as a chore to bring about the excretion of a little vile snivel accompanied with a kind of convulsion and considerable writhing."

"After being married twenty-six years, I do like being married, I love the woman and I always have. We've had some very severe marital problems, one and a half years separated, together again now for six weeks and so far it's better than it was. Sex in our marriage is not so good. Quite simply stated, I'm turned on, she isn't. In the last years I've felt depressed because of my feeling I'm not getting the fullest possible complete sexual experience. I sincerely feel that it couldn't really be much better and that I'm expecting more than is possible for any woman to give. I think also that I'm not physically well, something like low blood sugar which can cause symptoms of depression, indigestion, heartburn, tiredness, etc. But why doesn't she want it as much as I do?"

"I will be married twenty-four years next month. Overall I like it, but there is a slow, deadly erosion of sex. The affection lingers. I still love my wife in many ways. She does not like sex—she probably never really did—and I have tried just about everything, chiefly patience and gentleness and forbearance, with no real change. It is a sad thing. I wish it weren't that way. It never was that great, for us. I wish we could have kept moderately happy and gone to bed more often. We still sleep together in a double bed. In all these years I don't think she ever has asked for sex, in any form, and invariably has seemed relieved when I didn't want to. There is still a feeling of warmth and partnership, and we love our kids, but the spark, the magic, has long departed. She has her hobbies, I mine, and we don't communicate much except about routine matters. If the morning paper is late we never have much to say at breakfast. She is a fine person in most respects and I wish things were different. They just aren't. Yet I do not ever intend to leave her. I have many failings, but I am loyal. (Although I had two long-term affairs, over now.)"

"I live for sex and want it whenever I can get the chance. My wife is just the opposite. Marriage is a real screw-up, but even with a reluctant wife I think that I get more sex than if I were single trying to make out at some bar . . . I think that's why I've stayed married almost twenty-eight years to one woman; I mean, she's not perfection but what or who the hell is. I suppose I really in some way feel like I'm oversexed and some kind of a maniac and put myself down for always having sex on my mind."

"I have been married for twenty years. I like being married but live an essentially asexual existence. It may be my fault, but I don't think so. I put the burden on my wife's family and on her for not trying harder to modify her essentially negative, destructive attitude toward herself and her own sexuality. The initial contact sexually with my wife is, with few exceptions, almost always initiated by me—never by her. She is so repressed that physical contact is normally repugnant to her. I try to touch her, embrace her, kiss her. If she is receptive (seldom) she will feel warm, and force herself to go soft and cuddly. I then proceed to caress, eventually fondle her. Unfortunately my advances are usually rebuffed by a cold, rigid—don't touch me—reaction. But I never let a day or evening go by without reaching out to her and trying to comfort her (that's pretty hard work sometimes, no matter what the resolve). It is now mid-April. The last time I had intercourse with my wife was in mid-November."

"I'm a Ph.D., college professor, married for fourteen years. I prefer being married to being single, at least most of the time: after a period of fighting and sex deprivation I always add up the pros and cons of being married—so far being married seems best. I got married originally because it seemed about time, I was thirty-one—and because I loved my wife. In recent years, our sex has become routinized and largely without passion. It has been fourteen years since I've had sex with anyone except my wife. I have never told my wife of the joy I obtain from masturbation. She wouldn't be interested.

"I don't know how much she enjoys sex with me. She has orgasm no more than one-third of the times we have sex. I would very much prefer to have sex with a woman who has orgasm from coitus. In fourteen years of marriage that has never happened with my wife. She manages to orgasm through clitoral stimulation only, and for a long time I was resentful of this behavior. I thought if she would just try harder, she could orgasm with me, from the stimulation of my penis in her vagina. But reading *The Hite Report* convinced me that the need for clitoral stimulation is not uncommon, and that I am probably not the fault of her lack of 'normal' orgasm. Our life improved after this became known.

"With all its faults and shortcomings, I am probably happiest married as I am now. The best thing is that the relationship is stable. But I fear that we may be creating the setting for one of those later-life divorces. Once the children are gone, and retirement provides us with the time to do the things we always have wanted to do, I fear that we will discover just how incompatible we really are. The largest single problem in our marrige is that my wife's need for sex is about one-half or less than my need."

"We have been married for twenty-one years. When we were married I was twenty-two and she was twenty-one, both virgins. The first few years were great. But then we started a family, and all the pressures of raising my kids, buying a home and being successful stopped our communication. Eventually I felt that her lack of interest in anything outside of raising children was my fault. In addition, my wife as it turns out has a fairly difficult time achieving orgasm. She says that the orgasm is not necessary for her satisfaction.

"We reached a stage in our marriage where I felt that I was a 'sex maniac.' My wife is very easily sexually satisfied. I could not understand how she could be fulfilled without sexual gratification and eventually this became a great problem to me. I could not accept the fact that she was not as sensual as I—did not want sex as often or get as much pleasure. On occasion, I cried, thinking I was not the right person sexually for my wife. I felt totally inadequate and useless. I even planned on leaving and letting my wife find someone with whom she would be happy. We have talked this over many times, and my wife says she is totally fulfilled and is this not why two people share their lives? I guess I should feel contentment in the fact that she is happy and fulfilled. I don't always have this feeling though, and I get really tense and short-tempered if I go without sex for any time at all. If my wife is not interested in intercourse, then I get uptight.

"Finally, I found myself involved with a married mother of three, the wife of a co-worker. Our marriage was finished as far as I was concerned. I loved my wife, but she just didn't seem to give a damn. Whenever I brought up the topic of sex, I was told that I placed too much importance on it. I figured that I had failed my wife in not awakening the potential of her own sexual self. When she told me everything was fine and I would try to explain my feelings, we would come to an impasse. All other aspects of our marriage were good. We enjoyed the same things, the same people. No money problems plus my wife has always been a good mother and home-maker—but bed was very seldom a happy place.

"The woman I met had much the same problem. Without seeking it, a two-year affair ensued. We gave each other what we felt we were missing with our spouses. If anything, my love for my wife grew throughout this period. I never felt guilty (and still don't). Neither of us wanted our spouses to find out but I think deep down I really did. I didn't want to hurt my wife and yet I think I hoped that she would find out and realize that we did have a problem. The affair itself was totally satisfying—pure sexual bliss, fantastic. I discovered that I wasn't an oddball in bed—that my sexual appetites weren't abnormal—and yes, I could satisfy a woman. I felt as though I had been re-born.

"During this time, I tried to tell my wife what I felt and tried to find out what her feelings and expectations were. Our children were growing up and I started suggesting that she get out of the house and do something that she wanted to do. Not the bridge and coffee routine—but something that would make her more aware of herself, less dependent on me and give her a feeling of fulfillment outside the home. I have always read a lot but now I started bringing home 'dirty books.' Such books as *Joy of Sex, Human Sexual Response,* etc., were brought home and read—by me. Try as I would, my wife would only glance through them with pursed lips. I would read articles to my wife and she would agree with them—but that was it. I brought a vibrator home—it sounded like a Mack truck—so much for that—I was a sex fiend. But at least we were talking.

"One night after making love I told her that she was superb and when she said, 'How do you know? You're only saying that,' I told her that I did know because I had made love with another woman. The reaction was understandable. We stayed up all night talking and have been talking ever since. I bought her a Prelude 2* and we incorporate it into our lovemaking sometimes now. I bought *Getting Clear* and *For Yourself* but you don't change overnight. My wife went back to school and is getting a bachelor's degree. I have always done housework—cooking, etc.—but now I do a bit more and the kids are more involved around the house. I think we have a good home in which it is fun to be a family.

* This is a type of vibrator designed for use on the clitoris, and not inside the vagina.

"After the initial shock of not having Mommy home all the time, things settled down and I think our family is a healthier unit. But I found it very lonely at first and felt threatened. I have had one affair since she started to work. I'm not too sure why. I will never tell my wife about this one because it would really hurt her. The funny thing is that right now my wife is just completing a course in 'human sexuality' and we are talking and loving all the time. I don't feel that I am being unfaithful and truthfully can say that I hope my wife will be fortunate enough to share herself—enjoy herself with someone other than me. I don't think she will ever really realize what a total woman she is until someone else tells her. I wish this for her—not to ease my conscience—but for her sake so that she will know the feeling of being her own person. I would not like her to go through life feeling that she missed something. My one fear is that she would find someone she would rather be with but if that were the case—so be it.

"The only real problem left is that my wife still makes very few demands about having sex. If I look forward to bedtime and have helped my wife through the day and evening so that we can spend some leisurely time together—just loving—and then she sits in front of the TV set and comes to bed late, saying, 'Why don't you come in me, I don't want to come, I'm too tired,' I figure, 'Hell, what's the point.' And then I feel hurt that she can't be bothered enough to get involved. This to me is a real let-down. The same goes for the everyday little things like touching and kissing. When you get rebuffed because 'the kids might see,' I figure that something is wrong—and that's when I look for a relationship elsewhere. I feel so hurt when my advances are repulsed, and most of all when I am feeling particularly tender and loving."

Why don't women—or at least most women—want sex with men as much or as often as men want sex with women? It is valid to ask not only "Why don't women want more sex with men?" but also "Why do men want sex with women so much?" In essence, we did ask this question, and looked into the answers, in chapter 3; the answers involve understanding what sex means to men. Without these meanings, many of them culturally created, men might want it, as currently defined, less. However, in this chapter we will address men's assertion that women frequently lack interest in sex, and the reasons for this.

A related complaint: Women rarely make sexual advances, and frequently turn men's advances down.

"Do you usually make the initial sexual advance? How do you feel about it? How do you feel if the other person does not want to have sex with you? Do you ever initiate sex because the other person seems to expect it?"

Not only did men complain that women often do not want sex as frequently as they do, but similarly, men complained that women rarely initiate sex. Almost every man who answered said he was almost always the one who made the initial advance in heterosexual relations—and almost every man resented or felt uncomfortable about this fact (and the possibility of rejection), often expressing a strong emotional reaction:

"I usually make the initial advance and I definitely do not feel good about it. If the other person does not want to have sex, I feel quite hurt. My self-esteem is lowered considerably."

"I make the initial sexual advance, but I don't like to. If the other person doesn't want to have sex with me I get angry. I get tears in my eyes but I hide them."

"I do not like to always have to be the one who gets things rolling. Why should I always be the one to run the risk of being told no? Depending on who it is, I either roll over and go to sleep, or I feel rejected."

"I *hate* making sexual advances. It makes me feel vulgar and crude."

"I usually make the first advance, but I don't feel very good about it; in fact, I usually feel like a jerk trying to pick someone up at a party or something."

"If I'm 'rejected' I feel like a total fool. I feel like apologizing to the woman and slinking off to a corner like the lecherous scum she must think I am."

"I usually make the first sexual advance, and this has given me about twenty years of trouble: anxiety about asserting myself and expressing a desire for sex, trying to get what I want and still be considered a 'nice guy.'"

"I almost always make the initial sexual advance in all my relationships and I hate it!! I feel like I am stealing something or forcing her to do something she may in fact not want to do."

"If the other person does not want to have sex with me I feel alone and defeated."

"I usually make the initial sexual advance. How do I feel about it? *I feel precisely that I am less desirable to the woman than she is to me;* and fairly often I feel I'm frightening her. That is one hell of a way to begin. When the woman does make the sexual advance, that alone gives me very positive feelings. I hope she feels the same way when I make the sexual advance to her, but I seldom get that impression. If she does not want to have sex with me, I try not to, but do, feel hurt and rejected. I know this is unfair and not rational, but I can't help it."

The basic feelings most men reported when a partner didn't want to have sex were rejection, disappointment, and annoyance or anger. Here are some answers to "How do you feel if the other person does not want to have sex with you?":

"It's a humiliating experience, and I feel like I could never look that person in the eye again."

"That old monster, rejection, is the most painful remnant of my adolescent sexual attitudes. It's idiotic to feel that way, I just ignore it and hope it'll go away."

"I think, let's face it: I'm a geek. Women don't find me attractive. How come a sexual advance by me seems to be totally *un*expected, contrary to what seems to be the norm? Sure, it's expected from jock types, men who always have their way around women, but I must have been dropped from another planet."

"It doesn't hurt my feelings intellectually, as I can understand her reasons, but my body doesn't follow my brain. A refusal at bedtime often results in night-long insomnia and a bad day the next day. Fortunately, she loves me, likes to have intercourse, even passively, and it doesn't happen very often."

"I feel mildly rejected the first time she doesn't want it. Two or three times in a row are another story. I sometimes get angry and demanding and tell her she is inhuman to make me go so long without sex."

"Many times the girl will respond with a vehement 'No' and make me feel like a barbarian rapist by her facial expression. I generally get angry when I make an advance and am refused, because I don't attempt to initiate sex lightly or with just anybody."

Only a handful of men said they preferred always to be the aggressors:

"I'm old-fashioned. I like a man pursuing, woman coy. I like to chase, woo, and win. I like to be the aggressor, and only once in a while let her take me."

"I make the sexual advance. I feel somewhat celebrated about making the sexual advance as it brings me a lot of attention from my friends. It is fun and gratifying to be the one who gets the girl."

"I like it. I need that macho trip."

"I prefer it, because if the other person pursues *me*, I immediately start worrying about being trapped, dominated, etc."

A few men said it was ordained by nature that men be the aggressors:

"It's up to the man . . . since he has the strongest sex drive."

"God made men that way."

"It's great. I go right on to the next one until I get my score . . . make a killing and get my satisfied feeling like a Wolf or an Elk."

Although most men thought the tradition that they should have to take the initiative—and risk rejection—was unfair, some said they accepted it as just the way things are:

"I think that most women are rather shy of making advances; the customary ethic is that men are supposed to do that. Which is not fair; but there it is."

"I initiate the sex because I feel it is expected from the girl and it has always worked out to be the best to save time in many ways."

"I almost always initiate intercourse. I don't mind; I'm used to it."

Once again, there were many complaints that the man having to take the initiative made it seem women didn't want sex as much as they did:

"The feminist movement has made a big point of the fact that our society 'tells women they have no sexual desires.' There is another side of that coin. The same set of conventions, rules, and assumptions say to a man that he is not sexually desirable. They say that the intimacy and contact which he wants with women are something repugnant to her, something she considers degrading, something which *perhaps* he can get from her by bribery, persuasion, or trickery, but certainly not something which she would do for its own sake. This idea makes the man 'the enemy' to women. He must identify with the role of 'enemy,' 'out to score.' "

"I find I usually have to make the initial sexual advance because she can go for so long without sex. Sometimes I wonder if she is acquiescing to an advance because she feels she has to 'perform,' because it's 'her duty' or some other similar shit that women have been brought up to feel. I would feel much better if she would say, 'I have a sexual identity that is mine to explore, expand and enjoy. I haven't tried this. So let's do X Y and Z!' I would feel much better if I knew she was as interested in me for her own sake and gratification as I am in her for my own sake and gratification."

And more feelings of anger:

"This is the question I've been waiting for. *Yes,* I usually make the initial sexual advance—the initial advance and every other advance after that—and I'm damned tired of it. *I* make the first phone call, *I* make the first date, *I* kiss *her,* *I* touch *her,* and *I* fuck *her.* It's no wonder we grow up to think of women as objects, because that's exactly what many women act like. They give little indication that they are driven by the same motives, desires, and urges that we are. They operate under the assumption that they have something we want—why don't they ever act like *we* have something *they* want? When am I going to be treated like a sexual object?—I'd love it."

Others commented on the roles men and women are assigned to play by our culture:

"I usually make the first overt sexual advance. I am not too thrilled about the social norms that make this necessarily so. Because women are taught not to make advances, men are obliged to second-guess them, single-handedly carry the risk of rejection, and devise ingenious ways of signaling: 'I want you but I won't rape you, so say no if it's no.' "

"My wife used to be more aggressive sexually but since we have had kids, it's like she thinks somebody's mother shouldn't feel me up or try to turn me on. I guess once a kid or two comes you are locked into many traditional roles. Sometimes I'm not sure she wants sex but goes along with me because it's her role. This is so depressing to me . . . like something out of Queen Victoria's era."

"I have a great feeling of pressure on me to ask the girl for a date, to kiss her, to start a romantic conversation, to be the aggressor in sex and to dominate it, all because I feel it is expected of me to behave like this."

"I often feel that I should initiate sex with women because it's expected. Women often feel that I should, too, because it's expected. It's my job, my role, after all. I don't have much to do with women like that anymore. Whenever I feel that I 'should' be doing something or other because it's expected of me because of some role that I'm assumed to be playing, I start feeling really hostile. I try not to act on my hostility, and realize that they're being victimized by role playing too, but I am firm about not getting involved in situations in which my behavior is expected to follow some arbitrary pattern that has nothing to do with my needs."

Only a few men said they did not usually make the first advance:

"We decided a long time ago that anything goes. Whoever is horny or just happy will make it known and hopefully the other partner is ready and willing to accompany the initiator. Since we live apart we are both normally ready all the time. If she's preoccupied or in a down mood I'm still very content to just hold her. I'm more concerned with helping her than satisfying my sexual urge. I think it proves how much I care about her. I've masturbated beside her if I just have to release the internal pressure. She appeals so much to me I just always want her—I want her close by and sexually as much as possible. I love her."

Do men want women to make the first advance?

Over and over again, as we have seen, men said they wished the woman would make the first advance:

"I have read about men who do not want their wife making the first advance, but not me. I can remember about twenty years ago (we had been married three years) we checked into a motel on vacation in the middle of the afternoon. Soon after getting in our room, my wife pushed me onto the bed and climbed on top of me. The loving that followed was wild and torrid. How I wish she would act like that again."

"I'd like my wife to just outright ask me if she wanted to fuck, or just come over and grab me and caress me or when I'm sleeping wake me up blowing or fucking me or just come over to me and start playing with me when we're alone at night but she never does any of these. It gives me a sort of inferiority or not whole feeling in our marriage."

"I'd love to be a sex object at least for a while. I think I'd probably have a heart attack if some woman said to me, 'You turn me on and I'd like to make love with you.' "

"I often wish they'd be more up-front and tell me what they have in mind. I wonder if they tell Redford in advance."

And yet many men—sometimes the same men who wished women would make the first advance—had mixed or negative feelings about whether the woman should make the first advance or be sexually aggressive:

"When I suggested to my partner that she be more aggressive, she tried it and I back-pedaled. My initial reaction to any sexually aggressive woman is to move away."

"When a woman I'm not interested in makes an advance, I feel uncomfortable, as if advances from a woman were still so rare that it would be cruel to discourage her by not responding."

"I have felt that my wife was too passive. But maybe women are passive out of wisdom, since I am frequently unreceptive when she has been more aggressive."

"There *was* one occasion when I was living with a woman for a week, when I wanted to avoid sex after a few days. Amazing how my sex drive dropped; maybe it was a subconscious fear of getting trapped."

"As women become more direct in their sexual expression, I think more men are going to get scared. The times when I had to decline an invitation to sexual activity from a woman I am intimate with were annoying: first I tried to express disinterest by not responding physically. When asked outright 'How's about it?' I had to apologize and decline. I don't like having to apologize, and especially I don't think I should ever *have* to apologize. I should be ready, or as a man, I should be able to do it."

"It's strange, about having a woman make a pass at *me*

—I haven't gotten rid of the cliché that 'she might be a prostitute.' "

"As for having her make the 'pass' at me—that's one of my fantasies, but I 'choke up' (get real nervous) whenever there's the possibility that someone *is* making a pass at me. I feel that I've lost control of the situation, and although I *want* to be 'picked up,' I'm not yet comfortable enough with that feeling. I also get very confused. Is she serious, or is she just joking? Is that a 'meaningful' look, or am I reading too much into it?"

"It turns me off to have the woman be the aggressor (initially anyway). I can't stand being 'hustled' by a hooker or a female whom I am not attracted to."

"My fantasy is that I'd love to have someone make passes at me. The truth is probably, though, that I'd be scared to death. But I've had one really neat experience where I met a lady, we kissed long and sexually (birthday kisses) and she called me up that night to ask if I wanted to make love the next day. I said yes, and didn't sleep all night."

"I find I am resentful when women are too abrupt in initiating sex. If they wish to be 'seductive' I am delighted, however."

"I do not wish to be the one always expected to initiate sexual contact. At the same time, I find that I very much wish to be 'invited,' rather than seduced, teased, or played with. I freeze when suddenly gripped about the penis by my lover—the element of forcefulness in my lover's approach to me can be startling to the point of turning me off."

Conclusion

When men say they want women to be more "aggressive" sexually, what do they mean? Do they mean that they want the woman to assert her own sexual identity and uniqueness, to create sex in a new way, a way which might bring more pleasure to her, or do they mean that they want women to participate with more enthusiasm in the ritual of what our culture has come to regard as male sexuality? As one man put it, "I don't like to have a woman be passive with me, because I feel then that she is indifferent, and it endangers my potency. An active women showing her enjoyment and excitation in response to what I do to her excites me. But she shouldn't be demanding, and initiate sex when I don't want it either."

MEN'S DOUBTS, QUESTIONS, AND LACK OF INFORMATION ABOUT WOMEN'S ORGASMS

MOST MEN WERE NOT SURE WHEN A WOMAN HAD AN ORGASM

Many vague answers were received to the question "When/ how does your partner usually orgasm?":

"I suppose during coitus, if at all. Most of my partners have not told me, in words or actions, that they have orgasmed."

"She's usually too tired or harassed, with the kids and all."

"After five minutes."

"I assume she has them from intercourse. Sometimes she rubs her own clitoris then too—but I doubt whether she orgasms this way—she orgasms on top with me making slow ins and outs."

"I haven't usually asked, as long as they have enjoyed it."

"I think it's usually a combination of stimulation. I will have to ask."

"I imagine she has orgasm from my fucking her."

"Here's what we usually do, mainly to make it last. We start out slowly, both of us moving together. We find it easier if there's slow music playing, but if a fast song plays we just 'insert a beat' between every beat. No pun intended. After we've done this for a while, we change from a slow, kind of circular motion to a slightly faster in/out motion. When we

630

both near orgasm, she usually lies still (except for a little squirming) and I begin to alternate between driving it in as far as it will go to pulling it almost all the way out. The closer I come to orgasm, the faster and harder I pump, until I begin to ejaculate. Then we usually lie quietly for a while, before we either start again or leave if we have to."*

"Women's orgasms are always stimulated from some form of pleasant friction placed upon the clitoris, even the deep vagina orgasm is from clitoral stimulation. A good dickman will usually make even a woman suffering from the psychological ills of sexual frigidness melt into a most enjoyable orgasm."

"To be honest, I never really paid that much attention to her reactions before. I'm starting to, though. I don't know if she had orgasms. The girl I'm in love with told me, 'Oh thank you,' after I performed cunnilingus, so I guess she had one, maybe more. I'm going to become more aware from now on. Lots of times I'm too tired after I orgasm to go anymore. I feel so relaxed and almost dead."

"I am not sure if my wife has orgasms, and if she has I didn't notice the difference. She will not discuss it with me."

"Usually I enter her after I enjoy bringing her into an extreme state of arousal. Either she enjoys it as much as I do or she puts on a convincing show. I have a modicum of doubt, but will not ask. I feel that this would remove some of the mystique. We seem to communicate well without words, and the post-coital treatment (she often goes to sleep) would indicate a state of satisfaction."

"I haven't thought much about it, but I guess she has it coincidentally with mine."

"She does not tolerate any clitoral stimulation; probably she orgasms during intercourse, although she gives no sign of it."

"I am very rarely certain of my partner's orgasm; they seize up and spasm, but that could be voluntary, or they might have remembered the opening bars of 'Stardust.' "

And the following two answers were quite typical of many in that they expressed positive sentiments, but left one to wonder exactly when the woman did orgasm:

---

* Due to the lack of differentiation here between his feelings and hers, one wonders, based on women's statements in *The Hite Report* on female sexuality, whether the woman did actually orgasm.

"I'm not like most men. I feel I take into consideration the feelings of my partner. What should I do to make her feel good? I am a sensitive lover, I respect my lover's feelings as well as mine. I take my time and make each movement count. I love foreplay and during intercourse I usually take it nice and slow. I feel I am a sensitive lover who is aware of his partner's needs and wants."

"Some men just want to hop on and hop off with no regard for getting the woman ready or pleasing their partners. Most men don't really know how to please a woman."

"Can you usually tell without asking whether or not your partner has had an orgasm?* How can you tell? Are you ever in doubt? If in doubt, do you ask?"

Most men experienced a great deal of insecurity and confusion over knowing when—or whether—a woman had had an orgasm. (The overwhelming majority were looking for this orgasm during intercourse.) In fact, most men had great doubts about whether, or how frequently, women had orgasms with them; 61 percent of the men who answered said they usually could not tell when a woman had an orgasm, or could not be sure:

"I can't tell. She makes a fair amount of noise and such —but there is no clear division in the visible signs between her intense pleasure short of orgasm, and orgasm."

"This business of knowing when a girl comes is pretty vague and shadowy. It's open to a lot of misunderstanding, as well as out-and-out fraud. I would have to admit that I'm often not sure at all."

"I never really know. I probably hoped or thought that they did more often than they really did. I used to check their nipples to see if they were stiff. I didn't like doing it really, but otherwise I felt compelled to ask, and asking was such a drag. If you ask, it means that it is important to you, and if she's afraid to let you down (and herself), she will lie and say yes."

"Unless a woman has a strong reaction to her own orgasm, I don't always know for certain. Most women are absolutely quiet during their orgasms, like they're ashamed

---

* Although this question does not refer to orgasm during any particular activity, most answers refer to orgasm during intercourse.

of it. Sometimes I can feel it if I'm touching their vaginas or clitorises or abdomens or the insides of their thighs but usually, I have to ask."

"The subtlety of some women's orgasms can be deceiving. I usually try to tell by the partner's movements, a change of pace, quickening of breath, moaning, contractions, grip, affection, kisses, etc., but usually I am not sure."

"With my wife, sometimes I'll ask and she'll usually laugh and say something like 'Couldn't you tell?' or 'What difference does it make?' The crucial thing to her is, and she kids me about this, that her orgasms vary considerably. If she's having a 'big one,' I may be able to tell by the contractions, the waves I feel in her vagina. If I am eating her or masturbating her, I feel the contractions in her vulva and pubic area and her more obvious motions in the rest of her body. But often her coming is subtle, slow, soft."

"I cannot really tell, but with some there are actions that speak more than words. For some orgasm is not what it is all about. I never ask, and only ask if it was a joyful experience, and know if the female wants to see me again, then I could have done something right."

"I have found that the best way for me to know when a woman's orgasm is approaching is for her to tell me. Otherwise I must admit I am only guessing. I can feel that it's happening for her by her movements and groans, but I've been with enough women who have faked it to know that that is not enough."

"I can never tell for sure and it makes me very uneasy. I am always in doubt. I asked one woman but felt very awkward, foolish, and ignorant doing so. She seemed to give an honest reply and I believed her. But another woman felt that if men were sensitive enough, they would know. Well, goddamnit, I'm doing my best to develop that sensitivity, but right now, since each woman seems to be different, it seems thoroughly baffling to me."

Many men said they could only tell after a period of time with a regular partner:

"If we are well acquainted sexually, I can usually tell, otherwise not. I can tell because I know what she looks like during orgasm, how her muscles contract, etc."

"I can always tell when my wife has an orgasm. But I have had sex with a couple of other women who said they orgasmed, but I did not feel that they did. My wife is very obvious because she has intense, long spasms and moans and a sudden change in breathing and attitude."

"At first I couldn't tell but now I can easily. She tightens all her muscles (especially leg and abdominal) and trembles all over."

"I can tell with my present partner. She has a wonderful overall reaction—she tightens her legs and body and then holds, and finally lets go—it is great."

"I can often tell from her movements or the throbbing of her cunt when she has one. We talk about it quite freely. One of the advantages of long years of marriage (for us anyway) is the good communication. Nuances, tones, and actions are all familiar and add meaning to the spoken word."

"My present partner turns a lovely shade of pink from the neck up and virtually stops breathing for a few seconds (seems like longer). But in the past with shorter relationships it was hard to tell. One girl I knew just faded away upon orgasm like a small faint. It was hard to tell at one point if it was 'for real,' or lack of interest on her part."

And most men said they very often had to ask:

"I usually have to ask if my partner has had an orgasm. She is quiet and moves very little, beyond an upheaval and a subsiding . . . but that doesn't always mean she has come, either. I like to know, though. I like to know what I have to do . . . continue, switch to another activity, slow down, speed up . . . or even IF she wants to come."

"Usually I ask—even though I have a picture in my mind of an obnoxious clod who finishes fucking a woman (coming as fast as possible, of course) and then asks, 'Didja come?'"

"It's tough for me to tell, but I'm trying to become more sensitive about this. Meanwhile I ask."

"I can't always tell if my partner has orgasm. The only certain way to tell is to ask if she had an orgasm. She is honest and will tell me. We talk about sex and orgasms freely."

Some men did not like to ask because it pressured the woman to say yes, or they met with a negative reaction:

"If I am in doubt I do ask. Some women get upset and say, 'Couldn't you tell?' So sometimes I won't say anything and let her voluntarily say whether she did or didn't. Depending on the woman, it can be a touchy situation."

"I no longer ask, as my questions are taken as accusations—as they were once intended."

"I used to ask because I wasn't sure. I'm sorry now that I did because it was embarrassing for her. I also know she was faking it and lying about it."

"I'm sometimes in doubt, and I sometimes ask—but I hate it when they take my asking to be male ego and start massaging my ego. So I only ask when it's an easy relationship where 'performance' or worry about the other's own ego involvement in their 'performance' isn't an issue."

Some men stressed the importance of asking:

"If in doubt I do ask her. It is too serious a matter to be taken lightly and leave someone 'uptight.' "

"Asking sounds harsh and is, I suppose, sort of crude, but to be honest with someone means to admit you don't know, too. It is also a measure of showing you care. I do care. I ask and let her know *why* I ask."

"I ask did you achieve your goal. If not, what the hell, neither did I."

"The only thing that really irritates me about women is their resentment over being asked whether or not they have had, or are ready to have, an orgasm. When a man is concerned about this, it does not mean that he is nagging or imposing some sort of responsibility; it means, rather, that he *is* concerned. He is being considerate. And the women who imagine that the soft contractions of a moist, dilated vagina can be sensed by a penis urgently striving to release semen, while its owner is straining to hold the fluid in and stay rigid, are imagining one helluva lot."

Or were very sensitive in their manner of asking:

"If I'm ever in doubt, I ask obliquely—framing my question in perhaps a phrase like 'Be sure to tell me what you need from now on.' "

A few made a point of creating an open atmosphere in which both people could feel free to talk before and during:

"Sometimes when in doubt, I ask. But even this apparently considerate action is often taken for a form of demand.

So I prefer to be in a relationship where the woman feels free to express herself and ask for what she knows will be given freely."

"I usually encourage communication all during intercourse. If I don't know the woman very well, it is much more important to get feedback about what feels good to her than just asking if she came afterwards. In other words, I am more interested in if she is going to rather than if she did."

"I ask *first* what she likes, and then ask for feedback during."

But quite a few men stated they did not ask, because whether or not the woman had an orgasm was not that important:

"It is often difficult to tell when a woman has an orgasm. I don't ask, it's not that important."

"I can usually tell if my partner has had an orgasm by the way her body reacts. Sometimes I'm not sure, but I seldom ask, unless she has reacted much differently from the way I've come to anticipate women will react—then my curiosity is aroused. But as a rule, I feel that her orgasm or not is only important if she makes it important."

Some men did not think asking was worthwhile, since a woman might fake an orgasm or lie:

"I used to be easily fooled—I'm not anymore. Of course anyone can be fooled by a good actress. I ask when in doubt, but if she's that good an actress . . . ?"

"Once in a great while I'll ask if I don't know for sure, but that's a waste of time because I never know whether or not to believe the answer."

"There is no way a man can tell for sure if a woman has had an orgasm, and it's none of his business if the woman does not wish to tell him. 'Normal' female orgasms run the gamut from the barely discernible to the spectacular, so do the fakes."

"I can't feel a *thing* different, so how can I tell? There's no point in asking, because she might lie. She's free to fake it but if I ever find out, that's all. But I doubt if a gal who fakes it wants really to do it again. Maybe that's a good way of telling—who would want to keep faking orgasms, unless they were very, very lonely? and just wanted the closeness with the involvement."

But some men were more understanding of why a woman might fake an orgasm:

"When in doubt, if I'm comfortable enough, I'll ask. I've never doubted when she said yes. Even if she faked it. I don't want to get into that game. I deal with people honestly and I expect them to deal with me honestly. Actually I almost feel hypocritical saying that, since I've faked it twice. So I guess I understand the pressures that might make her fake orgasm. Still, I'd prefer that she be honest, and if she *does* fake it, I'd rather find out later than right then. I'd like to be able to talk to her about what feels good, what things she prefers (ways of manually stimulating her, positions and types of motion during intercourse), but she has trouble communicating these things—almost a block—and will only try if I specifically ask."

And one man was very upset when he learned his partner had faked orgasms:

"After hearing about *The Hite Report,* I asked my partner about faking orgasms and she lightly admitted faking a few with me. I cried like a baby and was deeply hurt to know that. The relationship ended soon thereafter."

Some men made the point that it was much easier to recognize a woman's orgasm during clitoral stimulation than during intercourse:

"Clitoral orgasms I think I can almost always tell by the facial contortions, blushing all over, erect nipples, and body convulsions. Vaginal orgasms are harder to tell."

"My wife gets so much joy from *my* orgasms that her cries of delight are not much different than her moaning when she actually comes. (She is not faking it when she doesn't come, she is just very happy when I come.) Of course, when I go down on her, there is never any question."

"I really get no feedback of an orgasm during coitus, only cunnilingus. Indications are a raising or stiffening of her body. Or when I have my fingers inside her, I can feel her muscle contractions. Also, her body tenses up at climax."

Many men had inaccurate ideas of the signs of female orgasm:

"My wife would get loud and occasionally, every third time or so, cry afterwards. All of the women I've ever known have uncontrollable erection of their nipples when they climax. Most women have told me that at orgasm they're out of control."

"Most women who have orgasms with me show it by losing control of their bodies. They do things they should not do otherwise. She does not hear a word I say. Some women make a lot of noise. Some sound as though they are crying like with a broken heart."

"When my wife is really hot and I can keep a hard erection, she will become short-breathed and many times will dig her fingernails into my shoulders. I really enjoy knowing she is having a climax."

"She rapidly moves her hips, makes a sound deep in her throat, and smiles."

"I can always tell, her breathing gets louder and she gasps, moans, and sometimes literally hollers."

Some men had more practical alternatives which they preferred to asking:

"Almost always the question 'What can I do to make you come?' is a better question that 'Did you come?' Also, when in doubt, it is more fun to proceed."

"I have been in doubt before. It's hard to have the courage to ask, so I usually start out by stimulating her to an orgasm manually or orally first. In these conditions it's easier to tell."

"If I'm not sure, I start to bring her up to another. I still feel she can always have one more! I continue and if she tells me she has had enough, then I have mine."

"For a while I had some doubts, so we talked about it. Now she's not afraid to help herself along so she can reach orgasm too."

"In our early years, when she had no orgasm and wanted one, she would relieve her tension by a torrent of tears and great sobs, and I would feel like some sort of monster. I always felt it had been my fault; that I had been too much in a hurry and had not brought her along thoroughly or patiently enough, or not given her enough foreplay. Now, if such should happen, we just use the vibrator to get her going (or she can, herself) to joy and relief."

"How does the woman's orgasm feel during intercourse?"

The difficulty most men had identifying a woman's orgasm was even greater during intercourse. In fact, men said the feeling of contractions in the vagina was usually very faint, if noticeable at all, and so orgasm during intercourse could be difficult to recognize—besides being rather rare.

Most men said they could not tell from feelings in the vagina whether the woman had orgasmed or not:

"I can't tell. I can't feel any difference."

"I never really noticed. Could it be that I never brought a woman to orgasm?"

"Can't say."

"Cannot feel it."

"I never could tell any difference."

"I cannot tell. Sometimes I think that the vagina may seem a little wetter, or that maybe there are some slight contractions—but if I had to bet on it—I wouldn't."

"I've never felt the vagina during orgasm."

"I am not certain that I've ever been in a woman when she was orgasming."

"I don't think I ever paid any attention to the way the vagina feels during her orgasm. I have just started to become really aware that she does have orgasms. I think a lot of men are in the dark about a woman's sexuality. It's like I was blind and now I can see very clearly. At least I'm trying to be more sensitive and understanding. It's nice to know what you're doing, and know how to make her happy and satisfied."

"To be quite honest, I don't very often notice any particular contraction sensations when my wife orgasms; I guess there is some squeezing, but it's minimal."

"The woman's orgasm (assuming one is obtained at all, which is not often in intercourse) is frequently hardly noticeable in the vagina."

A few men mentioned that they could feel her orgasm better if they were not at the same time thrusting or working toward their own orgasm:

"If I am not thrusting very hard I can feel the contraction of the woman's PC muscles during her orgasm—a gentle rhythmic squeezing around the vaginal opening."

"I have to stay still to feel it."

"If I am not too hard, I can feel the vagina pulsate better."

"I honestly cannot tell whether or not my partner has had an orgasm. After all, I am pretty much caught up in my own orgasm. If I were not going to orgasm myself and concentrated on my partner, I believe I could."

"I sometimes feel contractions. This varies according to how deeply and firmly inserted my prick is. I feel more of it if I'm only partially in."

Once again, it is notable that many of the men who were more certain of the woman's orgasm, and gave clearer descriptions of it, were describing orgasm not during intercourse but during some form of clitoral stimulation:

"I cannot feel a woman's orgasm during intercourse, but I can sometimes feel it with my finger."

"The only time I detected a vaginal orgasm was when I had my fingers in my partner's vagina and felt the quick, spontaneous contractions. To this day I don't know if I would feel the same contractions with my penis in her vagina. Until I have the experience, I won't know."

"With my penis, I can't feel the orgasmic contractions much, but I can feel them with my fingers when they are thrust (or actually held) into the vagina at the right moment. It just feels like a rhythmic tightening all around the opening."

Some men said they didn't know because the woman didn't orgasm from intercourse:

"I have not ever known a woman who had an orgasm while we were sharing intercourse. During cunnilingus or hand stimulus I often notice contractions."

"Since female orgasm and vaginal penetration are virtually mutually exclusive in my opinion, I wouldn't know."

"My wife *never* has orgasmed with my penis in her vagina."

"I don't know what it feels like during a woman's orgasm because my partner only 'comes' orally."

Many other men specifically expressed doubt about whether women were having orgasms with them during intercourse:

"I doubt that I have ever actually had intercourse with a woman who has had an orgasm with me. Several women have told me later that they only pretended to have orgasms."

"I am not sure if a woman has ever had an orgasm while

I was having intercourse with her. This tells you something about my technique (or lack, I guess)."

"To this day I have never known when a girl has had one. Girls have moaned and groaned and all that, had spasmodic pelvic movements, and the whole scene, but is that an orgasm? No girl has *ever* told me she had one."

"Women have told me they climaxed during intercourse, but I'm not convinced. I don't think they're always strictly honest about it."

"Clitoral stimulation is known to excite the woman to orgasm, but I must admit that in the past I would perform cunnilingus and penetrate and thrust—now I realize that this might be disastrous for the female orgasm. I had been used to perform coitus until she begged me to stop, which I interpreted as her orgasm(s) and resulting exhaustion. No woman has ever cared or dared to complain or clarify, probably for fear of insulting my ego. It seems many women enjoy being banged (thrusted) and the moans and grunts are genuine, but it doesn't have much to do with orgasm."

Others described the feeling of the vagina during various stages of arousal, confusing this with orgasm:

"Wide open."

"No change."

"Hotter and wetter."

"It seems to me that the vagina gets hotter."

"Sometimes notably during orgasm, her vagina expands so large as to effectively disappear and I am forced to alter the angle of thrusting to reestablish any stimulation. Apart from this, during orgasm (my wife and I are 98 percent simultaneous), there is too much else going on to focus externally very effectively."

"I think I can notice that the vagina is hotter during orgasm. This may or may not be imagined. But when she comes there is definitely more wetness in the vagina and it seems to be thicker and more slippery than the other wetness which I call the lubricant."

"I don't know. Tighter. I never really analyzed this, I enjoyed the fact that she was having pleasure."

"The inner wall of her vagina changes to an electric smoothness, a sweet fluid seems to drain around my penis and to exude around the opening as my penis moves in and out."

Other men said the feeling of orgasm varied from woman to woman—which may have reflected the reactions of different women, or the fact that some women were having orgasm and some not:

"Some have strong contractions, others seem to soften."

"Some vaginas are no different during a woman's orgasm, others contract with pulsating effect. I don't know how much control women have over this movement, whether it is voluntary or involuntary."

"Some just thrust harder, some seem to grab your penis. They are all different."

"When the emotion of orgasm in a woman is at a high pitch, her vagina in most instances closes on the penis. No two women are the same or react the same. Some scream, some laugh, some cry, some scratch."

"Some women contract their muscles and excrete a fluid when they orgasm. Some show no physical sign of orgasming at all. (I really believe that this is true even in spite of those that attempt to fake it.)"

A few answers were quite exaggerated:

"It becomes alive. It's like a writhing snake wrapped around my penis."

"It feels like a volcano."

"Screaming electric snakes in a warm barrel of furry honey."

"Her inside muscles are chewing on my dick—while her uterus is trying to knock the head off it. It's a wonderful feeling."

"Something doughnut-like begins clamping rhythmically on my monstrous engine—occasionally with such force as to eject me, if the contracting area is near the end of my great throbbing instrument."

But some men gave clear descriptions of how vaginal contractions felt to them:

"It opens up, hollows out at the back, and constricts around the penis."

"Her vagina starts squeezing my penis in pulses that remind me of my own orgasmic pulsations."

"Tremendously hot, moist, and clutches at my penis."

"At climax, her vagina lets go, and seems to open wide at the back. At the peak of her climax, she tightens at the opening in an abrupt, throbbing clasp that is utterly thrilling to me (I suspect the tensing of her legs and thighs rather than the vaginal walls imparts the feeling), holds a moment, then her vagina lets go, feels very soft, very open, sometimes still gently throbbing. I wish I had the skill to convey the heart-stopping beauty of it."

The faintness of the contractions was surprising to many men:

"To tell you the truth, I don't feel much difference at all when a woman's vagina is orgasming. I feel a little rippling along my penis. It has always puzzled me when I've read erotica stating that the author felt himself being 'milked' by a woman's vaginal muscles. I've never experienced that."

Most men found external body signs to be more helpful:

"I can feel no definite contraction in the vagina when a woman orgasms. But there is a stiffening—a temporary rigidity of her overall body as if she were having a seizure."

Other descriptions:

"She seems to exhibit the same sort of muscular tension that I do. Her legs will be like steel and she'll show remarkable strength with her arms."

"I hear a kind of breathless intensity that exactly mirrors how I feel at the approach of *my* orgasm. And then I feel that wild loss of control, that temporary joyous epilepsy . . . Unmistakable! Once in a while she's had one when we've been in a semi-public place (while camping with other people sharing a campsite, for example) and I know she'd be embarrassed to really let go. It's a bit like trying to sneeze quietly in church . . . I can feel the held breath, the sudden stiffening and quiet."

"She tightens all her muscles (especially leg and abdomen) and trembles all over."

"There is a tautness of her body, a sudden rigidity or 'freeze,' and then relaxation."

"During cunnilingus there is a raising or stiffening of the body."

"Her entire body goes rigid and spasmodic."

"Her body tenses and then stops breathing."

"She breathes hard and then holds her breath—her vagina contracts—and her legs must be together."

"She tenses and becomes quiet, with a look of ecstatic agony on her face."

MOST MEN STILL ASSUME WOMEN SHOULD ORGASM FROM INTERCOURSE AND LACK INFORMATION ABOUT THE CLITORIS

"I always assumed there was something wrong with them if they couldn't orgasm with each intercourse without clitoral stimulation. That prejudice dies hard. Although now I know what the truth is, doubts still remain, just below rational consciousness."

"One weekend my wife sent the kids off to their grandparents' house, and then she told me she had something to tell me. Well, what it was was that she didn't have orgasms the way I thought she did, that she didn't mean to hurt me, that she had really loved having sex with me all those years, but she just hadn't been honest. I was flabbergasted, I didn't know what to say. We started talking and she told me just how she did orgasm, and then, I couldn't believe my eyes, she showed me how she did it. I have never been the same since, I mean for the better. I fell in love with her all over again, or anyway, I got a case of the hots for her that didn't quiet down for about six months. She was *much* more interested in sex than before. I learned how to make her come with my hand and we started specializing in weekend-long sex sessions. It was just too much. Bliss. Heaven. I was ready to die."

"When I first read that women needed stimulation on their clitoris, and didn't usually orgasm with the penis, I thought, but what about all those women who had orgasms with me? Then I realized maybe they didn't really have orgasms, maybe they were just excited *with me*. I usually said something like 'Was it good?' and they would say yeah— but maybe they didn't orgasm at all. That thought really shoots my ego down. Why don't they tell men? Why put men in such a stupid position? It made me feel like a fool, not knowing all those years, and acting like such a big jock. Were the women laughing at me behind my back? Or feeling sorry for me, or thinking I was stupid? Did other men treat them different? It's all just too hard to believe."

We have seen that most men do not know, or are not sure, when a woman has an orgasm. Much of this uncertainty is due to the fact that men have wrongly been taught that women should orgasm from the thrusting of the penis, and have been told very little about clitoral stimulation, and so are looking for women's orgasm at the wrong time. The fact is that only approximately 30 percent of women do orgasm from intercourse itself* (usually from pubic area contact, rather than thrusting per se); on the other hand, most women orgasm easily from more direct clitoral stimulation.

Even today, most men still assume women should orgasm from simple thrusting during intercourse, and would greatly prefer that they do.

"Would you prefer to have sex with a woman who has orgasm from intercourse (coitus), rather than clitoral stimulation? When does your partner usually orgasm?"

Most men still assume women should/would orgasm from simple intercourse (coitus):†

"If she didn't come during intercourse I would wonder why she didn't."

"Some women will not orgasm from intercourse. Either they do not know how to make themselves orgasm or they do not want to. I feel a woman should orgasm during intercourse. She should try all different positions till she finds one that is best for her. If a woman can have fantasies when she is having intercourse and learn how to enjoy each movement, she will find that she will orgasm. I have taught this to many women and with good results. Of course, the man has to know how to fuck."

---

* This figure reflects the answers of 3,019 women in *The Hite Report* on female sexuality; similar figures were found when the study was replicated in three other countries.

† See also chapter 3. Answers seen here include men of all ages, points of view and backgrounds; younger and older men alike were just as likely to expect women to orgasm from intercourse, and to be unfamiliar with giving clitoral stimulation to orgasm.

"A lot of women have trouble reaching a climax. Some women should have surgery or go to a psychiatrist. I went with four women in a row that had to have manual stimulation to reach a climax. I was a little bit shaky, wondering if the entire sex had gone to pot."

"I believe that a woman's emotions play a large part in whether she has an orgasm. If I am tender and careful to be attentive to her during intercourse and still she doesn't have an orgasm, then the problem is in her head. She either doesn't love me enough or is preoccupied with something that's bothering her or something. If she wants to be orgasmic, I believe that a woman can be."

And the overwhelming majority of men* preferred the woman to orgasm from intercourse/coitus:

"I prefer to have sex with a woman who orgasms from intercourse to a woman who only orgasms from clitoral stimulation."

"Coitus, simply because that is how I have my orgasms. I enjoy it so much and it means so much to me that I feel they would be missing something."

"It matters a lot to me that my partner comes during intercourse. I'm sure I think it proves my manhood, and also just excites me. If she came some other way than intercourse, I'd feel kinda useless."

"I'd rather have sex with a woman who has orgasm from intercourse. It would be very frustrating and a deep hurt to not be able to stimulate her to orgasm with my penis. I hope I never meet a woman whom I can't satisfy with my penis."

"Vaginal orgasm is preferable 'cause it's easier for me —i.e., less for me to do."

"I like it if she get off when I do; I feel like that is the 'natural' and free way for me."

"I prefer intercourse because during intercourse you get the idea that you're both thoroughly involved at the same time."

"Coitus, because I want to feel her orgasm on my penis. Also, I think her orgasm would be more violent and all-encompassing."

"Coitus because otherwise it seems too one-sided."

"Yes, I prefer intercourse. She has orgasm whenever I want her to."

---

* Of those who understood the question.

"Coitus. I would like to feel that when we're having intercourse we're not just working toward an orgasm for *me*—at least, that we're doing it for me—it makes me feel selfish."

But most men in this study had not had the actual experience of giving a woman an orgasm from specific clitoral stimulation, and thus were answering theoretically.

An almost equally large number answered "either" or "both." Often they included the phrases "I don't care how she has orgasms—either way," or "It doesn't matter to me how she does it," or "Any way she wants to." These statements seemed to indicate less a willingness to try anything than a kind of lack of knowledge, or frustration with the "problem" of women's orgasms—or lack of interest. Perhaps it was easier for these men to say something like "It doesn't matter to me as long as she gets pleasure," than to really distinguish what it is their partners specifically require:

"It doesn't really matter—any way they want to get off is fine with me."

"It doesn't make much difference to me."

"It doesn't matter to me. They usually come during intercourse."

"I have only had intercourse with my wife. I don't care how she has orgasm, she can have it any way she wants to. If my wife wants to stimulate herself with a freight train she has my blessing. I will even be the conductor. But if my wife does not orgasm during intercourse I do not feel bad. In fact, I like it better when she does not orgasm because she will be warmer next time. She is best when she orgasms about once a week."

"I enjoy the freedom of stimulation in any manner. I dislike any limitations."

"I don't really prefer any certain way for the woman to get off. I don't think that much about whether she is getting off but I do what I can to make the experience the most exhilarating for the both of us."

"It doesn't matter to me. I prefer to have sex with women that are sexually uninhibited, with open minds, and have clear thoughts about themselves and their sexuality."

"Who cares? As long as she gets as much pleasure from me as I get from her, it shouldn't matter."

"It doesn't really matter to me where she gets her orgasmic sensations."

And several men said they would prefer "both"—as long as her orgasm during intercourse was the grand finale:

"I prefer a woman who has both. The best times are when I can create at least a couple of clitoral orgasms before we begin to have intercourse and then be able to make her climax vaginally three or four times."

"The woman who has orgasm first from clitoral, then again during intercourse with my orgasm is the best."

However, some men who gave "both" as their answer indicated a more complete understanding of the alternatives:

"Sometimes I would prefer to have her orgasm from intercourse rather than from clitoral stimulation, but not always. It's a different sort of enjoyment. When she orgasms from intercourse, I have to exercise more self-discipline. However, it does cause contractions in her vagina which give me a good deal of pleasure, as well as her body movements just prior to orgasm. But if she orgasms from clitoral stimulation, I can then fuck at my own speed knowing that she is not depending on me to last a certain length of time. Also when she has her orgasm prior to my entry, it makes her very loose and slippery and sensual, which I like."

"I do not care whether the woman gets her satisfaction from her clitoral area or from intercourse as long as she communicates what she wants and lets me be a participant in the action. I have only found one woman who would let me watch her masturbate and found this very stimulating."

"No preference. I aims to please. Kidding aside, everyone is different, looks different, feels differently. God, small matter for me to please her if I can. I have not had a great number of women in my time, but the majority have enjoyed masturbation clitoral style, some have enjoyed both."

"I don't feel it is very important whether the woman has orgasm from intercourse or clitoral stimulation. Most of the women I have known have had orgasms more readily, and apparently with as much pleasure, from clitoral stimulation. I get a big kick out of stimulating a woman to orgasm with my hand. Orgasm during actual intercourse is also nice. If I stimulate a woman with my hand during sex, it often is the case that the woman can experience more than one orgasm. If she only has orgasm during intercourse, it often excites me to the point of orgasm too, and the woman then has less chance of multiple orgasms, my potential for frequent orgasms being very small."

Many men avoided answering this question directly, often discussing the importance of feelings, while ignoring the issue of how the woman actually did orgasm:

"The partner's type of stimulation is not as important as that there be mutual physical satisfaction and love."

"How she orgasms is not as important as if she feels love in the act."

"This is a tricky question. Let's just say that I'll do whatever my partner needs to have done for an orgasm. I'm one of those fools who links sex and love as much as possible —in other words, I try just to make love to women I care a lot about—so giving a woman an orgasm is more important than the process of doing so. In summation of all this, I really don't have a preference."

"I prefer to have sex with a woman who has knowledge of how to stimulate me and no hang-ups about any part of her own anatomy."

"I guess it doesn't matter how they do it as long as they do it with me."

"The question is whether she had pleasure from going to bed with me and not whether she had an orgasm."

"I enjoy intercourse with a woman who also enjoys intercourse—however that is accomplished."

Others expressed confusion over whether intercourse itself actually provides indirect clitoral stimulation for the woman:

"Why separate orgasm from intercourse from orgasm from clitoral stimulation? Can't coitus also stimulate the clitoris? I do not really have a preference anyway—I want to give a woman what she wants, and as I observe orgasm, I can't tell any difference. Nearly all women can orgasm from finger/tongue stimulation directly to the clitoris. Some have a very hard time reaching orgasm from straight coitus."

"I try to have my woman get off first during foreplay,

---

* For a discussion of the differences between *The Hite Report* and Masters and Johnson on this issue, see *The Hite Report*, chapter 3. Basically, Masters and Johnson have said that women should get sufficient indirect clitoral stimulation from the penis's traction on the skin surrounding the vagina, which is indirectly connected to the skin covering the clitoris, to reach orgasm; however, *The Hite Report* on female sexuality, based on a much larger sample, found that, in practice, this was not effective for the large majority of women, who need more direct clitoral stimulation for orgasm.

then intercourse; both are clitoral stimulation just by different means—or am I mistaken? If they have an orgasm at all, I'm happy."

"Aren't they the same? Isn't *that* question settled yet?"

Or held the misconception that it did:*

"I believe clitoral stimulation is the only way a woman can reach orgasm. What most people feel is coital stimulation is really a very gentle and indirect clitoral stimulation."

A few men used the phrase "She gets clitoral stimulation from my penis," with no explanation given as to what the writer meant, or as to how this might be true—implying a possible misunderstanding of female anatomy:

"During intercourse I never had a woman stimulate herself other than to rub her clitoris against my inserted penis."

"I believe that a woman who has coitus orgasm can be easier stimulated to orgasm than one who has clitoral orgasm because of the location of the penis in the vaginal tract."

"Standing up against a wall allows the woman to get more stimulation of her clitoris. As the penis goes into the vagina the outer lips are pulled down and in slightly. This allows the swollen clitoris to contact the top of the penis and thereby stimulate the woman. However, if the woman is shorter than the man, he must either bend slightly at the knees or she must stand in a little higher on some support."

"All orgasms are from the clitoris. My penis comes in consistent contact with my wife's clitoris so she's really getting clitoral stimulation as part of our intercourse."

One man commented:

"Some women like to rub the shaft of the penis against their clitoris as I move in and out, but that is agonizing because it bends the shaft where it isn't supposed to bend."

* Women in *The Hite Report* on female sexuality who had orgasm during intercourse without the addition of manual clitoral stimulation usually got the needed clitoral stimulation from friction on their mons, in contact with the man's pubic area, and not from simple thrusting inside the vagina.

And some men assumed that a woman would get enough clitoral stimulation from "foreplay" before intercourse to finally have orgasm during intercourse:

"This is really a matter of definition. Theoretically, I understand that if a man moved his erect penis in the lubricated vagina of a woman who was not aroused in any other way, that she probably could/would not orgasm. But I believe that if intercourse or the sex act is defined so as to include foreplay, during play (actively kissing the partner's face, breasts, ass, and legs during penis-vagina intercourse), and after play, then a woman could/would orgasm from intercourse."

"I'm aware that the thrusting of the penis in the vagina does not of itself assure the woman's orgasm and that usually her clitoral area must be stimulated if she is to climax. However, I wouldn't feel that I had failed if she couldn't come in coitus after *foreplay,* provided I hadn't rushed her, and provided she had indicated she was ready for my penis. And I wouldn't feel it was my fault if she failed to orgasm thereafter, no matter what we both tried. Women do get hung up and get so uptight that they can't come. These things happen, and while a man should help a woman in any way possible—just as he would expect sympathetic help from her if the positions were reversed—in the last analysis the woman, like the man, has to accept the situation. This time it was a dud. Next time, better. And in most cases I think women can train themselves to be more responsive. But a man should be supportive in all cases."

Although this has been traditional wisdom, most women in *The Hite Report* on female sexuality said that this did not work for them.

Some men described ways in which women did get enough clitoral stimulation for orgasm during intercourse with them:

By the addition of manual clitoral stimulation during intercourse:

"I usually prolong intercourse about fifteen minutes and slip my fingers between us to stimulate her clitoris while moving my pelvis."

"Most of the time she orgasms by my stroking the clit with my finger while we are having intercourse."

"I always infinitely preferred being on the bottom, because it gave me a chance to manipulate my wife's clitoris much more easily, and because she acted much more wild. I would have liked only making thrusting movements into my wife's vagina, but I don't think that gave her pleasure."

"My wife had a non-orgasm problem for many years of our marriage, but now she usually has one when I get on top supporting my upper body high enough with arms straight so she can use her fingers while I am inside; this also holds me off until she is ready to come; we can usually always come at the same time this way."

"Lately I have been stimulating the clitoris as we are having intercourse. The results are tremendous."

"My wife very rarely climaxes in the old missionary position. However, she does enjoy masturbating herself to a climax in that position provided I'm in her fairly still."

"Our method for obtaining mutual orgasm is for me to enter from behind while she is lying down, applying a vibrator to the clitoris. My wife takes a long time to come this way, but it is one of the most reliable ways to cause her to have an orgasm. I wait for her climax and we time our orgasms so that they arrive at the same time."

By contact between the man's pubic bone and the woman's clitoral area—especially with the woman on top:

"Orgasm from my prick moving in and out of her cunt, with no effort on my part or hers to stimulate her clitoris? Though some women have told me their cunts are highly sensitive and that they can come by this stimulation only, I find in fucking that they sooner or later accompany their orgasms by spreading their legs wide and pressing me hard against them so they can rub their clitoral area against my mons. Gradually over the years I have changed my fucking technique, so that now, instead of my former in-and-out movement, I insert my prick all the way and then with my mons press hard against the clitoral region, moving it back and forth slowly and regularly until my partner has come as many times as she wants to. Then I come."

"She likes to be on top rubbing my pubic bone with my penis in her. She brings herself off fastest that way."

"The woman I am currently involved with usually has orgasm by being on top and humping me, therefore, as I see it, she is orgasming from both intercourse and clitoral stimulation, though it would seem her clitoris is not being stimulated 'directly' (i.e., with fingers), but rather by rubbing against the bone (mons?) above my penis."

"I use either a thrusting in-and-out motion or a rotary, grinding motion. Sometimes we lie quite still and press our pubic bones together. This works best with the woman on top and is most stimulating to her."

"The woman I have sex with most often orgasms always the same way—by my pressing my penis against her vulva (outside) to stimulate her clitoris. I enjoy this, too, and can orgasm the same way, although the ideal position of my penis for me is about one inch or so different than for her. I usually try to delay my own orgasm until after she comes so that I can move slightly. We always go into the position that is best for her since I can come either way, but my penis must be in a specific place for her to come."

"Each time she wants to come, she presses her hands down hard on my ass to bring my mons tight against her clitoral area, rubs hard against me, her muscles tense, and she moans and rolls her tongue on mine. I love it."

However, the fact that these methods can work for some women in some situations does not imply that all women "should" be able to make them work. For example, a great many women can orgasm only with their legs and thighs together:

"Before reading *The Hite Report* we generally used the missionary position. But with the insight on a woman's orgasm from the book I was able to prod my wife into revealing that her orgasms were very minor this way, limited to the vagina and very incomplete. When we tried a new position, her on top, legs closed and inside mine, she was able to bring us both off in a way she'd never felt before."

Most men who had done clitoral stimulation clearly thought of the clitoris as something there to fall back on if nothing else worked; for a woman to have an orgasm from clitoral stimulation was second best:

"If she is tired and had a hard day, some clitoral stimulation usually is necessary during foreplay. If she is really down and out, clitoral stimulation is used during coitus."

"When I have not been very good in intercourse, and she

doesn't come, I usually try some oral sex, or try to bring her to orgasm manually."

"With the exception of about two women I've been with, all will climax with some degree of frequency. One of the other women would with coitus and manual stimulation. The second couldn't even with oral or manual stimulation."

"I usually have intercourse and then follow up with clitoral stimulation and oral sex (fellatio and cunnilingus) if she didn't come yet."

"If it takes clitoral stimulation in addition to coitus to get her to enjoy it, O.K."

"I use clitoral stimulation only when my penis doesn't hold an erection."

"If I am with a woman who does not usually orgasm during intercourse, I will religiously stimulate her to orgasm before taking my own pleasure. But this seems rather a mechanical undertaking. And my own orgasm becomes a lonely thing."

"I prefer coitus. But any orgasm is better than none."

"Coitus is a much easier climax, but I don't mind if they orgasm by clitoral stimulation."

"I prefer coitus. Then clitoral stimulation if that doesn't work."

Many men also said, surprisingly, that they would still prefer the woman to orgasm from coitus—even though this was not the case or would be impossible:

"It would be nice to have sex with a woman who experienced orgasm as a result of intercourse, because then the physical feeling would be more synchronized and shared and there would be less of a split between the partners. However, some conversations have led me to believe that a climax resulting from intercourse is rarely experienced and commonly faked. The orgasms I have come to believe in are clitoral and often quite separate from my own. (Manually or orally induced, before or after intercourse.)

"The woman that I live with cannot have an orgasm from intercourse so she has to have them by other means, which is clitoral stimulation. I don't mind either aesthetically or psychologically, but of course things would be easier if she could have them while I was having mine. Maybe it would be more like a symphony than a conscious technique."

"This is a touchy question—but intercourse orgasm from my lover would probably make me feel better. After two years of infrequent sex, the other day my girl told me she'd only had one vaginal orgasm (i.e., during intercourse) in those two years. It made me feel quite frustrated——I'd gone through great lengths to make myself a good, long lover and I felt inadequate. I still love oral sex with her and love to stimulate her clit with my tongue——but the idea that I should be able to 'give' her orgasm through intercourse hangs over my head. My lover always orgasms through oral sex. I've tried to stimulate her clit during intercourse, but it's hard to twist my large hand around to get to her clit. I wish she'd do it herself if she felt the need."

"I prefer coitus. But that makes me sound like one of the 'cone heads'——brainwashed."

"Most women seem to respond most easily to oral or manual stimulation, with penile friction running a poor second. This is a pity because I do prefer to fuck a woman who can orgasm easily during intercourse. The primary reason for this is physical: watching a woman in the throes of orgasm is the most exciting thing in the world, and it often triggers my own orgasm. Watching a woman stifle a yawn during intercourse is a classic turn-off."

"Coitus, if such a woman exists. I wish I could say I could make them orgasm by my technique, etc. . . . but it just doesn't seem to work that way."

"I'd prefer coitus. But how is it possible? Clitoral stimulation is necessary. If I were God, I would have made women in such a way that they needed daily orgasm through vaginal penetration."

"I prefer coitus. But my wife has her orgasm from cunnilingus."

Some men truly resented the necessity of clitoral stimulation:

"I feel it is a shame the clitoris on a woman isn't inside somewhere. A man likes to go in and out so the head gets stimulated, but a woman wants it all the way in. Her orgasm never excited me in the slightest and sometimes by the time she got hers, I didn't give a damn if I got mine or not, and would quit and go clean up in the bathroom and wash off all her damn slime and get my cock clean and jack it off."

"I appreciate it when a woman tells me in advance that she has difficulty achieving orgasm and can tell me what she needs. But if it sounds like too much work, I won't even try it for fear of resenting her."

"I get fed up with masturbating my partner to orgasm."

"There would be a lot less problems if women all orgasmed easily through intercourse."

"I would much prefer to have sex with a woman (women) who has orgasm directly from intercourse, if such a woman exists. Clitoral stimulation is all right before or after intercourse but during intercourse it has always seemed distracting whether it was by my own hand or hers. Aside from that it was uncomfortable, which in no way implies that it is wrong if it pleases the woman. Also it seems to be very awkawrd for me to do, so if it must be done I would rather it be done by the woman herself, which gives her the control over technique that would seem more beneficial to her."

A few men said they didn't have enough experience with clitoral stimulation to know:

"I prefer coitus. I don't know anything about clitoral stimulation. I was married for fifteen years but we were never able to find her clitoris."

"I just recently came to the awareness of how important the clitoris is, and now I'm trying to become more familiar with it."

Some men said, "It doesn't matter what I like; clitoral stimulation is necessary":

"All women I have known, including my current partner, require clitoral stimulation to orgasm. This seems to me to be a simple fact of the female anatomy and not something about which I need to be asked my preference."

"I suspect there aren't any women who really have orgasm from intercourse. The only one I ever met who came close has perfected the technique of providing herself the needed clitoral stimulation during intercourse; basically, she's masturbating with my penis inside of her. That's fine. The important thing is (a) that she should have it, and (b) that we should share it. I find much the best way to share it is for me to produce her orgasm by caressing her vulva and clitoris, either very very lightly with my fingertips, or with the tip of my tongue. That's better than with the penis for the excellent reason that I have much more precise sensation in my fingertips, and very much better control. I'm able to be aware of the intricate details of her shape, of the immensely detailed texture of her reaction: in short, to participate in her orgasm in a way that's quite impossible during intercourse. Intercourse requires all that thumping and shoving with a blunt and rather insensitive instrument; *so much more is possible* with better tools."

Or that since the woman cannot be expected (nor should she want) to change her anatomy, it is the woman, not the man, who has the right to a preference:

"Whatever my wife wants is best. *She's* what I want."

"I love whatever she loves. I love *her*, not a 'type' of woman who orgasms from one thing or another."

"I want the best for her. I want to be sensitive and responsive to how she achieves her orgasm, because in doing so, my own buildup to orgasm is especially heightened and made more pleasurable."

"No preferences. You have to find what each woman prefers. I would simply adjust."

"Her choice."

"No preference. Trying out new ideas means more pleasure."

"My goal is to please her, who cares where she operates from."

"Whatever *she* likes best."

"I believe that it is the woman's right to have orgasm in whatever way she wants. For too long men have dictated what the 'right' way for a woman to act should be. Sex should be for mutual pleasure and should involve sharing. Each partner should get the maximum out of it that is possible. If a woman prefers clitoral stimulation, then it is her right to expect it."

Although almost no men said they preferred orgasm during clitoral stimulation to orgasm during coitus, a few men did say that not only is clitoral stimulation necessary but that they also enjoyed it:

"Clitoral stimulation is enjoyable because I can be 100 percent aware of what is happening to her—preceding, during, and after her orgasm—without having my orgasm distract me from my attention to her."

"I enjoy stimulating the clitoris and bringing on orgasm manually."*

---

* These statements are included here because, even though they seem unremarkable, they were very rare.

"It's fun to watch the pleasure build up in a sexual partner. I enjoy clitoral stimulation."

"Clitoral stimulation is fun because it gives the male more variety in the manner of stimulation."

"The thing I like about making oral and manual love to a woman is the feeling I am giving something to her, rather than the feeling I am taking something ('a piece of ass') from her. The result is, that when I bring a woman to climax just using my mouth, tongue, hands, and fingers (or sometimes *multiple* climaxes) she feels I have done something great for her and I seem to gain her affection and admiration. In other words, I have the feeling she views me as a true man. This bolsters my ego. It makes me feel *great*. The Bible says, 'It is more Blessed to give than to receive,' and this is just what I find."

There was an unfortunate tendency in some of the answers to this question to hope or assume, if the respondent was aware of the statistics of The Hite Report, that his partner was among the 30 percent of women who do get clitoral stimulation during intercourse (adequate to orgasm)—and a further tendency to believe that the most "mature" and "best" women are naturally among the 30 percent.

How do men feel when they first understand women's need for clitoral stimulation as separate from coitus?

Some men told how they had felt when they first realized that (contrary to cultural stereotypes) clitoral stimulation is more important for most women's orgasms than intercourse itself—that intercourse does not actually lead to orgasm for most women:

"I used to think I understood feminine sexuality—you know, I was gentle, patient, understanding, etc.—if they 'couldn't' orgasm, it was 'O.K.,' I let them get on top during intercourse and *everything* (a real sport, wasn't I?). Anyway, now I see that the sensitivity I had that I thought was about 90 percent was more like 10 percent." (Age twenty-two.)

"I guess I had personally observed in my own experience that the clitoris was the place of excitement in the female; I know that on many occasions I knocked myself out thrusting in the female with little effect. There was something wrong, but I must admit I was crestfallen when I finally became aware that what I had suspected was true—male thrusting of the penis in the female vagina is not what we males thought it was." (Age thirty-eight.)

"I didn't feel good when I heard it. I didn't feel good for them, like a car with a defect that the dealer wouldn't fix. You're stuck with it and have to work around it. Or don't drive." (Age thirty.)

"The other day a friend of mine told me that I was making a mistake expecting women to orgasm during intercourse with me, and that I should try to stimulate them some other way. This was radical news to me. It was odd, talking about it with another man like that. I have never really talked about sex with another man before, except the usual stories, etc. I wonder what he thought of my reaction, or if he thought I should have known or what. Anyway, I'm glad he told me." (Age thirty-one.)

"Through almost eleven years of marriage, I believed that orgasm through intercourse was the rule rather than the exception. I 'knew' that the clitoris was part of the female orgasm process—nothing more. In the last year a lover entered my life (I am still married) and it is with her and through reading *The Hite Report* that I began to understand the function of the clitoris and the importance of manual stimulation. It has opened up a whole new side of sexuality, an addition." (Age forty.)

Certain men had accepted the information with relief and a sense of pleasure—especially when it confirmed their own personal experience or when they thought that the "problem" had been their fault:

"My wife has never orgasmed from intercourse. I used to feel that something was wrong with my technique or with my wife's frame of mind (mental block). Now all that is gone and forgotten. She can always orgasm from clitoral stimulation, so we are not missing something." (Age forty-six.)

"I can't believe we have been deceived so long about the penis-vagina orgasm. I am sure my wife (and I) would have developed much more sensibly if we had known this fact thirty-five years ago. I often felt sad and puzzled that she did not orgasm from intercourse. I was relieved to find out that this is normal." (Age fifty-seven.)

One man had worried at first that the news that women needed more clitoral stimulation would mean even more work for him, and even more pressure to perform ("give the woman an orgasm"):

"At first I was worried because I thought this would mean more responsibility for me, that women needed more stimulation, not that it would make things easier in the long run. But that's how it worked out, really, because I don't have to strain so much during intercourse for a result that's impossible anyway—and besides, sometimes she helps me with her hand on top of mine stimulating her clitoris. I'm glad I learned." (Age forty-six.)

Some men voiced the difficulties of changing:

"I feel a great resistance in myself to the idea that a woman really needs direct clitoral or mons stimulation to orgasm. She *should* be able to orgasm during intercourse— that is what men have always said. And yet, if it isn't true, it isn't true. I know I should accept it, but it's really a revolutionary change in all my assumptions (and the way I've always behaved). I have to force myself to believe it. And yet, how egotistical can I be, with my very own love telling me it is so? Change is hard."

"It's a bit worrying to think of women not enjoying intercourse as we do—hope they're not going to lock us out of their vaginas forever. Still, the facts of female physiology can't be denied, even if they're not as men might wish. As Martin Luther declared: 'There I stand. I can do no other.' "

One man was grappling with the information and its implications—wondering how the woman felt about intercourse and how he himself should feel about it—and in the process re-thinking his own definition of sex:

"First of all, my partner, my wife, has never orgasmed during intercourse, or in my presence, while nearly every time we have had intercourse, I have come to orgasm and ejaculation. Never! Here is the way I feel about it. Besides expecting to orgasm during sexual intercourse, I rejoice in the fact that I can orgasm during intercourse. I consider orgasm during masturbation and during intercourse as two different types of orgasm: masturbatory orgasm, for me, is a selfish orgasm, a self-love orgasm, all for myself. Orgasm during intercourse, to me, is a mutual orgasm, that is, I feel that I have not brought myself to 'come,' but also that my wife has helped me to 'come.' The fact I am enjoying the physical contact and closeness with her, the fact she has allowed me to penetrate her, make love to her is an intricate/ intimate articulation of the fact my orgasm is in part a gift from her. To me, emotionally and psychologically, this is ultimate, this kind of orgasm means so much more to me than my own masturbatory orgasm. This is how I feel I am.

"But I feel bothered I cannot bring her to orgasm during a mutual experience of lovemaking and intercourse. I do *not* feel bothered because I feel responsible to bring her to 'come,' or that 'it is my job.' I have transcended this expectation. She is entitled to her orgasms as I am (masturbatorily). But, because I feel so much ecstasy when I have come while having coitus with her, I feel that I can be a part of an orgasm with her. I want to give or bring her to orgasm. Can you sympathize or empathize with me? When I come and she does not, I feel one-sided about the orgasmic ecstasy: I feel I have reached a plateau she has not, which does make me feel alone in ecstasy, sometimes lonely. I desire my body, myself, and my lovemaking to be in part hers, for her, the gift of myself to her.

"Since we are both aware of *The Hite Report* on female sexuality, my wife no longer feels the pressure or feels inferior about not being able to 'come' with me. Now, I feel good about this fact and more realistic about the reality of female orgasm. However, this fact does not exonerate my desire to be a part of her orgasm, especially in the knowledge of who I am to her.

"As for helping my wife (if she wants it) to come before or after I come, I feel all game and willing to participate in this. But she feels a bit embarrassed to stimulate herself 'in front of me.' This is O.K. What I wish to make clear is that I am quite willing to help her come, in whatever manner it takes.

"I have felt like a sore thumb having put so much emphasis on mechanics, performance. However, I feel this is only a stage, a learning period toward mutual liberation where our sexuality is concerned, and a period which our emotions for each other will enable us to work out."

FEELINGS OF ALIENATION, BLAME, GUILT, AND ANGER WERE CREATED IN MANY MEN WHEN THE WOMAN DIDN'T ORGASM

"How do you feel if the woman you are with does not have an orgasm at all in any way?"*

Doubts about how or if women were having orgasms frequently made men feel uncomfortable, guilty, inadequate, or defensive during sex—although some men said that they didn't care whether a woman had orgasms or not, since women's orgasms were not that important. But most men, still assuming women should orgasm during intercourse, all too often wound up feeling alienated, and either blaming themselves or blaming women for not achieving what really is very difficult or impossible to achieve.

Men had many ways of expressing this discomfort:

I accept it, but it is as if a part of her is not allowing itself to open to me.

Like a doctor who loses a patient on the surgery table.

Inadequate, a poor lover, a failure.

Sorry for her.

Pity her.

Depressed, disappointed. Feelings of self-hatred.

She says it's O.K., but I worry.

Disappointed with her.

Like I'm in bed with a cold dead fish.

Not concerned.

Disappointed because there was no mutuality.

Disgusted if it's a pattern.

Surprise—what was all that noise about?—uncertainty, disappointment. Does she mind? What did I do wrong? What should I have done? But she seems O.K.

Angry.

Defeated.

Lousy, but I don't worry about it.

I would lose interest in her.

Growing disillusionment.

Sorry—she helped me even though she didn't want it!

* The phrasing of this question was an attempt to refer not only to orgasm during intercourse but also to orgasm during manual clitoral stimulation or cunnilingus; nevertheless, most answers clearly refer to intercourse, as if this were the expected time for women to orgasm.

There's no point in making love.

A selfish pig.

With my first wife, I became indifferent.

Sensitive and hurt.

I feel parasitic or unexciting.

Disappointed for her—not for me!

I used to feel rejected.

Sorry for her—I ask what she likes for next time.

It's nicer if she does; it makes the air clearer after.

Lack of women's orgasm, mainly due to cultural imperatives which insist women should orgasm when men do, has been an unspoken source of alienation between men and women over the years. As one man put it, "I feel more respect for her and myself if I don't feel I am cheating her out of an orgasm—or I guess the word is 'using' her, since I have an orgasm and she doesn't. I feel relieved to be with an equal." And another man said, "I have been married for sixteen years. My wife reaches orgasm only with some difficulty. I have been trying all means of helping her gain confidence and relaxation during intercourse, but I believe that there is a shade of jealousy in her mind about my easy satisfaction."

Men's reactions to a woman not having an orgasm (usually the answers refer to during intercourse) generally fall into three categories:

I. "It's the man's fault"

Many men felt that it was their fault:

"I feel inadequate. Sometimes I wonder just how good a sex partner I am. But I guess we all have those doubts."

"I feel partially responsible."

"I feel I am at fault."

"I would feel that I had failed her."

"It's something I have done wrong."

"I have not done enough or the 'right' thing."

"I let her down."

"I failed her."

"I must be inadequate."

Or that women not having an orgasm reflected badly on them:*

* This group of answers especially seemed to reply exclusively in terms of orgasm during intercourse.

"If the person I am with would not orgasm, I'd feel inadequate, like I wasn't enough of a man for her or something. It'd put a big shattering strain on my confidence."

"Not having an orgasm too often implies failure—failure of the person who didn't come and failure of the partner to make it happen. At times, I fall into this trap and feel somewhat inadequate, particularly if the woman wants to come."

"I do feel a little inadequate. If I know I've done my best, her not orgasming doesn't *crush* my ego, but it doesn't help it either."

"It matters a lot to me that my partner comes. I'm sure I think it proves my manhood, but it also just excites me. I don't mind if she comes some way other than intercourse. But I feel a little let down (by myself or by her) if she doesn't come at all. I am anxious about premature ejaculations and don't like to feel that I haven't 'performed' well."

"Deep down inside I do feel that I must be doing something wrong; but I feel myself that some women take longer than others to achieve orgasm. I think it's important to talk to the woman. Ask her what she likes, where and how she likes it. This way, even if the woman doesn't have orgasm, at least I know I did my best."

"I used to feel really shitty if the person I was with didn't orgasm at all, because I had tried my best and it wasn't good enough. In recent discussions with partners, however, I've found that they aren't as upset about it as I was, and they feel that the emotional high they get is a good second to orgasm and means a lot to them. As long as I know they feel this way, I don't feel half as bad, although deep down I wish I could do more."

"This painful situation has led me to be angry in the past because of the implied slight on myself, that with another man she would have attained an orgasm."*

Many men felt guilty—"like I was using her":

"I felt sort of selfish, as if I got more out of it than she did."

"Women's orgasms are important to me, because otherwise I feel like I'm using the woman, not loving her."

* This is probably a reference to one typical impasse caused by the ideology that insists women should orgasm from intercourse: that a woman who has had sex all her life with one man feels that she would orgasm during intercourse with another one.

"Like I've ripped her off."

"I feel like they are being left out, that I am not being fair, and that I should not let that happen."

"It makes me feel selfish, especially if nothing I've done is effective. At that point I question my capability to please the woman, and wonder if I have done something wrong, or not enough, or too much."

"Greedy—since I probably want to or have had an orgasm, I feel as though I'm not doing my fair share for her."

"I feel that it was all my trip. Not fair."

"Guilty and selfish. My fault."

"Sometimes I feel I am taking advantage of her, or that she is 'putting up' with me."

"If she has no orgasm at all, I feel as if I am merely using her, or rather her cunt, to rub my cock in till I come, this despite the fact that she may tell me she has enjoyed it and has been satisfied."

"I feel I've been using her like a whore if she has no orgasm in any way. I feel bad—I can't help it."

In fact, some men said that they had or would quit seeing a woman who did not orgasm rather regularly:

"If it is a frequent thing with the same person, it is very unlikely that I will become aroused, and I will not feel inclined to promote further sexual activity with that person."

"One girl never orgasmed. I tried every trick in the book from straight intercourse, to masturbating her, to holding myself back and eating her out for half an hour, both on and off grass. Nothing worked. She could be stimulated, but no release. I couldn't stand the prospect of me getting my jollies off while she couldn't, so I broke off the relationship—hoping that she might find an answer to her problem. It obviously wasn't me, and I didn't want to stand in her way."

"If I were with a woman who was incapable of orgasming at all, no matter what I did, I would hold out little hope for any long-term relationship. We just are not suited to one another."

"I'd probably leave such a partner unless we loved one another very much. I believe women who can't have orgasms can love, too. If there's love, it doesn't matter. Of course such a love would have to be very strong."

There was an undertone of frustration and anger in many of these answers, although only a few men verbalized it directly:

"The only person I've ever been with sexually is my wife —in the first years of our marriage she really didn't get turned on to sex—never had an orgasm and I often felt frustrated and blocked because of her un-involvement. Because that is not any longer the case, it's hard to recall just what the feelings were—but, as I remember, anger, 'to hell with it,' bewilderment, and a sense of 'is that all there is to it?' "

"What's wrong with women that they have such difficulty having orgasm? I have screwed somewhere in the neighborhood of thirty-five to fifty different women, and most didn't know how to screw properly; only one felt like she had an orgasm."

A few men envisioned this as a "sexual challenge," and themselves as the skillful teacher:

"I'd enjoy going through a period with her in which I helped her to learn to have orgasms using masturbation, vibrators, and T.L.C. I've even had a fantasy or two about doing this. Underlying this, of course, would be my basic assumption that she *should* have them. If it never worked, I'd feel disappointed, and might well have to deal with some issues of somehow having failed in my role."

2. "It doesn't matter—women's orgasms are not that important"

Quite a few men said orgasms were not the point of sex for women:

"Her not having an orgasm cannot determine my manhood. I came into the world with my manhood. If I were inconsiderate about her orgasm, I would certainly be a poor human being. But so long as she was enjoying herself too, there would be no real problem. So many questions we ask about sex limit us, particularly if they promote our sense of sex as some kind of scorecard."

"To me, if the female is totally happy, satisfied, loving, understanding, enjoyable, responsive, I do not total up orgasms, or have much care about it, only if she is happy."

"Counting orgasms one's lover has is as farfetched as counting stars. Numbers do not a game make. Fulfillment, completeness, sleep, relaxation, tension relief, coziness, cuddling, kissing, a feeling of happiness—these are the things strived for, not for a numerical count. Counting is asinine. My orgasm spurts are not counted any more than the kisses."

"I now know from years of experience with my wife, and with a few other women, that women don't have to come like crazy in order to have pleasure."

Many men thought men's orgasms were more important than women's:

"Orgasm seems to be a part of physical and mental well-being. That may be more necessary for a man than a woman."

"Orgasms are very important. It's hard to feel satisfied without it. My partner's orgasm is not as important to me, but I do try to please my partner."

"A girl could never know how good an orgasm feels to a man."

"Orgasm isn't just important to a male, it is essential. He must discharge his semen or he cannot be satisfied and feel he's got the job 'all wrapped up.' This is hard to explain to a woman. Suffice it to say that the sex needs of a man are more physical than those of a woman, which are more emotional."

In fact, many men said they themselves could not enjoy sex without orgasm—but could take pleasure if their partner did not orgasm. Eighty-three percent of the men who answered "no" to "Can you enjoy sex without an orgasm?" still stated that they found sex pleasurable themselves if the woman did not orgasm:

"I can enjoy sex if my partner does not. I like to reach my peak and release the sperm as soon as I can and just lay there enjoying my partner."

"It's nice if my partners have lots and lots of orgasms, but I'm not going to hold off my pleasure due to the inefficiency of someone else's nervous system."

Some men warned against women insisting on having orgasm "every time"—"straining" to orgasm:

"I consider women to be culturally crippled sexually. If they try to jump in and keep up with men it will make it worse."

Others said it was only a problem if the woman complained:

"If the woman is happy and fulfilled without orgasm, that's fine. If she is bitter about not having one, then the relationship needs to be altered."

"If the woman complains, I feel awful. Otherwise, O.K."

But one man said:

"I am beginning to feel better about being the only one to have an orgasm because I think I would enjoy the reverse—i.e., me sometimes stimulating her clitoris manually so that she orgasms but that I don't. In that case I think it's all right that only one person orgasms."

Other men felt uncomfortable if the woman did not orgasm, but thought that they were not supposed to feel uncomfortable—that they were supposed to accept it—and yet they couldn't help feeling troubled somehow:

"I feel as if I've let her down. I feel as if I've failed her someplace. I feel 'sorry' for her, and frustrated. But, I know (or feel) that I shouldn't have feelings like that. But believe me, they are hard to overcome. I think totally frustrated is how I feel most of all. Kind of helpless. I feel as if somehow our sexual encounter is incomplete, unfinished. But I do appreciate honesty and if she wasn't satisfied I like to know that, and the reason why if possible."

"My wife told me that she almost never had an orgasm during intercourse, and this is something she had never told anybody before. Once she felt free, not having to fake orgasms nor prove anything, she started enjoying intercourse much more. She obviously liked sex, even with her orgasm problems, otherwise she would not have made love so often. Why should she feel bad about coming or not? She is not orgasmic all the time now, either, I am sorry to say, but she does not care much, nor do I. That is what sex is all about: a way to feel free, close to people, and an assortment of good physical feelings."

"I first assumed women should orgasm easily and felt inadequate when they didn't. I now know differently and try to please the girl I'm with to the greatest degree possible, whether she can have an orgasm or not. I'm learning that orgasm is not necessary for women all the time, that they enjoy sex without orgasm. This I must admit, makes it easier for me to relax and enjoy my own sexual excitement and orgasm without watching too close to see if the woman also has an orgasm. Sometimes sex is fun if it's all one-sided. To enjoy oral sex or being masturbated without any effort to please the woman can also be exciting. And it can work the other way also. I can stimulate a woman without needing it in return."

Some men said that sometimes they didn't care if the woman orgasmed or not:

"Sometimes when I get in a woman-hating mood, I just want pure-sex one-night stands, which I suppose is tantamount to rape. When in woman-hating moods, I could care less whether she enjoyed it or not."

"I never have been very concerned as to whether or not my lady partner had an orgasm. I am not always sure whether she came. Often I can tell, but if not I don't bother to ask her."

"It matters to me that a woman orgasms or be brought to orgasm *if* she desires orgasm. If she would rather just enjoy the buildup through touching and kissing that is all right too."

Finally, a very few men said that they had no feelings on the matter:

"No feelings on it."

"If she's not making me responsible for it, I would not care."

"Indifferent. Do not mind."

"The world won't end for me."

"If a woman was enjoying herself and never did, I wouldn't mind, as long as she lubricated."

"It would probably matter more to her than to me."

Conclusion

The point is well taken that orgasm is not necessarily the point of sex; however, over 97 percent of the men who answered reported that they did have orgasms always or almost always during sex, and most also reported that the women much less regularly did. As women in The Hite Report pointed out, although they did not for the most part want to make sex a "race for orgasm," still, if the man always had one and they did not, they felt cheated. This feeling of anger and frustration was compounded by the fact that so many women, although they knew how to orgasm by themselves during masturbation, did not feel free, or consider they had the right, to clearly show or state this during sex with a man. For men, it is not simply a question of "accepting" the woman's not having orgasm from intercourse, but of finding out how she does orgasm and making that an integral part of what we call "sex."

3. "It's the woman's fault"

While some men, as we have seen, felt it was "their fault," others felt it was "her fault":

"Some women just can't orgasm due to some head problem or hang-up."

"Who knows why—medical or psychological reasons."

"There have been occasions when the woman wasn't feeling up to par, but I was always satisfied."

"She may be in need of professional help."

"Sorry, but I can't understand why women don't orgasm, considering the lengthy activity. It borders on frigidity."

"I would consult a physician or psychologist."

"It's her fault—either a physical or psychological problem. She could be a lesbian. Or she's too uptight."

"I figure she did what she wanted to do and got what she wanted. I leave it as her problem."

"That only happened with one woman that I know of, my first. I later realized she had some problems."

"Sorry, perhaps she should have her clitoral sheath peeled."

"I enjoy sex each time, so if a woman doesn't enjoy it, I don't feel let down, but I do wonder where their head's at. She either has psychological hang-ups or an unconscious desire to put me down. I've heard that prostitutes seldom or never orgasm. And I further believe that a woman who uses her body like a prostitute (for personal gain of some kind) will never have a healthy sex life. I pity them."

"I never felt any guilt if my partner failed to have an orgasm. I liked to have her have that pleasure and I did all I could to help her, but after I ejaculate there is no more I can do about it.* I always felt that the fact that I could ejaculate was proof enough of my manhood. Now that I am

---

* This reply assumes erection and intercourse are necessary to help the woman orgasm.

eighty years old I still enjoy ejaculation, but if I am not able to shoot I simply blame it to old age. After all, I have ejaculated many, many times in the past sixty-five years."

Once again, many of these answers probably refer to intercourse, as the majority of them—citing "psychological problems" or "hang-ups"—present the standard theory which was used in the past to explain why a woman did not orgasm from intercourse (or was "frigid," as the terminology went).

As one man said:

"If the greatest environment for a man's penis pleasure is the woman's vagina, then the assumption which should amount to a hypothesis is that the greatest pleasure for a woman's sex is having a man's penis inside the vagina. Otherwise the assumption is that nature did something wrong, which must be nonsense. If some women, whatever the percentage is, are having problems with orgasm and satisfaction, we have to look for pollution in women's upbringing, or in society's inhibitions."

And another:

"The reason my wife can't orgasm is that she cannot let her mind get into the program. She was raised by a mother who thought sex was dirty or whatever, and it affected the lives of all three girls sexually."

A currently popular view is to say that the woman's orgasm is her own responsibility:

"It's her business. She is responsible for her own orgasms."

"I offer everything. If she doesn't accept, I'm clean."

"It's her decision."

"The problem would be more hers than mine. She needs to know what turns her on."

"It's not my problem. It's up to her."

"I consider myself ultimately responsible for providing my own orgasms. To be hard-nosed about it, I frankly consider a woman ultimately responsible for hers too. None of my relationships has ever been so lacking in respect, tenderness, and diplomacy that we degenerated to fighting about orgasms, but if it did happen, and I was accused of 'being not man enough,' I would counter righteously that it takes two, and it is more than likely that she wasn't woman enough."

Conclusion

These slightly defensive or hostile answers are certainly correct in one sense—that everyone does, finally, make his or her own orgasm. However, a woman's situation is different from that of a man. To imply that women are not taking their fair share of responsibility for what goes on overlooks the fact that most "sex" is still carried on according to the old rules—that is, the woman is supposed to orgasm from intercourse, intercourse *is* sex, it is assumed that intercourse will be included, and that the man has the right to the appropriate stimulation for his orgasm, i.e., intercourse. The man has society behind him, encouraging him to have his orgasm, but the woman has society telling her that what she needs—i.e., clitoral stimulation to orgasm, usually in the form of manual or oral stimulation—is not "normal," or that she has no right to assert herself. In other words, our pattern of sex does not put men in the position of having to ask for the stimulation they need; it is clear that "sex" should end with intercourse and male orgasm, whereas women must request "special" ("extra") stimulation, and/or stimulation not related to intercourse. As one man put it, "If the woman needs some special stimulation, she should let the guy know."

In summary, many men were very annoyed with women for not having orgasm more frequently or more easily during sex—feeling, "Why are women being so difficult? They could orgasm if they wanted to, if they would just try a little harder, or if they were not being overly emotionally complicated— why are they trying to make men feel bad?"—not realizing that it is the lack of adequate clitoral stimulation in traditional "sex" that makes orgasm difficult for most women, and not esoteric reasons. There was a great sense of annoyance, anger, and hostility in these answers—*why* are women so difficult after all?

"Women should speak up"

Other men felt the situation was the woman's fault in the sense that the woman should tell the man what she needs— and should especially speak up about her need for clitoral stimulation outside of intercourse—although here again, many answers seemed still to imply that the woman would speak up about some particular preferences during intercourse. Men were frequently angry if they felt women wouldn't tell them what they wanted:

"There is something wrong with me only if a woman lets me know that she can orgasm if I do a certain thing, and I refuse to do it. Nothing works all the time for everyone, and I'm not going to stake my manhood on my ability to read minds."

"I would prefer she would tell me anything she wants, rather than dead silence."

"It's her fault. I'm not a mind reader. She has to tell me what to do."

"I would help, if she would just *tell* me. It *really* pisses me off to think that a girl would tell me she had come when she hadn't and wanted to. Hell, that's what I'm there for!"

"If I have anything to say about it, I pretty well know what it takes for a woman to orgasm *before* I climb into bed with her. If she plays games, is consistently noncommittal, and won't talk straight about it, then I think she gets what she deserves; if she can verbalize a little about where she's at, then we'll probably do O.K. Women who are scared to tell a guy where they're at are usually too timid for me to really open up with either. I wish I knew what they were scared of."

"If I ever make love to another woman, I will insist that she express her feelings freely and tell me what she really wants. Then it's up to me to act on what she says."

"It's the woman's fault for *not telling!*"

"I assume that if she's not satisfied she'll tell me. But again, just try to find a woman this open—I think it's almost impossible. This is why I'm sick and tired of women's libbers telling everybody that men just like to 'love 'em and leave 'em.' This is bullshit. The truth is that women avoid being controlled by men by being secretive and unpredictable."

"Many women indicated that they could not even *suggest* that their male partner was not satisfying them because if they did he would just *fall apart*. I felt a little insulted by that. I'm a big boy. If I'm not stimulating your clitoris correctly or whatever, tell me. I can handle that. I think most men can."

Similarly, in answer to many other questions, men often made the same comment—that the problem was that women didn't speak up:

"I feel that too many demands are made on me in sex—the demand to take the lead, the demand to initiate sex, the demand to determine how far I want to go, and the demand to somehow—by ESP maybe—know exactly what the girl wants without having her tell me. Evidently they all think I'm used to making love to deaf-mutes."

"I have found that very few momen were willing to openly discuss the things that turn them on. This is a major problem in my eyes, because this means that these women may, somewhere down the road, complain that their men are only interested in rolling over and going to sleep after intercourse. In my own wife, when I have tried to talk with her about how I think our sex life should be better, she first gets defensive and then gets very depressed with a lot of crying. For this reason, I have written all of this while she was away. There are many things here I will never tell her."

"No woman has shown me her clit or how she masturbates. It seems that even though many of the women I've known are 'into the movement,' it is mostly on an intellectual and/or political level."

"If my partner moans and groans during the sex act, fakes an orgasm when I have mine, then says nothing and holds me tight afterward, I have no other recourse than to assume she's been satisfied too. I don't think men as a whole realize when and if women have orgasms—or that women hardly *ever* have them from intercourse. Men act out of ignorance rather than bullishness, so faking an orgasm won't get a damn thing accomplished! Men *must* be told when women want more satisfaction. It will *not* hurt their ego if told in the right way. I don't see how it could. Because it's really saying, 'Please love me more and more and never stop. It's not you that's not satisfying me, it's a lack of us really knowing each other and exploring what will do it.' I can't imagine myself being upset if my partner wants me to keep making love to her. What man would? It's just the way women ask for it, I think. As long as she realizes that it's a goddamned difficult thing to do to stimulate a clitoris perfectly, he'll understand."

"Men are brought up in just as much ignorance of women as women are, *at least*. And when it's added that he's *supposed* to know it all, too, it's a bit rough. Many women evidently require different things for orgasm than do men (i.e., *clitoral* stimulation, not just intercourse); but men are brought up to believe that if they're 'man enough' (sometimes this translates simply into 'big enough') then the woman will get off just fine with intercourse. And that message occasionally *is* transmitted by women too. Neither bunch seems ready to consider that maybe men and women simply require different things, and it's *not* that the man is necessarily inadequate. I wonder how many cold, uncommunicative men are simply responding to the belief that they're not masculine enough to 'please the lady like a real man could,' and simply withdraw from a situation where what he should do is drop a preconceived notion. And if that one preconceived notion could be dropped by *both* men and women, maybe we could get over something else: Most of the women who did not orgasm with a man placed the blame, or at least a lot of resentment, squarely on the man. And yet all the talk about how liberating masturbation is, how it allows a person to take control of one's own life and be autonomous. How about if women went to bed with men with a little of that attitude —that a man is not solely responsible for her orgasm? That you go to bed (with someone) actively *looking* for pleasure, not just to *receive* it from him. Debilitating ideas held by men and women:

"... that if a man is 'enough of a man,' the woman will naturally get off with intercourse alone.

"... that a woman's orgasm is a man's responsibility. If she doesn't come, he has invariably cheated her somehow, if in no other way than by not being masculine enough. (Bullshit!)

"... that it is a function of one's masculinity to fulfill a woman's femininity—that if she is happy in bed with him, *then* he is 'a man.' (I'm a man, regardless.)

"(My, aren't I getting defensive?)

"Brother! (oops, Sister!) I'm really getting wound up!"

"Lately from things I read I get the impression that women do not think men ever consider or think about women's sexuality—that men do not know what women want and need sexually. Well, this may be true in most cases, but did they ever wonder why? Maybe many of them are like my wife. Our sex life got to the point where we were just going through the motions until finally I didn't want to sleep with her, let alone have sex. Still she didn't say a word, she just let things ride, hoping they would get better.

"Finally I could take no more and we had it out. I couldn't stand this just getting my rocks off and nothing more, no emotional satisfaction. I asked her what I was doing or not doing that made sex so routine and dull. I asked her a lot of questions and had to pry out the answers. The answers I got are not important here but the fact that *I* had to ask the questions and then pry out the answers concerning her happiness and satisfaction is important. Many women seem to figure that men should know what women want instinctively. Well, ladies, sex is a skill, something to be learned, and no man can do what is expected unless he is taught. Also, since all women are unique and have unique wants and needs for satisfaction, each woman must teach her man, just as each man must teach his woman. Most women will not tell or show their men what they want because they are afraid of him or of hurting his feelings; either way, if this is the case he is not your man, there is obviously no communication. If my wife showed or told me what she wanted, it would make life a lot easier and much more joyous for both of us, I am sure. Some women may tell their men, once, what they want, then expect them to remember forever and a day every fine detail of what they said. My wife has a good memory, but she has forgotten most of what I have told her makes me happy. It's a two-way street, both men and women forget. It is not our fault that you women don't talk about sex except to complain. Why don't you speak up more?"

Other men were more sympathetic about why women did not tell them more openly what they wanted:

"I've been gradually becoming aware that most men seem to feel that if a woman can orgasm from whatever stimulation they offer, fine. If not, well better luck next time. Horseshit. I think women are partly to blame for this situation. I don't believe that society has allowed a woman to demand the sort of stimulation she needs for sexual fulfillment. You can ask nearly any man if he's a good lover and you'll get a leer and a wink and something like 'I never had any complaints.' Reason: in his experience women have been too intimidated or shy to speak up and tell him what she needs. Ladies, let him know that he doesn't know what the hell he's doing. Don't worry about his ego. If a woman cares enough about a man to go to bed with him, she should care enough about herself to demand fulfillment. If she doesn't get it then don't, don't see the guy anymore. I think the women's movement has been instrumental in changing this, however slowly."

"I believe that we as men have to consistently try to

block our tendencies to believe that women don't have orgasms. We have to really push women to *show* us what they like and how they orgasm—and not be satisfied with the first few things they say, but keep trying! It's hard for them to open up after centuries of repression. Also, we have to really *want* to know what they are going to say—it has to seem important."

"I feel cheated and hurt. I once had a lover that I cared very deeply about, and yet she wasn't open about how I could help her to orgasm. She seemed embarrassed about not being able to climax during intercourse and just didn't help me help her at all. I feel deprived that I could never give her all the pleasure that I wanted to give. Frankly, since she was by far my favorite lover, I still feel hurt and frustrated about it."

Some men made it a point to encourage dialogue:

"I used to feel it was my fault if the woman didn't come. Now I ask, 'Does this feel good? What will make it better? Will you do this to me?' If the woman doesn't enjoy herself I do not accept as much of the blame now."

"First I feel bad, then I ask questions."

"If it's a pattern, *I want to talk about it*."

"I would want to know why—I won't just overlook it— I want to know if there is anything I did not do, or if there is something bothering her."

"I discuss it right away to avoid hard feelings, and try to work it out. I want to help."

"If my partner could not have orgasm, I would ask her to tell me how to maximize her enjoyment. Once I knew, I would try to do what she told me in a sultry manner, to let her know that I respect her feelings and do not consider them unusual."

"I hug and kiss a lot, touch and *talk*—then use clitoral stimulation over a long duration of time."

"If a woman desires orgasm and I am not bringing her to it, then I will ask her guidance and advice on how best to stimulate her."

"Yes, I want her to orgasm. I try to find out what she likes best, position or stimulation. I'm not ashamed to ask her if what I'm doing is particularly good. I also ask if there is something in particular she wants me to do, or position my mouth, cock, or hands the way she likes it. I appreciate it if a woman tells me without having to guess."

One man expressed pleasure at having had a very communicative and active partner:

"Most women are too inhibited and centered around my needs. I had a girlfriend this year who was great; she had masturbated a lot, was not shy, and would talk to me when making love about what she wanted. Her favorite position was to be on top of me, because she could control intercourse best and feel me better, she said. I would stimulate her clitoris with one or two hands and she would come and come all over me—warm and wonderful."

MEN'S FEELINGS ABOUT GIVING A WOMAN CLITORAL STIMULATION TO ORGASM

HOW DO MEN FEEL ABOUT THE CLITORIS?

What were men's general attitudes toward the clitoris? When men were asked, "How do you feel about the clitoris?" many answers included jokes or satirical remarks:

"How do I feel about the clitoris? I feel in awe of the little bugger. It's gotten so much publicity and become the focal point of so much rancor that I have the urge to salute it when I see it."

"A woman's clitoris is the greatest thing since the mop —other questions redundant."

In many other answers, the importance of the clitoris was brought into question by the frequent use of diminutives:

"A woman's clitoris is a wonderful little thing."

"The clitoris is a mysterious little 'love button.' "

"I think it is cute as it peeps out from its hiding place. Sometimes girls call it the 'tickle button.' "

"Big surprises come in little packages."

"Cute little devil."

But there were enthusiastic and positive remarks too—some beautiful and serious, others containing some of the diminutives and humorous phrases mentioned before:

"It is the primary erotic center of her body, tender and sensitive, and has to be treated with great care and emotion."

"It's just as important to her as my penis is to me."

"Just as much fun to play with as a penis."

"That's *the* place."

"Beautiful, stimulating, the most sensual part of a woman's body."

"I like to suck her, lick it, kiss it, talk to it, and she thinks I do a super job in it all."

"The clitoris is the blasting cap on a stick of dynamite. It is the trigger mechanism which puts everything else into motion."

"The clitoris is the center of her emotional sexuality, and once I have it under my finger or tongue, I know she's mine!"

"Wonderful organ."

"All right!"

"It's the most important part of the vulva. A man that has loved a woman and cares for her knows these things."

"It amazes me. It's the center of my wife's entire sexual being. Every square micron must be packed with nerve endings because of her reaction when I touch it or even get near it."

"It's the key to a lot of enjoyment for her and every man should know how to use it to the woman's advantage. I think it's too much overlooked by most men."

* The exterior clitoris as we know it is only a part of a very large internal clitoral network. See the drawing on page 684.

"It's the area where I come most in contact with her sexual feelings."

"An amazing thing, because it's so hidden but has such a powerful effect on women."

"Very beautiful and mysterious."

A few men professed complete neutrality:

"What do I think about it? Nothing really."

"I never really felt anything about it emotionally."

"O.K., I guess."

"Nothing special."

"No particular feeling. I know where it is after medical anatomy courses."

"It is just a part of her that I caress now and then, but nothing to rave over."

"If that is the point she wants stimulated, I will stimulate it. But I don't have any special feeling about it any more than I have any special feeling about any other body part that isn't in plain sight. It's like asking me how I feel about her liver."

Some men regretted the location of the clitoris:

"I think it belongs at the bottom of the vagina where it could meet the glans of my penis during sexual intercourse."

"Women need two 'clits.' One where it is now, and one in the hole about four or five inches deep."

Or its size:

"A pity that it's not larger so I could find it easier—or orgasm would be easier for her."

Others had had no experience, or bad experiences:

"She won't let me touch it."

"My wife says my finger hurts it."

"The clitoris is a strange thing to me. It protrudes."

"I could never find my wife's. She doesn't seem to have one."

"I'm not sure what the clitoris is."

And one man said:

"I have no feelings about it. She shouldn't have one."

When men were asked, "What does the clitoris look like?" there was a wide range of replies—many containing elements of discomfort and unfamiliarity, and sometimes hostility, again often using diminutives:

Soft tissue.

About the shape and color of a pencil eraser and maybe half the size, usually glistening with moisture.

Like a large pimple.

It looks a bit like an extended nipple.

Like a pea caught under her skin.

A teeny weeny cock when erect.

A small nub of flesh. Even though the books call it a small penis, I have never seen one larger than maybe ¾ inch.

Sort of like a bud.

A bump or roll of flesh.

It looks like a piece of skin was accidentally partially cut.

A miniature penis.

Kernel-like.

A little finger.

A magic pink button.

A micro finger-like projectile.

It is a sort of a bump.

A pearl in a velvet pouch.

It looks like a nipple with a foreskin.

Like a skin fold or a vestigial penis.

It looks like a hooded bullet.

It looks like a small leaf.

It is sort of a little knob covered with loose skin.

A glistening pink jewel in its case of mahogany plush.

Some are large while others are smaller.

I call it a little pee hole.

A pinkish area—not very prominent.

Sorta pointed, whitish and so tender.

My wife's is so tiny it can only be seen when erect.

Cute.

A little pearl.

It looks like an ice cream cone in a raging storm.

A small, elongated mound or lump.

Like a bright pink knob or projection when erect and the hood is pulled back.

A small hooded pink bump which enlarges on arousal.

It looks like a tiny worm which needs sunlight . . . very pale.

It looks good and tasty.

When the hood is pulled back, it looks like a red pea coming out of its shell.

Like the tip of a male cat's penis.

It looks like a funny little critter peeping out of its house.

Pink and easily mistaken for another part if you are not careful.

A small pink mound.

A tiny titty jelly bean (I like the red ones).

Like a grapefruit seed in a translucent veil of tissue.
A shiny translucent pimple.
Small, round, pink, and sensitive.
Beautiful. A pearly little head. I have not seen it as illustrated in books.
Like a dog's penis.
Anything from an unnoticeable rise to a swollen wound.

Cute nubbin about an inch or so that's pink and smooth and tender—not fully developed. Concealed as a hard lump beneath the skin.
A small nipple—that's why I love to suck it.
It looks like a woman's helmet or something similar at the tip.
Why, it looks like a clitoris, of course.

But most men said they had never actually seen the clitoris:

"Never seen one in real life."

"Only seen them in books."

"I've never seen one because the lights are off or my eyes are closed."

"The female clitoris has something of a mysterious quality to me since it isn't visible. It is at the upper part of the opening just under the upper fold of skin. I don't know what it looks like or how to describe it."

"The clitoris remains somewhat of a mystery to me. I know what it is and where it is located from pictures and descriptions in my biology classes, but I have never been shown a girl's clitoris and I'm not sure I could find a girl's clitoris if I had to."

"I learned long ago that the top of a woman's cunt was very sensitive to touch from hand or tongue when she was aroused, but I had no idea of the location or name of the clitoris before reading about it. And I have never seen it."

"I can't remember when I first heard about the clitoris, but I always had a hunch it was there. No woman has actually hauled off and flashed her clitoris at me saying, 'Here now, fella, this is a clitoris.' "

"I've seen diagrams and photos but not my partner's clitoris—she admonished me not to 'play doctor.' Instead we have operated by verbal feedback, i.e., 'further up . . . a little to the right.' This seems to work O.K."

"The clitoris swells and is easier to find as a woman becomes aroused. But I have never turned on the lights, sat back, and examined one, so I am unclear about the exact description."

"I was never told about the clitoris, nor about the shape of a woman's vulva (apart from there being a hole there). Nor did I hear where the urethra was. So I've had some difficulty in finding my way in on various occasions. I haven't seen it or examined it in detail, but believe I know where it is. Just inside the top of the main slit. Incredibly high up in fact, right out of the region that I used to consider as cunt."

"I don't know much about a woman's clitoris, but I'd like to know more. I don't know exactly where it is or what exactly it looks like. It's never been important to any of my lovers yet. I would like to know more about it though. I wish one of them would make a point of educating me on it."

"I know where it's supposed to be according to the books but she's apparently fully hooded and it is never exposed. At the slightest pressure it rolls sideways and gets lost again."

And most men of every age said that they had gotten most of their information out of books:

"I have only learned about the clitoris from books on sexuality. No women have ever shared any information on their clitoris or masturbatory style with me." (Age twenty-five.)

"I took a course in college that filled me in about some of the intimacies of marriage, but real awareness about the clitoris came only in the last ten years when I picked up a book about it. No woman has ever *shown* me her clitoris. I took the liberty to explore my wife, once, not knowing if she would even approve." (Age fifty.)

"I learned about the clitoris from pornographic books." (Age thirty.)

"I had heard men joke about it but I didn't really know about its function and location until I read about it in a book." (Age twenty-eight.)

"I read about it recently in some anatomy literature." (Age seventy-four.)

"I first heard the word 'clitoris' on the radio, and then looked it up in a few books. I was surprised to find that so important a part of human anatomy and sexuality existed, that was spoken of so little." (Age twenty-eight.)

"I read in a book that it was the center of sexual stimulation for a woman and that its manipulation is necessary for her orgasm." (Age thirty-two.)

SIMILARITIES BETWEEN CLITORIS

Parts of the clitoris and penis

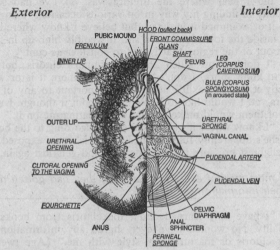

Exterior — *Interior*

PUBIC MOUND
HOOD (pulled back)
FRONT COMMISSURE
FRENULUM
GLANS
SHAFT
INNER LIP
PELVIS
LEG (CORPUS CAVERNOSUM)
BULB (CORPUS SPONGYOSUM) (in aroused state)
OUTER LIP
URETHRAL SPONGE
URETHRAL OPENING
VAGINAL CANAL
CLITORAL OPENING TO THE VAGINA
PUDENDAL ARTERY
PUDENDAL VEIN
FOURCHETTE
PELVIC DIAPHRAGM
ANAL SPHINCTER
ANUS
PERINEAL SPONGE

The clitoral system during arousal.

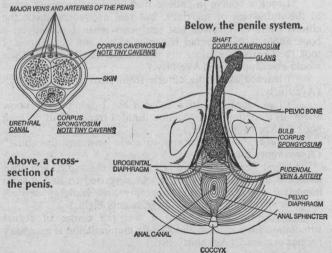

MAJOR VEINS AND ARTERIES OF THE PENIS

Below, the penile system.

CORPUS CAVERNOSUM NOTE TINY CAVERNS
SHAFT CORPUS CAVERNOSUM
GLANS
SKIN
URETHRAL CANAL
CORPUS SPONGYOSUM NOTE TINY CAVERNS
PELVIC BONE
BULB (CORPUS SPONGYOSUM)
UROGENITAL DIAPHRAGM
PUDENDAL VEIN & ARTERY

Above, a cross-section of the penis.

PELVIC DIAPHRAGM
ANAL SPHINCTER
ANAL CANAL
COCCYX

AND PENIS ANATOMY

systems are underscored.

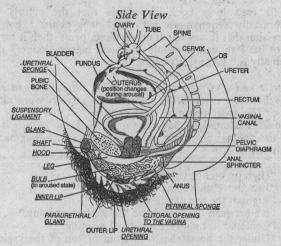

The clitoral system during arousal.

There is a widespread misunderstanding of women's sexual anatomy. What we usually think of as the "clitoris" is simply the exterior part of a larger interior structure. The extent of this interior clitoral network is quite large—comparable to the size of the penis and testicles in men. Inside the penis there are two cavernous bulbs the length of the shaft that fill with blood and thus cause erection. These same two cavernous bulbs exist in the female; however, in the female they are separate, each extending on one side of the vulva, beginning at the pubic area (the exterior clitoris) and going back on either side of the vagina. During arousal they fill with blood and cause the entire area to swell: this is why a woman's vulva becomes swollen and puffy, pleasurably sensitive to the touch. When orgasm occurs, the blood is sent out of these structures in waves by muscle contractions. In other words, the clitoral system is similar in size to the penis, but the clitoral system is *interior,* while the penis is exterior. Both systems are the same in the early embryo.

If men could understand the similarities of their structures to those of women, they could understand clitoral stimulation much more easily. For example, most men need stimulation at the top of their penis for orgasm, even though they feel the orgasm basically at the base of the penis and inside their bodies: stimulation at the sensitive tip and around the rim leads to sensations deeper inside the body. In the same way, stimulation of the exterior clitoral area causes sensations deeper in the body and vaginal area, culminating in orgasm.

"Until I read about it recently (my wife gave me a book), I didn't realize the importance of the clitoris, I just thought of powerful thrusting intercourse as the thing a woman would like." (Age sixty-two.)

"I read in a book in college that the clitoris was anatomically synonymous with the glans penis. I got the impression that it was much more 'like a penis' than it turned out to be. I thought it would be much bigger (longer) than it actually is." (Age thirty-three.)

When asked, "Where is the clitoris?," although most men knew basically where it is, many of the answers were rather vague. The most common answer was: "At the top of the vagina." It is unlikely that most men think the clitoris is inside the vagina; are these men using the word "vagina" to mean "vulva"?

"High up on her vagina."
"Just above the vagina."
"Right at the top of the vagina."
"It's between the lips above the vaginal opening."
"Centered just above the vaginal opening."
"Under the hood/sheath in front of/top of the vagina."
"Very top edge of the vagina."
"Top of the vaginal opening."

Clearer descriptions included the following:

"It's near the top of the 'crack.' "
"It is higher up than one would think—and farther away from the vagina."
"It's at the upper end of the outer lips, near the pelvic bone."
"In the folds of the lips, above the vagina."
"Above the genital slit, under the hood of skin descending from the mons."
"It's above the vagina toward the belly button."
"At the top (pubic bone) end of the vagina."
"Although I have never removed the hood from my wife's clitoris, I know where it is—at the point of the V of the inner lips."
"It's under the V-shaped hood in front of the vagina (I hope)."

"It's at the upper corner of the genitals. When it's stimulated, it hides under its hood."

"Right above the pee hole."

"At the base of the mons, sandwiched between several folds of flesh."

"Tucked in there amid the folds at the north end of the vulva."

"Hiding under the covers above the vagina."

Also notable is the emotional reaction this question created in some men:

"I could give an average location in centimeters from the top of the vagina, etc., but there are many more questions I could better spend the time on."

"I would rather show than tell."

"In the illustration on page 6 of 'Sex for Third Graders.'"

"Sure ain't in her nose."

A few men said they did not know for sure:

"I have never separated the clitoris from the whole genital area."

"To tell the truth, I am not quite sure where a woman's clitoris is."

"I was performing cunnilingus one time and all of a sudden I stopped and said to my girlfriend, 'Where the heck is your clitoris anyway?' I think she was a little embarrassed and just gave one-word answers, 'higher,' 'lower,' while I prodded with my finger. All of a sudden she said 'there.' I looked to see where my finger was, but I couldn't see anything special. I still don't know where it is. We've made a deal that sometime when we're really into it (horny) we'll tell each other exactly how to make the other orgasm. It's going to make me really self-conscious but deep down I want to do it."

And some men truly did not know where it was, stating that it was inside the vagina:

"It is inside the vagina."

"It is deep down inside."

"Between the lips up inside the vaginal opening."

"An inch or so inside the vagina."

"In the vagina just past the folds of skin."

"Just inside her pussy."

HOW DO MEN FEEL ABOUT STIMULATING A WOMAN CLITORALLY BY HAND?

"I hate to admit it, but my wife's way of having orgasm used to really irritate me in the beginning. She always clenches her legs together, sometimes even twists them together while I am supposed to rub her clitoris. After all I had heard about a woman spreading her legs meaning she wants you, I felt that this was a rejection, and really, that there was something 'weird' about her. It took a couple of years before we could talk about this. In the beginning, I just did what I thought she wanted, but I really resented it, and gradually I began to do it less and less enthusiastically, I guess. Finally, we had a fight about it. She said she thought I resented her orgasms, and I said I thought she was being selfish when she had them. She didn't need me at all. I wasn't involved, I wasn't inside her, and I wasn't getting stimulated (although I have to admit that sometimes it was a pretty sexy situation, with her doing all that moaning and groaning, writhing and getting hot and sweaty, saying she loved me and grabbing me after—wow, very passionate kisses). Anyway, I still resented it. She was very hurt that I didn't enjoy her orgasms, and didn't want to have sex for a while. That got me started thinking, what was the point of sex anyway? It's taken me a long time to begin to accept that this is how she (women?) has orgasm, and that it doesn't mean that there is anything wrong with me because she doesn't do it during intercourse. I mean, I know rationally that this is it, clitoral stimulation, and I really dig it, but at the same time, the myth of how it should be is still there."

Most men who had tried it expressed doubts about their expertise at giving manual clitoral stimulation. When asked, "Do you feel knowledgeable and comfortable stimulating a woman clitorally? How do you feel while giving clitoral stimulation with your hand?" most mentioned feelings of discomfort and said that getting feedback from the woman was essential:

"I don't feel sublimely confident when dealing with a clitoris; the orgasm seems very picky about what it likes and what it doesn't like, and it's hard to know, until you get to know a girl pretty well, just what the right thing is. I feel much better if my partner will indicate to me what feels good."

"Sometimes I can't find a woman's clitoris. I am either constantly getting lost—or else the damn thing moves around a lot."*

"I feel knowledgeable about touching a clitoris up to a point (get it?), and then I want her to communicate to me what she likes. I'm no mind reader, and different women like different pressures and motions, although I find that they often are so glad to have their joy button get any attention at all that they go up the walls."

"I don't think I'm doing it right. I've talked about it with the other guys, but all I hear are stories about 'sticking-your-whole-god-damn-fist-up-there' while 'she-was-getting-wet-to-her-ankles' crap."

"It's exciting to stimulate a woman clitorally and see her sexual arousal. My girlfriend told me I was too rough sometimes. I was never too gentle, or then she didn't say anything."

"Generally I feel knowledgeable about touching it, but some differ *so* radically in preferences that one can never be sure. And, like most humans, I am subject to errors of touch. I think that men tend to be too rough with female parts and women too gentle with men."

"After ten years my wife finally conceded to letting me touch her, but was very embarrassed in those days but not today. I enjoy giving my wife stimulation, but I have to keep myself stimulated too with my other hand because she cannot hold my penis during her stimulation—it distracts her and she can't come."

"Different women have such different size and shape clits that I have trouble understanding what pressure to apply. However, I try to do the job well. I depend a lot on communication from my partner. Basically, I will proceed until I'm redirected. I enjoy producing a manually developed orgasm. My favorite was during a movie at a theater. I reached up under her skirt and she melted in my hand."

"My present partner is hypersensitive to pain. Sometimes I hurt her when I am rubbing her clitoris. I feel guilty and confused when this happens. It sometimes happens even when I am being as soft as I can be."

"I never felt intimately knowledgeable on the subject—I

---

* Once again, these replies were much more likely to contain jokes than answers relating to intercourse or other topics.

knew the clitoris existed, but I didn't really know that it functioned separately from the vagina. My current lover has shown me how to masturbate her, and I have learned a lot about it from her. Before that, I had just heard about it from jokes (told by other men) and medical books."

"I guess my mom told me that women had a thing like a little penis that was their 'high.' I never really understood what exactly a clitoris was for a long time, slowly putting together reading and street information and finding out from my own experiences. I still don't quite know where it is or what it feels like."

"It's hard to know just what feels good for the woman unless she gives constant feedback as to what's feeling good and what's not. The clitoris is very sensitive and a little too much pressure in the wrong place can be more uncomfortable than pleasurable."

Many had never tried it, or had a mistaken idea of what it involved:

"I would sure like to try it. Haven't done it yet."

"I like women that are full round and curvaceous. I like to feel all the curves and kiss her all over her body, but I don't know if I have ever touched her clitoris."

"I enjoy and use the full range of touching, rubbing, caressing, kissing, licking, sucking, tonguing, biting, holding, snuggling, tickling, and anything else I am able to think of at the time, but I don't concentrate it in any one particular spot."

"I stick my finger up her clitoris and move it in and out."

"I don't understand the question."

"Never tried it."

"Twenty-four years ago with a girlfriend I would stimulate her with a finger usually inserted all the way."

"I start by just stroking her lightly, then as she starts responding, I penetrate her with my index and middle fingers. I keep going until she tells me to get in her and then finish up that way."

Many men had felt uncomfortable the first few times they tried it:

"The first time I was more concerned with finding her clitoris than anything else. Then I remember being worried that I would hurt her, by doing it too hard."

"It took me time to find the right motion but I found it.

It was great. When I first did it at the age of twenty-eight I was clumsy, but as I continued, I learned to love it."

"Success was not immediate. It took a few tries. At first I felt I was violating some private sanctity of hers, then I began wondering how long it would take, and if I was doing it right. It was tiring."

"When we first started making love, I would briefly stroke her breasts, then begin stroking her clitoral area. I was abysmally ignorant of why and how a woman became sexually stimulated—but at least she was willing to tell me what she liked. However, because I did not understand why I was doing a particular motion, I found it difficult to remember it from one session to another. I probably came across as somewhat insensitive, even though I am not. I was simply too inhibited and too unfamiliar to do it right."

"It requires a lot of concentration and an even, rhythmic motion of my fist. I felt unsure the first few times I did it, because she had to keep telling me that I wasn't doing it right. I felt great when I brought her to orgasm though."

"I did it with the first woman I slept with, because it seemed the right thing to do from what I'd heard and read. This was the first time a woman reached orgasm with me, and it blew me away to find out a woman could experience the same body feeling/explosion that I did."

One man described his first experience in detail:

"At the time I didn't know her real well, I'd only known her for six weeks. When I came over that afternoon, she said, 'Let's sit down for a while.' She sat down leaning her back against my chest, and I had my arm around her, with my hand resting on her stomach. I felt really close to her. We were sort of slouched down in the couch. She said, 'I want to have an orgasm. Look—I'll show you how to do it.' She put my hand on her pubic area, with hers on top, and started moving and pressing my hand against her, ever so slightly. Gradually she began to stiffen her body and she straightened her legs out in front of her. She started moving our hands really fast, getting even stiffer, then suddenly she came in a kind of jerking spasm. She smiled and said it was wonderful and would I mind doing it again! It was great, the way she was breathing, and the sounds, well I felt like there was a lot of revelations made that day to me. I felt like when I went home later on, I felt like I'd been doing something really special, really very beautiful that I didn't expect to be like that. I didn't know what to expect. I'd never really done anything like that.

"I felt like I was really close to her, but I was a little bit confused about my role—and my . . . orgasm—I didn't have one! (Except when I went home later and masturbated.) And she didn't seem to be interested at all if I had one, and it didn't have any bearing on my pleasure—so that gave me a little something to think about. But the thing that I thought about most was the fact that she had had those two orgasms really fast. On the one hand I felt really successful that I was able to masturbate her to orgasm, and also that she was so excited, but on the other hand, it seemed, judging from my own orgasms, she had had a much better one than I ever had. So it was really a surprise.

"Also I felt really complimented that she had an orgasm. Whatever I had to do with it I don't know, but it made me feel really really good that she had an orgasm, that I was with her and she had an orgasm—it made me feel real special to be there when she did that. I felt like I was really close to her."

A few men said they felt they were doing something "abnormal" that they should not need to do:

"I was glad to find out from *The Hite Report* that the need for clitoral stimulation is normal. It makes me feel a little less weird when I do it! I know it's ridiculous to feel so inhibited, but I just can't get over it."

"I always feel awkward about it when I'm doing it. I mean, I know this is what gives women orgasms, but do other men really do this? I have never seen a picture of one doing this, so it must not be too common. Maybe it's weird, a 'real man' shouldn't have to do it. I know it's not true, but that's how I feel. I wouldn't brag about it."

A few men connected manual clitoral stimulation with "teenage" behavior (calling it a "high school" activity, or even "adolescent" behavior*)—since it was something they had done only before intercourse was possible:

"I used to do clitoral stimulation—it was pretty much the male half of the exchange before we were old enough to screw."

---

* Of course, Freud, in his work on female sexuality, called the need for clitoral stimulation "immature."

"I did it in high school. My girlfriend loved it, but it doesn't seem so appropriate now."

One man had decided while in school that he didn't like it:

"The first time I did clitoral stimulation was when I was dating in college. I took the woman to orgasm, but I felt left out of the whole affair, even though I enjoyed watching. Now I still enjoy stimulating a woman's clitoris, but I enter her before she reaches orgasm."

Other men felt awkward initiating clitoral stimulation, wondering if it was appropriate or if the woman wanted it:

"Not knowing with a new partner what she wants, I have initiated it and if anyone objected I stopped. If it was/is agreeable I have given clitoral stimulation until orgasm."

"I usually include clitoral stimulation to orgasm in the sex act unless my partner asks me specifically not to, because it's better to offer than not. She can always say no."

"I always do clitoral stimulation or cunnilingus when engaging in sex, if the girl wants it done. I ask permission, and would never do it if the girl objected. I must say that I have never had a woman say no. I continue it until the girl says to stop. I leave it up to the girl, if she wants to have an orgasm or not."

"I can never decide whether to do it or not. Once I started trying and the girl jerked back and looked at me, and said, 'What are you doing?' I was like a freak or something. Now I always do it with my girlfriend—she's not afraid to ask me. But I'd rather not ask a new gal for sex than face that situation again."

"Yeah, I've heard about clitoral stimulation—I guess I should do it—but I just don't know, no girl has ever asked me to do it. What if I did it wrong or she didn't want me to do it?"

Deciding whether to stop or to go on to orgasm could also be difficult:

"I observe her breathing—her actions toward me. If she rubs her hands on me, my back or butt, she's still horny and wants to come this way. If she pulls me on top of her, she wants intercourse. Anyway, I keep stimulating her to see if she wants more, to make sure."

"Most women don't express this too explicitly, so I still finish her so that she doesn't have to say."

Clitoral stimulation for orgasm

But most men had never given a woman an orgasm with manual clitoral stimulation. When asked, "Have you stimulated a woman to orgasm through manual clitoral stimulation?" only 20 percent of the men said yes, this was a usual part of their sexual relations (this group contained men of all ages, backgrounds, and points of view); 39 percent did it infrequently, almost never, or never; 22 percent of the answers were so vague that their meaning could not be ascertained; and the remaining 19 percent did not answer.

"Please describe how you stimulate the clitoris with your hand or finger. Is it difficult to do, or uncomfortable or tiring?"

Some men mentioned practical difficulties with giving manual clitoral stimulation for orgasm:

"I make a fist and rotate it over her pubic hair. She keeps her knees together. I move my hand pretty fast. The important thing is to keep it rhythmic and not change the motion. I can get a tired arm from doing this if my arm is in a somewhat awkward position. I also do it left-handed sometimes when that hand falls into the natural position, but it's harder left-handed because I'm right-handed."

"Sometimes it takes too long and my wrist and arm can become fatigued, but a comfortable position at the start helps."

"It is tiring and boring when it takes fifteen minutes or longer."

"I am easily tired of it."

"The one time I did it, it took about ten minutes. It was uncomfortable and tiring."

"Clitoral stimulation is a nuisance if my efforts on my partner are not producing the desired responses. It can happen if a woman is not communicative either by telling me what she wants me to do or not to do. One example is the varying wanting of varying degrees of pressure on the clitoris, with fingers or tongue. If what I am doing is not producing results, I often ask why not and the best partners will explain why not. If they cannot or do not help me in this manner, then it is a nuisance."

"Stimulation is an up and down motion. There are times when we lose it, but as long as we're relaxed we seem to get back in gear fairly soon. She stays quite still during the early stages of stimulation. It took a few times to realize that this was her way of focusing on what was going on—not a signal that she didn't feel anything."

"I do it on occasion when she and I are feeling appropriately sure about the situation and our feelings are clear, but I feel clumsy. I work around the area and then rub it with my finger. It's difficult to find sometimes, or to stay on target."

But one man said:

"I don't care if I sit there till the cows come in or my arm goes numb (upon occasion) from masturbating her, time is irrelevant. I sincerely want her to get off—no matter what."

And another said:

"I've had mixed reactions to doing clitoral stimulation for her with my hand—excitement, boredom, resentment—it depends on other things, not the act itself."

A few men shared interesting and detailed descriptions of the clitoral stimulation they had worked out with their partners for orgasm; of course, there is no "one way" to stimulate the clitoris that will work for every woman, as the feelings are highly individual:

"I gently pull her pubic hairs, stroking gently and rhythmically—I prefer to use my thumb, which is softer, in a circular movement on the clitoris. After I feel and see that the arousal plateau is higher, I use my own lubrication on my index and middle finger so I can smoothly rub the labia minora. At all times I keep rubbing the clitoris. I encourage my wife to touch her breasts (if I'm not sucking her nipples)."

"My partner likes very light, rapid rubbing of the clitoris by my hand while she spreads her labia apart with her hands. Then when she comes, she grabs my hand and presses it tight to her without moving. Then she wants to do it all over again. We do, and we keep it up until I just can't hold off any longer and I get on top of her and we have wild intercourse until I come."

"The main way that I stimulate the clitoris is that I

gently move my finger up and down. The touch must be soft, but not to the point of tickling. I have asked my wife to guide my hand as to exactly how she wanted to be stimulated and this has been most helpful. I keep the pressure and rhythm constant, gradually increasing as orgasm nears. More pressure and more speed right at the point of orgasm. Once I begin clitoral stimulation I always go on to orgasm."

"I move my hand down through her bush until I find the clitoris. I usually use the tip of my index finger to flick the clitoris. Sometimes I have one or two fingers in the vagina, my little finger along or inside the anus, and my index finger rubbing the clitoris. Orgasm does not occur, however, until I substitute the vibrator. While using the vibrator I usually also use my fingers in the vagina, and think sexy things, like how I've got her in my power."

"Using two fingers, I stroke along and over the clitoris, in a circular motion, usually in a rhythm—easing off and then applying more pressure. I don't consider it difficult, but it can be tiring when I can't tune in with the woman's approach to orgasm."

"I start by caressing the entire pubic area with light pressure. I gradually increase the pressure until the vagina starts to lubricate. I then use the vaginal fluids to lubricate my fingers. From here on things vary according to my partner's response. Most commonly I'll use long strokes with an increase in pressure as my fingertip approaches the clitoris. This is alternated with sharp direct pressure on the clitoris. As my partner nears orgasm I'll use more direct pressure and quicker strokes. I will also roll the clitoris between my thumb and index finger. After orgasm, I will reverse the process ending with gentle stroking of the pubic area and rear. This will change at my partner's request or depending on her response. One of my current partners likes very hard, direct stimulation, another wants very slow, gentle pressure, others want different things at different times. I do not find it difficult to do or tiring."

"She likes it better if I apply pressure to her clitoris (and the area around it) with the palm of my hand than with my fingers. She says she needs more generalized stimulation. I tend to move the skin around over the underlying structures, sometimes pulling the skin upwards toward her navel (which also pulls the whole vulva tight). If at the same time, I tease her vaginal opening from behind with the fingers of my other hand, this seems to drive her crazy, and she often puts her hand on top of mine on the clitoris and moves it to orgasm. Her whole body gets rigid and after, she writhes around in pleasure, telling me how good it was and how much she loves me."

And a few men used their penis against the woman's clitoris:

"I enjoy so much to lay steady next to and hold my girl in my arms with very tender and steady kissing. In this position with her breasts pressing against me, I can feel her butt with my hands, and press my penis into her pubic hair. Sometimes too I hold my penis in my hand and stimulate her clitoris with the head. It makes her moan."

A few used a vibrator:

"A woman has to be much more cooperative if I am masturbating her with the vibrator than if I am masturbating her manually because I can feel the pressure of my own hand much more than I can the vibrator, and know how much pressure to use. She likes to use a towel with it because it softens it. If I am getting her close to an orgasm with the vibrator on her clitoris and then the machine moves out of place, this is really very frustrating, so she reaches down and puts it in the right place again for me. If I'm just stimulating her manually, I can feel the place where my hand should be, because I feel the position and the way that the flesh is moving. There's this top layer of flesh that moves over the one underneath—it's like massaging—you can feel the exact spot where you're supposed to be, you get real familiar with the area."

One man commented on getting his own stimulation while he was stimulating the woman:

"I usually tease myself when I'm stimulating her, so I get more energy. I have to be in a very active and aggressive state of mind if I'm masturbating her—I can't just lie there and do it mechanically. Usually I stay hard during the whole thing. But if I've had an erection for a long time, a couple of hours, and I'm stimulating her but getting tired or sleepy, then it might start going down, and so I tease myself. I like this because I like to keep that really itchy driving feeling going."

Some men, when asked, "Do you get sexually excited by stimulating your partner? Do you enjoy her orgasm physically? Emotionally?" were very enthusiastic, and commented on how much they enjoyed stimulating their partner to orgasm in this way:

"I have done it many times and I feel really great. It is beautiful to see a woman having orgasm out of your stimulation, your direct stimulation without being worried with your sexual performance. It is also very arousing, and together with the caressing that's possible (most people have two hands . . . and a mouth), it becomes a great experience."

"In the past I would say she had orgasm with me extremely rarely, partly due to her timidity and partly to my stupidity. During intercourse, almost never. Now playing with her clitoris with my finger or tongue always makes her come —I am glad that I have discovered the clitoris and what it means. I enjoy her excitement terrifically."

"I get very excited. When she orgasms I feel so good I feel we are flying. My girlfriend had multiple orgasms. It was marvelous. It seemed that the girl would have a breakdown. She breathed profoundly and rhythmically. I thought she'd go mad. During her orgasms she held me tightly. That was the best."

"I was somewhat clumsy and rough at first, but my girlfriend guided me and showed me how to go about it, as she had learned herself through masturbation. When I learned how, I enjoyed it immensely. I love to watch the blood rush to her face, her mouth open and eyes closed, her lips begin moving and pressing against my hand, and finally, hands holding on to me as she climaxed in pure joy. I love to give her pleasure! Her reaction, when she recovers, is usually to grab me and kiss me madly."

"When I'm masturbating her, I love the idea that she's getting really excited. It makes me feel like we're communicating, rather than if I'm always aroused by her, and having my orgasm, and she's not as aroused by me and not having orgasm. Sometimes she's had five or six orgasms in one time in bed, at which point she gets so worked up and I get so worked up my mind is going crazy. She's really a turn-on. I love the way she smells and feels when that's going on."

*And some men were even more enthusiastic about stimu-
lating their partner to several ("multiple") orgasms; when
asked how they felt about it, they said they felt great:**

"Proud!"

"An ego trip."

"The first orgasm is sort of a breakthrough leading to
more (two to three). I am a little envious, but also amazed
that until recently men knew so little about women's superior
capabilities."

"I feel flattered."

"I like it because the emotional sharing grows."

"Boosts my ego."

"It's fun for me."

"If she has dozens, it makes me feel wanted, desired,
needed, and very happy. I always want the woman to get more
out of sex, *so I can get more sex.*"

"I work at satisfying her to a state of blissful exhaustion.
It's good for my ego!"

"Many and multiple orgasms are beautiful to behold. We
only discovered after twenty years that my wife could have
multiple orgasms. What a breakthrough—and what a change
for us."

"Sometimes my wife has two or three, sometimes more,
after I'm through and soft, while I follow up by hand or
mouth. Am I envious? Should I be envious of the elephant
that has a trunk, the turtle that has a shell? God gave her
the capacity for many and God bless her because I have
fun helping out. All I know is her multiples often stimulate
me to having a new erection and often another orgasm,
especially when we have lots of time."

"I love it when she has more than one, feeling good and
being uninhibited, generally enjoying herself. I try to bring
her to as many as she wants, till she stops me."

"Ideally for me foreplay does not end until my partner
has had no less than one and hopefully many orgasms, to the
point where she is beautifully exhausted and more or less
demands that it is time for me to have an orgasm."

---

* These represent only a small fraction of the answers received, but are
included for their interest.

HOW DO MEN FEEL ABOUT A WOMAN STIMULATING HERSELF?

But can a woman also stimulate herself manually while she is with a man? In the same way that men said that women often don't give them the correct manual stimulation of their penis, isn't it difficult for one person (especially of the opposite sex) to know just how to stimulate another? Although learning to do just that with a specific partner can be very loving and exciting, it is also very important for men and women to feel that they can stimulate themselves during sex with a partner. This can be an extremely intimate activity, while at the same time removing many frustrations and pressures from both the woman and the man.

"How do you feel if a woman stimulates herself to orgasm with you? During intercourse?"

Most men had never experienced a woman stimulating herself (manually) while close to them; for most men, having the woman give herself an orgasm was a new idea. As one man said, "No woman has ever shown me how or even admitted to masturbation."

In fact, many men were shocked by the idea that their partner could masturbate to orgasm at all, even when alone; most men did not know how (or if) she did it. When asked, "Does your partner masturbate to orgasm? How? If you don't know, would you like her to share this information with you?" many gave answers similar to the following:

   "No. I don't think so."
   "No. Yes."
   "Yes—when alone."
   "I don't think she ever has."
   "Can't answer."
   "Don't know or care—probably on rare occasions."
   "She and I orgasm together if possible but I have a tough time holding mine."

Many men did not like the idea of the woman stimulating herself while with them:

"It's O.K. if she has to, but I would feel let down that I can't please her."

"I would feel inadequate if she did that."

"There would be a tinge of personal failure."

"It has never happened. I would feel very threatened."

"I would resent it."

"I hope it never happens. I would get up and leave."

"I feel very uncomfortable when she masturbates while I watch. I feel left out, an audience, unimportant, merely an afterthought on her part. I enjoy physically receiving and giving pleasure, and I don't really care whether hand or tongue or penis or vagina is the instrument of the other's pleasure. I also feel very uncomfortable when my partner enjoys more than one orgasm at a time. As much as I dislike the hang-up, I continue to feel inferior to her and also feel a kind of emotional impotence because there is apparently nothing comparable about my body and my sexual experience."

"Maybe *deep* inside my male ego would be wounded. It would depend on if there is malicious intent."

"It would be like I didn't satisfy her."

"Never happened. I've just been lucky."

"Why does she need me?"

"O.K. if she feels it's necessary. Any other way, what would she need me for? I'm not a voyeur."

And many had mixed feelings about it:

"It's O.K., provided it does not lead to a sense of separateness between us, or inadequacy on my part."

"It's good—but I would also feel slightly inadequate and hurt."

"It's O.K. if she uses my cock."

"It's not much fun being pushed out of the way, but I don't mind having expert guidance. And who more expert than the recipient?"

"It wouldn't hurt my ego but it would disturb me if she climaxed that way only."

"Great if she's willing to disclose this to me. I feel strange —happy that she'll reach orgasm, but unhappy because I'm not doing it to her liking."

"I don't feel too bad, as long as I'm the *mental* stimulation."

"I might feel left out; somewhat undesirable, unattractive,

inadequate. However, if the woman lets me know that she is doing it not because of my failure but because at this time it is necessary to meet her needs, I feel better. During intercourse—I suggested it to my partner after discussing and experiencing her non-orgasmic feelings. It doesn't upset me a lot, as long as she treats me as an important part of her pleasure."

"If I am feeling O.K. about myself, I feel O.K. when a woman reaches orgasm by stimulating herself on me. When I'm not feeling O.K., I tend to feel used."

"Well, I don't want to feel left out. I want to share her experience. If she were just sitting there doing her solitary thing and I'm just the substitute for an electric blanket, I'd be disappointed. On the other hand, obviously she's aware of just what she needs in the way I can't possibly be. If she needs her own stimulation in order to come, fine."

Quite a few men didn't understand the question at all:

"I don't understand this question. Anyway, I would be too embarrassed to masturbate in front of her."

"This question leaves me puzzled."

As to doing it during intercourse, some men thought manual clitoral stimulation would be O.K. during intercourse—as long as they did the stimulating:

"Let me help too—if it's gotta be."

"Hope I could handle the job myself."

"Happy to help."

"*I* do it."

"I would rather do it."

"Sometimes my wife has had to do it due to my clumsiness at it. (Just married.)"

"O.K., but I'd rather do it myself since I enjoy it."

"I would feel good if a woman stimulated herself to orgasm with me. At least I think that I would. But, of course, not during intercourse. Actually, to be honest, I think that *I* would rather stimulate her to orgasm."

And a few others said it would be all right, but not during intercourse:

"It could add an exciting dimension, but I wouldn't want her to do it regularly, and never during intercourse."

"I like to watch her masturbate, but it gets in the way during intercourse."

But some men expressed an open attitude toward trying it:

"I'd be relieved. It would be a great help in our case."
"I would appreciate her cooperation."
"It's never happened. But why shouldn't she?"
"It sounds very exotic. I wish she would do it."
"It would be nice, but she seems inhibited."
"I would not mind, but my wife will not try it."
"I have been trying to get her to do that."
"She has the right."
"I wish more women would feel free to stimulate themselves to orgasm at any time during the sex play—but especially afterward, if what we've done together doesn't work or I don't seem to have the right touch to bring her to orgasm."
"I would be greatly flattered if the woman felt relaxed enough with me to masturbate in my presence. I would consider it a tremendous compliment."
"Many women will gladly *show* me how they enjoy direct clitoral stimulation—but unfortunately, self-masturbation is still taboo."
"Although my wife is a marvelous, super partner, I have yet to observe her masturbating. Someday, I hope to have that opportunity—it would 'blow my mind.' A fantasy of mine would become a reality."

One man implied what many may have felt—that it sounded rather depraved:

"Sounds kinky but I'm for it."

And a few said they liked it very much; these answers are quoted at length for their interest:

"It makes me feel so super close to her. It's almost better sharing masturbation than intercourse because more of the false privacy is shared with one's lover."
"It's a great experience to share—it makes me freer."
"I love it and encourage it. Most women won't but I wish they would."
"Good, sometimes I fondle my balls at the same time."

"It is a beautiful sight. My job is to accompany her and to help her along the way."

"I feel very close that we can share in that way. It makes me feel included."

"One woman I know uses a vibrator during intercourse. It's great—I am thrilled."

"My relations with my wife have improved a great deal and I'm sure part of it has to do with the impact of the liberation movement if only indirectly. She does not read the literature—but the force of the women's movement creates an atmosphere, a social climate, that touches all or most of us. The message filters down—sex is O.K., it's O.K. to do it any way you like, express yourself. She, my wife, seems warmer, more responsive. All of a sudden, after thirty years, she feels free to masturbate in my presence without embarrassment and vice versa. That is significant and it has brought us closer together."

"It's great. It shows she knows herself as a person."

"My wife will masturbate using the head of my penis. This is great. I enjoy her masturbation, particularly when I participate by touching her."

"Looking at a woman having an orgasm blows my mind."

"I feel very good about it. She knows her own body better than I do. If it gives her pleasure then do it. Many men feel inferior when this happens. Why? Can a woman masturbate a man as well as he could masturbate himself?"

"She does orgasm with me, but only through my or her masturbation. She has told me that she could never, and has never with other lovers, orgasmed through intercourse. She also has 'breast orgasms' when I caress them while she masturbates—which is great, because I love a woman's breasts."

"I am twenty-nine, married to a beautiful girl, for five years. Our sex life has always been very open and active, but let me say my wife and I are enjoying sex even more now. About a year ago I started talking openly about masturbation with my wife. Well it didn't take long at all. With a little gentleness and common sense my wife and I now share our masturbation together. Sometimes she will masturbate for me and I for her. This is a wonderful turn-on. Sometimes we masturbate each other. I really get great pleasure in knowing my wife can have an orgasm anytime she wants. We're into sharing our fantasies and we really get turned on by this. I cannot believe that a husband would not be willing to share all of his wife's desires. I enjoy sex and I enjoy masturbation and I certainly wouldn't want my wife to miss out on all the fun."

"She is very beautiful when she stimulates herself with me."

"Great. I want to give her this space. I feel I am learning something, by watching."

"When my wife masturbates herself in our lovemaking sessions, I am delighted, because to watch her jack off is a turn-on for me. I often ask her to do so, just so I can enjoy watching her move and come. If she does it during intercourse, it means that she likes to have more intense pleasure, and it excites me no end to have a woman who likes the good feeling in sex. Sometimes she asks for my leg or hand to finish off a little 'corner' of an orgasm that had not quite got off, and this is just added pleasure for me."

"A woman stimulating herself to orgasm is highly arousing to me. A woman's self-stimulation is also useful in several ways: it shows me exactly the type and speed of stimulation she likes; it generally produces stronger and more consistent orgasms for her; with each of us in charge of our orgasms during intercourse it is much easier to pace our activity—for instance, if she wishes to have several orgasms or if we wish to climax together, etc. Even though I encourage female self-stimulation I have found that most women are very reluctant to practice it. Surprisingly this is even true for women who are very independent and self-assured."

"My wife frequently masturbates to orgasm when we are in bed. She says, 'Make an ice cream cone.' I cup her breast in both hands and suck her nipple. She has masturbated since age eight and habitually during our marriage. It is another happy way for us to be close. Sometimes she kisses my scrotum or sucks my penis after intercourse while masturbating. Occasionally I masturbate while she watches. It is *intimacy*."

"A really great turn-on for me, is some evening when we are going to bed early in expectation of making love, I may enter the bedroom to find her spread out on the bed masturbating with wild abandon—this is always arousing to me! Occasionally if I am in the bedroom first, I will do the same."

"I help my wife have an orgasm with my thigh between her legs and some gentle fondling of her breasts and some sexy whispering in her ear while she rubs against me. I'm not annoyed—just happy to be part of it."

"How do you feel if a woman stimulates herself to orgasm with a vibrator while with you? How do you feel about the use of a vibrator in sex?"

Most men seemed not to have had actual experience with a woman using a vibrator or with using one themselves. However, although often ridiculed, the vibrator can play an extremely helpful role. A woman who may feel shy and inhibited with clitoral stimulation from her partner, and a man who, due to inexperience, may feel uncomfortable and inadequate giving clitoral stimulation, can benefit greatly from a vibrator. The vibrator can be an excellent transitional solution because it can bring on an orgasm very quickly, without so much worry about technique, and it can be a great deal of fun. Beyond its transitional role, of course, a vibrator can be a very pleasing addition to sex.

Actually, the best kinds of vibrators for clitoral stimula are not shaped like a penis and are not battery-operated but are either the kind traditionally used for body massage that strap onto the hand or a kind made especially for the clitoral or other small (facial) areas, which simply have a handle and a small or medium-sized massaging head. Both of these are electric.

*Most men did not like the idea of vibrators at all:**

"I'd rather she came without a vibrator."

"A vibrator is cancerous, probably."

"Anything to make her come."

"It's not the end of the world if she stimulates herself, especially if she uses her own imagination to do it. I don't think I'd be crazy about her using a vibrator though."

"I only feel no good if she needs a vibrator to orgasm."

"Clitoral stimulation is O.K. but it's carrying it too far when she uses a vibrator!"

"I am very happy she does not use one."

"Something about vibrators bothers me, but I don't complain to the one person I know who likes to incorporate one into the act. The secondary vibration through the pubic bone is sort of a 'kick' but they tend to produce so rapid a

---

* Are some of these men thinking that the vibrator would be inserted vaginally? In fact, most women who use vibrators use them on the clitoral area or vulva, and they are almost never inserted.

climactic effect in women that I always feel a bit odd about coming afterwards—I can never 'keep up.' "

"If a woman stimulates herself to orgasm with me, I feel cheated. I would like to bring her to orgasm, and if I'm not, why am I her lover?! Vibrators are for shit as far as I'm concerned. Vibrators are the embryos which, taken to their logical end, have men and women getting off on machines instead of each other; each has become obsolete in the other's eyes."

But a few men expressed an open attitude toward trying one:

"I intend to buy a vibrator to see if we can enhance our sex life. I hear they're great."

"I never experienced it, but I would enjoy watching her use a vibrator."

"I would not mind my partner using a vibrator if I also took part, e.g., manipulating or helping manipulate the vibrator while kissing and fondling her breasts, etc."

"We don't have vibrators etc. as we don't know a reliable place to get any, but I would enjoy it."

And a few men enjoyed the use of the vibrator by a woman:

"I love to watch her body spasmodically orgasm while she uses her vibrator."

"My lover does not orgasm from intercourse—but we do many many things together besides intercourse. It is very exciting to masturbate together. She has orgasms when she wants to—she just grabs the vibrator."

"I really loved using the vibrator we had on my lover, as I could give her intense orgasms that way."

"Fine, anytime. If she uses it then she can use it on me, it feels good. It doesn't make me feel unmasculine."

"One woman uses a vibrator during intercourse. I am thrilled, frankly, that she is so into sex. She apologizes, and I have to keep supporting her, encouraging her. The nitwit. It's like me eating a whole meal, and her feeling she must nibble."

One man described how he had felt the first time a woman used a vibrator with him:

"Before knowing her, I wasn't familiar with vibrators. I didn't know what a vibrator was really for. I had heard all those jokes they make about vibrators. I thought that you put vibrators inside, and I still couldn't figure out why it should vibrate if you put in inside, because in-and-out was the motion, not vibrating. Anyway, it was a phallic-looking thing, is all I knew—I had never really seen one, to tell you the truth. I'd never touched one, I didn't know how they worked and what they did, but naturally I pretended like I knew all about them, just like every other man, of course! I didn't talk to women about it. I never really talked about them that much to men either, but if anyone ever said anything about one to me . . . I would laugh along with all the other guys, like "Yeah, I know all about those too." But really I don't think that very many men know either.

"When my lover said she wanted to use the vibrator with me for the first time I felt really apprehensive. I really didn't know how to use it, and I couldn't understand how it could feel good, or what it could accomplish. When she turned it on, and started massaging her clitoris, I felt inadequate, sort of rejected for the vibrator. I didn't want to seem unfriendly, but I did feel awkward and like a rookie. I was curious to learn about it, but I was nervous, and scared, I don't know why. I guess it was because I didn't know what to do. I didn't realize that it was to be used in a similar way as manual stimulation, which I knew how to do by now.

"When we first did it with the vibrator, I felt left out. I didn't like the vibrator. She was using it, and was able to have orgasms really fast with it, so I didn't know what to do. I didn't say anything, but tried to think positive. After a while, I started experimenting, and discovered that an exciting thing to do when the other person is masturbating (with or without a vibrator) is to talk to her and encourage her to have an orgasm. I love to touch her too, but talking about fantasies (I don't know if that's a good word, fantasies, but I mean sexy things you're thinking about), is the best. Like when she says sexy things to me when I'm going to have an orgasm, it just makes me go crazy wanting to have one. When I discovered how turned on the things I said made her, and how she loved them, that's when I felt like I had a really active role in the whole thing. Now I really like the vibrator sometimes, because it's variety—you know, a different way of doing it, plus it's fast. But sometimes it's more spontaneous without it because mechanically you don't have to grab the thing, and also it is more quiet."

MEN'S FEELINGS ABOUT CUNNILINGUS

Although most men liked cunnilingus, and were more familiar with it than manual stimulation, it was not a major way of giving women clitoral stimulation *to orgasm*. Only 32 percent of the men who answered said that they usually continued cunnilingus until the woman reached orgasm, with most others ignoring this part of the question.

However, most men were extremely enthusiastic about cunnilingus. For just over half of the men who answered who enjoyed sex with women, cunnilingus was the second most popular sexual activity, after intercourse. But a large number of men felt squeamish about cunnilingus—including many of those who were enthusiastic about it. There were very few in-between opinions about cunnilingus, and the answers show a much greater emotional reaction than those to almost any other subject.

Although most men thought of cunnilingus as "foreplay," they felt more comfortable with this form of clitoral stimulation than with manual clitoral stimulation. In fact, when asked about "clitoral stimulation," most men began discussing oral sex, not mentioning manual stimulation unless it was specifically referred to by the question. Still, the form of cunnilingus practiced by most men did not include much specific clitoral stimulation, but was more likely to concentrate on the general vulva and/or vaginal opening, rather than the clitoris. While this can be very pleasurable, both physically and emotionally, and even preferable to many women, lack of precise clitoral stimulation for orgasm is a drawback if no other provision is made for the woman's orgasm during sex.

"Do you enjoy cunnilingus with a woman? What do you like and/or dislike about it?"

Most men were extremely enthusiastic about cunnilingus:

"More than anything else I enjoy oral sex. If my partner wants, I will eat her all day long. I feel very happy, content, secure, and loving doing so. I adore the texture, feel, and taste, and also the lovely way a woman seems to respond. The women I have had oral sex with seem to relax and enjoy it. There seems to be a very open feeling between us."

"Oral sex is my favorite of all. I feel a great closeness, a deep intimacy burying my face in that dark secret place. I feel that she trusts me fully. I love to look up and see her eyes closed and her face contorted in exquisite agony. I love my face drenched in her secretions, and her clit dancing under my tongue and her rocking hard and arching her back. And especially her moaning, screaming, raising her arms above her head so I can see her armpits. I love the convulsive motions of her coming. I love it when it's over and I keep my face between her legs and it gets dry and sticky and our skin pulls when it peels apart. I orgasm quite often myself while performing cunnilingus, usually before she does. Oral sex is *the* way for me to get my lover to orgasm."

"I like to taste and feel her, her genitals are very beautiful. I embrace her clitoris with my mouth and tongue and I love to lick her inside. I do not mind swallowing, she tastes good!! I get aroused when I go down on her. I want to take her whole vagina in my mouth. I use my tongue on her clitoris and inside her. What I don't like—stopping!! If she handles my penis while I'm doing it, I have an orgasm, a very intense one, especially if she is coming at the same time. When she is coming she arouses me extremely. I watch her face and it really blows my mind. I love the way she puts her hand by her mouth, she closes her eyes, and sometimes at the last moment she goes wild. It used to scare me in the beginning because it reminded me of an epileptic attack. I used to think I was hurting her, but she explained it was the exact opposite."

"I love the way a woman's genitals look when I am close enough to see all of the features. When a woman begins to respond to the act of cunnilingus, her vagina opens like the petals of a flower—her lips fill and enlarge, just as a man's penis does. It tastes like ambrosia that only a woman's body could exude."

"She has gorgeous legs even at sixty-one. I usually start it. I could wish she would ask, or tell me to eat it, but she is bashful. I massage her with my tongue and she directs me. We have done this for forty-one years, and more frequently the last two years."

"I feel that the genital kiss given by a man to a woman is one of the most intimate expressions of love that there is. I often have dreams involving sex, most of which do not end with my orgasm or ejaculation but do include a protracted period of my kissing the woman's genitals."

"I enjoy the feel of her skin on my face, the wetness of

a slight taste of urine but it isn't bad at all. Once I've licked away the urine, it tastes pretty good."

"I love to stick my face in there and grab her butt or feel her breasts. Whatever smell is there to begin with usually becomes neutral within a few licks. I like to get my face wet. It's kind of decadent or something. The smell isn't bad, it just is. Most often something like fish. I guess I associate it with sex, so it's definitely more arousing than discomforting. I guess I enjoy eating the 'monkey' as much as I do the fucking."

Most men licked the clitoral and vaginal areas, but a few men said they only kissed the area "on top":

"I am usually reluctant to go 'whole hog' at cunnilingus. I do not swallow deliberately. I take the clitoral area between my lips and gently pull and suck on it. For the most part I avoid the vaginal area and stay above it, only occasionally sucking the lip fringes, and I have never put my tongue inside a woman's vagina."

"I like to kiss a woman's vagina, on top of the vagina. I don't like to go inside. I'd rather kiss her on top."

Some men did it just to please their partners, although they themselves did not like it that much:

"I do cunnilingus for *her*. I've only gone through this with my wife. Basically I do not like it for my own sake. I started this when I felt that I was too high and she was too cool. Initially she was very reluctant and several times I had to press the issue, but after the initial shock was over, she soon found out that behind this odd thing was a sure source of orgasms—after which time she stopped objecting to it."

"Cunnilingus can be enjoyable once you're used to it, but the joys of pardon my language 'eating pussy' are really blown out of proportion. I like it mainly for the pleasure it gives to the woman, though if she hasn't cleaned up lately it can be kind of a put-off. A stimulated, wet vagina took a little getting used to at first, pressing my lips to it. I could not do it at all if I did not care emotionally for my partner."

"I personally can take it or leave it, but my girlfriend *loves* it (she just starts moaning like crazy, and once when she came, she started to bang my head against the car wall!). Just to see her in this state makes me want to come. Sometimes the smell is bad, but human beings can get used to anything. I *hate* it when a woman, without asking, tries to *push* me physically down to do it. On those occasions I refuse out of principle. If she's warm and open about wanting it, I'll do it with pleasure."

For a few men it was connected to a feeling of subservience to the woman:

"It is a great turn-on for many women because it means they are so strongly desired that their man is willing to perform this almost sacrificial, servile act of love. It tells them much about his real feelings for them. It tells them that he desires them, *all* of them."

"It's the ultimate turn-on for me before coitus because she is confident enough in me and my feelings to allow me into what in most women is an area they are somewhat reluctant (if not outright ashamed) to show a man. It's both a feeling of power and dominance and submission and sacrifice."

"Eating pussy makes me feel subservient. I enjoy serving a woman in this manner. I would stay down on her for two hours if that is what it takes to make her come off. I love to have her stroke my shoulders, twirl her fingers through my hair, and put her feet on my body and head. What I detest is a quick orgasmic response that must be a fake. I am down on a woman because I enjoy servicing her."

But more men said the opposite—that causing such a strong response made them feel powerful:

"I sometimes get a feeling of power over my partner, when I am bringing her to multiple orgasms through cunnilingus. I feel like I'm toying with her entire body and mind."

"What's special about it is that it often elicits the most marvelous response. Some women who are bored by being played with are rapidly unbored by cunnilingus. (But other women won't allow it, seem repulsed, or shocked, or threatened by the idea.) It is eliciting that response, and almost glorying in what I'm doing to her, that sets cunnilingus apart."

Some men also mentioned the intimacy implied, in that the woman would trust the man to look at her there:

"I love cunnilingus very, very much. It is a close second to vaginal intercourse as my favorite sexual activity, and whatever is in third place is way, way back. I am not sure why I like it so much. There is something incredibly intimate about it. It requires a great deal of trust for a woman to lie back and separate her legs and expose her genitals completely to a man, to let him look at them so openly. I also like the opportunity cunnilingus gives to make my partner come, to see and experience her coming, while I am relatively calm and able to appreciate it and savor it, to really see what is going on with her as she is having her orgasm."

A minority of men said their wives or lovers did not like it or were embarrassed by it:

"I have never done it. The idea embarrasses my wife. Nine years ago I finally just started kissing her there at a tender time which seemed appropriate. She burst into tears. I date the end of something—not our marriage, for we shall be married twenty-four years in June—from that moment. I never brought it up again. She doesn't even want to talk about it, or anything else which she considers perversions. Since then I have had two long-term lovers, at separate times, and neither of them has seemed interested either."

"I offered it to my wife once when she complained of not coming, but she rejected it indignantly and thought me 'queer.' "

"One of my lovers was always most reluctant to permit cunnilingus, though she insisted on performing fellatio. Her reason: the belief that her genitalia were ugly, distasteful, and could not possibly appeal to any man, when in truth, to me performing cunnilingus with her was a massive turn-on, the quickest way to restore flagging powers, to build a new erection after recent ejaculation. And add to that, cunnilingus gave me almost as much pure personal pleasure, in the knowledge that it was giving deep pleasure to my partner, as the act of intercourse. And yet, she could not understand that and refused to believe that I was being truthful."

"My wife gets mad when I want to eat her. When she won't let me, I stick my penis in her and just poke her till I get tired and stop."

A few men had never tried it:

"I think a naked woman looks beautiful when all that is visible of her genitals is the pubic hair. But to look into her vulva, I don't like to look at it, it looks awful. I never have and never will have cunnilingus with any woman."

"I have not had cunnilingus with a woman and I have no desire to do so, but maybe if I tried it, I would like it? I have never had a very good look at a woman's genitals, but from the obscene pictures I have seen, I think it would be a pretty stimulating experience. My wife always changes clothes in the bathroom and always wears a bra and panties to bed plus."

"Although I never tried it, I daydream about it."

"I have never done cunnilingus with a woman. At age thirty-five and after ten years of marriage I am just now beginning to overcome my fear and hostility towards women's sexuality. It is not the physical aspects of taste, sight, and smell that have made me uncomfortable; rather, it is the *power* that women in my life have exercised over me that makes me both afraid and angry."

"I have never done this. Physically I find it repulsive because of the odor and unappetizing taste, but I have fantasized doing this many times."

"If I were with a beautiful woman who really aroused me and I sensed she was clean, I think I would try it. I find the pubic hair most repulsive. If a beautiful woman would shave all the hair, cleaned her vagina, and if I might use some fruit (I've heard a sliced peach works good) to rub on her cunt to offset the taste, I would do it. I would do it for psychological reasons—and to have the experience, a reality not just fantasy, and if I expect a woman to do oral sex on my penis, I should be prepared to have her ask me to return the favor. I hope I like to experience this."

And a few men said it was simply bad and they did not like it at all:

"It's ghastly. I tried it once and barfed all over my wife."

"Nobody in his right mind will do it unless the person is a dog and/or low-class animal. Human beings are high-class animals, not beasts."

"During the excitement of orgasm the woman might pee. That bothers me."

"I like oral sex done on me only."

"Only if a woman is attractive and young and insists on it."

"It makes me sick."

"It has no appeal to me at all—women's genitals are not attractive to me—only breasts!"

"I blot cunnilingus with a woman completely out of my mind. It isn't a block. It's a whole damned fortress!"

"I don't like oral sex. A woman's genitals smell. I sometimes kiss a girl's clitoris or vagina if I think it will turn her on. And, as an ol' male joke goes, 'You never eat 'em out after fucking, they smell and taste too bad.' Also, I dislike the wetness on my face."

"The idea of cunnilingus repulses me. Female genitals are very unattractive to me. There's a massive fear reaction in there somewhere. I'm working on it."

"Cunnilingus stinks! The smell is horrendous!"

"A cunt smells like stale fish and it looks raw—ecch!"

"Cunnilingus with a woman is nauseating. But I am making a real sacrifice for her pleasure, a demonstration of my love and devotion for her. Physically, it is sickening, although I must admit her genitals in my mouth makes me very excited. I put my tongue inside her vagina and suck and lick it. When I swallow it it tastes like warm blood or some other sick thing."

Are women's genitals "clean"?

At the same time that many men liked cunnilingus very much, almost half of those who answered were also preoccupied with whether the woman or the woman's genitals were "clean":

"I'm learning more and more to enjoy cunnilingus. It's been hard to do—I have uncomfortable feelings about oozing. I was raised clean clean clean. I like to take a shower after sex."

"If I want to have oral sex with a gal, I am saying to her, 'You are clean.' "

"I'm still kind of squeamish about cunnilingus, and still think of female genitalia as dirty. Most of my earliest sexual experiences were with women whose genitals *were* dirty and really did smell awful. I sometimes enjoy oral sex with women when I first establish that they're clean."

"My partner usually washes just before and is either tasteless or pleasantly scented. Stale, unwashed female genitals taste and smell bad to me."

"How does one ask a woman politely to wash?"

"My wife keeps very clean."

"Clean. I do not have the deviant's taste for stale accumulations, the same as I do not care for stinky armpits or for kissing a lip corrupted by a runny nose, or dirty hair, etc."

"I like everything about oral sex with my lover-wife as long as she has secretly showered (I like my partners 'clean')."

"I only like it after a bath. I don't like the taste of urine or stale secretions. Or the smell of feces. But a clean pussy tastes good, believe me!"

"This is a delicate point of etiquette: how do you tell a woman that you'd be only too glad to eat her out for the next hour and a half, if she wants, if she'd only go and use a touch of soap and water? I've only said it to one woman, a *very* good friend who was very candid and verbal about sex, and even she got a little offended, though she said she understood it in the spirit in which I had said it—trying to be helpful, not to offend."

"I appreciate it *if* the genitals on a woman are not filthy!"

Closely associated with this were comments that women's genitals smelled bad:

"You can rub and scrub and clean it well, but you can't get rid of that codfish smell."

"Sometimes the smell is bad but human beings can get used to anything."

"Her hair smells like urine."

"My wife repels me four out of five times. Sometimes her genitals smell like a chicken dinner."

"First you sniff it, if you wouldn't lick it, don't lick it. I am attempting to overcome the cultural conditioning that says women smell bad but for now, I agree."

"I recall one girl in my teens who smelled so terrible that from just fingering her I vomited."

Or that they smelled very strong:

"Some gals smell strong at first but if you just get going, it's like eating Limburger cheese. Smells rough but tastes great."

"As the taste and smell are strong, I sometimes have to be slightly deliberate about first contact, but no more so than when eating, say, a particularly ripe cheese or unusual fruit, drink, spice, etc.—once you get a good sniff or taste, then whatever the initial apprehensions, it's enjoyable. And anyway, it's her."

"Occasionally during a woman's cycle the smell is more of a turn-off than a turn-on initially. If I 'kiss' her anyway the smell soon becomes a turn-on."

"I haven't done cunnilingus much, but it tastes kind of bitter, smells like bad breath, and looks red, wrinkly, and wet."

Of course, yeast infections could disrupt the natural smell:

"Several minor vaginal infections, including trichomonas, produce an off odor. I'm confident that I can diagnose trichomonas by the odor-flavor. There are also some women who taste and smell beautiful at first, but develop an off odor as secretions from higher up trickle down after ten or fifteen minutes of cunnilingus. In such situations, I just cover the vulva with a loving, affectionate hand to block out most of the odor and continue on the clitoris."

"Once in a while she's had some sort of vaginal infection that produces a strong and definitely unpleasant smell, an odor of old sweat and decaying fish. I don't like it. She understands . . . but I've never found a way to tell her that without making her feel hurt. I wish I could say, 'Hey, you've got that symptom again,' without making it sound like a moral accusation. After all, *she* can't very well get down there to taste it."

Some men hadn't decided yet:

"Female genitals are fragrant. Taste wonderful and my only complaint is a really, really raunchy crotch that hasn't been washed. But it's not really a true complaint since I've never experienced one—I just think that if someone didn't wash for two weeks it would smell foul. But then smelly armpits (especially smelly) turn me on!"

"What I dislike is that some women have an offensive—well, not really offensive but strange—smell. I'm still trying to get used to it. The texture of the vulval lips and the clitoral region is often strange and quite alien to me."

But some men had none of these negative associations:

"Many men and women find a woman's sex to be unclean in some way. I enjoy showing the woman that not only do I find her sex not unclean, but in fact I find it extremely delightful. I like their taste and their smell and their look. It is superb in every way."

"Would you believe that some women are reluctant to engage in such an activity since a lot of them have hang-ups and prehistoric beliefs that they smell bad? Usually my partner showers before the activity and it smells clean and tastes great with all the woman juices."

"Many women have a tendency to push your face away from their genitals as though they feel they've done something wrong or smell bad. It is hard to convince them that I enjoy the smell and taste—and I do. In fact, a freshly washed vagina has lost much of its flavor appeal for me."

"My wife cleans too much."

"For me, cunnilingus is beautiful but only when the woman enjoys it. Some get pretty freaked out about it. The smell and taste is something exquisite. I like to put my whole mouth between her labia. The flavor is great and I swallow every drop. It can get a bit raunchy at times, but on the other hand, a freshly scrubbed cunt can be pretty tasteless, and lose a lot of appeal."

Some men emphasized that they liked the taste very much:

"Darndest thing: women taste so sweet down there. Without using anything added. Just reasonably clean. It's really nice."

"Tastes and smells always excite me. Tastes vary—sometimes they are sweet and sometimes a little salty or tangy. I guess it depends on her body pH level. But always wonderful."

"The taste is a very plain taste with just a slight distinctness which I like and which also arouses me."

"Most are sweet and creamy."

"I love the way my wife's genitals taste and smell, the way her pussy looks and feels, the heat and velvety wetness of it."

"I like, in fact, just adore, the taste of women's genitals. In other words, it tastes good—almost like men's sweat."

In fact, of men who mentioned "feminine-hygiene sprays" or flavored creams, most said they did not like them:

"Women taste great (if clean and if they're not using any of those hygiene sprays). Their odor is a definite sexual turn-on and the taste is superb."

"All the women I've gone with have been clean and washed. I like the natural woman taste and smell and do not like the use of the 'vaginal mouthwash' sometimes advertised."

"I generally like the smell of women's genitals—I like the smell of sweat too. I don't believe in all this hype about antiperspirants, etc. All that advertising serves to separate people from each other, makes them think they stink and are ugly, and uses sexuality for profit. A great deal of the troubles people have with sex stem from myths that are engendered by the profitization of human feelings."

And other men emphasized that they liked the smells:

"The taste is faintly salty; there's a delicate smell that's very distinctive, but I can't describe it. I like it. Sometimes I've gotten it in my fingers and long afterwards I can hold them to my nose and still get a trace of that lovely scent."

"The smells have become increasingly attractive to me with age."

"The taste is good but not as exciting as the smell."

"Smell is most important—not a real heavy odor, but some smell is essential."

Conclusion: Are women dirty?

One of men's most frequent "but's" about the vagina and vulva is related to whether the woman is clean or has washed recently. While the fact that all bodies need bathing rather regularly would seem to go without saying, no men mentioned the necessity for brushing teeth regularly to make kissing pleasant. The fact that so many men saw fit to stress this point with regard to women's vulvas seems to reflect the influence of the age-old patriarchal view of female sexuality (and women) as being "dirty," "nasty," or "not quite nice." Each child still learns this in the story of Adam and Eve: it was Eve's sexuality and "desire for carnal knowledge" which ruined the Garden of Eden and for which men and women are still being punished—especially women, who are told that they must henceforth bring forth children in pain and suffering. And of course women who are overtly sexual are often punished by society's double standard, which still categorizes women as "good women" and "bad women."

Unfortunately, for centuries in our society, women's sexuality has been considered "dirty": a sensual, sexual woman is a "tramp," "dirty," "filthy," and so on, whereas a sexual man is very masculine, admirable. The vulva, of which women are taught to be ashamed (the medical term for the vulva is "pudendum," a Latin word meaning "of which one ought to be ashamed"), has been hidden away for so long that few people really know what it looks like. The general impression many men have is of a dark wet place, with an unfamiliar smell, a kind of unknown space into which the penis ventures courageously. One of the early triumphs of the women's movement was to reclaim the beauty, strength, and dignity of women's bodies for women, and to emphasize that it is women who own women's bodies, and not men. Women for the first time felt that they had the right to explore their own bodies and look inside them. With a mirror and a light and a plastic speculum a woman could see her interior, suddenly finding it to be a beautiful glossy pink, clean and dazzling— as opposed to the dark and unpleasant place she might have been led to believe she would find.

Perhaps men who still feel they are affected by these stereotypes about women's genitals can overcome them by also looking inside a vagina once, with someone they care about. Some men have seen their wife's or partner's vagina during a joint physical examination, conducted by a gynecologist or sex therapist. This technique was originated by Drs. Leon and Shirley Zussman, and has had excellent results.

A few men commented on cunnilingus during menstruation:

"I like the warmth and moisture of my partner's genitals, and I enjoy the very pleasant odor of them. The only time I do not like cunnilingus is during her period, although I have done it and was surprised that I could not tell the difference in taste or odor. This was early in her period."

"I love the smell of my lover's vagina while she is menstruating. I want her to menstruate in my mouth and on my face—it tastes so sexy and smells so good. It's also sexy to have intercourse at this time. The bad thing is when she gets cramps—I hate her to have to go through that terrible ordeal every month."

"The smell and taste of a menstruating vagina does not appeal to me, though I have never tasted one. I have no desire to do so."

"Some women have a psychological hang-up of feeling dirty during this time. Why should they? Aren't they proud to have such sophisticated bodies? Aren't they proud that they are women? Could a man ever produce a living thing? Whether a woman does or does not have children, her body was still designed to have them. The menstrual cycle is just part of this design."

"As I grew up I was led to believe that this was the time of the month when a woman discharged all the poison and disease germs from her womb. I know better now, but still am hung up about it."

"Menstruation makes little difference to me. Oral sex with a tampon in place is just the same as when she is not menstruating. Without a tampon, I reserve the right to refuse but that is unlikely. There is nothing that I have done when she wasn't in her period that I haven't done when she was, I think. She is a woman and there is no time that it is more obvious. What's wrong with it?"

"I feel more 'afraid' of the vagina at that time. I'm less likely to play with it, to touch it or feel it. I rule out oral sex completely. She is hornier when menstruating. I will not hesitate to have intercourse. Once I felt this string hanging out of a girl, and I wondered what on earth it was. I only recently learned what a tampon looks like."

"I ate one girl who later said she was menstruating at the time, but I guess I was too wrapped up in it to care. Blood, blood, I had enough of it on me in Vietnam not to worry about it."

"How do women's genitals look?"

Not only were there misgivings about whether women's genitals were "clean," but also many men had ambivalent feelings about the looks of women's vulvas. On the other hand, some men liked them very much and offered beautiful descriptions. The range of answers covered every attitude imaginable:

"Objectively, ugly. But they turn me on."

"A ripe peach cut halfway across by a knife."

"Animal-like."

"Like lips."

"Like curtains on a stage."

"They look forbidden."

"Better than men's."

"I dislike the hair. A beautiful face and 'raw flesh' is a horrible mismatch."

"I wish they were dry. I dislike the loose lips."

"A big, wet marsh."

"What does a cock look like to you? Please don't say a sword."

"Moisture bothers me. It looks like the skin of an old woman on a young one."

"Female genitals are shaped to do the job intended."

"They smell and look like a sandwich."

"Gorgeous."

"They look O.K., I guess. Certainly no sillier than a penis."

"They look mysterious."

"Inviting."

"They look hairy, sensual, puffy, excited, red, and full."

"A pretty furry pet animal."

"Ugly but appealing and nice to touch."

"The look fascinates me—like a small penis that has been sliced open at the bottom side."

"Ugly and unfinished."

"Like a damp rose, petals blossoming."

"Strange and compelling, inviting and ripe for explorations."

"Female organs seem forbidden, a trace from childhood."

"I believe them to be fantastic beauty and power."

"Cunts look exquisite, haunting, dangerous, fascinating, infinitely desirable, edible, threatening, ominous, powerful."

Some men, in longer answers, described why they liked the looks:

"I love my wife's genitals. They look big, pink, wet, warm, ready for fun, ready to respond to me, mysterious, powerful, something to explore. Wow!"

"I think women's genitals are about as lovely as something on this earth can get. I love the way they taste and smell. There have been some genitals about which I held a near-religious feeling; this was because they were attached to women for whom I felt a deep love. At such times in my life, every fold, every nuance of a particular woman's genitals became very important and beautiful."

"I think a woman's—my friend's when I peeled off her pants—genitalia are so beautifully shaped and designed! What was very nice was that her pubic hair was very blond and the moon shone in the window as I put my head between her legs. There were shadows all over, quite an experience! But I'm not sure why I liked it and I can't really describe what the lips, folds, etc., looked like, though I can see them in my mind's eye."

"A woman's genitals are very attractive to me. They look like so many pairs of lips desiring to be kissed."

"I like the genitals' looks. They look basically lewd, 'dirty,' obscene, irresistibly inviting."

"I love the way a woman looks—the fold of flesh is as if the body were protecting something delicate and precious."

"Vaginas with the labia minor lips protruding are most attractive to me. I like the richness of the colors of the lips and canal."

"Every person in this world came out of a vagina so how could it be anything but beautiful. It never fails to amaze me in its odor, makeup, or complexity. To me it is the most marvelous set of nerves anywhere. I am an engineer and I do get carried away sometimes in analyses. However, a woman's body is more sophisticated than any computer system in the world."

"I like the look of a vagina, though I'd be hard-pressed to say why. It resembles nothing as much as a large, pink, waterlogged prune."

"I love everything. The shape, smell, and taste remind me of an exotic fruit which one savors. From the soft fuzzy thatch to the delicate lips to the rosy inner flesh tissue and ultimate clitoral seed. The smell drives me insane with desire and wantonness. There is no more magnificent fragrance on earth. The taste is like salty nectar that is indescribable."

Others emphatically disliked them:

"Women's genitals are plain old gross looking and smelling. They look like a dog had been chewing on them."

"I prefer those pussies that don't have lips hanging out like Monday morning wash flapping all over the place. I enjoy symmetrical lips and light rose-colored interiors."

"Cunts are really ugly—they look unfinished."

"I was twenty-two years old when I found out that women have pubic hair. Whatever I had read about sex assumed that everybody knew that, and had not mentioned it. My idea of no pubic hair for women was based on the general observation that on their bodies men are hairier than women. Maybe for this reason I hate pubic hair in principle. I must admit that sometimes it covers something that I like even less. The more the external genitals look like those of a young girl (a child), the more I like them. What I think is extremely ugly is when the labia minora hang outside the labia majora. But that was the case with the woman I loved most, and it did not affect my love."

"The purple color reminds me of bruises."

"I think the look of a pussy is scary at first and you have to get used to looking at what we're conditioned not to look at."

"I am inexperienced. It looks all right with a woman's legs together. With a woman's legs wide apart and up, it's not that attractive."

"They look too scar-like—smell too strong. They look like an exploded anus—they look like a device for urination and waste disposal."

"In looks it is a mixed blessing. For one part it is the most fascinating part, for the other it looks quite ugly. I dislike the looks when the bush is so big that the woman cannot wear a small bikini without hair looking out. I like when the outer lips cover the inner ones. I like when the clitoris peeps out. For me a woman's ass usually looks a lot more sexy than her vulva."

"Female genitals look like they previously had a penis, it was ripped out and now they have a gaping wound in their crotch that never healed."

"If a woman had to depend on the attractiveness of her genitals, the race would have died out long ago."

"As a friend of mine said of a woman's cunt: 'How could anything that feels so good look so awful?'"

Some men mentioned that they did not like the pictures of women's genitals in men's magazines:

"I do not like the appearance of a woman's genitals. It is particularly repulsive to see her genitals in photos such as *Playboy*. The pubic hair is a beautiful sight but I hate to see the pictures with her legs wide open and the inner part of her genitals showing."

"Women's genitals look interesting, fascinating shapes, colors, etc., but not beautiful; I like to look at them, in private, but I don't think they are attractive or sexually stimulating for public display as in the 'up the crotch' school of male magazine photography. They are truly private parts—reserved for use in very personal relationships (same goes for the penis)."

"I like the way a woman's genitals look when the woman is my partner. In most 'men's' magazines they contrive to make them look . . . I'm not sure what the word I want is. Salacious? It's like their approach is based on the assumption that sex is dirty, and 'look here, you horny bastard, there's a real *cunt* for you.' I don't feel like that looking at my partner's genitals. My reaction to them is part of the overall reaction to my partner's body and persona."

Most men had not been able to look carefully—and many might be more familiar with pictures in magazines than with their partner's appearance:

"How do a woman's genitals look to me? It is almost incredible that after thirty-five years of being the best there is at performing cunnilingus, I have never seen the inside of a woman's genitals. I part the hair of her vagina with my nose and tongue, and achieve facial penetration without ever seeing her vagina. Performing the entire act by feel alone."

"I find that most girls are very much embarrassed if you examine them too much in the genital area."

"My wife's genitals look pristine, pretty, and perfect. I seldom look at them, but if my memory serves me right, they look like nothing in the world except my lover's: a temple, a sacred place, an altar."

One gynecologist contributed his thoughts:

"As a gynecologist, I could literally write a book on how I view the world from the end of an examining table. Sometimes the experience is pleasant and sometimes repulsive from a couple of parameters—either visually or olfactorily. Though sometimes I find a vagina attractive and inviting in its own right, I generally must feel an attraction for the entire person and then most genitals look, feel, smell, and taste good."

A few men compared the vulva and the penis, most saying that the penis was more beautiful:

"As for women's genitals, I must admit that the old line about an 'unhealed wound' seems appropriate. I think my cock is a work of art, but have never cared for close-up views of cunts."

"I love a cock and I love mine—they have character. A cunt is two fat lips covered with hair."

"I don't think women's genitals are as beautiful, though, as I do a man's (this includes my wife's). They are just not as aesthetically pleasing to me."

But a minority preferred the vulva:

"I think female genitals are very attractive, sort of graceful. A penis is really kind of comical-looking, especially erect, it bounces around like an idiot puppy or something; but a cunt is more dignified, even more practical-looking. You could never say a cock is beautiful, but a cunt, with its symmetrical layers and nice color, is really aesthetically beautiful."

Techniques for stimulating a woman to orgasm by cunnilingus

Most men thought of cunnilingus as "foreplay"; many others mistook the woman's arousal and excitement for orgasm. Only a minority gave descriptions of the type of stimulation used during cunnilingus to lead to orgasm—stimulation which was highly individual and varied greatly from woman to woman:

"When I suck my wife, I do about everything I can think of—I start by spreading her cunt lips with my hands (or she may do it) and start gentle lip kissing all over the area. I also 'tongue-fuck' her by shoving my tongue in and out of her hole, and at the same time rub her clitoris a little bit with my fingertips. My wife's cunt tastes salty, musky, exciting, good. I love the smell and taste of her cunt. Sometimes she will put her hands down there and jack herself off at the same time I am sucking her. Then I lick her fingers and kiss them too. I feel wonderful to be able to enjoy her so much and to give her that much enjoyment."

"One of the prime reasons I like cunnilingus is that I can stimulate her clitoris better than with *any* other method. The thing that seems to really turn her on is to suck as much of the area around the clitoris into my mouth as possible and then massage the clitoris, its hood and lips with my tongue moving fast. It excites me a lot. I use the tip of my tongue mostly. Light, rapid flicking motions will always bring her to a climax. Occasionally I will insert my tongue in her vagina, but only for the sake of variety. I like it when she glides my head with her hands to the spot(s) she wants covered. It's also nice if she tells me 'gently, hard, fast, slow,' etc. (especially if I get carried away and press too hard); whatever she wants, she gets. I feel great doing this because this is a more intimate and personal way I can give my woman deep and intense orgasms without giving myself sexual gratification also."

"I prefer to be on the bottom so that my woman can control the exact amount of pressure that she wants brought to bear on her clitoris. If she is able to control the pressure, she can have an orgasm easier."

"I enjoy cunnilingus with my wife in every way. I like her taste, smell, my head squeezed between her lovely thighs, and licking her beautiful cunt and anus. I thrust my tongue as deep into her cunt as I can, then slowly lick her labia from the clitoris all the way to her anus and back again, settling on her clitoris finally, sucking it gently with my lips and tongue. When her hips begin to push her cunt against my mouth I know her orgasm is imminent. I then suck her clitoris a little harder until her whole body is in one beautiful orgasm. Her pelvis thrusts, her head moves from side to side, she gasps, moans, and grabs my head in her hands and pushes it against her cunt until her contractions and spasms end. Bringing her to orgasm this way makes me feel great. I really think she has her best orgasms from cunnilingus but she says she is more emotionally satisfied with orgasm from penile penetration. I believe she is still inhibited about oral sex from her upbringing and religious background."

Some men pointed out that orgasm is not always so easy to create:

"The only thing I don't like about it is that I've never been able to provide the constant rhythmic stimulation to help her to orgasm. Sometimes after she's had a few it may work but most of the time she gets impatient, probably due to my inability to maintain a constant stimulus. My tongue gets tired."

"Sometimes I put the clitoris between my lips softly and then suck on it for a while. Usually I run my tongue all around the clitoris. She seems to like a lot of pressure on the clitoris, rubbing hard against the pubic bone. Still as yet I haven't perfected the technique but I want to work on it."

"I don't make my lover orgasm very often through oral sex and I secretly wish I could more often. I can't move fast enough or provide the right kind of friction to do it. I guess I'd like her to feel as intense an orgasm with oral sex as I do when she has oral sex with me. But I don't worry about it."

"Women seem to hold back when I'm down there. And I hardly ever receive any directions. I do sometimes feel 'less than a man' when I can't bring a woman to orgasm by cunnilingus but I think it's partly her fault by not providing me with sufficient directions. Perhaps I'm missing the subtle hints women are said to give. If so, maybe they are using too much subtlety. Most men are not mind readers. And in the heat of passion, who listens to words, much less try to discern the subtlety behind them?"

Others emphasized that the type of stimulation varies greatly, depending on the woman:

"Cunnilingus depends on the female's preference. Some like to be sucked hard, others want motion with tongue, others many motions, some direct contact with the clitoris, others indirect contact. You really have to ask."

"Exactly what do I do? It really depends on the particular woman. Some women like it when my mouth is tight around the clitoris and my tongue moves back and forth over the clitoris. Some like up-and-down motion more; some like the whole area to be moved around without very much direct stimulation of the clitoris."

Some men stressed the importance of maintaining a sensitive awareness of the woman's reactions and desires during stimulation:

"I always encourage my partner to advise and guide me. I get a lot more out of it when I get positive feedback that I am touching the right place in the right way."

"Usually my wife will open her legs wide and draw her knees up to assure me of better access, and her of better stimulation. Sometimes she moves a little bit up or down or sideways to get special stimulation at one point or another. Sometimes she murmurs, 'That's good! That's good!' or 'I love that—just keep doing that. Don't stop.' "

"Sometimes she'll ask me to do certain things, like 'Just lick all the way up' or 'Lick around the clitoris.' Everything gets wonderfully wet and my mouth, tongue, and face are moistened with her juices."

"I enjoy being encouraged, directed, and urged on in my endeavors. She lets me know whether to go harder or lighter, since her sensitivity seems to change from one time to another."

"I watch her stomach rise and fall and try to get into her rhythm. By attempting to center on her movements, my feelings try to reach hers."

But another man said:

"I do it because it makes me feel like a "good' lover, i.e., skilled and caring, and it's an easy way to give her an orgasm. But if she complains I'm not doing it right, I hate it."

And finally, a few men expressed their great pleasure at watching and feeling the woman orgasm this way:

"Do I enjoy cunnilingus? I love it. The only thing that I can think of that is better than watching a woman have an orgasm, watching and feeling the lips move, hearing the gasps of ecstasy and watching her body contract and heave—is having an orgasm myself. It's just great. I like it because I can totally see the pleasure that I'm giving her. It's a very reassuring thing that she needs me as much as I need her for this particular event to happen."

"It's really a revelation to see a woman this way. I feel like I have total control over her orgasm and indeed over her entire body—especially when she clamps her legs tight around me and clutches me in great, spasmodic movements to her climax. It's an incredible turn-on to know I'm giving her such pleasure. I come very close to orgasm myself."

CONCLUSION: THE HISTORICAL DENIAL OF CLITORAL STIMULATION

Many men say they are frustrated and dissatisfied with sex with women, or have profoundly mixed feelings about it, even at the same time they say they want more. The reasons for this are deep and very ancient—but not unchangeable—in that they are tied to the basic social structure: the society has created a great inequality and separation between the sexes, which originally involved a struggle over the control of reproduction, and which now permeates almost every aspect of sexual relations between men and women. These attitudes are only slowly beginning to change.

WOMEN'S VIEW OF INTERCOURSE

Why haven't women been more enthusiastic about sex with men? It is not because women don't like "sex" and intercourse. It is, first, because women feel exploited sexually: they must help the man have his orgasm but must not take/make the stimulation they need for their own. Given our definition of sex, the fact that men usually want sex more than women should come as no surprise. Sex provides efficiently for male orgasm, and inefficiently and irregularly for female orgasm; sex is defined so that the woman expects to help the man orgasm every time, but the man is not realistically informed about how to help the woman orgasm, and the woman is told it is wrong to stimulate herself. Therefore, should we be surprised that men want "sex" more often than women do? Sex as we know it is a "male"-defined* activity, and women, in not showing enthusiasm for many aspects of it, are displaying resistance to participating in an institution which they have not had an equal part in creating.

And yet most men have believed that they were doing "what a man should" by performing intercourse, and that a woman should orgasm from their thrusting. They were taught that providing a woman with intercourse, especially for an extended period of time, would give her what she wanted and needed. However, somehow men have known on some level that it didn't, and this has led to deep, unspoken feelings of discomfort, alienation and guilt—which were often manifested as distrust of women's motives for having sex, and anger at women for not speaking up and being "honest" about sex.

Where did the belief arise that women should orgasm from intercourse? As discussed in chapter 3, the institution we know as "sex"—"foreplay" to intercourse ending with male orgasm —was first legislated into existence as the only acceptable form of sexual expression approximately 2,500 years ago, probably for purposes of increasing reproduction. But it did not take on the connotations we give it today until much later; intercourse was not always considered a romantic activity during which women were supposed to orgasm. In the late nineteenth century, in fact, women were considered vulgar if they did. However, in the early part of our century, with the increasing discussion of the rights of women, women's orgasm has begun to be considered important. Perhaps it seemed logical, in the beginning, to assume that women should orgasm from the same activity from which men orgasmed,† especially since participation in this activity was glorified as being a form of "natural law."

In addition, women's interior clitoral anatomy had not yet been studied. However, it was known that women did masturbate to orgasm clitorally and generally not with vaginal penetration. Refusal to accept women's testimony (how they

---

* That is, defined by "male" ideology, not male biology.

† Of course, men orgasm from other forms of stimulation too, but the "acceptable" time for men to orgasm was during intercourse.

stimulated themselves) was characteristic of the general attitude toward women as second-class in a male-dominated society: women were advised to learn to orgasm "the right way"—from vaginal penetration—and thus conform to supposed "male sexuality" needs, women's role being that of "helpmate." When, however, this often did not work in practice, who was to blame? Who was flawed? Was it women, or men, or both? Although generally it has been felt that *they* were to blame—that there was something deeply wrong with them or their penis when the woman did not orgasm. This oppressive expectation, then, has led to needless suffering, self-examination, and accusations between men and women.

Tragically, although most women have known how to stimulate themselves to orgasm easily during masturbation, they have not felt free to explain the stimulation they needed to men, or to stimulate themselves during sex with men. Being dependent on men, economically, socially, and politically, has kept women silent: women have not felt that they had the right to challenge the society's definition of sex or to assert their own needs and forms of sexual expression.

IS INTERCOURSE A CHOICE FOR WOMEN?

But on another level, women have been resistant to intercourse because intercourse has not been a choice. The legal structure in which women were owned by either their fathers or their husbands included (and still includes in many countries today) the provision that a man had a right to intercourse with his wife on demand; there was (is) no such thing as "rape" in marriage. Further, many women have felt unable to protect themselves against pregnancy by using birth control, when it was (is) against the rules of the state or church.* Thus, in a very real sense, women had no rights over their own bodies, as their husbands controlled them; and therefore many women, feeling that their husbands could do with them

---

* Today, women in some countries have the right to use birth control, but the forms available often make it difficult or dangerous; furthermore, the tradition of women's availability to men for orgasm inside the vagina is continued in the idea that the woman should have the entire responsibility for using birth control, and that she should use a form which does not interfere with the man's pleasure—invisible, if possible. As one man remarked, "Why, in all the movies or sex magazines, don't they ever show the problem of birth control? They make it too romantic."

whatever they pleased, and that any attempt at resistance or influence was futile, developed very passive and/or hostile attitudes about sexual relationships: they would participate in sex, but only when they had to, and would not be any more active during it than necessary.

Thus, intercourse, far from being a simple pleasurable activity, has for centuries* symbolized and celebrated male domination and ownership of women, children, and society. Conversely, it also symbolizes female subservience, or being owned. A woman, in having intercourse, especially in the traditional position with the woman on the bottom, helping the man have an orgasm but not having one herself, was reminded of her position vis-à-vis the man. It is obvious, in this context, why many men would feel much more drawn toward participating in this institution than would women.

Many women's resistance to "sex"—far from being simply negative "conditioning" about sex—can also be seen as a large-scale and healthy resistance to being dominated and to their bodies being owned. Saying no to "sex" has become, for many women, a way of maintaining dignity and integrity, and some control over their own identity.

INTERCOURSE AND WOMEN'S EMOTIONAL ALIENATION

A final related cause of many women's resistance to sex/intercourse is emotional alienation. If women feel that men think of them as second-class,† and value them only as "help-mates" and sexual partners, this is likely to lead to emotional alienation within the relationship—giving yet more cause for women's passive resistance (in the Gandhian sense) to having sex. One man embodied these attitudes quite clearly: "My wife is not perhaps the woman one might dream up, but she's steady, dependable, and consistent. She's the mother of my four kids, and in my way I love her, even though she doesn't like sex too much. She says the reason is because I don't show her enough kindness and affection throughout the day. She says if I did she'd be more active sexually. These things are not so bad that I can't live with them, but after twenty-seven years of marriage, they bug me if I don't watch out." Another man commented: "Most men are only attentive to women when they want sex, and women know it. From my experience

* But not always. See conclusion, chapter 3.
† See chapter 2.

as a minister listening to married women describe their sexual problems, men spend their time, energy, and interest elsewhere —then expect the women to want them when it's time for sex. This hurts the women considerably."

This emotional alienation can be directly traced to the inequality created by the society in giving men rights and privileges over women, and is aggravated by bringing up men and women with different psychological attitudes,* and re-warding them for different types of behavior. Owning (or having the tradition of owning) women can lead men to be condescending toward women, while valuing other men more. But if a woman is valued only sexually, sex (or not having sex) can be her only power. If a man only expresses a real desire to spend time with a woman when he wants her to have sex with him, is it any wonder that a woman often says no? In a society in which women are dependent on men, and in which men sometimes seem only to "need" women for sex, saying no is many women's only chance to gain recognition as an individual, or have some control in the relationship.† Despite this, many women still enjoy intercourse for its own sake or other reasons.

MEN'S VIEW OF WOMEN AS PASSIVE

How do men feel about all of this? We have seen in this chapter that men often feel angry with women who never initiate sex and too often don't want sex. But this anger has an undertone of alienation, guilt, and insecurity: men feel instinctively on some level that sex does not involve an equal sharing, especially when they are having an orgasm and the woman does not—and this puts them on the defensive. As one man remarked earlier in this chapter, "I feel more respect for her and myself if I don't feel I am cheating her of an orgasm— or I guess the word is 'using' her, since I have an orgasm and she doesn't. I feel relieved to be with an equal." But many men covered this feeling over by bragging, accepting their

---

* See chapters 1 and 2.

† As one man put it, "As a male, there is no question, we are always in control once she consents to love-making. We have the dick, that's all there is to it! We are the fucker and she is the fuckee. At the same time, in this society, the woman has the final choice as to sex or no sex. She can deny us (and herself) or she can engage in sex."

"aggressiveness" as inherently "male," and insisting that they were only behaving as their "natures" compelled them to.

Although many men are very angry with women and suffer profound discomfort due to women's "passivity" regarding sex—possibly because of buried feelings of guilt and defensiveness, knowing that somehow women are being exploited—most men do not overtly connect this with the need for improving women's status. Most men prefer to think that the problem is simply a lingering vestige of "Victorian morality"—and further prefer to believe that somehow women can be sexually "free" even though they are not also economically and politically free.

Men are encouraged to accept this "difference" between men and women, and not to question it. Although many men instinctively feel uneasy on some level about what is going on, they are told by society that this is "just the way things are." Even though many men feel that by their having an orgasm and the woman not, they are exploiting the woman, that the situation is unfair, or that the woman is somehow in an inferior position, they are told that it is men's "nature" to continue wanting intercourse and having orgasm, and that whether the woman does or not is "her own problem." Men's reaction to this is often to become alienated from women, to feel "different," superior, uncomfortable, hostile or insecure with them. But, they may still wonder, do women really accept their less privileged status, or are women angry?

Men are faced with the dilemma of either believing that (1) women are built differently than men, and do not always need orgasm to be satisfied, and further that women in fact do not mind simply watching/ helping the man have an orgasm while they do not; or (2) that women can indeed orgasm (through masturbation, for example) but that they have been oppressed economically and socially into a position in which they have been forced to accede to men's wishes in sex, and that women have a hidden residue of anger at men for this. In other words, either women are innately unequal, or women have been forced to submit. These are not pleasant options from which men may choose. If a man believes (1), he must accept the idea that women are somehow fundamentally different from men in their basic humanity. This point of view was implied by Freud's famous question, "What do women want?," which seemed to say that what women want is so fundamentally different from what men want, that it is mysterious and unfathomable. If a man accepts this position, then his ability to be truly close to a woman is quite limited, as he feels himself so different from her.* Their relationship may be quite distant and formal, as each views the other as truly "other." On the other hand, if a man believes (2), he is in a much better position for achieving a close and fulfilling relationship with a woman, even though he may have to re-examine how sexuality is defined, and re-think the basis of male-female relationships. But this process can lead to much greater fulfillment and happiness for a man in his own sexuality and life.

HOW CLITORAL STIMULATION AFFECTS MEN'S HAPPINESS

Is clitoral stimulation (whether by hand or mouth) something that men "should" learn to do because women need it, women "demand" it—or is clitoral stimulation an erotic and beautiful activity, as valuable and intense as intercourse? Is it pleasurable for men?

Most men know that women do not orgasm regularly during intercourse with them—and this often makes them feel insecure, defensive or "inadequate." There was an undertone of anger and frustration in many of the answers: "What's wrong with women that they have such difficulty having orgasm?" Or, "When she doesn't have orgasm during intercourse, I feel like I've ripped her off. I wonder whether I should be sticking myself in her, or not. What's in it for her? Is this some sort of martyr shtick?"

And yet, as we have seen, though most men realize that women do not orgasm with them regularly during intercourse, most still also assume women *should* orgasm from simple intercourse. Most men have very little understanding of women's need for clitoral stimulation outside of intercourse. The stereotype in our society that says that women have a "problem" having orgasm, is false: it is not women that have a "problem" having orgasm, but society that has a problem accepting how women do orgasm. Almost all women can stimulate themselves to orgasm easily, quickly, and with great

---

* Not only sexually, but also in what he wants out of life; he may feel he is more aggressive and demanding of life in general, in his career, etc., than women—who are "naturally" content with home and security. This can make him feel alienated, emotionally unconnected, isolated, and angry. (See chapter 2.)

physical pleasure. The implication of this is that this stimulation should be included as a regular part of sex between a man and a woman.

In fact, not understanding women's sexuality/sensuality and need for clitoral stimulation inhibits men's sexuality and pleasure. For example, if manual clitoral stimulation were accepted, men would no longer have to feel anxious about whether the woman had an orgasm, since adequate stimulation would always be available, whether by him or by her. During intercourse, a man could really let himself go, feeling free to enjoy his own feeings and orgasm, not worrying about whether he was "giving" the woman an orgasm too. As one man put it, "You're afraid to really let go during intercourse because you might get her mad if you're having too much fun. If your orgasm seemed too great, she might be envious."

But it is very hard for many men to accept that what they have been taught for so long—that their thrusting during intercourse should make the woman orgasm—is inaccurate, and also oppressive to women. And perhaps it is even harder for many men to learn, or admit they want to learn, new ways of stimulating women to orgasm.

The most important benefit of clitoral stimulation for men is that it is a very pleasurable activity. Men who are not familiar with clitoral stimulation sometimes react to the idea with displeasure, but this is a mistake: what man, on reflection, would not want to see a woman have an orgasm—to feel her body become tense and filled with ecstasy, to have her become as excited as it is possibie to be? It is a pleasure to excite another person to that point, and very exciting to see.

Of course, it is not only a question of orgasm—although this has been the focus of this chapter—but of women's equal input into sex, a new valuing of women's experience. If a woman has the freedom to be really herself with another person, it will bring increased love, respect, trust and happiness.

6

RAPE, PORNOGRAPHY, AND DOMINATION-SUBMISSION

Are the topics in this chapter fundamentally different from the basic definition of sexuality and the relationship between men and women endorsed by our culture? Where do pressuring women into sex, rape (of various kinds), and buying women in pornography fit into men's lives—if they do? Are they things only "abnormal" men are involved with, or do they in some way involve and affect all men's lives and relationships with women, because they somehow involve the basic underpinnings of the entire social structure?

In chapter 3, we saw that sex/intercourse has traditionally been the basic symbol of male domination and ownership of women (whether or not an individual man may feel this at any given time). Rape and buying women through pornography are basic extensions of this ideology—not biologic "urges" or part of a physical male "sex drive." It is what "sex" means to men that makes them sometimes want to rape women, not a desire for orgasm.

Men as individuals may transcend this definition, but the general culture—in movies, books, jokes, and popular sayings—reinforces the idea that men "get" or "take" sex from women, men "have" women, men conquer and possess women, women say "no" but mean yes, women "give in" to men—and penetration is the symbol of this victory. Men, brought up to feel that a vital part of being a man is to orgasm in a vagina, often resent women's "power" to withhold this "male need" from them—not realizing that this is in many ways the only "power" left to many women. It is this dynamic that sometimes leads men to say that women are "more powerful" than men.

If the culture can change its basic idea of the relationship between men and women, including concrete changes in the fundamental legal, social, and economic inequalities, then the definition of "sex" can change—and forcing women into sex (intercourse) will lose much of its appeal, since it will have lost its meaning. But it may take hundreds of years for this change to occur. Right now, forcible physical rape stands as an overwhelming metaphor for what has been the rape—physical, emotional, and spiritual—of an entire gender by our culture.

RAPE

DO MEN WANT TO RAPE WOMEN?

"Sometimes I've found myself getting excited watching a show in which a man is planning a rape. It bothered me that I was being aroused by it. I'm not sure I understand why."

"I have often wanted to rape a woman, and I fantasize about it a lot. But the idea disturbs me because it runs counter to my sense of mutual respect, humanism, feminism, etc. I'm really anxious to see what other men feel about rape."

What does the physical rape of a woman mean to men? Is the desire to rape sexual? A form of hostility and anger? Or a way to reassert an injured "masculine pride"? Is rape only direct physical force, or can it also be a form of pressure on women to have sex—either physical or economic?

How many men have thought about forcibly raping women, and how many have done it? How did men feel about pressuring women to have sex, and at what point (if any) did they feel that this took on overtones of rape? Or did most men believe that pressuring a woman into sex and intercourse was their necessary role? Or their "right"? And how many men were totally philosophically committed against the idea of raping, forcing, or pressuring a woman in any way into having sex?

Most men had never forcibly raped a woman, but sometimes wanted to:

Most men said they had never raped a woman, but could want to under certain conditions, usually connected with feelings of anger over rejection, and the idea "What right does she have to refuse me?":

Others said women are "asking for it," the implication being that women have no right to be sexual unless it leads to intercourse with men, and that men have the right to control women's sexuality:

"I've seen a lot of women who seem to be asking for it . . . just as a person with a fistful of money is asking for robbery by flaunting his money, especially in a gin mill or dark alley. I also feel sympathy for women. After all, when someone wants to protect one's money from being stolen, the money can be placed in a bank. But how does a woman protect her body from being raped? I wish I knew. A little more prudence, I guess. I'm glad I'm a man."

"There is the provocation of 'dry hustling.' Dry hustling is making oneself available for sex and then withdrawing or withholding it. The brassiere-less woman in a public place is a dry hustler. The bra-less look is attractive. It is supposed to be. *And it is a provocation*."

"Yes, I wanted to. She was and is the greatest tease I've ever known."

"What is the curious fascination that women have concerning rape? They write about it endlessly and read about it with repressed glee. And it is an endless source of amusement in conversation. They seem to want it."

And some said that women don't mean "no" when they say "no":

"I have thought about doing it to those who really want to get fucked but pretend they don't."

"I usually feel women are lying when they say no, and am tempted to just go ahead and take them."

"I have at times in my life had to do with the *demi-vierge* type, who plays with a man on the brink of orgasm, then coyly puts him off. On a number of such occasions I might well have proceeded, and been pretty well justified in proceeding to a 'rape.' (But would it have been?)"

A few men said they were afraid of being caught:

"I have often thought about it, fantasized about it. I might like it because of having a feeling of power over a woman. But I never actually wanted to through fear of being caught and publicly ruined."

"I have never raped a woman, but have at times felt a desire to—for the struggle and final victory. I'm a person, though, who always thinks before he acts, and the consequences wouldn't be worth it. Besides I don't want to be known as a pervert."

A few said rape was justified by the male "sex drive"* and the "failure" of women to meet that "need":

"I have never raped a woman but I have often almost wanted to. Women just don't understand what the sexual urge is to men. For many men the craving for sex is so powerful it is analogous to hunger for food. How would you feel if you were starving and someone made you jump through hoops, do tricks, and beg, for the possible promise of a meal, only to end up with a crumb of melba toast? No woman can conceive of what it's like to have 'blue balls' (a very painful condition of the balls resulting from unsatisfied arousal). No woman has ever woken up in the morning with balls so painful it's hard to get your pants on. In effect, a woman who stimulates a man without satisfying him is kicking him in the balls. If a guy did that to me I certainly would get violent with him."

"I've never raped a woman, but I've had fantasies about raping women in which physical desire is mixed up with anger at not having that desire met. Particularly annoying are salesgirls and other women who you know are using their attractiveness just to make money without really giving you anything."

Underlying the point of view of many of the replies just seen is the idea, strong in our culture and in all patriarchal cultures, that men own women's bodies. As one man said, "She is *mine.* I have a right to orgasm through intercourse. God gave me the right when he made women for men." A man should not have to masturbate for orgasm when sexual desire is not mutual, according to this point of view; he should have his orgasm through a woman at all times (only an orgasm had through intercourse with a woman is legitimate†), and it is women's duty at all times to help him do this.

* See page 351. However, as we have seen, most men do not rape for sexual pleasure, in fact, many rapists lose erection immediately after penetration (possession), and never ejaculate. A need for orgasm can, after all, be satisfied by masturbation.

† See chapter 3.

Also implicit in many of the replies we have just seen is the idea that a woman denying a man sex is somehow denying him his manhood and that by raping a woman a man is reasserting his masculinity—not only with the woman but in his own mind:

"I have never raped a woman and I do not intend to. However, I have considered it. The type of woman who will lead you on to a certain extent and then stop all of a sudden, and who does this consistently, shows no respect for her partner as a man or as a human being. In a case like this, I *might* conceivably rape her, and I would not feel guilty about it either."

"Once I was going with a woman (in high school) and she would not let me have sex. All my friends had done it with their girlfriends, and even did it with us when we went out on double dates and parked together after. I got to feel like a real reject. I could have lied to them about it, but then my girlfriend would have found out, and they probably wouldn't have believed me anyway, since I couldn't have described the feeling. This made me so angry I felt like raping her. Finally, without anybody knowing, I picked up a streetwalker and had intercourse. This did a lot for my feeling of confidence in my own masculinity. Soon after, I broke up with my girlfriend and started going with somebody else who would go all the way. Then I could tell the guys, and I felt like one of the group again."

A few men connected their desire to rape women to the teachings of the culture:

"Mentally to myself I've raped many women—just letting my sexist upbringing take over, and depersonalizing, objectifying women."

"Have I ever wanted to? Sometimes—with a particularly aloof woman, or a tease. It's pretty obvious that I have some hostility toward women that started way back—they have something I want, and I'm a 'bad boy' for wanting it—they're excluding me—they have a secret—they have a sex organ, but dirty little boys don't get any, etc., etc., ad nauseam. I have become aware of these feelings and know when they are active; when I feel them, I back off whatever situation is causing them and find something else to do. I've wasted a good hunk of my life on feelings based on the past and I'm not wasting any more—my life has to be now."

Some men said they wanted to rape women because of their generalized feeling of rejection—feeling left out of what "everyone else" was enjoying, or what other men were having:

"I have certainly wanted to. Usually this desire comes after I have been rejected by a very attractive woman e.g., at the office. Then I fantasize following her, putting a gun to her head (I own a revolver), and asking her something like 'Now tell me who you want to go to bed with.' In recent months, I have become more sympathetic toward rapists, because I see in myself the other side of the sexual revolution: it is all well and good for the Beautiful People to decide to bring their fantasies out of the closet and talk about the joys of sex in public—it is another to be tantalized day after day by the sight of beautiful women you desire but can't have. Apparently every one of them is experiencing the wildest sexual pleasures and fulfillment, because the media are everywhere saying so."

"I have never raped a woman. But I have been mad enough at women's behavior toward me to want to at least think about it. There is *provocation for the act of rape* in a man's life and it isn't necessarily the provocation of the rape victim. The provocation can be a generalized frustration and feeling of *personal* impotence. The media proclaim that everyone is having sex. If you are not having sex, these media statements mean *everyone but you.* As in propaganda, the Big Lie, if told often enough, begins to be believed. When it is believed, a man may start to wonder about himself—'What's wrong with me? Why aren't I getting any?' "

"I don't believe in rape, but I'm beginning to want to, just to find out what it's like to have sex with a woman. Maybe it's the only way I'm ever going to have sex. I'm already twenty-two and I still haven't had it. At least three times a week now I find myself crying, so depressed I think about suicide. I have only been on dates with one girl, and that was four years ago. I've been rejected so many times I couldn't even try to count them. Nothing is going right in my life, and I'm so damn lonely it hurts even to get up in the morning. Other guys seem to have no problem talking to and picking up girls, but I can't seem to do it. I'm slowly going crazy."

*Only a few men mentioned they would like to rape a woman for reasons connected to sexual pleasure or lust:**

---

* It seems that men in invading armies (such as in Bangladesh) rape to show dominance, possession, not out of "sexual need"—since they could, in any case, masturbate for orgasm.

"I have sometimes wanted to rape a woman, because of her body which I watched and the hard-on I got from watching it. But I can easily control myself. Still, very tight jeans or a beautiful body give me terrific arousal and desire to take the woman sexually."

"I respect the law and fear it. But if I were going to be a criminal, rape would be at the top of my list. Why? I like sex and sometimes feel like taking a woman and satisfying myself."

"Once I saw a woman I was really attracted to, a counter girl at an all-night strung-out restaurant, and I felt in me: push her open-handed in the chest, knock her down, splayed, take her. Cool, impersonal. It was a rush, you know, we all get that inside."

The image of being a rapist seemed to appeal to some men, who identified it with being a strong and virile, passionate and powerful man. Although the following answers are from both men who were interested in rape and men who were not, they all see the rapist as strong and powerful:

"I don't think I could. But I have been sort of impressed by people who pulled off what seemed to be an especially brilliant or daring rape."

"I never wanted to rape a woman. But trying not to get caught and the violence could add to the thrill, and make me feel pretty tough."

"I have *thought* about it. Why? The Power and Domineering aspects of it. To have that frail thing, cowering, to take what I want. I think I have the latent instincts of a Bastard!"

"I have had fantasies of doing it, as a form of 'proving' to the woman that I am really all 'man,' able to get and keep a hard-on and use it to force myself on her, whether she wants me or not."

And some men said that all "real" men have a desire to rape women because this is part of a male's innate makeup (a "natural" animal instinct*):

"Why do I want to rape women? Because I am basically, as a male, a predator and all women look to men like prey. I

---

* This is inaccurate, since animals do not rape. The implication in this answer is that rape is a "natural instinct," which only "civilization" can overcome. In fact, it is our "civilization" which has created the concept and encouraged it.

fantasize about the expression on a woman's face when I 'capture' her and she realizes she cannot escape. It's like I won, I own her."

"Yes, I want to. I think every man has had a desire to rape a woman at one time or another."

"I think there is in me a relatively small Attila the Hun quotient, but perhaps all men have some of this. Maybe it's taught by our culture, maybe it's congenital; but whether it's 'natural' to men or not, I believe it is a bad thing, and self-defeating."

"I must admit a certain part of me would receive some sort of thrill at ripping the clothes from a woman and ravishing her. But I would probably collapse into tears of pity and weep with my victim. Rape behavior in males today probably exists because it has been selected for (this would take precedence over selection by females) in the Darwinian model of natural selection; as much as our contemporary society despises the rapist, we must admit that in man's history the rapist's genes were naturally selected because the behavior had survival value."*

A few men wondered why they didn't have these feelings, and felt "abnormal":

"I have never raped a woman, or wanted to. In this I guess I am somewhat odd. Many of my friends talk about rape a lot and fantasize about it. The whole idea leaves me cold."

On the other hand, some men said raping was "unmanly":

"I have never raped a woman. I would not enjoy the idea of taking a woman against her will. It's an asinine way of trying to prove you are a man. A coward's way."

"I've wanted to, sure—most men do have feelings like these at one point or another—but raping a woman is like shooting fish in a barrel—no sport whatsoever!"

"I have never raped a woman and have no desire to do

* Darwin's theory concerned selection between different species, not within species. This is a misunderstanding and misuse of the concept of "survival of the fittest."

so. I think a man has to be very small-minded and unsure of himself to force himself sexually upon a woman."

"I feel rape is a feeling of sadism by a male who is basically inadequate and incapable, in sex and life."

In fact, despite the seeming secret admiration of some men for rapists as the ultimate "man," strong and powerful, the reality is usually just the opposite: it is the man with the lowest self-esteem who is most likely to rape women or pressure them for sex—the man who does not see himself as strong and powerful, the man who feels the most rejected, the most like a "loser":

"My wife's sexual ardor cooled off beginning with the honeymoon. Except for when she is 'horny,' she will have sex with me only because she feels an obligation or because she doesn't want me to have an excuse to seek sex elsewhere. She is uninterested most of the time. I am sure that the problems I have had with my professional life have resulted from the intense and constant frustration I have felt resulting from such deprivation. I can't get along with the people I work with, but it is only because she rejects me. I finally grew to hate my wife so much so that once, just after I had lost my last job, I decided to rape her. Had I not been given a powerful faith to hold on to by my extraordinary parents, I would have done it. Now I don't know what to do. Nothing has changed. This was two months ago."

"I am single, never married, never lived with a woman, and I am so alone that I am slowly going crazy. I am fifty pounds overweight, work as a clerk in a welfare office and as a security guard at nights. I find going out to meet women very frustrating. Going to dances and no one wanting to dance with me gets me pissed. I get very depressed and antisocial. I have a perverse but vicarious thrill in other people (usually men) who go berserk in public places and kill innocent bystanders, such as David Berkowitz (Son of Sam). When I was in college, I wanted to shoot good-looking coeds on campus with a concealed automatic pistol. They never look at me or acknowledge my humanity, so maybe I'm not good enough for them. I think they're afraid I'm going to rape them. I would never rape a woman because I don't think I could convince them I'm serious, they'd probably scream and I would run. Berkowitz's strategy was more direct, hostile, vengeful, and up-front. I admire Berkowitz, Son of Sam, for what he did."

Do most men fantasize about raping women? Many men
said they would not really want to rape a woman, but still
thought it was an exciting fantasy:*

"I never did and never will. However, lots of times I
fantasize that some beautiful woman done me extreme harm
and I rape her."

"The idea of rape is sometimes a turn-on. I've had rape
fantasies. There is a power to sex—a powerful sort of
exhilaration."

"Somehow, the animalistic taking of a woman you are
sexually attracted to is very exciting to me in fantasy. I
wouldn't want to physically or psychologically hurt anyone,
though—in reality."

"I have a fantasy of catching a woman bending over into
the trunk of her car and just walking up behind her and
pulling her dress up and pulling down her panties and telling
her don't look around I've got a gun (or something like that)
and having intercourse with her and her never even seeing
who did it."

"I sometimes fantasize about having some woman completely under my control. There are never any thoughts of
pain being inflicted, just being able to tell a woman to do
anything I want."

*The typical rape fantasy ends with the woman becoming
aroused and wanting it—a sort of romantic conquest:*

"In my fantasies, when I finally penetrate the poor
damsel, after the requisite roughness and violence, she
suddenly throws her arms and legs around me and enjoys
herself no end. I don't have enough ego in the real world to
believe that kind of shit."

"I have had fantasies of screwing a woman (or devirginizing one) who was initially unwilling or reluctant, or afraid,
but who became eager and hot after a little bit, and then
enjoyed it with me."

* However, most men did not regularly have violent fantasies; the most
common fantasies involved simply imagining various activities: "I just
imagine myself and another person performing the basic acts with each
other," or, "The things I fantasize are extensions of my own experience,
or sometimes imagining going to bed with some woman I have just met—
most often I imagine cunnilingus, or that we are having intercourse with
each other."

A few men had brutal fantasies of raping a woman:

"Yes, I have sexual fantasies like everyone else. Mine may be a bit more sadistic than average. It is dismembering the female while having sex and of course the usual rape. Though doubting I could actually do the first, I could do the second."

"There is one corner of my mind that gets off on fantasies of Nazi torture kind of scenes, and that scares the hell out of me. I try to keep it suppressed, and consider it a bad sign when fantasies like this begin to surface. I know my head is not in a good place, and that I'd better sit down and sort things out."

"I think there's a part of me that doesn't like women, and I would like to cultivate that side. Ropes, chains, power, threat, terror, torture, humiliation, bondage, submission, power, arrogance, inequality, and an end to petition and plea and negotiations and patience and politeness and coordination and accommodation and cultivation and concern. I think it's the mincy-pincy moral superiority of women and their one-dimensional emotional cloying inability to think clearly on sexual matters that particularly offends me."

"I always fantasize being the dominant. I would like to own a 'slave' for sex purposes. Actually the feeling that some-one cares enough to be my slave would be the most appeal-ing thing about it."

"One particularly exciting scenario is when I bind a play-ful girl-woman with her consent, indeed with her cooperative connivance, due to her own fascination with the thrill of it. Then I imagine the bound girl-woman pulling a cart, being ridden, being led on a leash, being tickled, etc., etc."

"I, like every man, fantasize complete domination over a woman. I feel that hidden in every man is domination and sadomasochism over some woman he despises—his wife, ex-wife, lover, etc."

Some men had forcibly raped a woman or women

A minority of men had raped a woman (women). Usually these men gave many of the same reasons for doing it as those who had wanted to but didn't, especially anger:

"Yes, I have. But it was slightly beyond my control. I just got tired of being rejected by a girlfriend of mine. Outside,

I felt terrible. But inside, I really enjoyed it. It really thrilled me and I met the greatest arousal I'd ever had."

"Yes, one time I raped a woman. She was a tease. But it did not appeal to my values."

"Once when I was very drunk and angry with another woman, I 'forced my attentions' on a woman. The next day my memory was very foggy but I apologized and she excused me for being drunk. But I felt terrible about it and pledged to never do such a thing again."

"My wife had died and I was miserable, physically lonely and vulnerable. A woman led me on sexually, playing on my obvious shell shock, and at the last moment repulsed me. It was not a last-minute realization that she didn't really want to, she had deliberately played with me for her own entertainment. My desire turned to rage and we grappled. I wanted to skin her. But I suddenly realized what I was doing and ran out of there. I felt sick at heart, disgusted and appalled and hating her for reducing me to such ugliness."

"My first girlfriend and I had a kind of strange thing going where she would come on like she wanted it, but sometimes really didn't. I just went ahead with it one time because I thought she just wanted to be 'taken' (nothing at all brutal, though). Afterward, I realized that I had really forced her and I felt really bad. From that point on, we began to communicate more honestly with each other."

"Yes, I did it, to find out what it was like. It was scary. I spent a long time afterwards calming her down. We both cried, and I didn't leave until she was beginning to get mad. I knew she'd be O.K. then. She never pressed charges, but we never saw each other again."

"Something that happened a few years back and still causes grave guilt feelings is the way I exposed myself to my daughters when they were developing into young ladies. As they were maturing into young women, I refused to deal with the fact that their bodies turned me on sexually and I touched them where I should not have. I'm thankful that this is over now and that it is in the open between my wife and I. It is especially difficult to rebuild trust between us but it is happening."

"One night I was mad and I pushed my partner's head down near my penis. I told her to perform fellatio or I would beat her until she was black and blue. I told her to suck it until I came and then swallow it all. I held her head and shoved my cock into her throat with no regard for her comfort. I came. I did not feel bad after either. She deserved it."

Other men who had committed a rape gave various justifications:

"I cannot claim never to have raped a woman. What I did was because of ignorance of how to please her, and of her rights in the matter. She just lay unmoving, unresponsive once I had forced her, and this made me lose my erection after a few strokes (no ejaculation), and I just lost my entire drive and inclination. It was quite strange, in a way."

"Not in the criminal sense of raping a woman who honestly doesn't want to have sex, but in the sense of forcing a woman who is denying her own sexuality to have sex, and thereby awakening her to her own potential for enjoyment, yes. I think that this is a kind of romantic rape, and is very different from actual forcible rape."

"I walked in on a woman who was lying on a couch passed out from liquor. I pulled her pants down and I fucked her, left, and never mentioned it to her. Rape?"

"Once. I picked up a woman in a bar, and subsequently forced her to submit. She enjoyed it and made a date with me for the next weekend. But I became frightened and never went back. (She may have been under eighteen.)"

"Once I picked up an 'amateur' in a bar and took her to a hotel room. More drinks and onto the bed—half undressed, quite sure everything was proceeding to a natural conclusion. Suddenly she hit me across the side of the head with a bottle which was on the bedside table. Damn nearly knocked me unconscious. I was enraged and inflamed at the same time. I slapped her hard across the face and forced myself into her. Don't think she really wanted this to happen, and when I released her she quickly got out of there—sobbing all the while. I was not at all proud of that behavior and worried about the consequences for some time. However, I was in the Army and soon moved on. Never forgot it and still feel badly about it."

"I let her know that if she was going to have a relationship with me, she was going to fuck when I wanted to. Sometimes I want to and she don't, if we are in bed I will get on top and force my way into her."

And a longer reply from a man currently in prison for rape:

"I am twenty-three. I am at present incarcerated here at the State Medical Facility prison for rape. I have been incarcerated for approximately four years.

"I turned myself in to the authorities after my fourth successful (if it can be properly termed as such) rape, I couldn't stand the pressure or the worry that I might seriously hurt or kill my next victim. I have since been in various therapy sessions, and am still attempting to glue my thoughts, feelings, and ideas to a more suitable state that is more acceptable to myself and society.

"I sincerely hope you can find that my feelings are honest, as I did my best. I'd like to say this before going on to the questions, that a rapist is tagged a Mentally Disordered Sex Offender (M.D.S.O.), but it's a question not so much of a sickness, but comparable to a building block. In most of our childhoods, we start learning and experiencing life, and it's our responsibility to build correctly foundational morals. If incidents happen, trauma, accidents, whatever, that tears down one's blocks, he must put it back together. I believe that when my 'blocks' were kicked over, I put them back up incorrectly and in a disordered fashion. It took twenty years to try and gain enough confidence and self-respect to try and reorder and rebuild my 'blocks.' An M.D.S.O. is not a diseased animal, but someone who has to get a thing straightened out in his own life and head before he can live acceptably to his peers.

"I'm presently a nurse's aide in this facility's hospital, specializing in emergency aid and the intensive care unit for the last two years. I have a G.E.D. with only tenth-grade backing.

"I was brought up in a broken home before my mother remarried my stepfather. I'm the oldest of five children. I suffered disrespect for myself, and feelings of guilt and helplessness since my father's divorcing when I was five, and have lived my life being a phony to get people's attention.

"I have raped women (four rapes with one attempt) for two major reasons: (1) to gain a feeling of absolute control over a woman I felt rejected me, and (2) to prove I was as worthless as my inner turmoil made me believe I was. A lot more is involved, but that's the basic cause for my acts. The acts themselves were frightening to both myself and my victim. I felt like I only wanted to be accepted, to have her say she understood me, I just didn't have enough on the ball, or the confidence to ask, or try and build the relationship because I had myself doomed in my own head towards rejection.

"When I was refused sex before, I usually felt rejected and then anger, and get pissed off to the point I feel justified to rape her and degrade her. I'm now at the point that I still feel rejection, but I try to understand women have their preferences, as I do, and they have desires and likes, as we all do.

"When I raped, I felt a commitment to finish intercourse after initiating my approach, though I didn't want sex (I was after that feeling of utter control and domination over someone else), but I felt I had to finish what I started. In normal sex with a willing partner, I usually desire intercourse, and I also like to just hold and hug and lightly pet with those women in my life I feel close to without the actual sex act, or having to go on to intercourse.

"I used to ejaculate immediately (three to five seconds after penetration) if the intercourse was forced on my partner. I feel this happened because when I'm forcing sex, I'm not into the act of sex, but only out to prove I can control my victim, and also to increase my inadequate feelings about myself. It used to bother me so much that the confusing act would in itself cause me to rape for a fourth time, eventually forcing me to turn myself in for help. I now have routed out most of my inadequacies to the point of I now realize I no longer have to be phony, which helps my self-confidence and allows me to be a bit more open with my relationships.

"I felt very inadequate and powerless when I raped. Most often and as often as I can feel powerful, I'll try and achieve the feeling. The point where I feel most powerful during non-forced sex is at the point I keep up my foreplay until they beg for me to enter them. I feel like I'm very much in absolute control.

"I would still like to live my fantasy in sex. I would like to have a partner who is at first unwilling (young; between fifteen and twenty-six) but is soon aroused by my tongue until she asks for my penis.

"My first sex experience was also the first time I was very aware of orgasm, I was nine and my partner thirteen. She dared me to first kiss her, and she manipulated me until I was performing intercourse. All I can recall is that when I came, I felt like a part of me had just left and went into her, and I neither understood it or wanted it. I was very much afraid someone (my mother) would discover its absence and hate me. I was extremely confused and very frightened.

"I had sex with a hooker once, and it was a mess. We did it in a motel room with her four kids not more than three feet away watching TV. I was feeling greatly inadequate, afraid, and guilty, plus I didn't have the agreed-upon price (ten dollars). This was when I was fifteen, my last of three previous sexual encounters before I met my wife in high school.

"I was still living at home with my family when my wife first came into my life during our high school days and it was simply assumed and accepted we were having sex. We never really discussed this until the question of marriage and children cropped up two years after we had been together. So we are common law. We have a seven-year relationship that has been broken up in pieces of time by army service and my present four-year incarceration period. I much like my long-standing relationship, am at this time in it, very much in love and comfortable and proud to have this woman who's lived with my mistakes and still loves me. Our sex is varied and pleasing, we know more or less just what we both want and how we need to express our sexual needs.

"I've had extramarital experiences and my wife has had two known to me. She knows of all of mine now, but didn't at the times they occurred, with the exceptions of when we were separated or traveling, or in the Army. At the time I felt I was being cute, with no regard to my wife's feelings, sometimes hoping she'll find out and force an issue. When she discovered my affairs and my rapes, she was very much hurt, confused, and very willing to accept *her* actions as the reasons I raped.

"I don't think I ever trusted myself with love enough to let it affect me until these last three years. I just used my wife for our first five years, I suspected and was wary of her reasons for loving me until two years ago when we started talking about fears and inhibitions we were trying to avoid concerning ourselves. After that, it seemed I just accepted her. By that I mean I didn't suspect her motives, I respect them. I don't worry about her leaving me. If it happens, I hope it's with a man she can be happier with. With this growth, my feelings for my family and friends is larger and a lot more comfortable.

"I've cried out front and without hindrance just these last three years. Also over my wife's and my near breakup, over a close friend's inability to express himself and his bottled-up emotions. I've never thought of suicide, and I consider it to be a weakness, and a very selfish act. Even when I turned myself in, I did it to stop hurting others and from tearing myself and my wife up further and to get help with my problem.

"Before, my wife and I only had a fairly content sexual relationship, with nothing else about it truly understood. Since I've started feeling good about myself, we've been talking a little more openly, and about our feelings and wants more than just saying mundane day-to-day talk. I think my first rape was sexually satisfying because it was one of my fantasies and it worked out, and because it was an on-the-spot encounter and I didn't have to communicate, or trust this woman, just have sex with her and no other responsibility.

"Now I have enough confidence and trust in my wife to tell her absolutely anything I feel or think or want, and don't worry about her rejecting me (my biggest fear is rejection), or laughing at me. Sometimes I don't feel my wife is as open with her feelings and thoughts as I'd like her to be, and she has difficulty expressing herself from what I feel she may be afraid I won't understand. She also can't bring herself to trust me as fully as I'd like for her to, due to my past actions and behavior. Hopefully she'll learn to trust and respect the changes I've tried to make in these last four years.

"I believe my sex life now will be completely altered from what it had been six years ago. I'm not into 'just sticking it in until I bust' no longer. I have to bring out my partner's fulfillment to enjoy my own. I no longer have the desire to 'take' my partner, she now has to be willing in order for me to gain my pleasure. I no longer feel women were made just to please me, but are individuals I must work with and for to gain their respect. I feel I've grown and matured in the past four years of incarceration to the point that I'm content with myself, which seems to reflect to my loved ones. I feel I have a great deal to offer now, it just hasn't been asked of me yet.

"I've gone these four years with no more sex than fantasy and masturbation. Not including the first nine years of my life, this is the longest I've abstained from sex. I sure as hell don't like it.

"I answered these questions because I felt a present need to express my feelings and to see if I could be honest with myself. I wanted to do it in a way I wouldn't be laughed at or misunderstood by assholes. I think, too, I secretly want a pat on the back. I also hope people will see that some rapists aren't just animals, but just confused and tightly locked up in their own fantasy worlds. As a whole, if a person has the balls to answer these honestly and openly, he may find quite a few surprises and insights. I found it an eye opener and I used it to get a little feeling out, it made me back up and take another look at aspects of sex that I had taken for granted."

Some younger men in groups had raped—or tried to rape—women to gain membership in the male "club":

"I never raped a woman, but once in college I entered a darkened room, the fifth or sixth man of a gang bang. The girl began crying, 'How many of you are there?' She got out of bed, turned on the light, and sobbed. I attempted to convince her to stay, as I was the last one. She declined, left the room, and there I was sitting on the bed in my shorts. When the others eventually entered, I felt compelled to tell them I was turned down. Actually, they never would have known, had I not."

"Yes, I have indirectly raped two different girls several times although intercourse never took place on any of these occasions. I guess the reason I did this was to follow the lead of my friends who were a year or two older. This took place when I was in ninth and tenth grade in high school. We were very attracted to two thirteen-year-old neighbors. We all knew these girls well. Over a period of a year, starting one summer, my friends and I would catch and hold the girls down, then strip her of her clothing. We would then fondle their breasts and insert fingers into their vaginas. They would struggle and sometimes scream, but we would not physically harm them. I think they secretly very much enjoyed being taken, but didn't want us to know."

"I'm almost fifteen. I was born in Minneapolis, and I live in a suburb. We're a middle-class family. I'm white. I've never had intercourse except one night this girl got high on spray paint. I came over there after she had gotten high. About ten boys jumped her, including me. I felt out her cunt and tits. She probably liked it 'cause she didn't fight it hardly at all."

Only a few men said they had actually raped women "just for the sex":

"Yes. Because I was horny, goddammit. It wasn't too great. Usually a little dry."

"Yes. I raped a woman. I did it just for the sex. It was quick and exciting."

And other men said yes, they had raped a woman—but "only my wife":

"Only my wife once, after about fifteen years of marriage from frustration and anger when she wouldn't verbalize with me. Once was too much."

"No, I've never raped a woman. Maybe sort of my wife once. I didn't want to hurt her. I guess I felt like she belonged to me. She was terribly upset and so was I, but within a short time we straightened things out."

"I've sometimes forced my wife to couple as one when she didn't want to; I think of that as sort of rape."

"No, unless you can call forcing myself on my wife after her continuous refusals over a long period of time, as rape. Maybe I should have gone outside the marriage."

"When I was drinking I forced my wife several times, but I didn't bash her around, and she could have stopped it at any time—it *was a destructive game and we were both players.*"

"I suppose that it could be considered rape. We were married at the time and I wanted sex and she didn't, she didn't even want to know. I forced her."

"The only woman I have ever 'raped' was my wife, and that was only a kind of bondage game I thought she'd enjoy."

"I would never think of taking it by force—except from my wife. I don't think I could get it up in a rape situation. It so appalls me that I couldn't do it. I have forced myself on my wife when she has repeatedly refused me and has led me to believe I could have some then closed up. This has only happened a few times and I feel bad afterwards. I would rather get a divorce than do it again."

And a few men had begun a sort of rape of their wives, but found it a very unhappy experience:

"I did something near it once and I felt like hitting myself or burning my hand off. One time she was not in the mood, so I picked her up and put her in the bed and got on top of her. I started to kiss her and move my body on her, then she started to cry softly, and all the wanting just went out of me. I think I'd have killed myself if I had a gun. My erection disappeared and I was not in the mood for sex. She cried for a while and I held her after a while, but I did not touch her again for the whole night. I only touched her after three days after she made the first move. She told me why she cried and I understood."

"I tried to rape my wife once, after we were married. We had an argument. I tore off her panties and tried to mount her. After we had a short fight, which was exciting to me, she gave in. She just lay there, spread her legs, and shut her eyes. I looked at her, my erection left, and I laid my head on her chest and cried. If she didn't want me, I didn't want her."

Some men said that it often felt like rape when they had intercourse with their wives:

"That all depends on how you define 'rape.' Something which was tantamount to rape for me was when I had intercourse with my first wife. She was very reluctant to have intercourse except maybe once a month or once every two months. When we had intercourse I always felt that I was forcing myself on her, which, considering the beautiful sharing marriage that I have now, I can only describe in very cold, unfeeling terms that would be to a degree 'rape.' Thank God that's all behind me."

"I used to fantasize about it after sex with my wife. I felt starved and guilty like I'd raped her because she never responded to me."

"I have never wanted to rape a woman. Sex with my wife feels bad enough for me when my wife makes love with me because she thinks it is her duty, rather than because she wants to."

And some had used their positions of power to pressure a woman into sex or acceptance of an inappropriate situation at work:

"She was an employee and I was the 'boss.' I don't think this is the only reason why she had sex with me, but it was an influencing factor. *Maybe* she felt that intercourse with me would give her some security in her job, but only maybe."

"I had a brief affair with a student of mine and it was obvious that the power I held over her must have affected her decision to have sex with me in some way."

"I have raped a woman, but never by beating her or that type. Rape by exorcism, firing her off the job, or not giving her a contract in business, etc."

And one man spoke about his feelings and desires—and his perceptions and fantasies of his daughter's feelings—while dancing close to her:

"I am in my sixties, but feel younger than my age. I have been married to the same woman for almost thirty-five years. I like being married, very much, although no man and woman can ever reach the perfection of 'the perfect marriage.' The effect of marriage on a sexual relationship is to provide a sanctuary for the enrichment of both.

"I have had extramarital sexual experiences which were unknown to my wife. They have decreased a tremendous amount of the disagreements, conflict, frustration, and tension that was a result of the wide difference in our sex drives. She may know about them and not mention them because of the realization that they have solved our most disappointing difference. I used to feel some guilt about it, but I don't anymore.

"I have two sons and one daughter. My daughter, who is sixteen, has shown abundant sexual response to me—for the last two or more years. She loves to sit on my lap, and does so whenever she gets a chance; and she puts her arm or arms around me and runs her fingers through my beard, or through my hair (especially the back of my neck), and I know she can feel my penis swelling and stretching and getting hard and pressing and throbbing against her buttocks and thighs, because she moves her buttocks around on my prick so that it will feel better to her and to me. Several times when I was lying down on the bed—resting, with nothing on but my underwear shorts (during the day or after supper at night)— she has come into the bedroom to 'ask me a question or two,' and while we talk she usually sits on the bed beside my waist and puts her hand on my chest and gradually moves her hand around to feel the hair on my chest, feel my breasts and nipples.

"Over a year ago she asked me to teach her how to dance, not any of the modern dances, but the dances we did when I was in my teens and twenties—the 'round dancing' of the Big Band Era; I have tape recordings of Glen Miller, Tommy Dorsey, and many others. She learned very quickly, and she initiated putting both arms around my shoulders or neck while we danced. I have led her in dancing (and she follows well) all around a room and from one room to another all over the house, dancing to that music. I'm sure she knows that I wear my penis on the right side—not on the left as most men do—and sometimes we dance like that for an hour or two. She likes for me to bend her over backwards in a spin—which I learned how to do many, many years ago— and keep our balance. While we are dancing, she keeps her pubic bone pressed close to mine and loves for me to lead her backwards pushing my thigh between her legs, and she can feel my hard prick against her thigh when I do that. In fact, I stay hard practically the whole time I'm dancing with her. She adds another bonus to our dancing by pressing and moving her breasts against my chest. Sometimes she seems to be moving her breasts around in circular motions on my chest. Sometimes I have felt her get very tense (with her chin on my shoulder), so that she seems to be having an orgasm. If that is true, then I can remember several times when she has had several orgasms, one right after another. She is usually the one who says she is ready to stop 'for the time being.' And she always looks at my bulging penis (through my pants, of course) when we stop dancing and separate, and always with a beautiful smile. That's been the extent of her sexual responses and feelings toward me and of mine toward her—to date."

Many men would not rape a woman

But a large minority of men said they would not even want to rape a woman, because they wanted the woman to want to be involved, and rape would not satisfy their desire to be wanted and accepted:

"No, it would disgust me. If the woman doesn't want me, I don't want her."

"I don't think I would want to really rape a woman because sex should be enjoyed by both parties and if she did not respond I would not enjoy it. I had a prostitute once and that was the next thing to rape. She just lay there like a limp dishrag holding the money in one hand and hurrying me to get done."

"It would not be at all self-assuring to have to force my attentions on a female. It's a woman's affections that I want—not just her body. I'd rather masturbate than have sex without affection."

"The most enjoyment that I get out of sex is to see my partner enjoy herself to the point of ecstasy. Knowing that I am causing this sensation for my partner is thrilling and exciting and it gives me a sense of power because *I know she wants me.* I don't believe these feelings would be possible for either partner in case of rape. A person who would rape a woman must be extremely emotionally unstable, a sick mind, irresponsible, one who has no consideration for the rights and feelings of another human being. I consider such a person a scum and reprobate."

"I would feel terrible and foolish—like what's the matter with me that no woman wants me? I could never do it."

"I do not comprehend rape. Why would anyone want sex with someone else who didn't desire sex with them? Stupid and insane. The act is beautiful only when shared by both people."

"The desire to rape comes from a woman choosing

whom she allows to enter her. This choice inevitably leads to rejection of the male or some males—and it is in males who have a strong fear of rejection that the desire to rape arises. When I experience rejection, it hurts, but I would never want to rape someone. I generally go off people who don't want me."

"If a woman resists me by being cold, let alone physically struggle with her, the act would be greater agony for me than her."

"One volunteer is worth six conscripts."

Quite a few men said they did not see how rape was physically possible:

"I wouldn't even be able to get an erection with somebody who is resisting."

"How could you rape a woman? First she would be dry and not sexually lubricated, which would hurt my penis as well as injuring her vagina and put her into sexual shock."

"For me, most of the thrill of lovemaking lies in the feedback: I love to excite a woman. Seems to me that the feedback I would get from a rape would be pretty uninspiring. I frankly doubt if I could maintain an erection. One other thing: getting into a dry vagina is difficult and painful. Does the average rapist go out armed with K-Y jelly? If not, how the hell does he achieve intromission?"

"I always thought it would hurt the rapist's penis because of no lubrication. I should think it would hurt him like hell, physically."

"If I were to hit a chick I would feel angry, not horny, so the force necessary to rape a woman would leave me without an erection to fuck her with."

"I have thought about raping women, when I was angry or frustrated, but I don't know if I could get an erection after pounding some poor small body into submission."

Some men said they would never consider raping someone, because it would hurt another human being:

"I am honestly appalled by and genuinely concerned with rape and the rape issue. I read Susan Brownmiller's book *Against Our Will* and thought it a powerful, extremely important book—and a neglected one in the mainstream culture."

"The idea makes me puke. Simple enough? I have seen

the results of rape, and what it does to a woman. I have had
a few women friends who have been raped, and I know the
emotional and psychological results. It's absolutely sickening
to me."

"The sexual act can be so beautiful and so delicate and
tender, that it seems particularly cruel to have it contaminated
with violence, pain, and humiliation. I might as well punch
her in the mouth."

*Some men said they would never do it because it would be
a violation of someone else's rights, a woman's ownership of
her own body:*

"I have never raped a woman nor have I ever *wanted* to
rape a woman, because I think violation of another human
being is an absolutely ridiculous thing. What could possibly
give me the right to decide for another person whether she
should have sex with me? Nothing could give me that right."

"Rape is a violent crime where one violates another and
this is sick behavior. My ideals relate to personal freedom and
the desire to be involved voluntarily."

"I cannot see rape as anything other than a dehumanizing brutalization of a person's rights, space, and body."

"I don't believe in rape because of the mental and psychological scars that can develop. A woman's body is her
precious commodity. If she wants to share it with me, fine.
However, if she will not give herself to me, I might be disappointed, but I would never forcibly take my pleasure with
her."

A few men said no, because the women would not enjoy it:

"The only way I could ever imagine raping a woman is
if I knew she would enjoy the sex. But the chances are kind
of against this, aren't they? It seems that if you rape a woman,
most would be so terrified that you could not tell how to make
her happy sexually."

*And few men said no, because their wives or lovers had been
raped and they realized the damage it could do:*

"Seven years ago my wife was raped by a man who we
both knew and who lived in our apartment building. She kept

this locked up inside her for a year because she was afraid that I would no longer want her or that I would blame it on her in some way. Fortunately, in spite of the feelings and rage that were boiling inside of me at this time, I did not direct my anger or hurt at her. When I realized how deeply hurt and confused she was because of this experience, I fell even more deeply in love with her than I had been. I was enraged that any person should be forced into submitting to being used by a slob for what could only be nothing more than masturbation, simply because she was physically unable to defend herself and had to submit in order to avoid physical harm and possibly worse. I couldn't see how my wife's unwilling body could be satisfying to him. His own right hand would have been more stimulating since it would at least do something other than just lie there like a lump. Her understanding of my feelings about it, and my understanding of her feelings and fears stemming from it all, combined to make us closer and more deeply in love than ever. Our deeper closeness and love also allowed us to have a far more satisfying sexual relationship as well."

"My wife was a rape victim when she was nineteen. A good part of our marriage so far has consisted of my, and our, attempts to pick up the pieces. The idea of rape is a complete and total turn-off to me; even the pseudo-rape sequences in X-rated movies fill me with the vilest hate. I sincerely believe (intend) that I would without hesitation kill any man who ever again touched my wife with this unspeakable atrocity. I at moments imagine my wife's screams on that night several years ago—I'm afraid that all the anxiety I've ever felt for the victim (my wife), I would unleash on a man if I heard a woman's call for help. It is my belief now, and she agrees, that this is a good part of the reason we cannot seem to get to a normal sexual functioning level in our marriage.

"She is a beautiful and intelligent girl, and it infuriates me to see all the ways that it has put kinks into her personality. She is afraid to be by herself, even somewhat in our house. She seems to want to be as unobtrusive as possible all the time. This whole rape fixation in the porno industry is a big bring-down for both of us . . . and at moments I wonder whether it is good that women's rape fantasies are stressed so frequently in the men's magazines, as they are. I mean, how many animals are there around?"

And a few men explained that they themselves had been raped:

"I have never raped a woman. I doubt that I could. I learned firsthand how quickly men can turn an innocent situation into rape and how helpless a woman can be against strong men. I escaped only because they had been drinking. I learned what it felt like to be held tightly and lifted off the ground so that my struggles were ineffective. The men made two other subsequent attempts and I reported them to the authorities. I was told they were only joking. When I insisted they were serious, I was told I must be doing something to attract them. I was warned that if something happened, I would have to prove I resisted. I was told mere verbal protests were not considered resistance. As a consequence I feel I could vote any man guilty of rape if I were ever on a jury."

"When I was a prisoner in an army stockade in 1970, I was beaten up and homosexually gang-raped. I was one of three inmates in a period of about a week that were subjected to this, before the brass finally took measures to put a stop to it. I was relatively 'lucky,' since only three of the group that attacked me went through with the sexual part, forcing anal penetration. Unlike with the other two victims, they didn't have time to force fellatio or drag out the humiliation for very long. One of the other two raped soldiers later attempted suicide."

"I have never raped a woman, though I have *wanted* to. I am going to tell you exactly why I have not. When I was a teenage punk I spent a summer on the streets of L.A. I was arrested and chucked into the county jail. There among the felonious criminals I learned almost at once how innocent my life had theretofore been. (I wasn't not guilty, merely innocent.) When I hit the cellblock I was: 5' 6" tall, 126 lbs., new in a jungle I did not yet perceive, friendless, white (the population was then about one-third each black, Chicano, and white, but the blacks ran the place). I was additionally: exhausted from previous weeks of dissolute existence, half asleep from the preceding fifteen hours in overcrowded intake bullpen, confused, numb, sick; in sum, so vulnerable as to constitute the Perfect Victim.

"The very first night, many of us sleeping in cellblock corridor due to overflowing cells, I feel the famed Stealthy Group. Dimly I perceive in the gloom two looming blacks, each roughly twice my weight and age, and heavily muscled, one with razor in hand. At once, razor is at my throat. I am turned over, stripped of underpants, sat on, informed that razor is now at my 'balls, baby.' My butt is raised, my knees spread, he is between them. Initial reaction to this point: uncomprehension, disbelief, denial, immobility; in retrospect probably luckly for me. Thence what might be termed in court asquiescence, penetration of anus (the pure shock of it), incredible pain, two to three minutes of being fucked (precisely the appropriate word), then flashlight beam, guard. Attackers flee as he approaches.

"I remember more vividly than the rape, the *after:* shame, shame beside which the outrage and pain of the during are nothing; guilt; longing for oblivion, wanting only to crawl into a hole and cease to be, only to *forget;* need to pretend it never happened, could not have happened (and guards only to glad to go along).

"So we all four groups of participants in the drama—predators, victim, silent witnesses in the gloom all around, and authority—all engaged in a 'cover-up conspiracy' to deny it ever happened, each for his own reasons, none so urgently as I. The attackers doubtless gloating, the victim guilt-ridden and ashamed (I have never, not even after all these years, spoken of it to anyone), without even the shower I so badly wanted.

"What it did to the body was so very less important, torn flesh, bleeding and all, than what it did to the mind. That, in fact, is what men don't grasp about raped women who 'haven't been hurt.' Nothing ever so damaged *me* as a *person*, nothing ever so violated the very integrity of my individuality, nor so truly *hurt* me as that rape. Not other times' concussion, broken bones, knife wounds, nothing. It must have been three or four years before I could let myself think about it. Though it no longer bothers me, I will sure as hell never forget it. That costly understanding explains the empathy that explains why I have never raped a woman (though I have wanted to) *and I never will.*"

Conclusion

Why do men rape women? Since orgasm is always available to a man through masturbation, what is the meaning of rape? As we have seen in this chapter, most men do not rape out of "lust," but because of feelings of anger, lack of self-esteem, and a desire to assert masculinity or male dominance and put a woman "back in her place." Thus, masculinity is, for some men, equated with dominating a woman. Dominating a woman can be a way for a man to feel more successful when other areas of his life are not going so well. As one man put it, "I fantasize rape most often when I've felt 'out of it'—raping someone would be a symbolic way of forcing myself into the awareness of other people."

As the typical rape fantasy of the men in this study goes, "I have had fantasies of screwing a woman (or devirginizing one) who was initially unwilling or reluctant, or afraid, but who became eager and hot after a little bit, and then enjoyed it with me." Many men do not think women have a right to reject them. After all, men are supposed to be superior to women; therefore, to have an inferior reject you is the greatest insult possible. Men are supposed to do the choosing ("pick a bride," "take a wife"). In addition, the society tells men that women should love men, and that this is one of their basic duties: women who do not "love" men are "bad" women. Therefore, if women do not make sex available, men have a right to take it. In other words, having sex with a woman is a large part of our society's definition of a "man"; therefore, if a woman denies a man "sex," she is "denying him his right to be a man." She has no "right" to do this, and therefore he has a "right" to take it (sex).

This is still true legally in marriage in most states in the United States. For this reason, the intercourse definition of sex has been called the *rape* definition of sex, since traditionally a wife was forced to have intercourse at her husband's demand, and was not permitted to use birth control. This effectively took away any control she had over her body. This situation continues today for many women, and there is still a widespread presumption on the part of many men that they own or have rights to women's bodies.

But rape has *not* always existed—because intercourse was not always seen as a symbolic and meaningful act. The myth of the "caveman" dragging "his" woman home by the hair is just that—a myth. Rape is not the satisfaction of a physical urge; rape is cultural. If we lived in a society in which men did not feel they should dominate women, and intercourse was not the primary cultural symbol it has become, would men see the forcing of women to have intercourse as a meaningful activity? What gives it its emotional appeal? It is the meaning of the act, the fact that it symbolizes acceptance and masculine status for many men.

In all too many cases, the combination of pressure to be a "man" and the alienation and loneliness sometimes created by this attempt leads to a pressuring of women to say "yes" to male "biological" (and therefore "manly," not "weak") needs. Many men attempt to make the physical act of sex a substitute for emotional contact (e.g., through conversation), as seen in chapter 3; the more a man finds this is the only way he is able to relate in a personal, emotional way to others, the more likely he is to complain that he doesn't get enough sex. These thought patterns can eventually lead some men to the feeling that they are completely justified in raping a woman.

On another level, it is important to point out that there are many kinds of rape—not only forced penetration of a woman's vagina, but also a kind of daily attempt to remind women of their place, a daily attempt to force penetration of a woman's self-respect and status as a fully respected member of the community, with rights equal to those of men. The idea of "taking" a woman, using a woman when she is under some kind of pressure to cooperate—whether the pressure is physical, psychological, legal, or financial—is only symptomatic of the attitude of the culture to women on every level.

OTHER KINDS OF RAPE: PRESSURING A WOMAN INTO SEX

Is sexual rape only direct physical force to have intercourse? Or are some forms of psychological pressure and coercion also rape?* Where is the line between initiating sex and pressuring a woman into sex?

When asked, "How do you define rape?"† some men pointed out that rape can include not only direct physical force but also seduction and pressure on a woman to engage in sexual intercourse against her will:

"Rape is having sex with a woman who does not want it. Any verbal, physical, or emotional trick that puts a woman in the position of having intercourse against her will is rape."

* And is economic pressure also a form of rape? See page 293.

† Other answers ranged from "Rape is any sexual act, even as mild as kissing, that is done against the will of the person it is being done to," to "Forced intercourse is only rape when the girl is hurt and violent acts are included." The most common answer was "forcible intercourse."

"Rape is the act of coercive sex upon another human being. It doesn't necessarily have to be violent. Most of the time it isn't violent and many people don't know they're participating in a rape when it's happening. But any time a human being has sex against her will, it's rape. Or—had sex because, if she didn't, sanctions of one sort or another, especially economic, would be imposed upon her directly by the man."

"Forcible intercourse including seduction. A means used by small (mentally or socially) men to show their contempt for or mastery over women."

"If I had sex with a woman just as if she was an object, not caring about her feelings, I'd be raping her."

These alternate definitions became an issue with the question "Have you ever pressured a woman to have sex with you when she didn't seem to want to? How did you do it? Did it succeed?"

Most men answered yes, they had pressured women into sex; do the following answers reflect the roles men and women are taught to play,* or do they sometimes amount to a form of rape?

"When I started out I busted my ass to get under her skirt. I would say anything if I thought that it would get me into her pants. This is corny but in high school I used to go to the five-and-ten and get a bunch of dollar initial rings and give them out with a line about it was my granddad's or the folks gave it to me for some sweet little reason. It worked a couple of times, believe it or not. I was full of bullshit, and had a number to say to her as soon as I had the car parked. I had special places to park. I got a lot of hand action, but that's about all."

"I have tried many times to talk it up. I did it according to the situation. If I did not have a rubber, I said I would pull it out or we could have oral sex. I told her I would never tell anyone else she gave it to me, I liked her very much, I loved her, she was the greatest, my nuts were bursting and would harm me, and it was her fault for working such a hot-blooded person like myself up with her feminine ways. It usually succeeded."

---

* And, in fact, is the role women are taught to fulfill in itself in many ways a form of rape—or a form of teaching women themselves to cooperate in their own rape?

"Of course. One can't avoid it. By all the means in the book—moving back and playing hard to get—being hurt and making her feel sorry—exacting her sympathy—the medical reasons—it's good for you—or it's bad for me—I'm in pain—my balls ache. Present buying. Alcohol to soften her. Or straightforward exciting her by kissing, fondling, petting. Some succeeded, some not."

"I have tried all sorts of things to say when I try to persuade a woman to let me make love to her. I like to be sincere. The most truthful thing I can tell her is that I do not know what got into me, and that I am afraid I may go out of my mind if she does not consent."

"Yes. Guilt is the best way to get what you want from a woman."

"Much fast talk—love, love, love—all pure bullshit!"

"Verbal intimidation. Example: 'We haven't done anything in several weeks. What's up? Tell me the problem. Let's talk, O.K.?' Success is low because I usually back out (feeling dishonest)."

"By using emotional tactics such as telling her how much it meant to me and how that if she didn't meet my needs, I would go to someone else. Most of the time the tactic works."

"I told a woman (several women) if she (they) did not give in I was not going to see her (them) anymore. That was the truth. I am not a monk. Yes, always succeeded. I have very pitiful eyes."

"Yes. Begged. Succeeded."

"Yes! I'd pout like a little boy, or make known to her that I'm angry. But the one that always works is 'economic blackmail.' "

"Regretfully, I plead guilty due to ignorance and lack of willpower. I played on emotions such as empathy, sympathy until they thought they really wanted me too. It succeeded physically but I seldom if ever have seen the person since then and probably lost out on at least a great friendship."

"Yes, I have pressured my girl to have sex with me when she didn't want to. I've done so by sulking, by explaining I'm horny and need sex (I am and do), and by talking about how we don't have much time left together before we separate again (which is the truth). They've all worked."

"One way is I would wrestle her; another I would not fulfill all of her immediate needs and trade favors and services from myself for sex and money, and I have made some feel guilty about things they were not supposed to be doing, but were doing behind closed doors of private rooms. Yes, it succeeded."

"I played on her sympathy, told her I had doubts about my heterosexuality because of a previous sexual failure and needed desperately some woman to help me."

"I told the woman I would tell her husband or get word to him that she had been screwing around. Yes, it succeeded."

"I use her 'love.' It succeeds depending on her 'love.'"

"Yes, by trying to elicit some kind of sympathetic feelings. Usually by trying to focus her attention on what appears to be strong affection for her from me (genuine or not). And by 'negative pressure,' i.e., telling her that I very much want to make love with her and then telling her that I don't expect any answer to that, I simply wanted to express what I was feeling. It works more often than not, but that has more to do with selection than technique."

"I probably have pressured a woman into having sex. I have responses of pouting, resentment, withdrawing—those tricks have done the job before."

"I have pressured a woman to have sex with me. We talked and petted and although she seemed reluctant she never really stopped me. I had the impression she found it easier to go along than to take the risk of my being angry by telling me she didn't want to. I was callous and horny and decided if she would go along with it, I could get what I wanted."

"Women are not exactly open books. There are times when a little 'pressure' changes their minds, or reveals that they *did* want to after all (very likely quite unknown to themselves). But I have never made any use of liquor in 'persuading' a woman down the primrose path. I just use all those same words, caresses, touches, gallantries, pleadings, suggestions, gaieties, display of manliness, etc., etc., which consist of 'wooing' a woman; sometimes I have just used a frank and direct request; sometimes, I almost feel ashamed to say, an appeal to her sense of pity at leaving me without relief, and most women do seem to have in them a tender considerateness and hate to be the cause of hurt to someone else, which may render such an appeal the turning point— like the line of one of Edna St. Vincent Millay's sonnets, '. . . I might as well be easing you as lie alone in bed.'"

"Not really rape, but I've put a little pressure on at times thinking that she really wanted sex but this was part of the act that some girls think they should do."

"I've never raped a woman in the classical sense of

using physical force, but I think I've forced women to engage in sexual activities with me psychologically. I have argued them into sex with me. The whole notion of sex involves—or did, during the bulk of my experience—men trying to secure it from reluctant women. Within this framework, where does persuasion end and coercion start?"

Other men told how they did it in marriage:

"When I was married, I accomplished that by laying some heavy guilt games down. Wifely duty, and that sort of thing. It made for some of the worst sex I've *ever* had. That is one factor that helped form the philosophy I adhere to now. First, *both* parties have the right to say no! without any bullshit coming from the other. Secondly, I will say no if I don't think the lady really wants to."

"I have, in the past, pressured my wife into having sex with me when she didn't seem to want to. I simply told her that I wanted her, right while she was in the midst of housekeeping. It was not bad, perhaps because my wife was tolerant of everything except rape."

"That's one of the reasons my wife left me."

"Only my wife. I 'talked' to her. Usually I was successful but it made me feel unloved, unwanted."

"I suppose many times my wife had sex with me when she didn't want to. I am not sure it would be called 'pressure.' More likely it was a feeling of 'duty' on her part."

"I wish I could say no to this but I will have to say yes. On occasion I have put pressure on my wife to have sex with me when she didn't want to. I guess you could call it a form of blackmail. I remember one instance in particular. My wife wanted me to go with her to an office party and she really wanted to go, but she wouldn't go without me because she would feel awkward. A couple of nights before the party I wanted to have sex but she did not, so I told her that if she would not do this for me I would not go with her to the party. I did not really want to go to her office party anyways because she is a secretary at the university and the professors she works with are a bunch of stuffy snobs who like to impress each other with the books they are in the process of writing and I think it is very boring. In a way it was a success and in another way it was a failure. She did have sex with me, but I did not enjoy it because she was not enjoying it. I felt like I was using her, but then again she was using me too because I did not want to go to the party."

"My wife. I would act like I was mad at her and she would give in. It works every time."

Some said they believed the woman liked it:

"I've learned to do this with my wife, and she likes it. For years, I took 'no' for an answer, and was unhappy, and she was too, but in more recent years, both of us have been making our desires known and it's much better. She likes to be pressured, as she says it makes her feel I really want her, which is a turn-on."

"I found that some women expected to be pressured into sex, as then they could tell themselves that it was not their complete doing. Others pretended to be hard to get, but all along wanted to see how much struggle they were worth. It is a high compliment to be desired and the harder a female is pursued, the grander it makes her feel. Women are coy, men are persistent. A wonderful combo."

"Who hasn't? I lied shamelessly to her. But then again, women seem to like to hear lies. Tell her how you love her to distraction, can't go a day without thinking of her, how your body aches for her, etc., etc. It works. Women's lib criticizes men for their desire to have their egos inflated but I've never found a woman who didn't like the same thing. The bigger the flattery, the more the woman likes it. Of course, it succeeds. I doubt if you'll get a negative answer to this question. We all like our egos stroked and caressed."

"Pressure was the name of the game in my early dating days. We used peer pressure—'Everybody's doing it,' 'Why not?' 'I won't date you anymore,' 'Don't you love me?' 'I'll tell everyone you did, if you don't,' etc., etc. It worked if the girl was hot enough and wanted to do it anyhow. It sort of justified it in her own mind. She could say, 'You made me do it!' and try to escape her own guilt feelings."

Quite a few men said it seemed a standard activity necessitated by male and female roles, but they wished it weren't necessary:

"I've pressured women to have sex with me. I think more times than not (for the first time). Mostly I've done it with gentle persistence and lots of patience. I hate that, too. It seems to me that most women have to make their first 'down-fall' with someone a forced event. Maybe they think they will be thought of badly if they 'give in too easily.' I don't know, but I've gotten awfully tired of it."

"It would seem that I have pressured every woman to have sex with me. If I had waited for them to do something, I would still be a virgin. It's so distasteful that I just refuse to 'hustle' anymore."

"Most of the time, I didn't realize it—believe it or not. My last lover felt 'obligated' to sleep with me because I was so nice to her and drove twenty-five miles to see her—those are *her* words! Now why the hell don't women say things like that *before* it happens? I thought she wanted to have sex with me."

"I have coaxed a woman into having sex with me when she really didn't want to do so, mainly because I was really horny and wanted to make love to her very much. And I thought she really wanted to make love to me although she said she didn't. But this is not something I do regularly. I know I would not like sex forced on me."

Others said they felt bad after:

"My wife and I have had sex without her wanting it. There wasn't much feeling in it for me, just a shallow feeling, a release of sexual pressures from within me."

"I have used pressure in obtaining sex, but being the devious sort, I have usually resorted to psychology. The best technique is to resort to some very subtle form of pity. It always works. However, the sex is somewhat lacking in feeling. I seldom engage in that, and have never had to do it with the woman I now go with. I guess it defeats the whole purpose of sex for me."

"I do it by trying extra hard to seduce her, by continuing to fondle and kiss her, by talking sexy, sometimes by taking off my clothes. This has worked more often than not for me, but I have usually been rather disappointed in myself afterwards. Every time this has occurred, I might add, I have been somewhat drunk."

One man was ashamed of having pressured women into sex, but nevertheless felt it was the women's fault:

"This is the only question that I answer with some shame. Yes, I have pressured girls into having sex with me a number of times by dint of great persistence and an inability to accept defeat gracefully. It usually works. But listen, I have to enter some plea in my own defense. The occasions when I have pressured a girl into having sex were usually during a prolonged period of celibacy when I met a girl who was eager to go out with me, and willing to make out and touch me all over afterward, but did not want to have sex. I believe that such bitchy behavior is a girl's prerogative, but it puts a hopeless strain on my willpower."

Some men said they used to, but it had turned out not to be very pleasurable:

"Not lately. In the old days, when I occasionally used verbal glibness to 'tame' a woman into having sex with me, it never turned out to be very satisfying sexually anyway. I have learned better."

"By verbal insistence. It was terrible! I was fifteen at the time and reasoned it was part of my learning curve. I have never done that since."

"Not lately, except my wife. I used to pressure her to experiment; sometimes I won and sometimes I didn't—I can't handle that anymore. There are a thousand ways to manipulate people—play on guilt, fear, weakness, but if you do, what have you won?"

And a few men said they would not do it:

"No. It's easier to find a new one."

"No. If a woman is not going to enjoy sex then there is no point to it."

"No. I don't scratch victim notches in my penile gun."

"No. I feel the same about that as rape."

"No. If it's not free it just ain't no good. It's the mutual giving that makes you feel good."

"I'm still unable to deal with the ragtime needed to con chicks in order to participate in the sexual revolution."

"Because our society puts a woman in a weak position regarding sex, I am extremely sensitive about abusing my more powerful position and forcing matters. To me sex is a mutual endeavor: I want to get the woman's approval or give her mine before we move to the next step."

PORNOGRAPHY

More men than ever before are reading and seeing pornography, and more than ever before are reading and seeing it at an earlier age. Most men now in their twenties and thirties had first seen pornography when they were very young, as shown in their answers to "Where did you first learn about sex?":

"My father always brought *Playboy* into the house, and sometimes some other, more graphic magazines, and it was cool for me to read them without any hassle. I remember loving it and getting impressions about male and female models from it."

"My father had a scrapbook of erotic pictures and poems I would sneak and take under the back stairs and masturbate to. A male friend would usually go down there with me. Parallel masturbation only. (We didn't touch each other.) This was age eleven or twelve."

"I saw my first 'men's' magazine at a grocery store at which I was working when I was in high school. Two young married men who owned the store and two or three other young men (married) who worked there made a habit of telling each other every day whether or not their wives had let them 'have any' the previous night. A couple of these men brought some porno storybooks to work and encouraged me to read them. They were stories without pictures, but very explicit."

"My father had *Playboy* on his nightstand hidden under the Bible. I discovered them when I was about ten."

"*Hustler* is my favorite now, but my father got me my first subscription to *Playboy* at age fifteen."

"I first saw it at a friend's house at about eleven years of age. I was turned on but at the same time turned off—it was a bondage and discipline picture book."

"I first saw a 'men's magazine' in the barbershop. They always had *Playboy*, which I would read attentively while waiting my turn to have my hair cut. Luckily, my father had a copy of the *Kinsey Report* he had hidden under his bed, which I found and read, saving myself some of the problems the misinformation in the magazines would have caused me."

"I saw my first hard-core porno when I was sixteen, at a summer camp where I was working. Also, there was a bit of hard-core 'written' porn circulating in high school."

"My father subscribed to *True* and to *Playboy*. I discovered his stash of *Playboys* on his closet shelf while looking for (I think) shoe polish, I think when I was about eleven or twelve. I knew it was 'naughty,' so I was aflutter about it."

"I saw my first men's magazine when I was eight or nine: some men tenants in our hotel left them lying around. I read them when I found them (had to sneak, though—Dad didn't approve of that trash), but would be bored by them now, I suspect."

Many men saw pornography later basically in a context of looking at it together with other men, at work, in socializing together (especially younger men), or in lounges, etc., as "entertainment":

"I had a friend on my bowling team. Every time after the game when we would be in the bar later, he would pull it out and we would all start looking at what some girl had to offer."

"In the airport, between flights, sometimes some of the rest of the crew and I buy the latest trash and make jokes about the girls and their poses. It's one way to pass the time."

It could serve the purpose of male bonding, rather than simple sexual stimulation:

"The barbershop seems like the place where men are supposed to get together and relax, and revel in their 'masculinity.' The last time I went to a barbershop I walked in, and there was the barber, and one customer he was working on. So I sat down, alone, in front of the big stack of magazines, with the *Playboy* on top of the pile. I felt like the other men expected me to reach for the porno magazines, and revel in them, because this was a place where us men can lust together over pictures of nude women. I felt like they expected me, the young stud, to show my approval and desire for these women in the magazines. I felt like I was expected to live up to the 'manly' image of the porno magazines. It is a point of understanding between men, even men who are strangers—we can all look at those pictures and understand each other. Anyone who doesn't like *Playboy* is obviously not a real man—must be a weirdo."

Other men used it to look at when alone, or as part of masturbation:

"My fantasies are often stirred up and heightened through the use of pornography. I have a collection of over a hundred magazines and about fifteen films."

"If I masturbate alone, I usually need visual stimuli (pictures of lovely ladies nude, pictures of sexual intercourse) or I must read about very explicit sexual experiences."

"Nude pictures from men's magazines turn me on, and when I finally ejaculate, I aim at the girl's breasts, pubic hair, or buttocks, whichever pleases me most. The more copious my output of sperm, the more satisfied I am."

"Sometimes if I get around to it, or have a magazine around (I don't subscribe to any), I sneak it into the bathroom—like when my wife is out shopping or working late—and really luxuriate in arousing myself, letting myself get really excited before I start getting ready to jerk off. But usually I don't have the time, or it's too much trouble."

But some men said that they looked at sexual magazines or pornography only irregularly, preferring their own fantasies:

"My eye is attracted to it when I chance upon it, but I don't buy it or ask to borrow it. I prefer to fantasize about women I know."

"I have looked at the magazines and been to topless bars, X-rated movies, and sex shops. None of these things turned me on, so I rarely do it now. What I can imagine is much better."

"Most pornography doesn't turn me on. I have never purchased any pornography. My wife turns me on."

"I used to be extremely turned on by 'hard core' porno, but lately I can 'take it or leave it.' It was never as good as my fantasies."

"Pornography I have seen, movies, cartoons, pictures, and stories, all seem to be aimed at a low level of mental development in that it is too explicit and leaves nothing for the viewer to add for his own enjoyment. For this reason pornography doesn't usually turn me on. I'd 'rather do it myself,' as the saying goes."

A few men said they never looked at it:

"I cannot stomach it and frequently pass up opportunities to indulge. I really look forward to home and my wife and the real thing."

"Even at twenty-seven I haven't looked at my first *Playboy* yet and I don't plan to. As you might guess, I've never been to a movie that would be rated more than GP either."

But some men were all in favor of pornography and men's magazines, and said that looking at them made them feel good, or was an ego boost:

"Yes, I look at pornography, I read *Hustler, Cheri, Chic,* etc. I go to nude girl shows (live) and to porno movies. My opinion of pornography is that I like it, and I hope that live nude sex shows will come to my area. I like it when the girls flirt with me."

"I haven't and never will see enough of it. I think it shows a lot of the animal that's really in all of us. Pornography should be legalized and used in high school sex education courses."

"It's great for me. It gives me new ideas to try and see, and it's always sexually exciting. It gives me a lift."

"I love pornography, both visual and written. The most beautiful sight I can ever imagine was Linda Lovelace fucking cocks with her mouth. She also seemed to enjoy it so much. I wish all women could or would see this show. Marilyn Chambers turned in a masterful job of cocksucking and fucking both in *The Green Door*. I would love to see more good movies along this line of entertainment. A woman could sure boost my ego with these things."

"When I get the new issue I go through all the pictorials, selecting for future reference those poses I find most exciting. I narrow them down to three or four, and then, like a beauty contest judge, I announce (to myself, of course) the first runner-up, and finally the girl of the month. I open my book to the page which features the winning pose, lie down beside it, and have my fantasy 'date' with her. Before the new issue hits the bookshelves I have honored the also-rans, the finalists, Wicked Wanda, Pusscake, and even those serious, antiseptic women in the condom ads."

WHAT KIND OF PORNOGRAPHY DO MEN LIKE?

The key to arousal for most men seemed, in photos, to be eye contact:

"My female (picture) must be looking straight into the camera lens (my eyes) to be most useful. The more intent her stare or gaze, the more suitable. There must be no other male present (in the picture) to interfere with my use of her. She and I have direct contact. As most of the best 'center-folds' are posed this way it would seem that my desires are quite universal and well understood by the publishers. The younger the model is and the more brazen (in a refined way), the more tantalizing she will be for me."

"I used to read pornography until recently, the *Playboy* or *Hustler* kind. The most salient feature of the kind of pornography I liked was that the subjects seemed to be missing me, that I was somehow their sex partner through the page. All the positions and expressions had a blank space for the man (me) to fill in."

"I like the pictures best where the woman is looking me in the eye, *smiling,* and showing her cunt, and touching it. It does me good to think she wants *me.*"

Most men preferred these pictures to be "soft core":

"A good-quality magazine, photographically, is O.K. *Playboy* magazine, which I look at rarely, still portrays the women as soft and desirable. They usually don't have crude photos. Some of the more recent publications are disgusting. Is a woman stretching her vaginal lips to the floor sexy? And the films are really crap. Sure, the photography is great and so is the action, but the actors stink. It all seems too mechanical. It's good to watch for a turn-on but a really romantic movie without the sex scene is more rewarding. I guess I'm just a damn romantic and not a humping machine."

"I enjoy heterosexual pornography that is presented in good taste, and shows a desire to enhance a woman's beauty through the right combination of seductive pose and beautiful and well-planned background. I consider this to be art. The purpose of the photographer is not just to photograph a woman's genitalia but to produce a piece of art. I enjoy looking at pornography which poses a woman in an innocent-looking way with just a bit of seduction. The innocent Sleeping Beauty photographs are my favorites. I dislike photographs that appear in *Hustler* or *Penthouse* magazines which pose women as prostitutes with their legs spread open as well as their cunts. The main objective in this type of pornography is simply to display the women's genitals so some guy can get his rocks off. I hate that kind of pornography."

But some men (a minority) liked more explicit sex:

"I love pornography, both visual and written. The most beautiful sight I can ever imagine was Linda Lovelace fucking cocks with her mouth. She also seemed to enjoy it so much. I wish all women could or would see this show. Marilyn Chambers turned in a masterful job of cocksucking and fucking both in *The Green Door*. I would love to see more good movies along this line of entertainment. A woman could sure boost my ego with these things."

Most men complained that most "hard core" pornography was degrading looking, and that they did not want to identify with it, even though they would still use it when nothing "better" was available:

"Once in a great while I like to see well-photographed 'foxy' women, but hard pornography I avoid. I can't identify with it. Looking at it makes me feel like someone undesirable."

"Most porno, like X-movies, is poorly done. I usually get a feeling of distaste after a few minutes. The people are not those you'd care to associate with—the women look bored. However, I saw *Deep Throat* and enjoyed it thoroughly."

"Some of it is well done, some trash, by trash I mean it made the participants seem degraded, ugly."

"Some if it—maybe most—is raunchy, unimaginative, repetitive, boring, and aesthetically wretched, but occasionally I see or read something that's above average, something that lifts up my heart with its beauty and sensitivity."

"Pornography can be done tastefully but most of it is just plain garbage. All they consist of is very short dialogue: 'Hi, my name is Mark.' 'Mine is Marcia, let's fuck!' and slurping sounds. I once saw a film that I thought was very sexually stimulating, but most of what is out today is garbage."

*But many men said they had very mixed and confused feel-
ings about their own reactions—even when they found
pornography degrading or offensive, they still felt excited:*

"What is my opinion of the pornography I've seen? A
mixture of anger, disgust, and fascination. I really find a
great deal of it offensive. I dislike seeing people displayed as
meat, or as whores, and that's how much of the porno
magazines seem to me. On the other hand, I also feel a sort
of unwilling turn-on to much of it. That's double annoying:
to feel this is done nastily, and also that it does grab my
attention."

"I think that it is sad and disgusting that they have
transformed such a beautiful act into something so base and
animalistic. Unfortunately it turns me on physically. I find
myself looking at it out of curiosity and getting aroused even
though I hate myself for doing it."

"I have used the pictures of naked women in that kind
of magazine to jerk off to, imagining I was fucking them, at
the same time knowing that I wouldn't like to relate to any
real woman on that mindless level."

"Looking at pictures of naked bodies is a real turn-on.
Dirty, but there's something appealing and exciting about
orneriness (sometimes). Pornography is *impressive* but I'm
not at all sure that it should be supported or even allowed.
Of course, just looking at porno can at times be really *depressing, disgusting; but exciting, nonetheless.*"

"As far as pornography goes, I look at it occasionally.
I am very ambivalent about it. Some of it does arouse me,
but most really does nothing because sex without affection is
cold and not very exciting. I also think it degrades women
and that definitely turns me off or makes me angry."

HOW DO MEN FEEL ABOUT
PORNOGRAPHY: WHAT DO THEY SEE
WHEN THEY LOOK AT IT, AND WHAT
DO THEY FEEL?

*While some men felt that pornography was exciting but they
shouldn't like it, others felt it wasn't exciting but they should
like it (since all "men" should like it); these men complained that the pornography they saw was boring—if only
the quality were improved, it would be stimulating, they
believed:*

"In my humble opinion, all the pornographic movies I have seen have been terrible. Usually I will have an erection for the first five minutes, then be bored to tears till it's over. The plots are moronic, the acting pitiful, and (most inexcusable) the girls unlovely, and the fucking mediocre. Girlie magazines are a little better. The best ones (notably *Playboy*) do, at least, find exquisitely beautiful girls, and photograph them with taste and skill."

"I wish they would make X-rated movies that have a good story with some tender, but explicit sex scenes. The couple of movies I've seen (e.g., *Deep Throat*) get boring very rapidly. In fact, when we went to see it, both my wife and I had no desire for sex that night, which is certainly unusual for me!"

"If I have not seen any in a long time I find it exciting. In any case it is at first interesting, later boring. I think the boredom sets in because the material is not well artistically constructed."

A few men spoke out definitively against pornography, saying that all pornography—whether "hard" or "soft" core—degraded and dehumanized men as well as women:

"I have a very depressed feeling about pornography because I believe it is degrading to both men and women and mankind in general. Yet I am very much against censorship—I just wish people would have higher ideals."

"Current pornography I find to be degrading to both men and women and to my concept of the sharing between a man and woman which can be expressed sexually."

"I think it's childish and degrading, both to women and men."

"My first hard-core movie made me want to give up sex altogether (and affected most of the other viewers the same way—it was a private showing of somebody's silent film to us fellows, all about twenty-two or twenty-three). I felt completely degraded to be in the same species as the things on the screen. They knew it, too, I think—had smirks on their faces like they were playing in their feces and knew Mommy would be home any minute. My first exposure, I think, to conscious evil. They agreed it was wrong—that was *why* they wanted to do it. I still shake my head in disbelief."

—And was sexist:

"I get hooked into the bookstore or movie theater by the aura of sex, the promise of sensual sight for the eyes. But then I get turned off because the sex is so lacking in warmth, tenderness—it's totally dehumanized and commercialized. The only sincere orgasms are the men's. In other words, it's another situation where the women get the shaft. Pornography is truly sexploitation."

Others, including men who liked pornography, commented that most pornography was too violent:

"Most porno turns me off. There is no feeling, caring, or tenderness in it. A lot of it seems to me to be sexual violence."

"I enjoy pornography, if they are engaged in something I've been similarly engaged in. But it's usually boring and too violent."

"I'm getting a little bored with porno, because it has deteriorated to the basest level of violence, sadomasochism, and abuse possible."

"I do object to the occasional SM themes worked into 'men's magazines,' because I feel they should reflect joy, pleasure, rapture, etc., and not pain, male dominance, force. I'm afraid these unwilled sexual themes may be moving all of us in the wrong direction."

"Most American films seem Mafia produced and therefore violent, perverse, and not very imaginative. I have seen some privately produced films that had a lot of caressing and affection and spontaneity."

"I've gone to a couple of X-rated movies to see love-making, and seen violence instead, which I don't like at all. I used to get off on *Playboy* and all that. Now I can't even do that, since the whole idea seems violent."

Or that they were tired of a "leering" quality:

"Thinking about pornography makes me angry. There is too much emphasis on 'kinky' sex, on sadomasochism and fetishes. Too much 'lust.' I am sick and tired of a leering, sniggering attitude toward sex, of 'dirty' jokes—I've lived through far too much of this already. This sort of thing is the flip side of childhood (and adult) sexual repression and scarcity."

Astonishingly, some men blamed women for the crudity of pornography. They didn't seem to be aware that pornographic magazines are owned and designed by males and edited by men to appeal to men:

"Raunchy provocative stuff turns me off. Seeing such contortions and misaligned anatomy makes me wonder how a woman doing that can expect me to get excited and still consider her a human being and not just a collection of flesh."

"*Hustler* is about as sick as anything I know of today. When will women be human beings? How can you love a woman who isn't human?"

DO MEN THINK PORNOGRAPHY IS EDUCATIONAL?

Some men alluded to the supposed benefits of pornography:

"I think it is educational to look at the various vaginas, clitorises, inner/outer lips, etc. I feel I have improved my sexual technique to some extent through porn books/movies."

"I firmly believe that there is a definite need for pornography for adult use. In many cases it fills the need for viewing the bodies of the opposite sex, thereby aiding masturbatory practices and fulfilling the fantasy world of many people who are alone in the world. Couples who share porno material generally enjoy a more liberal sexual life together and if they cooperate, a more fulfilling one."

"One thing I've noticed—when you find really great detail it's like a key to another world. Some extreme close-up open beaver shots give a real eyeball look at an organ seldom studied in such close range, and they—I think almost always accidentally—transform the female reproduction organ into a work of art."

But when asked, "Do you feel pornography represents certain elemental truths about how men and women really are —both psychologically and sexually?" only a very few men said yes:

"I enjoy pornography. I think it's very truthful. It's very real. I still cannot understand why almost all women who look at pornography utter the words 'gross' or 'filthy' when they do exactly the same things the pictures show."

Several men said that it represented truths only about men, since most pornography was made and bought by men:

"I think all porno is male-oriented and degrading to women. I honestly don't enjoy it. It leaves little doubt as to what most men do or would like to do to women."*

"Most of the porno I have seen is more men's fantasy; the women are just along for the ride."

"Most of the pornography I have seen seems to represent male fantasies about the women they would like to have but in reality are scared to ask out."

"It seems to me it should be possible to produce movies and magazines that both men and women could find exciting. On the other hand, I'm aware of how exciting men (myself included) find it to see women degraded sexually, and so most porno winds up being anti-female."

"It represents certain hidden needs, certain truths about how men and women—but especially men, because most porno is made by men—would like to be sexually and psychologically."

"My wife and I were persuaded to see *Deep Throat* by another couple. It was the 'in' thing to do when it came out. We sat through about half of it and then left. I didn't find it repulsive; in fact, I thought it interesting, cheaply clever, and interesting in a clinical sort of way. I liked the large cocks, I'll tell you that! But my wife said, and I believe her, that it was a rip-off emotionally and sexually and very sexist. I agree. The essential image is of a sex-hungry woman who can't get enough cock to eat. I find this obnoxious. My wife, and other women I have made love to, more or less enjoy sucking, but not as a central obsession. Still, I enjoyed seeing it."

And several men commented that pornography gives a very unreal picture of sexual relations; rather than being sexually educational, it gives sexual misinformation:

---

* Is this true, or is pornography produced by a minority who are giving men the message that this is what they *should* want to do to women?

"The characters are stereotyped and cater to the fantasies of sexual supermen. Just stick it in and they go wild with multiple orgasms."

"Pornography is a drag and is objectionable because it presents fantasy as fact and distorts the expectations of the gullible."

"If I made love the way they do in porno movies, every woman I've ever known would have left me after the first time in the sack. For example, they never show clitoral stimulation (or fumbling!), or how you have to explore with a new person to get things right, etc., etc. I could go on and on. Real stories would be just as erotic. Why do they have to play up the macho myth?"

"The ideas batted around in men's magazines are far from an accurate picture of what men and women are; they are basically fantasies in print."

"It's into infantile fantasies. It does not convey what real men and women are."

"I've seen some soft-porn movies, which seem to have the common theme that a great many women would really like to be raped, and after being thus 'awakened to sex' will become lascivious nymphomaniacs. That seems nasty, false, and possibly dangerous, because it provides a sort of rationale for rape: 'they want it, and anyway, it's really doing them a favor.'"

"It forces a man to think he should be Don Juan placed on earth to please women. And I think it forces a woman to feel she can't have a satisfactory sex life without being a goddess in velvet sheets. I do like informative magazines which are more mature and enlightening. But I don't think a person with a healthy sex life would waste money on today's pornography."

"Films I saw had nothing in common with my experience, past, present, or anticipated. I went mainly because it made me feel worldly to have seen them."

"Porn generally shows women ready to receive, hotter than cheap pistols, looking for a man to satisfy them. A glance, a feel, and the man has them turned on ready for cooking. I'm inclined to disbelieve this. In my limited experience, it's taken a full evening of togetherness and approaching before I felt she was ready to go. And in no case was the indicator the direct porn tearing-at-clothes. Rather, a coming towards me, a sighing and relaxing, a vague statement of admiration while holding hands. I don't believe a woman would respond to me as a porn film queen does."

"Pornography also pictures sex as the main thing in life. Though it may be one of the most important, it's not the most important. The most important thing in life is to love others and to receive love from them—this may include sex, but it also may not."

"It's pretty puerile stuff having little to do with human sexuality. I think it's the fitting, karmic response to a society which denies and invalidates basic human needs such as food and love."

"I don't believe in censorship, but I think someone should have the power to take the sleazy, crappy pornography off the market. The harm this crap has done in starting and perpetuating sexual myths in this country will take several lifetimes to eradicate. Good pornography is healthy and educational and coupled with good sex education would lead to more healthy attitudes in this country towards sex. Turn the pornography business over to the women in this country and the men would soon learn what it's all about."

A few objected strongly to the sexist nature of pornography:

"It is always depicting the woman screwing the man, it is very sexist. I think for the most part it has reflected the thinking of who spent the money which supports the business."

"I read most of the men's magazines as a teenager out of curiosity. I have since discovered them to be sexist, corrupting ego publications."

"I don't care for slick magazines like *Playboy* or *Penthouse*. I think they perpetuate bad attitudes toward women. Pretty boring and certainly sexist."

"I am definitely *not* turned on by ill-made movies of nameless one-dimensional nitwits fucking each other in all conceivable and inconceivable positions, by groups of pseudo-lesbians plunging giant dildos into each other and faking orgasms as though they expected an Oscar, photos of girls with breasts like watermelons, women in black garter belts and fetishist boots with eyes dilated and tongues lolling out, sadomasochist scenes, and any sexual exploitation of children. I respond negatively to all portrayal of people as sex objects. People are sexual, but if they are stripped of all other dimensions and attributes, they become grotesque. I think that pornography is mostly to blame for keeping alive the notion that sex is something a man *does* to a woman."

But again, men had very mixed feelings—even when they found pornography full of misinformation and sexist, they still found it arousing:

"As far as arousing the programmed sexual responses in me, most pornography is terrific. Whether the whole program and its arousal is a good thing is a different matter. Lately the whole thing repels me. I see it more and more as apart from who I'm trying to be. It becomes one more sticky strand of the web of lies that hold me prisoner. It represents certain elemental truths about how men and women are supposed to be—how men and women can be by learning the code by heart, and never thinking or doubting that they really are who someone else says they are. It's obvious that pornography tells us that men are powerful, eternally rigid, and will deign to take their pleasure from a woman. It's also obvious in most pornography that sex is a statement of power, that it is somehow never proper, that the whole damn thing is nothing more than forces directed towards the establishment of restrictive frameworks, and towards the corruption of those same frameworks. It no longer makes sense, but the program is still there inside me, the arousal still occurs, and still feels pleasurable."

Conclusion: Pornography and the definition of "male sexuality"

What is the reason for pornography's increasing importance in our society? According to *Forbes* magazine, by 1978, sex was a larger business than the record and film industries combined, amounting to $4 billion a year. Why do men use and look at pornography? Is it for sexual stimulation or male bonding and identification? What "turns men on" about pornography? Is it because of the viewing of female nudity or sexual activities? Or because of the fantasies of male power that accompany the viewing?

Certainly we all—men and women—have a right to see and read about intimate relationships between people—and in this way, to make more sense of our own lives and feelings. But pornography as we know it does not for the most part serve this purpose. In fact, much of pornography shows a woman submitting to a stronger, threatening, perhaps hostile and violent male.* Even in "soft-core" pornography, in which

---

* Pornography much more frequently shows women rather than men being dominated, tortured, and humiliated. Sadism against women is a cultural theme for the West which goes back to the "witch" burnings of the Middle Ages during which several million women were killed.

a woman is alone on the page, perhaps making eye contact with the viewer but almost always in a "come and get me" pose, the woman is being dominated too—not by a man in the picture, but directly by the viewer, who can use her in any way he pleases. Pornography as we know it—as, indeed, sex itself —is a reflection of the society, with women often being used for men's pleasure. The fact that men dominate women in most of these pictures is such a commonplace that it is not seen as remarkable.

Pornography also reinforces in men the idea that all women can be bought; as one man said, "Pornography is a cheap way of buying a woman." Pornography does not glorify women; most men have contempt for the women they see on the pages, no matter how beautiful. A common form of using pornography is for men to look at it together in a group and to make comments about the women. This is a form of male bonding and reinforces the idea of male ownership of women.* Pornography reminds one of slave markets and slave auctions: each man can appraise, select, and buy the body that suits him. House slaves are the younger, "prettier" women, while field slaves are the hard workers—domestics or wives. The economic pressures on women, especially poor women, to sell their bodies in this way are great.

The continued spread of pornography will make relationships between men and women much slower to change, because pornography reinforces in men so many of the old and stereotyped attitudes to women and toward themselves that have done so much damage—both to women and men—already. This is true just as much of pornography that shows the woman/women dominating men as it is of depictions of men dominating women, since this is only a role reversal and still centers on the same definitions of sex involving all the issues we have discussed in this book so far. Pornography keeps men believing women are the way they want women to be, or have been told women are (either submissive or dominant, "bitchy"), and fortifies men's belief in their own sex role. Men, reading and looking at pornography, know they are sharing in something other men see, and assume therefore that this is what all "real men" want, identify with, and enjoy.

---

* Most men do not look at pornography with a woman, as most women do not like the way women are portrayed in pornography. Also, men looking at pornography together also find that it is another way of proclaiming one's masculinity for other men to see, and a way for men to have sexual feelings together while still focused on a "heterosexual" object.

DOMINATION-SUBMISSION

But "taking" someone during sex, or "being taken"—although this is the basic definition of rape, and one of the most basic themes of pornography—can also have other, more positive meanings (as discussed in chapter 4).

MEN'S DESIRE TO BE TAKEN

Following are statements from a minority of men in this study, mostly regarding their experiences and desires to be dominated. Some men had tried and enjoyed being dominated, bound, spanked, or participating in other similar activities; a few of these men also mentioned playing "mock" rape with a woman or binding or restraining her.

Some men said they fantasized being raped by women—but their fantasies were not of rape* but of being sexually desired and pleased, often by more than one woman:

"I've often thought about being raped—not out in the street, but by my sexual partner. Such aggressiveness would make me feel aroused and desired by my mate. Also I sincerely have a strong religious conviction that premarital sex is a no-no, and rape would take away all pangs of guilt. Rather it would put me in the 'throes of ecstasy.' "

---

* Men can never be raped by a woman in the same way a woman can be raped by a man—or a man can be by another man—since cultural symbols do not allow female sexual aggression to be humiliating to a man.

"I've often had fantasies of being raped by women. A group of aggressive feminists catch me in an arm lock at the foot of the stairs and proceed to feel up my crotch and squeeze my arse,* saying, 'How do *you* like being treated as a sex object!' (Well, it's a nice fantasy anyhow.) Personally, I think that female rapists ought to get government grants. (But there should be the death penalty for a woman who just teases you.) Admittedly, I would not at all like being raped by another man."

"I have not been raped by a woman yet, unfortunately. But I am patiently waiting for such a moment because it could make me feel sexual if I caused a woman to attack me out of lustful desire. Female motorcycle gangs seem to fascinate me. If I were in a large city where female gangs existed I would like to flaunt myself in hope of being raped. I have not sexually attacked a woman and I never plan to."

A large number of men said they liked or thought they would like a woman to be aggressive and dominate them:

"During the heat of passion some wild ideas do occur to me. One that sure has is to be attacked and anally fucked, by a dildo or her finger inside me."

"When I get in the mood, I want my wife to do with my body what she desires, whether it be tie me up or put me over her knees and spank me, hard as she can—that really excites me and I have been known to have an orgasm like that—or she gets on top of me and rapes me. It makes me feel helpless but so secure. I get sexually excited just thinking about it. Also, when I can make my wife hurt and scream and feel helpless, that makes me feel sexual, super. When she says it hurts, I feel powerful and don't want to let her up."

"One of the most exciting things to me is when my lover ties me up, and stuffs my nose, ears, ass up with things—she blindfolds me and hits me—hard—and fucks me (up the ass) with things. She is in complete control. I beg her to stop, but she won't, and humiliates me further. This is very pleasurable and makes me feel ecstatic and reduced to a child. I allow her to control me completely."

---

* An interesting analysis of this type of plot in pornography is contained in the book *Pornography: Men Possessing Women*, by Andrea Dworkin.

"We play female domination, tease, talk, discuss her experiences with other people (she talks about what but not who) and anything else we read about or think up on our own—domination, whipping, nursing, urolagnia, licking her 'clean' when she comes home, paying her, being shut off and allowed to kiss it—or kneel in front of it and masturbate, be dismounted during intercourse and 'allowed' to watch her vibrate herself off and go to sleep—plus other things. You name it and we not only fantasize, we do it."

"I act out my fantasies with a prostitute I see regularly. She comes into the living room where I am seated to 'arrest' me. She handcuffs me. I am told to remove my shoes and socks before being handcuffed. She leads me by the arm to 'jail.' Often I am an unruly prisoner. That means that I get slapped in the mouth. If I really go too far, I am forced to kneel at the foot of the bed and get my butt whipped with a coat hanger. I do not want to be tortured, so I feel that I must stand up to her. Then she locks me up for an undetermined length of time in the closet, which is spacious enough to be a cell. When she is thoughtful, she pours water into a dish for me. I lie on the floor, helpless. When she releases me from the cell, I remain handcuffed. I must obey her orders or suffer consequences. Often I must eat her pussy or kiss her feet. The party is terminated with her getting on top of me and fucking me. My orgasms are fantastically explosive. Once I bust my nuts, our conversation gets cheerful and normal because the party is over."

Or fantasized being submissive to a woman:

"I have lots of sexual fantasies. Some I am tied up and whipped and mistreated and women smother me and use me poorly. I am their slave and eventually I am murdered for their pleasure. In others I am burned or tortured, etc. In others I am doing the torturing to beautiful young women. I wish I did not have these thoughts. I get excited about being mistreated when I feel worthless, and about mistreating a woman when I feel women have done me wrong—I feel if I actually did these things I'd get in trouble."

"Sadomasochism is not at all appealing to me, but being dominated by a woman is. I would like to experience being a sex slave to a woman who wears the traditional black sheer stockings, garter belt, 'merry widow,' etc. I wonder how I would react. Being forced by her to dress as a woman and act as one goes along with this fantasy."

"My fantasy concerns a very dominant female, an amazon of great beauty, clad in super erotic lingerie, leather or rubber, who is skilled in bondage and discipline along with excellent knowledge of sado masochism. I am tied, bound, forced to dress as a woman in lingerie, while she sodomizes me with fake penises she straps on. She inserts vibrators up my rectum and masturbates me to the point of climax without release for hours at a time. I am subjected to spankings and whippings without cause or notice."

Or being raped by men:

"I start off by fantasizing that my high school basketball team, which I'm on, has just finished an away game at an all-black school. We beat them by one basket over which there was a lot of question, there is a lot of name calling by both teams as we go to different parts of the locker room, and we're really happy because we beat them. To avoid any hassles each team uses different showers. I'm the last one to leave the showers, and on the way back I become lost in the maze of strange lockers. Then suddenly I turn a corner and I find myself in the middle of the black team, who are all drying off from the showers too. I quickly turn to leave but my exit is blocked. Their captain comes toward me, and he tells me that I should be taught a lesson for beating them. First he tells me to dry off his whole body. So, completely nude, I do this. Then he stands up on the bench, spreads his legs, and tells me to blow-dry his asshole, balls, and cock. I do this too. When I start on his cock, it starts to harden and he orders me to go down on it. I willingly do this. Just about when he is about to come, I feel a stiff prick going up my ass. This goes on till I've serviced and been fucked by all the team's cocks. With jism from a whole team dripping out of my ass and mouth, my arms and feet are tied. I am then made to get into a tall gym clothes locker, then one by one the team members piss, then jack off on me, while calling me names. Then the door is shut and locked on me. Later my teammates come looking for me, they hear my calls for help, force the door open, and find me there, tied, nude, abused, and covered with piss and come. The rest of the jocks agree that it was a vengeance against our team, which it was, but they'll never know how much I wanted it to happen."

Other men said they played "mock" rape:

"My wife and I have pretended rape as part of our love games."

"I have never done or wanted to do anything resembling rape. The rape-fantasy things that I have played around with with my primary lover have been acting-out episodes, harmless and void of the kind of hatred feelings which seem to accompany rape."

"I have *pretended* to rape my wife (ripped the clothes from her body; however, I know she was very willing and put up a token resistance). We got enjoyment from this, *not* because of cruelty, but she felt I had a passion for *her* that I couldn't control. It was only play, acting rough (tough on clothes) but being very careful *not* to hurt her. She got a big thrill from this if it was not expected and on rare occasions."

"I have enjoyed a kind of ruggedness (as well as softness) with my partner, wrapping her up in my arms and legs and wedging against her in such a way as to communicate that I have captured her and she is my prisoner. I may place my hands over her eyes. The contrast of being heavily masculine toward her at one time, and then very soft with her seems to heighten the whole experience."

"I have never literally raped a woman. But I have stripped (torn) clothes off of some of my lovers. It's fun."

Some men liked being bound:

"At ten, I had a strong feeling for a boy one or two years older; I provoked him; we struggled; I was aroused, especially by the constriction of my head and neck. From that experience on, I never could refrain from fantasies of being bound up: I kept it secret, not to be laughed at, or thought strange. I practiced bondage of myself at night. Ejaculation came at eleven, twelve, or thirteen, in bondage and fantasies of a mocking and dominating partner (probably the same boy). Today I still like it but I don't feel guilty—I like my lover to tie me and gag me, and clench his or her hand around my throat while jerking me off."

"I'm interested in both bondage and spanking occasionally. It is as much fun to be tied up as to be in control. I like the feeling of being tied up and subject to her will. I like mild spanking then—and unexpected things—like having my cock teased, a dildo forced in my ass all of a sudden, and so forth. We always leave the ropes loose—so you don't lose circulation, you could probably get loose by yourself, and when you have come and want to get free fast and hug and cuddle, the ropes can be off in a flash. It's the fantasy of being subject to someone's will that is the turn-on. There is no real pain. If there was I'm sure my wife would never submit. For myself, I like the feeling of not being able to stop her when it feels too good. When I tie my wife to the bed or a table, I like to eat her out until she comes, because she won't let me do it otherwise. I also like to tease her—by putting my cock in her vagina and getting her worked up—then pulling out abruptly, letting her ease down a bit, working up again, etc., to a big explosive orgasm."

And some wanted to try either being bound, or restraining their partner:

"I would like for me and my wife to be more forthright in saying and doing what we want. What we have is good, but we tend to do the same things time after time with only minor variations. Quite frankly, I'd like to do 'kinky things' like from time to time to indulge in bondage, and role playing."

"I have no desire to inflict pain on my lover—at least that I am aware of—but I have toyed with the idea, the fantasy, of restraining her so that everything is under my control. I'm not so sure I could work her up to the white heat that I'd like to see her in before I gratified myself, however, since I'm not so good at self-control sometimes. I guess one's partner would have to feel very comfortable—trusting and trusted—in order to 'let go' enough to engage in this kind of sexual activity."

"I would like to experiment with tying down or being tied down during sex to see how the situation of complete helplessness and the consequent complete trust in another can contribute to sexual excitement. Light spanking might be fun, too. So far I have not found a participating partner, perhaps because I haven't gotten around to asking. I have found it almost impossible to say this to someone."

Some men liked, or wanted to try, being spanked:

"I find a strange delight in lying on my stomach, being spanked with one hand while, with another, she has reached under and authoritatively gripped my balls. She knows them as my place of utter vulnerability, and when her hand is on them I melt. When my ass is spanked, I feel utterly submissive as well. She likes to be spanked too, and I have on a few occasions 'taken' her, by overpowering her with my strength, eating her out, spanking her, and then fucking her. We keep talking about tying each other up and teasing and lovingly dominating one another, but we never seem to get around to it, perhaps because we would each rather be tied."

"I am fascinated by spankings, willing either to give or take. A good spanking gives a hot, burning sting while giving sexual joy and pleasure at the same time."

"Spanking *most definitely*. Every man should be spanked now and then. It is sexually exciting—even the very thought of spanking excites me."

"To tell the truth, I am a little interested in violent sex. I think that I would like to be whipped, not too hard of course, with a broad leather belt, perhaps like a shaving strap."

Some men said that extreme physical sensations were fulfilling and satisfying to them:

"I love to get a good hard whack on the ass while I am fucking her. The harder the better, and I like it if it just grazes my balls, or it can even hit my asshole. I feel it all the way through to my cock, or the base of it inside the skin. It makes it feel like a fire is there."

"During masturbation, I sometimes stimulate my nipples with clothespins (which I also attach to the scrotum). It feels very good."

"I use body oils that burn the sensitive parts of my body, specifically my scrotum and armpits. The pain from the burn is sometimes so intense I almost scream. I love this pain nevertheless."

Other similar forms of sex men liked or were interested in included:

"Now that my wife and I are alone, we are less inhibited. I find it exciting to be there when she is urinating, for example, and have gone so far out as to try some 'golden showers.' She sits on me and lets go, and I can have a rather rapid erection that way. Again, the very personal touch and contact . . . always important . . . the coming near another human, as near as possible. I like her to hold my penis when I'm urinating sometimes. Or kneel before her when she is, and put my hand between her legs to feel the wet warmth touch my fingers. I like to tear down inhibitions, to know what I am really like, and what I really enjoy. I'm not afraid to accept what I find I like, nor to reject what I find I dislike. But I do want to continue exploring my own sexuality."

"I enjoy the silky feeling of my wife's nylon panties. They excite erotic feelings in me. Sometimes I rub her panties on my penis while masturbating, but I don't do it very often."

Are these fantasies of being dominated, and desires for other forms of violent sex built into the definition of sex and sexual relationships in our culture—or is there some other explanation for them? Is it possible they sometimes reflect a massive frustration with the lack of meaningful or close relationships, a frustration that turns to violence to break the tension?

Some men saw a connection between violent sex and anger or other strained feelings in the relationship:

"I have hit my wife but not in a lovemaking setting. I hated it both times and immediately wanted to take back the blow. It certainly didn't help our relationship and I felt servile —because of the uncontrolled act of anger, and the teeming frustration. But I can imagine her slapping me or me slapping her at other times, in a teasing way, and it might be quite exciting—kind of a release of tension which would allow us to love each other better, having gotten all our petty annoyances out."

"I used to fantasize doing horrible things to my wife and her lover—like putting needles through her nipples or having her stand with my sword between her legs, point in vagina, and then telling her to squat and she did. Sick stuff from a sick hurt person. I never wanted to act on these—the rational mind almost died but not quite ever lost control."

"My wife used to hassle me when I wanted to drink beer and watch television—she'd keep it up until I'd threaten to leave, then she'd stop me from leaving and I'd respond by saying that if she didn't get off my case I'd have to hurt her— and her answer always was 'Go ahead.' Then usually I'd undress her and squeeze her breasts as hard as I was capable of —drunk—then I'd slap her face and breasts—several times I raped her—I guess it was rape—although she could have ended it at any time by telling me to stop and she knew it. Several times instead of my hurting her, I'd say, 'If you hate me so much, hit me,' and she would—once with a poker and once repeatedly with a heavy leather belt, brass buckle end out—and I let her. One can get some legitimate thrills out of controlled pain, particularly if working off aggressive or hostile feelings—which people do get."

"I felt strong sexual desires when I started going with my lover. Then, as I fell more deeply in love, I started to feel many other emotions, like that I needed her, and this made me feel like raping her—just like attacking her at my will and doing just what I wanted to do with her. I resented needing her and her control over me because I needed and wanted her. We've worked through this now. I love her very much."

One man questioned why he felt these things:

"I wonder why I have these thoughts. Maybe it's because of the frustration. This isn't the kind of fantasy that I have about anybody—it is only about the one I love—and feel vulnerable to. Sometimes I'm afraid she doesn't love me as much as I love her. Maybe I fantasize that she forces me to have sex with her because I sometimes worry that she doesn't desire me as much as I desire her. If she forces me to screw her, it shows she wants me and needs me. Probably I fantasize her humiliating me, beating me, and being very rough because I feel insecure that she doesn't love me as much as I love her, or doesn't desire me as much as I desire her. It seems crazy that being humiliated would make me aroused, but it does."

But a few men defended the concepts of domination and submission in sex as being meaningful and serious exchanges in their own right:

"My fantasies usually consist of having the power to drive my partner mad with pleasure and I want her to be able to do that to me. Mutual submission is very important to me, it's a matter of ultimate giving and openness, to share the responsibility, the roles. In *Hiroshima, Mon Amour* she said in bed, 'Destroy me.' To me that meant destroy my inhibitions, my civility, transform me, become all feeling, all human animal."

"I find rapes in porno books repulsive. The only violence which is meaningful is a mutually shared violent ritual—i.e., agreed upon and ending in mutual intense consummation. Rape is to force someone else to let you fuck them, to threaten them with violence to submit, or to force someone to do things that they don't want to do, and don't want you to do to them. Rape is very traumatic. The difference between consent and rape is that the rapist doesn't care if the person wants him, he just forces and causes fear in the object of his attack. It is an act of hatred towards the person being raped. Mutually desired violence is different, somehow we pass beyond certain limits and forge deeper bonds together through certain acts involving trust."

"I've read the standard interpretation of the bondage fantasy, that tying up a woman removes her threatening aspect. Since she cannot reject anything, she can *only* passively accept whatever is done to her. But it feels good to me to be bound and helpless too. I know there's gratification for the bound as well as the binder. The standard interpretation of that: being bound frees one to accept what one really wants, but due to inhibition, cannot accept unless helpless, and so not responsible. I reckon these interpretations have some validity, but it feels to me like a lot more than that is involved. Sometimes it's really a magical feeling. There's a whole ethos, an entire aesthetic to it.

"There is such a thing as tender bondage, in which the prevailing emotional component is adoration, not the need to hurt. And from the other side, one can want to be bound without wanting to be treated sadistically. Sadomasochism and domination-submission partake of the same spirit, there is a common boundary where they meet (bondage may be that frontier), but at their extremes they are so effectively different as to place them in separate worlds. Domination-submission-humiliation role playing, or even tying and tickling, is light-years from severe pain, torture, mutilation, and murder. Pain and damage are the measure. The presence of the need to inflict or the need to receive pain distinguishes sadomasochism from domination-submission. But as meaningful as the effect of the play is the emotional content."

However, most men had never experimented with physical sadomasochism, violence, or bondage and discipline, and said that they were not interested in trying them; a few men explained their reasons:

"The whole sweep-me-away-with-your-frenzy syndrome, I think, is the other half of the desire to control, dictate, dominate. I don't like either part."

"A few years ago I had the brilliant idea that at a certain point pleasure and pain were indistinguishable. I decided that as she neared or was experiencing orgasm I'd give her a few sharp slaps on the face. After one or two tries I junked the idea. Hurting someone even if it thrills them ain't sex to me. Sex is tenderness and softness. The thought of inflicting pain during sex, or for that matter anytime, is obnoxious to me."

"I don't find violence sexually exciting, and in general violence and pain repel me. Sometimes I would like to knock hell out of somebody, but that is in anger. I don't see anything sexy about pain or about dominating, or about conflict."

7
SEX AND LOVE BETWEEN MEN

"I was almost seventeen years old when I first fell deeply in love. The intensity and the depth of the feeling frightened and overwhelmed me. At the time I was working as a cashier in a large supermarket. I enjoyed the work and enjoyed the close contact with people, especially the employees. After work we often got together and went bowling or played pool, etc. I was especially attracted to one of the fellows and we double-dated. It was on one of these double dates that I started having sexual fantasies. While he was making love to a girl in the back seat, I thought of him while I was kissing my girl in the front seat and wondered what it would feel like to be made love to by him. After the date I asked him to spend the night at my house and he accepted. I knew that something was happening to me but I wasn't sure what. After he fell asleep I got up, put my clothes on, and went to a nearby church. I knelt there and prayed, begging God for guidance. I cried, dried my tears, and returned home to bed and the strangest, most enduring relationship of my life began. I was surprised when he responded to me sexually and I discovered what his kisses were like. I was in a state of shock at what had happened to me when I realized I was in love.

"We both had feelings of guilt and fought the relationship. We stopped double-dating and avoided each other like the plague. Once or twice I visited the places that he frequented and remained in the background watching him. After a stint in the armed forces we got together one night. The feelings were still there but I had developed some self-control and we touched and kissed and that was it. After that we got together about twice a month for several years, but didn't touch. I always remember the magnetism of his body chemistry in relation to mine."

ATTITUDES TOWARD HOMOSEXUALITY

Has there been any change in attitude toward homosexuality? Although, judging from the answers received, there is still a great deal of homophobia, at the same time many men are beginning to realize that this attitude is based on prejudice and that each individual has a right to his or her own sexual preference.

The vilification of homosexual contacts has had a long history in our society. Kinsey put it quite well:

> The general condemnation of homosexuality in our particular culture apparently traces to a series of historical circumstances which had little to do with the protection of the individual or the preservation of the social organization of the day. In Hittite, Chaldean, and early Jewish codes there were no over-all condemnations of such activity, although there were penalties for homosexual activities between persons of particular social status or blood relationships, or homosexual relationships under other particular circumstances, especially when force was involved. The more general condemnation of all homosexual relationships (especially male) originated in Jewish history in about the seventh century B.C., upon the return from the Babylonian exile. Both mouth-genital contacts and homosexual activities had previously been associated with the Jewish religious service, as they had been with the religious services of most of the other peoples of that part of Asia, and just as they have been in many other cultures elsewhere in the world. In the wave of nationalism which was then developing among the Jewish people, there was an attempt to disidentify themselves with their neighbors* by breaking with many of the

---

* Especially their non-patriarchal neighbors.

customs which they had previously shared with them. Many of the Talmudic condemnations were based on the fact that such activities represented the way of the pagan, and they were originally condemned as a form of idolatry rather than a sexual crime. Throughout the middle ages homosexuality was associated with heresy. The reform in the custom (the mores) soon, however, became a matter of morals, and finally a question for action under criminal law.*

Kinsey, who was originally a biologist, also tells us that other animals routinely have homosexual relationships:

The impression that infra-human mammals more or less confine themselves to heterosexual activities is a distortion of the fact which appears to have originated in a man-made philosophy, rather than in specific observations of mammalian behavior. Biologists and psychologists who have accepted the doctrine that the only natural function of sex is reproduction have simply ignored the existence of sexual activity which is not reproductive. They have assumed that heterosexual responses are a part of an animal's innate, "instinctive" equipment, and that all other types of sexual activity represent "perversions" of the "normal instincts." Such interpretations are, however, mystical. They do not originate in our knowledge of the physiology of sexual response, and can be maintained only if one assumes that sexual function is in some fashion divorced from the physiologic processes which control other functions of the animal body. It may be true that heterosexual contacts outnumber homosexual contacts in most species of mammals, but it would be hard to demonstrate that this depends upon the "normality" of heterosexual responses, and the "abnormality" of homosexual responses.†

---

* Alfred C. Kinsey et al., *Sexual Behavior in the Human Female* (New York: Pocket Books, 1965), pp. 481–82.

† *Ibid.*, pp. 448–50.

In fact, even the defense of heterosexuality (as the only "natural" form of sexuality) as the basis for the family can be questioned on historical grounds. The earliest families were not the nuclear, "heterosexual" family as we know it, but included the mother, sisters and brothers, aunts, uncles, and so on in a loose grouping. There was no "father," and the relationship between mother and child was nowhere near as primary as we believe it to be today—in fact, sometimes children, mothers, and sisters became confused as to whose child was whose. However, it was not considered to be an important issue, as each would receive nurturance from various members of the group or from whichever members felt most sympathetic to one another. Indeed, for centuries, as mentioned earlier, the role of intercourse in causing pregnancy was not known. During these centuries, the clan-family was a viable social institution whose demise came only with the changeover to patriarchy and male ownership of children around 8000–5000 B.C.*

However, in our society, despite all the recent publicity regarding gay rights, there is still an enormous amount of prejudice, and gay men must, for the most part, hide their feelings. In this chapter, we will examine these attitudes, then look at who gay men are and how they feel about their sexual and personal lives.

"In our society you can go to war and kill a guy, but God help you if you're caught in bed with one."

"I have known for a long time that I have homosexual tendencies. This *used* to worry me until I fell in love with another man for a while. And it was just that. I wasn't gay or some screaming faggot, I just fell in love with someone and that person happened to be male."

"I see no real reason for homosexuality to be taboo. But like a lot of other things, it just did not fit into the society (openly, of course) that we were forced to enter (by birth). Before World War II, I can remember when mentally retarded children were kept in hiding from the public eye. When these children were big enough to cause a lot of trouble, they were taken to the *insane asylum* (as it was called then) and some of them were never seen again by the people who knew them. A homosexual was considered the same as mentally retarded except worse."

* See pages 481–487.

"Why has homosexuality been a taboo? Do you believe in homosexual marriage?" "If you have never had a physical or sexual relationship with another man, would you enjoy one?"

There is still a great deal of prejudice against homosexuality —and fear of being homosexual—in our society:*

"Homosexuality is sick and disgusting. It's against the laws of nature."

"It's unnatural and unclean."

"Homosexuals are defective human beings, mostly brought about by themselves and rejection by society because of their own tendencies. I object to homosexual marriages, homosexual teachers, homosexual anything where a queer is allowed to publicly boast about his abnormality, or influence anyone else to accept him."

"It is contrary to the laws of nature and of God. This is an abuse of the organs for their divinely ordained purpose."

"It is an unnatural act between two people of the same sex. Most homosexuals are gross and disgusting person-wise in addition to the acts they perform."

"I am a retired policeman and the only thing I liked to do with faggots was beat them up. I have no sympathy or understanding or tolerance of queers, gays, faggots, nor do I want to. They're all degenerates and dangerous."

"Homosexuality is a cop-out, likened to alcoholism. Both can be treated and cured. Reading of homosexuals and their experiences, you can smell the cop-out on the realities of life from the beginning. I know this, for I was a psychological cop-out for a long time (alcoholic) and only one cop-out can smell another one."

"Homosexuality is a taboo because it's repulsive to most people. I feel sorry for queers as I feel sorry for sick people and I feel they should be encouraged to try to change. As long as they limit their sex to consenting adults they remain merely pathetic creatures. Homosexual marriage is a farce."

And another, newer form of prejudice:

"Between men, it's revolting. Between women—it excites me."

* In fact, the majority of replies reflected this in some form.

Some men took advantage of this question to criticize and ridicule homosexual men:*

"Homosexuality is all a matter of a simple genetic flaw present at birth. Genetic homosexuality as opposed to learned or special situation homosexuality will be a part of society until genetic engineering becomes a reality."

"Homosexuality has been a taboo, and properly so, because it is a psychological aberration which threatens the family unit. The fact that the American Psychiatric Society recently declared homosexuality not to be aberrant says much more about the state of psychology today than it does about homosexuality. To their credit, I understand the declaration was made by a minority and the majority would like the chance to vote again!"

"Homosexuals are queers. A man is not a mother. A flat chest is not a pair of boobs. Sticking it into an ass is not the same as screwing a cunt. They should be treated for their disease."

"Homosexuality is strongly and positively related to the decline of Empire. Just look at the USA today."

Others saw it as an opportunity to insist on their own lack of interest in homosexual activities and to defend their own "heterosexuality":

"I can honestly say that I am 100 percent heterosexual. I have never had a remotest homosexual desire or inclination let alone experience. I have never been approached by a homosexual or desired to be. If I were to pass judgment I would say homosexuals are or have been emotionally and/or psychologically misdirected."

"I consider myself very broad-minded and liberated in MOST ways concerning sex, but I feel that our Creator made men with a penis and women with a vagina for a reason, and that's for intercourse, and male homosexuality in particular completely turns me off!!!"

"I'm a 100 percent lady's man. To me the idea of a man touching me makes me want to fight."

---

* In fact, as Kinsey pointed out, "homosexual" and "heterosexual" are more properly used as adjectives describing *activities*, rather than people. However, in this text, these terms are sometimes used, as above, for the sake of clarity and simplicity.

Many men, while stating that they believe the individual has a right to his own choices, still also felt that there was something "wrong" with homosexuality:

"I think homosexuality is an unnatural act but if the parties involved like it and don't force it on anyone else it's their business."

"Homosexuality is O.K. if you like it or are inclined toward it but I feel that they are mixed up in the mind."

"While I've never been gay, and probably won't be, and I even think to a degree it's unnatural and I do think it's irreligious, I feel strongly about the rights of individuals. Each to his or her own. It might strike you funny but when it comes to rights I'd never want to discriminate against or for a woman because of her sex preference, just her sex."

Several homosexual men pointed out that some men who consider themselves heterosexual can feel an attraction for other men from time to time, and fear these feelings:

"I think all men have homosexual feelings at one time or another and are terrified of them. In this sexually obsessed society, it seems inevitable that any 'threat' to the sexual status quo would be feared."

"The thought of two men having sex repulses people. I think men are afraid of it because they may secretly have those kinds of feelings. Men aren't supposed to be loving to one another. They are supposed to be competitive beings."

"People always want to categorize people to make them easier to deal with, more a label, less a person. Plus, most people have homosexual tendencies they want to suppress. They don't want to admit to their fantasies."

"Homosexuality has been a taboo because it's a temptation."

Indeed, some men recognized their own homosexual feelings, or had had isolated homosexual experiences, but found them distressing, because of their contempt for homosexuality:

"The greatest displeasure of my sex life is my own bisexuality, which I have yet to finally resolve. I lust to engage in what is morally reprehensible for me."

"I enjoy sex with men, but my upbringing leaves me with such guilt feelings that it is almost self-defeating. About twice a month, though, I nearly go up a wall, and just have to go out and scare up something! Even in a small town, gay sex isn't hard to find."

"I had my first recent homosexual experience three weeks ago. He was not a new partner. After a thirteen-year period of abstinence, I wrote him and he drove a hundred miles directly from the post office for a two-hour session—or honeymoon—of *physical* and *emotional* release. I hugged that man until we were exhausted and breathless. I cried, 'Oh, Tom, oh, Tom, oh, Tom.' I could barely reach around him but I tried to squeeze him in to me. We both married thirteen years ago and each has one child. Meanwhile, my life is in turmoil, my wife knows something is going on, I only know to go see my therapist. I don't know what's going to happen. I dread thinking that anyone would find out. The worst thing is that I half think I'm disgusting and disgraceful for doing it. Why do I crave men? Why don't I like my wife? I don't know. God help me."

One gay man* spoke at length about trying to change himself:

"One of my pet peeves is people who say of gays, 'Well, if you people want to choose to be like that . . .' I did not choose to be this way. Most of us did not choose to be this way. It's just the way we are. We did not choose to be gay any more than heterosexuals choose to be 'straight.' It's just the way we are by nature.

"Many of us have desired and wished and *prayed* to be changed, but as far as I can learn we cannot change or be changed either by psychology, psychiatry, or religion. Most people who thought they were changed by any of these means soon found that they were still gay.

"I would like to tell you one of my secular attempts at trying to make myself 'straight,' even though it did not succeed. I went to heterosexual porno movies and looked at

---

* Most men who preferred sex with other men used and accepted the word "gay"; however, one man said, "I don't like the word 'gay'; I don't identify with its connotations—though I don't deny liking sex with members of my own sex."

naked women, and said to myself such things as 'Look at that hot, tight, juicy pussy. Wow! I'd like to shove my hot, hard cock up there and fuck her good.' I looked at the women and said these kinds of things to myself, but I have to admit *I was lying to myself* as fast as I could talk or think. When the naked men with their erections entered the pictures I was excited by them without any attempts to try to make myself think I was.

"As I have learned to accept myself, I have realized that being gay is not bad, is not sad, is not something to try to avoid or change. Our only reason, my only reason for wanting to change in the past has been because of society's disapproval, because I know/knew my friends would not approve of it or accept it, or *me*. And because I had not accepted myself. I am finally learning to accept myself as and for who and what I am. I want to say, I am gay and I am proud. I'm almost there, I almost can."

In fact, most gay men said they still had to hide their sexual feelings for other men most of the time:

"No one at work knows that I'm gay, or at least not to my knowledge. My feedback on gayness hasn't been the best from my fellow workers, so I try to keep them in the dark. I have a 'romance' going on with a co-worker—but in reality we don't do much. My parents ought to be suspicious by now, but they have never said anything, and I haven't told them anything. No use causing an issue that isn't necessary. I don't go to great extremes to hide my gayness, and if they did find out, it wouldn't be that big of a deal. But why risk ill feelings."

"I don't take open stances on gay issues, except among my closest friends. For the most part I play the role of a straight man that just happens to have a roommate that is twenty-eight and has been living with him for four years."

"No one at my office knows. I don't think they need to know. My parents are in their late seventies and it would serve no purpose to tell them. Also, I want to appear straight to the world since I know that's where all *good* happens—I'm talking about salaries, grants, promotions, appointments. I don't feel compelled to tell anyone about the gay side of me. I do smart when I read about gay priests being asked not to participate in church life by bishops, or when churches say that gay people cannot serve on the clergy, or when I hear youngsters scream 'Fag!' at people."

"I used to be much closer to my mother than now. This has to do with my being gay. I feel bad about this—someday I'd like to just tell her and hope we can be honest and closer again, but I just don't know how she'd take it."

"My behavior is very reserved. Thus, few people guess that I am gay. My reserved behavior did not originate as a cover for my homosexuality, but now I use it as such—not so much as a conscious front or deception, but I just don't allow myself as much freedom or relaxation in my behavior as I really want. Often I'm not aware of how much self-control I am exercising until I'm in a situation where I feel free enough to allow myself to let my hair down. Then it comes as a great relief."

"When I was twenty-four my assistant was killed while standing next to me while we were in Vietnam. We had been partners (lovers) for six years. I have never felt so deeply attached to anyone. I thought I would explode inside from some tremendous pressure, but I never uttered a sound or shed a tear until ten years later. I was afraid people would know."

A minority of heterosexual men expressed a mixture of openness and negativity or ambivalence:

"I believe that homosexual feelings and contacts are O.K. and should be more open; but I don't think the gay world should be self-glorifying, as it tends to be often. I think the Anita Bryant bit is a horrible piece of invasion of human rights—sexual McCarthyism. But some parading by gays of their new freedoms is almost as repulsive. I have no problem with homosexuals as homosexuals. I do have problems with their claim to be untroubled. I have found them to be the opposite, generally."

"To me a homosexual is a man in all respects but for the fact that his deepest emotional needs and sexual needs are for another man. I have two daughters. How they will turn out I don't know. I do feel at this time that I hope they are happy, content, and fulfilled in their relationships. If this means lesbianism for them I hope I understand and accept it then. I had very miserable married years, so I think happiness with someone you love is more important than with one who is acceptable to others."

One man commented on his own prejudice:

"I am a devoted and tested heterosexual. But I do have an anecdote that may be of interest. While working on my master's at Columbia I rented a room in the apartment of a couple whose kids were away at college. The other available room was first rented by a young woman. When she moved out it was taken by a 'flaming faggot' studying at Juilliard School of Music. His behavior was so flamboyantly effeminate that I seized upon an opportunity to remark that, while I had no antagonism to another's preferences, I myself preferred girls. His response was terrific. In a loftily affected manner (patterned after an especially epicene George Sanders) he said: 'We-hull . . . *you* don't have to worry. You're not at all attractive anyway!' Obviously, I wouldn't have said to the girl previously ensconced in the room: 'See here, I don't want you trying to lay me because I've another lover already.' What this episode indicated to me was that I was actually guarding against my own unconscious impulses more than against a likely confrontation with this 'queer.' I am perfectly willing to accept a certain suppressed homosexual longing within myself. But that's as far as it goes."

Only a few men were neutral:

"I have had limited experience with men but would not now be interested nor have I been for a great many years. I do have some friends who are gay but this is merely a result of having met men and become friendly with them and later on happening to find out they were gay and this in itself would not change my friendship or dislike of them, for that matter."

Some men were trying to develop a more open point of view:

"I have not had a physical or sexual relationship with another man. In high school and college when our friendships got too close it was uncomfortable, we did not know how to deal with our feelings, so we let the friendship go. The taboo must still be with me, from time to time I have been attracted to a good-looking man and the feeling terrifies me. I want to get past that because until I do I may not be able to develop any male friendships."

A few heterosexual men made statements in favor of gay rights:

"I don't think my homosexual feelings are very strong. But I believe men need the right to show this kind of physical affection without fear of reprisal."

"I think men should be able to express strong friendships and affection however they want, including sexually."

A few men said they would like to have a closer physical relationship with another man/men:

"This question is forcing me to be honest. In my early twenties I had a friend. Two or three times we masturbated each other (two times drunk, once not). I enjoyed it—physically and the closeness. We were uptight though and *never* even talked about it. We never really let go. I haven't done anything with another man in about six or seven years. To be honest, I think about it sometimes. Not just masturbating—but really making love—emotional sharing—sexuality. Experiencing our masculinity. I haven't talked to anybody about this but I don't feel guilty about it. Perhaps because since my involvement with my friend I've experienced enough with women that I'm comfortable and confident. I don't think my feelings would go away if I let go with another man. I would love to kiss—French-kiss—with a lot of tongue with another man I felt close to. It feels good to write this. I enjoyed saying that about 'a lot of tongue.' I'd love to experience another man's body fully."

"On one or two rare occasions I have felt that a deep friendship needed some sort of consummation. But I never acted on it."

"I'm uptight about it, but I love my best male friend and I'd like to someday express it sexually."

"I have never tried sex with a man. I would like to try fellatio with a man. I think I will enjoy it both physically and psychologically. Physically I am fascinated with my own penis, the way it looks, smells and feels in my hand, these feelings projected on another man's penis let me assume that I will enjoy fellatio physically. Psychologically, I think that it will also be enjoyable. In my understanding, a sexual act with a woman satisfies my natural need to feel stronger, and to feel like making the pleasure happen. I do not think that I have a potential of pure homosexuality, but with the pressures of modern life I think even the strongest man in the world needs moments of security, which can be generated by the feeling that a strong man is giving him affection. I think that once in a while I may enjoy it. But I would never kiss a man in any way. If I will ever be affectionate to another man, I think that will only involve genitals and perhaps touching."

"I like an attractive male physique. As I have become older, I'm feeling more warmth toward men. It appears that my normal defensiveness toward men is declining. Right now, I seem to be immersed in a very complex set of feelings toward men. I'm seeking a 'father,' and I am also seeking 'brothers.' I am wondering if homosexuality is an issue with me. I don't know. When I first thought of this I was frightened. Now I am curious."

"I really don't think I'm gay, yet sometimes I *do* get off thinking about other men's penises—sometimes I think that if I met the right man, under the right conditions, I might enter into a gay relationship. But I *don't* want to make it, on a casual basis, with just *any* man. I think I *really* want a heterosexual relationship and I just fantasize about men, because it would be so easy for me to get a homosexual relationship, whereas a heterosexual one is so hard to get. Well, like I say, I don't really know where I'm at in this regard—I'm confused."

A few said they wanted to try a relationship with a man, but didn't know how to initiate one:

"My deepest secret, my most secret passion is to make love with another man. It has been a conflict of conscience and identity for years, but I have finally had to admit it. Performing fellatio for another man has very much appealed to me but I have never done so. Since I need an emotional warmth with a person to get involved sexually, I couldn't just do it with any Tom, Dick (no pun intended!), or Harry off the street. But, as far as I know, my male friends are 'straight'—confirmed and practicing heteros."

"I'm anally erotic, and masturbate that way sometimes (as I have since prepubescence). I'm ready for a male lover. But where to find a man—if you're not a cruiser and you're not, finally, looking that hard, that desperately? I never felt closer to women, and the women's movement, than when I really looked at men as potential lovers where I was in every sense vulnerable. Men don't know much about love."

And few "heterosexual" men talked about their first or only sexual experience with another man:

"I was afraid of sexual contact with other men (but increasingly desirous of such contact) until I was twenty-five. Then I fell in love with a man and went to bed with him. It was a difficult relationship but it also freed me up in many ways. I experienced that men could be sexually affectionate together, and I discovered that physical relations with men were as rewarding *and* as difficult as relations with women. Right now I still have a lot of questions of how to make a sexual relationship with a man really sing. When I was fearful of other men, no men approached me. Where I'm at now is I am more relaxed having oral sex done to me, but a penis still feels strange in my mouth. Where I'd like to be is: more relaxed in giving pleasure to other men. It's a self-appointed decision, and a part of this decision involves having more confidence in performing fellatio with other men."

"I usually have sex with women, but I once met a guy who I masturbated with out on a beach. He was a celibate and masturbated because he enjoyed it. He wasn't huggable but he shared a spontaneous moment with me."

"I've had a homosexual experience. Once this man, who was very scared and nervous, just wanted me to hold him closely. We lay down in bed, and I put my arms around him and tried to make him feel protected and secure. After a while he rubbed my chest and asked if he could kiss me. I said yes. All in all it was a beautiful experience. Instead of feeling like a weak, pansy, homo faggot as society told me I would feel, I felt just the opposite. I felt big, gigantic. I felt as strong and as masculine as I've ever felt, even more so. I became more of a man that day, I was proud of being a man, and I was proud of men. We can be brothers to other men, we can reach out and we can give, and it really has nothing to do with 'homosexuality.' It's a simple act of masculine tenderness, of brotherhood, of human love. Manhood is good, it's even better when we share it."

Conclusion: Strong male friendships and/or homosexuality

What is homosexuality? How close can men be without being "homosexual"? What is a close male friendship? There is no word in the language which recognizes this possibility—or for that matter the possibility of close friendships containing physical affection between women. The only word available to "describe" men's strong feelings or important relationships with each other is "homosexual." And yet this word is tied to an outdated view of the world which defines people by the gender of their sexual preference or their function in reproductive sex.

If we lived in a non-patriarchal, non-reproductively focused society, it is likely that the terms "heterosexual" and "homosexual" would be rather obscure and infrequently used. Kinsey pointed out in his works on male and female sexuality that the terms "heterosexual" and "homosexual" should be used not as nouns but as adjectives, and that they should be used to describe activities, not people. Kinsey also discussed the fact that in prepatriarchal societies, there was no anti-homosexual taboo. Even used as adjectives referring to activities, the words are vague, since as we have seen in previous chapters, many activities can be shared by either sex and are not gender-specific. Additionally, some men do not fit into either "category," as they like to have sex with both men and women. For them, the word "bisexual" has been devised, but this word is rather unpleasant; in fact, wouldn't the word "sexual" be sufficient for all of these categories?

"Homosexuality" is an anti-word—that is, it is known basically as the opposite of "heterosexuality." But the word "heterosexual" is hardly ever used to describe a person; a man is simply assumed to be "heterosexual" unless the prefix "homosexual" (i.e., "deviant") is placed before his name. The whole viewpoint which makes a fetish of gender is out of date. It developed out of the definition of "sex" as reproductive activity.

As has been true throughout this book, there is a need here for many more subtle descriptive and personal terms in our culture's vocabulary. What is a "homosexual" act? In one way, men are having sex with other men when they share pornography and discuss how they "have" sex with women, or go to topless bars together. They are enjoying sex together and joining in a form of sexually related bonding. Is caring for another man "homosexual"? In some ways, as we have seen earlier, it is considered even less manly to embrace or kiss a man than to have sex with him. Why can't men be close and affectionate? In fact, not only can men *not* touch each other and be close physically, even just as friends, but also they are not allowed to share real emotional intimacy, in most cases. What many men seemed to express a longing for, in this and in chapter one, was something new—the possibility that men can begin to see each other in a new way, and relate to each other differently, to become more open, more close, and more honest with each other.

SEX BETWEEN MEN

Eleven percent of the men who answered said that they preferred sex with other men.* What is sex between men like, both physically and emotionally? (See also chapters 1 and 4.) How is homosexual sex different from heterosexual sex? Is there a sequence or pattern of usual activities "performed" during sex between men, similar to that in sex between men and women? What are men's favorite activities during sex together?

"Most of the times you have had sex with men, what did you both do?"

Although men together usually started with "foreplay" and ended with orgasm, patterns between men were much less rigid than patterns between men and women; most sex between men was further distinguished by the fact that both partners almost always reached orgasm:

"With my male lover, our sex consists of a lot of conversation; affectionate kissing, holding; body contact—a great

* Two of these eleven percent also enjoyed sex with women; see page 857.

deal of oral exchanges—deep tongue kissing—tongue in ears, on neck—and all over the body—use of tongue, lips on penis —and hands all over the body—massaging—masturbating— lotion lubrication—on penis and hands—usually ending in anal sex—mutual or *quite often* 69."

"If we both have an erection and we are rubbing our rods together, it's the same as masturbating. I like to slow wrestle with an abdomen and pelvis locked tightly together. If possible I'll rub his chest softly. Then it'll turn into a wrestling match that grows more vigorous as we reach climax."

"There is the utmost tenderness shown between emotionally bonded homosexual men. There are all kinds of caresses, all sorts of kisses all over the body, deep, deep mouth kissing—kiss the lips, the nose, the eyelids, the forehead; be as tender as a butterfly. Of course, lying together nude is part of it—fellatio is very special; a lot of handling and caressing of the genitals, maybe mutual masturbation, some thrusting with the penis between his legs or against any part of his or my body, or thrusting during fellatio. Just fuse into one bonded relationship. After an hour or two of the above activities, we may wish to reach orgasm by either fellatio or penis-anal intercourse, or maybe finger fucking and fellatio simultaneously."

"In the gay world there's an unwritten code of tit for tat (you come, I come). Sometimes it is a relief for my partner to know it isn't essential for me to ejaculate, but unless I am very direct (which can feel a little awkward if you have not known them long) I will go into automatic pilot and orgasm. At those times it is more like masturbation with an audience for me, which I hate, because the potential for emotional connection is lost.

"What we usually do is: Overall body caressing, activities ranging from oral sex (most common) in a 69 position or otherwise. Close hugging and friction. If the mood was romantic (and I prefer that it is) dancing, petting, deep kissing, mutual fellatio, then 'milking' during the ejaculation, that is, swallowing the semen, sometimes mutual masturbation, or reaching orgasm by body friction in a variety of positions— chest to chest, chest to back, penis wedged between thighs, or chest to side. Or my favorite, anal penetration.

"If it's a very macho guy then he usually wants me to submit after some perfunctory petting. I refuse almost always. If the partner is a confirmed 'catcher' then the signals become clear that he wants you to penetrate him. I do not always want intercourse. There are times when I would be more than satisfied—satiated in fact—by simple petting and sleeping together. I do sometimes fellate someone or sodomize someone because it is expected. Sometimes I sense their appetite and comply out of compassion."

"Normally I like foreplay. I like to get sucked, I like to suck. Sometimes I shower with or without my partner (making sure they do) and then I love rimming a nice round, firm, hairy butt (analingus). My nipples are the most sensitive part of my body. I love grabbing and lightly slapping asses. *My nipples are most important.* But sometimes I like to just 'grease it up, stick it in, and fuck to my heart's content.'"

"I will tell you my favorite recent experience with someone I just met. (Picked him up at a bar.) The first night, I asked him to come home with me. When we walked into my living room, the first thing he did was strip to his birthday suit. I was a little surprised at the quickness of the action, but I followed suit and we sat down on the sofa with a drink. He had a nice body and I was ready, so I started to feel him on the leg. The minute I touched him—he was ready to trot. Went to the bedroom and in the privacy of darkness he really came to life. Rolled over on top of me and kissed me full-mouth. I thought he would suck my tongue out of my mouth. Then he sucked my breasts and went down on me. He wasn't very good but he tried some of everything. After a while, he worked back up to my face, and with a wet finger working into my asshole, he asked if I had ever had a piece of meat up there. I told him yes but if he wanted to do it, be gentle. He was and with me on my back—with the aid of a pillow—he really enjoyed it. After quite a while, he finally climaxed—with all of him in me and sucking my tongue out of me. I climaxed at the same time. It was such a close feeling. I shot up onto my chest and, holding me very close with both arms, he ran his tongue down to taste it. Sucked up some and brought it to my lips. We lay that way for a long time until my legs were going to break."

And one man described a special sexual relationship he had had with another man:

"There was a period of two years when I was orgasmically dysfunctional. The dysfunction manifested itself for two years after I 'came out' as a homosexual. The basic reason was guilt associated with my homosexuality. I had a lover (he is still my lover now) and we did a great deal of reading on sexuality. And he was very patient in bed. Together we worked at freeing my hang-ups in bed. I got to the point where I could masturbate in front of him. We began to enjoy mutual masturbation. We experimented with many positions and vicarious actings-out of fantasies. I saw a doctor for a period of a month also. The dysfunction waned and I began to have oral orgasms with my lover. Since that time I have experienced no problems with my orgasms. One of the greatest reading aids during that time was Sam Julty's book *Male Sexual Performance*."

"What are your favorite things about sex with men?"

Men's preferences were quite varied, but most answered with enthusiasm:

"My favorite thing about sex with men? Well, the only possible answer I can give is that I love their nude bodies to be next to mine and my nude body next to theirs."

"I enjoy holding and being held by a man-most of all. Fellatio comes in for a close second, but I need the physical contact most."

"I guess the best way is to say it feels good when my friend is fucking me. I want his body close to me, the warmth feels great. If he is on top of me, facing me, I like his head down close on my shoulder. Sometimes when I am really turned on, I want him to kiss me. I want to have his hot sperm deep within me."

"What do I like? My rod sucked."

"I just like being close with a *masculine* guy and turning each other on."

"My favorite sex thing is anal intercourse, especially with a nice, firm, hairy butt."

"My favorite is when I fuck my partner, especially if he comes at the same time by masturbating himself. Or the reverse. I also like the 'Princeton fuck' or the 'collegiate fuck' —just rubbing together face to face to the ecstasy of orgasm. Also, jerking off together can be very nice. This way I experience the warmth and closeness of my partner, while my own hand knows exactly what to do to my body."

"I like to take his clothes off real slow and watch him get horny and hot."

"The affections (hugs and kisses) are the best part."

"The touching. It makes me feel as if I were in contact with myself and my body is acceptable instead of just accepted. I feel as if I'm getting instead of just *giving*."

"The intrigue! It's also an ego trip to see that I successfully attract the well-built macho types."

"Well, I'm anally erotic and there doesn't seem much place to go with it *finally* without men."

"My favorite activity: cuddling together without any thought of erection or orgasm."

"I love rubbing our bodies together."

"I like feeling my lover inside of me and astride me—me on my back and my lover on top of me. The reason I like it this way is I enjoy the feeling of passivity."

"I like to have another guy gently holding my cock while I'm shooting sperm in my partner's ass. I definitely do not like anyone to touch my testicles—they are too tender."

"I like kissing where my partner and I lie together, bodies intertwined, mouth to mouth, tongues touching, moving tongues slowly together, advancing and retreating, kissing sometimes gently, sometimes vigorously."

"I like to make thigh-leg contact, to be held tightly and touched on the neck, back, tailbone, and buttocks. I love the feeling of closeness, tenderness, lack of expectations, the laughter and subtle communication. I *love* embracing men— to hold and be held tightly. Having sex with a man is like feeling a closeness deeper than a brother."

"My favorite thing in sex with men is anal intercourse. It is most rewarding emotionally, although I feel somewhat strange admitting that. Because after the act is completed what I remember most vividly and savor long afterward was the union, the tenderness, and the language that was established between my partner and myself. Just being inside of a man makes us a unit and for that one moment of anal intercourse we are a complete 'ONE' emotionally as well as physically. I love the feeling of his scrotum against mine. His manhood next to mine."

"What are the advantages and disadvantages of sex with men?"

Most men stressed social and psychological factors, the most frequently mentioned disadvantage being social disapproval:

"It is truly enlightening to find out what other men are like intimately. It brings you closer with other men. Disadvantages are social—it's highly dangerous to love another man for fear of social ostracism. I have found the safest affairs are with men who have something to lose if the affair is found out. That way the affair is secret, sacred, and safe."

"Advantages to gay sex: no fear of pregnancy; heightened pleasure from its 'illicit,' 'forbidden' aura; more flexible and enlightened attitudes towards fidelity, monogamy, and casual sex; perhaps better chances for deep communication and mutual understanding because of the physical and emotional similarities. Disadvantages: even today, and in this relatively enlightened society, we run the risk of losing our jobs, our housing, being fined, jailed, even *killed* for being gay."

"Advantages: availability, make new friends. But the primary disadvantage is that I would be very embarrassed if my family and most of my friends found out. Also many men are assholes and I want nothing to do with them, much less to share sex with them."

"Being able to love another man is the best part. The only disadvantage is the social stereotype and persecution gays still suffer, but this only makes gays more aware of other oppressed peoples, and strengthens you as a person."

"One advantage is not worrying about getting him pregnant! The roughest part is not being able to have a family."

"Advantages: physically, sex is better. One can also understand oneself better by reflection—it feels good, knowing what really feels good to a man. Disadvantages: specific health problems which are not that big of a deal, if one has knowledge of them; or no children. Most disadvantages are social."

"The only disadvantage of being gay is trying to convince non-gay people that you are a human being. Otherwise, I am very happy being gay. At the very best, a person can find a missing part of himself in a loving relationship with another man."

"There is nothing I don't like about sex with men, and I definitely prefer it to sex with women, but I am becoming very tired of the gay men's subculture in San Francisco—it is so exclusively male. I spent my high school years and half of my college years mainly with boys/men (they were boys'/men's schools) and I loved the male company and still feel easy and close with men most of all, but now men's groups, men's subcultures, etc., do not interest me. I am much more interested in women and in mixed groups. Being with men too much now gives me the same feeling I have when I spend too much time just with white people or Americans. It is too confining."

"It has advantages in that you can be freer and more emotional, and can do many things traditionally avoided by straight men. However, you have to be able to cope with the negative or anti-gay attitudes of society, and you have to deal with the potentially traumatic problem of what to tell your parents. It can also be a lonely life. Intimate relationships tend to last only a short time, which is sad, and many people have to be very careful on the job to keep their gayness a secret. If you're in a position to be able to accept your gayness and be open about it, the pressure is not too bad. I personally feel fewer personal restrictions on what I can and can't do in my private life—i.e., the so-called masculine and feminine things that a straight man might feel odd doing—but there is always that feeling of societal disapproval in the background."

"It is a very enjoyable and satisfying way of life. The advantages are friendship, sex, comradeship, and belonging to a special group of people . . . your own society. The only disadvantage is discrimination. It's something that every person should definitely experience at least once or twice in their lives."

"How is sex with men different from sex with women (if you have had sex with a woman)?"

Some men stressed that sex was physically better with men:

"Sex with men is different because men are more outgoing sexually. They want sex. Women will fight you off. Also men are better at 'sucking' than women, probably because they have cocks and know what they like. They have similar experiences. Finally, fucking a man is tighter than fucking a woman and in that sense is a more sensual, sexually attractive thing to me, and I respond to it physically and emotionally in a way I cannot generate with a woman. My wife considered me a fantastic sex partner, but to me sex with her and the three other women I was involved with has been less satisfactory, physically and emotionally, than masturbation."

"I find that sex with men is a much more responsive thing for me. I know what I like and how to please another man. Too many times when I have been with women, I found out that they were pretending to enjoy what I was doing, and afraid to do anything except just lie back and get screwed."

"It's far more relaxed, since men understand each other's bodies, feelings, reactions, and needs—we are all basically the same and it is a totally *natural* thing to me."

"Far more intense. More of a sharing experience. More fulfilling. A little more complicated deciding who does what to whom."

"Men are more exciting partners; they have less inhibitions and are more willing to sexually experiment; also I find there is less of a game or coyness about getting down to sex."

"The tight fucks are great. Plus, you can both fuck and be fucked (something you can't do with a woman). Also, men are better off psychologically than women."

"Cleaner, we know what to do with each other."

"I've found my male partners more responsive than my female partners, and they seem less inhibited about caressing my body than the women I've been with have been. I find more equality in action with another man."

"Roles are shifted easily and thus there is more variety. One is less likely to encounter a puritanical attitude towards all techniques except intercourse. Men are more vigorous and aggressive in sex than women, and almost always more muscular and rougher in action. The chief attraction of males over women is having a cock."

Others emphasized the emotional and psychological advantages—especially the lack of performance pressures, or the increased feeling of equality:

"Gay sex is relatively new to me. Still, it has been much easier to have sex with males than with females. There is no real question of 'performance': both parties are interested in having an enjoyable time, and take equal part in the 'process.' To be fair, however, the gay bar 'scene' is just as nerve-racking and creates the same kinds of questions in my head that having sex with a woman does (i.e., 'Is he attracted to me? Does he want to have sex with me?' Etc.)."

"Right now due to past emotional and sexual experiences with women, I feel contempt and hostility—most women I find boring, dull. I feel better with men."

"I think that the emotional involvement between two people of the same sex is qualitatively different than that between a man and a woman—the basis for their understanding of each other is broader since they come from the same place essentially."

"I never make love anymore with women, and haven't in five years. The reasons are as much psychological as physiological. I like women's bodies O.K. but don't like the heavy role playing that always seems to result from male-female sex—when I, the male, wasn't dominant, it generally seemed that the female took over the dominant role. We had so much trouble being equals that we finally gave up. It's much easier and more natural with another man."

"Men don't give you the horseshit women do—I don't like the rat race women lead you on. You know you're going to fuck her, but you must go through a long ritual. If a man is willing—you get it right now."

"With men it's honest. I like the honest level of the involvement."

"Sex with men is sex between equals. I understand and like the way men act because I am one. It is always a mutual affair—each being satisfied."

"I do enjoy sex with men best both psychologically and physically because I can relax passively in the strength of someone else, which I can only occasionally do in a heterosexual relationship."

"I think that in gay relationships there is more of a sharing of power in the sexual encounter than there tends to be in heterosexual relationships. For example, sometimes I'm in the mood to be the active partner and sometimes I'm not, and that's O.K."

"You don't have to worry about having to support her, or marry her."

"My favorite thing about sex with men is the freedom of it—freedom in many senses. There is much less emotional involvement with men in sexual encounters."

"Society expects me to be dominant in my work, in social affairs, in my spirituality (vis-à-vis the Catholic ideology of male supremacy), and also in my home life including bed. That is *too damn much* dominancy. I need to be able to feel 'catered to' emotionally at times too. Thus, I find a homosexual relationship much more rewarding in that I can have a healthy balance between dominance and submission in bed."

"My male partner does not find some of my body repugnant, as my wife sometimes makes me feel. Fucking men is not as competitive and I feel relaxed in the company of most men, although I never feel relaxed around aggressive macho men."

"Sex with a woman is nice, there is a physical release. However, the emotional release is not there. With a man the feeling of strength with strength is a fantastic feeling to me. Women are too soft and cannot give me the strength which I need. Being next to a man amplifies my own strength."

"Women I can take or leave as sex partners. I like them as people but I don't allow them or can't allow them to touch me emotionally the way a man can. With me, there is a great unclothed baring, revealing of the body/soul—the trying for intimacy which never seems to be there otherwise. I can be intimate with a woman without sex, but the closest I can come to it with a man is by nakedly relating physically in the so-called act of love. Then, for a moment, a man is vulnerable and drops his defenses and can almost be reached."

Some men did mention performance pressures that also existed in sex between men—although they were far fewer than in sex with women:

"In bed with men, most of the time I find that I am the active partner, too often I find that I have to lead, I have to perform the part that the male is expected to perform."

"I hate to say it, but sometimes there is a big silent competition between who has the biggest cock, can shoot the most come, and stay hardest the longest, etc."

"Sexual activity in the gay world is fraught with role playing, exaggerated postures, and too damn much emphasis on potency or 'masculinity.' Some of the rituals are unpleasant —the cruising routine in bars, for example, and heavy use of alcohol, marijuana, 'uppers.' Some of the bizarre interests are not too much fun either."

"Occasionally my sex partner tells me he is waiting to orgasm with me. This becomes a pressure when I'm just enjoying myself totally, and then am suddenly reminded I must orgasm or the sex act isn't complete. I resent this sometimes and tell him so."

"Sometimes I feel pressured by men to have an orgasm, especially in 'quicky' situations with strangers. It's often almost a contest as to who can make the other come first."

Some men also complained they felt they had to do more of the "work" or make more of the "advances":

"Yes, most of the work done in lovemaking is done by myself and this soon becomes something of a chore, in which I lose a lot of interest."

"Usually I am the one that makes the advances, due to my higher sex drive, I guess. I am unsatisfied if I have to make all the advances. It's as if your partner isn't interested. I like to be passive at least once in a while. I like to know that they are interested in me, and in my body. It makes me feel more loved when my partner is forward. I have often wanted other people to make a sexual advance, but they never have. It makes me feel empty and unloved when that happens."

"I think we all have wanted the other person to make an advance and not gotten it. But you could sit and wait and rot till it falls off if you wait for other people."

And some gay men complained that men were too genitally oriented and not affectionate enough:

"I don't like men who jump up after and have to leave right away, and don't like to show any affection."

"I'd like to change the attitudes of some men engaging in sex—a willingness to be open to real affection would be terrific, for example. I would like sex to have a greater emotional emphasis than most men are ready to give it, and for men to have a greater commitment toward mutual respect."

One man described his own hostile sexual behavior in this way:

"Sex between men is not always 'nice.' Recently I was drunk and feeling nasty. I was seduced by a friend of mine. We were in bed when I decided to turn the tables on him. I started to tear his clothes off (figuratively speaking). I got on top of him and used my whole body, rubbing against his to get him turned on. In a short time, he was so turned on he shook, he couldn't talk. Could hardly breathe. Then I left. It was a very sick thing I did. To this day I regret it and will never do it again. Human beings are not cheap. People are not playthings."

One man described in detail the differences he found between sex with men and sex with women:

"How is sex with men different from sex with women? Generally, I think men know exactly what physical stimulation works for each other. You do for someone else what you know you enjoy. Also, there is nothing like a cock. It's great to be able to *take* physically into your body the force of a man's passion—his body into your body. It's also great to be able to express the strong feeling you may have for a man in a sexual way. You have sex with someone not because they are this or that, but because you like or love them.

"I usually lose my erection if I am being fucked, but if I fuck another guy I usually orgasm. Fucking a guy is tighter—perhaps an advantage—and more awkward than fucking a woman. But the difference in feeling, emotionally, is hard to describe. Perhaps some of the enjoyment is feeling that a man is making himself vulnerable to you—something which goes against the clichés of how men normally react— so that you feel he is granting you a special kind of favor. Also there is some kind of feeling of safety or security in feeling a man's flesh all around yours. It's like you; there is no threat or danger from it. Perhaps the basic thing about it is the defusing of the potential threat that comes from sexual competitiveness among men. They fight each other basically because of sexual possessiveness. But if a man allows you to have sex with him, he is no source of threat to you."

LOVE, RELATIONSHIPS, AND MONOGAMY BETWEEN MEN

"Describe the time you fell most deeply in love. How did it feel? What happened?"

"Being in love is the most all-encompassing, overwhelming experience of my life: I feel ecstatically happy when I'm with him, when we're doing something together, or simply spending the evening together at home. He means more to me than anyone else in the world. I cried myself to sleep when at one point he said that he thought we were spending too much time together, and that we needed new experiences apart (including, potentially, other sexual things). I was desperately unhappy, both with him and when we were apart. I could barely stand seeing him be cold and unaffectionate with me. Although I agreed that we had become too isolated from other people, I didn't want our reaching out to new people to negatively affect our relationship. But we have more or less worked through this now, and the happiest period of my adult life has been the past year. Especially when we were away on holiday together, away from our work, doing new and exciting things together. Perhaps the closest I've ever felt to him was the last time I saw him, and we both cried on each other's shoulder about having to say even a temporary goodbye. Those tears were more expressive and real than any words could ever have been."

"Does feeling deeply in love really need description? I felt that the most important thing in my life was the happiness of the person I loved. I subordinated my own feelings and interests to the objective of my love's happiness. I felt (no doubt irrationally) that had it been necessary I might as well have sacrificed my very life for the preservation of my love. My whole experience for a couple of years was suffused with this all-important passion. What happened? The person I loved, who had reciprocated my feelings at first, grew less interested in me and by the end of three years of living together he was not any longer in love with me at all. It was a heartbreaking crisis for me, and the emotional agony and scars from that experience have left me permanently and clearly altered in my personality. I have never since had the same emotional capacity that I had before this experience. It is as though a part of my emotional capacity had been burned right out of my body or amputated. Eventually after many months I slowly resumed living. I have never, however, in the ten years since, been able to shed a single tear over anything. As I said, it is as if a part of my emotional capacity had been removed . . . cauterized away. I am basically a happy person. Only rarely do I feel a slight depression, but after that episode I think it must have been three years before I had a week when I could look at myself and say honestly, 'I am happy this week.' "

"The most deeply in love I have been was when I was nineteen, with someone I lived with for six years. There was a sexual attraction, but beyond this there was a sense of 'comfortability,' a tremendous joyful feeling of well-being. I don't like the gay term 'lover'; to me that denotes something risqué, spurious, without depth. This was a partnership, an equal sharing where we both used our talents to complement the other and shared the day-to-day responsibilities of living. There was no 'he' or 'she,' simply two people who happened to be male and who happened to fully enjoy and respect each other. I do not recall that either of us felt any need to be jealous even when one or the other would seek a sexual encounter outside. We were honest in our relationships with others as well as each other. I believe that the honesty in our relationship gave it a tremendous amount of security. I have never known such a sense of well-being or happiness since that time."

"I have been deeply in love twice . . . both times with straight men who loved me also but could not totally express that feeling, sexually or otherwise. I have kept close contact with both and have continued to love them, one for seventeen years and the other for fourteen. The two times I was in love it hit me like an electric shock—like having a bolt of lightning hit me. I knew at that instant that this was going to be 'the one.' I was relatively speechless and fumbled for words. I became flustered. I was enormously aroused sexually although not aware of having an erection. The first time the fellow touched my hand (by circumstance, not intentionally), it was so intense it was almost painful."

"I met my lover of two and a half years in a bar. I walked up to him and initiated conversation. There was immediately a strong attraction (physical). We returned to my apartment and had sex but it was more like making love. He was very considerate, and gentle in a way I had never really experienced before. After we had sex, we talked for a few hours, really candidly. I had to work the next morning and recall seeing him sleeping as I got dressed. He looked like a peaceful cherub. I knew this experience was a beginning, I knew it intuitively. We spent much time together, going to plays, movies, and art museums. I remember being turned on by his entering a room. Several times I couldn't tell whether I felt my penis or his. I missed him horribly when I was away. We became such good friends it permitted me to unlock much within myself and him. There was no question about the reciprocal nature of our relationship. There was a deterioration, however, when we took an apartment together. He became absorbed in his career and became distant, and very selfish about some things. I made all kinds of allowances and tried to talk things through. Still whenever things got rough for either of us we each supported the other strongly. When we began after two years to do fewer things together, I knew that my commitment was dying. So I decided not to move with him when he got a job offer in another city. He was surprised and hurt but made a fast recovery. I was upset, too. I still deeply love the guy. We visit each other at holidays, and have sex. But it is more out of a tribute to the past, I guess."

And many gay men expressed their desire for long-term relationships in very sincere and warm terms when asked, "What are your deepest longings for a relationship with another person?":

"My deepest longings are to find someone to form a life-long loving, give-take relationship based on love, trust, companionship, and understanding. It would be a physically and emotionally fulfilling relationship."

"I want a permanent relationship with someone who is 'always there.' The hardest thing in my life is ultimately being alone at night. I can have great days and good times at work and in a variety of traditional ways, but it always ends in going home alone. I wish there were someone there to go to bed with me for the night; someone who cared and who was not there necessarily for sex."

"To find a male sexual partner—a man I can share my life with and to whom I can express all my emotions, sexual passions, and drives—and most of all a man I can love."

"My hope is that I find someone who is attractive, a good person, happy, that likes or loves only me, faults and all. That I can be relaxed and giving with. Sex together would be very satisfying. That we both have satisfying careers and are comfortable financially. That I think of him a lot when he is away. Our relationship gets better and deeper as time passes. That we are monogamous. And share hobbies and common interests together. That we stay together until we are very old. That we both share a family of friends and contribute to the community. That we truly and deeply love each other. That he is also my best friend and lover. That my real family loves and accepts him as a son also."

"Is gay 'promiscuity' a myth or a reality? Do you prefer emotional closeness or casual sex or both?" "Are you in love? In a steady relationship? How many men have you had a sexual relationship with? Do you like monogamy?"

Many men said that "promiscuity" is a word with many negative connotations, which they preferred not to use. One man replied, " 'Promiscuity' is a ridiculous word!" Another pointed out that just as it is inappropriate to identify someone by sexual preference, it is also inappropriate to link the terms "gay" and "promiscuous":

"There seems to be a more basic sense of promiscuity in men that allows them to move from one to the other with a minimum of emotional attraction if desired. But I don't think one can talk about gay promiscuity any more than one can talk about heterosexual promiscuity. There are promiscuous people and there are those who are not, and that exists in both sexual preferences. I think that gay promiscuity is probably more obvious since homosexuals have been forced by society to identify themselves on a primary basis by their sexual preference, which is not a natural state to me. For example, I say 'I am a homosexual.' But that is not a word I would choose to use as a description of me, any more than if I were heterosexual I would state that as a descriptive term. But I find that it is important to other people's understanding of me to include that as a part of a definition of me, and so I do. But heterosexuals have the specific luxury of being able to place their sexual identities in a more realistic perspective, and therefore do not obviously function totally as sexual beings. But I know many heterosexual men who are as promiscuous as any gay man that I know. Given the opportunity I think many more would be. I do think that promiscuous sex is more available to the gay male, particularly, than perhaps it is for other men or even a gay female."

Many men preferred sexual freedom/non-monogamy:

"I've had sex with over 2,000 men. I love to fuck and look at all men's penises. I'm what they call a whore. I love group sex and going to the baths. I would be bored with monogamy."

"I am in love. I have a gay lover. I have had sex with probably 100 men in my lifetime, maybe more. I do not believe in monogamy. It's part of the thwarted Christian ethic."

"I'm in love with my lover, but I'm also in love with all men. I've had sex with several hundred men in my life, and don't intend to stop now."

"I am in love. However, I am not now in a steady relationship. To total the men that have wandered into my life would be foolish, but a conservative estimate would be 150 to 200. Monogamy doesn't work for me."

"I don't like the idea of being tied down to one person all the time. Right now I feel that I have enough love and affection within me that I can share it with more than one person, but if I ever do go into a relationship I hope it will be for an extended period of time, because for me to give a good meaning behind my love I would have to concentrate on just one person. Right now I prefer having casual relationships, it gives me a chance to meet and like many different kinds of people and it's helping me decide the type of person I would like to settle down with."

A minority were involved in, or preferred, long-term monogamous relationships:

"I have a steady male relationship. I do love him, but we don't talk about *love*. We enjoy each other's company and most of our talk centers about our careers. The relationship has been steady for one year. In my forty-four years I've only had sex with four men. I'm too busy to cruise and I don't feel safe in a multiple-relationship arrangement. The 'gay' men I know are monogamous and are far from promiscuous. If there is any promiscuity, it's in younger men. I never make passes at teenage men. I never contemplate sex with my college students. I've only had sex with men who are professional and are generally colleagues. I really like most men I work with and feel very close to them, even emotionally close."

"I am in love in a steady relationship. There are too many men to count to know how many men I've been with. I like monogamy. I don't have to worry all the time about finding someone."

"At the present moment I am monogamous. It is a steady relationship of six months' duration—but it is the most satisfying emotionally I have ever experienced."

"I am twenty-seven. I have been involved with more than one man at a time, and it's hell. Just one good relationship at a time, please."

"In my present life, homosexual promiscuity is a reality. It certainly was not so through most of my life until the age of sixty-nine. Even now I would greatly prefer emotional closeness with one person to casual sex."

One man said he had grown to prefer being monogamous as he became older:

"My earliest sexual credo was the more the better—quantity without regard to quality. Over the years my attitudes toward myself as a sexual being have metamorphosed. Now at fifty, I prefer sex as an expression of deeper feelings rather than the simple act of getting my rocks off. I guess this is a sign of maturity, at least I hope it is!"

One man described his attempts to come to terms with his lover having sex with others:

"I am twenty-four years old. I am just coming out of an important relationship that remained fairly constant and stable for two and a half years, and I'm still trying to evaluate it. Sex was great for the first six months. Gradually sex became less frequent but oddly enough the intensity was there for the duration. I was pretty satisfied with our sexual interaction but disturbed by its diminished frequency. My 'love,' so I came to find out, was considerably less complacent. Before we paired off I had considerably less 'experience' sexually than my lover, although we had both had periods of promiscuity before. This 'marriage' began with a tacit understanding about fidelity. However, within four months my lover, while I was hospitalized for three weeks, had several sexual encounters at the 'baths.' When he told me, I was disconsolate.

"Weeks later, to counter this terrible feeling of jealousy and being threatened, I forced myself to go to the baths while my lover was out of town. It was not an attempt on my part to seek revenge. I needed to understand the bath environment because my total ignorance of it gave rise to exaggerated fears regarding my sexual performance. I learned that depersonalized sex, in that manner at least, in no way detracted from my attraction or love of my lover. So I felt better—at least temporarily.

"A few months later, while we vacationed together at a resort that was predominantly gay, we innocently fell into an orgy situation. I most definitely did not want to participate but sensed my lover did, so I told him to go ahead. But it was more then I could handle observing, and I flipped out. After this crisis I resolved to moderate my relationship with my lover with casual encounters of my own. The impulse here was not sexual appetite primarily but my overwhelming need to come to terms with my sexual jealousy. Thereafter I had perhaps eighty very fleeting sexual encounters, unknown to my lover in our remaining two years together. They did not jeopardize my emotional fidelity to my mate—in fact they enhanced my ability to relate and interact with him. I did, however, experience guilt and took precautions that he would not discover anything.

"Now I am 'single' again for the last nine months. At first, after that relationship, I enjoyed being able to do exactly as I pleased, no longer finding it necessary to conceal any of my actions. I had two affairs (one lasting four weeks, the other two weeks). But I am very dissatisfied with what I have come to regard as insubstantial relationships. I wish more than I can convey to be involved in a strong commitment. Since there is no sanction for a gay bond, nothing societally that legitimizes the commitment I crave, I feel somewhat at sea. I hope to find (and I am expending plenty of energy searching!) a meaningful relationship that incorporates both sexuality and deep friendship. What is depressing about gay life is that as much as you hope to avoid the banal stereotypes, they are almost inherent in the nature of this subculture. I mean, you may wish a life mate but it is a rarity among those I know. You also may dislike the prevalent emphasis in gay bar society on conspicuous sexual attractiveness, but you are forced to play the game—the bar routines—in order to meet people. It becomes a vicious cycle. I have found myself becoming more adept at bar communication but I attempt to mix sincerity with bar suaveness. My 'success' (score) rate is high, but I do not pride myself in this, since my goal is a long-term relationship."

But most gay men believed in a style of life that was neither "monogamous" nor "promiscuous," suggesting that a non-monogamous but committed relationship was the ideal:

"I have a lover and we've been together for eight years. I occasionally have sex with other guys, but they are for sex only, usually, and there is little emotional entanglement. My lover does likewise. We have many gay friends, but they are comrades, confidants. Our love is not based on infatuation, but was something that took a period of years to build and nurture. There have been good times and bad times. Bad times (emotionally, financially, and sexually) have helped us grow and understand one another much better than if everything had been great always."

"Age forty-one. Homosexual. Married thirteen years. Got married for children and respectability (1960!). I loved my wife in a way but always had to fantasize males while making love. I also had lots of sex with males outside. I wanted children and had two, adopted two more. I love my children very much. Now I'm living with one lover and have occasional sex on the side. The present relationship is the happiest and the closest. We never fight and are neither exclusive nor consider our relationship to be eternal. It is nice and cool in that we accept what we have as long as it lasts."

"I am seventeen, and have had a lover for ten months. I like the permanence, but I think it dulls sex sometimes. I love my lover because he cares for me. I have had relationships on the side. The thrill of getting away with it is why—although my partner usually knows."

"I do not like extended periods of monogamy, which place too much pressure, emotional and sexual, on the partners involved. When I have a steady relationship, I enjoy casual sexual encounters. But casual encounters *alone* leave me all at sea, confused, and in a state of emotional need."

"Gay promiscuity is reality. I like to be especially close to someone with a little casual sex on the side."

"I prefer an open monogamous relationship, one in which we are primarily monogamous but realize that people do come and go that are attractive and friendly—those you might want to date for dinner or go out with."

"I have been married for five years (I'm twenty-five); however, we lived together at the same residence for a year, then I moved into my own separate home. I enjoyed very much our life together. My wife chose to work and I stayed home and took care of the household duties. We both love each other very deeply. However, we are both homosexual and did and do have our lovers as separate relationships from our marriage. I like to know a man well and this for me means one man at a time over a longer-term relationship (not necessarily monogamous)."

"I don't want monogamy now—can't predict if I'll want it in the future. Unquestionably, gay men have, on the average, more different sex partners than heterosexuals. However, the word 'promiscuity' is loaded with negative judgments that I don't share. I hunger for emotional *and* sexual closeness— don't know if I'm capable of casual sex without emotional closeness. But I think the term 'promiscuous' is best applied to heterosexual relationships. For gays I would prefer to use the phrase 'less sexually restricted.' "

But one man pointed out that perhaps the largest number of gay men were celibate:

"The so-called promiscuity of gay men is a myth in the sense that most gay men are living lives of quiet frustration. They are so closeted that they are afraid to come out and have sex with anyone, and thus are virtually celibate—or living as heterosexuals."

THREE GAY MEN DESCRIBE THEIR LIVES

In order to get a deeper understanding of relationships between men, of how men feel both physically and emotionally in a sexual relationship with another man, it is important to hear more complete replies. Following are three longer replies; Other complete replies from gay men ages eighteen to seventy-three can be found in chapters 5, 8, and 9.

"I am twenty-three, went to Princeton University one year, white, now work as an operator for the telephone company. I would say that I am 'reasonably good-looking.' I am no raving beauty, but I am not the Creature from the Black Lagoon, either.

"I work in an office of over two hundred people. My closest friends in that office know I am gay and I am pretty sure that all the supervisors and management personnel know. We even have an openly gay manager! We have one lesbian couple, several unattached lesbians, lesbians with lovers not in the office, and several gay males (attached and unattached). Yes, my parents know. I was so sexually confused and hurt for so long that when I got my head on straight and finally decided to come out and face the world with my homosexuality, I felt they *must* know. I never approved of sneaking around. Anyway, their acceptance of me really has made me feel like a whole person, because their opinion of me is just as high, if not higher because I leveled with them. Who can live a double life as some gays are forced to do without it taking some toll? Who needs the extra toll? Life is hard enough anyway.

"I went to the same school from kindergarten to ninth grade. I knew everyone—all sixty people. They always teased me and said I was probably a faggot because I didn't go out for football, which I thought was a crock of shit, but you just don't retort back to the 'clique.' Hell, I didn't want my head bashed in. My mother occasionally called me a sissy too, and it bothered me a lot. I guess even the most liberal mothers say that once in a while. Everyone is entitled to make a mistake now and then. By ninth grade, I started getting very withdrawn and becoming distant from everyone. My parents recognized this and that's when they sent me 1,200 miles away to live with my sister and go to public school. What a wonder that did for my head.

"But I got along with my mother pretty good—we became close especially during one particular episode of her life when I was about nine: she was a teacher in a parochial school and was discriminated against because she was a woman. She had tenure, more education, and yet a man was hired with less credentials, and paid more because he was a man. My mom challenged the school board for equal pay. Their reply? He is a man and has children to support. 'Well, what do you think I have? Four talking monkeys? I have kids, too.' From that point on I had a lot more sympathy for my mother and for women in general.

"I masturbated frequently and felt very guilty about it from about age sixteen to twenty-one. I had been pretty much indoctrinated in school: play with yourself and you will be damned to hell. But I wanted to save my sex with others, so I was a virgin until I was twenty-two (last year). So far I have found short-lived affairs but nothing substantial to speak of. I have never had a 'relationship' and I am dying to have one, but if you look for such a thing, you will never find it. It just has to happen.

"I like men's bodies. Beards, muscles, thighs, asses, sideburns, mustaches, weathered faces. Love kissing men. I had one experience with a woman, and I was fantasizing about sex with a man. I love a hard, toned body and the 'rough gentleness' of a man. I can fall in love with a woman probably emotionally. No, wait. Let me take that back. Well, yes, maybe I could. But physically, forget it. I just couldn't get it up and I just know I would be fantasizing about a man while making love. I enjoy women as friends, but I just love getting down with a man. Especially a gentle, but firm man. A hard body against another hard body.

"As to what I like sexually, I still masturbate (of course!) whenever I feel the need, and now it seems to me perfectly normal. If the President asked me if I masturbate, I would answer with a resounding *yes!* I used to feel awful about it, but as you grow older, you change. I enjoy masturbation but I sometimes would rather be with a partner and share my pleasure with him. I fantasize about receiving fellatio from certain gay stereotypes, such as the leatherman (although I am not involved in S&M) or by the Clone—jeans, plaid shirt, and boots.

"Foreplay is what I enjoy the most. I love to start with all of our clothes on, standing up, rubbing crotches, kissing lightly, soul kissing, swaying back and forth, hugging real close. I am sensitive anywhere. Usually I happen to click with people who enjoy a lot of foreplay. After a lot of foreplay, I don't feel the slightest bit disappointed even if I don't have an orgasm at all. Also I love just sleeping next to someone. If I am 'cruising' for sex, and I enjoy the person I am with, I don't even care if we 'have sex.' I just get off cuddling, fondling (not the genital area in particular, the whole body), and kissing, especially soul kissing. I love making love to men.

"I have tried anal penetration on two or three occasions. I would like to find someone who would take time to introduce me to it slowly and who would be very gentle with me. I just fear someone ramming their penis up my anus and hurting me internally or bruising my prostate. I haven't experienced it that much, but someday I will find someone (hopefully, my first real lover) who will show me how I can enjoy getting fucked.

"I enjoy fellatio very much and I always orgasm. (I prefer fellatio to anal intercourse.) One must be careful of an inexperienced fellator, because damage could be done if he clamps down on the penis with his teeth. I also enjoy giving a man fellatio, although the first time I swallowed semen was a bit weird—but now I like it. I am taking something of him into me.

"Manual stimulation is O.K.—but the partner usually stimulates me too fast or too rough, and I can lose my erection. I love for my partner to stimulate my balls lightly, and breathe on them, rustling the pubic hair. Sometimes, too, I rub my crotch to get myself stimulated before sex. Self-stimulation relieves some of the burden of the partner you are with. You should take it upon yourself to see that you and your partner have a good time, and sometimes with a partner, you need to show him how you like to be stimulated.

"If I am standing when having an orgasm, and I or my partner has been stimulating me for a long time, getting me close to orgasm and then backing off at the brink, I literally cannot stand when he brings me off. I go into slight convulsions and I have to lean against the wall or I will fall down. My face gets all screwed up, but there is a big smile on it. When I am with someone I care for very much, I feel as if I am in heaven.

"Am I worried about masculinity, my masculinity? Masculinity is a very difficult term, but the old thing that 'boys shouldn't cry' is pure bullshit, and thank God my parents never told me not to cry. Crying can be a great release for me sometimes, and I do feel much better displaying my emotions than bottling them up inside, causing major stress and tensions that could be destructive to my mental health and general attitude. I feel that I am masculine but I also feel that I am androgynous in some ways; anyway, we are all born with male and female hormones. If men weren't so hell-bent on displaying their machismo and trying to impress other men (who, in turn, are trying to impress the men that are trying to impress them), they would loosen up and display emotions that have always been termed 'female.' It is such a male-oriented white society, it really turns me off. Most men who are straight, in my opinion (and don't get me wrong—there are some men who are straight and have their head together), are usually looking for Mommy when the wife searching begins. They want someone to take care of them, nurture them, feed them, 'service' them, to root for them when the going gets tough, etc. No wonder women are leaving men in droves in this country. Why would anyone want to put up with that trip?

"Really being masculine means being masculine naturally. When someone thinks he isn't 'masculine enough,' he will try to emulate the 'masculine image' of that time—like the gay community has where the Castro Clone look (lumberjack shirt, tight Levi's jeans, and boots) is the look. They feel that this clothing is masculine, even if they are 'effeminate.' They somehow think that donning this attire is going to turn them into a supermasculine-butch-stud. I have seen many gay men who are masculine and many who tend to be more effeminate. But straight men seem to think all men who are effeminate are gay. Macho straights just love to gay-bait effeminate men. I think many machos have several sexual identity problems, and are fighting an inner battle, a battle only they can stop.

"I am not afraid of being called 'feminine,' 'effeminate,' 'womanly,' or 'girlish.' I could care less. I don't care what anyone thinks. If I should flutter my hand for a second, many would say, 'There's a queer, Martha.' As far as my own 'masculine' success goes, I feel I am successful in that I have accomplished everything I have wanted to do with my own funds and no support from my parents. I have always been fiercely independent.

"Finally, I think if more men were gay, there might be a little less hostility in the world. In fact, I think many men have secret homosexual feelings that they can never display. When one bottles up these feelings they can be transmuted into violent reactions. Perhaps this could lead to the abuse of wives and girlfriends? I don't know. I kinda like to be different—I don't want Joe Straight to find out what I have—I like being different."

"I'm twenty-five—a liberated faggot with leftist leanings. Youngest of four from a cracker family out of Alabama. My parents entrusted me to the public schools. I work in a theatrical company. Anglo all the way, southern Baptist. I've been out in the field researching male sexuality, and I'm glad somebody finally asked me to report back.

"I wasn't touched by another man until I was sixteen; he blew me in a moving car. It was dismal. I stayed celibate for about three years after that—during which I went through my classic queen phase, red hair and all—then I got spaced real bad and went to Colorado to look at the mountains. Then I moved in with the woman who gave me this questionnaire (who had been off running an abortion clinic while I was in rhinestones) and we lived together for about a year. Then I took a sleazy apartment while she went away to school and I started getting sleazier. Loved it. Still do.

"Things in men I like. Oafishness. Strength in repose. Wistfulness. Bravado. Physically?—I have an aversion (of which I don't approve) to fat. But I've enjoyed all sizes and shapes of men. A favorite type is a muscular little man shorter than me. But it really don't matter.

"I like kissing a lot; probably because I don't understand how my head is working during kissing; everything registers somehow, but it isn't memorable. It's all very subverbal. Like dreaming. After orgasm I usually like to snuggle and talk for a while and then go to sleep. Nothing is so relaxing as a good orgasm. Most of the time I'd rather have affection than sex, but it's harder to find—from a man.

"As far as penetrating my anus goes, half a dozen men had tried unsuccessfully to penetrate me over a period of about two years. When I first really became active sexually—let me see, maybe four years ago—I was real confused about the possibilities, and didn't really know what I wanted. I insisted I couldn't be fucked and only found out in the last

three months that I really don't mind it. My previous refusal
had even been a factor in the termination of a six-month
relationship. It's psychological, you bet. I particularly cannot
stand somebody coming at me from a position where I can't
see them. What does it feel like? Hm. It feels like being fucked,
it doesn't feel like anything else. If I'm in the right mood it
really can be almost comforting. Anyway, everybody likes to
fuck these days, so you can bet that it's going to be making
some man awfully happy; which, if you can find any reason
to do, you'd better do it, the way I figure. Men need help.

"I enjoy fellatio. A lot. But there's a new macho mood
afoot among men, and this is one act that has become kind of
a power thing. Except in rare circumstances—like love—I
don't like to perform fellatio—I have a gag reflex that won't
quit, after all these years. Interesting.

"I've gotten considerably rougher in the last six months,
maybe just because of who I've been running into. Or pursuing. Pain in sex really isn't pain, it now seems. I'm not into
a lot of it, and I certainly don't care to see blood—but I don't
mind a few bruises or abrasions. Again, it's just another
option. Maybe I'm schizoid, but then after all that I really
like to wake up cuddled like a teddy bear. Too too Disney.
The ingestion of urine is also getting to be quite the vogue,
but I haven't caught up to it yet. Don't understand it.

"I've never been sexually involved with or aroused by a
woman. Women have usually been my best friends, I think
women have taught me the only useful things I ever learned.
Men are crazy. (There; I've said it.) So why do I dislike
being touched by a woman? Gee, I'm not sure. There's a lot
of Freudian crapola I could throw in about that—the smother-
ing mother and seeing nobody but nurses my first three years,
etc. . . . But why *still?* I feel very backward about not relating
sexually with women. Can't think what to do about it. What's
to do?

"Well, about relationships, it seems all I can really relate
to is the dead-end affair—someone I know is leaving. There
was a hustler. Then I dumped my six-month lover (the record
holder)—because he went outa town for two weeks. The next
day I happened upon one of the finds of the decade in men,
who also happened to be moving outa town in two weeks. I
thought it would be a perfect fling while my lover was away,
but it turned out I couldn't go back to him. Just couldn't.
Then there was a fling with a black designer. What I'm not
telling so far is what these relationships really felt like.

"The hustler made me feel sane by comparison. That was

nice. Also he was market quality, which is why we didn't really have good sex. But he was a poet (of sorts) and wanted to be an actor, but was really marked not to grow up anyway. Intensely childlike person. The six-month man made me feel very crazy by comparision; he didn't smoke or drink or dance, and he was punctual and professional and real good sex. The one who distracted me from him was very nearly a Jesuit priest or a Mafia man but left town to go to hair school. His father was furious.

"Essentially what I have to say about relationships is that I don't want one. I enjoy my life. But when somebody falls out of the sky and strikes up the harmonious chord, well, what can you do? Honor it.

"Jealousy? Yuck. Nonproductive. Stifling. A ploy of the economic system. People are not property.

"Two nights ago I went to bed with a man who had never been to bed with a man before. I loved it. We were sitting there at the bar talking about how hard it is growing up male, and then I started yapping about growing up gay, and then suddenly he said, "Would you like to make love to me?" Honest. Perfect. So we went to his house and I kept giving him every out, in case he didn't really mean it, but he did, and we did, and he was Great. No hesitation, no bad ideas (mutual fellatio is what seemed natural to him)—and I was surprised because I would have expected some reluctance on the part of a first-timer to suck. Wrong-o. And he always referred to it as "making love," which, yes, is different. If I take him at face value—I mean, what he told me—he is exactly the kind of new man this society needs. Quiet; open; affectionate; articulate; and incidentally, a hell of a looker.

"I guess I can't really end this without telling you the whole thing about Jim, the 19-year-old hustler who committed suicide in New York. He was pushy as hell, and loud and demanding, and scared. He became a liberated faggot at age fourteen in a small town. He needed support desperately, so I'd feed him dinner and kiss him goodbye at the door as he went out to work the streets. Then he'd come home about two and make me walk to the Quik-Trip for burritos. Ick. But then he really did drive me crazy, too; by the time he left we just said, "Later," by which I meant give yourself a couple of years. Six months later—when I was having a fling with another farm-boy fairy with adjustment problems—he called up and said I have to come back. Now. I said nah, you don't mean now. He said please and I said no. So then a couple of weeks later he calls late one night and talks for a while, clearly drunk, asking for phone numbers, desperate to talk, and maybe not to me. He called back at some outrageous hour the next morning and told me stories and read a poem and laughed a lot and then got kinda spooky, but not more so than a lot of other times, saying "remember this conversation" (which I don't quite), but anyway we both knew that he was dying and he did a few hours later. Why was it love? A lot of it is energy, I guess. The energy flow between us, the amount of respect—respect—that can be expressed meaningfully. I come off sounding real hard when I talk about him because it was such a ludicrous situation. We thought we were the latest thing from MGM Productions. I gave him two oak trees in a small pot. His abandoned pet mice came to die on my dining-room rug—two floors below their home—after he left. After he died I felt stood up.

"I am happiest with strangers. I mean, none of these relationships was really balanced right sexually. So I really get into one terrific night. No phone numbers. Although— honorable mention goes to the two-week man who moved. Haven't heard from him since, but sleeping with him was a real treat. Couldn't go to sleep because he grinds his teeth; the noise was deafening, so I'd lie next to him and try to massage his jaw. Once he asked me to rub my stubbly chin on the nape of his neck. Good details, even if the big picture turned out to be not so attractive.

"My friends are permanent. Sex partners come and go. So do lovers. Love? Oh my. Really, it's like the ocean, it just goes on and on.

"Every sexual act I've performed was illegal. Am I pissed? Do you wonder if I'm pissed?

"Questions I have to ask myself: How much of my desire to fuck men is based on hostility? How far have I pushed myself *not* to become the upright Baptist Masons man I was born to be? How much further to go? And what *do* all those men think about themselves?

"Observation: Most straight men like me. They'll open doors or pat my ass or just any crazy thing because (I think) they're intrigued by my apparent "decadence." I don't mind.

"Gee, why did I answer? Well, gay men have a responsibility to help change the patterns, to ensure personal freedom *and* mass survival. Ain't gonna be easy. The Facts of Life, they used to say."

"I am sixty-nine years of age, white Anglo-Saxon Protestant (!) with DAR eligibility on both sides of my family.

I am retired from teaching art at the university. I was brought up as a strict Methodist, straightlaced—good people, you know, but awful tight.

"A few years ago, as I was approaching sixty, I went through a lot of fear of getting old and losing my sex, and losing my sex drive—and the fear was very debilitating. But what I perceive now is a lot of cyclical variation: sometimes a fairly high sex drive, sometimes (inexplicably) a very low sex drive. It's very curious.

"I was married for twenty-eight years, but on a lifelong basis I regard myself as bisexual. For the last year and a half I have had an ongoing relationship with a man ten years younger than I am. I don't know exactly where it's going, but I am happy with it, at least for now. But back to my marriage. I have three grown children and three grandchildren. Yes, I liked being married—that was the thing to do, wasn't it? And the marriage was certainly not without real strengths, rewards, and fulfillments, etc. Looking back, I probably married by default, or at least, the reasons were a bit less than totally free and wisely evaluated. (But I suppose that a great many marriages are undertaken in that way, perhaps the great majority: it is largely by chance that the things which draw two people together will continue, or that the two will grow parallel in the same direction throughout their lives. Obviously that sometimes happens. Those are the success stories.) The effect of my marriage on sex, in my case, was disastrous. Because of my early youth experiences with homosexuality, and the terrible guilt and confusion attached, I was very conscious of my contribution (or lack of it) to the sexuality of the marriage. The fear and confusion were tremendous, and in that time (1925-35) there just was no usable information or counsel to be had.

"In my twenty-eight-year marriage, the sex was disastrous. She evidently never had an orgasm until late in our married life. There was only one occasion that I am entirely sure of, although she may have reached orgasm sometimes after years and years of therapy and counseling. But, I loved my wife—in quite a few senses. If she had been comfortable enough with her own sexuality we could have had a great time together in the early years. Then we "grew apart." Maybe that was unavoidable. I look back now almost aghast to realize that I would have stayed with her without any sex at all if we could have worked out a minimum living arrangement. That was in 1967. Since then I have grown and changed tremendously. The divorce was final in 1968, after a bitter battle. I initiated the action, but followed the "chivalrous" convention of allowing her to press the charges.

"I masturbated whenever there was not enough sex with her. I felt guilty about it, and had to keep it secret from her.

"Originally we both believed in monogamy, and pretty much lived up to it. In fact, I had only one evening of extramarital sex during those years. I was foolish enough to confess it to my wife—which was partly due to the guilt that I carried from my religious upbringing—and partly a little punitive on my part, because that one night with my former lover, even though the sex wasn't all that great, rejuvenated me and made sex with my wife possible again—where it had been falling apart.

"The first child arrived quite unexpectedly for me, although I discovered much later that my wife knew exactly when it was conceived. I cannot say that she consciously planned it, but I feel that at some unconscious level she got pregnant to "save the marriage." It was psychological hell, all right! I wanted to be a father, but I was dismayed when I first heard that we were having a baby. It was not the right time. I was spending the first available year of my life giving full time to trying to be an artist, the highest goal of my life, and the scariest project. The child should have waited until after that year. Now I love each of my three children intensely, and I'm sure they know of my love for them, believe in it, and return it. I had to give up quite a lot to be married and have children.

"The main reason for our divorce—and it still holds up as the real reason—was to open up more space for all of us concerned. Although I am not now in any position to know close up where my former wife's head is at, or just how her happiness is being served, she maintains good contacts with the children, and I think is really in a much better place separated from me.

"I had a lot of problems with impotence after my divorce. This was understandably an aftermath. My dear ex-wife knew exactly how to get to me on this and that is one of the things that had been a real bummer. I used to be caught in the pressure trip of having to go ahead and *do* it. I did *all* the work in lovemaking, and when after ten years of marriage I was impotent in my wife's bed, this was a *horrendous* blow to me, just awful. But one short session with a psychotherapist (he turned out to be pretty good)—well, I guess two or three sessions it was—a little conversation, a little counseling, and Jesus, I was a horny bridegroom again—so I can look back and see that I was practically a superman to do all of the work in lovemaking for ten years. I had the feeling that I *had* to have a stiff prick and do it and that it just *had* to be. That was an awful pressure.

"Also with my wife I was obligated to perform hours of foreplay that never got anywhere. (I discovered after my divorce that cunnilingus is great, but I'm sorry to say my wife smelled and tasted awful, and there was twenty-eight years of that!) Well, I love foreplay, and if this is mutual . . . really, I'm good, I'm marvelous, and I can really turn on. But I've never been with a woman who returned the same kind of thing. I would love it, I would just love to have a partner turn me on. My breasts are sensitive, but through all the years of marriage, my wife "knew" that men's breasts were *not* sensitive, absolutely not! And so they weren't, I guess, I never discovered it, never had any idea, I never diddled with them myself, and she would certainly never touch them—but now I know I *love* to be touched, and my breasts are very sensitive.

"I think we American men are terribly burdened with performance failure. The whole male performance thing has been laid into us *heavy*. That whole dating game, just short of sex, heavy petting and so on. I was very, very sensitive to cock teasing women, who were playing everything but the last giving of sex, because of prestige, position, economics, and marriage. Women in my experience—aunts, older female relatives—seemed like they submitted to sex because that was the way that they got what they needed—money, prestige, whatever else—and this I found very demeaning *to men*—this quite aside from the women's side of it. There's no question of the oppression of women in that regard at the hands of men. But this reverse of the whole thing is terribly demeaning to men.

"I've been single now for twelve years, and in the past two years I have had sex with about six men. My ongoing relationship at the moment is really the equivalent of "going steady," in this case with a man about ten years younger than I am. We maintain our independent apartments in different parts of the city, live our own lives quite independently, but have a very significant emotional "primary" relationship between us, including sex and a good deal of mutuality, caring, and companionship. For my part, I would hardly call it "love," but I really do not know how to apply that word at this point in my life, for this relationship is surely "loving." Right now I have the feeling that this relationship, which has lasted more than a year and a half, is changing, just how I'm not sure. This is my first, and only, sustained intimate relationship with a man. My sex with men includes: four men between the ages of fifteen and twenty-five, the first a few times, the other three once each.

"Now I do not believe in monogamy. My present liaison is not exactly a marriage equivalent, but we are quite open in our mutual freedom. I have had occasional sex with other friends. My partner knows about them, in some cases quite explicitly, in other cases inferentially, when it is totally clear that our openness with each other is not threatened. The particular people involved are usually mutual friends, or at least mutual acquaintances.

"I am the happiest right now, of all the periods of my life, but not because of any single "someone." The reestablished closeness with my children is very important. Also the fact that I perceive myself as contributing a lot to my present partner is fulfilling to me at a deep level. (I very much value and enjoy his companionship and increasingly respect both his mind and his values. All I was implying above is that I think at the time we came together he was a bit more needful than I was. I am his first long-term, close relationship, and I contributed almost embarrassingly to his "happiest time in his life," which he has now managed to share openly with his lifelong friends, all of whom are married.)

"I am planning someday to get back to "dating" women. But at the present time I am giving myself "permission" to flow along, and not have to try to direct what is going to happen. The main feeling is that I am O.K., just as good, valuable, and loving a person as ever *even* if I am having sex with a man!

"When I started having sex with men, the most surprising thing to me was the fact that there are so many more similarities than differences! I had been brainwashed into assuming that it was something totally "other"! Most of it is the same, just varying according to which people are involved. The main difference is that the role indoctrination, the "battle of the sexes," is absent in my experiences of sex with men. Neither one is the dominant one, neither one controls socially sanctioned prerequisites, but, most important, the sex roles learned from early childhood just do not apply. Understandably, this probably does not apply in the same way to all men, but in my case it was possible to come together sexually with no strings attached, a thing still culturally impossible with women for me at the time of my courtship and marriage, and still very prevalent throughout the world. (The feminist battle is scarcely yet won.)

"My favorite thing about sex with men is surely the absence of the stereotyped roles and conflicts which I have experienced with women. And I would recommend homosexuality to other men almost entirely on the basis of exorcising that big bugaboo of homophobia. I think that is in the interests of all men, regardless of their sexual preferences and satisfactions. The surest way to challenge homophobia is to try loving men—all the way. I do not, however, make any sweeping recommendations. I suspect that bisexuality is where it's at theoretically, with a very wide range of preferences, experiences, and patterns. The advantage is more loving experience. Disadvantages are endless at the present time, practically all of them social, as far as I can see. Otherwise, to explore love with men would be ony a positive gain, even if it did not prove to be particularly satisfying to any particular person. But, at present, the social cost is very great, and, most difficult, a large part of that social oppression is internalized, and carried around with all of us.

"Most difficult is sexuality in relationship to one's children. One son, who is now very close, used my sexual disclosure as the excuse for a lot of hurt and abuse—but it really came from somewhere else, including his own homophobia.

"My sexual feelings for men are a part of brotherliness— I mean, this is a part of paternal closeness. Recently, the two or three men I've had contacts with initiated the relationship. I never would have initiated it. This was kind of mind-blowing for me, they being much younger. These younger men, good friends, partly represent the hero figure of youth and beauty, with a little of the sadness of aging, looking back at it. Partly they are just ageless and just dear, dear friends. Partly they are my delighted children, and I am wishing them the sexual freedom and openness that I missed when I was young. And I have had that kind of feeling for my own sons—that's the kind of feeling that shades off into relationships with good friends (they're students at the university—I've had lots of students who were sensitive people, and it would certainly have been easy to be sexual with them if they happened to feel like it— but I've never felt any overt, certainly no drive that ever led me to consider seducing anybody, or anything like that). As I say, the experiences that I have had with men in recent years have been initiated by the younger man, and those have been marvelous.

"About two years ago, I had a totally unbelievable relationship with a young man which was—it was sexual, but it didn't end up with completed sex—but it was from a person I would never have expected it from. We simply went through a love affair in a period of a couple of hours. I don't even know his last name. This was in my own home, and it was with friends—but a beautiful young man I had not thought I could even respect, we just tuned in to the same wavelength, and were very, very open physically—it did not end up with completed sex, I suppose you would say. The main thing is that it was a very deep feeling, right at the beginning, for no known reason.

"What I was told about sex by my parents consisted mostly of a YMCA booklet (this was about 1922 or 1923) which should not have been inflicted on anyone! The whole grim nineteenth-century scenario of masturbation causing decline, decay, softening of the brain, falling hair—naturally, virility *all* down the drain—total depravity! Otherwise all was silence on the subject from my parents. They were too uncomfortable about it to say anything. But the unspoken message, loud and clear, both from them and through the church and community, was that sex was a form of sin so unspeakable that it couldn't even be mentioned. Nothing was ever said about menstruation, and it remained a very puzzling and mysterious thing.

"When I was thirteen, I was taught to masturbate by a friend in junior high school. Very fine orgasm and ejaculation the first time. From then on I masturbated so regularly that I seldom had wet dreams, but masturbation was so fearful and awful a thing, so far as the grown-ups were concerned, that I sometimes tried not to do it.

"How does age affect sex? Over the years? Up and down! But for the last ten or twelve years steadily for the better. Yes, age affects sex, but in subtle ways, not obvious ones, once you get past the gross physiological ones of sheer energy, which doubtless peaks early, surely by mid-twenties. Exercise is very important. Although I am now reducing the amount of time I give to exercise as a part of balancing my whole schedule, I still give time to yoga and stretching exercises every day, with a yoga class once a week. Formerly I spent a lot of time with Tai Chih Chuan, and before that in jogging and a supervised physical fitness program.

"I am of medium height, medium build, wiry rather than bulky, and very well "preserved." In fact, I am a very handsome man. (A very few years ago I would not have been able to make such a confident claim, even though, physically, I was even better-looking when younger, of course.)

"I am very proud of my masculinity. When young I feared that I was not masculine enough. Everybody I knew really felt the same way. I'm sure, now, that the jocks and the studs when I was a kid were just as much prey to those fears as I was, very possibly even more than I! I used to think that well, heck, all those capable guys (!)—you know, the studs, the machos, the big men on campus—I figured they had it all wired! Now I know, God no! Probably, being a late bloomer, I was just plodding along and better than most of them. As I said earlier, looking back at it, and I didn't think so myself, but looking back at it, my performance was pretty damn good —it has been just damn good.

"Men can be proud of thought, art, science, craft, skill; but ashamed of the way they have bought into the myth of power. By this I mean basically the expectation that their greatest fulfillment will come through power over others, rather than through participation in the experience of life. Those who have chosen experience—artists, mystics, gourmands, drifters, clowns, fools, etc.—have been despised by the main-line machos who have imposed their forever unfulfilled notion of masculinity through the institution of patriarchy.

"The only heroic role I can see at the present time for men or anybody is an effective life bucking the inhumanity and injustice of the world we live in, thus contributing to the lives of people, whether now living or yet to be born.

"Just a few years ago my greatest fear was that I might not make it into old age on the sunny side. Now I know that I have already made it, and I am far from old! My enjoyment of sex has very greatly increased with my escape from the male performance roles, and I now have more sex, both interpersonal and solitary masturbation, than at any other time in my life.

"Wow! That was quite an experience! This seemed like a good time to undertake a kind of sexual inventory of myself and my life. I shall keep a Xerox among my own papers. My children can then know, direct from me, who I was sexually when they go through my papers after I am dead."

MEN WHO HAVE SEX WITH BOTH WOMEN AND MEN

Men who liked sexual relations with both men and women found there was little sympathy or understanding for their point of view:

"Bisexuality is nowhere in this society dealt with as a potentially open, valid, and acceptable option. My gay friends are annoyed that I'm 'half straight,' and my straight friends are waiting for me to 'come to my senses.' Talk about alienation."

"Because of my relationships with both men and women, people insist on trying to put me in a category. To some I am a closet homosexual who keeps his relationships with women only to hide his true personality from the outside world and himself. To others, I am a heterosexual who is disturbed by some childhood experience. In actuality I am a human being who enjoys sharing intimate experiences with other human beings with whom I feel friendship, love, or compassion. If the label 'bisexual' is slapped on my reply, I will be very disappointed."

"I think the work gay organizations are doing is heroic and necessary. But I often feel that I can't get behind gay stands on things because they tend to exclude people who have heterosexual interests. It seems you have to be labeled, you have to fit into somebody's stereotype or you don't count. What I think civilized society really needs is bisexual liberation."

"I refuse to be considered gay or straight. I want only to be accepted as a human being."

One man, age seventy-three, predominantly homosexual, explained the advantages he saw in "bisexuality":

"I like the muscularity of well-maintained male bodies, and especially a male organ that gets fairly hard. Nevertheless, I do not recommend exclusive homosexuality. Sex with women is not only functional for procreation, but it also provides its own varieties of sensual and emotional pleasure, and failure to engage in it handicaps one in fully understanding and appreciating half the human race. So my recommendation to young men who feel themselves to be exclusively homosexual is to try heterosexual relations before habit crystallizes their emotions to the point that their fear of nonperformance with women makes them reluctant to try. I believe that almost all males have considerable heterosexual as well as homosexual tendencies—at least until conditioning in our homophobic culture freezes most of them as heterosexual (but also some become frozen as homosexual). At the same time, having had pleasurable homosexual relations has benefits for those men who are predominantly heterosexual beyond the brief sensual and possibly emotional satisfactions of actual sex. It produces a useful sensitivity towards one's own sex, tends to reduce aggressive hostility and competitiveness—and makes for pleasanter situations (nonsexual) when males are together."

Four percent of the men in this study (plus an additional 2 percent who were previously included in the statistic on men who *prefer* sex with other men) had and enjoyed sex with both men and women. Most of them had had very infrequent sexual relations with men, while having most of their sex with women.

An extremely small minority of other men had very regular sex with both men and women as an ongoing part of their lives; most felt surprisingly comfortable about it. Following are two men's replies:

"I have always been bisexual, a tag I don't actually approve of, but for the sake of communication it will have to do. I spent a good deal of my life, about forty years, being ashamed of my love and attraction for men. I became, as I got older, more and more neurotic, and more and more withdrawn sexually from my wife, who was very much into being married, and particularly to me. My wife suffered terribly because of this, and was deprived because she hung on to the relationship sexually, despite the fact that we had practically stopped having sex together. I was a very successful businessman, but one day I just suddenly threw in the towel. As the gay movement was becoming more acceptable, I somehow had to come out, or I was going to have to walk out on my family, which I was very much attached to . . . I have four daughters.

"My wife suspected that I had homosexual desires, and confronted me with them, and that was the beginning of my doing something about it. I went to a therapist and like a bull in a china shop, I worked at myself. For the first time I was able to confront all the shit that had been put on me by society, by my parents, and by other men, and in the end by my wife's expectation of what I was supposed to be as a man. It took three years to fight our way through all the hang-ups, and all the expectations, and all the pressure that had been applied to us. It wasn't easy, it was full of pain, and a lot of suffering. We nearly parted about six times . . . but somehow there was a deep and real commitment between us. It's O.K. now—we live together, we enjoy each other, she has accepted what I am, and I have learned to understand her needs more. It's very much a middle-class monogamous relationship, but with me having the right to express my sexuality also with men, without her being offended or threatened. I don't think that in the end I would have been able to be fully homosexual, and I am very pleased that I have a sexual partner like my wife, with whom I have a real good understanding in bed.

"I got married because I did really fall in love with my wife. And after all the traumas of our life, we have a fantastic relationship, caring and sensitive. But I am sure that I married not only because I loved her, but also because it was expected of me that I would marry—any suggestion that I wouldn't was frowned on, and looked at suspiciously. With my attraction for men, it became, in a lot of ways, a method of escaping the judgment of society. I wish I had had the advantage of the openness or the near openness there is today about homosexuality. Then at least my wife and I would never have had the awful periods of pain we suffered in the 1950's and early 1960's.

"My feelings about sex have changed with time. For example, with regard to intercourse (which I love)—in my youth I just got in and came, without understanding anything about myself or my wife, or the guys that I went to bed with. It was as if intercourse, fucking, was just getting your prick active, and always having to come to prove that you were a man. But now—it's my sensitivity to my partners and to myself that has made the difference. I want sex, or intercourse, to consummate the fullness of my feelings towards another human being . . . it's the statement of my love and affection.

"I have learned that I can have an orgasm without an ejaculation, and in some ways that is mind-blowing, also that my wife doesn't feel that I have to come every time we have sex. What the hell—orgasm is not the whole story! But after orgasm, I feel fantastic, I want to hang on to my partner forever afterwards, the problem is that my wife wants to curl up on her side of the bed and go to sleep after we have hugged and tickled. I would like to sleep in the feeling of the sexual act itself, that is very close and touching.

"I like to take a long time with arousal, so does my wife. It's not that it's the best part of sex, but arousal is such an exciting and meaningful period because it is the statement of wanting and appreciating your partner. Touching and kissing is vital.

"I enjoy oral sex . . . it gives me a feeling that I can show my deepest affection not only through my prick. I like the look, and the feeling to my mouth. They seem to express the whole concept of life, the great tunnel of creation . . . it's warm and comforting. I put my tongue right into her vagina . . . it tastes salty. My throat feels open, I am doing it because there is a need in me. My partner will tell me when and how she wants it done.

"I think that men are more open to using their mouths, but that may simply be a physiological reason . . . I don't know, it's different—more passion, but less feeling. Women are much more caring about the way they use their mouths, men are a bit violent, or at least more aggressive.

"Sometimes I like anal penetration but it is a bit sore, I need to be very turned on by the guy to want to be fucked. I don't orgasm, in fact I lose my erection.

"I like men's bodies, and their smell. I like the feeling of their strength, and the feeling of their and my bodies together. I also like their penises. But by comparison I find the whole process of sex with women more meaningful. I am not sure that this may not be the taboo with which I was brought up, but somehow there is a deeper feeling of awareness with a woman than with a man . . . I know for sure that I could never live with a man in a monogamous relationship, but I have lived more or less with my wife for thirty years, and wouldn't change that experience for a homosexual 'marriage.' Actually I don't believe in marriage at all, I believe

that two people don't need the formality of a marriage ceremony but we have made a fetish of it in our society, society
needs the value judgment of the stamp of a certificate to value
human relationships. Plus, in our society, in marriage the
woman becomes the possession of the man by virtue of a
piece of paper with the approval of the Church. This is what
women are fighting to prevent. Men have to change the basis
of their attitudes before there is going to be meaningful status
for women on an equal basis for the future.

"I think that the women's liberation movement, however
unstructured it may be at the moment, is the most important
and significant political and social event since the French
Revolution, and certainly since the Russian Revolution. It has
this importance because for the first time women have said
clearly that any change in society has to acknowledge the
need for men to change their dominance, whether in a revolutionary situation or not. Thus the future of the world will
never quite be the same as the movement grows in strength,
and as the Western world accepts the equality of women,
let's hope the socialist world will also, not just in theory but
in reality.

"That's enough. I have enjoyed answering these questions. My wife and I went through the book together, and
we went through these questions together. It helped iron out
a whole lot of shit between us, and I hope what I have written
helps others too."

"There is one thing I must ask. Maybe it's just me. But
here it goes.

"I am thirty-one years old, my wife is twenty-six. We
have a fourteen-month-old baby girl. I myself have had a
lot of sexual contacts with both sexes. It started very early
in my life at the age of eight, with an older boy of fifteen
years. He did everything to me, from kissing me and making
me take off my clothing very slowly, then he would take my
penis in his hand and start kissing it, then sucking it. Then
he would turn me around and do the same to my rectum.
He told me not to tell anyone, 'cause if I did he would take
care of me in a way I wouldn't like. This went on for some
time, till I was around twelve. Then my family and I moved
to the other side of town. I didn't see that boy again, but
would always think how good he made me feel, then I would
masturbate while thinking of him.

"When I started high school I found a new friend, a

boy, we started sleeping over each other's homes. And before you knew it we were making it with each other and I liked it. We would make believe that one of us was the girl and then take turns going down on each other. And having intercourse with each other till we both would come. This went on for three years, we had other boys we would mess around with also. One night this boy and six others of us were staying at my house overnight while my mother and father were away for the weekend. Someone had gotten some girly books and we all got hot and picked partners, stripped, and played with each other. You name it and we did it. Then all of us would take a turn sucking each boy, and taking it up the ass. Then all eight of us made it with the other. This went on till four that morning, then we all fell asleep.

"After a few more gang bangs the club started to break up because we all started to date girls. I also would date girls, mess around with them. But yet I was still longing for a male partner and would make it with any boy that would.

"When I turned twenty I started to date more and now the girls would let me have intercourse with them. We would go down on each other, have sex, and then leave. That was until I met a girl around five years older than myself, with three kids and a man and ring. She was the first woman that had me doing all kinds of things to her. Things that I have never even seen in a skin book. And she would do the same things to me. Now in between our meetings I was going out with other girls and once more with other boys.

"Then five or six weeks later I was to meet my wife. We had intercourse and all that before we were made as one. And we knew that each of us had intercourse before we met. Our sex drives were hot until the baby came. Then for around eight months she slowed down, only having sex around one to two days a week. So before I started to run on her, I thought that we should have a talk. We both just came right out and told each other how we felt. And then for the next few weeks, we had intercourse three to four times a week. Then it started to happen again. She would go out with her grandmother and girlfriends at night to play bingo. Once, then three or four times a week. Leaving me home by myself to take care of the baby. So again I had a talk with her. And things were all right for a while. When it started up again, I started to run on her and would let her stay home to look after the baby. But I had to stop because I couldn't face her or when we did have intercourse I felt like hell. So I stopped running and now I am in the same spot I was in before.

"She says all I think about is sex and all the crazy things I would like her to do. She doesn't mind if I go down on her or eat her ass and she enjoys sometimes doing the same to me. But most of the time when I feel like having sex, if I take too long, say fifteen to twenty minutes, she gets mad at me, then in turn I get mad and I'll stop and she'll just turn over and fall asleep. Leaving me to play with myself till I make myself come. I don't know, maybe it is me. I do always think of sex, it's on my mind most of the time.

"Do I need help? Am I a sex nut because all I think of is making it with someone, male and female? But I don't— I just think about doing it, get myself all hot, and end up playing with myself till I come. Am I the only man that has these same feelings over and over? I hope not. One thing you must believe, I love my wife very much and I know that she loves me. She's a good mother, she keeps herself neat and clean, as I do. We both do the housework on weekends. But when it comes to sex, she does it when she gets ready, and when she does she goes all the way and holds nothing back. But that's only once or twice a month. Any other time she's cold. Can you help me?"

8

THE SEXUALITY
OF OLDER* MEN

* How old is "older"? Perhaps older includes all of us, since we all worry so much about becoming older. There is no real definition of "older," or no real cutoff age. Bodies (and minds and spirits) age at different rates; therefore the quotes in this chapter reflect a variety of ages.

Perhaps the cruelest stereotype about men is the idea that they are at their sexual peak when they are nineteen or twenty, and that they will only decline from then on.

Most younger men had heard and believed this "fact":

"I'm at the height of my sexual worth right now, I guess." (Age twenty-three.)

"I have been told that I am in the height of my sex life. Would you please tell me why it will decrease." (Age seventeen.)

"Seems like if you're past thirty, you're no longer considered virile enough, etc., at least from what one reads and hears. At least I'm not over the hill yet." (Age twenty-seven.)

Judging from the answers received from every age group, an enormous fear of aging accompanies most men throughout their lives:

"Whenever I see an old man, I get scared of what it will be like then for me—though I guess now people are saying sex doesn't need to cease with age. Sex is too great to do without." (Age twenty-one.)

"In this youth-oriented society I fear I will lose my sex drive in a few years, or no one will want to have sex with me because I'm too old. I know the day is not far off when I'll wake up one day and realize that the most recent experience will be the last—and that will be that." (Age forty-one.)

"One of the purposes of sex is a proclamation of self—a way of saying I enjoy and can be enjoyed. For this reason, having sex is one of the most vital activities of my life—I look upon advancing age with dread." (Age fifty.)

"When I reach the point where I can no longer have erections, I shall carry on, orally, digitally, or with the use of a penis substitute if my partner wishes penetration. I would like to know how most women feel about an impotent man using the above procedures. Of course, now we have surgical procedures such as the bypass and implants." (Age thirty-five.)

"A doctor friend of mine told me about my prostate gland: 'Don't let it grow old! Keep it young! Make use of it as often as you can!' My prostate gland causes me no real trouble yet, but I fear the day they will tell me 'you need to have it removed.' Well, I keep it going. Leaving it on the side track, I think, will see it rust to the point of requiring its removal out of the way to the garbage dump. I don't want it to happen!" (Age forty.)

"I doubt I will care to love if/when I become impotent or I can't find, or at least seek, a partner." (Age twenty-eight.)

Although men feared aging and its effect on their sexuality, actually men in this study replied that aging and maturing seem to improve sex, or at least the enjoyment of sex. In fact, *there was hardly a man in the entire study who did not report that his sex life was better in some way than it had ever been before*—except for those who were having difficulties in maintaining or achieving a relationship, which is a problem having little to do with aging. Of course, many of these men had also redefined sex over the years, making their answers even more interesting.

HOW DOES MEN'S SEXUALITY CHANGE WITH EACH DECADE?

"How does age affect sex? Does desire for sex increase or decrease with age? Enjoyment of sex? Is your sex life different now than it used to be? How?"

How do men feel in each decade of their lives? What, in fact, can one expect at the various stages of life? Following are answers from men divided by age group.

Ages 20 to 29

Many men in their twenties said that they enjoyed sex more than they had before because now they connected it with actual pleasure and an emotional feeling for the partner; some also mentioned that their own sexuality was more developed:

"For myself I have found that my sex gets better with each birthday. My desire grows accordingly. The only difference is that now I make love to someone, and they make love to me. In every sense of the word. Before all I did was fuck. Bang-bang-bang, come." (Age twenty-seven.)

"The older I get, the more I want to have sex, and the more comfortable I am in letting myself feel sexual feelings. I know more now of what turns me on." (Age twenty-five.)

"I am much more sexually sensitive now than I was when I started to have sex, and I continue to get more sensitive all the time." (Age twenty.)

"The older I get, the more emotionally, rather than physically, involved I get." (Age twenty-four.)

"The older I get, the better sex is. I am growing mentally. I have more confidence. I am becoming a more sensitive and expressive person, and being less macho." (Age twenty-four.)

"I would like to help dispel the myth that a man's sexual height is when he is nineteen (where this arbitrary age came from I don't know). All I can tell you is that when I was nineteen, women would find that I was a pretty lousy lover as compared to myself today. When I was nineteen, I lacked patience, and understanding of a woman's emotional and physical needs—and had no knowledge of the complex biological aspect of sexuality. Now, eight years later, I feel I am only beginning to understand that there is no 'formula' for sexual satisfaction and that men and women who look for one or think they have found one may only be trapped in a repetitious automatic routine." (Age twenty-seven.)

Ages 30 to 39

Most men in their thirties said that they were currently enjoying sex more because they were more comfortable with it: they knew more about both their own and their partners' sexuality, and felt freer to communicate about it. Also, most men stressed the increased importance of an emotional attachment to their partner. A few men mentioned noticing physical changes, but most said that they had not changed physically:

"My enjoyment is greater now because my wife and I can communicate more openly about sexual concerns than we could at a younger age. We are more willing to try different techniques and approaches to intercourse as we have matured in our marriage." (Age thirty-two.)

"I'm better because I'm less inhibited." (Age thirty-two.)

"As you grow from childhood and get married, you don't have the same free time raising and supporting a family, plus you have different psychological pressures you didn't have. These I believe come with age and can change your sex life, but age alone, no. My enjoyment of sex hasn't changed except now I feel better knowing you can give pleasure instead of just receiving it. On the whole I get half my enjoyment from the fact my wife is getting some enjoyment also." (Age thirty.)

"I do not think age has any effect on sex, but my sex life is more enjoyable now because it has changed from heterosexual to homosexual." (Age thirty-seven.)

"I find that as one gets older and more mature, sex is more enjoyable and satisfying. I have an increased desire for a better quality of sex life and increased frequency. I wonder if it will continue to improve or reach a plateau and level off." (Age thiry-eight.)

"I'm probably a little less capable of having multiple acts of intercourse in short periods of time than I was fifteen years ago, but I also think that I'm a better lover now than I was then. I don't think age is nearly as important as caring and knowledge of how to act on that caring for the other person." (Age thirty-four.)

"Most change is emotional. I grew weary of casual sex because it was considerably less exciting." (Age thirty-seven.)

"Everyone says it does. I haven't noticed a physical change. But I think I'm getting better at it—more adventuresome." (Age thirty-seven.)

"The older I get, the better it gets . . . the more I know, the more I dig it. Perhaps each encounter is less intense than when I was a teenager on the physical level, but on overall levels it's more fulfilling—maybe less 'getting off' and more 'getting into.' " (Age thirty-six.)

"In my case, it is more enjoyable. I really never knew how to completely satisfy a woman until this year. I read many books, and learned more about the female body, plus the patience a male needs to make a woman enjoy sex also." (Age thirty-four.)

"Age seems to diminish libido a bit, I think. At the same time the potential for enjoyment is greatly multiplied by experience. The two things which time and experience bring are the ability to control ejaculation and the growing appreciation of the varieties of sexual experience beyond penis-in-vagina." (Age thirty-two.)

"Very much improved. I've developed courage." (Age thirty.)

"I am thirty-five and sex seems more satisfying, interesting, and humane than at twenty-one. The hurry is gone and relationships more important. The whole body is appreciated. I'm more delighted with personalities." (Age thirty-five.)

"It keeps getting better. I don't have the dumb guilt feelings and hang-ups I had when I was younger." (Age thirty-seven.)

"As I get older I feel that I enjoy sex more. I need less of it, but of a better quality. The genital aspect of sex is less important; I look more for affection and understanding. Also, jobs, housework, and raising our daughter take their toll and give us less time and energy for sexual (or other) activities." (Age thirty-four.)

"When I was in my late teens, I was egotistical, continuously horny, and preoccupied with getting laid. Now I can take it or leave it, mostly leave it, in spite of the bombardment of erotic advertising. I can ejaculate by masturbating, so now I look at sex as an adjunct to communication and conversation with a woman—more a means of friendship than the prior physical necessity." (Age thirty-seven.)

"I believe age very definitely affects sex. The older (or perhaps more experienced) the person is, the more they seem to want to 'make love' rather than being screwed. Anyone can screw someone else, but to make love takes either age or experience. My desire for lovemaking has *increased* over the years. When I first started I was a screwer and not a lovemaker; there is all the difference in the world between the two." (Age thirty-five.)

"The older I get, the more I want to connect spiritually, instead of just sexually, with a potential sex partner. Companionship, common interests become more important; passion less so. I find myself thinking of my sexual partners as friends rather than lovers." (Age thirty-three.)

And a few men said:

"From age nineteen to thirty-two, sex has become generally less important as I've come to derive increasing pleasure from other activities like work or my own self-development." (Age thirty-two.)

"I think we learn as we grow older that sex does not have to be the dominant thing in our life, and can be put on the back burner for a while, especially if it is a problem." (Age thirty-seven.)

Ages 40 to 49

The height of worry over "performance" and aging occurred in men in their forties. But while often mentioning a difference in their frequency or the timing of ejaculation, most said—almost without exception—that they enjoyed themselves more than ever, except for those who were bored or unhappy with their relationships; also, men in their forties stressed again the even increased importance of an emotional relationship with their sexual partner for complete enjoyment of sex:

"As I get older it takes longer between sessions to get to the stage where I 'really get horny'—and getting horny is fun in and of itself. Desire for frequency of sex seems to diminish somewhat, but sex overall is much more fun as more variety of activities are tried—but it only works with someone like my wife who loves me like I love her and enjoys sex and is free and open to talk about it—and experiment— without fear that what we're about to try may ruin our sex life. With both of my previous wives it was very 'straight,' 'boring,' 'non-experimental,' and unloving." (Age forty-four.)

"Over the years my sex life has improved by virtue of greater ease of communication, with less misunderstandings of feelings, wants, and needs. There has also been removal of tension about possible conception, especially since my vasectomy, and an increase in the frequency of intercourse. It has improved and become more natural with less taboo aspects. Attitudes are more easygoing—nudity, four-letter words, cunnilingus, etc.—hence our activities have a wider scope, but I am too well-satisfied to be very energetic about the expansion of activities." (Age forty-nine.)

"I get more satisfaction now at the age of forty-eight, but whether that is as a result of my age or simply from doing it oftener is hard to say—either one might explain slower erections and the ability to retain them longer." (Age forty-eight.)

"I am forty-nine years old and only feel the difference of the years in the frequency of sex, not the pleasure of sex. Sex is still great, I masturbate as often as when younger. Sometimes in bed with my partner my mind might be saying 'screw,' but my penis doesn't get the message. But if I place my partner's hand on my penis and she plays around for a little while, wham, bang, there is my erection. I have encouraged her to take the aggressive role and really enjoy being 'king for a day.' " (Age forty-nine.)

"I cannot see any slowing down. I enjoy sex more now, as I have the experience and a good control over my ejaculation, which, like most men, I did not have in my early years." (Age forty-six.)

"I have not noticed any change in my 'sex life' at the age of forty-five, except that younger women think of me more as a 'father image' than before." (Age forty-five.)

"There is no doubt that age reduces ability in any physical activity, but then, sex is not an Olympic performance. Quality in communication is more important than anything else." (Age forty.)

"About a week ago I discovered that because of the sedentary nature of my business, I got very little exercise and, without realizing the slow decline, had almost become a semi-invalid. Just woke up one morning and realized that I couldn't even walk through the house without stopping to lean on something. Also I just couldn't seem to stand up straight. Began doing stretching exercises and taking walks around the block every hour or so. It was very painful at first, but in this short time I have seen dramatic results. My sexual feelings and ability have returned rapidly, plus the ability to breathe more comfortably. I'm beginning to think that what I thought were my sexual problems are more physically based than I realized." (Age forty.)

"At the present time I am not married and do not have a steady partner, but I masturbate every day. I am in my best physical shape ever, after having exercised heavily for the last fifteen years. I exercise and jog for an hour a day, and I am careful with my meals. As a result, my sex drive and stamina are the strongest they have ever been in my life." (Age forty-five.)

"I am having more fun (e.g., intercourse, etc., etc.) at forty-seven than at twenty. For fifteen years of my marriage, 'sex' was a seldom item with my wife; I tried 'others' but found cheating not my bag for full enjoyment. I masturbated frequently. Now my second marriage is idyllic in every way, emotionally, psychologically, and physically." (Age forty-seven.)

"Age has not affected my desires, or enjoyment for sex except to give me perhaps greater enjoyment. But my sex life is different now, as my wife is through the menopause and does not seem to get very much from sex anymore."* (Age forty.)

"Orgasms are better than ever. Intercourse is more fulfilling, lovelier, longer-lasting. Desire is the same, but no longer obsessive—if that makes any sense. When I didn't have as much as I wanted, I was half crazy to get it. I have all I want now. It's very nice." (Age forty-two.)

"I think I still have as much desire but I am honestly bored and frustrated by having the same partner for twenty years." (Age forty-six.)

"You slow down a little, come more slowly, don't spurt as much—but you savor it more and appreciate it more, too. Desire decreases, enjoyment increases. At seventeen it was an automatic reaction; at forty-three it is a joyous celebration of life." (Age forty-three.)

"I'm in better shape emotionally, and my life isn't so complex. I just have to never forget I must keep in better shape physically, watch the liquor and what I eat, and keep active. If not, you'll get so fat and sloppy it'll make your eyes water. I'm still capable of three big long erections a day for several days in a row, and for as long as I want them. Orgasms are just as intense although I guess I don't ejaculate as hard. Other than that, I don't feel I'm slowing down." (Age forty-three.)

"Age affects sex the same way it affects everything. If you've been paying attention and actually learned something about life, sex gets better and better. I can't generalize about desire, because my lover has such an incendiary effect on me that I attribute my near-perpetual state of desire to my relationship with her. And my sex life is different now because it is predicated on love and is a continuing thing. Before—that is, up till five years ago—my sex life varied according to the nature and duration of the relationships. Now, it is the best I've ever known, both sensually and emotionally. I think I am twice the lover I was ten years ago, in my thirties, and most assuredly more giving and loving than I was in my twenties. Part is simply a modicum of

---

* Actually, this stereotype is untrue, as discussed in *The Hite Report* on female sexuality.

maturity, knowing who I am, and the largest part is the good fortune of meeting a woman who is right for me (and I for her)." (Age forty-two.)

"The desire for sex remains strong but I've found that my social/political interests have overshadowed much of my drive. I'm in the process of rechanneling much energy into these fields." (Age forty-six.)

"I think that the real desire for sex doesn't decrease with age, but the ability (physical endurance, tiredness, etc.) can affect the success of sexual experience. When success is achieved, the enjoyment is just as strong as it was when I was 'twenty.' My sex life is different only in that I have come to terms with accepting my homosexuality, whereas I have previously tried to think that it did not exist and tried to hide it. I have as many lovers now as I have ever had. And as long as I have something special to offer, I know I always will." (Age forty-five.)

Ages 50 to 59

By their fifties, most men were pleasurably engaged in re-creating their sex lives (and often their lives in general)— either to make them more what they had always wanted or to adjust to their changing physical/muscular (overall body) reactions, or both; most said they were enjoying sex and their relationships more than ever:

"With age came understanding of myself and my lover's wants and needs. I am not as intent in just pursuing penetration and ejaculation. I have learned to enjoy it more and not waste energy on anxiety and pressures that are set by books on performance. I have learned to use the ideas presented, but let the mood determine the way for that occasion. I enjoy my sex life ever so much more. I know what it takes to bring my lover to orgasm via the breasts, clitoris, and vaginal activities with confidence. I have been very fortunate in learning, with the help of my lover, to read her emotional level by her response and body movements. This takes lots of worry and guesswork out of sexual love foreplay. I have learned how to match her need with my capabilities. By that I mean if she has a real horny need, I use more preliminary orgasms in love play before using my energy all up in thrusting with my penis. Thus allowing me to bring her to satiation, if that is what she indicates she wants." (Age fifty-seven.)

"I'm fifty and my sex drive is stronger than at any

previous time. I believe this is the result of education and accepting my sensuality and sexuality rather than being ashamed of them. I was afraid and ashamed of them before. My sex life is different because I have insisted on improvement in our marriage or I want out. We have had five years of all kinds of therapy, group therapy, seminars, love-learning, sex therapy, etc. Almost all of it nonsexual, but aimed at making our marriage more complete; and our least complete area has been sex. At this point I am unsure whether we will make it or not." (Age fifty.)

"For me, age increases the importance of sex in my life —the children are grown and gone, retirement looms, and I've acquired some wisdom, I learned to put first things first. At the same time that capacity for performance decreases, desire has *increased*, along with and because of enjoyment. My sex life has changed radically from its onetime nature: it's freer, less guilt-ridden, less anxious, less exploitative of my partner, and much more joyful—ecstatic—for both of us." (Age fifty-five.)

"My sex life is very different because I am doing the things I always wanted to do, am less inhibited about speaking openly about sex, and find that women are of the same mind also." (Age fifty-seven.)

"In my case, desire for sex has increased with age, as has enjoyment of sex. My sex life is different and better now than it used to be because all of my relationships with people are better, and because my self-love is greater than at any point in my life." (Age fifty-six.)

"My sex life is better now (at over fifty) than it was. Since my vasectomy, my wife and I seem more compatible— she seems to feel less 'victimized' or 'used' by my desires for sex, which are more frequent." (Age fifty-six.)

"I have less ability at fifty-three (started about forty-nine or fifty) to erect and maintain it. But I actually have a stronger sex drive now, or maybe it is because I have eliminated some guilt that I had when younger. My enjoyment of sex is much greater now—partly because I have admitted I like sex with men better—and partly because the fear and guilt have lessened." (Age fifty-three.)

"I desire about half the sex now at fifty-four that I did in my twenties. It is about twice a week now and I can 'do with' once if that is all there is. But I enjoy sex much more now than when I was younger because it is different: (a) I can control myself much better now and, therefore, prolong the enjoyment. (b) I know a lot more about women and what they want and need than I used to, and this allows me to provide them with better sex, and that in turn enhances my own enjoyment. (c) My orgasms seem to be better than they were when I was younger. I believe that is because I can build up to them for a longer time. (d) One difference that I *don't* like is that sometimes I can fail. I am not as vigorous as I used to be and, if I try to prolong things too long, I can louse up the whole deal by tiring myself to the point that I lose my erection." (Age fifty-four.)

"Age slows sex down. But this isn't bad. Both partners enjoy a higher level of pleasure because it no more needs to be wham, bam, thank you, ma'am." (Age fifty-three.)

"It does slow down a lot with age. I am more satisfied now, and less 'horny' than when I was twenty-five, but I know more and can do more for a partner and understand a lot more now than then. I have had two heart attacks and still have a very active sex life." (Age fifty-three.)

"You just cannot get the fast hard erections anytime you want them. As you get older and older it takes much longer to get the full erection. My desire is as high as it was when I was in the twenties, but you just cannot respond as fast and it is discouraging. Also, for some unknown reason, as I get older and older, I feel I like and would like to have the services of a male, and male genitals look better and better to me. They are just beautiful in men from nineteen to fifty-five." (Age fifty-eight.)

"The desire for sex becomes more meaningful, is longer-lasting and more enjoyable, and a greater masterliness in the overall sex act is achieved. Women 'come back for more,' because now I have the staying power and give them repeated orgasms. When I was younger there were many 'quick bangs,' which I'm sure was not all that completely satisfying to the girl. My sex life now is saner, more selective, more exquisite, and more enjoyable." (Age fifty.)

"I thought maybe I was having age trouble, but then I met some new women! I had lost 80 percent of my interest for about four years. It may have been partly health and partly depression. Now I have lost about twenty pounds and feel much better. I'm not the stud I used to be, but I'm not bad either. Desire and enjoyment seem to be nearly un-affected. The number of orgasms per night is down, and the stimulation needed to reach orgasm is up—but orgasm isn't the objective anyway, release of tension is. I'm firmly con-vinced that psychological factors account for something like 90 percent of sex. 'It's all in your head.' " (Age fifty-one.)

"Past the forties, the realization strikes that this way is passed only once. The enjoyment of sex does increase with age because there seems to be increased participation with the partner. My sex life is somewhat different than it used to be because I have learned to give more to my partner (wife) in the way of sensual release than I did at an earlier age. Therefore, it might be said that I have become more loving, and willing to spend more time in preparation for the culmination than when I was much younger." (Age fifty-one.)

Following are two longer replies from men in their fifties, to give a broader perspective on how men are experiencing their sexuality in the context of their lives as a whole:

"I am fifty-two. I am short, overweight, and gray. I suppose I used to be what some people would call handsome but right now I would consider myself bordering on ugly. I have been in fire department work (administrative) off and on for twenty-eight years. The last twelve in positions of authority. I am Catholic from a religious family but I don't practice my religion. I never graduated from high school because I joined the Navy in 1944.

"My biggest worries are my four youngest children (we have eleven children) and the daily problems I encounter on my job. I am holding a political position and there are times when I am pressured by deadlines, administrative duties, politicians, the news media, and the general public. Sometimes all at once. I am at the top of my profession and earn an adequate salary. I would feel useless if I didn't work. My job has been satisfying for the most part, but I am becoming cynical and disgusted with people. I believe I should receive more recognition because I am doing an outstanding job and have the statistics to prove it.

"I have been married almost thirty-two years. I guess I like being married but I have the best of two worlds—I am single during the week and married on weekends. I have an apartment 125 miles away from my wife, so when we see each other on weekends it's a pleasure. Maybe this is the way we all should live. We got married because my wife was pregnant but we were engaged at the time. (Engaged is going out of style, isn't it?) During thirty-two years, sex reaches so many peaks and valleys that it's difficult to say what effect the years have on it. I will say that right now sex with my wife is at its greatest. She seems to get better with age and both of us are probably without any inhibition. This was not really true until the past ten or twelve years but she is more attractive and better in bed than she ever was.

"I love my wife, and I'm sure she loves me, despite both our many faults. She is very orgasmic, contrary to our earlier lives, but probably that was as much my fault as hers, or more. She never really entered the outside world until twelve years ago because she was busy having and raising children. I love her but I also like and admire her tremendously. She is something else. In my own field, politics, I would like to see many more women hold political offices. Men should be ashamed because they have refused to allow women to be equal.

"I believe in monogamy. Who in the world wants two wives? I have had extramarital experiences—three or four but only one for any length of time (one and a half years). I am not now having one and doubt if I ever will again. The long one very nearly ruined my life and my wife knew about it.

"We have eleven children (really ridiculous, isn't it?) but we didn't 'decide' to have them. My wife kept getting pregnant. I guess I wasn't too upset the first time, since we were engaged and were ready for marriage. I love my children, but there are times when I could have murdered some of them. We gave up a lot by having so many children but it never really hurt my career. There are people who don't have much faith in some idiot who fathers eleven children but I guess I've been lucky. We probably would have been able to enjoy the finer things in life but what the hell! We all make our own bed, don't we? We're reasonably happy."

But one of these two men's replies illustrates a problem many men in this age group were having; even though they could enjoy sex just as much as ever, their wives did not often want to have sex with them, and negative sexual patterns had developed over the years (see chapter 5):

"I am age fifty-seven. I am a millwright in the steel mills. I was brought up in a Mormon home in Utah with good moral standards. I served four years in the Army during World War II in Africa and Italy.

"I was most deeply in love when I first got married. It was the best feeling of contentment I ever had. I slept better at night and felt more energetic when I was awake. But it didn't last for long, and I don't think my wife or any other woman ever had a very deep feeling for me, that I was number one in their life. About two years after I was married, my wife turned from me one day when I tried to kiss her and never gave me an affectionate kiss since. I was so deeply hurt then that I couldn't sleep no matter how hard I tried.

"I enjoyed sexual relations with my wife when I was first married, but I don't feel that I ever really had a good one compared to what I have read about. It was mostly a 'get it over with if you have to' thing. She wouldn't communicate on what felt best to her. When I would try to talk to her about it, she would say 'just don't do it' felt best to her. I did good to get her nightgown up enough and her panties down far enough to get it in. I feel that having sex with the clothes on is worse than taking a bath with them on.

"We have been married twenty years. I would like to be married to a more loving and affectionate woman that felt like I was good enough for her and wasn't always complaining because I don't have a million dollars for her to spend. I am married now because of obligation to my children. Once you're married and have children, with the laws they have you her slave forever. If I was free of all my obligations, I would hurry and try to find a more compatible woman to start a new life. I got married originally because I wanted to have a family-type life with children. I never dreamed my great dream would turn into such a nightmare. Sex also played an important part in my desire to get married. I would as soon been dead as to have lived without it like I have.

"Rather than cheat on her if she won't take care of my needs, I would rather get divorced and marry someone who is willing to take care of me. Sex with myself only is better than nothing, but I about climb the walls without some relief. Plus I get prostate gland trouble. When I relieve myself two or three times a week I don't have a pain in my prostate.

"I would like my wife to be more affectionate. And even if it weren't for my religious attitudes, it seems that if a man is supporting a wife and family, she should feel some obligation to the marirage. I feel that my wife should be willing to have sex often enough to satisfy my need for it. If occasionally she didn't feel like it I think I could accept it. It would be a woman's right to refuse if she wasn't married to the man, if she didn't lead him on too far. I think it is a wife's obligation to keep her husband satisfied.

"I do have a problem having an erection at times, or other times I can get an erection and not be able to have an orgasm. I really seem to have a problem getting an erection sometimes, but I can usually get sexual release by masturbation. I have never had fellatio stimulation of my penis and haven't much desire to—it doesn't seem right. I know I would not want to do it to anyone else.

"I hadn't worried much about her orgasm before I read *The Hite Report,* especially when she would not discuss the problem and try to cooperate. It would be all right with me if she stimulated herself to orgasm if it makes her feel better. I would even help if she would let me know what felt best. I would like to cooperate to make it as enjoyable as possible for her. I have not had cunnilingus with a woman and I have no desire to but maybe if I tried it I would like it? Also, my wife will not allow me to do it manually to her. When I try to give her a little foreplay she just says quit bugging me and get over on your own side of the bed. I am not sure if my wife has orgasms and if she has I didn't notice the difference. She will not discuss it with me.

"I have only had sex with my wife. She is one year younger than me and there is certainly much to be desired that she doesn't offer. She is a poor cook, can't sew, hates housework, a poor sex partner, and complains all the time. I think a woman is infringing on the rights of a man when she marries him and refuses to take care of his need for sex and the other obligations of a family life. She should stay single if she doesn't want to take care of her marriage duties. It is kind of late for her to change her mind when there are children.

"I believe in equal rights both ways. I have shared everything I have with her, but she hasn't shared everything she has with me. I bring my paycheck and hand it to her to put in the bank for our family use. I do not smoke, drink, or gamble."

Ages 60 to 69

Most men in their sixties could enjoy sex as much as they had when they were younger—often to their own surprise—even though physically they were different sexually than they had been in their twenties, and might have sex or orgasm less often:

"This is a myth, of course, that older people do not like sex. In my own experience I find I orgasm somewhat less frequently than I did in the past, but in other ways my activity has increased, as I have been less inhibited in later years." (Age sixty-four.)

"As one gets older, sex becomes more beautiful! My sex desire at sixteen was almost nil. At twenty-six it was quite active. At thirty-six it was good. At forty-six it was great. At fifty-six it was the best. Now—over sixty it's about the most important thing in life." (Age sixty-one.)

"The intensity of sexual desire and the ability to produce semen and to discharge it forcefully do gradually decrease with age, although usually not as much as you younger people think and perhaps worry about." (Age sixty-four.)

"My sex life has been a succession of peaks and valleys. Between eighteen and twenty-two I enjoyed the apogee of my sexual activity with the partner who was the great love of my life. After we separated there was a long period of five or six years marked by only intermittent episodes and long intervals of celibacy. A powerful resurgence came with courtship and marriage and lasted perhaps twenty years until female complications caused my wife pain and discomfort, and sex activity became sporadic. After a hysterectomy my wife became a cipher in sexual matters and I was practically celibate for almost fifteen years. At age sixty-three I met my present companion, who is twenty-five years younger than I, and I have been functioning on all cylinders ever since. I'm approaching age sixty-nine with very litle diminution in interest or activity in sex." (Age sixty-eight.)

"I think desire for sex increases with age. It is a mistaken notion that old folks don't need sex any longer; that they should 'settle down and act their age.' But my sex life at sixty is much poorer than it was in my earlier years, despite my sex drive being the same. This is due to a poor marital situation. I would prefer to be with someone who wants to mutually share a life together, but unfortunately I can't see my way clear to do this." (Age sixty.)

"My enjoyment of sex is as great as it ever was, perhaps more so because my wife has become more knowledgeable with age; she is not shocked or repelled as she may have been when we were first married forty-four years ago. Because we have become more sophisticated, our sex life is different and more enjoyable than it was. There is definitely more variety to it, less embarrassment and reluctance, more acceptance." (Age sixty-eight.)

"I enjoy sex more now than I did when I was young. There was too much hassle then, too much uncertainty, too many fears and expectations. Now I know what to do, and it always works just about perfectly." (Age sixty.)

"Age is a slowing-down process. This includes sex. I

have found that with increasing age, my desire for sex has also decreased. But it has also increased the emotional aspect of sex in every way: feelings are more important than physical pleasure. Physical enjoyment may decrease, but the emotional pleasure increases. My sex life is different now in that it entails less fucking and more 'sensuality,' more time spent just enjoying each others' bodies in a physical way, caressing, kissing, stroking, etc." (Age sixty-three.)

"Lovemaking is my chief desire and interest—offset by long brisk walks—not jogging—just for reverie, no destination." (Age sixty.)

"As I age, I find it harder to (1) meet women and (2) become interested and active with women who will, I think, generate pleasant feelings. But I can enjoy orgasm just as much." (Age sixty-five.)

"I vaguely remember hearing someone quote someone to the effect that it's a pleasure to reach an age where sex is an occasional source of enjoyment instead of a constant source of annoyance. I have slowed down from six or more ejaculations a day at sixteen to five or six a week at sixty-four. The change in attitudes and activities has been the continuing increase in options." (Age sixty-four.)

"I enjoy penile-vaginal intercourse and I always have orgasm although I am sixty-five. But it *does* take a bit longer, and I don't have as much semen as I formerly had, or eject it as forcefully as fifteen years ago. This means milder orgasms. I have intercourse with my wife two or three, sometimes four times per week. I could use more, but my wife is aging faster than I, although she is four years younger." (Age sixty-five.)

"Too many people feel that only physically young, beautiful people enjoy sex and that isn't so. Sex can be great with sagging breasts, flabby muscles, wrinkles and paunches. People should realize this. *Desire* does decrease but enjoyment should not!" (Age sixty-three.)

"Sleeping with an old man seems a sort of obscenity to many people, but senior citizens are much sexier than younger people like to think." (Age sixty-six.)

"My wife and I missed many years of exciting sex because of her inhibitions and refusal to frankly talk sex with me from the beginning of our marriage. When I tried any type of foreplay she would say, 'Just put it in, that's what I want.' I felt that I was being masturbated in her vagina and was not satisfied with my orgasms even though they were intense. I knew that we were not getting all there was out of sex. I finally succeeded in getting her to discuss her needs with me. I had to almost force oral sex on her even though she would orgasm each time to some degree and would not admit that it was that good. She is still too inhibited to ask for cunnilingus unless I suggest it. I am gradually learning to read her mind by her actions during the buildup to our sexual foreplay. Erotic sex-oriented stories are good to arouse her. We also have some good sex movies that arouse me more than her. We don't respond to exactly the same scenes. She is doing her best to be frankly and openly honest with me, and with patience and love we hope to disprove that sex after sixty is not good." (Age sixty +.)

And a few longer replies from men in their sixties:

"I'm sixty, religious and active in my congregation, serving on the worship committee. I love my work (I'm an engineering consultant), people, and sex. I especially enjoy hosting parties with my new partner. I enjoy getting up in the morning and look forward to going to bed at night. My mother told me: 'You're certainly not good-looking; you'll probably never be rich; but there's no reason you can't be punctual.'

"My father told me that women were the most precious elements in the world, and that the greatest joy I could experience would be sharing life with a woman and caring for her and our children. I grew up feeling women were wonderful, mysterious, powerful, gorgeous, and desirable. I couldn't wait to get married. But my mother felt I might never marry, and should, therefore, learn how to care for myself completely. Therefore, I'm an excellent cook, and a demon housekeeper. My partner thinks I'm a jewel to live with, because I believe chores get done by whoever is handiest, not by any sex role definitions.

"I've been living full-time with my new partner for only two months. She is someone I've known for perhaps twenty years. Her children and mine were in class together throughout grammar and high school. She'd been widowed for about two years when, one summer when my wife took off on an extended cross-country vacation, I borrowed a book from her. She asked a routine social question: 'I suppose you miss Marjorie.' To my surprise, I answered honestly: 'Not at all.' At that moment, her telephone rang, and she went off to answer it; I departed with borrowed book in hand. Several nights later I invited her to dinner to discuss the book. We met each other off and on throughout that summer. When my wife returned, I told her of what had happened. Her reply: 'I'm not at all surprised; you were always sweet on her.' (Which was news to me.) We talked about our marriage and then made one final major effort to salvage something with professional help. That failed, and shortly after that I moved out. I gradually established a 'regular' pattern with my present partner, during the early stages of which I occasionally dated someone else—occasions which seemed flat and non-interesting.

"We enjoy life together, doing things we each always wanted to. We enjoy our children (all grown) and my grand-children. We look forward to being together, and we find ourselves wondering specifically how we'll manage with the dwindling sexual drive which is supposed to accompany the aging process. (So far, we're doing great!) We are happy and content as we are, taking life day by day. Perhaps we'll marry in a few years when it will not adversely affect the amount she will get from social security.

"Cuddling and caring for children is a big part of my life. My father, when he ushered at church, was always pick-ing up the babies and cuddling them. I've always done it. My son has always done it. Being a father is great, from the act of conception through living with the children as they become independent adults in their own right. Close physical contact, stroking, nuzzling, kissing, and the like are impor-tant—with my partner, my children, and my grandchildren. Looking out for others is a part of life, and probably one of the reasons I've been a good manager in my work, and was a good troop commander in World War II."

"I've had intercourse with only three women. The sec-ond was my wife. Our sex life was unsatisfactory, and it extended over more than a quarter of a century. Toward the end of our marriage, during the final series of marriage counseling sessions with a therapist (selected by my wife), my wife dropped out, claiming there was nothing she need do. The therapist expressed surprise that I had never actively thought about divorce. He felt that if I chose divorce as a course of action he could be helpful to me, but otherwise, he suggested termination with him. About six months later, I discovered another marriage therapist, but my wife refused to go with me. That summer, when she took off for an ex-tended vacation, I consulted a therapist on my own. In our first session he hit me right between the eyes with the question: 'How come you've considered suicide, but you haven't considered divorce?' That was the turning point, and a year later the divorce was an accomplished fact.

"Until five years ago, I had to find all my warmth and closeness with my children, and with some selected friends; the past five years my life has been so much improved because I'm now with a woman who wants to be close to me, and who isn't turned off by my continuing expressions of affection and desire. Our sex is great. In fact, we fit together sexually, physically, intellectually, emotionally, financially, spiritually, and on just about any other level you could name. It seems as if our prior lives were simply apprenticeships to prepare us to enjoy each other in our present relationship.

"My partner now has discussed her sexual feelings at length, telling me what she likes and doesn't like, sharing the feelings, describing what happened. She feels comfortable in doing this, something she'd never been able to do before. She's amazed that she can tell me what she wants done to her at a given moment without having me go defensive. As a result, sex gets better and better, if that's possible.

"I know where the clitoris is, how to find it, and thanks to my partner, how to treat it the way she wants it at that particular moment (which changes from time to time). I seem to need the active element of stimulating her, appreciating her, stroking her, before I even begin to reach a real level of arousal within myself. The higher she builds, the higher I go. Often I guide my partner through a series of orgasms, and I have no strong urge for orgasm myself—my delight is in what we can accomplish for her and it leaves me totally satisfied. At other times I feel as if I'm about to explode from the first moment.

"After thirty-some-odd years of living with a woman who was not interested in sex, and after all the time of trying to find something she'd like, I'm delighted to be with a woman who enjoys sex, and I do my level best to find everything that feels good to both of us.

"Sex may not be the most important thing in the world, but without it, everything else loses its luster. When work, and companionship, and learning, and doing, and sex all come together in a mutually reinforcing matrix—then God's in His heaven and all's right with the world, as Browning put it."

"I am sixty-six years old, retired—was a manufacturing executive, an Ivy League graduate. I was brought up with high moral standards—virginity was saved for marriage. I am Jewish. Forty-three years married. It is the greatest institution on earth. Sex is a beautiful part of it. No extra-marital experience. I am married to my first girl (known since about thirteen years old), started getting really serious at about eighteen, married after she graduated Seven Sisters. We have had all our sexual experience with each other and have enjoyed each other mentally, physically, and every other way. Our two children are long gone on their own and prac-tically every day is pleasant—a really wonderful time of life. I think our relationship sexually only with each other has had a positive effect on our marriage.

"In youth I had no difficulty with strong erections last-ing as long as necessary (twenty-five minutes to half an hour average). Now erections take longer and are not as hard as in former years. Also erections do not last too long at this age, but we have adjusted by more manual and oral stimula-tion, and faster orgasms by my wife. However, even if erec-tion is lost, my partner can orgasm by rubbing my quite soft penis against her clitoris, and I do ejaculate even though not hard.

"Our intercourse is mostly penis against clitoris with, in youth, withdrawal at climax if I did go inside. We found this method exciting but still safe for birth control. Going against her clitoris and vagina lips, ejaculating into her pubic hair and on her stomach, was very satisfying to us both. At the present age, I go off inside of her if I am still hard—otherwise against her. We average once a week now for me—once in ten days average for wife. When my partner holds the penis herself and uses it to rub against her clitoris, she holds the sides mostly, as too much pressure on the bottom of the penis causes too great an excitement for me. She rubs the head against her clitoris and the entire length against her vagina lips and clitoris.

"Most of the time, or let us say the majority of the time during our life, I think I've made the initial move. However, just two nights ago I fell asleep reading in bed. Awoke at 11:45 p.m. and was propositioned by a lovely old lady in the next bed. Sometimes, in our early years, I felt rejected when my wife preferred to wait until another time. However, the feeling soon passed. But I believe our sex has been just about all we could want. Probably the only addition I'd enjoy would be to watch my wife masturbate to orgasm.

"I could be attracted to younger women—youth is so attractive to healthy older people. However, I am not a big enough fool to think that a young woman would want an old man, even though I still weigh what I did twenty-five years ago and have not completely lost my 'looks.' I'll stick to what I know and have—unless some young beauty attacks me! And then I'd probably run for the hills."

"On Sunday morning we do what we have done since the early years of our marriage: I usually wake first and go down to make coffee. I put the urn and cups on a tray and bring it up to the bedside. When she wakens we sit up on the edge of the bed and chat while we have coffee. Then she goes to the bathroom, voids and washes thoroughly, as I already have done, and we get each other in the mood for sex. I tell her what a good wife she is and get specific—how clean she always keeps her body, how pretty she is, how I like her responsive kisses, the taste of her passionate tongue, the response of her nipples to my kissing, how I like to have her play with my penis and her expertise at oral sex, and the sweet joy of sucking her labia and then bringing her to first orgasm by sucking her clitoris, how I like to have her tickle and tongue my balls, how I like to have her squeeze her breasts to encircle my hot penis, and many other things we have done. Then she tells me again what gives her pleasure. Maybe she says she'd like to sit astride me this time and take her time to give us the maximum of pleasure. Maybe she is gently caressing my penis all that time—up to an hour or more if it's raining—while I'm kissing and caressing her all over.

"Early in marriage my penis hardened instantly at her touch; now it may take me several minutes to erect and for her to come to a hot-passion arousal. A very few times while watching television she has aroused my desire for sex with her by pulling up her dress and masturbating in front of me while saying something like 'Let me see what your John Henry is doing about that sexy blonde on the screen.' She is one year older than I am—sixty-one. Her few wrinkles are beautiful to me. I love her.

"Yes, indeed, we do feel affection and touching are important. We often kiss while she is near me. She knows I like to pat and rub her fanny without wanting her to have immediate sex. And after a movie or party we often play with each other's sex just for a minute or two, then kiss and turn over to sleep. Once in a while she goes to sleep with my penis in her hand.

"A woman's desire for sex doesn't really develop fully until she is thirty-five to forty years old. Her performance increases in intensity and total response until she is well past childbearing age, because she no longer has to fear pregnancy. My enjoyment of sex probably was most intense from age seventeen to twenty-five years of age. It has declined rather steadily since then but when my wife really turns me on we have a ball. It just takes longer for me to come to orgasm. It's still great at sixty.

"To be more specific about the changes in my sex life, orgasm time is slower, my penis takes longer to get firm enough for insertion, I can't make it jerk as vigorously as of yore, the amount of ejaculate is greatly diminished, the spurts and pleasure are reduced, my testicles hang lower and more loosely in my scrotum, the head in erection does not swell to as dark a purple but stays more on the dark red side, nor does my penis spring to erection every time a pretty girl swings her fanny temptingly past my window. But when my wife takes it in her warm hand and flips it around for a couple of minutes, then plops it into her mouth for a hot tonguing, it comes alive for Lady Godiva's Sunday morning ride. Later at our buckwheat cakes and maple syrup or honey, she leans across the corner of the breakfast table and says something like 'Darling, your hair is gray but you still have what surely must be one of the nicest cocks in the whole world. You made my pussy so happy she's still singing.' But if the grandchildren are visiting us she just reaches over, pats my hand, her eyes twinkle, and I just grin like a happy idiot and nod.

"The pleasure of orgasm is less than half what it was when I was seventeen. But still, orgasm at sixty is the greatest pleasure in my life and every night I thank God I can still have a good erection, even though it may take me sometimes five minutes' stimulation to achieve effective hardness. If the erection is only partial I can still achieve insertion by pinching the penis at the base, then after inserting it, my wife's hot vagina does the rest—I'm soon fully erect. In other words, if my penis does not erect after the normal preliminaries, I just place my hand on my pubic area, squeezing the base of my penis between my forefinger and the middle finger, and trap the blood until the penis is firm enough to slide into her previously excited and naturally lubricated vagina, and when inserted the natural heat of her vagina sufficiently restores my virility, and we proceed with intercourse. If that fails we have 69 to orgasm. Lack of erection is no sign of disinterest. If, after ejaculation, my wife informs me she has not reached orgasm, I kiss and caress her sex parts, especially her engorged clitoris, to orgasm. Sometimes twice before she's ready to stop.

"For the last few years we have had intercourse only on Sunday morning because we find the orgasmic pleasure is more intense at that interval. Orgasm is usually followed by a nice afterglow, then a shower together, then we get breakfast together. For variety we sometimes have 69 instead. Same routine follows. If it's raining we may laze abed until I can get it up again. On rare occasions, in midweek.

"What does my wife's vagina feel like to my penis? It feels like the velvety feet of a thousand honey bees must feel to a cattail swaying in a stiff tropical breeze. It feels like spring sliding up into an Alpine valley full of daffodils. (Ah, how sweet her kisses when I've told her that!) It feels like summer's pillar of smoke being withdrawn from a Flanders field where all-seasons perfume is made. It feels, and feels, and feels! Alas, that my penis cannot speak with its lovely little mouth. My penis, any penis, can only probe, and probe for the hidden bell that only the Song of Solomon tells so beautifully well . . .

"How does my darling's vagina feel to my penis and to me when she is in orgasm? I can tell you this: If she is sitting astride my hips and doing most of the moving, both circular-horizontally and vertically, and I am almost totally quiescent and almost in total possession of my faculties, fondling her breasts and watching the red 'measles' blotches spread from her lower belly to her neck and finally to her breasts, my penis feels the outer third of her vagina contracting to about two-thirds of its excitement size, inviting my penis to make violent thrusts to overcome the resistance of her muscular rings. Head thrown back, she lifts her eyes blindly upward, throws her torso forward, her fingers digging into my upper arms, gasps and groans as she grinds her pubic area against mine. Through my penis I feel her half dozen orgasmic contractions. Suddenly she thrusts her tongue into my mouth and goes into a coital frenzy. She has two more orgasms in rapid succession. I'll try to sum it up: It makes my penis feel pretty damn *good!*"

*And once again, some men found that, although they felt the same pleasure in sex as always, their partners or wives were not as interested in having sex with them:**

---

* Possible reasons for this are explored in chapter 5.

"My wife and I are over sixty and have been married for thirty-five years. At first, I was terrified by getting married. It wasn't that I didn't like having a home and having sex. But the expense and duties of one and the duties and difficulties of the other were more than I expected. However, one thing was sure. I knew I loved the girl and wanted to be with her.

"In sex, when we were first married, just getting used to being together and trying positions for the pleasure of them was the main thing—and also, just trying to get her to be able to come. This took several months, and it was more nearly a year before satisfaction was reached.

"One of the big problems has always been that she will not say what she likes or doesn't and it leaves a big guessing area. I still don't realize when she's too dry for intercourse, and when we were first married, I did not know about the necessity of lots of lubrication with rubbers. A druggist explained, after he asked if I needed K-Y cream with them. There was a rather long time when our usual would be a little play, then a long joined period, ending too often when I came and she didn't.

"What we've worked out in sex usually takes an hour or a little more, and most of that is what I try to do to charge her up. I could bang off in a few seconds most of the time. I call it the missionary position, but very little of our bodies meet while she's working because I am fairly still and braced over her. Then when she's coming, or a little while after, when she's easing off, I settle down. That's when I get a very short, but very rewarding, big time.

"By now we are settled (against my will) into sex once a week and one position—'missionary' as I described. Somehow along the years when small children and different schedules made it awfully hard to get a chance to 'be together alone,' my wife set firmly against any more experimenting. Even at first she liked mainly a few positions. She has never agreed to give me head (so I've never had any) and the one or two times I experimented with cunnilingus were disasters. At different times we have had brothers or sisters from either side staying with us for rather long times, and once my mother. This caused a lot of tension. Also I agreed to her stipulation of lights out and only at night, but I do know that a lot of mornings or afternoons would have delighted me.

"Also, our sex life now is set a lot more by when the kids are likely to be out late than by when we want to do what. I've suggested motels, and not joking either, but it makes my wife mad. I like to make more noise than I can with kids in the next room. And I'd like to get more than we can.

"A funny thing is, now, for the last ten years or so, my erection is much slower to go down after orgasm, especially after a lot of foreplay, and sometimes I come more than once without having separated myself from her! This was a surprise since I had thought that age would bring less orgasms, not more. Also, I can keep an erection a lot longer. But if I have been cross or worried, I do sometimes come as fast now as when I was a teenager. You would think this would make my wife try to arouse me again fast, so she could get satisfaction, but it has the opposite effect, and just makes it harder for me to get her again. I guess this is the sort of thing which leads to divorce.

"But no matter what the problems, it is always wonderful to be with my wife. I like to go to sleep holding her or at least with one arm over her shoulder, and when I wake up in the night, I like to be able to reach out and touch her. During most nights I cuddle her spoon fashion for some of the time. She doesn't give back much, but I love her anyway."

As we saw in chapter 5, men tended to complain of women's lack of interest in sex more frequently when they were in relationships which did not contain enough emotional give-and-take, and/or did not develop beyond traditional sexual patterns which do not provide the woman with sufficient stimulation for orgasm, or leave space for the woman to feel free to express herself sexually.

And finally, age was no guarantee against ageism and sexism:

"I personally find very few women my own age that turn me on either mentally or physically, while younger women do. This is a youth-oriented society and there is a very small proportion of younger women who want to make it with an 'older' man. I don't think that age, per se, diminishes the capacity for fucking as much as it diminishes the opportunity." (Age sixty-two.)

"Even at the age of seventy-eight a man likes a firm buttock, breast, good skin, and the absence of flabbiness that some but not all elderly women are cursed with. He may and probably does have flabbiness, dentures, and wheeziness himself. Eventually he'll have to go to a prostitute and get a job a step above masturbation." (Age seventy-eight.)

Ages 70 to 79

In their seventies, most men—but not all—although they might be having less regular or predictable erections and/or orgasms, were still enjoying sex, with or without intercourse. A few men mentioned a decline in interest in sex. Almost all found that emotional relationships (or lack of them) played a crucial and increasingly important role in their ability to enjoy sex. General good health, of course, was the key to continued sexual enjoyment. Overall, a kind of peace seemed to have settled in on many men in their seventies that wasn't apparent in the earlier age ranges—a quiet happiness:

"These days, my erections tend to come and go a bit unpredictably, but it doesn't particularly matter. It usually comes back again pretty soon if stimulation is continued. And in any case, it only affects vaginal intercourse, and sex can be very good by other techniques." (Age seventy-nine.)

"We have slowed up some. We are both seventy-four years old and still very passionate." (Age seventy-four.)

"Age, I have noticed, makes sex better and better. It takes a little longer to ejaculate, but this simply prolongs the pleasure. The enjoyment of sex has increased for me. When I was young, I thought mostly of gratifying myself. Now I find more pleasure in gratifying my partner, thereby increasing my own gratification. I believe too many men think they are finished with sex when they hit sixty or sixty-five, and thereby let their organs atrophy. Constant use will keep them active." (Age seventy-one.)

"Age affects sex. I *cannot* get a good erection anymore, and I have had no coitus since age sixty. I'm now age seventy-one and I masturbate two or three times a week. I have accounting jobs with two organizations, am very busy working, and I'm very happy. All a man needs is a job to do, and a woman to love. I have a girlfriend, age over sixty, who is married, but we have a good time petting." (Age seventy-one.)

"I have found that age affects sex very little. I enjoy it just as much or even more than when I was a young man. I take longer to come, but that is a pleasure not a trouble." (Age seventy.)

"With me I have observed first a diminution of libido, then a diminution of the amount of semen. Desire for sex is the same as it was when I was thirty. Enjoyment is also equal. My sex life is different now only because I am a widower. Not having a woman around forces you to abstinence, and I use masturbation as a last resort." (Age seventy-one.)

"Age has made sex better because I do not come so fast. It has reduced the requirements in frequency. We make love on an average once a week and I would like to double that. My sex life is better now than when I was young, because we love each other more." (Age seventy.)

"Desire does come less often now, unless it is stimulated by my spouse. But the urge is strong when it does come. The act takes longer, the orgasm is more physical effort, but very satisfactory and relaxing." (Age seventy-four.)

"Desire remains—no increase or decrease—but impotence has eliminated all intercourse." (Age seventy-nine.)

"Orgasm is always desired, but is of diminishing importance to me. Due to prescribed medication, I am impotent except on rare occasions. Sex is *very* enjoyable even without orgasm, but obviously less enjoyable." (Age seventy-one.)

"Many times I become hard but do not ejaculate before my penis gets soft. This is not the most enjoyable sex, but I still find it very nice sex." (Age seventy-two.)

"I still desire sex but since I can't stand so much, I require less. Bare female flesh still brings blood rushing to my pecker, my heart goes fast. I enjoy sex just as much as I ever did when I get it. But my sex life is a lot different now, I have no interested partner. I have learned to live with it, to take care of myself as best I can. When I am alone or with my wife I hide nothing from her, if I'm hot with a hard-on I just go ahead and play with it—watching TV, riding in the car, or in bed. I like walking naked around the house and in the backyard with a stiff prick. The breeze feels so good on it. Sometimes I stop and shoot in the grass." (Age seventy.)

Here are a few longer replies:

"We are in our seventies and been married five years, and I doubt there is another couple in this country that kisses and hugs each other more times in the average day than we do. We want to be together all possible. This is my wife's third marriage and my second, due to deaths. Sex is always with my wife, I am no woman chaser. I like to lay close to my wife. I love to have my wife lie with her head on my shoulder and her leg laying across my stomach, both satisfied.

"I have my greatest difficulty in obtaining full erection. It is not my wife's fault. She is a willing partner, in fact she loves it. I can't play around for extended periods of time, when I do get an erection, I have to get there fast and go or not go, I soften down. When my wife is really 'hot' and I can keep a hard erection, she will become short-breathed and many times will dig her fingernails into my shoulders. I enjoy knowing she is having a climax. She will often have a sort of vacuum or should I say it feels like her vagina is sucking my penis in. It is wonderful. The ultimate pleasure is ejaculation in my wife to orgasm.

"Many times I have told my wife that I just can't wait till she gets her passion up sufficiently to climax and she tells me to go ahead and climax, ejaculate, she wants me to ejaculate in her even though she hasn't reached that point herself.

"Why I can't get an erection when I want one takes a lot of explaining, due mainly to my late wife, who flatly refused me for over eight years before her death, and she had no justifiable reason except to punish me. It is a long story.

"I never have and don't intend to try cunnilingus.

"I would like to know why I can't obtain an erection, nothing especially wrong with me physically, I cannot obtain an erection while fondling my wife, but must, unbelievable as it is, I must wash my penis and genitals with cold water, which seems to bring on a partial erection, hurry to my wife, who is in readiness, before my penis becomes flaccid. I have the desire strong enough."

"Greetings. My age is seventy-two. I graduated twelfth grade, I'm Protestant, Caucasian, work in bus transportation (driver and superintendent of operations), forty-five years on the job. Retired now, don't like it.

"My wife has been sick and we have all we can do to keep even, sometimes we need to make them wait. Social security and small company pensions is not enough. Now I am happy because she is gaining her health back and to me that is heaven.

"When my wife was sick, I had sex out of the house, unknown to her. I think it took care of a lot of tension, but I felt guilty. Generally we have sex about once a week—I always orgasm—it's not often enough, but my wife only wants it two or three times a month.

"I'd lie if I said I didn't like casual sexual relations, but I think God meant for us to stay with one woman. Marriage is good. After fifty-five years, this is love commitment—no one can kill or change *real* love—it goes far beyond the grave. We 'fight' when we have a problem and then iron it out—then kiss and make up like we did fifty years ago."

"I am a single male, age seventy-one, and have led a very active sex life since the age of fourteen. But in 1970 I underwent amputation of one leg, which suddenly brought an end to my opportunities of meeting women and I have not had intercourse since, even though I am physically able to perform. As a shut-in, being deprived of sex is an ever-present reality I am unable to solve except by masturbation. I live by myself in a nice apartment and have many interesting hobbies, but about twice a week I take an hour or two to enjoy my body, examine my genitals very thoroughly, admire my growing penis, fondle it into a terrific erection, and prolong the arousal, enjoying every moment as the tension builds. The longer it takes to ejaculate, the more intense the pleasure when it does occur."

"I am almost seventy-three years old, and currently very active homosexually—for the past three of four years far more active sexually with others than at any previous time in my life. I am a bachelor, living alone in a large city, holding a doctorate from a leading university, semi-retired, but still professionally active and useful, and highly regarded by my colleagues. By temperament I am cheerful, vigorous, and lively, and although I have sustained some serious illnesses, currently for my age I am in pretty good health, and look much younger than my years.

"So far as I know, all my near relatives and friends are heterosexual (they are almost all married), and so I have not revealed my orientation to any of them. Doubtless some friends and relatives suspect my sexual orientation, for although I like and get along well with women, I have dated them very infrequently. Anyway no one has ever mentioned the matter to me, and I am treated with respect, regard, and often with affection. The contempt, or at least uneasiness, with which most avowed homosexual males are regarded by the average American heterosexual I have avoided by my 'closeted' status.

"My most satisfying and deepest love relationship ('falling in love') was the mutual, truly loving friendship that developed between myself and a friend with whom I first had sex when he was eighteen, and with whom I continued to have sex on the infrequent occasions when business brought him to my city until his untimely death in middle age. He was heterosexual, and our relationship, regarded by his family only as a close friendship dating from boyhood, in no way interfered with a very successful and happy business life and an affectionate marriage to a wife who idolized him.

"Having had only one satisfying love relationship, it is evident that my friendships, while very few, have been close, and more satisfactory. I get along well with people, am outgoing and good-humored, but I reveal my basic personal emotions to very few. I am on very good, if not deep, terms with my family, brothers and sister, and their children.

"For the last three years I have had a more active sex life than I did in my entire life up to now. My sex life is with the patrons of the back rooms of all-male porno cinemas. Anonymous, generally with no verbal preliminaries, and most often in the dark. I suspect I have had sex, that is to say hand to penis, being fellated, or some form of anal contact, with at least five hundred men. With most there was no orgasm on either side, but I am not counting the almost countless instances of feeling each other through clothes, or flesh contacts that were only momentary. When visiting the back rooms, from 7:30 to almost midnight, I may have sexual relations of some sort with from six to a dozen or more individuals. Usually I have one orgasm during the evening, less frequently two, and very rarely three. This depends in part on how early in the evening I have the first orgasm, and in part how much activity I engage in. Almost always I bring from one to three partners to orgasm, but some pull away to avoid ejaculation when very 'close.' Invariably I engage in mutual masturbation; I am always willing to masturbate and aim for mutuality, but some partners avoid masturbating me (hoping I will fellate), while others do not wish to be masturbated. Usually, but not always, I get fellated (without asking) at least once, not infrequently by two or three men. Less often I am entered anally and about half the time my partner comes. I have achieved orgasm by anal entry, usually only when my partner has assisted manually or been attractive and shown enthusiasm.

"Being single has advantages in freedom of action, availability for one person of one's financial resources, avoiding the inevitable annoyances and criticisms of one's home companion. The great disadvantage is occasional loneliness, lack of someone to care if one is ill, lack of someone to talk with in important situations, and concern of what will happen in the weakness of old age. Lack of love is the main problem, but many married people lack love and are emotionally (even economically) abandoned in old age. Although I am almost seventy-three, I have sexual relations (usually with orgasm) about twice a week as explained. A number of men find me attractive and tell me so.

"I would prefer to have sex with attractive social friends or certain relatives, but not wishing to risk loss of friendship, I stick to sex with strangers, which I find much more emotionally satisfying than masturbation, though far from ideal. I would no longer wish to share an apartment with another man as lover or sexual friend, for I have become too used to freedom. But I would enjoy a friendship that included sexual intimacy and the ability to talk with utmost openness.

"I should like to be able to work openly for the cause of full and equal justice to homosexuals. I feel, however, that the disadvantages to myself, chiefly social, would counterbalance whatever satisfactions I could derive from helping a good cause. Professionally my prestige depends on my reputation for good judgment, at least in part. Right or wrong, the public view of homosexuals is that they are temperamental, unreliable, and overly emotional. If I avowed my homosexuality, the very fact of my doing so would raise questions about the soundness of my judgment and reliability. Further, friends and relatives with adolescent sons might feel uneasy about their friendships with me.

"Doubtless many 'gay lib' activists would dislike my views and consider them damaging to 'the cause,' but I believe truth is best in the long run. I felt that my life might be worth making available to sociologists, and for the future."

"How old am I? I am seventy.

"Am I in love? Yes, with my wife, to whom I have been married for over thirty years. I am happy with my wife, but I don't get everything I want and neither does she, I'm sure. But by and large I find it the most satisfying relationship I've had. It's spiced with enough excitement to keep it from growing stale and it's solid, stable, despite occasional ups and downs, and it's loving in a practical way. The worst part for me is that my wife finds it hard to accept me for what I am. Specifically, she disapproves of what she considers my inordinate interest in sex as exemplified by my masturbation or the pleasure I take in erotic material. Maybe she feels threatened, though why I don't know, since my erotic interests only help to keep alive my sexual interest in her. Anyway, she reacts with hostility and censoriousness. Previously I would openly show her such material—for example, books—but it got so that to keep the peace I now usually keep such things to myself, thereby incurring the accusation that I'm ashamed

of them and am 'sneaky.' I don't like it this way, I'd rather
she'd share my interests or at least learn to accept them. But
I know that isn't to be, although foolishly occasionally I try
to make overtures in that direction and invariably emerge
with more scars. Exposing one's nakedness to another—
especially one dearest to you—is not always a rewarding experience. I must emphasize, however, that my wife is no
shrew. She is a person of much understanding and generosity,
and this is really our only seemingly insoluble problem. It's
a familiar sort of bind, I suppose. I could—and may—
eliminate from my life all the activity she finds objectionable,
but if I do just because she doesn't like it, it won't change *me*
or the way I *think* or *feel*. And that is what she really wants,
I suppose. What else would have any point? Certainly not
pretending that I *had* changed inwardly when, in fact, I had
not.

"I *love* intercourse. We usually have it once a week,
sometimes not as often if we have guests staying with us. Our
house is small and we are self-conscious about being over-
heard at our sex activities. My wife is usually much less often
in the mood for intercourse to orgasm than I am. She's simply
not as 'horny' as I am. She desires intercourse at rare intervals
—a month or even two months.

"I masturbate, and enjoy it, although there's sometimes
an after feeling of guilt—which I don't feel is reasonable
(after all, I don't hurt anybody by it or deprive anyone of
anything) but which still persists because of the sex taboos
and brainwashing we've received. I masturbate (to orgasm)
three or four times a month—or more if I don't have intercourse about once a week. In addition, I fondle my genitals
and stroke my penis when the mood strikes me. Like my
masturbation, this is usually done in front of a mirror.

"There are a lot of things I'd like to change about my
current sex life but my wife knows about them and feels
differently about them, so I'm not going to make an issue over
them. What good does that do? But here they are: I'd like
occasional fellatio to orgasm in my wife's mouth or at least
kissing, licking and sucking of the penis as foreplay before
coitus or as a means of inducing orgasm without coitus (that
is, my wife could remove my penis from her mouth just as
I'm about to orgasm). I'd enjoy doing more manual fondling
of her vulva and more cunnilingus, not only as foreplay, but
to have my wife orgasm in my mouth, as it were. I'd like my
wife occasionally to stretch out naked on the bed, spread her
legs wide, bring her knees up, and masturbate to orgasm

while I kneel between her knees and also masturbate to orgasm. I'd like my wife to read erotic books with me and discuss them. I'd like to see erotic films—maybe have some at home—and discuss them. I'd like to make genuine, spontaneous caresses a part of our everyday life. I'd like her to put aside the idea that she can only orgasm at long intervals and let me try to arouse her (or have her try to arouse herself) more often than once every month or so. I'm not afraid to tell her such things, but when I try to break through—and I often have tried—I meet resistance, refusal, and the charge that to ask her to change her ways makes her self-conscious. This is the ultimate put-down since, if true, it would destroy all hope of any spontaneous mutual sexual enjoyment. The result of all this is that I keep most of my sexual interests to myself rather than disturb our relationship when no good can result. I am a vigorous man, my interests are varied, I lead an active life, I love my wife and have no thought of leaving her. I enjoy all of her that she will give, and if I want more and can't get it, I take that philosophically. She's got to be her own person and do what she feels is best for her."

Ages 80 and over

Men in their eighties and nineties were having fewer erections and orgasms, depending on overall physical health, but almost all said that enjoyment does not automatically decrease. Many had made interesting discoveries and innovations in their ways of relating. Once again, whether a man was happy or not depended much more on the state of his relationships than on his ability to "function":

"Age decreases your ability and you get fewer erections and orgasms, but your mental desire increases and your enjoyment does too, when sex is available. Hell, yes, I still like it." (Age eighty-three.)

"Sex gets better with age, if health is good. Also, the desire for sex increases with age if health is excellent, and if you remain physically active and mentally active, and are free of taboos, old wives' tales, and inhibitions about what you should and should not feel like. Retired people have more time to enjoy sex at its best." (Age eighty-one.)

"I have just been reading my grandson's sex education book he brought home from college for the holidays. Pretty interesting. Think I'll try some of this stuff with my wife when he leaves." (Age eighty.)

"It feels just as good as ever but not as often. Sex life no different." (Age eighty-six.)

"I still have the desire, only to a lesser degree." (Age eighty-two.)

"Time has left me a castaway on an isle of tropical desires, where my only companions are sirenic memories and the fantasies I can conjure up from the mellowing moonlight on the little waves that lap at the evening shore. But still my head and my hands find a way to celebrate Saturday nights and the quivering dawn of a Sunday morning. Really, God still is very good to me." (Age ninety-two.)

And four final long replies:*

"My age is eighty. I am in love with my wife. We have been married fifty-nine years, happily. I prefer sex with my wife. No one else could be as satisfying. Married life is fine. I like it. We were married because we have liked each other's company since we were eight years old. Monogamy is the best plan. I have no extramarital experience. I could not enjoy anyone else half as much as my wife.

"Sexual desire has not been affected by age. We do different things now than we did when younger, but I think we enjoy each other more. My first real sexual experiences were with my wife. We were over twenty years old at the time. I never had any sex with anyone else. I learned about sex the hard way. No parental instruction.

"Bathroom privacy is advisable until a couple has lived together about fifty years, then it doesn't matter. Sleeping with your wife is very pleasant. Celibacy would be horrible. Also I would be very jealous if my partner had sex with anyone else. I hope it never happens.

"Orgasm is important to me. I would not like to go without it, but I don't think I can describe it. I can orgasm and enjoy sex without erection. Then we enjoy closeness after sex, and resting together. Touching and discussing sex is very important.

"I enjoy masturbation. I usually masturbate once a day, but not to orgasm. I only go all the way to orgasm once a week or so.

"We had intercourse often when younger, but not often now. The vagina feels so lovely to the penis. I never had my

---

* Other longer replies from men in their eighties and nineties can be found in chapter 9.

penis in but one, my wife's. At my age erection does not come easily (encouragement by manual or oral stimulation is necessary) but I do not have premature ejaculation. I can have penis/vagina intercourse for three-quarters of an hour without ejaculation.

"I am pleased to have my wife experience orgasm by any of the sex techniques we use. She prefers cunnilingus and having me manually stimulate her clitoris beforehand. If my wife does not have orgasm from cunnilingus I am disappointed. I do enjoy it, but I do it more to please my wife since it feels good to her. I enjoy looking at her. I rub my tongue along the labia, in the vagina, and rub her clitoris as well with my tongue. Her reactions are exciting. The clitoris is a handy area of stimulation.

"I greatly enjoy fellatio. I do not allow the penis to discharge during it, but after a reasonable time my wife stops the stimulation and I masturbate, sometimes to orgasm, but usually just a short time because it feels good. I also like my wife's manual stimulation, it is a delightful feeling but I do not discharge. I like long-time foreplay. My wife plays with the penis, rubbing it and patting the glans, commonly for half an hour. Our sex life is satisfactory. We communicate well. I usually make the advances. If my wife does not want to have sex she says so, and I do not press the point. This works out fine for us."

———

"My wife died about three years ago. We were married for fifty-two years. I don't feel that I am really in love at this time, but I do have a seventy-two-year-old lady living with me. She is very sexy, and I was also during the majority of my life. I still love to try having sex with my roommate. I am not able to get an erection like I used to, but we do have intercourse four or five times a week. She almost always has an orgasm; I have a good ejaculation at least once a week and often twice.

"Orgasm or ejaculation sends a pleasant feeling all through the body, but it was much stronger when I was younger. When I was younger orgasm and ejaculation seemed to be one and the same; but now I enjoy intercourse until I seem to have an orgasm and my penis goes soft even though I did not ejaculate. At that time I am all through. I must rest a day or more before having an erection again.

"But the *desire* to have sex does not decrease or increase with age, just the ability to achieve and hold an erection. Also the ability to discharge a nice large charge of semen. Orgasms

seem to be milder now. When younger I did enjoy masturbation, as it relaxed my testicles. Now I only have orgasms
during intercourse.

"I have been single nearly three years. I don't like to
live alone. But I don't expect to marry again. The woman I
am living with and I enjoy each other in many ways. Especially in bed. She likes fucking fully as well as I do or ever did.
I wish I could do it as often as she would like. We both
enjoy sleeping together very much. She is good company, a
good cook, and very good in the bedroom. I also had sex
with an eighty-five-year-old woman and she loved it very
much.

"It is not likely that you will get many replies from
eighty-two-year-old men. I would like to read them if you
do. Perhaps they have a solution to my problem about erections."

"I am eighty years old (born in February 1900), but
feel much younger and do not look my age. I am a white,
Anglo-Saxon Protestant, brought up in a small town (5,000
population) in the Midwest. I was valedictorian of my high
school class, and editor in chief of the high school annual.
Graduated college Phi Beta Kappa.

"At twenty-three, I married another student with whom I
had fallen in love during my senior year. We both entered
graduate school then, she in social work and I in theological
seminary. We remained married (no children) for fifteen
years, until I was thirty-eight, while I did graduate work,
served as pastor of two churches, then switched careers to
teaching. My wife continued her social work career, changing
jobs when I did. After fifteen years, she abruptly decided to
terminate our marriage, much to my distress at the time.

"Within two or three months I recovered my equilibrium,
fell in love with a faculty colleague (previously unmarried),
and after a six-week engagement we were married. That was
forty years ago, and we are still *very* happily married. She
continued her career in teaching except for two maternity
leaves. Thirteen years ago, when I was sixty-seven, she sixty-
one, we both retired, and since then have enjoyed life (and
each other) even more than before!

"I am reasonably handsome, white-haired, partly bald
above my forehead, a bit above average height, somewhat
overweight (around 200 pounds), erect posture, fairly brisk
walk—but not quite as brisk as a few years ago. I could pass
for ten years or so younger. I have blue eyes—real 'Irish

blue,' my wife says, and she quite often makes complimentary remarks about them.

"I have the respect and affection of my family and a wide circle of friends—and my own self-respect—and a comfortable and happy home life. One of the great advantages of being retired, and living by ourselves in our own home, is now we have complete leisure to spend in loving and caressing each other. We typically have sex about three times a day.

"I might add that during the first fifteen months of our marriage (until our first child was four months old), we lived in an apartment with an exceptionally roomy bathtub and we loved taking our baths together in the same tub. I would sit behind her with my legs straddling her buttocks, and much enjoyed lathering her back and sponging it off—also in reaching from behind and lathering her breasts and massaging them in the soap suds. Since then our tubs have not been wide enough for both of us to climb in at once, but we would if we could. The nearest we can come to it is for me to kneel beside the tub and lather her back and sponge the lather off with a soft sponge.

"I suppose that, without our saying so, my wife and I are increasingly aware of our mortality—aware that we don't know how much longer we shall have together. That awareness makes each day more precious. We want to make the most of every day we have. Our affection and enjoyment of our mutual love (not just sex, but everything else, too) increases all the time, and is not at all diminished by the fact that our reflexes are slowing down, and that orgasms occur less often now. We are both in good health, but one never knows what the future holds. We like the Latin motto 'carpe diem,' and mention it now and then.

"As I have become older, there have been some interesting changes. My enjoyment of sex is certainly no less (probably more), and the amount of time we spend making love in bed is much greater since we both retired thirteen years ago. We seem to have become *more and more* uninhibited and free with each other—although we were always anything but inhibited. For example: During the day, every now and then we take a notion to sit on the sofa and open my fly so she can fondle my penis, while I reach inside her panties and stimulate her. Many times a day, every day, we give each other deep 'soul kisses' just on the spur of the moment. (I guess this was always true to some extent, but it has gotten even more frequent in recent years.)

"Meanwhile, our sex activities in bed have tended to become less oriented toward vaginal intercourse and more toward mutual masturbation (not necessarily to orgasm, although we do orgasm that way, sometimes simultaneously and sometimes not) and cunnilingus-cum-masturbation, with my wife frequently coming that way, and with me coming with the combination not very often, but being 'on the brink' every time. There have been times when, after my wife got up after our siesta, I have masturbated myself to orgasm, especially if she came during either cunnilingus or mutual masturbation and I did not. On occasion, she has seen me masturbating while she was getting dressed, but she has never seen me actually produce my own orgasm that way.

"My childhood was entirely asexual. I had three younger brothers and a sister (the youngest). I was nine when my sister was born. I never saw her naked. I did not know how babies came. I vaguely remember when my youngest brother was born at home, when I was five and a half, but my sister was born at the hospital and all I knew was that Mother went to the hospital with no baby and came home with one. I guess I knew that the baby was expected, but I don't remember knowing anything about pregnancy as such.

"I guess my first sexual experience was when I had my first wet dream at about thirteen years of age. I thought I had wet the bed, but I knew it was somehow different and talked to my father about it. He told me that it was different from urine, but it was all right, that it happened to boys around my age, and not to worry if it happened occasionally, 'so long as you don't make it happen yourself.' I did not understand what he meant, and puzzled about it for several days.

"When I was maybe fifteen, I decided that I wanted to find out about babies and so on, but I did not feel that I could ask my parents about it, and at that time there weren't books about sex as there are today. (This was about 1915.) I finally found that the *Encyclopaedia Britannica* in my grandparents' front parlor had a rather detailed article on 'Reproduction,' and I spent several hours pouring over it. There was an anatomical diagram showing how ancient Chinese depicted anatomy, and it showed what looked like two penises. Actually, it was their way of showing the urinary system separately from the reproductive system, but I couldn't understand it at all, and asked my mother about it. She did not give me any clear answer and I learned nothing about intercourse. I was having occasional erections by then, but did not understand them at all, and thought they were probably a sign that I needed to urinate.

"I remember my mother telling me that when a boy is with a girl at a party, or on a date, that particular girl is likely to seem to him at the time like the most attractive girl in the world; but that the feeling should be expected to be temporary, and the boy will feel the same way about the next girl he takes out. But as to actual sexual behavior, how mothers get pregnant, etc., nothing. I only learned about menstruation at the age of twenty-three after I married my first wife.

"I first masturbated to orgasm when I was nineteen years old, a junior in college. For maybe a year before that, I had masturbated some and enjoyed the erections that occurred, but (believe it or not) I did not know about orgasms, so I had not continued the masturbating long enough to have one. I finally learned about orgasms and about producing them by masturbation from books that were assigned for a college psychology course. Also somewhere I read that some people masturbate while taking a tub bath, so I decided that would be a good thing to try—and it worked. I enjoyed it so much that I did it again then and there, running more hot water into the tub so it wouldn't cool off too much. The semen just floated off in the water. From then on, I kept a handkerchief under my pillow and masturbated in bed every night, and I've been an enthusiastic masturbator ever since—especially *before* my happy second marriage.

"My senior year in high school, a girl who went to the same Congregational church and Christian Endeavor Society that I did was my steady date for maybe six months. We did some hugging and kissing for fairly long stretches at a time, but it never went further than that. In college, I dated several girls, but not with any sophisticated petting until my senior year. At that time, I was masturbating heavily, and with one girl I discovered the pleasure of mutual masturbation. I was not in love with her, however, and when she started hinting about getting engaged, we had a very frank talk in which it was made clear that we were *not* going to become engaged, but we could continue our sex play strictly for fun, since we both enjoyed it, but with no further complications. She was agreeable to that, and we continued.

"*Marriage I:* It was in the midst of this pseudo-affair that I fell in love with the girl that became my first wife two and a half years later. This marriage lasted for fifteen years, but it never really 'took' with her, although it did with me. The courtship started when I fell 'madly' in love with her, but she did not respond much, as she was already half-engaged to a fellow at another college to which she moved about a month later. I deluged her with letters, to only a few of which she replied. Before long, she became engaged to the other fellow, and we were virtually out of touch for a year and a half. But then her romance cooled and we began corresponding more and more intensely. Entirely by mail, without seeing each other or even talking by telephone, we became engaged. Looking back, I can see that for her it was a 'ricochet romance,' a getting even with her former fiancé by getting engaged to me and getting married. We were married in her parents' home. I never had intercourse before marriage.

"The marriage was always one-sided. I continued (I wonder why, now) to dote on her. I let her make most of the day-to-day decisions—although we both accepted the fact that where we lived depended on where my job was. I consciously tried to be considerate of her in every way, and especially sexually. She was never responsive, was increasingly reluctant and standoffish and on the rather rare occasions when she tolerated intercourse, she would urge, 'Finish it quickly; I don't want to go on and on.' I guess I was sort of afraid of her—specifically afraid that if I offended her she would leave. Eventually she left anyway, of course.

"When my first wife abruptly terminated our marriage, I was deeply hurt, and resented it very much for a time. But my very happy second marriage has eclipsed all that—in fact, I became grateful to 'number one' for walking out, for that is what made my later happiness possible.

"Almost from the beginning of the first marriage I resumed masturbating, which I had been doing daily for the previous four years. I considered that I was doing her a favor by masturbating myself, because that way she did not have to be 'bothered' about it, and I didn't 'pester' her too much about it. I enjoyed masturbating, so it did not bother me, except that I wanted the intimacy with her, and her aversion to sex with me symbolized a basic estrangement. She insisted on twin beds, and even separate bedrooms when possible, almost from the start, although I protested. I never did masturbate in her presence, although one night when we had not seen each other for some time and were sleeping in a double bed at a friend's summer cottage, she refused to respond at all, and after she went to sleep I masturbated while in bed, and pretended I had had a wet dream and got up to change my pajamas. (She insisted that I wear pajamas.) She 'woke up' then, but I suspect she may have been feigning sleep.

"There were stretches as long as six months when my only outlet was masturbating. Toward the end of our marriage, I was becoming more open about it, but still not in her presence. I would put one or two check marks on a wall callendar to indicate the number of ejaculations I had had that day. And while masturbating in the bathroom I would leave the door open, use soap suds on my penis to make audible swishing noises, and even stand before a light in such a way that the shadow of my penis and my hand masturbating could be seen from her bed. We never discussed it, except that she asked me not to check the calendar. (But I still checked it.)

"All those fifteen years, I was 'monogamous.' It really didn't occur to me not to be. I never had an affair with another woman (until after our separation), and was satisfied with masturbating.

"My first wife and I had no children. For the first four years she used a diaphragm. Then she decided she would like to have a child, and so did I, but she did not conceive. After a few months, my sperm was examined and found to be normal (although below average motility). On medical advice, my wife had a cervical dilation to facilitate impregnation, and she did become pregnant, but after two or three months she spontaneously aborted after running to catch a train, and she never became pregnant again. The failure to conceive was probably due largely to the infrequency of intercourse. I don't remember any particular emotional reaction to her brief pregnancy or to her spontaneous abortion. Looking back, I am very doubtful whether my first wife would have made a good mother. I had no conscious thoughts to that effect at the time, but unconsciously I may have. It would certainly have complicated the divorce, and I am very happy, as things turned out, that we did not have any.

"*Marriage II:* My second marriage began when I was thirty-nine, and has lasted so far for forty-one years—and, we hope, for a fair number more. We were ecstatically happy when we found each other, and have been more and more so ever since. Our marriage is about as nearly perfect as I can imagine—and we both feel that way about it.

"We had been fellow members of the same college faculty (different departments) for about three and a half years, but had hardly known each other—until about four months after my first wife walked out. For six or eight weeks after she did, I was 'celibate' and even stopped masturbating, then I started dating. My wife was the sixth woman I dated. Immediately after we started noticing each other, we 'clicked' emotionally and felt, right away, that we were 'meant for each other.' I stopped dating the other five, and we became engaged, setting a wedding date about six weeks in the future. From the start, we did a great deal of passionate kissing, hugging, caressing, and continual hand holding. Within three weeks we began mutual masturbation, and in another week intercourse. At that point, she gave up her apartment (just three blocks from mine) and moved in with me. (That was ten days or so before the wedding.)

"The 'effect on sex' was explosive. My wife, who was thirty-three, had thought of herself as an 'old maid' and as basically asexual. She was a virgin. A few years before, briefly, she had been rather tentatively engaged, but without any real affection. With me, she found herself quite a 'sexpot,' learned to enjoy multiple orgasms, and wanted intercourse at least once (often twice) every day. When she was menstruating, we masturbated each other daily (or occasionally she performed fellatio). As for me, this was a delightful contrast to my first marriage. For the most part, the only occasions for self-masturbation now were while she was in the hospital giving birth, and during two later hospital stays for surgery (hysterectomy and a broken hip).

"We did not always orgasm simultaneously and we never made a fetish of that, but it did often occur, both in intercourse and in mutual masturbation. She also orgasmed with cunnilingus, and sometimes at the same time she would masturbate me to orgasm—or almost to orgasm, followed by intercourse during which she would have a second orgasm while I had my first one. Whenever I orgasmed first, I would bring her to orgasm by cunnilingus or (more often) by masturbating her. If she orgasmed first, we would continue intercourse (or mutual masturbation) until I came also, while she would have another (or several more). This remained our sexual pattern for many years, and is essentially our pattern now—except that at our ages (eighty and seventy-four) we orgasm only occasionally (once a week or so), but *almost* come every day, and we spend more time in sex play even than when we were honeymooners. (We often say to each other that we are still honeymooners.)

"Since we retired thirteen years ago, we have formed

the habit of taking a siesta every afternoon for two hours or so. We spend the siesta naked in each other's arms in bed—sometimes sleeping part of the time and sometimes not. These siestas are in addition to an hour of sex play between waking up and getting out of bed every morning, and half an hour to an hour most evenings after we go to bed. We used to take orgasms for granted almost every day, although even then it was the touching and the closeness and intimacy that meant the most to us. Now, the orgasms are the exception, but the touching and closeness are as precious as ever—even more so.

"As for having children, my present wife and I definitely wanted children, and would have adopted some if we had not had any. We discussed this at the time of becoming engaged. Having been childless in my fifteen-year first marriage, I was not at all sure that I could produce children. However, she became pregnant within two months. Our sex life continued unabated. When we resumed vaginal intercourse (instead of mutual masturbation, fellatio, etc.) not long after the first baby arrived, she was fitted for a diaphragm and used it (plus spermicidal jelly) every day, except when menstruating, from that time until two years later, when we decided to have another child. After our second child, she used the diaphragm and jelly for two years or so. We might have decided to have a third child, but before we reached a decision she was advised to have a hysterectomy (fibroid tumors, not malignant), and of course that relieved us of thinking about the diaphragm. (It had never bothered us, anyhow.)

"I was forty when our daughter was born and forty-three when our son arrived. I was very happy about the children. We both loved our children very much. We employed a series of full-time cook-housekeepers after my wife's first maternity leave ended, so that she could return to her college teaching, but our teaching schedules were such that we could usually be at home from mid-afternoon on, and after the children started school, one or both of us would be there when they came home after school. We loved doing things as a family.

"Sex is very important, and not overrated; rather, I would say it is more often underrated. But, it needs the context of a stable family life or stable partnerships, of having and/or bringing up children (adopting if necessary), of intimate companionship and friendship and interdependence. In that context, sex is probably the most interesting aspect of life. As to what other things are more important, there are a few but not many. Personal integrity would perhaps head the list, and closely related to that is playing a mature, responsible role in one's community. Friendships with both men and women are important, but less important than sex, I think. The *ideal* friendship situation is when a husband is his wife's dearest friend and the wife her husband's dearest friend—which is the situation I am privileged to enjoy.

"Sex does have a spiritual significance for me. It symbolizes the closeness, the intimacy, the psychological identification with the other person that a real marriage basically is. By sex, I mean more than intercourse and orgasm (but not to underestimate them). I include all the touching, fondling, hand holding, admiring each other's naked bodies, and all the other intimacies of living together as complete partners.

"Orgasms are very important to me, but somewhat less important at present than when I was younger. Since seventy-five, sex without orgasms is the norm, and sex with orgasm the exception (for both of us). In a way it is even more pleasurable, since sex play sometimes continues for a couple of hours or so without any orgasm that would, in effect, mean the end of the play. Of course, orgasm is a special pleasure, and there is always in the background, I suppose, the thought that maybe this time one or both of us will come. And every now and then we do. But we don't feel too much sense of frustration when we don't. Sex is still the most enjoyable activity there is, and the most satisfying way of expressing our mutual love.

"When the orgasm comes when we are together it is like a flood of unspeakable warm affection, intimacy, oneness with the other, and being intensely aware of her as a person as well as of her body. Everything just said applies equally when the orgasms are by intercourse or by mutual masturbation or by cunnilingus/fellatio, except that 'Felix's' (my penis's) pulsations and 'Felicia's' (her vagina's) contractions are felt and enjoyed by the other's fingers or tongue, as the case may be. The feeling here is: 'Whee! Wow! Hurray for nature! Hurray for double beds! Hurray for us! You're wonderful and I'm wonderful and being married is wonderful. Let's do it some more!' We often play a game of pretending we aren't married, and I'll say, 'Let's get married,' and she'll say. 'But this is so sudden; I've only known you for forty years,' and so on. If we have both come, we feel especially affectionate, and often lie entwined, naked, talking affectionately for an hour or more (except before breakfast, when we start to get hungry).

"I have also thought of comparing orgasm to the building up and bursting forth of a summer thunderstorm—with the increasing darkness, gusts of wind, lightning and thunder, false starts with a few drops of rain but only tentative and preliminary, and then with a *big* gust of wind the 'heavens open' and the 'cloudburst' is there and the ground is drenched, even though the storm is soon over.

"When I have sex with my wife, our left hands are sometimes intertwined (with my left arm under her neck and her left hand raised on mine) as we lie on our backs and use our right hands to manipulate the other; and on such occasions, when we relax after orgasm (either one, or both together) we may find our left hands almost cramped from the self-forgetful clenching of the intertwined fingers.

"I should add that when my wife is masturbating me, I sometimes *help* her to do it with my right hand, while continuing to masturbate her with my left hand. I do this when her stimulation of my penis is too gentle or absentminded and I lose my erection. The only disadvantage of mutual masturbation is the absence of the pleasure (and symbolism) of penetrating, but my wife and I have found that long-continued, deep 'soul kisses' while masturbating each other or just lying facing each other are a very satisfying alternative to genital penetration. An advantage of mutual masturbation over intercourse is that there need be no concern whatever about maintaining erection.

"When I was fifty-nine, I had a complete prostatectomy (no malignancy), and since then have had no sperm to ejaculate. This made no difference whatever in my sex life, except for no longer needing a handkerchief to use after masturbation. (Also, of course, there was no longer any semen for my wife to swallow after fellatio.) When fully erect, my penis is quite beautiful, I like to stand naked in front of a full-length mirror (even when not masturbating, but especially when masturbating). When it is strongly erect, really hard, I can make it 'wave' by contracting the muscles and I like to watch myself do this in the mirror. I also like to 'wave' my erect penis this way at my wife (when she is undressing, perhaps, while I am already on the bed).

"I used to orgasm during fellatio sometimes, but in recent years never, but this does not make it really much less pleasurable. Our usual position for fellation is with me lying on my back, and her kneeling or partly reclining at right angles to me.

"I enjoy the way my wife's genitals look, very much. She

washes them daily, even when not taking a full bath. I have never done cunnilingus while she was menstruating, and it would hardly occur to me. I would object to trying it. But I am crazy about cunnilingus with my wife. It gives me enormous pleasure to observe her buildup of sexual excitement and her orgasm—or, more likely, her series of orgasms.

"I am crazy about 'foreplay,' and we do it by the hour every day. I also love to hold hands—whenever and wherever we can. Tight, tight hugging face to face, preferably without clothes on, whether standing up or lying down, is also important to me.

"We have intercourse now mostly as episodes in between the other things we do. At various times we have tried several positions for intercourse. Our favorite position is a kind of 'flanquette' position with her half on top, facing me, her right leg on the bed between my legs, and her left leg, knee bent, straddling my left flank. Her head is turned toward me, so our faces are together, and passionate kissing is continuous. Sometimes, after my right hand on her buttocks has pulled her as close as possible, I insert my middle finger as far as I can into her anus.

"I do not remember ever refusing sex with my wife, and can't imagine doing so. The only times she has sort of 'refused' my approach have been when I would start to get affectionate on first waking up, maybe at 5:30 or 6 a.m., and she says, 'It's too early. Go back to sleep. Seven o'clock is early enough, and we'll get up at eight.' And that doesn't bother me, because of course she's right!

"At night, we have tried going to sleep face to face, but she finds that too stimulating to be able to relax, so she generally turns her back and we 'fit,' with my right arm around her until we both drop off to sleep. Often, when she has gone to sleep and I am about to, I also turn my back, with my buttocks fitting more or less into the small of her back.

"My main reason for answering is that I feel that this uninhibited report from a 'sexy senior citizen' (I accept that label) will fill a slot in the total picture that might otherwise be inadequately covered. I hope that some other older men will also be among your respondents, to confirm (or modify) my report.

"I have been as honest as I know how in my answers, really trying (and very successfully, I think) to shed all inhibitions, and at the same time not exaggerate or yield to the temptation to brag or color my answers for effect. I have enjoyed writing all this down."

"I am almost eighty-six years old.

"I was in love with my wife until she died just a month ago. We live in Arkansas.

"Through working hard to preserve our marriage it became stronger. Though our marriage began with my 'love' being mostly sexual attraction, I also appreciated her strong character and had a poetic appreciation of her personality and physical beauty. Now I'm sure love was an achievement from a life shared with our daughter, our friends, but especially our shared faith in God and the influence of the *true* and *beautiful*. I had a large heart carved on our gravestone. Inside the outline is carved:

TOGETHER
FOREVER

"My father was a schoolteacher. Mother divorced him for cruelty and became a dressmaker to support her four children when I was three and a half. I only attended high school one year—but have never stopped getting my own education. Occupations: printer, carpenter, rancher, dishwasher in lumber camp, cigar maker, poet, copyreader on two metropolitan newspapers; last job: editor on the largest afternoon newspaper in the U.S. for thirty years. Mother was a strict Presbyterian. My ancestors have all been Presbyterians, so I must really have been in love when I proposed to a *Methodist* girl. She said she would marry me *if* I joined her Methodist church. I did. She is the wife who died just a month ago. The Sunday before she had her fatal stroke (on a Friday) we had slept all night (after intercourse) in the new bedroom which I was building and had just completed.

"I was married for sixty-five years. Until she died last month, yes, I liked being married. I got married because I was in love and wanted to get married and have children. Marriage transforms sex into a joyful part of God's plan for Creation. Marriage isn't an easy life. You have to work hard at it, love Good (God), subordinate your ego to a desire for harmony, and *hope* your wife and God will understand what you are doing.

"Orgasms are important, but prolonging the preceding pleasure is even more important, and the belief that I am giving pleasure to my partner is most important of all. I have had sex without orgasm in actual intercourse and the pleasure was intense because my partner had told me she would enjoy it most if she did not have to worry about getting pregnant. After she had three unmistakable orgasms she gave me relief orally.

"We had been married about twenty years before my wife asked me to show her how I masturbated so she could give more pleasure. After she learned about variations of tempo our intercourse pleasure was greatly intensified, and so were our orgasms. This instruction also lengthened duration of our foreplay. She learned how to get me really excited; and in mutual masturbation (short of my having orgasm) I found she had always wanted to go off a couple of times before intromission but had not dared to tell me so.

"The pleasure of the entire buildup was always much greater if she takes the initiative before dinner and recalls some incident of our courtship, follows up with one of my favorite dishes, acts and talks seductively till bedtime—all this puts a recurrent tingle in my testicles and penis, and a lot of get-up-and-go-after-her in my love for her.

"As I write this I find it hard to believe that she died of a stroke just four weeks ago. Even in memory her touch is still so warm and exciting. My pleasure was greatest when she took the initiative. Her hugging, sighing 'oo-oo,' and pelvic thrusts that accented her deep kisses, her pulling up of her nightie and putting my hand on her sex, her whispering, 'She wants you to play with her, darling!'—all this heated my blood, hardened my penis in a crescendo until her hand slid down between us, gave 'it' a brief but comforting pat and clasp, then tenderly cupped my testicles. It felt like they were being bounced around by a springtime breeze playing with a hummingbird nest."

CONCLUSION

Older men have a very important contribution to make to our understanding of what sexuality can be. It is only our society's biased viewpoint about sexuality that has caused older men to be scorned as "less than men," and even asexual. Older men in this study often transcended the stereotypes they had learned and practiced in their youth, and developed more mutual, open, and receptive ways of relating to their partners. The assumption that younger men enjoy sex more and give more pleasure is based on the belief that a better erection or more intercourse equals better sex.

Is "impotence" inevitable with age? No; loss of erective ability has to do with certain degenerative physical conditions, which can occur at any age but which often accompany the decline in health many older people experience. Actually, most men continue to have regular erections through their sixties, although perhaps not as frequently. During the seventies, it can be more difficult, once again depending on general health. Older men often simply need more direct physical stimulation to achieve erection.

One of the most difficult stereotypes which older men and women have to face is the idea that they should not fall in love —they should not feel passionate or romantic about their partners, whether new or long-term, and they should not develop intense new attachments as they did when they were younger— and especially, they should not display any of these feelings in public or be seen holding hands or kissing. Sex and romantic or physical love are for "young people." But in this study, most older men said that sex for its own sake was no longer very interesting, and that they now saw sex basically as an important accompaniment to a strong emotional attraction or feelings for another person. Thus—ironically, in view of the cultural assumptions just mentioned—strong emotional relationships (both new and old) are crucial to men's happiness and sexual pleasure in later years. In fact, the older a man became, the more likely he was to connect sex with emotions and feelings for his partner—to *need* them to make sex interesting and worthwhile, or even possible.

A very obvious example of this attitude toward older people is the general refusal of most nursing homes to let their clients have even the simplest privacy for kissing or lying in bed together. Consider, also, the attitudes of children (of any age) toward their parents. Most children never think of their parents as sexual, or know much about their parents' intimate lives; conversely, most parents believe that it is their duty to ensure that the children do not think of them as sexual, or know what their sexual lives are like—or even that they have sexual lives. This hurts both the parents and the children: it hurts the parents in that they must present themselves as less than complete human beings (and also lie to their children), while it hurts the children because it prevents them from having a chance to see physical affection or sexual attraction in a loving, ongoing, daily context with which they could identify.

There are many organizations working now to change these stereotypes about older people and to change their status in the society in general. One such organization, the Gray Panthers, in Philadelphia, Pennsylvania, has chapters all over the country. Basically an organization by and for older people, it also, however, fights ageism in any form, that is, discrimination against anyone because of age, including not only older people but children and teenagers as well.

9

NINE MEN SPEAK ABOUT THEIR LIVES

Following are long excerpts from nine men's replies. These replies were chosen not necessarily for representativeness but because they were some of the most interesting and emotionally involving material received and show the great range and variety of points of view expressed.

I am twenty-nine, living off and on with my lover. I work as an electrician. Every day is a real struggle, both with work and with our relationship together, but I love her and we have the best sex life I've ever had—the greatest. I've been thinking a lot about my life lately, being together so intensely with my lover has made me have a lot of thoughts, but none of the men I know ever talk about these things. That's why I'm answering this questionnaire. I would really like to know how other men feel, and I want to tell about myself.

For me, being in love is not exactly the fairy-tale sugar-coated happily-ever-after story of the movies, novels, and "great" moments in history. At times it has been painful, and a lot of times I have felt unsure of what was going on and my role in it.

When I was in my teens I thought love always implied settling down, getting married, having children, and me getting a job and supporting the lot of them, like my father and grandfather before me. It meant sacrificing one's true feelings to put on the appearance of being happy all the time. I also believed that marriage was inevitable, as everyone just gets married finally, and forgets about what they really want to do. This idea of marriage is security-oriented rather than passion-oriented. I guess I really disliked the idea of traditional marriage on many levels, but felt like a weirdo for not liking it. I thought there was something wrong with me for not liking the "normal" way of life for couples.

However . . . !!! I found myself feeling lots of new feelings when I got my lover. When we first met I had decided never to go out with or get involved with anybody again, as it was always such a nightmare in the past, including one very difficult relationship which ended in disaster. But I felt this unbelievable sexual, physical, and personality attraction to her. I was extremely afraid of getting involved, because I thought it would be painful, complicated, and wouldn't last. However, she was so irresistible and sexy I couldn't control myself. I have never desired someone's body as much as I desire hers. I can never believe how exciting it is when we make love.

When I fell in love with her I felt as if I had discovered my emotions—but immediately I was also in turmoil. Although she made me feel alive and exhilarated and more sexually excited than I ever thought I could get, and made me experience all kinds of feelings that I didn't know I had, this "great love" also made me fear obligations. I was afraid. When my lover told me she needed me, I got scared, because I thought a lot was expected of me. I thought that now I would have to be a "husband" like my father and tied to her. The result was the relationship was very rocky because I felt so torn. I felt that I was getting into something really serious, something that demanded a great deal of sacrifice from me. It seemed burdensome, so I would rebel against this feeling of restriction by saying or doing something to hurt her, since I thought she was the cause of my tension. Really it was not her expectations of me but *my idea* of her expectations of me that was burdensome. I assumed she *needed* me and me only—that only I could fulfill her needs, and that I was trapped, because she said she loved me.

I also assumed she couldn't hurt me, or wouldn't hurt me, even if I hurt her. I refused to believe she was in control of her life and could solve her problems without me or leave me if I made her unhappy. It's funny I thought this way because she is independent and successful, more than I am. I didn't want to believe that she could hurt me if she wanted to, or could break up with me, or could reject me. I didn't want to accept her as an equal (emotionally), and I didn't want to be vulnerable. (But I wanted her to be vulnerable.) But if you want to really feel close to somebody you must become vulnerable. It's the chance you have to take.

Men think they please women by just being around and letting the woman please them. They can't really love a woman because they either put her on a pedestal or treat her like a mommy or a child. Very condescending no matter how you look at it. The way I was raised, I thought I was God's gift to women. Men think of themselves as being really interesting—everyone is interested in what they have to say—people want to listen to them. But who wants to listen to a woman? Some are married to women they don't even know—they only know who they want to believe she is—they never ask her *who she is.*

Most men's mothers treated them like kings, and so men feel like any other woman should too. Certainly it's not worth fighting very much with a woman to make the relationship better, since another woman will be glad to please me—at least that's the way I used to think. But fighting with my lover helped me develop as a person. Even though the fights were terrible, really, I felt I was growing in an important way.

Every time I decided to give up my lover, I became physically ill, and couldn't eat, my stomach felt like it had been stomped on, and I had tension headaches. Finally I realized that I need her love—she makes me feel happy, warm, alive—like living and doing positive things rather than negative things. I need her, and I need her love, and I want to show her that I love her any way I can, because the thought of being alone again is the worst thing I can imagine. It's funny, because before I met her I thought I was happy alone.

One thing I never knew about before her was clitoral stimulation. I used to think that my role was to fuck until I had an orgasm, or my performance would not be up to par—I thought she could feel my orgasm. I thought it would disappoint her if I didn't have an orgasm. I thought I wasn't a man if I didn't have orgasms. Fucking would make me sweat, and make my beard grow faster! Furthermore, I thought the very best possible thing was to orgasm simultaneously—and I would time my orgasm till she had hers (during coitus) and try to come at the same time she did. I thought any vaginal spasms were the contractions of female orgasms—they felt great to me. I was sure (at the time—this is with an ex-lover) that I knew when she was orgasming, and that she knew when I was (she could feel the hot sperm, I thought), even though we didn't ask each other very often. I never masturbated her to orgasm—I didn't know how to, didn't ask, I thought sticking a finger in her vagina was masturbating her. Sometimes during intercourse I realized she didn't orgasm. I would feel that I didn't fuck as good that day (or long enough), but I believed that intercourse was the only way to achieve female orgasm—the only right way! So I felt I had let her down, but we never discussed it, we just went to sleep. The thing I have wondered about since we broke up is whether or not she had orgasms as often as I assumed she did, and also whether she faked them regularly, as some of the women in *The Hite Report* said they did. At the time my masculinity and ego would have been miniaturized beyond comprehension and I'm sure I would have developed a huge complex if I thought I wasn't giving her orgasms.

When I read that women usually didn't orgasm from intercourse, my face fell—imagine that—I believed all this time that I could give women an orgasm by fucking them—suddenly this fundamental belief of mine was shattered, and I wondered if women had been faking it all along or what. I felt helpless and really embarrassed upon learning this. I had been taking this huge credit for giving women orgasms, when I didn't even know how to! It seems so funny now, but it was really a crisis when I found this out. A complete ego crisis. Not only was my ego shot, but now I had to face the problem of how to give my lover an orgasm.

The first time my lover asked me to give her an orgasm, she told me to hold my hand in a fist and put it on her pubic mound and to move it. I wasn't in a real comfortable position. But I had read *The Hite Report* at that point, so I wanted to try. Even though if you read the book you think you know a lot, but, still, to actually do it is really interesting because I'd never felt anyone's body that way before. She had shown me exactly what to do, which was so straightforward, all of a sudden I felt really enlightened.

But I also felt nervous because I kept changing the rhythm, and wasn't doing it the same way all the time. I'd speed it up and slow it down and move in different directions. Then she told me not to do it like that. I started feeling kind of insecure, because I thought, well, I don't know if I'm really doing this right, plus I couldn't anticipate when she was going to have an orgasm—I didn't know how long I was going to have to keep doing this. I didn't know if I was doing it right, I didn't know if someone else could do it better than me, or what. My confidence was on the line. I felt if I didn't do it good, if I failed . . . if I couldn't do it, she could easily humiliate me for not knowing how to do it—by criticizing me, like "Hey, man, haven't you ever done this before?" or "You're not doing it right at all!" She didn't say anything. She just moved my hand back down there and told me to just do one thing, don't move around. Even though I was getting kind of worried, don't get me wrong, I really loved it! Since it was the very first time I was doing it, I was trying to make sure I was doing it right. But the thing that was really exciting was that she showed me exactly what to do—that meant she was very excited too, excited enough to want me to do it to her. It made me feel really close to her and special since nobody ever did that before—really intimate, because I always thought of masturbation as a very private thing. If she wanted me to masturbate her, that seemed *really* private. I felt, how could we be any closer?

Men never talk about masturbating women, at least I've never heard them talk about it. They talk about women masturbating *them* a lot, but they never talk about themselves masturbating women, or there being thirty-two different ways women masturbate! And I didn't even know one. I thought women masturbated by putting something inside. Masturbation had still for me a real pejorative context, like it's not the real thing, or that's just what women do when they don't have a man. A frustrated woman would want to stick something in her, I thought, but it could never be as good as a cock. I guess that's why men think that a woman needs a man, that she could never masturbate herself as well as a man could —I've heard that said so many times. But really, a woman can just put a vibrator or her hand on her mons and just come and come and come.

Anyway, getting back to the first time I gave her clitoral stimulation, after a while when I kept trying, she was really excited and breathing heavy, her whole body was tensing up with her legs tight together and straight out—and then she got *really* tense and tight and moaned and held herself like that for a few minutes. Then she told me she came. It was a revelation for me.

Of all the things we had done before that—like when we were kissing and I could hear her moaning, her head is right by my ear sometimes, and I'm listening and I can feel her breathing—never was it that exciting, it was so thrilling during her orgasm. I felt like she was really strong! That was my first reaction to the whole thing—that she had a tremendous strength—a really powerful energy that was inside her. Also I felt really small next to her when she had an orgasm and I didn't!

I also felt like—well, I used to believe that the idea was to fuck until you both had orgasms together, but all of a sudden I realized it was a really good feeling to enjoy someone else's orgasm, even if I didn't have one. Plus, to discover that she could have one that made me envious—plus I think she had another one about a minute later—well, I was really amazed! Later, after we did it a lot, I really got to enjoy it. She feels energetic and powerful and independent when she orgasms, and it makes me feel good to be next to someone so strong and active and alive.

Do you know the difference between being next to a really passive person and someone that's really excited? It makes me feel great, it makes me feel really excited, aroused, like having orgasms, really strong, it makes me feel like an animal. I just want to hop on and screw her at that point, and I often do.

But I consider my masturbating her one of the major things that we do. I don't consider it as a warm-up thing. Sometimes when we don't do it I miss doing it. Sometimes she's said things to me while I'm doing it that make me feel really good, or really hot. I get sweaty when I'm doing it, and I like that feeling a lot. I'll usually be really close against her body while I'm doing it, so I'll rub myself on her or I'll rub myself on the bed, or if my arm is in the right position I can rub it on my arm. I feel really wild when she's having the orgasm—she feels really wild to me, like she's breaking away from all physical restraints of any kind.

I've never told my friends or anybody else any of this. I never tell the guys much of anything I do. I don't know what their reactions would be. But, since most of the guys I know are always boasting about their exploits and I never do, then they boast all the more because they think I'm a prude, because I don't talk about my sex life.

But if I told them about this whole clitoral stimulation thing, they'd probably just say it's "kinky." Or couldn't she make it any other way? They'd probably be really freaked out, because I've never heard anybody tell a story like that. I don't think most men know how to do it, and then the ones who do would be afraid to be ridiculed for talking about it. It seems like all men ever talk about is how they fuck. It would make me very nervous to talk about clitoral stimulation to the guys. When you're working with other men, for example, the first topic that comes up during the lunch break is "Wow, I really fucked a lot last night!" Somebody will start boasting about what he's done, and then they expect you to come up with an equally macho story—the more graphic, the better, of course. And I never do come up with any stories. Then they think you can't get laid, or you're too sensitive or whatever. They don't like to talk about it in emotional terms. Of course, mostly they're not talking about their wives—sometimes they are, but usually they're trying to say they are having affairs with somebody. Most of the time that they are bragging, they are also bragging that they are seeing more than one person. But sometimes people will say, "I'm going home to fuck my wife!" I've heard that. I thought it was really nice when I heard it. It was somebody that I didn't know very well, and he said, "I'm going home and fuck my wife!" (He was really drunk.) It sounded like a great thing to do. I should have wished him a happy time. But most men seem to think that anything outside of intercourse is a deviation from the norm, or it's not the "real thing." All I know is, that seems to me now like a really limited way of seeing things.

Another thing I've always heard was that you weren't supposed to have sex when the woman was having her period. Women are always supposed to hide it, and not let anyone know they're having it, and men aren't supposed to know about it, and everyone is supposed to pretend like it doesn't happen.

One time we were making out, lying in bed, she didn't have any clothes on, and we were thinking about intercourse, but she still had the Tampax in. I said I wanted to take it out for her. She was going to take it out herself in the bathroom, and then wash herself, but I wanted to take it out. And it was really sexy to take it out. I wanted to look at it while it was coming out—not just reach around and pull it out—I wanted to watch it, I wanted to see the colors on it. I thought it would be really great to look at it and watch the thing come out. It seemed really beautiful to watch it come out. It was part of her on the Tampax—I just wanted to watch it, I don't know why. It was really sexy. When I took it out, I had it and I didn't want to throw it away. I wanted to keep it. It smelled good. So I put it in my mouth. It was great to be chewing on it, tasting it.

It smelled strong but it smelled really good, it was really sexy the way it smelled, plus it was part of her. It smelled sweaty, kind of, a sharp and kind of sweaty smell, just like regular blood and mucus together, but also with some kind of a sharp, strong odor—the more, the better.

It is very exciting to just mess around sometimes. I like kissing, squeezing, my cock fondled and stroked, I like to be licked, and stroked on the neck and back, and be bitten on the chest. I like to be sucked. We both make advances, because we both love to mess around. If I want to get her excited, I make an advance. When she makes an advance, it gets me very excited.

I love to masturbate my lover to orgasm and feel her

tremble when she orgasms. But also just caring for her is lots of fun. I like to give massages to my lover and bathe her. I wasn't raised to do this—quite the contrary—I was raised to keep distant from others physically.

If I'm with my lover I sometimes have orgasms, sometimes not. Making love doesn't require having orgasm to be beautiful. I like to get more and more excited, and to stay like that. Why end it? The building *up* of feelings is much more exciting than having an orgasm and going to sleep. My lover often drives me crazy, to the point that my desires get very strong and uncontrollable. I love her for making me feel that excited. I crave her, need her, and it feels great to really want someone like that—it makes me feel real, alive. I like to let my desire build up to a frenzy. It gets painful, it's such a gnawing, craving desire. As the excitement builds up we get rougher. Orgasms that come from frenzy are the best—they are uncontrollable. This is very different from "timing my orgasm with hers"—what a conceited practice—and boring! My lover doesn't orgasm from intercourse, but she is a great fuck, because she makes me crave her. I want to fuck her in every part of her body, and cream all over her. To feel *this* way is the best feeling in the world.

I love intercourse. It feels great physically. Emotionally it is very satisfying and soothing. We have intercourse several times a week. Sometimes I come very soon upon entering, and it feels good when this happens involuntarily. But I'd rather build up the excitement. Knowing that I don't have to make her orgasm from intercourse makes intercourse less traumatic, and I don't feel obligated to orgasm myself. I can enjoy being inside her for various lengths of time, and go back in later, and do other things meanwhile.

I have only orgasmed once from fellatio. It is very pleasant but too gentle to orgasm. I need harder pressure to orgasm, or a huge amount of penis stimulation beforehand to orgasm this way. I love it when my lover masturbates me, but it takes a long time to bring me to orgasm. I like my balls rubbed, and a finger up my ass sometimes.

The first time my lover stuck a finger up my ass, it hurt and felt good simultaneously. I didn't really like it; it made me feel like a little baby being punished, and brought tears to my eyes. But it also felt sort of like an orgasm—a continuous orgasm, not like a regular quick, pleasurable, painless ejaculation. Sometimes it feels like I am regressing to childhood—I feel like I am unlearning sphincter control, because sphincter discipline is the definition of being an individual, a responsible person. With a finger up my ass, I feel utterly help-less, like a child, like I can't control my shitting, like my partner has complete control over me. Ironically it is very pleasurable. I feel completely out of control, compared to in-tercourse, where I feel in control, powerful, like a man, an adult, in control of my body. And penetration makes me feel free and like I am being filled.

I usually have at least two orgasms a day from masturbation if I'm alone. Sometimes I masturbate one to five times a day, usually two to three. I like to do it, but I don't talk about it much. It relieves tension, but it makes me a little depressed later. I like it because it is a quick way to have an orgasm. I don't like it because it doesn't really satisfy me or make me happy, the way making love does.

To be a man means to come out on top. Or like my mother used to say, "I don't care what you are, just be the best at whatever you do." Competition begins at an early age—kin-dergarten, where kids try to outdo each other in everything they do. Of course, the boys have boy games and girls have girl games. The emphasis is on excelling: who can run fastest, play harder, play rougher. I always felt insecure about it, be-cause I wasn't very aggressive and didn't want to be—on the physical level, that is. I was deathly afraid of getting into a fight. I was paranoid all the time that somebody would pick a fight with me. In order to survive, I had to develop and excel somehow. So in grade school I excelled in my classes. At least people respected me from being smart in class.

It seems like people love to take out their frustration and hatred for the system on an individual who doesn't succeed. Especially in high school, where individuals are outright ostracized for dressing "funny," being slow, being quiet, in-troverted, "square," "prudish," "ugly," fat, you name it, the group can tease someone to death. I survived a lot of this somehow, and now I've even learned to get the group's respect —but I feel really bad that this harassment and pressure is so prevalent. I've seen guys actually drop out of school because the rest of the class teased them so much.

This cruel quality in men seems to be a big part of mascu-linity—to be able to inflict pain on weaker, slower individuals is the tough, macho way to show your superiority. Men justify cruelty by emphasizing that the victim is a "weak" person, who deserves it. And this mentality also says, "Why not? I deserve everything I got, I earned it—the slobs deserve everything they get too (punishment)." I don't understand this competition fully, except I do know it is prevalent in every aspect of my life, and I do it myself too. But I hate it—I feel "on guard" all the time around other men.

Only *men* work where I work—lately we are repairing dangerous telephone wires and lines that have been cut, etc., and other electrical wiring. The most macho ones are the meanest, sweatiest, most foul-mouthed, drink more beer, smoke bigger cigars, and tell the "dirtiest" jokes, very abusive towards women. When a woman passes by where we are working, every man becomes self-conscious of his macho image. They light up a cigarette, stop working, and stare at her, undress her mentally, very aware that the others are doing the same thing, and will nod to each other if she is sexy, or make a face if they don't think she is. Men in groups are hostile, edgy, and like to show that they don't have feelings—feelings of tenderness, caring, or friendship (except under the rules of bonding), or feelings of pain, be it emotional or physical. Men pride themselves among each other on their ability to not flinch while in pain. Many jobs we do involve exposure to dangerous live wires, or require us to work at dangerous heights, but most macho men won't wear safety equipment unless it is required or the situation is *extremely* dangerous, because macho men like to show each other that they don't feel any pain.

Macho men comment to each other about female passersby, and if you don't have a comment to support the group's opinion you are considered (1) a fag, (2) a mama's boy, (3) a prude, (4) a real jerk, (5) a jerk-off. Then you draw the next round of insults from the group, and become the victim of their further abuses and hostile comments. It's very child-like, the way children ostracize and tease the kid with glasses or a stutter or any physical weakness. The thing is, this whole macho group-bonding thing is actually *taught* in the high schools and trade schools, as the students who are studying skilled trades like plumbing and electricity and carpentry must also withstand the nonstop group harassment and teasing that goes on in the classroom. Even the instructors do it, and humiliate and abuse slow or weak students. "You gotta be a *real man* to get into the Brotherhood of the Plumbers Union!" To keep a job one must deal with this horrible social system. The foreman is typically the very most macho, grouchy, cursing, angry-looking person on the site. There is never any positive reinforcement for good work, only criticism for bad or slow work. One never admits ignorance in one's job just as one never does about women, because that would bring the roof down on your own head and all the humiliation that goes with it.

Most of the men I work with get paid very well for their work, and resent women who try to break in as equals. They really don't want women as equals, only as a fuck, or a "mommy," or a cute daughter. They want to protect the "poor things," be a big hero all the time, and bring home more money than the women. Men act very different among themselves than they do in groups with women. They don't talk about women among themselves as equals or humans— they say stuff like "She likes cock," "She's frigid," and especially "She loves my ass." They don't say, "I love her," "I respect her," "I need her," or "I hope she is feeling good." The worst part of it is that I don't do anything to change this really. I just put up with their attitudes because I want the money. And to be perfectly honest, I also want to be accepted.

My father always expected the women in the family to do certain *daily* things, like clean the house, cook, take care of the children, and the boys and men to do other, more *special* things, like shovel snow, fix cars, clean the garage and basement. I'm sure he expects me to know more about the world than my wife and to make more money than her. He believes his role is to support the family and wife. He's worked seven days a week, fourteen hours a day (as a plant maintenance supervisor) to do this since I can remember. He doesn't spend time with his family. I never got to know my father till I began working with him. He is a workaholic, and doesn't understand how anyone *feels* about anything. I hate him but I also love him very much. My mother always listened to me, and trusted me to make my own decisions, even though we never talked heart to heart or were never really physically close.

It was my sister I was really close to (one year older). She was my "best friend" in second, third, and fourth grades. We did things together as equals with no sexual (role) barriers. We were *friends*. As a child I remember that boys were supposed to play with boys' toys, and girls with girls' toys. Girls played "house," "dolls," and "shopping," and boys played army men, fort games, snowball fights, and more strenuous games. But there were some games that boys and girls could play together, like cards and table games, ride bikes. There were times when I felt torn between playing with my sister, who was my best friend, and playing with the boys. Especially skating—the girls did figure skating, and boys played hockey. Of course, it was an honor to be accepted into the group of boys as a hockey player; I remember feeling like I had betrayed my sister when I went to the rink with her but didn't play with her once we got there. I didn't want to be a sissy, so I let her play with her girlfriends and I played with the boys.

It was never the same after that. We took off on our respective masculine and feminine roles. As an adult, it is almost impossible for a man to be "friends" with a woman or "best friends." The roles we are assigned don't allow it. Men have their wives, and their friends (other men). Men don't see women as equals; perhaps they did as children, but when they follow their roles, they begin to feel guilty for leaving women behind, and later feel contempt for women who are not their equals, since they didn't let them be. Men show contempt for women because they are not able to treat them with respect and honesty, because they consider themselves superior.

My lover is a feminist—and I respect her for it. She is honest and courageous. She won't stand to be treated like a second-class person. She is very strong. But I used to think that the women's movement was a minority of women radicals who were very bitter people, who were overly critical of society, and generally too extreme to be taken seriously. I never thought of it as if I were a woman, nor did I ever experience what it's like to be a woman, to be stared at by men, discriminated against on the job level, the educational level, and even in conversation. Feminists made me nervous: I felt I was innocent—I never intentionally was unfair to women—I was nice to them—why should they be mad at me?

Of course, I didn't understand. The weird thing is that even though I wasn't satisfied with society's definition of me as a "man," I was not inspired by the group of women who were rebelling against the society's definition of them as women.

I have discovered that the most important thing for keeping our relationship on an even keel is a daily sharing of feelings, how we feel. I never grew up thinking this was important. I thought I was always supposed to be objective, and that I should suppress any other feelings, to express them would be weak. One result of this was that, sometimes she would get very angry and upset because I didn't express my feelings to her. Other times, too, she would tell me her feelings about something that had happened, but I just sat silently and she would get mad. When she got upset at me I felt very nervous, upset, afraid, angry, mean, and confused. But I never expressed this either, nor did I ask her why she felt so angry. My basic impulse was just to get out of that situation; I wanted to avoid situations in which I felt anything other than loved, confident, wanted, happy, and stable. I though her anger was just a waste of time. I thought to myself, "I love her—doesn't she understand that? Why doesn't she let me love her?"

It really helped when I finally realized that communication about feelings and moods is something that has to be kept up every day. Even now, if we are not really communicating and keeping in touch and sharing with each other how we feel, I get confused, estranged, and insecure about where I stand. Then I get paranoid and pretend that everything is O.K., instead of saying the truth, like "I feel weird, we're drifting apart. Why? Aren't I communicating, or aren't you?"

I answered this because I want to know how other men feel about these things. I haven't been able to talk these things over with anybody, and they are very important to me. And at the same time, I wanted to tell other men what I have experienced. I also found it a relief to say I find some of my friends' behavior really revolting sometimes. But I could never say this to their faces. It's really crazy, but at the same time I like them.

At age seventy, with the awareness that death and oblivion are much closer now than ever before, I have become much more conscious of the essential loneliness of the human condition and of an increasing desire for a warm, close, and loving relationship with another person, and, for me as of now, sex is an essential component of such a relationship. The physiological aspects of sex and achievement of orgasm, while still very enjoyable, are not as strong or compelling a part of my sex life as formerly, while the psychological components as expressed in hugging, kissing, and caressing are now much more important. In retirement, with the interests and challenges of my work no longer demanding my concern, my need for this latter type of sex seems to have greatly increased.

My wife and I have been married thirty-nine years, during most of which we struggled to overcome a sexual incompatibility deriving from our mutual ignorance of female sexuality.

From adolescence on my wife has been obsessed with the conviction, probably derived from the many romantic novels that she has read, that the highest peak of sexual ecstasy that a woman can reach is in experiencing a vaginal orgasm, and any woman who goes through life without having them has only half lived. She has also long been convinced that the main obstacle to her achievement of this blissful experience was my inability to maintain an erection and continue "pumping" indefinitely. Having a smaller than average penis, I was preconditioned to feelings of inadequacy, and with no basis for disputing her faith in vaginal orgasms (*The Hite Report* came thirty-five years too late to salvage our sex life!), our sexual encounters became sessions of frustration, bitter recriminations, and mutual hostility so distasteful that I eventually became impotent and we stopped having sex altogether. At my suggestion, we recently adopted open marriage and she now at age sixty-five has a "young" lover in his forties with whom she can continue to pursue her will-o'-the-wisp, the vaginal orgasm, and I have found a warm, hugging, kissing, caressing, oral-sex-oriented woman who has revitalized my sex life and with whom I have fallen deeply in love.

I am quite sure that, although I was in love several times before marriage and a few times (at a distance) since, I have never been as deeply in love as I am right now with my lover. Although of very different backgrounds and with a sixteen-year difference in our ages, we seem to be made for each other in the unprecedented degree to which our tastes, interests, likes and dislikes, coincide. I'm in seventh heaven while we're together and miss her terribly when we're apart. I certainly never expected to fall so deeply in love at this age! It's a moot question whether the delights of being together outweigh the pain of separation and the near-hopelessness of our ever being able to get together permanently. However, I find our relationship very deeply satisfying emotionally, and it adds a whole new dimension to my life. Also, as she says, the delightful periods that we do spend together are like a permanent honeymoon taken on the installment plan, with the periods of separation ensuring the permanence of our enchantment with each other. My relationship with my lover is essentially a monogamous one on my part, although not on hers, since she still has sex with her husband.

I am white, in good health, and the father of three grown children. My parents were of the lower middle class with only grade school educations. They were loving and moderately religious. I have an M.A. in chemistry, worked thirty-six years for a major oil company doing technical work that I enjoyed, retired, taught chemistry in school for a few years, and again retired. In religion I am a humanist. I had no sexual experiences until around age twenty-two, when I finally rejected the brainwashing of my parents regarding the terrible effects of "playing with oneself," and began to masturbate regularly.

After marriage to my wife, a sexually quite inhibited woman, the sequence of operations gradually evolved to include (1) imbibing two or three cocktails to relax my wife's inhibitions, (2) insertion of a diaphragm by my wife, (3) preplay in the form of kisses and caresses applied to various supposedly sensitive areas of my wife's head and body, (4) finger or tongue massage (usually the former, with which she felt less embarrassment) of the clitoris to near or incipient orgasm, (5) hasty mounting "missionary" style, and thrusting in and out with the penis in a consistently unsuccessful effort to convert the near-orgasm to what my wife has always firmly believed must be the epitome of ecstasy for any woman, but after thirty-nine years of trying has not yet achieved: a vaginal orgasm, (6) rapid fading of my wife's sexual excitement of the near-orgasm to a feeling of bitter disappointment and frustration while I pumped away and eventually had my orgasm, the pleasure of which, however, was tempered by the knowledge that I had somehow again failed to achieve for my wife the one thing that she felt was essential for a woman's happiness, (7) finger massage of the clitoris to complete (though sometimes only simulated) orgasm, and (8) a "postmortem" of the operation which usually constituted the final scene of this little comedy-tragedy, with my wife, sometimes in tears, agonizing over her failure once again to attain vaginal orgasm and ascribing the failure at times to some lack within herself, at times to my inability to continue the in-and-out thrusting indefinitely on the chance that her sexual excitement might eventually again be stimulated to the desired orgasm. Gradually these always disappointing and, for me, guilt-laden sexual encounters acquired such consistently negative associations that they became distasteful to me, I had increasing difficulty obtaining erections, and eventually, after thirty-nine years of married life, became impotent.

Although my sex life with my wife has always been very unsatisfactory to both of us, in other respects we enjoy a good, even if unexciting relationship. In fact, aside from our sexual difficulties, our married life has been surprisingly harmonious, and it is especially so now that we are no longer fighting "the battle of the sexes." I think I can truly say that we still respect and love each other in a nonsexual way.

As I grow older, I find that the greatest pleasure in sex, for me, is the feeling of closeness or "oneness" with my loved one that it gives me. I enjoy being touched and kissed and petted as much, or perhaps even more, than genital sex because the sensual pleasure and feeling of intimacy is more prolonged. Still, although having orgasms is not as important to me now at age seventy as when I was younger, they are important. I certainly would feel deprived if my partner did not help me to an orgasm every other day or so of our lovemaking, if only as a demonstration of her concern that I should get as much pleasure as possible from our sexual relationship.

I enjoy masturbation when I am separated from my loved one and feel "in the mood." But psychologically it induces a certain feeling of loneliness and regret that my loved one is not present to make the moments of pleasure complete. When we are separated, I may masturbate from one to three times per week. Masturbation, with me, always leads to orgasm. I usually masturbate in the shower, with a hard jet of hot water hitting against the underside of my penis. I usually fantasize variations of cunnilingus.

I enjoy cunnilingus with any woman sexually atttractive enough that I could enjoy kissing her on the mouth, but even more with the woman I deeply love. The pleasure is both physical in the warmth and softness of her parts and the stimulating "femaleness" of the taste and odor, and psychological in that cunnilingus comes closer than anything else to satisfying the strong desire I have for attaining the greatest possible intimacy with her. Another important and pleasurable aspect of cunnilingus is the intense satisfaction I feel when my partner achieves orgasm, as she normally does.

I also very much enjoy fellatio and always orgasm this way. Even at age seventy I'm sure that I could orgasm every day this way if I had the opportunity. However, since my lover and I are only able to get together for two or three days at a time and only in the daytime, these occurrences are limited to two or three times every week or so. With my lover's fellatio, I never have difficulty having an orgasm.

If I love the person I am with, I want physical closeness and lovemaking to go on and on after orgasm. I think if I didn't I would interpret it as an indication that the "bloom is off" our romance. With a partner whom I love, ejaculation is just one episode in an extended period of loving and caressing. In a shallow, physical sense I feel momentarily satisfied, but in a much deeper sense I have the feeling that I could never really be fully satisfied unless our bodies could somehow be melted and fused together into a single unified being. For me kissing, hugging, and caressing seem to bring me closer to this ideal state than simply ejaculating. This life is a very lonely place when one has no one with whom to share human closeness and warmth and love, and for me the sense of mutual caring and concern are much more important than a mere orgasm.

When I was about twelve, for a reason that quite escapes me, most of my fantasies involved anal penetration. I possessed a treasure of antique *National Geographic* magazines, through which I pored anxiously looking for articles on primitive tribesmen. The naked breasts left me quite cold, but occasionally there was a hint of a phallus to be seen, which would fascinate me no end. Using the pictures as a base, I would fantasize being ritually sodomized by the tribe's warriors, one after the other. This fantasy was infused by a longing that I did not at all understand, or want to. This was a recurrent and very powerful fantasy. I also, because I loved science fiction, imagined sex as it might occur on other planets. I drew crude pictures of strange beasts with incredible sexual appurtenances. One that I recall involved a twelve-foot-long "fertilizing tube" that wrapped around before penetrating the female (who interested me so little that she was not even drawn).

I fantasized endlessly about the unattainable bodies of the seventeen- and eighteen-year-old Adonises that I could see in the changing rooms of our swim club. Their thickly sprouted pubic hair, lithe movements, and firm bodies haunted my imagination—particularly was I tortured by their casual rapport with one another. I was certain that I, a lowly twelve-year-old with but the most tentative fuzz on his balls, would never attain to their estate. When I masturbated I frequently held the image of one or another of them in my mind.

When I was fourteen I made a momentous discovery. My mother possessed an unexpurgated set of Burton's *Arabian Nights*. I almost slaveringly read the too brief references to sodomy, and cursed the passages in Latin and French for eluding me. A few I laboriously translated but as I would read these books in conjunction with masturbating, I seldom held out long enough. Through the influence of these books a new picture emerged in my mind—an Arabian boy, only slightly older than myself, but all-experienced, who served as my sexual initiator. Together, he and I did everything. He was a prince, and knew his way around the palace like one would, but he was also on friendly terms with the lowliest workman. He had a roguish delight in pranks that disturbed social proprieties, and a very clever wit. Usually, he sodomized me, but a few times he offered himself to me as tears of gratitude filled my eyes and tenderness my heart. How I loved him . . . I imagined doing everything with him that boys might do. Together, he and I did everything, whether sexual or not. My most consistent image of him was of him sitting nude on his luxurious bed, an exotic desert landscape out of his open window, semi-erect, smiling gently at me. Writing this, I realize that I have not even now satisfied the longing that caused me to form his image. I am surprised that I never named him, but I may have been waiting for him to name me.

When I was sixteen, out of crazy desperation I drove to an area of the city in which I lived with my family which some instinct—I have no idea how I knew this—told me was a place where one could encounter gay men. This was a beach. I stood on the boardwalks between the parking lot and the sand and gazed at the athletic young men lounging and playing volleyball in the sun. I was consumed with longing and sexual desire. Soon, sure enough, I was approached but by an effeminate, slight, and somewhat shabby young man who struck up a conversation and soon asked if I would like to go for a coffee with him. I accepted, and we left in my car. On the way to the restaurant, I pressed him for the reason behind his interest in me, and to my mingled horror and satanic glee he gripped my thigh and suggested that we have our coffee at his place. Somewhat faintly, I agreed, casting surreptitious glances at his crotch.

My terror was great. What if he had a disease? Visions of my cock rotting off at its base flooded my mind. I vaguely wondered aloud whether he had a disease, and said perhaps I'd rather go back. But he assured me that things were O.K. if you looked closely, and we soon arrived at his house, a nondescript cracker box complete with a strip of lawn and two ailing palm trees. Inside, things were plain, tentative, and rather bare. His roommate sat typing at a card table in the living room, and we went immediately to my acquaintance's bedroom, not even stopping to have the promised coffee.

The bedroom was likewise plain and depressing. It seemed a kind of sex den to me—I imagined this man to be a slave of his sexual appetite, such as I had an absolute horror of becoming (and in fact was, at that very moment). A crusty washcloth on the floor beside the bed—a mattress and box springs resting directly on the floor—rounded out my impression of decadence.

He unceremoniously unzipped my pants without even giving a friendly hug, and took out my penis, squished the tip around, trying to look up the little hole. I suppose that this was somehow related to the strained discussion of disease in the car fifteen minutes earlier. Then, we removed our clothes. I avoided looking at his body, except for his penis, at which I stole frequent glances, and which was more uninspiring. Compared to the beautiful adolescent dongs I was seeing every day in P.E. and which had inspired my desire in the first place, this was no treasure. It was small and covered by too black and too straight hair. It did not have pleasing lines. I wanted to flee but felt there was no going back.

We sat facing each other cross-legged on the bed, and he reached directly for my genitals and began to manipulate them. I was hard right away, because of my state of need, and to my horror he smiled and made an idiotic show of little grins and smacking noises. I asked him if he was going to suck me—then I could lie back, close my eyes, and have my orgasm without having to touch the guy. But, no, he would not. He "did not do that." But his roommate did. Should he call him? No . . .

He moved beside me on the bed and put his arm around me and began jerking me off. I came very quickly, and immediately withdrew from his touch. I was revolted and had been obsessed the entire time with having as little physical contact with him as I possibly could. He seemed not to mind all that much and actually smiled at me. I apologized for coming so soon, and said, "But whaddya expect, I'm so young." I told him my age and felt myself some sort of feather in this guy's cap—a lucky strike for him, something he might crow about. I imagined him scrawling his triumph on the seamy walls of public lavatories.

I got out of there as quickly as I could, and once home plunged into the shower and did not emerge for at least an hour. During that time I soaped my entire body at least three times, and my genitals a good dozen. I was determined never to do anything like that again, and reflected that although fantasizing about sex with males might be exciting, the reality was not.

I did not have another sexual experience with another person for two years, although I was frequently out of my mind with desire. When I was eighteen I got together with a boy whom I met through friends. We formed a quick friendship that had an erotic undercurrent that I did not acknowledge to myself, and told myself that he was not sexually desirable. He seemed unusually eager to get to know me, and I began to wonder consciously if he had desires similar to mine. We knew each other for a few months, and finally got around to spending the night together, at my place. Nothing happened. We sat up almost the entire night together, talking, he clad only in his shorts, and me with my shirt off. We spent the following night together as well, went skinny dipping in the pool, and as we were drying off, he grabbed me. Before I knew what was happening we were all over each other, kissing, stroking, sucking, and shortly afterwards, coming. It was very sweet. I recall realizing that I was not disgusted—somehow it had been O.K. The guy had been a friend of mine, and it was a secret that we held between us—not a ghastly public spectacle like my first experience. I often thought of this experience later when I desired other boys. I cannot remember how often or even whether we made love again after that, because I soon left the city and we saw each other very infrequently. I visited him a few years later and we had become quite different sorts of people, and yet there was a very good feeling between us.

I recall another first experience, which occurred the summer that I turned eighteen—my first casual blow job. I was hitchhiking in Belgium and a very young man picked me up who pointedly put his hand on my thigh every time he offered to light my cigarette. It is the intensity of this memory that causes me to wonder whether he did indeed fellate me during our experience together. I clumsily indicated to him that I did not find his advances objectionable—there was a rather formidable language barrier to be overcome—and he almost immediately brought his exploring hand up to my genitals. Soon he had turned off the highway and into a field, where, both hands free, he unzipped my fly and brought my penis out into view. He then unzipped himself, and stroked the both of us simultaneously. Again, I was loath to touch, and when he took my hand and firmly placed it on his penis I stroked it tentatively for a while, trying to block the strangeness of the sensation from my mind. I found the angry red knot of his uncircumcised penis to be a beacon of distate, but also of fascination. I soon withdrew my hand—if I could have somehow explored his penis without having to deal with *him*, however, I would have done so. Then, without warning, he bent over and put his mouth on my penis. I was shocked. I had no idea that might happen. I remember being astonished at the unusual and incredibly pleasurable sensation. He placed my hand on

his penis again, and began to move his head up and down so
that my penis slid in and out of his mouth just as if it were a
vagina. When I began to near orgasm I was frantic to let him
know, so that I would not come in his mouth, which "must
not" be allowed to happen. I moaned and tried to lift his head
with my hands, but to my amazement he insisted on stroking
away until I discharged. Now I was *really* amazed, as he
swallowed and sat up with a bleariness and air of uncertainty
that I found distasteful. I considered him a pervert (I, of
course, was not). He did not have an orgasm, or at least I do
not recall it. He was really rather good-looking, in his middle
twenties, and I was excited in spite of myself. We drove off
hurriedly, as he was late for an appointment—to photograph
a wedding.

I had very mixed feelings about this experience. I was far
more sophisticated than I had been at sixteen, and did not
consider anything evil to have happened. But I was very confused and wondered for the first time about my own capacity
for degradation. I had liked it. I thought of some of the men I
had been longing for for two years. I wondered whether I
might not lose myself in a maelstrom of homosexual, or
"queer," activities. I busily, tirelessly denied to myself the
implications of my compelling, real desire for other males.

When I was nineteen a girl I had known from high school
visited the city in which I was then at university, and we
spent a few days together. We went one afternoon to an
enormous and wild park and found a quiet spot. I felt very
strange; I had been leading the way, and doing many other
things because I felt it was expected of me, but I wasn't sure
by whom. She was both incredibly voluptuous and incredibly
naive, also very intelligent. I had crudely planned it all, and
sensed myself uncomfortable working under a compulsion. I
felt that if I had a sexual experience with her I would be
certified "all right." (All the way through my teens I was
constantly aware of my "late," "disturbed" development. I
cursed my environment but also suspected a flaw within myself.) I was unbelievably tense the entire time, yet I was erect
as we fondled each other. I believe that it was the first time
that either of us had ever fondled the genitals of the other sex.
What we did was very tentative. My penis was much larger
than she'd been expecting an erection to be. She stroked it
very lightly, and I kept hoping that she would squeeze, but she
didn't. She hardly touched my balls, which I was dying for. But
when I put my hands in her genitals, an odor escaped that
totally unmanned me. I was shocked. I have never smelled

anything like it since. I guess on vacation she wasn't washing. I've no idea what she experienced at that moment. I wilted and we mumbled something which I have forgotten. We kissed a little bit but we didn't tongue-kiss. And we left.

That experience was something of a setback. The odor really unnerved me. The penis seemed so clean by comparison, and I began to suppose that I preferred them after all.

My first complete sexual experience with a woman or girl or whatever occurred when I was nineteen and a student at a large university. I met her at a coffeehouse near the absurdly enormous dormitory building in which I "lived." I was drawn to her because she seemed so very unsure of herself, a bit frozen inside. Confident and warm young women baffled and terrified me, but I felt that here was one who would make no demands that I explain myself—she would not "see through me." I may have vaguely hoped to have found someone as lost as I was. I was the "sophisticate," to an extent. We became friends as I pestered her for attention, and asked her out from time to time. I frightened her as much as she did me. Things developed very slowly, and sometimes we would get around to clumsy and tentative necking. She was also a virgin. I can't remember the precise details, but late one evening, after this sort of thing had been going on for some time, I pressed her to stay the night and make love with me. Silence, then a frightened and somewhat placatory O.K. I told her I didn't want to do it if she was not sure, so she struggled to say O.K. in a tone that would be acceptable to me. Vaguely I thought that this was not it either. At any rate, we went on with it. I can remember very little about it, except that I was not terribly impressed by the uniformity of the sensation. We were utterly unadventurous, and did little preliminary necking. I avoided her breasts. She experienced some pain, and I tried to remember everything I could from the pathetic fifties sex manuals that I had sent away for in plain brown wrappers in the past. I can remember almost nothing about my thrusting. She hardly moved at all. I think I orgasmed fairly soon, and withdrew, thinking, Huh? Was *that* it? What's so great about it?

I thought of the illicit fires that fueled my desires for men and of how pale this had been. But I had almost entirely forgotten the occasional rushes of real erotic curiosity and romantic longing I had experienced in my early teens. This approved activity, surrounded by so many do's and don't's and rules of etiquette and expectation, was too heavy for me. We continued our relationship for about six months, but we had intercourse seldom, and I cannot remember anything about it. Finally she went home for summer vacation and we lost contact—we didn't even write.

My first experience of receiving anal intercourse was with a pickup at a local bar. He was black (I am white). His easy confidence put me more at ease than I usually was. We talked like friends. I must have been twenty-one or twenty-two, and by then freely admitted to myself my homosexual desires. (The confusion of my late teens had culminated in a crisis which resulted in my leaving college, taking a job at manual labor, and beginning to hang around the gay scene in the city.) And so I was not the least bit surprised to find myself in a graceful, witty, handsome young black man's apartment, being thoroughly seduced. Halfway through the night, he managed to titillate my asshole so sensitively that I decided to let him in. He was very sensitive, taking a very long time to work his well-greased, long but not too thick tool in. Then he waited even longer, only moving slightly, until I began to grow comfortable and until he was thrusting away without hurting me in the least. I enjoyed the sensation enormously, but he grew very passionate and could not get enough. He had one orgasm, and went on to another. Then he wanted to go on to another, but I had to beg off. He immediately desisted. It can be a very powerful experience. I thought everything from, now I'm really degraded, to what would my mother think of me now, to ohh, this is really *it!*

I can't remember precisely when I first slipped my penis inside of another guy. It must not have made too big an impression on me, or it happened at a time when many other important things were happening. Also, my passive experiences seem to make a bigger impression on me than do my active ones.

After that for a few years I had many casual sexual relationships. They served a very useful purpose, and I regret almost none of it. I certainly learned to be comfortable with the most outrageous people, and with people of widely different backgrounds. In bed with at least one hundred boys and men I received a composite picture of their essential humanity and of their male sexuality. (I once heard a story—secondhand—of a twenty-nine-year-old fellow from Chicago, encountered at a loose gay party in Toronto, who admitted to keeping a list of the cocks he'd sucked, and that he had a goal of reaching two thousand by his thirtieth birthday. This guy was doing postgraduate work in psychology at the University of Chicago.) At any rate, I have accumulated in my mind a rich store of memories of late-night confessions of many boys and men—sometimes difficult to draw out, but more often *wanting* to talk, and very happy to be able to really relax with another male. In some very important way, I feel as if I have made love with the entire male sex—that I transcended the bonds of individuality. This may have been my own way of exploring my own maleness.

The time I felt the most deeply in love was last summer, when things between my lover and I were going rather well. We had a cottage in the country, and I was on vacation from school. I put in a beautiful vegetable garden, and it all felt so sweet, right, and healthy to have him in mind, and have the time to read and reflect to my heart's content, as well. The good physical exercise mellowed and relieved me. I wanted only him for lovemaking, and to think of my future as involving him. However, it had taken me rather a long time together with him to grow into this state, and after three years his patience was shot. And we were still not really sharing each other's interests. He considered the garden mine, for instance, which hurt me deeply. I was never the tidy mothering homebody that he longed for (he, incidentally, has since found a man who just fits the bill). He wanted nothing less than 100 percent service and devotion. So we argued a lot. At the end of the summer when we moved back to the city, things became impossible. There were some painful scenes. We argued frequently and sometimes almost violently. I would find the tenderest concerns of my heart torn into little shreds. Who knows why . . . I have buried my feelings and not altogether disinterred them. Where am I now? I'm drifting.

My clearest recent fantasy involved my own son—I do not have a son, but I imagined that I had a son who was just at puberty. I was going to help him celebrate his accession to biological manhood by taking him on a backpacking trek somewhere in British Columbia, where we would each do a small amount of LSD and I would initiate him into the mysteries. I would share my experience and awe and humility before life with him, and then we would masturbate into separate moss, feather, and seaweed amulets, which we would then sew up. These we would carry to the top of a prominent hill, climb the tallest tree, and hang these amulets there just at dawn, so that our male kinship with the steady burning and brilliant sun would be sealed. Or ogasm just as the sun's disc broke the horizon. Thus would my son be impressed with the pure atavism of sex, and thus would he experience something in the vast realm beneath that petrified one of rational veneer. An animistic ceremony.

I am ninety-three. I was born March 15, 1885, on a farm and was later a Yellowstone stagecoach driver in 1905 and 1906. Later I owned large tracts of land and became something of a capitalist. I have attended two colleges and have paid for a scholarship in a state university so that some other person may also get as good an education as I have. I am a Methodist and of course an Aryan. Every member of the family became outstanding and a leader.

I am just an average-looking fellow, not handsome and I guess not ugly. Folks who know me marvel at my virility and the fact that at my age my voice has no quiver and I have all my teeth, not bald, and capable to look after caring for 400 parcels of real estate still.

I am not big but, like my father, pretty masculine. I am able to grow a beard and I generally am the dominant person even though my wife tries often to be boss. I have been a successful man and women have contributed little to it.

I know what it is to be masculine but I know nothing about what a macho is. I have a deluxe edition of Webster's Dictionary in three volumes but Webster's doesn't dignify the word by mentioning it. I suppose it is a slang word sometimes used by youths and morons.

My father didn't marry until he was forty and Mother twenty. He died at seventy-one and divorce has been absent in the family for the past 200 years. Father was a stern man and lectured his sons but little. I think he felt all he really needed to do to have good boys and girls was to set an impeccable example. The two girls more than made good and his seven sons was every inch a *man*. Father was very respectful to women and was the only farmer I knew in northern Illinois who raised his hat to a woman near a hundred years ago. Yes, he was gallant but we boys knew he had no use for a man who was dominated by a woman.

[The following are answers to the questions given on pages 995–1008]

1. I was twenty and she was a high school girl of nineteen.

2. I am ashamed to say sometimes I did this when alone, perhaps nine or ten. No one coached me and I learned by myself.

3. After a time, perhaps about twelve, I observed a little watery semen shoot out but it was very little. Yes, I would say

I came to a climax before there was any sign of juice discharge. No, have never enjoyed touching my skin. I had no wet dreams before seventeen or perhaps eighteen.

4. We were born and reared on a farm in Illinois and my parents were very stern. They never told us anything about sex but they knew always where their boys were. But my brothers were all older than I, for I was the seventh son, and they were very smart and told me a great deal about sex, whores, clap, syph, women menstruating, etc. I heard these things by the time I was seven.

5. I was always very passionate and I always had an erection but we were reared to be terribly afraid we might get a girl pregnant or get a venereal disease. Those fears precluded illicit relations. And Mother was strict.

6. Very definitely it should be repressed. There are many good reasons why parents oppose their children marrying or having intercourse without marriage. There is grave danger of venereal disease but more especially people under thirty are not sufficiently experienced to choose a lifetime mate. The generation I enjoyed in my youth had practically no divorce and many are still married at eighty and ninety.

7. No, there is no appreciable change in my sex life and at ninety-three I am about as keen as I was at forty. However, at ninety-three my penis is not as responsive as I would prefer nor does my blood replenish it as quickly as it should.

8. Funny, I like or care for no sports. I was born on a farm and had to work from 4 a.m. to 8 or 9 p.m. and my only recreation is either reading or gardening. And at the latter I am a prize winner. Of course, I am civic-minded and serve various city boards and aid many Republican conservatives.

9. I have been married over sixty years, of course do not masturbate nor allow sex to interfere with my business.

10. I have never told my friends how much I loved them nor they don't tell me such silly things. I am a sort of hardboiled guy and I scarcely tell my wife how much I love her. I have, I think, the respect of thousands but I don't think any love me.

11. I guess family life is important to me, as I am never in saloons and always home at night. I am a poor lodge man or club man—just an old farm boy or man.

12. No, I can't say I enjoy especially caring for or petting children.

13. I must confess I never longed to become a mother. I didn't feel any inferiority in the knowledge that the Lord ordained I be a *man*. And I might add I am grateful.

14. I think it a mighty important role to be a father and especially every boy sorely needs one. I and my brothers are fathers and I think good ones. Girls need them also. I think these homosexuals are the result of too much momism!

17. No, I was the youngest boy of seven brothers and there was but a little girl younger than I of nine children. I never was taught or trained to look after children or old people and I would not be too adept.

18. I never pined for love nor even much warmth and I feel well satisfied.

19. I have all the time to myself I want. As to that I am satisfied.

20. I feel proceeding to the bathroom should be a strictly private affair and I close the door and lock it. No, I definitely was not reared to have a wife watch me take a leak and I don't want it. Also I don't want to see my wife urinate nor any other woman, for it is too reminiscent of the days of my youth on the farm when a cow would urinate. The operation is painfully reminiscent and let us say analogous.

20–24. (See his introduction page 945.)

25. Father read a great deal to Mother, for she was educated and so was he. He had a lot of respect for her judgment, and I must say sometimes he made a mistake not to heed her judgment. But in the main I know he didn't feel them anything near the equal of men.

26. I think a young, virile, and fearless young man can distinguish himself by showing up Woodrow Wilson and Franklin Roosevelt for bringing on two useless wars and the loss of thousands of young lives and billions in property. The Jews wanted war and England wanted to defeat Germany because Germany had taken much of their commerce. Roosevelt, I think, was a throwback to his Jewish ancestry when the name a few generations ago in Holland responded to name of Rosenfeldt. And we had such disreputable Presidents as Kennedy, Truman, and Johnson, all of whom aided in advocating a damnable institution called busing and tearing down the integrity of the pure Caucasian race. Mixing the races was a no good idea and I feel sure only fostered by liberal Democrats for the sole purpose of pandering to the Negroes so they would vote the Democratic ticket. The most heinous crime was Johnson's so-called Civil Rights Laws. Instead of now punishing the criminal blacks, the politicians turn them loose and appoint them to fill spots for which they are often unfit. God knows I bear the Negro no ill will and my father being a friend of Lincoln's risked his life to help

free the Negro. But the latter has forgotten that, and 90 percent vote for the giveaway liberals. We need a hero citizen and an orator to awaken the people. I grieve for the youth of our land.

27. The young conservative men who were elected to Congress last November can be very proud. They made a great fight and I helped some thirty. We have a liberal Democrat who is willing to make every concession to remain in power but he will see these young Republican conservatives will largely turn the tide. You ask what men can be ashamed of. We can be ashamed that the men we elected to office have plunged this nation into debt and we owe more than the total of the entire wealth of the nation, with Carter buying votes by supporting more and more welfare. Jackson was the first Democrat and a rogue who murdered the Indians of the Five Civilized Tribes and gave their lands to his friends in Virginia and the Carolinas.

28. I think I have no worry or problem of note. I of course have pernicious anemia and that can be handled and now must use a cane since arthritis has shown me scant respect and has invaded my tailbone by depositing calcium.

29. Of course success is important. I was a millionaire at forty. I had worked my way for a college education. I have never been sued or debased in any way and they have given me at least three plaques for meritorious city achievements and service on city boards.

30. No, I am never ruthless and have never been criticized or abused by the populace. I never had a fight and I have stayed out of saloons and gambling houses. I avoid trouble-quarrels. I don't think my father was ever ruthless and I just can't imagine being involved in a situation where I had to be ruthless.

31. Of course in my youth I often felt hurt when the girl I wanted to date went with another boy or I was turned down at a party, but I don't think I felt like a robot.

32. In my youth that would have hurt me sorely but not now at all. There are many intelligent women and I would not be averse to the comparison.

33. No, I don't think I was ever called a sissy. My mother and my two sisters were outstanding persons but the average woman is dumb, given to small talk, chitchat. And I feel our women have slipped in the matter of drinking, swearing, and the rearing of worthwhile children.

34–35. I have no resentment at all toward women in general.

36. Yes, my first wife and I lived together forty-two years and she died at seventy-five. Certainly I feel at times I was not sufficiently considerate and kindly. Certainly had I known I would get rich, I would have spent more money on her. She was a wonderful woman and she loved me dearly.

37. I have never subscribed for a magazine containing naked men or women but of course in waiting in the offices of other persons I have looked at these pictures. I have a big library and many papers and magazines but I would feel like a fool to spend money to look at pictures of naked women or men. Father had nothing like *Playboy* around. I think perhaps momism has tended to produce homosexuals and perhaps tended to foster the dissemination of lewd magazines.

38. I am not qualified to give an opinion. However, I don't think they are filling an important role, for the world got along pretty well for centuries without them.

39. I think the sexual revolution is certainly reprehensible. The widow next to my friend's house came from the North and bought a house for $200,000 so her three daughters would have a home, but as they became eighteen each wanted a separate apartment, and when all had left, the lady sold the house and bought a unit in a condominium. I feel sure the morals of our people have deteriorated.

40. My present wife still gets along after twenty-two years but I think women's so-called liberation is and was a mistake. Men have lost a good deal of the respect they had for them and I see in the future a woman President that I think will prove a calamity. But personally I am not affected.

41. I am not attracted to nor do I admire a masculine woman nor have I ever seen one that I felt my superior in executive ability.

42. I get along well with all my wife's friends, but I am essentially a man's man and men treat me with deference and respect. I would say I have more men friends.

43. When I want sexual intercourse I try to seduce my wife, and failing that I am not averse to having intercourse with some other female, but of course always circumspect as to clap or syph. No man ever fooled with me nor I with them.

44. I think sexual intercourse essential to all males, man or beast. But there are also other important things and I don't think folks should become a prey to it, nor go to whorehouses or commit rape or look on every woman as a prospect.

45. I am not as religious as I should be, and I would admit that spiritual significance is not of paramount importance.

46. I have been married sixty-seven years. It has its good

points, such as right in your home a degree of safety and satisfaction (maybe) in intercourse. And you have a female to produce children for you and perhaps she might be a cook and housekeeper. But the really big thing is to have safety in marriage from venereal disease.

I loved my first wife because she loved me and did everything a wife should do. She felt so long as I was satisfied she was happy.

I have no extramarital experiences nor never did have.

My first wife was very anxious to have one or two children. My father was one of six very important children and my mother one of six and I was one of nine children. I thought I could afford to have one or two and so why not. No, I don't feel having a wife or a couple of children were deterrent factors. Cancer took my first wife after we were married forty-two years and neither I nor any of the other nine children ever got a divorce or was a victim of one. I am not a homosexual and I would feel ashamed to have a friend who was or is one.

You ask how we get our sex education. Why, you can't look at television, hear radio, or listen to a schoolteacher without their expounding on its virtues and tribulations. Sex is crammed down our throats at every opportunity until it all has become disgusting. I listened to a damn fool woman the other day declare children should be taught to masturbate and she said every child at puberty should have plenty of fucking when they begin to get the urge a couple years before puberty. If one reads history they will find such conclusions caused the downfall of Rome, Greece, and all other nations who made screwing and alcohol important.

48. I fell in love at twenty with a girl of sixteen. I was in college and she was in high school. Nothing especially happened. I knew better than to have sex with her, for I wanted to make a stake before I got married and I knew my folks would have compelled me to marry her.

49. No, never.

50–53. I am a poor lover. Never been too happy with anyone and I have no longings for a "relationship" with anyone. My family ties are fairly strong because our old-fashioned folks taught all us children we must get along together and not quarrel and always we have abided by their admonitions. I don't drink and have no partying friends.

54. Well, I feel sure every man wants his wife or his sex partner to come to a climax, but my first wife often could not do so, as she worked so hard she was tired. My second wife

is amorous but it takes her so long to come to orgasm that I must delay action for a long time until she is ready. But when she really goes off she is in such raptures you can hear her holler a block away. A short rest and again she is ready and anxious and a few strokes and she is off a second time.

55. A man who served in the Civil War with my father gave us boys long before we married the best description I ever heard of an orgasm. The phrase may seem crude but certainly it is descriptive. Said he, "When your gun (penis) goes off it feels just like a flock of quail flew out of your ass." My present wife is very selfish about orgasm and insists on doing it her way. If I am to avoid a spat I dare not go off till *she* is ready.

56. With my first wife she probably only came to climax half the time, maybe less.

57. Now, of course, I am an old man and not as active as when young but I don't think I ever moved around much after orgasm and I never did it twice the same night. I had lots of semen and once I spent I was ready to turn over and go to sleep.

58. If I have sex I of course always ejaculate. When I was fifty I could maintain an erection an hour and refrain from coming to a climax, trying to get a woman's "gun off." But a certain woman who was crazy to screw couldn't come to a climax in six months. But always after ejaculating I was through for the night.

59. No, I never did. The first two years I was married we had sex or rather I had sex once every night except for about four days each month when my wife was unwell, but never more than once a night.

60. No, erection is not necessary for arousal but you better have a good hard prick if you try any funny business with your wife. A soft prick burns my second wife up yet I feel just as amorous as ever and try things with a soft penis but she won't stand for it.

61. Certainly it's embarrassing, but I would try to use it anyway, but my present wife won't stand for it. At my age I might not have any semen. This wife is selfish.

62. Yes, I would say that I was always aroused when I had an erection.

63. No, I don't like being aroused unless the situation is propitious and I am able to immediately have intercourse. Well, I think when you get flushed, all heated up, and your penis is hard and you have had no sex for a week, you are aroused.

64. When I was young I did masturbate but not now. I am decidedly ashamed of those puerile habits. Of course, I was secretive about it and never until this letter did I ever tell anyone I did such nasty things.

65. It's of course unsatisfying and I think every boy who ever practiced it has been ashamed of it. I think very few ever admitted doing it. When I was a boy, folks were told boys addicted would go crazy. But now I know little girls do those things too.

68. Yes, when younger I have partially aroused myself to erection by stroking my penis a few times and then inserting it in a woman. When a man gets older his penis is not as responsive as it should be and women insist it must be in proper condition. But I consider masturbating a mighty poor substitute for screwing.

69. Masturbating was never important in my life. I feel sure every boy or man who practiced it was ashamed and depressed afterward.

70. No, I see nothing attractive about my genitals and I never tasted them nor smelled them. I have nothing to brag about. My cock is smaller than I would have it and one testicle is a good deal smaller than the other one.

71. I have been circumcised. Had it done when I was twenty-seven because the foreskin was too long. And at the same time had some varicose veins cut out of my scrotum and that made a suspensory unnecessary. In my case I am well satisfied but as to another person I cannot advise.

72. I have been told it is a part of the Jews' religion. There is a sort of "cheese" gathers around the head of the penis. I think some mothers think it more sanitary to have a boy circumcised. And again many persons feel there is less danger of getting a dose of clap if they have this done.

73. I guess I heard about it when I was about ten. I was told by some who knew about the Jewish custom. I don't remember any reaction on my part. I wanted the varicocele operation, that to me was important, and I thought as long as I took the anesthetic I would have that long foreskin shortened up. And also thought I would have a little more fun with orgasm and I guess it was fruitful.

74–76. Circumcision hasn't affected my sexual capabilities and I've heard no complaints from women. I don't show myself purposely, but I feel I have nothing I need be ashamed of.

77. I never indulged in oral stimulation of genitals and also never with boys or men or girls or women and certainly with

either wife. No man or women ever sucked me off nor did any female do this.

78. Never h d sex with or by way of anal with any human being, nor by way of mouth.

79. I never had a partner who would indulge in manual stimulation of genitals. Both wives were definitely opposed to such practices and I never had intercourse with anyone else unless they were gone visiting for months. No woman ever played with my cock to the point I came to a climax.

80. I never masturbated before anyone nor did any person masturbate in my presence or even admit they ever masturbated. Folks are sensitive about it and ashamed.

81. I of course have never felt or had a penis in my rear nor anyone's finger except a doctor's in making an examination of my prostate gland. No, I would not like it nor would I tolerate doing this to me. I would be ashamed for my part and definitely ashamed for my partner in this dirty business.

82. I really am not anxious to be touched or petted or kissed, and my breasts and buttocks and ears are not sensitive. Of course, a few times young girls of, say, ten or twelve have been curious, touched my cock or testicles, and I can't stand that without ejaculating and so I always try to avoid an encounter.

83. All I want.

84. No.

85. Nearly always I make the sexual advance as becomes a male. Very rarely did my first wife make the advances. My second wife is passionate even at seventy and always ready. No, I don't think love has anything to do with sex. A woman that is passionate I think will let a Negro screw her if no white man is available. I hate to say it, however.

86. I have been refused plenty of times. It didn't anger me nor did I blame them. Yes, I have refused whores because I felt it unfair to my wife, even though she was 3,000 miles away for months, and also due to fear of venereal disease. And I have refused little girls of ten to thirteen for the reason I was unwilling to pollute a child's morals and of course the danger she might tell on me. But they liked me and begged to see my cock. The danger of their telling was very slight.

87. I have never experienced a low in sexual exuberance. I have been the same for over seventy years except of course my penis lacks the "authority" it once did.

88. Nothing in particular except perhaps men are stronger than women, are smarter, and are far more truthful than women.

89. I would make a mighty poor homosexual. I care nothing about a man's body and really not very much about a woman's body except to fuck them.

90. I don't care much about sports and waste no money on expensive games and don't even play golf, checkers, or shuffleboard. And I don't care to have any contact with men's bodies. My recreation is my library, newspapers, magazines, and of course garden. On trips I visit the museums and art galleries and zoos.

91. I don't care for them and don't frequent them except on rare occasions with a nephew. I get my baths in the privacy of one of my baths in my home.

92. I am reasonably proud of my body, for I have no birthmarks, warts, ingrown toenails, or any ugly features. I am not bowlegged, not bald nor do I have a low forehead indicating lack of intelligence. I like to be nice and clean but I am not a crank about a daily bath—there are other things more important.

93. I never kissed a man in my life except when my father died I bent over and I kissed him on the forehead. I would look askance on a man who kissed other men.

94. I never saw another man screwing or masturbating and I don't want to see a man ejaculate.

95. I know a few gay fellows but they know such monkey shines are anathema to me and I am never solicited. I definitely do not want a homosexual relationship.

96. I have never had any.

97. I never had any illicit relations with a man but my father used some physical contact when he whipped me as a boy. I was reared amongst the farmers of northern Illinois and when I grew up I doubt we had a homosexual in the county. Everybody in the county knew every other person, and everybody would have shunned a homosexual almost as vehemently as a massasauga rattlesnake.

98–99. Don't know anything about nor waste my time to consider it.

100. Personally I know nothing about it but it seems some men are crazy to "corn-hole" boys. I pity such fools but I hope they hang them.

101. No man or woman ever sucked me off and I never asked anyone to do this. Besides I never had a man or woman to ask me to suck them off.

102. I suppose in my youth I could have done this but I never indulged in such puerile practices. If I got a piece of

tail lined up I wanted to get to the real activity and soon get it over.

103. I have been in love with girls but never with men. To me sex with men is disgusting.

104. I do what is in good taste in relationships with men.

105. No, not at ninety-three.

106–107. I am opposed to homosexuals to be permitted to teach school or have contact with children, and I contribute to Anita Bryant's organization.

108. I had two sisters and have some fairly close friends amongst my wife's friends but I am having sex with none of them.

109. My mother was a stern woman. Married at twenty and died at eighty. Had an intellect that would have done honor to a man. She tolerated no foolishness. But she had a keen sense of humor.

110. I admire a woman who is living with a man she married, is a good mother, a good cook and housekeeper, and believes in education and attends parent-teacher meetings, garden clubs, church, hospital auxiliary, etc. I don't like women who mistreat their husbands, gad around in cars, flirt with men, or neglect their children. I am opposed to the ERA and I think it will likely become the downfall of the nation. I admit, some women are smart but I have a deep prejudice against career women. The noblest calling for a woman is to be a good and virtuous wife, good mother, cook, and housekeeper.

112. No, I am living with my second wife and I have no amorous connection with any other woman.

113. I talked at times with women about their sexual likes and dislikes. Certainly I was interested and asked them. Sometimes they have been candid and truthful but I would not generally consider the answers neither truthful, nor candid nor even lucid. Most of them are dumb, and lie.

114. I can't say I was inordinately impressed at the sight of a woman's genitals and I never tasted them. They smell all right if they frequently bathe and don't smell too much of urine. One woman's uterus is like another's, and when I am having intercourse it doesn't matter who my partner is, at least not too much.

115. Of course I know what the clitoris is and I know women who just won't let me have intercourse who love to have me use my big finger in place of a penis and they like to have that continue for an hour or several hours. I don't know

if they came to a climax or not. They all lie about an orgasm anyway. I never was told I was too rough nor too gentle. They just don't talk but like it.

116. I have answered this previously, no woman ever sucked me off nor I them.

117. Some are afraid of venereal disease or pregnancy but seem to love you to sort of give them a screwing with your finger. Of course, that hardly satisfies a man but if they refuse to let him screw them properly and if he likes the woman he just goes along with her—she is the boss.

118. Certainly you like to see a woman you love or are friendly with come to orgasm. They all know a man wants them to go off, and so if you ask them they will lie if they think they can get away with it. You kiss them and you feel of their breast or even gently pinch her ass.

119. I never had intercourse with a woman menstruating if I was aware of it. No oral sex ever, even with my wife.

120. Sure I like women's bodies and I like to kiss their lips, face, and breasts, but to taste I know nothing. I like a little odor of sex but don't like a strong odor of urine.

121. Generally money means much more to the average woman than sex. Once in a long time a woman who is over-sexed will really beg you to go to bed with her. If they have sex with a man they want a man very masculine and with a stiff cock.

122. We never go in for any fancy positions or circumstances. I am not heavy or fat. When we are in bed I am on top. But once in a while when my wife is anxious for intercourse she will feel over and get hold of my penis and get it hard and say nothing but gently roll on top of me and then she wants to do the heavy work, which is generally the male's province, and she may just come to climax.

123. Any way my wife elects doing is fine, it's all good.

124. I like intercourse because if I don't have it I am not satisfied. And too it is nature.

125. Oh, no, there is no discomfort after screwing. Really gives one great satisfaction.

126. When folks are in a loving mood, if they are not tired we generally get our things together. If a wife loves you enough even though she don't want it she will let you have intercourse.

127. I would define sex as intercourse. It sort of disgusts me to see folks lallygagging around and spooning. I don't want to get all stirred up and get no intercourse. Have your sex and get busy on other things—that's my motto.

128. My first wife rarely came to a climax, as she worked too hard and got too tired. My second wife wants to come to a climax every time but it takes way too long for me. But she gets furious if I go off before her. She never wants to unless she can do it her way.

129. With my first wife always I was in doubt if she reached climax and same with other women, but with my second wife she is very passionate and she won't screw unless she goes off. She hollers in rapture. They all lie and tell you they went.

130. Of course I prefer to have a woman have orgasm when having intercourse and go off. I don't know whether or not they ever come to climax if you screw them with your finger.

131. We never used a vibrator and I never saw a woman try to get herself worked up to the point of orgasm. No, I don't feel myself at fault if they don't come to a climax, for I have heard other men tell of their experiences and read doctor books. I have known women so quick on the trigger you couldn't get your cock in over an inch till they went off and would go off perhaps a dozen times and panting while I went off once.

132. I have learned long since I am not to blame whatever their peculiarity in sex.

133. No, I never made it an important factor in my life whether or not a woman came to a climax or not. And my wives and I never tried any special means to bring about their coming to a climax. Screwing has been important but not the main feature of my life.

134. Nearly always I am ready to go off before either of my two wives but it's true nearly all apologize if they are slow in coming to a climax and try hard to please a man.

135. I knew one woman, when my wife was gone for nearly a year, to have sexual intercourse covering a period of over an hour and in six months was never able to go once. In those days I could keep my penis hard and not go off for an hour.

136. I don't let it bother me too much. I work maybe an hour and try to satisfy them and in the end I go off, get up, and call it a day—or a night.

137. Up to the time I was sixty I could control time of coming to a climax but now I am unable to keep an erection but for a short time. Of course it is disturbing.

138. Intercourse is of primary importance to her and she can't tolerate a soft penis and though it takes long to go off she is furious if I don't wait for her.

139. When I was younger I sometimes went off too soon. No, if I ejaculated into a woman I felt refreshed and rather

good about it even if they failed to come to a climax. But I
was distressed when I dreamed off and soiled the bed.

140. No, I use no method to delay coming to a climax and
I don't observe any lessening of sensitivity of feeling in penis.

141–142. My second wife is beyond childbearing age. She
likes to have intercourse but she insists I give her a good
prolonged fucking before she is able to go off. But at that point
she wants me to also go off. I think she likes to feel a lot of
good hot semen shot into her and she hollers in ecstasy. But
now that I am getting old the penis becomes too soft and she
has no patience with that nor will she aid in getting it hard.
The wife decides when sex is over. During my prime, say,
forty to sixty, I did control the situation.

143. Never bothered much until at about eighty. Hot water
tended to produce an erection.

144. No, I would not like to change the false meaning of
sex. "Sex" is not a nasty word and most folks feel "screwing"
is and also "fucking."

145. It is natural women don't want sex often like men
because in all animal life the female will only permit a male
to fertilize when she is in heat. All animals have intercourse
in order to procreate. But the situation is different with the
human race. They screw for the fun of it. Women don't want
to become pregnant every time they have intercourse and so
don't screw when menstruating. In all animal life the male is
the aggressive one but with nearly all the farm animals I have
observed the males don't bother the females unless the latter
are in heat. Women rarely come to climax and screwing is not
so important to them as to men. Often they have intercourse
only to please men.

146. With my first wife we never used any, as she wanted
a baby and had two sons. However, she menstruated but little
and stopped completely at thirty-five. My second had just
stopped menstruating a month before we married. I never got
another woman pregnant and never took any precaution.

147. Oh yes—I read a great deal and folks are duly warned.

148. Answered above. Never used a condom nor pursued
any other method.

149. Certainly I would protect a woman. If I was to have
intercourse with a woman who just might be susceptible to
pregnancy.

150. Nearly always I have intercourse only with my wife
and she is beyond the age.

151. Answered above.

152. I am only in favor of abortion if her life is in danger.

I never got a woman impregnated save my wife. No, I never furnished the money for an operation nor did I ever go with one to consult a doctor.

153. Never had a vasectomy. Yes, my wife and I had two sons. I am ignorant of results.

154. Not at my age. And anyway I don't believe I would want any young man to do it.

155. No, I have never witnessed it and it would be repulsive to me.

156. No, I think violence in sex is a terrible abberration. I could never condone it nor in fact understand it.

157. I am a man of peace and I never had a fight with a boy, a man nor a woman.

158. If I had struck a person I loved I certainly would regret it terribly.

159. I never spanked anyone and such actions certainly would give me no thrill.

160. No, I never got satisfaction to force someone to my will.

161. I never kissed anyone's feet nor indulged in golden showers and I am willing to forgo the pleasure of both.

162. Women tell me rape is a terrible thing. Most women are virgins who are raped and they are badly torn generally. Even if an older woman is raped who is not a virgin she is still likely to be torn, for the rapist cares nothing for her feelings or welfare and in fact now it appears rape is not so much an intercourse satisfaction to the rapist as a satisfaction to him that he has punished a woman.

163. No, I never had intercourse with a very young person.

164. I of course never raped a woman and never had a desire to. Always I have never wanted to screw if she didn't want to do it. I feel there should be affection and a little petting and she should come to a climax when I do.

165. Surely I think all men have pressured women to have sex. I have and been turned down pretty regularly. No, I don't care much to do it unless they want to. But if a girl or woman really wants sex I certainly get great satisfaction in acceding.

166. I get no fun in being rough or forcing and my first wife was entirely submissive about sex but my second wife is very definitely the boss. It's got to be done her way or not at all. I dare not go off until she is able to.

167. My present wife insists the job must be consummated her way. The penis must be hard and remain so for a long time while she works diligently to arrive at orgasm and she wants

me to come to a climax exactly when she does. She is then in raptures and you can hear her holler a block away.

168. Sex is not political, for all denominations and sects indulge.

I took the questions seriously and I wanted you to have a truthful résumé. No, I never read *The Hite Report* but I have read Kinsey's and others. I was honest and truthful and I think other men will be—at least more truthful than women.

This covers the field pretty well and I have nothing to add. I feel sure all my father's seven sons pursued intersexual activities in the same old-fashioned method I did.

I am twenty-eight, an independent television producer. I have been disabled with cerebral palsy since birth. The disability affects my speech, dexterity, and walking. I use a wheelchair.

My biggest problem is that I don't have a relationship. I haven't even had a date since my engagement broke off. This was the biggest emotional disturbance of my life, breaking off my engagement to someone I loved very much this January second. Last May I met her—she also has cerebral palsy. She was twenty-five years old. We dated all summer and became engaged. We had some problems, but I felt that we could work them out. The problems mainly dealt with her lack of maturity. She was unable to make a decision for herself, and I caught her lying to me or not telling me the complete truth on a number of occasions. Still, for the first time in my life I had someone who really loved me, and I didn't want to give that up.

Sex was a bone of contention. She told me many times she didn't want to wait until marriage. In December, I finally found a night when she didn't have cramps or a headache, or any other physical problem. I pushed the point, and she eventually said OK. About the time I was half undressed and getting into the appropriate frame of mind, she starts whimpering and says, "I was always taught to wait until marriage." I was mad. I told her that if that was how she felt that was OK, but she picked a lousy time to tell me! Especially after telling me the opposite many times. Still, I loved her and didn't want to break it off.

On Christmas Eve, Dad and I had a private talk. I told him that, even though I knew it was a bad reason, one reason for my not wanting to break the engagement was that I didn't want to have to start all over again from ground zero trying to find someone else. I said that the problem was not lack of love on either side. Dad agreed, but asked me if her love was a mature love. I said I didn't know.

My fiancée and I continued to discuss our problems when I visited her in Baltimore, for Christmas. On January second, she called me to ask about some papers she thought she had left in my apartment. She was going to a job interview that morning and was up-tight. I told her that I had looked for them after the call the night before but hadn't found them. She told me to look again and mail them if I found them. When I tried to say that she would get them faster if I kept them and gave them to her when she came down that weekend, she hung up on me. I was angry. I called her up, yelled at her, then I hung up. Not exactly the most mature thing I've ever done! All day I tried to find a reason not to break the engagement. That evening, as I picked up the phone to call her I was still hoping she would say something that would make me feel that we could still continue the engagement. I began the conversation by apologizing for hanging up on her that morning. Then I paused, hoping she would reciprocate. There was an awkward silence. Then I began, "I guess if it has come to the point where we do things to each other like this morning, it's time we . . . we kind of have to . . ."

"Call off the engagement?" she asked.

"Yes," I said. She said that she had come to the same conclusion, and that if I didn't call her that night, she was going to call me the next day to say the same thing. I choose to believe this. I think the writing was on the wall for both of us.

For three weeks after this I was extremely depressed. The phone calls between us were tense, and I always seemed to say the wrong thing. Finally, I wrote her a letter telling her that I still cared for her and that I would be there if she wanted anything. However, I said I wouldn't contact her until she contacted me—she had asked me for time to think things out. That letter was like a pressure valve. I felt I had freed myself and slowly began to pull out of my depression.

Now, three and a half months after the engagement was broken, I'm back at ground zero—looking for, but not finding dates. In retrospect, in answer to my father's question, I can say that her love for me, while sincere, was not a mature love. She seemed at times unwilling or unable to put me first in her life over her family, and unwilling to sacrifice for me. She's a beautiful, intelligent, and charming lady; she just doesn't have the maturity to make it all work for her. If and when she gains that maturity, she'll be a wonderful woman, and make some man a dynamite wife. I don't blame her for her lack of maturity. When she was a teenager, she spent several years laid-up with surgery. She missed whatever it is that people get from peer associations. Add to this a family who was always there to make decisions for her, and you've got a situation that would stunt anyone's development.

As for me, I still think about her and remember nights lying beside her having someone warm and soft to curl up with. I do call her occasionally—my self-imposed silence lasted a month. I sometimes wish we could get things back the way they were, but realize that many things have to change before that happens. I still care about her and what happens to her. I think I always will, even if we marry other people. I learned a lot from this experience—it's just a shame to pay such a high price for the knowledge.

I didn't have such a normal upbringing either. As a disabled teenager, I didn't get out as much as I would like. For example, whenever teachers planned field trips, they would ask my parents to chaperone because they (the teachers) didn't want to take responsibility for someone in a wheelchair. My parents always said yes because the implication was, "If you don't come, neither does he!" So my attempts to get away from my parents were often foiled, as were their attempts to get rid of me and have time to themselves. Consequently, I was very happy to leave home for college, and they were very happy I was able to. It was like a graduation of a sort. I was told the year before that unless I learned to be totally independent in terms of my personal needs, I would not be admitted to the University where I spent my first two years. In one year I learned to feed myself, wash my hair, clean my teeth, take a bath, and do most personal-care activities. These may seem simple tasks to one who learns them in childhood; they are frustrating and time-consuming when you learn them at age eighteen. My leaving home was a declaration to those who knew me and would come to know me of my complete personal independence. A triumph.

While my parents did miss me, they were very happy for me. This was brought out most poignantly at Dulles Airport one time as I left for school. Mom kissed me good-bye, and Dad took me out to the plane. A man came up to my mother and asked, "How can you let him go like that?"

"You'll never know how many times I've prayed that he would be able to go off on his own," was my mother's reply. The man was looking very sad and bewildered so my mother added, "Don't think I don't miss him. I miss him terribly! But he has to go!"

"Oh, my! Oh, my!" the man exclaimed as he drew back and walked away, undoubtedly failing to comprehend the significance of the moment. Did I feel guilty about leaving home? No. It was a sense of accomplishment and total freedom.

As a child, I always knew I was loved by both my parents, but was and still am, closer to my mother. As a teenager, Dad and I had a lot of fights about many things—right now I couldn't tell you what. Mom says we were two bullheaded Irishmen who were too much alike in many of the wrong ways. But in the last ten years, since I left home for college, we have both mellowed. I was somewhat surprised when I came home from college and he asked me if he and I could go see the movie *Patton*. He said he wanted to see it, but Mom didn't. We went and we both enjoyed it. Dad is an intelligent person with a sense of humor and a fettish for being well-organized and efficient. In fact, he becomes very tense and disgruntled if those around him are not as organized as he is. He works for the government in a field that is extremely technical. Perhaps, this is why we were never super close. I would ask him about his work and get an answer I didn't understand. When I tried to follow up with other questions, I got even more confused, so I gave up. I know very little and care even less about his field, and while Dad cares about whether I'm doing O.K., he knows little and cares less about my field. Also, there have been times when I haven't been organized enough to satisfy him. I can talk to Dad about my problems but often don't. I guess this goes back to my teen years when I was having girl problems and would ask him what to do. He never seemed to have any better ideas than I did, so I got out of the habit of asking him about my problems.

In high school, since I couldn't excel in sports and I didn't have much luck with the girls, I poured my energies into getting high grades. Even though I now realize that grades are not as important as I had thought them to be, everyone needs an ego-builder. That was mine. Sometimes I was taunted with words like "cripple" or "retard." It made me extremely angry and I felt like less of a person. Sometimes I took it out on others. I remember one day when I was coming home on the bus, sitting next to a cerebral palsied boy who was weaker than I. I started talking to him and every once in a while I punched him in the stomach. I did this three or four times. I wasn't sure why I was doing it, and to this day I don't know why. I guess

I needed to feel stronger than someone that day. I was nine or ten at the time. Evidently, no one saw and the boy didn't say anything, because I never was punished for it.

Today I have a good male friend whom I have known for four years. He is also disabled, blind, and works in the media, specifically as a radio journalist. We have worked together on a number of media activities on behalf of disabled activist groups—setting up press conferences, demonstrations, etc. We sometimes have dinner, go drinking, or engage in other similar activities.

There are many hassles to face when you are handicapped. What makes me maddest is not being treated like a real human being. This takes many forms. There are those I get on the telephone who tell me, "Call me back when you're sober!" Others just hang up without trying to find out what I want. When I'm out, I am sometimes asked if my mother knows where I am. Some people ask if I know where I live! Then there are those who park in front of the curb-cuts so I can't get up or down the curb. If I'm out late at night, I'm sometimes asked what I'm doing out late, all alone. This question usually comes from other people who are out alone late at night! If I go to a singles bar, I suddenly become invisible. When I do start talking to a woman, she usually says she has a boyfriend. Now I ask you, what is a woman who already has a boyfriend doing in a singles bar? There are many other manifestations of people's inability to treat disabled people as equal human beings. I guess I have to learn to allow for the able-bodied!

I really miss my fiancée. Being in love added a warmth to my life that replaced the intense loneliness that I had felt before, and have felt since the engagement was broken. It made me feel needed, and I felt a keener sense of responsibility. I have never spent Christmas without a family, yet 1979, was, perhaps, the first Christmas in many years when I didn't feel lonely.

This question made me think a lot: "Are love and personal relationships as important to your life as your work? What is the most important and satisfying part of your life?" To be honest I just don't know. Through the years I was growing up, I built a stubbornness and determination to succeed despite anybody or anything. Now I am doing well in my career, and it would be hard for me to give that up. On the other hand, I don't want to spend the rest of my life alone. My biggest fear right now is that ten years from now, when half my hair is gone, and the other half is gray, when I've got middle-aged spread, I'm pushing forty, and most of my sexual prime has passed, I will still be looking for someone.

I have tried to give my answers as a single, disabled man, struggling to find someone. But allow me to warn you about overlooking something: while the physical aspects of sexual intercourse are important, and a difficult problem for many disabled people, many of us are still stuck at the more basic levels, such as how to get a date. And if we do get a date, how do we keep it from being the first and last? I have heard it said, "Well, that's everybody's problem." That's true, but it begs the point that many in our society have negative attitudes toward the disabled. Some believe we are all impotent. Others seem to feel that if we're not impotent, we should at least have the common courtesy not to do anything about it! I feel very strongly that all able-bodied persons should ask themselves some of the following questions: "Maybe you're willing to hire a handicapped person, but would you be willing to go out on a date with one? Would you feel comfortable introducing a handicapped lover to your friends? To your family?" "Do you think disabled men ask women for their phone numbers for the same reason able-bodied men do, or do they just want to be friends?" Remember, it is estimated that 17 percent of the disabled population were born with their disabilities. We don't really understand how able-bodied people think relative to disability, any more than able-bodied people understand what it's like to be disabled. I look at myself as a person, like any other person, with my disability being one of many characteristics. I don't see why other people can't do the same.

I am forty-two, a physicist with a master's degree. I work in the aerospace industry and teach part time. I was born and raised a Catholic. I have been married more than twenty-two years. My wife is an excellent cook—I prefer her cooking to any restaurant you can name—and she is a terrific housekeeper. I appreciate these things very much, and she actually likes to be in the home doing these things. She is not a "libber." We also have a good social life together, especially since taking up dancing a few years ago. Unfortunately I am extremely unhappy with our sexual relationship, both in quantity and quality. This, I realize, is not really her fault. The greatest factor in inhibiting our sexual life is the teaching of the Catholic Church.

Because of religious influences, my wife is prejudiced against foreplay, and will not allow manual or oral stimulation of her clitoris. (She responds only to my rubbing my penis on her clitoris.) She has never attempted masturbation, she says, because it is sinful. Here I disagree with the Church. I do not believe that female masturbation in a marital situation is a mortal sin.

Before I go further, I want to set the record straight on a couple of things. My answers to many of these questions seem to present the teachings of the Catholic Church in an unfavorable light or even to criticize them. In fact, I hesitated for a while about sending this material in, but I realized that others would probably say the same, or worse, things and not defend the Church's teachings. I am in favor of the Church's code of sexual morality regarding its main points on adultery, homosexuality, premarital sex, solitary masturbation, and birth control by artificial means. In addition, however, there are some gray areas on which I am not sure whether the Church and I would agree. Masturbation in a marital setting (husband and wife watching each other stimulate themselves in preparation for intercourse, or a woman learning what stimulates her to help guide her husband) is hard to believe to be sinful. Strict adherence to ejaculation only in the vagina even when the woman is infertile also seems too rigid, although I admit I generally confess it as birth control when this happens.

A second area I would like to set straight is my attitude toward my wife. My answers to most of these questions might seem to indicate dissatisfaction with my wife. But I love her and, while there are a lot of things wrong with our sex life, I do not entirely blame her. Many of our problems are my fault, some are in her upbringing (I remember hearing her mother say that only tramps enjoyed sex), some come from being Catholic, some come from the fact that she has been very sick most of the time for at least the last ten years, and some come from the difficulties we have with our children. So far I have always maintained the hope that things will improve, especially after the children have gone and menopause is complete.

Meanwhile I tend to use masturbation as an occasional outlet. In our religion this is sinful, but I think it is a lot less evil than adultery, for example, which my moral principles inhibit—therefore my only sexual partner has been my wife. Masturbation is my only illicit outlet and I have taken much pleasure in it. Anyway, I always repent.

I can usually achieve the fullest possible arousal and the best orgasm through masturbation, provided I take the time to do it right. Sometimes inadvertent arousal, such as the morning erection, is the trigger. Rejection of serious sexual advances towards my wife is another occasion when I may fall into masturbation. Many times the fall is gradual. One day I will find it hard to stop washing my penis and a battle between my hand and my conscience will ensue. My conscience wins the first time but it has a harder time the next day since arousal without orgasm leads to easier arousal each time. Soon I am playing a game of brinkmanship and before many episodes I get so close I can't avoid coming. Sometimes I stop at just the right point near the brink and have an orgasm with several contractions but only a few drops of emission, and I immediately resume masturbating and have a second, marvelous orgasm in a minute or so. Once I have fallen, the floodgates are open and I average about once a day with orgasm every time until I get hold of myself and go confess my sins to the priest. But in these times between the fall and the repentance I have had some fantastically good sex with myself.

My wife is very "turned off" on intercourse. My wife does not orgasm if I penetrate her. We have only had intercourse about three times in the past fifteen months. Usually she will say something like "If you want to do it hurry up and get it over with because I'm tired. You have one minute." Then she will lie still on her back and avert her face while I climb on and come. Then I have to get off immediately and help clean her up. She has always said that the Church has ruined sex for her by its teaching on birth control. She says that she does not get aroused at the "safe" times of the month and that penetration, which the Church says is the only morally acceptable end to the sex act, turns her off. Needless to say, I would welcome a change in this pattern of intercourse. It would be nice to use a variety of positions and to have her move also. I have read about and seen pornographic movies of women sitting on it and thrusting it in and out by bouncing up and down. I would love to take the passive role, at least occasionally.

I like cunnilingus very much. I think women's genitals are very beautiful to look at, as are their entire bodies. Unfortunately my wife will not permit cunnilingus anymore. I think she considers her genitals unclean. About twenty years ago she permitted it for a while after one night when her genital area was extremely dry and I had offered to wet it with my tongue. But, except for those few months, she has always opposed it.

I have never had anyone lick or suck my penis. My wife will not do it. This is the one thing I yearn for the most.

The usual pattern of our sex is, after we are in bed, for me to kiss and hug my wife. We kiss with mouths closed since she does not like tongue contact. I pull her nightgown up and start feeling her thighs, belly, breasts, and mons. If I try to touch her vulva or clitoris, she reminds me that she doesn't like to be touched there. I try to get her to pet me also by taking her hand and placing it on my penis, or by saying, "Rub me," or "Play with me." She almost always says, "I don't feel like it," although sometimes she reluctantly holds it in her hand and moves a finger on it. If I accidentally get some of the fluid which drips from my penis on her hand, leg, or belly, she gets angry. At some point I usually turn her on her side facing me and reach around to rub her back and her buttocks. I think she likes this. Often I will kiss and suck her breasts but I am pretty sure it gives her no pleasure. Sometimes I kiss her belly, thighs, and buttocks but if I get too close to her crotch she gets angry and often will tell me to go away. The great majority of times we will not even get to this point, since she will have said several times, "Look, what are you doing this for? We can't do anything. It's not safe." (We are permitted only the rhythm method of birth control by the Church's teaching.) Eventually she will roll over and say, "Go away." If it is a time when she is sure it is safe, and I am persistent enough, she will sometimes say, "All right. Go get something to put under me and go ahead, but make it quick. I'm tired." I go get a towel and arrange it under her, spread her legs apart, and take my position between her legs. I take my penis in one hand and move the head back and forth in between her labia, using the fluid which drips from the penis to lubricate her. Then I place the head in her vaginal opening and slowly penetrate. (If I push it in too fast or without making sure it is lubricated, she scolds me for hurting her.) Once in her, I come as fast as I can, by thrusting. She makes me pull out and get off as soon as it is over, and then I help her clean up the semen which seems to flow out almost as rapidly as I put it in.

Another pattern is followed if she decides to attempt orgasm. After getting a towel, which is even more important to her in this situation since I will certainly wet the sheets and her also, I put my penis between her legs and use it for clitoral stimulation. I thrust back and forth trying to push it up against her clitoris. We do this in a variety of positions, me on top, side by side, or her on top. Sometimes we have her legs tight together, sometimes slightly apart. I feel very unsure of myself in this activity, though, because I have no way of knowing if I am stimulating her. I have gone on like this for a long time (once it was all the way through the Johnny Carson TV show) only to have her say at the end, "I hope you had a good time because you weren't even touching me." If I take my penis in my hand and rub the head on her clitoris, she accuses me of masturbating and won't believe otherwise.

Many times I use some strenuous positions to ensure no-hands contact between penis and clitoris. On top, I keep it between her legs and draw my knees up so I am sitting on her upper thighs and then I bounce up and down, causing it to thrust between her legs. On the bottom I get into a similar position. Sometimes I talk her into joining in with synchronous movements. I will say something like "Use it. Move until you touch it." When we are really trying to do it, we will often roll over from top to bottom several times. After an amount of time which may vary from about five minutes to over an hour, I begin to come. Then one of two things happens. If it is "safe" and we have decided to obey the Church's teachings, I will quickly insert it and ejaculate in her vagina since it is a sin to deposit the semen anywhere but the vagina. If we are defying the Church, which is not often either, I will continue simply shooting off into space beyond her buttocks while thrusting. But she insists on quitting as soon as I come, even though I do not lose my erection for quite some time and, if stimulation continues, can keep it up for a very long time. Many times she will get violent and bite me or hit me with her fists. Once she gave me some bad scratches with her fingernails. I admit I sometimes come too soon, but I am certain it is caused by anxiety over my inability to satisfy her.

I do not feel adequate to perform no-hands clitoral stimulation by my penis. We have not succeeded for more than about once in ten or twenty attempts in recent years. I don't think my wife believes me when I say my penis can't tell where it is touching her. My penis is not a magic wand! It is unfortunate my wife will not permit manual or oral stimulation of her clitoris, both of which I actually desire.

If I could change things, I would like sex to involve mostly playing, where no part of our bodies would be off limits for caressing, kissing, licking, and sucking. I would like it to last for hours, with her having multiple orgasms and with me being brought to the brink without coming, over and over again, orgasming only occasionally (every couple of hours) and only when arousal reaches unbearable peaks.

I want to repeat that although I have said some things here which might seem to indicate dissatisfaction with my wife, I love her and I hope that someday she will read my answers to these questions, or at least let me tell her about them. Fortunately, she is wonderful in other ways, and our marriage is based on all these things, sex being only a small part. I have come to realize that love is something you work at over a long period of time. Although it starts more in the form of sexual attraction, real love wins out in terms of satisfaction, excitement, lovingness, and longevity. Marital love is much better and more important than any other kind of closeness in life.

P.S. I just asked my wife and she told me that she will not read what I have written—too much trouble. And she often says *I* don't communicate! I think she defines communication as entertaining her with small talk. But whenever I try to have a serious discussion of sexuality, she says I am obsessed or "hung up" about sex. I guess I must face the fact that we are sexually incompatible, not only in terms of my inability to satisfy her in the way she prefers but especially in terms of attitudes. I think the sex organs are beautiful and wholesome, worthy of all kinds of physical contact. She acts as though they are disgusting and obscene, especially her own. She seems to think it is sick to seek sex more often than once a week, best to go for much longer periods (months or more) without it. I can understand why she has this attitude but I feel sorry for her.

The first time I was married (I've been "married" twice) was a real bona fide American Dream type. It lasted for two years. My current marriage was the result of more human forces. I met this woman. I loved and liked her, and wanted to spend much more time with her than our vacations allowed. Because of various job situations, we decided that she should move to where I lived, rather than me moving to where she lived. For various reasons, we are formally married, but otherwise we'd just as soon be living together. Our relationship is pretty much day-to-day. We have quarterly evaluations of the relationship, and decide each six months (every other quarter) whether we'll go on living together for the next half year.

I know that sounds rigid and silly. In fact, the evaluations are more fun than serious, but the observation of our own and each other's happiness does occur. I like being married. I mean that I like living with this person. I don't want any kind of security, or live-in maid. I do want to find out how it could be possible for two people (or more) to live together for prolonged periods of time. I don't think that marriage has any appreciable effect on sex or on anything else, except for the way other people view you. There is an overwhelming tendency for people to couple-bind us and themselves. Everything gets done in couples. People want to help you find someone to couple with, if you're alone.

When the crush went out of my first marriage and the sex stopped almost altogether, I thought there was something wrong with the relationship. When it happened again in my second marriage with a considerably more suitable companion, I thought it must be something about my character, some part of my persona that I didn't want to accept or admit, that didn't want sex with a female companion. I think now that it's just a slow evolution from one appropriate form of sexuality to another appropriate form of sexuality. Some part of me screams, "Please let it be that, please let a new sexuality develop to fill this void."

I love my wife. I don't usually call her my wife, though. I love her because she's the first and only woman I've met who can see the world the way I see it. She's the first person I've met who had something new, completely new, to say about anything. I love her because she can surprise me and make me laugh. I love her because she is my peer, and because her body is female. It allows some nice dancing.

I don't believe in monogamy in the sense that one person is expected to fill all your needs. I haven't had any extra-marital sexual experiences in this marriage yet, but at the same time I consider our relationship to be non-monogamous. I have a healthy web of personal interdependencies and intimacies with my friends. At the beginning of our relationship, before we were married, I was involved with another couple, only sexually, for a few brief times. This did put a strain on us, we both had to grow really rapidly to accommodate the situation. Later, my wife became sexually intimate with a close friend of mine, eventually all of us experienced sex together. It put one hell of a strain on me, because at the time our couple sexuality was cooling off, and I became really confused as to what was happening.

I don't think being married has circumscribed my life, but rather has made it explode in a frenzy of development, feeling, thought, and rich sharing. My life might have been directed toward different goals if I had continued to live alone after my first marriage, but I'm pretty sure that this is the beter way to get where I want to get.

The time I fell most deeply in love was the last time, with the woman I now live with, and am married to. This is tricky too, because I've only learned to associate the word "love" with other things than infatuation recently. About the infatuation, though . . . It felt wonderful. There are no words for it. I went around for weeks and months seeing the world as a place of beauty and hope, rather than ugliness and despair. I spent hours being enchanted by the presence of the woman. Every little nook and cranny of my head was comprehended fully and cherished for the first time in my life. Now there were two of me. It was as if the One decided to give itself a rare treat, by splitting into two, then seeing how tenuous it could make the split. What happened? I would like to know myself what happened. What always happens. I suppose the nature of infatuation is transitory. Anyway, we went through a lot of bad times, and came out the other side intact. I'm still learning to call what we have now "love."

But during it all I cried myself awake and shaking through crawling, dark hours. Yes, and walked miles and miles, and actually drank myself into stupors. And pictured myself dead and her remorse-drowned. Why? What else can you do when it's here in you and not there in the other? I guess I've cried for release from the pain, for attention and sympathy if not love, and because I knew I had to change again to stay with someone. Probably the most hurt has come from the set of unrealistic expectations I have about love and marriage. I wish I'd been told the truth, or if there is no timeless truth, at least the tools to find my own truths.

I think of the happiest times as those of infatuation. It seems that at any stage in my growth and development, infatuation has been able to raise me to the height of joy. This means that the happiest was the last, that's when I was able to be most happy in my life. The next should be even happier. The closest times seem to be during intercourse, or immediately after, when the cuddly mist falls over you. But now I'm trying to find a completely new way to experience my lovers' bodies. Damn it, it's bloody confusing. The woman that I live with does not make love with me in any of the old recognizable ways, the ways we made love when first we loved.

During the early years of my sex life, the myths were nearly at one with the reality. The first change was my inability to be erect almost constantly. I associated this with some emotional problems I'd had with a particular woman who would not make love with me. In retrospect I see this as a natural development, but made traumatic by the way the myths taught me to ignore the reality of my sensory experiences, and focus on what I was "supposed" to feel. The next change was the conflict between myth and reality as the women I found as lovers and friends became more individuals and less inclined to follow the roles prescribed for them. The next change was my heightened awareness of and attention to my partner's needs. The next was abandoning the myths and searching for some kind of new reality. And this is where I am now.

Now, when we have sex, orgasms are not as important as they once were. At first, when I was growing up, there was a long time of necking and fondling without orgasm, with my first girlfriends. I remember those activities as being complete and exciting in their own way, mainly the adventure of new experiences. Then there was a period within the last few years when my partner's orgasms assumed a large role in sex. Until the trends to liberation and to outspoken searching for mutual satisfaction, I never really considered my mate's orgasm as being somehow my concern or responsibility. Then a lot more information about female orgasm was available to me, and I grew overly concerned about my partner. I operated on the basis that my orgasms were her responsibility, and hers were mine.

I am trying to get past the myth-drivers (romance for women, eternal lust and erection for men) and into some kind of experience that is possible for two clear-eyed grown adults who are no longer infatuated. So the orgasm is far in subordinance to the politics, the psychology, and the feeling. This reduction of the emphasis on orgasm is purposeful and deliberate, to examine the neglected areas of sexuality. I have found I can enjoy sex without an orgasm, and without penetration. It seemed amazing at first.

I've freed myself of the notion that I as the man am responsible for the success of the experience. I've also freed myself of the definition of sex as being penetration with the erected male member. This eases a difficulty I have with erection in the initial sexual exchanges with a new partner. Since I'm not responsible anymore, and since I don't *have* to penetrate anymore, I don't have a problem anymore. It doesn't help me stay any harder, but it does help me worry less. Unfortunately, it doesn't help the female who is frustrated by lack of penetration. How strange that is. She doesn't get very frustrated by her own lack of orgasms, but by my lack of penetration. And how nice it is to be able to shrug and say, "Don't worry, it'll work when the time is right." Whee.

Although I like intercourse, I'm in a period of reevaluation now, so I'm not too sure how I feel about it emotionally. It took us a while to find the most satisfactory position for stimulation of her clitoris during penetration. When she kneels over me, straddling my legs, she can regulate the amount of pressure for my pubis on hers. (The number one favorite for her orgasms is with my tongue.) Unless she kneels over me, she really doesn't have enough control over the pressure and contact areas of our genitals. She can orgasm in this position from the friction between my pubic bone and her clitoris. Actually it is only with my current partner that intercourse has really become interesting.

It took two weeks of experimentation and discussion (Lord, it was sweet), when we first started living together, to develop these methods, or ways I could give her orgasms manually or with my mouth. Then it seemed like we orgasmed in intercourse, nearly simultaneously, for a long period. Then we experienced a long period of abated sexual activity. Lately, she comes from oral stimulation, as we don't have intercourse.

I'd also like to hold and kiss and fondle my partner while she masturbates, but no one has been able to do this with me yet. It seems like it would be O.K. for her to masturbate in front of me, the important point would be that she would be under her own control. This sits well with me now. But I still get a rush out of someone placing herself in my charge and letting me lead her to an orgasm.

I always like fellatio and I also like to watch manual stimulation as well as feel it. I orgasm this way quite frequently of late. I also like my partner to touch my scrotum and anus, the flesh at the top of my legs, and the dividing line between my legs in general. I like anal penetration with my own finger. I've never experienced it with anyone's else's finger/penis.

I'm interested in violence as a valid part of the human experience in sexuality. I'm not interested in actual violence so much as symbolic violence. This is the kind of soft violence that is self-aware, and done with deliberation on the part of the participants. For example, one partner might agree to feign resistance while the other acted out a rape, either gender taking either role. Or one partner might agree to remain passive and submit to the will of the other, trusting that the other would not actually abuse the submissive partner. I think little pains, like a strong bite, can be nice, especially when the lovemaking is frenzied.

I've never deliberately physically hurt someone, but I've done a kind of "playing rough." This feels all right. There is some sort of connection between sexual frenzy and strong (painful) sensation, but I don't know how much is simply natural (like cats fighting each other) and how much is bound up in my subconscious or semi-conscious sexual politics.

I don't like men's bodies sexually, because I haven't been taught to. All those years and years of practice in the bathroom with porno: here is a naked woman, become aroused. But I like the sight of erect penises. I like the feeling of the turgid penile tissue, extending far into the body of the erectee.

Cuddling and sharing body warmth works best with women. The feelings are present in the same activities with men, but the whole thing is clouded with concerns about homosexuality, and transgressing the approved patterns of behavior. It's a real treat to find men who are not afraid of hugging and resting with bodies touching. If you and a friend are lying on the floor, talking or listening to music, or watching television, it should be the simplest thing in the world to rest your head on his legs or lap. It should be easy to let a stranger on a bus sleep with his head on your shoulder. It should be, and everyone knows it, but it isn't. Consummate cowards all.

Either we develop our own special rules for touching or follow the established ones. Warmth and closeness should also be found in animals and wind and trees and sunshine. I'm sure it's there, but I can't find a good way to remember that I'm not separate from all these things, that all these things are as sentient as am I.

When I was five or so, I slept with a large assortment of dolls, puppets, and stuffed animals. About age nine, my parents decided that I should grow up, and forbade my sleeping with my "fellows." My father gave me the old pep talk about acting like a little man. I was sad to lose the playthings. I couldn't understand the point of it all. It was just part of the big mystery, the senseless code that grown-ups followed, and enforced.

I was about eleven when I first masturbated. I thought that masturbation was all my own discovery but it's obvious that I did get some pointers from my peers. I also had some notion from friends that sex meant that the man was supposed to put his penis inside the woman. It seems really sinister that my first notion of sex was that about penetration of the woman by the man. Maybe the fixation on intercourse (penetration) started with wanting a simple answer to what sex was. It seems really strange now.

I remember another incident when I was about twelve. I had a new friend down the street. We used to pretend that we were a family. Sometimes he was the father, sometimes he was the mother. We hugged and embraced. One night my mother came into my room as I was preparing to sleep. She told me that I shouldn't hug and kiss this friend anymore. I asked her why. She told me that there were such people in the world as fairies. For one heartbeat the world was filled with magic again. Would the fairies come and steal away little boys that hugged each other? Did they have wings and horns? Then she began the weary and senseless explanation about men who liked other men instead of women. She said it was wrong. Why, Mom, why? The magic was gone again, flattened into dust by another stale rule of the code.

My father sent away for a book because his father died when he was eleven. All that he knew was from "the street" or from armed forces films. We sort of learned the stuff in the book together, he a chapter ahead of me. The book was a cheery Ann Landers sort of Healthy Approach to Manhood. The only valuable stuff in it dealt with physiology. The first thing I heard about menstruation came from my mother. She simply told me that girls sometimes bled between their legs when they got older. I remember it as a time of secrets. It seemed a whole and complete second world was opening up around me.

At this time I was involving pornographic pictures and magazines in my masturbation routines, and I also began to incorporate the girls in my class into my fantasies. In high school I associated with girls, but not much. I was a shy person, creepy too! My first steady girlfriend was the first girl I kissed. We went together for five years, and learned about sexuality together. There was the shocking discovery that our lovemaking didn't feel in the least "wrong." There was the satisfaction of trying on the various roles available to us as a male-female couple. There was the emotional storm of a first love, which I believe is mostly doubting your feelings. That's not right.

When I think of masculinity, or of masculine people I've met, I think of cold power. Masculine is the life of doing as opposed to the life of being. Masculine is bull-headed vigor. Then again, there's a kind of masculine that's not quite so frightening. That's where a dancer of life chooses for a while to put on the role of masculinity, in order to play against another dancer's feminine role. This way, masculinity is a body of attitudes, gestures, postures, behaviors, that forms a complex costume that's fun to fool around with. I get a bit confused here. But when you get to that point the gender stuff doesn't apply anymore. All that's left is the silent clear strength of being. The purity of disinterested action.

Macho is when the posturing and behavior of the male role are acted out by a clumsy dancer who isn't even aware that he/she is only acting a role. There are times when I still get caught up in the role and lose sight of who I really am. Those are the times when I get furious because the women in my life won't make love when I demand it. Those are the times when I will not give up trying to get the car out of a snowbank, and end up putting it in up to the axles.

My father told me not to cry. Fatherhood, at least as I know it from my father, seems a shitty and thankless job. The stupid authoritarian posturing, the painful bids for affection, all seem a caricature of human life. I suppose the real problem is the difficulty in deviating from accepted standards of fatherly behavior. I've never seen a model of fathering that looked reasonable. I think there must be one, though.

I like to comfort upset people. It's fulfilling. But I wasn't prepared by my parents to nurture myself, let alone the others. I think that they assumed there would be a woman to replace my mother and her nurturing skills. I miss a lot of living skills that fall into the category of nurturing myself —food, clothing, etc.—which were not a valid part of being a male.

I was educated to be an industrial engineer. I've never used any of the things I learned in school, but the degree has gathered me an amazing variety of jobs. All the jobs have been in industry, and totally devoid of social significance. I'm a systems engineer. This is fun to tell people, because by and large they don't have any better idea of what I'm supposed to do than have I. But the title is too grandiose to query. The thing that's nice is that systems don't really exist, so here I am, engineering the void.

Am I successful? I have more than enough material wealth to meet my needs. I have influence in the sense that my ideas and contributions are usually accepted gladly. The only area where I feel unsuccessful is in the creative work I do. I think that I have something to say, and a nice way of saying it, but I haven't done much about saying it yet. My potential lies far beyond the objective bounds of man, husband, engineer. It's nice in a way that it does. Nobody but me knows that I am a failure. That means that I can be pretty gentle with myself in struggling on towards my dreams.

Talking with friends is a rare event. I have trouble finding people who are aware and intelligent enough to have anything to say for themselves, or who are capable of hearing what I'm trying to say. When there are no such friends available, I often keep a journal. I guess verbalizing my experiences is essential to my well-being, but try to find a man who can be told "I love you" by another man without flinching.

I answered these questions because I knew it would be a wonderful exercise for me. I've taken developmental swipes at this area of my conditioning before, but never with focused consciousness. I attribute this to a quietly waxing personal integrity and a loudly alive partner. "My" wife is very alive and growing. She's brilliant. She is a singer, my partner. Sometimes she seems hard and aggressive. I don't like these things, but we can usually tolerate each other's point of view. What I like most about her is that she is still open, and developing. She can always surprise me. It's the first satisfying relationship I've ever had. It's excruciating at times but always very stimulating.

I also answered because I think the vehicle you provide is a much needed chance to communicate with each other. The greatest obstacle to my development has been this working alone, in the dark. I can struggle to develop the new thoughts and behavior I need, but it is so much easier when we can discuss our experience with others.

I obviously hope that other men will contribute their thoughts and experiences. I also think that they will be very honest. What could be disappointing would be the lack of depth or thought or evaluation, or attempt at change in the general male population. I'm glad you asked about the honesty. It reminds me to tell you one of he nicest benefits I've gotten from answering. I caught myself wondering about my honesty as I replied to the questions. I often thought I saw myself carried away on my own profundity, my own pompous verbosity. Then I wondered if the man I was describing was really me, or some ideal that I held. I came to realize that this was a basic feature of all my growth. I can evaluate and discard (avoid, recondition) some thinking and behavior. I have to conceptualize much of this new material before I can act on it. So in the end I don't know how truly I am this new person, but I know that he is who I have described.

Goodbye.

Thank you!

My age is forty-two. I am a factory worker. My education is high school plus. I am black and my religion is Baptist. I consider myself handsome. I am married ten years. I like being married sometimes. I got married because I had a very strong feeling for the girl I married, and I wanted to have children with her. The sex with my wife is less than I would like for it to be, however I feel that with time it would get better.

My wife is stubborn, beautiful, intelligent, sometimes thoughtful and sometimes lazy. I like her because I can communicate with her and we have a lot in common mentally and materialistically—also she doesn't nag me a lot. I love being a father too, not only can I be part of their learning and development, but it is a great feeling to have someone say, "Hi, Dad!" My biggest worry is the security of my family should I die at an early age.

Sports and exercise play an important part in my life too. The more active I am with some type of exercise, the better I feel. I like football, baseball, basketball, and golf, but playing baseball is the No. 1 thing.

My father told me that having intercourse was a natural part of life and as I got older I would learn more. Mother also told me that I would have a lot of sexual experiences because I was aggressive. I did not understand what they meant at the time. I was close to my mother. She would not let my father whip me a lot of times. She was affectionate and considerate. I think she was the best mother a child could have, although she spoiled my kid brother and me. We were the last two of twelve children. I am still close to all my sisters.

My playmates and me talked about females a lot and that is when I first learned about masturbation. We were about ten. We all agreed that masturbation was something that made you feel good. I first had orgasm with sperm at age fourteen. Sexuality is repressed in children by those who control our society and their reasons for doing so are many. My opinion is that they do so to impose their belief upon every young person they can. I feel that a parent should always be available to honestly discuss sex with their children because the child will always have questions to ask, and if they can't ask the parent then they will rely on their peers and may not get the true words or understanding.

I fell most deeply in love during my high school days. I felt good walking with my girlfriend, talking to her on the telephone, and just seeing or being with her. I was going to summer school and she came to the school to have lunch with her boyfriend. He was not present and I just went from there.

When I was younger I did not understand women as well as I do now, and I may have acted in a wrong manner, but I do not feel guilty. Today I enjoy sex more because I have learned more and will experiment more. Both my attitude and activities have changed for the better. I think sex is important. But it does not have a spiritual meaning.

I like foreplay. I like the rubbing of the body, kissing the lips, kissing the breast's nipples, and being in tight embrace. But I do not get enough foreplay from my wife. Also I always seem to make the advances. I think it would feel great for my wife to make the advance.

We have intercourse three times a week. I like it from the rear. It's all right with her because she told me she likes it. I am only bored when she is not affectionate during intercourse. She orgasms sometimes. I can tell because of her body reaction, and she makes noises, also she is very limp afterward. I know where her clitoris is and I feel knowledgeable about touching it. I have been told that I am too rough but never too gentle. Also, sometimes she told me she was sorry she took so long to have an orgasm while I was stimulating her. I can enjoy sex without orgasm if my partner is enjoying the sex play, but I want to satisfy her.

When I am in bed for the night sometimes I cannot get an erection. I do not know why and it does not happen very often. I just try and go to sleep.

I like fellatio, but have never reached a climax or had orgasm that way. I do not especially care for manual stimulation, as it has never done anything for me. I have never experienced mouth-anal contact, and I would not like to be rectally penetrated. I can't remember the last time I masturbated.

I read *Playboy, Chic, Hustler, Penthouse,* etc. Women are more likely to be exploited than men in all of the magazines, using females as an attraction for sales.

If I were described being "like a woman," I would feel disappointment and ask the person who said it to qualify that statement. But the things I admire most about women are their grace, hearty intelligence, sexual behavior, and their ability to express themselves as well as solve problems. I do not like women that lie, as well as ones that always make an excuse as an answer when they are not certain about the question. I do not like women who do not want to make sexual advances and who do not enjoy sex to the fullest. Women have contributed much to society, mainly education, invention, technology, medicine, and have made us all think about and be aware of the total universe.

I am twenty-five. French Canadian, Roman Catholic. From a family of twelve children, I am the youngest. My parents were very poor farmers, I was raised in the countryside. My father was fifty and my mother was forty-two when I was born. My brothers and sisters had to quit school and go to work to provide help to the family. The two last ones were the only ones to get a decent education. Our upbringing was very straight: Roman Catholic. Sex was a sin. Nothing else was ever said about it. But it gave place to a lot of things: incest, rape, etc., in the family.

My parents are dead now. I had been wishing their death for a long time. I was ashamed of them and I felt that when they would die, I would finally start to live my own life my own way. I respected them more than I loved them because they had been through a lot of trouble for us. I looked at the older kids as my parents more than my parents.

As a child, I can remember getting very high by brushing my hands on nearly any part of my body. Even lifting the bed sheet and letting it come back down was giving me very strong feelings. Many wet dreams. I also remember showing and feeling penises and asses with young neighbor friends in the barn at four or five years old.

My parents never talked of anything sexual. I first learned about intercourse from a school friend who told me the penis penetrated the vagina. I was intrigued, but I refused to believe it for a very long time. I first learned to masturbate by seeing older boys just mocking the gestures, so I decided to try it and it worked. This was at twelve. I saw my first men's magazine in the stable when I was around thirteen—I ran into my older brother's books he hid in the hay. I must have been fourteen or fifteen when I first heard about menstruation. It was very late to learn about all that.

I was very attracted to men, as they were always the ones who would joke about sex and they would also pee outside, which gave me a chance to look sometimes. It was very stimulating for me to hear men tell dirty jokes, but women would always be put down for telling some. Sex to me appeared very young as a man's world. I didn't understand why women were excluded from it the open way (questionable, but that was the way I thought then, I thought men were very open to sex) men dealt with it.

In childhood, I slept with my brothers and sisters, sometimes up to five in the same bed, but even if I was very curious I was never too interested in sexual games with them, probably due to the fact that I was the youngest one and a bit a basket case.

In high school my fantasies were directed towards a couple of physical education teachers. I would masturbate just thinking about them. One was a blond guy with hard muscles, beautiful eyes, and a very sensuous mouth, and the other was a slim woman with well-developed breasts, big dark eyes, and long hair that she would tie in all kinds of ways or let loose. I very seldom talked to them, for I was very complexed for not talking English too much (I am French Canadian) but they were always present with me in my head for my sexual activities—repeated masturbations. But I do not think they ever noticed me in any special way.

I left home at eighteen and that's when I started feeling less pressure on me. It took a good two years to get rid of my nervous tics; nail-biting, occasional bed-wetting which had been continuous till fourteen, interrupted sleep. My mother died when I was eighteen and my father when I was twenty. Till then I had used theater in college to tell what I had to say. After my father died I left for Europe (one year), and one year in Central America. I felt I couldn't be myself at home because I was too contradictory with my milieu and with myself. But I learned it's not the place, it's the person.

My sex life was masturbating till eighteen. Before sixteen,

the contacts I had were shaking hands or pushing around when wrestling. Some necking occasionally from eighteen to twenty. First heterosexual experience completed at twenty. First homosexual experience completed at twenty. About women, at first I had to demystify them a lot and eliminate the mother picture which was so omnipresent for me in women at large. How could I make love to my mother? That was hard to suppress—though I guess it's never done completely. And after passing that, I had to learn how to enjoy it together and not take your fun, period. I was always ejaculating too soon but kept going to give joy to the girl, but I felt I never satisfied girls. I was very preoccupied by it, but very ill at ease to discuss it. It finally improved a lot but there is always some left.

With men the physical relation was easier because I had learned quite a bit about a man's body through my own masturbation. But emotionally it was very tough. I felt I could never get to men, to their feelings, even if the sexual relation was working well. I still am very reticent facing anal intercourse. I have still a long way before being relaxed. It works only with one man I am in love with now, but for one-night stands it does not work. It was always torture to have sex that way.

I have about the same amount of male and female friends. Very close friends I have only two—one male and one female.

A lot of women took me as a confidant during the past four years. I inspire their trust as they don't feel I'm trying to seduce them or impress them. I never asked anyone about his problems but quite a few men opened themselves to me too, to a point that I felt crushed at hearing other people's problems. It was putting me on low gear for long periods of time. Now I don't talk so much anymore.

I prefer sex with men because it is more relaxed, since we are both alike and know our bodies more totally. It is easier also due to the organs that are external. I love sex with women too but it takes me a while to adjust and get to know each other. The clitoris leaves me perplexed very often because it is hard to feel. I am not as relaxed with a woman that I met for one night as with a man, it only comes after many encounters. Sex with women appears to me as more technical than with men. I like having sex with myself too. To me it is marvelous.

I do not define myself as gay but my parents never knew

I had sexual relationships with men. Only one of my brothers knows and we never talk about it. He has gay friends and it seems O.K. with him.

It seems like I can never have enough sex. Now I am in love with a man and a woman and I cannot have enough sex with both of them. I even go for outside sex sometimes and masturbate. Sick? Maybe, but I just follow what I feel. Maybe it is my Latin side that comes up. Nothing in life is more important to me than sex with the ones I love.

The woman I am in love with and I will be leaving together on a six-week bicycle tour pretty soon, and I'll be away from my male lover for that time. Women are as important to me now as men are. I need both in order to feel balanced emotionally. Physically sometimes I feel I could go without both and just have casual sex, but emotionally it's different.

She is marvelous, very strong morally, physically attractive, very intelligent, and talented for the arts. Perceptive, sensuous, and comprehensive. I love her because she loves me as I am and permits me to be myself wholly, not without protesting very often, but always accepting what I am. I love her because she is open, simple, and doesn't want to get satisfied with less than she knows she deserves. She doesn't have stopped ideas on things but gives them a chance to evolve, and I get the same chance with her. She brings me a lot and we really get along well together. No jealousy, no overprotection, just fair play. No one is trying to put the hook on the other person and we love each other.

I enjoy being single. I choose to remain so. Advantages: no ties, I would have to be unfaithful even if I was married because I don't believe one person can fulfill me (sexually, at least). I have learned not to expect to fulfill the other person and to leave room for the ones he or she will need to fill the spots I am not suited for. I don't believe in marriage anyway, an institution where the woman says no to the few rights she had. Disadvantages: no possibility of adopting a child. I do not plan to marry. My sex life is quite busy.

Orgasms are not of prime importance. To me, the most important is to give pleasure and enjoy sex liberally without focusing on orgasm all the time and be tense, etc. I do often have sex without orgasm and it is very enjoyable. To me it seems that orgasm is very often a way out. People just want to turn around and be left alone or dive into sleep. I do enjoy sex too if my partner does not have orgasm. I am lucky enough to have partners who share my views on that point.

During orgasm I lose control totally. It starts from my toes like a tidal wave until I ejaculate. Then my penis is so sensitive it's almost hurting. The line between joy and pain is very thin. During the climax, all my muscles go in a spasm. My heart beats fast and my body becomes very sensitive all over. Just being touched makes me jump or roar. During the climax it's like I don't have any contact with reality, or I have complete contact because I feel all the parts of my body reaching out, a bit like the pores of the skin opening up during a sauna.

I masturbate very often—two to three times a week. Sometimes more. Sometimes I'm angry with myself but not more than when I eat an extra piece of cake. I am satisfied but sometimes frustrated when I just do it to get rid of an erection without going deep into providing myself pleasure. I am secretive about it with people at large, even with my partners. (I was going to lie here and say I was open with them about it.)

I do enjoy it physically. Emotionally, I think I keep doing it because I lack something but I don't know. To me it's like people smoking cigarettes. Before being a physical need it was an emotional need. It's satisfying in a way that it releases tension, but unsatisfying in the way that I can't go without it. It's always time to start over again.

My genitals look O.K. to me, though they're small and one testicle hangs lower than the other. The size used to give me complexes for years. I would never show my genitals. I'd even put my jock strap over my shorts for the phys. ed. class and I always refused to shower, giving as excuse that I'd miss my bus back home. But now I am very at ease. Their size looks fine, even when it is shrinked down after swimming. For the last two or three years, I have been very active physically. Swimming, biking, and dancing. And I have never been in such shape. It's a lot easier to deal with problems when your physical strength seems to reflect on your morale.

Foreplay is of prime importance—any kind: petting, kissing, just being there and fondling each other, or squeezing each other. My favorite one is to lick and suck the other all over, but certain spots are essential depending on the person. I like to be touched gently all over my body, but the spots with hair on them—legs, waist, arms—are more sensitive. And the spots with joints, like behind the knees, where the elbows fold, between the toes and fingers, the neck . . . The sensation of someone's mouth on my anus, penis, neck, and breasts is the most exciting. But if the mouth is really wet and emits a lot of saliva, it is really exciting for me to be kissed anywhere and get really high.

My breasts are sensitive especially when they are erected. My buttocks are sensitive too but mostly the space between them. My testicles are sensitive when sucked or manipulated, but they hurt if pressed or fingered too roughly. Mouth is extra-sensitive—that's why I enjoy so much the foreplay I do on others, mostly with the mouth because it arouses so much.

I give a lot more foreplay than I get. I never considered I had enough with anyone. I don't know if something is wrong with me but most of the time I get partners who are not the most active and do very little participation in the foreplay. For this reason I prefer to get on to real sex because that is where I get my real share of the action. Otherwise I'd always be giving. I don't dare suggest they do more because I'm afraid the way one makes love is very personal and it is not another one's business really. They love what I do and they always tell me it feels great, so they are not without knowing that it would feel great on me too. At least that is the way I see it.

In most cases I make the initial advance with the woman. With the man, it is shared. If the other person makes the advance I feel good, relieved of a burden because I am always afraid to be too sexual. Once with the girl I am with now, I didn't make any advance till she finally phoned me up to know if I'd like to sleep with her. It required a lot of her to do it and she felt good after. But every time it's as hard because she is so used to be asked for it that's it's the easy way out to just wait and see. With me she had to change that because we did not have that type of relationship where the man initiates and takes over the dominating role through the whole sexual act. It was hard, but she got to love it and now it's more balanced, though it's not always easy for her.

With the man, at first he would make an advance only when he'd see I was ready for it, because otherwise he was afraid of being turned down. I never did but it frustrated him when he was really turned on and I wouldn't show any interest and would eventually walk out on him or push him to the wall to get to the point, because I didn't want to fall in the trap of always being the initiator.

Often when I wasn't sure with a man of his homosexuality, bisexuality, or multisexuality I'd wish him to make the first step and it happened quite often that I wouldn't get it—and wouldn't make it myself due to the fear of losing face or losing what had been built up till then. With women I never really expected any advance, and I got very bitter. I felt so weird with women. I was always afraid they would consider me as the nth male who tried to grab their ass or to get them in bed just to score, to abuse them, take their body and leave them there without really caring for their pleasure. How could they know I wanted to offer more and receive more? So I'd always freeze and get nowhere.

I do feel the coward sometimes for not making the advance because you can feel by the vibrations and actions of someone if you're wanted or not. It is to me a lack of guts, a fear of being turned down.

I like everything about men. Their body, their way of acting, dressing, eating. Anyway there's the penis that the woman doesn't have that attracts me in men. Disturbing for me are the overdeveloped stereotyped feminine traits which are not essentially feminine but that the normal society we live in decided to call feminine. In short, the effeminated men disturb me.

I like hugging and touching men in contact dancing, which is a type of dance where you improvise from your own body or from the bodies that are around you.

I love fellatio. I can always orgasm this way. With my boyfriend I come a good 60 percent of the time, with my girlfriend very seldom.

I like to be penetrated in the ass, but only when it is done very gently and is smooth. My rectum has to be lubricated first and worked on gradually. If it is not done tenderly, it just stresses me and hurts very badly. I usually don't go for it when I'm not rather sure about the essence of the relation, because I end up feeling frustrated and hurt. It's a bit like being raped when it's not done gently. By a finger to start with, by a penis if not too big. It feels very bizarre, but I get really high having someone else inside me. It wakes up the whole rectal area, which contracts and comes to life. After a good heating up and being very relaxed (with poppers, it helped to get there the first times I tried out), it seemed I could never get enough of it. And when my partner would ejaculate I'd find a way of stimulating him again to get more. But at first I am always reluctant and afraid of being hurt. Very often the feeling is so intense in itself that it is disconnected from the penis and I do not orgasm unless my partner stimulates me with his hand at the same time, or unless I do it myself. So far it was too much for me to connect both together.

I love being penetrated but penetrating a man is rather hard for me. It feels so tight compared with a woman, and the lubrication and the control on the muscles make a lot of difference. This tightness either gets me to orgasm prematurely or to lose my erection, and it makes me feel guilty, because I can't give back what I feel when I am penetrated. With a man you can also simulate penetration very often just by lying chest to chest, one on top of the other, and doing the rocking movement as for coitus. The penises rubbing together or on the belly of the partner can be very sensual, especially when lubricated with saliva.

For me, though, it is harder to arouse a woman, as I do not possess as well the anatomy of her body. The clitoris is not always easy to find or to stimulate during intercourse. Often with me women appear to be more passive than men, and passivity tends to turn me down. I do not like imposing my power trip on anyone and I become nervous when I feel I'm given too many responsibilities. With men, they seem more determined concerning what they want and more ready to go after it. This is a general rule in my limited experiences. For me one kind of sex is as stimulating and satisfying as the other, as long as I can give satisfaction in return. This satisfaction is usually easier to bring to men than women, greatly due to the fact that the orgasms are external and are like my own. To me, again in my limited experiences, men appear to be more prompt to try new things whereas women are less inventive or more shy. They seem to be self-conscious very often of their actions.

Having sexual relationships with other men opens you up to yourself. It makes you understand yourself better, physically at least, because emotionally due to the state of things socially concerning homosexuality, emotionally it can sometimes be hard to take. The disadvantages take form in the social repression exercised towards homosexuality, because homosexuality is not only physical, it is not only in bed. When you fall in love and you would like to show affection to your partner, you know you'll be judged socially and receive a ton of bad vibrations—that is where the real disadvantages are. Even if you are not afraid of being stamped or pointed at as homosexual, the reactions you get from people at large are disturbing. It frustrates me to be able to walk and kiss and hug and hold hands with my female partner, when I don't feel free to do it with my male partner. We develop another system of communication for these things which is very personal, but we get the feeling we have to hide our true nature and cheat ourselves for others.

With my woman lover right now I have intercourse once or twice a week, as we both work. My relationship with my male lover takes a few nights a week too. Intercourse is always the most intense moment of the day. To come so close to another person is comforting for me.

I like her genitals. Very intrigued. To me it's still a mystery. I can't assimilate it—every time, it is a discovery, all hidden away. I always have a hard time locating the clitoris and very often am not sure if I'm on it or beside it or too low. As a matter of fact, the woman I'm in love with right now never had a vaginal orgasm. They were always clitoral, so I stimulate her clitorally with my mouth or other parts of my body, fingers, nose, knees, toes . . . Sometimes when I finger her clitoris I am told I am too rough.

I do really enjoy cunnilingus. I enjoy it most when the woman is really lubricated and shows she enjoys it by sounds and words and movements. Her orgasm throws me way up. I like the texture and moisture and warmth. Sometimes I dislike the strong smell of urine. I often orgasm while doing it.

At first when she was menstruating, I was reluctant to have intercourse because I thought it might cause her cramps. But I found out it was easier due to the lubrication the menstrual flow brings automatically. It felt funny after to look at my penis all bloody. Orally, I had no fear, I was anxious to try it just to test myself. It didn't repel me at all. I felt O.K. about it.

I had a vasectomy three years ago. I decided for myself. (Wasn't implicated with my actual partner then.) I know the pill has bad side effects. That is why I would not like any woman I love to have to take it, but there's not much choice for lots of them if they don't want abortion later. It's a pity nothing better than the pill that fucks a woman's body up has been invented. Very few efforts have been directed toward men. Anyway, could women really rely on men? Big deal!

Before I was vasectomized, I would refrain from having intercourse if the woman would not take the pill. Anyway, I never focused on only intercourse as sex. There are many other ways, even if it is super enjoyable for the woman to have a penis inside her. I can't make a woman pregnant now.

Since the so-called "sexual revolution," women can have

pleasure too while having sex but they are still the ones who have to watch out not to get pregnant while they're at it. Pleasure killer. Is that revolution? Males still continue to control the job market. Big revolution.

My vasectomy brought a lot of freedom to my sexual activities. I wasn't blocked anymore by the fear of impregnating a woman or by the thought of imposing all the responsibility of contraception on a woman. My female partners always responded very well to it though some commented on my age, and one even said she would refrain from getting involved any longer with me because she wanted a man who could give her children. She did nonetheless admit that she felt very free having sex with me because the pressure of worry could finally be removed. My female partner now is glad about it, because she couldn't take the pill due to complications and always rejected sterility. She does not want to have kids either. But she is in a dilemma when she has sexual relations with other men because not all of them can consider sex still being sex without intercourse. And if she wants to be penetrated it is a problem. I never wished yet to have it reversed. I would recommend it to other men.

Masculine means you can stand by yourself. Macho needs the power of oppression to survive. I would rate myself very low on the macho scale. Masculinity has to be defined by femininity. One would not go if the other would not exist. It's hard to define such a thing without falling into clichés, etc., but I'll try. Masculinity to me appears as more rational, more logical, has pride and self-esteem. I don't know. I consider I have some masculine traits in me but I also have some feminine ones. However, I look very masculine though not "macho."

My father never talked to me, but by his attitudes he said a lot. A man has all rights and a woman has none. A man is all possibilities. Almighty. A man is weak but should never show it. A woman is too weak. It shows. Whenever I'd cry or do anything a boy on a farm should not do: e.g., cross legs, shout out of joy or surprise, play girl games, I felt frustrated and I'd very often run away and express myself as I wanted to but in front of no one.

For me the role of a father doesn't correspond to the image the "American way of life" shot at us. A father is a friend, a support. The role as it is now or as my father played it: *shits*. To see someone engross his ego through kids which are his property and were made by him—no to that. Authority—no. A minimum but not necessarily from the father as the high-ranking person in the family. I am not a father.

I like noncompetitive sports: swimming, bicycling, skating, cross-country skiing, snowshoeing. I don't enjoy participating in body contact sports when they turn out to be aggressive and violent, or "manly," as so many men describe them. I don't like watching them either.

I am not unhappy even if I am not fulfilled. I have till now attained what I wanted to do.

The thing I envy the most about women is the fact that they can freely show marks of affection (in moderate ways for other women, *bien entendu*). Also, sometimes, I would like to have the choice of someone supporting me. I envy the choice but not the fact that most of them don't even have the choice due to their education, e.g., my own sisters. With the instruction they received, they could not get a job that would permit them to live and eventually support children if they wanted any without having to be dependent on a man's salary.

I can't stand the type of woman that plays the role of sexual object.

I constantly feel guilty for men in general for their behavior towards women. Personally too I have some guilt. I lack patience with women. I'm hot about seeing them become autonomous, but very often do not provide them with the understanding they would need to do it—e.g., nail and hammer. Instead of showing it twice, you do it the second time. Small details like this, but a cumulation.

One thing I admire about women is their power to give birth. Their generosity and irrationality. Their sensitivity and sensuality that they are freer to express than men. Women are the less alienated members of this world. I see women's lib as very political at the same time as social and personal. Let's hope it will eventually bring man out of his rut too and make him realize that crushing and dominating does not help anyone. Man is choking in this world, he is inevitably bound to blow up.

What helped me see clearer in women and understand what they were living was seeing the extremes in the Arab world, Muslim wives and women. Also me in that world being all of a sudden transformed into a very highly prized sexual object for the Arab men. For the Arabs I was like the women for men here—the prey over which they consider they have every right, or at least the right to try their chances with.

Rape is imposing or trying to impose one's will on another person. To me pinching someone's ass going by is a kind of rape. It is intruding in the other's world without being invited. Whistling at someone is another form of rape. It's stupid that rape is considered just forced sexual intercourse. Someone can be brutalized and ripped off of her clothes, but if penetration is not successful, there has not been rape. Silly!

Pornography is cheap thrills. Brainwashing in roles and types of people. The models are always super something, super boobs or ass or chest or muscles, but there is always an ideal part of it. You never see the real confusion, the mother or the beer-belly man. It's always a symbolic representation of the human race physically. Roles, roles, roles. Man—macho. Woman—submitted or passive, but beautiful by certain standards. It's just to keep the system in place.

I answered this for many reasons:

1) to clear up my mind on what I am sexually.
2) for myself.
3) to demystify the man's image I always felt was forced down on me being a man.
4) to go deeper in my inner self to seek answers to my own sexual and emotional problems.
5) because a girlfriend of mine talked to me about *The Hite Report* (I haven't read it) and told me there would be one on male sexuality and asked me if I was interested in answering a questionnaire for it. I hesitated at first but it was very pleasurable.

Will men be honest? I don't see why they wouldn't if they accepted to answer it. But I myself corrected the thing where I cheated in the question on masturbation where I wrote down I was open about it with my partners, which is not true. It must still be very taboo for me. It is still to suppress. I guess I still see it as shameful even if do enjoy it. But I was so honest with the rest that I had to come back at the end and correct that lie or I wouldn't have been able to send my answers. It was only one word but to me it would have destroyed the whole thing, and especially my own credibility facing myself.

Now I feel so relieved that I am crying. It required me a lot of strength to be honest all the way and to be placed in front of reality, denuded of all the masks. Very relieving and at the same time very stressing because I feel it is a combat I am delivering, trying to live up to what I feel should be or is for me.

APPENDIXES

This section represents an abridged version of the appendixes; the complete text is available in the hardcover edition of this work.

QUESTIONNAIRE FOR MEN (IV)—1979–81

This study was based on essay-type questionnaires like the following:

The purpose of this questionnaire is to better understand how men feel about their lives. Since so many of our society's ideas about who men are and who men should be (perhaps made most explicit in "sex") are so stereotyped, it is hard to know what men as individual human beings really feel.

It means so much to us that you will answer, and perhaps help us develop a more positive and caring way of relating to one another.

The results will be published as an extended discussion of the replies, including many quotes, in the same format as *The Hite Report* on female sexuality. The replies are anonymous, so don't sign your answers.

It is NOT necessary to answer every single question. Answer only those which interest you, because otherwise you may not have the time to finish. But *please* answer!

We are looking forward to hearing from you. Send answers to S. Hite, F.D.R. Station, Box 5282, New York, New York 10022, U.S.A. THANK YOU.

I. TIME

1. What is the earliest sexual experience you can remember? How old were you?

2. How old were you when you first masturbated? To orgasm? How did you learn—by yourself, from someone else, or from books or movies?

3. At what age did you first orgasm? First ejaculate? Did you orgasm before you were old enough to ejaculate? Did you

get intense pleasurable feelings from touching yourself? Have wet dreams?

4. Were you told about sex by your parents? What did they tell you? What did your friends tell you? What did you first hear about menstruation?

5. What were your sexual feelings as you grew up? In childhood? In grade school? In high school?

6. Do you think childhood or teenage sexuality should be repressed? Why or why not? Why *is* it repressed?

7. How has your sex life changed over the years? Does age affect sex? Has your enjoyment of sex changed? Have your attitudes and activities changed?

8. How big a part do sports and exercise play in your overall feeling of physical well-being and pleasure? What sports and exercise do you like? Swimming? Football? Running? Other?

9. How big a part do activities like sunbathing, cuddling up in a bathrobe on the couch, sleeping next to someone's warm body, petting your animals, etc., play in your overall bodily joy? What do you like especially?

10. How big a part does what we generally call "sex" (genital sex) play? Masturbation?

11. How big a part does talking to friends play in your overall feeling of well-being? Do you ever tell your friends how much you care about them?

12. Does home and/or family life play a part in your overall feeling of physical well-being? (This includes *everyone,* of course, not just those who are married.)

13. Do you enjoy touching and holding children? Do you enjoy snuggling with them? Wrestling? Giving them baths? Holding them? Rocking them? Feeding them?

14. Have you ever wished you could be a mother? How did you feel when you found out you couldn't bear children? How did you find out? How do you feel about it now?

15. What do you think of the role of being a father (whether or not you are a father)?

16. Do you enjoy physically caring for another human being, whether child or adult? How do you do it? Do you baby them? Is it fun? Were you prepared by your parents to nurture others?

17. Have you found the warmth and closeness in your life that you want? Where?

18. Would you like more time to yourself?

19. How do you feel about privacy in the bathroom? Do you close the door? Do you sometimes like for your partner

to be in the bathroom with you during urination or defecation? Do you like to see your partner urinating, etc.?

II. MASCULINITY

20. What is your age, and your background—occupation, education, upbringing, religion, and race, or anything else you consider important?

21. What do you look like? Do you consider yourself handsome, pretty plain, ugly—or no comment? (Please forgive these words!)

22. How would you define masculinity? Are you masculine? How masculine are you?

23. What is the difference between masculine and "macho"? How high or low would you rate yourself on the "macho" scale?

24. What qualities make a man a man? That is, what qualities do you admire in men? Are you proud of your masculinity?

25. What did your father tell you about how to be a man? What did he tell you about women?

26. How can a man distinguish himself today? What is heroic in our time?

27. What can men as a group be proud of today? Ashamed of?

28. What is your biggest worry or problem in general in your life?

29. Is success important? Are you successful? In what way?

30. Do you believe in being ruthless when you have to?

31. Do you often feel hurt or sad when you don't show it? Do you force yourself to behave like a robot? Do you ever *feel* like a robot?

32. How would you feel if you were described as having something—anything—about your behavior or views that was "like a woman's"?

33. Were you ever called a "sissy"? Told to "be a man!"? What was the occasion? How did you feel?

34. Do you envy women's freedom to be gentle or emotional, or to have a temper? Do you envy them the choice of having someone support them, or the seeming lack of pressure on them to make money?

35. Do you have any strong resentments against women, or against ways any women have hurt you?

36. Are there ways in which you feel guilty for how you

have behaved toward women, or toward a woman in particular?

37. Do you look at pornography? What kind? Did your father read pornography when you were growing up? Where/when did you see your first "men's magazine"?

38. What is your opinion of pornography you have seen? Do you feel it represents certain elemental truths about how men and women really are—both psychologically and sexually?

39. What do you think of the "sexual revolution"?

40. What do you think of women's liberation? How has it affected your relationships?

41. What do males need from females? What do you get from women that you don't get from men?

42. Do you have more male or female friends? Why?

III. RELATIONSHIPS

43. Do you prefer sex with women, men, or either—or with yourself, or perhaps not at all?

44. Do you think sex is important, or is it overrated? Is it interesting or is too much made of it? What other things in life are more important?

45. Does sex have a spiritual significance for you?

46. Answer *one* of the following:

A. *If you are married*, how many times have you been married? Do you like being married? Why did you get married originally? What is the effect on sex?

Do you love your wife? In what sense? Does she orgasm with you? From what stimulation? If you masturbate, does she know?

Do you believe in monogamy? Why or why not? Have you had/do you have "extramarital" sexual experiences? If so, how many and how long? Are you having one now? What was/is the effect on you as an individual and on your marriage? Did/does your partner know about them?

If you have children, why did you decide to have them? Did you want to be a father? How did you feel when your wife first told you you were having a baby? Do you love your children?

Do you feel you had to give up some things in order to be married and/or have children? Did being married/having children circumscribe your job and career opportunities? How would your life have been different?

B. *If you are divorced,* what are the reasons? How do you feel about it? Also please answer any of the questions above which apply.

C. *If you are homosexual,* please answer any of the previous questions that may apply to you and also: How long have you had physical and emotional relationships with men? How do they compare with relationships with women, if you have had any? Emotionally and physically? Are you involved with more than one man? Do you want to, or do you, live permanently with one man?

D. *If you are "single,"* do you enjoy being single? What are the advantages and disadvantages? Do you plan to marry eventually? What is your sex life like?

E. *If you are still living at home with parents or family,* what rules are set up concerning your sexual and dating activities? Would you like more or less restrictions? Have your parents or relatives discussed sex realistically with you? Where have you gotten most of your knowledge of sex? From friends? Teachers? Books? Sex magazines? Family? Have you had problems getting accurate information on sex? If you have had a sexual relationship, do your parents know? If so, how did they react?

F. *If you have not yet had sex with a partner,* what do you imagine it will be like? Does it interest you, or does too much seem to be made of it? What physical activities have you enjoyed so far?

G. *If you are living with someone,* please answer any of the questions above which apply, and also how long have you been living with them? Would you rather be married? What are your plans for the future?

H. *If you are currently uninterested in sex* (except perhaps for masturbation), how do you like this way of life? How long do you plan to remain "celibate"? How long have you felt this way? Do you think this could be beneficial to other men? Do you find you relate more to nature or your pets or music when you are living alone?

47. Perhaps you do not feel that any of these categories describe your life. If so, please describe yourself in your own way.

IV. LOVE

48. Describe the time you fell the most deeply in love. How did it feel? What happened?

49. Did you ever cry yourself to sleep because of problems with someone you loved? Contemplate suicide? Why?

50. What was the happiest you ever were with someone? The closest? When were you the loneliest?

51. How do your friendships compare with your love relationships?

52. Do you feel you can truly love someone?

53. What are your deepest longings for a relationship with another person?

V. ORGASM

54. How important are orgasms to you? Can you enjoy sex without an orgasm? Can you enjoy sex if your partner does not have an orgasm?

55. Please describe what an orgasm feels like to you—during the buildup? Before orgasm? During the climax? After? Which moment feels best? How does the very best moment feel?

56. How often *do* you have sex without orgasm? Do you ever feel pressured to have orgasms? If so, when?

57. How does your body react when you are having an orgasm? Tighten up? Move a lot? Stop moving? Go out of control? What happens to your arms and legs? Your face?

58. Do you always ejaculate when you orgasm? How often do you orgasm or experience a sensation close to orgasm without ejaculating? Do you sometimes ejaculate without experiencing orgasm? How often? Or does orgasm *mean* ejaculation? Did you orgasm as a boy before you started ejaculating?

59. Do you like more than one orgasm during sex? Do you ejaculate each time? How do successive orgasms feel? Have

you ever continued on to a second orgasm without losing your erection?

60. Is erection necessary for sexual arousal? Have you ever felt sexual without an erection? Did it bother you not to have an erection? What was your partner's reaction?

61. Is it O.K. to have sex with a soft penis? Are you embarrassed to continue sex with a soft penis if you don't have an erection?

62. Are you always aroused when you have an erection, or are there other causes of erection?

63. Do you like feeling aroused for extended periods of time, or do you prefer to go on to orgasm relatively quickly? Could you describe what arousal feels like?

VI. MASTURBATION

64. How often do you masturbate? How do you feel about it? Are you pleased? ashamed? satisfied? Are you secretive or open about it?

65. Do you enjoy masturbation? Physically? Emotionally? What do you find satisfying and unsatisfying about masturbation?

66. How do you masturbate? Please give a detailed description. For example, do you hold your penis with your hand and move your hand on your penis, or do you move your whole body—rubbing against something? Is stimulation important at the top or bottom of your penis? Do you mind the wetness of ejaculation? Is there any specific position you like to be in? Are there specific thoughts or fantasies you use?

67. Can you delay your orgasm during masturbation? Does this make it more or less exciting? What specific ways do you use to delay your orgasm?

68. Do you always want an orgasm when you masturbate? Do you ever stop short of orgasm when you masturbate to heighten your sexual feelings? Do you masturbate (but not to orgasm) to arouse yourself before sex? How often?

69. What is the importance of masturbation in your life?

VII. YOUR BODY AND YOUR FEELINGS

70. Do you like the way your genitals look, taste, and smell? Do you like the size and shape of your genitals? Your balls?

71. Are you circumcised? Do you like it, or wish you weren't? Did you, or would you, have your son circumcised?

72. What were your feelings when you found out about circumcision? About your own circumcision? Were you shocked? Pleased? Do you have a physical reaction in your genitals when you think about it?

73. Do you remember anything about the procedure? How old were you?

74. Has circumcision affected your attitude about exposing your penis to others? How? Does having or not having a foreskin affect your sexual activities?

75. Why are men circumcised?

76. Does your partner like your genitals? Has a partner ever commented adversely about your genitals? How? How did you feel about this?

77. Do you like fellatio (oral stimulation of your penis)? Can you orgasm this way always, usually, sometimes, rarely, or never? How often *do* you orgasm this way? How do you like it to be done?

78. Do you like mouth-anal contact?

79. Do you like manual stimulation of your penis by your partner? Do you often orgasm this way? What other parts of your genital area do you like your partner to touch?

80. Do you enjoy masturbating with another person present? Do you like having your partner masturbate him/herself when with you?

81. Do you like (or would you like) to be rectally penetrated? By a finger? By a penis? How does it feel? Do you orgasm this way? Exactly what does anal intercourse feel like —both physically and emotionally?

82. Do you like "foreplay"? What kind of "foreplay" is important to you for *yourself*? How do you like to be touched, and where? Kissed? Petted? Are your breasts sensitive? Your buttocks? Your testicles? Your mouth? Your ears?

83. Do you get enough foreplay from your partner? Does your partner touch and fondle *you* enough?

84. Do you sometimes like making out without having "real sex"? Do you prefer it?

85. Who makes the initial sexual advance? How do you feel if the other person makes the advance? Have you ever wanted the other person to make the advance and not gotten it? Do you feel unloved if your partner never makes the advance? Unwanted?

86. Have you ever approached someone about sex and been

refused? How did you feel? Have you ever refused someone else? Why?

87. Are there certain times when you're not interested in sex? Is it O.K. to be celibate? Do you experience periodic highs and lows in your sexual interest? How often?

VIII. FEELINGS ABOUT MEN

88. Describe your best male friend. What do you like about spending time with him?

89. Do you belong to, or socialize with, a group of men? What do you enjoy/like about it? What do you do? What do you talk about?

90. Do you value your men friends? Is it important to have male friends—or relatives you are close to? What do you value about their friendship? What do they mean in your life?

91. Were you in the Army or another branch of the military? Did you like the camaraderie? Did you have any close physical or sexual experiences with men during this time?

92. Do you like sports? Which kinds? Do you enjoy participating in sports with other men? Do you like the closeness with men in these activities?

93. Did you have a best friend in high school or college? What were your feelings for him?

94. Are you or were you close to your father? In what way? What was/is he like? What do you think of him?

95. Describe the man you are or were closest to in your life. In what ways are/were you close? Do/did you spend time together? Why is he valuable to you? Why do you like him?

95A. If you have not had a physical or sexual relationship with another man, would you enjoy one?

IX. SEX WITH MEN

96. How old were you when you had your first gay experience?

97. What was the first time you ever had physical contact with a man? Your father? A relative?

98. How is sex with men different from sex with women (if you have had sex with women, or based on what you think it would be like)?

99. What are your favorite things about sex with men? Why

would you recommend homosexuality to other men? What are the advantages? Disadvantages?

100. Do you like anal intercourse? Exactly what does it feel like—both physically and emotionally? Do you orgasm this way?

101. Do you like giving a man fellatio? Do you swallow the seminal fluid? Do you like it?

102. Can you orgasm from just lying down together and kissing and rubbing crotches together?

103. Are you in love? In a steady relationship? How many men in your life have you had a sexual relationship with? Do you like monogamy?

104. Is gay "promiscuity" a myth or a reality? Do you prefer emotional closeness or casual sex or both?

105. Would you ever fall in love with a woman (again)? Why or why not?

106. Do people at work know you are gay? Do your parents?

107. Would you take an open stand on gay issues? Are you working for gay liberation? Or do you prefer the adventure of being gay in a straight world, the pleasure of belonging to a secret, elite society?

X. FEELINGS ABOUT WOMEN

108. Do you have any close women friends? A sister you are close to?

109. Are you or were you close to your mother? In what way? What was she like? What do you think of her?

110. What things about women in general do you admire? Dislike? What do women contribute to society?

111. What do you think about women's liberation?

112. Are you currently in a relationship with a woman? What is she like? Why do you like her?

XI. SEX WITH WOMEN

113. Has any woman discussed sex and her sexual feelings seriously and openly with you? Did you ask?

114. When did you first learn about the clitoris? What did you hear from other men? From women? From books?

115. Do you like clitoral stimulation? Why or why not? When did you first do it? To orgasm? How did it feel? Do you feel comfortable now giving clitoral stimulation?

116. What kind of clitoral stimulation do you give? Please describe how you do it. Describe how you stimulate the clitoris with your hand or finger. Do you do this to orgasm?

117. Does your partner masturbate to orgasm? How does she do it? If you don't know, would you like her to share that information with you?

118. When did you first hear/realize that most women don't orgasm from intercourse (coitus) alone? What was your original reaction?

119. Do you enjoy cunnilingus with a woman? What do you most like and dislike about it? Does it depend on your feelings for your partner?

120. Do you get sexually excited by stimulating your partner? Do you enjoy her orgasm? Physically? Emotionally? What aspects of touching, feeling, and kissing your partner(s) do you enjoy most? Least?

121. How do you give the woman an orgasm? Do you prefer the woman to orgasm from coitus?

XII. INTERCOURSE

122. Do you like intercourse (penis/vagina)? Physically? Emotionally? How often do you have intercourse?

123. What position is most satisfying to you? Is this position all right with your partner? What position does she like? Do you like this position?

124. Why do you like intercourse?

125. Do you ever experience physical discomfort during intercourse? Afterwards? Do you ever experience boredom during intercourse?

126. After sex has begun, do you assume intercourse is expected next? Do you assume that every time you have sex, it will include intercourse?

127. Would you be willing to replace intercourse with other activities during some sexual encounters? How often? Or do you *always* want to define sex as intercourse?

128. Does your partner orgasm during sex with you always, usually, sometimes, rarely, or never? During intercourse? During other activities? Which ones?

129. Can you always tell if your partner has an orgasm? How can you tell? Are you ever in doubt? If in doubt, do you ask? If you ask and she says "yes," do you believe her? Do you talk about it?

130. Would you prefer to have sex with a woman who has orgasm from intercourse (coitus) rather than from clitoral stimulation? When does/do the woman/women you have sex with usually orgasm?

131. How do you feel if a woman stimulates herself to orgasm with you? During intercourse? How do you feel if she uses a vibrator?

132. Do you feel there is something wrong with your "performance," technique, or sensitivity if the woman does not orgasm from intercourse itself? That you're "not *man* enough," or at least that you did not do it right?

133. Does it matter to you if a woman orgasms during sex with you? Do you try to find out what stimulation an individual woman needs to have an orgasm?

134. Who usually orgasms first? You or the woman? During which activity? Do you orgasm when you want to? If not, why?

135. Has a woman ever expressed anxiety or been apologetic to you about how long she takes to orgasm or become ready for intercourse?

136. How do you feel if your partner does not have an orgasm at all, in any way?

137. Can you control when you come to a climax? How long can you hold off without losing your erection? Does it disturb you to lose your erection?

138. Are you embarrassed to have sex with a soft penis (i.e., if you don't get an erection)? Do you stop physical closeness and other activities if you can't have intercourse?

139. Do you ever ejaculate or orgasm "too soon" during intercourse? How long are you talking about? Is this ejaculation/orgasm satisfying to you? When does this happen? Why? Does it bother you?

140. Do you use any particular method to have intercourse longer without orgasming? Does prolonged thrusting dull the sensitivity or feeling of your penis?

141. When should a man ejaculate? Should the woman be consulted? Who decides when sex is over?

142. Do you control which activities sex consists of? Do you control when you come and how you have an orgasm?

143. Do you sometimes have difficulty having an erection at a time you desire one? When? Why? How often does it happen? What do you do at such times?

144. Do you talk to other men about sex? What do you talk about? Do you or other men tend to brag or exaggerate your exploits with women? Do you share practical information (how-to)? Feelings of insecurity?

145. What are the reasons why many women traditionally have not wanted sex as much as men? What kind of sex do women want most?

XIII. BIRTH CONTROL

146. What contraceptive methods (birth control) do you use? Who decides what contraception will be used? Which kind do you prefer?

147. Are you aware of the possible side effects of the birth control pill?

148. Have you ever experienced physical discomfort from any form of birth control? Condom? The diaphragm? IUD? Foam? Have you ever used a condom to delay orgasm?

149. Do you feel responsible for discussing birth control before intercourse? If you are having a sexual relationship with a woman, do you protect her from becoming pregnant? Who is responsible if she does become pregnant? Do you ask a woman if she has taken measures to prevent conception before intercourse?

150. Do you fear impregnating someone? Does the possibility of pregnancy cause you problems in a sexual relationship?

151. Have you ever been a party to an unwanted pregnancy? What did you do about it?

152. Are you in favor of abortion? Have you ever impregnated a woman who subsequently had an abortion? Have you ever been involved in helping a woman secure an abortion? Did you share the expenses? Go with her? What was the outcome?

153. Do you have a vasectomy? (Do you have children?) How has having a vasectomy affected your sexual activities? What do your partners think about it? Have you ever wished to have it reversed? Would you recommend it to other men?

154. Do you know what vasectomy involves? Would you be willing to get one, and under what circumstances?

155. Have you ever witnessed childbirth?

XIV. VIOLENCE

156. Are you interested in violent sex? Has violence been part of a sexual relationship you had? What kind? How did you feel about it?

157. Have you ever been excited by a physical struggle or combat, or a fight—with a man or woman? Please describe.

158. Have you ever deliberately struck or hurt your lover? Why? What effect did it have on the relationship? Did you feel good when you did it?

159. Are you interested in bondage? Spanking? Why or why not? How does it feel?

160. Is it fun to force someone to your will?

161. Do you find kissing feet sexual? Golden showers?

162. Would you or have you had a sexual relationship with a very young person? How did you feel about it?

163. How do you define rape? Is it disturbing to you? How? How not? Where do you draw the line between consent and rape?

164. Have you ever raped a woman? If not, have you ever *wanted* to rape a woman? Why?

165. Have you ever pressured a woman to have sex with you, when she didn't seem to want to? How did you do it? Did you have a line? Did it succeed? Did you enjoy sex?

166. Is being forceful with your partner fun for you in sex? Do you usually control your partner during sexual activities? How do you develop the sexual relationship in the direction you desire? Is it easy to remain in charge of the situation?

167. If there is a power relationship involved in sex, who has the most power—you or your partner?

168. Is sex political?

THANK YOU FOR ANSWERING THIS QUESTIONNAIRE!

QUESTIONNAIRE FOR WOMEN 1982–84

The purpose of this questionnaire is to hear many women's points of view on questions that were left unanswered in the original *Hite Report* on female sexuality. For example, how women feel about love, relationships, marriage, and monogamy were not covered, due to lack of funds. We would very much like to hear your thoughts and opinions on these subjects now, as well as anything else you would like to add. The results will be published as a large-scale discussion of what was said, with many quotes.

The questionnaire is anonymous, so do not sign it. Feel free to skip around and answer only those questions you choose; don't feel you have to answer every question. You may answer on a tape cassette if you wish, or use as much extra paper as you need.

We are looking forward to hearing from you!

1. Who are you? What is your own description of yourself?
2. What makes you happiest in your life? Your work? Your love relationship? A hobby or side career? Music? Going places (travel, concerts, or dinner with friends)? Your children? Family? How happy are you on a scale of one to ten?
3. What do you want most from life?
4. What was your greatest achievement to date?
5. What was the biggest emotional upset or disturbance that ever happened to you—the greatest crisis, the thing you needed the most courage to get through?
6. Are you in love? Who is the person you are closest to?
7. What is your favorite way to "waste time"?

I. GROWING UP FEMALE

8. Growing up, were you close to your parents? Your mother? Father? What did you like most and least about them? Did your parents love you? In what way?

9. What was your relationship with your mother like? Were you close? Physically? Was she affectionate with you? What was she like? What do you think of her today? Do you like to spend time with her? Were there clashes between you?

10. Were you close to your father? Was he affectionate? Did you talk? Go places together? Did you like him? Fear him? Respect him? What do you think of him today? What did you and he argue about, if anything?

11. What did you learn from your father was the proper attitude toward your mother? What did you learn from your mother was the proper attitude toward your father? Were they affectionate in front of you? Did they argue?

12. Were there ways in which your mother showed you how to be "feminine"—how to act like a girl or a "lady"? Did you and your mother do things your brothers (if any) were not expected (or invited) to do?

13. Were you ever a "tomboy"? What was it like? Were you warned against being a "tomboy," or acting too rough, playing "boys'" games, not acting "ladylike" enough?

14. Did your father tell you to be a "good girl"? Your mother? What did they mean?

15. Did you masturbate as a child? How old were you when you started? Did your parents know?

16. Did your parents discuss menstruation with you? Your mother? Your father? Were you prepared for it when it started?

17. Did you have a pet as a child?

18. Was there great pressure to conform—be like the other girls—in high school? To dress like the other girls? Be popular?

19. Did you like high school? What did you like and dislike about it? Did you belong to any particular group? Have a hobby or special interest?

20. Did you have a best friend? What was she like? Did you spend the night at each other's houses? What did you do

that was most fun together? What did you talk about? Are you still in touch?

21. Was there an age at which you began to want, or feel pressured to, date boys? How old were you? How did you feel about this?

22. What was your mother's attitude when you started dating? Your father's? Did you discuss with your parents what happened when you went out on dates? Did you tell your best friend (if you had one)?

23. When was the first time you held hands with someone? Kissed? Made out? Said "I love you"?

24. Was it difficult leaving home? Declaring your independence?

II. FALLING IN LOVE

25. Describe the time you fell the most deeply in love. How did it feel? What was the person like? Did the relationship last? What happened?

26. What was the happiest you ever were with someone? The closest?

27. When were you the loneliest? Did you every cry yourself to sleep because of problems with someone you loved? Contemplate suicide? Why?

28. Do you/did you like being in love? Is being in love a condition of pleasure or pain? Learning? Enlightenment? Ambivalent feelings? Frustration? Joy?

29. How do your friendships compare with your love relationships? Which are closer? More rewarding? More enduring? Have love relationships followed any particular patterns that you can see?

30. Do you think falling in love is important?

31. What is your favorite fictional love story—the greatest love story you have ever seen or heard? Was it a book or a movie? What was the story about?

32. Are you good at giving love? Is it easy for you to be loving? When and with whom were you the most loving in your life?

33. How would you define love? Is love the thing you work at in a relationship over a long period of time, or is it the strong feeling you feel for someone right from the beginning, for no known reason?

III. YOUR CURRENT RELATIONSHIP

34. Are you in a relationship now? If so, with whom and how long have you been together? Do you live together? Are you married? Do you have children?

35. What is the most important part, the basis, of this relationship? Is it love, passion, sexual intimacy, economics, daily companionship, or the long-term importance of children and family? Other?

36. What do you like best about this relationship? Least? Are you happy? Is your partner happy?

37. Are you "in love" with the person you are with? Or is it more that you love them, rather than being "in love" with them? In what way do you love them?

38. Do you love your partner as much as he/she loves you? More? Does one of you need the other more? Is one of you more dependent? Is the way your partner loves you satisfying to you? Do you feel loved? Does your partner say you make him or her feel loved?

39. Do you agree or disagree with the following statement: "It is quite possible to be in a heavy emotional relationship with someone you are *not* in love with, or don't love—it's just a kind of familiarity or friendship."

40. What is the biggest problem in your current relationship? How would you like to change the relationship, if you would? Could it be better? How?

41. What do you enjoy doing together the most? Talking? Having sex? Being affectionate? Daily life together? Sharing children? Hobbies? Going out? Other?

42. How does your partner act toward you in intimate moments? Does your partner tell you he or she loves you? That you are wonderful or beautiful? That you are very sexually desirable? Talk tenderly to you? How do you feel at these times?

43. What things does your partner most often criticize about you? What do you most often criticize about him or her?

44. What is the worst thing your partner has ever done to you? The worst you have done to him/her?

45. Is it easy to talk? About everything? Who talks more? Would you like more intimate talk—about feelings, reactions and problems?

46. Does the relationship fill your deepest needs for closeness with another person? Or are there some parts of yourself

that you can't share? That aren't accepted or understood? How well do you think your lover or husband knows you? Or do you prefer not to share every part of yourself?

47. Is the kind of love you are giving and receiving now the kind of love you would most like to share? Have you seen a type of love in a friend's relationship or in a film or novel that you would like to have? How was that love better than your relationship?

48. Is your lover and your relationship with your lover the center of your life? How important is the relationship to your life? More important than work? Children?

49. What are the practical arrangements? Who does the dishes? Makes the beds? Does the cooking? Takes care of the children? What is daily life like?

50. How do you share the money? Who controls the money? Do you both work outside the home? Who pays the rent or the mortgage? Buys the groceries? What is your financial arrangement? How do you feel about it? Do you feel it affects the relationship?

51. What is the best way you have found to make a love relationship work? How did the most successful relationships you have seen/been in work? What were the inner dynamics?

52. If you are married, how many years have you been married? Do you like it? What is the best part of being married? The worst? Before you got married, did you think it would be different than it is? Do you like or dislike the term "wife"? Do you like using your husband's name (if you do)?

53. What were your reasons for getting married originally? Were they romantic? Social? Economic? Sexual? Would you do it over again? Do you plan to stay married? Why or why not?

54. If you have children, do you like having them? How did you feel when you first knew you were going to have a baby? Did you have to give up some things in order to be married and/or have children? How would your life have been different? What did you gain?

55. Did having children change your relationship with your husband? How?

56. Do you believe in monogamy? Why or why not? Are you monogamous? Have you had/are you having sex outside of the relationship, or "extramarital affairs"? If so, how

many and for how long? What was your reason (if there was one)? What is/was the effect on you as an individual and on your relationship or marriage? Did/does your partner know about them?

57. What is/was the affair like? Is/was it serious? How did you feel about your lover? What did you (or are you) getting out of it?

58. Has your partner been "faithful" to you? How do you feel about this? Do you want your partner to be monogamous?

59. Have you ever (as a single person), or are you now, going with a married man? What is it like?

60. Describe the biggest (or most recent) fight you had with your husband or lover—no matter whether the fight was over something trivial or important.

61. How do you feel about fighting? What do you most frequently fight about? Who usually wins (if anybody)? How do you feel during? After?

62. How do conflicts or arguments usually get resolved—or at least ended? Who usually says they're sorry first after a fight? Who usually initiates talking over the problem? Making up?

63. How do you feel about the following statement: "You don't try hard enough to find out what's inside of me."

64. What does your partner do that makes you the maddest?

65. If you are in a very long relationship or marriage, have you found that certain disagreements or conflicts continue to be present over the years, or do old ones gradually get resolved and new ones take their place? Did you argue more at any particular period you can remember?

66. Describe the time recently when you were the happiest with your lover or husband, or your most joyous occasion? The closest or most intimate?

IV. BEING "SINGLE"

67. If you are not in a relationship, or if you have ever gone for long periods of time without a sexual relationship, how do or did you feel about it? Do you like being "single," or do you prefer to be in an intimate relationship with someone, part of a couple? Why are you "single"?

68. What are the advantages of being "single"? Disadvantages? Do you like going out alone (to a party, restaurant, shopping, etc.)? Do you sometimes get the impression people think there is something wrong with you when you are not in a relationship? Or do they envy you being single?

69. What is your sex life like? Do you enjoy periods of celibacy, or no sex with another person?

70. Is it easy or difficult to find or meet someone you like and are attracted to and have respect for?

71. Do you feel there is pressure to choose between being married and having children, or having a career or full-time job working outside the home? If so, which would you choose on a permanent basis?

V. BREAKING UP, OR GETTING A DIVORCE

72. If you have ever gotten a divorce or broken up with someone who was important in your life, what was it like? Who wanted to break up, you or the other person? Why?

73. How did you feel about it? Were you glad or did you have regrets? Did you feel like a failure, or did you feel freer, or both? Did you hate the other person? Cry a lot? Or feel you could start living again? Did you talk to friends? Hide from them? Work harder?

74. How did you get over it, if you didn't want to break up? How long did it take you?

75. Did your mother or friends encourage you to stay in the relationship when you were having difficulties? Support you in leaving it? Or were they no help at all? Did you tell them about your feelings?

76. After breaking up in general, would you tend to look for a new love to replace the old, or shy away from love altogether for a while?

77. While breaking up or getting the divorce, what did you feel was the most permanent solid thing in your life? Your relationship with your parents or relatives? With friends? With your children? Your work? Yourself? Nothing?

78. Was there a time at which you gave up on love relationships as not being as important as you once had thought? Decided to give less time and importance to them? Or

do you basically believe that a rewarding life comes mainly by working through a love relationship and developing it over time?

VI. LOSING A HUSBAND OR LOVER THROUGH DEATH

79. Have you ever lost a loved one through death? What was your reaction? How did you feel about it?
80. What did you miss most about the person?
81. Was a part of you not sorry? How did this make you feel? Were you angry at him for "deserting" you?

VII. SPECIAL PROBLEMS IN RELATIONSHIPS WITH MEN

The following are random questions that have been suggested by women. There is no particular order and no attempt to imply any particular point of view. The questions are just a way of opening the subject up for discussion. Answer only the questions you want, or add your own.

82. What do you like best about men? Least? What qualities do you admire in men? Dislike?
83. What do women need from men, if anything? Is there something you get/want from men that you can't get from women? From women that you don't/can't get from men?
84. Do you think men take love and falling in love with a woman seriously? What part does it play in their lives?
85. Were you ever financially dependent on a man you lived with? Was this a problem? How did you feel about it? Did/does it affect your relationship?
86. How do you think men feel about women working outside the home? If you work, and are married or living with someone, how does he feel about it?
87. Does your husband or lover see you as an equal? Or are there times and ways when he seems to treat you as an inferior? Leave you out of decisions? Act superior?
88. How do most men you know feel about the women's movement? How does your husband/lover feel about it?
89. Have you ever been deeply hurt by a love relationship? What happened?
90. Did you ever enter therapy to try to solve personal problems related to your love relationships? What were they? Did therapy help? What were your conclusions?

91. If you had one overall grievance about your relationship(s) with the man/men you have loved, what would it be?

92. Do you have a comment on the following statement: "I would like a study of the emotional trips a woman goes through in a sexual relationship with a man."

93. Do you think you pick the "wrong" men? What kinds of men do you pick?

94. Do love relationships in general make you feel good?

95. Do you ever feel your loved ones are suffocating you? Holding you down?

96. Are you jealous? Of friendships? Career? Other men or women?

97. Did you ever grow to hate a lover? Did you act violently toward him? Scream at him? Hit him?

98. Describe the man you hated the most. Why did you hate him? Did you do anything about it? Did you remain angry or become depressed? Did you tell your friends?

99. Is there any way you have hurt a man in the past, for which you are now sorry? Or gotten revenge—for which you were *not* sorry?

100. Did a lover ever strike you or beat you up? Why, and when? How did you feel?

101. Did someone you loved ever grow to despise you?

102. Did you ever have a sense of having to work to keep someone with you? Keep the relationship together? Did you have a fear of his leaving you? Losing his love? That he would grow tired of you? Do you feel a lover usually becomes less attentive over a period of time? Loves you less?

103. Are you honest with men, or do you find it necessary to manipulate them to get what you want?

104. Do you have a nagging fear of being deserted by your lover or husband? Are you afraid he will stop loving you? Why? Because you are getting older? For reasons you don't understand?

105. Who usually breaks up the relationship first—you or the other person?

106. Did you have long periods of depression after the break-up with an important lover in your life? Did you think of suicide? How did you manage?

107. Have you ever loved someone who hurt you deeply, in spite of what had happened, and in spite of your desire not to love them any longer?

108. Do you sometimes feel at the mercy of the other person to either accept you or reject you?

109. Does it help to keep them by being beautiful or seductive? To be better than other women in some way?

110. Have you ever pretended to a man you cared less than you did? That he was less important to you than he was? Put up a front? Why? Did it work?

111. How do you feel about the following quote: "She was afraid that if she showed a man she loved him, he would consider her inferior and leave her."

112. Do you find you have to employ "a streak of manipulative coldness," to keep your distance, keep things "cool"?

113. Do you ever feel you have "unhealthy" needs and cravings for love, or dependency? As one woman put it, "My love has usually been too blind, too desperate." Do you ever feel you have an "excessive" need for affection?

114. Are you afraid of clinging to a man? Making him feel tied down, unfree? Did you ever feel like a "clinging vine"? Feel you were too emotionally dependent?

115. Do you feel more insecure and self-doubtful when you are in love?

116. Do women need love more than men do? Do women need affection more than men do?

117. Do you feel as strong as the person you are in a relationship with—emotionally? intellectually?

118. How do you feel if a man is very emotionally dependent on *you* in a relationship? Needs you more than you need him? Complains that you do not love him enough?

119. Have you ever felt that you were "owned" in a relationship so that you wanted out?

120. Do you think that most men, underneath the surface, are more emotionally dependent than women are?

121. Does your partner look at pornography? Men's magazines? How do you feel about this?

122. Do you think love is a problem for most women? Why or why not?

VIII. SEXUALITY

123. What is sex with your partner (or in general) usually like? Do you enjoy it? Do you usually orgasm? During which activity? Does he know how you masturbate? What is the worst thing about sex with him? The best?

124. What part does sex play in your current relationship (or in your last important relationship)?

125. Have you read *The Hite Report* on female sexuality? Which issues or chapters do you most agree with? Disagree? Which parts were most important for you? Least? Most emotional?

126. Has your sexuality, or your style of relating sexually, changed over the last few years? In what way? Why?

127. Which is the easiest way for you to orgasm: through masturbation? clitoral stimulation by hand from your partner? through oral sex? intercourse/coitus? with a vibrator?

128. If you orgasm during intercourse (coitus), how do you usually do it?

    A. By added clitoral stimulation from your partner? Please explain.

    B. By your own clitoral stimulation/masturbation during intercourse?

    C. By being on top and rubbing against your partner?

    D. Other? (Please describe.)

129. When did you first orgasm, during sex with a partner or masturbation?

    A. Did you first discover masturbation on your own, or did you read about it? How old were you? How did you feel? Did your parents know about it? Friends?

    B. When you had your first orgasm with another person, what activity was it during? Did you learn to make it happen, or did it happen without trying?

130. Have you told a man you do not (if you don't) orgasm from intercourse? What did he say? Did you tell him most women don't? How did you feel?

131. Have you masturbated with a partner? During intercourse? During general caressing? Was it hard to do the first time? How did you feel about it? What was his/her reaction?

132. Have you told a woman friend you don't orgasm from intercourse (if you don't)? Explained your sex life in any detail to her? What did you say? How did she react?

133. Have you talked with other women, or your mother, sister, or daughters about some of the issues in *The Hite Report* on female sexuality? Do they know if you masturbate? Do you know if they do? What else have you talked about? What else would you like to talk about?

134. Does sex with the same partner change—and if so, for better or worse—over a long period of time? Does it become boring, or more pleasurable? Or does it depend on the relationship?

135. How often do you like to have sex? Do you think sex is important, or is it overemphasized?

136. Do you feel a choice has to be made between a passionate relationship and a more stable relationship? Is there a contradiction between sexual passion and a long-term relationship? Do the daily details of living and working at a relationship conflict with, or make impossible, feelings of passion? Cool them? How important is feeling passionate?

IX. FRIENDSHIPS BETWEEN WOMEN

137. Describe your best woman friend. What do you like about her? What do you do together? When do you see her? Has she helped you through difficult times in your life? How do you feel when you are with her? How much time do you spend together, or talking on the telephone? What does she do that you like least?

138. What is or has been your most important relationship with a woman in your life? Describe the woman you have loved the most. Hated the most.

139. Were you close to your mother? Physically? Emotionally? Are you now? What was she like? Did she work outside the home, or was she a full-time mother and "house-wife"? What did you think of her? What is she like now, and what do you think of her today?

140. Are you like her?

141. Were there other women in your family you were/are close to, or particularly liked or admired? A grand-mother? An aunt? Do/did you have a sister(s)? What were some of your relationships like?

142. Do you have a daughter? What do you think the role of being a mother (whether or not you are a mother) should be?

143. What things about women in general do you admire? Dislike? What do women contribute to society?

144. Is it easier to talk to women than to men? How do you feel about the following statement: "I wish I could talk to my husband like I can to my best friend"?

145. What do you think of women's liberation? Do you consider yourself a feminist, or in favor of the women's movement? Or are you against some of these ideas?

146. Have your feelings about the women's movement and its ideas affected your life? Your relationships with women? With men?

147. Do you enjoy being "feminine"? How would you define "femininity"? ("Masculinity"?) Do you enjoy beautiful clothing? Dresses and lingerie? Do you spend time on your hair and make-up? How do you feel about the way you look?

X. CONCLUSION

148. Looking back, who have you loved most in your life—man, woman, child, friend, pet, parents, or lover—who was it?

149. Who made you feel the most alive, the most *you*, in your life? The most excited? The most loved? Happiest?

150. Have you found what you are looking for in love and family, or are the kinds of love and relationships you want yet to come?

151. Was there anything you would like to say but didn't?

THANK YOU!

WHAT DID YOU THINK OF THIS BOOK?

The author would like to hear from both male and female readers.

Please share your thoughts and opinions on what you have read by answering the following questions (use extra paper if you wish):

1. In general, what did you think of what men said in this book?

_____

_____

2. Were there any chapters or sections which you in particular agreed or disagreed with?

_____

_____

3. Did you read The Hite Report on female sexuality? What did you think of it?

_____

_____

4. Is there anything that you would like to add?

_____

_____

5. Please give your

   age _____

   male or female _____

   married, living with someone, or single _____

Do not sign your name; this questionnaire is anonymous.
Mail to Shere Hite, P.O. Box 5282, F.D.R. Station,
New York, New York 10022.

THANK YOU FOR ANSWERING!

INDEX

1023